Luigi Lacchè

History & Constitution

Developments in European Constitutionalism: the comparative experience of Italy, France, Switzerland and Belgium (19th–20th centuries)

Studien zur
europäischen Rechtsgeschichte

Veröffentlichungen des
Max-Planck-Instituts
für europäische Rechtsgeschichte
Frankfurt am Main

Band 299

Vittorio Klostermann
Frankfurt am Main
2016

Luigi Lacchè

History & Constitution

Developments in European Constitutionalism: the comparative experience of Italy, France, Switzerland and Belgium (19th–20th centuries)

Vittorio Klostermann
Frankfurt am Main
2016

Bibliographische Information der Deutschen Nationalbibliothek
Die Deutsche Nationalbibliothek verzeichnet diese Publikation in der Deutschen Nationalbibliographie; detaillierte bibliographische Daten sind im Internet über *http://dnb.dnb.de* abrufbar.

Druck und Bindung: docupoint GmbH, Barleben
Typographie: Elmar Lixenfeld, Frankfurt am Main

Gedruckt auf Alster Werkdruck der Firma Geese, Hamburg.
Alterungsbeständig ISO 9706 und PEFC-zertifiziert

Printed in Germany
ISSN 1610-6040
ISBN 978-3-465-04285-3

To my sons Giulio, Alessandro and Francesco

Contents

When history meets the constitution 1

Chapter I
Constitution and federalism: the Swiss experience

Costituzioni e federalismo nella Svizzera del XIX secolo.
Note sui caratteri originari della democrazia 17

Una "mobile complessità": l'istituzione parlamentare, la democrazia rappresentativa e i "diritti popolari" nella Svizzera post-quarantottesca ... 49

Chapter II
Constitution, Monarchy, popular sovereignty: the Belgian experience

La costituzione belga del 1831 77

Constitución, Monarquía, Parlamento: Francia y Belgica ante los problemas y "modelos" del constitucionalismo europeo (1814–1848)... ... 115

Chapter III
Constitution, Monarchy, representative Government: the French experience

Coppet et la percée de l'Etat libéral constitutionnel 201

Granted Constitutions. The Theory of *octroi* and Constitutional Experiments in Europe in the Aftermath of the French Revolution 227

La garanzia della Costituzione. Riflessioni sul caso francese 259

Governo rappresentativo e principio parlamentare: le *Chartes* francesi del 1814 e 1830 303

La razionalizzazione ottocentesca: il problema dell'affermazione del modello parlamentare nell'età delle *Chartes* 329

«Gouverner n'est point administrer. Régner est encore autre chose que gouverner». Le rétour d'un vieillard: P.-L. Roederer et le problème du «gouvernement» pendant la Monarchie de Juillet (1835) 355

Chapter IV
Constitutional developments and discourses: the Italian experience

Responsabilità ministeriale 381

L'ordine costituzionale liberale nel XIX secolo. Fondamenti e caratteri ... 391

Il "discorso" costituzionale nell'opera di Giuseppe Pisanelli 407

Il potere giudiziario come «potere politico» in Attilio Brunialti 427

Argumente, Klischees und Ideologien: Das „französische Verwaltungsmodell" und die italienische Rechtskultur im 19. Jahrhundert 447

L'opinione pubblica nazionale e l'appello al popolo: figure e campi di tensione 467

Per una teoria costituzionale dell'opinione pubblica. Il dibattito italiano (XIX sec.) 489

Lo Stato giuridico e la costituzione sociale. Angelo Majorana e la giuspubblicistica di fine secolo 509

Il nome della libertà. Tre dimensioni nel secolo della Costituzione (1848–1948) 533

La *lotta per il regolamento*: libertà politiche, forma di governo e ostruzionismo parlamentare. Dalle riforme Bonghi al regolamento Villa del 1900 ... 553

«Personalmente contrario, giuridicamente favorevole». La "sentenza Mortara" e il voto politico alle donne (25 luglio 1906) ... 577

Il limite, la garanzia, l'arbitro. La Corte e il costituzionalismo ... 617

Il tempo e i tempi della Costituzione ... 639

Chapter V
Comparative constitutional History and European perspectives

Europa *una et diversa*. A proposito di *ius commune europaeum* e tradizioni costituzionali comuni ... 659

The Italian Constitutional Tradition and the Debate around a European Constitution ... 689

Index of Authors ... 707

When history meets the constitution

1. A journey across twenty years and twenty-five essays

This volume contains a selection of twenty-five essays published during the last twenty years (1995–2013). It is therefore the result of a personal journey across the continent – or, more modestly, in certain areas – of modern constitutionalism traversed and seen through the lens of constitutional history. In the guise of the modern *flâneur* invented by Charles Baudelaire and conceptualised by Walter Benjamin, I wandered through the ruins of the past and anticipations of the future. It has been a voyage of exploration unhampered by any excessively burdensome programmes.

This journey is in turn the outcome of a mixture of chance and necessity. I started in Switzerland and made my way through France, Belgium and Italy. What in fact connects these four different constitutional experiments, which I observed above all in a most unusual *Sattelzeit*, between the nineteenth and the twentieth centuries? At the beginning my interest in a European liberal jurist and politician, Pellegrino Rossi,[1] born in Italy, then a Swiss citizen in Geneva, a naturalised Frenchman in 1834 (he was the first to teach a university course in constitutional law), finally murdered in Rome in 1848 when he was the premier of the "constitutional" government of the Pope, led me to study constitutionalism and liberalism, constitution and freedom, as one of the most important issues of the nineteenth century. That was the element of chance, following the adventurous life of Rossi around Europe after the Restoration and the age of reform and revolution. But this journey was also a necessity,

1 P. Rossi, *Per la Patria comune. Rapporto della Commissione della Dieta ai ventidue Cantoni sul progetto d'Atto federale da essa deliberato a Lucerna il 15 dicembre 1832*, edited and with an introduction by L. Lacchè, Manduria 1997; L. Lacchè (ed.), *Un liberale europeo: Pellegrino Rossi (1787–1848)*, Milan 2001; L. Lacchè, *"All'antica sua patria". Pellegrino Rossi e Simonde de Sismondi: relazioni intellettuali fra Ginevra e la Toscana*, in *Sismondi e la civiltà toscana*, ed. by F. Sofia, Florence 2001, 51–91; L. Lacchè, *Pellegrino Rossi*, in *Il contributo italiano alla storia del pensiero*, ottava appendice, *Diritto, Enciclopedia italiana di scienze, lettere ed arti*, ed. by P. Cappellini, P. Costa, M. Fioravanti, B. Sordi, Rome 2012, 302–306.

prompted as it was by an awareness of the epochal significance of the modern language of the constitution, considered as a crucial framework ordering the complex social life of men.

Constitutions and constitutionalism were at the center of a scientific project which has taken shape in my own University in the years since 1992.[2] In perfect continuity with this experience, in 2001 we founded the *Journal of Constitutional History*,[3] which, in fifteen years, has become a reference point for research into constitutional history and the methodological issues involved – a journal known for its international perspective, its multilingual approach, its pronounced interdisciplinary orientation, and its interest in comparison. Gathering together a collection of individual essays published over the years also offers an opportunity to ascertain what has been achieved. The objectives pursued by the *Journal of Constitutional History* have been by and large my own. Only by combining "History" and "Constitution", the two terms of my title, can we hope to address the complexity of the constitutional issue, and thereby tackle the major challenges that we now face.

2. Looking at the present: protean constitution and fragmented constitutionalism

At the (provisional) end of my journey I observe that the concept of constitution and the borders of constitutionalism have never been so blurred. Scholarly debate suffers at times from imprecise and disparate definitions; the concept of constitution bears a striking resemblance to the Greek God Proteus.

The third generation of constitutions after the Second World War had announced a new era. These constitutions have confirmed the original vocation for mutual self-restraint between democracy and constitutionalism. They have embraced the idea of the constitution as an act of national and democratic

2 I refer to the "Laboratorio di storia costituzionale A. Barnave" founded by Roberto Martucci. This Centre organised many conferences, seminars, editorial series, a PhD Programme, a highly specialised library. See R. Martucci, *Laboratorio di storia costituzionale "Antoine Barnave" dell'Università di Macerata, 1992–2001*, in *Historia Constitucional* (revista electrónica), 2, 2001, http://hc.rediris.es/02/index.html.

3 The *Giornale di storia costituzionale / Journal of Constitutonal History*, six-monthly review, is directed by Luigi Lacchè, Roberto Martucci and Luca Scuccimarra (edizioni università di Macerata). It is indexed in Scopus and in the other main international databases. See L. Lacchè, *Un nuova rivista italiana ed europea: il "Giornale di storia costituzionale"*, in *Historia Constitucional* (revista electrónica), 3, 2002, http://hc.rediris.es/03/index.html; L. Lacchè, R. Martucci, L. Scuccimarra, *For constitutional history, ten years later*, in *Journal of Constitutional History*, 19, 1, 2010, 9–14.

foundation, according to a strong concept of constituent power generating political power.[4] In this context, the constitution emerges "as a symbolic marker of a great transition in the political life of a nation".[5] This idea of constitution remained anchored to the State, its territory and political sovereignty. But it had to work now within a pattern of "welfare state constitution" that emphasised functional complexity. Within the democratic "interventionist" states, constitutions contain basic principles and values serving to orient the principal societal challenges (fundamental rights, pluralism, multiculturalism, etc.). Outwardly, constitutions have had to deal increasingly with at least two major "external" phenomena. On the one hand, I have in mind here Europe's transformation within Community coordinates. Multilevel constitutionalism, treaties and Bills of Rights, common constitutional traditions, the jurisprudence of the European Courts, the European *demos*, and European constitution-making are some of the topics that have dominated the debate during the last two decades.

On the other hand, modern territorial sovereignty and its legitimacy[6] no longer meets the challenges of the post-national constellation. With the advent of a global society perspective, the traditional paradigms of the constitution have entered into crisis. The European Union has been seen as presaging a post-national "constitution," and has led scholars to ponder the utility of the conceptual tools and operating practices of "national" constitutional theory.

But while constitutionalism was attaining a high level of legitimacy, this period of maturation "coincides with the erosion of some of the basic conditions on which those achievements have rested". Whatever name is attached to this erosion, "constitutionalism can be understood to be entering a twilight zone".[7] We can see – as has been correctly observed[8] – a singular blend of triumph and decline.

In fact, most scholars agree as to the extent of the gap between the state and the forms of politics and constitutionalism evident in the new global order.

4 M. Loughlin, N. Walker (eds.), *The Paradox of Constitutionalism. Constituent Power and Constitutional Form*, Oxford 2007. "We sought to demonstrate that what connects our constitutional past, present and future, and what links the state as the traditional site of constitutional government to new subnational and transnational sites, is a constant preoccupation with the question of the relationship between authorization and authority, politics and law, *pouvoir constituant* and *pouvoir constitué*" (V). See also M. Loughlin, *The idea of Public Law*, Oxford 2003, 113.

5 B. Ackerman, *The Rise of World Constitutionalism*, 1996, *Occasional Papers*. Paper 4, http://digitalcommons.law.yale.edu/ylsop_papers/4.

6 N. Walker (ed.), *Sovereignty in Transition*, Oxford 2003.

7 P. Dobner, M. Loughlin, *Introduction*, in *The Twilight of Constitutonalism?*, ed. by P. Dobner and M. Loughlin, Oxford 2010, XI.

8 Ibidem.

Constitutionalism beyond the state is the central issue. On one side, the constitutional law developed in states is increasingly "open" and concerned to take account of global phenomena. Distant events can produce practical effects within states. The intention is now to subject the relevant causes and effects to the law by resorting to a sort of common / global constitutional law composed of different elements. Europe's experience and European constitutionalism beyond the state[9] have been seen as very important but controversial "construction sites". Constitutionalism "in an age of diversity"[10] should make us more aware of the limits of nominalism under "common labels" but "we should [also] resist the temptation of a provincial particularism".[11] The new "global constitutionalism" cannot respond on a global level to the "canonical" chain state / sovereignty / constitution. Constitutionalism was born from the internal conflicts in the processes of building modern states, and yet there does exist a platform based on principles common to the written and unwritten constitutions, universal declarations, conventions and treaties, constitutional courts jurisprudence, and the constitutional theory of law. These phenomena can be observed from different points of view. The acknowledgement and construction of an essential core for a cosmopolitan constitutional law[12] based on the protection of fundamental rights can be seen as the major goal of the worldwide academic community and of the judges in the courts. But, at the same time, this gave rise to concerns and criticisms relating to the supranational transfer of power from representative institutions to judiciaries by dint of a more extensive and active judicial review in a global perspective.[13]

It is true: "Constitutionalism is changing – that is beyond question. But the direction of change remains an open issue".[14] Global constitutionalism is ever more attached to international law and global governance.[15] The age of globalisation has posed the problem of the efficacy of constitutional theory centred on the nation-state. Can it really be useful? Global law without a state[16] points to

9 J. H. H. Weiler, M. Wind (eds.), *European Constitutionalism Beyond the State*, Cambridge 2003.

10 J. Tully, *Strange multiplicity. Constitutionalism in an age of diversity*, Cambridge 1995.

11 B. Ackerman, *The Rise of World Constitutionalism* cit.

12 Q. Camerlengo, *Contributo ad una teoria del diritto costituzionale cosmopolitico*, Milan 2007.

13 R. Hirschl, *Towards Juristocracy. The Origins and Consequences of the New Constitutionalism*, Cambridge 2004; Id., *The New Constitution and the Judicialization of Pure Politics Worldwide*, in *Fordham Law Review*, 75, 2, 2006, 721–753.

14 P. Dobner, M. Loughlin, *Introduction* cit., XVI.

15 J. L. Dunoff, J. P. Trachtman (eds.), *Ruling the Word? Constitutionalism, international law and global governance*, Cambridge 2009.

16 G. Teubner (ed.), *Global Law without a State*, Aldershot 1997.

the pulling down of the traditional pillars of the theory of the state: territory, people, sovereignty. In the transnational perspective there are new and fragmented "social constitutions", "private regimes", "constitutional actors" who take part in the social constitutionalisation of the world.[17] This means that in a transnational world constitutional problems arise beyond the limits of the nation-state, often in the 'private' sectors of global society. Transnational constitutionalism requires new "constitutional" regulatory regimes, a global constitutional law based on the governance of fragmentation and of collisions between plural regimes and systems. According to this vision,[18] collisions between the diverse regime constitutions might be coped with by a selective process of networking that normatively strengthens already existing empirical networks between the regime constitutions: the linkage of regime constitutions with autonomous social sectors; and, more importantly in this context, the linkage of regime constitutions with one another.

So, if constitutionalism is changing, and in unforeseen directions, one thing is certain: the complexity of the new landscape requires a science that is fully aware of its task and able to govern the systemic complexity of the new "constitutional" processes and structures. When we speak of a need for a worldwide jurist, we are invariably referring to this dimension. Pluralism, coexistence / tension between unity and diversity, and constant comparison must be handled with the appropriate sensitivity, with a critical spirit and with a readiness to explore less well-worn paths.

17 For a critical survey see B. Clavero, *Globalización del Constitucionalismo? Transnacionalidad de empreas entre poderes y derechos por tiempos postcoloniales (1947–2011)*, in *Quaderni fiorentini per la storia del pensiero giuridico*, 41, 2012, 483–580.

18 On this position see G. Teubner, *Global Private Regimes: Neo-spontaneous Law and Dual Constitution of Autonomous Sectors?*, in K.-H. Ladeur (ed.), *Globalization and Public Governance*, Oxford 2003, 71–87; G. Teubner, A. Fischer-Lescano, *Regime-Collisions: The Vain Search for Legal Unity in the Fragmentation of Global Law*, in *Michigan Journal of International Law*, 25, 4, 2004, 999–1046; Ch. Joerges, I.-J. Sand, G. Teubner (eds.), *Transnational Governance and Constitutionalism*, Oxford and Portland Oregon 2004; G. Teubner, A. Fischer-Lescano, *Regime-Kollisionen. Zur Fragmentierung des globalen Rechts*, Frankfurt am Main 2006; G. Teubner, *Verfassungsfragmente. Gesellschaftlicher Konstitutionalismus in der Globalisierung*, Frankfurt am Main 2012. On Teubner's perspective see A. Febbrajo, F. Gambino (eds.), *Il diritto frammentato*, Milan 2013.

3. Making a polyptych: a comparative constitutional history in a global perspective

These new and controversial constitutional horizons adumbrate a very complex landscape. How are we to deal with these issues? Constitutionalism, as I noted above, seems to have two grand frameworks in mind. The first is the idea of a *ius commune europaeum* based on «constitutional traditions that are common to member States», thus generating a series of decisions focused on the protection of fundamental rights. It was in the ambit of principles and "common constitutional traditions" that it was possible to develop a "new *ius commune*", and this on two levels: on the one hand, a "heritage" that consolidated the past and which was therefore rooted primarily in national traditions, and on the other a *space of communication*, which made it possible to look to the future independently of the evolution of law as defined by treaties or, from another perspective, by a Constitution-Treaty. The second framework concerns worldwide constitutionalism, seen from different points of view, oriented to the building of a *ius cosmopoliticum* characterised by uncertain boundaries. In our attempts to address such matters, we probably need a multidisciplinary and integrated approach. In this context, constitutional history, understood as a discipline situated at a crossroads and therefore requiring a wide range of different tools, may be able to offer a useful contribution. Constitutionalism can be seen as a new *ius commune*[19] built during the last few centuries. In 2008 the European Parliament, the European Council and the European Commission have pointed out the need for interaction between constitutional process and public debate as a crucial prerequisite for democratic participation in the Union. Faced with the weakening of the integrative power of constitutions, constitutional history may well have considerable heuristic potential. If this history is, in some respects, yet to be written,[20] it is also true that in the last two decades, coinciding with the European and global metamorphoses, constitutional history has fostered a number of different initiatives. I refer here to certain dedicated journals, websites and book series.[21]

19 F. Tomás y Valiente, *El «ius commune europaeum» de ayer y de hoy*, in *Glossae. Revista de Historia del derecho europeo*, 5–6, 1993–1994, 13–14.

20 H. Dippel, *Modern Constitutionalism. An introduction to a history in need of writing*, in *Tijdschrift voor Rechtgeschiedenis*, 1–2, 2005, 153–169.

21 I refer above all to some series of works published between Germany and Italy, for example P. Schiera and M. Kirsch (eds.), *Denken und Umsetzung des Konstitutionalismus in Deutschland und anderen europäischen Ländern in der ersten Hälfte des 19. Jahrhunderts*, Berlin 1999; H. Dippel, *Executive and Legislative Powers in the Constitutions of 1848–49*, Berlin 1999; P. Schiera and M. Kirsch (eds.), *Verfassungswandel um 1848 im europäischen Vergleich*, Berlin 2001; G. Manca, W. Brauneder (eds.), *L'istituzione parlamentare nel XIX secolo. Una prospettiva*

One of the major challenges faced by constitutional history is that of putting at the heart of its concerns the idea of a common ground connecting different research perspectives and scholars using different tools and languages. Constitutional history is a set of routes leading to one and the same territory. Each follows a particular path.[22] There is no such thing as a single, "true" constitutional history. Each feels that his specialism is essential but at the same time he needs to enter into dialogue, to engage with other scholars coming from other disciplines. Constitutional history is like a river with an estuary delta formed by the debris carried downstream by its various branches. Constitutional history is a *quid pluris*,[23] composed of different ingredients, although but the set is greater than the sum of its component parts. Constitutional history should serve to "open up" and to connect the individual research fields. Its "autonomy" is the result of a critical process.[24] This "autonomy" is a point of view, *un certain regard*. The metaphor of the polyptych comes to mind here.[25] Our "constitutional" painting is just like a huge polyptych. At the centre the "ancona" may portray the *Maestà* or the crucifixion of Jesus Christ, but polyptychs are ambitious works and so are enriched with predellas, *cimase*, cusps, panels with lives of the Saints, angels, miniature landscapes, the whole enclosed by massive gold frames. Those who cultivate constitutional history resemble art historians trying to reconstitute polyptychs whose parts have been scattered across different sites and museums.

comparata, Bononia, Berlin 2000; M. Kirsch, A. G. Kosfeld, P. Schiera (eds.), *Der Verfassungsstaat vor der Herausforderung der Massengesellschaft. Konstitutionalismus um 1900 im europäischen Vergleich*, Berlin 2002; G. Manca, L. Lacchè (eds.), *Parlamento e costituzione nei sistemi costituzionali europei ottocenteschi*, Bononia, Berlin 2003. Regarding the European constitutional history we have to remember at least two handbooks: P. Brandt, M. Kirsch, A. Schlegelmilch (eds.), *Handbuch der europäischen Verfassungsgeschichte im 19. Jahrhundert. Institutionen und Rechtspraxis im gesellschaftlichen Wandel*, vol. 1: *Um 1800*, Bonn 2006; W. Daum, P. Brandt, M. Kirsch, A. Schlegelmich (eds.), *Handbuch der europäischen Verfassungsgeschichte im 19. Jahrhundert. Institutionen und Rechtspraxis im gesellschaftlichen Wandel*, vol. 2: 1815–1847, Bonn 2012; and the four volumes of the *Handbuch Ius Publicum Europaeum* (2007–2011), ed. by A. von Bogdandy and P. M. Huber. Among the relevant Journals, see *Historia Constitucional*, open Journal founded by J. Varela Suanzes-Carpegna, published in Oviedo since 2000 and the already mentioned *Journal of Constitutional History* (see *supra* nt. 3).

22 J. Varela Suanzes-Carpegna (ed.), *Historia e historiografía constitucionales. Entrevistas con Ernst-Wolfgang Böckenförde, Michel Troper, Maurice J. C. Vile, Maurizio Fioravanti*, Madrid 2015.

23 M. Fioravanti, *Sulla storia costituzionale*, in *Journal of Constitutional History*, 19, 1, 2010, 29–32.

24 M. Troper, *L'autonomie de l'histoire constitutionnelle*, Ibidem, 33–43.

25 L. Lacchè, *Tra storia e comparazione*, in *Giornale di storia costituzionale*, 1,1, 2001, 5–6; Id., *Ripensare vecchi temi con nuove idee*, in *Giornale di storia costituzionale*, 14, 2, 2007, 5–6.

Each "part" makes "sense", has *value*, and can be looked at in its own right, but the "constitutional frameworks" and the "constitutional factors" are the continuous composition and decomposition of the parts in the whole, between past, present and future. We can observe each predella as if it had a certain autonomy, but everything changes once our gaze takes in the polyptych as a whole. Now we can see the internal dialogue, the cross-references, the multiplicity of perspectives. The ancona of our polyptych is what we call constitution (our *Maestà*) and all around there are the forms of society, politics, the economy, anthropology, culture and so on. For reading the "constitutional polyptych" we need, today more than ever, an integrated interdisciplinary approach, new perspectives and an ever vigilant self-criticism.[26]

The historicity of constitutions is an integral part of the new cultural history.[27] Constitutional culture can be grasped through a vision transcending institutional devices[28] and a merely formal idea of constitution.[29] The concept of constitution seeks to identify the constitutional factors that continuously interact in order to define a principle of social and political unity. Constitution is always process, conflict, movement,[30] change. It finds equilibrium points but lives between reform and revolution, chance and grand design.[31] Every *Verfassungsbedarf* is historically determined.

Today we need a comparative constitutional history approach[32] in a global perspective.[33] "... we definitely can say that the times of national constitutional histories are over."[34]

26 B. Clavero, *Constitución europea e historia constitucional: el rapto de los poderes*, in *Historia constitucional*, revista electrónica, http://www.historiaconstitucional.com, 6, 2005.

27 P. Häberle, *Verfassung als öffentlicher Prozess: Materialien zu einer Verfassungstheorie der offenen Gesellschaft*, Berlin 1978; Id., *Verfassungslehre als Kulturwissenschaft*, Berlin 1982.

28 R. Blänkner, *La storia costituzionale come storia culturale*, in *Memoria e Ricerca*, 35, 2010, 13–30.

29 P. Schiera, *Dall'amministrazione alla comunicazione. Profili di storia costituzionale europea*, in *Scienza & Politica*, 41, 2009, 35–47.

30 See the interesting project, funded by the European Research Council, *Reconsidering Constitutional Formation* (Advanced Grant 2013), directed by Ulrike Müßig, University of Passau.

31 R. C. van Caenegem, *Constitutional History: Chance or Grand Design?*, in *European Constitutional Law Review*, 5, 2009, 447–463.

32 K. Å. Modéer, *Is European Comparative Legal History Running Wild? From Function and Texts to Perspectives and Contexts*, in K. Å. Modéer, P. Nilsen (eds.), *How to teach European comparative legal history*, Lund 2011, 16–18.

33 Th. Duve, *European Legal History – Global Perspectives*, Working paper for the Colloquium *'European Normativity – Global Historical Perspectives'* (Max Planck Institute, September, 2nd–4th, 2013), n. 2013-06, http://ssrn.com/abstract=2292666; M. Vec, *National and transnational Legal Evolutions – Teaching History*

4. History & constitution

The articles published in this collection are not designed to give a systematic account of European constitutional history. They can hope to do no more than represent one particular way, one path allowing the reader to attain a deeper understanding of a series of different profiles studied over the years. They share a common inspiration but they cannot provide a comprehensive framework. In fact they concern above all four constitutional areas: France, Belgium, Switzerland and Italy. This is thus the history of four important constitutional experiments, but it does not neglect crossroads, contaminations, transfers. What comparative constitutional history offers us is precisely the possibility of subjecting already established positions and perspectives to critical review. This approach can serve to shed new light on familiar themes, and to help us to jettison stereotypes and unduly schematic interpretations. We need to be aware of the fact that myths and traditions are part and parcel of constitutional history building. Demystification and critique of the excessive and ahistorical use of "constitutional" models are important elements in the fashioning of a renewed history. In this way constitutional history can enhance other research outlooks, for example comparative constitutional law and political science.

One of the issues of constitutional history is about the "making" of constitutional texts. Not infrequently this history has been reduced to a sort of history of mere genealogies. The use of "models" as prescriptive frameworks suggests that there are "original" and "derivative" constitutions. Sometimes we chance to read that in a constitution a significant proportion of its articles are copied from texts or principles coming from other nations. But what does it mean to transpose or copy some articles? It is evident that to copy really means to invent or to reinvent. Texts move, they are compared and also "copied" and yet every text becomes specific and "original" once again, because contexts, circumstances, times, places, authors, factors change every time. A constitution is at one and the same time a factor of sharing and of separation, of identity and of difference. A constitution is always a *patchwork* composed of different elements. A constitution is not a fixed design because it always lives through discourses, languages, the transnational exchange of ideas, and the interplay of constitutional stakeholders. A constitution has long been a means of communication between State and society, institutions and social classes. For this reason constitutional history needs different and integrated research approaches able to combine or at least to take account of the history of public law, legal scholarship about the State,

of International Law, in K. Å. Modéer, P. Nilsen (eds.), *How to teach European comparative legal history*, cit., 37.

34 M. Stolleis, *Concepts, models and traditions of a comparative European constitutional history*, in *Journal of Constitutional History*, 19, 1, 2010, 53.

political doctrines and institutions, the science of administration, political and social conditions.[35] This approach can serve to avert the ever-present risk of anachronism.

The articles published in this volume study four constitutional experiments, but in reality they had a wider purview. The myth of the English constitution pervades the discourses and languages of the French liberals, especially during certain moments in the nineteenth-century constitutional history. In Italy Belgium is known as "Little England". The *Modell Deutschland* is more and more an object of fascination to Italian public law scholars. In the 1830s Alexis de Tocqueville analyses the situation in Switzerland, comparing the different kind of federalism in America and in Europe. These and many other intersections show how complex the attempt to study national experiments in terms of *Sonderwege* may prove to be.

The twenty-five essays here published in Italian, French, English, Spanish and German, consider above all some developments in European constitutionalism in the nineteenth and twentieth centuries. But I should emphasise that the focus is upon the experiments and developments of the nineteenth century. I refer to a *Sattelzeit* – associated with Reinhart Koselleck's concept – extending from 1814 to the outbreak of the First World War. This volume takes the Restoration seriously, not least the pivotal role played by the category of granted constitution in European constitutional history. This kind of constitution is something more than simply a transitional phenomenon, or an 'interval' (albeit an important one) between the novel and strategic idea of the eighteenth-century constitution based upon the constituent power of the people and the full realisation of democratic constitutionalism in the course of the twentieth century. The intrinsic interest of this approach lies in its capacity to portray granted constitutions as instruments serving to preserve ancient forms of sovereignty alongside post-revolutionary innovations. 'Monarchical constitutionalism' established an important and long-enduring workshop in which we can observe 'old' and 'new', tradition and change, reform and revolution, conflicts and mediations, ancient words and new concepts, the ideology of *octroi* and parliamentary experiments. Constitutions and parliamentary processes are by no means as linear as they have been made out to be. Nation-building, popular sovereignty, constitutional monarchy, parliament, science and public opinion are the fundamental concepts of our point of view.

The monarchical constitution was, for a century, common ground for developments and applications which were far from predictable. The deliberate vagueness and flexibility of the constitutional formula, which was an intrinsic

35 J. Varela Suanzes-Carpegna, *L'histoire constitutionnelle: quelques réflexions de méthode*, in *Revue française de droit constitutionnel*, 68, 2006, 676.

feature of the constitutionalism of the Restoration, was in fact a *programme*, to interpret and flesh out at will. The political theology elaborated by the reactionary writers of the Restoration was undoubtedly a powerful tool in the analysis of the *undecided* constitution, a constitution shaped by the contradictions of a liberal constitutionalism which accepted the *octroi* and the idea of the autonomous will of the monarch and, at the same time, sought to limit, if not annul, the originally personal dimension. As a consequence the difficult separation of *régner* from *gouverner* was destined to be one of the greatest political-constitutional problems of the nineteenth century. Constitutionalism was for a long time a key factor of composition and synthesis between Revolution and Restoration.[36] At the same time we cannot underestimate the administrative dimension of the constitution. Administration is the *lebendige Verfassung* that accompanies the social developments of the State.

A European comparative constitutional history, in a global perspective, can help us to better decipher two very important issues in our times: first of all assessing the identity and the constitutional substance of a European living common core of the constitutional traditions; then considering constitutional history as a useful tool to address different levels of global constitutionalism and new trends of governance.

History & Constitution will, I trust, offer not only insights into the past, but also some guidelines for the future.

Over the years, working in the area of constitutional history, I have contracted a debt of gratitude to many colleagues and friends. I would like to thank here at least some of them: Robert Roth, Alfred Dufour, Giovanni Busino, Michel Porret, Victor Monnier, Alexis Keller; Michel Pertué, Lucien Jaume, Michel Troper, Marcel Morabito, François Burdeau (†); Michael Stolleis, Heinz Mohnhaupt, Thomas Duve, Dian Schefold, Dieter Grimm, Reiner Schulze, Thomas Vormbaum, Francis Delperée, Alain Wijffels; Antonio Manuel Hespanha; Martti Koskenniemi; Bartolomé Clavero, Marta Lorente, Carlos Petit, Joaquin Varela Suanzes-Carpegna, Ignacio Fernandez Sarasola; Martin Loughlin, Joseph H. H. Weiler, Bruce Ackermann; Paolo Grossi, Pietro Costa, Maurizio Fioravanti, Paolo Cappellini, Bernardo Sordi, Giovanni Cazzetta, Luca Mannori, Stefano Mannoni, Claudia Storti, Floriana Colao, Aurelio Cernigliaro, Giulio Cianferotti, Gian Savino Pene Vidari, Giacomo Pace Gravina, Cristina Vano, Pierangelo Schiera, Luca Scuccimarra, Roberto Martucci, Piero Aimo, Paolo Colombo, Anna Gianna Manca, Cesare Pinelli, Sabino Cassese, Alessandro Pace, Massimo Luciani, Roberto Bin, Alessandro Torre, Marina Calamo Specchia, Nicola Lupo, Andrea Simoncini, Giulio Salerno, Giovanni Di Cosimo.

My work in Macerata owed much to my colleagues Mario Sbriccoli (†), Paolo Marchetti, Massimo Meccarelli, Monica Stronati, Ninfa Contigiani, Antonella Bettoni. Giuseppe Mecca and Martin Thom helped me a great deal with the task of revising and editing this volume. I am grateful to Karl-Heinz Lingens and his team at the Max Planck Institute for European Legal History for having typeset and edited this volume. Many thanks finally to Thomas Duve, Director of the Max Planck Institute for European Legal History, for having agreed to publish this volume in the series "Studien zur europäischen Rechtsgeschichte".

36 P. Schiera, *El constitucionalismo como discurso politico*, Madrid 2012, 18.

The essays contained in this volume have already appeared in the following publications.

Costituzioni e federalismo in Svizzera. Note sui caratteri originari della democrazia, in *I viaggi di Erodoto*, Milan, Bruno Mondadori, 25, 1995, 130–143 (The text given here is more extensive than in the original version).

Una «mobile complessità»: l'istituzione parlamentare, la democrazia rappresentativa e i «diritti popolari» nella Svizzera post-quarantottesca, in *L'istituzione parlamentare nel XIX secolo. Una prospettiva comparata*, ed. by A. G. Manca and Wilhelm Brauneder, Bologna, Il Mulino, Berlin, Duncker & Humblot, 2000, 149–174.

La Costituzione belga del 1831, in *Storia Amministrazione Costituzione. Annale dell'Isap*, 9, 2001, 71–112.

Constitución, Monarquía, Parlamento: Francia y Belgica ante los problemas y «modelos» del constitucionalismo europeo (1814–1848), in *Fundamentos. Cuadernos monográficos de teoría del Estado, derecho público e historia constitucional*, 2, 2000, *Modelos constitucionales en la historia comparada*, 467–557.

Coppet et la percée de l'Etat libéral constitutionnel, in *Coppet, creuset de l'ésprit libéral. Les idées politiques et constitutionnelles du Groupe de Madame de Staël*, ed. by L. Jaume, Paris, Economica, Aix-Marseilles, Presses Universitaires, 1999, 135–155 (published also in Italian: *Il circolo di Coppet e gli orizzonti liberali dello Stato costituzionale*, in *Rivista trimestrale di diritto pubblico*, 2, 1999, 529–556).

Granted Constitutions. The Theory of the octroi *and Constitutional Experiments in the Aftermath of the French Revolution*, in *European Constitutional Law Review*, 9, 2013, 285–314 (published also in Spanish and Italian: *Las Cartas Otorgadas. La teoría de l'octroi y las experiencias constitucionales en la Europa postrevolucionaria*, in *Fundamentos*, 6, 2010, 269–305; *Le carte ottriate. La teoria dell'octroi e le esperienze costituzionali nell'Europa post-rivoluzionaria*, in *Giornale di storia costituzionale*, 18, II, 2009, 229–254).

La garanzia della costituzione. Riflessioni sul caso francese, in *Parlamento e costituzione nei sistemi costituzionali europei ottocenteschi*, ed. by L. Lacchè and A. G. Manca, Bologna, Il Mulino, Berlin, Duncker & Humblot, 2003, 49–94 (published also in *Annali della Facoltà di Giurisprudenza*, Università degli Studi di Macerata, 2000/2002, Milano, Giuffrè, 2004, 41–93).

Governo rappresentativo e principio parlamentare: le Chartes *francesi del 1814 e 1830*, in *Giornale di Storia costituzionale*, n. 8, II, 2004, 99–120.

La razionalizzazione ottocentesca: il problema dell'affermazione del modello parlamentare nell'età delle Chartes, in *La Costituzione francese. La Constitution française*, ed. by M. Calamo Specchia, Turin, Giappichelli, 2009, 125–147.

«Gouverner n'est point administrer. Régner est encore autre chose que gouverner». Le rétour d'un vieillard: P.-L. Roederer et le problème du «gouvernement» pendant la Monarchie de Juillet (1835), in *Etudes à la mémoire de François Burdeau*, Paris, Litec, 2008, 125–145 (published also in Italian: *«Gouverner n'est point administrer. Régner est encore autre chose que gouverner». Il ritorno di un vegliardo: P.-L. Roederer e il problema del 'governo' durante la Monarchia di Luglio*, in *Giornale di storia costituzionale*, 12, II, 2006, 111–132).

Responsabilità ministeriale, in *Atlante culturale del Risorgimento. Lessico del linguaggio politico dal Settecento all'Unità*, ed. by A. M. Banti, A. Chiavistelli, L. Mannori, M. Meriggi, Rome, Bari, Laterza, 2011, 359–371 (also published, with minor modifications, in *Scienza & Politica*, 40, 2009, 13–23).

L'ordine costituzionale liberale nel XIX secolo. Fondamenti e caratteri (published, with minor modifications, as *Il costituzionalismo liberale*, in *Il contributo italiano alla storia del pensiero*, ottava appendice, *Diritto*, *Enciclopedia italiana di scienze, lettere ed arti*, ed. by. P. Cappellini, P. Costa, M. Fioravanti, B. Sordi, Roma, Istituto della Enciclopedia italiana, 2012, 294–301).

Il "discorso" costituzionale nell'opera di Giuseppe Pisanelli in *Giornale di storia costituzionale*, n. 10, II, 2005, 87–103 (published also in *Giuseppe Pisanelli. Scienza del processo cultura delle leggi e avvocatura tra periferia e nazione*, ed. by C. Vano, Naples, Jovene, 2005, 149–173).

Il potere giudiziario come "potere politico" in Attilio Brunialti, Commento a A. Brunialti, *La funzione politica del potere giudiziario* (1870), in *Storia Amministrazione Costituzione. Annale dell'Istituto per la Scienza dell'Amministrazione Pubblica*, 7, 1999, 1–45.

Argumente, Klischees und Ideologien: Das "französische Verwaltungsmodell" und die italienische Rechtskultur im 19. Jahrhundert, in *Rheinisches Recht und Europäische Rechtsgeschichte*, ed. by R. Schulze, Berlin, Duncker & Humblot, 1998, 295–313.

L'opinione pubblica nazionale e l'appello al popolo: figure e campi di tensione, in *Burocracia, poder politico y justicia*. Libro-homenaje de amigos del profesor José Maria García Marín, Madrid, Dykinson, 2015, 455–473.

Per una teoria costituzionale dell'opinione pubblica. Il dibattito italiano (XIX secolo), in *Giornale di storia costituzionale*, n. 6, II, 2003, 273–290.

Lo Stato giuridico e la costituzione sociale. Angelo Majorana e la giuspubblicistica di fine secolo, in *Il "giureconsulto della politica". Angelo Majorana e l'indirizzo sociologico del Diritto pubblico*, Macerata, edizioni Università di Macerata, 2011, 23–53.

Il nome della libertà. Tre dimensioni nel secolo della Costituzione (1848–1948), in *Un secolo per la Costituzione (1848–1948). Concetti e parole nello svolgersi del lessico costituzionale italiano*, Florence, Accademia della Crusca, 2012, 29–50.

La lotta per il regolamento: *libertà politiche, forma di governo e ostruzionismo parlamentare. Dalle riforme Bonghi al regolamento Villa del 1900*, in *I regolamenti parlamentari nei momenti di "svolta" della storia costituzionale italiana*, numero monografico del *Giornale di storia costituzionale*, 15, I, 2008, 31–51.

«Personalmente contrario, giuridicamente favorevole». La "sentenza Mortara" e il voto politico alle donne (25 luglio 1906), in *Donne e diritti. Dalla sentenza Mortara del 1906 alla prima avvocata italiana*, ed. by N. Sbano, Bologna, Il Mulino, 2004, 99–151.

Il limite, la garanzia, l'arbitro. La Corte e il costituzionalismo, in *Giornale di storia costituzionale*, n. 11, I, 2006, 5–22.

Il tempo e i tempi della costituzione, in *Dalla Costituzione "inattuata" alla Costituzione "inattuale"? Potere costituente e riforme costituzionali nell'Italia repubblicana*, ed. by G. Brunelli and G. Cazzetta, Milan, Giuffrè, 2013, 365–386.

Europa una et diversa. *A proposito di* ius commune europaeum *e tradizioni costituzionali comuni*, in *Teoria del diritto e dello Stato. Rivista europea di cultura e scienza giuridica*, 1–2, 2003, 40–71.

The Italian Constitutional Tradition and the Debate around a European Constitution, 2007, English version unpublished (published in Italian: *La tradizione costituzionale italiana e il dibattito sulla "costituzione europea"*, in *Giornale di storia costituzionale*, n. 16, II, 2008, 71–83).

Chapter I
Constitution and federalism: the Swiss experience

Costituzioni e federalismo nella Svizzera del XIX secolo. Note sui caratteri originari della democrazia

«Perchè la Svizzera, che ha tre lingue, due religioni, tre o quattro razze, è una nazione, mentre la Toscana, per esempio, che è così omogenea, non lo è?».[1] La domanda di Ernest Renan è del 1882, ma conserva una viva attualità. L'interrogazione è suggestiva: continua a far riflettere sulle ragioni che hanno fatto prosperare una comunità nazionale in un contesto, all'apparenza, non proprio favorevole. Alla domanda si possono dare molte risposte, tutte legittime e significative. Proverò ad evidenziare alcuni dei tratti che sembrano meglio caratterizzare la moderna evoluzione delle strutture costituzionali, cantonali e federali, della Confederazione svizzera.[2]

Le «anomalie» e i «paradossi» offrono forse una chiave di lettura per dar conto del rilievo e della persistenza storica di vicende ritenute «peculiari». Gli svizzeri hanno contribuito all'affermazione di immagini e di argomenti che sono all'origine dello spirito di convivenza civile e sono oggetto – sino al presente – di ininterrotta riflessione critica. Il *Sonderfall*, il mito della separatezza, l'idea di una storia peculiare – tra eventi reali e aspetti immaginari – rappresentano alcune costanti della rappresentazione storica. I territori politicamente organizzati, gli *Orte*, sono l'emblema della conquista di un'antica libertà. La vicenda-mito, universalmente nota, di Guglielmo Tell è un esempio di scuola del Romanticismo: da Lumirre a Schiller, da Rossini a Lamartine. Proprio il poeta francese sottolinea, nel 1869, l'arcaicità del carattere nazionale del popolo elvetico. Lo svizzero elettivo è ancora il montanaro, il pastore-contadino: devoto, diligente, patriota, soldato, da sempre uomo libero.[3] Il paradigma drammatur-

1 E. Renan, *Che cos'è una Nazione?, e altri saggi*, con introduzione di S. Lanaro, Roma 1993, 9.

2 W. Martin, *Histoire de la Suisse. Essai sur la formation d'une Confédération d'Etats*, Parigi 1926, 8, reputa (con ironia) più semplice riassumere la storia di Francia o d'Inghilterra che la «duplice» storia (federale e cantonale) della Confederazione svizzera.

3 S. Widmer, *Sonderbundskrieg und Bundesreform von 1848 im Urteil Frankreichs*, Bern 1948, 108 ss.

gico, in realtà, serve, nel corso dell'Ottocento, a compensare – in un paese già protagonista di un significativo percorso di modernizzazione – la perdita dell'innocenza contadina, ricordando agli Svizzeri di onorare quell'indipendenza di spirito che alimenta l'amore per la libertà.[4] Ma nel 1869 gli Svizzeri possono oramai «rivedere» la pur appagante leggenda dell'eroe nazionale: il mito democratico della storia patria, «spogliata degli ornamenti che l'avevano falsata»,[5] gli affianca la volontà paziente di tutto un popolo artefice dei proprî destini. L'immagine della Svizzera come nazione-volontà[6] riposa sull'antica forma costituzionale del patto-giuramento. È l'*Eidgenossenschaft*, la convenzione giurata[7] a caratterizzare – in maniera del tutto singolare – la lunga storia della sovranità politica svizzera, almeno sin dal celebre patto del Grütli allorché le genti di Uri, Svitto e Unterwaldo, nell'agosto del 1291, vollero sottoporsi «in eterno» a regole comuni, per sancire non solo un regime di mutua difesa ma anche un «modello» di convivenza civile tra i confederati, nel rispetto dell'autonomia di ciascun corpo politico.

Il gesto del giuramento ripete «un archetipo contrattuale antichissimo».[8] Il *Giuramento dei tre confederati svizzeri*, dipinto a Londra, fra il 1779 e il 1781, dallo zurighese Johann Heinrich Füssli, coglie nell'unione armata delle braccia il senso più profondo di un gesto che possiede un'indubbia trascendenza epica.[9]

La mitologia storico-figurativa si è impadronita del giuramento del 1291 sino a farne, a torto o a ragione, la data di nascita della Confederazione svizzera.

Il patto siglato dai *Waldstätten*, cioè dai «luoghi» o cantoni forestali (il cuore tradizionale dell'immaginario svizzero), è importante anche perché simboleggia il paradigma fondamentale della storia elvetica: la scrittura solenne di principî (di rappresentatività della giurisdizione, di maggioranza – anche nelle dispute fra Stati –, di reciprocità, della forza giuridica delle consuetudini) destinati a rafforzare la «costituzione».[10]

La tradizione del patto-giuramento è il motore profondo dell'evoluzione storica. È il meccanismo «tecnico» che ha trasformato le *anomalie* in *regole*.

4 J. Steinberg, *Why Switzerland?*, Cambridge 1976; A. D. Smith, *Le origini etniche delle nazioni*, Bologna 1992, 424–425.

5 H. Hungerbühler, *Etude critique sur les traditions relatives aux origines de la Conféderation suisse*, Genève 1869.

6 E. R. Papa, *Storia della Svizzera dall'antichità ad oggi. Il mito del federalismo*, Milano 1993, 6.

7 Su questo tema è adesso fondamentale il lavoro di P. Prodi, *Il sacramento del potere. Il giuramento politico nella storia costituzionale dell'Occidente*, Bologna 1992.

8 J. Starobinski, *Il giuramento: David*, in *1789. I sogni e gli incubi della ragione*, Milano 1981, 59.

9 *Ibidem*. Dello stesso autore vedi *Johann Heinrich Füssli*, in *1789*, cit., 73–80.

10 E. R. Papa, *Storia della Svizzera*, cit., 28.

L'accordo federativo racchiude in sé parecchi elementi dello spirito svizzero, è il germe di una religione civile, di una cultura strettamente legata alla posizione geopolitica della Svizzera.

I paradossi, nella storia di questo paese, rappresentano un punto di forza.

Si pensi, per esempio, al singolare destino di una lunga e gloriosa tradizione militare (evidente nell'immagine del montanaro bellicoso e gran soldato)[11] che ha ceduto spazio, progressivamente, alla cultura della neutralità (ben armata),[12] sino ad associare – invertendo i colori – l'emblema della croce bianca su campo rosso (già simbolo di Svitto, l'antico cantone forestale) alle vicende di quella grande istituzione umanitaria che è la Croce rossa.

La Svizzera è, del resto, una nazione che, in uno dei momenti più drammatici della propria storia (1847), ha sofferto una guerra civile che è però durata solo poche settimane, con un centinaio di morti: un esito singolare se lo si paragona ai lutti e ai traumi di altri eventi «comparabili» (per esempio la guerra civile americana).

È una nazione che ha saputo conservare la forma repubblicana (nella diversità dei regimi politici) e confederale pur[13] trovandosi al centro – come in una sorta di assedio – di un'Europa gremita di monarchie e di aggressive potenze militari.

11 Carattere tempestivamente «codificato», per esempio, nell'*Helvetiorum respublica. Diversorum autorum ...*, Lugduni Batavorum 1527, e, in particolare, da I. Simler, *La Republique des Suisses*, Anversa 1579, 158 ss. Il «mito» potrà invece diventare, nel XIX secolo, oggetto della preconcetta ironia di Arthur de Gobineau: «La vanità degli Svizzeri è una caratteristica di tutti i piccoli popoli, inesorabile e senza confini; l'idea di giocare un ruolo grandioso sulla scena politica europea blandisce oltremodo la loro intorpidita immaginazione e l'ebbrezza è così forte (119) da fargli ammettere con fierezza l'idea di far paura all'Europa dando asilo ai suoi nemici. Gli Svizzeri si reputano nel giusto, preparano i loro cannoni, tengono in esercizio le loro milizie e vantano l'abilità senza rivali del generale Dufour. Infine, di fronte alle rimostranze straniere, ecco un diluvio di rodomontate» (M. Degros, a cura di, *Correspondance d'Alexis de Tocqueville et d'Arthur de Gobineau*, introduzione di J.-J. Chevallier, Paris 1959, t. IX delle *Œuvres complètes*, 118–119). Sull'immagine mitizzata del contadino svizzero e sulla sua ideologia politica conservatrice, vedi M. Weishaupt, *Bauern, Hirten und «frume edle puren». Bauern und Bauernstaatsideologie in der spätmittelalterlichen Eidgenossenschaft und der nationalen Geschichtsschreibung der Schweiz*, Basel 1992. Sull'immagine romantica, patriottica del montanaro svizzero – nell'esaltazione della natura forte e selvaggia delle Alpi – si ricorderanno anche alcune belle pagine di F. Chabod, *L'idea di nazione*, Bari 1993, 6ª ed., 26 ss.

12 Oltre al fondamentale lavoro di Edgar Bonjour (*Geschichte der schweizerischen Neutralität*, Basel 1965–1970, 6 voll.), vedi F. W. Dame, *Continuity and change in Swiss neutrality from 1815 to 1980: an analysis*, Saarbrücken 1981.

13 Tocqueville direbbe «grazie» «alle gelosie dei suoi vicini» (A. De Tocqueville, *La democrazia in America*, Milano 1992, lib. I, cap. VIII, 154).

Non deve quindi stupire l'atteggiamento che accomuna molti osservatori: è la meraviglia per il senso di indipendenza, di autonomia, di libertà; è l'ammirazione (da Machiavelli a Montesquieu, da Voltaire a Tocqueville) per la saggezza e la natura moderata della comunità svizzera. L'essere *Willensnation, mixtum compositum,*[14] sapiente combinazione e sintesi compromissoria[15] di antichi pluralismi e di un più recente senso comune di appartenenza, rappresenta la costante forse più significativa e ricca di spunti per una riflessione sul tessuto connettivo delle istituzioni e della società. Il patriottismo costituzionale (d'impianto ottocentesco), attraverso la condivisione consapevole di valori e di tradizioni, ha generato un nucleo di identificazione nazionale.[16] «Osservando più da vicino questo piccolo stato, mi accorgo che non mi trovo davanti ad una realtà omogenea, ma davanti ad un insieme di piccole aree differenti, per clima e territorio, ma specialmente per lingua e cultura. Ciò che tiene uniti gli abitanti è solamente la loro volontà di formare un'unica nazione. Devo ammettere che questo fatto mi ha sempre colpita: come far stare sotto un unico cappello tutte queste idee diverse? Penso che sia stata adottata l'unica soluzione possibile: formare una Confederazione di cantoni che pur conservando in parte ancora la propria autorità, si rifanno ad un centro comune.»[17]

Questa soluzione, tuttavia, deve essere separata dall'immagine idilliaca che tende a coprire, dietro una facciata mistificante, il *mito* svizzero.[18] Anche la storia della democrazia elvetica non è priva di contrasti e di antagonismi (che proprio le Costituzioni hanno cercato di comporre e di eliminare). Essi non sono (come in ogni sistema democratico) transitori ed eccentrici. Anzi, il regime costituzionale svizzero si basa sulla vitale, incessante, dialettica fra poteri, istituzioni e popolo.

14 Cfr. P. Saladin, *Zur Einleitung. Die Schweizerische Eidgenossenschaft am Anfang ihres achten Jahrhunderts*, in *Zeitschrift für Schweizerisches Recht*, 110, 1991, n. 1, 5. La rappresentazione del *Corpus Helveticum* come «Repubblica mista» è risalente: vedi I. Simler, *La Republique des Suisses*, cit., 157.

15 Sulla valenza costituzionale della nozione di *compromesso* – principio inscritto nelle istituzioni e condizione di esistenza del sistema politico svizzero, indispensabile per integrare le radicatissime identità linguistiche, confessionali, culturali in un'unica comunità nazionale, riducendo i punti di attrito e di conflitto –, vedi A. Auer, *Problèmes fondamentaux de la démocratie suisse*, in *Zeitschrift für Schweizerisches Recht*, 103, 1984, n. 2, 94.

16 D. Sternberger, *Verfassungspatriotismus*, Frankfurt am Main 1990; J. Habermas, *Cittadinanza e identità nazionale*, in *MicroMega*, 5, 1991, 132.

17 B. Luscieti, *Il nostro paese non è altro che un fazzoletto di terra nel cuore dell'Europa*, in J. Gemperle (a cura di), *Der Bund der Eid-Genossen. Modell oder Denkmal? Beiträge zur Zukunft der 700jährigen Eidgenossenschaft*, Luzern 1990, 169.

18 Cfr. le interessanti osservazioni di P. Caroni, *Il mito svelato: Eugen Huber*, in *Zeitschrift für Schweizerisches Recht*, 110, 1991, n. 1, 385.

Senza dubbio la Svizzera federale, fondata su una grande varietà di istituzioni democratiche, offre l'esempio di una nazione nata dallo spirito di libera convivenza fra popoli. Gli eventi degli ultimi anni – il crescente processo di integrazione europea, la fine della Guerra fredda fra le due superpotenze, la disintegrazione della Jugoslavia – propongono alla coscienza della Confederazione elvetica nuovi interrogativi e insinuanti inquietudini. Friedrich Dürrenmatt ha affermato – rispondendo ad una domanda («Basler Zeitung», n. 162, 14 luglio 1990, p. 3) sul possibile scenario prossimo venturo –: «Le ragioni che hanno determinato la fondazione della Svizzera sono venute meno. La Svizzera non è più minacciata». L'alleanza sancita dal patto-giuramento è destinata a sciogliersi e a invertire il cammino della storia svizzera? La risposta provocatoria dello scrittore elvetico non manca, certo, di far riflettere.

1. Le antiche istituzioni e il momento francese

Non è affatto semplice dover riassumere i tratti essenziali della storia costituzionale svizzera. Non è difficile, tuttavia, indicare nel secolo XIX il periodo più fecondo e significativo del costituzionalismo svizzero: nei dibattiti e nelle concrete realizzazioni. L'Ottocento è il secolo di fondazione delle basi costituzionali della Svizzera contemporanea, dagli interventi compiuti nell'età della dominazione francese alla Costituzione del 1874 che, malgrado le tante revisioni subite, è ancora l'attuale carta fondamentale.

Detto questo, è però bene ricordare che il federalismo svizzero non ha mai reciso le radici profonde che – attraverso il patto di alleanza – conducono all'età medievale. L'*Eidgenossenschaft* fra i tre cantoni già evidenzia taluni elementi del futuro regime politico svizzero: l'affermazione dell'indipendenza, il riconoscimento dell'individualità dei cantoni, la promessa di un soccorso vicendevole e la reciproca garanzia dell'esistenza di ciascuna comunità. La struttura confederale si è sviluppata nei secoli tenendo insieme un numero crescente di entità politiche. Tale organizzazione si basava su un sistema flessibile, a «geometria variabile»: i cantoni hanno aderito in momenti successivi e dando vita a rapporti differenziati. Il cosiddetto «Corpo delle Leghe elvetiche» era formato dall'insieme dei tredici cantoni sovrani aderenti (*Corps Helvétique*), dagli alleati-satelliti (*Verbündete, Zugewandte*), dai paesi soggetti (cioè i territori conquistati e dominio di uno o più cantoni: *gemeine Herrschaften, Vogteien*). Al vertice di questa *Confederazione di Stati*, intrico di complessi legami giuridici, non c'era un'autonoma autorità centrale, ma una semplice Dieta (*Tagsatzung*) formata dai delegati-ambasciatori dei cantoni, chiamati a deliberare in riunioni temporanee.

L'origine del *Corps Hélvetique* fa vedere il grande ruolo svolto dai cantoni nel disegnare le strutture portanti dell'edificio costituzionale. Non si dovrebbe dimenticare che l'origine storica e sociale della Federazione attuale è comunque il cantone. Qui ci si rivela uno dei nodi più problematici della storia svizzera: la dialettica sempre viva fra il desiderio di preservare le particolarità di ciascuna delle sue componenti (*Heimat*) e la ricerca di efficacia politico-istituzionale garantita – almeno in una certa fase storica – dal progetto di unificazione (*Nation*). L'equilibrio tra questi due poli, entrambi essenziali, non è stato trovato se non in virtù di compromessi sempre rinnovati.

La *république fédérative* – osserva Montesquieu[19] riferendosi anche all'esperienza svizzera – composta da piccole repubbliche gode, all'interno, della moderazione di ciascun governo e all'esterno, grazie alla forza dell'alleanza, di tutti i vantaggi delle grandi monarchie.[20]

Ma sul finire del XVIII secolo la debolezza della Confederazione risiede nella sua stessa struttura, ovvero in un'organizzazione politica formata da cantoni sovrani (con forme di governo di natura democratica, *Landsgemeinde*, o oligarchica)[21] e da un governo centrale pressoché inesistente e quindi incapace anche di far rispettare le comuni deliberazioni. La Confederazione appariva debole e divisa (dal XVI secolo la Riforma religiosa – è bene ricordarlo – aveva accentuato

19 Ch.-L. de Secondat de Montesquieu, *Lo spirito delle leggi*, Milano 1989, lib. IX, capitoli I–II–III. «É [la repubblica federativa] una società di società che ne formano una nuova, la quale si può ingrandire con altri associati» (cap. I, 283). Il giudizio di Montesquieu è in parte ripreso da Tocqueville (*La Democrazia in America*, cit., lib. I, cap. VIII, p. 160). Cfr. T. Fröschl, *Federal structures, single-chamber systems, and bicameralism in the eighteenth century: the Unites States of America, the Holy Roman Empire, the Helvetic Confederation, and the United Provinces of the Netherlands in comparative perspective*, in H.W. Blom, W.P. Blockmans, H. de Schepper (a cura di), *Bicameralisme. Tweekamerstelsel vroeger en nu*, 's-Gravenhage 1992, 87–99.

20 Meno positivo è il giudizio di Hamilton e di Madison: «Qualunque possa essere stata l'efficienza dell'Unione svizzera nei casi di ordinaria amministrazione, quando sono comparse delle questioni tali da mettere a dura prova la sua forza, essa non è stata all'altezza del compito» (A. Hamilton, J. Jay, J. Madison, *Commento alla Costituzione degli Stati Uniti, Il Federalista*, Pisa 1955, n. 19, 124).

21 A. De Tocqueville, *Voyage en Suisse. 1836*, in *Angleterre, Irlande, Suisse et Algérie*, edizione del testo a cura di J.-P. Mayer e A. Jardin, in *Œuvres complètes*, sotto la direzione di J.-P. Mayer, tomo V, 2, Paris 1958, 173–174, Berna, 15 agosto 1836, *Remarques sur l'histoire suisse. Division des cantons entre eux, impossibilité de les réunir*, sottolinea come i cantoni abbiano voluto conservare la loro fisionomia individuale: «Nei primi secoli la Confederazione annoverava Stati composti da piccoli villaggi e Stati governati da grandi città; Stati in cui regnava una semplicità di costumi prossima alla grossolanità e all'ignoranza e Stati fra i più civilizzati e illuminati d'Europa; Stati dediti al commercio più che alle attività guerresche, e Stati essenzialmente guerrieri e per nulla mercantili; Stati dove la democrazia era, per così dire, senza limiti, e altri dove l'aristocrazia conservava un grande potere».

le ragioni di divisione), chiusa in un conservatorismo corporativo ormai sterile, e, per altri versi, potenzialmente sensibile alle idee di progresso sociale e di eguaglianza civile diffuse allora, «a mano armata»,[22] dai francesi. E l'invasione dei transalpini non avrebbe potuto essere più traumatica sul piano costituzionale.

La Costituzione elvetica del 12 aprile 1798 (esemplata sulla Costituzione francese dell'anno III) sancisce il passaggio da una Confederazione di Stati – mal coordinati da una Dieta – ad una Repubblica una e indivisibile. I cantoni diventano poco più che circoscrizioni amministrative. L'esercizio del potere legislativo è diviso fra il Senato (quattro rappresentanti per ciascun cantone) e il Gran Consiglio (formato da un numero di deputati proporzionale all'entità della popolazione). I deputati sono eletti a suffragio universale e col metodo del doppio turno. Il potere esecutivo è affidato a un Direttorio di cinque membri. Il governo è rappresentato dai prefetti nei cantoni e dai sottoprefetti nei distretti.

Questo tentativo di introdurre un sistema di accentramento politico-istituzionale ebbe scarso successo, anche perché non rifletteva le reali volontà degli Svizzeri e si inseriva nel contesto di una politica di conquista che era sempre più arduo nascondere dietro i grandi messaggi della Rivoluzione. Si comprendono allora la grande instabilità politica e il carattere permanente del dibattito costituzionale. I due progetti della Malmaison (elaborati, appunto, in uno dei castelli di Napoleone) segnano, pur senza particolare chiarezza, l'inizio di un *revirement* e cercano di meglio armonizzare le competenze federali e cantonali. La Costituzione del 2 luglio 1802 (la prima ad essere votata, con referendum, dal popolo) distingue le competenze dello Stato centrale e dei cantoni. Il bilancio di questi anni, tuttavia, non è solo negativo. La Svizzera non è più un singolare insieme di entità politiche differenziate: gli alleati e i paesi soggetti acquistano, con l'affermazione del principio di uguaglianza, il pieno *status* cantonale. Il dibattito fra centralisti e federalisti è anche l'occasione per il radicamento di una più matura cultura politico-costituzionale (principio della separazione dei poteri). Lo sguardo è rivolto verso meno consueti modelli culturali (è il caso, per esempio, del bicameralismo americano); si afferma l'idea del governo collegiale (modulo direttoriale);[23] emerge il meccanismo fondamentale del voto referendario.[24]

22 A. De Tocqueville, *Relazione sull'opera di A.E. Cherbuliez intitolata: «La democrazia in Svizzera»*, in N. Matteucci (a cura di), *Scritti politici*, Torino 1988, vol. I, 254.

23 T. Fleiner-Gerster, *Le Conseil fédéral: Directoire de la Confédération*, in *Pouvoirs*, 43, 1987, 49–63.

24 «La Svizzera, diciamolo pure, non è la patria né del referendum obbligatorio né del referendum facoltativo. Ma è in Svizzera che questi istituti sono stati

Nel breve spazio di cinque anni la Repubblica Elvetica, che avrebbe dovuto essere una e indivisibile, ritrova il più famigliare lessico confederale. Nel 1802 Bonaparte rimprovera gli irrequieti cittadini svizzeri, divisi in fazioni (centralisti / federalisti); si presenta loro come l'*arbitro* che pacificherà il paese. «Sarò il mediatore delle vostre controversie» scrive nella lettera (30 settembre) con cui convoca a Parigi le autorità politiche dei cantoni. Questo *Mediatore* – come è stato osservato – ha più i tratti dell'istitutore. Gli svizzeri sono come scolari da far rigar diritto.[25] Ma a parte questo, quel che interessa è il nuovo atteggiamento napoleonico. «La natura ha fatto il vostro Stato federalista. Voler ignorare questa realtà non sarebbe cosa da uomo saggio. Per paesi diversi, diversi governi». L'universalismo rivoluzionario cede il passo al *Sonderfall*. È un modo, questo, per far rifiorire non pochi elementi della tradizione costituzionale di antico regime e assegnare alla risorgente Confederazione lo scomodo ruolo di protettorato francese e di paese semi-neutrale. L'*Atto di Mediazione* è un singolare documento costituzionale. Al testo delle diciannove costituzioni dei singoli cantoni fa seguire un ventesimo capitolo intitolato *Atto federale* che descrive l'organizzazione centrale. I cantoni, così come la Confederazione, non possono modificare i rispettivi regimi senza il consenso del Mediatore. Fra gli organi ritroviamo la Dieta, il Landamano (una sorta di fiduciario dell'imperatore: è il borgomastro del *Vorort*, cioè il cantone che di anno in anno ha la guida della Confederazione) e altri tratti della «costituzione» prerivoluzionaria. L'assetto costituzionale del primo decennio dell'Ottocento palesa un legame «federativo» più stretto rispetto al passato (a prima cioè del 1798), ma nondimeno la Repubblica Elvetica rimane una Confederazione di Stati. Questi affidano, sulla base di un contratto politico, alcuni poteri – intangibili senza il consenso di tutti i contraenti (i cantoni) – a organi comuni.

L'uguaglianza fra i cantoni diventa una solida base del costituzionalismo svizzero. Nel 1813 si torna a discutere di revisione della Carta fondamentale. La Dieta prende il nome di *Assemblea federale*.

2. La "Restaurazione" e il Patto federale del 1815

Anche la Svizzera ha di fronte a sè il dilemma che turba quasi tutti i governi europei: si deve ritornare al passato o intraprendere un'azione di cauto rinnovamento? I progetti si susseguono (1814) e solo dopo una *Lunga Dieta* si giunge all'approvazione del *Patto Federale* (7 agosto 1815).

consacrati in modo più fedele e coerente, e ciò a tutti i livelli dell'organizzazione statale» (A. Auer, *L'esperienza del referendum in Svizzera e negli Stati Uniti*, in *Quaderni costituzionali*, 3, 1990, 473).

25 J.-F. Aubert, *Traité de droit constitutionnel suisse*, Paris 1967, t. I, 10.

Il Congresso di Vienna sancisce la neutralità perpetua della Svizzera. Questa nazione, naturale barriera tra alcune delle maggiori potenze continentali, non deve essere, in fondo, né troppo debole né troppo forte. Il *Patto* (*Bundesvertrag*) ha anche la funzione di conservare un duraturo equilibrio. La nuova Confederazione assomiglia molto alla vecchia. Per alcuni aspetti, il vincolo confederale appare ancora più debole di quanto non fosse nell'*Atto di Mediazione*. Il preambolo (§ 1) e la norma di chiusura (§ 15) consacrano un «contratto» fra i ventidue Stati sovrani (i cantoni), per difendere la libertà e l'indipendenza contro ogni attacco esterno ed assicurare la tranquillità all'interno, nella reciproca garanzia delle singole costituzioni. Il *Patto* viene siglato dai deputati e dai consiglieri di legazione degli Stati confederati. L'alleanza ha, innanzitutto, natura militare, secondo la più radicata tradizione del patto-giuramento. Tale carattere convenzionale (fra Stati) è accentuato dalla previsione di una procedura di *arbitrage* che dovrebbe esaminare – entro una sorta di *spazio neutrale*: il diritto confederale – le pretese e le contestazioni insorte fra i cantoni su materie non comprese dal Patto federale (§ 5). Il paragrafo VII riveste una qualche valenza «federale» poichè codifica il principio di uguaglianza dei cantoni e stabilisce che il godimento dei diritti politici non può essere un privilegio esclusivo di una classe di cittadini.

Il potere esecutivo federale risulta indebolito. Venuta meno l'ambigua figura del Landamano, è la Dieta che dovrebbe dirigere gli «affari generali» della Confederazione. La Dieta è composta dai rappresentanti dei ventidue cantoni (§ 8). I deputati votano con mandato imperativo, cioè secondo le istruzioni recevute dai rispettivi governi. La Dieta è presieduta dal borgomastro del cantone-direttore (*Vororte*: tali cantoni-guida sono Lucerna, Berna, Zurigo). Per gli affari di Stato (guerra, pace e alleanze con potenze straniere) occorre la maggioranza dei tre quarti dei voti. Ai cantoni è restituita la libertà di concludere alleanze fra di loro, purchè non pregiudizievoli al Patto federale (§ 6), e con i governi stranieri, per le capitolazioni militari e su materie economiche e di polizia, purchè tali convenzioni non contrastino col Patto federale e coi diritti costituzionali degl'altri cantoni (§§ 6 e 8). Il cantone-direttore può ricevere, in circostanze straordinarie (§ 9), poteri speciali e qualora la Dieta non sia riunita può dirigere gli affari generali con le stesse attribuzioni esercitate anteriormente al 1798 (§ 10).

La struttura costituzionale del 1815 riposa su un legame confederale che non intacca, se non in misura ridotta, la sovranità originaria dei cantoni. Il Patto istituisce un vincolo comune che «tiene insieme» i cantoni nella misura meno impegnativa. Ma si comprende poco della Svizzera di quegli anni se non si getta almeno uno sguardo sulle costituzioni cantonali. Il *leitmotiv* è il ritorno alla politica conservatrice: sistemi elettorali censitari e / o capacitari a più turni, un diritto di voto riservato ai soli cittadini, garanzie deboli dei diritti individuali e delle libertà. Anche nei cantoni dove vige un regime di più ampia rappresentatività è un numero ristretto di famiglie a monopolizzare il governo. La restaurazione di privilegi a favore del patriziato, delle borghesie o del culto religioso prevalente segna il periodo storico inaugurato dal Patto del 1815.[26]

Alexis de Tocqueville giudica il Patto troppo «vago», basato su una concezione «medievale» della divisione dei poteri. Il viaggiatore francese rovescia un giudizio comune: la Dieta non è debole perché ha esigue attribuzioni ma, al contrario, perché ne ha – in teoria – addirittura troppe. «Gli Svizzeri hanno dato al loro governo federale il *mezzo* per eseguire tutto ciò che essi gli hanno dato il *diritto* di fare?».[27] La risposta è negativa. La confusione dei poteri determina non pochi inconvenienti. Il potere legislativo dipende dal meccanismo del mandato imperativo. Ciò fa sì che la Svizzera abbia non una Dieta soltanto ma ben ventiquattro (quanti sono i cantoni e i semi-cantoni). Il potere esecutivo confederale sconta molte contraddizioni: la Dieta può essere dispotica nelle situazioni di emergenza e, al contempo, incapace di portare a termine i più ordinari affari amministrativi; il potere esecutivo è troppo instabile; il potere federale non possiede una vera autonomia ma si identifica, di volta in volta, col potere esecutivo cantonale (di uno dei tre cantoni guida). Ma la causa principale della debolezza del governo confederale risiede nel fatto che esso non ha il diritto di eseguire ciò che ha il diritto di ordinare. La dipendenza dai cantoni è pressoché assoluta. Se i singoli Stati si rifiutano di obbedire ecco aprirsi la prospettiva della guerra civile, se invece oppongono una resistenza passiva (come succede il più delle volte) il governo centrale non sa più che fare e cade nell'inerzia.

Le osservazioni (1836) di Tocqueville[28] aiutano a comprendere le cause dell'evanescenza del governo confederale lungo gli anni della Restaurazione. Non ci si deve dimenticare però del baricentro della storia costituzionale svizzera, ovvero delle dinamiche cantonali. Nella seconda metà degl'anni Venti[29] – nonostante il

26 «La verità è che gli Svizzeri, come gli altri popoli del continente, vennero trascinati da questa reazione passeggera ma generale, che ravvivò all'improvviso in tutta Europa la vecchia società; e, dato che la restaurazione presso di loro venne compiuta non da dei principi, il cui interesse, dopo tutto, era distinto da quello degli antichi privilegi, ma dagli antichi privilegi stessi, essa fu più completa, più cieca e più ostinata che nel resto d'Europa. Non fu tirannica, bensì esclusivista» (A. de Tocqueville, *Relazione sull'opera*, cit., 255).

27 A. de Tocqueville, *Voyage en Suisse. 1836*, cit., 178.

28 Tocqueville riprenderà queste osservazioni nella *Relazione*, cit. (1847), su *De la démocratie en Suisse* di Cherbuliez.

29 La storiografia tende a suddividere la storia svizzera del primo Ottocento in due fasi distinte: la Restaurazione (1815–30) e la Rigenerazione (1830–48) (ma c'è

controllo (sulla stampa, sulla libertà di opinione, sulle società segrete, sui rifugiati politici) esercitato dalla Santa alleanza nei cantoni svizzeri – si notano i primi segni di un risveglio della coscienza liberale. Acquista forza il movimento che si batte per la revisione, in senso democratico, delle costituzioni cantonali. Le prime riforme le scorgiamo nei cantoni di Appenzello, Lucerna, Vaud, Ticino, fra il 1829 e il 1830. La cultura liberale si irradia in una buona parte della Svizzera. È una cultura che ha forti radici autoctone ma sa recepire – anche attraverso l'apporto dei rifugiati politici – stimoli esterni. È un liberalismo variegato. Alla tradizione delle antiche libertà politiche e al mito romantico dell'indipendenza nazionale si affiancano le dottrine del costituzionalismo liberale (si pensi al celebre circolo di Coppet, nel castello di Madame de Staël, frequentato da Constant, da Victor de Bonstetten, da Sismondi ...) che divulgano il principio della separazione dei poteri, il regime del parlamentarismo rappresentativo, il pieno riconoscimento dei diritti e delle libertà fondamentali dell'individuo. L'impetuosa rivoluzione industriale, infine, inizia a trasformare l'economia e la società di alcuni cantoni e si collega strettamente alla pratica del libero scambio, nonostante la politica protezionistica adottata da quasi tutte le nazioni vicine.

3. La Rigenerazione e il "Patto Rossi"

La sovranità popolare è invocata, soprattutto dai radicali, quale titolo fondante la legittimità costituzionale. La volontà di tutti i cittadini – senza distinzioni di ceto, di confessione religiosa, di domicilio – deve diventare la base della democrazia svizzera. L'apprendistato politico e il patriottismo del cittadino svizzero si rinvigoriscono grazie anche al diffuso associazionismo,[30] dalla Società elvetica[31] alle feste nazionali di tiro (il cd. «Tiro federale»).

Su questi fondamenti ideologici, in un compromesso fra proposte radicali e un più moderato liberalismo, riposano le dodici costituzioni cantonali revisionate dopo il 1830. Ma la *Rigenerazione* non investe soltanto i singoli cantoni. Già sul finire degli anni Venti il problema cantonale si intreccia con la richiesta di

chi, ad esempio, fa iniziare questa seconda fase nel 1798). Lo schema – come ogni altro tentativo di sintesi e di semplificazione – può essere utile strumento di lavoro, salvo poi considerare la maggiore complessità del dato reale.

30 Tocqueville tende a sottovalutare la forza e il significato politico dell'associazionismo elvetico. Cfr. *Voyage en Suisse. 1836*, cit., 176.

31 Sulla Società Elvetica, v. O. Zinniker, *Der Geist der helvetischen Gesellschaft des 19. Jahrhunderts besonders zwischen 1807 und 1849. Ein Beitrag zur Geschichte des Liberalismus in der Schweiz*, Biel 1932; U. Im Hof, F. De Capitani, *Die Helvetische Gesellschaft. Spätaufklärung und Vorrevolution in der Schweiz*, Frauenfeld, Stuttgart 1983.

riforma del Patto. Un coro a più voci si leva per affermare – soprattutto dopo i mutamenti istituzionali del 1830–31 – che il Patto del 1815 non rappresenta più la situazione reale. Già nel 1830 circola un progetto[32] che auspica un rafforzamento del potere federale: si ispira al modello presidenziale americano per raggiungere un più efficace equilibrio fra la sovranità cantonale e l'azione del governo federale. Il liberale Kasimir Pfyffer (del patriziato di Lucerna) propone[33] nel 1831 di rivedere il Patto: disegna un *Bundesstaat* munito di più incisivi poteri federali. L'uguaglianza dei diritti, la libertà di stabilimento, l'istituzione di una Camera rappresentativa sono gli ulteriori capisaldi della riforma da realizzare.

Il «Journal de Genève» (15 settembre 1831) sottolinea il nesso sempre più stretto che deve esistere fra la prosperità e l'indipendenza e la necessità di rafforzare il vincolo confederale. Per allontanare dal paese le tempeste europee «occorre, così come rapidamente si è fatto nelle riforme politiche di alcuni cantoni, creare, per la Svizzera, un centro di deliberazione e di azione che esprima le vere opinioni popolari, che dia alla federazione la coscienza di ciò che essa è realmente [...]. Bisogna creare per questo un centro regolare di azione e non aspettare il momento dell'attacco per dar vita a un sistema di finanze e di amministrazione».[34]

Le rivoluzioni costituzionali spezzano antichi equilibri. In alcuni cantoni, la lotta fra Città e Campagna mostra i bagliori della guerra civile (Basilea, Svitto, Neuchâtel). Nel 1831 la questione della riforma del Patto fa il suo ingresso nella Dieta. Alcuni deputati reclamano la libertà di stabilimento e di commercio su tutto il territorio confederale, maggiori competenze per la Dieta e i suoi deputati, la garanzia federale da accordarsi alle costituzioni cantonali. La domanda di revisione, pur contrastata da alcuni cantoni (Uri, Svitto, Unterwaldo, Appenzello e Vallese), ottiene 9 voti.

In una lettera (8 marzo 1832) ad Alphonse Nicole Du Pan, primo deputato del Vaud, Pellegrino Rossi paventa due pericoli: l'ulteriore indebolimento del legame federale, la reazione dei partiti retrogradi. Rossi indica quattro «tipi» di atteggiamento politico: ci sono gli scontenti o retrogradi, gli «immobilisti», gli unitari e, infine, i progressisti che lottano per la revisione del Patto. Gli unitari

32 W. Rappard, *Un projet volontairement oublié de réforme du Pacte de 1815 (1830)*, in *Revue d'histoire suisse*, 21, 1941, 229–249.

33 Soprattutto in *Zuruf an den eidgenössischen Vorort Luzern bei Übernahme der Leitung der Bundesangelegenheiten*, Zürich 1831, e in *Über die Folgen der neuesten Staatsreform in der Schweiz*, Zürich 1831. Sempre del 1831 sono le *Observations sur les changements demandés au Pacte fédéral helvétique*, Genève, opera del deputato liberale ginevrino Fazy-Pasteur.

34 Cfr. H. Wild, *Das Ringen um den Bundesstaat. Zentralismus und Föderalismus in der schweizerischen Publizistik von der Helvetik bis zur Bundesrevision*, Zürich 1966, 95–96.

sembrano a Rossi i più pericolosi. L'esule italiano[35] considera la prospettiva unitaria e la Svizzera realtà incompatibili. «La Svizzera, dacchè c'è stata una Svizzera, fu uno Stato federativo e sin tanto che esisterà una Svizzera essa non potrà essere un'altra cosa».[36]

Nel 1832 i cantoni rigenerati hanno bisogno, con urgenza, di vedere garantite le loro nuove costituzioni. Il 17 marzo i cantoni di Zurigo, Berna, Lucerna, Soletta, San Gallo, Argovia e Turgovia concludono, a tale effetto, il cd. concordato dei Sette. La reazione dei cantoni d'Uri, Svitto, Unterwaldo, Vallese e Neuchâtel non si fa attendere. Nel giugno si dichiarano contro il concordato dei Sette e

35 Pellegrino Luigi Odoardo Rossi (Carrara 1787 – Roma 1848) visse in Svizzera per più di un quindicennio sino a diventarne uno dei protagonisti della vita politica e culturale. A Ginevra trovò asilo e soccorso: la sua brillante carriera di avvocato e di professore bolognese si era interrotta nel 1815 allorchè, Commissario Civile (Dipartimento del Reno, Rubicone, Basso Po e Pineta) nella sfortunata impresa murattiana, era stato costretto all'esilio per fuggire i rigori della persecuzione austriaca. A Ginevra (che conosceva e aveva frequentato sin dal 1813) Rossi iniziò a vivere una «seconda vita». Nella città di Calvino il giovane Rossi si fece ben presto apprezzare per la raffinata intelligenza, per la brillantezza di spirito, per la profonda cultura. Accompagnato dalla fama di «rivoluzionario» – in una città più incline a umori conservatori – seppe invece dimostrare moderazione ed equilibrio. Intellettuale liberale, fu accolto nei salotti più vivaci: annoverò amici ed estimatori in uomini di vaglia, da Sismondi a Bonstetten, da Pictet de Rochement a Bellot, da Dumont a Rigaud, da Prevost a de la Rive. L'ascesa di Rossi fu, insomma, irresistibile: primo cattolico ad insegnare (1819) – per un vasto e appassionato uditorio – nell'Accademia della città (dapprima diritto romano e diritto criminale, poi diritto costituzionale, diritto internazionale, economia politica, storia nazionale svizzera), ricevé nel 1820 la cittadinanza, prese in moglie una ginevrina, venne eletto nel Consiglio rappresentativo dove fece risuonare per più di un decennio la sua voce sempre più influente e ascoltata. Le straordinarie qualità oratorie e dialettiche, l'acume e la chiarezza di ogni intervento fecero di Rossi uno dei *leader* del Consiglio. «Non appena domandava la parola, tutti si facevano attenti, le conversazioni cessavano ...» (A. E. Cherbuliez, *Pellegrino Rossi*, in *Bibliothèque universelle de Genève*, 10 (1849), 143). L'eclettismo culturale di Rossi convergeva, attorno al 1830, verso l'analisi politica delle questioni costituzionali e federali. Nel 1831 tenne un corso di storia svizzera e fu il fondatore del giornale politico *Le Fédéral* (qui l'assonanza con il *Federalist* americano è evidente), importante tribuna moderata nel dibattito sul federalismo svizzero. Non è certo un caso, quindi, se Rossi fu designato prima tra i rappresentanti ginevrini alla Dieta (1832), poi membro della Commissione di revisione del Patto del 1815, infine *rapporteur* del progetto e ambasciatore in Francia (1833) per diffondere e difendere la causa del federalismo liberale svizzero.

36 G. Dolt, *Lettres politiques de Pellegrino Rossi au syndic Jean-Jacques Rigaud, 1832–1841 (Avec une préface de M. le Professeur Charles Borgeaud)*, Genève 1932, 20–21.

minacciano di dar vita ad un'alleanza qualora l'accordo, contrario al Patto federale (sostengono loro), non venga sciolto.

Il tema della revisione è ormai al primo posto nell'agenda politica svizzera. La Dieta ordinaria (formata da tredici cantoni) nomina il 17 luglio una *Commission de revision du Projet de Pacte*. Il clima politico è incandescente: il cantone di Basilea è scosso dalla guerra civile fra Città e Campagna; nel novembre i cantoni dissidenti danno seguito alla minaccia: la Lega di Sarnen (così chiamata dall'Assemblea riunita nella capitale di Obwaldo, semicantone di Unterwaldo) istituisce una Dieta separata e si impegna a non riconoscere gli scissionisti di Basilea Campagna e di Svitto Esterno. La Svizzera è divisa in due, da una parte – in buona sostanza – i cantoni liberali e radicali (attorno al Concordato dei Sette), dall'altra gli Stati cattolici e più conservatori: il paese è sull'orlo di una guerra civile, le potenze straniere sono pronte ad intervenire.

Dal luglio al dicembre 1832 la Commissione nominata per riformare il Patto lavora alacremente nella città di Lucerna. Alcune lettere di Pellegrino Rossi[37] a Jean-Jacques Rigaud (esponente di spicco del liberalismo ginevrino) descrivono con rara efficacia i lavori della Commissione, le diverse posizioni politiche e lo stato d'animo dei quindici componenti. Tra i rappresentanti dei cantoni che partecipano all'opera di revisione scorgiamo alcuni dei nomi che hanno lasciato un'impronta duratura sulla scena politica svizzera. Si pensi, per esempio, a Edouard Pfyrrer (fratello del citato Kasimir), primo magistrato del cantone di Lucerna e presidente della Commissione, a Joseph Munzinger, membro del consiglio esecutivo di Soletta, a Gallus-Jacob Baumgartner, rappresentante del Piccolo Consiglio di San Gallo, ai professori Charles Monnard del Vaud e Pellegrino Rossi di Ginevra. Il progetto elaborato alla fine del 1832 deve molto al delegato Baumgartner, ma è da rimarcare certamente il contributo di Rossi (*rapporteur* del progetto) all'intero dibattito. Il progetto, a dire il vero, fu ribattezzato «Progetto Rossi» – «per discreditarlo agl'occhi dei conservatori tedeschi»[38] in quanto opera di un *welsche*, un dottrinario ginevrino – ma il riferimento costante a Rossi rende omaggio all'attività dell'esule italiano. Il progetto del 1832 nasce – come si è detto – dalla necessità di adeguare il Patto ai bisogni della Svizzera del 1832.

Rossi – nel suo *Rapport* – insiste sul carattere moderato del progetto: opera di conciliazione improntata a realismo. In alcune Confederazioni domina, come pensiero generale, l'idea di una delega limitata fatta al potere centrale dalle sovranità particolari. In altre, invece, la sovranità locale riveste un ruolo subal-

37 *Ibidem*.

38 G.J. Baumgartner, *Die Schweiz in ihren Kämpfen und Umgestaltungen von 1830 bis 1850 ...*, Zürich 1865, t. III, 368.

terno. Si deve scegliere, pur entro molte graduazioni, tra una di queste forme. La Commissione ha ritenuto che l'idea dominante in Svizzera, per tradizione politica e culturale, è quella della sovranità cantonale. Fra le opposte posizioni «il solo mezzo per arrivare ad un successo consiste nel non accontentare alcuno. La forma della proposizione è paradossale; la sostanza è una verità innegabile».[39] Il progetto è in linea con la peculiare storia svizzera; non presenta un modello astratto, teorico. Del resto, privilegiare il principio cantonale non significa affatto negare il principio nazionale. C'è un legame comune, la nazionalità svizzera: «una forza segreta, un cemento morale, che nulla può dissolvere, nè le sventure dei tempi, nè le follie degli uomini». Il dato di fondo del sistema federale svizzero è questo: coesistono il cantone e la patria comune, la sovranità cantonale e il potere centrale. «É nella sovranità cantonale che si ricerca la regola: nel potere centrale non si scorge che l'eccezione. La prima è la fonte, il secondo è il derivato».

Muovendo da tali premesse, la Commissione ha cercato di trovare il giusto equilibrio tra la salvaguardia della sovranità originaria dei cantoni e l'esigenza di rafforzare la sovranità federale. I cantoni ripetono il patto-giuramento (*Un pour tous, tous pour un*) per riconfermare le antiche tradizioni di libertà, di indipendenza, di mutuo soccorso. Essi sono sovrani e, come tali, esercitano tutti i diritti che non hanno espressamente deposto nelle mani del potere federale. La struttura della Confederazione di Stati è controbilanciata dall'aumento delle deleghe al potere centrale. La Confederazione garantisce le attribuzioni cantonali, come dire le singole Costituzioni, ma a patto che queste non contengano principî contrari all'Atto federale, assicurino l'uguaglianza dei cittadini nell'esercizio dei diritti politici, vietino l'assoggettamento di una parte del cantone ad un'altra parte dello stesso, prevedano la possibilità e i modi di revisione delle forme costituzionali (anche per prevenire le violente crisi «interne» che avevano segnato la storia più recente). È previsto, inoltre, un sistema obbligatorio di arbitrato per dirimere le controversie insorte fra i cantoni ed evitare ogni ricorso alle vie di fatto. Come si può notare, queste disposizioni fanno quasi da contrappunto regolativo a tutte quelle dinamiche politico-istituzionali che mettevano a repentaglio la vita stessa della Confederazione.

Il processo di rafforzamento del potere federale riguarda gli interessi fondamentali della comunità svizzera. Il principio della libera circolazione di tutti i

39 P. Rossi, *Rapport sur le Project d'Acte Fédéral délibéré à Lucerne le 15 décembre 1832*, in *Mélanges d'économie politique, de politique, d'histoire et de philosophie* ..., Paris 1867, t. II, 435.

cittadini svizzeri in tutti i cantoni e la libertà di stabilimento trovano così un pieno riconoscimento. Le ragioni del liberalismo orientano molte delle scelte: il mercato unico dovrebbe garantire sia lo sviluppo politico che quello economico. Le merci potranno circolare più liberamente: le dogane esterne sono di competenza federale, i pedaggi intercantonali riguardano solo i consumi. La moneta è unica; unico il sistema dei pesi e delle misure. Taluni servizi (le poste, per es.) sono gestiti in regime di monopolio. La politica internazionale (diritto di pace e di guerra, conclusione di alleanze e di trattati politici e di commercio; i cantoni possono stipulare convenzioni ma a patto che non contengano nulla di contrario all'Atto federale) e la difesa nazionale sono di competenza confederale.

Il progetto si prova poi a meglio definire i rapporti fra i poteri federali. Le autorità nazionali sono la Dieta, il Consiglio federale, la Corte federale. La Dieta rappresenta il potere supremo federale: è composta da 44 membri (due per cantone). Il problema della rappresentanza (se eguale o, invece, differenziata in base a criteri demografici ed economici) era stato molto a lungo dibattuto. La soluzione prescelta riflette gli umori compromissorî. Ben difficilmente i cantoni avrebbero acconsentito ad una soluzione che non fosse quella contrattuale. Il modello bicamerale americano (con una Camera di rappresentanti eletti in proporzione al numero dei cittadini di ciascun Stato) è respinto da Rossi sulla base di molteplici argomenti,[40] ma la questione pratica (la mancanza di un consenso cantonale) appare alla fine prevalente nella scelta di un sistema che fa dei cantoni i soli membri della Confederazione. I delegati cantonali deliberano secondo tre procedure distinte: nelle materie riguardanti i rapporti internazionali, nei casi di conflitto fra cantoni, nelle questioni di guerra o di pace seguendo le istruzioni ricevute (è confermato lo schema della delegazione diplomatica); in regime di libertà di discussione e di voto (senza istruzioni, quindi) in ordine, per esempio, ai trattati con l'estero che non hanno natura politica o alle garanzie delle Costituzioni cantonali, ma le decisioni assunte sono poi sottoposte alla ratifica dei cantoni; in tutta libertà (senza bisogno di istruzioni o di ratifica) nelle trattazioni puramente legislative (in materia di bilancio, per es.).

Il Consiglio federale è composto da quattro membri – eletti dalla Dieta – che dirigono i dipartimenti dell'Interno, degl'Esteri, della Difesa, delle Finanze e dal Landamano della Svizzera, eletto dai cantoni, nel ruolo di presidente del Consiglio. Il nuovo organo esecutivo sostituisce il sistema del *Vorort*. «La Confederazione deve avere un proprio governo, responsabile verso di essa e da essa eletto». La rotazione dei cantoni-guida non assicurava stabilità e continuità di governo: incapace di armonizzare le istanze federali con i bisogni

40 Rossi insiste su due argomenti: l'eccessiva onerosità di una rappresentanza numericamente ragguardevole; l'incompatibilità fra il bicameralismo e il sistema basato sulle istruzioni dei delegati cantonali.

del cantone. Il Consiglio, invece, sembrava garantire una gestione permanente, specifica e impegnata da una responsabilità personale ed effettiva. La Corte federale (9 membri eletti per 6 anni dalla Dieta) ha competenza sulle contese intercantonali e su alcuni delitti politici. Al potere giudiziario, reso indipendente, si affida una funzione di garanzia. L'indipendenza è assicurata anche dal fatto che la Corte non risiede (secondo il modello americano) nella capitale. Lucerna viene designata come centro politico confederale: la scelta di una città cattolica e prossima ai più restii cantoni montani ha lo scopo di ammorbidire l'opposizione di questi ultimi. L'Atto federale prevede, infine, la possibilità di revisione. La procedura rende questo obiettivo non poco difficoltoso, ma è comunque il primo abbozzo di quell'insieme di istituti destinato a caratterizzare il movimento costituzionale svizzero.

Il progetto è la base su cui costruire il «nuovo edificio». «Volete imprimere sull'alleanza federale – domanda Rossi – il sigillo nazionale, svizzero, nient'altro che svizzero?». «L'anno 1833 sarà l'anno santo, l'anno solenne e storico della Svizzera moderna». Ma la realtà è amara. L'auspicio di Rossi e degli altri commissari rimane lettera morta. Nel marzo 1833 la Dieta, riunita a Zurigo, esamina il progetto. Ma è una Dieta a ranghi ridotti, vista l'assenza dei delegati della Lega di Sarnen e di altri cantoni. I veti incrociati, malgrado i tentativi di conciliazione, hanno la meglio. Le decisioni assunte dalla Dieta, in verità, sono giuridicamente valide (sono infatti presenti sedici cantoni e mezzo); il progetto viene scrupolosamente esaminato, ulteriormente revisionato e infine approvato all'unanimità dai delegati dei cantoni aderenti. Mentre Rossi difende a Parigi la necessità della revisione costituzionale, il progetto è respinto. Occorrevano dodici voti, l'Atto federale ne ottiene undici e mezzo. Ironia della sorte: proprio i comuni rurali della capitale designata, Lucerna, rifiutano il progetto obbedendo alle indicazioni del partito clericale.

Lo spirito moderato che anima il progetto del 1832/1833 non riesce a raccogliere i consensi necessari. Ragioni contingenti e ragioni più profonde si intrecciano fra loro. I rapporti conflittuali fra i cantoni (cattolici e protestanti, ricchi e meno ricchi, grandi e piccoli, conservatori e radicali) condizionano il destino dell'Atto federale. Il progetto, benchè compromissorio, non riesce ad avere la meglio sull'intransigenza delle diverse posizioni politiche. I conservatori – ripiegati entro i loro cantoni[41] – paventano ogni rafforzamento del potere federale (e la soppressione delle disposizioni del 1815 che garantivano i conventi determina una più dura opposizione). Si teme la formazione di una costosa burocrazia

41 Cfr. N.-L. Bonaparte, *Politische und militärische Betrachtungen über die Schweiz*, Zürich 1833, 19.

federale e il declassamento dei cantoni[42] a poco più che consigli provinciali. L'istituzione di una Corte federale produrrebbe – si sostiene – effetti negativi sulla sovranità cantonale. «É un'attribuzione mostruosa, che da sola distruggerebbe la libertà, l'indipendenza, la sovranità dei cantoni!».[43] Se i federalisti moderati (Cherbuliez o Monnard,[44] per esempio) apprezzano, in generale, la «filosofia» che ispira il progetto, i radicali criticano proprio il nodo delle forme (irrisolte) della sovranità. Lo Stato federale nasce dalla sovranità popolare: i diritti esercitati direttamente dal cittadino devono trovare riconoscimento in un'assemblea nazionale che rappresenti, proporzionalmente, la popolazione.[45] «Nelle questioni federali non c'è sovranità cantonale; i cantoni e la loro sovranità sono obbligati a piegarsi dinanzi alla sovranità nazionale, costretti a sottomettervisi».[46]

Il progetto del 1832–33 – con la sua veste moderata, mediana – si colloca fra il Patto del 1815 e la successiva Costituzione del 1848. Il tentativo di rafforzare il potere federale senza prevaricare l'autonomia cantonale è avversato dagli opposti estremismi. Il *juste milieu* non è l'espressione magica che possa risolvere, in quel momento, i problemi della Svizzera. Certo è che tutte le questioni di fondo rimangono irrisolte. L'Atto federale prefigura, pur con le sue indubbie contraddizioni, alcuni dei meccanismi e delle soluzioni destinati a caratterizzare la Costituzione del 1848. «Ho l'intima convinzione che il bisogno di centralizzazione si farà presto o tardi sentir di nuovo [...]. L'Atto federale del 1832 non è che un'opera transitoria. L'immensa parte che lascia alla sovranità cantonale non è che una concessione temporanea».[47]

Cherbuliez è facile profeta. Vagheggiamenti del passato, ristrettezza di vedute, sterili intransigenze: tutto ciò mentre le questioni scottanti son lì a reclamare una ben più incisiva iniziativa politica. L'immobilismo non serve. Le pressioni esercitate sulla piccola Repubblica dalle potenze europee (a cominciare dal

42 G. M. De Seigneux, *Du principe fédératif en Suisse et de son application au projet d'acte fédéral*, Lausanne 1833, 10 ss.

43 J. Muret, *Quelques observations sur l'Acte fédéral proposé*, Lausanne 1833, 11.

44 A. E. Cherbuliez, *Essai sur les conditions de l'alliance fédérative*, Genève 1833; Ch. Monnard, *Le Pacte, la Suisse et le Canton de Vaud. Opinion émise dans le Grand-Conseil du Canton de Vaud, le 5 juillet 1833*, Lausanne 1833.

45 Cfr. P. I. V. Troxler in *Politische Schriften in Auswahl*, a cura di A. Rohr, Bern, Stuttgart 1989. Sull'influenza americana, cfr. E. His, *Amerikanische Einflüsse im Schweizer Verfassungsrecht*, in *Festgabe der Basler Juristenfakultät und des Basler Juristenvereins zum Schweizerischen Juristentag, September 1920*, Basel 1920, 81–110. Si veda anche D. Schefold, *Volksouveränität und repräsentative Demokratie in der schweizerischen Regeneration. 1830–1848*, Basel, Stuttgart 1966.

46 H. Druey, *Discours pour la Constituante féderale*, Lausanne 1835.

47 A. E. Cherbuliez, *Essai sur les conditions*, cit., 44.

pretesto dei rifugiati politici) delineano uno scenario ben poco rassicurante: ne va di mezzo l'integrità del paese. Lo sviluppo industriale sollecita interventi capaci di conformare i cantoni a una politica comune. La centralizzazione e le autonomie cantonali sono i poli di ogni dibattito costituzionale. I conflitti fra cantoni conservatori e liberal-radicali assumono una forte connotazione confessionale. Tutto ruota attorno alla lotta politica sul modello di Stato (fra *statu quo*, federalismo, centralizzazione) cui dare concreta forma istituzionale.

4. Verso il '48 e la Costituzione federale

Non è possibile, in questa sede, riassumere la fitta trama di avvenimenti, di «microstorie» cantonali fra gli anni Trenta e Quaranta dell'Ottocento. C'è un filo comune, ma dipanare la matassa richiederebbe ben altri approfondimenti. Un dato però merita di essere sottolineato: la frattura politica che aveva diviso la Confederazione fra il 1832 e il 1833 non solo non è ricomposta ma diviene sempre più profonda. Due diverse visioni – per semplificare – s'affrontano: governo oligarchico e democrazia rappresentativa, Stato confessionale e Stato laico, autonomismo cantonale e forza del numero, fiere tradizioni elvetiche e nuove prospettive di federalismo nazionale.

Al centro del dibattito troviamo – e non potrebbe essere diversamente – il problema della rappresentanza e della sovranità politica. Si dia integrale applicazione al Patto del 1815[48] o si giunga a un compromesso «all'americana» (bicameralismo) per ricercare un equilibrio fra la necessità di rappresentare tutti gli Stati (indipendentemente dalla loro «taglia») e la sempre più pressante richiesta di dar voce «federale» ai cittadini che in quegli Stati vivono: questa alternativa è ben chiara a Tocqueville. L'aristocratico francese giudica pericolosa l'instaurazione – auspicata dai più radicali – di una repubblica unitaria. I cantoni svizzeri sono troppo diversi fra loro per poter sopportare un governo centrale «forte».[49] Ma la soluzione suggerita da Tocqueville è poco persuasiva.

48 «Il patto ha voluto che il potere federale allora creato potesse essere esercitato dalla minoranza della nazione rappresentata nella dieta dalla maggioranza dei cantoni» (A. De Tocqueville, *Voyage en Suisse. 1836*, cit., 181).

49 «La costituzione svizzera ha diviso la popolazione in ventidue nazioni differenti, ma la natura e i pregiudizi avevano determinato, prima ancora di quella legge, qualcosa di analogo. La Svizzera racchiude, entro un piccolo territorio, paesi che differiscono profondamente per origine, lingua, religione, ricchezza, culture, stili di vita. La natura sembra dunque indicare che ognuna di queste popolazioni deve avere un proprio governo. Non sarebbe possibile sottomettere popoli cosi dissimili ad uno stesso governo, guidarli secondo uno stesso corpo di principî, piegarli alle stesse misure se non violentando molte volontà, creando grandi problemi e, di conseguenza, grandi resistenze» (*ibidem*, 182).

La conservazione dell'esistente (migliorato, se possibile),[50] il gradualismo (la lenta uniformazione fra cantoni) non potevano essere la via di salvezza per una nazione segnata da continui rivolgimenti.

Alla metà degl'anni Quaranta la storia svizzera è ancora storia di settarismi e di leghe. D'un lato l'alleanza dei cantoni liberali, dall'altro il *Sonderbund* (un patto segreto concluso, nel dicembre 1845, dai cantoni di Lucerna, Uri, Svitto, Obwaldo, Nidwaldo, Zugo, Friburgo, Vallese). Il *Sonderbund* viola il Patto del 1815. Nel 1847 una Dieta straordinaria è investita del problema. La strada del compromesso non pare percorribile. La maggioranza dei cantoni (dodici più due semicantoni) vota lo scioglimento dell'alleanza cattolica. Il *Sonderbund* non solo non si piega al diktàt ma decide di mettere insieme una cospicua forza militare. La risposta della Dieta è conseguente: ha inizio la cosiddetta guerra del *Sonderbund*. Guerra davvero singolare. Condotta senza spirito di vendetta e di crudeltà – da ambo le parti – rivela la perizia del generale Dufour che in poche settimane fa capitolare i separatisti. Una soluzione militare tanto repentina non consente alle potenze straniere di intervenire nel conflitto. Una nota diplomatica (26 gennaio 1848) diffida la Confederazione dall'intraprendere una revisione del Patto violando gli impegni assunti nel 1815. Le rivoluzioni del 1848 bloccano però possibili iniziative militari.

Nel febbraio 1848 una Commissione è già al lavoro per offrire alla Confederazione una nuova carta costituzionale. L'impronta radicale è evidente (basta scorrere i nomi dei commissari). Il Patto federale in vigore non prevede una procedura di revisione. È però ragionevole, trattandosi di una Confederazione di Stati, presumere una manifestazione di consenso da parte di tutti i cantoni. I costituenti sanno bene che tale consenso è una chimera. L'espediente usato per superare l'impasse è formalizzato nelle disposizioni transitorie della nuova Costituzione. I cantoni determinano le forme per pronunciarsi sul testo costituzionale. Sarà poi la Dieta (organo costituito in base alle disposizioni del Patto del 1815) a dire – come «giudice» della sua legittimità – se la nuova Costituzione federale è stata accolta. Questa è, in effetti, accettata da 15½ Cantoni contro 6½ (Uri, Svitto, Obwaldo, Nidwaldo, Zugo, Appenzello interno, Ticino e Vallese) ed in votazione popolare (con applicazione anticipata di una nuova misura costituzionale) da 169.743 voti contro 71.897. Il 12 settembre 1848 la Dieta proclama – come suo ultimo atto – l'accoglimento (scontato) della nuova Costituzione. Non restava, a questo punto, che eleggere, applicando le nuove regole, l'Assemblea federale. I parlamentari si riuniscono a Berna –

50 «... concludo affermando che ogni persona che ragiona sulla Svizzera deve argomentare così: 1º Migliorare la costituzione federale, se è possibile. 2º Altrimenti cercare di conservarla. 3º E comunque non dar vita, mai, alla repubblica unitaria» (*ibidem*, 185).

capitale federale – il 6 novembre ed eleggono i sette membri del primo Consiglio federale.[51]

La Carta fondamentale è intitolata «Costituzione federale della Confederazione Svizzera». La Svizzera è adesso uno Stato federale. Se l'uso della parola Confederazione (cioè alleanza, per via convenzionale, di Stati sovrani) è, sul piano giuridico-formale, contraddittorio, nondimeno esso si spiega con la volontà di rendere omaggio alla plurisecolare tradizione elvetica. Tale scelta appare importante anche per un'altra ragione. La Costituzione è senz'altro ispirata dai principî del radicalismo liberale, del federalismo, della democrazia rappresentativa, dell'egualitarismo, dello Stato di diritto. I modelli ideali però non sono troppo ingombranti, non producono rotture col passato. La rivoluzione si compie nel nome di un sapiente realismo: la nuova struttura costituzionale rivela profondo rispetto per lo spirito di radicata autonomia che, nelle forme più diverse, aveva caratterizzato da sempre la vita politica dei cantoni e dei comuni. Del resto, il progetto del 1832–33 – nella sua veste programmaticamente compromissoria – è sotto gli occhi dei costituenti, documento capace di suggerire talune soluzioni e, comunque, di far riflettere sulle priorità della revisione. Il federalismo ha la funzione di conciliare le tradizioni particolari con il bisogno rinnovato di unità. La «rivoluzione democratica» ha fatto prevalere nei cantoni istituzioni e massime di governo conformi. Ciò fa accrescere il loro spirito d'indipendenza ma elimina anche gran parte delle cause di resistenza e «senza dare ai governi cantonali maggior voglia di obbedire al governo federale, rende loro infinitamente più facile obbedire alla sua volontà».[52]

Il Preambolo alla Costituzione illustra la *ratio* della riforma federale. «La Confederazione svizzera, volendo consolidare l'alleanza dei Confederati, mantenere e accrescere l'unità, la forza e l'onore della nazione svizzera, ha adottato la seguente Costituzione federale».[53] L'art. 3 stabilisce uno dei principî fonda-

51 Furrer (Zurigo, presidente), Ochsenbein (Berna), Druey (Vaud), Munzinger (Soletta), Naeff (San Gallo), Frei-Hérosé (Argovia), Stefano Franscini (Ticino).

52 «La confederazione ha cambiato natura – osserva Tocqueville prima ancora del 1848 –. In Europa essa è divenuta qualcosa di nuovo; una politica di azione si è sostituita ad una di inerzia e di neutralità; da puramente municipale la sua esistenza è divenuta nazionale; un'esistenza più laboriosa, più turbata, più precaria e più grande» (*Relazione*, cit., 267–268). Queste affermazioni – a distanza di più di un decennio – modificano quanto Tocqueville aveva scritto ne *La Democrazia in America*, cit., lib. I, cap. VIII, 163: «Fra la civiltà del cantone di Vaud e quella del cantone di Uri vi è una differenza come dal secolo XIX al XV: perciò la Svizzera non ha mai avuto veramente un governo federale».

53 La necessità di dare maggiore forza al governo federale, senza inclinare alla forma della repubblica unitaria, era stata più volte sottolineata da Tocqueville. In un

mentali: «I cantoni sono sovrani sin dove la loro sovranità non è limitata dalla Costituzione federale e, come tali, esercitano tutti i diritti che non sono devoluti all'Autorità federale». Scartato il modello della repubblica unitaria, l'ambito della sovranità è ridisegnato nel senso di una accentuazione federalista. L'organizzazione dei poteri nel rispetto dell'autogoverno e della autonomia cantonale avviene entro il quadro definito delle attribuzioni enumerate a livello federale. La teoria classica dello Stato federale americano – recepita soprattutto attraverso l'opera di Tocqueville – propone all'esperienza svizzera il tema della sovranità «divisa» fra lo Stato centrale e gli Stati membri. La Confederazione garantisce ai cantoni il loro territorio, la loro sovranità nei limiti indicati dall'art. 3, le loro Costituzioni, la libertà e i diritti del popolo, i diritti costituzionali dei cittadini, così come i diritti e le attribuzioni che il popolo ha conferito alle Autorità (art. 5). I cantoni non possono concludere alleanze e trattati speciali di natura politica (art. 7). La Confederazione si riserva poteri esclusivi in materia di relazioni internazionali (salvo eccezioni) e di organizzazione militare (opportunamente centralizzata) (artt. 18–20). L'Autorità federale dispone i lavori pubblici di interesse generale e le necessarie espropriazioni dietro versamento della giusta indennità (art. 21); sovrintende alla politica doganale (art. 23 ss.), ha il monopolio sulla moneta (art. 36), sulle poste (indennizzando i cantoni) (art. 33); esercita l'alta sorveglianza sulle vie di comunicazione (art. 35). Le finanze della Confederazione sono costituite dalle entrate federali e dalle contribuzioni cantonali disposte su base proporzionale (art. 39). La Costituzione garantisce il libero diritto di stabilimento in ogni cantone (salvo i limiti indicati dall'art. 41), la piena eguaglianza fra tutti i cittadini (art. 42), il libero esercizio delle confessioni cristiane (art. 44), la libertà di stampa (art. 45).

L'autorità suprema della Confederazione è l'Assemblea federale con i suoi due Consigli, il Consiglio nazionale e il Consiglio degli Stati (art. 60). Tale soluzione può richiamare alla mente il sistema bicamerale già adottato nella Costituzione della Repubblica elvetica, ma, senza dubbio, è qui il modello americano a suggerire i principî fondamentali.[54] Il Consiglio nazionale (come la Camera dei Rappresentanti) è formato dai deputati eletti dal popolo (uno per ogni 20.000 abitanti) (art. 61). Il Consiglio degli Stati (come il Senato) riunisce i

articolo apparso su il *Commerce* (21 aprile 1845) Tocqueville faceva l'esempio della federazione americana che disponeva dei mezzi adeguati per dare seguito alle sue decisioni. «... il governo americano è forte, regolare, rispettato, mentre il governo svizzero ha un'esistenza contestata e, per così dire, nominale» (in *Ecrits et discours politiques*, a cura di A. Jardin, t. III, vol. II delle *Œuvres complètes*, Paris 1985, 469).

54 U. Marti, *Zwei Kammern, ein Parlament: Ursprung und Funktion des schweizerischen Zweikammersystems: sämtliche Nationalräte und Ständeräte seit 1848*, Frauenfeld 1990.

44 deputati dei cantoni. Con l'introduzione di tale forma di bicameralismo, i costituenti hanno voluto bilanciare la sovranità popolare con il principio di indipendenza dei cantoni, il principio del federalismo con una più accentuata centralizzazione, il principio conservatore con gli ideali radicali della democrazia diretta.

Il potere legislativo domina – in linea teorica – gli altri poteri. L'art. 74 enumera le materie di competenza dell'Assemblea federale. L'analogia con il sistema americano non deve però ingannare. Le differenze, infatti, sono numerose e significative. A cominciare dalla diversa origine delle due federazioni, dal ruolo del popolo nella democrazia svizzera, dalla specializzazione delle due Camere negli Stati Uniti, dal differente peso costituzionale dei rispettivi presidenti (si pensi, per esempio, al diritto di veto del presidente americano). Il Consiglio degli Stati non ha mai avuto la forza del Senato americano e il Consiglio nazionale ha sempre sostenuto la maggioranza di governo. Peculiare, in effetti, è il rapporto fra l'Assemblea e la suprema autorità esecutiva, il Consiglio federale.[55] I membri del Consiglio, oltre alle attribuzioni di natura esecutiva, hanno funzioni consultive nelle due sezioni dell'Assemblea nonchè il diritto di fare proposte su un oggetto in deliberazione (art. 89). Uno dei tratti più caratteristici del rapporto fra Governo e Parlamento risiede nel fatto che il Consiglio federale non è soggetto a voto di sfiducia. Un eventuale conflitto – ma le crisi di gabinetto sono ignorate dal diritto e dalla prassi federale – metterebbe a repentaglio le stesse istituzioni. Questo meccanismo anomalo ha garantito una notevole stabilità di governo, dal 1848 ad oggi.

Il giudizio contraddittorio dato da Arthur de Gobineau sul primo governo federale riflette una situazione politica ancora incerta. Se de Gobineau insiste sull'impotenza del Consiglio federale (come se nulla fosse cambiato[56]), Tocqueville osserva con il consueto acume: «La Svizzera, malgrado la febbricola cronica della sua democrazia, mi sembra avere una salute più robusta e un avvenire più tranquillo che la maggior parte degli Stati che la circondano».[57]

55 Tale istituzione ha i suoi precedenti nel Direttorio della Costituzione del 1798 e soprattutto nel Consiglio federale delineato dal progetto del 1832. L'Assemblea federale nomina i sette membri che compongono il Consiglio e, fra questi, il Presidente della Confederazione che dura in carica un anno (art. 86).

56 «Più il tempo passa, più l'impotenza del governo federale si manifesta pubblicamente e di conseguenza aumenta. Questa impotenza è certamente causata, soprattutto, dalla costituzione stessa di siffatto meccanismo di governo; ma essa è, per così dire, raddoppiata dalla personalità degli uomini che sono incaricati della funzione eminente di rappresentare la Confederazione», lettera di A. De Gobineau a A. De Tocqueville, Berna, 24 febbraio 1850, in *Correspondance d'Alexis De Tocqueville et d'Arthur de Gobineau*, cit., 115.

57 Lettera di A. De Tocqueville a A. De Gobineau, Parigi, 14 maggio 1850, *ibidem*, 137.

La Costituzione del 1848 si basa sul principio della democrazia rappresentativa. Solo in materia di revisione costituzionale è consentito ai cittadini (50.000) di chiedere una modifica della Carta fondamentale.[58] La Costituzione del '48 propone un disegno moderato: si cerca di raggiungere – nella prospettiva radical-liberale – un equilibrio fra la tendenza al rafforzamento del governo federale e le autonomie cantonali. Ma la Costituzione non poteva certo risolvere tutti i problemi. La frattura tra progressisti e conservatori (per usare una semplificazione) – culminata nella guerra del *Sonderbund* – mantenne un rilievo non secondario. Le istituzioni federali poterono, tuttavia, radicarsi nella vita politica del paese. I «luoghi» del potere federale (la capitale Berna, il Tribunale federale a Lucerna, ecc.) definirono stabilmente l'immagine più «visibile» del nuovo Stato federale.

Se c'è un pericolo che minaccia – ed è una costante della storia svizzera contemporanea – l'integrità della vita democratica, esso risiede nella formazione di un ramificato, possente, sistema politico-finanziario. L'intreccio di politica, amministrazione e affari (banche, ferrovie, ecc.) favorisce la formazione di forti oligarchie locali e nazionali. Il potenziamento delle forme di partecipazione democratica si propone anche come antidoto capace di limitare gli effetti negativi derivanti da quell'intreccio. Il movimento democratico segna le vicende che preparano la Costituzione del 1874. Una prima, assai limitata, revisione – con voto popolare – si verifica nel 1866: la confessione isrealita è equiparata a quelle cristiane. Ancora una volta la conquista di più cospicui diritti politici in alcuni cantoni (in materia di iniziativa legislativa, di referendum legislativo obbligatorio) determina un contraccolpo sul piano federale. L'accentuarsi della politica anticlericale (*Kulturkampf*) e la necessità di un rafforzamento dello Stato centrale[59] sono poi fra le ragioni che più contribuiscono a inquadrare lo sforzo compiuto per modificare la Costituzione del 1848. Nel 1872 l'Assemblea federale[60] elabora un vasto progetto di revisione totale che viene però respinto, con uno scarto esiguo, dal voto popolare e dai cantoni. L'Assemblea, tuttavia, non vi rinuncia. Una nuova mozione riceve un quasi unanime consenso. Il

58 «Quando una sezione dell'Assemblea federale decreta la revisione della Costituzione federale e l'altra sezione non vi consente, oppure quando cinquantamila cittadini svizzeri aventi diritto al voto domandano la revisione, la questione di sapere se la Costituzione federale deve essere revisionata, è, nell'uno come nell'altro caso, sottoposta al voto del popolo svizzero» (art. 113).

59 La guerra franco-prussiana del 1870 aveva rivelato, di riflesso, la debolezza del dispositivo militare elvetico. L'unificazione della Germania e dell'Italia ponevano, inoltre, la Svizzera in una posizione geopolitica ancor più delicata.

60 R. Haeberli, *Die Revision der Bundesverfassung 1872/1874 im Lichte der öffentlichen Meinung*, Bern 1949; A. Steiner, *Der Versuch einer Bundesrevision 1870/72 im Spiegel der Innerschweizer Presse*, Stans 1959.

progetto costituzionale modera le tendenze centralizzatrici (concessioni alla Svizzera romanda) e adotta misure di più spiccato segno anticlericale.[61] Il dato numerico dell'approvazione popolare e cantonale è, questa volta, piuttosto consistente (340.199 sì contro 198.013 no, 14½ cantoni contro 7½: il voto riproduce ancora la frattura del *Sonderbund*).

La nuova Costituzione del 29 maggio 1874 ripete la struttura e i principî fondamentali della Carta del 1848. Si tratta quindi di una revisione parziale. Lo Stato federale – secondo la tendenza più volte sottolineata – accresce le proprie competenze,[62] nei settori tradizionali (difesa militare) ma anche nell'ambito del governo dell'economia e delle prime politiche sociali. Il diritto di stabilimento è ulteriormente rafforzato, così come lo spazio delle libertà e dei diritti politici. Il Tribunale federale diventa struttura permanente: ha, in particolare, giurisdizione su tutte le controversie di diritto pubblico rientranti fra i compiti dello Stato federale e assicura l'uniforme applicazione del diritto federale.

La complessa architettura costituzionale attribuisce un ruolo privilegiato – non riscontrabile, in pari misura, in altri ordinamenti – agli istituti di democrazia diretta. Si è già detto delle singolari dinamiche che caratterizzano i rapporti fra l'Assemblea e il Consiglio federale. Non bisogna dimenticare però che anche il corpo dei cittadini attivi può determinare direttamente – partecipando, nelle forme previste, alle funzioni legislative e di governo – gli indirizzi di politica generale. L'ampio raggio di azione di tali istituti ha eroso, nel tempo, l'originaria centralità dell'Assemblea federale, finendo col rafforzare, entro certi limiti, il ruolo e l'efficacia del potere esecutivo (Consiglio federale). Anche in considerazione di ciò, non devono meravigliare il crescente astensionismo che caratterizza le elezioni politiche svizzere, il ruolo singolare dei partiti politici,[63] la rielezione di consiglieri federali che abbiamo promosso atti senza poi ricevere il consenso dell'Assemblea. La dialettica forse più significativa è quella che riguarda il «potere minoritario di governo» e il «potere maggioritario di controllo».[64]

La democrazia attiva o pura è, del resto, una forma di partecipazione politica assai radicata nella storia svizzera. Ancora oggi alcuni cantoni (Appenzello, Unterwaldo, Glarona) conservano la *Landsgemeinde*, cioè l'assemblea (di antica ascendenza germanica) dei cittadini attivi chiamati a votare, per alzata di mano,

61 Per una critica a questo processo di accentramento, v. V. Du Bled, *Histoire de la Monarchie de Juillet de 1830 à 1848 avec une introduction sur le droit constitutionnel aux États-Unis, en Suisse, en Angleterre et en Belgique*, Paris 1877, t. I.

62 Si veda P. C. Von Planta, *Die Schweiz in ihrer Entwickelung zum Einheitsstaate*, Zürich 1877.

63 D.-L. Seiler, *Enjeux et partis politiques en Suisse*, in *Pouvoirs*, 43(1987), 115–138.

64 Cfr. M. Hauriou, *Précis de droit constitutionnel*, Paris 1929, 2 ed., 174 ss.

sulle questioni di interesse comunitario. Ma a parte queste reliquie, è alla moderna teoria della sovranità popolare che bisogna guardare per definire il quadro ottocentesco della democrazia svizzera.[65]

Il principio del voto popolare ha conosciuto uno sviluppo significativo. La Costituzione del 1848 ha introdotto il referendum obbligatorio in materia costituzionale, la Carta del 1874 il referendum facoltativo in materia legislativa.[66] Nel 1891 è stato inserito l'importante diritto di iniziativa popolare per la revisione della Costituzione.[67] Poichè questa non fissa un criterio obiettivo di differenziazione tra le materie riservate all'intervento costituzionale e quelle riservate alla legge ordinaria, la sovranità popolare si trova ad avere virtualmente una posizione che sovrasta alla funzione legislativa dell'Assemblea. Il ripetuto ricorso al meccanismo delle revisioni ha consentito di sviluppare, poco a poco, il diritto costituzionale della Confederazione, tanto da far sopravvivere, a tutt'oggi, l'impianto complessivo della Costituzione del 1874. Lo Stato si è avvalso dell'iniziativa di revisione per dare forma e legittimità alla crescente politica di

65 J.-D. Delley, *La démocratie directe. Un système politique aux portes ouvertes*, in *Pouvoirs*, 43 (1987), 101.

66 «Le leggi e i decreti federali di portata generale devono essere sottoposti al popolo per l'accettazione o il rifiuto quando 30.000 [50.000 a partire dal 1977] cittadini attivi o otto cantoni ne fanno richiesta» (art. 89, II). L'applicazione di questa misura è stata estesa (nel 1977) ai trattati internazionali. L'adesione ad organizzazioni di sicurezza collettiva o a comunità sopranazionali deve essere sottoposta al voto popolare e dei cantoni per l'accettazione o il rigetto (1977). Parimenti, 50.000 cittadini o otto cantoni possono richiedere di votare sui decreti federali di carattere obbligatorio emanati in caso d'urgenza (art. 89 bis, introdotto nel 1949).

67 «L'iniziativa popolare consiste nella domanda presentata da 50.000 [100.000 dal 1977] cittadini svizzeri aventi diritto di voto e richiedenti l'adozione di un nuovo articolo costituzionale o l'abrogazione o la modifica di determinati articoli della Costituzione vigente [...]. La domanda d'iniziativa può assumere la forma di una proposta generale o la forma di un progetto elaborato in tutti i suoi aspetti. Se la domanda d'iniziativa è concepita in termini generali e le Camere federali l'approvano, queste procedono alla revisione parziale nel senso della domanda e sottopongono il progetto all'adozione o al rigetto del popolo e dei cantoni. Se, al contrario, le Camere non approvano la domanda, la questione della revisione parziale sarà sottoposta alla votazione del popolo; se la maggioranza dei cittadini svizzeri votanti si pronuncia affermativamente, l'Assemblea federale procederà alla revisione conformandosi alla decisione popolare. Se la domanda d'iniziativa è in forma di progetto già elaborato e l'Assemblea federale vi aderisce, il progetto sarà sottoposto al popolo e ai cantoni per l'adozione o il rigetto. Se l'Assemblea federale non è d'accordo, può essa stessa elaborare un proprio progetto o consigliare al popolo il rigetto del progetto presentato e sottoporre alla votazione il suo controprogetto o la sua proposta di rifiuto e al contempo il progetto di iniziativa popolare» (art. 121).

accentramento; i cantoni, al contrario, ne hanno fatto lo strumento per limitare e «rinegoziare» gli ambiti di intervento del potere federale. La flessibilità dell'istituto ha poi consentito alle varie istanze della società civile di promuovere – in una prospettiva di grande stabilità – l'adeguamento del quadro politico-istituzionale alle più pressanti necessità sociali ed economiche. Tale tecnica di revisione non ha però lasciato indenne la compattezza, la coerenza e l'unità del documento costituzionale. «Non si può dire – ha scritto Bastid – che la Costituzione federale brilli per elegante semplicità».[68] L'azione referendaria ha svolto una valida funzione di apertura del sistema politico, di crescita democratica, di ampliamento dei temi oggetto del dibattito politico. Certo, i fenomeni dell'astensionismo, il rischio di strumentalizzazioni lobbistiche esistono e non devono essere sottovalutati. D'altro canto, il referendum e l'iniziativa popolare innescano dinamiche complesse, non etichettabili *a priori* secondo gli schemi politico-ideologici del «progressismo» o del «conservatorismo».

La piccola patria svizzera si è «ritagliata», nel tempo, una veste politico-costituzionale «su misura». L'ideale della separatezza, cioè di un'identità che non sa pienamente riconoscersi nei principali modelli europei, appare l'effetto di un destino singolare e la ragion d'essere dell'esistenza *appartata* di una nazione che è, tuttavia, il cuore geografico del continente, una delle sue più ricche e sviluppate regioni, uno dei luoghi deputati alla rappresentanza degli organismi internazionali. Il federalismo svizzero – cornice di riferimento per le istituzioni politiche e per i meccanismi costituzionali – non ha nulla di artificiale; è sinonimo, per eccellenza, di storie, tradizioni, culture profondamente radicate nelle sue unità cantonali e nelle articolazioni federali. Il federalismo si è rivelato il mezzo «naturale» per dar forma a politiche di solidarietà reciproca e di raccordo di comuni interessi, la filosofia politica e lo strumento concreto per ricercare un equilibrio fra l'unità e la diversità. La coscienza del patto (*foedus*, appunto), del giuramento, della sintesi comune di valori ha guidato il cammino *dal basso* dei comuni e dei cantoni – per «addizioni» successive – verso quella complessa struttura federativa che si è impegnata a salvaguardare l'originario e variegato patrimonio delle comunità locali immettendolo in uno scenario più vasto e articolato.

Le definizioni di federalismo quasi non si contano; i diversi significati sono utilizzati, nel comune linguaggio politico, confondendo, non di rado, piani distinti. Le forme storiche di federalismo – e tra queste *soprattutto* quella che si identifica con la realtà svizzera – rappresentano al tempo stesso una teoria della Stato, un complesso di ideologie politiche, una dottrina sociale di ampia portata,

68 P. Bastid, *Gouvernement d'assemblée*, Paris 1956, 271.

un vero e proprio metodo capace di individuare le istituzioni necessarie al governo della collettività. È quindi difficile enucleare principî generali – applicabili alla generalità delle situazioni – dalle singole esperienze federali. L'astrazione fonda i necessari modelli, ma non si deve dimenticare la complessità (storicamente determinata) di ogni esperienza.[69] Il caso svizzero – come si è detto – è tra i più esemplari e dovrebbe far riflettere sull'uso spregiudicato o disinformato di parole estrapolate dal loro specifico contesto. È abbastanza paradossale che l'assetto politico-costituzionale svizzero, pur così peculiare storicamente e per niente segnato da astrattezza (ideologica) abbia finito per essere considerato un modello da imitare e da assumere, quasi fosse possibile ridurre a schema concettuale ciò che è il risultato di un lenta, graduale, specifica evoluzione.

Le tappe della storia costituzionale svizzera – dalla Confederazione di antico regime allo Stato federale del 1874 – fanno ben risaltare la diversa intensità del legame federale nelle successive configurazioni della forma statale elvetica. La Costituzione dello Stato federale regola le rispettive competenze degli organi collettivi e delle comunità singole. I cantoni partecipano alla formazione della volontà federale.[70] Dalla ripartizione delle competenze tra gli Stati membri e la Confederazione deriva la concreta fisionomia della struttura federale.[71] La distribuzione del potere su base territoriale circoscrive gli spazi della «sovranità» dei cantoni quali organi dello Stato federale.

69 «Non esistono due Stati federali che siano simili. Non c'è neppure una definizione che si applichi a tutti gli Stati che si definiscono federali. La soluzione più semplice per i giuristi sarebbe, allora, di lasciare questa parola ai letterati, ai giornalisti e agli uomini politici. Questi soli possono esprimere, con tutte le sfumature necessarie, lo stupendo equilibrio che è proprio del federalismo; mentre i professori di diritto, abituati a rinchiudere i fatti sociali entro caselle ben precise, non ne trovano di adeguate a un fenomeno tanto complesso. Questa conclusione la riteniamo più giusta che sensata. In effetti, l'uso della parola "federale" risponde ad una tradizione così risalente che sarebbe vano pretenderne oggi la proscrizione. Conserviamo dunque la nozione, ma attribuendogli d'ora in poi un significato quantitativo piuttosto che qualitativo». (J.-P. Aubert, *Traité de droit constitutionnel suisse*, cit., t. I, 201).

70 Questo è il carattere che sembra differenziare (a detta di autori come His, Giacometti, Bridel, Aubert), più di altri, la federazione dallo Stato centralizzato. Le parti costitutive hanno un diritto di co-decisione nel processo di ripartizione delle competenze. In Svizzera, dippiù, l'autorità originaria dei cantoni dà ulteriori, peculiari indicazioni sul modo di essere dello Stato federale. Cfr. B. Knapp, *Le féderalisme*, in *Zeitschrift für Schweizerisches Recht*, 103 (1984), n. 2, 300–301.

71 B. Knapp, *Confédération et cantons. L'influence des crises sur l'évolution de leurs relations*, in *Pouvoirs*, 43 (1987), 31–47.

Il federalismo americano – dal «Federalist»[72] alla «divulgazione» tocquevilliana[73] – ha rappresentato senza dubbio un modello importante, ma, come si è detto, il federalismo svizzero ha saputo conservare una fisionomia aderente ai caratteri originari della sua storia. Nel corso del XIX secolo la teoria della divisione della sovranità ha suscitato largo interesse fra i giuristi. In seguito, si è preferito far cadere l'accento sulla teoria tradizionale della sovranità come *summa potestas* appartenente alla sola federazione,[74] salvo poi riconoscere ai cantoni una autonoma autorità statale interna (*eigene Herrschaftsgewalt*), nei limiti della sfera di attività costituzionalmente garantita, quale elemento di differenza rispetto ad una mera potestà di autoamministrazione.

Il modello federale si è andato trasformando nel corso di un secolo e mezzo di storia delle istituzioni svizzere. Il federalismo ottocentesco si riconosce nei principî fondamentali che hanno continuato ad ispirare l'azione riformatrice dell'assetto costituzionale. L'equilibrio, il cauto adeguamento, la conciliazione delle diverse esigenze hanno caratterizzato lo sviluppo del costituzionalismo svizzero. Il federalismo non è rimasto fermo all'Ottocento. Il dibattito degli ultimi decenni sul federalismo cooperativo[75] (per distinguerlo da quello co-

72 Sulla formulazione americana della teoria dello Stato federale, vedi A. Hamilton, J. Jay, J. Madison, *Il Federalista*, cit.

73 Non senza dimenticare R. Mohl, *Das Bundes-Staatsrecht der Vereinigten Staaten von Nord-Amerika*, Stuttgart, Tübingen 1824.

74 Per la dottrina della divisione della sovranità, in area tedesca e svizzera, v. soprattutto G. Waitz, *Das Wesen des Bundesstaates*, in *Allgemeine Monatsschrift für Wissenschaft und Literatur*, 1853, 494 ss.; J. Dubs, *Das öffentliche Recht der Schweiz. Eidgenossenschaft*, Zürich 1878, 23 ss.; J. J. Rüttimann, *Das Nordamerikanische Bundesstaatsrecht verglichen mit den politischen Einrichtungen der Schweiz*, Zürich 1867, vol. I, 71. La teoria della sovranità federale è invece legata, in special modo, a G. Meyer, *Staatsrechtliche Erorterungen über die deutsche Reichsverfassung*, Leipzig 1872; P. Laband, *Das Staatsrecht des Deutschen Reiches*, Tübingen 1911, vol. I, 55 ss.; G. Jellinek, *Dottrina generale del diritto dello Stato*, Milano 1921, vol. I, 738 ss.; F. Fleiner, *Schweizerisches Bundesstaatsrecht*, Tübingen 1923, 54. Cfr. J. J. Schollenberger, *Das Bundesstaatsrecht der Schweiz. Geschichte und System*, Berlin 1902; E. Deuerlein, *Föderalismus. Die historischen und philosophischen Grundlagen des föderativen Prinzips*, München 1972.

75 Tale formula sottolinea l'indirizzo che privilegia la collaborazione tra il potere centrale federale e i cantoni e intende promuovere – anche attraverso speciali accordi fra lo Stato e le associazioni intercantonali – un più efficace e razionale funzionamento dello Stato federale. Cfr. U. Haefelin, *Der kooperative Föderalismus in der Schweiz*, in *Zeitschrift für Schweizerisches Recht*, 1969, II, 549–741; Ch. Dominicè, *Fédéralisme coopératif*, ivi, 743–893; L. Neidhart, *Föderalismus in der Schweiz*, Zürich 1975; J. Theiler, *Föderalismus, Voraussetzung oder Ergebnis rationaler Politik*, Berne 1977. Sul «principio di concordanza» quale matrice del *corporativismo democratico liberale*, v. Ch.-A. Morand, *La formation et la mise en œuvre du droit*, in *Pouvoirs*, 43 (1987), 74.

siddetto competitivo) e le discussioni e i progetti di riforma totale della Costituzione dimostrano, in ultima analisi, la vitalità del modello svizzero.

La sfida che incalza più da vicino la Svizzera federale si chiama Europa. La Confederazione ha sempre avuto con l'Europa un rapporto singolare ed è oggi chiamato a scelte difficili. Nel 1992 il popolo svizzero ha rigettato la proposta di entrare nello spazio economico europeo, prima tappa di un possibile ingresso nella Comunità. Alcune delle motivazioni che hanno portato a questo voto negativo sono il riflesso moderno di paure e di inquietudini più antiche. Certo è che il problema appare soltanto rinviato. E comunque le relazioni fra il federalismo svizzero (che si articola al suo interno in forme diverse) e la politica «unitaria» europea devono ancora trovare – anche a livello costituzionale – una convincente soluzione.[76] La federazione europea non può restare insensibile – *mutatis mutandis* – alla complessa esperienza costituzionale svizzera. Il popolo elvetico (pur con uno scarto minimo) e la maggioranza dei cantoni hanno respinto – ancora un paradosso? – la possibilità di un legame, non soltanto economico, con l'Europa. Ma probabilmente il federalismo europeo è apparso ancora troppo incerto e distante dallo spirito del federalismo svizzero.

Per un ulteriore percorso bibliografico

Non è agevole proporre al lettore un percorso bibliografico, per quanto conciso, che dia conto (nella prospettiva del saggio) della variegata storia svizzera e delle sue tante ramificazioni cantonali. Il compito è arduo anche perchè la letteratura rispecchia il peso diverso delle comunità linguistiche e la lingua italiana occupa uno spazio abbastanza esiguo. Poche sono le traduzioni italiane (di casa nostra) delle opere più rappresentative e ciò conferma, in ultima analisi, una tradizione di sporadico interesse. Qualcosa forse sta cambiando ed è merito dell'attualità del dibattito sul federalismo. I riferimenti all'esperienza elvetica non sono però sempre appropriati ed è quantomai auspicabile un'attenzione più equanime ed approfondita.

Una sintesi piuttosto efficace la dobbiamo a E. R. Papa, *Storia della Svizzera. Dall'antichità ad oggi. Il mito del federalismo*, Milano 1993, cui si rinvia anche per l'itinerario bibliografico. Tra gli autori di ricostruzioni compendiose e generali bisogna almeno ricordare W. Martin, *Histoire de la Suisse. Essai sur la formation d'une Confédération d'Etats*, Paris 1926 (trad. it. del 1928); U. Im Hof, *Geschichte der Schweiz*, Stoccarda 1974 (trad. it. 1983); Aa.Vv., *Nuova storia della Svizzera e degli svizzeri*, Bellinzona 1983, 3 voll.; Ch. Gilliard, *Histoire de la Suisse*, Paris

76 B. Knapp, *Quel fédéralisme demain?*, in *Revue de droit suisse*, 110, 1991, 83–101.

1991, 10 ed. (trad. it. 1989); U. Im Hof, *Mythos Schweiz: Identität, Nation, Geschichte, 1291–1991*, Zürich 1991. Un eventuale approfondimento non può eludere le grandi storie otto-novecentesche – ricche di profili politico-istituzionali e costituzionali – di Baumgartner, Bluntschli, Blumer, Meyer, Dändliker, Droz, Oechsli, Dierauer, Gagliardi, Nabholz, Bonjour.

Agli scritti di personaggi come Tocqueville, Cherbuliez, Rossi (vedi nelle note) sono da affiancare, tra i classici del diritto costituzionale svizzero, il commentario di W. Burckhardt, *Kommentar der schweizerischen Bundesverfassung vom 29. Mai 1874*, Bern 1905; i trattati di F. Fleiner, *Schweizerisches Bundesstaatsrecht*, Tübingen 1923; F. Fleiner, Z. Giacometti, *Schweizerisches Bundesstaatsrecht*, Zürich 1949; l'opera di E. His, *Geschichte des neuen schweizerischen Staatsrechts*, Basel 1928–1938, 3 voll. Si considerino inoltre J. Dubs, *Das oeffentliche Recht der Schweizerischen Eidgenossenschaft*, Zürich 1878 (trad. it. coeva, *Il diritto pubblico della Confederazione Svizzera*, vol. VI della *Biblioteca di Scienze Politiche*, Torino); J.J. Schollenberger, *Das Bundesstaatsrecht der Schweiz. Geschichte und System*, Berlin 1902. Un lavoro non privo di interesse è quello di B. Bertoni, A.O. Olivetti, *Le istituzioni svizzere nel diritto pubblico e privato della Confederazione e dei cantoni. I. Diritto pubblico. Saggio storico-critico*, Torino 1903.

Per completare il quadro della storia costituzionale e delle istituzioni politiche svizzere cfr. C. Hilty, *Le costituzioni federali della Svizzera*, Bern 1891; C.G. Picavet, *Une démocratie historique. La Suisse*, Paris 1920; A. Heusler, *Histoire des constitutions suisses*, Lausanne 1924; la vecchia collana di testi e documenti costituzionali (promossa dal Ministero della Costituente) edita da Sansoni, contiene tre opere non prive di utilità per il lettore di oggi: G. Bergmann, *Costituenti e Costituzioni svizzere*, Firenze 1946; V. Gueli, *Il sistema elettorale elvetico*, Firenze 1946; Id., *La Costituzione federale svizzera*, Firenze 1947; inoltre A. Siegfried, *La Suisse, Démocratie-Témoin*, Neuchâtel 1948; J.- Ch. Biaudet, *Les origines de la Constitution fédérale de 1848*; M. Bridel, *L'esprit et la destinée de la Constitution fédérale de 1848*, Lausanne 1949; W.E. Rappard, *La Constitution fédérale de la Suisse*, Neuchâtel 1948; N. Jaeger, *Lezioni di diritto svizzero. Diritto pubblico e teoria generale*, Milano 1951; K. Schumann, *Das Regierungssystem der Schweiz*, Köln 1971; A. Buitta, *Decentramento dei poteri nel sistema costituzionale svizzero*, Milano 1973. La «Revue de droit suisse» ha dedicato il numero 93 del 1974 al centenario della Costituzione svizzera. L'opera recente, a nostro avviso, più importante e più utile sul diritto costituzionale svizzero, provveduta anche di puntuali profili storici, si deve a J.-F. Aubert, *Traité de droit constitutionnel suisse*, Paris, Neuchâtel 1967–1982, 3 voll. Questi è autore, inoltre, dell'agile *Petite histoire constitutionnelle de la Suisse*, Bern 1974 e di *La constitution, son contenu, son usage*, in *Revue de droit suisse*, 110, 1991, n. 2, 9–141. Da ricordare, infine, R. Ruffieux, *Les données de l'histoire constitutionnelle*, in *Handbuch politisches Systems der Schweiz*, Bern 1983, vol. I, 119–211; U. Häfelin, W. Haller, *Schweize-*

risches Bundesstaatsrecht. Ein Grundriß, Zürich 1984; O. Sigg, *Le istituzioni politiche in Svizzera*, Zürich 1985; J. Rohr, *La démocratie en Suisse*, Paris 1989; il numero 110, 1991, della *Revue de droit suisse* (*Zeitschrift für Schweizerisches Recht*) che ha inteso celebrare i 700 anni di storia della Confederazione elvetica; A. Kolz, *Neuere schweizerische Verfassungsgeschichte. Ihre Grundlinien vom Ende der Alten Eidgenossenschaft bis 1848*, Bern 1992; A. Pirro, *Federalismo e democrazia in Svizzera*, in *Nuovi studi politici*, 2, 1994, 127–137.

Sull'esperienza della «democrazia diretta» (o «semi-diretta»), v. J.-F. Aubert, *Le référendum populaire*, in *Revue de droit suisse*, 91, 1972, n. 1, 481–506; P. Saladin, *Le référendum populaire en Suisse*, in *Revue internationale de droit comparé*, 1976, 331 ss.; J.-D. Delley, *L'initiative populaire en Suisse. Mythe et réalité de la démocratie directe*, Lausanne 1978; E. J. Grisel, *Initiative et référendum populaires: traité de la démocratie semi-directe en droit suisse*, Dorigny 1987; J.-F. Flauss, *Le nouveau mode de vote sur l'initiative populaire et le contre-projet en droit fédéral suisse*, in *Revue du droit public*, 104, 1988, n. 6, 1555–1573; A. Lombardi, R. Wertenschlag, *Formen der Volksinitiative im Bund: heute und morgen*, Basel 1990; Th. Tanquerel, *La Suisse doit-elle choisir entre l'Europe et la démocratie directe?*, in *Revue de droit suisse*, 110, 1991, 187–200, con ampia bibliografia; A. Auer, *Le référendum populaire: histoire et avenir*, in *Plädoyer. St. Gallen*, 9, 1991, n. 2, 54–60; Id., *L'esperienza del referendum in Svizzera e negli Stati Uniti*, in *Quaderni costituzionali*, 10, 1990, n. 3, 463–477.

Le prospettive del federalismo elvetico – con riguardo, soprattutto, al processo di integrazione europea e al nuovo ordine politico-economico internazionale – sono al centro di un vasto e vivace dibattito. Cfr. D. Sidjanski, *La Suisse face à la Communauté européenne*, in *Pouvoirs*, 43, 1987, 139–149; *La Suisse et l'échéance européenne de 1992*, Paris 1989; R. Ruffieux, A. Schachtschneider Morier-Genoud (a cura di), *La Suisse et son avenir européen: une analyse des positions suisses face à l'intégration de l'Europe*, Lausanne 1989; R. E. Germann, J. D. Muller, *La dynamique fédéraliste suisse*, Bern 1989; O. Jacot-Guillarmod, D. Schindler, Th. Cottier, *EG-Recht und Schweizerische Rechtsordnung*, Basel 1990; D. Schindler, *Die Europaverträglichkeit des schweizerischen Rechts*, Zürich 1990; J. Gemperle (a cura di), *Der Bund der Eid-Genossen. Modell oder Denkmal? Beiträge zur Zukunft der 700jährigen Eidgenossenschaft*, Luzern 1990; J.-F. Flauss, *La Constitution suisse face à l'espace économique européen. Chronique d'un aggiornamento manqué*, in *Revue du droit public*, 6, 1993, 1501–1519; *Europäische Union. Gefahr oder Chance für den Föderalismus in Deutschland, Österreich und der Schweiz?*, Berlin 1994.

Una «mobile complessità»: l'istituzione parlamentare, la democrazia rappresentativa e i «diritti popolari» nella Svizzera post-quarantottesca

«Rien de plus difficile que de fixer, de préciser les caractères de la constitution suisse; pareille aux divinités hindoues, cette constitution change sans cesse d'aspect, de forme, de figure, et il devient presque impossible de la suivre dans ses avatars [...] il est aussi téméraire de vouloir les analyser dans leur mobile complexité, que d'essayer de se faire jour au travers des forêts vierges du nouveau monde, tant elles se succèdent avec rapidité. Ceci peut s'accorder avec les vœux de l'école radicale, qui voit dans le *provisoire perpétuel* l'idéal du gouvernement, mais cette instabilité blesse un des sentiments les plus profonds et les plus légitimes de l'humanité, le besoin d'assurer la durée à ses œuvres, de pouvoir compter sur un lendemain».[1]

Questo rapido giudizio, espresso da un francese, nostalgico della monarchia orleanista, illustra taluni aspetti importanti della Costituzione svizzera nel corso dell'Ottocento. Costituzione cangiante, eppure formalmente «ferma» al 1874, caratterizzata da una «mobile complexité» che sembra assecondare il progetto radicale di una «perpetua provvisorietà», ma che assicura invece un grado notevole di stabilità politica.

In un volume dedicato all'istituzione parlamentare nel XIX secolo, in una prospettiva comparata, è legittimo aprire una "finestra" sulla complessa esperienza svizzera? Molti elementi, infatti, sembrerebbero allontanare inesorabilmente il *Sonderfall Schweiz* da quel "minimo comun denominatore" che in genere si assume come base per un'analisi "comparativa". In effetti, risaltano subito le differenze più marcate: nel *Modell Schweiz* non possiamo certo ritrovare il principio monarchico né, ovviamente, quel processo di parlamentarizzazione

1 V. Du Bled, *Histoire de la Monarchie de Juillet de 1830 à 1848, avec une introduction sur le droit constitutionnel aux Etats-Unis, en Suisse, en Angleterre et en Belgique*, I, Paris 1877, XXXIII–XXXIV.

che, su scala europea, si è sviluppato attorno al delicato e contraddittorio rapporto monarca / parlamento né, ancora, la forma più tipica del governo parlamentare. La domanda che sorge spontanea è se i paradigmi del costituzionalismo svizzero siano a tal punto "singolari" da impedire una qualsiasi forma di confronto storico-critico con le esperienze costituzionali di Stati che pur confinano con la Confederazione. Credo che per comparare l'esperienza elvetica occorra, anzitutto, avere profonda consapevolezza delle peculiarità del suo disegno costituzionale, senza cercare di ricondurla a tutti i costi dentro gli schemi offerti abitualmente dai costituzionalisti e dai politologi. Ciò vorrebbe dire annullare o sminuire il *proprium*, l'irriducibilità, della storia costituzionale svizzera. Un altro errore, tuttavia, non si vorrebbe commettere: ovvero leggere la costituzione come un dato puramente formale, "positivo", come se ciò che oggi è la costituzione svizzera dovesse guidare l'analisi del suo passato e della sua genesi. Ricollocare, dunque, il sistema costituzionale svizzero nell'alveo delle sue coordinate storiche appare il primo passo per proporre ipotesi e paradigmi capaci di rivelare il volto storicamente più probante della Costituzione federale nel suo sviluppo ottocentesco. Si tratta, perciò, di gettare lo sguardo al di là dell'immagine attuale e consolidata del "modello svizzero" per restituirgli la sua più complessa dimensione diacronica.

1. «Il y a des cantons; il n'y a pas de Suisse»?

La modernizzazione del sistema costituzionale a partire dal 1848 non deve far dimenticare i tratti «permanenti»[2] della storia elvetica. L'interrogazione di Ernest Renan non ha perduto di attualità e ripropone l'"enigma" della Costituzione svizzera: «Perché la Svizzera, che ha tre lingue, due religioni, tre o quattro razze, è una nazione, mentre la Toscana, per esempio, che è così omogenea, non lo è?».[3] La struttura costituzionale non può così prescindere dal patto-giuramento, dall'*Eidgenossenschaft*, dall'essere *mixtum compositum*,[4] *Willensnation*,[5] da un legame federale che, nelle varie epoche, ha cercato di far convivere unità e

2 Cfr. J. Gemperle (ed.), *Der Bund der Eid-Genossen. Modell oder Denkmal? Beiträge zur Zukunft der 700jährigen Eidgenossenschaft*, Luzern 1990, in particolare i saggi di G.-A. Chevallaz e O.K. Kaufmann.

3 E. Renan, *Qu'est-ce qu'une nation?*, in *Œuvres complètes*, I, Paris 1947, 887–906 (trad. it. *Che cos'è una nazione? E altri saggi*, Roma 1993, p. 9). Cfr. anche J.K. Bluntschli, *Die schweizerische Nationalität*, Zürich 1915 (ed. orig. 1875).

4 J. Simler, *Helvetiorum respublica. Diversorum autorum, quorum nonnulli nunc primum in lucem prodeunt*, Lugduni Batavorum 1527.

5 P. Saladin, *Zur Einleitung. Die schweizerische Eidgenossenschaft am Anfang ihres achten Jahrhunderts*, in *Zeitschrift für schweizerisches Recht*, 110, 1991, 5.

diversità,[6] e ancora dalle profonde tradizioni democratiche e repubblicane. Non deve quindi stupire l'atteggiamento che accomuna molti osservatori: è la meraviglia per il senso di indipendenza, di autonomia, di libertà; è l'ammirazione (da Machiavelli a Montesquieu a Tocqueville ecc.) per la saggezza e la natura moderata della comunità svizzera che attraverso una sapiente combinazione e una sintesi compromissoria[7] di antichi pluralismi e di un più recente senso comune di appartenenza ha generato un nucleo di identificazione nazionale.

La Costituzione del 1848 (e più ancora la revisione totale del 1874), scritta con l'intento di dar forma ad una Svizzera più unita e più moderna (sul piano politico ed economico) non intende certo distruggere il patrimonio «premoderno»[8] la cui filosofia politica ritroviamo nelle istituzioni elvetiche, privilegiando più il principio del consenso che, in apparenza, quello della pura e semplice maggioranza. « [...] Oasi repubblicana in mezzo a Stati monarchici»,[9] la Svizzera ha perseguito lungo tutto il XIX secolo la via della fondazione e dello sviluppo del proprio sistema costituzionale, a partire, dunque, da un tessuto connettivo e da tradizioni di libertà e di autonomia che formano varie stratificazioni.[10]

6 Il principio di fondo, osserva Pellegrino Rossi nel primo Ottocento, è la «variété sans fusion, l'unité avec une profonde variété; elle a trouvé la solution de ce problème dans le lien fédéral ... En Suisse la séparation est naturelle, la fusion rationelle, son histoire est le développement de ce principe: ni séparation complète, ni fusion absolue». Si veda L. Lacchè, *Un italiano a Ginevra, alla ricerca della patria comune*, introduzione a P. Rossi, *Per la Patria comune. Rapporto della Commissione della Dieta ai ventidue Cantoni sul progetto d'Atto federale da essa deliberato a Lucerna il 15 dicembre 1832*, Manduria, Bari 1997, XLII.

7 Sulla valenza costituzionale della nozione di "compromesso" – principio inscritto nelle istituzioni e condizione di esistenza del sistema politico svizzero, indispensabile per integrare le radicatissime identità linguistiche, confessionali, culturali in un'unica comunità nazionale, riducendo i punti d'attrito e di conflitto –, cfr. A. Auer, *Problèmes fondamentaux de la démocratie suisse*, in *Zeitschrift für schweizerisches Recht*, 103, 1984, 94.

8 T. Fleiner, *La democrazia consensuale della Confederazione Elvetica*, intervista di R. Notarangelo, in *Democrazia e diritto*, XXXVII, 1998, 67 ss.

9 A.-E. Cherbuliez, *De la démocratie en Suisse*, Paris, Genève 1843, (trad. it. *La democrazia nella Svizzera*, [Biblioteca di scienze politiche e amministrative VI/2], Torino 1891, 249). Jakob Dubs scrive: «Ciò che ci sembra affatto particolare alla Svizzera, ciò che si riflette nella nostra stessa denominazione politica, è la nostra esistenza come Confederazione politica libera e repubblicana. Questa idea non appartiene in Europa ad alcun altro Stato all'infuori del nostro; è dunque essa che forma il nostro speciale carattere politico.» (J. Dubs, *Das öffentliche Recht der schweizerischen Eidgenossenschaft, dargestellt für das Volk*, Zürich 1877, trad. it. *Il diritto pubblico della Confederazione Svizzera*, in [Biblioteca di scienze politiche e amministrative, VI/2], Torino 1891, 777–778).

10 Z. Giacometti, *Das Staatsrecht der schweizerischen Kantone*, Zürich 1941.

È vero, come scrive Jakob Dubs, che «Uno svolgimento sistematico più completo della vita costituzionale non si ebbe che dopo il 1848; sotto questo riguardo quell'anno è l'inizio d'una nuova epoca nella nostra Confederazione»,[11] tuttavia il cinquantennio che precede la nascita della moderna Costituzione svizzera fu uno straordinario banco di lavoro dal quale emersero categorie e principi destinati a confluire, in una sintesi efficace, nel documento del 1848. La parificazione dello *status* giuridico cantonale, la sovranità popolare e l'idea rappresentativa, il modulo di governo direttoriale affermati con la Costituzione della Repubblica Elvetica del 12 aprile 1798; il definitivo riconoscimento del *Sonderfall* con l'Atto di Mediazione napoleonico del 1803;[12] il debole compromesso raggiunto nel Patto del 1815; l'importante tentativo di revisione costituzionale tra il 1832 e il 1833: queste, a voler semplificare, sono le tessere principali del mosaico costituzionale elvetico nella prima metà dell'Ottocento.[13] In pochi decenni, la Costituzione muta di forma e di contenuti, conservando alcuni elementi condivisi e destinati a durare, ma oscillando pericolosamente tra gli estremi della costituzione repubblicana *une et indivisible* (1798) e il confederalismo *ancien régime* del 1815.

Unitari e federalisti si affrontano senza mai trovare una soluzione capace di conciliare efficacemente la volontà di rafforzare il centro federale con la salvaguardia delle infinite peculiarità cantonali. Se le costituzioni di età francese nascono col sigillo della "dipendenza", anche il Patto del 1815 ha origine sotto il segno del "controllo" straniero. La Svizzera, nei decenni successivi, crederà sempre più ad una costituzione integralmente "nazionale". Non v'è dubbio, la "nuova" Svizzera può trarre origine soltanto dal codice genetico federale: resta da vedere quale possa essere, concretamente, la formula più efficace. C'è poi un'altra "certezza": il Cantone è il motore profondo della storia svizzera; lo

11 J. Dubs, *Il diritto pubblico della Confederazione Svizzera*, cit., 567.

12 «La Svizzera – osserva Napoleone rivolgendosi alla Consulta dei rappresentanti dei Cantoni a Parigi – non rassomiglia ad alcun altro Stato, sia per gli avvenimenti che vi si sono svolti durante parecchi secoli, sia per la sua posizione geografica e topografica, sia per le differenti lingue, le diverse religioni e per l'estrema differenza di costumi che si verifica fra le sue diverse parti. La natura ha fatto federativo il vostro Stato. Volerla vincere non può essere cosa saggia».

13 Per una sintesi delle vicende che hanno caratterizzato la storia costituzionale elvetica tra il 1798 e il 1848 ci permettiamo di rinviare, anche per ulteriori riferimenti bibliografici, *supra*, in questo volume, *Costituzioni e federalismo nella Svizzera del XIX secolo*, 21–35 e L. Lacchè, *Un italiano a Ginevra, alla ricerca della patria comune*, cit. Per una originale e puntuale lettura dei principi-guida del costituzionalismo storico svizzero sanciti dall'art. 2 della costituzione del 1848 si veda adesso V. Monnier, *Les origines de l'article 2 de la Constitution fédérale de 1848*, in *Société suisse des juristes. Rapports et communications*, 132, 1998, 415–490.

«svolgimento sistematico», a cui accenna Dubs, ha nell'esperienza cantonale il punto imprescindibile di riferimento.

La strada, tuttavia, non è agevole. La descrizione che, nel 1836, Tocqueville fa della Costituzione materiale, vigente il Patto del 1815, è impietosa: «[...] il y a des cantons; il n'y a pas de Suisse».[14] Basterebbe leggere il Rapporto della Commissione di riforma che Pellegrino Rossi aveva presentato alla Dieta nel dicembre del 1832 per trovarvi un elenco completo dei difetti della costituzione svizzera.[15] Tocqueville, nei suoi *carnets* di viaggio, sottolinea i punti critici: osserva le istituzioni confederali inforcando gli occhiali della democrazia americana e delle libertà inglesi, occhiali che, a dire il vero, non sempre si addicono alla specificità elvetica.[16] Il bilancio è presto fatto: un Patto dai termini troppo vaghi e dai tratti "medievali", che ignora il principio di separazione dei poteri; un governo federale estremamente debole[17] diviso tra una Dieta che,

14 A. De Tocqueville, *Œuvres complètes*, V/2: *Voyages en Angleterre, Irlande, Suisse et Algérie*, a cura di J.-P. Mayer, A. Jardin, Paris 1958, 181. Non è improbabile che una delle «fonti» utilizzate da Tocqueville per i suoi appunti sulla Svizzera sia stato l'importante scritto di A.-E. Cherbuliez, *Essai sur les conditions de l'alliance fédérative en général et sur le nouveau projet d'Acte fédéral*, Genève 1833. Jean-Charles Biaudet riporta un passo significativo di una lettera del giurista lucernese Ph.-A. von Segesser ad A. Heusler-Ryhiner in data 9 febbraio 1848: «La Suisse n'a d'intérêt pour moi que parce que le canton de Lucerne, ma patrie, y est situé. Si le canton de Lucerne n'existe plus en tant que membre libre et souverain de la Confédération, la Suisse m'est aussi indifférente que la Grande ou la Petite Tartarie» (J.-Ch. Biaudet, *Les origines de la Constitution fédérale de 1848*, Lausanne 1949, 8).

15 P. Rossi, *Per la Patria comune*, cit.

16 Sull'intelligenza storica di Rossi, messa a confronto con taluni pregiudizi e schematismi interpretativi di Alexis de Tocqueville, cfr. le acute osservazioni di A. Dufour, *Histoire et Constitution. Pellegrino Rossi et Alexis de Tocqueville face aux institutions politiques de la Suisse*, in *Présence et actualité de la constitution dans l'ordre juridique* ..., Bâle et Francfort-sur-le-Main 1991, 431–475. Sul punto cfr. anche L. Lacchè, *Un italiano a Ginevra, alla ricerca della patria comune*, cit., XXXVI ss. Su Tocqueville e la Svizzera, cfr. L. Monnier, *Tocqueville et la Suisse*, in *Alexis de Tocqueville. Livre du Centenaire, 1859–1959*, Paris 1960, 101–113; Id., *Alexis de Tocqueville et Auguste de la Rive à travers leur correspondance*, in *Mélanges offerts à P.-E. Martin*, Genève 1961, 610–623.

17 A. De Tocqueville, *Œuvres complètes*, III/2: *Ecrits et discours politiques*, a cura di A. Jardin, Paris 1985, 469: «Il nous parait incontestable que la plus grande partie des maux de la Suisse vient de son gouvernement, le plus misérablement faible de tous ceux qui existent dans le monde ... L'extrême faiblesse du gouvernement suisse ne tient donc pas à la limitation imprudente de ses pouvoirs. A quoi tient-elle donc? A ce qu'en lui donnant de grandes attributions, on ne lui a pas accordé le moyen d'en faire un usage habituel et facile. Comment cela? Le gouvernement fédéral suisse ne commande jamais directement aux citoyens. Il n'agit sur eux que par l'intermédiaire des gouvernements cantonaux. Voilà la raison principale

rappresentando solo i Cantoni, non assume autonome deliberazioni essendo vincolata ai mandati imperativi dei singoli deputati e un governo, il *Vorort*, che altro non è se non il Cantone (Zurigo, Berna, Lucerna) che, a cadenza biennale, "dirige" la politica svizzera, ingenerando grave confusione tra gli interessi confederali e gli obiettivi del Cantone-direttore; un potere giudiziario federale, infine, inesistente.

Tocqueville dice ciò che gli Svizzeri più avvertiti sanno già: o si raggiunge un compromesso per migliorare la Costituzione (ma il fallimento del 1833 è un segnale minaccioso) o la debolezza delle istituzioni non impedirà certo il sorgere di violenze e del pericolo della dissoluzione. La "Rigenerazione" attorno al 1830 è il movimento culturale e politico che, pur nella diversità delle singole esperienze, pone con forza, tra liberalismo moderato e proposte più radicali, la questione della riforma della società. Non è un caso che l'ordine imposto nel 1815 subisca le prime lacerazioni non appena, fra il 1829 e il 1830, il movimento per la revisione costituzionale investe i primi Cantoni. Il liberalismo si irradia in Svizzera, con radici autoctone e declinazioni europee, richiamando i grandi temi del costituzionalismo: la separazione dei poteri, il regime rappresentativo, i diritti fondamentali di libertà. Il fallimento del c. d. Patto Rossi sembra sbarrare la strada ad un riformismo moderato, graduale. Come scrive Tocqueville, anche in Svizzera va in scena la lotta tra «les deux grands partis aristocratique et démocratique qui divisent le monde [...]». Tutto ciò, sommato alle profonde differenze che caratterizzano la Svizzera, «[...] peut-il mener à autre chose qu'une crise finale?».[18]

Le dure lotte politiche e confessionali che si svolgono in alcuni Cantoni, tra gli anni Trenta e Quaranta, denunciano l'indebolimento del legame federale e la precarietà del governo (Dieta e *Vorort*). Da un lato lo spettro ricorrente della guerra civile, dall'altro «[...] un mouvement d'assimilation très sensible se fait sentir entre toutes les parties de la Suisse, malgré les vices de sa constitution fédérale [...]».[19] Il conflitto e il movimento di rigenerazione "nazionale" sono, a ben vedere, le facce di una stessa medaglia. La debolezza del sistema costituzio-

de son impuissance». L'articolo, apparso nel *Commerce* del 21 aprile 1845, contiene una comparazione tra i sistemi di governo americano e svizzero. Una sintesi ulteriore del pensiero di Tocqueville sulla Svizzera si trova in Alexis De Tocqueville, *Relazione sull'opera di A. E. Cherbuliez intitolata: «La democrazia in Svizzera» (1848)*, in N. Matteucci (ed.), *Scritti politici*, Torino 1988, I, 251–268. È utile seguire anche Cherbuliez nelle pagine dedicate al sistema di governo ne *La democrazia nella Svizzera*, cit.

18 A. De Tocqueville, *Œuvres complètes*, V/2, cit., 187.

19 «... que les Suisses de différents pays se voient davantage, qu'ils échangent leurs idées, qu'ils se communiquent leurs habitudes, que, par des concordats (ou traités volontaires entre les cantons), un grand nombre de cantons parvient à établir une législation uniforme ...» (*ibidem*, 183).

nale di governo, tuttavia, non riesce a tenere insieme le due tendenze, contraddittorie ma non necessariamente inconciliabili. L'affermazione di Tocqueville – «il y a des cantons; il n'y a pas de Suisse» – denuncia tale contraddizione, ma disgiunge i due aspetti. La frattura politica che aveva diviso la Confederazione fra il 1832 e il 1833 non solo non viene ricomposta ma si aggrava. Due diverse visioni s'affrontano: governo oligarchico e democrazia rappresentativa,[20] Stato confessionale e Stato laico, autonomismo cantonale e forza del numero, fiere tradizioni elvetiche e nuove prospettive di federalismo nazionale. Al centro del dibattito troviamo – e non potrebbe essere diversamente – il problema della rappresentanza e della sovranità politica. Già nel 1833, osservando la rigidità del modulo confederale, Cherbuliez aveva scritto:

> «On peut bien, à la vérité, essayer des médiations, des arbitrages, et d'autres moyens conciliatoires; mais le véritable moyen, le moyen extrême d'exécution, c'est la guerre entre la majorité des états et la minorité».[21]

20 Cfr. D. Schefold, *Volkssouveränität und repräsentative Demokratie in der schweizerischen Regeneration. 1830–1848*, Basel, Stuttgart 1966.

21 A.-E. Cherbuliez, *Essai sur les conditions de l'alliance fédérative*, cit., 12, ripreso poi in *La democrazia nella Svizzera*, cit., 257. Il progetto di revisione federale (1832–1833) fu preceduto e seguito – come accade di solito – da un considerevole dinamismo progettuale. Alcuni degli scritti dell'epoca (tra il 1830 e il 1838 soprattutto le *brochures* e i progetti "privati", di vario orientamento, delle società patriottiche e di personaggi come Cherbuliez, James Fazy, Fazy-Pasteur, Roger, de Sellon, Monnard, Muret, de Seigneux, Franscini, K. Pfyffer, Zschokke, Troxler, Schnell, Kasthofer, Baumgartner, Bluntschli ecc.) meriterebbero di essere riletti e meditati, anche per meglio comprendere le coordinate storico-concettuali della Costituzione del 1848. Non di rado, infatti, il testo del 1848 viene visto – non senza coloriture ideologiche e storiche – sotto una luce di eccessiva "novità", volendo porre l'accento sui profili di maggiore distacco dal Patto del 1815, poco o nulla insistendo sulla importante pubblicistica degli anni Trenta. Per qualche riferimento, cfr. L. Lacchè, *Un italiano a Ginevra, alla ricerca della patria comune*, cit., XXVI ss. Si possono, inoltre, consultare O. Lauber, *Das Bundesstaatsbegriff in der schweizerischen Publizistik und Praxis*, Luzern 1911, 20 ss.; J. Dierauer, *Geschichte der schweizerischen Eidgenossenschaft*, Bern 1967 (ed. orig. 1922), 574 ss.; W. E. Rappard, *La constitution fédérale de la Suisse 1848–1948, ses origines, son élaboration, son évolution*, Neuchâtel 1948; H. Wild, *Das Ringen um den Bundesstaat. Zentralismus und Föderalismus in der schweizerischen Publizistik von der Helvetik bis zur Bundesrevision*, Zürich 1966, 91 ss.; e soprattutto A. Kölz, *Der Verfassungsentwurf von Ludwig Snell als Quelle der Regenerationsverfassungen*, in W. Haller (ed.), *Festschrift für Ulrich Häfelin zum 65. Geburstag*, Zürich 1989, 299–322; A. Kölz, *Neuere schweizerische Verfassungsgeschichte. Ihre Grundlinien vom Ende der Alten Eidgenossenschaft bis 1848*, Bern 1992, 374 ss.; A. Kölz (ed.), *Quellenbuch zur neueren schweizerischen Verfassungsgeschichte, I: Vom Ende der Alten Eidgenossenschaft bis 1848*, Bern 1992, 369–380, progetti di James Fazy (*Projet de Constitution fédérale*, 1837) e di I. P.V. Troxler (*Entwurf eines Grundgesetzes für die schweizerische Eidgenossenschaft*, 1838).

Quella rigidità viene spezzata sul finire del 1847 dalla cosiddetta guerra del *Sonderbund* con la sconfitta dei Cantoni forestali e dei loro alleati.[22] Lo scontro tra la Svizzera dei *Waldstätten*, in prevalenza cattolici e conservatori, e la Svizzera più ricca, dinamica e popolosa ha molte radici: confessionali, politiche, economiche, sociali. Occorrerà del tempo per lenire la ferita, ma proprio l'adozione di un sistema costituzionale "aperto" offrirà ai "vinti" – come vedremo – una possibilità concreta di integrazione.

2. La «rivoluzione democratica»

La «rivoluzione democratica»[23] – con le sue lontane premesse nell'Elvetica e nel movimento di "Rigenerazione" – può adesso fare il suo ingresso nell'età della «costruzione». Partita dai Cantoni – ancora una volta «laboratori di sperimentazione»[24] – tale rivoluzione «ha creato degli interessi comuni, delle passioni comuni che, per soddisfarsi, hanno sentito il bisogno di un potere generale e comune che si estendesse contemporaneamente a tutto il paese. Il governo federale è quindi entrato in possesso, per la prima volta, di una grande forza, che gli era sempre mancata; ha potuto appoggiarsi su un partito; forza pericolosa, ma indispensabile nei paesi liberi dove il governo, senza di essa, non può quasi nulla».

Tocqueville fa questa osservazione prima ancora che si realizzi la revisione costituzionale. Ciò che conta è la metamorfosi in atto della "Costituzione materiale": il governo federale è destinato ad aumentare, di fatto, il proprio potere. «Ciò che è certo è che ormai, qualunque siano le modifiche apportate alla lettera del patto, la Costituzione federale svizzera è profondamente e irrevocabilmente alterata. La confederazione ha cambiato natura. In Europa essa è divenuta qualcosa di nuovo; una politica di azione si è sostituita ad una di inerzia e di neutralità; da puramente municipale la sua esistenza è divenuta nazionale; un'esistenza più laboriosa, più turbata, più precaria e più grande».[25]

La Costituzione del 12 settembre 1848 sancisce e consolida la «rivoluzione democratica», rende concreta quella "chimera" che Cherbuliez, nel 1843, aveva identificato nell'«idea di un popolo elvetico sovrano». Il movimento costituzionale è quasi integralmente monopolizzato da quella coalizione di correnti e di tendenze politico-ideologiche accomunate da un progetto progressista, misto di federalismo moderato, di democrazia parlamentare, d'*esprit* liberale. Il «partito»,

22 Uri, Svitto, Obwaldo, Nidwaldo, Zugo, Lucerna, Friburgo e Vallese.

23 Espressione utilizzata da Tocqueville in *Relazione sull'opera di A. E. Cherbuliez*, cit., 253.

24 R. Ruffieux, *Les données de l'histoire constitutionnelle*, in *Handbuch politisches System der Schweiz*, Bern 1983, I, 119–211.

25 A. De Tocqueville, *Relazione sull'opera di A. E. Cherbuliez*, cit., 266–268.

cui si riferiva Tocqueville, formatosi nel corso degli ultimi quindici anni nasceva, in realtà, da un *mélange* inestricabile di elementi liberali (le libertà dell'individuo, la separazione dei poteri, ecc.)[26] e di taluni profili più spiccatamente radicali (sovranità popolare, eguaglianza, ecc.).[27] La costituzione del 1848 rappresenta in buona misura i valori e gli interessi dei vincitori e dei padri fondatori;[28] al tempo stesso, però, formula regole e principi che "parlano" anche ai vinti.

Definita un capolavoro di moderazione e di saggezza,[29] essa crea un nuovo Stato federale senza però pretendere una rottura con il passato: opera più dell'esperienza che della teoria, concepita da uomini dei Cantoni ben attenti a misurare e a bilanciare i sacrifici imposti agli Stati.[30] La procedura prevista dall'art. 113[31] consente a una delle due Camere che formano l'Assemblea

26 Il «partito» liberale – formatosi nel corso della Rigenerazione – «... domandava la libertà della stampa, l'allargamento dei diritti elettorali, la separazione dei poteri, l'amovibilità dei funzionari ...». Sui 'partiti' degli anni Trenta e Quaranta, cfr. L. Lacchè, *Un italiano a Ginevra, alla ricerca della patria comune*, cit., XXIII ss. Sul punto cfr. B. Van Muyden, *Essais historiques. La Suisse sous le Pacte de 1815*, Lausanne 1892, II; J.-Ch. Biaudet, *La Suisse et la Monarchie de Juillet 1830–1838*, tesi di dottorato, Lausanne 1941, 69 ss.; E. Grüner, *Die Parteien in der Schweiz. Geschichte, neue Forschungsergebnisse, aktuelle Probleme*, Bern 1977, 2 ed., 47 ss.

27 Cfr. J.-F. Aubert, *Traité de droit constitutionnel suisse*, Neuchâtel 1993, 20 ss. Nel 1847 Henry Druey aveva detto: «La verità è che la maggioranza vuole organizzare la Confederazione più democraticamente ... Infatti noi abbiamo così di fronte i due principii che dividono il mondo: da una parte la democrazia e il liberalismo, l'eguaglianza, la fratellanza, il progresso, la luce, la fede; dall'altra, l'assolutismo, l'aristocrazia, i privilegi, l'abbruttirsi delle masse, le tenebre, l'egoismo» (cit. da W. E. Rappard, *L'individu et l'Etat dans l'évolution constitutionnelle de la Suisse*, Zürich 1936, 261). Su Druey, una delle figure preminenti del primo radicalismo svizzero, cfr. A. Lasserre, *Henry Druey, fondateur du radicalisme vaudois et homme d'Etat suisse*, Lausanne 1960.

28 Tra i fondatori troviamo molti dei radicali e liberali che hanno dominato la scena politica tra l'età della Rigenerazione e il consolidamento dello Stato federale: i due relatori H. Druey (Vaud) e C. Kern (Turgovia), i commissari J. Furrer (Zurigo, presidente del Consiglio degli Stati nel 1848 e primo presidente della Confederazione), Ulrich Ochsenbein (Berna, presidente della Dieta nel 1847–1848 e poi del Consiglio nazionale), J. Munzinger (Soletta), W. M. Näff (San Gallo), F. Frei-Hérosé (Argovia) ecc. Per i profili biografici, cfr. U. Altermatt (ed.), *Die Schweizer Bundesräte. Ein biographisches Lexicon*, Zürich 1992, e soprattutto *L'Assemblée fédérale suisse 1848–1920*, I, E. Grüner, K. Frei (edd.) *Biographies*, Berne 1966, 805–806, 704–705, 71, 209–210, 426, 575–576, 649–650.

29 W. E. Rappard, *La constitution fédérale de la Suisse*, Neuchâtel 1948, 104.

30 Cfr. W. Martin, *Histoire de la Suisse. Essai sur la formation d'une Confédération d'Etats*, Paris 1926, 263.

31 Il testo in A. Kölz, *Quellenbuch zur neueren schweizerischen Verfassungsgeschichte*, II: *Von 1848 bis in die Gegenwart*, Bern 1996, 479.

federale (quando l'altra non è d'accordo) o a cinquantamila cittadini di chiedere che la revisione della costituzione sia sottoposta al voto popolare. Se la maggioranza è favorevole, le due Camere saranno rinnovate per poi procedere alla revisione. Infine, la costituzione riformata entra in vigore se accettata dalla maggioranza dei cittadini che prendono parte alla votazione e dalla maggioranza dei Cantoni (art. 114, Cost. 1848).[32] La rigidità del Patto del 1815 – che naturalmente non prevedeva alcuna procedura di revisione – è ora un ricordo. La Costituzione è modificabile in ogni tempo (art. 111, Cost. 1848),[33] dà spazio all'iniziativa e al voto popolare, prevede infine, nella logica federale, il doppio voto (del popolo e dei Cantoni), il che significa che anche i Cantoni del *Sonderbund* potranno giocare un ruolo significativo nel nuovo sistema.

I modelli ideali non sono quindi ingombranti, la rivoluzione si compie nel nome di un sapiente realismo: la nuova struttura costituzionale rivela profondo rispetto per lo spirito di radicata autonomia che, nelle forme più diverse, aveva caratterizzato da sempre la vita politica dei Cantoni e dei comuni. È una Costituzione che ha avuto il merito della moderazione, mentre avrebbe potuto essere, considerato il contesto storico, più radicale.[34]

3. La repubblica dei radicali è un tipo di democrazia rappresentativa

Il testo del 1848 riuscì nell'impresa di conciliare la realtà poco incoraggiante, conseguenza della guerra civile, con un progetto costituzionale originale che, alla prova dei fatti, si rivelerà solido e lungimirante, in grado di consolidare la democrazia e il federalismo, cioè i due fondamenti dell'esperienza svizzera, senza dover rinunciare a rafforzare il "potere generale e comune". I costituenti utilizzarono il lavoro svolto nel 1832–1833, ma spingendosi ben oltre; tennero presente il modello americano,[35] ma calandolo nello specifico elvetico.

Uno dei rischi che corre – non da solo per la verità – lo storico della costituzione svizzera è quello di applicare alla fase di fondazione categorie che si sono andate formando nel tempo e, non di rado, nel corso del nostro secolo. Allontaniamo un primo possibile equivoco. La Repubblica del 1848 si muove nel solco della democrazia rappresentativa, mentre la forza della democrazia diretta, se si eccettua la pur importante procedura di revisione costituzionale, è ancora allo stato potenziale. La Repubblica del 1848 è altrettanto lontana

32 *Ibidem.*

33 *Ibidem.*

34 Cfr. G. De Reynold, *La démocratie et la Suisse*, Bienne 1934, 228.

35 Cfr. il classico J. J. Rüttimann, *Das nordamerikanische Bundesstaatsrecht, verglichen mit den politischen Einrichtungen der Schweiz*, 3 voll., Zürich 1867–1876, e E. His, *Amerikanische Einflüsse im Schweizerischen Verfassungsrecht*, in *Festgabe der Juristischen Fakultät*, Basel 1920.

dall'essere un modello – come si dice oggi – di *Konkordanzdemokratie*. La ferita della guerra civile è così viva che sarebbe davvero irragionevole pensare ad una soluzione del tutto irenica. La Costituzione del 1848 resta la Costituzione dei radicali vincitori. La dimensione del consenso è di là da venire.

Il perno del sistema politico-costituzionale è l'Assemblea Federale[36] composta dal Consiglio Nazionale (*Nationalrath*) i cui membri sono eletti, per tre anni, dal popolo svizzero e dal Consiglio degli Stati (*Ständerath*) i cui deputati, due per ogni Cantone (uno per i semi-Cantoni), sono nominati in base al sistema elettorale appositamente prescelto da ciascun Stato. L'assemblea federale è «l'autorità suprema della Confederazione» (artt. 60 e 73, Cost.1848)[37] dominata, sin dal 1848, e per parecchi decenni a venire, dalle forze radicali e liberali di varia tendenza. La sinistra radicale, nel 1848, raccoglie 82 dei 111 seggi a disposizione del Consiglio Nazionale, lasciando al centro liberale e ai conservatori il resto. La presa del radicalismo è salda.[38] Il sovrano della Costituzione – le forze politiche costituenti – ha nell'Assemblea lo strumento per determinare l'indirizzo generale dell'attività dello Stato. Questi *homines novi*,[39] borghesi reclutati soprattutto nel mondo delle professioni (anzitutto giuridiche), della funzione pubblica (professionale e onoraria), dell'economia, sono i patrioti che si sono formati politicamente nei Cantoni – dove hanno sèguito popolare –, nelle associazioni

36 Cfr. U. Marti, *Zwei Kammern, ein Parlament: Ursprung und Funktion des schweizerischen Zweikammersystems: sämtliche Nationalräte und Ständeräte seit 1848*, Frauenfeld 1990.

37 Cfr. A. Kölz, *Quellenbuch zur neueren schweizerischen Verfassungsgeschichte*, I, cit., 465, 468.

38 Non esistendo, all'epoca, una chiara definizione dei 'partiti', è assai difficile – soprattutto rispetto al complesso mosaico svizzero (circuito Cantoni-Confederazione, vita politica locale-nazionale ecc.) – fornire un quadro di sintesi. Il notevolissimo tentativo compiuto da Erich Grüner, su base biografica, sociologica e statistica, rappresenta un modello importante per le analisi di sociologia parlamentare. «... de 1848 à 1893, nous n'établissons que *trois grands groupes*: la droite, le centre et la gauche; pour la droite nous distinguons entre les conservateurs catholiques et les conservateurs réformés. A partir de 1896, nous nous en tenons aux groupes et partis existants et nous établissons notre classification d'après le groupe de politique sociale, les radicaux-démocrates, libéraux-conservateurs (centre) et les conservateurs catholiques. A partir de 1911, il existe un groupe socialiste autonome; jusqu'à ce moment-là les socialistes étaient unis au groupe de politique sociale» (*L'Assemblée fédérale suisse 1848–1920*, II: *Sociologie et statistique*, Berne 1966, 83). Si veda anche E. Grüner, *Die Parteien in der Schweiz*, cit. Le forze d'ispirazione radicale e liberale manterranno la maggioranza parlamentare sino all'introduzione, nel 1919, del sistema elettorale proporzionale. Nel 1890, per esempio, i radicali e i democratici hanno 89 seggi sui 147 del Consiglio Nazionale; nel 1911 la maggioranza è fortissima: 135 seggi sui 189 a disposizione.

39 Si veda *L'Assemblée fédérale suisse 1848–1920*, II, cit., 148.

studentesche, patriottiche e militari (*Helvetia*, Società svizzera degli studenti ecc.), nelle formazioni massoniche e che si accingono ora a conquistare la ribalta nazionale.[40] Questa *élite* politica, una volta elaborata la Costituzione, si impegna ad approvare leggi organiche,[41] che rendono operante e consolidano il nuovo ordinamento politico.

4. L'istituzione parlamentare e il Governo

La prima fase di quella che potremmo definire la "Costituzione dei radicali" instaura un sistema di rappresentanza politica (con un regime elettorale maggioritario a più turni) che favorisce la creazione di forti maggioranze liberal-radicali e lascia alle ancora titubanti forze conservatrici, che si identificano in linea di massima con i Cantoni dello sconfitto *Sonderbund*, uno spazio ridotto nell'Assemblea Federale. Nella Costituzione del 1848 troviamo definite, nella loro veste moderna, sia l'istituzione parlamentare che la forma di governo (Consiglio Federale). Il sistema bicamerale di tipo federale opera una brillante e saggia mediazione tra il programma radicale della rappresentanza nazionale e unitaria e la valorizzazione delle antiche sovranità cantonali.[42] Il modello americano è il referente obbligato. Personaggi come il ginevrino James Fazy o lo zurighese Jakob Rüttimann[43] si fecero banditori della soluzione "all'americana" la quale, per la verità, nel 1848, pur se accolta, non suscitò soverchi entusiasmi.

40 Cfr. R. Ruffieux, *La Svizzera dei radicali (1848–1914)*, in *Nuova storia degli Svizzeri*, Lugano-Bellinzona 1983, 15 ss., e soprattutto *L'Assemblée fédérale suisse 1848–1920*, II, cit., *passim*, per l'analisi generale e le statistiche.

41 Basti pensare ai regolamenti del Consiglio degli Stati (7 dicembre 1849) e del Consiglio Nazionale (9 luglio 1850), alle leggi sui rapporti tra le due Camere (21 dicembre 1849), sul governo (16 maggio 1849), sul Tribunale federale (5 giugno 1849), sull'amministrazione (9 dicembre 1850), sull'organizzazione militare (1° maggio 1850).

42 Il Consiglio degli Stati, tra l'altro, poteva esser considerato come l''erede' storico della Dieta. Su questo *Kardinalproblem* della Costituzione del 1848, cfr. la sintesi di A. Kölz, *Neuere schweizerische Verfassungsgeschichte*, cit., 554–567.

43 Fazy aveva pubblicato nel 1833 un interessantissimo *Projet de constitution fédérale*, Genève, Pelletter, 1833, dove il sistema americano veniva indicato come il modello da seguire: «Le mode des Etats-Unis d'Amérique est le seul qui remplisse ces conditions: depuis cinquante ans qu'il est en vigueur, il a concilié tous les intérêts, organisé un pouvoir central formidable ...» (S. 4). Rüttimann, importante uomo politico zurighese (cfr. *L'Assemblée fédérale suisse 1848–1920*, I, cit., 99–100), scriverà, a partire dagli anni Sessanta, il suo fondamentale lavoro sulla Costituzione americana (cfr. *supra*, nota 35). Si vedano anche R. Van Berchem, *De la chambre unique au système bicaméral*, Zurich 1924; M. L. Tripp, *Der schweizerische und der amerikanische Bundesstaat*, Zürich 1942.

Il Consiglio degli Stati svolge una funzione "moderatrice" – alla stregua di ogni Camera Alta – ma nella logica più propriamente federale: la sovranità cantonale, in tal modo, entra in «contatto vivo e continuo colla rappresentanza della sovranità nazionale»,[44] prevenendo possibili attriti tra le due componenti organiche dello Stato. Il Consiglio dei Cantoni svolge le stesse funzioni del Consiglio Nazionale: partecipa all'attività legislativa di competenza federale, può prendere parte al processo di revisione della Costituzione federale, elegge in seduta comune i consiglieri federali, i giudici federali. Non v'è dubbio, però, che al Consiglio degli Stati si assegni, già nella Costituzione del 1848, una posizione istituzionalmente "subordinata" rispetto alla Camera Nazionale: basti pensare solo al fatto che nelle votazioni dell'Assemblea Federale a Camere riunite, il Consiglio Nazionale, in forza del numero,[45] ha un peso specifico ben più cospicuo che quello dei quarantaquattro rappresentanti dei Cantoni. Malgrado ciò, è da notare come nei primi decenni la Camera cantonale attragga le più eminenti personalità politiche: sei membri[46] su sette del primo Consiglio Federale provengono dal Consiglio degli Stati. La più breve durata del mandato (in genere un anno) e l'indebolimento del nesso funzionale tra i governi dei Cantoni e il Consiglio degli Stati ha spinto, nei decenni successivi, gli uomini politici più influenti a farsi eleggere nel Consiglio Nazionale.[47] Già nel corso degli anni Settanta Jakob Dubs propone una «specializzazione» (sul modello del Senato americano) e un rafforzamento della seconda Camera proprio per non svilire la logica dello Stato federale.[48]

44 J. Dubs, *Il diritto pubblico della Confederazione Svizzera*, cit., 574.

45 Numero che, nel corso degli anni, è cresciuto: dagli originari 111 deputati si è giunti agli attuali 200. Dubs critica questo squilibrio che contraddice il principio costituzionale dell'uguaglianza tra le rappresentanze delle due sovranità (ivi, 589–590).

46 Jonas Furrer (presidente del Consiglio Federale nel 1848, 1849, 1852, 1855, 1858), Druey, Munzinger, Frey-Hérosé, Näff, Franscini.

47 Questa impressione è ancora evidente in James Bryce, *Démocraties modernes*, Paris 1924, t. I, 392. L'equilibrio è stato, in seguito, ristabilito: cfr. J.-F. Aubert, *Traité de droit constitutionnel suisse*, cit., 472.

48 «Se dunque si volesse assegnare al Consiglio degli Stati la posizione che gli conviene, si dovrebbe incorporarlo completamente nell'organismo federale come parte essenziale e integrante, abbandonando naturalmente ai Cantoni la composizione personale del Consiglio, prolungando la durata delle funzioni, pur concedendo libero diritto di revoca [...] Se il Consiglio degli Stati fosse tolto dalla falsa posizione in cui si trova e pienamente riconosciuto come organo federale altrettanto legittimo che il Consiglio Nazionale, certamente esso renderebbe al paese maggiori servizi di quello che non faccia ora» (J. Dubs, *Il diritto pubblico della Confederazione Svizzera*, cit., 585–586). Questa visione è stata poi superata – come vedremo – a seguito del processo di democratizzazione della

L'istituzione parlamentare, così delineata, deve essere esaminata in relazione all'organo cui si assegna, nella Costituzione, la funzione di «suprema autorità esecutiva e direttoriale».[49] È proprio nel rapporto singolare tra Parlamento e Consiglio Federale che possiamo cogliere il dato costituzionale più caratteristico del sistema svizzero e della sua forma di governo. Il Consiglio Federale è «l'architrave, il compromesso ideale, il punto d'equilibrio di tutto l'assetto federale [...]».[50] Organo collegiale, formato da sette membri, nominati per tre anni (quattro a partire dal 1931) e scelti, non più di uno nello stesso Cantone, dalle Camere riunite tra tutti i cittadini svizzeri eleggibili al Consiglio Nazionale, rappresenta un elemento di notevole singolarità, tanto da porre ai costituzionalisti e ai politologi numerosi problemi classificatori. Il pensiero corre al regime direttoriale della Costituzione francese dell'anno III ("importata" in Svizzera nel 1798) e, soprattutto, alla prefigurazione del Consiglio Federale nel Patto Rossi.[51]

rappresentanza cantonale. Oggi Thomas Fleiner può affermare: «Il nostro *Ständerat*, mutuato nel 1848 dal modello americano, è la soluzione più democratica perché non rappresenta i governi cantonali, ma il popolo. I cittadini svizzeri non accetterebbero mai l'ipotesi del *Bundesrat* tedesco. Riconosco che il dibattito sul neofederalismo delle future istituzioni politiche dell'Unione europea tende a privilegiare il modello *Bundesrat*. Ma questo perché la concezione dello stato moderno, nella cultura politica europea, è di tipo gerarchico, dominato dall'esecutivo. La Svizzera ha un sistema politico che non funziona come negli altri stati europei» (T. Fleiner, *La democrazia consensuale della Confederazione Elvetica*, cit., 69).

49 Il principio di separazione dei poteri rappresenta, nel sistema svizzero, una categoria assai "relativa" e poco rispondente alle più classiche modellizzazioni. Sul governo, v. J. Dürsteller, *Die Organisation der Executive der schweizerischen Eidgenossenschaft seit 1798 in geschichtlicher Darstellung*, Zürich 1912; K. Schumann, *Das Regierungssystem der Schweiz*, Köln 1971.

50 T. Fleiner, *La democrazia consensuale della Confederazione Elvetica*, cit., 77. «L'uomo di governo per la Confederazione dev'essere quello che sa convergere ad un fine le diverse tendenze particolari, che sa prevedere gli avvenimenti, che sa preparare i movimenti dell'opinione pubblica, che sa condurre di lunga mano il disegno di un determinato vantaggio» (B. Bertoni, A. O. Olivetti, *Istituzioni svizzere nel diritto pubblico e privato della Confederazione e dei Cantoni*, vol. I, *Diritto pubblico. Saggio storico critico*, Torino 1903, 140).

51 «È tempo, o Signori, che la Confederazione abbia un governo suo proprio, unicamente occupato delle cose federali, e che non sia obbligato di dirigere nel tempo stesso gli affari di uno stato particolare». Il Consiglio federale, nel progetto del 1832, è formato da quattro membri – eletti dalla Dieta – che dirigono i dipartimenti dell'Interno, degli Esteri, della Difesa, delle Finanze, e dal Landamano della Svizzera (eletto dalle legislature cantonali), in qualità di presidente. Tale Consiglio mostra evidenti legami con l'esperienza direttoriale e con le costituzioni dell'età francese, ma presenta già diversi tratti del "modello" che sarà accolto nel 1848. Cfr. L. Lacchè, *Un italiano a Ginevra, alla ricerca della patria comune*, cit., XLVIII.

Ma non bisogna dimenticare che il regime collegiale di governo è anche un'antica consuetudine nella maggior parte dei Cantoni, dove un Piccolo Consiglio (o Consiglio di Stato o di Governo)[52] esercita alcune attribuzioni proprie del potere esecutivo.

Il Consiglio Federale segna il superamento del sistema precedente del Cantone-direttore che non assicurava né stabilità, ne continuità di azione, e in modo particolare ingenerava una pericolosa confusione tra gli organi e l'attività del Cantone-guida e della Confederazione. In realtà, vigente il Patto del 1815, l'organo preminente era la Dieta che assommava in sé le diverse funzioni dello Stato confederale e il *Vorort* non aveva alcuna autonomia se non in circostanze straordinarie (art. 9, Patto 1815).[53]

Il Presidente, eletto dall'Assemblea tra i consiglieri, dura in carica un anno ed è il Presidente del Consiglio Federale più che della Confederazione: è in realtà un *primus inter pares*, anche se gli si riconoscono alcune prerogative onorifiche e di rappresentanza.[54] Come gl'altri consiglieri, è a capo di un dipartimento che, in origine, è quello politico.[55] Gl'altri sei consiglieri sono al vertice di altrettanti dipartimenti (difesa, finanze e dogane, interno, giustizia e polizia, ferrovia e commercio, poste e telegrafi). Questa ripartizione risponde all'esigenza di "specializzazione" e di funzionalità del governo, ma le decisioni emanano dal «Consiglio federale come autorità».[56] La collegialità è dunque un elemento

52 A. E. Cherbuliez, *La democrazia nella Svizzera*, cit., 170 ss.; J. Dubs, *Il diritto pubblico della Confederazione Svizzera*, cit., 416 ss. Sono senza dubbio molto importanti le analogie tra il sistema di governo nella maggior parte dei Cantoni (Gran Consiglio, Piccolo Consiglio, Presidente) e il sistema federale.

53 Non a caso, nel 1840, fu avanzata una proposta di revisione parziale degli artt. 9 e 10 del Patto (v. A. Kölz, *Quellenbuch zur neueren schweizerischen Verfassungsgeschichte*, cit., vol. I, 199–200) per rendere permanente l'affiancamento al *Vorort* di sei rappresentanti federali.

54 Ha anche poteri di presidenza e il suo voto, in caso di parità, è decisivo. Firma le decisioni del Consiglio e può, in caso di urgenza, assumere decisioni che dovranno poi essere ratificate dal collegio.

55 Sino al 1887 il Presidente era anche il ministro degli esteri. Per ovviare al cambio annuale e alla conseguente discontinuità della linea politica, a partire dal 1887 si cominciò ad affermare il cd. sistema Droz, dal nome del presidente Numa Droz che tenne per alcuni anni di seguito il dicastero degli esteri. Tale sistema si affermerà definitivamente nel 1920. Su Droz v. *L'Assemblée fédérale suisse 1848–1920, Biographies*, cit., vol. I, 893–894.

56 Questo principio venne attenuato dall'*arrêté fédéral* del 21 agosto 1878 che prevedeva la possibilità, per il Consiglio, di delegare talune materie ai dipartimenti, con riserva espressa di un diritto di ricorso al Consiglio. Nel 1914, a seguito di votazione popolare, tale meccanismo fu introdotto nella Costituzione (art. 103, II, in A. Kölz, *Quellenbuch zur neueren schweizerischen Verfassungsgeschichte*, cit., vol. II, 206).

fondamentale. Il Presidente non è un primo ministro, non ha alcuna influenza sulla composizione del collegio; il capo dello Stato è dunque l'intero consiglio che assume le proprie decisioni a maggioranza (con almeno quattro consiglieri presenti).

I membri del Consiglio Federale hanno voto consultivo nelle due Camere e possono avanzare proposte sulle materie in discussione. Tra le attribuzioni del Consiglio, oltre quella generale di direzione e di sorveglianza, bisogna ricordare il diritto di presentare progetti di legge all'Assemblea e di dare il proprio avviso sulle proposte avanzate dalle Camere e dai Cantoni, nonché l'obbligo di dare conto della propria gestione all'Assemblea Federale ad ogni sessione ordinaria, presentando una relazione sullo stato della Confederazione e raccomandando le misure ritenute utili per accrescere la "prosperità comune".

Ciò che caratterizza in modo particolare la forma di governo nella Confederazione non è soltanto la collegialità. Di grande interesse è il tipo di rapporto che si è instaurato tra il Consiglio Federale e l'Assemblea. Nella prassi costituzionale post-quarantottesca il Consiglio Federale persegue una linea di governo che riflette "docilmente" l'indirizzo politico di un'Assemblea a forte maggioranza radicale. Questo fatto non meraviglia, se si pensa che fino al 1891 nel Consiglio Federale siedono solo esponenti di tendenza liberale e radicale. Arthur de Gobineau nel 1850, diplomatico francese a Berna, nelle lettere che indirizza a Tocqueville, è molto critico verso il Consiglio Federale. Il giudizio è viziato dalla sua idiosincrasia per la «rivoluzione radicale»: scrive così di «[...] sept hommes sans influence, sans appui, sans considération réelle [...]»;[57] tuttavia questo giudizio registra il maggior peso costituzionale dell'Assemblea. In effetti, la maggior parte dei casi di dimissione e di non rielezione di consiglieri – non più di una decina – si situano proprio tra gl'anni '60 e '70,[58] gli anni del monocolore radicale. Forse si potrebbe anche sostenere che in questi decenni l'elemento "parlamentare" sia, date le circostanze, più marcato. Ma, detto questo, non possiamo spingerci troppo oltre: non si può infatti parlare di "subordinazione" politica o di vera e propria "dipendenza" funzionale. Il Consiglio non è soggetto a voto di sfiducia né è costretto a dimettersi collegialmente nell'ipotesi di censura parlamentare o popolare (bocciatura di una proposta di legge, ecc.). A sua volta, il Governo non può sciogliere il Parlamento. In caso di conflitto o di messa in minoranza, «[...] le Conseil se soumet, et ne se démet pas».[59] La regola è che i consiglieri restino al loro posto, instaurando un "dialogo" assai complesso con l'istituzione parlamentare.

57 Alexis De Tocqueville, *Œuvres complètes*, IX: *Correspondance d'Alexis de Tocqueville et d'Arthur de Gobineau*, a cura di M. Degros, Paris 1959, 146.

58 Per la casistica v. J.-F. Aubert, *Traité de droit constitutionnel suisse*, cit., 530.

59 *Ibidem*, 37, 531.

Il Consiglio federale è eletto per un periodo determinato – come il potere esecutivo nei regimi presidenziali – ma dal Parlamento e non direttamente dal popolo.[60] Come nei regimi presidenziali non sono previsti né le dimissioni forzate, per ragioni politiche, del Governo né il potere di dissoluzione del Parlamento in capo al potere esecutivo. Pur derivando dal Parlamento, la durata in carica del Consiglio dipende dalla Costituzione e non dalla volontà dei deputati.[61] In questo ambito si può notare uno degli aspetti più interessanti della costituzione elvetica sul punto del rapporto tra la Costituzione formale e la Costituzione materiale. Il Consiglio Federale – come abbiamo detto – deve per esempio dare conto del suo operato all'Assemblea; altri ancora sono i collegamenti istituzionali tra Governo e Parlamento. A rigor di logica, non si può dire che il Consiglio Federale sia irresponsabile; è piuttosto l'Assemblea che ha – di fronte al silenzio del testo costituzionale – rinunciato di fatto a sanzionare la responsabilità del Governo.[62] Da questo tipo di prassi discendono la stabilità e l'autorità del sistema di governo: in ottant'anni si sono succeduti appena 50 consiglieri, con una durata media della carica che si aggira attorno ai dieci anni; così come discendono il ruolo arbitrale del Consiglio e il suo progressivo rafforzamento.[63]

> «Questi benefici sono dovuti ad una pratica o ad una convenzione, non concretata in alcuna disposizione della Costituzione, ma formata dall'uso e raccomandata dai risultati. Siamo in presenza di un esempio importante della misura, fino alla quale le norme legali di una Costituzione giungono ad essere modificate, nel loro funzionamento, da quella che il professor Dicey [*The Law of the Constitution*] ha chiamato "le Convenzioni di una Costituzione", ossia gli usi azionati da una specie di intesa, intervenuta tra uomini politici, e così bene organizzati nella pratica da divenire, virtualmente, sebbene non legalmente, imperativi».[64]

60 Proposte in tal senso, sempre respinte, furono avanzate dai socialisti nel 1900 e nel 1942.

61 «Non è un Gabinetto, perché non dirige il Parlamento, né è amovibile da parte sua [...] Neppure è indipendente dal Parlamento, come il potere esecutivo degli Stati Uniti e delle repubbliche, le quali ne hanno mutuato il cosiddetto sistema presidenziale; e, per quanto, il Consiglio Federale abbia qualcuna delle linee di entrambi questi sistemi di governo, differisce da entrambi per non avere un distinto carattere di partito. Esso si colloca a parte, non è scelto per sviluppare un'attività di partito, non dà vita ad una politica di partito; eppure non è completamente privo di un colore di partito» (J. Bryce, *Democrazie moderne*, Milano 1949–1953, vol. I, 267–268).

62 Cfr. le osservazioni puntuali di J.-F. Aubert, *Traité de droit constitutionnel suisse*, cit., 539–540.

63 «Questa indipendenza dalle vicende parlamentari ha contribuito a dare stabilità ed autorità al Consiglio Federale e continuità ed efficacia alle funzioni governative» (G. Bergmann, *Costituenti e costituzioni svizzere*, Firenze 1946, 89).

64 J. Bryce, *Democrazie moderne*, cit., 375.

Hanno carattere convenzionale – oltre quelle che "disciplinano" i rapporti tra Parlamento e Governo – regole fondamentali come la rielezione, più o meno integrale, del Consiglio Federale di tre anni in tre anni; il fatto che il vicepresidente del Governo prenda il posto del Presidente uscente; l'elezione in Consiglio Federale, sin dalle origini, di un consigliere di Berna, uno di Zurigo, quasi sempre uno del Vaud, e con almeno due rappresentanti *welsches*.

Le "anomalie" della forma di governo elvetica – ovvero la sua irriproducibile "tipicità" – sono il risultato di una graduale costruzione che nulla ha di artificiale. Non sono mancate neppure proposte diverse o tese a riformare aspetti "critici". Se Bluntschli ha insistito sui presunti limiti della collegialità (mancanza di unità ed armonia) suggerendo una figura di Presidente di Gabinetto, con un diritto di proposta sull'elezione dei consiglieri o di veto contro le «nomine disarmoniche»,[65] lo stesso Dubs ha suggerito una distinzione tra il Governo vero e proprio (3/5 membri che sovrintendono alla direzione politica) e l'amministrazione posta nelle mani di direttori – una sorta di "segretari di Stato" –, recuperando una misura già operante nella Repubblica Elvetica e soprattutto il modulo americano di direzione politica unitaria adattandolo, però, alla collegialità svizzera.[66] Quasi mai, tuttavia, il riferimento ai regimi parlamentari o, più spesso, al sistema americano, giova alla piena comprensione dell'istituto parlamentare e della forma di governo confederale. Ogni divergenza dal "modello americano" viene vista sovente come una «debolezza»[67] del Consiglio Federale, mentre invece in quella radicale diversità risiedono la stabilità e la funzione di equilibrio[68] tra i poteri esercitata da tale organo.

65 J. K. Bluntschli, *Diritto pubblico universale*, Napoli 1873, vol. II, 44. Su Bluntschli, v. W. Hochuli, *Johann Caspar Bluntschli (1808–1881)*, in *Zeitschrift für Schweizerisches Recht*, 101, 1982, 87–104.

66 J. Dubs, *Il diritto pubblico della Confederazione Svizzera*, cit., 594–595. Non di rado il Consiglio federale è paragonato al *bureau* di direttori scelti tra i membri di una grande società per azioni: cfr. A.V. Dicey, *Introduction à l'étude du droit constitutionnel*, Paris 1902, 438.

67 Per restare agli osservatori italiani, G. Padelletti, *Nuova fase della democrazia in Svizzera*, in *Nuova Antologia*, serie II, X, 1869, 460–510, e soprattutto L. Palma, *Costituzioni moderne. La Confederazione svizzera*, *ibidem*, serie II, XXXVI, 1882, 239–278, 458–499, che fa riferimento al veto presidenziale.

68 Non è esatto, come sostiene Vincenzo Gueli, affermare che «se, infatti, si ravvisasse nel Consiglio Federale un organo corrispondente al gabinetto di un governo parlamentare tipico, l'assenza nell'ordinamento svizzero di un organo corrispondente al Capo dello Stato fa sì che non vi si possa stabilire quell'equilibrio di poteri che caratterizza tale forma di governo» (V. Guelfi, *La costituzione federale svizzera*, Firenze 1947, 87–88). Il Capo dello Stato esiste, ma è collegiale ed esercita una specifica funzione di equilibrio dei poteri.

5. La democrazia in Svizzera e i «diritti popolari»

Nel periodo compreso tra il 1848 e il 1874, ovvero l'anno della revisione totale della Costituzione, la democrazia rappresentativa appare come la forma più congeniale alle forze costituenti radicali e liberali. Non si comprenderebbe però la trasformazione dell'assetto costituzionale restando dentro il recinto del solo, tipicissimo, circuito Parlamento-Governo. Jakob Dubs dedica una pagina assai interessante del suo lavoro sul diritto pubblico svizzero al ruolo dell'opposizione inteso come metodo di controllo del Governo e, in generale, delle autorità politiche. Ebbene, il concetto di alternanza dei partiti al governo del paese è davvero salutare in Inghilterra. «Presso di noi non si seppe ancora elevarsi a un tale concetto, si crede anzi che perisca il mondo se avviene un tale cambiamento».[69] Questa osservazione – fatta da uno dei pochissimi consiglieri federali ad aver dato le dimissioni[70] – coglie alcuni profili importanti. Il sistema politico svizzero nasce e si sviluppa dopo una guerra civile: c'è una parte, pur minoritaria, del paese che porta avanti una politica "difensiva" e resta fuori della "stanza dei bottoni". Non esistono ancora, a livello federale, meccanismi efficaci di "controllo" e di "proposta" azionabili "al di fuori" del circuito Parlamento-Governo, se si escludono la complessa procedura "eccezionale" di revisione totale della Costituzione e il ruolo appena abbozzato del Tribunale Federale. Bisogna attendere la revisione del 1874 per compiere un passo decisivo.

È a partire dagl'anni Sessanta che in Svizzera si comincia a parlare di riforma, parziale, della Costituzione. A quasi due decenni dall'entrata in vigore della prima costituzione di stampo moderno è possibile fare un primo bilancio. I liberali, con Dubs in testa, sollecitano un consolidamento dello Stato federale, senza spingersi troppo oltre sulla strada dell'uniformità; i radicali di sinistra propongono invece una più decisa "nazionalizzazione" e l'introduzione, a livello federale, dei «diritti popolari»; i conservatori, infine, respingono i due distinti programmi. Se nel 1866 la revisione parziale può riguardare solo la libertà di domicilio degli ebrei, è perché la distanza tra federalisti e radicali resta grande. Nel 1872, quando si giunge ad una nuova votazione[71] – ma stavolta per la revisione totale – la spaccatura non si è affatto ricomposta[72] e l'esito negativo

69 J. Dubs, *Il diritto pubblico della Confederazione Svizzera*, cit., 507.

70 Cfr. G. Ermatinger, *Jakob Dubs als schweizerischer Bundesrat von 1861 bis 1872*, Zürich 1933.

71 Si veda A. Kölz, *Quellenbuch zur neueren schweizerischen Verfassungsgeschichte*, cit., vol. II, 128.

72 È in questo frangente che Dubs lascia il Consiglio Federale per meglio sostenere la sua campagna contro il progetto di revisione ritenuto troppo radicale. È da segnalare, al riguardo, lo scritto *Zur Verständigung über die Bundesrevision*, Zürich

sancisce l'inasprimento del conflitto. La divisione non vede semplicemente i radicali e i democratici centralizzatori da un lato e i federalisti dall'altro. La vicenda è più complessa: l'opposizione di molti radicali romandi – che temevano l'egemonia tedesca – illustra bene la segmentazione degli schieramenti. È nel 1874 che si riesce ad operare una "sintesi" tra le diverse posizioni. L'impulso democratico, la rivendicazione centralizzatrice, il tono anticlericale (*Kulturkampf*) confluiscono nel testo della revisione totale del 1874, l'odierna Costituzione elvetica. Un testo, questo, che pur rafforzando ulteriormente le competenze del centro, non manca di fare alcune concessioni ai federalisti.[73] Il sistema federale rimane il perno della democrazia. L'Assemblea Federale perde alcune attribuzioni a vantaggio sia del Consiglio Federale che del Tribunale Federale, il cui statuto di indipendenza viene irrobustito.

Se nella costituzione del 1848 trovavamo la procedura di revisione della Costituzione (senza distinguere tra revisione totale e parziale), nella Costituzione del 1874, nel corpo stesso delle attribuzioni dell'Assemblea Federale, scorgiamo una disposizione destinata ad incidere in maniera profonda sul sistema politico svizzero.

> «Le leggi federali, come pure le risoluzioni federali di carattere obbligatorio generale e che non sono di natura urgente, devono essere sottoposte al popolo per l'accettazione o il rifiuto, quando ciò sia richiesto da trentamila cittadini aventi il diritto di voto, oppure da otto Cantoni» (art. 89, II, Cost. 1874).[74]

1871. Si veda, soprattutto, E. Kaufmann, *Bundesrat Jakob Dubs und die Bundesrevision von 1872–1874 im Lichte seiner Zeitung "Die Eidgenossenschaft"*, Freiburg 1957, diss.phil.-hist. Su tutta la vicenda è fondamentale R. Haeberli, *Die Revision der Bundesverfassung 1872–1874 im Lichte der öffentlichen Meinung*, Bern 1949. Per ulteriori indicazioni, v. *L'Assemblée fédérale suisse 1848–1920, Biographies*, cit., vol. I, 61–62.

73 «Ma se più davvicino si considerino le cose, si scorgerà che nell'evoluzione del diritto pubblico svizzero, già a partire dal movimento liberale del 1830, un pensiero, o meglio un sentimento è dominante. L'accentramento e il decentramento non sono più considerati come due principii avversi ed inconciliabili, di cui uno debba distruggere l'altro, ma piuttosto come due forze egualmente necessarie, dal cui giusto equilibrio dipende il benessere del paese. Si riconosce, per ragione o per istinto, che l'accentramento politico non deve essere il portato di una concezione metafisica e di un atto arbitrario, ma la corrispondente conseguenza di quell'altro accentramento che si opera nei costumi, negli interessi economici e nella coltura per effetto della progredita civiltà e dell'aumento dei traffici. [...] L'unificazione del diritto pubblico e privato non è stata guidata dal preconcetto di un fine necessario, ma dal verificarsi di successive contingenze di fatto e dal consecutivo spostamento degli interessi» (B. Bertoni, A. O. Olivetti, *Istituzioni svizzere nel diritto pubblico*, cit., 71–72).

74 Cfr. A. Kölz, *Quellenbuch zur neueren schweizerischen Verfassungsgeschichte*, cit., vol. II, 176. Per l'attuazione di questo articolo, cfr. la legge federale del 17 giugno 1874 sulle votazioni popolari delle leggi e dei decreti federali.

Il fatto che la previsione del referendum facoltativo si trovi nella sezione dedicata alle attribuzioni dell'Assemblea, sottolinea il carattere di sanzione, eventuale ma strategica, dell'intervento popolare sull'attività legislativa del Parlamento. Di conseguenza l'Assemblea esercita il «potere supremo della Confederazione [...] sotto riserva dei diritti del popolo e dei Cantoni» (art. 71, Cost. 1874).[75] Il Parlamento non è più, come nella Costituzione precedente, l'«autorità suprema della Confederazione». Nel 1874, dunque, la democrazia diretta fa il suo pieno ingresso nella vita politica federale. Ancora una volta, il banco di prova è offerto dai Cantoni nei quali le decisioni del popolo-sovrano – guidate dal movimento democratico più critico verso il sistema rappresentativo – hanno creato molteplici forme di partecipazione diretta, sia nel campo delle revisioni costituzionali che in quello del potere legislativo. Se il fenomeno tradizionale della *Landsgemeinde* tende progressivamente a ridursi nei Cantoni forestali, è soprattutto il referendum a guidare lo sviluppo dei «diritti popolari». Nato nei Grigioni e nel Vallese, trova a Neuchâtel una prima applicazione come referendum finanziario (Cost. 1858), seguito poi dal Vaud (Cost. 1861) e soprattutto da Basilea-campagna (Cost. 1863) che introduce il referendum obbligatorio su «tutte le leggi, come pure le decisioni e i contratti che contengono una obbligazione generale», e rafforzato nel 1869 da Zurigo, Turgovia, Soletta e Berna[76] per giungere infine, in forma facoltativa, alla Costituzione federale del 1874.[77]

Lo sviluppo del referendum e dei diritti popolari è stato accolto non senza apprensioni e critiche. Se Cherbuliez, nella prima metà dell'Ottocento, loda il sistema «organico» e «conservatore» della *Landsgemeinde* e esprime un giudizio fortemente negativo sul veto e sul referendum come strumenti di degenerazione democratica,[78] Dubs riconosce il necessario fondamento «sovrano» del sistema referendario ma critica alcuni difetti di «organizzazione» a cominciare dal fatto che i Cantoni, pur potendo chiedere il referendum, non hanno il diritto di

75 Il testo *ibidem*, 171.

76 Il referendum obbligatorio e l'iniziativa legislativa furono introdotti nei primi tre Cantoni, mentre a Berna il solo referendum.

77 Cfr. J. Dubs, *Il diritto pubblico della Confederazione Svizzera*, cit., 468 ss.; J.-F. Aubert, *Traité de droit constitutionnel suisse*, cit., 46; dello stesso autore si vedano inoltre *Le referendum populaire*, in *Zeitschrift für Schweizerisches Recht*, 91, 1972, 481–506; *Le referendum populaire dans la revision totale de 1872/1874*, *ibidem* , 93, 1974, 409–431.

78 A. E. Cherbuliez, *La democrazia nella Svizzera*, cit., 179: «In Isvizzera non v'ha che una sola opinione circa il *referendum*: che è un grave ostacolo ad ogni sviluppo razionale delle istituzioni politiche e civili, ai più urgenti miglioramenti, alle riforme più giustificate nel sistema delle leggi organiche dal quale dipende lo stato intellettuale e morale di una nazione».

votarlo (come invece avviene nell'ipotesi di revisione costituzionale: doppio voto).[79] Dubs vede il referendum legislativo più nell'ottica dello Stato federale che della supremazia dei diritti popolari: il pericolo, a suo dire, sarebbe quello di dar vita a un referendum «inorganico» che, senza la guida e il contrappeso delle autorità cantonali, favorirebbe le decisioni negative (veto). Chi, poi, scorge nel sistema rappresentativo l'unico in grado di assicurare realmente il «governo dei migliori», non può non guardare con occhio critico al referendum quale forma di «capacità politica» delle masse, strumento che nei Cantoni avrebbe trasformato i Gran Consigli in comitati legislativi, asservendoli all'«inorganico» capriccio popolare.[80]

Malgrado i dubbi, l'espansione democratica prosegue dopo il 1874. A parte i tentativi sempre falliti di introdurre l'iniziativa popolare legislativa, nel 1891 fa il suo ingresso nella costituzione l'iniziativa (cinquantamila cittadini) per la

79 J. Dubs, *Il diritto pubblico della Confederazione Svizzera*, cit., 702: «Evidentemente questa è un'anomalia, in contraddizione con tutto il sistema federale, che poggia sull'eguaglianza della Confederazione».

80 G. Padelletti, *Nuova fase della democrazia in Svizzera*, cit., discute gli scritti di J. Dubs, *Die schweizerische Demokratie in ihrer Fortenwicklung*, Zürich 1868; E. Tallichet, *La démocratie suisse et son évolution actuelle*, in *Bibliothèque universelle et Revue suisse*, juillet, août, septembre 1868; J. Gengel, *Die Erweiterung der Volksrechte. Besprechung im Verein der Liberalen Bern's herausgegeben*, Bern 1868; C. Hilty, *Theoretiker und Idealisten der Demokratie*, Bern, Solothurn 1868; cfr. anche L. Palma, *Costituzioni moderne. La Confederazione svizzera*, cit. e G. Crivellari, *Il referendum nella Svizzera e la sua introduzione nel diritto amministrativo italiano*, in *Archivio giuridico*, XXXIV, 1885, 399–400: «Per tutte queste ragioni si è operata nell'opinione pubblica svizzera la inversione delle parti, già osservata da Cherbuliez per il referendum cantonale, che i fautori, radicali, ne sono in gran parte divenuti avversari; e i conservatori viceversa. Né gli uni né gli altri sembrano avessero o abbiano ragione di preferire al sistema strettamente rappresentativo quello che abbassa la sapienza legislativa sino alla massa popolare e nuoce alle funzioni elettive senza garantire il progresso politico e civile». Sul punto v. J. K. Bluntschli, *La politica come scienza*, Napoli 1879, 310. Il sistema costituzionale elvetico ha attirato l'attenzione, a partire dalla seconda metà dell'Ottocento, degli studiosi italiani. Oltre agli autori già citati, si deve ricordare almeno – non potendo in questa sede sviluppare oltre il profilo comparativo – Attilio Brunialti la cui prelezione al corso libero di diritto costituzionale comparato, tenuta nel 1872 (*Le istituzioni politiche della Svizzera*, Roma 1872), fu poi ampliata nello scritto *La democrazia in Svizzera*, in *Le moderne evoluzioni del governo costituzionale. Saggi e letture*, Milano 1881. Brunialti faceva risaltare, fin dalla prolusione del 1872, il sistema politico-costituzionale elvetico – considerato anche «nella vita del popolo» – come uno straordinario «campionario» delle varie forme di democrazia. Il giovane costituzionalista italiano aveva già trattato del tema della rappresentanza e della democrazia in Svizzera (con specifico riferimento ai Cantoni di Ginevra e di Neuchâtel) in *Libertà e democrazia. Studi sulla rappresentanza delle minorità*, Milano 1871, 225 ss. e *passim*.

revisione parziale[81] della Costituzione. Fu il Consiglio degli Stati a chiedere che alla semplice proposta concepita in termini generali si affiancasse la possibilità di presentare un progetto già redatto nella sua interezza (art. 121, IV, Cost. 1874). Questa disposizione attribuiva ai proponenti un importante potere di determinazione tecnica della revisione costituzionale e soprattutto alle minoranze (nella circostanza conservatori e socialisti) la possibilità di entrare "in competizione" con l'indirizzo politico emanante dal Parlamento (ancora dominato dai radicali).[82] Numa Droz, nel 1894, criticava questa evoluzione:

> «On peut diviser l'histoire contemporaine de la Suisse en trois périodes: celle du parlamentarisme, qui s'étend de 1848 à 1874; celle de la démocratie, issue de la révision fédérale de 1874, qui a établi le référendum facultatif; et celle de la démagogie, qui s'est ouverte il y a deux ans avec l'introduction du droit d'initiative en matière de revision partielle de la Constitution».[83]

Lo spettro della demagogia non può tuttavia essere invocato per liquidare o sminuire il ruolo "strategico" degli istituti di democrazia diretta nella storia svizzera. Il referendum legislativo e l'iniziativa di riforma parziale della Costituzione si affermano, nell'ultimo quarto del XIX secolo, come strumenti di integrazione e di controllo. Tra il 1875 e il 1879 il popolo appoggiò l'operato del Parlamento 3 volte su 7, tra il 1880 e il 1884 5 furono i rifiuti su 5 votazioni.[84] Questo tipo di risultato sembrerebbe dare ragione a Dubs che considerava il referendum troppo «inorganico», privo di una guida, considerata la relativa debolezza dei partiti[85] e l'assenza di un voto cantonale. Tuttavia, ciò che Dubs definisce «inorganico» altro non è se non il carattere di autonomia della democrazia diretta rispetto al circuito della democrazia rappresentativa dominato dai radicali e dai liberali di centro. Figlio della spinta democratica, di matrice radicale, nei Cantoni prima e nella Confederazione poi, il referendum

81 Adozione di un nuovo articolo costituzionale ovvero abrogazione o modifica di articoli della Costituzione (art. 121, II, Cost. 1874). Cfr. A. Kölz, *Quellenbuch zur neueren schweizerischen Verfassungsgeschichte*, II, cit., 191–192.

82 La Costituzione non fissa un criterio obiettivo di differenziazione tra le materie riservate all'intervento costituzionale e quelle riservate alla legge ordinaria. Ciò spiega anche l'ampio utilizzo della procedura di revisione parziale. Sino al 1940 furono approvate 41 modifiche e 30 non raccolsero la maggioranza dei votanti. Non tutte le aggiunte e le modifiche hanno "dignità" costituzionale. Tale tecnica di revisione, che ha il merito della flessibilità, non ha lasciato indenne la compattezza, la coerenza e l'unità della Costituzione. «On ne peut pas dire – ha scritto Bastid – que la Constitution fédérale brille par une élégante simplicité» (P. Bastid, *Gouvernement d'assemblée*, Paris 1956, 271).

83 In *Bibliothèque universelle*, 4, 1894, 225. Sul punto cfr. J.-F. Aubert, *Traité de droit constitutionnel suisse*, cit., 67.

84 Tra il 1874 e il 1920 il Parlamento ha approvato 320 leggi; 33 sono state sottoposte a referendum: 20 sono state respinte e 13 accolte.

85 Sul sistema dei partiti, si rinvia a E. Gruner, *Die Parteien in der Schweiz*, cit.

fu utilizzato dai conservatori e più tardi dai socialisti per contrastare il «blocco» Parlamento-Governo monopolizzato dalle forze costituenti. Le minoranze parlamentari poterono ricorrere agli istituti della democrazia diretta per frenare l'attività legislativa. Tali istituti funzionarono spesso da contrappeso, tanto più in un sistema nel quale non poteva affermarsi un regime di alternanza; in altre occasioni furono uno stimolo per il Parlamento.

I diritti popolari contribuiscono a porre dei freni sia al potere centrale che alle *élite* politiche. In assenza di un veto moderatore nelle mani del potere esecutivo – come negli Stati Uniti – il corpo elettorale può esercitare un "controllo di merito" sulle leggi federali. Si tratti di sanzionare l'oligarchia affaristica (industria-banche-ferrovie) che ha un notevole peso in Parlamento (si pensi al cd. sistema Escher, potente industriale e deputato zurighese),[86] di limitare i difetti della repubblica notabiliare, di sconfessare le Camere su provvedimenti fiscali o di altra natura, la democrazia diretta svolge una funzione "fisiologica". Il ricorso alla partecipazione diretta non è, quindi, una sorta di "deviazione"; al contrario, è parte integrante e fondamentale del codice genetico del "sistema" costituzionale svizzero. Le "parti" di democrazia diretta e di democrazia rappresentativa interagiscono, controbilanciandosi a vicenda. Il referendum legislativo produce effetti "preventivi", condiziona le autorità legislative, elide l'opera della rappresentanza, interviene sul rapporto tra legislativo ed esecutivo, limita lo sviluppo del governo di partito, esercita un «potere maggioritario di controllo».[87] La democrazia diretta va ad integrare quella forma peculiare di democrazia rappresentativa che contraddistingue il sistema costituzionale svizzero dopo il 1848. A partire dall'ultimo quarto dell'Ottocento sono «utili compagni di viaggio».[88] Sino all'avvento del sistema proporzionale (legge 14 febbraio 1919), il referendum legislativo e l'iniziativa costituzionale svolgono la funzione di opposizione-integrazione delle minoranze parlamentari (nel 1891 Joseph Zemp diventa il primo consigliere federale conservatore), contribuendo a legittimare il sistema nel suo complesso e a consentirne un costante adeguamento all'evoluzione della società.

Successivamente, la democrazia diretta ha potuto svolgere una pluralità di funzioni, non previste nella fase di fondazione (1848–1891), a testimonianza della flessibilità dei suoi istituti.[89] Ma l'analisi della moderna Costituzione

86 Cfr. E. Gagliardi, *Alfred Escher, Vier Jahrzehnte neuerer Schweizergeschichte*, Frauenfeld 1919. Vedi anche *L'Assemblée fédérale suisse 1848–1920, Biographies*, cit., vol. I, 63–65.

87 M. Hauriou, *Precis de droit constitutionnel*, Paris 1929, 174 ss. Cfr. anche M. Bridel, *L'esprit et la destinée de la Constitution fédérale de 1848*, Lausanne 1949, 47 ss.

88 T. Fleiner, *La democrazia consensuale della Confederazione Elvetica*, cit., 228.

89 Cfr. supra, in questo volume, *Costituzioni e federalismo nella Svizzera del XIX secolo*, 42–43.

svizzera rivela per tempo la “mobile complessità” – per riprendere l’espressione dalla quale eravamo partiti – che ne caratterizza la sua lunga fase genetica. Il corpo elettorale (*Aktivbürgerschaft*) è in grado di esprimere l’ultima parola (votazione) sulla determinazione dell’indirizzo politico generale. Il principio della sovranità popolare è dunque a fondamento dell’assetto costituzionale elvetico: sia nella forma della rappresentanza che in quella della diretta partecipazione dei cittadini politicamente attivi. Le due forme funzionano insieme e il successo e la stabilità dell’intero sistema dipendono dall’equilibrio e dall’integrazione raggiunti. Il concetto di democrazia semi-diretta, se lo si vuole applicare a questa decisiva fase ottocentesca, è da interpretare in tal senso. Aveva comunque ragione Tocqueville, nel 1850, a scommettere sulla Confederazione: «La Suisse, malgré la petite fièvre chronique de sa démocratie, me parait pourvue d’une santé plus robuste et avoir un avenir plus tranquille que la plupart des états qui l’environnent».[90]

90 Alexis de Tocqueville, *Œuvres complètes*, cit., 137.

Chapter II
Constitution, Monarchy, popular sovereignty: the Belgian experience

La costituzione belga del 1831

1. Premessa

Il Belgio è stato protagonista negl'ultimi trent'anni di una profonda e originale metamorfosi istituzionale. La revisione costituzionale del 5 maggio 1993 ha 'completato' un complesso e sofferto processo di trasformazione avviato nei primi anni Settanta per rispondere a diverse, seppur convergenti questioni. Il *fédéralisme à la belge* si è identificato con uno *work in progress* di cui ancora oggi è difficile immaginare l'esito ultimo. Non deve quindi meravigliare l'interesse per il lessico istituzionale del 'laboratorio' belga in virtù sia della ricchezza tematica che, al tempo stesso, della sua irriducibilità ad ogni altra esperienza costituzionale. Se «Le istituzioni belghe sono un vestito su misura ...»,[1] è impossibile offrirne un'immagine che non sia rigorosamente tagliata sulle specificità storiche e sulle concrete dinamiche politiche, sociali, culturali ed economiche.

Da Stato unitario a Stato composito,[2] infine a Stato federale, e ancora dalla costituzione del 1831 alle revisioni del 1893 e 1920–1921 sino alla radicale riforma del 1993. Tra questi termini si svolge la storia costituzionale del Belgio lungo più di un secolo e mezzo. In apparenza questa è la storia di un 'paradosso': se la costituzione del 1831 è stata raffigurata e a lungo percepita come un vero e proprio 'modello', l'esempio per eccellenza di un determinato assetto politico-istituzionale, quella del 1993 (o meglio il processo pluridecennale di riforma dello Stato) è definibile *a priori* come un non-modello che – alla ricerca di un difficile punto di equilibrio e di compromesso tra istanze e valori diversi – ha investito in maniera profonda la più antica e conservata[3] Costituzione scritta del

1 M. Leroy, *Il federalismo belga*, in *Quale, dei tanti federalismi?*, a cura di A. Pace, Padova 1997, 110.

2 F. Delpérée, *Droit constitutionnel*, t. I, *Les données constitutionnelles*, Bruxelles 1987, 440.

3 La Legge Fondamentale olandese del 1815 e la costituzione svedese del 1809, benchè più antiche, hanno subìto nel corso del XIX secolo modifiche ben più profonde di quelle che investirono la costituzione belga (regime elettorale e Senato) nel 1893 e nel 1920–1921.

continente sino a farne una forma costituzionale *sui generis* di Stato federale. Le riforme successive, gli aggiustamenti, lo *choc* istituzionale conseguente all'approvazione del testo nel 1993 hanno dunque radicalmente trasformato la costituzione belga e più in generale l'assetto complessivo dello Stato.[4] Si potrebbe forse osservare che il testo della costituzione del 1831 rappresenta ormai solo una grande pagina di *storia* del Belgio e del costituzionalismo europeo, ma proprio per questo appare quanto mai attuale interrogarsi sulle ragioni e sui caratteri che hanno fatto di quel documento un paradigma di lunga durata e un vero e proprio mito storiografico. Non ci si può avvicinare alla straordinaria complessità delle istituzioni odierne senza uno sguardo retrospettivo che ritorni alle origini ed alle successive determinazioni politico-costituzionali.

> Il piccolo paese del Belgio, con quattro milioni e mezzo di abitanti, ha tentato di sciogliere uno dei più difficili problemi politici dei tempi moderni, quello di accordare le stabili e sicure guarentigie della libertà colla monarchia rappresentativa. Gli Inglesi lo chiamano *la piccola Inghilterra*, ed è questo il più bell'onore di lodi ch'esso possa ambire; anzi, se piuttosto dei costumi, nei quali l'Inghilterra è institutrice dei popoli, si consideri la libertà nelle leggi, il Belgio si può dire una piccola Inghilterra corretta da molti abusi ed immune dai maggioraschi e dalle reliquie dei privilegi feudali. La sua costituzione, *investigata sotto l'aspetto teorico*, è un modello di popolari franchigie ed accoglie senza alcun temperamento quasi tutti i principii del diritto pubblico proclamati dai più illustri scrittori.[5]

4 Sul pluridecennale processo di revisione e sul testo del 1993 mi limito a segnalare – nell'ambito di un'ampia bibliografia – almeno i seguenti lavori: A. Lijphart, *Conflict and Coesistence in Belgium*, Berkeley 1981; P. Lauvaux, *Parlementarisme rationalisé et stabilité du pouvoir exécutif. Quelques aspects de la réforme de l'Etat confrontés aux expériences étrangères*, Bruxelles 1988; il numero 54, 1990, della rivista *Pouvoirs* dedicato al Belgio; L. Primicerio, *La riforma dei sistemi costituzionali. Il caso belga*, Salerno 1991; M. Uyttendaele, *Le fédéralisme inachevé: réflexions sur le système institutionnel*, Bruxelles 1991; A. Alen (a cura di), *Treatise on Belgian constitutional law*, Deventer, Boston 1992; *La constitution fédérale du 5 mai 1993*, con introduzione di F. Delpérée, Bruxelles 1993; F. Delpérée (a cura di), *La Belgique fédérale*, Bruxelles 1994; F. Delpérée, *La nouvelle constitution belge*, in *Revue française de droit constitutionnel*, 17, 1994; R. Senelle, *Il Belgio federale*, in *Federalismo e regionalismo in Europa*, a cura di A. D'Atena, Milano 1994; E. Cerexhe, *La réforme de l'Etat belge sur la base du texte coordonné de la constitution*, Bruxelles 1995, 2 ed.; *L'ordinamento federale belga*, raccolta di scritti coordinata da Francis Delpérée, con saggi introduttivi di G. Guiglia, G. Peccolo, R. Orrù, Torino 1996.

5 L. Luzzatti, *Lo Stato e la Chiesa nel Belgio con alcune applicazioni alla questione religiosa in Italia. Saggio storico e critico*, Milano 1867, 1–2.

Così Luigi Luzzatti sintetizza, poco oltre la metà del XIX secolo,[6] un giudizio che fa della Costituzione belga un modello e al tempo stesso un mito,[7] e l'uso dell'espressione «piccola Inghilterra» è al riguardo denso di significati. Proprio per questa ragione – oltre che per l'intrinseco valore storico-costituzionale – le istituzioni belghe sono assurte lungo il XIX secolo a fondamentale punto di riferimento e di stimolo per numerose altre esperienze. Un'*idée reçue* – in verità con fondamenti non sempre ben argomentati – vuole la Costituzione del 1831 tra le più accreditate matrici dello Statuto albertino. Pare più utile, però, rivolgere lo sguardo verso la dimensione ordinamentale (i regolamenti parlamentari, le leggi elettorali,[8] l'organizzazione amministrativa centrale e periferica,[9] il problema della cd. giurisdizione unica[10]) per trovare elementi che rendano più attendibile l'analisi comparativa. E comunque, che il Belgio dia vita, nel corso dell'Ottocento, ad una delle più significative esperienze istituzionali su scala europea, appare fuor di dubbio.

Con legittimo orgoglio Edouard de Laveleye può constatare, a cinquant'anni di distanza, la 'prova di resistenza' della legge fondamentale, tanto più se confrontata alla proverbiale instabilità costituzionale francese. «Non seulement,

6 Sull'interesse comparativo di Luzzatti per il Belgio v. adesso M. Galizia, *Gli esordi di Luigi Luzzatti negli studi di diritto costituzionale*, in *Il Politico*, 1, 2000, 5 ss. Sulle tradizioni del liberalismo e sulle relazioni tra gl'intellettuali dei due paesi, v. M. Dumoulin, *Italie–Belgique, 1861–1915, Rélations diplomatiques, culturelles et économiques*, Dissertation, Louvain-la-Neuve 1981.

7 Sul punto v. in particolare P. Schiera, *La costituzione inglese fra storia e mito*, in *Il modello costituzionale inglese e la sua recezione nell'area mediterranea tra la fine del 700 e la prima metà dell'800*, Atti del seminario internazionale di studi in memoria di Francisco Tomás y Valiente, Messina, 14–16 settembre 1996, a cura di A. Romano, Milano 1998, 39–58 e A. Romano, *Cadice come modello costituzionale per l'Europa liberale e antinapoleonica. Nota introduttiva*, premessa a *Costituzione politica della Monarchia Spagnola tradotta dall'originale*, a cura di A. Romano, Messina 2000, XVII, nt. 1.

8 S. Furlani, *L'influenza della Costituzione e dell'ordinamento costituzionale belga del 1831 sulla stesura dello Statuto e di altri testi istituzionali fondamentali del Regno di Sardegna nel 1848*, in *Bollettino di informazioni costituzionali e parlamentari*, 2 (1986), 111–201.

9 A. Petracchi, *Le origini dell'ordinamento comunale e provinciale italiano …*, Venezia 1962, vol. I, 172 ss.; A. Taradel, *Analogie e differenze tra la riorganizzazione dell'amministrazione centrale del Regno del Belgio del 1846 e la riforma dell'amministrazione centrale del Regno di Sardegna del 1853–54*, in *Rivista trimestrale di scienze dell'amministrazione*, 2, 1985, 31–56.

10 J.-C. Escarras, *Les expériences belge et italienne d'unité de juridiction*, Paris 1972; B. Sordi, *Uno sguardo all'Europa: il legislatore del 1889 di fronte ai modelli continentali di giustizia amministrativa*, in *Studi per il Centenario della quarta sezione*, Roma 1989, 188–190; P. Aimo, *La giustizia nell'amministrazione dall'Ottocento a oggi*, Roma, Bari 2000, 58.

notre constitution a duré, mais elle a servi de modèle à la plupart de celles qui ont été adoptées par les pays qui se sont affranchis du despotisme: l'Italie, la Roumanie, la Grèce, l'Espagne, le Portugal».[11] Il discorso genealogico e derivativo ha contribuito a fare della costituzione belga uno dei più significativi crocevia del diritto costituzionale europeo del XIX secolo. Tale Costituzione trae la sua struttura e gran parte dei suoi contenuti da altri testi precedenti – si tratti della Legge Fondamentale olandese o della *Charte* del 1830 o ancora della costituzione francese del 1791[12] – e diventa poi il modello *par excellence* di un tipo costituzionale destinato a influenzare innumerevoli altri testi.[13]

La Costituzione belga del 1831 si rivela di particolare interesse anche per le questioni che solleva in termini di modellistica, di morfologia istituzionale, di comparazione dei sistemi costituzionali. Il problema della composizione di un testo costituzionale – con tutte le specificità del caso – è stato a lungo affrontato ricorrendo alla nozione di *modello* inteso come dato normativo che definisce e prescrive una regola (regolarità) che si pretende essere, in senso gerarchico, originaria o derivata.[14] Ma che cosa significa recepire e 'copiare' il titolo di un capitolo, di una o più norme costituzionali, assemblare testi diversi modificando spesso la 'posizione' degli articoli, amputando, aggiungendo, in una sorta di fantasioso gioco alchemico? È evidente che 'copiare' significa in realtà inventare e re-inventare, ricostruire un ordine costituzionale che all'apparenza è 'derivato' e che tuttavia può tramutarsi in qualcosa di assolutamente originale ed unico. I testi circolano, vengono messi a confronto, si 'copiano', si aggiornano in un laboratorio comune nel quale è certo possibile individuare le matrici fondamen-

11 E. De Laveleye, *Quelques considérations sur la constitution belge*, in Th. Juste, *Le Congrès National de Belgique 1830–1831*, Bruxelles 1880, a–b.

12 Sul punto v. *infra*, paragrafo 2.1.

13 «La costituzione belga del 1831 stabilirà infine un nuovo tipo perfezionato di monarchia parlamentare, e tale costituzione farà il giro del mondo esercitando sull'Europa continentale un'influenza assai maggiore di quella esercitatavi dalla prassi inglese ...» (B. Mirkine-Guetzevitch, *Le costituzioni europee*, Milano 1954, 24). Si ricordano in particolare le costituzioni di Spagna (1837), Grecia (1844, 1864), Romania (1866), Paesi Bassi (1848), Lussemburgo (1848), Regno di Sardegna (1848)), Prussia (1850), Bulgaria (1881), ecc. Per tutti vedi J. Gilissen, *La constitution belge de 1831: ses sources, son influence*, in *Res publica*, 10, 1968, 107–141.

14 Su questa linea vedi C. Bornhak, *Genealogie der Verfassungen*, Breslau 1935 e più recentemente H. Gangl, *Der deutsche Weg zum Verfassungsstaat im 19. Jahrhundert*, in *Probleme des Konstitutionalismus im 19. Jahrhundert*, a cura di E.W. Böckenförde, Berlin 1975, 23–58. Su questa impostazione vedi adesso le puntuali osservazioni di G. Manca, *Introduzione* a *L'istituzione parlamentare nel XIX secolo. Una prospettiva comparata. Die parlamentarische Institution im 19. Jahrhundert. Eine Perspektive im Vergleich*, a cura di G. Manca e W. Brauneder, Bologna, Berlin 2000, 9–45.

tali e consolidate nonché le regole e i principi condivisi; e tuttavia, nello stesso tempo, ogni testo è proprio e diverso[15] perché cambiano i contesti istituzionali, le condizioni, i tempi, i luoghi e quant'altro. Il testo costituzionale è al contempo fattore di 'comunione' e di distacco, di identità e di differenza. Lavorare senza ricorrere alla modellistica, ovvero a un pur minimale *outillage* concettuale, è all'evidenza impossibile. Ma, d'altra parte, non bisogna dimenticare la complessa commistione di discorsi e di ricostruzioni ideologiche che hanno finito sovente per fuorviare la comparazione storico-costituzionale, confondendo realtà e miti, concreti percorsi genealogici e perniciosi, quasi inattaccabili, luoghi comuni, alla ricerca di un ordine gerarchizzato che aiuta ben poco a penetrare le culture storiche, le strutture mentali, l'indefinibile *esprit* che alimenta e fa vivere, o meno, di vita propria un sistema costituzionale.[16] Il 'gioco dei testi', nel ricordato circuito imitativo, non può quindi giovare all'analisi se ad esso non si accompagna poi lo sforzo di cogliere dall'interno[17] le ragioni profonde[18] che fanno esistere e durare, funzionare o fallire quei *patchwork* costituzionali di cui è possibile, articolo per articolo, segnalare avi e discendenti.

La Costituzione del 1831 è paradigmatica della coesistenza di un forte carattere imitativo – se si resta al dato numerico degli articoli 'derivati'[19] – e di una pronunciata originalità, tali da contribuire entrambi alla sua 'mitizza-

15 «... quel che circola è una carta, un sistema costituzionale compiuto, e quindi un modello, oppure circolano princìpi, valori costituzionali, e quindi una cultura del costituzionalismo?» (M. Sbriccoli, *Sintesi conclusiva*, in *Il modello costituzionale inglese*, cit., 1074).

16 Utili indicazioni metodologiche si leggono in F. Rugge, *Una "storia costituzionale" tra filosofia ed istituzioni*, in *Amministrare*, 3, 1991, 431–432; Id., *Storia dello Stato: istituzioni e dottrine giuspubblicistiche*, in *Storica*, 7, 1997, 128–129.

17 Sui profili di «filosofia della conoscenza» e sulle alternative metodologiche, cfr. E. Zoller, *Qu'est-ce que faire du droit constitutionnel comparé?*, in *Droits*, 32, 2000, 134: «Ou bien nous persistons à étudier les systèmes constitutionnels étrangers de manière séquentielle et juxtaposée en nous appliquant à faire des typologies et à construire des modèles par rapport auxquels nous situons avec plus ou moins de bonheur nos propres institutions, ou bien nous attelons à étudier les systèmes constitutionnels, politiques et juridiques étrangers comme nos grands comparatistes – songeons à Montesquieu ou à Tocqueville – savaient les regarder autrefois, de l'intérieur, en eux-mêmes et pour eux-mêmes».

18 «Gli studi di diritto costituzionale comparato rivelano la relatività dei testi, delle fomule, dei dogmi; i testi non creano le democrazie, ma i veri fattori determinanti di un regime sono gli uomini e le idee, i partiti e i princìpi, le mistiche e le affermazioni, i costumi e le tradizioni. I testi creano soltanto talune condizioni favorevoli all'evoluzione, alle trasformazioni, alle realizzazioni politiche» (B. Mirkine-Guetzevitch, *Le costituzioni europee*, cit., 11–12).

19 Si veda J. Gilissen, *La constitution belge de 1831*, cit. e infra, al paragrafo 2.1.

zione'.[20] Capace di dare forza e unità al movimento di indipendenza, tale documento ha saputo offrire una sintesi sufficientemente equilibrata e soprattutto «appropriée au caractère et aux mœurs de la nation»,[21] contribuendo a garantire, attraverso una provvida evoluzione, stabilità e durata al meccanismo costituzionale.[22] Il nesso tra indipendenza e costituzione, il carattere originario di ordinamento eterocefalo,[23] la scelta della monarchia costituzionale rappresentativa, il consolidamento dello Stato liberale di diritto[24] – insieme ad altri importanti fattori – renderanno agevole il processo di imitazione 'a valle' e la cristallizzazione dell'immagine della «piccola Inghilterra» in grado di trasfondere vita e dare continuità al regime monarchico-parlamentare, operando un'ipotetica mediazione culturale tra lo straordinario successo della mitica e sfuggente costituzione britannica e il fallimento dei regimi politici della Francia alla continua ricerca di un sicuro approdo costituzionale.

Ed è proprio avendo riguardo a quest'ultimo aspetto che si deve ridimensionare un altro luogo comune: considerare la Costituzione belga (e la rivoluzione che la precede) come un fenomeno *naturaliter* 'riconducibile' alla Rivoluzione di Luglio e alla *Charte* dell'agosto 1830. Al di là delle apparenze, l'accostamento è piuttosto artificiale e risponde ad una logica tipicamente

20 Numerose saranno le ricostruzioni tese a ricollegare la costituzione del 1831 alle antiche istituzioni e alle libertà delle province belghe, rintracciando 'precedenti', tradizioni e quindi una linea pressoché ininterrotta di 'originalità': «Plus d'une fois on a vu, dans les temps modernes, des peuples qui, après s'être émancipés, copiaient ou adoptaient servilement des institutions étrangères; l'assemblée constituante de la Belgique, plus fière ou plus éclairée, ne voulut copier personne. Elle produisit une œuvre originale ...» (Th. Juste, *Le Congrès National de Belgique*, t. I, cit., 295).

21 *Ibidem*. «La costituzione belga pare conforme ai principii d'equità, ai bisogni del paese, ai progressi della ragione, garantisce largamente ogni specie di libertà e consacra pienamente tutti i principii di diritto pubblico e privato» (C. Montalcini, *L'istituzione regia e la responsabilità ministeriale*, in *Biblioteca di scienze politiche*, diretta da A. Brunialti, vol. V, Torino 1890, 756).

22 Cfr. A. Mast, *Une constitution du temps de Louis-Philippe*, in *Revue du droit public et de la science politique en France et à l'étranger*, LXXIII, 1957, 988–992.

23 Ph. Lauvaux, *Les monarchies: inventaire des types*, in *Pouvoirs*, 78, 1996, 30.

24 «La révolution belge de 1830 a fait une nation, une dynastie et une constitution. Si elle s'était bornée à ce dernier acte, tout en remuant de grandes questions d'organisation intérieure, elle aurait pu ne pas attirer l'attention universelle; mais ébranler le droit public européen, appeler un peuple à l'existence, lier cette existence à celle d'une dynastie nouvelle, c'est prendre place dans l'histoire générale» (E. Huyttens, *Discussions du Congrès National de Belgique, 1830–1831*, Bruxelles 1844, t. I, I). Francis Delpérée osserva, giustamente, che sarebbe stato più esatto dire: «Une constitution, une dynastie, une nation» (*Droit constitutionnel*, t. I, cit., 458).

'francocentrica'.[25] Tale pretesa derivazione è da ripensare criticamente:[26] il legame "famigliare", come si può intuire, è meno forte di quanto non si sia spesso sostenuto.

Ernest Vandenpeereboom, nella sua classica opera sul governo rappresentativo in Belgio, mette in guardia il lettore che si aspetti una "narrazione" romanzesca alla de Carné.[27] L'autore francese

> «... a rencontré, sur sa route, l'échafaud d'un roi; deux autres rois marchant vers l'exil; des républiques renversées par des despotismes militaires; les guerres les plus glorieuses et les desordres les plus honteux; dix constitutions arrachées, avant qu'elles aient pu prendre racine; la tribune, passant de la brillante liberté à la plus humiliante contrainte; la presse, ce guide des peuples libres, menée à la lisière!... Mais le régime parlementaire de notre heureuse Belgique présente des faits plus tranquilles et des leçons plus modestes. Avec notre dynastie intelligente et aimée; avec notre Constitution, vierge de toute atteinte; avec nos libertés, que rien ne restreint et que nul ne menace, les faits ne sont, pour ainsi dire, que des souvenirs de famille, – *domestica facta*. M. de Carné a écrit les péripéties des drames qui ont agité une grande nation: je n'ai eu à tracer que le tableau du paisible intérieur d'un peuple libre.»[28]

Ben diversi sono i presupposti delle due Rivoluzioni del 1830: i fatti di settembre ebbero come conseguenza la rigenerazione del Belgio e la conquista della sua indipendenza. La costituzione del 1831 è il documento solenne di una rivoluzione nazionale e della creazione di un nuovo Stato.[29]

In questo saggio, dell'esperienza costituzionale belga si cercherà di far emergere anzitutto i caratteri fondativi, i principi ispiratori, le ragioni di un successo che merita di essere analizzato distinguendo i pur importanti profili mitografici dai reali presupposti e sviluppi di una costituzione destinata a lasciare tracce tanto profonde nella storia e nell'evoluzione istituzionale del Belgio e nel comune diritto costituzionale europeo.

25 Per G. Antonetti, *Les monarchies constitutionnelles*, in *Les monarchies*, a cura di Y.-M. Bercé, Paris 1997, 429, «D'ailleurs cette Constitution belge était, en 139 articles, une copie développée des 70 articles de la charte révisée d'août 1830».

26 Cfr. in questo volume infra *Constitución, Monarquía, Parlamento: Francia y Bélgica*, 180 ss.

27 L. De Carnè, *Etudes sur l'histoire du gouvernement représentatif en France*, Paris 1855, 2 voll.

28 E. Vandenpeereboom, *Du gouvernement représentatif en Belgique (1831–1848)*, Bruxelles 1856, t. I, XIV–XV.

29 E. De Laveleye, *Quelques considérations sur la constitution belge*, cit., III ss.

2. La rivoluzione belga del 1830 e il processo costituente

2.1 La nascita del Regno dei Paesi Bassi e la *Grondwet* del 1815. Alle origini dell'opposizione belga

Gli avvenimenti rivoluzionari del 1830 e la Costituzione del 1831 sono stati messi in relazione con i passaggi cruciali della storia dei territori che formano il Belgio contemporaneo. Si può così risalire, a seconda del punto di vista privilegiato, alle varie forme della costituzione politica e sociale dell'antico regime, all'età francese o alla pretesa influenza del Luglio parigino sulla rivoluzione belga. Al di là di tali riferimenti, non sembra però possibile avvicinare gli eventi del 1830 prescindendo da una pur breve analisi delle vicende di maggior significato politico-costituzionale che seguirono alla riunione del Nord (Paesi Bassi) e delle province belghe sotto le insegne di Guglielmo I d'Orange-Nassau, figlio dell'ultimo *stadhouder* olandese. La principale preoccupazione delle Potenze alleate (soprattutto Inghilterra e Prussia) rispondeva a ragioni geopolitiche, dar vita cioè ad un regno che formasse una sorta di 'barriera' di contenimento in funzione anti-francese. Come per le altre 'sistemazioni' territoriali dell'epoca furono i trattati delle potenze vincitrici a determinare i caratteri fondamentali dei nuovi assetti istituzionali e la soluzione, consacrata dal Trattato di Parigi e confermata poi a Vienna, assunse le forme di un'annessione delle province belghe al regno degli Orange.

Guglielmo aveva dichiarato, nel dicembre del 1813, di accettare la sovranità sui Paesi Bassi nel quadro di una «saggia costituzione». Riprendendo e sviluppando uno schema (*Schets eener Grondwet*) elaborato nel 1812 dal più importante uomo politico olandese, Karel van Hogendorp, un'apposita commissione redasse il testo della costituzione del 29 marzo 1814,[30] non certo priva di elementi liberali[31] ma con evidenti radici nel costituzionalismo cetuale di antico regime.[32] Tra il 1814 e il 1815 nasceva dunque un nuovo Stato su basi

30 Cfr. J. Gilissen, *Le régime représentatif belge depuis 1790*, Bruxelles 1958, 56–57.

31 La Legge Fondamentale conteneva disposizioni avanzate in tema di libertà di coscienza, di eguaglianza delle confessioni religiose, di libertà di stampa e di petizione, di libertà individuale, di inviolabilità del domicilio, di inamovibilità dei giudici, di autonomie locali (Stati provinciali e reggenze locali). Su quest'ultimo profilo, cfr. S. Mannoni, *L'autonomia locale in Belgio: dalle riforme giuseppine (1787) alle leggi del 1836*, in *Storia amministrazione costituzione*, 3, 1995, 87–112. Più in generale, v. L. Hymans, *Histoire politique et parlementaire de la Belgique de 1814–1830*, Bruxelles 1869, 76 ss. e 200 ss.

32 Gli *Etats généraux* erano formati da due Camere, l'una di membri nominati a vita dal sovrano, l'altra di deputati degli Stati provinciali. Cfr. E.-C. De Gerlache, *Histoire du Royaume des Pays-Bas, depuis 1814 jusqu'en 1830*, Bruxelles 1859, 3 voll.

essenzialmente politiche, ma l'unione non poteva certo occultare i più gravi fattori di tensione. Le culture nazionali, le pratiche linguistiche e religiose dividevano le diverse province. Il dualismo era quindi nella realtà delle cose:[33] l'Olanda aveva una struttura in prevalenza agricola e commerciale e disponeva di vasti territori coloniali, il Belgio conosceva già un'importante sviluppo industriale; se l'una era più favorevole ad una politica di libertà commerciale, l'altro lo era verso politiche di più forte segno protezionistico. Infine, non era affatto secondaria la questione demografica, con i Belgi ben più numerosi degli Olandesi (quasi tre milioni e mezzo contro due).[34]

Le disposizioni[35] che gli Alleati avevano imposto a Guglielmo come condizioni per salire sul trono non erano del tutto sorde verso i problemi che – com'era facile prevedere – avrebbero potuto ostacolare l'«amalgama» tra le due parti del regno. Nel protocollo di Londra, ribadito il principio dell'unione «intima e completa» basata sulla Costituzione olandese, si diceva però che tale testo avrebbe dovuto essere modificato «di comune accordo» (art. I). Si confermavano i principi liberali presenti nella *Grondwet* del 1814 che garantivano pari libertà di culto e di accesso alle pubbliche funzioni (art. II) e si stabiliva una «conveniente» rappresentanza delle province belghe nell'assemblea degli Stati generali da tenersi alternativamente nelle due parti del regno (art. III).[36] Queste ed altre prescrizioni rivelavano l'indirizzo da seguire ma anche tutte le difficoltà del caso.

La revisione «di comune accordo» della costituzione olandese doveva rappresentare l'occasione per porre le basi del nuovo Stato. Una commissione paritetica di ventidue membri,[37] presieduta da van Hogendorp, si mise al lavoro per adattare il testo alle mutate condizioni. Non fu, come ci si potrebbe aspettare, la divisione tra olandesi e belgi a segnarne l'elaborazione, quanto piuttosto la

33 «La creazione del regno dei Paesi Bassi, la quale aveva accoppiato il Belgio all'Olanda, era stata a malincuore sofferta dalla grande maggioranza del primo paese. Malgrado la costituzione, liberale anziche no, di cui il re di Olanda aveva dotato il nuovo regno, la preponderanza della parte olandese di esso era troppo nella natura delle cose, per non emergerne e non ferirne la parte belga» (G. Arrivabene, *Memorie della mia vita, 1795–1859*, Firenze 1880, 2 ed., 177–178).

34 Sulle ragioni del distacco e sugli sviluppi rivoluzionari, cfr. la *Lettre sur la révolution belge, son origine, ses causes et ses conséquences*, attribuita a Sylvain Van de Weyer, pubblicata a Londra in lingua inglese nel 1831. La lettera è riportata da E. Huyttens, *Discussions du Congrès National de Belgique, 1830–1831*, cit., t.V, 376–386.

35 Si tratta dei cosiddetti VIII Articoli stipulati a Londra il 21 giugno 1814.

36 Cfr. L. Palma, *Le costituzioni dei popoli liberi*, in *Biblioteca di scienze politiche e amministrative*, diretta da A. Brunialti, II serie, vol. II, Torino 1894, 111.

37 Si veda H.T. Colenbrander, *Ontstaan der Grondwet*, 's-Gravenhage 1908–1909.

dialettica, non necessariamente di segno 'nazionale', tra 'conservatori' e 'progressisti'. I commissari belgi diedero un apporto non irrilevante alla nuova costituzione che si arricchì – rispetto a quella olandese del 1814 – di quasi cento articoli (234 contro 146) e introdusse un sistema bicamerale, e la Prima Camera di nomina regia fu patrocinata soprattutto dai membri belgi della commissione.

Il testo della Legge Fondamentale fu sottoposto all'approvazione di un'assemblea che per la parte belga era formata da 1604 notabili designati dal re. Il ruolo svolto dal clero, escluso dall'assemblea, e l'influenza esercitata sui cattolici fiamminghi contribuiscono a far capire l'esito del voto: 796 suffragi negativi, 527 positivi, 281 astensioni. Il testo veniva quindi respinto, ma il sovrano non esitò a considerare voti favorevoli sia le astensioni sia i voti di coloro che avevano motivato il loro diniego «per causa religiosa». La singolare «aritmetica olandese» – come si disse allora – rovesciò il risultato e fece nascere la *Grondwet* del 24 agosto 1815. Il voto, al di là del dato numerico, aveva però evidenziato una spaccatura della classe dirigente belga: infatti se i liberali trovavano nella Legge Fondamentale garanzie e principi tipici del costituzionalismo liberale, i conservatori clericali ne temevano, per ragioni speculari, i possibili effetti negativi soprattutto in tema di libertà ed eguaglianza religiosa e di istruzione pubblica.

Sotto il profilo dei diritti e delle libertà la *Grondwet* del 1815 era per l'epoca una delle costituzioni più liberali d'Europa.[38] La seconda Camera era sì formata da 110 membri eletti dagli Stati provinciali sulla base di un complesso e opaco meccanismo elettorale a vari gradi e di tipo censitario, ma essa – malgrado il nome – aveva ormai poco da spartire con l'organizzazione cetuale di antico regime.[39] Il vero problema politico nasceva invece dalla ripartizione paritaria dei seggi pur in presenza del maggior peso demografico dei Belgi. D'altra parte, il criterio proporzionale avrebbe messo in discussione la sovranità olandese. Costituzione liberale per alcuni versi, la Legge Fondamentale era tuttavia informata ai dettami del «principio monarchico», dando vita ad una «monarchie tempérée et représentative».[40] Entravano così in gioco sia il profilo istituzionale della Corona e la forma di governo, sia la personalità di Guglielmo I. Il re sanzionava le leggi dopo aver sentito il parere di un influente Consiglio di Stato di nomina regia. I ministri erano poco più che *grands commis* al servizio del sovrano e pertanto li si riteneva non responsabili dinanzi alle Camere. In virtù del potere regolamentare il re disponeva di un vasto campo di prerogative e le

38 Non è certo isolato il giudizio dell'esule italiano Giovanni Arrivabene: «Il governo dei Paesi Bassi, una specie di Toscana del Nord, ma ancora più tollerante ...» (*Memorie della mia vita*, cit., 169).

39 J. Gilissen, *Le régime représentatif belge depuis 1790*, cit., 60 ss.

40 O. Orban, *Le droit constitutionnel de la Belgique*, t. I, *Introduction et théories fondamentales*, Liège, Paris 1906, 109.

spese ordinarie venivano sottoposte al controllo e all'approvazione degli Stati Generali una sola volta ogni dieci anni.

La *Grondwet* del 1815 fu utilizzata da Guglielmo I più per affermare il suo stile personale di governo[41] che per assecondare uno sviluppo più equilibrato del sistema politico-costituzionale del Regno. Il sovrano non esitò ad interferire, come nel 1815, nella formazione della Camera elettiva, a limitare poi la libertà di stampa, ad abolire la giuria e colpire il clero riottoso, a privarsi del consiglio dei ministri migliori e più indipendenti quali Hogendorp, Falck, Roëll. Malgrado le due Camere, Guglielmo governò in molte circostanze confidando nel solo potere regolamentare (tra il 1815 e il 1830 i decreti regi furono 1700 a fronte di meno di 400 leggi votate dagli Stati Generali).

Nel corso degl'anni Venti i territori belgi furono interessati da un graduale processo di trasformazione politica. Da un lato, i conservatori cattolici che dalla nascita del regno avevano rappresentato la più battagliera opposizione cominciarono – in virtù anche della positiva influenza delle idee di Lamennais – a mettere in correlazione la libertà dei culti (in una prospettiva separatista), la libertà di insegnamento e la libertà di stampa.[42] Dall'altro, i progressisti, che per alcuni anni avevano giudicato con favore la politica anticlericale di Guglielmo I nel ricordo del 'giuseppinismo' laicizzante, si avvicinarono a posizioni meno radicali.

L'accelerazione dello sviluppo industriale contribuì – favorito dalla politica guglielmina – a irrobustire una classe dirigente borghese che rimase tuttavia legata a forme e concezioni di tipo "superiore" e aristocratico. La piccola e la media borghesia si rivelò la più "attrezzata" a guidare il movimento politico di indipendenza e di riforma costituzionale, composta in gran parte da intellettuali, insegnanti, giornalisti, funzionari, mercanti in grado di elaborare un programma politico-ideologico su fondamenti liberal-democratici e con valenza costitu-

41 Per un rapido ritratto di Guglielmo, cfr. H. Pirenne, *Histoire de Belgique des origines à nos jours*, s. l., 1974, t. IV, 241 ss. «Il Re era uomo taciturno, pedante, irritabile, ma educato nell'avversità era laborioso, aveva coraggio e istruzione; semplice ne' suoi gusti pareva un capo repubblicano, e preferiva nei posti ai patrizi i plebei; amava e curava il progresso intellettuale ed economico; pareva quindi il principe più illuminato, e in Olanda era amato. Ma voleva esser Re, governar personalmente lui; tanto che fra i suoi stessi Olandesi lasciò da parte i migliori ministri, Hogendorp e Falk, uomini dell'antico partito oligarchico come i liberali odierni ... Si reputava di giudizio infallibile, ed era fermo sino alla più cieca ostinazione. Calvinista, era inoltre abituato all'idea che lo Stato doveva esercitare un potere supremo sulla Chiesa. Sicché volle venire a capo di ogni opposizione, del clero e dell'altiera nobiltà, come dei liberali e di tutta la nazione belga, che non seppe intendere ...» (L. Palma, *Le costituzioni dei popoli liberi*, cit., 113).

42 F. Perin, *Histoire d'une nation introuvable*, Bruxelles 1988, 82 ss.

zionale (le libertà fondamentali, l'autonomia politica, il regime parlamentare, le autonomie locali ecc.).[43] Dalla tribuna del «Courrier des Pays-Bas» di Bruxelles i giovani e brillanti Ducpétiaux, Sylvain Van de Weyer, Louis de Potter (il più vecchio, appena quarantenne) e dalle pagine del «Mathieu Laensberg» di Liegi Joseph Lebeau, Paul Devaux, Charles Rogier, Jean-Baptiste Nothomb si battevano per ripristinare in tutta la sua estensione la libertà di stampa. Il grido «La libertà in tutto e per tutto» sedusse anche i cattolici delle più grandi famiglie, i de Mérode, i de Gerlache, i Surlet de Chokier, i Robiano, i Vilain XIV.[44]

La frattura tra Olandesi e Belgi, nel corso degl'anni Venti, si allargò anziché ricomporsi, rivelando così il carattere velleitario dell'«amalgama» tra i due popoli.[45] Un'amministrazione ad assoluta prevalenza olandese (in un regno a maggioranza belga), l'uso obbligatorio della lingua neerlandese nelle attività pubbliche, la politica autoritaria di Guglielmo I favorirono il formarsi di un movimento politico sempre meno frammentato. La radicalizzazione consentì ai gruppi politicamente più attivi e consapevoli del proprio ruolo di influenzare in maniera crescente l'opinione pubblica. Tra il 1827 e il 1828 mosse i primi passi quell'alleanza «mostruosa» (come fu definita da taluni) o «mariage de raison» tra i cattolici e i liberali che spezzava definitivamente la politica del *divide et impera* perseguita da Guglielmo I. L'8 novembre del 1828 Louis De Potter lanciò sul «Courrier des Pays-Bas» l'appello per l'Unione dell'opposizione cattolica e liberale nella camera elettiva e nel Paese. Il sovrano, esitante, adottò una linea di condotta equamente divisa tra minacce e promesse. Le petizioni toccavano i fondamenti stessi del regime costituzionale: la piena libertà di stampa, la responsabilità politica dei ministri,[46] il suffragio diretto. L'11 dicembre del 1829 Guglielmo – nel suo celebre messaggio agli Stati Generali – restò fedele alla contraddittoria politica di concessioni e di rifiuti, respingendo ogni richiesta che avesse come obiettivo l'evoluzione della forma di governo in senso parlamentare. De Potter, a nome dell'opposizione, rispose al sovrano esigendo uno «Stato rappresentativo costituzionale».[47]

43 Cfr. E. Witte, J. Craeybeckx, *La Belgique politique de 1830 à nos jours. Les tensions d'une démocratie bourgeoise*, Bruxelles 1987, 3 ss.

44 Cfr. F. Van Kalken, *La Belgique contemporaine (1780–1930). Histoire d'une évolution politique*, Paris 1930, 36.

45 Cfr. H. Pirenne, *Histoire de Belgique des origines à nos jours*, cit., t. IV, 233 ss., 267–269.

46 Nel 1829 l'opposizione belga riuscì a far respingere un progetto di legge di bilancio mettendo in minoranza il governo del re. Sul tema della responsabilità politica dei ministri, vedi *infra*, paragrafo 3.5.

47 L. De Potter, *Lettre de Démophile au roi sur le nouveau projet de loi contre la presse et le message royal qui l'accompagne*, Bruxelles 1829. Nel 1830 de Potter sarà perseguito e costretto all'esilio.

2.2 Le giornate rivoluzionarie e il governo provvisorio

Le giornate insurrezionali tra l'agosto e il settembre 1830 sono state spesso messe in correlazione alle «gloriose giornate» del luglio parigino,[48] ingenerando un equivoco anche di natura costituzionale che ha fatto ripetere a lungo la *vulgata* di una "naturale" filiazione della costituzione belga del 1831 dalla Charte del 1830. Come si è già osservato, la derivazione è tale più per ragioni apparenti ed estrinseche che per caratteri sostanziali. Ciò non vuol dire che le due costituzioni appartengano ad un diverso genere, tuttavia le differenze sono qualificanti e destinate a tracciare percorsi peculiari. Non si tratta dunque di due costituzioni e di una sola "tappa". Semmai i testi e la pratica costituzionale rivelano punti di colleganza, talune "parentele", dettati da antiche familiarità storiche e culturali oltre che dalla prossimità cronologica degli eventi. Il carattere esteriore della monarchia «elettiva», il lessico del «governo parlamentare», il sistema elettorale censitario, le condizioni socio-economiche, talune preoccupazioni ideologiche[49] avvicinano le due esperienze, ma bisognerà andare oltre tutto ciò per cercare di cogliere gli elementi che realmente caratterizzano il sistema costituzionale belga.[50]

Malgrado la crescente radicalizzazione politico-nazionale tra il 1829 e il 1830, l'alleanza tra i liberali e i cattolici restava legale e dinastica, chiedendo riforme costituzionali e concependo tutt'al più un processo graduale di separazione amministrativa tra il Nord e il Sud. Gli eventi dell'agosto 1830 furono in non piccola misura inattesi e misero in moto un processo irreversibile. L'ostinazione di Guglielmo I, l'attendismo e poi la reazione militare nel mese di settembre, la resistenza belga e le numerose vittime, le tardive concessioni e infine il drammatico bombardamento olandese di Anversa (27 ottobre) allontanarono i contendenti sino a spezzare il filo che univa le due parti del regno. Le ragioni profonde di divisione diventavano adesso il presupposto di legittimità del governo provvisorio e di una nuova nazione.

Il 4 ottobre 1830[51] il governo provvisorio[52] delle province belghe aveva già deciso di dar vita a uno Stato indipendente, invitando il comitato centrale ad

48 «Seul un petit groupe de démocrates, admirateurs passionnés de la France, sous la conduite de l'avocat montois Alexandre Gendebien, aurait voulu déclancher une insurrection, avec le concours des Lamarque et des Maguin. Mais le prudent Louis-Philippe avait supplié ces conspirateurs de surseoir à leurs projets» (F. Van Kalken, *La Belgique contemporaine (1780–1930)*, cit., 41).

49 F. Delpérée, *Droit constitutionnel*, t. I, cit., 90.

50 Si pensi, per esempio, a come il problema della «sovranità nazionale» sia differentemente affrontato e risolto nella Francia orleanista e in Belgio.

51 Sulle vicende costituzionali, cfr. E. Vandenpeereboom, *Du gouvernement représentatif en Belgique*, cit., t. I, XIV–XV; Th. Juste, *Le Congrès National de Belgique*, cit.

52 Sul governo provvisorio, v. J. Gilissen, *Le caractère collégial des premières formes de*

occuparsi al più presto di un progetto di costituzione da sottoporre al Congresso nazionale. Le prime riforme furono abbozzate dallo stesso attivissimo governo che svolse un'importante funzione di "indirizzo". L'esecutivo fece cadere con una serie di decreti le restrizioni alle «libertà dei cattolici» ed alle «libertà dei liberali»: basti pensare alla libertà personale, di associazione, dei culti, di insegnamento, di stampa, nonché ai primi interventi nel campo dell'organizzazione giudiziaria.

2.3 La redazione del progetto di costituzione e il Congresso nazionale

Il Comitato Centrale, il 6 ottobre 1830, nominò una *Commission de Constitution* affidandole il compito di redarre un progetto. La grande maggioranza dei suoi membri era formata da giuristi e i due più giovani, Jean-Baptiste Nothomb (25 anni), segretario, e Paul Devaux (29 anni) furono i redattori materiali del progetto.[53] In soli cinque giorni il testo fu approntato e il 27 ottobre lo stesso Nothomb ne diede lettura al governo provvisorio.[54] La Commissione (e soprattutto Nothomb) stabilì inoltre le condizioni – poi recepite con due decreti (10 e 12 ottobre) dal governo provvisorio – per poter votare ed essere eletti al Congresso nazionale. Il sistema del censo differenziato[55] secondo il precedente sistema olandese venne "temperato" da una serie di «capacità».[56] Il voto fece

gouvernement et d'administration de l'Etat belge (1830–1831), in *Revue belge d'histoire contemporaine*, XII, 1981, 609–639.

53 I processi verbali della Commissione, redatti dal segretario Nothomb, sono stati ritrovati qualche decennio fa tra le carte dell'uomo politico e pur nella loro laconicità sono molto utili per ricostruire le fonti e i caratteri fondamentali della costituzione belga. Si veda al riguardo W. Van Den Steene, *De Belgische Grondwetscommissie (oktober–november 1830): tekst van haar notulen en ontstaan van de Belgische Grondwet*, Bruxelles 1963. Per l'analisi di questa fonte cfr. soprattutto J. Gilissen, *La constitution belge de 1831*, cit. e Id., *Jean-Baptiste Nothomb et les origines de la constitution belge*, in *Jean-Baptiste Nothomb et les débuts de la Belgique indépendante*, Wetteren 1981, 80–95.

54 J.-B. Nothomb, *Essai historique et politique sur la Révolution belge*, Bruxelles 1834, 3 ed., 77.

55 Il censo poteva oscillare dai 13 tredici fiorini dei piccoli centri del Lussemburgo ai 30–50 delle città medie sino ai 130 di Anversa e ai 150 di Bruxelles. Nelle campagne il censo, in origine più elevato (da 50 a 150), fu ampiamente ridotto. L'età per essere eletti fu abbassata da 30 a 25 anni, sembra per consentire al venticinquenne Nothomb di entrare al Congresso. Si veda J. Gilissen, *Le régime représentatif belge depuis 1790*, cit., 82–84; G. Eeckhout, *Nos institutions représentatives*, in *Histoire de la Belgique contemporaine, 1830–1914*, Bruxelles 1930, 351–404.

56 I deputati del Congresso nazionale furono eletti a suffragio diretto, ammettendo alle urne circa 38.000 elettori per censo e 7.500 per capacità, ovvero circa l'1% del

nascere un Congresso nel quale le tendenze conservatrici e moderate erano meglio rappresentate delle forze democratiche e progressiste che avevano svolto un ruolo di primo piano durante la rivoluzione. Il carattere moderato segnò le aspirazioni e i lavori del Congresso nazionale sino alla stesura della carta costituzionale. Il 10 novembre i 200 deputati si riunirono a Bruxelles.[57] Il Congresso era formato da una maggioranza di borghesi di estrazione relativamente modesta: non a caso si parlò di «habits râpés et mauvais parapluies».[58] Gli orangisti – abbastanza numerosi tra l'aristocrazia e i grandi industriali e negozianti di Gand e Anversa – non parteciparono compatti al voto. Alla fine furono le varie anime della tradizione liberale e cattolica ad essere maggioritarie, anche se appare difficile attribuire coloriture 'partitiche' a un'assemblea dominata dal centro moderato e dalla politica di «unione».

Il Congresso nazionale proclamò subito l'indipendenza del Belgio (18 novembre), decise poi di adottare la forma della monarchia costituzionale rappresentativa e di escludere gli Orange-Nassau dalla successione al trono.[59] La discussione del progetto durò due mesi, dal 4 dicembre 1830 al 7 febbraio 1831. Il testo della Commissione, redatto nella sostanza da Nothomb e Devaux – malgrado la non buona accoglienza da parte della stampa e dello stesso Congresso – funzionò da 'canovaccio' e da struttura portante per il testo definitivo. La gran parte delle questioni più delicate furono affrontate e risolte dalla Commissione, anche se non si può negare l'importanza dei dibattiti parlamentari e delle soluzioni originali[60] emerse dal lavoro delle sezioni e dell'aula.[61]

popolo belga. I redattori del progetto avevano seguito in particolare la legge elettorale francese del 5 febbraio 1817. Cfr. J. Gilissen, *Jean-Baptiste Nothomb et les origines de la constitution belge*, cit., 83.

57 Il Congresso nazionale si riunì sino al 21 luglio 1831.

58 F. Van Kalken, *La Belgique contemporaine (1780–1930)*, cit., 45–46. John Gilissen invece quantifica le varie 'componenti' del Congresso: *Le régime représentatif belge depuis 1790*, cit., 84–85. Cfr. inoltre P. Errera, *Traité de droit public belge. Droit constitutionnel. Droit administratif*, Paris 1909, 11.

59 Per il testo dei tre decreti cfr. Th. Juste, *Le Congrès National de Belgique*, cit., t. II.

60 Il Congresso – suddiviso in dieci sezioni e in una sezione centrale – conobbe tre progetti: il primo redatto dalla Commissione nominata dal governo provvisorio, il secondo presentato da alcuni deputati (Forgeur, Barbanson, Fleussu, Liedts), il terzo elaborato dalla sezione centrale. I testi così come i dibattiti costituenti del Congresso sono stati riuniti nel 1844 dal barone Huyttens de Terbecq, cancelliere della Camera: v. E. Huyttens, *Discussions du Congrès National de Belgique, 1830–1831*, cit. Il Congresso non seguì sempre il progetto della Commissione: fu così per esempio nella scelta dei senatori e nella disciplina dei rapporti tra Stato e Chiesa. Sul Congresso si veda inoltre L. De Lichtervelde, *Le Congrès National de Belgique*, Bruxelles 1922.

61 Secondo Gilissen più dell'80% del testo finale deriva dall'opera di Nothomb e Devaux, con gl'apporti minimi della Commissione governativa. I punti sui quali

Se vi era un forte consenso a contenere i pericoli «assolutistici»[62] insiti nella forma di governo, nondimeno la monarchia costituzionale ereditaria appariva come la scelta obbligata per assicurare stabilità ed equilibrio. La rivoluzione – si disse – era stata fatta non contro la monarchia bensì contro gli abusi, le umiliazioni patite.[63] La soluzione repubblicana, pur avendo una pattuglia di sostenitori nel Congresso, conquistò alla fine solo pochi voti a fronte della maggioranza schiacciante favorevole alla monarchia (174 contro 13).[64] Il dibattito costituente contribuì a dipingere la forma monarchica come la più adatta alle esigenze del Belgio. Non bisogna dimenticare che la repubblica rappresentava nell'Europa di allora una mera eccezione[65] o peggio una pericolosa utopia, come l'esperienza francese aveva dimostrato: «Comme monarchie – affermò Nothomb – vous serez une puissance, comme république un épouvantail».[66] La monarchia avrebbe messo fine alla rivoluzione, la repubblica ne avrebbe innescata un'altra. Il Belgio aveva due possibilità di esistenza: o riunirsi alla Francia, o istituire una monarchia nazionale. Rigettata la prima ipotesi, non restava che una sola scelta. Riprendendo la 'profezia' di Burke sulla transizione francese dalla repubblica al dispotismo militare, Nothomb prediceva la stessa sorte per un Belgio repubblicano: «... nous traverserions la république pour tomber sous la domination étrangère».[67] La monarchia rappresentativa sembrava invece poter conciliare al meglio la stabilità e il movimento, l'ordine e la libertà. Alla forma repubblicana si imputavano gli eccessi rivoluzionari, e

la Commissione si era più divisa al suo interno sono segnalati da J. Gilissen, *Jean-Baptiste Nothomb et les origines de la constitution belge*, cit., 88–89.

62 Cfr. J. Lebeau, *Observations sur le pouvoir royal, ou examen de quelques questions relatives aux droits de la couronne dans les Pays-Bas*, Bruxelles 1830.

63 Th. Juste, *Le Congrès National de Belgique*, cit., t. I, 123.

64 In seno alla Commissione la forma monarchica era stata adottata con 8 voti, mentre il solo Tielemans aveva votato per la repubblica. Fu questa una delle ragioni che determinò la stampa, di prevalente fede repubblicana, ad apprezzare con riserva il testo da sottoporre al Congresso. Pare che Louis de Potter, il prestigioso leader democratico, abbia detto: «Ce n'était pas la peine de verser tant de sang pour si peu de chose» (J.-B. Nothomb, *Essai historique*, cit., 77–78).

65 Gendebien disse: «Dans mon opinion personnelle, la république est le meilleur des gouvernements ... mes concitoyens sont dignes de vivre sous un régime républicaine; mais dans la position où nous sommes placés ... la république n'aurait pas trois mois d'existence». Sul dibattito in seno al Congresso cfr. E. Huyttens, *Discussions du Congrès National de Belgique, 1830–1831*, t. I, cit.

66 Sull'intervento di Nothomb v. J. Gilissen, *Jean-Baptiste Nothomb et les origines de la constitution belge*, cit., 93–94. Nell'*Essai historique* Nothomb insisté a più riprese sul legame necessario tra scelta monarchica, indipendenza e riconoscimento delle Potenze europee.

67 Cfr. E. Huyttens, *Discussions du Congrès National de Belgique, 1830–1831*, cit., t. I, 193.

anche se associata all'esempio americano faceva emergere preoccupazioni di varia natura, dalla 'destabilizzante' elettività del presidente alla lotta fra i partiti (Lebeau, Devaux).[68]

Scelta la forma di governo, bisognava trovare ed eleggere un re. La nascita del nuovo Stato aveva suscitato le interessate apprensioni e la costante tutela delle grandi potenze europee. Il conflitto tra Belgio e Paesi Bassi aveva rimesso in discussione l'equilibrio sancito dal Congresso di Vienna e la rivoluzione aveva suscitato non pochi allarmi dopo che già la Francia era insorta contro Carlo X. Non bisogna dimenticare che le manovre diplomatiche e militari, basate su alleanze e interessi contrastanti, ebbero una decisiva influenza sulle scelte del Congresso nazionale e dei primi governi.[69] «La Belgique offrait un spectacle jusqu'alors unique dans les annales de l'Europe moderne. L'assemblée nationale, dépositaire de la souveraineté populaire, allait briser les traditions de la legitimité et nommer au scrutin le chef de l'Etat, après avoir discuté publiquement ses titres ...».[70] La scelta, contro la volontà delle potenze alleate e della stessa Francia, cadde sul duca di Nemours,[71] figlio di Luigi-Filippo. Il 21 febbraio 1831 il Congresso ebbe la notizia ufficiale del rifiuto francese. Il contesto internazionale, che non poteva tollerare un Belgio così manifestamente legato alla Francia – pena la minaccia di una guerra – ebbe la meglio sulla determinazione del Congresso. Bisognava rivolgere lo sguardo altrove, alla ricerca di un principe "disponibile" e in grado di tenere in equilibrio gli interessi confliggenti delle potenze dell'Europa centrale, della Francia e dell'Inghilterra.

La delusione fu grande e si vide la necessità di eleggere un reggente, facendo entrare in vigore da subito la costituzione (22 febbraio 1831). L'anziano barone Surlet de Chokier, già personaggio di spicco della dirigenza politica belga, venne eletto reggente. Bisognerà però attendere il giugno successivo perché il voto favorevole del Congresso faccia di Leopoldo di Saxe-Cobourg-Saalfeld (1790–1865)[72] il re dei belgi. Principe luterano, appartenente a uno dei rami di una numerosa famiglia tedesca, imparentato con i reali inglesi e forte di una

68 *Ibidem*, 208–215.

69 Cfr. H. Pirenne, *L'Europe et l'indépendance belge (1830–1839)*, Bruxelles 1990.

70 Th. Juste, *Le Congrès National de Belgique*, cit., t. I, 238.

71 Al primo scrutinio il duca di Nemours ebbe 91 voti, 67 il duca di Leuchtenberg; 35 l'arciduca Carlo d'Austria. Nessun candidato ottenne la maggioranza di 101 voti. Si procedé al secondo scrutino cui parteciparono 192 deputati. Con 97 voti de Nemours divenne per qualche giorno virtualmente re del Belgio. Sulle relazioni franco-belghe, tra il 1830 e il 1832, cfr. la sintesi di G. Antonetti, *Louis-Philippe*, Paris 1994, 621–624, 641–643, 663–667.

72 Leopoldo aveva sposato nel 1816 Charlotte, erede al trono di Inghilterra morta di parto nel 1817. Nel 1830 fu eletto re degli Elleni ma rinunciò subito di fronte ai problemi insorti in Grecia.

vasta rete di alleanze dinastiche,[73] stimato per capacità politica e conoscenza del regime parlamentare (inglese), appariva il soggetto più adatto a salire sul trono belga. Il 21 luglio Leopoldo I prestava giuramento solenne nella piazza reale di Bruxelles dinanzi al popolo, quasi a voler ricordare, in forma moderna, quella *Joyeuse Entrée du Brabant*[74] che per secoli aveva unito il principe ai distinti territori del Belgio.

L'indipendenza, la costituzione, il re. «Cette constitution, après avoir d'abord surpris et inquiété l'Europe, devait quelques années plus tard lui servir d'enseignement et quelquefois même de modèle».[75]

3. La costituzione del 7 febbraio 1831

3.1 Un «mosaico costituzionale»

L'opera di redazione del 1830–1831 rivela con innegabile evidenza le fonti ispiratrici e le relative imitazioni. John Gilissen ne ha con particolare cura ricostruito – dopo i lavori ottocenteschi di Descamps[76] – i percorsi, le genealogie, le variazioni. La Costituzione belga è forse l'esempio più significativo di «mosaico costituzionale» e di composizione di un testo che risulta infine profondamente «nuovo» e originale[77] e pertanto ben diverso dalle Costituzioni francesi del 1791 e del 1830 e soprattutto dalla *Grondwet* del 1815 da cui trarrebbe più ampia ispirazione.[78] Come si è detto all'inizio,[79] è di indubbia

73 Leopoldo si risposerà, nel 1832, con Marie-Louise sorella del duca di Nemours, ristabilendo quindi quel rapporto di "alleanza" con la Francia orleanista che a molti sembrava "naturale", oltre che necessario. Cfr. Th. Juste, *Léopold Ier et Leopold II Rois des Belges. Leur vie et leur règne*, Bruxelles 1878, 4.

74 Nell'ambito di una letteratura assai vasta, cfr. almeno Ch. Fader, *Etudes sur les constitutions nationales. Pays-Bas autrichiens et Pays de Liège*, Bruxelles 1847 e E. Lousse, *La Joyeuse Entrée brabançonne du 3 janvier 1356*, in *Schweizer Beiträge zur Allgemeinen Geschichte*, 10, 1952, 139–162.

75 Th. Juste, *Le Congrès National de Belgique*, cit., t. I, 295–296.

76 Cfr. E. Descamps, *Code constitutionnel belge, contenant la Constitution, comparée aux sources modernes antérieures et aux anciennes constitutions nationales*, Louvain 1887; Id., *La mosaïque constitutionnelle. Essai sur les sources du texte de la constitution belge*, Louvain 1892.

77 É però molto significativo il giudizio di de Gerlache in merito al progetto: «Il ne renferme rien ou presque rien de nouveau; et c'est ce qui en fait, selon moi, le mérite. Il ne faut rien donner à l'aventure quand il s'agit des institutions d'un pays. Et personne de nous n'a été assez osé pour improviser des nouveautés», in E. Huyttens, *Discussions du Congrès National de Belgique, 1830–1831*, cit., t. I, 324.

78 Gilissen ha quantificato percentualmente le rispettive influenze. La costituzione belga sarebbe tributaria per il 40% dal Grondwet del 1815, per il 35% dalla

utilità conoscere le ascendenze, gli influssi, i circuiti e i processi di imitazione che nell'ambito costituzionale sono da sempre terreno di indagine e di discussione; e tuttavia questo tipo di analisi comparativa testuale e sinottica non può prescindere dalla successiva fondamentale ricerca delle tradizioni, delle forme e delle tecniche di elaborazione dottrinale, delle determinazioni politico-costituzionali, dei *Sonderwege*.

Non si sbaglia ad affermare che il Belgio è sul Continente «le pays où les faits correspondent le mieux avec l'idée, le fond avec la forme, les principes avec leur application».[80] La Costituzione è il risultato di un'impresa solida, coerente, equilibrata, capace di sciogliere preventivamente i principali nodi problematici che in tante altre costituzioni restarono nell'ambiguità e nell'indeterminatezza. La Costituzione è intimamente associata all'indipendenza, è realmente fondatrice di un ordine politico e giuridico. I costituenti vedono in essa un inizio assoluto e credono al valore eminente della legge espressione della volontà generale.

Non di rado si usa avvicinare la costituzione belga ad altri testi – a cominciare dalla Carta orleanista – nel presupposto che vi sia una forte identità "filosofica". In questo ambito tuttavia non sovvengono categorie troppo generali incentrate sul consolidato binomio dualismo / monismo. Talvolta si scambia l'evoluzione con le premesse di un sistema costituzionale e le apparenze possono risultare, come si è osservato,[81] fuorvianti. Così, per esempio, all'ambiguità politico-filosofica della Carta di Luigi Filippo fa da controcanto nella Costituzione belga una chiara definizione del potere costituente originario. Il Congresso fa la Costituzione e solo dopo sceglie ed elegge il monarca.[82] La Costituzione è inequivocabilmente l'alfa e l'omega dei poteri pubblici. «Tous les pouvoirs –

Charte constitutionnelle del 1830, per il 10% dalla Costituzione del 1791 e per il 5% dal diritto pubblico inglese (senza considerare, naturalmente, l'influsso dei principi e delle regole che si possono far risalire al costituzionalismo britannico). Resterebbe dunque solo un 10% da mettere sotto la rubrica delle norme propriamente "originali" (*La constitution belge de 1831*, cit., 132–133).

79 Si rinvia *supra*, *1. Premessa*.

80 V. Du Bled, *Histoire de la Monarchie de Juillet de 1830 à 1848 avec une introduction sur le droit constitutionnel aux Etats-Unis, en Suisse, en Angleterre et en Belgique*, Paris 1877, t. I, XCV.

81 Cfr. *supra*, *1. Premessa*, 80–81.

82 «Quand l'assemblée constituante de 1830 reçut la haute et dangereuse mission de fixer l'organisation politique du pays, le trône était vide et le peuple, rentré dans la plénitude de ses droits, pouvait librement disposer de ses destinées. Le Congrès national n'hésita pas à admettre et à proclamer que la souveraineté réside dans la nation belge» (J.-J. Thonissen, *La constitution belge annotée offrant sous chaque article l'état de la doctrine, de la jurisprudence et de la législation*, Bruxelles 1879, 3 ed., 110).

recita l'articolo 25 – émanent de la nation. Ils sont exercés de la manière établie par la Constitution».[83] Questa è la norma-matrice e la sovranità nazionale – come la si intendeva nel Belgio del 1830[84] – rappresenta il fondamento dottrinale incontestato e da essa discendono i principali caratteri della costituzione, dallo statuto del Parlamento alla forma di governo e al ruolo del monarca, dalla definizione del potere giudiziario alla disciplina dei diritti e delle libertà.

«La Constitution de 1831, – afferma Jean-Baptiste Nothomb – expression d'un état social, n'a été ni une théorie philosophique, ni le manifeste d'un parti triomphant. C'est pour cela qu'elle a duré ...».[85]

3.2 I diritti e le libertà dei Belgi

«Novateur parce qu'il était prévoyant, le Congrès belge eut la gloire de décréter le premier, sur le continent, la séparation complète de la société religieuse et de la société civile, en même temps qu'il consacrait l'alliance intime du principe monarchique avec la liberté républicaine».[86] L'indipendenza nazionale aveva trovato, come si è detto, nella difficile alleanza tra il cattolicesimo liberale e il liberalismo politico la pietra angolare per un innovativo progetto costituzionale. Proprio in quell'alleanza possiamo scorgere l'ideale del «patto costituzionale» tra le due principali "famiglie" politiche della storia del Belgio moderno e una caratteristica fondamentale del «modello belga».[87] La libertà dei culti, nelle sue varie espressioni, veniva strettamente collegata alla libertà di pensiero (art. 14),[88] ribadendo la comune matrice «liberal-costituzionale» e la

83 L'articolo 130 recita: «La Constitution ne peut être suspendue en tout ni en partie». Sull'articolo 25 v. J. Gilissen, *La constitution belge de 1831*, cit., 126–127.

84 A. Mast, *Une constitution du temps de Louis-Philippe*, cit., 989. Cfr. H. Van Impe, *Le régime parlementaire en Belgique*, Bruxelles 1968.

85 Cit. da O. Orban, *Le droit constitutionnel de la Belgique*, t. I, cit., 119.

86 Th. Juste, *Le Congrès National de Belgique*, cit., t. I, 295.

87 Sull'evoluzione e sulla crisi dell'«Unione», si rinvia a C. Lebas, *L'Union des catholiques et des libéraux de 1838 à 1847. Etude sur les pouvoirs exécutif et législatif*, Leuven, Paris 1960.

88 «La liberté des cultes, celle de leur exercice public, ainsi que la liberté de manifester ses opinions, en toute matière, sont garanties, sauf la répression des délits commis à l'occasion de l'usage de ces libertés» (art. 14). Cfr. Th. Juste, *Le Congrès National de Belgique*, cit., t. I, 327 ss. I principi fondamentali sono stabiliti dagli articoli 14, 15 e 16. Sul dibattito in sede costituente, v. E. Huyttens, *Discussions du Congrès National de Belgique, 1830–1831*, cit., t. I, 525 ss. («La liberté des cultes, la liberté d'enseignement et celle de la presse ont été justement rapprochées dans les articles du projet de constitution: elles sont en quelque sorte identiques. C'est toujours la manifestation de la pensée, sous des formes

volontà di superare il regime ben più restrittivo della Legge Fondamentale del 1815 e il principio di asservimento[89] della Chiesa allo Stato (con conseguente sottoposizione dell'esercizio pubblico del culto ai regolamenti di polizia) stabilito dagli articoli organici della legge del 18 germinale dell'anno X rimessi in vigore da Guglielmo I nel 1816.

Una volta affermato dall'articolo 14 il principio-guida (la libertà di manifestare le opinioni, escludendo ogni intervento preventivo volto a limitarne la portata), seguono i corollari della libertà di insegnamento (art. 17),[90] di stampa (art. 18),[91] di riunione (art. 19) e di associazione (art. 20).[92] Le libertà primarie – assieme a quella fondamentale della libertà individuale (art. 7) – appaiono la necessaria condizione per dare vita ad un robusto regime parlamentare. Basta insomma confrontare il titolo della costituzione dedicato ai diritti dei Belgi o al potere giudiziario (in particolare in tema di giurisdizione giudiziaria dei diritti civili e dei diritti politici, artt. 92 e 93) con le corrispondenti sezioni delle Carte francesi[93] o dello Statuto albertino[94] per rendersi subito conto della maggiore

diverses», intervento di de Gerlache, ivi, 574); J.-J. Thonissen, *La constitution belge*, cit., 44 ss.; O. Orban, *Le droit constitutionnel de la Belgique*, t. III, cit., 587 ss.

89 «L'Etat n'a le droit d'intervenir ni dans la nomination, ni dans l'installation des ministres d'un culte quelconque, ni de défendre à ceux-ci de correspondre avec leurs supérieurs, et de publier leurs actes, sauf, en ce dernier cas, la responsabilité ordinaire en matière de presse et de publication ...» (art. 15).

90 Per l'importante e acceso dibattito sulla libertà di insegnamento, v. E. Vandenpeereboom, *Du gouvernement représentatif en Belgique*, cit., t. I,166 ss.; t. II, 36 ss.; P. Errera, *Traité de droit public belge*, cit., 485 ss.; O. Orban, *Le droit constitutionnel de la Belgique*, t. III, cit., 476 ss.

91 «Il fallait considérer la liberté de la presse comme la clef de voûte de l'édifice constitutionnel, parce qu'elle protège et sauvegarde toutes les autres libertés» (Th. Juste, *Le Congrès National de Belgique*, t. I, cit., 363).

92 Cfr. E. Huyttens, *Discussions du Congrès National de Belgique, 1830–1831*, cit., t. I, 621 ss.; J.-J. Thonissen, *La constitution belge*, cit.

93 «Se vuolsi infatti paragonare questo Statuto con quello che i Francesi imposero alla monarchia di Luglio si vedrà di leggieri quanto l'opera fiamminga superi in larghezza quella francese. I Belgi proclamando coll'art. 18 la piena libertà della stampa, affrancano da ogni cauzione gli scrittori e gli editori. Lo Statuto francese non esclude la cauzione, e la legge obbliga a questo dovere. I Fiamminghi hanno il diritto di riunione. I Francesi son dispogliati di cotesto diritto, e le antiche leggi penali su questa materia rimangono in vigore. In Francia al solo re spetta il potere esecutivo. In Belgio il re non ha altri poteri per l'art. 78 che quelli che gli conferisce formalmente la Costituzione. Dal re francese emana ogni giustizia, e si distribuisce in suo nome dai giudici che egli presceglie. In Belgio per l'art. 25 tutti i poteri emanano dal popolo, e al re non si concede che il diritto di nominare i giudici di pace e quelli di prima istanza. In Francia il Parlamento non può che congregarsi che per ordine del principe. In Belgio si riunisce ogni anno di pieno diritto per l'art. 70 il secondo martedì di novembre. Lo Statuto francese

completezza della disciplina costituzionale e del carattere decisamente liberale delle disposizioni.[95] Migliorando il buon impianto della *Grondwet*, il costituente belga si è spinto ben oltre, inserendo articoli assenti in molte costituzioni coeve[96] dove, anche quando il principio è presente, è però spesso limitato nella sua portata.[97]

3.3 «Tutti i poteri emanano dalla nazione»

Se dal titolo II consacrato ai Belgi e ai loro diritti l'analisi corre al titolo successivo sui poteri, la peculiarità del sistema belga non potrà, ancora una volta, che risaltare. L'articolo 25 assegna ai tre poteri costituzionali una piena sincronicità di origine. Nessuno di essi, emanando a pari titolo dalla nazione, può vantare diritti anteriori o superiori alla costituzione né può arrogarsi un diritto di imperio sugli altri.[98] Il potere legislativo è esercitato collettivamente

stabilisce l'età di anni trenta per essere eligibile, e prescrive un censo pei deputati. Il Fiammingo richiede per l'art. 50 l'età di anni venticinque, e non impone alcun censo. Il Francese porge il dritto al re della nomina dei pari, vuole che sia a vita, ed il numero illimitato. Il Fiammingo sottopone i senatori all'elezione popolare, ed il numero lo restringe alla metà di quello dei deputati. Il Francese nelle disposizioni per lo ordinamento municipale e provinciale si attiene al principio elettivo, ma non passa più oltre delle disposizioni generali. Il Fiammingo per l'art. 108 determina le condizioni e stabilisce: l'elezione diretta; la pubblicità delle sedute; quella dei conti e delle rendite; ed il diritto esclusivo ai Consigli comunali e provinciali su gli interessi della comune e della provincia ...» (C. Gemelli, *Storia della rivoluzione belgica dell'anno 1830*, Bologna 1867, 2 ed., 410–411).

94 Naturalmente, il confronto potrebbe essere fatto con tutte le costituzioni europee del XIX secolo.

95 «Le Congrès national de 1831 prit pour mot d'ordre cette généreuse devise: *Liberté en tout et pour tous*. Il consacra de la manière la plus nette et la plus audacieuse ces quatre libertés *cardinales* qui n'existent chez aucun peuple européen à un degré aussi illimité: liberté de la presse, liberté des cultes, liberté de l'enseignement, liberté d'association. C'est là le côté le plus original, le plus extraordinaire de cette constitution de 1831, votée dans un pays en voie de formation, au lendemain d'une révolution ...» (V. Du Bled, *Histoire de la Monarchie de Juillet de 1830*, cit., XCVII).

96 Basti pensare alla libertà di insegnamento, di riunione, di associazione, all'abolizione della morte civile, ecc.

97 Sui diritti dei Belgi v. J. Gilissen, *La Constitution belge de 1831*, cit., 123–125 e soprattutto J. Vanderlinden, *Aux origines du titre II de la Constitution belge de 1831. Essai d'histoire constitutionnelle comparative*, in *Présence du droit public et des droits de l'homme. Mélanges offerts à Jacques Velu*, Bruxelles 1992, 1193–1209.

98 J.-B. Bivort, *Commentaire sur la Constitution belge*, Bruxelles 1858, 15; J.-J. Thonissen, *La constitution belge*, cit., 113.

dal re, dalla Camera dei rappresentanti e dal Senato (art. 26), appartenendo a ciascuno il diritto di iniziativa, fermo restando la precedenza della Camera nell'esame delle materie di bilancio e del contingente dell'esercito (art. 27).[99] Queste norme – e le conseguenti determinazioni costituzionali – vengono interpretate secondo la logica propria dell'equilibrio e della collaborazione necessari alla monarchia costituzionale: i poteri devono conciliare i rispettivi diritti, moderare le reciproche pretese. Secondo il figurino tradizionale ogni soggetto rappresenta in prevalenza un elemento: il monarchico, il conservatore (il Senato), l'elemento popolare (la Camera dei rappresentanti).

3.4 La rappresentanza nazionale: la Camera dei rappresentanti e il Senato

È significativo il fatto che nella costituzione belga, diversamente dalle Carte francesi o dallo Statuto sabaudo, le due sezioni dedicate al parlamento precedano il capitolo sulle prerogative regie e sulla funzione esecutiva. Come si è già sottolineato la centralità politico-costituzionale del parlamento trova conferma nell'ampia competenza esclusiva del legislatore anche in materie che precedentemente rientravano nel campo dell'amministrazione.[100] La Costituzione fissa in dettaglio i principi che fondano il sistema censitario, sia per la Camera dei rappresentanti che per il Senato.[101] Le norme comuni alle due sezioni del parlamento (cap. I del tit. III) si distinguono egualmente per la cura dei singoli 'dettagli' (artt. 33, 34, 37, 38, 39, 40, 41, 42) e non poche regole del moderno diritto parlamentare vi trovano un esplicito riconoscimento. Una norma come quella che prescrive la decadenza dall'ufficio del parlamentare nominato dal governo ad un incarico retribuito[102] o che ne tutela le libertà connesse alla funzione non si riscontrano, nella stessa misura, in altri testi.[103]

99 «Un principe fondamental, et propre à maintenir chaque branche du pouvoir législatif dans bornes naturelles, c'est que la connaissance première des lois les plus importantes, pour le bien-être matériel du pays, doit appartenir à la partie de la législature qui représente plus spécialement le mouvement et le contrôle en être réservé à la partie conservatrice; tel est le but de l'art. 27 de la constitution» (*Répertoire de l'administration et du droit administratif de la Belgique*, s.v. *Amendement*, par C. de Brouckère et F. Tielemans, Bruxelles 1834, t. II, 181). Sull'attribuzione ex art. 27 c. 2, vedi la critica di O. Orban, *Le droit constitutionnel de la Belgique*, t. II, cit., 418 ss.

100 Cfr. per es. gli articoli 3, 17, 23, 66, 67, 108, 110.

101 Si vedano gli articoli 47–50 e 53, 55, 56. Sul censo elettorale cfr. s.v. *Cens éléctoral*, in *Pandectes Belges. Encyclopédie de législation, de doctrine et de jurisprudences belges*, Bruxelles 1885, t. XVII, 1–451. Sui sistemi elettorali v. *infra*, paragrafo 4.

102 «Le nombre de l'une ou de l'autre des deux chambres, nommé par le gouvernement à un emploi salarié, qu'il accepte, cesse immédiatement de siéger, et ne reprend ses fonctions qu'en vertu d'une nouvelle élection». Cfr. E. Vandenpeereboom, *Du gouvernement représentatif en Belgique*, cit., t. I, 33. L'obbligo di

La discussione più approfondita e più accesa in seno al Congresso riguardò senza dubbio la struttura del Parlamento. Il dibattito[104] sull'istituzione o meno del Senato ripropose gli argomenti che la tradizione ha forgiato tra la fine del Settecento e gli inizi dell'Ottocento. I fautori (per es. Defacqz) di una sola Camera potevano invocare Rousseau, Sieyès e negare la legittimità di una Camera del 'privilegio' giudicata in constrasto con le premesse e i principi fondamentali della Costituzione. I sostenitori del Senato, invece, si richiamavano alle esperienze 'positive' (Gran Bretagna, Stati Uniti) ricordando viceversa i fallimenti del monocameralismo *à la française*.

rielezione riguardava anche i ministri nominati tra i parlamentari e ciò era una incongruenza rispetto alla logica di un regime parlamentare. La rielezione divenne così una sorta di mera formalità. Tale obbligo fu eliminato nel 1893 a seguito della prima revisione costituzionale. Si veda J. Gilissen, *Le régime représentatif belge depuis 1790*, cit., 111.

103 È sufficiente la comparazione degli articoli 44–45 con i corrispondenti articoli della Carta francese del 1830 e dello Statuto albertino.

104 Cfr. E. Huyttens, *Discussions du Congrès National de Belgique, 1830–1831*, cit., t. I, 393 ss. (per es. gli interventi del conte De Celles (camera unica) e del conte de Baillet (seconda camera), *ibidem*, 393–398) e t. IV, 75–82 (rapporti di Devaux a nome della sezione centrale). Si vedano inoltre E. Vandenpeereboom, *Du gouvernement représentatif en Belgique*, cit., t. I, 12 ss. e 359: «Le Sénat n'est donc pas et ne peut pas être, à cause de l'infériorité du nombre de ses membres, le contrôleur, le réviseur de toutes les décisions de la Chambre. Il est un corps *modérateur*, chargé de mettre, en certaines circonstances, un obstacle législatif aux dangereux entraînements de la chambre populaire: il doit servir de bouclier au pouvoir royal, contre les périls auxquels celui-ci pourrait être exposé par l'action directe et trop vive d'une assemblée unique. Qu'on nous permette le mot. Le Sénat est comme le ressort de la machine représentative; il rend les secousses moins sensibles, les choses moins brusques. Ses fonctions, pour être passives plutôt qu'actives, n'en sont pas moins salutaires. Mais si le ressort est trop mou, il se fausse: s'il est trop roide, il risque de se briser ... L'utilité, la nécessité constitutionnelle du Sénat reposent sur cette combinaison: avec deux Chambres, le pouvoir royal est plus couvert, sa responsabilité est moins engagée»; Th. Juste, *Le Congrès National de Belgique*, cit., 157 ss., 392–393: «Le Sénat devait avoir la même origine que la Chambre des représentants, c'est-à-dire l'élection directe par le même corps électoral. Mais comme le Sénat était établi pour représenter l'élément aristocratique et conservateur, on exigea de ses membres l'âge de quarante ans et un cens d'éligibilité consistant dans le payement en Belgique de mille florins au moins d'impositions directes; en outre, on refusa tout traitement ou indemnité aux sénateurs. Une autre disposition fixa le nombre des sénateurs à la moitié des députés de l'autre Chambre: cette limitation était la conséquence nécessaire de l'adoption du principe de l'élection directe et la condition première de la représentation réelle de l'aristocratie. Enfin, le mandat des sénateurs reçut une durée double de celle du mandat des membres de l'autre Chambre: cette prolongation se rattachait au caractère même du Sénat, destiné surtout à maintenir la stabilité des institutions».

Al termine del dibattito ebbe la meglio la soluzione bicamerale (128 a 62). Il Congresso non intese vedere nel Senato una forma di organizzazione sociale fondata sulla diseguaglianza delle condizioni (J.-B. Nothomb), una sorta di transazione tra l'aristocrazia e la democrazia, o creare una Camera alta analoga alla paria inglese.[105] «Il a simplement admis le Sénat comme un fait d'organisation politique, un rouage utile à la marche prudente et sûre du pouvoir législatif. Il l'a composé d'éléments propres à assurer à la discussion des lois plus de lenteur, de calme, de modération et de maturité».[106] Nel corso del dibattito furono avanzate varie proposte sul modo di composizione del Senato: doveva essere di nomina regia e vitalizio, formato dai Consigli provinciali o addirittura cooptato dalla stessa Camera dei deputati? Dopo aver scartato queste possibili soluzioni, il Congresso votò l'emendamento Jottrand (130 a 40) che stabiliva il principio elettivo. Organo moderatore, meccanismo di stabilità, risulta formato da senatori che abbiano almeno quarant'anni e un censo superiore ai mille fiorini; ricevono un mandato di otto anni e non godono di alcuna indennità.[107] Più che l'esempio inglese, si deve forse tenere presente quello americano.

> On peut dire des deux Chambres belges ce que Rossi disait des deux Chambres américaines: "Nous avons une Chambre à principes progressifs, l'autre à principes conservateurs, l'une qui a mission de donner l'impulsion, l'autre qui a mission de régler cette impulsion, l'une pousse, l'autre retient dans une juste mesure, et c'est ainsi que par la combinaison de cette double force, la société marche sans courir et que vous réalisez l'idée d'un progrès sage et continu."»[108]

105 «Messieurs, je ne veux point de la pairie anglaise, point de fidéicommis, point de droit d'aînesse; je ne veux point de la pairie française, point d'hérédité, point de majorats; mais je ne veux pas non plus faire courir à mon pays les dangers d'une chambre unique: je veux un système mixte. Que l'on prenne ce qu'il y a de bon sur l'institution, en France, en Angleterre, en Amérique; que l'on fasse de tout cela un éclectisme politique, en le conciliant avec les intérêts bien entendus de notre pays» (v. l'intervento di Joseph Lebeau, assai ricco di riferimenti dottrinali, seduta del 13 dicembre 1830, in E. Huyttens, *Discussions du Congrès National de Belgique, 1830–1831*, cit., t. I, 412–416, 416).

106 J.-J. Thonissen, *La constitution belge*, cit., 133.

107 I deputati – per i quali non è previsto alcun censo di eleggibilità – sono eletti per quattro anni (art. 54) e dispongono di una indennità mensile se provengono da una località diversa da quella nella quale si tiene la sessione (art. 52). Cfr. J. Gilissen, *Le régime représentatif belge depuis 1790*, cit., 88–89.

108 J.-J. Thonissen, *La constitution belge*, cit., 134. Cfr. P. Rossi, *Cours de droit constitutionnel professé à la Faculté de Droit de Paris …*, Paris 1867, t. IV, 56.

3.5 Una «monarchie constitutionnelle représentative, sous un chef héréditaire»

Il Congresso nazionale con decreto del 22 novembre 1830 ha adottato la forma di governo monarchica costituzionale rappresentativa ed ereditaria. La costituzione assegna al monarca il potere esecutivo, «tel qu'il est réglé par la Constitution» (art. 29). I costituenti – accantonata l'opzione repubblicana – si resero ben conto della necessità di affidare al re il potere esecutivo, ma nello stesso tempo, coerentemente col principio posto dall'articolo 25, ne vollero riaffermare a più riprese (e, si può dire, attraverso l'intero sistema delle norme costituzionali) la natura di potere costituito. La costituzione nasce per volontà della nazione e il monarca – che significativamente sarà eletto[109] solo in un secondo tempo – ne accetta il testo.[110]

> «Les pouvoirs du roi sont tellement limités, que, à part l'hérédité et le droit de faire grâce, ainsi que de conférer des titres de noblesse, cette partie de notre pacte fondamental aurait pu s'appliquer, sans changement, au président d'une République. C'est ce qui a fait dire, avec raison, que nous vivons sous un régime démocratique, avec un chef héréditaire; "plutôt sous une république royale que sous une monarchie républicaine", comme le disait M. Le Hon ...»[111]

Questo giudizio – che si può ricollegare idealmente alla riflessione tardo settecentesca sul ruolo problematico del «capo dello Stato» – può rivelarsi semplificante, ma non v'è dubbio che in Belgio – più nettamente che nella Francia orleanista – la monarchia diventi «un elemento organizzatorio nell'equilibrio dei poteri dello Stato di diritto liberale».[112] La delimitazione del potere

109 Sull'interferenza dell'elezione nello sviluppo dinastico delle monarchie «costituzionali», v. Ph. Lauvaux, *Les monarchies: inventaire des types*, cit., 26 ss.

110 «Il est vrai qu'il se forme un contrat entre lui [il capo dello Stato] et la nation, mais la constitution ne forme pas la matière de ce contrat, c'est l'acceptation du mandat que lui confère la nation. Le mandant est ici un être collectif de la nation constituée» (Van Meenen, seduta dell'8 febbraio 1831, in E. Huyttens, *Discussions du Congrès National de Belgique, 1830–1831*, cit., t. II, 492).

111 E. Vandenpeereboom, *Du gouvernement représentatif en Belgique*, cit., t. I, 7.

112 Sulla scorta di F. J. Stahl, vedi C. Schmitt, *Verfassungslehre*, Berlin 1928, tr. it. *Dottrina della costituzione*, Milano 1984, 381. Sul tipo di monarchia costituzionale nata in Belgio nel 1831, in rapporto soprattutto al cd. *monarchische Prinzip* della tradizione prussiana, cfr. R. Smend, *Die Preussische Verfassungsurkunde im Vergleich mit der belgischen*, Göttingen 1904; O. Hintze, *Das monarchische Prinzip und die konstitutionnelle Verfassung*, in *Preussische Jahrbücher*, 144, 1911, 381–412, tr. it. *Il principio monarchico e il regime costituzionale*, in *Stato e società*, a cura di P. Schiera, Bologna 1980, 29; *Beiträge zur deutschen und belgischen Verfassungsgeschichte im 19. Jahrhundert*, a cura di W. Conze, Stuttgart 1967; E. W. Böckenförde, *Der deutsche Typ der konstitutionnellen Monarchie im 19. Jahrhundert* (1967), in *Staat, Gesellschaft, Freiheit. Studien zur Staatstheorie und zum Verfassungsrecht*, Frankfurt am Main 1976, 112–145.

regio viene vista come una delle condizioni fondamentali della monarchia costituzionale belga, e in particolare come il profilo che le garantisce un carattere «essentiellement modérateur».[113] Il re può dunque esercitare le prerogative[114] formalmente attribuitegli dalla costituzione e da leggi particolari (art. 78). Il re ha il diritto di convocare, prorogare e sciogliere le Camere (artt. 70–72), ma la costituzione prevede che queste si riuniscano «de plein droit» ogni anno il secondo martedì di novembre, a meno che il sovrano non le abbia convocate anteriormente (art. 70). Le Camere si devono riunire per almeno quaranta giorni l'anno. Il re può aggiornare le Camere, tuttavia tale atto non può eccedere il termine di un mese, né essere rinnovato nella stessa sessione senza il consenso del parlamento (art. 72).[115] Il monarca sanziona e promulga le leggi (art. 69), ha il comando dell'esercito, dichiara la guerra, stipula i trattati di pace, di alleanza e di commercio (art. 68), è la fonte degli onori e concede la grazia (artt. 73, 75, 76), partecipa al «potere costituente derivato» nel procedimento di revisione costituzionale (art. 131). «La puissance et l'influence que ce commandement lui procure ne sont pas à redouter dans un pays qui possède des institutions parlementaires largement organisées. La responsabilité ministérielle, jointe au vote annuel des impôts et du contingent militaire, suffit pour écarter tous les périls qu'on pourrait justement redouter sous le régime du pouvoir absolu».[116] Se il potere regio è al centro delle relazioni con l'estero, i trattati di commercio devono però essere sottoposti all'approvazione delle Camere e i trattati di pace ricevere l'assenso dell'assemblea allorché si ritiene possano danneggiare lo Stato o gravare sui cittadini belgi.

Il re fa i regolamenti e i decreti necessari per l'esecuzione delle leggi, ma senza poter mai sospenderle o dispensare dalla loro esecuzione (art. 67). Questa disposizione deriva testualmente dal riformato articolo della Carta orleanista del 1830 (art. 13), ma la costituzione belga assicura ulteriori garanzie: l'articolo 107 stabilisce infatti che le corti e i tribunali non applicheranno i decreti ed i regolamenti generali, provinciali e locali, se non quando saranno conformi alle leggi; l'articolo 64 imputa la responsabilità dell'atto al ministro che avrà controfirmato il regolamento o il decreto che viola l'articolo 67. È sufficiente scorrere le norme che regolano la successione o l'istituto della reggenza (artt. 60–62, 79–85), il potere giudiziario o le istituzioni provinciali e comunali

113 Th. Juste, *Le Congrès National de Belgique*, cit., 394.

114 Sul concetto di potere e di prerogativa nel diritto pubblico belga, v. J. Velu, *La dissolution du Parlement*, Bruxelles 1966, 54 ss.

115 Sulle sessioni, sull'aggiornamento e sui casi di scioglimento obbligatorio delle Camere (artt. 85 e 131), vedi P. Errera, *Traité de droit public belge*, cit., 166.

116 J.-J. Thonissen, *La constitution belge*, cit., 219.

per poter ancora una volta constatare come la monarchia sia constantemente pensata in rapporto al parlamento e all'intervento limitativo della legge.[117]

> «Dans la monarchie limitée, tout ce qui n'est pas prévu appartient au gouvernement; dans la monarchie constitutionnelle, tout ce qui n'est pas réglé appartient au législatif, mais ce qui est prévu comme dépendant de l'autorité exécutive est ou doit être suffisant pour faire d'elle encore une plénitude de puissance, une somme de pouvoirs déterminés sans doute, mais un ensemble, une généralité assez vaste pour être opposée aux pouvoirs spéciaux de juger et de légiférer».[118]

Si racconta che Leopoldo I abbia espresso ai deputati del Congresso che gli offrivano la Corona il rammarico per la sua "posizione" costituzionale: «Messieurs vous avez rudement traité la royauté qui n'était pas là pour se défendre».[119] E, tuttavia, non poco del successo e della durata del sistema belga si deve alla capacità di combinare prerogative e limiti, instaurando un gioco ben calibrato di interdipendenze. Se la camera dei rappresentanti ha il potere di accusare i ministri, il giudizio è tuttavia svolto dinanzi alla Corte di Cassazione (art. 90) e non al Senato, come avviene in altri sistemi bicamerali, poiché l'elettività dei senatori è vista come possibile fattore di «turbativa politica» e la Cassazione, formata da giudici autorevoli e inamovibili, sembra poter offrire più ampie assicurazioni di 'neutralità'.[120] Il costituente belga ha infatti manifestato un'ampia fiducia verso il giudiziario, facendone un potere autonomo e indipendente,[121] assistito da cospiscue garanzie in termini di inamovibilità, trattamenti, divieto di cumulo ecc. Non stupisce quindi il controllo di legalità sui decreti e regolamenti non conformi alla legge (art. 107) né che la Corte di cassazione – i cui consiglieri sono scelti dal re su due liste presentate dal Senato e dalla stessa corte suprema (art. 99)[122] – giudichi i ministri per i reati commessi nell'esercizio delle loro funzioni.

La costituzione afferma l'inviolabilità della persona del re e la correlativa responsabilità dei ministri (art. 63). Escluso ogni riferimento alla «sacralità» del

117 «... Il faut seulement tenir en mémoire que cette royauté est parlamentaire, que ses pouvoirs sont d'attribution, sans qu'elle puisse se prévaloir de ce qu'on appelle le résidu de souveraineté, c'est-à-dire que le Roi ne peut faire ce que la Constitution et les lois lui permettent de faire (art. 29 et 78) et non tout ce qu'elles ne lui défendent pas» (P. Errera, *Traité de droit public belge*, cit., 112).

118 O. Orban, *Le droit constitutionnel de la Belgique*, t. II, cit., 245–246.

119 F. Van Kalken, *La Belgique contemporaine (1780–1930)*, cit., 55.

120 O. De Kerchove De Denterghem, *De la responsabilité des ministres. Mémoire couronné*, Gand, Paris 1867, 158 ss.; J.-J. Thonissen, *La constitution belge*, cit., 198 ss., 398 ss.

121 «En 1830, les Belges vinrent dans la justice le palladium, l'égide de la liberté individuelle et politique; aussi ont-ils fait le pouvoir judiciaire très-fort ...» (V. Du Bled, *Histoire de la Monarchie de Juillet de 1830*, cit., XCII).

122 «... à bien des égards, nous nous rapprochons ici plutôt des idées anglo-saxones» (P. Errera, *Traité de droit public belge*, cit., 221 ss.).

re, si sottolinea il carattere razionalizzato della massima *the King can do no wrong.*[123] L'immagine che viene proposta dai costituzionalisti belgi è quella, di matrice constantiana,[124] di una *royauté* intesa quale elemento essenziale della costituzione, sottoposta al vincolo assoluto della responsabilità dei ministri ma non priva di prerogative penetranti (a cominciare dal procedimento legislativo), personificazione dell'unità nazionale, capace di rappresentare la tradizione, la continuità, la durata. «Institution vivante, elle a été placée par la Constitution dans une sphère supérieure, d'où elle veille sur les mouvements de l'opinion, d'où elle interroge et écoute la pensée des autres grands pouvoirs de l'Etat».[125] Ma la posizione di inviolabilità del re, «position exceptionnelle au dessus de la région des orages»,[126] non è pericolosa perché il Capo dello Stato non può compiere alcun atto senza che un ministro se ne assuma la responsabilità.

Come si è visto, durante il regno di Guglielmo I, il principio della responsabilità parlamentare non era riuscito ad imporsi.[127] Nel 1828 il ministro olandese Van Maanen aveva dichiarato nella seduta del 2 dicembre: «Je ne suis pas responsable devant vous, je ne suis responsable que devant le Roi».[128] E proprio alla vigilia della rivoluzione tale questione aveva assunto una primaria importanza sia nel dibattito parlamentare che nella pubblicistica.[129] La Costituzione del 1831 affermò il principio (art. 63) prevedendo l'obbligo di controfirma dei

123 «Notre système constitutionnel, dont l'inspiration est démocratique, a fait de cette fiction un principe constitutionnel. Il lui a donné une base rationnelle par l'effet de la règle que le Roi ne peut agir seul. Ainsi l'adage que le Roi est incapable de mal faire ...» (*Rapport de la Commission chargée d'émettre un avis motivé sur l'application des principes constitutionnels relatifs à l'exercice des prérogatives du Roi et aux rapports des grands pouvoirs constitutionnels entre eux*, 6 août 1949, riportato da F. Delpérée, B. Dupret, *Nul ne peut decouvrir la Couronne*, Louvain-la-Neuve 1989, 60).

124 Sul punto v. in questo volume *infra Coppet et la percée de l'Etat libéral constitutionnel*, 219–226.

125 J.-B. Bivort, *Commentaire sur la Constitution belge*, cit., 32.

126 Th. Juste, *Le Congrès National de Belgique*, cit., 395.

127 L. Hymans, *Histoire politique et parlementaire de la Belgique de 1814–1830*, cit., 202–203, 214 ss. Già durante i lavori della Commissione mista belga-olandese l'introduzione della responsabilità ministeriale – non prevista dalla Legge Fondamentale – era stata oggetto di contrasto, e comunque auspicata da alcuni commissari belgi. Cfr. O. De Kerchove De Denterghem, *De la responsabilité des ministres*, cit., 38.

128 *Ibidem.*

129 A. Castiau, *De la responsabilité et de la mise en accusation des ministres en Belgique*, Gand 1829; J. Lebeau, *Observations sur le pouvoir royal*, cit.; F. Tielemans (Anonimo), *Lettre à Van Maanen sur la responsabilité ministérielle*, Bruxelles 1830. Cfr. P. Harsin, *La constitution belge de 1831 et la responsabilité ministérielle*, in *Revue d'histoire politique et constitutionnelle*, I, 1937, 164–177.

ministri quale condizione di validità degli atti del re (art. 64).[130] Anche in questo caso la legge fondamentale del Belgio si distingue per aver cercato di organizzare più in dettaglio il principio,[131] affiancando alla responsabilità politica quella giuridica dei ministri (artt. 90, 91, 134) in attesa che una legge organica ne definisse i casi di responsabilità, le pene e la procedura.[132] Che la Costituzione del 1831 cerchi però di 'delimitare' il problema politico-parlamentare della responsabilità lo si coglie anche da un altro indizio: in caso di vacanza del trono i poteri costituzionali del re sono esercitati dai «ministres réunis en conseil, et sous leur responsabilité» (art. 79).[133]

Se taluni commentatori considerano i ministri anzitutto come «ministri del re» dal quale ricevono formalmente il mandato (art. 65) che sarà revocato allorché non godranno più della sua fiducia,[134] è da osservare come la consuetudine secondo cui il re non può nominare come ministri che gli uomini

130 Cfr. W. J. Ganshof Van Der Meersch, *Des rapports entre le chef de l'Etat et le gouvernement en droit constitutionnel belge*, in *Revue de droit international et droit comparé*, 1950, 181–197.

131 Cfr. gli articoli 24, 63, 64, 79, 89, 90, 91, 134, 139.

132 In attesa della legge organica, la disciplina transitoria di cui all'art. 134 prevede che la Camera elettiva abbia un potere discrezionale nell'accusare un ministro e che la Corte di cassazione proceda a definire il delitto e ne fissi la pena che non potrà però eccedere quella della reclusione. Sui progetti presentati sin dal 1831 (de Brouckère, ecc.) sino alla legge del 19 giugno 1865, vedi O. De Kerchove De Denterghem, *De la responsabilité des ministres*, cit. e C. Montalcini, *L'istituzione regia e la responsabilità ministeriale*, cit., 861, 885–886.

133 P. Errera, *Traité de droit public belge*, cit., 208, osserva che «C'est un régime coutumier; il est dans l'esprit de la Constitution; la lettre ne dit rien à cet égard», ma poi scorge nell'art. 89 la conferma della responsabilità dei ministri non dinanzi al re ma ai rappresentanti della nazione (*ibidem*, 210). Sulla esistenza giuridica e di fatto della presidenza del consiglio vedi sempre *ibidem*, 212–213; O. Orban, *Le droit constitutionnel de la Belgique*, t. II, cit., 292 ss.; L. De Lichtervelde, *Le Conseil des ministres dans le droit public belge*, in *Bulletin de l'Académie royale de Belgique, Classe des lettres et des sciences morales et politiques*, 1947, 21–44; P. Wigny, *Droit constitutionnel. Principes et droit positif*, Bruxelles 1952, t. 2, 677 ss.; J. Velu, *La dissolution du Parlement*, cit., 59 ss.

134 «Comme aucun acte du roi ne peut avoir d'effet qu'autant qu'il est contre-signé par un ministre, il est évident que le pouvoir exécutif, en réalité, enlevé au chef de l'Etat, à l'instant même où le libre choix des ministres ne serait plus envisagé comme une partie intégrante de ses attributions» (J.-J. Thonissen, *La constitution belge*, cit., 212). Ancora in pieno Novecento è stata avanzata (in concomitanza con la scelta di Leopoldo III di non seguire il governo in esilio a Londra) da Louis Wodon la tesi – del tutto minoritaria in dottrina – della cd. "préeminance royale". Cfr. *Sur le rôle du Roi comme Chef de l'Etat dans les cas de défaillances constitutionnelles*, in *Bulletin de l'Académie royale de Belgique, Classe des lettres et des sciences morales et politiques*, t. XXVII, 1941, 207–219, 250–253; *Considérations sur la séparation et la délégation des pouvoirs en droit public belge*, *ibidem*, 1942.

ai quali il parlamento accorda la *confiance* si affermerà in modo regolare solo nel corso del tempo. Anzi, la libera scelta dei ministri da parte del re è vista come una conseguenza necessaria del regime parlamentare:

> «Sous un régime franchement constitutionnel, en présence de deux chambres électives, avec la discussion publique de toutes les lois, et une véritable responsabilité ministérielle, le chef de l'Etat est le plus intéressé au bon choix de ses ministres ... L'intérêt personnel du prince est son meilleur garant. Gardons-nous, en cédant à la crainte d'un danger invraisemblable et même chimérique, de frapper d'exclusion temporaire quelques capacités utiles au pays.»[135]

4. Politica e costituzione: continuità ed evoluzione

La costituzione del 1831, frutto di un compromesso di alto profilo, ha rappresentato il pilastro istituzionale attorno cui costruire il Belgio indipendente. Non bisogna però dimenticare quanto difficili furono gli anni successivi in virtù della persistente minaccia militare olandese, delle agitazioni orangiste, della crisi finanziaria, e si dovette attendere il 1839 – con la controfirma del Trattato dei XXIV articoli – per regolare i rapporti con i Paesi Bassi, rinunciando definitivamente ai territori del Limburgo e del Lussemburgo[136] e dovendo accettare uno statuto di neutralità assoluta.

Le regole del gioco politico-costituzionale si imperniano anzitutto sul sistema elettorale. La costituzione belga fissa il censo minimo (20 fiorini) e massimo (100 fiorini) (art. 47) per i deputati. Il costituente Forgeur aveva osservato durante il dibattito che «Ce point est grave, messieurs; car si vous n'avez pas dans la constitution une disposition qui fixe le cens électoral, comme c'est là-dessus que repose tout l'édifice constitutionnel, il se pourrait que les législatures à venir, en le modifiant, renversassent tout notre ouvrage».[137] Se il cittadino per essere

135 Charles de Hon, seduta del 20 gennaio 1831, in E. Huyttens, *Discussions du Congrès National de Belgique, 1830–1831*, cit., t. II, 220. Il deputato Hubert-Joseph Masbourg ha dato un contributo importante alla definizione della funzione ministeriale. «Les ministres sont, dans les Etats représentatifs, les véritables dignitaires du pouvoir. Si d'un côté la responsabilité ministérielle confère une garantie à la nation contre des infractions manifestes à la constitution, d'un autre côté cette même responsabilité transfère la souveraineté réelle entre les mains des conseillers de la couronne» (*ibidem*, 221). Si vedano anche i *rapports* di Joseph Raikem sul capo dello Stato (7 gennaio 1831) e sui ministri (10 gennaio 1831), *ibidem*, t. IV, 83–93.

136 Il Belgio dovette rinunciare a una parte dei territori sulla Mosa (compresa la fortezza di Maastricht) e del Lussemburgo. Il testo del trattato del 15 novembre 1831 è riportato da J.-B. Nothomb, *Essai historique*, cit., 463–475. Cfr. Van Kalken, *La Belgique contemporaine (1780–1930)*, cit., 56 ss.

137 Cfr. E. Huyttens, *Discussions du Congrès National de Belgique, 1830–1831*, cit., t. II, 28. Defacqz aveva insistito sulla necessità di fissare il censo nella costitu-

elettore deve dimostrare il censo richiesto,[138] l'eleggibilità, invece, è sottoposta alla condizione di possedere la cittadinanza, di godere dei diritti civili e politici, di avere 25 anni di età e il domicilio in Belgio. Questa distinzione cerca di mediare tra la prevalente concezione moderata che domina il Congresso nazionale e le forze liberal-democratiche che hanno avuto un ruolo importante in seno al movimento rivoluzionario.

La costituzione si basa, se così si può dire, su due principi: l'uno è la sovranità nazionale, l'altro è l'equilibrio tra le due Camere e il re titolare del potere esecutivo, tra il potere di scioglimento del monarca e il vincolo di fiducia tra parlamento e ministero. Formule come quella di «république royale» o di «monarchie républicaine» possono apparire suggestive ma non aiutano a capire l'evoluzione del sistema costituzionale. Il mito della Costituzione belga – a cui, per la verità, è difficile resistere – deve essere messo alla prova delle vicende politico-parlamentari. Se l'intervento personale del monarca – in ordine al potere esecutivo – è anzitutto sottoposto alla disciplina della controfirma ministeriale, il profilo politico di influenza e di capacità "attiva" non deve essere sottovalutato. Se la dinastia chiamata sul trono ha per lungo tempo tenuto un atteggiamento di integrità costituzionale, non bisogna certo dimenticare le condizioni che hanno accompagnato la nascita e lo sviluppo del sistema rappresentativo in Belgio dopo il 1831.

zione. «Je pense aussi qu'à raison de l'importance de cette condition il ne faut pas la laisser à l'arbitraire d'une loi mobile et changeante; il ne faut pas que les législatures qui nous succéderont puissent en disposer à leur gré, et peut-être selon les caprices du pouvoir ...» (*ibidem*). Cfr. anche *ibidem*, 640 ss. Sul dibattito si veda inoltre E. Vandenpeereboom, *Du gouvernement représentatif en Belgique*, cit., t. I, 25 ss.

138 La legge elettorale fu approvata il 3 marzo 1831 (101 voti a favore contro 31). Se il governo provvisorio aveva ammesso, per l'elezione dei membri del Congresso nazionale, anche i capacitari presunti (magistrati, ministri dei culti, ufficiali superiori, laureati), la legge del 3 marzo 1831 prevedeva solo un censo differenziato, che cambiava cioè a seconda delle circoscrizioni le quali, in buona misura, coincidevano con gli *arrondissement* dell'età francese. Il censo raggiungeva il *maximum* previsto dalla costituzione nelle grandi città, era meno alto nelle circoscrizioni d'importanza media, toccava il minimo per gli elettori delle campagne. Tale principio fu votato con uno scarto di due soli voti (63 a 61). È evidente il carattere conservatore di questa misura: nelle città solo l'alta borghesia aveva il diritto di voto; nelle campagne avevano maggiore influenza la media e piccola borghesia e i contadini più agiati. Il *pays légal* restava però molto ristretto, poiché il diritto di voto spettava a 46.000 cittadini, cioè ad un elettore ogni 95 abitanti. Sulla disciplina elettorale, cfr. J. Barthélemy, *L'organisation du suffrage et l'expérience belge*, Paris 1912; D. De' Cocci, *La legislazione elettorale belga*, Firenze 1946; J. Gilissen, *Le régime représentatif belge depuis 1790*, cit., 90–94; P. Harismendy, *Il caso belga*, in *I sistemi elettorali in Europa tra Otto e Novecento*, a cura di M. S. Piretti, Roma, Bari 1997.

Che la *royauté* – come scrive Vandenpeereboom – sia rimasta «consciencieusement dans les limites qui lui avaient été primitivement assignées ...»[139] è affermazione da valutare con più senso critico. Leopoldo I era in effetti il principe "ideale" per la fondazione nazionale del Belgio, ma non si può dire che la sua attività abbia mancato di influenzare la dinamica costituzionale e lo sviluppo del sistema politico. La costituzione del 1831 lascia comunque ampi margini "letterali" ad un monarca che, pur "eletto", rimane personalmente legato ad una concezione "conservatrice" e non certo "repubblicana" dell'autorità regia. Il barone Stockmar dice che Leopoldo I era «ein menschlicher Fürst», dotato di qualità non comuni.[140] È del resto celebre il giudizio comparativo di François Guizot sulla condotta di Luigi Filippo e del genero Leopoldo I: quanto l'ingerenza del primo era "apparente", tanto la prudenza del secondo sapeva tradursi in una reale «influence personnelle».[141]

I re belgi non hanno esitato a 'piegare' in senso monarchico la logica del governo parlamentare.[142] Del resto, nella storia della monarchia belga il sovrano esercita le attribuzioni costituzionali e svolge diverse funzioni,[143] di stimolo, di mediazione, di simbolo. La durata dei regni[144] rivela l'importanza di un fattore ereditario di stabilità.[145] Non è un caso se la monarchia, ovvero la sua funzione costituzionale e politica, sia stata fatta oggetto nel dopoguerra[146] di una

139 E. Vandenpeereboom, *Du gouvernement représentatif en Belgique*, cit., t. II, 299–300.

140 «Tuttavia, come vedemmo il potere della Corona essere mutabile a seconda delle qualità personali del monarca, le doti dei Leopoldi attribuirono loro tutta quell'influenza che la Costituzione pare avrebbe voluto limitare ...» (C. Montalcini, *L'istituzione regia e la responsabilità ministeriale*, cit., 756).

141 F. Guizot, *Mémoires pour servir à l'histoire de mon temps*, Paris 1872, t. VIII, 95: «Je suis convaincu que son gendre, le roi Léopold, infiniment plus prudent et plus réservé dans son attitude et son langage, a exercé, dans le gouvernement de la Belgique au dedans et au dehors, plus d'influence personnelle que le roi Louis-Philippe dans celui de la France; mais l'un en évitait avec soin l'apparence, tandis que l'autre se montrait toujours préoccupé de la crainte que la justice ne fût pas rendue à ses desseins et à ses efforts».

142 «A l'interprétation républicaine que le Parlement donnait à la constitution, il (Leopoldo) est arrivé à substituer son interprétation monarchique et, tout en respectant scrupuleusement le pacte fondamental qu'il avait juré d'observer, a réussi à doter le gouvernement des prérogatives indispensables au maintien de l'Etat» (H. Pirenne, *Histoire de Belgique*, cit., t. IV, 387–388).

143 Su questa distinzione v. F. Delpérée, B. Dupret, *Le roi des Belges*, in *Pouvoirs*, 54, 1990, 15–24 e F. Delpérée, *La fonction du Roi*, in *Pouvoirs*, 78, 1996, 43–54.

144 Leopoldo I (1831–1865), Leopoldo II (1865–1909), Alberto I (1909–1934), Leopoldo III (1934–1951), Baldovino I (1951–1993).

145 Si veda l'ottima sintesi di L. Domenichelli, *Il ruolo della Corona nella costituzione federale belga del 1993*, in *Il Politico*, 4, 1994, 691–726.

146 In particolare sono due i momenti che hanno contraddistinto tale discussione: la

particolare attenzione, sulla scia di un processo storico che ne avrebbe limitato i margini di manovra. Il concetto di influenza della Corona rimane però alla base dell'interpretazione dominante. Ciò si deve sia a fattori storici che a fattori istituzionali. Il dato internazionale ha inciso profondamente sulla conformazione del regime costituzionale: Leopoldo I ha supplito, specie negli anni Trenta, all'inesperienza della classe dirigente mettendo a disposizione del paese la sua autorità 'dinastica' nell'ambito della diplomazia europea; Leopoldo II ha condotto una politica coloniale 'personalistica'; Alberto I e Leopoldo III hanno dovuto confrontarsi con i dilemmi e le tragedie degli eventi bellici. Parimenti, la natura del sistema politico ha giocato un ruolo di primo piano: dall'unionismo iniziale al conflitto tra le forze politiche costituenti sino al processo di democratizzazione avviato tra le due revisioni costituzionali (1893, 1921–1922) per arrivare infine alla frammentazione politico-partitica che ha caratterizzato la scena degl'ultimi cinquant'anni. Contingenze e dati strutturali si sono pertanto strettamente intrecciati, favorendo comunque – specie nel corso del XIX secolo – un certo grado di 'influenza personale', più o meno visibile. La dottrina belga può ammettere la massima inglese, rivitalizzata da Thiers nel 1830, del «re regna e non governa» solo se con essa si intende sottolineare il ruolo di una monarchia che ha determinate attribuzioni giuridiche ed è istituzionalmente influente, ma «elle doit toujours paraître ne s'occuper que des intérêts essentiels et permanents du pays».[147] Certo, la distinzione non è agevole, se anche nelle attività più sensibili (la nomina e la revoca dei ministri e lo scioglimento delle Camere) il confine tra 'giuridico' e 'politico' presenta margini di ben nota indeterminatezza.[148]

cd. "question royale" (1949–1950) in merito alla condotta di Leopoldo III durante l'invasione nazista del Belgio e il dibattito che ha accompagnato il rifiuto di Baldovino I nell'aprile del 1990 di sanzionare la legge che depenalizzava parzialmente l'aborto, ricorrendo all'art. 82 della Costituzione e dando vita ad un singolare meccanismo di sospensione-reintegrazione nelle funzioni di regnante.

147 O. Orban, *Le droit constitutionnel de la Belgique*, t. II, cit., 273. Sul concetto di influenza cfr. W. J. Ganshof Van Der Meersch, *Des rapports entre le chef de l'Etat et le gouvernement*, cit.; R. Fusilier, *Les monarchies parlementaires*, Paris 1960, 419; J. De Meyer, *Réflexions sur la monarchie parlementaire*, in *Res Publica*, 2, 1961; R. Senelle, *Le monarque constitutionnel en Belgique*, in *Res Publica*, III, 1962, 51–65; A. Molitor, *La fonction royale en Belgique*, Bruxelles 1979 (1994, 2 ed.); Id., *Réflexions sur la fonction royale*, in *Nous, Roi des Belges ... 150 ans de monarchie constitutionnelle 1831–1981*, Bruxelles 1981, 18; F. Delpérée, B. Dupret, *Nul ne peut découvrir la Couronne*, cit., 24 ss.

148 Si vedano, per i vari profili ed interpretazioni, J. Velu, *La dissolution du Parlement*, cit.; B. Waleffe, *Le roi nomme et révoque ses ministres*, Bruxelles 1971; F. Delpérée, B. Dupret, *Le roi des Belges*, cit.; J. Stengers, *L'action du roi en Belgique depuis 1831. Pouvoir et influence. Essai de typologie des modes d'action du*

L'evoluzione della forma di governo in Belgio non può essere raffigurata come un agevole percorso rettilineo di parlamentarizzazione del sistema. Se tale percorso rappresenta una linea tendenziale di sviluppo, la logica dell'equilibrio tra la «sfera di autonomia» del monarca e il «primato giuridico del potere legislativo» continuerà a produrre lungo il XIX secolo (e oltre) oscillazioni in un senso o nell'altro in virtù delle contingenze politiche e della personalità dei monarchi.[149]

Leopoldo I non disdegna un'"alleanza" strategica con il blocco conservatore cattolico che risulta favorito dal sistema elettorale.[150] Nei primi anni di regno, per aumentare la sua autorità e non potendo contare solo sulle forze di ispirazione cattolica, cerca di favorire la creazione di governi «unionisti», ovvero governi di centro-destra basati sulla compresenza di cattolici e di liberali moderati. Negli anni di *imprinting* – come si è detto – il re non poteva svolgere una mera funzione 'moderatrice'. Del resto nella tradizione monarchica belga – in analogia con altre esperienze europee[151] – si affermò, almeno sino ad Alberto I, un potere, più o meno incisivo, di 'riserva' nel campo della difesa e della politica internazionale. Se si osserva lo sviluppo del regime politico in Belgio lungo l'Ottocento si ricava un'immagine vigorosa della funzione monarchica impegnata a regolare e moderare il fondamentale gioco di equilibri tra l'esecutivo e il legislativo, in virtù sia del potere di scioglimento[152] che del potere di nomina e di revoca dei ministri.[153] Non bisogna infine dimenticare che uno dei grandi *clivage* della storia belga consiste – dopo l'iniziale «periodo unionista» – nel conflitto / competizione[154] tra cattolici e liberali, tra tentazioni di predomi-

roi, Paris, Louvain-la-Neuve 1992 (Bruxelles 1996, 2 ed.); R. Ergec, M. Uyttendaele, *La monarchie en Belgique. Reflet du passé ou nécessité nationale?*, in *Présence du droit public et droits de l'homme. Mélanges offerts à Jacques Velu*, Bruxelles 1992, vol. III.

149 L. Domenichelli, *Il ruolo della Corona*, cit., 716 ss.

150 Il censo differenziato, infatti, favorisce nei collegi rurali più i cattolici che i liberali.

151 Per quella italiana disponiamo ora di un'ampia ricostruzione monografica: v. P. Colombo, *Il re d'Italia. Prerogative costituzionali e potere politico della Corona (1848–1922)*, Milano 1999.

152 Si veda l'ampia e accurata ricerca di J. Velu, *La dissolution du Parlement*, cit.

153 R. Senelle, *Le monarque constitutionnel en Belgique*, cit., 56 ss.; J. Stengers, *Evolution historique de la royauté en Belgique: modèle ou imitation de l'évolution européenne*, in *Res Publica*, 1, 1991; J. Stengers, *L'action du Roi en Belgique en 1831*, cit.

154 Cfr. A. Miroir, *La Belgique et ses clivages: contradictions structurelles et familles politiques*, in *Pouvoirs*, 54, 1990, 6–7. Si vedano inoltre F. Van Kalken, *La Belgique contemporaine (1780–1930)*, cit., 54 ss. e E. Witte, J. Craeybeckx, *La Belgique politique de 1830 à nos jours*, cit., 21 ss.

nio confessionale[155] e contraccolpi anticlericali che si riflettono su tutte le grandi questioni: il sistema elettorale, l'insegnamento, le autonomie locali, la politica linguistica ecc. E l'influenza di Leopoldo I e Leopoldo II fece leva non di rado proprio sul conflitto che opponeva i due schieramenti su questioni di grande rilevanza politica e costituzionale.

Il 1848 rappresenta in Belgio una tappa fondamentale del processo di consolidamento dello Stato e delle istituzioni nate nel 1831. Il fallimento dei movimenti insurrezionali di matrice democratica e repubblicana assestò un duro colpo alle speranze di una trasformazione del regime politico. Il governo liberale profittò[156] della situazione guidando un processo riformatore cauto ma di indubbia efficacia. L'insegnamento francese non sfuggì alla classe dirigente belga. La legge elettorale fu riformata abbassando per tutti (anche a livello comunale) il censo al *minimum* di venti fiorini facendo quasi raddoppiare il numero degli elettori (da 46.000 a 79.000) e andando incontro alle istanze progressiste della piccola borghesia urbana. L'abolizione del diritto di timbro sui giornali rese effettiva la libertà di stampa pilastro del regime parlamentare. Infine, fu reso incompatibile il mandato elettivo con lo statuto di funzionario.[157] Nei decenni successivi, la lotta tra cattolici e liberali si incentrò soprattutto sul regime delle elezioni locali, potenziando il criterio capacitario o abbassando quello censitario. Bisognerà attendere la prima revisione costituzionale[158] del 1893 per vedere modificati gli articoli 47 e 53 della costituzione. La transazione raggiunta tra le forze politiche produsse un sistema complesso che affiancava al suffragio universale e diretto, il cd. voto plurale, nonché forme di regime timocratico e di *household suffrage*.[159] L'evidente carattere compromissorio di

155 Si vedano L. Luzzatti, *Lo Stato e la Chiesa nel Belgio*, cit.; A. Miroir, *La Belgique et ses clivages*, cit.

156 Nel 1847 i liberali avevano ottenuto la loro prima vittoria elettorale. Il governo guidato da Charles Rogier e dal giovane Hubert Frère-Orban accelerò l'azione riformatrice dopo i fatti del febbraio 1848, ma le linee guida erano state definite nel corso del primo congresso del "partito liberale" svoltosi nel 1846. Cfr. F. Van Kalken, *La Belgique contemporaine (1780–1930)*, cit., 75 ss.; J. Gilissen, *Le régime représentatif belge depuis 1790*, cit., 96 ss.

157 Un quarto del parlamento era composto, prima della riforma, da funzionari. La legge del 26 maggio 1848 vietò il cumulo tra mandato parlamentare e ogni impiego statale retribuito. Sul punto si veda l'analisi di A. G. Manca, *I funzionari-deputati tra Parlamento e amministrazione in una prospettiva comparata*, in *L'istituzione parlamentare*, cit., 391–429.

158 Sulla procedura di revisione prevista dall'articolo 131 e sulle revisioni del 1893 e del 1920–1921 v. A. Mast, *Une constitution du temps de Louis-Philippe*, cit., 990 ss. Per quanto riguarda l'evoluzione del sistema elettorale in Belgio, tra '800 e '900, si veda l'ampia sintesi di P. Harismendy, *Il caso belga*, cit.

159 Nel 1893 fu rivista l'organizzazone del Senato con la previsione di tre categorie di senatori (i membri di diritto, i senatori eletti dai consigli provinciali, i senatori

questa riforma sarà definitivamente superato con la revisione del 1920–1921 che introdusse il suffragio universale senza più correttivi.[160]

La costituzione del 1831 è all'epoca, in Europa continentale, quella che meglio definisce i principi del regime costituzionale rappresentativo, organizzandone i congegni fondamentali. Appare, tuttavia, anacronistico voler retrodatare[161] agli anni Trenta del XIX secolo il pieno dispiegamento del regime parlamentare, con maggioranze politiche solidali, disciplina di partito, responsabilità politica dei ministri, rapporto fiduciario e via dicendo.[162] In realtà, come si è detto, la pratica consuetudinaria[163] non offre ancora una soluzione univoca al problema dell'equilibrio costituzionale e in particolare sul punto decisivo della responsabilità dei ministri e dell'inviolabilità / irresponsabilità politica del sovrano.[164] Del resto basta leggere – e siamo agli inizi del Novecento – le pagine nelle quali Orban tratta del rapporto tra monarchia parlamentare e governo di gabinetto o del carattere della «doppia fiducia»[165] per constatare come fino al

eletti direttamente). Cfr. O. Orban, *Le droit constitutionnel de la Belgique*, t. II, cit., 430 ss. Sul sistema elettorale riformato – che accrebbe il numero degli elettori sino a circa 1.370.000, ovvero il 22% della popolazione – v. soprattutto P. Errera, *Traité de droit public belge*, cit., 135 ss. Vedi anche G. Beltjens, *La constitution belge révisée*, Liège 1894.

160 Il riformato articolo 48 sancì nella costituzione il principio della rappresentanza proporzionale e del voto segreto. L'età per essere elettori fu abbassata a 21 anni. Il voto delle donne fu ammesso per le elezioni provinciali e comunali.

161 Si tratta – come è noto – di una tendenza comune a molte tradizioni storiografiche, ovvero desumere l'esistenza *reale* del governo parlamentare dall'interpretazione del testo costituzionale e cristallizzare *ab origine* un tipo di regime politico che è invece il risultato di evoluzioni storiche spesso contraddittorie, di equilibri precari e variabili, di coloriture e differenze nazionali.

162 Pur con talune riserve, si veda il giudizio in tal senso di J. Gilissen, *Le régime représentatif belge depuis 1790*, cit., 112 ss. Secondo Mirkine-Guetzcvitch la costituzione belga ha creato un tipo di monarchia parlamentare con un potere regio limitato e il ruolo decisivo del parlamento anche rispetto al governo. «Le parlement qui gouverne, c'est la grande conquête de 1830» (*L'histoire constitutionnelle comparée*, in *Annales de l'Institut de droit comparé de l'Université de Paris*, 2, 1936), 95). Nel corso del dibattito costituente prevale senza dubbio l'interpretazione 'parlamentaristica': «La chambre élective ... tient dans sa main la destinée du cabinet; elle impose à la couronne ses exclusions et ses choix; elle élit donc en réalité, quoique indirectement, le ministère tout entière» (Joseph Lebeau, in E. Huyttens, *Discussions du Congrès National de Belgique, 1830–1831*, cit., t. I, 208).

163 «Qui pourrait, par exemple, – osserva Paul Errera – à la seule lecture des constitutions belge et prussienne, sonder l'abîme politique qui sépare les deux royaumes? Les notions mêmes de monarchie constitutionnelle et parlementaire sont toutes coutumières ...» (*Traité de droit public belge*, cit., 5).

164 L. Domenichelli, *Il ruolo della Corona*, cit., 717–720.

165 O. Orban, *Le droit constitutionnel de la Belgique*, t. II, cit., 274 ss.

primo dopoguerra la logica dell'equilibrio dualista[166] venisse ancora realisticamente messa in evidenza. Anche un autore come Paul Errera, certo più orientato ad una lettura storico-parlamentare dello sviluppo costituzionale, mostra i profili di "permanenza" e di specificità.[167]

La progressiva estensione del suffragio contribuì – come in altri sistemi costituzionali – a ridefinire la dialettica tra le esigenze di stabilità e durata delle istituzioni politiche e le inesorabili ragioni del cambiamento e della democratizzazione.[168] Il Belgio continuava però a confidare in quel cauto «principio di aderenza» tra Costituzione e società che ne aveva accompagnato la nascita e la successiva evoluzione.

166 Qui bisogna distinguere tra il piano istituzionale della struttura dualista dell'esecutivo e il piano effettivo delle determinazioni politico-costituzionali. Sul principio di unità dell'esecutivo nel sistema costituzionale belga contemporaneo (dopo il 1949), vedi F. Delpérée, B. Dupret, *Nul ne peut découvrir la Couronne*, cit., 14 ss.

167 P. Errera, *Traité de droit public belge*, cit., 208 ss. e 194–195: «Il résulte de là que des opinions personnelles peuvent être exprimées par le Roi, sans engager la responsabilité des ministres. Ce système, contraire au strict parlementarisme tel qu'il est compris en Angleterre depuis le règne de Victoria, se rapproche non seulement du régime allemand, mais encore de celui des Etats-Unis, surtout sous le président Roosevelt …». Per le differenti interpretazioni vedi C. H. Hojer, *Le régime parlementaire belge de 1918 à 1940*, Uppsala, Stockholm 1946; F. Perin, *La démocratie enrayé. Essai sur le régime parlementaire belge de 1918 à 1958*, Bruxelles 1960.

168 Cfr. J. Gilissen, *Gouvernés et gouvernants en Belgique, depuis 1815*, in *Gouvernés et gouvernants*, Ve partie, *Recueils de la Société Jean Bodin*, Bruxelles 1965, 95 ss.

Constitución, Monarquía, Parlamento: Francia y Bélgica ante los problemas y «modelos» del constitucionalismo europeo (1814–1848)[1]

> «*Le Métaphysicien.* [...] Vous prononcez les noms de Roi, de Roi légitime, de monarchie pure, de monarchie constitutionnelle, de république, de droit à la couronne; voudriez-vous m'expliquer le sens de chacun de ces mots?»
> (Anónimo, *Des sectes politiques. Dialogue entre un Royaliste pur, un Royaliste constitutionnel, un Républicain et un Métaphysicien*, en *Le Censeur, ou examen des actes et des ouvrages qui tendent à détruire ou à consolider la constitution de l'Etat*, Par M. Comte, A Paris, Marchant, 1814, tome premier, n. 2, 47)

1. Premisa

El constitucionalismo del siglo diecinueve nunca se ha cansado de preguntarse sobre el *nombre* de las *cosas*. Operación necesaria y obligada, se dirá, pero al mismo tiempo difícil y para algunos vana. Formalizar los conceptos, las categorías, las palabras; atribuirles un significado, un sentido, una dimensión concreta. «Voudriez-vous m'expliquer le sens de chacun de ces mots?». El personaje metafísico del diálogo imaginario llega a una conclusión: es inútil entablar batallas nominalistas, porque lo que realmente importa es defender la *Charte*. Pero, ¿se puede «defender» la constitución sin tener bien claro lo que es, cuál es la organización de los poderes y de los órganos que prefigura, cuál es la «forma» dentro de la cual los sujetos políticos – en un cuadro de pluralismo incierto – son llamados a jugar su partida? Una buena parte del *problema constitucional* a lo largo del siglo XIX, a escala europea, deriva justamente de la dificultad de hallar un «terreno común» que permita a los protagonistas de la vicisitud constitucional convenir sobre las palabras para atribuirles un significado aceptable, dentro de márgenes más o menos amplios de compromiso.

1 Traducción del italiano a cargo de Ignacio Fernández Sarasola, Profesor Asociado de Derecho Constitucional de la Universidad de Oviedo.

El problema de las palabras es, evidentemente, el problema de las cosas, de la fluida realidad concreta, tan difícil de fijar y definir. La formalización jurídico-constitucional trata de hallar soluciones, pero la tarea es ardua. Defender la *Charte* puede no resultar suficiente, y el contexto de las circunstancias, dentro de las que situaré dos experiencias distintas, la francesa y la belga, está fuertemente condicionado por luchas y resistencias. El carácter decididamente político de las constituciones del XIX es un dato que no debe meterse entre paréntesis,[2] sin olvidar el específico lenguaje que entre los siglos XVIII y XIX busca dar contornos más ciertos y «formales» al vasto fenómeno constitucional.

La «etapa» de la historia constitucional que me propongo estudiar – en sus líneas necesariamente esenciales – comprende las Cartas francesas de 1814 y 1830, así como la constitución belga de 1831. A pesar de algunas apariencias arraigadas, esta proximidad es más que nada extrínseca. Desde mi punto de vista, el binomio debe leerse críticamente, superando aquel nexo cronológico y formal que pretende que la constitución belga es una especie de «heredera» más o menos directa de las doctrinas y prácticas constitucionales francesas de la Restauración, y, en particular, del texto orleanista. El ligamen «familiar», como se puede intuir, es menos fuerte de lo que a menudo se ha sostenido. En todo caso, tal binomio puede utilizarse legítimamente en el momento en que se pasa a afrontar el campo conceptual de la monarquía constitucional y del gobierno representativo en la primera mitad del siglo pasado. En este ámbito, las cartas francesas y la constitución belga – leídas desde la perspectiva articulada y compleja de la historia constitucional comparada – parecen representar los «modelos» continentales que durante algunos decenios del siglo XIX han representado tanto en Europa, inspirando un buen número de otras constituciones y ofreciendo, se podría decir, casi todo el *inventario* de las formas constitucionales que definen la gama de relaciones entre el principio monárquico y el principio representativo.

«Sin embargo, en materia constitucional, – reproduciendo aquí las célebres palabras de Mirkine-Guetzevitch – hay que desconfiar de las fórmulas, de los dogmas, de la terminología ... Hoy, los viejos términos han traído consigo, y han introducido en el vocabulario constitucional moderno, ficciones, malentendidos y un peligroso verbalismo».[3] Esta advertencia nos introduce en el delicado

2 H. Boldt, *Einführung in die Verfassungsgeschichte. Zwei Abhandlungen zu ihrer Methodik und Geschichte*, Düsseldorf 1984, 7 ss.

3 B. Mirkine-Guetzevitch, *Le costituzioni europee*, Milano 1954, 10. «Los estudios de derecho constitucional comparado – prosigue el autor – revelan la relatividad de los textos, de las fórmulas, de los dogmas; los textos no crean las democracias, sino que los verdaderos factores determinantes de un régimen son los hombres y las ideas, los partidos y los principios, las místicas y las afirmaciones, las

problema de los «modelos» en la historia constitucional comparada (aun cuando tal discurso reviste evidentemente una valencia que traspasa el tema específico). Que no se puede hacer de menos a los «modelos» es algo que se halla fuera de toda duda, pero no sin un pellizco de sana desconfianza. Tal instrumento resulta de hecho útil siempre que sea empleado con mesura y sentido crítico; si por el contrario se convierte en vehículo de lugares comunes y de certezas acríticas, es, sin más, nocivo. La historia constitucional comparada busca – más allá de las diferencias – las identidades, y un núcleo común de principios y de valores. Pero no puede olvidarse de los *Sonderwege* del constitucionalismo europeo. Para poder comprender la urdimbre común de una experiencia, se debe tener en cuenta ante todo algunos caminos diversos trazados y recorridos en Europa a lo largo del Ochocientos.[4] Partiendo de esta conciencia será después posible elaborar un método eficaz para superar artificiosas barreras nacionales y comprender el auténtico alcance general del fenómeno constitucional.

La construcción del modelo debe tener en cuenta tanto el momento doctrinal e institucional como aquel – de una catalogación todavía más difícil – propiamente «dinámico» del funcionamiento concreto da cada sistema constitucional. En definitiva, «¿... lo que circula es una carta, un sistema constitucional terminado, y, por tanto, un modelo, o, por el contrario, circulan principios, valores constitucionales, y por consiguiente una cultura del constitucionalismo?».[5]

Las constituciones de las que pretendo tratar ofrecen, en este sentido, una serie significativa de paradojas y de interesantes circunstancias. Ernest Vandenpeereboom, en su obra clásica sobre el gobierno representativo de Bélgica, pone sobre aviso al lector que pueda esperarse una «narración» novelesca como la de Carné.[6] Ésta «... a rencontré, sur sa route, l'échafaud d'un roi; deux autres rois marchant vers l'exil; des républiques renversées par des despotismes militaires; les guerres les plus glorieuses et les desordres les plus honteux; dix constitutions arrachées, avant qu'elles aient pu prendre racine; la tribune, passant de la

costumbres y las tradiciones. Los textos crean sólo algunas condiciones favorables para la evolución, las transformaciones, las realizaciones políticas» (11–12).

4 Véanse al respecto las oportunas observaciones de A. G. Manca, *El constitucionalismo europeo y el caso prusiano: especificidad y concomitancias*, en *Constitucion en España: origenes y destinos*, editado por J. M. Iñurritegui y J. M. Portillo, Madrid 1998, 309–342.

5 M. Sbriccoli, *Sintesi conclusiva*, en *Il modello costituzionale inglese e la sua recezione nell'area mediterranea tra la fine del 700 e la prima metà dell'800*. Atti del seminario internazionale di studi in memoria di Francisco Tomás y Valiente, Messina, 14–16 settembre 1996, edición de A. Romano, Milano 1998, 1074.

6 L. De Carné, *Etudes sur l'histoire du gouvernement représentatif en France*, Paris 1855, 2 voll.

brillante liberté à la plus humiliante contrainte; la presse, ce guide des peuples libres, menée à la lisière!... Mais le régime parlementaire de notre heureuse Belgique présente des faits plus tranquilles et des leçons plus modestes. Avec notre dynastie intelligente et aimée; avec notre Constitution, vierge de toute atteinte; avec nos libertés, que rien ne restreint et que nul ne menace, les faits ne sont, pour ainsi dire, que des souvenirs de famille, – *domestica facta*. M. de Carné a écrit les péripéties des drames qui ont agité une grande nation: je n'ai eu à tracer que le tableau du paisible intérieur d'un peuple libre».[7] El escritor belga expone así las diferencias profundas y bosqueja las respectivas historias constitucionales, remachando *topoi* desde las sólidas raíces y el mito de la «pequeña Inglaterra».[8] La historia constitucional de Francia a partir de la Revolución es la historia de un personaje colectivo, una suerte de Sísifo que cada vez se somete a la terrible fatiga, casi siendo ya consciente del éxito improductivo de su esfuerzo. Al tema de la inestabilidad francesa parece posible poner el contrapunto de la Bélgica *felix* y estable que nace con la constitución del '31. Si la historia constitucional francesa es una continua «novela», rica sobremanera en aventuras y cambios, la de Bélgica aparece, por el contrario, como un modesto oasis de paz y prosperidad, como subraya Emile de Lavelaye. La constitución de 1831 no se convierte en un «trozo de papel» – por decirlo en palabras de Burke y de Maistre. Estos autores pensaban en Francia, naturalmente. Bélgica ha sido más afortunada, ha embocado de pronto la vía de las instituciones más adecuadas,[9] convirtiéndose en un ejemplo de duración y un «modelo» para los países que

7 E. Vandenpeereboom, *Du gouvernement représentatif en Belgique (1831–1848)*, Bruxelles 1856, t. I, XIV–XV.

8 «El pequeño país de Bélgica, con cuatro millones y medio de habitantes, ha intentado desentrañar uno de los problemas políticos más difíciles de los tiempos modernos; el de poner de acuerdo las estables y seguras garantías de la libertad con la monarquía representativa. Los Ingleses la llaman *la pequeña Inglaterra*, y éste es el más bello elogio que pueda ambicionar; si más que a las costumbres, en las que Inglaterra es maestra de los pueblos, se considera la libertad en las leyes, puede considerarse que Bélgica es una pequeña Inglaterra enmendada por muchos abusos e inmune a los mayorazgos y a las reliquias de los privilegios feudales. Su constitución, *estudiada en el aspecto teórico*, es un modelo de franquicias populares y acoge sin ninguna modulación casi todos los principios del derecho público proclamados por los escritores más ilustres». (L. Luzzatti, *Lo Stato e la Chiesa nel Belgio con alcune applicazioni alla questione religiosa in Italia. Saggio storico e critico*, Milano 1867, 1–2).

9 «... l'assemblée constituante de la Belgique, plus fière ou plus éclairée, ne voulut copier personne. Elle produisit une œuvre originale, appropriée au caractère et aux mœurs de la nation ... Cette constitution, après avoir d'abord surpris et inquiété l'Europe, devait quelques années plus tard lui servir d'enseignement et quelquefois même de modèle» (Th. Juste, *Le Congrès National de Belgique 1830–1831*, Bruxelles 1880, 295–296).

se han liberado del despotismo[10] y han conquistado la independencia nacional. «La révolution belge de 1830 a fait une nation, une dynastie et une constitution. Si elle s'était bornée à ce dernier acte, tout en remuant de grandes questions d'organisation intérieure, elle aurait pu ne pas attirer l'attention universelle; mais ébranler le droit public européen, appeler un peuple à l'existence, lier cette existence à celle d'une dynastie nouvelle, c'est prendre place dans l'histoire générale».[11]

Duración frente a cambio: ésta parecería una primera cuestión diferencial. Cuestión estrechamente conectada con la búsqueda incesante de un punto de equilibrio en la forma de gobierno que caracteriza la historia francesa post-revolucionaria. Las razones adoptadas son múltiples y heterogéneas, comenzando por la concepción «filosófica», en vez de histórica, de la libertad, como dirá Ernest Renan. El mito inglés de la libertad radicada en la historia está siempre preparada para sugerir cualquier cosa, según declinaciones que se extienden desde Burke a de Maistre, desde la escuela histórica hasta los liberales de la Restauración. «C'est que la souveraineté du peuple ne fonde pas le gouvernement constitutionnel. L'Etat, ainsi établi à la française, est trop fort, loin de garantir toutes les libertés, il absorbe toutes les libertés; sa forme est la Convention ou le despotisme».[12] El péndulo de la historia política y constitucional no acaba de pararse, corre de un extremo a otro. La predominante visión estatal de las libertades ha influido ciertamente en dicho éxito. El liberalismo ha tenido que arreglar cuentas con una cultura y una práctica de gobierno que no pueden menos que buscar un punto de encuentro entre «les droits et libertés de l'individu moderne avec la légitimité de l'Etat souverain».[13] En Francia, el Estado[14] existe antes que la Constitución y esta precedencia histórica y «filosó-

10 E. De Laveleye, *Quelques considérations sur la constitution belge*, en Th. Juste, *Le Congrès National de Belgique 1830–1831*, cit., a–b. *Cfr.* G. Gilissen, *La constitution belge de 1831, ses sources, son influence*, en *Res publica*, X, 1968, 107–141.

11 E. Huyttens, *Discussions du Congrès National de Belgique, 1830–1831*, Bruxelles 1844, t. I, I.

12 E. Renan, *La monarchie constitutionnelle en France*, en *Revue des Deux Mondes*, 1er novembre 1869, después publicado en *La réforme intellectuelle et morale*, Paris 1872, 3 ed., 240.

13 L. Jaume, *L'individu effacé ou le paradoxe du libéralisme français*, Paris 1997, 16. Para algunas observaciones, *vid. infra Coppet et la percée de l'Etat libéral constitutionnel*, 211 ss.

14 También un escritor como de Cormenin subraya este perfil: «En este país siempre se quiere gobernar mucho, administrar mucho, hacer muchas leyes, muchas cosas. La libertad trata, sobre las primeras, de retener el río entre sus diques; pero éste los rompe, se esconde, corre tan rápido y desciende por tantos riachuelos que rápidamente no le queda nada de su estrépito y de su caudal». (L. M. De Cormenin, *Studi sulla eloquenza parlamentaria e ritratti de' principali oratori della Camera di Francia*, Firenze 1841, 2 voll., vol. I, 137).

fica» acaba por suponer una pesada hipoteca para la misma definición de un orden liberal-constitucional. El «artificialismo» constitucional es una de las cuestiones más recurrentes: hacer y deshacer las constituciones es, en suma, un «vicio» francés. No se trata de inventar, de hacer *tabula rasa*: la constitución es un edificio que se construye poco a poco, partiendo de un núcleo histórico, añadiendo después, si es necesario, una estancia tras otra.[15] No basta, por otra parte, introducir las libertades en la Carta, tener dos Cámaras, una ley electoral, para que la obra sea completa:[16] la constitución debe poder «vivir», convertirse en costumbre, práctica social y política. De otra forma la constitución se arriesga a reducirse al célebre «trozo de papel» que no vale ni tan siquiera la pena garabatear.[17] Tarea ardua, ésta, en una nación que ha hecho de la cultura política del conflicto su elemento característico.[18]

Por otra parte, no puede tampoco olvidarse la peculiar actitud francesa para definir – al tiempo de las constituciones – el *espacio del código civil*. El derecho del código civil posee una indudable vocación constitucional[19] y una fuerte

15 «Or, à l'épreuve, nous n'avons jamais été contents de la nôtre; treize fois en quatre-vingt ans, nous l'avons démolie pour la refaire, et nous avons eu beau la refaire, nous n'avons pas encore trouvé celle qui nous convient. Si d'autres peuples ont été plus heureux, si, à l'étranger, plusieurs habitations politiques sont solides et subsistent indéfiniment, c'est qu'elles ont été construites d'une façon particulière, autour d'un noyau primitif et massif, en s'appuyant sur quelque vieil édifice central plusieurs fois raccommodé, mais toujours conservé, élargi par degrés, approprié par tâtonnements et rallonges aux besoin des habitants. Nulle d'entre elles n'a été bâtie d'un seul coup, sur un patron neuf, et d'après les seuls mesures de la raison». (H. Taine, *Les origines de la France contemporaine*, t. I, *L'ancien régime*, Paris 1880, II).

16 E. Laboulaye, *Histoire des Etats-Unis*, Paris 1877, 6 ed., 3 voll, vol. I, V–VI.

17 «Qu'est-ce qu'une Charte, une Constitution, aux yeux d'une majorité toute souveraine qui, aux jours de trouble, fait et défait les lois? Une feuille de papier morte souvent. Nous avons sur ce point quarante ans de tristes exemples. L'Angleterre a peu de lois écrites, mais des corps puissants en eux-mêmes, des agrégations qui défendent leurs privilèges pied à pied, parce qu'ils sont inhérents au pays» (J. B. H. Capefigue, *Le gouvernement de juillet, les partis et les hommes politiques. 1830 à 1835*, Bruxelles 1836, 2 tomos, t. I, 162).

18 *Cfr.* P. Rosanvallon, *La Monarchie impossible. Les Chartes de 1814 et de 1830*, Paris 1994, 179–180. François Furet ha definido a los Franceses como «fondamentalistes de la politique», lo que deja «très peu d'espace à la réflexion constitutionnelle proprement dite, et à ce minimum d'empirisme inséparable de l'étude d'institutions ajustées au paysage tourmenté offert par l'opinion» (*L'idée de tradition révolutionnaire dans la France du XIXe siècle*, en *Pouvoirs*, 50, 1990, 12).

19 *Cfr.* D. Corradini, *Garantismo e statualismo*, Milano 1971; G. Tarello, *Storia della cultura giuridica moderna. Assolutismo e codificazione del diritto*, Bologna 1976, 22 ss.; B. Clavero, *Codificacion y constitucion: paradigmas de un binomio*, en *Quaderni fiorentini per una storia del pensiero giuridico moderno*, 18, 1989, 79–145; Íd., *Lo spazio dei diritti e la posizione dei giudici tra costituzione e codice*,

pretensión de estabilidad y autonomía. Los principios informadores, las fuentes del derecho, los conceptos de ciudadanía, de libertad, de igualdad, de propiedad, de voluntad – por no recordar los mismos pilares – son, en la perspectiva del estatalismo liberal, una *parte* primaria de la constitución material del Estado. La certeza del derecho y la igualdad formal resultan garantizados por el derecho del Estado y, en particular, a través del código civil, que establece las «reglas del juego».

La tensión constante entre la idea liberal de constitución y la fuerza dominante de la democracia delimita el campo de batalla durante todo el siglo (y aún más allá). En él, la experiencia francesa se percibe como el «modelo» *par excellence*, en negativo o en positivo, según la perspectiva adoptada. Estado y constitución, centralismo y libertades locales, *esprit* jacobino o mitología inglesa, monarquía y república, liberalismo y democracia: parejas conceptuales inspiradas todas ellas en una tensión que hace incontestablemente de la Francia postrevolucionaria un *laboratorio* extraordinario de ideas y de categorías imprescindibles para la formación del universo ideológico contemporáneo.

La historia de las *Chartes* de 1814 y de 1830 reproduce, con todas las diferencias del caso, el problema-dilema ya experimentado después de 1789: hacer compartir la soberanía regia con otros órganos constitucionales conservando la unidad de la dirección y acción del gobierno. Los *monarchiens* habían lanzado la mirada al otro lado del Canal de la Mancha, sin poder comprender el *esprit* de las instituciones inglesas. En 1814 se asiste en Francia a una *reinvención* de un modelo de ambigua co-soberanía que tenía unas raíces muy frágiles o inexistentes,[20] y la constitución de Luis XVIII refleja bien la dificultad de conciliar el lenguaje constitucional del antiguo régimen con la razón moderna de la constitución-acto. El Prevost-Paradol de *La France nouvelle* – en los

en *Materiali per una storia della cultura giuridica*, 1, 1989, 95–129; Íd., *Origen constitucional de la codificacion civil en España (Entre Francia y Norteamérica)*, en *Derecho privado y revolucion burguesa*, dirigido por C. Petit, Madrid 1990, 53–85. *Vid.* también P. Ungari, *L'età del codice civile. Lotta per la codificazione e scuole di giurisprudenza nel Risorgimento*, Napoli 1967, 7 ss.; D. Grimm, *Die verfassungsrechtlichen Grundlagen der Privatrechtsgesetzgebung*, en *Handbuch der Quellen und Literatur der neueren europäischen Privatrechtsgeschichte*, vol. III, Parte I, dirigido por H. Coing, München 1982, 17 ss.; P. Caroni, *Liberale Verfassung und bürgerliches Gesetzbuch im 19. Jahrhundert*, Bern 1988; G. Cazzetta, *Responsabilità aquiliana e frammentazione del diritto comune civilistico (1865–1914)*, Milano 1991; M. Fioravanti, *Appunti di storia delle costituzioni moderne. Le libertà fondamentali*, Torino 1995, 117 ss.; L. Lacché, *L'espropriazione per pubblica utilità. Amministratori e proprietari nella Francia dell'Ottocento*, Milano 1995.

20 *Cfr.* F. Furet, *Introduzione* a *L'eredità della Rivoluzione francese*, dirigido por F. Furet, Bari 1989, 6.

umbrales de la Tercera República – ya ha comprendido que el problema más grave de la historia constitucional de Francia (y que reproduce en clave «técnica» las tensiones que hemos referido brevemente) se refiere a la relación entre el poder ejecutivo y el poder legislativo. Walter Bagehot, reflexionando sobre los mecanismos constitucionales británicos, observa que «Le pouvoir exécutif ne doit donc pas, en France, être séparé du pouvoir législatif ni mis en face de lui ...».[21] De esta forma se retornaba al nudo fundamental de la historia constitucional de más allá de los Alpes: ¿cómo articular la relación entre los poderes «iguales» del Estado e impedir de esta forma la absoluta preponderancia de uno sobre otro?[22] «Les constitutions, les lois, la pratique du gouvernement ont été dirigées tour à tour, comme des machines de guerre, vers l'un ou l'autre dessin ...»,[23] escribirá Guizot, quien desde la Restauración se había convertido en uno de los autores que había captado con mayor lucidez la sustancia del problema constitucional.

De Prevost-Paradol *au rebours*: hasta Constant, Madame de Staël, Sismondi, Necker ... El cerco parecía poderse cerrar, finalmente. Y el pensamiento, desde entonces, no podía dejar de volver a la edad de la Restauración, la verdadera «cuna» de esta larga búsqueda. Para mantenernos en el campo de la metáfora mitológica: si el Sísifo francés se ha esforzado no poco – saliéndose del mito – para encontrar una solución para sus problemas, el bifronte Jano ofrece una imagen sugestiva de las Cartas constitucionales y, más en general, del constitucionalismo europeo del XIX: las *Chartes* poseen al menos dos caras que reflejan la ambigüedad del diseño constitucional de la Restauración: de un lado, la autoridad tradicional, el rostro del principio monárquico, la *lettre* del texto; de otro, las libertades hijas de la Revolución, el rostro del principio representativo, el *esprit* del texto. Se trata – como veremos – de principios que no son necesariamente antitéticos, pero tampoco abocados a encontrarse *naturaliter* sobre el terreno del compromiso.

Las Cartas de la «monarquía imposible» – por una paradoja recurrente en la historia constitucional-, incapaces de «terminar» la Revolución y de fundar un sistema institucional estable capaz de garantizar las libertades modernas en el cuadro de la monarquía constitucional, elaboradas en lo general con precipi-

21 W. Bagehot, *La constitution anglaise*, Paris 1869, *Introduction*, I–II.

22 Sobre esta cuestión insiste Marcel Morabito, en *Le chef de l'Etat en France*, Paris 1996; *Il comando negato. Rivoluzione francese e potere esecutivo*, Roma, Manduria 1997; (con D. Bourmaud) *Histoire constitutionnelle et politique de la France (1789–1958)*, Paris 1998, 5 ed. Unas consideraciones más breves en *infra Coppet et la percée de l'Etat libéral constitutionnel*, 216–219.

23 F. Guizot, *De la démocratie en France (janvier 1849)*, Paris 1849, 106.

tación,[24] estaban destinadas a ofrecer a Europa una importante *silhouette* de extraer principios y mecanismos singulares, contando en realidad a menudo más como discurso ideológico[25] que por el mérito de las soluciones que proponen.

Por otra parte, la comparación entre las Cartas francesas y la constitución belga revela, como ya se ha señalado, la falacia de las «apariencias».[26] Los presupuestos de las dos Revoluciones de 1830 son muy distintos: los acontecimientos de septiembre trajeron como consecuencia la regeneración de Bélgica y la conquista de su independencia. La constitución de 1831 es un documento solemne de una revolución nacional y de la creación de un nuevo Estado.[27] La elección de una asamblea constituyente, la elaboración de un texto constitucional, resultado de un compromiso de alto perfil entre las dos grandes fuerzas constituyentes, la católica y la liberal, texto que precede y teoriza el nacimiento de una «monarquía democrática», son sólo algunos de sus elementos distintivos.

2. La Restauración y la idea de constitución

«Notre administration date de l'Empire; notre politique date de la Restauration».[28] Esta contundente afirmación de Joseph Barthélemy aprehende icásticamente el carácter «fundador» de la Restauración. Verdad, ésta, que no se les escapó a los protagonistas de aquella renovación intelectual; basta recordar a Guizot, o al Chateaubriand de las *Mémoires d'outre-tombe*. El movimiento de las ideas acelera, hace reflorecer todas las formas de expresión del pensamiento.[29] En el cambio de ritmo político, el constitucionalismo liberal ocupa el centro de la escena y busca dar fuerza institucional a la difícil alianza entre las libertades modernas y la autoridad tradicional.

24 «A parcourir ainsi d'un coup d'œil toute notre histoire constitutionnelle contemporaine, il se confirme donc bien que les Constitutions ne sont pas des œuvres systématiques conçues par la raison arbitraire de leurs auteurs, mais des œuvres vivantes produites par l'histoire» (M. Deslandres, *Histoire constitutionnelle de la France de 1789 à 1870*, Paris 1933, t. II, 734).

25 *Cfr.* P. Colombo, *Costituzione come ideologia. Le rivoluzioni italiane del 1820–21 e la costituzione di Cadice*, comentario a J.-M. Portillo Valdés, *La Nazione cattolica. Cadice 1812: una costituzione per la Spagna*, Roma, Manduria 1998, 129–157.

26 G. Antonetti, *Les monarchies constitutionnelles*, en *Les monarchies*, dirigido por Y.-M. Bercé, Paris 1997, 429, considera la constitución belga una copia ampliada de la orleanista.

27 E. De Laveleye, *Quelques considérations sur la constitution belge*, cit., III ss.

28 J. Barthélemy, *L'introduction du régime parlementaire en France sous Louis XVIII et Charles X*, Paris 1904, 1.

29 Véase, en particular, A. Omodeo, *Studi sull'età della Restaurazione. La cultura francese nell'età della Restaurazione* …, Torino 1974, 2 ed.

En general, la atención se centra sólo sobre la *Charte* de junio de 1814, pero es preciso no olvidar que el constitucionalismo de la Restauración no se agota con ella. De un lado hallamos textos más efímeros, pero no por ello prescindibles, como la Constitución senatoria del 6 de abril de 1814, el Acta Adicional del 22 de abril de 1815 y los proyectos de junio-julio de 1815, elaborados por la Cámara de los diputados;[30] de otro, es preciso subrayar que más allá del omnipresente modelo inglés, los redactores de la constitución francesa podían ya tomar en consideración también las constituciones, de distinta inspiración liberal, de Suecia (1809), España (1812), Sicilia (1812) y Noruega (1814).[31] Por consiguiente, se puede hablar de un *corpus* constitucional relativamente coherente y homogéneo bajo el perfil de la forma monárquica y de algunos mecanismos abstractamente pactados (sufragio censitario, bicameralismo de tipo aristocrático, sanción regia de la ley, derecho de disolución de la Cámara electiva, responsabilidad de los ministros de naturaleza fundamentalmente «penal», etc). Existe un núcleo duro de ideas y principios compartidos por liberales y conservadores moderados, hasta el punto que Guizot – con un léxico típicamente doctrinario – afirmaba que la Carta «était écrite d'avance dans l'expérience et la pensée du pays; elle sortit naturellement de l'esprit de Louis XVIII revenant d'Angleterre, comme des délibérations du Sénat secouant le joug de l'Empire; elle fut l'œuvre de la nécessité et de la raison du temps».[32] Sin embargo, si el análisis de estos aspectos hace pensar justamente en una cultura constitucional compartida, no puede tampoco dejar de observarse la diversidad de «inspiraciones» de las constituciones bajo el aspecto, muy relevante para el funcionamiento concreto de aquellos mecanismos, de la legitimidad «constituyente», de orden histórico-providencial o, por el contrario, de naturaleza voluntarista-popular.

En 1814 sólo una perspectiva «ecléctica» parece ser capaz de inspirar un texto constitucional. Se mantiene, sin embargo, con una solución dudosa el problema de las *premisas* – de orden histórico-político – que puedan dar unidad y coherencia a la constitución. Si la constitución-acto, esto es, fruto de un diseño constituyente y racional, aparece como la única constitución posible en Francia, la apelación a la historia tiende, sin embargo, a reforzarse. Justamente de la imposibilidad de conciliar la historia con la Revolución derivaba el desesperado

30 En la línea ya trazada por Stéphane Rials, sostiene el justo relieve de estos textos A. Laquièze, *Les origines du régime parlementaire en France (1814–1818)*, thèse pour le doctorat en droit, Université de Paris II, 1995, 2 tomos.

31 *Cfr.* G. Antonetti, *Les monarchies constitutionnelles*, cit., 389 ss.

32 F. Guizot, *Mémoires pour servir à l'histoire de mon temps*, Paris 1858–1867, vol. 1, 36.

proyecto de salvar la monarquía del antiguo régimen implantándola en el espacio hostil de la soberanía popular. Ahora se busca, más bien, «corregir» la rigidez de la constitución artificial, fundada sobre la preeminencia de la dirección política, releyéndola a la luz de una «racionalización» historicista. El Sismondi de las *Recherches*[33] no concibe la constitución fuera de la historia. La constitución – como la libertad – es un producto de la historia, o bien del desarrollo social en un determinado momento histórico; no es ni un resultado arbitrario, ni un producto casual. El mismo Constant, aun siendo en sustancia fiel a una idea racional de constitución, tratará de hallar un punto de equilibrio entre la razón y la historia. Ya en los escritos directoriales, la doctrina de la perfectibilidad eleva a una cuestión general el problema de la vinculación entre ideas e instituciones, con el tiempo *a fare da bilanciere*. En los *Principes* de 1806, Constant pretende conjugar la reflexión sobre la historia como fundamento de la teoría política. «Le temps, dit Bacon, est le grand réformateur. Ne refusez pas son assistance. Laissez-le marcher devant vous, pour qu'il aplanisse la route. Si ce que vous instituez n'a pas été préparé par lui, vous commanderez vainement ...».[34] Al principio de la Restauración, Constant tenderá a equilibrar el elemento racional («Les constitutions se font rarement par la volonté des hommes») con el de la historia («Le temps les fait»). «Elaborar» la constitución es tal vez indispensable, pero una vez constituidos los poderes debe dejarse el espacio justo a las «deux puissances réformatrices»,[35] el tiempo y la experiencia. Tal discurso no puede reconducirse simplemente a la concepción de la constitución histórica. El discurso se traslada desde la mera contraposición constitución racional / constitución histórica, hasta una perspectiva mucho más compleja sin la que es difícil imaginar el proceso de racionalización de la monarquía constitucional. El concepto de «máquina constitucional» vive en la historia, pero opera en el cuadro de un diseño racional (*pouvoir neutre*, responsabilidad ministerial, segunda Cámara, gobierno representativo, etc.), con el modelo inglés destinado a hacer de principal, aunque controvertido, paradigma.

En el campo liberal se distinguen claramente ecos «conservadores» y perspectivas eclécticas en la busca de supremo compromiso entre el antiguo y en nuevo

33 J. C. L. Sismondi, *Recherches sur les constitutions des peuples libres*, edición e introducción de M. Minerbi, Genève 1965. La concepción historicista sismondiana de la constitución material (social) y del legislador conservador resulta todavía más acentuada en los posteriores *Etudes sur les constitutions des peuples libres*, Bruxelles 1836.

34 B. Constant, *Principes de politique*, ed. Hofmann, Genève 1980, 412.

35 B. Constant, *Réflexions sur les constitutions, la distribution des pouvoirs et les garanties, dans une monarchie constitutionnelle*, Paris 1814.

régimen:[36] de la *prescription* de Burke[37] a la concepción anti-constructivista de de Maistre o de otros tantos[38] – como se decía –, hasta el más vasto movimiento de la escuela histórica. Ineludiblemente permanece la ardua cuestión del babel del lenguaje: ¿es posible dar vida a una especie de léxico común a fin de concebir una idea suficientemente unitaria de constitución? La *Charte* de 1814 y los restantes textos constitucionales coetáneos se resienten todos – en diversa medida y partiendo cada uno de una *premisa* específica – de tal dificultad. El discurso de la historia constituye una forma de reacción al constitucionalismo revolucionario, pero no puede prescindir totalmente de él; por otra parte, los excesos reconocibles en la abstracción racional de la época revolucionaria han hecho reflexionar con más favor «... à l'aide du temps, le plus doux et le plus puissant des auxiliaires».[39] A pesar de la voluntad y los proyectos de los protagonistas del acontecimiento político-constitucional de la Restauración, el terreno de enfrentamiento (y de difícil conciliación) es precisamente el de la *idea de constitución*.[40] Sin una concepción suficientemente compartida, parece difícil, sino imposible, poder fundar un sistema constitucional capaz de asentar raíces.

3. *La bella Angélica*, o la constitución inglesa

Aparentemente, el enlace entre el lenguaje empírico y la racionalización de la forma constitucional es – o más bien *debe ser* – el del imperante «modelo inglés».

36 Sobre este extremo *vid.* sobretodo L. Diez Del Corral, *El liberalismo doctrinario*, Madrid 1945; y las precisiones de J. Varela Suanzes, *El liberalismo francés después de Napoleón (de la anglofobia a la anglofilia)*, en *Revista de Estudios Políticos*, 76, 1992, 29–43.

37 *Vid.* por todos P. Lucas, *On Edmund's Burke doctrine of prescription or an appeal from the new to the old whigs*, en *The Historical Journal*, XI, 1968, 33–63.

38 *Cfr.* P. Manent, *Il liberalismo francese e inglese*, en *L'eredità della Rivoluzione francese*, cit., 53; M. Boffa, *La Rivoluzione e la Controrivoluzione*, *ibídem*, 82 ss.; S. Chignola, *Società e costituzione. Teologia e politica nel sistema di Bonald*, Milano 1993, 141 ss.; B. Fontana, *Benjamin Constant e il pensiero post-rivoluzionario*, Milano 1996, 64–65; J.-P. Clément, *Introduction: de Chateaubriand à Jules Ferry*, en *Liberté, libéraux et constitutions*, J.-P. Clément, L. Jaume, M. Verpeaux (edit.), Paris, Aix-en-Provence 1997, 13.

39 «Tant qu'on n'a pas essayé d'une constitution par la pratique, les formes sont une lettre morte: la pratique seule en démontre l'effet et en détermine le sens. Nous n'avons que trop abattu l'édifice sous prétexte de le reconstruire: profitons désormais des lumières qui ne s'acquièrent que par les faits, afin de pourvoir graduellement à tous les besoins partiels, avec mesure, avec lenteur, à l'aide du temps, le plus doux et le plus puissant des auxiliaires» (B. Constant, *Principes de politique applicables à tous les gouvernements représentatifs et particulièrement à la constitution actuelle de la France* (1815), en *Œuvres*, texte présenté et annoté par Alfred Roulin, Paris 1957, 1126).

40 Sobre esta expresión, *vid.* P. Bastid, *L'idée de la constitution*, Paris 1985.

Sin embargo, pronto aparecerá la dificultad de conciliar un modelo de fuerte implantación histórica, que institucionaliza la dinámica de las fuerzas sociales en la organización del gobierno mixto de soberanía «fraccionada» (las tres formas «puras» del Estado), con la concepción post-revolucionaria con predominio racionalista, que tiene en su código genético la idea prevalente de la soberanía «absoluta» (el espacio nuevo de la soberanía popular en lugar de la soberanía monárquico-tradicional). En definitiva, moderar el constitucionalismo mecanicista y necesariamente «artificial», apelando a otro asentado sobre una lógica histórica natural de los contrapoderes[41] resulta un arduo cometido. En el complicado juego de espejos, formado por observaciones e influencias, que se desarrolla a partir del Setecientos, la mirada al otro lado del Canal de la Mancha es con frecuencia fuente de malentendidos y de interpretaciones abusivas. Pero la constitución británica – más allá de su real virtualidad práctica en el debate francés – se convierte en el paradigma de la constitución histórica, un modelo peculiar – podría decirse – de «perfectibilité constitutionnelle» caracterizado por el principio de la moderación: evitar, por ello, cualquier innovación violenta y por tanto peligrosa, así como cualquier actitud obstinada de clausura. «Chaque parti, depuis vingt-cinq ans, a repoussé et regretté tour à tour la constitution anglaise, suivant qu'il était vainqueur ou vainçu [...] On dirait que la constitution anglaise, ou plutôt la raison, en France, est comme la belle Angélique dans la comédie du *Joueur*: il l'invoque dans sa détresse, et la néglige quand il est heureux».[42]

Vitrolles, en sus Memorias, describe la difusión de la anglomanía en la Restauración como si se tratase de una epidemia, de una fiebre contagiosa.[43] Mirar más allá del Canal de la Mancha nunca había estado tan *à la mode*[44] en Francia como en la época del llamado «Quindicencio inglés»[45] (1814–1830).

41 Sobre este punto véase la eficaz síntesis de M. Barberis, *Constant e Montesquieu: liberalismo e costituzionalismo*, en *Sette studi sul liberalismo rivoluzionario. Con una introduzione metodologica e un'appendice bibliografica*, Torino 1989, 219 ss.

42 G. De Staël, *Considérations sur les principaux événements de la Révolution française*, en *Œuvres posthumes*, Paris 1861, réimpression Genève 1967, t. III, 104.

43 E.-F.-A. De Vitrolles, *Mémoires de Vitrolles*, E. Forgues y P. Farel (edit.), Paris 1950–1951, vol. 2, 53–54. *Cfr.* J. Barthélemy, *L'introduction du régime parlementaire*, cit., 15.

44 P. Bastid, *Les institutions politiques de la Monarchie parlementaire française (1814–1848)*, Paris 1954, 33.

45 Véase, en particular, Th. Zeldin, *English Ideals in French Politics during the Nineteenth Century*, en *The Historical Journal*, 2, 1959, 40–58; P. Reboul, *Le mythe anglais dans la littérature française sous la Restauration*, Lille 1962; J. R. Jennings, *Conceptions of England and its Constitution in Nineteenth-Century French Political Thought*, en *The Historical Journal*, 1, 1986, 65–85; P. Rosanvallon, *Le moment Guizot*, Paris 1985; A. Laquièze, *Les origines du régime parlementaire en France*, cit., t. 1, 147 ss.; L. Jaume, *L'individu effacé*, cit., 283 ss.

La Constitución británica parece poder ofrecer – según una imagen estereotipada y necesariamente vaga[46] – un cuadro tranquilizador del que sacar un buen número de «enseñanzas»: la quintaesencia de la constitución histórica, pero no privada de algunas sabias intervenciones racionalizadoras, la prosperidad de la nación inglesa y la estabilidad de sus instituciones, la forma de gobierno capaz de conciliar orden y libertad, y así sucesivamente. El examen de la constitución británica permite también reconocer el valor más importante, a lo largo de una línea de desarrollo que en Francia va desde Necker a Constant:[47] la eficaz combinación-vínculo del poder legislativo y el ejecutivo, en la lógica de los contrapoderes. «Ce problème de la solution duquel dépendaient et la stabilité des gouvernements et le repos des peuples, a été résolu par les Anglais».[48]

Si el modelo inglés es una especie de arsenal del cual extraer argumentos y motivos de reflexión pera introducirlos en el debate y en la lucha política en Francia (de Constant a Vitrolles, de Chateaubriand a Guizot ...), son preponderantes las visiones «imaginarias» que a menudo hacen ver sólo los aspectos externos de las instituciones inglesas. El anglófobo Fiévée es impiedoso: «Nous croyons pouvoir imiter la constitution anglaise; la connaissons-nous? Nous ne connaissons de cette constitution que ce qui se voit; comme on ne juge, au premier aspect, un bâtiment que par la partie qui s'élève au-dessus des fondations».[49] Pero no debemos creer que el escepticismo sea una prerrogativa exclusiva de los escritores realistas. Royer-Collard pudo utilizar el mismo argumento, por razones también tácticas, en un célebre discurso de 1816, para mostrar la gran diversidad de *premisas* y de condiciones entre el régimen de la

46 P. Rosanvallon, *La monarchie impossible*, cit., 62.

47 Para constatarlo, *cfr. infra*, § 8. Véase *sobretodo* H. Grange, *Les idées de Necker*, Paris 1974, 307 ss. y L. Jaume, *L'esprit de Coppet et l'organisation du pouvoir exécutif*, en *La Constitution de l'an III ou l'ordre républicain*, Colloque de l'Association Française des constitutionnalistes, Dijon, Paris 1998.

48 Anónimo, *D'une des principales causes de l'inactivité du gouvernement*, en *Le Censeur*, 4, 1814: «Un des problèmes les plus difficiles que la politique présentât à résoudre était de constituer le pouvoir législatif et le pouvoir exécutif, de manière que l'un formât toujours un obstacle aux usurpations de l'autre, sans que de leur action et de leur résistance il pût jamais résulter un choc assez fort pour mettre l'un des deux en péril» (133).

49 J. Fiévée, *Correspondance politique et administrative, commencée au mois de mai 1814*, Paris 1815–1819, parte primera, carta I, 3. Sobre la anglofobia, entre otros autores citados, *cfr.* G. Bonno, *La constitution britannique devant l'opinion française de Montesquieu à Bonaparte*, Paris 1932; F. Acomb, *Anglophobia in France. Essay of constitutionalism and nationalism*, Durham 1950; A.-J. Tudesq, *Les grands notables en France (1840–1849)*, Paris 1964, 2 vols., vol. 2, 745 ss.; F. Burdeau, M. Morabito, *Les expériences étrangères et la première constitution française*, en *Pouvoirs*, 50, 1989, 97–112.

Charte y la mítica constitución inglesa.[50] Era preciso, en definitiva, convertir a los franceses en ingleses, ejercicio verdaderamente imposible además de, obviamente, no deseado. La «harmonie laborieuse»[51] que hacía posible el gobierno constitucional resultaba una quimera.

En realidad, el verdadero problema de Francia había sido – como dirá lúcidamente un atento estudioso de las instituciones inglesas como Prosper Duvergier de Hauranne[52] – considerar a la Restauración como una especie de Minotauro – para retomar aquí la metáfora mitológica – formado de una «cabeza inglesa» y de un «cuerpo francés», es decir, del gobierno representativo y de la monarquía administrativa.[53] Duvergier descubre en la preexistencia de un robusto y radicado *système administratif* (el Estado *antes* de la Constitución) la huella más visible del peculiar camino francés a la construcción del Estado moderno.[54] La diferencia de implantación obligaba entonces a seguir un acercamiento diferenciado, yendo más allá de la estéril llamada al «mito» inglés. ¿Cómo se podía pretender – escribía por esos mismos años Louis de Cormenin – que un país fanático de la igualdad pudiese recibir instituciones nacidas a partir del interés de la aristocracia? «A esto se llama verdaderamente injertar ficciones sobre ficciones …».[55]

50 «[…] Si vous voulez substituer le gouvernement anglais à notre Charte française, donnez-nous donc la constitution physique et morale de l'Angleterre; faites donc que l'histoire d'Angleterre soit la nôtre; mettez dans notre balance politique une aristocratie puissante et honorée […]» (P. De Barante, *La vie politique de M. Royer-Collard. Ses discours et ses écrits*, Paris 1863, 2 voll., vol. 1, 217).

51 La expresión es de F. Guizot, *Pourquoi la Revolution d'Angleterre a-t-elle réussi? Discours sur l'histoire de la Révolution d'Angleterre*, Paris 1850, 114. Sobre Guizot y el modelo inglés, *vid.* A. Kahan, *Guizot et le modèle anglais*, en *François Guizot et la culture politique de son temps*, Colloque de la Fondation Guizot-Val Richer, M. Valensise (edit.), Paris 1991, 219–231.

52 En el opúscolo de 1827 *De la nouvelle révolution ministérielle en Angleterre*, Paris, donde ya ha dado luz a la cuestión de la reforma parlamentaria.

53 «Les Anglais – escribe Charles His – ont établi une république, et cependant ils ont une monarchie. Si nous adoptons leur mécanisme constitutionnel, nous n'obtiendrons que la république, et notre monarchie sera détruite» (*Du danger pour la France, d'adopter le mécanisme constitutionnel de l'Angleterre*, Paris 1814, 4).

54 «Mais c'était oublier que chaque forme de gouvernement a ses principes, ses tendances, ses conditions propres, et que le rapprochement de deux systèmes si divers devait donner lieu à bien des difficultés, à bien des conflits» (P. Duvergier De Hauranne, *De l'état actuel des partis en France et de la nécessité d'une transaction*, en *De la politique extérieure et intérieure de la France*, Paris 1841, 214–215).

55 L. M. De Cormenin, *Studi sulla eloquenza parlamentaria*, cit., vol. I, 141. De Cormenin atribuye a Constant – que en realidad tiene una posición mucho más compleja y articulada – tal ilusión.

4. El constitucionalismo de 1814–1815

La época de la Restauración halla – como dirá Victor Hugo en *Les Misérables* – un país cansado, en el que «todos piden un lecho», un asilo. Los Franceses desean paz y reposo después de veinticinco años de vicisitudes extraordinarias. Los Franceses estan cansados pero la libertad política descubierta – a pesar de la tutela ejercida por las potencias aliadas y que durará hasta 1818 – devuelve vigor a la verdad de la palabra después de los años del silencio y de la difidencia. Años que, sin embargo, no habían transcurrido en vano, permitiendo percibir, por vez primera, mediante la Revolución, un *discurso público de la libertad*, con las distintas «familias» de liberales y de conservadores moderados destinados a desarrollar un papel de primer orden. Finalmente «... un peu de tolérance et de respect pour leur droits réciproques ...».[56] La cultura y la política pasaban a formar una unidad,[57] y para un Constant novelista había un Chateaubriand que se deleitaba con política constitucional. La mirada dirigida a la forma de gobierno representativa[58] devolvía al centro de todo la (siempre vigilada) libertad de imprenta, piedra angular de todo sistema constitucional. Entonces no sorprende que Francia se convirtiese en el escenario de una «guerra» de *pamphlets*. «Il n'est pas un écrivain, quelque chétif qu'il soit, qui ne veuille dire son mot sur le gouvernement qui convient à la France».[59]

El engarce entre los sucesos histórico-constitucionales y la reflexión doctrinal resulta tan fuerte que se corre el riesgo de confundir los dos órdenes distintos del discurso constitucional. En el transcurso de poco más de un año cinco textos constitucionales revelan – como ya se ha observado[60] – la existencia de un debate vivo pero también toda la dificultad de encontrar un punto de equilibrio entre el *fin* que la constitución debe perseguir (tutelar las libertades de los individuos a través de una organización eficaz de los poderes del Estado) y la *legitimidad-forma* de la constitución. Si respecto del primer elemento es posible apreciar un cierto grado de encuentro entre *técnicas* y mecanismos de funcionamiento del régimen constitucional (poniendo el acento, por ahora, más sobre las notas comunes que sobre las diferencias), respecto del segundo elemento los distintos textos y

56 F. Guizot, *Mélanges politiques et historiques*, *Préface*, Paris 1881, XIII.

57 A. Omodeo, *Studi sull'età della Restaurazione*, cit.

58 «Mais avec la liberté de la presse, le gouvernement représentatif est le seul qui puisse aujourd'hui concilier la liberté la plus entière avec la soumission aux lois et prévenir les révolutions violentes [...]». (Anónimo, *Du système représentatif*, en *Le Censeur*, 3, 1815, 77).

59 Anónimo, *Des sectes politiques. Dialogue entre un Royaliste pur, un Royaliste constitutionnel, un Républicain et un Métaphysicien*, en *Le Censeur*, 2, 1814, I, 43.

60 Véase *supra*, § 2.

proyectos se dividen a partir del punto de la legitimidad fundadora y, por tanto, sobre la naturaleza de la soberanía para «constitucionalizar».[61]

La Carta senatorial del 6 de abril de 1814 resulta elaborada en menos de una semana, inaugurando un *estilo* de redacción extremadamente apresurado que el constitucionalismo francés no abandonará hasta 1830. La operación senatorial se desarrolla – como lo haría, por otra lado, gran parte del movimiento constitucional de la Restauración – bajo el signo de la emergencia. Las tropas extranjeras, desde el 31 de marzo, dominaban París y el vacío de poder, tras la caída de Napoleón, amenaza con agravar la situación. Resulta preciso intervenir rápidamente. El príncipe de Benevento, Talleyrand, da el impulso, después de que el Senado ha recibido la investidura «constituyente» por las potencias aliadas.[62] El Senado es el protagonista del acontecimiento pero también, para ser exactos, su factor de debilidad. En realidad, dicho órgano invoca – yendo más allá de la dicción constitucional – el art. 54 del senado-consulto orgánico del 16 de termidor del año X (4 de agosto de 1802) que le permite regular «todo aquello que no esté previsto en la Constitución, y que sea necesario para su funcionamiento». El asidero es evidentemente frágil, pero el estado de necesidad y urgencia consiente no ser demasiado sutiles.[63]

Las líneas que establece el texto del 6 de abril se hallan ya presentes en la declaración del Senado del 1 de abril de 1814 que revela el intento «conservador». Se trata ante todo de establecer garantías de supervivencia y de poder salvaguardar los «derechos adquiridos» y las libertades fundamentales (de culto y de imprenta). El texto viene por tanto prefigurado como un *salvoconducto* dirigido a transportar a la «nouvelle France» dentro del nuevo orden constitucional. Todavía más significativa es el Acta de caída de Napoleón (3 de abril),[64] con el cual el Senado denuncia las violaciones constitucionales cometidas por el emperador, considerando «que dans une monarchie constitutionnelle, le monarche n'existe qu'en vertu de la Constitution ou du pacte social».[65] La intervención – en su redacción – de personajes como Lambrecht, Destutt de Tracy o Lebrun, y más en general de senadores que habían formado parte de las asambleas revolucionarias, hacía inclinarse la balanza de la parte del constitucionalismo post-revolucionario. La constitución senatorial, en fin, trata de lograr un compromiso entre el constitucionalismo liberal y el principio de soberanía nacional

61 Véase *infra*, § 7.
62 Declaración de las potencias aliadas, 31 de marzo de 1814. El texto se ha tomado de P. Rosanvallon, *La monarchie impossible*, cit., 187–188.
63 *Cfr.* A. Laquièze, *Les origines du régime parlementaire en France*, cit., t. 1, 218 ss.
64 El texto está publicado en P. Rosanvallon, *La monarchie impossible*, cit., 191–193.
65 J. De Soto, *La Constitution sénatoriale du 6 avril 1814*, en *Revue internationale d'histoire politique et constitutionnelle*, oct.–déc., 1953, 268 ss.

asociado a la forma monárquica. La yuxtaposición del art. 1, con sabor *ancien régime* («Le Gouvernement français est monarchique et héréditaire de mâle, par ordre de primogeniture») y de los artículos 2 y 29[66] revela la desviación entre la voluntad de reprender la dirección de marcha del constitucionalismo revolucionario y la legitimidad de la monarquía tradicional. Esta «alianza» se había intentado en 1789,[67] y había diso mal concebida en 1791: en 1814 parecía al fin posible realizar un *pacto* que devolviese a la soberanía de los Franceses, el llamamiento al trono del nuevo monarca.[68] Los senadores deseaban «*instaurer* – et non *restaurer* – la monarchie traditionnelle, extraordinaire paradoxe dans les termes. Ils se refusaient à la reconnaître ou à la *déclarer*: ils voulaient la *constituer*».[69]

Esta elección de fondo es la verdadera razón del fracaso de la constitución y también el motivo que explica mejor la dificultad de poner de acuerdo las dos historias de Francia después de 1789.[70] La constitución senatorial se sumerge de pronto entre una avalancha de *pamphlets* que critican los aspectos de legitimidad y las disposiciones más marcadamente dirigidas a perpetuar los privilegios del Senado.[71] El descrédito que alcanza a los senadores es tal que oculta de inmediato los aspectos más duraderos y positivos de la carta senatorial que, no al caso, serán recibidos en parte en la *Charte* posterior.

66 «Le peuple français appelle librement au trône de France Louis-Stanislas-Xavier de France, frère du dernier Roi ...» (art. 2); «La présente Constitution sera soumise à l'acceptation du peuple français, dans la forme qui sera réglée. Louis-Stanislas-Xavier sera proclamé *Roi des Français*, aussitôt qu'il aura juré et signé par un acte portant: *J'accepte la Constitution; je jure de l'observer et de la faire observer*. Ce serment sera réitéré dans la solennité où il recevra le serment de fidelité des Français» (art. 29).

67 P. Duvergier De Hauranne, *Histoire du gouvernement parlementaire en France, 1814–1848*, Paris 1857, vol. 2, 99, observa que «La Constitution du Sénat consacrait et réalisait tous les principes, toutes les idées qui avaient été défendus par les membres les plus sages et les plus éclairés de l'Assemblée constituante, par Mounier, par Lally-Tollendal, par Mirabeau».

68 Sobre la constitución senatorial véase J. De Soto, *La constitution sénatoriale*, cit.; S. Rials, *Constitution sénatoriale*, en *Dictionnaire Napoléon*, J. Tulard (edit.), Paris 1989, 504 ss.; P. Rosanvallon, *La monarchie impossible*, cit., 15 ss.; A. Laquièze, *Les origines du régime parlementaire en France*, cit., t. 1, 218 ss.; M. Morabito, D. Bourmaud, *Histoire constitutionnelle et politique*, cit., 165–169.

69 S. Rials, *Une grande étape du constitutionnalisme européen. La question constitutionnelle en 1814–1815: dispersion des légitimités et convergence des techniques*, en *Révolution et contre-révolution au XIXème siècle*, Paris 1987, 130.

70 *Cfr.*, por ejemplo, H. Gregoire, *De la Constitution française de l'an 1814*, Paris 1814.

71 *Vid.* la reconstrucción de la polémica en P. Rosanvallon, *La monarchie impossible*, cit., 21–28.

En realidad, durante algunos días el documento senatorial parece poder superar la prueba de la lectura *royaliste*: el conde de Artois, hermano de *Monseigneur* que todavía permanecía en Inglaterra, declara, el 14 de abril, que lo acepta, haciendo pensar en que existe un probable sentimiento análogo de su «augusto hermano». ¿Pero qué es lo que acepta el conde de Artois, elevado por el Senado al rango de Lugarteniente general del Reino? En realidad aquella parte del proyecto que diseña un gobierno representativo de monarquía templada, formado por dos Cámaras que consienten libremente en los impuestos y que aseguran la garantía de las libertades y derechos adquiridos.[72] Entonces se habría dicho, con el lenguaje voluntariamente vago propio del «compromiso», que se aceptaba un «modelo inglés» de inspiración liberal o, por el contrario, un reenvío genérico a la monarquía limitada. Comenzaba, así, aquella estación de la ambigüedad – y de la confusión terminológica – que nunca más habría de abandonar a la *Charte*. Como se ha observado con certeza, el conde comprende que ante todo necesita regresar a Francia para poder después representar un papel más activo y eficaz.[73]

La palabra oficial de Luis XVIII no se hace esperar: la declaración del 2 de mayo[74] (la llamada declaración de Saint-Ouen) redactada por tres consejeros, Blacas, La Maisonfort y, sobre todo, Vitrolles, cambia el brazo de la balanza del Senado al monarca. Si las «bases» del proyecto senatorial eran suficientes para dar vida a una constitución liberal, muchos artículos, a causa también de la extrema rapidez con la que se habían redactado, debían modificarse. Luis XVIII, «par la grâce de Dieu, Roi de France et de Navarre», afirmaba de esta manera que la constitución era un asunto suyo y situaba el discurso dentro del esquema de la concesión. La posibilidad de un *pacto jurado* que hiciese de Luis (y de sus sucesores) el *rey de los Franceses* queda así definitivamente eclipsado. Antes aún que un problema sobre la forma que debía darse a la monarquía (que también tenía su relevancia evidente), había una cuestión preliminar de legitimidad que había de resolverse. Los pasos sucesivos son consiguientes y de nuevo con precipitación se llega a redactar el nuevo texto constitucional presentado a las Cámaras reunidas el 4 de junio.[75]

Los aspectos ceremoniales y procedimentales que acompañan al texto del Preámbulo muestran en qué medida en este caso la forma es también la

72 Para el texto de la declaración *vid.* P. Rosanvallon, *La monarchie impossible*, cit., 198–199.

73 *Ibídem*, 31–32.

74 El texto se encuentra en P. Rosanvallon, *La monarchie impossible*, cit., 209–210.

75 Sobre el proceso de redacción y sus diversos proyectos, *vid.* en particular, P. Simon, *L'élaboration de la Charte constitutionnelle de 1814 (1er avril – 4 juin 1814)*, Paris 1906; P. Rosanvallon, *La monarchie impossible*, cit., 29 ss.; A. Laquièze, *Les origines du régime parlementaire en France*, cit., t. 1.

sustancia. De hecho sería un error ver en la Carta borbónica una especie de *tributo de la apariencia,*[76] o bien un texto compuesto de la suma de dos «partes», una formal, de aparato, y otra, por el contrario – mucho más importante y duradera – destinada a los espíritus liberales de la nación, estipulando aquel «tratado de paz» que se halla ciertamente ínsito en la misma idea de Restauración, pero que no debe, sin embargo, convertirse en argumento de interpretación de la *Charte.* El *arcaismo*[77] del texto debe por tanto subrayarse como dato esencial y no meramente accesorio. Puede parecer paradójico que un texto, destinado a convertirse en uno de los modelos más influyentes del constitucionalismo europeo del siglo XIX, se inscriba más en la tradición racionalizada del antiguo régimen que en el surco del constitucionalismo del, también lejano, carácter revolucionario. En realidad, la Carta de 1814 conserva de este último lo estrictamente indispensable, comenzar con algunas disposiciones del *Droit public des Français* para finalizar con los *Droits particuliers garantis par l'Etat.* Toda la parte que se refiere a la organización de los poderes posee la seña de la monarquía limitada y de la centralidad constitucional de la *royauté.*[78]

En el Preámbulo, la filosofía inspiradora de la Carta está expuesta eficazmente por su autor, el conde Beugnot.[79] Después de la referencia inicial a la divina Providencia, se halla la soberanía regia como única fuente de la legitimidad política: a pesar de que toda la autoridad resida en la persona del monarca, éste decide, por el bien de Francia, conceder una constitución «libre et monarchique» que conserve los derechos y las prerrogativas de la Corona. Sólo la autoridad suprema «peut seule donner aux institutions qu'elle établit, la force, la permanence et la majesté dont elle est elle-même revêtue ...». Reanudando la «chaîne des temps», Luis XVIII ha buscado los principios de la Carta constitucional en la

76 Esta es la tesis de P. Bastid, *Les institutions politiques*, cit., 139 ss.

77 Este aspecto, ya evidenciado por J. Bonnefon, *Le régime parlementaire sous la Restauration*, Paris 1905 y por Ch. Rohmer, *Le droit d'ordonnance et l'esprit de la Charte de 1814*, Paris 1931, ha sido aclarado ulteriormente por S. Rials, *Essai sur le concept de monarchie limitée (autour de la Charte de 1814)*, en *Révolution et contre-révolution*, cit. y retomado, con abundancia de argumentos por A. Laquièze, *Les origines du régime parlementaire en France*, cit., t. 1, 131 ss. No puede tampoco olvidarse que ya Luis-Felipe de Orléans, en sus recuerdos dedicados a 1814, había puesto el acento sobre el carácter arcaico, *ancien régime*, de la Carta. Sobre el manuscrito *vid.* H. Robert, *Louis-Philippe constitutionnaliste*, en *Commentaire*, 63, 1993, 577–580.

78 Sobre la naturaleza jurídica y sobre las formas de la monarquía constitucional, *vid. infra*, § 8.

79 Sobre la redacción del Preámbulo véase P. Rosanvallon, *La monarchie impossible*, cit., 46 ss., que utiliza algunos importantes documentos contenidos en los *Papiers Beugnot* (Archives Nationales).

tradición francesa y hace libremente de ellos «concession et octroi» a sus propios súbditos. La lógica jurídica que inspira el texto tiene raíces antiguas. Junto a términos tales como *ordonnance de réformation* o *édit*, la expresión *Charte* se consideró finalmente – al lado de la adjetivación *constitutionnelle*[80] – la más idónea para expresar el carácter de libre concesión del soberano, y de acto de garantía de libertades (individuales, y no ya de clase). Luis XVIII, posteriormente, databa la concesión de la Carta en el año decimonoveno de su reino, es decir, en el momento en el cual había sucedido, en 1796, a Luis XVII. El Preámbulo, sin embargo, excluye cualquier posible reenvío a la soberanía nacional entendida como entidad jurídica distinta de la autoridad suprema que se identifica con la persona del rey. El Preámbulo representa una verdadera y auténtica teoría de la monarquía del antiguo régimen en el contexto de una modernización de la forma de ejercicio del poder que bosqueja los aspectos elementales del gobierno representativo, pero que a duras penas permite reconocer una verdadera dinámica pluralista de los órganos. La centralidad y la unidad del poder regio representan el dato característico del texto de 1814. El monarca se reserva un papel preponderante: ejerce de forma exclusiva el poder ejecutivo e hipoteca fuertemente el poder legislativo, del que controla todo el proceso de formación legal (iniciativa, sanción, promulgación).

La paradoja de la Carta de 1814 es sin duda transparente, aun cuando en el preámbulo se pretende matizar los tonos: si de un lado se garantiza el catálogo de los derechos y de las libertades de carácter revolucionario, comenzando por el principio de igualdad, por otro, hallamos como premisa un acto de concesión, esto es, la negación de aquellos derechos en términos filosóficos. La distancia entre la *práctica de la Revolución* y la *teoría de la Restauración* es el nudo más difícil de desatar.[81]

Como pondrá de manifiesto Barante en una memoria (julio de 1815) sobre las instituciones políticas y constitucionales de Francia,[82] los gobiernos de la primera Restauración, privados de unidad y cohesión, no habían sabido crear un clima favorable al retorno de los Borbones. El descontento se difundía rápidamente antes del desembarco de Napoleón, y habría debido afrontarse mediante «... la formation d'un ministère uni et solidaire, une réorganisation de la maison

80 Un acertadísimo análisis sobre la forma arcaica de la *Charte* corresponde a A. Laquièze, *Les origines du régime parlementaire en France*, cit., t. 1, 181 ss.

81 Nadie mejor que Charles de Rémusat ha visto en profundidad la "mortal contradicción" de la Carta y de la Restauración: *vid.* sobretodo *Politique libérale*, Paris 1860, 207 ss.

82 El texto de esta memoria, solicitada a de Barante por las potencias aliadas, está en los *Souvenirs du baron de Barante*, Paris 1890–1901, vol. 2, 169–176, hoy publicado también por P. Rosanvallon, *La monarchie impossible*, cit., 268–273.

militaire du roi, plus conforme aux idées et aux mœurs nouvelles, enfin quelques modifications essentielles à faire à la Charte».[83]

El efímero retorno de Napoleón pone a un lado la *Charte*, pero no la idea de constitución. También en esta ocasión es necesario «actuar rápido». Después del inicial reclamo intenso a la tradición revolucionaria y a la soberanía nacional, el emperador hace suya la fórmula de la monarquía constitucional[84] y confía la redacción de un proyecto a una comisión especial formada en gran parte por notables del Imperio. En el temor de no poder llegar rápidamente a un resultado concreto, Napoleón ofrece el encargo, el 14 de abril, a Benjamín Constant, sin duda el escritor político francés más grande de la primera parte del siglo XIX. No es éste el lugar de analizar las razones que llevaron a aquella compleja figura de héroe romántico que es Benjamín Constant, a pasar en pocos días del ataque violento contra el Atila francés, a una colaboración activa. Hay que señalar el dato de que la contribución no es secundaria, aunque tampoco cabe infravalorar ni los trabajos de la Comisión, ni la *aportación* del emperador.[85]

Así como la *Charte* buscaba en la «chaîne des temps» la continuidad histórica de la monarquía en Francia, el texto napoleónico acudía expresamente, desde su título – *Acte additionnel aux constitutions de l'Empire* – a la tradición constitucional del Imperio. El contraste entre Constant y Napoleón sobre un aspecto que tocaba de cerca a la frágil legitimidad de la restauración imperial, pone de manifiesto la dificultad, también en este caso, de injertar técnicas del constitucionalismo en el cuerpo de un régimen *ab origine* autoritario. Conservar las constituciones imperiales (art. 1), salvo las modificaciones establecidas en el Acta adicional, significaba dar vida a una especie de confuso *hipertexto constitucional*, caracterizado por una legitimidad heterogénea y ambigua, con reclamos cesarísticos al pueblo francés, de herencia revolucionaria y de continuidad dinástica.[86]

En verdad el mito de Napoleón se halla comprometido. «Pululan por todas partes opúsculos en los que se le alecciona, se le recuerdan sus errores pasados, el desconocimiento de los derechos de la naciones y los pueblos ... Lo tutean, y le

83 *Ibídem*, 271.

84 Napoleón inaugura la sesión parlamentaria el 7 de junio de 1815 diciendo «Je viens commencer la monarchie constitutionnelle» (*Archives parlementaires*, 2 serie, vol. XIV, 403).

85 Sobre este punto véase la equilibrada reconstrucción de A. Laquièze, *Les origines du régime parlementaire en France*, cit., t. 1, 305 ss. *Cfr.*, además, L. Radiguet, *L'acte additionnel aux constitutions de l'Empire du 22 avril 1815*, Caen 1911; S. Rials, *Acte additionnel*, en *Dictionnaire Napoléon*, cit., 32 ss.; D. De Bellescize, *L'acte additionnel aux Constitutions de l'Empire (22 avril 1815): une constitution mal nommée pour un régime sans nom*, en *Revue du droit public*, 4, 1993, 1043–1077.

86 *Cfr.* S. Rials, *La question constitutionnelle en 1814–1815*, cit., 139–143. *Vid.* también F. Bluche, *Le bonapartisme*, Paris 1980, 26 ss. y 119 ss.

enseñan los primeros elementos de la nueva ciencia ...».[87] De esta «nueva ciencia» existe una amplia huella en el Acta adicional, pero innovando muy poco respecto de la Carta senatorial o de la *Charte*, gesto que Napoleón no estaba dispuesto a «conceder» más de lo que lo hubiera hecho Luis XVIII. Lo que se ha definido como una «competición virtuosa»[88] entre el emperador y el Borbón, un juego en alza[89] para obtener la patente del liberalismo, no llega nunca más allá del límite trazado por la Carta o el Acta adicional.[90]

Durante, y después, de los Cien Días, en la «competición» entre Luis XVIII y Napoleón, asume un papel importante la Cámara de representantes. Hasta junio de 1815 la Cámara manifiesta la intención de «mejorar» el Acta adicional y elegir una comisión en la que descuellaba el diputado liberal Manuel. El objetivo es preparar un texto constitucional[91] que contemple una legitimidad distinta de la que fundamenta la Carta: un texto discutido por la representación nacional y aceptado por el pueblo. Luis XVIII, de vuelta a París, ignora dicho proyecto y con él la idea de constitución «pactada». Justamente en torno a esta *querelle* originaria se desentrañará la *estrategia interpretativa* diferenciada de la *Charte* hasta 1830.

5. Interpretar la *Charte*

En 1815, Luis XVIII había realizado, con la Proclama de Cambrai, del 28 de junio, una interpretación «auténtica» del espíritu liberal de la Carta. Este texto, junto al previo juramento de fidelidad hecho por el rey ante los diputados (16 de marzo), representa uno de los documentos más citados por las fuerzas liberales a lo largo de toda la Restauración para reforzar la interpretación «pacticia» de la Carta. Por otra parte, no deja de ser interesante la *Adresse* que la Cámara de diputados había enviado al monarca el 6 de junio de 1814 para atribuir unilateralmente a la *Charte* un sello «nacional». «Aussi avons-nous, Sire, l'intime confiance que l'assentiment des Français donnera à cette Charte un caractère tout à fait national».

No hay duda de que la mencionada ambigüedad de la Carta es en realidad obra de dos interpretaciones prevalentes del documento. La Restauración se

87 A. Omodeo, *Studi sull'età della Restaurazione*, cit., 52.

88 P. Rosanvallon, *La monarchie impossible*, cit., 68.

89 Se refiere en particular a la declaración de Luis XVIII del 16 de marzo de 1815 (publicada por P. Rosanvallon, *La monarchie impossible*, cit., pp. 265–266) y a la de Napoleón del 7 de abril.

90 Para un análisis de los mecanismos de funcionamiento de los órganos constitucionales en el Acta adicional, véase A. Laquièze, *Les origines du régime parlementaire en France*, cit., t. 1, 333 ss.

91 S. Rials, *Constitution de la Chambre des représentants (projet)*, en *Dictionnaire Napoléon*, cit., 503 ss.

caracteriza por una continua polémica entre dos formaciones, una que afirma el carácter unilateral, concesorio (*octroi*) de la *Charte*, otra que insiste en su intrínseca naturaleza «contractual», pacticia. Está claro que las dos tesis son difícilmente conciliables porque confrontan elementos excluyentes: la cuestión de la legitimidad, el tipo de soberanía constitutiva, la prefiguración del régimen político. La radicalización progresiva del desencuentro, que culmina con los acontecimientos de 1830, ha terminado – como a menudo sucede – por simplificar sobremanera los términos de una contienda ideológica que amenaza con anular también los matices que son distinguibles en las dos «formaciones». Ciertamente, la polémica se lleva al terreno que resulta más favorable: los *royalistes* – y no necesariamente los *ultras* – se atrincheran detrás del bastión de la *lettre* y de la forma concesoria; los liberales insisten sobre el presunto carácter liberal del *esprit*, concepto en realidad un poco vago, sino inconsistente, en el plano jurídico. Los unos poseen entonces un fuerte argumento *jurídico*, los otros creen poder hacer palanca sobre un argumento *político* que sin embargo necesitan cultivar y difundir. El uno es un argumento *estático*, el otro *dinámico*.

El equívoco de fondo nace de la doble naturaleza de la Carta: acto jurídico concesorio y forma establecedora de un cierto grado de colaboración entre el principio monárquico y el principio representativo encarnado en la Cámara de los diputados. La ambigüedad de la operación residía en la inevitable e insuperable confusión entre el elemento jurídico – relativamente fuerte bajo el perfil de la legitimidad – y el elemento político, más fluido y dinámico. El aspecto jurídico-formal (la tradicional prerrogativa regia, fuente de la constitución) fue contaminado y progresivamente agredido por la idea de que el acto constitucional era la sanción de un «compromiso», esto es, de un pacto entre el soberano y los súbditos. Sobre este frente se entretejen una pluralidad de perfiles heterogéneos, el histórico, el sociológico, el político, capaces de desvirtuar la fuerza presunta del aspecto jurídico-formal. Además, el esquema pacticio podía gozar de dos teorías distintas de referencia: la propia del «constitucionalismo medieval», que reconocía como legítimos modos y formas de obligación del soberano ante los señores feudales y las clases, y la del «constitucionalismo moderno» que, en su declinación británica – la que se halla entonces más en boga – podía leerse como forma racionalizada de equilibrio entre los poderes políticos «compartidos» por el monarca y los cuerpos representativos.[92]

«La France passera donc éternellement du despotisme à l'anarchie, et de l'anarchie au despotisme, sans qu'il lui soit possible de se fixer à aucun état. … On ne peut se dissimuler que les Français sont partagés en deux classes

92 Para una reconstrucción del debate, *véase* P. Pasquino, *La teoria costituzionale della "Monarchia di Luglio"*, en *Materiali per una storia della cultura giuridica*, 2, 1988, 382 ss.

essentiellement opposées. Ceux qui composent la première, tendent continuellement à renverser tout ce qui s'est fait depuis vingt-cinq ans; ceux qui composent la seconde, s'opposent à ce renversement, parce qu'ils craignent de voir consommer leur ruine ou rétablir les anciens abus».[93] La Francia dividida de la Restauración quiere hallar en la Carta el punto de equilibrio, el «compromiso» que permita salir de la espiral de la anarquía o del despotismo. Es Chateaubriand uno de los primeros en hablar de la *Charte* como un «traité de paix signé entre les deux partis qui ont divisé les Français, traité où chacun abandonne quelque chose de ses prétentions pour concourir à la gloire de la patrie».[94] Considerar la Carta como obra de transacción[95] contribuye a difundir la idea de que representa la sanción de un acuerdo alcanzado entre los dos «partidos» que han dividido Francia. El problema estriba en que mientras los *royalistes* tienden a ver el «compromiso» desde la óptica de la contingencia histórica, los liberales yuxtaponen el dato ulterior del carácter «contractual» de la Carta. En el primer caso, la referencia no posee contenidos jurídico-constitucionales, es decir, no implica que el «traité de paix» se refleje en la naturaleza concesoria de la *Charte*, mientras en el segundo caso el objetivo reside en que prospere una especie de «constitución imaginaria» que sobrepase la *lettre* de la Carta y reenvíe, en última instancia, a la *práctica del sistema político*, esto es, a las relaciones concretas de fuerza y al circuito de la *opinion*.

La interpretación que Guizot ofrecerá en sus Memorias es ejemplificativa de la actitud liberal. La Carta «se présenta comme une pure concession royale, au lieu de se proclamer ce qu'elle était réellement, un traité de paix après une longue guerre, une série d'articles nouveaux ajoutés, d'un commun accord, au pacte d'ancienne union entre la nation et le roi».[96] La monarquía constitucional volvía a confirmar la antigua alianza, el constitucionalismo moderno se reunía con el medieval. La metáfora de la *apariencia* contribuía a reducir el espacio de la originaria *real* coherencia de la *Charte*. Los dos «partidos» usaban el mismo

93 Ch. Comte, *Adresse à la Chambre des députés, sur les deux ordonnances de M. le Directeur-général de la police, du 7 juin 1814, relatives à l'observation des fêtes et des dimanches*, en *Le Censeur*, 1, 1814, I, 19.

94 F.-R. De Chateaubriand, *Réflexions politiques sur quelques écrits du jour et sur les intérêts de tous les Français*, Paris 1814, 70.

95 Esta tesis la afirma como "real" J. Barthélemy, *L'introduction du régime parlementaire en France*, cit., 12: «Les interprétations les plus opposées de la Charte étaient possibles parce qu'elle était avant tout une œuvre de transaction. Le roi pouvait regretter certaines prérogatives existantes dans l'ancienne monarchie; les intérêts nouveaux pouvaient regretter certaines garanties que leur reconnaissaient les précédentes Constitutions. La Charte consacrait des sacrifices réciproques à la réconciliation commune».

96 F. Guizot, *Mémoires pour servir à l'histoire de mon temps*, cit., vol. 1, 34.

lenguaje para decir cosas distintas. El éxito de la lucha estaba, sin embargo, condicionado por la distinta posición de las fuerzas en el campo. Mientras los *ultras* perseguían una *táctica*, los liberales, aun en medio de incertidumbres y dificultades de diverso género, poseían una *estrategia*, incluso si entre las «ficciones» y juegos de las partes, como evidenciará la actuación de la *Chambre introuvable*,[97] que hará decir a Guizot: «C'est dans le traité de paix qu'ils vont chercher des armes pour recommencer la guerre».[98] El tratado de paz es, en realidad, una tregua que se verá violada en repetidas ocasiones. El conde Beugnot, que tanta importancia ha tenido a la hora de poner las bases de la filosofía inspiradora de la *Charte*, expresa la fragilidad del «compromiso»: «La Charte ne sera jamais pour nous un évangile politique où l'on s'efforcera d'un côté, de tuer l'esprit par la lettre et de l'autre, de la sauver de la lettre par les inductions tirées de l'esprit. Elle a été donnée de bonne foi, elle doit être entendue de même ...».[99]

La imagen del bifronte Jano acompaña por tanto a la Restauración y a la naturaleza de la Carta. Sin embargo, esta connotación más que ser el contenido de la *lettre* del documento – que, sin duda, por laconismo y por incompleto, daba cabida a numerosas dudas interpretativas – es el éxito del conflicto *político* entorno a la *Charte*. El problema fundamental, como se ha dicho, se refiere a la superposición de imágenes entre sus contradictorios. La «cabeza inglesa» sobre «cuerpo francés» – como dirá al inicio de los años Cuarenta Duvergier de Hauranne – daba vida a un Minotauro del que huían comportamientos y actitudes.

El desarrollo del régimen político en Francia no es ni continua ni necesariamente progresivo.[100] Sin duda, la disputa sobre la interpretación de la Carta es el *fil rouge* que acompaña al período 1814–1830. Cada uno tiene *su* Carta: los *ultras*, en el curso de los años Veinte, sienten el peligro de un gradual desliz hacia un régimen de «influencia» de la Cámara de los diputados sobre la dirección política del «gobierno del rey» y, por tanto, se afanan en «restaurar» el significado «auténtico» de la *Charte*; los liberales, moderados y de «izquierda», por el contrario, ponen el acento sobre el carácter «contractual» y consideran la constitución desde el punto de vista «material».

Sin embargo no debe considerarse que los dos esquemas sean perfectamente claros y coherentes. El problema de la modificabilidad (en todo o en parte) o

97 *Cfr. infra*, § 9.

98 F. Guizot, *Du gouvernement représentatif et de l'état actuel de la France*, Paris 1816, 8.

99 J.-C. Beugnot, *Mémoires du comte Beugnot, ancien ministre (1783–1815)*, publiés par le comte Albert Beugnot, Paris 1889, 3 ed., 653.

100 Véase *infra*, § 9.

inmodificabilidad de la Carta, del cómo y a través de qué procedimientos hacerlo, revela una notable confusión. Si prevalece la tesis de la revisión por vía legislativa,[101] permanece sin embargo la cuestión del poder de ordenanza previsto en el artículo 14[102] de la *Charte*. Poco debatida durante el proceso de redacción, adquirió un relieve notable al final del reino de Carlos X, cuando la «radicalización» de la lucha política entre liberales y *ultras* hizo del artículo 14 el emblema de las respectivas posiciones, tocando el problema de si el poder constituyente era originario o derivado.

El debate sobre el artículo 14 adquiere un significado particular en el momento en el que las posibilidades de diálogo entre el monarca y la Cámara de los diputados – en la forma del procedimiento legislativo – se reducen drásticamente. Las elecciones de 1827 (17–24 de noviembre) confirman la distancia entre la mayoría parlamentaria y el gobierno Villèle, que dimitirá pronto. La sucesiva prueba de fuerza, con el nacimiento del ministerio *ultra* del príncipe de Polignac, y la posterior disolución de la Cámara (16 de mayo de 1830), reproduce, agravándolo, el mismo problema hasta la crisis final derivada de las ordenanzas del 25 de julio. La «apelación al pueblo» por parte de Carlos X podría hacer pensar en la fisiología del régimen parlamentario. Sin embargo, no pueden anticiparse los tiempos, confundiendo técnicas constitucionales afirmadas convencionalmente y reconducibles a la forma, abstractamente comprendida, del régimen parlamentario,[103] con la existencia concreta de tal régimen. La *Adresse* de 221 diputados al rey (18 de marzo de 1830) interpreta la Carta como un acto que consagra «comme un droit, l'intervention du pays dans la délibération des intérêts publics». La lógica es la del gobierno representativo en

101 En el preámbulo de la ordenanza del 13 de julio de 1815 – tras el retorno de Luis XVIII, exiliado a Gand durante los Cien Días – con la que se modificaba el régimen electoral, se lee: «... mais voulant cependant que, dans aucun cas, aucune modification à la Charte ne puisse devenir définitive que d'après les formes constitutionnelles, les dispositions de la présente ordonnance seront le premier objet des délibérations des Chambres. Le pouvoir législatif dans son ensemble statuera sur la loi des élections, sur les changements à faire à la Charte dans cette partie, changements dont nous ne prenons ici l'initiative que dans les points les plus indispensables et les plus urgents, en nous imposant même l'obligation de nous rapprocher, autant que possible, de la Charte et des formes précédemment en usage» (cit. da A. Laquièze, *Les origines du régime parlementaire en France*, cit., t. 1, 193, a la que nos remitimos para la correcta reconstrucción de la cuestión relativa al poder constituyente). Sobre el tema, *cfr.* además M. Roux, *Le pouvoir constituant sous la Restauration*, Paris 1908; J. Barthélemy, *La distinction des lois constitutionnelles et des lois ordinaires sous la Monarchie de Juillet*, en *Revue de droit public*, 26, 1909, 5–47.

102 «Le roi ... fait les règlements et ordonnances nécessaires pour l'exécution des lois et la sûreté de l'Etat».

103 Este importante aspecto se desarrollará más ampliamente en § 9.

el cuadro de una monarquía moderada por el «concours permanent des vues politiques de votre gouvernement avec les vœux de votre peuple ...».[104] Tal concurso tiene como presupuesto un sabio equilibrio entre la *opinion du pays* y el ministerio. Carlos X, al contrario, se convence de que el artículo 14 es el *lit de justice* para superar la oposición de la mayoría parlamentaria. El monarca cree poder disponer del «derecho a la última palabra» como si debiese hacer frente a un estado de emergencia que no es otro, en realidad, que la reivindicación de la regla fundamental del gobierno representativo. Promulgando las ordenanzas, Carlos X rehusa a aceptar tal lógica porque usa un instrumento *legal* (el artículo 14) para obtener un resultado contrario a la letra y al espíritu de la *Charte*.[105] Por ese motivo, en el *Rapport du Roi* del 25 de julio de 1830 Polignac declara el venir a menos de las «conditions ordinaires du gouvernement représentatif». El cuadro sombrío que traza – todo él centrado sobre el uso destructivo de la imprenta – niega en sus raíces los caracteres esenciales de tal forma de gobierno.[106]

104 El texto de la *Adresse* puede verse en P. Rosanvallon, *La monarchie impossible*, cit., 281–282.

105 No resulta imaginable que mediante ordenanzas se pueda modificar partes fundamentales de la *Charte*. «Quelque que soit notre respect pour la liberté des opinions, nous ne pouvons nous défendre de penser que ceux qui, par une fausse interprétation de l'art. 14 de la Charte, soutiennent qu'une simple ordonnance royale rendue sur l'allégation de la sûreté de l'Etat, peut déroger à la Charte et aux lois, se rendent coupables du délit prévu par l'art. 4 de la loi du 17 mai 1819, qui punit les *attaques formelles contre l'autorité constitutionnelle du Roi et des Chambres*» (A. Mahul, *Tableau de la Constitution politique de la monarchie française selon la Charte, ou Résumé du droit public des Français, accompagné du texte des lois fondamentales et des documents authentiques*, Paris 1830, 239). Sobre el aspecto del control jurisdiccional y de la "inconstitucionalidad" de las ordenanzas regias, *vid.* J.-L. Mestre, *Les juridictions judiciaires et l'inconstitutionnalité des ordonnances royales de la Restauration au Second Empire*, en *Revue française de droit constitutionnel*, 15, 1993, 451–461; *Íd.*, *Données historiques*, en *La Cour de Cassation et la Constitution de la République*, Actes du Colloque des 9 et 10 décembre 1994, Aix-en-Provence 1995, 35–67.

106 «... Nul gouvernement sur la terre ne resterait debout, s'il n'avait le droit de pourvoir à sa sûreté. Ce pouvoir est préexistant aux lois, parce qu'il est dans la nature des choses. Ce sont là, Sire, des maximes qui ont pour elles et la sanction du temps et l'aveu de tous les publicistes de l'Europe. Mais ces maximes ont une autre sanction plus positive encore, celle de la Charte elle-même. L'article 14 a investi Votre Majesté d'un pouvoir suffisant, non sans doute pour changer nos institutions, mais pour les consolider et les rendre plus immuables. D'impérieuses nécessités ne permettent plus de différer l'exercice de ce pouvoir suprême. Le moment est venu de recourir à des mesures qui rentrent dans l'esprit de la Charte, mais qui sont en dehors de l'ordre légal, dont toutes les ressources ont été inutilement épuisées» (en P. Rosanvallon, *La monarchie impossible*, cit., 290). Para la definición del cuadro conceptual resultan importantes algunas *brochures* del jurista *ultra* Charles Cottu, publicadas a partir de 1828, entre ellas *Des moyens*

La Revolución de 1830 muestra cómo el *régime représentatif* había conquistado en el curso de la Restauración fuerza y consenso crecientes. En realidad es una confrontación de *cultura política*: Carlos X y sus *ultras* no han tenido éxito en sostener – en la lógica del compromiso – la *cultura* del gobierno representativo que se convierte en otra cosa si está privado de la *opinión* y del uso legítimo de la imprenta y la publicidad.[107] El principio monárquico ha permanecido *más allá* de la Carta cuando, en cambio, Francia hace tiempo que daba signos de impaciencia y de voluntad de cambio. Carlos X no ha sabido abordar el núcleo del problema, derrotado por la más eficaz máquina propagandista de los liberales.[108]

Los artículos del joven Thiers aparecidos en *Le National*[109] desde su primera publicación en enero de 1830, contienen afirmaciones de indudable eficacia: la monarquía definida como «parlamentaria» es aquella en la que la mayoría debe poder prevalecer contra el ministerio vinculado políticamente por un todavía incierto y mal definido principio de responsabilidad. Reivindicaciones de naturaleza parlamentaria se difunden por los diarios de la oposición y por la tribuna.[110]

El argumento que – como una avalancha – adquiere un peso aplastante al día siguiente de las ordenanzas de Carlos X, es que éstas son inconstitucionales por

de mettre la Charte en harmonie avec la royauté, Paris 1828; *Du seul moyen de sortir de la crise actuelle*, Paris 1829; *Des devoirs du roi envers la royauté*, Paris 1830.

107 Observa justamente Pierre Rosanvallon que «Alors que le régime parlementaire consiste en un jeu subtil de contre-pouvoirs, d'influences réciproques, faisant appel à une chimie complexe de l'interaction des différents pouvoirs publics, les ultras ne pensaient qu'en termes de physique élémentaire» (*La monarchie impossible*, cit., 99). Charles Hello observa que «La conscience de son être constitutionnel manquait à Charles X» (*Du régime constitutionnel dans ses rapports avec l'état actuel de la science sociale et politique*, Paris 1848, 3 ed., t. II, 180).

108 Resulta de cierto interés la conversación entre Carlos X y el duque de Orléans que tuvo lugar el 14 de junio de 1830 – en las dos transcripciones distintas, la de Luis-Felipe y la de Vatout, bibliotecario y confidente del rey – por cuanto revela la distancia entre *orden legal* y *orden político*. *Cfr.* G. Antonetti, *Les monarchies constitutionnelles*, cit., 423–425. *Cfr.* también H. Robert, *Charles X au travers des souvenirs du duc de Chartres*, en *Revue de la société d'histoire de la Restauration*, 1, 1987, 78–80.

109 *Cfr.* D. L. Rader, *The Journalists and the July Revolution in France. The Role of the Political Press in the overthrow of the Bourbon Restauration, 1827–1830*, La Haye 1973.

110 Resulta interesante la toma de posición del general Sébastiani, consejero del duque de Orléans. Aunque la Corona posee el derecho de escoger libremente a los ministros, tiene algunos límites. «Les choix de la couronne doivent nécessairement tomber sur des hommes qui inspirent assez de confiance pour rallier autour de l'Administration l'appui des Chambres» (cit. por G. Antonetti, *Les monarchies constitutionnelles*, cit., 421).

violar el «pacto que unía al pueblo francés con su rey» (Bérard). «Le régime légal est donc interrompu: celui de la force est commencé».[111] La interpretación pacticia de la Carta que había sido motivo de constante polémica durante la Restauración, y todavía más a partir de 1828,[112] conquistaba entonces el campo y asentaba las premisas para fundar un régimen político que precisamente partiendo de tal idea debía cobrar vida. Lo imaginario se convertía en realidad, la ideología se transformaba en derecho. Tal interpretación de los hechos de 1830 hacía nacer aquella *Vulgata* que no habría de abandonar más la historia de la Monarquía de Julio: la Revolución había sido una respuesta legítima a una «insurrection du pouvoir», o sea, el acto que restablecía el orden legal violado.[113] La necesidad – como dirán más o menos todos los protagonistas, de Guizot a Thiers – ha hecho surgir la monarquía de Julio para escapar de la anarquía y de los dos abismos: «La France, en se donnant ce gouvernement, n'a cédé ni à un entraînement révolutionnaire, ni à un engouement pour un homme ...».[114] Thiers y Laffitte, entre el 29 y el 30 de julio, ya han «comprometido» al duque de Orléans, que no podrá echarse atrás. El evento y la necesidad han hecho a Luis-Felipe el rey de los Franceses.[115]

111 *Protestation de MM. les Redacteurs des feuilles périodiques*, 27 juillet 1830, en P. Rosanvallon, *La monarchie impossible*, cit., 298. El 25 de julio, Thiers había proclamado: «Les ministres ont violé la légalité, nous sommes dispensés d'obéir».

112 *Cfr.* P. Rosanvallon, *La monarchie impossible*, cit., 93 ss.

113 A.-M. Dupin aîné, *Révolution de Juillet 1830. Caractère légal et politique du nouvel établissement fondé par la Charte constitutionnelle acceptée et jurée par Louis-Philippe 1er, roi des Français, en présence des deux Chambres le 9 août 1830*, Paris 1833, 1 ss. «La révolution de 1830, on le sait, eut deux causes principales, l'une directe et immédiate, la violation du pacte constitutionnel par le prince et par les ministres qui avaient juré de le maintenir; l'autre, moins apparente, mais pour le moins aussi efficace, le souvenir de 1815 et l'impatience de la domination étrangère» (P. Duvergier De Hauranne, *De l'état actuel des partis en France*, cit., 153). «[...] on doit dire que la révolution française de 1830 a été parfaitement légitime, quoique non légale à son principe, parce qu'elle n'a été qu'une juste résistance à la violation de la Constitution jurée par le chef du gouvernement» (D. Serrigny, *Traité du droit public des Français, précédé d'une introduction sur les fondements des société politiques*, Paris 1846, 2 tomos , t. I, 52). Carlos X – con el ministerio Polignac – rechaza la lógica del gobierno representativo: «[...] le roi est-il indépendant ou non de la majorité des chambres? Peut-il choisir ses ministres hors de cette majorité?». Éste es el verdadero problema, dirá Thiers (*La monarchie de 1830*, Paris 1831, 10).

114 A. Thiers, *La monarchie de 1830*, cit., II.

115 H. Robert, *Louis-Philippe, duc d'Orléans et la Révolution de Juillet 1830: hasard et nécessité*, en *Revue de la société d'histoire de la Restauration et de la monarchie constitutionnelle*, 6, 1992, 37–56.

6. *Vive la Charte!* La constitución orleanista del 14 de agosto 1830

Vive la Charte! es el grito que acompaña a la Gloriosa jornada de julio y refuerza la idea de que la Revolución se ha hecho para afirmar la Carta violada por Carlos X y sus ministros. «La Charte désormais sera une verité» es la célebre fórmula que cierra la proclama del duque de Orléans (31 de julio) y es inmediatamente recogida por los diputados (proclama del 31 de julio). Un elemento parece ser común desde el inicio a las fuerzas políticas que han participado en el acontecimiento revolucionario: el carácter pacticio del nuevo régimen político. Sin embargo, tal referencia no basta por sí para aclarar las distintas implicaciones y el significado político-constitucional. La idea genérica del contrato como acto jurídico de fundación contribuye a unir a los diversos «partidos», pero apenas se profundiza, se revelan las distintas posiciones.

Los doctrinarios tienden constantemente a circunscribir los efectos de la Revolución de Julio. Son ellos quienes utilizan por vez primera «ce chiffre de 1688, qui devient l'évangile symbolique d'une nouvelle école ...».[116] La *Glorious Revolution* es el paradigma al que referirse:[117] como en el caso inglés, es preciso restaurar las antiguas libertades violadas entronizando al príncipe que ofrezca adecuadas garantías políticas y constitucionales y que sea, sobretodo, desde el punto de vista dinástico el más «próximo» posible al monarca que ha quebrado el *trust*. Es el ideal de una revolución *popular* en los principios y en los resultados, pero *aristocrática* en la ejecución que da vida a un «hereux melange de hiérarchie et d'harmonie dans l'ordre social».[118] La Revolución de Julio tiene, sobretodo, la finalidad de restaurar el *esprit* liberal de la Carta optando por la rama caída de la dinastía, buscando limitar al máximo la «fractura» con la edad de la Restauración. Luis-Felipe – dirán de Broglie y Guizot – sube al trono «parce que Bourbon», es decir, en cuanto primo de Carlos X, y porque es el único capaz de retomar los hilos del discurso liberal de acuerdo con la nación. La teoría de la *casi-legitimidad* elaborada con esfuerzo y no excesiva convicción por Guizot, revela la originaria debilidad de la interpretación doctrinaria.[119] La monarquía orleanista no debía su investidura a la legitimidad popular porque estaba dotada de una «legitimidad» originaria propia. El «contrato» se ponía entre dos legitimidades distintas: «Nous ne choisissions

116 J. B. H. Capefigue, *Le gouvernement de juillet, les partis et les hommes politiques. 1830 à 1835*, Bruxelles 1836, 2 tomos, t. I, 65.

117 *Cfr.* también D. Johnson, *Guizot et l'Angleterre*, en *Actes du colloque François Guizot*, Paris 1974, 111–120; O. Lutaud, *Guizot historien, politique, écrivain devant les révolutions d'Angleterre*, *ibídem*, 239–272; Ph. Raynaud, *La Révolution anglaise*, en *François Guizot et la culture politique*, cit., 69–81.

118 F. Guizot, *Pourquoi la Révolution d'Angleterre a-t-elle réussi?*, cit., 162–163.

119 *Cfr.* M. Valensise, *Introduction*, en *François Guizot et la culture politique*, cit., 23 ss.

point un roi; nous traitions avec un prince que nous trouvions à côté du trône et qui pouvait seul, en y montant, garantir notre droit public et nous garantir des révolutions».[120]

Evidentemente la cuestión de la «continuidad» estaba destinada a sufrir las críticas de quienes, por el contrario, sostenían la tesis del cese respecto del antiguo orden político. Tal y como en el proyecto de de Broglie y Guizot se sustentaba sobre la filosofía doctrinaria de la legitimidad, en el mismo modo el proyecto de Bérard – destinado, en sus líneas principales, a prevalecer[121] – hacía eco de la tesis de la paligenesia dinástica. Siguiendo tales disposiciones, el duque de Orléans toma el nombre de Luis-Felipe I, y no de Felipe VII, es el *rey-ciudadano* no por «apariencia», sino porque deriva sus derechos del pueblo fuerte y valiente que – con sangre – ha depuesto a Carlos X. Luis-Felipe ha sido elegido «quoique Bourbon»[122] porque había combatido a los enemigos de la Revolución.[123] Sin retornar a la soberanía nacional del 1791 (como propuso por ejemplo Persil) se buscó resaltar el peso de la legitimidad popular. «Il a été librement choisi, librement accepté par le vœu national; c'est là sa légitimité, pas *quasi*, mais pleine et entière, la plus pure, la plus honorable, la plus vraie, la plus éloignée de l'usurpation; cette légitimité est toute populaire, elle lui a valu le beau titre de *Roi-Citoyen*».[124] En consecuencia el gobierno de Julio «Ce n'est pas un gouvernement usurpé ni imposé, c'est un gouvernement *convenu*; il repose sur un *pacte débattu*, sur un *contrat librement consenti*, qui confère ses droits et impose des devoirs à la royauté; contrat *également obligatoire* pour le roi et pour les citoyens; qui oblige ceux-ci à respecter la prérogative sans laquelle le gouvernement du roi ne pourrait pas maintenir son autorité, et qui réciproquement oblige le roi à respecter les droits et les libertés qu'il est appelé à protéger de tout son pouvoir; car il règne pour notre utilité, et non pour son agrément ou son bon plaisir».[125] La Declaración de la Cámara de los diputados del 7 de agosto que registra todos los elementos constitutivos del «pacto» y el acto de aceptación

120 F. Guizot, *Mémoires pour servir à l'histoire de mon temps*, cit., t. 2, 26.

121 *Cfr.* A. Laquièze, *Les origines du régime parlementaire en France*, cit., t. 1, 263 ss.

122 Como se ha puesto de manifiesto, la rama caída de los Orléans tuvo que superar la actitud de sospecha y el no muy velado ostracismo por parte de los Borbones.

123 Sobre el juicio de Luis-Felipe acerca de la *Charte* de 1814 y de los errores cometidos por Luis XVIII, *vid.* Archives Nationales, 300 AP III 13, *Souvenirs de 1814*, manuscrito de 1849, citado por G. Antonetti, *Les monarchies constitutionnelles*, cit., 400 ss. Al mismo autor se debe la imponente biografía *Louis-Philippe*, Paris 1994. *Cfr.* también H. Robert, *Louis-Philippe constitutionnaliste*, cit.

124 A.-M. Dupin aîné, *Révolution de Juillet 1830*, cit., 35. Una posición "intermedia" es la de Thiers: Luis-Felipe quería decir la «royauté nouvelle fondée sur un droit nouveau», más popular, liberal, sabia (*La monarchie de 1830*, cit., 31).

125 *Ibídem*, 38.

de la Carta por parte de Luis-Felipe[126] representan el momento de encuentro de las voluntades.

Dupin, Bérard y los exponentes de la izquierda liberal rechazan tanto la teoría doctrinaria de la doble legitimidad como la doctrina republicana de la monarquía orleanista. «Parlera-t-on encore de ce fameux *Programme* dit de l'Hôtel-de-Ville, que personne n'a ni vu ni lu, et dont un parti cependant aurait voulu faire la véritable constitution de la France? *Une monarchie entourée d'institutions républicaines!* Chose aussi absurde qu'*une république entourée d'institutions monarchiques*, puisque dans le premier cas la prétendue monarchie serait en réalité une république, comme dans le second la prétendue république ne serait, au fond, qu'une monarchie! C'est donc une contradiction dans les termes, introduite pour amener une confusion dans les choses».[127] La monarquía «republicana», a pesar de tales críticas, conservará un espacio propio en el discurso de la etapa orleanista. Agostada – incluso probablemente nunca nacida – la hipótesis «presidencial» ligada a la figura de todos modos autorizada de La Fayette, los republicanos buscan introducir en la Carta su «imaginario» hecho de símbolos (desde el tricolor al «patriotismo» y al coraje de las guardias nacionales) y de técnicas constitucionales que podían convivir con el diseño contractual de la monarquía «parlamentaria». El sentimiento de la «revolución traicionada» por los doctrinarios del *canapé* y por los liberales *royalistes* acabó por tener un valor retórico. Si la revolución del '89 había sucumbido bajo la espada de un soldado, la de 1830 había caído bajo el azote de los doctrinarios.[128] La Revolución de Julio no era una paz, sino una tregua. Francia habría debido hacer como Bélgica: convocar una asamblea constituyente, un Congreso nacional.[129] Sólo así habría dado bases sólidas al nuevo régimen. El «vice radical de la charte et l'inconstitutionnalité des pouvoirs de la chambre»[130] no se habían sanado por la con-

126 *Cfr.* los textos en P. Rosanvallon, *La monarchie impossible*, cit., 345–350. V. anche Ph. Vigier, *Louis-Philippe roi des Français*, en *L'élection du chef de l'Etat en France de Hugues Capet à nos jours*, Paris 1987, 99–106.

127 A.-M. Dupin aîné, *Révolution de Juillet 1830*, cit., 41.

128 L. M. de Cormenin, *Studi sulla eloquenza parlamentaria*, cit., vol. II, 141. Sobre el tema de la "revolución confiscada", véase también B. Sarrans, *Louis-Philippe et la contre-révolution de 1830*, Paris 1834, 2 vols.

129 «La Belgique, encore toute brûlante des feux de la guerre, après avoir chassé Guillaume, n'a-t-elle point dissous ses Chambres législatives et rassemblé un congrès? Pourquoi la France paisible n'aurait-elle pu faire ce qu'a fait la Belgique agitée?» (L. M. de Cormenin, *Cinq lettres sur la Charte, la pairie et le pouvoir constituant*, *Réponse de M. de Cormenin à la lettre de MM. Kératry et Devaux*, Paris 1832, 12).

130 *Ibídem*, *Lettre sur le pouvoir constituant*, 1. Este argumento *fuerte* lo contrastaron los doctrinarios y Thiers recurriendo a argumentos *débiles*, sofismas variados: el carácter popular de la jornada de Julio, el asentimiento repetidamente manifes-

sagración popular de Luis-Felipe. Sólo el pueblo – y no la Cámara de los diputados – habría podido, apoyado en el poder constituyente originario, fundar la nueva legitimidad orleanista.

La *Charte* del 14 de agosto de 1830 – consideradas así las diferentes posiciones que animaron la Revolución e influyeron después sobre la redacción del texto constitucional – acabó por ser una transacción entre lo viejo y lo nuevo, y entre las diversas expresiones políticas. Totalmente nueva, bajo el perfil de la legitimidad[131] – cualquiera que fuese la interpretación que se hiciera de ella – , la Carta orleanista aportaba sin embargo modificaciones y adiciones importantes, prevaleciendo la tesis de la reforma del texto de 1814 con el fin de eliminar los aspectos incompatibles con el nuevo régimen.[132]

Entre las disposiciones más significativas, cabe recordar la que priva a la religión católica del carácter de religión del Estado (art. 6) y que establece la prohibición de censura a la prensa (art. 7). El célebre artículo 14 – en el capítulo dedicado a las «Formas de gobierno del rey» – está modificado, en el sentido de confirmar al monarca el poder reglamentario («hace los reglamentos y las ordenanzas necesarias para la ejecución de las leyes»), pero «sans pouvoir jamais ni suspendre les lois elles-mêmes ni dispenser de leur exécution» (art. 13). La función legislativa – dando continuidad a la práxis constitucional ya madurada durante la Restauración – se divide entre el monarca y las Cámaras: la proposición de las leyes no pertenece ya sólo al rey, sino también a las Cámaras (art. 15) y la eliminación del artículo 46[133] devuelve el derecho de enmienda

tado, etc. Argumentos, estos, que tenían como referencia la categoría de la *soberanía nacional. Cfr.* A. Thiers, *La monarchie de 1830*, cit., 35 ss. «La souveraineté populaire rappelle dans le gouvernement l'intervention des masses, qui n'y ont jamais paru que pour le bouleverser, le rendre anarchique, violent et sanguinaire. La souveraineté de la majorité rappelle au contraire un fait vrai, naturel, légitime; c'est que la nation, consultée non en masse, ce qui est impossible, mais consultée successivement dans la personne des électeurs, des députés, des pairs, qui tous en représentent l'élite, la nation répond et exprime un vœu qui est le vœu public ...» (46–47).

131 Comenzando por la eliminación del Preámbulo de 1814 sustituido por la breve fórmula que se refiere al texto enmendado por las dos Cámaras.

132 Berriat Saint Prix ha contabilizado las diferencias e identidades entre las dos *Chartes*: en la Carta de 1830 halla 46 artículos de la antigua, 18 artículos modificados, 11 eliminados, 4 añadidos (*Commentaire sur la Charte constitutionnelle*, Paris 1836, 32–33).

133 «Aucun amendement ne peut être fait à une loi, s'il n'a été proposé ou consenti par le roi, et s'il n'a été renvoyé et discuté dans les bureaux». Sin embargo, es preciso observar que ya el 23 de agosto de 1839, la Cámara de los diputados subordinó la lectura de una propuesta de ley individual a la previa autorización de tres de los nueve oficios de la Asamblea. También los Pares, el 7 de septiembre, intervienen para limitar la previsión de la libre iniciativa legislativa. *Cfr.*

libre de desarrollarse sin condiciones. Por tanto, el monarca no tiene más el monopolio del procedimiento legislativo (iniciativa, sanción, promulgación). La Cámara de los diputados resulta así reforzada del nuevo texto constitucional: se disminuye la edad del electorado activo y pasivo (respectivamente 25 y 30 años) (arts. 34 y 32), el presidente de la Cámara no es ya elegido por el rey, sino por la propia Cámara (art. 37); los presidentes de los colegios, igualmente, resultan designados por el cuerpo electoral (art. 35). Por otra parte, las leyes del 19 de abril de 1831 (ley electoral basada sobre el principio censitario pero con una pequeña aportación capacitaria) y del 29 de diciembre de 1831 (supresión de la heredabilidad de la condición de par, cuya investidura se reservaba sin embargo al rey) tienden a reforzar, aunque de forma bastante limitada, el principio «democrático». La ampliación del *pays légal* – hasta alcanzar en el curso de los años alrededor de docientos cuarenta mil electores – no logra de ningún modo eliminar del régimen político el carácter rígidamente censitario y nobiliar.

Todos los proyectos[134] que en los primeros días de agosto contribuyen a alimentar el debate sobre la «revisión» de la *Charte* se acompañan de la previsión de un elenco de materias que se deben regular cuanto antes con leyes ordinarias orgánicas.[135] Se trata de materias importantes por cuanto son capaces de cualificar e integrar de forma decisiva el «sentido» político-constitucional de la *Charte*. Mientras el texto de 1814 era tendencialmente *cerrado*, el de 1830 era necesariamente *abierto*, reenviando a un futuro más o menos próximo la solución de cuestiones relevantes que ya habían sido objeto de disputa durante la Restauración, baste pensar en la aplicación del jurado a los delitos de imprenta y a los delitos políticos, en la responsabilidad de los ministros y de los funcionarios, en la incompatibilidad entre las funciones públicas y políticas, en la organización electiva de las guardias nacionales, en el sistema electoral para formar instituciones representativas departamentales y municipales, en la instrucción pública y en la libertad de enseñanza, en la ley electoral política con la

M. Morabito, D. Bourmaud, *Histoire constitutionnelle et politique*, cit., 201. Véase también A. Laquièze, *Les origines du régime parlementaire en France*, cit., t. 2, 407 ss.

134 Los textos de los distintos proyectos (la llamada Proclama del Hôtel de Ville, los textos elaborados por Bérard, el proyecto de De Broglie y parcialmente de Guizot, el de Rémusat) se pueden consultar en P. Rosanvallon, *La monarchie impossible*, cit., 305 ss.

135 «Dans la mémorable séance du 7, la Charte fut révisée, et purgée de toutes les expressions qui, sous le précédent gouvernement, avaient entrainé abus ou fait équivoque; on y ajouta des dispositions nouvelles; enfin elle fut complétée par l'insertion d'un article qui place les couleurs nationales dans la constitution, et par l'engagement pris de porter différentes *lois organiques* qui devaient en assurer la marche et le développement» (A.-M. Dupin aîné, *Révolution de Juillet 1830*, cit., 25).

eliminación del doble voto. Algunas de estas cuestiones no recibieron nunca una regulación legislativa (es el caso, por ejemplo, de la responsabilidad de los ministros y funcionarios), otras, por el contrario, fueron objeto de múltiples intervenciones.[136] Sería imposible realizar la historia constitucional de la Monarquía de Julio sin tener en cuenta esta verdadera y auténtica *agenda* política fijada por el artículo 69. En 1830 era preciso «actuar rápido» y establecer las modificaciones absolutamente necesarias y «compartidas». Pero el éxito completo de la Carta dependía mucho del tipo de selecciones que se realizasen después en aplicación del artículo 69. Para ciertos aspectos esta norma dejaba abierta, como una herida o como una promesa, la cuestión del poder constituyente y de las determinaciones políticas de la constitución. Aquí, en la interpretación y en la aplicación concreta, se habrían de jugar las suertes del nuevo régimen político.

7. Soberanía y constitución

El constitucionalismo francés de la primera mitad del siglo XIX – como se dijo al inicio – debe al menos una parte de su interés al hecho de haberse percibido, en la escala europea continental, como un *laboratorio* rico de experiencias y eventos. Las constituciones francesas que han acompañado al desarrollo de la monarquía constitucional y a los primeros pasos inciertos y controvertidos del «régimen parlamentario»[137] han estado incluidos entre las primeras tentativas para «trasplantar» sobre el Continente algunos principios y mecanismos derivados de la historia constitucional británica. De la gran dificultad de unir la *sustancia* histórico-tradicional de la constitución del otro lado del Canal, con los principios inspiradores del modelo francés ya se ha hecho referencia. Falta analizar ahora la relación decisiva entre el concepto moderno de soberanía y la idea misma de constitución, nudo problemático de cuya falta de solución depende la toma de posición del constitucionalismo francés del '800.

La monarquía transalpina se ha encontrado durante algunos siglos en el centro de un conflicto de época. De un lado hallamos la perviviente idea medieval de constitución, o sea, la de *ancient constitution*, fundada sobre la necesaria pluralidad de fuerzas y de poderes que operan en el interno del cuerpo político, y articulado bajo la forma, también notable, de aquel «gobierno mixto» que asocia «príncipes» y clases sociales diversas, todas necesarias para el pacífico logro del bien común. Un sistema complejo e *históricamente* fundado en pactos y lazos cautiva a las distintas «partes» del Reino e impide que una de ellas pueda

136 El elenco de ellas en P. Rosanvallon, *La monarchie impossible*, cit., 119–121.

137 Véase *infra* el § 9.

pretender una primacía absoluta sobre las restantes. El «lugar de la soberanía» se identifica por tanto, con la única forma legítima de recomposición de los sujetos políticos en la forma más amplia y general de comunidad política compuesta por el monarca, las clases y los estados y sus magistraturas.

En la marejada de las guerras de religión – en la fase más crítica de la segunda mitad del siglo XVI – comienza a tomar forma en Francia la segunda idea de constitución, destinada a suplantar, aunque nunca del todo, a la idea medieval.[138] La forma moderna se aleja de esta última por, al menos, dos razones fundamentales: una contingente, a fin de neutralizar el terrible conflicto y superar la anarquía que amenaza la misma existencia de la comunidad política, la otra, «estructural» que acompaña al dificilísimo pero inexorable proceso de concentración de los poderes públicos dispersos en un único sujeto político. Este sujeto es obviamente el monarca, que no se considerará más en comparación con una parte cualificada y provista de especial *dignitas* como sucedía en la constitución medieval, sino como el ostentador originario de la *summa potestas*. Es como si el rey hubiese comenzado a romper aquella red de vínculos que le costreñían a *compartir* las prerrogativas que desde entonces serán definidas como «soberanas» y que tradicionalmente estaban divididas en el ámbito del *gubernaculum* y de la *jurisdictio*. Resulta ocioso señalar a Jean Bodin y *Les six livres de la République* (1576) para referirse a la teorización fundamental del concepto moderno – en presencia, sin embargo, de muchos aspectos muy arraigados en el universo medieval, comenzando con la idea de *gouvernement* – de soberanía originaria, perpetua, absoluta, indivisible que se identifica con el régimen político (el *éstat*) y establece la titularidad de las prerrogativas soberanas.[139]

No es éste el lugar para afrontar un problema de tanta enjundia. Es cierto que la historia de la monarquía francesa, del proceso de centralización político-administrativa, de la tentativa de afirmar una concepción «absoluta» – en sentido bodiniano – del poder representa una trama de unitaria complejidad.[140] En el momento de la Revolución – como más tarde dirá Tocqueville – los protagonistas afirmaron una ideología de *tabula rasa* y de cambio radical, silenciando y a menudo no comprendiendo que eran los verdaderos y solitarios herederos – bajo el perfil conceptual – de la pretensión de soberanía absoluta encarnada en los

138 *Cfr.* N. Matteucci, *Organizzazione del potere e libertà. Storia del costituzionalismo moderno*, Torino 1988.

139 La reflexión más apreciable y equilibrada sobre el concepto de soberanía en relación con los principales modelos constitucionales se debe a Maurizio Fioravanti, en particular en *Costituzione e popolo sovrano*, Bologna 1998, 47 ss. y *Costituzione*, Bologna 1999, 71 ss.

140 Véase la amplia reconstrucción de S. Mannoni, *Une et indivisible. Storia dell'accentramento amministrativo in Francia*, Milano 1994–1996, 2 vols.

monarcas.[141] El constitucionalismo revolucionario nacía de una raíz teórica tributaria, con otras «fuentes», de la reflexión realizada entre los siglos XVII y XVIII por Hobbes y Rousseau, los cuales, aun moviéndose de presupuestos y condiciones muy distintas, representan el punto de partida y de llegada de la categoría inequívocamente moderna de la soberanía política. La constitución es la imagen refleja de la soberanía: no es concebible – en su forma más radical – como atributo *diverso* o *distinto* de la soberanía. Ésta representa el único fundamento del acto constitucional. La idea de constitución que deriva de ella es profundamente distinta si no directamente antitética respecto a la que propone el *constitucionalismo.*

Éste es el tema central del que tomará cuerpo la obsesión de los liberales del siglo XIX, esto es, cómo hacer que los valores de libertad afirmados por la Revolución puedan sobrevivir (poniendo un «término» a la misma Revolución) a las amenazas más graves: por un lado, el absolutismo de la soberanía popular, por otro, la amenaza «tradicional» del monarca o la que ofrece la experiencia napoleónica. La cuestión de los dos «extremismos», vehículos potenciales ambos del «despotismo», acompañará a toda la reflexión liberal que, sin embargo, no estará todavía en condiciones, durante mucho tiempo, de transformar la obsesión en un argumento productivo para alcanzar el puerto seguro de una forma estable y eficaz de sistema institucional.[142] Los liberales deberán afrontar una de las paradojas de las doctrinas individualistas de la libertad que acompañan a la formidable concentración del poder en el Estado post-revolucionario que ha absorbido las libertades de clase, ha desarrollado una función «modernizadora» (lucha contra los privilegios), y sin embargo restablece en formas ulteriores el problema del abuso y del arbitrio.[143]

La referencia constante a la experiencia constitucional inglesa – a partir de Montesquieu para continuar con las tentativas de los *monarchiens* anglófilos en 1789 (ya «derrotados» en las premisas constitucionales de la *Declaración de derechos del hombre y del ciudadano*) y alcanza, en fin, al «Quindicencio inglés» de la Restauración (y aún más allá) – debe mucho a la búsqueda, a menudo confusa, de una distinta articulación histórica del problema de la soberanía. El blanco, más que Hobbes, será Rousseau, acusado, con razón o injustamente, de haber proporcionado el instrumental ideológico utilizado por los revolucionarios. El lugar de la soberanía se identifica íntegramente con la voluntad popular que se expresa a través de la ley y reconduce cualquier cosa a la voluntad general. En tal

141 *Cfr.* F. Furet, *Penser la Révolution française*, Paris 1978; Id., *L'idée de tradition révolutionnaire*, cit., 5–13.

142 Sobre estas reflexiones véase supra, § 1.

143 Véase al respecto, M. Fioravanti, *Appunti di storia delle costituzioni moderne*, cit., 28 ss.

sentido, el soberano puede quererlo todo, excepto limitarse a sí mismo a través de una constitución que limite «para siempre» la *summa postestas*.

Es preciso dirigir la mirada a Constant y otros escritores ligados a la experiencia de Coppet, desde Necker a Madame de Staël, a Sismondi, para aprehender correctamente el perfil liberal originario. En los *Principes de politique* (1806) Constant critica ya sea a Rousseau, ya a Ferrand y Molé, teóricos, por vías distintas pero convergentes, de aquella idea de *soberanía ilimitada* que conduce a un idéntico éxito tiránico: «L'obsession de Benjamin – se ha afirmado justamente – c'est la digue, la barrière, la borne, la limite, le préservatif (son vocabulaire est inépuisable sur ce sujet) contre n'importe quel risque de débordement de toute autorité ...».[144] Si la teoría de la soberanía popular es «optimista», en el sentido de considerar como «bien» la expresión de la voluntad general, siempre y cuando se realice de forma directa e inmediata y, por ello, lógicamente infalible,[145] la concepción de los liberales de Coppet[146] es tendencialmente «pesimista». «Une constitution est par elle-même un acte de défiance puisqu'elle prescrit des limites à l'autorité ...».[147] La autoridad social, aunque sea legítima, no es nunca ilimitada. No es suficiente el pesado sello de la voluntad general, para que los actos de la *suprema potestas* se conviertan, como tales, en legítimos. «La souveraineté n'existe que d'une manière limitée et relative. Au point où commence l'indépendance de l'existence individuelle, s'arrête la juridiction de cette souveraineté. Si la société franchit cette ligne, elle se rend aussi coupable de tyrannie que le despote qui n'a pour titre que le glaive exterminateur».[148] Limitar la soberanía y, por tanto al poder, significa establecer, ante todo, la línea infranqueable de la «libertad de los modernos» que garantice a los ciudadanos *contre le pouvoir*.[149] El «liberalismo de

144 E. Hofmann, *Les "Principes de politique" de Benjamin Constant. La genèse d'une œuvre et l'évolution de la pensée de leur auteur (1789–1806)*, tomo I, Genève 1980, 315 y *passim* para la interpretación constantiana de la obra de Rousseau. Resulta ciertamente interesante seguir esta huella en la obra precedente de Sismondi, *Recherches*, cit., 88 ss.

145 Sobre el concepto de infalibilidad, véase en este volumen *Il potere giudiziario come «potere politico»*, 435 ss.

146 Para el significado de esta expresión véase en este volumen *infra Coppet et la percée de l'Etat libéral constitutionnel*, 201 ss.

147 Sobre esta *Opinion* de Constant (15 nevoso del año VIII, 5.I.1800), *cfr.* L. Jaume, *L'individu effacé*, cit., 106.

148 B. Constant, *Principes de politique*, ed. Hofmann, cit., 49.

149 «C'est là ce qu'il faut déclarer, c'est la vérité importante, le principe éternel qu'il faut établir. Aucune autorité sur la terre n'est illimitée, ni celle du peuple, ni celle des hommes qui se disent ses représentants, ni celle des rois, à quelque titre qu'ils règnent, ni celle de la loi, qui, n'étant que l'expression de la volonté du peuple ou du prince, suivant la forme du gouvernement, doit être circonscrite dans les

la regla«[150] no puede prescindir de la *constitution-défiance*, y nadie mejor que Constant – después de Locke, probablemente – ha sabido expresar esta idea fuerte del liberalismo dirigido a tutelar los derechos individuales. Que un inmenso poder pertenezca a uno o a todos poco importa, puesto que siempre es un mal. De aquí la exigencia de limitar la autoridad social «au strict nécessaire»,[151] es decir, a las funciones indispensables a la jurisdicción de la sociedad. «Les droits individuels se composent de tout ce qui reste indépendant de l'autorité sociale». En realidad, son los derechos que una constitución bien dispuesta debe tutelar: los derechos de libertad religiosa, la libertad de expresión del pensamiento, la publicidad, las garantías judiciales, las formas tutelares.[152] Así diferenciados de los derechos «du gouvernement et de la societé», los derechos individuales adquieren evidencia indicando «[...] les objets sur lesquels le gouvernement et la société doivent s'abstenir de prononcer et laisser les individus parfaitement libres».[153]

Si los conceptos de resistencia y de equilibrio son comunes a la cultura liberal, hay que tomar en cuenta, sin embargo, cómo es su articulación concreta para dar forma a las diversas propuestas de organización constitucional. La limitación de la autoridad social es – en la perspectiva constantiana – difícil, pero posible. «Elle sera garantie d'abord par la même force qui garantit toutes les vérités reconnues, par l'opinion. L'on pourra s'occuper ensuite de la garantir d'une manière plus fixe, par l'organisation particulière des pouvoirs politiques. Mais avoir obtenu et consolidé la première garantie sera toujours un grand bien». Una vez determinado el *prius* lógico, esto es, la delimitación de la esfera de intervención legítima del poder social, queda sólo por dar el segundo paso: definir la organización y división de poderes.[154] El problema de la división de poderes no adquiere el

mêmes bornes que l'autorité dont elle émane [...]» (B. Constant, *Principes de politique applicables*, cit., 1075).

150 B. Manin, *Les deux libéralismes: la règle et la balance*, en *La famille, la loi, l'Etat: de la Révolution au Code civil*, I. Théry y C. Biet (edits.), Paris 1989, 372–389.

151 B. Constant, *Principes de politique*, ed. Hofmann, cit., 57. Sismondi observa: «[...] une nation ne put jouir de son entière liberté démocratique qu'autant que le gouvernement n'obtint aucune prérogative au-delà de celles qui sont nécessaires à son existence [...]» (*Recherches*, cit., 84).

152 «Les droits des citoyens sont la liberté individuelle, la liberté religieuse, la liberté d'opinion, dans laquelle est comprise sa publicité, la jouissance de la propriété, la garantie contre tout arbitraire. Aucune autorité ne peut porter atteinte à ces droits, sans déchirer son propre titre» (B. Constant, *Principes de politique applicables*, cit., 1075).

153 B. Constant, *Principes de politique*, ed. Hofmann, cit., 58.

154 «Nous dirons seulement qu'il nous semble possible de découvrir des bases d'institutions politiques, qui combinent tellement les intérêts des divers dépositaires de la puissance, que leur avantage le plus manifeste, le plus durable et le plus assuré soit de rester chacun dans les bornes de leurs attributions respectives

mismo relieve que tiene en la tradición constitucional más ligada a la lógica de los pesos y contrapesos (gobierno mixto, *checks and balances*) y a menudo referida, un poco genéricamente, al padre noble Montesquieu.[155]

Algunas afirmaciones de Constant parecen revelar una actitud prudente contra la dinámica, casi siempre elogiada, de los contrapoderes. «On peut, dira-t-on, par des combinaisons ingénieuses, limiter le pouvoir en le divisant. On peut mettre en opposition et en équilibre ses différentes parties. Mais par quel moyen fera-t-on que la somme totale n'en soit pas illimitée? Comment borner le pouvoir autrement que par le pouvoir?».[156] Sin una limitación preventiva de la autoridad social, la división de poderes amenaza directamente con convertirse en «un danger et un fléau».[157] En un célebre pasaje de sus *Principes* de 1815, Constant es todavía más claro: «Vous avez beau diviser les pouvoirs: si la somme totale du pouvoir est illimitée, les pouvoirs divisés n'ont qu'à former une coalition, et le despotisme est sans remède. Ce qui nous importe, ce n'est pas que nos droits ne puissent être violés par tel pouvoir sans l'approbation de tel autre, mais que cette violation soit interdite à tous les pouvoirs».[158] También en el joven Sismondi, que deja un espacio más amplio a la teoría de la *balance des pouvoirs*, el objeto de una constitución liberal es ante todo el de imperir a la nación «confondre la souveraineté avec la toute puissance …», y sólo después el de «régler les divisions de la nation, de répartir les pouvoirs, et d'établir l'équilibre entr'elles …».[159]

Me he detenido en Constant porque considero su concepción – junto a la de autores muy próximos a él – particularmente significativa para comprender qué arduo ha sido en la historia del constitucionalismo francés, hacer «convivir» el concepto de soberanía de carácter revolucionario con la cultura constitucional del liberalismo. La *constitution-défiance* y la lógica de los contrapoderes y del pluralismo no han sido capaces de dotar de sentido común y de impregnar en profundidad las instituciones. De nuevo la mirada al otro lado del Canal evidencia la búsqueda de un «modelo» que parece haber resuelto de un solo golpe el problema de la continuidad histórica, del rendimiento institucional y de la limitación de la soberanía. En un primer momento es el *gobierno mixto*[160]

et de s'y contenir mutuellement. Mais la première question n'en est pas moins la limitation de la somme totale de l'autorité. Car avant d'organiser une chose, il faut en avoir déterminé la nature et l'étendue», *ibídem*, 55–56.

155 «M. de Montesquieu d'ailleurs, dans sa définition de la liberté, a méconnu toutes les limites de l'autorité sociale», *ibídem*, 27.

156 *Ibídem*, 55.

157 *Ibídem*, 54.

158 B. Constant, *Principes de politique applicables*, cit., 1074.

159 J. C. L. Sismondi, *Recherches*, cit., 91.

160 Sobre el problema me limito a recordar las obras de W. Nippel, *Mischverfassungstheorie und Verfassungsrealität in Antike und früher Neuzeit*, Stuttgart 1980 y

el que atrae la atención debido a que es capaz de dar vida a un sistema constitucional que modera la acción de los poderes, garantiza la pluralidad y refleja el orden social despotenciando el carácter absoluto de la soberanía.[161] En la experiencia británica la constitución es el *prius* lógico respecto de la soberanía, que por tanto ejercerá unitariamente el cuerpo político de la nación representada por el *King in Parliament*. La extraordinaria y misteriosa combinación de «antiguo» y «nuevo» que guía la evolución de la constitución inglesa no puede – como ya se ha visto[162] – dejar de llamar la atención de los liberales franceses que lo encuentran el ideal del gobierno moderado y equilibrado, «prescrito» por el tiempo, pero aconsejado por la razón.

Afirmar esto en Francia significa tener que proponer un modelo de orden constitucional que, sin poder renegar de los fundamentos de la edad revolucionaria, debe, sin embargo, hallar el antídoto al veneno de los excesos que mina la historia constitucional. «Qu'est-ce en général qu'un gouvernement simple? C'est celui qui n'admettant pas une division de la souveraineté, des droits réciproques, des moyens de résistance, et une balance politique, ne peut séparer la toute-puissance de la souveraineté, et en gratifie toujours une partie de la nation, aux dépens de tout le reste. Qu'est-ce aussi qu'un gouvernement mixte et libre? C'est celui où pour qu'aucune partie de la nation ne devienne toute-puissante, aucune n'est revêtue de la souveraineté; pour qu'aucune partie de la nation ne soit opprimée, aucune n'est dépouillée de tout droit politique et de toute part au pouvoir suprême ...».[163] El ideal sismondiano, hasta la era termidoriana, sintetiza eficazmente el de otras generaciones de liberales que ponen el acento sobre uno u otro elemento sin salir por ello de un terreno común de reflexión. «La gestion de la complexité – como ha sido brillantemente subrayado – constitue la tekné de l'esprit libéral, dont la vertu de modération forme la face morale: il faut combiner en vue du meilleur possible».[164]

Las Cartas de 1814 y 1830 representan – junto con las otras experiencias más breves de la Restauración – el intento de dar voz a este *esprit* liberal, sin poder hallar un punto de equilibrio entre soberanía y constitución. La naturaleza *democrática* de la soberanía, que se expresa a través del poder constituyente, se ve como una fuerza bruta, un río rebosante que no parece reconocer ni diques, ni barreras, que derriba el pluralismo de los poderes, nivela las condiciones, reduce

de N. Doe, J.-M. Blythe, *Ideal Government and the Mixed Constitution in the Middle Ages*, Princeton 1992.

161 Sobre la noción británica de soberanía, me remito a la brillante síntesis de J. Varela Suanzes, *La soberanía en la doctrina británica (de Bracton a Dicey)*, en *Fundamentos*, 1, 1998, 87–165.

162 Véase *supra*, § 3.

163 J. C. L. Sismondi, *Recherches*, cit., 126.

164 L. Jaume, *L'individu effacé*, cit., 546.

el espacio de autonomía de los individuos, niega las diferencias y los rangos sociales. Las *Chartes* revelan una debilidad intrínseca: la dificultad de «afrontar» el problema constitucional de la soberanía. Una buena muestra de la ambigüedad «estructural» que caracteriza a las Cartas deriva precisamente de este límite originario que se refiere a la cultura política. Los liberales buscan de varias formas «neutralizar» la soberanía porque saben por experiencia directa que ésta tiende a concentrar el poder en un solo «lugar».[165] La topografía liberal se funda – como se dijo – sobre una pluralidad de localizaciones del poder, divididas pero colaboradoras, moderadoras una respecto de otras, dirigidas a un mismo fin. Los mecanismos institucionales que se pretende poder hallar en otras experiencias constitucionales – comenzando por Inglaterra – no llegan a sentar raíces en Francia, o si lo hacen, éstas son demasiado frágiles para resistir el choque de la soberanía.

Los liberales como Constant reconocen la soberanía popular pero limitan siempre rigurosamente el alcance tomando en seria consideración la inviolabilidad de los derechos del individuo. Los doctrinarios, por el contrario, tienden en el curso de la Restauración a calificar la soberanía en términos puramente negativos, tratándose para ellos de una «controversia teológico-jurídica».[166] Es Guizot quien afirma en 1820 la equivalencia entre toda forma de soberanía (popular o de derecho divino) y la usurpación de la fuerza,[167] para llegar más tarde a afirmar que la soberanía popular es una forma de tiranía, es decir, el poder absoluto de la mayoría numérica sobre la minoría.[168] Guizot establece en la célebre fórmula de la *soberanía de la razón* el punto de convergencia de las teorías doctrinarias de la representación y de la distinción fundamental entre origen y ejercicio de la soberanía.[169] Sin embargo, el carácter

165 «Il n'y a de souveraineté absolue nulle part ...» (Discurso de Chateaubriand a la Cámara de Pares, 7 de agosto de 1830, en *Archives parlementaires*, 2ª serie, t. 63, 85–87).

166 A. Omodeo, *Studi sull'età della Restaurazione*, cit., 66.

167 F. Guizot, *Du gouvernement de la France depuis la Restauration et du ministère actuel*, Paris 1820, 201.

168 F. Guizot, *Philosophie politique: de la souveraineté*, en Id., *Histoire de la civilisation en Europe depuis la chute de l'Empire romain jusqu'à la Révolution française*, P. Rosanvallon (edit.), Paris 1985, 309 ss. (*Présentation* de Rosanvallon) y 374.

169 Sobre este aspecto, además de los trabajos de Rosanvallon ya citados, véanse también del mismo autor *Les Doctrinaires et la question du gouvernement représentatif*, en *The French Revolution and the Creation of modern political Culture*, t. 3, *The Transformations of Political Culture 1789–1848*, F. Furet y M. Ozouf (edits.), Oxford 1989, 421 ss.; *Guizot et la question du suffrage universel au XIXème siècle*, en *François Guizot et la culture politique*, cit., 129–145; *Le sacre du citoyen. Du suffrage universel en France*, Paris 1992; y también A.-F. Perny, *Le pouvoir constituant sous la monarchie de Juillet*, Paris 1901; M. Barbè, *Etude historique des idées sur la*

artificial[170] de la teoría de la soberanía se refleja en la teoría constitucional de los doctrinarios. Royer-Collard debe igualmente referirse a una «soberanía de la Carta» que acaba por trasladar el problema sin resolverlo.[171] Justamente el debate sobre el poder constituyente durante la Monarquía de Julio – si se excluye la posición lineal republicana y, por distintas razones, la legitimista – revela el antagonismo entre la centralidad política y sociológica del sistema censitario (también visto desde una perspectiva meramente funcional) y la teorización de preeminente colorido doctrinaria. Incluso un jurista como Serrigny, que también criticaba el concepto de soberanía de la razón, avanzaba después a lo largo del sendero de la neutralización del poder constituyente visto como forma anómala, latente[172] o pasajera[173] de ejercicio de la soberanía. Juristas y políticos volvían a encontrarse en el terreno de la *soberanía nacional*, la única verdaderamente legítima, «... exercée par le roi et les deux Chambres ... La volonté nationale, ou la souveraineté politique, est exprimée par le concours de ces trois branches d'un même pouvoir».[174] Serrigny cita el célebre pasaje del discurso pronunciado en 1842 por Guizot,[175] con ocasión del debate sobre el proyecto de ley sobre la regencia, cuando el ministro de asuntos exteriores recupera de modo neto y claro la concepción de la soberanía nacional «organizada» en la forma de gobierno constitucional. «Soyez tranquilles, messieurs; nous, les trois pouvoirs constitutionnels, nous sommes les seuls organes légitimes et réguliers de la

souveraineté en France de 1815 à 1848, Paris 1904; J. Barthélemy, *La distinction des lois constitutionnelles*, cit.; Ch. Pouthas, *Guizot pendant la Restauration, préparation de l'homme d'Etat*, Paris 1923, 313 ss.; G. Bacot, *Carré de Malberg et l'origine de la distinction entre souveraineté du peuple et souveraineté nationale*, Paris 1985, 120 ss.; L. Jaume, *Guizot et la philosophie de la représentation*, en *Droits*, 15, 1992, 141–152.

170 «De ces trois systèmes, il faut d'abord écarter le dernier, comme ne faisant que déplacer la question sans la résoudre. En effet, personne ne nie que les pouvoirs préposés à la tête d'une société politique ne doivent prendre pour guide dans leurs actes la raison et la justice» (D. Serrigny, *Traité de droit public*, cit., t. I, 25).

171 P. De Barante, *La vie politique de M. Royer-Collard. Ses discours et ses écrits*, cit. *Cfr.* G. Remond, *Royer-Collard. Son essai d'un système politique*, Paris 1933, 36 ss.

172 «D'une part, la constitution donnerait le commandement en dernier ressort et le droit de représenter la société politique au pouvoir établi; d'autre part, les volontés individuelles qui ont concouru à le former, voudraient continuer l'exercice anormal d'un droit qu'elles ont abdiqué dans l'intérêt de la communauté. N'est-il pas clair que cette souveraineté latente réservée serait en opposition avec l'établissement de la constitution? On voit par-là comment le pouvoir constituant meurt à l'instant où naît la constitution, pour revivre au décès de celle-ci» (D. Serrigny, *Traité de droit public*, cit., t. I, 37).

173 F. Laferriere, *Cours de droit public et administratif*, 2 ed., Paris 1841–1846, 5.

174 D. Serrigny, *Traité de droit public*, cit., t. I, 72.

175 Para la teoría de Guizot y los doctrinarios véase P. Rosanvallon, *Le moment Guizot*, cit., 76 ss.; Íd., *La monarchie impossible*, cit., 134–135.

souveraineté nationale. Hors de nous, il n'y a, je le répète, qu'usurpation ou révolution».[176] La obsesión liberal – aunque en este caso puede decirse sobretodo doctrinaria – no logra concebir en la constitución un equilibrio entre, por una parte, la estabilidad y la solidez de la obligación política y, por tanto, de las instituciones y, por otra, la exigencia dinámica del cambio y de la integración política de la sociedad.[177] La constitución que pretende englobar la soberanía (nacional) debe confiar en ella misma, según lo había expuesto ya Royer-Collard durante la Restauración. La *Charte* de 1830 había nacido – según dijeron los doctrinarios – de una revolución, o del principio que ella habría debido combatir. «Le principe qui a présidé à notre révolution en doit pas présider à notre gouvernement», había afirmado Guizot, con la acostumbrada eficacia, en 1830.[178] Pero la *Charte* – a pesar del intento de positivización confiado a los juristas[179] – era en realidad demasiado frágil para alejar de sí el espectro de la revolución.

176 *Cfr. Le Moniteur*, 19 de agosto de 1842, 1811.

177 Se revela como una ilusión la pretensión de un «[...] équilibre *conceptuellement trouvé* (et non plus pragmatiquement élaboré comme en Angleterre et en Amérique) entre le libéralisme et la démocratie» (P. Rosanvallon, *La monarchie impossible*, cit., 284).

178 Discurso del 9 de noviembre de 1830.

179 En la tentativa de afirmar la plena *legitimidad* del nuevo régimen, Guizot, en 1834, había querido que se estableciera una cátedra de derecho constitucional, confiándola a Pellegrino Rossi, a fin de reconducir los distintos aspectos de la historia constitucional francesa en torno de las instituciones políticas de la *Charte*. La cuestión de la *casi-legitimidad* del régimen orleanista hacía urgente una "solución" que otorgase a Luis-Felipe el título pleno – nuevo Guillermo de Orange – en un diseño de difícil y ambigua "continuidad". La cátedra de derecho constitucional nacía en un clima necesariamente "militante". «L'objet et la forme de l'enseignement du droit constitutionnel – se lee en el *Rapport au Roi* de Guizot – sont déterminés par son titre même; c'est l'exposition de la Charte et des garanties individuelles comme des institutions politiques qu'elle consacre. Ce n'est plus là, pour nous, un simple système philosophique livré aux disputes des hommes, c'est une loi écrite, reconnue, qui peut et doit être expliquée, commentée aussi bien que la loi civile ou toute autre partie de notre législation. Un tel enseignement, à la fois vaste et précis, fondé sur le droit public national et sur les leçons de l'histoire, susceptible de s'étendre par les comparaisons et les analogies étrangères, doit substituer aux erreurs de l'ignorance et à la témérité des notions superficielles des connaissances fortes et positives» (*Rapport au Roi sur la création d'une chaire de droit constitutionnel*, 22 août 1834). Exponer científicamente la Carta, «comme M. Demante explique le Code civil ...» (*Journal des débats* del 30 de novembre de 1834), "neutralizar" la "filosofía", la "opinión política" de la *Charte*: ésta es la paradoja a la que Rossi dará sólo parcialmente continuación. (*cfr. Mémoire pour MM. Bugnet, Demante, de Portets, du Caurroy et Duranton*, Paris 1834). Sobre la cátedra de derecho constitucional de Rossi, *vid.* G. Colmet-Daage, *M. Rossi à l'école de Droit*, notice lue par Ernest Glasson à

8. ¿Qué *tipo* de monarquía constitucional?

Las Cartas francesas de 1814 y 1830 aparecen usualmente rubricadas bajo la noción genérica de monarquía constitucional. El problema definitorio, sin embargo, va mucho más allá de esta primera aproximación y representa para el caso francés – como he observado al principio[180] – un significativo *problema constitucional*. Aquella que se ha definido como la «monarquía imposible» no alcanza a conquistar un estatuto jurídico preciso y sufre una «vaguedad» de implantación que deriva de la dificultad de concebir la relación entre monarquía y constitución en el interior de la teoría de los regímenes políticos. La monarquía, por su naturaleza histórica, simbólica, política, debería ser el arquitrabe, el «motor» y el momento de síntesis del orden constitucional: y sin embargo, a pesar de los esfuerzos, en Francia falla su «encuentro» moderno con la constitución.

Tras las tentativas de 1789–1791, la monarquía reaparece en 1814, como se ha visto, bajo la forma de «monarquía limitada»[181] que asigna al soberano – según la lógica de la unidad del poder estatal – una posición de supremacía respecto de los restantes poderes que derivan sus atribuciones de la Carta *octroyée*.[182] En 1824, Royer-Collard dice que no basta definir el gobierno como «une monarchie

l'Académie des Sciences morales et politiques, séance du 22 mai 1886; P. Lavigne, *Le comte Rossi, premier professeur de droit constitutionnel français (1834–1845)*, en *Histoire des idées et idées sur l'histoire. Etudes offertes à Jean-Jacques Chevallier*, Paris 1977, 173–178; P. Rosanvallon, *Le moment Guizot*, cit., 285 ss.; Íd., *La monarchie impossible*, cit., 162 ss.; L. Lacchè, *Politica e diritto: Rossi e la Monarchia di Luglio*, en *Un liberale europeo: Pellegrino Rossi. (1787–1848)*, Luigi Lacchè (edit.) Milano 2001.

180 *Cfr. supra*, § 1.

181 Sobre la elaboración teórica de la noción de "monarquía limitada" – en relación con la noción genérica y de dudosa autonomía conceptual de "monarquía constitucional" – nos remitimos a S. Rials, *Essai sur le concept de monarchie limitée*, cit., 112 ss. *Cfr.* también, del mismo autor, *Une doctrine constitutionnelle française?*, en *Pouvoirs*, 50, 1990, 81–95. En relación con el debate en Francia en el marco de la teoría jurídica (Barthélemy, Carré de Malberg ecc.) *vid.* además Ph. Lauvaux, *Le principe monarchique en Allemagne*, en *La science juridique française et la science juridique allemande de 1870 à 1918*, O. Beaud y P. Wachsmann (edit.), Strasbourg 1997, 65–78; A. Laquièze, *Les origines du régime parlementaire en France*, cit., t. 1, 205 ss. Sobre la Monarquía de Julio *vid.* P. Pasquino, *La teoria costituzionale*, cit. Más en general, *vid.* H. O. Meisner, *Die Lehre vom monarchischen Prinzip im Zeitalter der Restauration und des deutschen Bundes*, Aalen 1969 (Breslau 1923).

182 «Le gouvernement établi par la Charte est, de tous les gouvernements à *institutions représentatives*, le seul où le pouvoir monarchique soit *principe* de l'organisation sociale et *source* de la vie politique» (Ch. His, *De la monarchie représentative*, Paris 1829, 4–5).

mixte, appelée Gouvernement représentatif, où la Chambre élective concourt avec le monarque et une Chambre héréditaire à la formation de la loi et à la direction des affaires publiques …». El «poder regulador» es el que imprime al gobierno un carácter específico. En el caso francés es el rey de la Carta, que conserva «une éclatante primauté entre les pouvoirs qui l'entourent. Seul il représente l'unité morale de la société; seul il agit, seul il commande, seul il est l'auteur de la loi dont l'initiative lui est exclusivement réservée. Cette dernière circonstance exprime qu'à son égard, les autres pouvoirs ne sont proprement que des limites; mais ce sont des limites vivantes et capables de se mouvoir …».[183] Royer-Collard, desde los primeros pasos de la monarquía restaurada – junto a los doctrinarios de su generación, de Serre y Jordan – había asumido las preocupaciones de Necker y de los *monarchiens* respecto del necesario reforzamiento del poder ejecutivo.[184]

Las cuestiones del equilibrio, de la modernización y del compromiso se hallan sin duda fuertemente ligados al diseño constitucional de la monarquía. Hay un acuerdo en decir que tal forma es difícil de realizar, basada como está sobre dispositivos delicados y complejos (del mismo modo que la «compleja» cultura política del liberalismo) que deben ponerse en movimiento con sabiduría y particular capacidad de visión política. El figurín del gobierno mixto acompaña al desarrollo de la monarquía constitucional, pero evocándolo de un modo estereotipado, a partir de la referencia noble del otro lado del Canal, o más frecuentemente, indicando una forma más o menos genérica de colaboración de los poderes «…avec la participation des éléments aristocratique et populaire aux actes les plus importants de ce pouvoir».[185] Pero la referencia al carácter mixto del gobierno – que se evocará durante la Monarquía de Julio como forma de «compromiso» entre los distintos principios – no es suficiente por sí para traducir los ideales del equilibrio y de la moderación en una forma autónoma y completa de régimen político.

183 P. De Barante, *La vie politique de M. Royer-Collard. Ses discours et ses écrits*, cit., t. 2, 216–217. Justamente A. Laquièze, *Les origines du régime parlementaire en France*, cit., t. 1, 237, pone de relieve este pasaje de la obra de Royer-Collard. Sobre esta cuestión *cfr.* también G. Remond, *Royer-Collard*, cit., 47. Sobre la noción de "principio monárquico" a partir de la Carta de 1814, *cfr.* también E. Kaufmann, *Studien zur Staatslehre des monarchischen Prinzipes*, Leipzig 1906 y L. Diez Del Corral, *El liberalismo doctrinario*, cit., 62 ss. que pone acertadamente de relieve – a diferencia de Kaufmann – la ambigüedad de dicha noción en el país de origen. «La doctrina del poder constituyente no se podía trasladar a la Monarquía sin incurrir en contradicciones o vaguedades» (66).

184 *Cfr.* B. Yvert, *Aux origines de l'orléanisme. Les doctrinaires, "Le Globe" et les Bourbons*, en *Revue de la société d'histoire de la Restauration et de la monarchie constitutionnelle*, 7, 1994, 41.

185 D. Serrigny, *Traité de droit public*, cit., t. I, 100.

La historia constitucional francesa muestra un desarrollo de la forma monárquica que, desde la «monarquía limitada» de la *Charte* de 1814 – aun en presencia de un gradual y vacilante proceso de «parlamentarización» – llega hasta el acto de redistribución de los poderes en 1830, acto que conserva en el rey el poder ejecutivo (con la mengua del poder reglamentario) pero en una lógica de reequilibrio total en beneficio de la Cámara electiva. A lo largo de todo este recorrido, apenas esbozado – al que no resulta extraño el cambio de los paradigmas de la legitimidad política – falta centrar el problema de la naturaleza constitucional del poder monárquico. También en este caso me parece que debe «retomarse» a Constant y a su reflexión al respecto (1795–1830). Constant tiene una clara deuda con Necker: piénsese en el poder ejecutivo como *force motrice* del sistema constitucional, en la necesaria «... liaison constitutionnelle entre le pouvoir exécutif et le pouvoir législatif ...», en la unión de los poderes más que de la lógica de los contrapesos, en la *royauté* como recurso simbólico distinto de la acción del poder ministerial.[186] No sorprende que se puedan divisar en los razonamientos «republicanos» de Madame de Staël, y sobretodo de Constant, lógicas y argumentaciones que provienen del arsenal de la práctica constitucional inglesa a través de la mediación neckeriana y de otros autores. ¿Cómo reproducir, entonces, el «mystérieux de ce nuage»,[187] donde está asentado el monarca inglés, en un contexto tan radicalmente distinto como es el directorial? ¿Cómo pueden convivir y cooperar las razones de la inviolabilidad y de la responsabilidad? ¿Cómo dirimir las controversias entre legislativo y ejecutivo?

Ciertamente, el constitucionalismo republicano no es pobre en propuestas. Sin embargo, las instituciones y los procedimientos son tan maquinales y «artificiales» que revelan una fuerte incomodidad y una afanosa tentativa para asegurar estabilidad y equilibrio. Después de las tentativas del año III, y la célebre propuesta de Sieyès de dar vida a un *jury constitutionnaire*, el *pouvoir neutre et préservateur* de Constant sitúa el problema central del constitucionalismo republicano: el monismo constitucional y los defectos intrínsecos de las constituciones de la etapa revolucionaria causantes de conflictos, abusos e ilegalidad. La teoría constantiana[188] – como se ha visto – está descrita en muchos lugares de su obra y responde a una idéntica exigencia que se presenta en formas y

186 Sobre estas cuestiones véase en este volumen *infra Coppet et la percée de l'Etat libéral constitutionnel*, 217–219.

187 G. De Stael, *Réflexions sur la paix intérieure* (1795), en *Œuvres*, cit.: «En Angleterre, le roi pourrait rester toute sa vie dans un nuage sans que la marche du gouvernement s'en ressentît. Il faut connaître seulement jusqu'à quel point le mystérieux de ce nuage est nécessaire pour étouffer toutes les ambitions particulières» (52).

188 *Cfr. infra Coppet et la percée de l'Etat libéral constitutionnel*, 219 ss.

condiciones distintas entre la etapa directorial y la restauración monárquica. Justamente esta situación permite a Constant conducir el concepto de *pouvoir neutre et préservateur* al interior de la más favorable «condition monarchique». La descripción es clara: el «pouvoir royal» es el poder neutro; el «pouvoir ministeriel», un poder activo. El monarca-relojero interviene «desde el exterior» cuando el «mouvement général» se para: «... quand ces ressorts dérangés se croisent, s'entre-choquent et s'entravent, il faut une force qui les remette à leur place».[189] Si el vicio más grave de las constituciones precedentes ha sido el de no haber creado un poder neutro, el «pouvoir royal» parece asegurar «... une sphère inviolable de sécurité, de majesté, d'impartialité, qui permet à ces dissentiments de se développer sans péril ...». El conflicto se convierte así, dentro de ciertos límites, en un recurso, y el «pouvoir royal» interviene sólo si es necesario «... y met un terme par des moyens légaux, constitutionnels, et dégagés de tout arbitraire ...».[190]

Este esquema existe – dice Constant – en la realidad y por tanto no es una mera hipótesis: la monarquía inglesa ha dado forma a «... ce pouvoir neutre et intermédiaire ... le pouvoir royal séparé du pouvoir exécutif».[191] La neutralidad del «pouvoir royal» es la «... condition indispensable de toute monarchie constitutionnelle, à laquelle je reviens sans cesse, parce que toute la stabilité de l'édifice repose sur cette base ...».[192] Si Madame de Staël había hablado del «mystérieux de ce nuage», Constant define al monarca «... pouvoir neutre et abstrait, au-dessus de la région des orages».[193]

La vehemencia que pone Constant en la «sacralización» del jefe del Estado, sin embargo, no debe hacer que se relegue a un segundo plano la complejidad de la teoría del poder neutro. No debe olvidarse que las fórmulas más coherentes son de un lado, la de origen republicano del «pouvoir neutre et préservateur», de otra la fórmula utilizada por la Restauración de «pouvoir neutre et inter-

189 B. Constant, *Principes de politique applicables*, cit., 1079. Constant describe el poder neutro también en los siguientes términos: «Le dépositaire du pouvoir suprême, siégeant au haut de la hiérarchie politique, modérant les mouvemens de tous les pouvoirs, rétablissant l'harmonie entre eux, et du haut de sa sphère, au-dessus des agitations et des orages, dissipant ces orages et appaisant ces agitations [...]» (*De l'état constitutionnel de la France*, en *La Renommée*, n. 1, martes, 15 de junio de 1819, en *Recueil d'articles. Le Mercure, la Minerve et la Renommée*, II, Introduction, notes et commentaires par E. Harpaz, Genève 1972, 1232–1233).

190 B. Constant, *Principes de politique applicables*, cit., 1082. Los mecanismos legales son la destitución de los ministros, la disolución de la cámara electa y el uso del veto, el derecho de gracia.

191 *Ibídem*, 1083.

192 *Ibídem*, 1180.

193 *Ibídem*, 1137. «Le monarque est dans une enceinte à part et sacrée».

médiaire». El soberano «préservateur» es el órgano de la unidad nacional y de la continuidad del Estado: apoyado en su «majesté» e «impartialité», encarna la «puissance publique», es el «être à part, supérieur aux diversités des opinions», el guardián que garantiza el equilibrio en caso de excepción, cuando la colaboración entre los poderes se halla amenazada. Pero el poder «intermédiaire» inviste al monarca también del encargo, históricamente arduo, de «pacificar» – a través de su neutralidad – un pueblo profundamente dividido entre visiones distintas del futuro (más que del pasado), atendiendo a la formación y al desarrollo de un sistema constitucional capaz de «disciplinar» la lucha política (vínculo con la opinión), de garantizar un gobierno unido y políticamente responsable (en el sentido en el que entonces se entendía), permitiendo formas de disenso y de pluralismo. El poder preservador, fundando un gobierno que responda ante la nación por sus actos, contribuye a mantener en equilibrio orden y libertad, garantizando, en última instancia, la seguridad de los ciudadanos.

Esta doble función, sin embargo, no puede asegurarse sólo mediante las atribuciones «negativas». También por esta razón el modelo inglés que Constant demuestra conocer bien – y resultado de un largo y complejo desarrollo histórico – no puede coincidir *tout court* con la idea constantiana del poder neutro. Los *ultras* de la *Chambre introuvable*[194] habían «instrumentalizado» la doctrina del poder neutro y de la responsabilidad de los ministros para dar relevancia a las prerrogativas parlamentarias. Tal episodio demuestra que la teoría de Constant es más compleja – e incluso más contradictoria – de lo que suele pensarse. El peligro de una literal «neutralización» del «pouvoir royal» como juicio de los poderes constitucionales «activos» estaba bien presente para Constant y no sólo en el Guizot del *Du gouvernement représentatif et de l'état actuel de la France* (1816).[195] La rectificación, en las *Additions* de 1818 (reedición de las *Réflexions sur les constitutions*),[196] sirve a Constant para replicar al vizconde de Chateaubriand

194 Véase *infra*, § 9.

195 Sin embargo, en Guizot resulta explícito el carácter "coyuntural": «Il serait étrange, en vérité, que la nature du gouvernement représentatif nous prescrivît de périr en nous défendant l'usage du moyen de salut le plus efficace; c'est en avoir une bien fausse et misérable idée; il y a, dans les principes mêmes de ce gouvernement, une étendue, une latitude qui laisse aux dépositaires du pouvoir la faculté de porter leurs forces et de diriger leur action, tantôt vers un point, tantôt vers un autre, selon occasion et la nécessité: aujourd'hui c'est vers l'affermissement et vers l'exercice plein et régulier de l'autorité royale qu'il faut tendre; tous les intérêts et toutes les passions qui menacent le bonheur de la France menacent en même temps l'autorité royale; elle seule peut les réprimer; c'est donc autour d'elle qu'il faut nous réunir, afin que, sûre de sa force, elle use librement de tous ses moyens» (66–67).

196 Citado por M. Barberis, *Benjamin Constant. Rivoluzione, costituzione, progresso*, Bologna 1988, 227.

que, interpretando maliciosamente la idea de poder neutro, había descrito al rey casi como un «espectador».[197] Constant dice que el monarca no puede permanecer «impasible» ante un ministro que se aleja de la «opinion» y por ello «il le renvoie avant que la faute en soit commise». La reflexión de Constant sobre el poder neutro no se limita al debate sobre la prerrogativa regia y sobre la interpretación que debe darse a la *Charte* de 1814.

El poder neutro no es, por consiguiente, impasible. Constant está casi obligado a repetirlo, pero emerge de sus escritos precedentes. En la neutralidad existe un núcleo de influencia y de determinación de la dirección política. El rey no gobierna, pero debe poder «choisir».[198] Esto lo ve desde el momento que Constant no pretende introducir en Francia el mecanismo formal, de carácter inglés, de la *motion of censure* o *Vote of no confidence*, porque contradiría la facultad regia de nombrar y revocar los ministros; esto es, Contant no hace depender la disolución de la Cámara (otro «medio legal y constitucional» de «apelar a la nación») de la práctica también inglesa del *in accordance with ministerial advice* y del refrendo del primer ministro, sino de una exclusiva, aunque no arbitraria, decisión fundada sobre la idea de oportunidad política. No sorprende, por tanto, el hecho de que Constant no dedique un tratamiento sistemático a la figura del primer ministro, tan importante en el constitucionalismo inglés desde Robert Walpole.[199]

El poder neutro de Constant es por consiguiente una forma de «poder de reserva». Cuanto más el sistema asegura fisiológicamente «la stabilité de l'édifice», más puede el monarca «retraerse», quedando el «être à part, supérieur aux diversités des opinions». Pero las prerrogativas que Constant asigna al «pouvoir royal» le consienten, en caso de un mal funcionamiento del sistema, salir del «sagrado recinto» y asumir un papel no privado de una dimensión «activa». Constant, aun inspirándose en el modelo inglés, parece querer «racionalizar» un aparente anacronismo: no mira al sistema inglés que opera de forma efectiva desde la segunda mitad del siglo XVIII, sino el pleno desarrollo de la monarquía hannoveriana.[200] El anacronismo de Constant revela un diseño lúcido y realista,

197 El mismo Chateaubriand, sin embargo, dice en el capítulo XII de *La Monarchie selon la Charte*, Paris 1816, que el rey no es un "vano ídolo". «Seul il nomme et déplace les ministres à volonté, sans opposition, sans contrôle: toute administration découle donc de lui, il en est donc le chef suprême».

198 B. Constant, *Souvenirs historiques à l'occasion de l'ouvrage de M. Bignon. Première lettre*, en *Revue de Paris*, XI, février 1830, 120.

199 Sobre estos aspectos *vid.* la excelente síntesis de D. Baranger, *Parlementarisme des origines. Essai sur les conditions de formation d'un exécutif responsable en Angleterre (des années 1740 au début de l'âge victorien)*, Paris 1999.

200 Considero en este punto fundamentales las observaciones de J. Varela Suanzes, *La monarquía en el pensamiento de Benjamin Constant (Inglaterra como modelo)*, en

aun cuando no esté privado de contradicciones y de interpretaciones forzadas. Rechazada la hipótesis de la monarquía limitada (a pesar de la *Charte*), Constant cree que el poder neutro no puede limitarse en Francia, en el momento de la Restauración (cuando el sistema constitucional todavía está por construir), sólo a la esfera de la *auctoritas*. El monarca debe poder, si es necesario, ejercitar todas sus *potestades*. El «pouvoir royal» debe ser suficientemente neutral, pero, en ocasiones, tener la fuerza legal para ser realmente «préservateur» e «intermédiaire». El rey poder neutro debe tener la capacidad y la voluntad – y aquí está el problema – para mantener en equilibrio la opinión y el «pouvoir ministeriel», las Cámaras y la función del gobierno, representando el punto variable del compromiso. El rey – podría decirse – tiene el difícil cometido de fijar el mutable punto de equilibrio entre la constitución formal y la constitución material.

El rey[201] de la Carta de 1814 no tiene en realidad la categoría del «poder neutro» como guía de sus operaciones. Se trataba de una *interpretación* de la monarquía constitucional que presuponía – como en el caso inglés – una sólida cultura política y que necesitaba, por tanto, de tiempo para convertir en práctica de gobierno. Faltaban todavía muchas cuñas para que pudiera convertirse en algo de uso común. El concepto sacaba a la luz – como ningún otro – la gran complejidad de la *máquina* constitucional que se necesitaba para el correcto funcionamiento de un jefe del Estado bivalente: por encima de las luchas políticas contingentes, pero severo y atento «regulador» activo del sistema constitucional. El riesgo de que la noción constantiana resultase instrumentalizada (como de hecho sucedería entre 1815 y 1816) era elevado, finalizando por simplificar y banalizar una construcción ingeniosa y capaz de proporcionar un «sentido» a la monarquía constitucional.

No es de extrañar que tal concepto vuelva a escena – aunque con elementos nuevos – en la víspera y durante la Monarquía de Julio. A menudo, la fórmula «Le roi règne et ne gouverne pas» se ve como la síntesis del pensamiento de Thiers. Sin embargo, no puede olvidarse el contexto y la articulación de su elaboración que precede a las jornadas de Julio. Thiers ya sigue la lógica de la

Revista del Centro de Estudios Constitucionales, 10, 1991, 121–138. Sobre la elaboración de la "teoría del poder moderador" *vid.* las originales reflexiones de L. Diez Del Corral, *El liberalismo doctrinario*, cit., 101 ss.

201 *Cfr.* J. Barthélemy, *L'introduction du régime parlementaire*, cit., 83 ss., que considera que Luis XVIII fue el único que se aproximó al ideal de jefe de estado parlamentario. Aparte de este juicio, parece improbable la tesis según la cual el monarca de la *Charte* – a lo largo del proceso de parlamentarización del sistema constitucional – sea un "rey parlamentario". El mismo Constant parece desear establecer una "mediación" entre la imagen mayestática del soberano y la "activa" de las prerrogativas.

«monarquía representativa»[202] fundada sobre el nexo de reciprocidad y de «contrapeso» entre dos *vetos*: el derecho del rey de disolver la Cámara y el derecho de la Cámara de solicitar la dimisión del ministerio. Thiers interpreta – en la polémica con los *ultras* – la prerrogativa regia como derivada de la Carta interpretada en sentido «contractual». Sólo desde febrero de 1830 el director del *National* fija la teoría ulterior del «rey reina, pero no gobierna». La filiación constantiana[203] resulta evidente, y sin embargo la diferencia del contexto y la naturaleza particular de la lucha política llevan a Thiers a utilizar la teoría del «poder neutro»[204] dentro de una pronunciada dinámica parlamentaria, prefigurando una más clara escisión del poder ejecutivo entre el poder de reserva del soberano y el «poder activo» del ministro y, en consecuencia, el derecho de la Cámara-mayoría a participar, con su poder de *veto*, en la elección de los ministros. El poder ejecutivo lo ejerce el ministro: «... il gouverne, en un mot, et comme il a la confiance des chambres, car il n'existerait pas sans cela, il ne fait que des choses qu'elles approuvent ... Ainsi, le roi règne, les ministres gouvernent, les chambres jugent».[205]

9. Entre el rey y el parlamento: el problema constitucional del gobierno. El «régimen representativo», el «régimen parlamentario» y sus condiciones políticas

La Carta de 1814, en su laconismo, no contempla sino con carácter genérico, el principio de la responsabilidad político-parlamentaria de los ministros (arts. 13, 55, 56). Sin embargo, desde 1814 resulta evidente el relieve que reviste tal

202 En la monarquía representativa la mayoría debe prevalecer sobre el ministerio sin que ello determine una "disminución" de la *royauté* que «... choisit les ministres, il n'y a pas de doute; mais la majorité des chambres les renverse. Il n'y a pas d'outrage, pas même d'offense envers le roi. Le roi rend la pareille au pays au moyen de la dissolution. La nation nomme la chambre, le roi la renverse, en la dissolvant. C'est un *veto* réciproque que le pays et le roi exercent l'un envers l'autre» (*Le National*, 8 de enero de 1830, 1, col. 3). Sobre la reflexión de Thiers véase la reconstrucción de A. Laquièze, *Les origines du régime parlementaire en France*, cit., t. 1, 241 ss.; Íd., *Adolphe Thiers, théoricien du régime parlementaire*, en *Revue française d'histoire des idées politiques*, 1, 1995.

203 Thiers, utiliza todavía en 1831 (*La monarchie de 1830*, cit., 6–7) la metáfora del sistema «qui, transportant la royauté dans une région supérieure, au dessus de toutes les attaques, laissait au dessous une région agitée où des ministres attachés à des partis divers se succédaient de l'opposition au pouvoir, du pouvoir à l'opposition ...». Por lo demás, Thiers describe el régimen representativo de la etapa borbónica a través de todas su potencialidades "parlamentarias".

204 Sobre la posición de Constant en 1830, *vid.* P. Rosanvallon, *La monarchie impossible*, cit., 99–100.

205 *Le National*, 4 de febrero de 1830, 2, col. 1.

principio para la configuración del gobierno representativo. El aspecto textual, como es notorio, no resulta de gran ayuda porque toma el originario carácter «penal» e individual del *impeachment* británico, con la acusación por parte de la Cámara baja para las hipótesis «extremas» de traición y concusión, y el juicio atribuido a la Cámara alta. ¿Ministros del rey, o *también* ministros dependientes *en alguna manera* de la mayoría parlamentaria?[206] Me parece que no resulta posible dar a esta cuestión una respuesta unívoca. En el período 1814–1848 no se afirma en Francia, sobre la base convencional, un mecanismo que imponga automática y «obligatoriamente» al gobierno a dimitir cuando pierda el apoyo mayoritario de las Cámaras. La ausencia de tal regla – más tarde afirmada en el régimen parlamentario racionalizado – parecería por tanto excluir la posibilidad de hablar de «régimen parlamentario al menos durante el período de la Restauración. Si, por el contrario, se ha hablado, y se habla, de «régimen parlamentario» en el período considerado, es, a decir verdad, más para afirmar un origen, un momento de arranque, que para sostener la tesis de una plenitud del sistema parlamentario. Sin embargo, no resulta suficiente encontrar algunas técnicas constitucionales de inequívoco sabor parlamentario (compatibilidad ministro / parlamentario; libre acceso de los ministros a las Cámaras y correlativo derecho a la palabra; refrendo ministerial; principio de unidad y homogeneidad del consejo de ministros; formas de «control» del Parlamento sobre la acción ministerial: desde la *adresse* a la discusión y al voto de los presupuestos ...) para llegar a la conclusión antedicha. Tiene razón Guizot cuando, en sus meditadas Memorias, compara el régimen parlamentario con una delicadísima planta de invernadero.[207] El régimen parlamentario no es simplemente la suma aritmética de técnicas y de principios. Existe un *quid* difícil de definir que informa el *esprit* de tal compleja experiencia. En los años de la monarquía constitucional es posible apreciar una fuerte *tensión* para reconocer en la responsabilidad de los ministros el problema constitucional *par excellence* de cuya solución depende, en última instancia, la definición de la forma de gobierno.

Si la Carta es ambigua y con lagunas, la publicística, por el contrario, es muy abundante, hasta el punto de intentar «colmar» el vacío del texto constitucional. En Benjamín Constant, la cuestión de la responsabilidad se halla estrechamente

206 A. Laquièze, *Les origines du régime parlementaire en France*, cit., t. 1, 24 ss. considera las obras de Joseph Barthélemy, *L'introduction du régime parlementaire*, cit. (1904) y de Joseph Bonnefon, *Le régime parlementaire sous la Restauration*, cit. (1905) como los dos modelos de interpretación de los orígenes históricos del régimen parlamentario en Francia. De notable interés son las páginas que Laquièze dedica a los éxitos del *Prix* Rossi, en los comienzos del '900, para la afirmación de la tesis de Barthélemy (t. 1, 12 ss.).

207 *Ibídem*, *passim*.

ligada a la idea de «poder neutro» que le permite convertir en dual al poder ejecutivo, imputando a la responsabilidad ministerial los actos que constituyen un «mal uso» del poder legal.[208] Constant tiende a configurar tal responsabilidad según el modelo tradicional de acusación penal, y sin embargo demuestra conocer muy bien el carácter «político» ínsito en la acusación que concierne a acciones que por su naturaleza son complejas y discrecionales, y busca una apreciación también «político» y discrecional también por parte de las asambleas. Lo que verdaderamente cuenta es, según la práctica inglesa del *impeachment*, la destitución del ministro y la afirmación del principio del gobierno representativo fundado sobre el control de la opinión acerca del gobierno que se manifiesta a través de la imprenta y las formas de publicidad. Estamos todavía lejos de una formalización de la responsabilidad, de un procedimiento jurídico-político fundado sobre un automatismo. Constant, que conoce bien la práctica inglesa del voto de desconfianza, no pretende introducirlo en Francia para no asignar a las asambleas una prerrogativa que podría entrar en conflicto con el «poder neutro» del monarca y en particular con el poder de libre designación de los ministros. Constant observa la situación francesa y no considera factible introducir *sic et simpliciter* los mecanismos propios de la experiencia inglesa. La constatación es otra: «Lorsque nous aurons ce que nous n'avons point encore, mais ce qui est d'une nécessité indispensable dans toute monarchie constitutionnelle, je veux dire, un ministère qui agisse de concert, une majorité stable, et une opposition bien séparée de cette majorité, nul ministre ne pourra se maintenir, s'il n'a pour lui le plus grand nombre des voix, à moins d'en appeler au peuple par des élections nouvelles. Et alors, ces élections nouvelles seront la pierre de touche de la confiance accordée à ce ministre ...».[209]

«Cuánto tendremos de lo que ahora carecemos», escribe Constant. Ésta es una cuestión muy importante porque evidencia el nexo necesario entre las condiciones de la cultura política (mayoría / oposición, papel de los partidos, unidad y homogeneidad del ministerio) y el desarrollo del régimen parlamentario. Entre tanto que las condiciones existan sólo en parte o en absoluto es una veleidad imaginar un determinado éxito constitucional. En este asunto no faltan, sin embargo, las paradojas.[210] Son los *ultras* quienes, de hecho, en el comienzo de la

208 B. Constant, *De la responsabilité des ministres*, Paris 1815, en *Cours de politique constitutionnelle ...*, Paris 1872, t. I, 405. Constant volverá a utilizar el concepto de "abus du pouvoir légal" en un artículo de 1830 (*Le Temps*, 31 de mayo de 1830), sin salir por ello del ámbito del *impeachment*.

209 B. Constant, *De la responsabilité des ministres*, cit., 408.

210 Sobre el concepto de "paradoja" respecto al problema de la ejecución de un texto constitucional *vid.* R. Remond, *La gestion des Constitutions*, en *Pouvoirs*, 50, 1990, 43–51.

Segunda Restauración, en el período de la llamada *Chambre introuvable*[211] (hasta septiembre de 1816), abordan con fuerza el tema de la relación entre la mayoría de la Cámara y la acción ministerial, afirmando una sensibilidad de tipo parlamentario. Disfrutando de una fuerte mayoría en la Cámara, los *royalistes* insisten en el tema del control parlamentario y de la participación en la dirección política del gobierno. Esta cuestión encuentra sólidos argumentos en obras de gran peso teórico que reenvían a personalidades de primerísimo plano, basta pensar en Vitrolles[212] y en Chateaubriand.[213] Si los originarios adeptos de la monarquía limitada se convierten en partidarios de una evolución «parlamentaria» del régimen político, los liberales – en este singular «juego de las partes» – se ven en la necesidad de mantener una postura defensiva y se atrincheran en torno a la *prérogative royale*. El debate de 1815–1816 tendrá, no obstante, el mérito de difundir en el país, incluso entre quien en principio poco o nada favorable a la idea de un orden constitucional,[214] un léxico esencial «común» a las dos tendencias políticas principales.[215] Probablemente es el análisis de Vitrolles

211 *Cfr.* M. S. Corciulo, *Le istituzioni parlamentari in Francia. Cento Giorni e seconda Restaurazione (1815–1816)*, Napoli 1979; Íd., *La Chambre introuvable et les principes du régime parlementaire*, en *Parliaments, Estates and Representation*, 1, 1981; C. Cassina, *I lavori parlamentari della Chambre introuvable*, en *Critica storica*, 4, 1989, 573–610; P. Rosanvallon, *Les Doctrinaires et la question du gouvernement représentatif*, cit., 412 ss.; E. De Waresquiel, *Un paradoxe politique: la Chambre "introuvable" et la naissance du parlementarisme français (octobre 1815–avril 1816)*, en *Commentaire*, 15, 1992, 409–416; P. Rosanvallon, *La monarchie impossible*, cit., 75 ss.; A. Laquièze, *Les origines du régime parlementaire en France*, cit., t. 1, 356 ss.

212 *Du ministère dans le gouvernement représentatif*, Paris 1815.

213 *De la Monarchie selon la Charte*, cit. (1816).

214 A. F. Villemain, *Le roi, la Charte et la Monarchie*, Paris, s. d., 7: «Les plus grands ennemis de la constitution sont désormais condamnés à l'invoquer toujours; leur triomphe l'aurait détruite; leurs attaques ne peuvent que l'affermir, en les forçant de jouer un rôle qui ne trompe personne, mais qui est un hommage rendu aux principes de la liberté, et qui complète l'unanimité nationale en faveur de la Charte. Nous le disons avec joie et confiance. Le gouvernement représentatif est donc naturalisé en France. Une puissance irrésistible y pousse également toutes les opinions. Les publicistes les plus opposés par leurs sentiments et leurs vœux, se rencontrent dans ce point commun. M. de Chateaubriand consacre son talent à reproduire et, si l'on veut, à réhabiliter les théories si bien exposées par M. Benjamin Constant: et *Jerusalem* parle comme *Samarie*».

215 Ch. Saint-Simon, *Lettre de M. le comte de Saint-Simon, sur l'établissement du parti de l'opposition*, en *Le Censeur*, 3, 1815, 334–356, se refiere a la necesidad de que a la «... division de l'opinion publique en deux partis: le parti ministériel et le parti de l'opposition ...» (335) corresponda un común *Verfassungspatriotismus*: los dos partidos, que se dividiran en todo, deben ser "constitucionales". «Les idées que j'ai présentées ne sont que les idées anglaises étendues et généralisées; il s'agit d'en faire l'application à l'état présent des choses. La France a un gouvernement parlementaire; ce gouvernement ne peut avoir une marche régulière sans un

sobre la unidad del ministerio responsable ante la «opinión» y el «partido» de la mayoría, sobre la distinción entre monarca irresponsable y gobierno, la más eficaz y avanzada[216] en la vía del régimen parlamentario. Chateaubriand, a su lado, y contrariamente a lo que sostenían los liberales, convertía al monarca – con evidentes referencias constantianas – en el punto de equilibrio del sistema. Los ministros no tenían la obligación de dimitir ante las solicitudes de la mayoría porque – en la lógica de la monarquía limitada – al rey le correspondía la decisión última,[217] aun cuando sostener el carácter político de la responsabilidad[218] significaba afirmar una fuerte influencia de la «opinión» sobre la elección y revocación de los ministros.[219]

El carácter «instrumental» de la polémica en los años 1815–1816 revela un dato «estructural» de la lucha política. Quien conquista la mayoría de la Cámara de los diputados tiende a acentuar la naturaleza «parlamentaria» del régimen. En el fondo, la actitud de los *ultras* de la *Chambre introuvable* tiene un débil eco en el comportamiento de los liberales a partir de 1827, desde la caída del ministerio Villèle. Esto significa que la lucha política corre un velo sobre la estabilidad y la compartición del marco constitucional. Es un elemento que no debe asombrar en absoluto si se piensa en los pocos años que han transcurrido desde el inicio de la experiencia constitucional en Francia. La «planta de invernadero» se esfuerza en crecer y debe prestarse mucha atención para no ponerla en contacto con un clima inadecuado. El «juego de las partes» entre *ultras* y liberales – por permanecer en la simplificación de los dos «partidos» – es también la expresión de una sicología constitucional que deriva de la interpretación de la *Charte* y de su régimen político. Quien tiene la mayoría, se decía, hace palanca sobre el carácter parlamentario y dualista; quien está a la defensiva tiende a encontrar en

ministère et une opposition: y a-t-il en France un ministère et une opposition? Je regarde et je vois des ministres et point de ministère, des opposants et point d'opposition des deux côtés, point d'union, point de principes fixes et précis, tout est encore à créer. D'après ce que j'ai dit ci-dessus, c'est le parti de l'opposition qui doit s'organiser le premier. L'organisation de l'opposition ne peut se faire que par la force de l'esprit public» (344–345).

216 E.-F.-A. De Vitrolles, *Du ministère dans le gouvernement représentatif*, cit., 61 ss.

217 F.-R. De Chateaubriand, *De la Monarchie selon la Charte*, cit., cap. XII.

218 «Si l'on dit que les ministres peuvent toujours demeurer en place, malgré la majorité, parce que cette majorité ne peut pas physiquement les prendre par le manteau et les mettre dehors, cela est vrai. Mais si c'est garder sa place que de recevoir tous les jours des humiliations, que de s'entendre dire les choses les plus désagréables, que de n'être jamais sûr qu'une loi passera, tout ce que je sais alors, c'est que le ministre reste et que le gouvernement s'en va» (*Ibídem*, cap. XXXIX).

219 Los liberales – basta pensar en Guizot (*Du gouvernement représentatif*, cit., 34–35) o en Villemain (*Le roi, la Charte et la Monarchie*, cit.) – critican la pretendida existencia constitucional del ministerio y del principio de responsabilidad.

el monarca – que ciertamente no tiene la intención de representar la figura de «espectador» – un sujeto dotado de preeminentes prerrogativas cuyo uso legal puede reconducir a la mayoría dentro de un ámbito más conforme con el esquema «monista» de la *Charte*. Es evidente que el debate de finales de los años Veinte coloca de nuevo a los *ultras* y liberales en sus posiciones «naturales», pero este carácter no abandonará – aunque con formas posteriores y distintas – el sistema constitucional en Francia hasta después de 1830.

El esfuerzo dirigido a disciplinar la responsabilidad de los ministros – recurriendo, sin embargo, a una conceptualización de naturaleza penalista[220] – revela no obstante la necesidad de aclarar un problema fundamental. Es cierto que, aun con las mencionadas incertidumbres, la insistencia sobre la legislación electoral y sobre la relativa a la imprenta[221] – que acompaña a las principales articulaciones políticas de la Restauración – muestra distintamente la convicción de que resulta posible gobernar y «durar» sólo con el apoyo de la «opinión» (que prospera por la libertad de imprenta), esto es, de aquella potencia que es «más fuerte que los ejércitos, que el legislativo, que el rey; más rápida, más vasta que el espacio, más inteligente que el pensamiento».[222] Otro aspecto debe subrayarse: el control del parlamento[223] (a través de la contienda electoral y las hornadas de pares) es la condición esencial para influir sobre la naturaleza del régimen. En ausencia de un verdadero y definido régimen parlamentario, se comporta «como si» éste fuese operativo en todos sus complejos engranajes. Pero no debe olvidarse que ningún voto de censura – como tal – hace caer un gobierno, y la disolución sigue siendo la manifestación de la prerrogativa regia, aun cuando en algunos casos es evidente y decisiva la postura repetidamente hostil del parlamento (así ocurre con ocasión de la caída del segundo ministerio Richelieu en 1821). En otros casos el ministerio recurre al monarca para pedir la disolución de la Cámara en la que existe una mayoría solidaria pero a través de tal acto se

220 *Cfr.* F. Perrin, *De la responsabilité pénale du chef de l'Etat et des ministres en France depuis la chute de l'Ancien Régime jusqu'à nos jours*, Paris 1903; P. Desmottes, *De la responsabilité pénale des ministres en régime parlementaire français*, Paris 1968.

221 Estos dos aspectos revisten enorme importancia para la configuración del gobierno representativo y merecerían un profundo tratamiento específico. El problema de la imprenta es fundamental. *Cfr.* en particular Ch. Ledré, *La presse à l'assaut de la monarchie, 1815–1848*, Paris 1960; *Guizot, les doctrinaires et la presse (1820–1830)*, D. Roldan (edit.), Paris 1994; L. Jaume, *Heurs et malheurs de la liberté de presse*, en *Liberté, libéraux et constitutions*, cit., 43–59; M. Morabito, D. Bourmaud, *Histoire constitutionnelle et politique*, cit., 183 ss.; L. Jaume, *L'individu effacé*, cit., 407–444.

222 L. M. de Cormenin, *Studi sulla eloquenza parlamentaria*, cit., vol. I, 150.

223 «Néanmoins, et toujours, dans un gouvernement représentatif sincère et libre, nul ministère n'existe s'il n'a la majorité dans la Chambre élective» (A. Mahul, *Tableau de la Constitution*, cit., 476).

intenta contrarrestar el progresivo afianzamiento de la minoría (Villèle en 1824 y 1827). Las elecciones revisten entonces un papel decisivo y se convierten en un «appel au pays» para arbitrar en la contienda política. El rey no puede ser «partidario» y «neutral»: la inteligencia política se le solicita para «interpretar» el sentimiento de la *opinion*. En un régimen de tendencia parlamentaria el monarca no puede utilizar sistemáticamente los medios legales para cambiar el resultado deseado por la opinión, so pena de una crisis constitucional de final incierto.

Se puede decir, por tanto, que el régimen parlamentario, en forma terminada, no existe jurídicamente, pero se halla ya en presencia – más allá de episodios aislados que pueden interpretarse de diversas maneras – desde un punto de vista *político-general*. El régimen parlamentario es al mismo tiempo el «campo de juego» (en la forma del régimen representativo) y la «partida» que hay que jugar:[224] una confusa superposición, ésta, que parece poder desvanecerse en 1830.

La Carta orleanista establece de hecho, sobre la base de igualdad, los dos poderes fundamentales del Estado, pero sin lograr deshacer el nudo teórico de la monarquía constitucional y el problema del régimen parlamentario. Paradójicamente, mientras que la monarquía de 1814 es coherente respecto del texto de la *Charte*, el documento de 1830 – por la ambigüedad ínsita a los orígenes del nuevo régimen «bastardo», monárquico pero con fuertes inserciones republicanas – es reticente respecto de muchas cuestiones comenzando por aquella fundamental del estatuto jurídico del gobierno y su responsabilidad. La Carta de 1830 que habría debido en teoría resolver las dos cuestiones más controvertidas durante la Restauración no plasma *en el texto*, sino de manera muy parcial, el debate que a finales de los años Veinte y en la víspera de la Revolución había abordado con decisión el problema del papel del monarca, la relación de «unión y colaboración» entre el ministerio y la mayoría parlamentaria, los mecanismos constitucionales de resolución del conflicto entre los órganos. Los constituyentes de 1830 no han logrado proporcionar a las instituciones una clara dirección de marcha, prefiriendo reenviar a la práctica y al tejido convencional y, en última instancia, a la lucha política, el éxito de la vicisitud constitucional. El año 1830, a pesar de compresión del proceso de parlamentarización de la monarquía, no puede resolver los problemas y atesorarse del debate de la Restauración. Luis-Felipe ya desde 1809, en la tentativa de subir al trono de España, había madurado la idea avanzada de la monarquía representativa y de la relación de colaboración entre ejecutivo y legislativo. Sin embargo, el fracaso en España, y la postura de

224 «... et en même temps le gouvernement représentatif fut énergiquement réclamé, discuté, commenté et fondé par la lutte même dont il était à la fois le théâtre et l'objet» (F. Guizot, *Mélanges politiques et historiques*, *Préface*, cit., XV).

las *Cortes* le dejaron una marca indeleble que después de 1830 se reflejará en sus posiciones «conservadoras» y en el rechazo del principio de la soberanía popular.[225]

Este límite – que incidirá mucho sobre las ausentes reformas de los años Cuarenta – se refleja sobre el pleno y definitivo desarrollo del régimen parlamentario. La Carta de 1830 había afrontado – como ya se ha visto[226] – el problema del reequilibrio de los poderes, pero la teoría de la «continuidad» sustancial respecto del texto de 1814 termina por hacer pasar a un segundo plano la adecuación constitucional al instituto del gobierno y de la responsabilidad de los ministros y de los funcionarios.[227] Si es cierto que una característica fundamental del régimen parlamentario – aun más en referencia al caso inglés – es justamente la «flexibilidad» que desaconseja toda formalización jurídica rígida, es también cierto que las Cartas francesas se caracterizan por una excesiva indeterminación. En la etapa orleanista era posible servirse – a diferencia de lo que ocurrió en 1814 – de la experiencia madurada a lo largo de la Restauración. El artículo 69 de la Carta no se valoró plenamente para desarrollar ulteriormente las condiciones políticas del régimen parlamentario (sistema electoral, reforma parlamentaria, etc.). La Monarquía de Julio permaneció, se podría decir, en medio del vado: sin poder obviamente retornar atrás, pero incapaz también de alcanzar la orilla de un régimen parlamentario más eficaz.

Para ser exactos, al final de los años Treinta vuelve a oírse la cuestión que había acompañado a la dinámica constitucional de la Restauración: en caso de conflicto entre los poderes, ¿quién debía tener la última palabra? ¿La Cámara electiva o el rey? La cuestión de la soberanía se entretejía estrechamente con el problema de la forma monárquica y del régimen político. La situación sugerida entre 1814 y 1830 era, para los *ultras*, que fuese el rey quien tuviese la última palabra *selon la lettre de la Charte*; para los liberales, por el contrario, la última palabra del rey debia sin embargo tener presente el *concurso* de la opinión representada por la Cámara *selon l'esprit de la Charte*. Esta segunda tesis, como se ha visto, prevalece y se convierte en *sentido común* en 1830. Sin embargo, la pregunta conserva intacta su significado también en la etapa orleanista. La lucha político-constitucional de 1838–1839 ofrece importantes puntos de reflexión. En diciembre de 1838 se forma contra el segundo gabinete Molé una *coalición* (Thiers, Guizot, Odilon Barrot) que acusa al ministro de ser sólo el «testaferro» de Luis-Felipe, y de gobernar independientemente del «concurso» parlamenta-

225 En relación con el episodio español, *cfr.* G. Antonetti, *Louis-Philippe*, cit., 364 ss.; Id., *Les monarchies constitutionnelles*, cit., 390–394.

226 Véase *supra*, § 6.

227 Ésta fue una de las materias previstas en el artículo 69 que no fue seguido por una disciplina orgánica.

rio. La disolución de la Cámara en febrero de 1839 – después que el fatigoso debate sobre el discurso de la corona[228] había desembocado en un *adresse* menos crítico que en su formulación original – y la dirección electoral el marzo sucesivo, con éxito negativo para Molé, le obligan a dimitir (8 de marzo). De nuevo el recurso al «pueblo» dirigido a reforzar la mayoría ministerial determina un contragolpe sobre el gobierno. Tal asunto suscitó un vivo debate sobre las prerrogativas constitucionales de los poderes, sobre la forma de la monarquía constitucional y sobre la naturaleza del régimen político.[229] Es preciso, por otra parte, recordar que el «personalismo»[230] es el estilo prevalente de Luis-Felipe hasta el inicio de los años Treinta.[231] Casi siempre es el «auténtico» presidente del Consejo; asume un papel decisivo en la caída de algunos gobiernos (piénsese en Thiers en 1836 y 1840) y tiene un peso igualmente considerable en la elección de los ministros. El «personalismo» – con el corolario de «gobierno del rey» más o

228 El discurso de Luis-Felipe había, en realidad, utilizado, respecto del pasado, un tono menos "personalista".

229 *Cfr.* G. Antonetti, *Louis-Philippe*, cit., 797 ss.; P. Rosanvallon, *La monarchie impossible*, cit., 158 ss.; A. Laquièze, *Les origines du régime parlementaire en France*, cit., t. 1, 365 ss.; G. Antonetti, *Les monarchies constitutionnelles*, cit., 462 ss.; M. Morabito, D. Bourmaud, *Histoire constitutionnelle et politique*, cit., 203 ss.

230 Guizot, en su *Préface* a los *Mélanges politiques et historiques*, cit., además de en diversos pasajes de sus Memorias, insiste mucho en el significado que debía darse a la expresión *pouvoir personnel* y al célebre «le roi règne et en gouverne pas». Guizot admite una cierta predisposicion de carácter de Luis-Felipe hacia el «intervencionismo» político, pero rechaza la idea de que el «personalismo» del rey haya asumido nunca los caracteres de un comportamiento extra-legal. Guizot rechaza la tesis del «trono vacío» retomando – al menos en el aspecto teórico – la concepción constantiana del poder neutro como poder de influencia. «Quelque limitées que soient les attributions de la royauté, quelque complète que soit la responsabilité de ses ministres, ils auront toujours à discuter et à traiter avec la personne royale pour lui faire accepter leurs idées et leurs résolutions, comme ils ont à discuter et à traiter avec les Chambres pour y obtenir la majorité … Partout où la monarchie constitutionnelle a existé, la personne du monarque, ses opinions, ses sentiments, ses volontés n'ont jamais été des faits indifférents, et les plus indépendants, les plus exigeants des ministres en ont toujours tenu grand compte» (*ibidem*, XXXVII–XXXVIII). De nuevo (Guizot había expuesto su pensamiento en un célebre discurso de mayo de 1846) emerge con toda evidencia el problema de la monarquía constitucional y del régimen representativo, es decir, de la dificultad de pensar y definir la medida y el grado de reparto de la influencia política necesaria para mantener en equilibrio los poderes del Estado. Sobre el concepto de «ejecutivo monárquico» en la teoría guizotiana de finales de los años '40, *vid.* L. Diez Del Corral, *El liberalismo doctrinario*, 356–357. Sobre el concepto de «poder personal» *cfr.* también Ch. Hello, *Du régime constitutionnel*, cit., t. II, 188–189. Hello dice que «Le roi influe sur le gouvernement, il ne gouverne pas» (*ibidem*, 196).

231 *Cfr.* R. Hayem, *Le Conseil des Ministres sous Louis-Philippe*, Paris 1939.

menos apoyado en una mayoría parlamentaria – acabará por asociar hasta tal punto la política ministerial de los años Cuarenta a la *deseada* por Luis-Felipe, que llega a comprometer después a la monarquía en la imprevista caída del régimen.

Las «recomendaciones» de Prosper Duvergier de Hauranne – el más lúcido intérprete liberal de la evolución jurídico-constitucional de la monarquía orelanista – no surtirán el efecto esperado. Sus artículos de 1838[232] se insertan en la polémica concreta pero poseen también un valor teórico más general. El marco de referencia no puede ser otro que el sistema institucional que deriva de la *Charte* de 1830 con el principio de la necesaria colaboración / "unión" de los tres poderes como centro. Tal convicción, que también es común a los que sostienen la prerrogativa regia, se resiente de la tradicional y genérica teoría del gobierno mixto, pero trata de enuclear una auténtica y verdadera doctrina del gobierno representativo. Si tal esfuerzo común existe,[233] también es cierto que en el paso de la teoría de la colaboración a la de la resolución del conflicto institucional emergen los dos campos de interpretación del «régimen parlamentario», uno obviamente centrado sobre la preeminencia del «principio parlamentario», el otro sobre la primacía del «principio monárquico». Un régimen como el representativo, basado en la necesaria colaboración entre los poderes, puede tolerar conflictos sólo en cuestiones de gran relevancia político-constitucional, y debe poderlas resolver rápidamente. La pregunta de la Restauración se halla en parte modificada pero permanece en esencia: ¿quién debe tener la «última palabra» en caso de conflicto, según la lógica de la colaboración? Para Duvergier será la Cámara de los diputados,[234] en cuanto es *más representativa* que los otros dos componentes, el rey y la Cámara de pares, pero negando así la

232 Publicados en la *Revue française* y después recogidos en *Des principes du gouvernement représentatif et de leur application*, Paris 1838.

233 Basta recordar a Charles His y su distinción entre el rey como «pouvoir dominant» y a las Cámaras como «pouvoirs-limites» tomando en consideración la dinámica del "concurso" (*Réponse à Monsieur Duvergier de Hauranne*, Paris 1838) (His ya había publicado *Des ministres dans la monarchie représentative*, Paris 1837) o a Henri Fonfrède, *Du gouvernement du roi, et des limites constitutionnelles de la prérogative parlementaire* (1839), en *Œuvres*, Bordeaux, Paris 1844, t. 6.

234 «Dans l'état normal, participer indirectement, mais efficacement au choix de la direction politique et à la formation du cabinet; puis, si la lutte s'engage entre les pouvoirs constitutionnels, exercer l'influence décisive, telles sont, à mon sens, les attributions essentielles de la chambre élective; telle est la prépondérance qu'il me paraît juste de réclamer pour elle … Ce n'est pas sans quelque surprise que j'ai pris la plume pour combattre une théorie que je croyais morte en 1830; la théorie qui attribue au roi la toute-puissance, et aux chambres le simple droit de contrôle et de conseil …» (*Des principes du gouvernement représentatif et de leur application*, cit., 24).

misma teoría de la *soberanía nacional*. Para autores como His, Fonfrède o Pepin, el equilibrio se inclinará en favor del «gouvernement du roi», invirtiendo los factores pero cayendo en el mismo equívoco. Duvergier invoca una teoría actualizada del «poder neutro» de ortodoxia constantiana. El monarca no tiene sólo los atributos simbólicos y ceremoniales, sino que debe hacer un uso sabio de sus conspicuas prerrogativas.[235] En tal sentido Duvergier no niega al soberano un inevitable derecho de *influencia* sobre la dirección política, pero la influencia debe ejercitarse más sobre el conjunto que sobre los detalles – esto es, en el plano de las grandes decisiones – y los ministros, después de haber escuchado respetuosamente las objeciones del rey, permanecen en su puesto totalmente libres de actuar hasta el día de su destitución.[236] Frante a un monarca «intervencionista», De Hauranne invocará uno más «discreto»: «... il est bon, il est nécessaire que son opinion personnelle apparaisse le moins possible, et qu'on ne le fasse pas descendre dans l'arène des partis».[237]

235 «Dans un discours récent, discours que les Ministres du 15 avril ont accueilli comme un hommage et comme une réparation, M. Guizot, après avoir reporté à la Couronne l'honneur de la politique aujourd'hui dominante, s'est élevé de toute force de son talent et de sa conviction contre cette idée absurde et inconstitutionnelle, selon lui, que «le Roi ne peut rien faire». Ce sont de grands efforts pour un bien petit résultat. Je ne sache personne, en effet, que ait dit pareille sottise. De par la Charte, le Roi est investi de prérogatives constitutionnelles qui supposent nécessairement une pensée, une volonté. Tel est l'appel à la Chambre contre un ministère qui a perdu la confiance du Roi. Tel est l'appel au pays contre une Chambre dont il croit les opinions fausses et la marche dangereuse. Dans ces deux cas, au moins, le Roi, très-constitutionnellement, très-légitimement, manifeste sa façon de penser. Pour soutenir le contraire, il faudrait n'avoir jamais lu la Charte» (P. Duvergier De Hauranne, *De la politique extérieure et intérieure de la France*, cit., XCIII–XCIV).

236 *Ibídem*, XCIV. Ya Chateaubriand había escrito: «Que fait le roi dans son conseil; il juge, mais il ne force point le ministre. Si le ministre obtempère à l'avis du roi, il est sûr de faire une chose excellente et qui aura l'assentiment général. S'il s'en écarte et que pour maintenir sa propre opinion il argumente de sa responsabilité, le roi n'insiste plus, le ministre agit, fait une faute, tombe et le roi change son ministre» (*De la Monarchie selon la Charte*, cit., V).

237 P. Duvergier De Hauranne, *De la politique extérieure et intérieure de la France*, cit., XCIV. Duvergier refiere una comparación entre la monarquía inglesa y la francesa realizada en el *Times*: «La Constitution française, disait-il, présente avec la Constitution anglaise un contraste évident. C'est à peine si chez nous les qualités personnelles du possesseur héréditaire de la Couronne peuvent influer sur le repos du pays, sur sa prospérité, et surtout sur la conduite de ses affaires au dehors. Le sort de l'Angleterre ne dépend point d'un tel accident, et les trois pouvoirs dont se compose la législature britannique ont, avec le temps, fondé et consolidé un système en vertu duquel il devient à peu près indifférent que le Souverain soit un homme d'Etat médiocre ou supérieur. En France, c'est le contraire; tout dans ce noble royaume dépend de la sagesse, de l'habilité, de l'influence personnelle du prince qui gouverne» (XCVIII–XCIX).

El jurista liberal prefigura un régimen parlamentario en el cual el ministerio sea el nexo vivo entre los poderes. «Pour tout dire en un mot, le ministère représente le roi dans l'enceinte des chambres, les chambres dans le cabinet du roi».[238] La elección de los ministros será el resultado del «concurso» de las Cámaras y el rey. Duvergier es probablemente el hombre político que, en el período 1814–1848, demuestra haber comprendido mejor la absoluta necesidad de *condiciones políticas*[239] para el nacimiento y la afirmación durable del régimen representativo de carácter parlamentario. De aquí deriva la insistencia sobre la homogeneidad de una mayoría parlamentaria estable («sistemática») capaz de actuar junta en las grandes decisiones y bajo la guía del verdadero *leader*, dejando aparte, si es necesario, el amor propio y los egoísmos; sobre una oposición también cohesionada; sobre el principio de responsabilidad política correctamente entendido.[240] La reflexión de Duvergier de Hauranne atiende al «deber ser» del régimen parlamentario, pero al mismo tiempo atiende a los problemas estructurales que impiden el pleno desarrollo del sistema parlamentario: el papel del rey logra «cubrir» el poder ejecutivo (favorecido por la ambigüedad de la Carta de 1830) porque la mayoría parlamentaria es débil, dividida, conflictiva.[241]

Paradójicamente son los escritores liberal-conservadores – Fonfrède, Pepin – quienes aciertan con el nudo del problema. Su reconstrucción atiende a los «males» de la representación parlamentaria: la debilidad de los «partidos», el particularismo de los intereses, el «localismo», el transformismo, la unión político-institucional de los diputados-funcionarios y de los pares. El monarca representa el interés general del pueblo, los diputados sólo a los concretos

238 P. Duvergier De Hauranne, *Des principes du gouvernement représentatif*, cit., 15.

239 «Le gouvernement représentatif n'existe véritablement qu'à trois conditions: 1° Que la couronne, couverte par un ministère *qui gouverne*, reste toujours dans la haute sphère où la constitution l'a placée; 2° Que la Chambre élective, indépendante et jalouse de sa prérogative, soit, en fait comme en droit, le centre réel du gouvernement et le pouvoir prépondérant; 3° Que les élections soient libres et pures, et qu'elles produisent ainsi une assemblée qui représente, dans de justes proportions, les droits, les intérêts, les opinions du pays. Hors de ce trois conditions, on peut avoir l'apparence du gouvernement représentatif; on n'en a pas la réalité» (P. Duvergier De Hauranne, *De la réforme parlementaire et de la réforme électorale*, Paris 1847, 2 ed., 249).

240 «Dès lors, il est bien évident que, de gré ou de force, et sauf le droit de dissolution, tout ministère doit se retirer lorsqu'il perd la majorité, c'est-à-dire lorsque la majorité se prononce, non contre quelques-uns de ses actes, mais contre leur ensemble; non contre telle ou telle loi, mais contre l'esprit général qui préside à la marche des affaires» (P. Duvergier De Hauranne, *Des principes du gouvernement représentatif*, cit., 12).

241 Como la lucha política de la *coalición* pone de manifiesto. *Cfr.* L. Girard, W. Serman, E. Cadet, R. Gossez, *La Chambre des députés en 1837–1839. Composition, activité, vocabulaire*, Paris 1976.

colegios electorales. Emerge – como ha sido observado – un régimen de equilibrio de los poderes, pero de ejecutivo monárquico,[242] en la convicción de que la estrecha relación entre monarca y gobierno (afirmado en el *texto* de la Carta) deba contrastar – también en funciones conservadoras – la pretensión de la Cámara electiva de «absorber» el poder ejecutivo y de asumir una posición de preponderancia en contradicción con el principio del «concurso» y del equilibrio de los poderes. Estas consideraciones ilustran las razones de fondo de la falta de afirmación de un auténtico régimen parlamentario durante el reino de Luis-Felipe. Los juristas como Rossi, Foucart, Serrigny, no acudieron al camino del «deber ser» del régimen parlamentario, sino que buscaron adaptar la realidad a un modelo de monarquía representativa que, apoyada sobre los frágiles fundamentos de la *soberanía nacional*, no desea modificar las *condiciones políticas*, sobre todo el régimen electoral y, con él, la forma de la representación.[243] Se ceba, así, un peligroso círculo vicioso: el particularismo de los intereses es cultivado por el ministerio (que en los años Cuarenta se identifica más con la «persona política» del rey) que usa la influencia administrativa para condicionar el principio electoral y tal uso condiciona a su vez al ministerio. «Le ministère, qui ne reçoit point la règle, la fait, et la fait à l'aide de la majorité. La majorité change alors de caractère; elle n'exprime plus le droit; elle le constitue; elle n'est plus un signe, mais un criterium. On n'a pas la majorité parce qu'on a raison; on a raison parce qu'on a la majorité. La majorité étant un chiffre cabalistique avec le quel tout est légitime, l'important n'est pas de la mériter, mais de la conquérir; on ne la recherche pas par l'opinion publique, on l'achète ...».[244]

Luis-Felipe trató de reforzar el régimen parlamentario sobre el terreno de la *práctica política*, consciente de la debilidad del principio monárquico desde el punto de vista de la legitimidad. El rey de los Franceses se afanó en devolver autoridad al trono con un sistema dualista que para funcionar necesitaba de la colaboración de los poderes del Estado, comenzando por el principio electivo. «Je tentais de reconstituer l'Autorité. Si j'avais pu le faire, j'aurais

242 A. Laquièze, *Les origines du régime parlementaire en France*, cit., t. 1, *passim*.

243 Todavía es la reflexión de P. Duvergier De Hauranne, *De la réforme parlementaire et de la réforme électorale*, cit., la que aprecia con mayor lucidez el dilema de la Monarquía de Julio: o se procede por la vía de las reformas (parlamentaria, administrativa, electoral), que permitirían hacer vivir a un régimen representativo, o se arriesga al decaimiento y la crisis.

244 Ch. Hello, *Du régime constitutionnel*, cit., t. II, 327–328. «Dans le gouvernement représentatif normal, le ministère et l'Etat sont choses très-distinctes, qui peuvent se séparer, qui se séparent; l'un passe, l'autre reste, et tout est dans l'ordre. Mais le ministère qui fait la règle ne se distingue point de l'Etat; il le résume en lui, il se l'assimile; l'Etat, c'est lui. Aussi n'est-il-rien qu'il n'immole à sa propre conservation. Toute réaction du dehors sur lui est un désordre ...» (ibidem, 328).

renoué la chaîne des temps qu'une terrible secousse venait de rompre. J'ai essayé ...».[245]

Al final, la *raison* no podrá nada contra la *force*.[246] El derecho no podrá hacer nada contra aquel elemento *político* que se quería neutralizar: la soberanía popular, el sufragio universal, la democracia, la revolución ... La tensión suma del siglo hará valer sus derechos. El «... procédé naturel pour extraire du sein de la société la raison publique, qui seule a droit de la gouverner» no podrá nada contra la «máquina aritmética».[247] «La maladie dont mourut le gouvernement de juillet fut de même si légère, qu'il faut admettre que sa constitution était des plus chétives ... Comment, avec toutes les apparences de la santé, le gouvernement de juillet se trouva-t-il faible? C'est qu'il n'avait pas ce qui donne à un gouvernement de bons poumons, un cœur vigoureux, de solides viscères; je veux dire la sérieuse adhésion des parties résistantes du pays».[248] La monarquía de Julio – como se comprendió a menudo en la teoría y en la dinámica de los sistemas constitucionales[249] – había escuchado más a las exigencias del pasado que a los dilemas del porvenir, condenándose a la caída.

10. La revolución belga de 1830

Las jornadas insurreccionales de septiembre de 1830, las barricadas del Parc de Bruselas, se han puesto a menudo en «correspondencia» con las Gloriosas

245 *Abdication du roi Louis-Philippe racontée par lui-même et recueillie par M. Edouard Lemoine*, Paris 1851, 88.

246 Chateaubriand, en un célebre discurso a la Cámara de los Pares el 7 de agosto de 1830 dice: «Très bien: vous proclamez la souveraineté de la force. Alors gardez soigneusement cette force: car si dans quelques mois elle vous échappe, vous serez mal venus à vous plaindre. Telle est la nature humaine! Les esprits les plus éclairés et les plus justes ne s'élèvent pas toujours au-dessus d'un succès. Ils étaient les premiers, ces esprits, à invoquer le droit contre la violence; ils appuyaient ce droit de toute la supériorité de leur talent, et au moment méme où la vérité de ce qu'ils disaient est démontrée par l'abus le plus abominable de la force, et par le renversement de cette force, les vainqueurs s'emparent de l'arme qu'ils ont brisée!».

247 F. Guizot, *Histoire des origines du gouvernement représentatif en Europe*, Paris 1851, t. 2, 150. «Le problème est évidemment de recueillir partout, dans la société, les fragments épars et incomplets de ce pouvoir, de les concentrer et de les constituer en gouvernement. En d'autres termes, il s'agit de découvrir tous les éléments du pouvoir légitime disséminés dans la société, et de les organiser en pouvoir de fait, c'est-à-dire de concentrer, de réaliser la raison publique, la morale publique, et de les appeler au pouvoir. Ce qu'on appelle la *représentation* n'est autre chose que le moyen d'arriver à ce résultat» (*ibídem*).

248 E. Renan, *La monarchie constitutionnelle en France*, cit., 264–265. *Cfr.* A. Jardin, *La chute du régime de Juillet*, en *François Guizot et la culture politique*, cit., 203–217.

249 O. Duhamel, *Histoire constitutionnelle de la France*, Paris 1995, 51.

jornadas del julio parisino, generando un equívoco también de naturaleza constitucional que ha provocado que se repitiera por mucho tiempo la *vulgata* de una «natural» filiación de la constitución belga de 1831 respecto de la *Charte* de 1830. Como ya se ha observado, tal derivación es más derivada de razones aparentes y extrínsecas que por caracteres sustanciales. Esto no quiere decir que las dos constituciones pertenezcan a un distinto *género*, sin embargo las diferencias son relevantes y destinadas a trazar recorridos peculiares. No se trata, por tanto, de dos constituciones y de una sola «etapa». Si acaso los textos y la práctica constitucional revelan algunos puntos de contacto, algunas «parentelas», derivadas de antiguas familiaridades históricas y culturales más que de la proximidad cronológica de los eventos. El carácter exterior de la monarquía «electiva», el léxico del «gobierno parlamentario», el sistema electoral censitario, las condiciones socio-económicas aproximan las dos experiencias, pero se deberá andar más allá de todo ello para tratar de aprehender los elementos que realmente caracterizan al «modelo belga de constitución».

La Revolución de agosto-septiembre de 1830 es importante sobre el plano del cumplimiento «político» del proceso de independencia, pero el episodio no parece que deba sobrevalorarse. Las premisas y las condiciones históricas requieren dar algún paso atrás. Los territorios belgas viven ya desde hace algunos decenios una difícil transición: de un lado, el antiguo régimen de clases y de los *Standen* privilegiados que fundan las propias razones de supremacía sobre una base social y económica de fuerte componente inmobiliario y sobre la estrecha unión con un clero tradicionalmente influyente; de otro lado, divisamos nuevos «modelos» de organización de la sociedad que hallan en una compuesta y rampante burguesía su elemento principal. La aceleración del ya fuerte desarrollo industrial contribuye – favorecido por la política de Guillermo I – a robustecer a una clase dirigente burguesa que sin embargo permanece ligada a formas y concepciones de tipo «superior» y aristocrático. Se puede decir que es la pequeña y la media burguesía la más «preparada» para guiar el movimiento político de independencia y de reforma constitucional, ya que está formada en gran parte por intelectuales, profesores, periodistas, funcionarios y comerciantes que sienten el peso de la «exclusión» política y que se hallan en posición sobre todo de elaborar un programa político-ideológico con fundamentos liberal-democráticos y valor constitucional (las libertades fundamentales, la autonomía política, el régimen parlamentario, las autonomías locales, etc.).[250]

Sin embargo, sólo la convergencia de múltiples intereses consigue alcanzar un objetivo que se ha ido definiendo poco a poco en el curso de la Restauración.

250 *Cfr.* E. Witte, J. Craeybeckx, *La Belgique politique de 1830 à nos jours. Les tensions d'une démocratie bourgeoise*, Bruxelles 1987, 3 ss.

La reunión política del Norte (Países Bajos) y de las provincias belgas bajo el reino de Guillermo I de Orange-Nassau – decidida en Viena y en función antifrancesa – afirma la forma de una anexión, dando vida de hecho a una subordinación de Bélgica a Holanda. El reino se regía por una Ley Fundamental (*Grondwet*) del 24 de agosto de 1815 que tenía sus orígenes en la constitución holandesa del 29 de marzo de 1814, no por cierto privada de elementos liberales,[251] pero con evidentes raíces en el constitucionalismo de clases del antiguo régimen.[252] La constitución había sido «concordada» por una comisión mixta (protestantes / católicos) pero conservó en sustancia los caracteres de aquella *octroyée* de 1814. A pesar de que después fue rechazada por una fuerte mayoría (796 votos contra 527) de los delegados belgas en los Estados Generales, fue igualmente promulgada por el monarca, que consideró las ausencias como favorables a la constitución ... El dualismo, en lo demás, estaba en la realidad de las cosas: protestante Holanda, católica Bélgica, más agrícola la primera, ya más industrial la segunda. La fractura entre los holandeses y los belgas, en el curso de los años Veinte, se amplió más que recomponerse, revelando así el carácter veleidoso de la «amalgama» entre los dos pueblos.[253] Una administración de absoluta preeminencia holandesa (en un reino de mayoría belga), el uso obligatorio de la lengua neerlandesa, las disposiciones, desde 1816, limitativas de la libertad de imprenta y más en general la política autoritaria de Guillermo I[254] favorecieron la formación de un movimiento político cada vez más interesado en la independencia. La radicalización permitió a los grupos políticamente más activos y conscientes de su propio papel influir de manera creciente en la opinión pública.

Entre 1828 y 1829 la alianza «monstruosa» (como la definieron algunos) entre los católicos y liberales refuerza las reivindicaciones belgas que revelan más concreción y apoyo popular. Uno de los principales exponentes políticos del

251 La ley fundamental contenía disposiciones de carácter liberal en relación con la imprenta, libertades individuales, inviolabilidad del domicilio, inamovilidad de los jueces, derecho de petición, autonomía local. Sobre este último asunto *cfr.* S. Mannoni, *L'autonomia locale in Belgio: dalle riforme giuseppine (1787) alle leggi del 1836*, en *Storia amministrazione costituzione*, 3, 1995, 87–112. Más en general, *vid.* L. Hymans, *Histoire politique et parlementaire de la Belgique de 1814–1830*, Bruxelles 1869, 76 ss. y 200 ss. Sobre la inadecuación política de la *Grondwet* respecto a las reivindicaciones de los Belgas, *vid.* H. Pirenne, *Histoire de Belgique des origines à nos jours*, s. l., 1974, t. IV, 236–237.

252 Los *Etats généraux* estaban integrados por dos cámaras, una de miembros vitalicios elegidos por el soberano, y otra de diputados de los Estados provinciales.

253 *Cfr.* H. Pirenne, *Histoire de Belgique des origines à nos jours*, cit., t. IV, 233 ss., 267–269.

254 Para un rápido retrato de Guillermo *cfr. ibídem*, 241 ss.

movimiento, Louis De Potter, lanza, junto con otros, el programa decisivo, la unión de los católicos y liberales en función nacional. El régimen constitucional se invoca como fundamento de la libertad y de los poderes públicos.[255] El problema religioso ocupa un puesto importante en el proceso político-constitucional en Bélgica, y representa por tanto uno de los caracteres fundadores de la «nacionalidad» y capaz de influir sobre el desarrollo de la vida política y social. La alianza entre católicos y liberales reviste naturaleza estratégica pero tampoco se halla privada de perfiles tácticos: el primer objetivo es la independencia y una constitución compartida; serán después la lucha política, el activismo, la radicalización popular los que determinen las reales relaciones de fuerza.

El 4 de octubre de 1830[256] el gobierno provisional estableció que las provincias de Bélgica deseaban formar un Estado independiente y que el comité central debía ocuparse de inmediato en realizar un proyecto de constitución que debía someterse a un Congreso nacional. El Comité Central, el 6 de octubre de 1830, nombró una *Commission de Constitution*. El 10 de octubre el gobierno provisional fijó los criterios para ser elegido miembro del Congreso nacional. El sistema censitario (electores con al menos 25 años y cuota de contribución fijada en las distintas localidades) aparecía «moderado» por las «capacidades»:[257] se lograba así un primer compromiso entre conservadores y grupos profesionales de la clase media liberal preludio de un más general *modus vivendi* dentro de la asamblea constituyente. El éxito de la votación hizo nacer un Congreso en el cual las fuerzas conservadoras y moderadas eran más numerosas que las democráticas y progresistas, que habían desempeñado un papel de primer plano durante la revolución. El carácter burgués moderado caracterizó las aspiraciones y los trabajos del Congreso nacional hasta la redacción de la carta constitucional.

Las primeras reformas constitucionales fueron esbozadas por el gobierno provisorio que desempeñó una importante función de «dirección»: basta pensar en las resoluciones en materia judicial, en la institución de la guardia cívica, en la libertad de culto, de imprenta, de asociación. En este contexto se introduce la opción tomada en la comisión constituyente en favor de la forma monárquica (8 votos contra 1). El 16 de octubre la Comisión encargó a los abogados Paul Devaux y Jean-Baptiste Nothomb redactar un proyecto según las bases por ella establecidas. El 10 de noviembre los diputados se reunieron en Bruselas.[258] Entre

255 L. De Potter, *Lettre de Démophile au roi sur le nouveau projet de loi contre la presse et le message royal qui l'accompagne*, Bruxelles 1829.

256 Sobre las vicisitudes constitucionales, *cfr.* E. Vandenpeereboom, *Du gouvernement représentatif en Belgique*, cit., t. I, XIV–XV; Th. Juste, *Le Congrès National de Belgique*, cit.

257 Los diputados del Congreso nacional fueron elegidos por sufragio directo, accediendo a las urnas unos 38.000 electores por censo y 7.500 por capacidad.

258 El Congreso nacional se reunió el 21 de julio de 1831.

las primeras decisiones se tomaron la relativa a la independencia del pueblo belga (18 de noviembre) y la confirmación de la forma monárquica. Si existía un fuerte consenso en contener los peligros «absolutistas»[259] ínsitos a tal forma de gobierno, no en menor medida la monarquía constitucional hereditaria aparecía como la elección obligada capaz de asegurar estabilidad y equilibrio. La revolución – se dijo – se había hecho, no contra la monarquía, sino contra los abusos, las humillaciones padecidas.[260] La solución republicana, aun teniendo un grupo de partidarios en el Congreso, conquistó finalmente sólo unos pocos votos frente a la mayoría aplastante favorable a la monarquía.

Elegida la forma monárquica, era preciso designar un rey. El nacimiento del nuevo Estado no se había producido sin las aprensiones y la atención constante de las grandes potencias europeas. El conflicto entre Bélgica y los Países Bajos ponía en discusión el equilibrio sancionado en el Congreso de Viena y la revolución había suscitado no pocas alarmas después de que ya Francia se había revelado contra Carlos X. La revolución belga de 1830 debe, sin embargo, encuadrarse dentro de los grandes juegos diplomáticos y militares, hechos de alianzas e intereses contrapuestos, que tendrían una influencia decisiva en la elección del Congreso nacional y de los primeros gobiernos.[261] «La Belgique offrait un spectacle jusqu'alors unique dans les annales de l'Europe moderne. L'assemblée nationale, dépositaire de la souveraineté populaire, allait briser les traditions de la légitimité et nommer au scrutin le chef de l'Etat, après avoir discuté publiquement ses titres ...».[262] La elección, contra la voluntad de las potencias aliadas y de la misma Francia, cae sobre el duque de Nemours,[263] hijo de Luis-Felipe. El 21 de febrero de 1831, el Congreso recibió la noticia oficial de la negativa por parte de los Orléans. La política internacional, que no podía tolerar una Bélgica tan manifiestamente «ligada» a Francia – debido a la amenaza de una guerra – se llevó la mejor parte con la determinación del Congreso. Era necesario dirigir la mirada a otro lugar para buscar un príncipe «disponible» y en situación de mantener en equilibrio los intereses en conflicto de las potencias de la Europa central, de Francia y de Inglaterra.

259 *Cfr.* J. Lebeau, *Observation sur le pouvoir royal, ou examen de quelques questions relatives aux droits de la couronne dans les Pays-Bas*, Bruxelles 1830.

260 Th. Juste, *Le Congrès National de Belgique*, cit., 123.

261 *Cfr.* H. Pirenne, *L'Europe et l'indépendance belge (1830–1839)*, Bruxelles 1990.

262 Th. Juste, *Le Congrès National de Belgique*, cit., 238.

263 En el primer escrutinio el duque de Nemours obtuvo 91 votos, 67 el duque de Leuchtenberg 35 el archiduque Carlos de Austria. Ningún candidato obtiene la mayoría de 101 votos. Se procedió al segundo escritinio en el que participaron 192 diputados. Con 97 votos de Nemours, se convierte en el potencial rey de Bélgica. Sobre las relaciones franco-belgas, entre 1830 y 1831, *cfr.* la síntesis de G. Antonetti, *Louis-Philippe*, cit., 621 ss. y 662 ss.

La desilusión fue grande y se vio la necesidad de elegir un regente, haciendo entran en vigor rápidamente la constitución. El anciano barón Surlet de Chokier, un personaje ya de relieve de la dirección política belga, fue elegido regente. El 7 de febrero de 1831, la constitución se votó por entero y se aprobó por unanimidad. Sin embargo, será necesario esperar el junio siguiente para que el voto favorable del Congreso haga de Leopoldo de Sajonia-Coburgo[264] el rey de los Belgas. Príncipe perteneciente al ramo católico de una numerosa familia alemana, emparentado con la realeza inglesa y apoyado en la trabada red de alianzas dinásticas,[265] estimado por su capacidad política y por su conocimiento del régimen parlamentario (inglés), parecía el sujeto más idóneo para subir al trono belga.

La independencia, la constitución, el rey. «Cette constitution, après avoir d'abord surpris et inquiété l'Europe, devait quelques années plus tard lui servir d'enseignement et quelquefois même de modèle».[266]

11. La constitución de 1831 y el régimen parlamentario en Bélgica

El perfil de «ambigüedad» que acompaña a la elaboración de la *Charte* francesa de 1830 y que deriva de la falta de solución al problema de la legitimidad y del ejercicio de la soberanía política[267] no se encuentra en los albores de la experiencia belga.[268] De hecho, la cuestión del poder constituyente se halla claramente resuelta en favor de una asamblea, el Congreso nacional, expresamente elegida para examinar, enmendar y aprobar la constitución. No hay un sujeto político identificable en la persona de un monarca (o de un aspirante soberano) que haya actuado para influir en la dinámica constitucional, si bien desde el inicio ha sido fuerte la determinación de conservar el principio monárquico. El Congreso *hace* la constitución y sólo después opta por elegir al monarca.[269] La constitución es inequívocamente el origen y la fuente de los

264 Leopoldo se había casado en 1816 con Charlotte, heredera al trono de Inglaterra y que falleció en 1817 dejando una heredera femenina. En 1830 fue proclamado rey de Grecia pero dimite rápido ante las fuertes oposiciones.

265 Hay que señalar que Leopoldo contraerá matrimonio en 1833 con la hermana del duque de Nemours, estableciendo entonces una relación de "alianza" dinástica también con la Francia orleanista.

266 Th. Juste, *Le Congrès National de Belgique*, cit., 295–296.

267 *Cfr. supra*, § 7.

268 «... c'est avec l'Angleterre, le pays où les faits correspondent le mieux avec l'idée, le fond avec la forme, les principes avec leur application» (V. Du Bled, *Histoire de la Monarchie de Juillet de 1830 à 1848 avec une introduction sur le droit constitutionnel aux Etats-Unis, en Suisse, en Angleterre et en Belgique*, Paris 1877, t. I, XCV).

269 «Quand l'assemblée constituante de 1830 reçut la haute et dangereuse mission de fixer l'organisation politique du pays, le trône était vide et le peuple, rentré dans

poderes públicos. «Tous les pouvoirs – expresa el célebre artículo 25, emulando la constitución francesa de 1791 – émanent de la nation. Ils sont exercés de la manière établie par la Constitution».[270]

«Novateur parce qu'il était prévoyant, le Congrès belge eut la gloire de décréter le premier, sur le continent, la séparation complète de la société religieuse et de la société civile, en même temps qu'il consacrait l'alliance intime du principe monarchique avec la liberté républicaine».[271] La independencia nacional había hallado, como se ha dicho, en la difícil alianza entre el catolicismo liberal y el liberalismo político la piedra angular y la base para un innovador proyecto constitucional que, aun derivando algunos principios e instituciones de la Ley fundamental de 1815, del constitucionalismo francés (las constituciones de 1791 y 1830 en particular), y del derecho público inglés, alcanzaba al final una solución ponderada y original.[272] Justamente en aquella alianza podemos divisar el ideal de «pacto constitucional» entre las dos «familias» políticas principales de la historia de la Bélgica moderna y la característica fundamental del «modelo belga». La influencia de Lamennais y del catolicismo liberal profesado por *L'Avenir* no dejó de hacerse sentir durante los trabajos del Congreso nacional para afirmar la libertad de conciencia y de culto que encontrarán en el texto constitucional plena afirmación hasta el punto de establecer la independencia de la Iglesia y su completa separación del Estado.[273] La libertad de cultos estaba estrechamente ligada a la libertad de pensamiento (art. 14) remachando el común carácter «liberal-constitucional» y la voluntad de superar el régimen mucho más restrictivo de la Ley fundamental de 1815 y el principio de sujeción de la Iglesia al Estado (con el consiguiente sometimiento del ejercicio público del culto a los reglamentos de policía)

la plénitude de ses droits, pouvait librement disposer de ses destinées. Le Congrès national n'hésita pas à admettre et à proclamer que la souveraineté réside dans la nation belge» (J.-J. Thonissen, *La constitution belge annotée offrant sous chaque article l'état de la doctrine, de la jurisprudence et de la législation*, Bruxelles 1879, 3 ed., 110). El 22 de noviembre de 1830, el Congresso se había expresado a favor de una forma de gobierno basada en la monarquía constitucional hereditaria.

270 El artículo 130 establece: «La Constitution ne peut être suspendue en tout ni en partie».

271 Th. Juste, *Le Congrès National de Belgique*, cit., 295.

272 *Cfr.* E. Descamps, *La constitution belge comparée aux sources modernes et aux anciennes constitutions nationales*, Bruxelles 1887; Íd., *La mosaïque constitutionnelle. Essai sur les sources du texte de la constitution belge*, Louvain 1892.

273 Th. Juste, *Le Congrès National de Belgique*, cit., 327 ss. Los principios fundamentales los establecen los artículos 14, 15 y 16. Sobre la discusión en sede constituyente *vid.* E. Huyttens, *Discussions du Congrès National de Belgique, 1830–1831*, cit., t. I, 525 ss.; J.-J. Thonissen, *La constitution belge*, cit., 44 ss.

establecido por los artículos orgánicos de la ley del 18 germinal del año X, restablecidos en vigor por Guillermo I en 1816.

Una vez afirmado por el artículo 14 el principio-guía (la libertad de manifestar las opiniones, excluyendo cualquier intervención previa dirigida a limitar su capacidad), surgieron después los corolarios de la libertad de enseñanza (art. 17), de imprenta (art. 18), de reunión (art. 19) y de asociación (art. 20).[274] Las libertades primarias – junto a la fundamental de la libertad individual (art. 7) – se presentan como la condición necesaria para dar vida a un robusto régimen parlamentario. «Il fallait considérer la liberté de la presse comme la clef de voûte de l'édifice constitutionnel, parce qu'elle protège et sauvegarde toutes les autres libertés».[275] En definitiva, basta confrontar el título de la constitución dedicado a los derechos de los Belgas o al poder judicial (en particular el tema de jurisdicción judicial de los derechos civiles y de los derechos políticos, arts. 92 y 93) con las secciones correspondientes de las Cartas francesas o del Estatuto albertino[276] para darse cuenta en seguida de la mayor plenitud de la disciplina constitucional y del carácter decididamente liberal de las disposiciones.[277] En este sentido, la constitución belga establece verdaderamente las premisas para una «íntima alianza entre el principio monárquico y la libertad republicana». Alcanza el éxito allí donde la *Charte* de 1830 ha fallado. Como se ha observado, las premisas histórico-políticas pueden engañar mostrando algunas analogías. En realidad, ya en los respectivos textos constitucionales es posible apreciar las condiciones que favorecen el menor desarrollo del discurso constitucional (comenzando justamente por la disciplina de los derechos y libertades).[278]

274 *Cfr.* E. Huyttens, *Discussions du Congrès National de Belgique, 1830–1831*, cit., t. I, 575 ss.; J.-J. Thonissen, *La constitution belge*, cit.

275 Th. Juste, *Le Congrès National de Belgique*, cit., 363.

276 Naturalmente la comparación podría hacerse con todas las constituciones europeas del siglo XIX.

277 «Le Congrès national de 1831 prit pour mot d'ordre cette généreuse devise: *Liberté en tout et pour tous*. Il consacra de la manière la plus nette et la plus audacieuse ces quatre libertés *cardinales* qui n'existent chez aucun peuple européen à un degré aussi illimité: liberté de la presse, liberté des cultes, liberté de l'enseignement, liberté d'association. C'est là le côté le plus original, le plus extraordinaire de cette constitution de 1831, votée dans un pays en voie de formation, au lendemain d'une révolution …» (V. Du Bled, *Histoire de la Monarchie de Juillet de 1830*, cit., XCVII).

278 «Si se quiere sin embargo comparar este Estatuto con el que los franceses impusieron a la Monarquía de Julio, se verá hasta qué punto la obra flamenca supera con mucho a la francesa. Los Belgas, proclamando con el artículo 18 la absoluta libertad de imprenta, libran de toda caución a los escritores y editores. El Estatuto francés no excluye la caución, y la ley obliga a este deber. Los Flamencos tienen derecho de reunión. Los Franceses están despojados de tal derecho, y las antiguas leyes penales sobre esta materia permanecen en vigor.

También la constitución belga establece en el artículo 139 una serie de materias que deberán, en el menor plazo de tiempo posible, convertirse en objeto de leyes orgánicas (imprenta, jurado, finanzas, organización provincial y comunal, responsabilidad de los ministros y agentes del poder público, organización judicial, etc.), pero la mayor coherencia y capacidad de «dirección política» que se aprecian ya en el texto representan una garantía segura para el desarrollo del sistema constitucional.

Si a continuación se dirige la mirada hacia la organización de los poderes, la peculiaridad del modelo belga sólo podrá resaltarse también. El artículo 25 asigna a las tres funciones constitucionales una plena sincronización de origen. Ninguna de ellas, emanando con un idéntico título de la nación, puede alegar derechos anteriores o superiores a la constitución, ni puede arrogarse un derecho de imperio o de control sobre los restantes.[279] El poder legislativo lo ejercen conjuntamente el rey, la Cámara de representantes y el Senado (art. 26), correspondiéndole a cualquiera de ellos el derecho de iniciativa, termina estableciendo la precedencia de la Cámara en el examen de materias presupuestarias y del contingente del ejército (art. 27).[280] Estas normas – y las sucesivas

En Francia el poder ejecutivo corresponde sólo al rey. En Bélgica (411) el rey, en virtud del artículo 78, no tiene otros poderes que aquellos que le confiere formalmente la Constitución. Del rey francés emana toda la justicia, y se distribuye en su nombre por jueces que él elige. En Bélgica, por el artículo 25, todos los poderes emanan del pueblo, y al rey no se le concede más que el derecho de nombrar los jueces de paz y los de primera instancia. En Francia el Parlamento no puede congregarse más que por orden del príncipe. En Bélgica se reúne todos los años de pleno derecho el segundo martes de noviembre, según el artículo 70. El Estatuto francés establece la edad de trenta años para resultar elegible, y prescribe un censo para los diputados. El Flamenco exige a través del artículo 50 la edad de venticinco, y no impone ningún censo. El Francés otorga al rey el derecho de nombrar pares, y determina que serán vitalicios y en número ilimitado. El Flamenco sujeta a los senadores a elección popular y restringe su número a la mitad de los diputados. El Francés, en las disposiciones de ordenamiento municipal y provincial se atiene al principio electivo, pero no va más allá de las diposiciones generales. El Flamenco, en el artículo 108, determina las condiciones y establece: la elección directa; la publicidad de los cargos; la de las cuentas y rentas; y el derecho exclusivo de los Consejos comunales y provinciales sobre los intereses del municipio y la provincia ...». (C. Gemelli, *Storia della rivoluzione belgica dell'anno 1830*, Bologna 1867, 2 ed., 410–411).

279 J.-B. Bivort, *Commentaire sur la Constitution belge*, Bruxelles 1858, 15; J.-J. Thonissen, *La constitution belge*, cit., 113.

280 «Un principe fondamental et propre à maintenir chaque branche du pouvoir législatif dans bornes naturelles, c'est que *la connaissance première* des lois les plus importantes, pour le bien-être matériel du pays, doit appartenir à la partie de la législature qui représente plus spécialement le mouvement; et *le contrôle* en être réservé à la partie conservatrice: tel est le but de l'art. 27 de la Constitution»

determinaciones constitucionales – resultan interpretadas según la lógica propia del equilibrio y de la colaboración necesarias para la monarquía constitucional: los poderes deben conciliar sus derechos respectivos, moderar las pretensiones recíprocas. Según la figuración tradicional, cada sujeto representa principalmente un *elemento*: el monárquico, el conservador (el Senado), el elemento popular (la Cámara de representantes).

La constitución afirma el principio de la monarquía hereditaria, de la que organiza y disciplina los delicados aspectos referentes a la sucesión y al instituto de la regencia (arts. 60–62, 79–85). Al monarca se le atribuye formalmente el poder ejecutivo, pero con los límites establecidos por la constitución (art. 29). En efecto, las condiciones históricas que han llevado a la configuración del texto de 1831 favorecen una solución que permite insertar la monarquía en el espacio tradicionalmente «hostil» de la soberanía nacional, mostrando al mismo tiempo la posibilidad de alcanzar un compromiso aceptable sobre el plano de la organización política liberal-burguesa. Los constituyentes – arrinconada la opción republicana – se dieron cuenta de la necesidad de asignar al monarca el poder ejecutivo pero, al mismo tiempo, coherentemente con el principio establecido por el artículo 25, quisieron afirmar repetidamente (y, si puede decir, a través de todo el *sistema* de normas constitucionales) la naturaleza del monarca como *poder constituido*. La constitución nace de la voluntad de la nación y el monarca – que significativamente será elegido[281] sólo en un segundo momento – acepta plenamente todas las consecuencias no siendo ni poder constituyente ni parte del pacto constitucional. La constitución belga da vida a un tipo de monarquía constitucional[282] fundada exclusivamente sobre el principio de la soberanía nacional y derivada de ella. «Les pouvoirs du roi sont tellement limités, que, à part l'hérédité et le droit de faire grâce, ainsi que de conférer des titres de noblesse, cette partie de notre pacte fondamental aurait pu s'appliquer, sans

(Tielemans, *Répertoire de l'administration*, *Amendement*, t. II, 181, cit. da E. Vandenpeereboom, *Du gouvernement représentatif en Belgique*, cit., t. I, 33).

281 Sobre la interferencia de la elección en el desarrollo dinástico de las monarquías «constitucionales», *vid.* Ph. Lauvaux, *Les monarchies: inventaire des types*, en *Pouvoirs*, 78, 1996, 26 ss.

282 Sobre el tipo de monarquía constitucional nacida en Bélgica en 1831, sobretodo en relación al llamado *monarchische Prinzip* de la tradición prusiana, *cfr.* R. Smend, *Die Preussische Verfassungsurkunde im Vergleich mit der Belgischen*, Göttingen 1904; P. Errera, *Das Staatsrecht des Königsreichs Belgien*, Tübingen 1909; O. Hintze, *Das monarchische Prinzip und die konstitutionelle Verfassung*, en *Preussische Jahrbücher*, 144, 1911, 381–412; *Beiträge zur deutschen und belgischen Verfassungsgeschichte im 19. Jahrhundert*, editado por W. Conze, Stuttgart 1967; E. W. Böckenförde, *Der deutsche Typ der konstitutionellen Monarchie im 19. Jahrhundert* (1967), en *Staat, Gesellschaft und Freiheit. Studien zur Staatstheorie und zum Verfassungsrecht*, Frankfurt am Main 1976, 112–145.

changement, au président d'une République. C'est ce qui a fait dire, avec raison, que nous vivons sous un régime démocratique, avec un chef héréditaire; plutôt sous une république royale que sous une monarchie républicaine», comme le disait M. Le Hon ...».[283] La limitación del poder regio se ve como una de las condiciones fundamentales de la monarquía constitucional belga, y, en particular, como el perfil que garantiza a la monarquía un carácter «essentiellement modérateur».[284] El rey puede, por tanto, ejercer sólo las prerrogativas que le son formalmente atribuidas por la constitución y las leyes particulares aprobadas en ejecución del texto de 1831 (art. 78). El examen de la constitución revela un poder regio «moderador» pero, sobre todo, un poder que primero viene sistemáticamente limitado por la intervención de las Cámaras y por la reserva de ley. La figura del monarca, si no coincide – como ha menudo se ha observado – con la de un «primer funcionario del Estado», está sin duda sujeta a un fuerte «adelgazamiento» bajo el perfil de las prerrogativas formales.

El rey tiene derecho a convocar, prorrogar y disolver las Cámaras (arts. 70–72), pero la constitución prevé que las Cámaras se reúnan «de plein droit» todos los años el segundo martes de noviembre, a menos que el soberano no las haya convocado anteriormente (art. 70). Las Cámaras deben reunirse durante al menos cuarenta días al año. El rey puede prorrogar las Cámaras, sin embargo tal acto no puede exceder el término de un mes, ni renovarse en la misma sesión sin el consentimiento del parlamento (art. 72). El monarca sanciona y promulga las leyes (art. 69), tiene el mando del ejército, declara la guerra, negocia los tratados de paz, alianza y comercio (art. 68). Investido con el poder ejecutivo, el rey se halla consiguientemente dotado de tales prerrogativas. «La puissance et l'influence que ce commandement lui procure ne sont pas à redouter dans un pays qui possède des institutions parlementaires largement organisées. La responsabilité ministérielle, jointe au vote annuel des impôts et du contingent militaire, suffit pour écarter tous les périls qu'on pourrait justement redouter sous le régime du pouvoir absolu».[285] Si el poder regio es el centro de todas las relaciones exteriores, sin embargo los tratados de comercio deben recibir el asentimiento de la asamblea cuando puedan perjudicar al Estado o imponer gravámenes a los ciudadanos belgas.

El rey hace los reglamentos y decretos necesarios para la ejecución de las leyes, pero no puede suspender las leyes ni dispensar su ejecución (art. 67). Esta disposición deriva textualmente del reformado artículo de la Carta orleanista de 1830 (art. 13), pero la constitución belga asegura ulteriores garantías: el art. 107 establece de hecho que las cortes y tribunales no aplicarán los decretos y

283 E. Vandenpeereboom, *Du gouvernement représentatif en Belgique*, cit., t. I, 7.
284 Th. Juste, *Le Congrès National de Belgique*, cit., 394.
285 J.-J. Thonissen, *La constitution belge*, cit., 219.

reglamentos generales, provinciales y locales, más que cuando sean conformes con las leyes; el art. 64 imputa la responsabilidad del acto al ministro que haya refrendado el reglamento o el decreto que viola el artículo 67. Es suficiente con recorrer las normas que regulan la sucesión o el instituto de la regencia, el poder judicial o las instituciones provinciales y comunales para poder de nuevo comprobar cómo la monarquía ha sido constantemente concebida en relación con el parlamento y la intervención limitativa de la ley.

Es significativo que en la constitución de Bélgica, a diferencia de las Cartas francesas, las secciones dedicadas al parlamento precedan a la relativa a las prerrogativas regias. En la dinámica constitucional y en el debate constituyente aparece con fuerza la centralidad político-constitucional del parlamento. En todo caso la discusión más encendida se refirió al carácter monocameral o bicameral del parlamento. El debate[286] sobre el establecimiento o no del Senado puso en el campo los argumentos a favor o contrarios que ya habían acompañado la historia del constitucionalismo francés. En particular, los adversarios del

286 *Cfr.* E. Huyttens, *Discussions du Congrès National de Belgique, 1830–1831*, cit., t. I, 393 ss. (por ejemplo, las intervenciones del conde De Celles (cámara única) y del conde de Baillet (segunda cámara), *ibídem*, 393–398) y t. IV, 75–82 (informes de Devaux en nombre de la sección central). Véase también E. Vandenpeereboom, *Du gouvernement représentatif en Belgique*, cit., t. I, 12 ss. e 359: «Le Sénat n'est donc pas et ne peut pas être, à cause de l'infériorité du nombre de ses membres, le contrôleur, le réviseur de toutes les décisions de la Chambre. Il est un corps *modérateur*, chargé de mettre, en certaines circonstances, un obstacle législatif aux dangereux entraînements de la chambre populaire: il doit servir de bouclier au pouvoir royal, contre les périls auxquels celui-ci pourrait être exposé par l'action directe et trop vive d'une assemblée unique. Qu'on nous permette le mot. Le Sénat est comme le ressort de la machine représentative; il rend les secousses moins sensibles, les choses moins brusques. Ses fonctions, pour être passives plutôt qu'actives, n'en sont pas moins salutaires. Mais si le ressort est trop mou, il se fausse: s'il est trop roide, il risque de se briser ... L'utilité, la nécessité constitutionnelle du Sénat reposent sur cette combinaison: avec deux Chambres, le pouvoir royal est plus couvert, sa responsabilité est moins engagée»; Th. Juste, *Le Congrès National de Belgique*, cit., 157 ss., 392–393: «Le Sénat devait avoir la même origine que la Chambre des représentants, c'est-à-dire l'élection directe par le même corps électoral. Mais comme le Sénat était établi pour représenter l'élément aristocratique et conservateur, on exigea de ses membres l'âge de quarante ans et un cens d'éligibilité consistant dans le payement en Belgique de mille florins au moins d'impositions directes; en outre, on refusa tout traitement ou indemnité aux sénateurs. Une autre disposition fixa le nombre des sénateurs à la moitié des députés de l'autre Chambre: cette limitation était la conséquence nécessaire de l'adoption du principe de l'élection directe et la condition première de la représentation réelle de l'aristocratie. Enfin, le mandat des sénateurs reçut une durée double de celle du mandat des membres de l'autre Chambre: cette prolongation se rattachait au caractère même du Sénat, destiné surtout à maintenir la stabilité des institutions».

Senado negaban la utilidad y, sobretodo, lo veían como una Cámara aristocrática en contraste con las premisas y principios fundamentales de la constitución. Si, finalmente, prevalecieron los partidarios de la segunda cámara (128 a 62), no debe sobrestimarse en exceso el significado de esta votación. El Congreso no ha visto en el Senado un modo de organización social fundada sobre la desigualdad de condiciones, una especie de transacción entre la aristocracia y la democracia, no ha querido crear una Cámara alta análoga a la pairía inglesa.[287] «Il a simplement admis le Sénat comme un fait d'organisation politique, un rouage utile à la marche prudente et sûre du pouvoir législatif. Il l'a composé d'éléments propres à assurer à la discussion des lois plus de lenteur, de calme, de modération et de maturité».[288] Previendo un censo de elegibilidad para los senadores (art. 56) no se ha deseado crear una verdadera y auténtica cámara aristocrática asignando al monarca el poder de nombramiento más o menos limitado. Más que el ejemplo inglés, se debe tener presente el americano. «On peut dire des deux Chambres belges ce que Rossi disait des deux Chambres américaines: "Nous avons une Chambre à principes progressifs, l'autre à principes conservateurs, l'une qui a mission de donner l'impulsion, l'autre qui a mission de régler cette impulsion, l'une pousse, l'autre retient dans une juste mesure, et c'est ainsi que par la combinaison de cette double force, la société marche sans courir et que vous réalisez l'idée d'un progrès sage et continu"».[289]

La constitución afirma la inviolabilidad de la persona del rey y la correlativa responsabilidad de los ministros (art. 63). No se hace referencia al carácter «sagrado» del rey – como en las Cartas francesas – pero tiende a subrayarse el carácter racionalizado de la máxima *the King can do no wrong*. La irresponsabilidad del titular del poder ejecutivo se convierte en esencia de todo gobierno constitucional. La imagen que proponen los constituyentes belgas es aquella, de derivación constantiana, de una *royauté* entendida como elemento esencial de la constitución, sujeta al vínculo absoluto de la responsabilidad de los ministros, pero no privada de prerrogativas penetrantes (comenzando por el procedimiento legislativo), personificación de la unidad nacional, capaz de representar la

287 «Messieurs, je ne veux point de la pairie anglaise, point de fidéicommis, point de droit d'aînesse; je ne veux point de la pairie française, point d'hérédité, point de majorats; mais je ne veux pas non plus faire courir à mon pays les dangers d'une chambre unique: je veux un système mixte. Que l'on prenne ce qu'il y a de bon sur l'institution, en France, en Angleterre, en Amérique; que l'on fasse de tout cela un éclectisme politique, en le conciliant avec les intérêts bien entendus de notre pays» (Joseph Lebeau, sesión del 13 dicembre 1830, en E. Huyttens, *Discussions du Congrès National de Belgique, 1830–1831*, cit., t. I, 416).

288 J.-J. Thonissen, *La constitution belge*, cit., 133.

289 *Ibídem*, 134. *Cfr.* P. Rossi, *Cours de droit constitutionnel professé à la Faculté de Droit de Paris* ..., Paris 1867, t. IV, 56.

tradición, la continuidad, la duración. «Institution vivante, elle a été placée par la Constitution dans une sphère supérieure, d'où elle veille sur les mouvements de l'opinion, d'où elle interroge et écoute la pensée des autres grands pouvoirs de l'Etat».[290] Pero la posición de inviolabilidad del rey, «position exceptionnelle au dessus de la région des orages»,[291] no es peligrosa porque el Jefe del Estado no puede realizar ningún acto sin que un ministro asuma la responsabilidad.

Durante el reino de Guillermo I, el principio de la responsabilidad parlamentaria no logró imponerse.[292] La constitución de 1831 trató de resolver el problema, afirmando el principio (art. 63) y previendo la obligación de refrendo ministerial como condición de validez de los actos del rey (art. 64). Tal responsabilidad no puede limitarse o excluirse por una orden del monarca (art. 89). Si la combinación establecida por los artículos 63 y 64 parece poder favorecer una lectura «política» de la responsabilidad ministerial, los artículos 90–91 y 134 sugieren una lectura «penal», con la Cámara de representantes como titular del derecho de acusación y la Corte de casación con el derecho de juicio hasta que una ley defina los casos de responsabilidad, las penas y el procedimiento.[293] Que la constitución de 1831 trató sin embargo de resolver el problema político-parlamentario de la responsabilidad se aprecia también a través de otro indicio: durante el período de vacancia del trono los poderes constitucionales del rey los ejercen «ministres réunis en conseil, et sous leur responsabilité» (art. 79).

Si algunos comentaristas consideran a los ministros ante todo como «ministros del rey» del que reciben fundamentalmente el mandato (art. 65) que será revocado en el momento en que no disfruten más de su confianza,[294] hay que observar cómo se ha ido formando rápidamente la costumbre conforme a la cual

290 J.-B. Bivort, *Commentaire sur la Constitution belge*, cit., 32.

291 Th. Juste, *Le Congrès National de Belgique*, cit., 395.

292 L. Hymans, *Histoire politique et parlementaire de la Belgique de 1814–1830*, cit., 202–203, 214 ss. Ya durante los trabajos de la Comisión mixta belga-holandesa, la introducción de la responsabilidad ministerial – no prevista en la Ley fundamental – había sido objeto de controversia, auspiciada por los comisarios belgas y negada por los holandeses. *Cfr.* O. De Kerchove, *De la responsabilité des ministres. Mémoire couronné*, Gand 1867, 38.

293 Hasta la aprobación de la ley orgánica, la disciplina transitoria del artículo 134 preve que la Cámara electiva tenga un poder discrecional para acusar al ministro, y que la Corte de casación proceda a definir el delito y a fijar la pena, que no podrá sin embargo exceder de la reclusión.

294 «Comme aucun acte du roi ne peut avoir d'effet qu'autant qu'il est contre-signé par un ministre, il est évident que le pouvoir exécutif, en réalité, enlevé au chef de l'Etat, à l'instant même où le libre choix des ministres ne serait plus envisagé comme une partie intégrante de ses attributions» (J.-J. Thonissen, *La constitution belge*, cit., 212).

el rey no puede designar como ministros más que a los hombre a los que el parlamento concede su confianza. Si ésta viene a menos, los ministros deberán dimitir, a menos que el rey haga uso de la facultad de disolver las Cámaras y haga una apelación al pueblo (art. 71). La libre elección de los ministros por parte del rey se ve como una consecuencia necesaria del régimen parlamentario: «Sous un régime franchement constitutionnel, en présence de deux chambres électives, avec la discussion publique de toutes les lois, et une véritable responsabilité ministérielle, le chef de l'Etat est le plus intéressé au bon choix de ses ministres ... L'intérêt personnel du prince est son meilleure garant. Gardons-nous, en cédant à la crainte d'un danger invraisemblable et même chimérique, de frapper d'exclusion temporaire quelques capacités utiles au pays».[295]

Si la intervención personal del monarca – en referencia al poder ejecutivo – está sobretodo sujeta a la disciplina de refrendo ministerial, el perfil político de influencia y capacidad «activa» no debe ser infravalorado, sobretodo durante el reino de Leopoldo I. Si la dinastía llamada al trono ha tenido durante mucho tiempo una actitud de integridad constitucional, no pueden olvidarse las condiciones que han acompañado al nacimiento y desarrollo del sistema representativo en Bélgica entre 1831 y 1848.[296]

La constitución de 1831 representa bien el compromiso alcanzado entre los moderados y los conservadores durante los trabajos del Congreso nacional. Es una constitución, por tanto, que refleja de un lado la estructura socioeconómica y política del país, pero, por otro, es capaz de trazar perspectivas más generales. No puede olvidarse que el nuevo Estado debió esperar hasta 1839 – con la ratificación del Tratado de los XXIV artículos – para regular sus relaciones con los Países Bajos, renunciando definitivamente a los territorios de Limburgo y Luxemburgo. La crisis financiera sumergió al país en la situación de tener que contratar créditos onerosos con los grandes grupos financieros internacionales,

295 Charles de Hon, sesión del 20 de enero de 1831, en E. Huyttens, *Discussions du Congrès National de Belgique, 1830–1831*, cit., t. II, 220. El diputado Hubert-Joseph Masbourg ha proporcionado una contribución importante en la definición de las funciones ministeriales. «Les ministres sont, dans les Etats représentatifs, les véritables dignitaires du pouvoir. Si d'un côté la responsabilité ministérielle confère une garantie à la nation contre des infractions manifestes à la constitution, d'un autre côté cette même responsabilité transfère la souveraineté réelle entre les mains des conseillers de la couronne» *(ibidem*, 221). Véanse también los *rapports* de Joseph Raikem sobre el jefe del Estado (7 de enero de 1831) y sus ministros (10 de enero de 1831), *ibídem*, t. IV, 83–93.

296 Sobre el papel, presente y pasado, de la monarquía en Bélgica, nos remitimos a A. Molitor, *La fonction royale en Belgique*, Bruxelles 1979; F. Delperée, B. Dupret, *Le roi des Belges*, en *Pouvoirs*, 54, 1990, 15–24; J. Stengers, *L'action du roi en Belgique depuis 1831. Pouvoir et influence. Essai de typologie des modes d'action du roi*, Paris, Louvain-La-Neuve 1992.

comenzando con Rothschild. El plano de la política interna, sin embargo, se entretejía estrechamente con el de la diplomacia europea. El compromiso alcanzado con la constitución de 1831 era un valor que había que proteger. La tendencia moderada y conservadora que había prevalecido en la constituyente continuó para regular el conflicto con las fuerzas democráticas y republicanas que no rehusarán a modificar, en breve período, la dirección de marcha del sistema político-constitucional. Igualmente, la oposición orangista anti-belga, fuerte en algunos sectores de la gran burguesía industrial y comercial, fue una espina en el costado hasta la firma del Tratado de 1839.

La constitución refleja eficazmente el punto de equilibrio alcanzado entre liberales moderados y católicos de distinta tendencia en torno al proyecto unionista de monarquía constitucional hereditaria y parlamentaria. Las reglas del juego se fijaron ante todo en el sistema electoral que no se deja, como en Francia, a la sola determinación legislativa. La constitución belga fija el censo electoral mínimo (20 florines) y máximo (100 florines) (art. 47). El constituyente Forgeur había observado durante el debate que «Ce point est grave, messieurs; car si vous n'avez pas dans la constitution une disposition qui fixe le cens électoral, comme c'est là-dessus que repose tout l'édifice constitutionnel, il se pourrait que les législatures à venir, en le modifiant, renversassent tout notre ouvrage».[297] Si el ciudadano, para ser elector, debe demostrar el censo requerido,[298] la elegibilidad, sin embargo, está sujeta a la única condición de poseer la

297 *Cfr.* E. Huyttens, *Discussions du Congrès National de Belgique, 1830–1831*, cit., t. II, 28. *Cfr.* también *ibídem* 640 ss. Sobre el debate véase además E. Vandenpeereboom, *Du gouvernement représentatif en Belgique*, cit., t. I, 25 ss.

298 La ley electoral se aprobó el 3 de marzo de 1831 (101 votos a favor y 31 en contra). Es interesante comprobar cómo la elección de los miembros del Congreso nacional estuvo regulada por una ordenanza del gobierno provisional del 10 de octubre de 1830, que admitía como base del derecho de voto ya el censo, ya la capacidad presunta (magistrados, ministros de culto, oficiales superiores, graduados). La ley del 3 de marzo de 1831 preveía un censo diferenciado que cambiaba según las circunscripciones, las cuales, en buena medida, coincidían con los *arrondissements* de la etapa francesa. El censo alcanzaba el *maximum* previsto por la constitución en las grandes ciudades, siendo menos alto en las circunscripciones de importancia media y llegaba al mínimo para los electores del campo. Tal principio se aprobó con una diferencia de tan solo dos votos (63 a 61). Es evidente el carácter conservador de esta medida: en las ciudades sólo tenía derecho al voto la alta burguesía; en el campo tenían mayor influencia la burguesía media y pequeña y los campesinos más acomodados. El *pays légal* quedaba muy restringido, ya que el derecho de voto correspondía a 46.000 habitantes, es decir, a un elector por cada 95 habitantes. Sobre la disciplina electoral, *cfr.* J. Barthélemy, *L'organisation du suffrage et l'expérience belge*, Paris 1912; D. De' Cocci, *La legislazione elettorale belga*, Firenze 1946; J. Gilissen, *Le régime représentatif belge depuis 1790*, Bruxelles 1958;

ciudadanía, disfrutar los derechos civiles y políticos, edad de 25 años y domicilio en Bélgica.[299] Esta distinción busca mediar entre la preeminente concepción moderada que domina el Congreso nacional, y las fuerzas liberal-democráticas que han desempeñado un papel importante en el seno del movimiento revolucionario.

El régimen parlamentario, a pesar de las premisas constitucionales, de todos modos ha intentado hacerse camino y funcionar según mecanismos propios. No debe creerse que la constitución de 1831, aun representando una etapa de avance del principio parlamentario, pueda haber estado por sí sola en disposición de orientar el proceso de parlamentarización. El *mito* de la constitución belga – al que, en realidad, es difícil resistirse – debe ponerse en relación con los reales acontecimientos político-parlamentarios. Que la *royauté* – como escribe Vandenpeereboom – permanezca «consciencieusement dans les limites qui lui avaient été primitivement assignées ...»[300] es una afirmación que ha de valorarse con más sentido crítico. Leopoldo I era en efecto el príncipe «ideal» para la fundación nacional de Bélgica, pero no se puede decir que su acción haya dejado de influir la dinámica constitucional y el desarrollo del sistema político. La constitución de 1831 deja amplios márgenes «literales» a un monarca que, aun «elegido», permanece personalmente ligado a una concepción fuerte de la autoridad regia. De ahí deriva un «activismo» que tuerce en sentido monárquico la lógica del gobierno parlamentario.[301] El diseño del rey, por otra parte, trata de impedir la formación de «partidos» en disposición de expresar cohesión y homogeneidad ministerial. Leopoldo I establece una «alianza» estratégica con el bloque conservador católico que se favorece del sistema electoral.[302] Al mismo tiempo, para aumentar su autoridad y no pudiendo contar sólo con las fuerzas de inspiración católica que a menudo expresan una visión autónoma, busca favorecer la creación de gobiernos «unionistas», esto es, gobiernos de centro-derecha basados en la unión de católicos y liberales moderados. Los gobiernos de los años Treinta revelan ya un proyecto «unionista», ya la necesidad de afrontar

P. Harismendy, *Il caso belga*, en *I sistemi elettorali in Europa tra Otto e Novecento*, M. S. Piretti (edit.), Roma, Bari 1997, 131–180.

299 Por el contrario, para los senadores se requería el censo de almenos 1000 florines y la edad se elevaba a un mínimo de 40 años (art. 55).

300 E. Vandenpeereboom, *Du gouvernement représentatif en Belgique*, cit., t. II, 299–300.

301 «A l'interprétation républicaine que le Parlement donnait à la constitution, il (Leopoldo) est arrivé à substituer son interprétation monarchique et, tout en respectant scrupuleusement le pacte fondamental qu'il avait juré d'observer, a réussi à doter le gouvernement des prérogatives indispensables au maintien de l'Etat» (H. Pirenne, *Histoire de Belgique*, cit., t. IV, 387–388).

302 El censo diferenciado, de hecho, favorece a los católicos en los colegios de predominio agrícola.

los graves problemas internacionales. El gobierno liberal – ya no «unionista» – formado por Lebeau y Rogier en 1840 tuvo que presentar la dimisión en abril de 1841 tras un voto de censura del Senado. El siguiente gobierno Nothomb (1841–1845), liberal moderado, estuvo obligado a hacer concesiones al rey y a los conservadores católicos. No puede, así, olvidarse que las circunstancias de política internacional y de política interna han permitido a Leopoldo I gozar de una libertad de acción funcional en el proceso de consolidación del régimen constitucional en Bélgica.

En el período que va desde finales de los años Veinte hasta la mitad de los años Cuarenta, el compromiso y la «unión» entre católicos y liberales parece poder garantizar un mínimo de cohesión política y constitucional. La organización «unitaria» de las fuerzas liberales en 1846 abre la estación del alejamiento y del conflicto / competición.[303] Por otra parte, justamente las relaciones entre católicos y liberales – relación compleja y transversal – representa, como se ha dicho, el elemento fundamental en la definición del discurso político-constitucional en Bélgica en el curso del siglo XIX. La constitución de 1831, de indudable implantación liberal, ha debido, en consonancia, asignar una posición de autonomía a la Iglesia; esta posición ha representado después el punto de partida para consentir a la Iglesia afirmar su propia hegemonía, tanto en el campo de la autoridad moral y religiosa, como en el politico-parlamentario.[304] Es suficiente constatar la pretensión de dar a la enseñanza un carácter confesional (ley orgánica de 1842) para darse cuenta de la naturaleza del proyecto político. La lucha parlamentaria se organizó en torno a las distintas instancias católicas y liberales, no sin diversas connotaciones anticlericales. La influencia de Leopoldo I sirvió de estímulo en el conflicto que oponía a las dos formaciones en cuestiones de gran relevancia política y constitucional, buscando reforzar su posición. El largo debate sobre la ley comunal muestra la tentativa del monarca para que se le reconozca el poder de nombrar y revocar a las autoridades locales. En 1842, Leopoldó rehusó obtener una ley que potenciaba, sin embargo, su prerrogativa permitiéndole nombrar los burgomaestres – considerados como los naturales «agentes ministeriales» a nivel local[305] – fuera del consejo comunal electo. Los conservadores católicos, a cambio del apoyo que dieron a la aproba-

303 *Cfr.* A. Miroir, *La Belgique et ses clivages: contradictions structurelles et familles politiques*, en *Pouvoirs*, 54, 1990, 6–7.

304 Véase L. Luzzatti, *Lo Stato e la Chiesa nel Belgio*, cit.

305 Ya en el curso del debate parlamentario de los años Treinta, Devaux había observado que «Le véritable système représentatif est celui où le pays a des organes libres et légaux qui viennent contrôler le pouvoir. Le pouvoir n'est pouvoir qu'autant qu'il choisit librement ses agents, ce n'est qu'à cette condition qu'il peut avoir force et unité», en *Moniteur Belge*, n. 209, sesión del 26 de julio de 1834, cit. de S. Mannoni, *L'autonomia locale in Belgio*, cit., 108.

ción de la ley comunal, obtienen el ver aprobada una medida legislativa que repartía las secciones electorales a fin de garantizar un mayor peso electoral en las ciudades.[306]

Es el gobierno liberal de Rogier y de Frère-Orban, formado en agosto de 1847, el que abre la estación del liberalismo político que, no sin sucesivas golpes de arresto, constituirá el carácter predominante de la escena política belga al menos hasta 1884. Si en Francia 1848 marca el derrumbe y la desaparición de la monarquía constitucional, en Bélgica, por el contrario, supone una etapa fundamental para el proceso de consolidación del Estado y de las instituciones surgidas de la constitución de 1831. El fracaso de los movimientos insurreccionales de carácter democrático y republicano asestó un durísimo golpe a las esperanzas de una transformación del régimen político. El gobierno liberal se aprovechó de la situación guiando un proceso reformador cauto pero de indudable eficacia. La «enseñanza» francesa no se le escapó a la clase dirigente belga. La ley electoral se reformó disminuyendo para todos el censo al *minimum* de veinte florines, haciendo así duplicarse el número de los electores y yendo al encuentro de las instancias democráticas de la pequeña burguesía urbana. La abolición del derecho de timbre sobre los periódicos hizo efectiva la libertad de imprenta, pilar del régimen parlamentario. En fin, se estableció la incompatibilidad del mandato electivo con el estatuto de funcionario.[307] Durante sesenta años la constitución no se modificará más.[308] En realidad, la norma-matriz de la constitución, el artículo 25, había preanunciado los tiempos, alejando a Bélgica de la ambigüedad de Jano y del esfuerzo de Sísifo.

306 *Cfr.* E. Witte, J. Craeybeckx, *La Belgique politique de 1830 à nos jours*, cit., 21 ss.

307 Una cuarta parte de los parlamentarios estaba integrado, antes de la reforma, por funcionarios.

308 Hasta 1893, momento en el que se utilizó el procedimiento de revisión previsto en el artículo 131.

Chapter III
Constitution, Monarchy, representative Government: the French experience

Coppet et la percée de l'Etat libéral constitutionnel

En étudiant les différents aspects du constitutionnalisme du groupe de Coppet, il est tout d'abord nécessaire de fixer les limites qui définissent le domaine de notre contribution. Un thème si vaste ne peut pas être traité entièrement, cela est certain, dans une synthèse qui veut privilégier quelques aspects seulement du discours constitutionnel. Ce thème contient déjà, du reste, en soi, un problème: s'il est en effet possible de déterminer les éléments forts et les bases politico-philosophiques de la doctrine constitutionnelle de Coppet, il est par contre plus compliqué de relever les images «concrètes» de l'Etat libéral constitutionnel.

«Nous sommes une génération de passage. Nés sous l'arbitraire – dit Benjamin Constant – nous sommes pour la liberté».[1] Si la liberté, en tant qu'objectif, est le phare constant de la philosophie politique du Groupe de Coppet, il est tout aussi fondamental de s'interroger sur le «moyen», c'est-à-dire sur la constitution en tant que forme d'Etat, capable avant tout de garantir les libertés imprescriptibles de l'individu. Mais, bien que le chemin qui mène de l'arbitraire à l'ordre politique libéral puisse être inscrit dans un projet rationnel de *perfectibilité*, il est rempli de bonnes intentions, mais non sans obstacles et sans pièges. La génération des «têtes politiques»[2] du groupe de Coppet (Necker, Mme de Staël, Constant, Sismondi ...) contribue considérablement, en ce qui concerne les idéaux et la pratique, à la «percée» de l'Etat constitutionnel. La «génération de passage» ne peut entrevoir que quelques développements, mais elle a une grande capacité de préfiguration: en définitive, il s'agit d'un legs généreux qui voit déjà les inquiétudes et les problèmes qui, à partir de ce moment-là et en peu de temps, émergeront d'une façon plus évidente. C'est justement la définition d'une grammaire, d'un langage, d'un ensemble suffisamment cohérent de solutions qui révèle un discours commun, au-delà de tant de différences: bref, ce qui a été

1 Cf. N. King, *Chevalerie et liberté*, dans *Sismondi européen*, Genève, Paris 1976, 243.

2 P. Thompson, *L'image de la Révolution chez les écrivains de Coppet: contribution à une redéfinition du groupe*, dans *Le Groupe de Coppet*. Actes et documents du deuxième Colloque de Coppet, 10–13 juillet 1974, Genève, Paris 1977, 50.

défini comme «[…] un corpus coppétien d'une remarquable unité […]».[3] Mais le constitutionnalisme de Coppet est une présence forte qui a donné à plusieurs générations de libéraux et autres – même chez ceux qui n'étaient pas disposés à le confesser – les éléments pour une réflexion plus méditée. Sous plusieurs aspects la richesse et la solidité de l'architecture culturelle – de la philosophie à la religion, de l'esthétique à la littérature … – caractérisent le constitutionnalisme de Coppet, comme, peut-être, bien peu d'autres mouvements libéraux du XIXème siècle. Sa théorie constitutionnelle en tire, au cours de cette longue période, un bénéfice certain et la veine apparemment «minoritaire» – dans la pratique institutionnelle française – finit par en préserver les aspects que nous admirons le plus: la sagacité critique et la rare capacité de perspective historique.

Dans l'itinéraire que nous voulons parcourir pour réfléchir sur les «images» de l'Etat libéral constitutionnel dans la réflexion de Coppet, l'auteur-guide sera Benjamin Constant, mais le cadre de référence doit comprendre au moins Necker, Mme de Staël et Sismondi, c'est-à-dire les écrivains les plus experts dans le domaine de la doctrine constitutionnelle. La donnée chronologique est, naturellement, très importante, ainsi que les différents contextes et il est de plus impossible de faire abstraction des caractères et des attitudes propres à chaque auteur. D'autre part, lorsque l'on est à la recherche de l'«esprit» d'un cénacle intellectuel comme celui de Coppet, il est inévitable que l'on ait tendance à comprendre davantage les aspects qui unissent plutôt que les différences qui séparent.

1. Années d'exil

Il est difficile de définir le «projet» constitutionnel de Coppet par un mot-clé ou par un paradigme. De nombreux efforts ont été faits dans ce sens, mais le résultat que l'on veut obtenir dépend, comme cela est connu, de nombreuses variables: du type de catégories interprétatives employées, du niveau plus ou moins élevé d'abstraction, de la coupure chronologique, du choix des interlocuteurs et ainsi de suite. Le discours pourra paraître plus ou moins cohérent et unitaire suivant le point de vue que l'on voudra préférer. Le risque de la synthèse est celui de forcer, à l'intérieur de schémas conceptuels unitaires, les fragments et les thèmes d'une réflexion bien plus fluide qui hésite encore à assumer les traits appartenant à une doctrine constitutionnelle jouissant d'une structure juridique robuste. Mais, dans la perspective d'un bilan, plus on a besoin de rechercher le fil rouge qui semble relier les différentes expériences, plus la synthèse devient nécessaire.

3 H. Grange, *Introduction* à B. Constant, *Fragments d'un ouvrage abandonné sur la possibilité d'une constitution républicaine dans un grand pays*, édition par H. Grange 1991, 30.

Ce sont tout particulièrement les «années d'exil» – pour reprendre un titre de Mme de Staël[4] – les années au cours desquelles l'on sent davantage l'urgence de rechercher (dans des œuvres souvent fondamentales mais restées inédites à l'époque) les «principes» qui devraient gouverner l'Etat constitutionnel. Tous les protagonistes, de Necker à Mme de Staël, de Constant à Sismondi, ont été marqués, à différents moments de leur vie, par l'expérience difficile de l'exil. Nous voyons en cela un lien étroit entre la culture politique et la donnée existentielle. Ceux-ci transforment leur dimension de l'exil en attitude politique, en en faisant un point de force paradoxal sur le plan de la théorie politique. L'échec ou l'insuccès tactique peut constituer le moment pour s'engager dans une analyse plus lucide. Le «libéralisme d'opposition»[5] n'est pas seulement la forme politique pouvant être rapportée à la division intérieure de l'homme moderne. Le «libéralisme d'opposition» est contingent, mais il fait, en même temps, partie intégrante d'un processus de maturation plus profond. L'«exil» est presque l'expression symbolique d'une condition commune: la difficulté, plus ou moins accentuée, de trouver un «lieu» où il est possible d'exprimer un idéal politique. Le fait que de nombreuses œuvres importantes n'aient pas été publiées – ou ne l'aient été qu'en partie – au cours de la vie de leurs auteurs ne surprend pas.[6] L'étude des œuvres inédites a désormais modifié le point d'observation de l'historiographie sur l'œuvre de Constant ou sur celle de Mme de Staël, et il faut continuer à réfléchir sur cet aspect.

Le «creuset de l'esprit libéral» distille une vision de cet Etat «imaginaire» qu'aucun modèle «concret» ne peut représenter totalement. La période cruciale (1795–1815) pour l'élaboration d'une doctrine libérale constitutionnelle est effectivement celle qui stimule le plus la pensée constitutionnelle, mais non sans contradictions. La génération de Constant est amenée à vivre l'héritage difficile d'une génération «forte, nouvelle, enthousiaste» et pourtant «engloutie»[7] dans le tourbillon de la Révolution. L'espace, vide au «centre», est désolé, et les extrémismes opposés, n'arrivant pas à arrêter le pendule de l'histoire française,

4 *Dix années d'exil*, éd. critique par S. Balayé et M.V. Bonifacio, Paris 1996. Sur la dimension existentielle de l'exil, voir également le très bon article de S. Balayé, *Absence, exil, voyage*, désormais dans *Madame de Staël. Ecrire, lutter, vivre*, Genève 1994, 47–60.

5 Sur cette catégorie, voir de P. Manent, *Histoire intellectuelle du libéralisme. Dix leçons*, Paris 1987 et *La Révolution française et le libéralisme français et anglais*, dans F. Furet (dir.), *L'Héritage de la Révolution française*, Paris 1989.

6 Voir B. Fontana, *Benjamin Constant and the Post-Revolutionary Mind*, New Haven 1991.

7 B. Constant, *Des effets de la Terreur*, dans B. Constant, *De la force du gouvernement actuel de la France et de la nécessité de s'y rallier. Des réactions politiques. Des effets de la Terreur*, ed. Ph. Raynaud, Paris 1988.

semblent prévaloir. La recherche d'un équilibre et d'un ordre libéral est l'œuvre que la génération de Coppet s'efforce d'accomplir.

Face à la menace de l'acte arbitraire – qui est souvent l'emblème et la conséquence d'une organisation du pouvoir défectueuse – le libéralisme de Coppet commence à définir ses positions, tout d'abord pendant le Directoire, puis sous le Consulat. La parole contre le silence; le droit constitutionnel à manifester l'opposition[8] contre le chemin de traverse autoritaire. Ce courant du libéralisme «n'a en effet rien d'une doctrine triomphante».[9] La célèbre déclaration *ex post* de Constant sur la défense «cohérente» de la «liberté en tout» se réfère à un triomphe constamment poursuivi: «[...] et par liberté j'entends le triomphe de l'individualité, tant sur l'autorité, qui voudrait gouverner par le despotisme, que sur les masses, qui réclament le droit d'asservir la minorité à la majorité».[10] Comme cela a été récemment observé, le chemin vers le triomphe de l'individualité représente une tradition noble, mais certainement incapable de prévaloir sur la vision du libéralisme du XIXème siècle où l'Etat était prédominant. Le «libéralisme du sujet»[11] a dû s'accommoder à une culture orientée vers la recherche d'un point d'équilibre entre «les droits et libertés de l'individu moderne avec la légitimité de l'Etat souverain».[12]

Il n'y a pas de doutes que les thèmes centraux du libéralisme de Coppet tendent à coïncider avec le modèle plus classique – certains diraient «utopique» – du libéralisme politique: l'individu, la liberté, le pluralisme, la délimitation du pouvoir politique. A propos de cela, il a été question du libéralisme «pur», radical, d'intellectualisme,[13] d'une forte charge d'idéaux. A travers ces définitions, il est certainement possible d'entrevoir des aspects importants, mais c'est peut-être justement du côté du constitutionnalisme que l'on peut apercevoir l'effort, inévitable, développé de sorte que le «système de la liberté [...] complet

8 La référence rapporte surtout à l'*opinion* de Constant du 15 nivôse an VIII (5.I.1800) exprimée devant le Tribunat. Cf. E. Hofmann, *Les "Principes de politique" de Benjamin Constant. La genèse d'une œuvre et l'évolution de la pensée de leur auteur (1789–1806)*, tome I, Genève 1980, 187–241; B.W. Jasinski, *Benjamin Constant tribun*, dans E. Hofmann (dir.), *Benjamin Constant, Madame de Staël et le Groupe de Coppet*, Voltaire Foundation, Institut Benjamin Constant, Oxford, Lausanne 1982, 63–88.

9 E. Hofmann, *Les "Principes de politique"*, cit., tome I, 211.

10 B. Constant, *Préface, Mélanges de littérature et de politique*, dans *Œuvres*, texte présenté et annoté par A. Roulin, Paris 1957, 801.

11 L. Jaume, *L'individu effacé ou le paradoxe du libéralisme français*, Paris 1997.

12 *Ibidem*, 16.

13 Cf. de M. Barberis, *Benjamin Constant. Rivoluzione, costituzione, progresso*, Bologna 1988, 144 ss.; *Madame de Staël o dell'intellettualismo politico*, dans *Sette studi sul liberalismo rivoluzionario*, Torino 1989, 123–143.

et régulier»[14] ne soit pas violé et que les individus puissent jouir «[...] d'une liberté d'action complète pour toutes les actions innocentes ou indifférentes [...]».[15]

2. Entre raison et histoire

Le groupe de Coppet est amené à imaginer sa constitution lors d'un des moments de l'histoire du constitutionnalisme moderne les plus extraordinaires et les plus dramatiques. Ses représentants suivent, l'un après l'autre, les échecs des constitutions de la Révolution et du Directoire qui n'arrivent jamais à amorcer le cercle virtuel constitution-pouvoir-liberté. Partant de l'idée d'une constitution prescriptive, la réflexion se déroule dans l'alvéole du constitutionnalisme révolutionnaire, de ses grandes révélations et de ses insuccès. En ce moment-là, la confiance dans la constitution «artificielle», rationnelle, est encore bien forte. «[...] l'histoire d'un pays qui se gouverne par des institutions, et non par la volonté d'un despote, – observe Mme de Staël dans *Des circonstances actuelles* – dépend entièrement de la nature et de la combinaison de ces institutions».[16] Si cette idée de constitution reste, bien qu'avec plusieurs nuances, un point ferme, il est pourtant vrai que la dimension volontariste s'inscrit dans un discours de transition.

L'admiration de Necker[17] – et son influence, plus forte, sur Madame de Staël, moins forte sur Constant – pour la «Happy Constitution»[18] britannique se trouve au centre d'une réflexion incessante sur l'«invention», en France, d'une culture constitutionnelle considérée «artificieuse» et produisant des conséquences pendant une longue période. Dans le jeu compliqué des miroirs, fait d'observations et d'influences, qui se déroule au cours du XVIIIème siècle, le regard tourné Outre-Manche représente parfois une source d'incompréhensions et d'interprétations abusives. Mais la constitution britannique – au-delà de sa

14 B. Constant, *Principes de politique*, ed. Hofmann, Genève 1980, t. II, 495.

15 *Ibidem*, 459.

16 G. De Staël, *Des circonstances actuelles qui peuvent terminer la Révolution et des principes qui doivent fonder la République en France*, édition critique par Lucia Omacini, Paris, Genève 1979, 194.

17 «La perfection serait donc un Gouvernement, qui, par sa Constitution, se trouverait en état de maintenir les lois de propriété, d'ordre et de liberté, sans avoir la faculté de les enfreindre lui-même. Et cette perfection me paroît représentée par la Constitution politique de l'Angleterre» (J. Necker, *Du pouvoir exécutif dans les grands Etats*, s. l., 1792, t. II, 356). Cf. H. Grange, *Les idées de Necker*, Paris 1974, 307–349.

18 Cf. B. Clavero, *Happy Constitution. Cultura y lengua constitucionales*, Madrid 1997.

possibilité réelle d'être utilisée d'une façon pratique dans le débat français[19] – devient le paradigme de la constitution historique, l'on pourrait même dire un modèle de «perfectibilité constitutionnelle» ayant comme caractéristique le principe de la modération: il faut donc éviter toute innovation violente, par conséquent dangereuse, ainsi que toute attitude obstinée de fermeture. «L'unique moyen de les éviter, c'est de se prêter aux changements insensibles qui s'opèrent dans la nature morale comme dans la nature physique [...]».[20] Ce thème est, au fur et à mesure que les années s'écoulent, de plus en plus pris en considération par les écrivains politiques de Coppet, et cela est dû à un processus de détachement face au système constitutionnel qui pensait construire, tout en ignorant les données de l'expérience. Inventer la constitution, une véritable culture constitutionnelle: voici le grand problème.

Si la constitution-acte, c'est-à-dire la constitution qui est le fruit d'un dessein constituant et rationnel, semble la seule constitution possible en France, l'appel à l'histoire tend pourtant à se renforcer. C'est justement de l'impossibilité de concilier l'histoire avec la Révolution que avait suivi le projet désespéré de sauver la monarchie d'ancien régime, en l'établissant dans l'espace hostile de la souveraineté populaire. Le groupe de Coppet en est conscient et essaie plutôt de «corriger» la rigidité de la constitution artificielle, fondée sur la prééminence de l'orientation politique, en l'étudiant de nouveau à la lumière d'une «rationalisation» historique. Sismondi, dans les *Recherches*,[21] ne conçoit pas la constitution au dehors de l'histoire. La constitution – de même que la liberté – est un produit de l'histoire, c'est-à-dire du développement social dans un moment historique déterminé; il n'est ni un résultat arbitraire ni un produit fortuit. Constant lui-même, tout en restant en fait fidèle à une idée rationnelle de constitution, essaiera de trouver un équilibre entre la raison et l'histoire. La doctrine de la perfectibilité pose déjà, dans les œuvres du Directoire, le problème de l'adhérence entre les idées et les institutions, le temps jouant le rôle de balancier. Dans

19 G. De Staël, *Considérations sur les principaux événements de la Révolution française*, dans *Œuvres posthumes*, Paris 1861 (réimpression Génève 1967), t. III, 104: «Chaque parti, depuis vingt-cinq ans, a repoussé et regretté tour à tour la constitution anglaise, suivant qu'il était vainqueur ou vaincu [...] On dirait que la constitution anglaise, ou plutôt la raison, en France, est comme la belle Angélique dans la comédie du *Joueur*: il l'invoque dans sa détresse, et la néglige quand il est heureux».

20 B. Constant, *De l'esprit de conquête et de l'usurpation dans leurs rapports avec la civilisation européenne*, dans *Œuvres*, cit., 1579.

21 J. C. L. Sismondi, *Recherches sur les constitutions des peuples libres*, édition et introduction de M. Minerbi, Genève 1965. La conception historique de la constitution matérielle (sociale) et du législateur conservateur est, en Sismondi, beaucoup plus accentuée dans les *Etudes sur les constitutions des peuples libres*, Bruxelles 1836.

les *Principes* de 1806, Constant prouve qu'il est d'accord avec la réflexion sur l'histoire en tant que fondement de la théorie politique. «Le temps, dit Bacon, est le grand réformateur. Ne refusez pas son assistance. Laissez-le marcher devant vous, pour qu'il aplanisse la route. Si ce que vous instituez n'a pas été préparé par lui, vous commanderez vainement ...».[22] Au début de la Restauration, Constant essaiera d'équilibrer l'élément rationnel («Les constitutions se font rarement par la volonté des hommes») avec celui de l'histoire («Le temps les fait»). «Faire» la constitution est quelquefois indispensable, mais, une fois que les pouvoirs sont constitués, il vaut mieux laisser l'espace nécessaire aux «deux puissances réformatrices»,[23] le temps et l'expérience. Ce discours ne peut pas être tout simplement réduit à la conception de la constitution historique. Le constitutionnalisme de Coppet, et en particulier la réflexion de Constant, déplace le discours du simple contraste constitution rationnelle / constitution historique, à une perspective beaucoup plus complexe sans laquelle il est difficile d'imaginer le processus de rationalisation de la monarchie constitutionnelle. Le concept de «machine constitutionnelle» vit dans l'histoire, mais il opère dans le cadre d'un dessein rationnel (pouvoir neutre, responsabilité des ministres, seconde Chambre, gouvernement représentatif etc.), le modèle anglais servant de paradigme principal, mais controversé. Ce qui compte vraiment, c'est la constitution en tant qu'ensemble fixe de principes, en tant que structure ne servant qu'à régler les parties «essentielles»: les attributions des pouvoirs et les droits civils et politiques. La constitution ne doit pas se perdre dans les détails (sources de violations futures), prétendre assigner le statut de rigidité à des matières[24] que l'on peut ramener au libre jeu des sujets constitutionnels. «La circonscription sévère d'une constitution dans ses bornes est mille fois préférable à la vénération superstitieuse [...]».[25]

3. Comme les généraux d'Alexandre

Le groupe de Coppet affronte un des paradoxes des doctrines individualistes des libertés qui s'accompagnent de la concentration formidable du pouvoir dans l'Etat post-révolutionnaire, lequel a absorbé les libertés propres aux différentes classes, a joué un rôle «modernisateur» (lutte contre les privilèges), mais propose, toutefois, de nouveau, sous des formes ultérieures, le problème de l'abus et de

22 B. Constant, *Principes de politique*, ed. Hofmann, cit., 412.

23 B. Constant, *Réflexions sur les constitutions, la distribution des pouvoirs et les garanties, dans une monarchie constitutionnelle*, Paris 1814.

24 "De ce qui n'est pas constitutionnel" est le titre d'un des chapitres les plus significatifs des *Réflexions sur les constitutions*, cit.

25 B. Constant, *Principes de politique*, ed. Hofmann, cit., 116.

l'arbitraire.[26] Aucun autre courant du libéralisme n'a placé ce thème, si important pour la configuration du libéralisme du XIXème siècle, au centre de son attention avec tant de force. Comment est-il possible de concilier l'individualisme libéral – dont il est impossible d'oublier, en France, les racines révolutionnaires – avec la légitimité de l'Etat souverain? La rigueur et la singularité avec lesquels le groupe de Coppet élabore son constitutionnalisme sont les aspects qui méritent le plus d'être pris en considération.

L'Etat constitutionnel de Coppet a comme base une conception «forte» du constitutionnalisme entendu comme technique de la liberté[27] pour limiter un pouvoir qui tend, naturellement, à dépasser ses limites. La constitution est le lieu de la garantie des droits et des libertés de l'individu, ainsi que des attributions des principaux pouvoirs. Ce sont les «douze Articles» dont parle Necker comme «bases fondamentales de la liberté civile et politique d'une Nation»,[28] les quelques «vérités politiques»[29] et les «trois ou quatre principes»[30] de Madame de Staël, les principes du gouvernement constitutionnel de Sismondi dans les *Recherches*,[31] les «principes positifs et immuables» de Constant.[32] Chacun de ces écrivains privilégie certains principes, mais les bases de la constitution représentent le terrain commun des garanties et des droits. Tout comme une seule déviation détruit le système des libertés, ainsi «[...] si une seule partie de l'ordre social est sans garantie, la garantie de tout le reste s'anéantit [...]».[33]

Cette idée centrale de la constitution en tant que garantie des droits et des libertés est une des idées les plus productives dans le constitutionnalisme de Coppet, et de Constant en particulier. L'une des faiblesses – ou mieux des

26 Voir, à ce propos, M. Fioravanti, *Appunti di storia della costituzioni moderne. Le libertà fondamentali*, Torino 1995, 28 ss.

27 Sur ce sujet, N. Matteucci, *Organizzazione del potere e libertà. Storia del costituzionalismo moderno*, Torino 1988.

28 J. Necker, *Du pouvoir exécutif*, cit., t. II, 314 ss.

29 «La division du corps législatif, l'indépendance du pouvoir exécutif, et avant tout, la condition de propriété: telles sont les idées simples qui composent tous les plans de constitution possibles [...]» (G. De Staël, *Réflexions sur la paix intérieure* (1795), dans *Œuvres posthumes*, cit., t. I, 56). Madame de Staël reprendra les "douze Articles" de son père dans les *Considérations*, cit., 156–157.

30 «[...] l'égalité politique, la garantie des formes judiciaires, et le droit de représentation, et la division du pouvoir exécutif, et la constitution de la seconde Chambre [...]» (G. De Staël, *Des circonstances*, cit., 196).

31 J. C. L. Sismondi, *Recherches*, cit., 99.

32 «[...] que nul ne doit être arrêté arbitrairement, puni sans avoir été jugé, jugé qu'en vertu des lois et selon les formes, empêché de manifester son opinion, d'exercer son industrie, de disposer de ses facultés d'une manière innocente et paisible» (B. Constant, *Principes de politique*, ed. Hofmann, cit., 115).

33 *Ibidem*, 67.

différences – du constitutionnalisme français par rapport au constitutionnalisme anglo-saxon, et en particulier à celui américain, est la perspective du garantisme. Dans la réflexion de Coppet, il y a une idée que nous considérons, de nos jours, fondamentale, c'est-à-dire que l'Etat constitutionnel tend à séparer les droits de la sphère de la loi. Coppet entrevoit ce point essentiel, sans pouvoir le développer complètement. Le paramètre est le droit, non pas la loi. C'est justement sur ce versant que la pensée de nos auteurs acquiert une forte valeur constitutionnelle. Si, dans la tradition du constitutionnalisme de l'Europe continentale, la loi est un acte fondamental de garantie des droits (légalité des droits), dans le constitutionnalisme de Coppet, cette tradition est analysée d'une façon plus critique.

«Les législateurs – écrit Constant – se partagent l'existence humaine, par droit de conquête, comme les généraux d'Alexandre se partageaient le monde».[34] Le Législateur qui prétend régler chaque aspect de la société, qui multiplie, sans que cela soit nécessaire, ses interventions, qui «crée» des liens et des besoins, est donc le sujet emblématique d'une conception extensive de l'autorité sociale. Ce n'est pas un hasard si Constant, dans ses *Principes* de 1806, étudie le problème de la multiplicité des lois après avoir pris en considération le thème général de l'extension de l'autorité sociale et ceci avant la section consacrée aux mesures arbitraires. La pensée consacrée, avec des accents propres à Montesquieu, au culte de l'uniformité n'étonne pas non plus: «Il est assez remarquable que l'uniformité n'ait jamais rencontré plus de faveur que dans une révolution faite au nom des droits et de la liberté des hommes». «[...] l'uniformité, c'est du mécanisme. La variété, c'est la vie [...]».[35]

La déclaration des droits et surtout leur garantie effective avaient représenté un point critique du discours révolutionnaire.[36] En effet, les droits avaient été constitutionnalisés, mais le législateur, en tant qu'interprète de la volonté générale, avait dicté l'orientation politique et avait envahi la sphère des droits imprescriptibles de l'individu. Le constitutionnalisme de Coppet propose donc

34 *Ibidem*, 84. Ce genre d'observations – et le discours devrait certainement comprendre de nouveau Mme de Staël et Sismondi – prouve combien le cercle de Coppet anticipe des thèmes et des motifs de discussion (par ex. la loi en tant que phénomène politique de "découverte" du fait social (historique) qui l'on attribue habituellement à l'influence de l'école historique du droit et en particulier de Savigny. Les écrits de la fin du XVIIIème siècle et des toutes premières années du XIXème siècle révèlent combien ces racines sont fortes chez des auteurs comme Constant. A ce propos voir P. Rosanvallon, *Le moment Guizot*, Paris 1985, 44–45, qui unifie pourtant ce discours à l'intérieur d'une perspective libérale plus générale.

35 B. Constant, *De l'esprit de conquête*, cit., 980 et 984.

36 J. M. Redor, *De l'Etat légal à l'Etat de droit. L'évolution des conceptions de la doctrine publiciste française*, Paris 1992.

fortement le problème de la constitution comme norme fondamentale de garantie capable de limiter et de restreindre l'action du législateur. C'est en partant du problème de l'extension de l'autorité sociale que ce constitutionnalisme offre l'une des contributions théoriques les plus significatives.

4. La constitution-défiance

«Une constitution est par elle-même un acte de défiance puisqu'elle prescrit des limites à l'autorité [...]».[37] C'est ainsi qu'en 1800 Constant synthétise le sens profond de la constitution en tant qu'acte instituant le rapport entre le sujet et l'autorité sociale. Celle-ci, bien que légitime, n'est jamais illimitée. L'accord de la volonté générale n'est pas suffisant pour que les actes de la *suprema potestas* deviennent légitimes en tant que tels.[38] A travers la lecture critique de Rousseau, l'écrivain de Lausanne accentuera, au cours des années, les intuitions qui étaient déjà présentes dans les écrits thermidoriens et encore liées aux vicissitudes de la République. «La souveraineté n'existe que d'une manière limitée et relative. Au point où commence l'indépendance de l'existence individuelle, s'arrête la juridiction de cette souveraineté. Si la société franchit cette ligne, elle se rend aussi coupable de tyrannie que le despote qui n'a pour titre que le glaive exterminateur».[39] Limiter la souveraineté, donc le pouvoir, signifie avant tout tracer la ligne infranchissable de la «liberté des modernes» qui garantit les citoyens «contre le pouvoir». Les généraux d'Alexandre n'ont aucun droit à la conquête: l'existence humaine, celle qui est au-delà de la ligne, doit être garantie par la constitution «acte de défiance».[40]

37 Sur cette *Opinion* de Constant (15 nivôse an VIII, 5.I.1800), cf. L. Jaume, *L'individu effacé*, cit., 106.

38 «En un mot je regarde comme tyrannique toute loi qui prétend prescrire à chacun comment il doit se conduire pour sa propre utilité [...]», J. C. L. Sismondi, *Recherches*, cit., 112.

39 B. Constant, *Principes de politique*, ed. Hofmann, cit., 49. Constant (*ibid.*, 45–46) s'inspire à un passage d'un discours prononcé par Sieyès à la Convention le 2 Thermidor de l'an III. Cf. E. Sieyes, *Opinion sur plusieurs articles des titres IV et V du projet de constitution*, dans P. Bastid, *Les discours de Sieyès dans les débats constitutionnels de l'an III*, Paris 1939, 17–18.

40 «C'est là ce qu'il faut déclarer, c'est la vérité importante, le principe éternel qu'il faut établir. Aucune autorité sur la terre n'est illimitée, ni celle du peuple, ni celle des hommes qui se disent ses représentants, ni celle des rois, à quelque titre qu'ils règnent, ni celle de la loi, qui, n'étant que l'expression de la volonté du peuple ou du prince, suivant la forme du gouvernement, doit être circonscrite dans les mêmes bornes que l'autorité dont elle émane [...]» (B. Constant, *Principes de politique applicables à tous les gouvernements représentatifs et particulièrement à la constitution actuelle de la France* (1815), dans *Œuvres*, cit., 1075).

L'Etat, en tant que construction du corps social, donc corps artificiel, n'a de sens que dans la perspective du gouvernement légitime parce que limité. Ce qui a été défini le «libéralisme de la règle» qui limite le pouvoir en fixant la ligne infranchissable,[41] trouve, sans aucun doute, dans la doctrine de Constant une de ses expressions les plus emblématiques. Délimiter le pouvoir est le *prius* logique, la prémisse conceptuelle; mais la distinction naturelle et nécessaire entre la société civile et la société politique – présente dans la perspective de Coppet – n'est jamais portée à ses conséquences les plus extrêmes. La distinction société/Etat est une des plus rigoureuses, mais la *défiance* n'est pas une fin en soi, c'est plutôt l'interrogation critique sur la nature indéchiffrable du pouvoir.[42] «Le degré seul de pouvoir social, en quelques mains qu'on le dépose, fait une constitution libre ou un gouvernement oppressif [...]».[43] Qu'un pouvoir immense appartienne à un seul ou à tout le monde, cela a peu d'importance, il reste toujours un mal. D'où la nécessité de limiter l'autorité sociale «au strict nécessaire»,[44] c'est-à-dire aux fonctions indispensables à la juridiction de la société. «Les droits individuels se composent de tout ce qui reste indépendant de l'autorité sociale». Si l'on observe bien, ceux-ci sont les droits qu'une constitution bien organisée doit sauvegarder: les droits de liberté religieuse, les droits de manifester librement la pensée, la publicité, les garanties judiciaires, les formes tutélaires.[45] Distincts de la sorte des droits «du gouvernement et de la société», les droits individuels deviennent plus clairs en indiquant «[...] les objets sur lesquels le gouvernement et la société doivent s'abstenir de prononcer et laisser les individus parfaitement libres».[46]

Si les idées de résistance et d'équilibre sont communes à la culture libérale, il faut toutefois remarquer que c'est leur articulation concrète qui donne forme aux différentes propositions d'organisation constitutionnelle. La limitation de l'autorité sociale est – selon le point de vue de Constant – difficile, mais possible. «Elle sera garantie d'abord par la même force qui garantit toutes les vérités

41 B. Manin, *Les deux libéralismes: la règle et la balance*, dans *La famille, la loi, l'Etat: de la Révolution au Code civil*, sous la dir. de I. Théry et C. Biet, Paris 1989, 372–389.

42 Sur confiance/défiance, v. L. Jaume, *L'individu effacé*, cit., 106–108.

43 B. Constant, *Principes de politique*, ed. Hofmann, cit., 38.

44 *Ibidem*, 57. Sismondi observe: «[...] une nation ne put jouir de son entière liberté démocratique qu'autant que le gouvernement n'obtint aucune prérogative au-delà de celles qui sont nécessaires à son existence [...]» (*Recherches*, cit., 84).

45 «Les droits des citoyens sont la liberté individuelle, la liberté religieuse, la liberté d'opinion, dans laquelle est comprise sa publicité, la jouissance de la propriété, la garantie contre tout arbitraire. Aucune autorité ne peut porter atteinte à ces droits, sans déchirer son propre titre» (B. Constant, *Principes de politique* (1815), cit., 1075).

46 B. Constant, *Principes de politique*, ed. Hofmann, cit., 58.

reconnues, par l'opinion. L'on pourra s'occuper ensuite de la garantir d'une manière plus fixe, par l'organisation particulière des pouvoirs politiques. Mais avoir obtenu et consolidé la première garantie sera toujours un grand bien». Une fois que le *prius* logique est reconnu, c'est-à-dire la délimitation de la sphère d'intervention légitime du pouvoir social, il n'y a plus qu'à faire le second pas: définir l'organisation et la division des pouvoirs.[47] Le problème de la division des pouvoirs n'obtient pas la même importance qu'il a dans la tradition constitutionnelle laquelle est davantage liée à la logique des poids et des contrepoids (gouvernement mixte, *checks and balances*) et qui est souvent ramenée, d'une façon un peu générique, à Montesquieu, son noble père.[48]

Certaines affirmations de Constant semblent révéler une attitude prudente envers la dynamique, presque toujours emphatisée, des contre-pouvoirs. «On peut, dira-t-on, par des combinaisons ingénieuses, limiter le pouvoir en le divisant. On peut mettre en opposition et en équilibre ses différentes parties. Mais par quel moyen fera-t-on que la somme totale n'en soit pas illimitée? Comment borner le pouvoir autrement que par le pouvoir?».[49] Sans une limitation préventive de l'autorité sociale, la division des pouvoirs risque même de devenir «un danger et un fléau».[50] Dans un célèbre passage des *Principes* de 1815, Constant est encore plus clair: «Vous avez beau diviser les pouvoirs: si la somme totale du pouvoir est illimitée, les pouvoirs divisés n'ont qu'à former une coalition, et le despotisme est sans remède. Ce qui nous importe, ce n'est pas que nos droits ne puissent être violés par tel pouvoir sans l'approbation de tel autre, mais que cette violation soit interdite à tous les pouvoirs».[51] Chez le jeune Sismondi aussi, où l'espace laissé à la théorie de la *balance des pouvoirs* est plus vaste, le but d'une constitution libre est avant tout celui d'empêcher à la nation de «confondre la souveraineté avec la toute puissance [...]» et, par la suite seulement, celui de «régler les divisions de la nation, de répartir les pouvoirs, et d'établir l'équilibre entr'elles [...]».[52]

47 «Nous dirons seulement qu'il nous semble possible de découvrir des bases d'institutions politiques, qui combinent tellement les intérêts des divers dépositaires de la puissance, que leur avantage le plus manifeste, le plus durable et le plus assuré soit de rester chacun dans les bornes de leurs attributions respectives et de s'y contenir mutuellement. Mais la première question n'en est pas moins la limitation de la somme totale de l'autorité. Car avant d'organiser une chose, il faut en avoir déterminé la nature et l'étendue», *Ibidem*, 55–56.

48 «M. de Montesquieu d'ailleurs, dans sa définition de la liberté, a méconnu toutes les limites de l'autorité sociale», *Ibidem*, 27.

49 *Ibidem*, 55.

50 *Ibidem*, 54.

51 B. Constant, *Principes de politique* (1815), cit., 1074.

52 J.C.L. Sismondi, *Recherches*, cit., 91.

Le pouvoir est un effet de l'opinion, c'est aux idées «[...] que l'empire du monde a été donné».[53] C'est l'opinion, invisible et puissante, qui délimite le rayon d'action du gouvernement. La presse libre est la voix de l'opinion. La liberté de la presse est la garantie par excellence: en son absence «Toutes les barrières civiles, politiques, judiciaires deviennent illusoires».[54] La liberté des modernes et le gouvernement représentatif ne peuvent vivre sans l'opinion publique. «Ce ne sont point les formes des constitutions qui les conservent; il n'y a point de durée pour une constitution, sans opinion publique, et il n'y a point d'opinion publique, sans liberté de la presse. Quand cette liberté est étouffée, les grands corps de l'Etat sont des masses isolées de la nation, sans vie et sans force véritable ...».[55] Si le lien entre l'opinion, la liberté de la presse et de publicité se desserre, alors la communication entre les gouvernants et les gouvernés risque, elle aussi, de se perdre.

5. La liberté des modernes

«La division des pouvoirs est excellente – écrit Constant – en ce qu'elle rapproche autant que possible l'intérêt des gouvernants de celui des gouvernés».[56] Mais ces intérêts sont bien différents. L'«autant que possible» est une expression significative: en réalité la division des pouvoirs a ses limites et «Il ne faut pas toutefois se faire illusion sur l'efficacité de ces moyens ou se flatter que l'on parvienne jamais à amalgamer complètement ces deux intérêts».[57] Bien qu'il soit le gouvernement des meilleurs et le seul possible pour la *commercial society*, le système représentatif,[58] «ne lève point cette difficulté»,[59] c'est-à-dire qu'il ne résout pas, en dernière instance, la difficulté de «communication» entre les gouvernants, qui exercent le pouvoir légitime, et les citoyens-propriétaires dotés des droits

53 B. Constant, *De la force du gouvernement actuel de la France et de la nécessité de s'y rallier*, dans B. Constant, *De la force du gouvernement*, cit.

54 B. Constant, *Principes de politique*, ed. Hofmann, cit., 136.

55 B. Constant, *Observations sur le discours prononcé par S.E. le ministre de l'Intérieur en faveur du projet de loi sur la liberté de la presse* (1814), dans *Œuvres*, cit., 1261.

56 B. Constant, *Principes de politique*, ed. Hofmann, cit., 54.

57 *Ibidem*, 465. Sur la «[...] lutte entre les gouvernans et les gouvernés qu'est une conséquence nécessaire de tout ordre social», cf. J. C. L. Sismondi, *Recherches*, cit., 146.

58 «Vous créerez, me dira-t-on, un nouveau genre d'aristocratie. Aristocratie ne veut-il pas dire le gouvernement des meilleurs? Et qu'est-ce qu'un gouvernement représentatif, si ce n'est le gouvernement du petit nombre et le pouvoir remis entre les mains des plus éclairés, des plus vertueux, des plus braves, tandis qu'on s'en remet ailleurs à la naissance du droit qu'on ne devait confier qu'au mérite personnel?» (G. De Staël, *Des circonstances*, cit., 188).

59 B. Constant, *Principes de politique*, ed. Hofmann, cit., 464.

politiques. «[...] la liberté politique, c'est-à-dire les précautions des gouvernés contre les gouvernants» sembleraient «[...] peu nécessaires. Mais cette assertion n'est point exacte».[60] A l'image simplifiante du gouvernement des meilleurs, fondé sur l'intérêt propriétaire et sur la possession des lumières, doit au moins être ajoutée celle de la liberté politique dans le but de réaliser un droit de contrôle et de surveillance, c'est-à-dire de jugement, dont l'individu moderne ne doit certainement pas se défaire.

L'on aperçoit, dans le gouvernement représentatif, un double aspect: d'un côté le «gouvernement des modernes», «[...] né de la nécessité [...]», «[...] une invention moderne, par laquelle on avoit cherché à communiquer aux grands Etats la liberté qu'auparavant étoit l'appanage des petits»,[61] de l'autre l'instrument qui permet d'atteindre un équilibre plus grand entre la jouissance des libertés de l'individu et l'exercice de la liberté politique. Les lignes d'influence dans la formation de la dichotomie «liberté des anciens» – «liberté des modernes» sont bien connues. Le développement des idées qui va des premières définitions de Madame de Staël à la célèbre formulation de Constant de 1819 semble important. Si, chez la dame de Coppet, la distinction,[62] en fait, «[...] paraît issue d'une véritable phénoménologie de l'opinion publique du Directoire»[63] et si, chez Sismondi, le sentiment de la liberté dans les petits Etats modernes, et en particulier dans les Républiques italiennes, est – à travers la lecture de Smith – fort,[64] c'est chez Constant que le gouvernement représentatif devient, entièrement, le système d'équilibre des libertés.

60 *Ibidem*.

61 J. C. L. Sismondi, *Recherches*, cit., 142 et 162.

62 Madame de Staël introduit ce thème dans les *Réflexions sur la paix intérieure* (1795), mais la formulation la plus célèbre, "partagée" avec Constant, se trouve dans *Des circonstances*, cit., 111–112: «En France, il faut sans doute former, autant qu'on le pourra, un esprit national, mais ne pas perdre de vue que l'opinion publique sera fondée sur l'amour du repos, le désir d'acquérir de la fortune, le besoin de la conserver, qu'on s'intéressera toujours plus aux idées administratives plutôt qu'aux questions politiques, parce qu'elles touchent davantage aux existences privées [...] Mais en France, où c'est le contraire, c'est le respect de l'existence particulière, de la fortune privée qui seul peut faire aimer la République. La liberté des temps actuels, c'est tout qui garantit l'indépendance des citoyens contre le pouvoir du gouvernement. La liberté des temps anciens, c'est tout ce qui assurait aux citoyens la plus grande part dans l'exercice du pouvoir».

63 M. Barberis, *Thermidor, le libéralisme et la modernité politique*, dans *1795. Pour une République sans Révolution*, sous la direction de R. Dupuy et M. Morabito, Rennes 1996, 137. Cf. surtout S. Holmes, *Benjamin Constant et la genèse du libéralisme moderne*, Paris 1994, 30–31.

64 Cf. M. Minerbi, *Introduzione* à J. C. L. Sismondi, *Recherches*, cit., 43 ss. La liberté moderne, pour Sismondi, ne peut pas faire abstraction ni du processus de civilisation (processus historiquement complexe d'affirmation de la liberté) ni du

Il est également possible de lire une mise au point graduelle dans l'œuvre de Constant: des *Principes* (1806), en passant à travers le *De l'esprit de conquête*, jusqu'à la conférence *De la liberté des anciens comparée à celle des modernes*, prononcée le 14 février 1819 à l'Athénée Royal. Constant aborde déjà, en particulier, dans les *Principes*, le problème de l'équilibre entre la liberté civile et la liberté politique. Bien que reconnaissant le caractère essentiel de la liberté capable d'assouvir le besoin des modernes pour le «repos» et les «jouissances», la liberté politique, conservée à l'intérieur des limites absolument nécessaires, est la garantie de la liberté civile.[65] «La conséquence que je tire des différences qui nous distinguent de l'antiquité, ce n'est point qu'il faille affaiblir la garantie, mais c'est qu'il faut étendre la jouissance. Ce n'est point à la liberté politique que je veux renoncer, c'est la liberté civile que je réclame avec d'autres formes de liberté politique». Les gouvernements doivent toujours respecter l'indépendance des individus. «Ils doivent porter chaque jour sur ces objets sacrés une main plus prudente et plus légère».[66]

Mais le système représentatif[67] – dit Constant en 1819 – n'est pas simplement le «gouvernement des meilleurs» basé sur une procuration indéfinie. Au contraire, il demande, justement à cause de la distance irréductible qu'il y a entre les gouvernants et les gouvernés, une surveillance active et constante. Le danger de la liberté moderne est son caractère privé, l'image, qui sera par la suite propre à Tocqueville, de l'*homo oeconomicus*, isolé, replié sur ses intérêts personnels. Mais les «jouissances» ne peuvent pas rester séparées des garanties, et surtout de la liberté politique. Celle-ci est «[...] le plus énergique moyen de perfectionnement

problème fondamental du "gouvernement" de l'économie. Cfr. F. Sofia, *Sul pensiero politico-costituzionale del giovane Sismondi*, in *Rassegna storica del Risorgimento*, LVIII, 1981, 136 ss. et P. Schiera, *Presentazione* à J.-Ch.-L. Simonde De Sismondi, *Storia delle Repubbliche italiane* (1832), Torino 1996, XXVI ss.

65 «La liberté politique offrait moins de jouissance qu'autrefois et les désordres qu'elle peut entraîner étant plus insupportables, il n'en faut conserver que ce qui est absolument nécessaire. Prétendre aujourd'hui consoler les hommes par la liberté politique de la perte de la liberté civile, c'est marcher en sens inverse du génie actuel de l'espèce humaine. Loin d'opposer l'une de ces libertés à l'autre, il faut ne présenter la première que comme garantie de la seconde» (B. Constant, *Principes de politique*, ed. Hofmann, cit., 435–436). Mme de Staël avait déjà posé le problème de la liberté politique en tant que fonction de la liberté civile: «Le droit politique doit être considéré comme un tribut qu'on paie à la patrie; c'est monter la garde, c'est exercer les devoirs des citoyens; mais le fruit de ces sacrifices, c'est la liberté civile [...]» (*Réflexions sur la paix intérieure* (1795), dans *Œuvres*, cit., t. I, 58).

66 B. Constant, *Principes de politique*, ed. Hofmann, cit., 436.

67 Cf. P. Pasquino, *Emmanuel Sieyès, Benjamin Constant et le "gouvernement des modernes". Contribution à l'histoire du concept de représentation politique*, dans *Revue française de science politique*, 2, 1987, 214–228.

que le ciel nous ait donné». «Loin donc, Messieurs, de renoncer à aucune des deux espèces de libertés dont je vous ai parlé, il faut, je l'ai démontré, apprendre à les combiner l'une avec l'autre».[68] L'éloge de la liberté politique devient l'éloge de la politique *tout court*, de la participation à la chose publique, de la dynamique du contrôle à travers les institutions qui fortifient les libertés et les droits (jury, pouvoir municipal, etc.). Il ne suffit pas que le peuple reste tranquille. Les institutions doivent compléter l'éducation morale des citoyens, sans oublier d'avoir une main prudente et légère, mais en leur donnant la possibilité de «[...] concourir par leurs déterminations et par leurs suffrages à l'exercice du pouvoir, leur garantir un droit de contrôle et de surveillance par la manifestation de leurs opinions [...]».[69] Le gouvernement des modernes n'est pas le gouvernement fondé sur la liberté définie comme «négative». Ce gouvernement est plutôt, comme le montre Constant, la recherche d'un équilibre-combinaison difficile, précaire,[70] entre la liberté civile et la liberté politique, entre le problème de la liberté et celui de la démocratie. A travers cette «fuite en avant» de Constant, il est à peine possible d'apercevoir le grand thème qui traverse le constitutionnalisme de Coppet et qui mûrit au cours du XIXème siècle: il y a, ici, l'intuition, dans le domaine des libertés, du problème qui touche le rapport individu-Etat, avec la conscience de devoir «combiner» – et cela est bien difficile – les deux libertés.[71] Il faut pouvoir concilier l'idée d'Etat basée sur la stabilité et sur la durée des institutions et des profils formels avec l'idée d'«enthousiasme» civique et de participation politique pour éloigner le risque d'un repli excessif de l'individu à l'intérieur de sa propre sphère privée. La frontière ambivalente entre le public et le privé dans la théorie constitutionnelle de Coppet apparaît donc comme une utile clé de lecture.[72]

6. Les pouvoirs et l'Etat

Le problème de l'extension de l'autorité sociale et, donc, de la séparation entre la société et l'Etat représente le point de départ et d'arrivée de la réflexion constitutionnelle de Coppet. Mais il reste à prendre en considération, pour

68 B. Constant, *De la liberté des anciens comparée à celle des modernes* (1819), dans *De la liberté chez les modernes*, publ. par M. Gauchet, Paris 1980, 514.

69 *Ibidem*.

70 Cf. en particulier B. Hasselrot, *Introduction* à B. Constant, *Lettres à Bernadotte. Sources et origine de l'Esprit de conquête et de l'usurpation*, Genève Lille 1952, LVIII; S. Holmes, *Benjamin Constant*, cit., 46 ss., 216–217; M. Barberis, *Benjamin Constant*, cit., 301 ss.; L. Jaume, *L'individu effacé*, cit., 82–86.

71 Pour quelques suggestions, v. M. Gauchet, *Benjamin Constant: l'illusion lucide du libéralisme*, introduction à B. Constant, *De la liberté chez les modernes*, cit., 9–91.

72 Cf. S. Holmes, *Benjamin Constant*, cit., 334–359.

conclure, le thème complexe de l'articulation du pouvoir de l'Etat, c'est-à-dire, comme l'on pourrait dire, du «lieu» et de l'espace légitime qu'il convient d'attribuer aux pouvoirs de l'Etat.

Limiter le pouvoir de l'Etat, cela ne veut pas dire affaiblir l'instance de gouvernement. Après avoir défini son rayon d'action, il faut se poser le problème de l'efficacité, de la force, de la dignité. L'expression «Pouvoir de l'Etat» est une expression synthétique, mais nécessairement complexe, parce qu'elle contient en elle-même, pour les doctrines du constitutionnalisme, l'idée de l'articulation des pouvoirs et de la division des fonctions (division du travail). L'Etat libéral constitutionnel de Coppet aborde l'idée reçue de la division des pouvoirs d'une façon critique. La réflexion de Necker à ce propos est fondamentale. Ce n'est pas en séparant les pouvoirs, en détruisant les mécanismes de raccord, de dialogue institutionnel, d'influence réciproque, que l'on fait fonctionner sagement une constitution. «Ce sont donc les liens, plus que les contrepoids, les proportions, plus que les distances, les convenances, plus que la vigilance, qui contribuent à l'harmonie des Gouvernemens; et si l'on arrête continuellement l'attention des Législateurs sur la nécessité de balancer une force par une autre, et non sur l'avantage de les réunir avec sagesse et par des moyens naturels [...]».[73]

Mme de Staël s'approprie le discours de son père sur l'union des pouvoirs. «Un penseur éloquent l'a dit, c'est à l'union des pouvoirs qu'il faut tendre; et l'on confond sans cesse la séparation nécessaire des fonctions avec une division des pouvoirs qui les rend forcément ennemis les uns des autres».[74] Le pouvoir est, comme Necker l'avait bien compris, «unitaire», bien qu'il soit exercé ensuite sous des formes différentes, c'est-à-dire sous une forme exécutive ou législative. En réalité, c'est la modalité de l'action – donc la forme – qui change, mais cela n'influe pas sur la nécessité de poursuivre un projet unitaire. «On doit chercher à établir une liaison constitutionnelle entre le pouvoir exécutif et le pouvoir législatif; on doit songer que leur prudente association, leur ingénieux entrelacement seront toujours la meilleure caution d'une circonspection mutuelle et d'une surveillance efficace».[75] Necker réfléchit sur le pouvoir de l'Etat et affirme

73 J. Necker, *Du pouvoir exécutif*, cit., t. I, 81.

74 G. De Staël, *Des circonstances*, cit., 179. Dans une lettre de juin 1795 à Pierre-Louis Roederer, Madame de Staël parlait déjà de l'unification des pouvoirs: P.-L. Roederer, *Œuvres complètes* ..., Paris 1853–1859, vol. VIII, 646.

75 Le passage continue: «Cependant, je l'ai déjà dit, les législateurs français ont pris à tâche de séparer en tous sens les deux autorités suprêmes, et ils se sont imposé cette obligation sur la foi périlleuse d'un axiome absolu trouvé en quelques livres, et au mépris des instructions fournies par l'expérience». La citation de Necker est extraite de *De la Révolution française*, dans *Œuvres complètes de M. Necker*, Paris 1821, t. X, 133–134. Cf. également *Dernières vues de politique et de finance*, *Ibid.*, t. XI, 125–126. Sur le sujet, voir l'importante analyse de

que la collaboration entre le «pouvoir exécutif» (action / impulsion) et le «pouvoir législatif» (contrôle / surveillance) est nécessaire. C'est sur cette distinction fonctionnelle que le discours polémique envers le principe-guide de l'organisation révolutionnaire du pouvoir s'inscrit: la prééminence du législatif (jusqu'à l'omnipotence)[76] sur la fonction de gouvernement. La constitution de 1791 et les décrets successifs en sont la preuve immédiate: la question du veto, le refus du bicaméralisme, l'ablation systématique de la royauté, le manque de communication entre les pouvoirs, le rôle des ministres, ainsi que de nombreux autres aspects, sont, on le sait, les grands thèmes de discussion. Le système anglais fait fonction, ici, de contre-chant. Ce que Necker considère dégradé, ou ne voit pas du tout en France, il le retrouve, renforcé par la longue tradition, en Grande Bretagne.

L'intérêt de la réflexion de Necker réside dans le fait que, bien qu'ayant comme objet le monarque «nationalisé», pouvoir constitué et désacralisé, elle prend en considération en réalité le plus vaste problème du pouvoir de l'Etat. Il n'est pas surprenant, donc, que cette réflexion puisse se développer au cours des années successives, toujours avec Necker comme témoin direct, face aux transformations du régime politique et au trône désormais vide. Bien plus, le problème du pouvoir exécutif devient le *leitmotiv* de l'analyse du banquier de Genève. Pouvoir exécutif vu comme «force motrice» du système constitutionnel, «puissance mystérieuse». Cela sonne presque comme une hérésie de dire que la chose la plus difficile, dans une constitution, c'est d'organiser le pouvoir exécutif.[77] Ce n'est pas en démembrant ce pouvoir que l'on prévient les abus et que les libertés se trouvent renforcées;[78] au contraire, la faiblesse est l'antichambre naturelle de l'arbitraire.[79] Un pouvoir de gouvernement muni des attributions indispensables n'est pourtant pas suffisant. C'est justement le principe de l'union des pouvoirs qui conseille des formes de dialogue, d'«association» entre les pouvoirs. L'initiative législative appartenant au Roi et aux Chambres, le veto, le pouvoir de dissolution, la présence des ministres dans

H. Grange, *Les idées de Necker*, cit., 272 ss. Cette idée sera reprise, de nombreuses années plus tard, par Sismondi: *Etudes sur les constitutions*, cit.

76 Sur cet aspect, nous renvoyons tout particulièrement à M. Morabito, *Le chef de l'Etat en France*, Paris 1996 et à la synthèse remarquable du même auteur *Il comando negato. Rivoluzione francese e potere esecutivo*, Roma, Manduria 1997.

77 J. Necker, *Du pouvoir exécutif*, cit., t. I, 14 ss.

78 *Ibidem*, 342 ss.

79 La synthèse de Constant est très claire: «Or en affaiblissant le gouvernement, vous le forcez à envahir. Ne pouvant atteindre son but nécessaire avec les forces qui lui appartiennent, il aura recours pour l'atteindre à des forces qu'il usurpera [...]» (B. Constant, *Principes de politique*, ed. Hofmann, cit., 462).

l'Assemblée, le pouvoir de contrôle des Chambres, le bicaméralisme, etc. sont quelques-uns des mécanismes d'«union» et de rééquilibre.

Les scénario changent, mais le problème reste avec toute son ampleur.[80] Nous trouvons encore Necker lire les constitutions du Directoire sur cette ligne, Madame De Staël partager l'analyse de son père,[81] essayant, ensuite, tous les deux, de résoudre la pesante hypothèque révolutionnaire, Benjamin Constant s'interroger sur la nature de la constitution républicaine.[82]

7. L'horloge et la balance: à propos de l'équilibre constitutionnel

Le débat que nous venons de rappeler nous amène à l'un des éléments les plus significatifs de l'Etat constitutionnel «imaginaire» de Coppet: si l'«union» et la collaboration des pouvoirs sont les piliers d'une constitution cohérente et efficace, il reste à comprendre comment il est possible de garantir et de conserver une condition d'équilibre durable, en d'autres termes quelle est la force «mystérieuse» capable de garantir la vertu de la «modération». C'est sur ce problème que la réflexion constitutionnelle de Coppet – en particulier dans sa formulation faite par Constant – a laissé, en héritage, aux théoriciens de l'Etat libéral de droit, un projet riche et stimulant.

L'on peut dire, plus simplement, que le débat sur le rôle et les fonctions du monarque entre 1789 et la constitution de 1791 représente le point de départ. Le passage du monarque absolu[83] au «premier citoyen du Royaume» (Sieyès) pour arriver ensuite au «premier fonctionnaire public» (art. IV, Constitution du 3 septembre 1791)[84] prouve le caractère radical de la transformation. Jacques Necker s'inspire, au sein d'une discussion très vaste et variée, du fondement historique de la royauté pour prouver, au contraire, comment celle-ci peut se révéler «utile» et nécessaire pour la re-construction du système constitutionnel en France. Un monarque séparé de la royauté perd tout ce qui «peut servir à dominer l'imagination».[85] Il n'y a pas que le pouvoir effectif qui compte, car

80 Cf. H. Grange, *Les idées de Necker*, cit. et L. Jaume, *L'esprit de Coppet et l'organisation du pouvoir exécutif*, dans *La Constitution de l'an III ou l'ordre républicain*, Dijon 1998.

81 Dans les *Réflexions sur la paix intérieure* (1795), cit. et, en particulier, dans *Des circonstances*, cit. Ce problème sera aussi abordé plus tard dans les *Considérations*, cit.

82 B. Constant, *Fragments d'un ouvrage*, cit.

83 Pour quelques suggestions, v. P. Viola, *Il trono vuoto. La transizione della sovranità nella Rivoluzione francese*, Torino 1989.

84 Voir la synthèse remarquable de R. Martucci, *1789, la Repubblica dei foglianti. Dal re d'antico regime al primo funzionario dello Stato*, dans *Storia, amministrazione, costituente. Annale I.S.A.P.*, 1, 1993, 87–104.

85 J. Necker, *Du pouvoir exécutif*, cit., t. I, 260 ss.

celui-ci est inséparable de l'«appareil», de la machine symbolique.[86] Une constitution garantit l'équilibre, la modération, la régularité si elle arrive à faire une «synthèse» entre ses organes et ses pouvoirs. La constitution anglaise révèle, d'après Necker, cette «vérité» fondamentale. La «sacralité» et la «magie» du trône sont tout à fait compatibles avec un système efficace. Necker est, sans aucun doute, un des observateurs les plus attentifs et les plus lucides du système britannique car il sait en tirer la logique de l'«union des pouvoirs». Necker en désarticule les mécanismes de fonctionnement, en cherchant à aller au-delà des apparences. Si le roi conserve des prérogatives importantes, il est également vrai que celles-ci n'acquièrent une signification particulière seulement si l'on considère que l'irresponsabilité / inviolabilité du chef de l'Etat n'est pas séparable de la responsabilité du pouvoir ministériel. La monarchie permettrait, donc, mieux et plus que toute autre forme d'organisation politique, de réaliser cette scission fondamentale.[87]

Dans le miroir anglais, les défauts de la constitution française semblent correspondre, en négatif, aux qualités de la constitution d'Outre Manche. Les constitutions changent, mais ce sont les principes – dit Necker dans sa lecture monarchique, et répètent Madame de Staël et Constant avec un point de vue républicain – qui se révèlent «structurellement» défectueux. Pendant le Directoire, la réflexion constitutionnelle est en grande partie centrée sur le rapport problématique qu'il y a entre le pouvoir exécutif et le pouvoir législatif. C'est ici que l'on saisit ce noyau profond de convictions qui rend la réflexion du groupe de Coppet cohérente et qui pousse ses principaux représentants vers une conception relativiste des formes de gouvernement.

Il n'est pas surprenant que l'on puisse découvrir dans les raisonnements «républicains» de Mme de Staël et surtout de Constant des logiques et des argumentations qui proviennent de l'arsenal de la pratique constitutionnelle anglaise, à travers la médiation de Necker et de bien autres auteurs. Comment, donc, reproduire le «mystérieux de ce nuage»,[88] dans lequel le monarque anglais est situé, dans un contexte si radicalement différent qu'est celui du Directoire? Comment les raisons de l'inviolabilité et celles de la responsabilité peuvent-elles

86 Sur la dimension symbolique, voir les observations de M. Morabito: *Necker et la question du chef de l'État*, dans *Coppet, creuset de l'esprit libéral. Les idées politiques et constitutionnelles du groupe de Madame de Stäel*, sous la dir. de L. Jaume, Aix, Marseille 2000, 41–54.

87 Cf. H. Grange, *Les idées de Necker*, cit., 307 ss.

88 G. De Staël, *Réflexions sur la paix intérieure*, cit.: «En Angleterre, le roi pourrait rester toute sa vie dans un nuage sans que la marche du gouvernement s'en ressentît. Il faut connaître seulement jusqu'à quel point le mystérieux de ce nuage est nécessaire pour étouffer toutes les ambitions particulières», 52.

cohabiter et coopérer? Comment mettre fin aux controverses entre le législatif et l'exécutif?

Le constitutionnalisme républicain n'est certainement pas pauvre en propositions. Les institutions et les procédures sont toutefois si compliquées et si «artificielles» qu'elles révèlent une forte gêne et une tentative difficile pour garantir stabilité et équilibre. Les plusieurs centaines de citoyens privés qui adressent, au cours de l'an III, un grand nombre de lettres à la *Commission des Onze* et même de vastes projets constitutionnels ont fait penser à une «république d'horlogers»[89] qui ne manquent pas d'une vive imagination: le «lieu» de la résolution des conflits constitutionnels est occupé d'organes appelés «Conseil de censure», «Sénat réviseur», «Pouvoir conservateur des lois et des droits».[90] La culture politique thermidorienne est déjà orientée, et cela avant que Sieyès ne présente sa célèbre proposition de *jury constitutionnaire* à la Convention,[91] de façon à s'interroger sur le problème de l'équilibre et de la stabilisation des pouvoirs. Le *corps conservateur* de Madame de Staël en sera une confirmation ultérieure, dans la tentative d'unir la logique «aristocratique» et la fonction tendant à mettre fin aux controverses entre le législatif et l'exécutif.

La réflexion de Sieyès est sans aucun doute au premier plan: de la métaphore de l'horloger à la garantie de la constitution en tant que forme suprême de garantie des droits.[92] Si la constitution est un corps de lois «on se demande où sera le gardien, où sera la magistrature de ce code? Il faut pouvoir répondre».[93] Le *pouvoir neutre et préservateur* de Constant cerne le problème central du con-

89 S. Luzzatto, *L'Autunno della Rivoluzione. Lotta e cultura politica nella Francia del Termidoro*, Torino 1994, 304. Sur l'horloge comme métaphore politique, O. Mayr, *Authority, Liberty and Automatic Machinery in Early Modern Europe*, Baltimore 1986.

90 Cf. S. Luzzatto, *L'Autunno della Rivoluzione*, cit., 310–312. Voir aussi F. Brunel, *Aux origines d'un parti de l'ordre: les projets de constitution de l'an III*, dans J. Nicolas (dir.), *Mouvements populaires et conscience sociale, XVIe–XIXe siècles*, Paris 1985, 687–696.

91 Cf. les discours des 2 et 13 Thermidor An III, dans P. Bastid, *Les discours de Sieyès*, cit. A ce propos, v. P. Bastid, *Sieyès et sa pensée* (1939), Paris 1970, 433 ss.; J.-D. Bredin, *Sieyès: la clé de la Révolution française*, Paris 1988, 366.

92 Cf. S. Mannoni, *Une et indivisible. Storia dell'accentramento amministrativo in Francia*, Milano 1994, t. I, 284 ss.

93 Cf. P. Bastid, *Les discours de Sieyès*, cit. Constant, dans les *Souvenirs historiques à l'occasion de l'ouvrage de M. Bignon. Première lettre*, dans *Revue de Paris*, XI, février 1830, 120, paiera son dû à Sieyès: «Ainsi, par exemple, on pourrait dire, quelque bizarre que paraisse l'assertion, quand on se retrace toute la vie de Sieyès, qu'il a contribué plus que personne, à poser les bases de la monarchie constitutionnelle. Il a le premier, en France, établi et prouvé que le chef, placé au haut de la hiérarchie politique, devait choisir, mais non gouverner [...]».

stitutionnalisme républicain: le monisme constitutionnel et les défauts intrinsèques des constitutions de l'époque révolutionnaire générateurs de conflits, d'abus et d'illégalités. Ce pouvoir est représenté comme neutre (comparé au rapport législatif-exécutif); il est de plus préservateur car il a comme but de conserver, en cas de conflit, la *machine* constitutionnelle, en jouant le rôle d'une sorte de valve de sécurité.[94] Constant construit ce pouvoir «tiers» et «impartial» avec des «matériaux» qui sont davantage déduits du «dépôt» historique de la monarchie constitutionnelle[95] (hérédité, faculté de dissolution du législatif, faculté de destitution du pouvoir exécutif) que de l'univers conceptuel du discours républicain, bien que dans le domaine de la légitimité légale de la nation. Dans les *Fragments*, Constant analyse, en observant l'expérience anglaise, le problème de la responsabilité politique. Constant rappelle qu'«Un des plus grands avantages de la Royauté, c'est d'avoir en quelque sorte constitué le droit de destitution entre les mains du roi [...]», en attribuant à Stanislas de Clermont-Tonnerre[96] la théorie de la double nature du pouvoir monarchique: «pouvoir exécutif investi de prérogatives positives» et «pouvoir royal» vu en tant que pouvoir neutre «entre le peuple et le pouvoir exécutif proprement dit qui est toujours délégué à des ministres».[97]

La définition ultérieure de la théorie du pouvoir neutre dans les écrits de la Restauration est une conséquence logique de la réflexion qui avait déjà mûri à l'époque républicaine. Le retour à la forme monarchique permet à Constant de «ramener» l'idée de pouvoir neutre et préservateur à l'intérieur de la «condition monarchique» qui est plus favorable.[98] Les attributions peuvent être confiées au

94 A propos de tout cela nous renvoyons aux observations importantes de M. Barberis, *Benjamin Constant*, cit., 173 ss.

95 «Le pouvoir préservateur doit être ce qu'est le pouvoir monarchique en Angleterre, avec les différences exigées par la nature du gouvernement républicain» (B. Constant, *Fragments d'un ouvrage*, cit., 403). Sur la pluralité des "sources" et des modèles utilisés par Constant – par ex. le Conseil des Dix vénitien dont parle Sismondi – v. H. Grange, *Introduction*, cit., 46–47.

96 En réalité, la position de Clermont-Tonnerre contredit l'attribution de Constant. Sur les raisons de cette attribution singulière, cf. la thèse de M. Barberis, *Benjamin Constant*, cit., 220 ss. Carl Schmitt s'était déjà interrogé sur ce point, *Der Hüter der Verfassung*, dans *Archiv des öffentlichen Rechts*, XVI, 1929, 2, 161–237, puis, avec le même titre, Tübingen 1931; enfin Berlin 1969, nt. 1 du chap. III.

97 B. Constant, *Fragments d'un ouvrage*, cit., 398.

98 «N'oublions donc jamais cette grande vérité, cette vérité qui établit l'unique supériorité de la monarchie, mais de la monarchie constitutionnelle seulement, sur le gouvernement républicain, dans lequel il a été impossible jusqu'ici de séparer le pouvoir exécutif du pouvoir suprême, et de résister à l'un sans ébranler l'autre [...]» (B. Constant, *Observations sur le discours prononcé*, cit., 1248–1249). «[...] ou sous le régime républicain dont le grand défaut est de ne placer nulle

pouvoir royal. Dans les *Principes* de 1815, Constant reprend la théorie des cinq pouvoirs et les raisonnements de l'époque républicaine, ainsi que, surtout, ce qu'il avait déjà dit dans les *Réflexions sur les constitutions* et dans *De la responsabilité des ministres*.[99] La description est bien connue: le pouvoir royal est le pouvoir neutre; le pouvoir ministériel est un pouvoir actif. Le monarque-horloger intervient «de l'extérieur» quand le «mouvement général» se bloque: «[...] quand ces ressorts dérangés se croisent, s'entre-choquent et s'entravent, il faut une force qui les remette à leur place».[100] Si le vice, le plus grave, des constitutions précédentes a été celui de ne pas avoir créé un pouvoir neutre, le pouvoir royal semble garantir «[...] une sphère inviolable de sécurité, de majesté, d'impartialité, qui permet à ces dissentiments de se développer sans péril [...]». Le conflit devient ainsi, dans certaines limites, une ressource, et le pouvoir royal n'intervient que lorsque cela est nécessaire et «[...] y met un terme par des moyens légaux, constitutionnels, et dégagés de tout arbitraire [...]».[101]

Ce schéma existe – dit Constant – dans la réalité, ce n'est donc pas une simple hypothèse: la monarchie anglaise a donné forme à «[...] ce pouvoir neutre et intermédiaire [...] le pouvoir royal séparé du pouvoir exécutif».[102] La neutralité du pouvoir royal est la «[...] condition indispensable de toute monarchie constitutionnelle, à laquelle je reviens sans cesse, parce que toute la stabilité de l'édifice repose sur cette base [...]».[103] Si Madame de Staël avait parlé du «mystérieux de ce nuage», Constant définit le monarque «[...] pouvoir neutre et abstrait, au-dessus de la région des orages».[104]

L'emphase faite par Constant sur la «sacralisation» du chef de l'Etat, ne doit toutefois pas faire passer en second plan la complexité de la théorie du pouvoir neutre, à la compréhension de laquelle n'a été favorable ni l'utilisation successive

part l'inviolabilité, condition indispensable pour la liberté, pour le repos et pour la durée» (B. Constant, *De l'état constitutionnel de la France*, dans *La Renommée*, n. 1, mardi, 15 juin 1819, dans *Recueil d'articles. Le Mercure, la Minerve et la Renommée*, tome II, Introduction, notes et commentaires par E. Harpaz, Genève 1972, 1233).

99 Paris 1815.

100 B. Constant, *Principes de politique* (1815), cit., 1079. Constant décrit également le pouvoir neutre dans les termes suivants: «Le dépositaire du pouvoir suprême, siégeant au haut de la hiérarchie politique, modérant les mouvemens de tous les pouvoirs, rétablissant l'harmonie entre eux, et du haut de sa sphère, au-dessus des agitations et des orages, dissipant ces orages et apaisant ces agitations [...]» (*De l'état constitutionnel*, cit., 1232–1233).

101 B. Constant, *Principes de politique* (1815), 1082. Les moyens légaux sont la destitution des ministres, la dissolution de la chambre élue et l'utilisation du veto, la concession de la grâce.

102 *Ibidem*, 1083.

103 *Ibidem*, 1180.

104 *Ibidem*, 1137. «Le monarque est dans une enceinte à part et sacrée».

et instrumentale dans d'autres contextes – il suffit de penser à la polémique que l'on cite toujours entre Kelsen et Schmitt[105] – ni le fait qu'elle a été proposée de nouveau comme catégorie interprétative qui pouvait être appliquée immédiatement à l'époque contemporaine. Au besoin, c'est justement son caractère problématique historique qui représente sa véritable force.

Il ne faut pas oublier que les formules les plus cohérentes sont, d'un côté, celle, d'origine républicaine, du pouvoir neutre et préservateur, et de l'autre, la formule utilisée à la Restauration, du pouvoir neutre et intermédiaire. Le souverain «préservateur» est l'organe de l'unité nationale et de la continuité de l'Etat: fort de sa «majesté» et de son «impartialité», il incarne la puissance publique, il est l'«être à part, supérieur aux diversités des opinions», le gardien qui garantit l'équilibre en cas d'excès, quand la collaboration entre les pouvoirs est menacée. Mais le pouvoir «intermédiaire» investit aussi le monarque du devoir, historiquement ardu, de «pacifier» – à travers sa neutralité – un pays profondément partagé entre des visions différentes de l'avenir (outre que du passé),[106] contrôlant la formation et le développement d'un système constitutionnel capable de «discipliner» la lutte politique (lien avec l'opinion), de garantir un gouvernement uni et responsable du point de vue politique (contrôle), en permettant des formes d'opposition et de pluralisme. Le pouvoir préservateur, en fondant un gouvernement qui répond de ses actes à la nation, contribue à garder un certain équilibre entre l'ordre et la liberté, en garantissant, en dernière instance, la sécurité des citoyens.

Toutefois, cette double fonction ne peut pas être garantie seulement par les attributions «négatives». C'est aussi pour cette raison que le modèle anglais que Constant fait preuve de bien connaître – et qui est le résultat d'un long développement historique complexe – ne peut pas coïncider tout court avec l'idée de Constant sur le pouvoir neutre. Les *ultras* de la *Chambre introuvable* avaient faits de la doctrine du pouvoir neutre et de la responsabilité des ministres un «instrument» pour emphatiser les prérogatives parlementaires. Cet épisode prouve combien la théorie de Constant est plus complexe – et peut-être aussi

105 Je me réfère, naturellement, à C. Schmitt, *Der Hüter der Verfassung*, cit. et à H. Kelsen, *Wer soll der Hüter der Verfassung sein?*, dans *Die Justiz*, VI, 11–12, 1930–1931, 576–628. Sur les différents points de vue dans le débat entre Schmitt et Kelsen, v. P. Pasquino, *Gardien de la constitution ou justice constitutionnelle? Carl Schmitt et Hans Kelsen*, dans *1789 et l'invention de la constitution*, sous la direction de M. Troper et L. Jaume, Paris 1994, 143–152.

106 Sur la Charte comme «transaction avec le passé» et forme «d'un gouvernement futur» (Guizot 1816) ou comme «traité de paix signé entre les deux partis qui ont divisé les Français» (Chateaubriand 1816), v. P. Rosanvallon, *La Monarchie impossible. Les Chartes de 1814 et de 1830*, Paris 1994, 83.

plus contradictoire – que l'on ne pense. Constant, et non pas seulement le Guizot du *Du gouvernement représentatif et de l'état actuel de la France*,[107] était conscient du danger d'une «neutralisation» littérale du pouvoir royal comme juge des pouvoirs constitutionnels «actifs». La rectification, dans les *Additions* de 1818 (réédition des *Réflexions sur les constitutions*),[108] sert à Constant pour répliquer au vicomte de Chateaubriand qu'en interprétant un peu malicieusement l'idée de pouvoir neutre, il avait presque représenté le roi comme un «spectateur». Constant dit que le monarque ne peut pas rester «impassible» face à un ministre qui s'éloigne de l'opinion et c'est pour cela qu'«il le renvoie avant que la faute ne soit commise». La réflexion de Constant sur le pouvoir neutre ne se limite pas au débat sur la prérogative royale et sur l'interprétation à donner de la Charte de 1814.

Le pouvoir neutre n'est donc pas impassible. Constant est presque obligé de le répéter, mais cela émerge de ses écrits précédents. Dans la neutralité, il y a un noyau d'influence presque «secrète», mais dont on ne peut pas douter, et de partage nécessaire de l'orientation politique. Le roi ne gouverne pas, mais il doit pouvoir «choisir».[109] L'on constate cela alors que Constant ne pense pas à introduire en France le mécanisme formel, de matrice anglaise, de la *motion of censure* ou de *Vote of no confidence*, parce que cela contredirait la faculté royale de nommer et de révoquer les ministres; ou bien là où Constant ne fait pas dépendre la dissolution de la Chambre (autre «moyen légal et constitutionnel» d'«appel à l'opinion») de la pratique, anglaise elle aussi, de l'*in accordance with ministerial advice* et du contreseing du premier ministre, mais d'une décision, solitaire, bien que non pas arbitraire, fondée sur l'opportunité politique. De plus, le fait que Constant ne consacre pas d'étude systématique à la figure du premier ministre, laquelle est si importante dans le constitutionnalisme anglais depuis Robert Walpole, n'est pas étonnant.

Le pouvoir neutre de Constant est donc une forme de «pouvoir de réserve». Plus le système garantit physiologiquement «la stabilité de l'édifice», plus le monarque peut faire «marche arrière», en restant l'«être à part, supérieur aux diversités des opinions». Mais les prérogatives que Constant assigne au pouvoir royal lui permettent, au cas où le système fonctionnerait mal, de sortir de l'«enceinte sacrée» et d'assumer un rôle qui n'est pas sans une dimension «active». Constant semble, bien qu'en s'inspirant au modèle anglais, vouloir "rationaliser" un anachronisme apparent: il ne se tourne pas vers le système anglais qui est effectivement opérant à partir de la seconde moitié du XVIIIème

107 Paris 1816.
108 Cité par M. Barberis, *Benjamin Constant*, cit., 227.
109 Voir plus haut nt. 93.

siècle, mais vers le développement de la monarchie de Hanovre.[110] L'anachronisme de Constant révèle un dessein lucide et réaliste, même s'il n'est pas sans contradictions interprétatives. L'on ne peut pas construire l'Etat constitutionnel en oubliant l'élaboration anglaise, complexe et séculaire. Ayant repoussé l'hypothèse de la monarchie limitée (malgré la Charte), Constant pense que, au moment de la Restauration (alors que le système constitutionnel est encore entièrement à construire), le pouvoir neutre ne peut pas être enfermé en France dans la seule sphère de l'*auctoritas*. Le monarque doit, si cela est nécessaire, pouvoir exercer ses *potestates*. Le pouvoir royal doit être suffisamment neutre, mais il doit, à l'occasion, avoir la force légale lui permettant d'être réellement «préservateur» et «intermédiaire». Le roi pouvoir neutre doit avoir la capacité et la volonté – et c'est ici que réside le problème[111] – de garder un certain équilibre entre l'opinion et le pouvoir ministériel, les Chambres et la fonction du gouvernement, en reconnaissant le point variable du compromis. Le roi – pourrait-on dire – a le difficile dévoir de fixer le point d'équilibre, toujours instable, entre la constitution formelle et la constitution matérielle.

L'on comprend pourquoi l'idée de pouvoir neutre est à proprement parler la vraie architrave du système, le problème théorique sans lequel il n'est pas possible de concevoir l'architecture de l'Etat constitutionnel libéral comme le voit Coppet. Le problème est que presque personne – rois ou conseillers, ministres ou constitutionnalistes – n'a su, pendant une bonne partie du XIXème siècle, interpréter le message «chiffré» de Constant, en relevant les avertissements, plus ou moins implicites, contenus dans son discours.

110 Je considère, à ce propos, fondamentales les observations de J. Varela Suanzes, *La monarquia en el pensamiento de Benjamin Constant (Inglaterra como modelo)*, dans *Revista del Centro de Estudios Constitucionales*, 10, 1991, 121–138.

111 Le débat parlementaire de 1830 et l'Adresse des 221 – avec l'intervention significative de Constant – semblent offrir une intéressante confirmation. Sur le point voir P. Rosanvallon, *La Monarchie impossible*, cit., 99–100.

Granted Constitutions. The Theory of *octroi* and Constitutional Experiments in Europe in the Aftermath of the French Revolution

Le mot octroyer et tous ses dérivés doivent être bannis à jamais de la science politique (E.-J. Sieyès, *Vues sur les moyens d'exécution dont les représentants de la France pourront disposer en 1789*, s. l., 1789, 47)

Nous avons volontairement, et par le libre exercice de notre autorité royale, accordé et accordons, fait concession et octroi à nos sujets, tant pour nous que pour nos successeurs, et à toujours, de la Charte constitutionnelle (*Charte constitutionnelle*, 1814, Preamble)

M. Constant: Comme tous les pouvoirs, en France, émanent de la Charte ...
(Voix a droite): Non, ils émanent du roi ...
M. Josse de Beauvoir: Ce n'est pas la Charte qui a donné le roi, mais le roi lui-même qui a octroyé la Charte.
M. Constant: Tous les pouvoirs ne sont légitimes que par la Charte ...
M. de Vogué: Non, par le pouvoir du roi ...
M. Benoit: La Charte n'est légitime que parce que le roi l'a donnée ...
M. Constant: Il me paraît que c'est faire au monarque la plus grande injure [...] de déclarer que ses pouvoirs ne viennent pas de la Charte (11 January 1822, *Discours de M. Benjamin Constant à la Chambre des députés*, Paris, Dupont, 1828, II, 3–4)

Und man kann hinzulegen: eine bloß octroyierte Verfassung ist gar keine Verfassung (K. Welcker, *Octroyierte Verfassungen*, in K. von Rotteck und K. Welcker, *Das Staats-Lexikon. Encyklopädie der sämmtlichen Staatswissenschaften für alle Stände*, Leipzig, Brockhaus, 1864, vol. X, 735)

Il demande quelle est la ligne à suivre par le Ministère? Si S. M. juge inévitable une Constitution, ainsi que tout porte à le croire, il faudrait tout préparer pour la donner, avec le plus de dignité possible pour la Couronne, avec le moins de mal possible pour le pays. Il faut la donner, non se la laisser imposer; dicter les conditions, non les recevoir; il faut avoir le temps de choisir avec calme les moyens et l'opportunité, après avoir promis de les employer (Count G. Borelli, Ministry of Interior, *Conseil de Conférence*, 3 February 1848)

1. Introduction

The category of the 'granted constitution' occupies an important place in constitutionalism in the era of the Restoration; indeed, the years between 1814 and 1848 may be said to be its Golden Age. During this period, political processes and constitutional debates hinged on the significance of granting a constitution, on the general constitutional form which derived from it and, more particularly, on its actual impact upon the form of government, upon the guaranteeing of rights, and upon the rules and procedures established for changing the constitution itself. The phenomenon of the 'granted constitution' can be clearly demarcated both temporally and spatially. In terms of space, this phenomenon was restricted to a triangle consisting primarily, but not exclusively, of France from 1814 until 1830; secondly, of the German lands from the Congress of Vienna and the emergence of the so-called *Frühkonstitutionalismus* onward; and thirdly, of the Italian States, in particular, the Kingdom of Sardinia. How was it possible for one and the same constitutional form to apply to so many different contexts and yet to spark markedly similar reflections and experiences? What was the common ground, and what were the points of divergence, that characterised the era of the granted constitution? What model (or, indeed, models)[1] informed the constitutional policies of the Restoration?

This essay is intended to be a preliminary contribution to the study of this phenomenon, and to stimulate theoretical debate concerning a topic which is in need of more systematic scrutiny. I propose to interpret nineteenth-century constitutionalism in terms of the function of the monarch (or the monarchy) within the different constitutional systems, considering this question on a European scale.[2] My intention here is to scrutinize the pivotal role played by

1 Regarding the use of models in comparative constitutional history, see *supra* in this volume *La Costituzione belga del 1831*, 80–83. In the present work, by monarchical constitutionalism and monarchy I simply mean that which is intrinsic to the dynastic authority and hereditary power of the king. While it is certainly possible (and for other reasons, necessary) to broaden this category, in the sense of including every form of domination exercised by a single subject (which M. Kirsch proposes in *La trasformazione politica del monarca europeo nel XIX secolo*, in *Scienza & Politica*, 34, 2006, 21–35; and, more broadly, Id., *Monarch und Parlament im 19. Jahrhundert. Der monarchische Konstitutionalismus als europäischer Verfassungstyp – Frankreich im Vergleich*, Göttingen 1999, it seems just as necessary to be aware of the profound diversity of forms and sources of sovereignty, legitimacy/legitimisation, constitutional organization, forms of power, etc.

2 See A. G. Manca, *La monarchia costituzionale nell'Europa del lungo Ottocento: da forma a strumento di governo*, in L. Blanco (ed.), *Dottrine e istituzioni in Occidente*, Bologna 2011, 151–184.

the category of granted constitution in European constitutional history. This kind of constitution is something more than simply a transitional phenomenon, or an 'interval' (albeit an important one) between the novel and strategic idea of the eighteenth-century constitution based upon the constituent power of the people and the full realisation of democratic constitutionalism in the course of the twentieth century. The intrinsic interest of this approach lies in its capacity to portray granted constitutions as instruments serving to preserve ancient forms of sovereignty alongside post-revolutionary innovations. 'Monarchical constitutionalism' established an important and long-enduring workshop in which we can observe 'old' and 'new', tradition and change, conflicts and mediations, ancient words and new concepts, the ideology of *octroi* and parliamentary experiments.

From a common starting-point, namely, the concern to reconcile monarchical "machinery" with the new aspirations towards constitutionalism and parliamentary representation, the model of granted constitutions led to a range of different outcomes. This model fostered the development, by a number of routes, of the constitutional idea of democracy founded upon popular representation and legal guarantees. Conversely, it sometimes justified a new form of monarchical constitutionalism, thereby bolstering authoritarian regimes. What is peculiarly fascinating about granted constitutions is their capacity to lead to more than one outcome.

2. The *Charte* and the *octroi*: the origins of the 'model'

The Spanish, German and Italian languages have each traced the use of the word and concept (*otorgar / otorgado*; *oktroyren / oktroyert*; *ottriare / ottriato*)[3] to the French term *octroyer/octroi*. In the Preamble to the *Charte constitutionnelle* of 4 June 1814 granted by Louis XVIII, we thus read:

> We have, willingly and by virtue of the free exercise of our royal authority, consented to and consent to, have conceded and granted the Constitutional Charter to our subjects, both for us and for our successors, and forever.[4]

'Faire concession et octroi' is, therefore, the constitutional formula which defines an entire era. Upon landing in France on 2 May 1814 after his exile in

3 It is important to note that the French term *octroi* could at times lose something in the translation. In German, for instance, *oktroyiern* has a somewhat stronger sense, implying 'to impose upon' rather than 'to grant'. The various renderings of the word *octroi* thus create a semantic field that is both complex and nuanced.

4 'Nous avons volontairement, et par le libre exercice de notre autorité royale, accordé et accordons, fait concession et octroi à nos sujets, tant pour nous que pour nos successeurs, et à toujours, de la Charte constitutionnelle'.

England, the future king, Louis XVIII, issued the Declaration of Saint-Ouen,[5] in which he stated that he would retain a number of important features of the Napoleonic era, among them the civil code and the sale of *biens nationaux* (confiscated land). One month earlier, on 6 April, after the Fall of Napoleon, what remained of the Napoleonic Senate had hastily approved the 'outlines' of a constitutional project.[6] The senators wanted to '*instaurer* – et non *restaurer* – la monarchie traditionnelle, extraordinaire paradoxe dans les termes. Ils se refusaient à la reconnaître ou à la déclarer: ils voulaient la constituer'.[7] However, Louis XVIII, 'par la grâce de Dieu, Roi de France et de Navarre', stated in a proclamation of 2 June that the constitution was his affair, a thing that he alone might grant. The possibility of a sworn pact to make Louis and his successors the kings of the French people seemed thus to have evaporated. Even before the important question of the form to be imparted to the monarchy was addressed, there was the basic issue of legitimacy to be resolved. The king's advisers set to work, and a new constitutional text was hastily drafted and presented to the Senate in the session on 4 June 1814.[8]

3. Theory of the *octroi*: the tale of the king-patriarch

The *octroi* was the instrument employed to affirm the constitutional position of 'restored' sovereigns, or of sovereigns whose political authority was under threat. By this means, the restored monarch endeavoured to bring a fundamental element of the new 'political theology'[9] within his sphere of influence:[10] a political theology that was hostile and dangerous, that had risen up against the monarchy and was summed up in the idea of the constitutional act. The

5 The text is in P. Rosanvallon, *La monarchie impossible. Les Chartes de 1814 et 1830*, Paris 1994, 209–210.

6 On the senatorial constitution, see J. De Soto, *La Constitution sénatoriale du 6 avril 1814*, in *Revue internationale d'histoire politique et constitutionnelle*, 3, 1953, 268–304; S. Rials, *Constitution sénatoriale*, in J. Tulard (ed.), *Dictionnaire Napoléon*, Paris 1989, 504–506; P. Rosanvallon, *La monarchie impossible*, cit., 15; M. S. Corciulo, *La constitution sénatoriale française du 6 avril 1814*, in *Parliaments, Estates and Representation*, 18, 1997, 139–150.

7 S. Rials, *Une grande étape du constitutionnalisme européen. La question constitutionnelle en 1814–1815: dispersion des légitimités et convergence des techniques*, in Id., *Révolution et contre-révolution au XIXème siècle*, Paris 1987, 130.

8 As regards the composition of this text, and the various drafts, see now: P. Rosanvallon, *La monarchie impossible*, cit., 29 ff.; A. Laquièze, *Les origines du régime parlementaire en France (1814–1848)*, Paris 2002, 38.

9 C. Schmitt, *Definition der Souveränität*, in Id., *Politische Theologie. Vier Kapitel zur Lehre von der Souveränität*, Berlin 1934, 2 ed.

10 See P. Colombo, *Con lealtà di Re e con affetto di padre. Torino, 4 marzo 1848: la concessione dello Statuto albertino*, Bologna 2003, 37.

Restoration thus attempted to neutralise that most terrible of powers, the constituent power of the people. In the second half of the eighteenth century *We the People*, *Nous la Nation* served to define – albeit with a wide range of different outcomes and in markedly different forms – a new conceptual order destined to leave an indelible mark upon modern constitutional doctrine. It was the people who defined and represented themselves as a totality, as a political unity that was conscious of its own existence and of having the capacity to act politically. All 'extraneous' bodies – extraneous, that is to say, to the nation – could no longer exist save by merging with popular sovereignty. The French Revolution was the stage upon which this momentous drama had been enacted.

In granting the *Charte*, Louis XVIII and his entourage intended to assert the monarch's uncontested paternal rights over the constitution. Count Beugnot – the principal author of the 'Charte' – observed that every deliberation of the two Houses which aimed at making the king dependent upon the will of the nation was inadmissible, 'especially as regards the constituent power'.[11] The sovereign, though reluctant to grant the *Charte*, ended up using the constitution as an ideological instrument; he declared that he was granting the constitution because he wished to do so, and because he thereby reasserted his authority against all attempts at restricting it.

In actual fact, granted constitutions were often issued following vague promises, partial reforms and constitutional 'outlines'. A constitution granted by royal fiat could not escape the paradox of having appropriated the 'artificial' voluntarism of revolutionary constitutionalism, but behind it there also lay a pragmatic strategy. The Congress of Vienna (1 November 1814 – 8 June 1815) was seen as the natural context for inaugurating in Europe a new era based on the political ideologies of the Restoration. It is true that the idea of the 'restored' sovereign emerged from the Congress of Vienna, but it only in part reflected the standard image of dynastic legitimacy (widely paraded though it was). The monarch had now to perform a range of functions, namely to reintegrate the nation, to pacify, to mediate, to defend the interests of a ruling caste and, indeed, to pre-empt unwelcome developments within the state.[12] Thus, the figure of the *rational* monarch came into being, one that was soon to oust the old forms of royal divinity. One could therefore be 'king by function', as in the case of the monarchies of Scandinavia or, in certain cases, of Eastern Europe, and this while adhering to a strictly political logic.

11 Quotation from A. Laquièze, *Les origines du régime parlementaire en France*, cit., 56.

12 An interesting new analysis of the Restoration period can now be found in S. Chignola, *Il tempo rovesciato. La Restaurazione e il governo della democrazia*, Bologna 2011.

At the same time, however, and here the monarchy still had the capacity to express a *surplus* of extra-juridical dimensions, even the monarch who had been enthroned, more or less ambiguously, with the explicit consent of popular sovereignty (for example, Louis-Philippe after the July Days in France, or Leopold I in Belgium, in 1831), would not willingly renounce being the sovereign. This was the case especially with regard to specific spheres of governance. Such circumstances clearly had a major impact upon the decision to adopt one form or other of government, or at any rate upon the way in which it was subsequently to develop.

I refer here to the situation in France, or to that of the monarchies of Southern Germany, where a return to the *ancien* régime, to a time in which there had been no written and 'perpetual' constitution-guarantee, no longer seemed possible. In the case of Italy in 1848, however, it seemed politically expedient to provide a constitution rather than submit to one under duress. During the early days of February 1848, Count Borelli in Turin remarked to King Charles Albert of Savoy who, though undecided, saw how things stood: 'we have to provide it [the constitution], not let it be imposed; dictate terms, not suffer them to be dictated to us; we need time to choose calmly what approaches to adopt and in which circumstances to act …'.[13] Only thus could the king retain most of his authority and powers.[14]

The granted constitutions should, first and foremost, be read from the perspective of the *ancien régime* and the Revolution. Once again, Count Beugnot[15] proved to be remarkably perspicacious. Urging Louis XVIII to follow

13 'Bisogna darla [la costituzione], non lasciarsela imporre; dettare le condizioni, non riceverle; bisogna avere il tempo di scegliere con calma i modi e l'opportunità, dopo aver promesso di impiegarli'. The text is in G. Falco (ed.), *Lo Statuto albertino e la sua preparazione*, Rome 1945, 180. See also E. Crosa, *La concessione dello Statuto. Carlo Alberto e il Ministro Borelli "redattore" dello Statuto (con lettere inedite di Carlo Alberto)*, Turin 1936, 68 ff. Regarding this constitutional episode, see R. Ferrari Zumbini, *Tra idealità e ideologia. Il Rinnovamento costituzionale nel Regno di Sardegna fra la primavera 1847 e l'inverno 1848*, Turin 2008.

14 Count Borelli observes 'That, in his view, the Constitution is without doubt a misfortune, but that they have reached the point of choosing the lesser evil, in order to avoid more serious ones' ('Qu'à son avis la Constitution est sans doute un malheur, mais qu'on est arrivé au point de choisir le moindre mal, pour en éviter de plus grands') (G. Negri and S. Simoni (eds.), *Lo Statuto albertino e i lavori preparatori*, Turin 1992, 47). Count Ferrand, one of those who had drafted the 1814 French *Charte*, had already considered the constitution, which he nevertheless was opposed to, as a 'lesser evil'. See A.-F.-C. Ferrand, *Mémoires du comte Ferrand, ministre d'Etat sous Louis XVIII*, Paris 1897, 73.

15 For a very short biography, see A. Laquièze, *Les origines du régime parlementaire en France*, cit., 44–45. See V. Sellin, *Die Erfindung des monarchischen Prinzips. Jacques-Claude Beugnots Präambel zur Charte constitutionnelle*, in A. Heinen and D. Hüser

the 'sovereign' path of promulgating the *Charte*, he reminded him that 'The plan proposed by the Chancellor has this rare, indeed, very rare, merit, of absorbing the Revolution into the Monarchy; whatever is contrary to this plan, and tends to bring either the Senate or the Legislative Body or else the electoral colleges into deliberation, tends, on the contrary, to absorb the Monarchy into the Revolution'.[16] Absorbing the Revolution into the Monarchy: this is one of the strongest messages relayed by the category of the granted constitution. The Revolution was still indubitably the French Revolution, but in the course of the nineteenth century it was destined to become that set of principles and values which founded the new middle-class society and engendered the liberal constitutional State.[17]

The granted constitutions were often preceded by preambles. Contrary to what one might suppose, these were not 'celestial prologues', ornamental flourishes put there only for show.[18] The ceremonial and procedural aspects that accompanied the promulgation of the texts produced symbolic effects that were not devoid of substance. Divine Providence upheld the hands of the sovereigns who 'bestowed' the constitutions upon their grateful peoples. A monarch's intentions were still construed as paternal, for was he not a good father to his beloved and faithful subjects? '*Il ne veut être*' – said Chancellor Ferrand – '*que le chef suprême de la grande famille dont il est le père*'.[19] It was 'with the loyalty of a King and with the affection of a Father'[20] that Charles Albert of Savoy granted his Constitution (*Statuto*) in 1848. The king-patriarch was

(eds.), *Tour de France. Eine historische Rundreise. Festschrift für Rainer Hudemann*, Stuttgart 2008, 489–497.

16 'Le plan proposé par Monsieur le Chancelier a ce rare et très rare mérite d'absorber la Révolution dans la Monarchie; tout ce qu'on oppose à ce plan et qui tendrait à faire délibérer ou le Sénat ou le Corps législatif ou les collèges électoraux tend au contraire à absorber la Monarchie dans la Révolution', *Rapport de Beugnot au Roi sur la forme de promulgation de la Charte*, 2 June 1814, in P. Rosanvallon, *La monarchie impossible*, cit., 241.

17 From the German perspective, see E.-W. Böckenförde, *Entstehung und Wandel des Rechtsstaatsbegriffs*, in *Recht, Staat, Freiheit. Studien zur Rechtsphilosophie, Staatstheorie und Verfassungsgeschichte*, Frankfurt am Main 2006, 143 ff. For some valuable insights see P. Schiera, *Nuovi elementi di statualità dall'Ottocento*, in A. de Benedictis (ed.), *Costruire lo Stato costruire la storia*, Bologna 2003, 11–29.

18 Thus P. Bastid, *Les institutions politiques de la Monarchie parlementaire française (1814–1848)*, Paris 1954, 139.

19 *Discours du chancelier Ferrand précédant la lecture de la Charte* (4 Juin 1814), in *Archives parlementaires*, 2nd series, vol. 12, 32–33, quoted from P. Rosanvallon, *La monarchie impossible*, cit., 248. Regarding the patriarchal dimension, cf. S. Rials, *Monarchie et philosophie politique: un essai d'inventaire*, in Id., *Révolution et contre-révolution*, cit., 84.

20 'Con lealtà di Re e con affetto di Padre'.

depicted as having returned to the throne, as in France, or as having reluctantly placed himself at the head of the 'constitutional' movement in order to 'satisfy the wishes of our faithful subjects'[21] or to find 'the safest means of reinforcing the ties of indissoluble affection which bind the people to our Italian Crown'.[22] The peace, prosperity and well-being of the subjects as well as of the Kingdom were the objectives the Monarchs said they wished to pursue. The royal 'we' was designed to enhance will, autonomy and *puissance*: We, We, We. 'For this reason, by Our certain knowledge and Royal Authority, having heard the opinion of Our Council, We have ordered and We do order, in execution of the Statute and Fundamental Law of the monarchy, which is perpetual and irrevocable.' (Statute of the Kingdom of Sardinia). In the preamble to the Charter its author, Count Beugnot,[23] underlined the fact that royal sovereignty was the sole source of political legitimacy: even though all authority resided in the person of the monarch, the king had decided, for the good of France, to grant a 'free and monarchical' constitution that interpreted the transformations under way in society and conserved the rights and prerogatives of the Crown. Only the supreme authority 'can give the institutions that it has founded, the power, permanence and majesty in which it itself is clothed'.[24] Reconnecting the 'chain of time', sundered by years of anarchy and violence, Louis XVIII had sought in French tradition for the principles of the constitutional Charter, in order to ensure peace and security to his long-suffering people.

4. How many different words to say 'constitution'

Can we speak of a constitution, even when the text in question does not call itself one? Between 1814 and 1848 this seems to be the case. In this regard, the texts of granted constitutions testify to the use of words being not just descriptive but often 'performative' also.[25] So far as the French ultras and moderate conservatives were concerned, the very mention of a constitution brought with it a

21 Constitution of the Grand Duchy of Württemberg, 25 September 1819.

22 'un mezzo il più sicuro di raddoppiare coi vincoli d'indissolubile affetto che stringono all'itala Nostra Corona un Popolo', Statute of the Kingdom of Sardinia, 4 March 1848.

23 On the drafting of the preamble (in the first version written by Fontanes), see P. Rosanvallon, *La monarchie impossible*, cit., 46. There is an accurate and exhaustive reconstruction in S. Rials, *Essai sur le concept de monarchie limitée (autour de la charte de 1814)*, in Id., *Révolution et contre-révolution*, cit., 103–105.

24 'Peut seule donner aux institutions qu'elle établit, la force, la permanence et la majesté dont elle est elle-même revêtue …'.

25 Concerning 'doing things with words', I hinted at this in *Una Convenzione per l'Europa*, in *Giornale di storia costituzionale*, 3, I, 2002, 6.

disquieting association with Revolution, and with the constituent power of the nation. It was not only Metternich who did not want to hear so insidious a word uttered. Indeed, this taboo had a more general relevance. Are the *Charte constitutionnelle*, the *Landständische Verfassung* and the (fundamental) *Statuto* linguistic devices employed to express the sense of a controversial word without actually voicing it, or, conversely, do they represent a 'new' category of constitutionalism? The answer is not so simple as one might suppose. My own conviction is that the lexicon used has to be taken seriously, since it has a manifestly communicative and ideological dimension.[26] We are concerned here with a manoeuvre which 'by itself acquires a politically "cooling" meaning, one of reformist moderation which *a priori* excludes the overthrowing of the established order'.[27]

The lexicon in question smacks of feudal privileges, parliaments based on medieval dispensations and free medieval Communes, and calls to mind diplomatic formulas of the distant past and concepts of the ancien régime. The semantic ground covered implies the notion of privilege, the concepts of bestowal and imposition, but also those of disposition and agreement. Once terms such as *acte constitutionnel*, *ordonnance de réformation* or *édit* had been ruled out, the expression *Charte*,[28] combined with the epithet *constitutionnelle*, came up for consideration. The intention was to capture the nature of the sovereign's free bestowal of a political settlement while at the same time guaranteeing individual freedom: 'the name used in ancient times, consecrated by the history of several peoples and by ours, is that of Charte'.[29] Louis XVIII dated the granting of the *Charte* to the nineteenth year of his reign, or rather from the very moment he had succeeded Louis XVII, in 1795. The preamble therefore excluded any and every reference to national sovereignty in the guise of a juridical entity distinct from the supreme authority vested in the person of the king. The archaism[30] of the text is therefore not contingent but intrinsic to it. It may seem

26 Supra in this volume *Constitución, Monarquía, Parlamento: Francia y Belgica*, 115 ss.

27 P. Colombo, *Con lealtà di Re e con affetto di padre*, cit., 95. On this point L. Ciaurro (ed.), *Lo Statuto albertino illustrato dai lavori preparatori*, Rome 1996, 45.

28 On the "category" *Charte*, see the critical comments in K. von Rotteck, K. Welcker, *Charte*, in Idd., *Das Staats-Lexikon*, Leipzig 1859, III, 491–497.

29 '... le nom anciennement utilisé, celui consacré par l'histoire de plusieurs peuples et par la nôtre est celui de Charte', J.-C. Beugnot, *Mémoires du comte Beugnot*, Paris 1866, II, 219.

30 This aspect, already emphasised by J. Bonnefon, *Le régime parlementaire sous la Restauration*, Paris 1905 and by C. Rohmer, *Le droit d'ordonnance et l'esprit de la Charte de 1814*, Paris 1931, has been studied in depth by S. Rials, *Essai sur le concept de monarchie limitée (autour de la charte de 1814)*, cit., 88–125 and

paradoxical that a text destined to become one of the most influential models of European constitutionalism in the nineteenth century, falls more within the rationalised tradition of the ancien régime than within the purview of revolutionary constitutionalism. In reality, the 1814 *Charte* retained what was strictly indispensable to the latter, starting with some measures regarding the *Droit public des Français* and ending with the *Droits particuliers garantis par l'Etat*. The whole of the section devoted to the organisation of powers reflects the concept of limited monarchy and expresses the constitutional centrality of *royauté*.

5. The 'historical' constitution

Eighteenth-century constitutionalism had introduced the idea of constitution-making or, in other words, the notion that it was the sovereign people that made the constitution. In the early nineteenth century the appeal to history reflects a concern to temper so radical a notion. As is well known, the difficulty of reconciling the French Revolution with history gave rise to the somewhat desperate project of saving the monarchy of the ancien régime by grafting it on to the hostile space of popular sovereignty. Then, in 1814, the task was to 'correct' the rigidity of the artificial constitution by rereading it in the light of historicist 'rationalisation'. Charles de Sismondi, in his *Recherches,*[31] does not conceive of the constitution as existing outside of its historical context. The constitution, like freedom, is a product of history, or rather of social development within a specific historical period; it is neither an arbitrary result nor is it a fortuitous outcome. Another Swiss liberal intellectual, Benjamin Constant, although loyal to a rational idea of the constitution, tried to find a point of balance between reason and history. In his works written after 1794, the doctrine of perfectibility already posed the question of the relationship between ideas and institutions, with time acting as a balance wheel. In the *Principes* of 1806, Constant plainly endorses the notion that history is the foundation of political theory. 'Time, says Bacon, is the great reformer. Do not refuse its assistance. Let it march in front of you; it will smooth your path. If what you establish has not

especially by A. Laquièze, *Les origines du régime parlementaire en France*, cit. We should not, however, overlook the fact that Louis-Philippe d'Orléans in his memoirs of 1814 had already emphasised the archaic character of the Charter. Regarding the manuscript, see H. Robert, *Louis-Philippe constitutionnaliste*, in *Commentaire*, 63, 1993, 577–580.

31 J. C. L. Sismondi, *Recherches sur les constitutions des peuples libres*, edited and introduced by M. Minerbi, Geneva 1965. The historicist concepts of Sismondi are particularly emphasised in the late *Etudes sur les constitutions des peoples libres*, Brussels 1836. See also the *Introduction* to his *Histoire des Français*, Paris 1821, vol. I.

been prepared by it, you will command in vain'.[32] At the beginning of the Restoration, Constant was inclined to balance the rational fact ('Constitutions are rarely made by the will of men') with that of history ('Time makes them'). 'Making' the constitution is sometimes indispensable, but once the powers are constituted, it is as well to leave the appropriate space for the 'two reforming powers',[33] time and experience. This stance cannot be traced back simply to the concept of the historical constitution, for Constant's argument had shifted from a simple contrast between rational constitution and historical constitution, to a rather more complex perspective, without which it is difficult to see how the rationalisation of the constitutional monarchy could ever have been undertaken.

The monarch of 1814 wanted to reconnect the 'chain of time', to take up where he had left off, and to reconcile archaic 'form' and content with 'modern' experience, prescribed by time, beginning with the prevailing British model, though reinterpreted in the light of its historicity, its capacity to develop as a historical constitution able to produce a felicitous combination / interweaving of legislative and executive power.

6. The *Landständische Verfassung*

If the language of the *Charte constitutionnelle* immediately raises the issue of terminological ambiguity,[34] the formula adopted in 1815 in Article 13 of the constitutive Act of the German Confederation (*Die deutsche Bundesakte*)[35] is still more 'open' to interpretation. 'In every federal State an estates-based constitution will be established',[36] states Article 13. Member states were to provide themselves with a constitution, or better still, a representative regime.[37] In the

32 'Le temps, dit Bacon, est le grand réformateur. Ne refusez pas son assistance. Laissez-le marcher devant vous, pour qu'il aplanisse la route. Si ce que vous instituez n'a pas été préparé par lui, vous commanderez vainement ...', B. Constant, *Principes de politique*, ed. by E. Hofmann, Geneva 1980, 412.

33 B. Constant, *Réflexions sur les constitutions, la distribution des pouvoirs et les garanties, dans une monarchie constitutionnelle*, Paris 1814.

34 See R. Car, *La genesi del cancellierato. L'evoluzione del potere governativo in Prussia 1848–1853*, Macerata 2006, 41.

35 The Act of the German Confederation was signed by representatives of 38 German states at the Congress of Vienna. This Act established the general framework under which the negotiations took place at the Ministerial Conference which ended with the Final Act (*Wiener Schlussakte*) on 15 May 1820, qualified as 'Fundamental Law that has the same force and validity as the federal Act' of the German Confederation of 1815.

36 'In allen Bundesstaaten wird eine Landständische Verfassung statt finden'.

37 J. Hummel, *Le constitutionnalisme allemand (1815–1918): le modèle allemand de la monarchie limitée*, Paris 2002, translates the German phrase as 'representative

course of the debate, both the time limit of one year in which to comply and its more strongly prescriptive character ('es soll') disappeared from the formula. The 'regime', in reality, postulated the need for 'some' form of collaboration by the estates in the exercise of political power.[38] This provision would seem to be designed to steer the debate both towards medieval forms of representation in a constitution structured in terms of the estates and towards types of assemblies which could be primarily traced back to the French model of the *Charte*. The semantic ambiguity of the laconic Article 13 is reflected in the first constitutions written in Southern Germany after 1815. It would seem difficult to trace back the preoccupations and constitutional dynamics, particularly in this phase, to a dialectic between the 'liberal-representative' and the 'monarchic-constitutional' models.

The preamble to the Bavarian constitution of 1818 'tells' a story that cannot but be different from the French story of the *Charte*. In the former narrative we can perceive the monarchic reformism which pervades the second half of the eighteenth century and which proceeds 'from above' and through administrative channels. We also catch a glimpse of the promises of *landständische Verfassungen* which the vicissitudes of the early nineteenth century, and later certain political decisions, nipped in the bud. We can sense the emergence of the German nation and its federated 'peoples', who, like the Bavarians, proved themselves to be sublime both 'in their misfortunes and on the field of battle'. We discern a 'continuity'[39] which, by contrast with events in France, had not been irreparably interrupted by the social and political Revolution. The task was to transform the old corporate structure by 'attuning' it to the 'new' political order.[40] Although German representative constitutions share the conceptual

constitution'. On this aspect, see the observations of R. Car, *Tra Pacta e Charte. Per una visione unitaria del costituzionalismo tedesco della Restaurazione*, in *Giornale di storia costituzionale*, 7, I, 2004, 115; Id., *La genesi del cancellierato*, cit., 40.

38 See W. Mager, *Das Problem der landständischen Verfassungen auf dem Wiener Kongress 1814/1815*, in *Historische Zeitschrift*, 222, 1973, 296–346; B. Wunder, *Landstände und Rechtsstaat. Zur Entstehung und Verwirklichung des Art. 13 DBA*, in *Zeitschrift für historische Forschung*, 5, 1978, 139–185.

39 Upon this controversial issue, see M. Kirsch and P. Schiera, *Einleitung*, in M. Kirsch, P. Schiera (eds.), *Denken und Umsetzung des Konstitutionalismus in Deutschland und anderen europäischen Ländern in der ersten Hälfte des 19. Jahrhunderts*, Berlin 1999, 9–10.

40 Otto Hintze, in the constitutional system based on estates, saw a socio-political structure which was not completely different from nor hostile to the modern idea, in brief a general stage of transition towards modern constitutionalism (O. Hintze (1930), *Typologie der ständischen Verfassungen des Abendlandes*, in Id., *Gesammelte Abhandlungen, I. Staat und Verfassung*, ed. by G. Oestreich, Göttingen 1970, 120–139. Regarding the acceptance by German Liberals of the monarchic

configuration of monarchic constitutionalism[41] (limited royalty) with the 1814 *Charte*, nevertheless the conditions for the existence of a constitutional monarchy are more deeply rooted in German history.[42] What in France was defined as the 'impossible monarchy',[43] a sort of 'phase' in French history fated soon to pass,[44] in Germany became 'possible' and assumed a concrete form in the guise of a predominantly monarchic structure which was destined to last a century and to find its own 'solution' in the 'neutralising' of sovereignty in the context of the organic theory of the State.[45] The Bavarian "Constitution" of 1818 contained an effective synthesis of what would be called the *monarchisches Prinzip*. 'Das Königreich Baiern in der Gesammt-Vereinigung aller ältern und neuern Gebietstheile ist ein souverainer monarchischer Staat nach den Bestimmungen der gegenwärtigen Verfassungs-Urkunde.'[46]

In these very years, in France, the *Charte* (especially in the 1830 'national' version) became the alpha and omega, the strategic resource exploited to address two convergent threats, namely, the spectre of the constituent power embodied in the sovereignty of the people and the absolute sovereignty of the monarch (a notion by then disempowered). It was Pierre-Paul Royer-Collard after the Restoration who reaffirmed that the sovereignty of the people was simply the 'souveraineté de la force'. In 1820, François Guizot likewise declared that there was an equivalence between the usurpation of force and every form of sovereignty that sought to be absolute, whether of the people or of divine right. He then added that popular sovereignty was a form of tyranny, in that it was the absolute power of the numerical majority over the minority.[47] 'I believe in the

principle also in the light of the difficulty of making the voluntaristic dimension of popular sovereignty their own, see H. Hofmann, *Repräsentation. Studien zur Wort- und Begriffsgeschichte von der Antike bis ins 19. Jahrhundert*, Berlin 2003.

41 M. Kirsch, *Monarch und Parlament im 19. Jahrhundert*, cit.

42 Now see M.J. Prutsch, *Making Sense of Constitutional Monarchism in Post-Napoleonic France and Germany*, Basingstoke 2013; Id., *The 'Legal Model' of the Charte constitutionnelle and the 1818 Baden Constitution*, in L. Beck Varela, P. Gutiérrez Vega, A. Spinosa (eds.), *Crossing Legal Cultures*, Munich 2009, 383–398.

43 From P. Rosanvallon, *La monarchie impossible*, cit.

44 Hintze had already spoken of a brief transitional phase (O. Hintze, *Das monarchische Prinzip und die konstitutionnelle Verfassung*, in Id., *Gesammelte Abhandlungen, I.*, cit., 360.

45 See E.-W. Böckenförde, *Der Staat als Organismus. Zur staatstheoretisch-verfassungspolitischen Diskussion im frühen Konstitutionalismus*, in Id., *Recht, Staat, Freiheit*, cit., 263–272.

46 Bavarian Constitution, 26.5.1818, tit. I, art. 1.

47 F. Guizot, *Philosophie politique: de la souveraineté*, in Id., *Histoire de la civilisation en Europe depuis la chute de l'Empire romain jusqu'à la Révolution française*, edition

sovereignty of reason, justice and law: such is the legitimate sovereign the world is in search of, and always will be in search of; because reason, truth and justice are not to be found total and infallible anywhere'.[48] The constitution was becoming itself a parameter of reason and to it was assigned the attribute of a sovereign entity, so that neither the prince, the people, the monarchy nor democracy could invoke a monistic conception intertwined with the exercise of the intimidating constituent power.[49] This led to an idea of an autopoietic constitution, sovereign within and for itself, fallen from the heavens. The theory of the sovereignty of the constitution,[50] and in Germany, the gradual, organicist construction of the *Staatslehre*, although differing in outcomes and methodologies, aimed at neutralising the conflict and hypostatizing an idea of constitutional compromise.

If the *Charte* circumscribes clearly both the ideology of the *octroi* and the theory of the limited monarchy, thus acquiring 'categorial' importance,[51] the experience of the German 'granted' constitutions reveals foundations[52] that can only partially be explained using the transalpine model. Inspiration[53] is one thing, concrete developments on the ground quite another.[54] The constitutions granted in 1848 show even greater differences. In terms of political culture, they

by P. Rosanvallon, Paris 1985, 309 (*Présentation* by Rosanvallon) as well as 374.

48 'Je crois à la souveraineté de la raison, de la justice, du droit: c'est là le souverain légitime que cherche le monde et qu'il cherchera toujours; car la raison, la vérité, la justice ne résident nulle part complètes et infaillibles', F. Guizot, *Du gouvernement de la France depuis la Restauration, et du ministère actuel*, Paris 1820, 201. Regarding the French debate, see *infra* in this volume *La garanzia della Costituzione. Riflessioni sul caso francese*, 270 ss. Cf. also H. Hofmann, *Repräsentation*, cit.

49 See C. Schmitt, *Verfassungslehre* (1928), Berlin 1993, 7–53.

50 Friedrich Julius Stahl's interest in, and, in balance, positive judgement regarding the pragmatic and conservative line taken by Guizot through his doctrine of the *juste milieu* is not accidental. On this point, see G. Bonacina, *Storia e indirizzi del conservatorismo politico secondo la dottrina dei partiti di Stahl*, in *Rivista storica italiana*, CXV, 2, 2003, 617–618.

51 Cf. the dissertation of Erich Kaufmann, *Studien zur Staatslehre des monarchischen Prinzipes: Einleitung. Die historischen und philosophischen Grundlagen*, Wiesbaden 1906.

52 O. Meisner, *Die Lehre vom monarchischen Prinzip im Zeitalter der Restauration und des deutschen Bundes*, Breslau 1913.

53 For example, R. Oeschey, *Die bayerische Verfassungsurkunde vom 26. Mai 1818 und die Charte Ludwig 18. vom 4. Juni 1814: ein Beitrag zur Lehre vom monarchischen Prinzip*, Munich 1914.

54 See P. Schiera, *Konstitutionalismus und Vormärz in europäischer Perspektive: Politische Romantik, Integrationsbedarf und die Rolle des Liberalismus*, in M. Kirsch and P. Schiera (eds.), *Verfassungswandel um 1848 im europäischen Vergleich*, Berlin 2001, 16.

were born 'older' than those that followed the Restoration[55] and their archaism corresponds to the experience of a 'constituent' monarchy which was trying to take the heat out of the question of sovereignty in a context of contested political legitimacy.[56]

The political lexicon of the Restoration refers both to the monarchic principle,[57] which grants the 'constitution' (theory of the constituent power of the king), and to estates-based representation, with outlines that are compatible with the model of the pact and of an agreement expressed in the form of legislative 'collaboration'.[58] The constitution granted by Maximilian Joseph in Bavaria in 1818, envisages a 'special' procedure for modifying or adding to the text 'with the consent of the states' (Title X, Article 7, Of the constitution guarantee). The constitution of the Grand Duchy of Hesse-Darmstadt (1820) also follows this model. The Prussian constitution of 1850 allows for the modification of the text 'by ordinary legislative methods' (Article 107).

7. Limited monarchy and the monarchic principle: the granted constitution as context of legitimacy

As has already been pointed out, the preamble to the *Charte* of 1814 had delineated an 'updated' theory of Ancien Régime monarchy within the framework of a 'modernisation' of the mode of exercising power centred on the characteristics of representative government. The 1814 text hinges upon the centrality and unity of royal power. The monarch reserves a predominant role for himself: he alone wields the executive power and has a strong claim on the right to make laws, the process whereby they are created (initiating, sanction, enact-

55 G. Rebuffa, *Lo Statuto albertino*, Bologna 2000, 47.

56 See V. Sellin, *„Heute ist die Revolution monarchisch". Legitimität und Legitimierungspolitik im Zeitalter des Wiener Kongresses*, in *Quellen und Forschungen aus italienischen Archiven und Bibliotheken*, 76, 1996, 335–361. Also H. Becquet, B. Frederking (eds.), *La dignité du roi. Regards sur la royauté au premier XIXe siècle*, Rennes 2009.

57 M. Stolleis, *Geschichte des öffentlichen Rechts in Deutschland. Zweiter Band 1800–1914*, Munich 1992, 102–105.

58 For these dilemmas see K. Welcker, *Octroyierte Verfassungen*, in K. von Rotteck and K. Welcker, *Das Staats-Lexikon. Encyklopädie der sämmtlichen Staatswissenschaften für alle Stände*, Leipzig 1864, vol. X, 735–738. Cf. C. Schmitt, *Verfassungslehre*, cit., 51. Regarding the 'middle-class' vision of the written constitution as sworn pact and as law, see *Ibidem*, 29. Concerning the theme of *konstitutionelle Verfassung* as political compromise, see E. W. Böckenförde, *Geschichtliche Entwicklung und Bedeutungswandel der Verfassung*, in Id., *Staat, Verfassung, Demokratie. Studien zur Verfassungstheorie und zum Verfassungsrecht*, Frankfurt am Main 1991, 34 ff.

ment) being wholly under his control. The self-limitation of the sovereign[59] allows for the attainment of a compromise between the conflicting legitimacies which the revolutions of the eighteenth century had bequeathed to the history of constitutionalism: on the one hand, the traditional *plenitudo potestatis* of the sovereign, on the other, the constituent power of the people.[60] The use, implicit or otherwise, of the category of constituent power on the part of post-revolutionary monarchies reveals not only its strength but also the underlying theoretical paradox. The paradox of the 1814 *Charte* is evident, although in the preamble an attempt is made to tone it down a little. If, on the one hand, the catalogue of rights and freedoms originating in the French Revolution, first and foremost the principle of equality, is guaranteed, on the other hand, we find as premise an act of concession, which in philosophical terms is a negation of those selfsame rights and freedoms. In the French context, the gap between *Revolutionary practice* and *Restoration theory* remains the thorniest problem to solve.[61]

> De facto this could not succeed. The monarch, whose position rests upon an institution with a juridical structure, that is upon the monarchy with a determined law of succession to the throne, cannot himself be also conceived as foundation and source, as the formless former (das Formlos-Formende) of the politico-social order which is outlined in the constitution.[62]

By means of the above-mentioned concession, the monarch sought to retain, while at the same time recasting, the substance of his original power. 'The king',

59 Regarding the theoretical elaboration of the notion of "limited monarchy" – as a distinct concept from the broader, but too generic one of "constitutional monarchy" – see S. Rials, *Monarchie et philosophie politique*, cit., 87; Id., *Essai sur le concept de monarchie limitée*, cit., 112. See also, by the same author, *Une doctrine constitutionnelle française?*, in *Pouvoirs*, 50, 1990, 81–95; A. Laquièze, *Les origines du régime parlementaire en France*, cit., 66; P. Lauvaux, *Les monarchies: inventaire des types*, in *Pouvoirs*, 78, 1996, 26.

60 Regarding the transformations and centrality of the concept of sovereignty, see M. Stolleis, *Souveränität um 1814*, in U. Müßig (ed.), *Konstitutionalismus und Verfassungskonflikt*, Tübingen 2006, 102–115.

61 The commentator who had best grasped the "mortal contradiction" of the Charte and of the Restoration, was Charles de Rémusat, see in particular *Politique libérale où fragments pour servir à la défense de la Révolution française*, Paris 1860, 207 ff. Concerning this aspect, see A. Craiutu, *Le Centre introuvable. La pensée politique des doctrinaires sous la Réstauration*, Paris 2006, 75.

62 ‚In der Sache konnte das nicht gelingen. Der Monarch, dessen Stellung auf einer rechtlich geformten Einrichtung, nämlich der Monarchie mit einer bestimmten Thronfolgeordnung, beruht, kann selbst nicht auch als Urgrund und Quelle, das Formlos-Formende der politisch-rechtlichen Ordnung, wie sie in der Verfassung Gestalt gewinnt, gedacht werden‘ (E.-W. Böckenförde, *Die verfassungsgebende Gewalt des Volkes. Ein Grenzbegriff des Verfassungsrechts*, in Id., in *Staat, Verfassung, Demokratie*. cit., 95–96).

we read in Title II, Article 1 of the 1818 constitution of Bavaria, 'is the supreme head of State: he unites in his person all the rights of supreme power and exercises them following those resolutions, which were established by himself, with this constitutional act'. Without impairing the principle of the unity of state power, the granted constitution is, at the same time, both 'a juridical act' and a 'political act': a unilateral act of constitutional determination and an act of political expediency entailing a compromise (the theory of the agreement) which mediates between the interests of executive-monarchic legitimacy and political principles of a liberal complexion. It could be said that the granted constitution is not, to use a term from political theology, a *constituent constitution*. In its 'full' meaning, the monarch's constitution is the monarch himself (like the historical constitution embodied in the fundamental laws). It is not the paper constitution that gives the sovereign his legitimacy and discretionary powers over the *Staatsgewalt*.[63] The constitution is a limit which does not establish the monarchy,[64] rather, it founds competences and rules which the sovereign solemnly undertakes, through specific procedures, to respect and guarantee, as may be seen in the first constitutions of Southern Germany. The monarchy, in this way, comes *before* the constitution (essence), but is *within* the constitution (implementation) once it assumes the *octroi* as an instrument for the 'modernisation' of a historical continuity and a monarchic reformism. 'The government established by the *Charte* is of all governments with representative institutions, the only one where monarchic power is the principle of social organisation and source of political life'.[65] Showing great perspicacity, Royer-Collard observed in 1824 that it was not enough to define the system as 'a mixed monarchy, called representative Government, where the elective Chamber combines with the monarch together with a hereditary Chamber to make law and to administer the affairs of state'. Indeed, it was the 'regulatory power' which imparted a specific character to this form of government. In the French case, in and through the *Charte* the king retains

> a dazzling primacy among the powers which surround him. He alone represents the moral unity of Society; he alone acts, he alone rules, he alone is the maker of the law, the right to initiate which is exclusively reserved for him. This last

63 J. Hummel, *Le constitutionnalisme allemande*, cit., 55. See also V. Sellin, *Gewalt und Legitimität. Die europäische Monarchie im Zeitalter der Revolutionen*, Munich 2011.

64 O. Hintze, *Das monarchische Prinzip*, cit.

65 'Le gouvernement établi par la Charte est de tous les gouvernements à institutions représentatives, le seul où le pouvoir monarchique soit principe de l'organisation sociale et source de la vie politique', Ch. His, *De la monarchie représentative*, Paris 1829, 4–5.

circumstance means that, with regard to him, the other powers are strictly speaking only limits; but they are limits which are living and liable to shift'.[66]

Nevertheless, within the context of the secularised state order, the *ex gratia Dei* monarch found himself in the hostile space of the constitution and beset by an 'insurmountable difficulty'.[67] The *sacre* of Charles X in Reims in 1825, accompanied by the practice of touching and 'healing' the scrofulous in the name of St. Marcolph, was an awkward ritual, a gesture of unmitigated political romanticism.[68] It was as if a medieval monarchy existing by divine right had absorbed the 'law' into the space of the legitimacy of the sovereign, thaumaturge and representative of God on Earth. The Restoration did its utmost to reunite legitimacy and legality, an operation doomed to failure, and yet – as we know – the monarchy of the *octroi* continued to play a pivotal role in the history of the socio-political organisations of the nineteenth century.

The monarch of the granted constitutions is the sovereign in the true sense of the term, but at the same time, through the representative constitution – understood as a functional tool in the exercise of single and limited spheres of the *Staatsgewalt* – it is he who stipulates agreements with non-unitary representatives of the people. The king, supreme head of State, is the person who 'makes the rules and ordinances which are necessary for the execution of laws and for the security of the State'. Article 14 of the *Charte* was considered by Carl Schmitt to be an exemplification of the decision mechanism on the 'state of exception'.[69]

66 'Une monarchie mixte, appelée Gouvernement représentatif, où la Chambre élective concourt avec le monarque et une Chambre héréditaire à la formation de la loi et à la direction des affaires publiques ...'. The monarch retained 'une éclatante primauté entre les pouvoirs qui l'entourent. Seul il représente l'unité morale de la Société; seul il agit, seul il commande, seul il est l'auteur de la loi dont l'initiative lui est exclusivement réservée. Cette dernière circonstance exprime qu'à son égard, les autres pouvoirs ne sont proprement que des limites; mais ce sont des limites vivantes et capables de se mouvoir ...', P. de Barante, *La vie politique de M. Royer-Collard. Ses discours et ses écrits*, Paris 1863, II, 216–217. With regard to the constitutional vision of Royer-Collard, and his interpretation of the *Charte*, see M. Pertué, *Royer-Collard et la Charte de 1814*, in *Revue administrative*, 382, 2011, 341–357.

67 H. Heller, *Staatslehre*, edited by G. Niemeyer, Munich 1934. L. Diez Del Corral, *El liberalismo doctrinario*, Madrid 1945, 66, observes: 'The doctrine of the constituent power could not be transferred to the Monarchy without running into contradictions and vagueness'.

68 M. Bloch, *The royal touch. Sacred monarchy and scrofula in England and in France*, London 1973 (1924). On the representation of this ritual on the stage by Gioacchino Rossini, see M. Schnettger, *Il viaggio a Reims oder die Restauration auf der Opernbühne*, in *Majestas*, 12, 2004, 161–194.

69 C. Schmitt, *Definition der Souveränität*, cit., 12–13. On this point, see H. Hofmann, '*Souverän ist, wer über den Ausnahmezustand entscheidet*', in U. Müßig (ed.), *Konstitutionalismus und Verfassungskonflikt*, cit, 270–284.

Although not discussed during the rapid drafting of the *Charte*, the question of the 'power of ordinance' acquired noteworthy importance during and at the end of the reign of Charles X, when the 'radicalisation' of the political struggle between liberals and ultras made Article 14 the emblem of their respective positions on the issue of constituent power. Charles X held that Article 14 was his *lit de justice* for overcoming the opposition of the parliamentary majority. The monarch thought he was entitled to wield the 'right of the last word', as if he were facing a state of emergency, although this latter was simply the liberals' demand for the fundamental rule of representative government. When enacting the ordinances, Charles X refused to accept such a logic, resorting to a legal instrument (Article 14) in order to obtain a result, which by that date was contrary to the letter and spirit of the *Charte.*[70] It was not by chance that in the *Rapport au Roi* of 25 July 1830, the king's minister, Polignac, declared that the 'normal conditions of representative government' had broken down. The sombre picture which he draws – focused entirely upon the subversive use of the press – negates the essential characteristics of such a form of government.

> [...] No government on earth would stand, if it did not have the right to provide for its safety. This power pre-exists the law, because it is in the nature of things. There are, Sire, maxims which have, on their side, both the sanction of time and the endorsement of all the European public law jurists. But these maxims have another still more positive sanction, that of the *Charte* itself. Article 14 invested His Majesty with a power sufficient, without doubt, not for changing our institutions, but for strengthening them and rendering them more immutable. Imperious necessities do not permit us to delay any longer the exercise of this supreme power. The moment has come to resort to measures which are within the spirit of the *Charte*, but which are outside the legal system, whose every resource has been exhausted and to no avail.[71]

70 For a fuller account of the events surrounding the ordinances of Charles X and the July Days, see L. Lacchè, *La Libertà che guida il Popolo. Le Tre Gloriose Giornate del luglio 1830 e le 'Chartes' nel costituzionalismo francese*, Bologna 2002.

71 '[...] Nul gouvernement sur la terre ne resterait debout, s'il n'avait le droit de pourvoir à sa sûreté. Ce pouvoir est préexistant aux lois, parce qu'il est dans la nature des choses. Ce sont là, Sire, des maximes qui ont pour elles et la sanction du temps et l'aveu de tous les publicistes de l'Europe. Mais ces maximes ont une autre sanction plus positive encore, celle de la Charte elle-même. L'article 14 a investi Votre Majesté d'un pouvoir suffisant, non sans doute pour changer nos institutions, mais pour les consolider et les rendre plus immuables. D'impérieuses nécessités ne permettent plus de différer l'exercice de ce pouvoir suprême. Le moment est venu de recourir à des mesures qui rentrent dans l'esprit de la Charte, mais qui sont en dehors de l'ordre légal, dont toutes les ressources ont été inutilement épuisées'.

8. Interpreting the granted constitution

The Revolutionary days of July 1830 put an end to the concept of the *octroi* and to the attempt to establish a general *monarchisches Prinzip* along French lines. They did not, however, satisfactorily consolidate a form of government whereby the king remained the 'supreme head of State'.

As we have seen, the claim made in the following years by the liberals, to the effect that the Bourbon Charter was two-dimensional in nature – the two dimensions being the formal one of the granting and the "true" one, calculated to appeal to the liberal-minded, of a "peace treaty" between the monarchy and the French people – does not bear scrutiny. As has already been observed, the theory of the *octroi* developed from the *Charte* was not merely a decorative flourish. Viewing the Restoration as an age of 'transition' does not, however, provide us with a proper interpretation of the granted text. The Second Restoration set in motion in France events that were destined to leave their mark upon the subsequent fifteen years. The liberal forces immediately took advantage of the Proclamation of Cambrai of 28 June 1815, through which Louis XVIII had given, in their opinion, an 'authentic' interpretation of the 'liberal' spirit of the *Charte*. Together with the oath of loyalty sworn by the king before the parliamentary representatives (16 March), even as Napoleon was marching on Paris, the Proclamation was one of the documents most frequently quoted by liberals intent upon reinforcing the interpretation of the *Charte* as being in essence a pact. On the other hand, on 16 June 1814, the Chamber of deputies had directed its *Adresse* to the monarch in order to unilaterally assign a "national" stamp to the *Charte*. 'We therefore, Sire, have the firm conviction that the assent of the French people will give this Charte a wholly national character'.[72]

The so-called ambiguity of the Charter, which is often emphasised, stemmed from the hermeneutic apparatus forged through the theoretical debate and the political-parliamentary struggle. The Restoration is characterised by an unceasing clash between two groups, one of which insisted upon the granted (indeed, unilaterally granted) nature of the *Charte*, while the other harped upon its intrinsically 'contractual' features. Needless to say, these two contrasting interpretations gave rise to arguments that are hard to reconcile, since they raise crucial issues touching upon legitimacy, the form of sovereignty and the nature of the political regime. The progressive radicalisation of the dispute, which culminated in the events of 1830, ended up – as is often the case – by grossly oversimplifying the terms of an ideological quarrel, obscuring nuances that

72 'Aussi avons-nous, Sire, l'intime confiance que l'assentiment des Français donnera à cette Charte un caractère tout à fait national'.

were, nonetheless, discernible in the two 'parties'. Each side without a doubt chose to view its own position in the most favourable light: the *royalistes* – but not necessarily the ultras – entrenched themselves behind the bulwark of the *lettre* and of the form of the concession; the liberals insisted on the presumed liberal character of the *esprit*. One 'party' therefore possessed a strong juridical case, while the other thought it could deploy a political argument that needed, however, to be nurtured and circulated. The former was a static, defensive argument, whereas the latter was dynamic and oppositional.

The basic misunderstanding stemmed from the dual nature of the Charter, namely the juridical act of granting, on the one hand, and on the other hand a form establishing a measure of collaboration between the monarchic principle and the representative principles (as embodied in the Chamber of Deputies). The ambiguity of the procedure lay in the inevitable and insurmountable confusion between the juridical element – relatively strong from the point of view of legitimacy – and the political element, which was more fluid and dynamic. The formal and juridical aspect (the traditional royal prerogative, the ostensible source of the constitution) was contaminated and progressively undermined by the notion that the constitutional act was underwritten by a 'compromise', or rather by a new pact between the sovereign and his subjects. On this front, a whole host of heterogeneous aspects, variously historical, sociological and political, together served to deprive the formal and juridical aspect of its presumed force. Moreover, the contractual scheme could be said to rest upon two distinct theoretical foundations, on the one hand, that of 'medieval constitutionalism', which accorded legitimacy to the sovereign's obligations, performed in ceremonies sanctioned by time, towards feudal lords and estates and corporations, and on the other, that of modern constitutionalism, which, in its (then fashionable) British form, could be read as a rationalised form of balance between political powers, 'shared' by the monarch and the representative bodies.

Chateaubriand was among the first to speak of the *Charte* as a 'peace treaty signed by the two parties which divided the French people, a treaty whereby everyone gives up some of their claims in order to contribute to the glory of the nation'.[73] To consider the Charter as an attempt at compromise[74] bolsters the notion that it represents the sanctioning of an agreement reached by the two

73 'Traité de paix signé entre les deux partis qui ont divisé les Français, traité où chacun abandonne quelque chose de ses prétentions pour concourir à la gloire de la patrie', F.-R. De Chateaubriand, *Réflexions politiques sur quelques écrits du jour et sur les intérêts de tous les Français*, Paris 1814, 70.

74 This thesis is affirmed as "royal" by J. Barthélemy, *L'introduction du régime parlementaire en France sous Louis XVIII et Charles X*, Paris 1904, 12.

'parties' that had divided France. Yet, the problem is that while the *royalistes* tended to see the 'compromise' in the light of historical circumstances, the liberals insisted upon its intrinsically 'contractual' nature. In the first case, the reference does not possess any juridical-constitutional content, or rather does not imply, where the concessionary nature of the *Charte* is concerned, any echo of the putative "traité de paix", whereas in the second case the aim would seem to have been to launch a sort of "imaginary constitution" which went beyond the *lettre* of the Charter and referred in the last analysis to the practical workings of the political system, or to concrete power relations and to the ebb and flow of *opinion*.

The interpretation that Guizot offers in his Memoirs exemplifies the liberal attitude. The Charter 'appeared as a purely royal concession, instead of proclaiming what it really was, a peace treaty following a long war, a series of new articles added, by common accord, to the pact of ancient union between the nation and the king'.[75] Thus the constitutional monarchy reaffirmed the old alliance; modern constitutionalism was reunited with the medieval. But the peace treaty was, to all intents and purposes, a truce that was to be broken on several different occasions. Count Beugnot, who had played such a major role in laying the foundations of the philosophy which inspired the *Charte*, had a clear grasp of the basic problem:

> The Charter will never be, for us, a political gospel where on the one hand, there will be an attempt to kill its spirit by means of the letter, on the other, there will be an attempt to save it from the letter by means of the inferences drawn from its spirit. It has been given in good faith, it must be understood in the same.[76]

If the French *Charte constitutionnelle* is undoubtedly the main theoretical / practical reference point of German *Frühkonstitutionalismus*, it is equally true that the first important constitutional experiments in Bayern, Baden, Württemberg and Hessen-Darmstadt (to mention a number of different *landständische Verfassungen* promulgated in 1818–1820)[77] exemplify contexts and developments which, in

75 'Se présenta comme une pure concession royale, au lieu de se proclamer ce qu'elle était réellement, un traité de paix après une longue guerre, une série d'articles nouveaux ajoutés, d'un commun accord, au pacte d'ancienne union entre la nation et le roi', F. Guizot, *Mémoires pour servir à l'histoire de mon temps*, Paris 1858–1867, I, 34.

76 'La Charte ne sera jamais pour nous un évangile politique où l'on s'efforcera d'un côté, de tuer l'esprit par la lettre et de l'autre, de la sauver de la lettre par les inductions tirées de l'esprit. Elle a été donnée de bonne foi, elle doit être entendue de même ...', J.-C. Beugnot, *Mémoires du comte Beugnot, ancien ministre (1783–1815)*, publiés par le comte Albert Beugnot, Paris 1889, 3 ed., 653.

77 For this stage of the German constitutionalism of the Restoration, see L. Gall, *Der Liberalismus als regierende Partei. Das Großherzogtum Baden zwischen Restau-*

the first German constitutional wave, although ascribable to common categories, inevitably present their own particular characteristics. From the *Charte*, these first constitutions draw principles and institutions like the discretionary power of the monarchic executive over legislative initiative, and, more generally, over the procedure for drafting legislative acts, as well as over mechanisms of convocation, extension of mandate and dissolution of the 'Parliaments'; the principle of ministerial (criminal) responsibility; bicameralism; the royal prerogative in spheres of international and military politics. Article 13 of the constituent act of the German Confederation institutionalises the semantic and political ambiguity which is a distinctive trait of this phase of European constitutional history. In view of the ambiguity and vagueness of the formulas, the interpretation (and the consequent acts) acquire an indubitable importance as well as a strong 'performative' capacity.

A key role is played by the concept of 'representation'.[78] Faced with the risks entailed by *ständisch* and *repräsentativ* seeming to be equal in status, Metternich, the Austrian chancellor, commissioned Friedrich von Gentz to write the memorial *Über den Unterschied zwischen den landständischen und Repräsentativverfassungen*,[79] addressed in 1819 to the ministers of the Member States of the German Confederation, who had been invited to the conference of Karlsbad. Gentz's text was intended to be a kind of 'authentic' interpretation of Article 13, offering an overview of developments since the promulgation of the first constitutions in Germany. The German 'model', Gentz argued, was not compatible with *Repräsentation*, understood as unitary popular-parliamentary representation, but only with the *landständische Verfassung*, interpreted as a form of

ration und Rechtsgründung, Stuttgart 1968; M. Stolleis, *Oktroi, oktroyierte Verfassung*, in A. Erler and E. Kaufmann (eds.), *Handwörterbuch zur Deutschen Rechtsgeschichte*, Köln 1984, III, 1230; M. Stolleis, *Geschichte des öffentlichen Rechts*, cit., 187 ff.; H. Brandt, *Parlamentarismus in Württemberg 1819–1870: Anatomie eines deutschen Landtags*, Düsseldorf 1987; Id., *Von den Verfassungskämpfen der Stände zum modernen Konstitutionalismus. Das Beispiel Württemberg*, in M. Kirsch, P. Schiera (eds.), *Denken und Umsetzung des Konstitutionalismus in Deutschland*, cit., 98–108; D. Götschmann, *Bayerischer Parlamentarismus im Vormärz: die Ständeversammlung des Königreichs Bayern 1819–1848*, Düsseldorf 2002; C. Schulze, *Frühkonstitutionalismus in Deutschland*, Baden Baden 2002; J. Hummel, *Le constitutionnalisme allemande*, cit., 47 ff.; J. Weitzel, *"Von den Rechten der Krone trete ich keinen Zoll ab". Das monarchische Prinzip und die Fortbildung der Verfassung in Bayern von 1818 bis 1848*, in U. Müßig (ed.), *Konstitutionalismus und Verfassungskonflikt*, cit., 117–126.

78 E. W. Böckenförde, *Der deutsche Typ der konstitutionellen Monarchie im 19. Jahrhundert*, in Id., *Recht, Staat, Freiheit*, cit., 281.

79 Cf. in H. Brandt (ed.), *Restauration und Frühliberalismus 1814–1840*, Darmstadt 1979.

Vertretung predicated upon a concept of socio-political order immanent in the particularistic caste structure. The following year, in 1820, when the 'Schlußakte der Wiener Ministerkonferenzen' was passed, Metternich ensured that Article 57 was ratified.[80] This article, placed under the tutelage of the Confederation, endorsed the centrality of the monarchic principle within the German area.

The monarchic principle, sometimes a juridical dogma and sometimes an historico-political postulate, raised to the level of fundamental constitutional norm in Article 57 of the final Act of the Conference of Vienna of 15th May 1820, had thereby consolidated the distinction, fated to survive up until the Weimar constitution, between German constitutionalism and Western European parliamentarianism. The monarchic principle, which was destined to a speedy decline in France, its country of origin, thus became in Germany during a period of over a century, the principle of legitimisation of the political power. Whereas the 1814 French Charter sought to reconcile the return to the principle of royal legitimacy with the social progress that had followed the Revolution, Article 57 of the final Act of the Conference of Vienna constituted something closer to a "prophylactic" tool ....[81]

This theory of the monarchic principle is designed to assign to the sovereign a general presumption of discretionary power within the constitution. According to this thesis, the monarch alone – and not the 'representatives' – can draw on this 'pre-constitutional' space, which tallies with the conceptual paradox, recalled above, of *das Formlos-Formende*. The ideological, "restoration" reading of Article 13 and the development of the *monarchisches Prinzip*, which enhanced the image of the granted constitution as 'constitution of the sovereign',[82] was opposed by the liberals, who gave it a contractual interpretation. In 1824 Johann Christoph von Aretin wrote that, after all, even a granted constitution

80 'Since the German confederation, with the exception of the free cities, is made up of sovereign princes, then in accordance with the here given fundamental principle all State power must lie in the supreme head of the State, and the sovereign can be bound to co-operate with the estates only in the exercise of specific powers' ('Da der deutsche Bund, mit Ausnahme der freien Städte, aus souverainen Fürsten besteht, so muß dem hierdurch gegebenen Grundbegriffe zufolge die Gesamte Staats-Gewalt in dem Oberhaupte des Staats vereinigt bleiben, und der Souverain kann durch eine landständische Verfassung nur in der Ausübung bestimmter Rechte an die Mitwirkung der Stände gebunden werden').

81 J. Hummel, *Le constitutionnalisme allemande*, cit., 71. On this point, see P. Schiera, *Dahlmann e il primo costituzionalismo tedesco*, in *Quaderni fiorentini per la storia del pensiero giuridico moderno*, 13, 1984, 397–400; G. Goderbauer, *Theoretiker des deutschen Vormärz als Vordenker moderner Volksvertretungen*, Munich 1989.

82 E. W. Böckenförde, *Geschichtliche Entwicklung*, cit., 36 ff. See Id., *Der deutsche Typ der konstitutionellen Monarchie im 19. Jahrhundert*, cit., 277.

was agreed upon, 'because only with the acceptance of the people does it become a real Constitution'.[83] Karl Theodor Welcker was likewise to claim, a decade later, that granted constitutions were not 'genuine' constitutions[84] and would only become such when the people accepted them with good will on the basis of a contract. The moment the sovereign had granted the constitutional law, as representative of the constituent power, it could no longer be revoked.[85]

If we consider another context, this time in the Italian peninsula, we can see that the Piedmontese liberals had adopted a similar stance, immediately after the *Statuto del Regno*, the constitution granted by King Charles-Albert in March 1848. Here too, the late rehabilitation of the model of the 1814 *Charte* – defined as the 'most monarchic'[86] – did not preclude rejection of the theory of the sovereign's right of repeal. The Statute as fundamental law, which is 'perpetual' and 'irrevocable', undoubtedly had its origins in the will of the sovereign, but did not impede the initial signs of institutional 'dialogue'. By having recourse to the category of parliamentary omnipotence, Count Cavour, in a famous article in "Il Risorgimento" of the 10th of March, said that once the path to 'self-limitation' has been chosen, 'the King is no longer in possession [of the unilateral power]. A minister who advised him to make use of it, without consulting the nation, would violate constitutional principles, and would incur the most grave responsibility'.[87] In a text such as the *Statuto*, drafted in the aftermath of

83 Quotation from D. Grimm in H. Mohnhaupt, D. Grimm (eds.), *Verfassung: Zur Geschichte des Begriffs von der Antike bis zur Gegenwart. Zwei Studien*, Berlin 2002.

84 K. Welcker, *Octroyierte Verfassungen*, cit.

85 K. von Rotteck, K. Welcker, *Charte*, cit.

86 See H. Ullrich, *The Statuto Albertino*, in H. Dippel (ed.), *Executive and Legislative Powers in the Constitutions of 1848–49*, Berlin 1999, 137; E. Rotelli, *Le Costituzioni di democrazia. Testi 1689–1850*, Bologna 2008, 114.

87 'Il Re non [lo] possiede più. Un ministro che gli consigliasse di farne uso, senza consultare la nazione, violerebbe i principii costituzionali, incorrerebbe nella più grave responsabilità'. 'The word *irrevocable*, as used in the preamble to the Statute, can only be applied literally to the new and great principles proclaimed by the same, to the great fact of a pact which is destined to unite in an indissoluble union both the people and the King. However, this does not mean that the particular conditions of the pact are not susceptible to gradual improvements, put into action by the common accord between the contracting parties. The King, together with the contribution of the nation, will always in the future be able to add to it all necessary modifications which will be indicated by the experience and reason of the times' ('La parola *irrevocabile*, come è impiegata nel preambolo dello Statuto, è solo applicabile letteralmente ai nuovi e grandi principi proclamati da esso, ed al gran fatto di un patto destinato a stringere in modo indissolubile il popolo e il Re. Ma ciò non vuol dire che le condizioni particolari del patto non siano suscettibili di progressivi miglioramenti operati di comune accordo tra le parti contraenti. Il Re, col concorso della nazione, potrà sempre nell'avvenire introdurre in esso tutti i cambiamenti, che saranno indicati

Orleanist constitutionalism and the Belgian charter, the dualistic reading of the *King in Parliament* proposed from that time on, was useful for delineating a *rigid* structure, the pact, which was designed to limit and temper the opposing causes and interests by offering reciprocal guarantees.[88]

9. The fate of the monarchic constitution

If the model of a granted constitution is indissolubly linked to 'monarchic constitutionalism', the destiny of the 'constitutional' monarchy within the European context is not univocal. We have seen, not by chance, just how strong the 'argument of ambiguity', as it might be termed, proved to be. This ambiguity is an intrinsic feature of 'granted' constitutionalism. We should not forget that the reference texts are at the same time both archaic and modern, with elements of estates-based *ancien régime* rationalisation called upon to 'integrate', to differing degrees, with post-revolution liberal constitutionalism: the *Verfassung* and the *Constitution* – to use the German terms – are less opposed than one might suppose, and tend rather to contaminate one another.[89] The monarch exists 'before' the constitution and this fact is too deeply rooted to be neutralised by the process of constitutionalisation. The constitutional integration of the institution of the Crown is the dilemma which pervades the history of European constitutionalism.[90] Nineteenth-century constitutional history is, therefore, characterised by a long process of *civilisation constitutionnelle* of the royal prerogative.

The constitutional monarchy is a general formula, a complex political order, a conceptual space which, during the course of the nineteenth century, took on a variety of characteristics and conditions that nonetheless sprang from the same basic assumptions and causes. On the Continent, the granted constitution was its main starting-point. The outcomes, however, are not easily predictable. The dualism between the monarchic and representative principles gave shape to the general terms of a form of government whereby the monarch was the supreme head of State and wherein at least part of the legislative power was exercised by elected representatives. French constitutional history displays a

dall'esperienza e dalla ragione dei tempi', C. B. di Cavour, *Il Risorgimento*, 10 March 1848).

88 M. Fioravanti, *Per una storia della legge fondamentale in Italia: dallo Statuto alla Costituzione*, in Id. (ed.), *Il valore della Costituzione. L'esperienza della democrazia repubblicana*, Rome, Bari 2009, 7.

89 See the observations of M. Meriggi, *Verfassung/Constitution: la "confusione babilonese" del medio Ottocento*, in *Giornale di storia costituzionale*, I, 1, 2001, 63.

90 P. Colombo, *Il re d'Italia. Prerogative costituzionali e potere politico della Corona (1848–1922)*, Milan 1999, 194.

development of the monarchic form which, from the 'limited monarchy' of the 1814 *Charte*, led in 1830 to an act of redistribution of powers. This 1830 *Charte* was a text of constitutional 'revision' stemming from a revolution and was later adroitly watered down by the moderate liberals and conservatives. It reverted to certain political and ideological presuppositions of a 'democratic' nature, namely the promises contained in Article 69. However, it did not solve the problem of governance and, more particularly, of the relationship between monarchy, government and parliamentary representation. In order to understand the monarchic function in its long and laborious constitutional transformation, the concept of *influence* is of fundamental importance, a key, albeit elusive concept. It is enough to read the thoughts of Prosper Duvergier de Hauranne,[91] or of constitutionalists like Pellegrino Rossi,[92] Charles Hello or François Guizot from the 1840s ('Le trône n'est pas un fauteuil vide') in order to become aware of this aspect.[93] In France, a regime predicated upon a balance of powers and with a monarchic executive[94] emerged, in the conviction that the close relationship between the monarch and the government affirmed by the text of the Charter would conservatively counterbalance the claim of the elective Chamber to 'absorb' the executive power and assume a position of predominance in contradiction of the principle of 'co-operation' and balance of powers. The 'republican' Benjamin Constant, at the time of the Restoration, had lucidly reassessed the constitutional potential of the 'condition monarchique'.[95] In his complex reflection on 'neutral power' (often misunderstood),[96] conceived as both 'pouvoir neutre et préservateur' (neutral and preservative power) and 'pouvoir neutre et intermédiaire' (neutral and intermediary power), the sovereign was the organ of national unity and continuity of the State, an organ which, by deploying its 'majesty' and 'impartiality', embodied the 'puissance publique'.

It was therefore the historical task of the nineteenth century to mediate between these two great forms of independent legitimacy, the sovereign and the 'representatives of the moderns'. The failure of the French experiment in limited

91 *Infra* in this volume *Governo rappresentativo e principio parlamentare: le Chartes francesi*, 314–319.

92 L. Lacchè, *Pellegrino Rossi e la Monarchia di Luglio*, in Id. (ed.), *Un liberale europeo: Pellegrino Rossi (1787–1848)*, Milan 2001, 69–108.

93 L. Lacchè, *La Libertà che guida il Popolo*, cit., 188 ff.

94 A. Laquièze, *Les origines du régime parlementaire en France*, cit.

95 B. Constant, *Observations sur le discours prononcé par S. E. le ministre de l'Intérieur en faveur du projet de loi sur la liberté de la presse* (1814), in *Œuvres*, ed. A. Roulin, Paris 1957, 1248–1249; Id., *De l'état constitutionnel de la France*, 1, mardi 15 juin *La Renommée* (1819), in *Recueil d'articles. Le Mercure, la Minerve et la Renommée*, II, ed. E. Harpaz, Geneva 1972, 1233.

96 In this volume see *supra Coppet et la percée de l'Etat libéral constitutionnel*, 222 ff.

monarchy did not, as we have seen, lead to the problem of the granted constitution being shelved. One misguided approach, which has long influenced the interpretation of European nineteenth-century constitutional systems, has been to consider them only from the standpoint of 'parliamentarisation'. This led to a progressive, linear and inexorably determinist interpretation of such systems, and one that did indeed rely upon the parliamentary paradigm.[97] The nineteenth century did not turn its back upon the conflagration of the French Revolution. If anything, it was the century in which the two great unresolved problems of constitutional history, the question of the head of State in the person of a hereditary monarch and that of the form and structure of the government, occupied a central position.

More recent historiography has advanced a more careful and nuanced analysis of this complex, hybrid and fiercely contested constitutional constellation. Representative government is a battlefield and the outcome seemingly always in doubt.

In Germany, the modernisation of the *monarchisches Prinzip*[98] proposed in 1845 by Friedrich Julius Stahl postulated the definitive abandonment of its class-territorial[99] nature, which had influenced the vagueness of the organising formulas of what the liberals of the *Vormärz* derogatorily termed *Scheinkonstitutionalismus*. The idea of State (*Rechtsstaat*) had, as a principle, to be constructed around the legitimate monarch and no longer around an 'absolutist' vision. The political-ideological character that pervaded this reinterpretation tended, in its later variants, to give rise to a monarchic-constitutional synthesis[100] which in practice was able to discipline and govern the antagonisms and conflicts occasioned by socio-economic dynamics.[101] Even amongst liberals, 'parliamen-

97 Regarding this profile, for a more detailed discussion, see *infra* in this volume *Governo rappresentativo e principio parlamentare: le* Chartes *francesi*, 303–327.

98 On the constitutive elements, see C. De Pascale, *Sovranità e ceti in Friedrich Julius Stahl*, in *Quaderni fiorentini*, 13, 1984, 431 ff.

99 Regarding class transformation in *Reichsstände* see *Ibidem* 428.

100 On this concept, see O. Hintze, *Das monarchische Prinzip*, cit.; O. Brunner, *Vom Gottesgnadentum zum monarchischen Prinzip*, in *Das Königtum*, Lindau 1957, 279 ff.

101 Cf. especially H. Brandt, *Landständische Repräsentation im deutschen Vormärz. Politisches Denken im Einflußfeld des monarchischen Prinzips*, Neuwied und Berlin 1968; H. Boldt, *Zwischen Patrimonialismus und Parlamentarismus. Zur Entwicklung vor-parlamentarischer Theorien in der deutschen Staatslehre des Vormärz*, in G. Ritter (ed.), *Gesellschaft, Parlament und Regierung. Zur Geschichte des Parlamentarismus in Deutschland*, Düsseldorf 1974, 77–100; Id., *Deutsche Staatslehre im Vormärz*, Düsseldorf 1975; H. Brandt, *Der lange Weg in die demokratische Moderne. Deutsche Verfassungsgeschichte von 1800 bis 1945*, Darmstadt 1998; R. Wahl, *Die Bewegung im labilen Dualismus des Konstitutionalismus in Deutschland. Möglichkeiten und*

tarianism', feared as a political-constitutional evolution liable to reflect the 'democratic' development of the wider society, caused apprehension and hesitation. 'A true monarchy exists – wrote Stahl in 1848 – only where the Prince possesses a power, albeit limited, but autonomous, where his personality and his personal will have a meaning for public order'.[102] To call to mind a theory dear to Donoso Cortès, the unity of powers in pure monarchy is a way of weakening what is manifold and contradictory and inevitably postulates the theme of conflict and constitutional pluralism.

The constitutional profile of the Belgian monarchy is significant in this regard also, serving as it does as a counter-example. After the Belgian Revolution of 1831, the new constitution, destined to become an important 'model' for later constitutions,[103] unambiguously affirmed the principle of national sovereignty. Article 25 established that 'All power emanates from the nation. They are exercised in the manner established by the Constitution'.[104] The political-constitutional centrality of parliament was confirmed in the exclusive and wide-ranging competence of the legislature even with regard to matters which had previously come within the scope of administration. By assigning executive power to the monarchy, the constitution led to the establishment of a 'representative constitutional monarchy, under a hereditary head'. It has been observed that the monarchy in Belgium became 'an organising element in the balance of the powers of the liberal State'.[105] The limitation of royal power is seen as one of the fundamental conditions of the Belgian constitutional monarchy, and in particular as the feature that guarantees it an 'essentially tempering' character.[106]

Grenzen einer Entwicklung zugunsten des Parlaments, in Lacchè, Manca (eds.), *Parlamento e costituzione nei sistemi costituzionali europei ottocenteschi*, Bologna, Berlin 2003, 95–126.

102 F. J. Stahl, *Die Revolution und die constitutionelle Monarchie, eine Reihe ineinandergreifender Abhandlungen*, Berlin 1848, 66–67.

103 See *supra* in this volume *La Costituzione belga del 1831*, 98–99.

104 'Tous les pouvoirs émanent de la nation. Ils sont exercés de la manière établie par la Constitution'. On Article 25, see J. Gilissen, *La constitution belge de 1831: ses sources, son influence*, in *Res publica*, X, 1968, 126–127.

105 Following F. J. Stahl, see C. Schmitt, *Verfassungslehre*, cit., 289. On the type of constitutional monarchy created in Belgium in 1831, especially in relation to the *monarchisches Prinzip* of the Prussian tradition, cf. the dissertation of R. Smend, *Die Preussische Verfassungsurkunde im Vergleich mit der Belgischen*, Göttingen 1904; O. Hintze, *Das monarchische Prinzip*, cit.; W. Conze (ed.), *Beiträge zur deutschen und belgischen Verfassungsgeschichte im 19. Jahrhundert*, Stuttgart 1967; E. W. Böckenförde, *Der deutsche Typ der konstitutionnellen Monarchie im 19. Jahrhundert*, cit., 278–279; in this volume *supra Constitución, Monarquía, Parlamento: Francia y Belgica*; and also *La Costituzione belga del 1831*.

106 Th. Juste, *Le Congrès National de Belgique, 1830–1831 précédé de quelques considérations sur la constitution belge*, Brussels 1880, 394.

The king may, therefore, exercise those prerogatives[107] formally attributed to him by the constitution and by special laws (Article 78).

Yet, notwithstanding these and other institutional characteristics of the Belgian monarchy, at the dawn of the twentieth century, Oscar Orban wrote that

> in limited monarchy, everything for which provision has not been made pertains to the government; in constitutional monarchy, everything which is not regulated pertains to the legislature, but everything that is deemed to depend on the executive authority is or should be enough to render it a plenitude of power, a sum of determinate powers, certainly, but a whole, a sufficiently broad generality to be opposed to the special powers of judging and legislating.[108]

This was because the Belgian kings did not hesitate to 'bend' the logic of parliamentary government to the advantage of the monarchy:

> He [Leopold] went as far as replacing the republican interpretation which the Parliament gave to the constitution, with his monarchic interpretation and, respecting scrupulously the fundamental pact which he had sworn to observe, he managed to endow the government with indispensable prerogatives to maintain the State.[109]

The concept of the *influence* of the Crown is at the basis of the prevailing interpretation. Not even in Belgium can the evolution of the form of government be portrayed as a smooth, straightforward process of parliamentarisation of the system. If such a process represents an intrinsic line of development, the logic of the balance between the 'sphere of autonomy' of the monarch and the 'juridical primacy of legislative power' continued to produce, throughout the nineteenth century (and beyond), swings from one side to the other, in line with shifting political circumstances and the diverse personalities of the individual monarchs.

The granted constitution, understood as a monarchic constitution, was, for a century, common ground for developments and applications which were far

107 On the concept of power and prerogative in Belgian public law, see J. Velu, *La dissolution du Parlement*, Brussels 1966, 54.

108 'Dans la monarchie limitée, tout ce qui n'est pas prévu appartient au gouvernement; dans la monarchie constitutionnelle, tout ce qui n'est pas réglé appartient au législatif, mais ce qui est prévu comme dépendant de l'autorité exécutive est ou doit être suffisant pour faire d'elle encore une plénitude de puissance, une somme de pouvoirs déterminés sans doute, mais un ensemble, une généralité assez vaste pour être opposée aux pouvoirs spéciaux de juger et de légiférer', O. Orban, *Le droit constitutionnel de la Belgique*, Paris 1906–1911, II, 245–246.

109 'A l'interprétation républicaine que le Parlement donnait à la constitution, il [Leopold] est arrivé à substituer son interprétation monarchique et, tout en respectant scrupuleusement le pacte fondamental qu'il avait juré d'observer, a réussi à doter le gouvernement des prérogatives indispensables au maintien de l'Etat', H. Pirenne, *Histoire de Belgique des origines à nos jours* (1974), IV, 387–388.

from being predictable. The deliberate vagueness and flexibility of the constitutional formula, which was an intrinsic feature of the constitutionalism of the Restoration, was in fact a *programme*, to interpret and flesh out at will.[110] The political theology elaborated by the reactionary writers of the Restoration was undoubtedly a powerful tool in the analysis of the *undecided* constitution, a constitution shaped by the contradictions of a liberal constitutionalism which accepted the *octroi* and the idea of the autonomous will of the monarch and, at the same time, sought to limit, if not annul, the originally personal dimension.[111] As a consequence the difficult separation of *régner* from *gouverner* was destined to be one of the greatest political-constitutional problems of the nineteenth century.[112]

110 See in this volume *Responsabilità ministeriale*, 389.

111 C. Schmitt, *Zur Staatsphilosophie der Gegenrevolution (De Maistre, Bonald, Donoso Cortés)*, in Id., *Politische Theologie*, cit., 75–77.

112 Regarding this theme, see in this volume *'Gouverner n'est point administrer. Régner est encore autre chose que gouverner'. Le rétour d'un vieillard: P.-L. Roederer et le problème du 'gouvernement' pendant la monarchie de Juillet*, 355 ss.

La garanzia della Costituzione. Riflessioni sul caso francese

> «Toute constitution qui a été violée est prouvée mauvaise. Car, de trois choses, une est démontrée. Ou il était impossible aux pouvoirs constitutionnels de gouverner avec la constitution, ou il n'y a avait pas dans tous ces pouvoirs un intérêt égal à maintenir cette constitution; ou, enfin, il n'existait pas dans les pouvoirs opposés au pouvoir usurpateur des moyens suffisants de la défendre ...».[1]

In questa notazione di Benjamin Constant non si intravede soltanto un profilo di teoria costituzionale: è soprattutto la recente storia francese dell'idea stessa di costituzione a balzare in primo piano con tutti i suoi drammatici interrogativi e dilemmi. È come se Constant volesse richiamare alla memoria della Restaurazione il serrato dibattito e il travaglio dell'età post-rivoluzionaria alla ricerca di quell'organizzazione dei poteri che, garantendo la costituzione, potesse salvaguardare al meglio i diritti e le libertà degli individui. Per Constant gli «interessi» e i «mezzi» – ovvero le garanzie – dovevano ancorare la costituzione (*constitution-défiance*) ad una antropologia non certo ottimistica dell'esercizio del potere. Se da un lato sembra voler credere alla necessità della garanzia costituzionale, dall'altro è ben consapevole dei limiti e dei pericoli insiti in ogni sua assolutizzazione.

L'impossibilità di costituzionalizzare la Rivoluzione se non ha certo impedito la nascita di uno straordinario laboratorio di forme, modi, tecniche di organizzazione del potere e di instaurazione dell'ordine politico, ha tuttavia dato l'abbrivio a quel complesso discorso strutturale sulla mutevolezza e sull'instabilità costituzionale destinato ad incunearsi ben dentro il nostro più ravvicinato orizzonte temporale. C'è chi come Walter Bagehot ha chiamato in causa il "carattere francese" (lungo un percorso che ci riporterebbe a Burke) perché inadatto al governo costituzionale: gli insuccessi a catena gli fanno sorgere a

1 B. Constant, *Cours de politique constitutionnelle ou collection des ouvrages publiés sur le gouvernement représentatif ... avec une introduction et des notes par M. Edouard Laboulaye, Additions et Notes*, 1818, Paris 1872, t. I, 380. Questo profilo era stato affrontato da Constant nel capitolo IX delle *Réflexions sur les constitutions et les garanties*, Paris 1814, e ancor prima nello scritto direttoriale *Des réactions politiques* del 1797.

metà dell'Ottocento il sospetto che «... un numero così grande di bancarotte suggerisca un po' d'inadeguatezza al commercio ...»,[2] che addirittura l'eccesso di ingegno – di ingegneria costituzionale si direbbe oggi – sia poco adatto a fortificare i principi costituzionali e a radicarne le istituzioni.

Non stupisce allora che l'«artificialismo» costituzionale sia uno dei temi più ricorrenti: fare e disfare le costituzioni sarebbe insomma un "vizio" tipicamente francese. Un tema, questo, che si istituzionalizza alla Restaurazione e che non lascia più il campo per buona parte del secolo. Prevost-Paradol, quasi alle soglie della Terza Repubblica, lo dirà con formula efficace: «... la Révolution française a fondé une société, elle cherche encore son gouvernement».[3] Questa ricerca non è stata mai tanto pressante e necessaria come dopo la Restaurazione. Qual è il valore, lo statuto politico e normativo della costituzione? Quale idea di Costituzione accompagna la storia francese in un arco cronologico che ripropone più diluita nel tempo la metamorfosi – come nel primo ciclo rivoluzionario – dalla monarchia costituzionale all'Impero passando per la Repubblica? Se certo non è possibile scorgere una linea di sviluppo "rettilineo",[4] in termini di storia "progressiva", sarebbe però insufficiente affidarsi a generici schematismi che enfatizzano elementi esteriori e non riescono a penetrare le ragioni più profonde del costituzionalismo francese. Una prima impressione infatti potrebbe favorire un'immagine eccessivamente riduttiva del valore della costituzione, segnata da una sorta di minimalismo costituzionale, da una prospettiva essenzialmente eclettica, da una intrinseca debolezza sul piano della legittimità. Pur convivendo con tali profili, si potranno però scorgere al contempo vicende storico-concrete e significative linee di riflessione dottrinale che sollecitano un più adeguato uso, in chiave di contestualizzazione storica, delle categorie di analisi che appartengono alla teoria costituzionale. Non giova infatti alla comprensione né un approccio appiattito sulla ricerca retrospettiva di ciò che è patrimonio esclusivo del XX secolo e che quindi non si potrà ritrovare se non

2 Bagehot scrive, non a caso, dopo il colpo di Stato di Luigi Bonaparte: *Napoleone III. Lettere sul colpo di Stato francese del 1851*, a cura di M. Griffo, Roma 1997, 94–95. Cfr. inoltre P. Rosanvallon, *La Monarchie impossible. Les Chartes de 1814 et de 1830*, Paris 1994, 179–180. François Furet ha definito i Francesi «fondamentalistes de la politique» che hanno concesso «très peu d'espace à la réflexion constitutionnelle proprement dite, et à ce minimum d'empirisme inséparable de l'étude d'institutions ajustées au paysage tourmenté offert par l'opinion» (F. Furet, *L'idée de tradition révolutionnaire dans la France du XIXe siècle*, in *Pouvoirs*, 50, 1990, 12).

3 L.-A. Prevost-Paradol, *La France nouvelle*, Paris 1868, 296.

4 Ph. Ardant, *Le contenu des Constitutions: variables et constantes*, in *Pouvoirs*, 50, 1990, 31.

forzando il dato storico, né escludere *a priori* la presenza di logiche, di meccanismi e di categorie che riteniamo appannaggio altrettanto esclusivo del nostro bagaglio culturale. Senza dubbio ci troviamo di fronte una categoria di costituzionalità che è presente in alcuni momenti, senza riuscire tuttavia a conquistare uno statuto di regolarità e di ordine sistematico. É una vicenda dunque che si può cogliere più nella prospettiva fluida e propositiva della politica costituzionale che in quella «normativa» del diritto costituzionale.

1. Tra «esprit» e «lettre», ovvero come interpretare la costituzione

Dopo il 1814, in concomitanza con l'*octroi* della *Charte constitutionnelle* e con altre più effimere ma importanti esperienze costituenti,[5] una babele di linguaggi sembra invadere la Francia. È possibile dare vita ad un lessico comune al fine di concepire un'idea sufficientemente unitaria di costituzione? La *Charte* del 1814 e gli altri testi costituzionali coevi risentono tutti – in varia misura e muovendo ciascuno da una premessa specifica – di tale difficoltà. Il discorso della storia costituisce una forma di reazione al costituzionalismo rivoluzionario, eppure non può più prescindere da esso; d'altro canto, gli eccessi riconoscibili nell'astrattezza razionale di epoca rivoluzionaria hanno fatto ripensare con più favore «... à l'aide du temps, le plus doux et le plus puissant des auxiliaires».[6] Malgrado le volontà e i progetti dei protagonisti della vicenda politico-costituzionale della Restaurazione, il terreno di scontro (e di arduo incontro) è appunto quello dell'idea di costituzione.[7] Senza una concezione appena condivisa, appare difficile se non impossibile poter fondare un sistema costituzionale capace di mettere radici. «Quando nel 1814 la Carta fu concessa, gli ultra s'illudevano, e i liberali temevano, che la costituzione fosse una formalità a cui momentaneamente ci si piegasse, salvo poi lasciarla cadere o a obliarla come le costituzioni

5 Mi riferisco alla costituzione senatoriale del 6 aprile 1814, all'Atto addizionale del 22 aprile 1815 e ai progetti del giugno–luglio 1815 elaborati dalla Camera dei deputati. Per una sintesi e per più ampi riferimenti bibliografici v. *supra* in questo volume *Constitución, Monarquía, Parlamento*, 130–137.

6 «Tant qu'on n'a pas essayé d'une constitution par la pratique, les formes sont une lettre morte: la pratique seule en démontre l'effet et en détermine le sens. Nous n'avons que trop abattu l'édifice sous prétexte de le reconstruire: profitons désormais des lumières qui ne s'acquièrent que par les faits, afin de pourvoir graduellement à tous les besoins partiels, avec mesure, avec lenteur, à l'aide du temps, le plus doux et le plus puissant des auxiliaires» (B. Constant, *Principes de politique applicables à tous les gouvernements représentatifs et particulièrement à la constitution actuelle de la France* (1815), in *Œuvres*, texte présenté et annoté par Alfred Roulin, Paris 1957, 1126).

7 Su questa espressione, v. P. Bastid, *L'idée de la constitution*, Paris 1985.

dell'Impero».[8] Nonostante la critica radicale dei più reazionari, l'ambigua "sopportazione" dei realisti moderati, l'esaltazione ideologica dei liberali, la Carta non fu lasciata cadere. Tutti parlavano di costituzione – nel bene e nel male –, ma il problema era poi definirne i tratti essenziali e di conseguenza il suo valore. Non bisogna dimenticare del resto come alla Restaurazione il Codice civile da un lato e la legge del 28 piovoso dell'anno VIII dall'altro continuassero a fissare i contorni costituzionali senza i quali sarebbe del tutto riduttivo leggere la vicenda delle Carte e del costituzionalismo ottocentesco. Essi rappresentano i due principali baluardi delle libertà borghesi "materiali" garantite dal diritto statuale. Le costituzioni leggere non sono insomma concepibili senza questa parte pesante che si identifica con lo spazio del Codice civile e con il governo burocratico-razionale dello Stato.[9]

Nell'arco di poco più di un anno i testi costituzionali rivelano – come si è già osservato – l'esistenza di un dibattito vivace ma anche la difficoltà di trovare un punto di equilibrio tra il fine che la Costituzione deve perseguire (tutelare le libertà dell'individuo attraverso una efficace organizzazione dei poteri dello Stato) e la legittimità-forma della costituzione. Se rispetto al primo elemento è possibile constatare un certo grado di condivisione delle tecniche e dei meccanismi di funzionamento del regime costituzionale (mettendo qui l'accento più sulle identità che sulle differenze), rispetto al secondo elemento i vari testi e progetti si dividono sul punto della legittimità fondatrice e dunque sulla natura della sovranità da costituzionalizzare.[10]

Non è del tutto corretto vedere nella Carta borbonica anzitutto un «tributo all'apparenza»,[11] ovvero un testo composto dall'assemblaggio di due "parti", l'una formale, d'apparato, l'altra invece – ben più importante e duratura – destinata agli spiriti liberali della nazione. L'«arcaismo»[12] del testo deve essere

8 A. Omodeo, *Studi sull'età della Restaurazione. La cultura francese nell'età della Restaurazione ...*, Torino 1974, 2 ed., 63, dove riporta l'efficace testimonianza del barone de Barante (*Souvenirs du Baron de Barante, de l'Académie française [1782–1866], publiés par son petit fils Claude de Barante*, 8 voll., Paris, Calmann-Lévy, 1890–1891, Paris 1880, II, 36).

9 Sul punto si rinvia a L. Lacchè, *L'espropriazione per pubblica utilità. Amministratori e proprietari nella Francia dell'Ottocento*, Milano 1995.

10 Si rinvia *infra*, par. 3.

11 É la tesi di P. Bastid, *Les institutions politiques de la Monarchie parlementaire française (1814–1848)*, Paris 1954, 139 ss.

12 Questo profilo, già evidenziato da J. Bonnefon, *Le régime parlementaire sous la Restauration*, Paris 1905 e da Ch. Rohmer, *Le droit d'ordonnance et l'esprit de la Charte de 1814*, Paris 1931, è stato chiarito ulteriormente da S. Rials, *Essai sur le concept de monarchie limitée (autour de la Charte de 1814)*, in S. Rials, *Révolution et contre-révolution au XIXe siècle*, Paris 1987, 88–125 e ripreso, con dovizia di

quindi sottolineato come dato essenziale e non meramente accessorio. Il Preambolo rappresenta una vera e propria teoria della monarchia di antico regime nel contesto di una modernizzazione della forma di esercizio del potere che abbozza i tratti elementari del governo rappresentativo ma stenta però a riconoscere una vera dinamica pluralista degli organi.

Considerate queste premesse, non deve sorprendere che la Carta del 1814 appaia una costituzione volta più a delimitare i confini del "compromesso" raggiunto al momento della Restaurazione che a "promettere" equilibri politico-programmatici da realizzare nei tempi a venire. La cosiddetta ambiguità della Carta è l'opera di due prevalenti interpretazioni del documento: i *royalistes* – e non necessariamente gli *ultras* – si trincerano dietro il baluardo della *lettre* e della forma concessoria; i liberali insistono sul significato dell'*esprit*, concetto a dir poco vago sul piano giuridico. Gli uni possiedono quindi un forte argomento "giuridico", gli altri pensano di poter far leva su un argomento "politico" che bisogna però coltivare e diffondere. L'uno è un argomento statico, l'altro è dinamico. Per i conservatori la Carta sembrerebbe un punto di arrivo, per i liberali un dato di partenza da potenziare e sviluppare. L'equivoco di fondo nasce dalla duplice natura della Carta: atto giuridico concessorio e forma istitutiva di un certo grado di collaborazione tra il principio monarchico e il principio rappresentativo incarnato dalla Camera dei deputati. L'ambiguità dell'operazione stava nella inevitabile ed insuperabile confusione tra l'elemento giuridico – relativamente forte sotto il profilo della legittimità – e l'elemento politico, più fluido e dinamico. L'aspetto formale-giuridico (la tradizionale prerogativa regia fonte della Costituzione) fu contaminato e progressivamente aggredito dall'idea che l'atto costituzionale fosse la sanzione di un "compromesso", ovvero di un patto tra il sovrano e i sudditi.

Le due prevalenti posizioni sembrerebbero dunque assestarsi attorno a questi poli argomentativi: per gli uni la Carta è un baluardo costruito attorno al monarca, per gli altri una prospettiva di interpretazione, prevalentemente ideologica, in grado di suggerire un determinato sviluppo-integrazione del testo.[13] Nel concreto della lotta politica, tuttavia, le posizioni e gli schieramenti

argomenti, da A. Laquièze, *Les origines du régime parlementaire en France (1814–1848)*, Paris 2002, 59 ss. É da notare che già Luigi-Filippo d'Orléans aveva, nei suoi ricordi del 1814, posto l'accento sul carattere arcaico, *ancien régime*, della Carta. Sul manoscritto si veda H. Robert, *Louis-Philippe constitutionnaliste*, in *Commentaire*, 63, 1993, 577–580.

13 È nella fase costitutiva del 1814–1815 che si vede la dimensione progettuale e di "avanzamento" costituzionale, anche nelle proposte meno provvedute sul piano concettuale: «La charte constitutionnelle qui vient de paraître, a déjà rallié tous

stentano a mostrare coerenza e sufficiente coesione. La vicenda della cd. *Chambre introuvable*[14] – tra il 1815 e il 1816 – mostra un paradossale scambio di "ruoli": gli *ultras*, che godono di una forte maggioranza nella Camera dei deputati, insistono sul tema del controllo parlamentare e della partecipazione all'indirizzo politico del governo. Vitrolles[15] e Chateaubriand[16] ne sono i più lucidi interpreti. Se gli adepti della monarchia limitata diventano i fautori di una evoluzione "parlamentare" del regime politico, i liberali – in questo "gioco delle parti" – sono "costretti" a tenere un atteggiamento difensivo e si fanno scudo della *prérogative royale*. Per uno Chateaubriand[17] che censura l'atteggiamento dei liberali, ecco un Guizot[18] o un Villemain[19] denunciare la singolare "metamorfosi" degli *ultras*.

les gens qui pensent bien autour du trône. Nous attendons encore peu de lois, mais de lois bonnes, durables, des lois organiques et générales qui en seront le développement et comme le complément; alors l'Etat de la France sera fixé» (L. Domeny De Rienzi, *Tableau de la France, telle qu'elle a été, telle qu'elle est, telle qu'elle peut être ou aperçu politique et impartial sur sa Restauration*, Marseille 1814, 42–43).

14 Cfr. M. S. Corciulo, *Le istituzioni parlamentari in Francia. Cento Giorni e seconda Restaurazione (1815–1816)*, Napoli 1979; C. Cassina, *I lavori parlamentari della Chambre introuvable*, in *Critica storica*, 4, 1989, 573–610; P. Rosanvallon, *Les Doctrinaires et la question du gouvernement représentatif*, in *The French Revolution and the Creation of modern political Culture*, 4 voll., Oxford 1989, vol. 3, a cura di F. Furet e M. Ozouf (edd.), *The Transformations of Political Culture 1789–1848*, 412 ss.; E. De Waresquiel, *Un paradoxe politique: la Chambre «introuvable» et la naissance du parlementarisme français (octobre 1815–avril 1816)*, in *Commentaire*, 15, 1992, 409–416; P. Rosanvallon, *La monarchie impossible*, cit., 75 ss.; M. S. Corciulo, *La «Chambre introuvable» e i principi del regime parlamentare (agosto 1815–settembre 1816)*, in A. G. Manca, W. Brauneder (edd.), *L'istituzione parlamentare nel XIX secolo. Una prospettiva comparata* (Annali dell'Istituto storico italo-germanico in Trento. Contributi/Beiträge, 10), Bologna 2000, 119–137.

15 E. F.-A. De Vitrolles, *Du ministère dans le gouvernement représentatif*, Paris 1815.

16 F.-R. De Chateaubriand, *De la Monarchie selon la Charte*, Paris 1816.

17 «Quelle pitié d'entendre aujourd'hui les *constitutionnels* nier l'existence des gouvernements représentatifs, soutenir qu'une chambre de députés doit se réduire à la passive obéissance, combattre la liberté de la presse, préconiser la police, enfin changer entièrement de rôle et de langage! Ils traitoient d'esprits bornés, d'esclaves, d'ennemis des lumières, ceux qui professoient les principes qu'ils adoptent aujourd'hui. Sont-ils convertis? Non, c'est toujours le même *liberalisme* ...» (*ibidem*, 81).

18 «Ainsi la Charte elle-même est devenue leur champ de bataille; c'est dans le traité de paix qu'ils vont chercher des armes pour recommencer la guerre; et, partant des points les plus opposés, se proposant les buts les plus contraires, ils semblent se concerter pour porter les mêmes coups au gouvernement et à la nation, qui, l'un et l'autre, n'ont rien à démêler avec eux» (F. Guizot, *Du gouvernement représentatif et de l'état actuel de la France*, Paris 1816, 8).

19 A. F. Villemain, *Le roi, la Charte et la Monarchie*, Paris s. d., 7: «Les plus grands ennemis de la constitution sont désormais condamnés à l'invoquer toujours; leur

Il carattere strumentale della polemica negl'anni 1815–1816 rivela però un dato strutturale della lotta politica. Chi conquista la maggioranza della Camera dei deputati tende ad accentuare la natura "parlamentare" del regime. In fondo, l'atteggiamento degli *ultras* della *Chambre introuvable* ha una pur debole eco nel comportamento dei liberali a partire dal 1827, dalla caduta del ministero Villèle. Ciò significa che la lotta politica fa velo sulla stabilità e condivisione del quadro costituzionale. È un elemento che non deve certo meravigliare se si pensa a quanti pochi anni siano trascorsi dall'avvio dell'esperienza costituzionale in Francia. Il "gioco delle parti" tra *ultras* e liberali – per restare alla semplificazione dei due «partiti» – è anche l'espressione di una psicologia costituzionale che discende dall'interpretazione della *Charte* e del suo regime politico. Chi ha la maggioranza, si diceva, fa leva sul carattere parlamentare e dualistico; chi è sulla difensiva tende a ritrovare nel monarca un soggetto dotato di prevalenti prerogative il cui utilizzo legale può ricondurre la maggioranza entro un ambito più consono allo schema «monistico» della *Charte*. È evidente che il dibattito di fine anni Venti rimette *ultras* e liberali nelle loro "naturali" posizioni, ma questo carattere non abbandonerà – seppure con forme ulteriori e diverse – il sistema costituzionale in Francia neppure dopo il 1830.

Anche il problema della modificabilità (in tutto o in parte) o immodificabilità della Carta, del come e con quali procedure farlo, rivela una notevole confusione.[20] Se prevale la tesi della revisione nella forma della legislazione ordinaria, nondimeno da un lato i liberali cercano di affermare la teoria secondo cui la modifica legislativa avrebbe dovuto seguire ad un mandato speciale (per es. a

triomphe l'aurait détruite; leurs attaques ne peuvent que l'affermir, en les forçant de jouer un rôle qui ne trompe personne, mais qui est un hommage rendu aux principes de la liberté, et qui complète l'unanimité nationale en faveur de la Charte. Nous le disons avec joie et confiance. Le gouvernement représentatif est donc naturalisé en France. Une puissance irrésistible y pousse également toutes les opinions. Les publicistes les plus opposés par leurs sentiments et leurs vœux, se rencontrent dans ce point commun. M. de Chateaubriand consacre son talent à reproduire et, si l'on veut, à réhabiliter les théories si bien exposées par M. Benjamin Constant: et *Jerusalem* parle comme *Samarie*».

20 Tale confusione dipende in molti casi dalla più scomoda posizione in cui si trovano i liberali rispetto agli *ultras*. Un esempio evidente si ha nell'atteggiamento di Benjamin Constant. Se questi nel 1814 elabora una chiara distinzione tra un nucleo rigido e ben delimitato della costituzione, non soggetto a revisione legislativa, e le materie «non costituzionali» ordinariamente modificabili, nel 1824 è costretto, di fronte all'uso strumentale ma inappuntabile delle sue stesse parole da parte di Castelbajac (in occasione del dibattito sul mandato settennale dei deputati), a contrastare tale tentativo senza però potersi avvalere della tesi della integrale immutabilità della Carta. Cfr. sul punto M. Barberis, *Benjamin Constant. Rivoluzione, costituzione, progresso*, Bologna 1988, 198 ss.

seguito di nuove elezioni),[21] dall'altro la maggioranza conservatrice nega che anche le più vistose modificazioni apportate alla Carta – basti pensare alle leggi sul doppio voto e sull'estensione del mandato elettorale (da 5 a 7 anni) – integrino l'ipotesi di "incostituzionalità". Nello stesso tempo, malgrado le indecisioni e le debolezze del sistema, è innegabile constatare la centralità della *Charte* nel discorso e nella lotta politica della Restaurazione. In fondo tutti gli schieramenti "difendono" la *Charte*: la differenza sta nei parametri di interpretazione del testo. Ognuno ha la "sua" Carta: gli *ultras*, nel corso degli anni Venti, sentono il pericolo di un graduale scivolamento verso un regime di "influenza" della Camera dei deputati sull'indirizzo politico espresso dal «governo del re» e quindi si adoperano per «restaurare» il significato «autentico» della *Charte*; i liberali, moderati e di «sinistra», invece, mettono l'accento sul carattere «contrattuale» e considerano la costituzione dal punto di vista «materiale».

2. «La Charte désormais sera une verité»

Sul finire del regno di Carlo X, la "radicalizzazione" della lotta politica tra liberali e *ultras* fece dell'art. 14[22] il punto di rottura, toccando esso il problema del potere costituente (tanto originario che derivato). Il dibattito sull'art. 14 acquista un significato particolare nel momento in cui le possibilità di dialogo tra il monarca e la Camera dei deputati – nella forma del procedimento legislativo – si riducono drasticamente. Le elezioni del 1827 (17–24 novembre) ribadiscono la distanza tra la maggioranza parlamentare e il governo Villèle che si dimetterà di lì a poco. La successiva prova di forza, con la nascita del ministero *ultra* del principe di Polignac e l'ulteriore scioglimento della Camera (16 maggio 1830)

21 Nel preambolo dell'ordinanza del 13 luglio 1815 – dopo il ritorno di Luigi XVIII esule a Gand durante i Cento Giorni – con la quale si modificava il regime elettorale, si legge: «... mais voulant cependant que, dans aucun cas, aucune modification à la Charte ne puisse devenir définitive que d'après les formes constitutionnelles, les dispositions de la présente ordonnance seront le premier objet des délibérations des Chambres. Le pouvoir législatif dans son ensemble statuera sur la loi des élections, sur les changements à faire à la Charte dans cette partie, changements dont nous ne prenons ici l'initiative que dans les points les plus indispensables et les plus urgents, en nous imposant même l'obligation de nous rapprocher, autant que possible, de la Charte et des formes précédemment en usage» (J. B. Duvergier, *Collection complète des lois, décrets, ordonnances, règlemens, avis du Conseil d'Etat*, Paris 1837, t. 20, 4–5). Sul tema, cfr. inoltre M. Roux, *Le pouvoir constituant sous la Restauration*, Paris 1908; J. Barthélemy, *La distinction des lois constitutionnelles et des lois ordinaires sous la Monarchie de Juillet*, in *Revue de droit public*, 26, 1909, 8 ss.; P. Rosanvallon, *La monarchie impossible*, cit., 130.

22 «Le roi ... fait les règlements et ordonnances nécessaires pour l'exécution des lois et la sûreté de l'Etat».

ripropone, aggravandolo, lo stesso problema sino alla crisi finale innescata dalle ordinanze del 25 luglio. L'*Adresse* che 221 deputati rivolgono al re (18 marzo 1830) vede nella Carta un atto volto a consacrare «comme un droit, l'intervention du pays dans la délibération des intérêts publics». La logica è quella del governo rappresentativo nel quadro di una monarchia temperata dal «concours permanent des vues politiques de votre gouvernement avec les vœux de votre peuple ...».[23] Tale concorso ha come presupposto un saggio equilibrio tra «l'opinion du pays» e il ministero. Carlo X, al contrario, si convince che l'art. 14 sia il «lit de justice» per superare l'opposizione della maggioranza parlamentare. Il monarca pensa di poter disporre del «diritto di ultima parola» come se dovesse fronteggiare uno stato di emergenza che non è altro, invece, che la rivendicazione della regola fondamentale del governo rappresentativo. Promulgando le ordinanze Carlo X rifiuta di accettare tale logica perché usa uno strumento legale (l'art. 14) per ottenere un risultato incostituzionale, contrario sia alla lettera che allo spirito della *Charte*.[24] Non a caso nel *Rapport au Roi* del 25 luglio 1830 si dichiara il venir meno delle «conditions ordinaires du gouvernement représentatif». Il quadro fosco che traccia – tutto incentrato sull'uso eversivo della stampa – nega alla radice i caratteri essenziali di tale forma di governo.[25]

23 Per il testo dell'*Adresse* si veda l'appendice in P. Rosanvallon, *La monarchie impossible*, cit., 281–282. Sulla rivoluzione del luglio 1830 e sulle dinamiche politico-costituzionali del regime orleanista rinvio a L. Lacchè, *La Libertà che guida il Popolo. Le Tre Gloriose Giornate del luglio 1830 e le Chartes nel costituzionalismo francese*, Bologna 2002.

24 Non è infatti immaginabile che si possa, con ordinanza, modificare parti fondamentali della *Charte*. «Quelque que soit notre respect pour la liberté des opinions, nous ne pouvons nous défendre de penser que ceux qui, par une fausse interprétation de l'art. 14 de la Charte, soutiennent qu'une simple ordonnance royale rendue sur l'allégation de la sûreté de l'Etat, peut déroger à la Charte et aux lois, se rendent coupables du délit prévu par l'art. 4 de la loi du 17 mai 1819, qui punit les *attaques formelles contre l'autorité constitutionnelle du Roi et des Chambres*» (A. Mahul, *Tableau de la Constitution politique de la monarchie française selon la Charte, ou Résumé du droit public des Français, accompagné du texte des lois fondamentales et des documents authentiques*, Paris 1830, 239).

25 «... Nul gouvernement sur la terre ne resterait debout, s'il n'avait le droit de pourvoir à sa sûreté. Ce pouvoir est préexistant aux lois, parce qu'il est dans la nature des choses. Ce sont là, Sire, des maximes qui ont pour elles et la sanction du temps et l'aveu de tous les publicistes de l'Europe. Mais ces maximes ont une autre sanction plus positive encore, celle de la Charte elle-même. L'article 14 a investi Votre Majesté d'un pouvoir suffisant, non sans doute pour changer nos institutions, mais pour les consolider et les rendre plus immuables. D'impérieuses nécessités ne permettent plus de différer l'exercice de ce pouvoir suprême. Le moment est venu de recourir à des mesures qui rentrent dans l'esprit de la Charte, mais qui sont en dehors de l'ordre légal, dont toutes les ressources ont

L'argomento che acquista un peso schiacciante all'indomani delle ordinanze di Carlo X è che esse siano incostituzionali e tali quindi da violare il «patto che univa il popolo francese al suo re» (Bérard). «Le régime légal est donc interrompu: celui de la force est commencé».[26] La Rivoluzione, si disse, era una risposta legittima ad una «insurrection du pouvoir», insomma l'atto che ristabiliva l'ordine legale violato.[27] Il 1830 è dunque una reazione per affermare la Carta come verità, respingendo il tentativo di far rivivere poteri pre-costituzionali e facendo trionfare quella «meta-costituzione» o «Costituzione materiale» che aveva trovato nell'*Adresse* dei 221 la definitiva sanzione.
Vive la Charte! è il grido che accompagna le Gloriose giornate di Luglio e rafforza l'idea che la Rivoluzione sia stata fatta per affermare la Carta violata da Carlo X e dai suoi ministri. «La Charte désormais sera une verité» è la celebre formula che conclude il proclama del duca di Orléans (31 luglio) ed è immediatamente ripresa dai deputati (proclama del 31 luglio). Come nella *Glorious Revolution* occorre restaurare le antiche libertà violate intronizzando il principe che offra adeguate garanzie politiche e costituzionali e sia, soprattutto, dal punto di vista dinastico il più "vicino" possibile al monarca che ha infranto il *trust*. È l'ideale di una rivoluzione popolare nei princìpi e nei risultati ma aristocratica nell'esecuzione, che dà vita ad un «heureux melange de hiérarchie et d'harmonie dans

été inutilement épuisées» (in P. Rosanvallon, *La monarchie impossible*, cit., 290). Importanti, per la definizione del quadro concettuale, sono alcune *brochures* del giurista *ultra* Charles Cottu, pubblicate a partire dal 1828, tra cui *Des moyens de mettre la Charte en harmonie avec la royauté*, Paris 1828; *Du seul moyen de sortir de la crise actuelle*, Paris 1829; *Des devoirs du roi envers la royauté*, Paris 1830.

26 *Protestation de MM. les Redacteurs des feuilles périodiques*, 27 juillet 1830, in P. Rosanvallon, *La monarchie impossible*, cit., 298. Il 25 luglio Thiers aveva proclamato: «Les ministres ont violé la légalité, nous sommes dispensés d'obéir».

27 A.-M. Dupin aîné, *Révolution de Juillet 1830. Caractère légal et politique du nouvel établissement fondé par la Charte constitutionnelle acceptée et jurée par Louis-Philippe 1er, roi des Français, en présence des deux Chambres le 9 août 1830*, Paris 1833, 1 ss. «La révolution de 1830, on le sait, eut deux causes principales, l'une directe et immédiate, la violation du pacte constitutionnel par le prince et par les ministres qui avaient juré de le maintenir; l'autre, moins apparente, mais pour le moins aussi efficace, le souvenir de 1815 et l'impatience de la domination étrangère» (P. Duvergier De Hauranne, *De l'état actuel des partis en France et de la nécessité d'une transaction*, s. l., s. d., 153). «... on doit dire que la révolution française de 1830 a été parfaitement légitime, quoique non légale à son principe, parce qu'elle n'a été qu'une juste résistance à la violation de la Constitution jurée par le chef du gouvernement» (D. Serrigny, *Traité du droit public des Français, précédé d'une introduction sur les fondements des sociétés politiques*, 2 voll., Paris 1846, t. I, 52). Carlo X – con il ministero Polignac – rigetta la logica del governo rappresentativo: «... le roi est-il indépendant ou non de la majorité des chambres? Peut-il choisir ses ministres hors de cette majorité?». Su tale problema, si veda A.-L. Thiers, *La monarchie de 1830*, Paris 1831, 10.

l'ordre social».[28] La Rivoluzione di Luglio ha avuto lo scopo di restaurare l'*esprit* liberale della Carta optando per il ramo cadetto della dinastia e cercando di limitare al massimo la "frattura" con l'età della Restaurazione. Ma la fragile legittimità del nuovo regime costituzionale, consiglia, tra l'altro, di rinviare ad un momento successivo la disciplina di alcune materie. Tutti i progetti[29] che nei primi giorni di agosto contribuiscono ad alimentare il dibattito sulla «revisione» della *Charte* sono infatti accomunati dalla previsione di un elenco di materie da regolare quanto prima con leggi ordinarie organiche.[30] Si tratta di materie di primaria importanza perché capaci di qualificare ed integrare in maniera decisiva il "senso" politico-costituzionale della *Charte*. Mentre il testo del 1814 era tendenzialmente chiuso, questo del 1830 era necessariamente aperto rinviando ad un futuro più o meno prossimo la soluzione di questioni rilevanti che erano già state oggetto di contesa nel corso della Restaurazione. Basti pensare all'applicazione della giuria ai delitti di stampa e ai reati politici, alla responsabilità dei ministri e dei funzionari, alle incompatibilità tra funzioni pubbliche e politiche, all'organizzazione elettiva delle guardie nazionali, al sistema elettorale per formare le istituzioni rappresentative dipartimentali e municipali, all'istruzione pubblica e alla libertà di insegnamento, alla legge elettorale politica con l'eliminazione del doppio voto. Alcune di tali questioni non ricevettero mai una disciplina legislativa (è per esempio il caso della responsabilità dei ministri e dei funzionari), altre furono invece interessate da molteplici interventi.[31] Sarebbe impossibile fare la storia costituzionale della Monarchia di Luglio senza tenere conto di questa vera e propria agenda politica fissata dagli articoli 68 e 69.[32] Nel

28 F. Guizot, *Pourquoi la Révolution d'Angleterre a-t-elle réussi? Discours sur l'histoire de la Révolution d'Angleterre*, Paris 1850, 162–163.

29 I testi dei vari progetti (il cosiddetto Proclama dell'Hôtel de Ville, i testi elaborati da Bérard, il progetto di de Broglie e parzialmente di Guizot, quello di Rémusat) sono consultabili in P. Rosanvallon, *La monarchie impossible*, cit., 305 ss. Si veda inoltre D. H. Pinkney, *La Révolution de 1830 en France*, Paris 1988 (ed. orig. 1972), 222 ss.

30 «Dans la mémorable séance du 7, la Charte fut révisée, et purgée de toutes les expressions qui, sous le précédent gouvernement, avaient entrainé abus ou fait équivoque; on y ajouta des dispositions nouvelles; enfin elle fut complétée par l'insertion d'un article qui place les couleurs nationales dans la constitution, et par l'engagement pris de porter différentes *lois organiques* qui devaient en assurer la marche et le développement» (A.-M. Dupin aîné, *Révolution de Juillet 1830*, cit., 25).

31 L'elenco è in P. Rosanvallon, *La monarchie impossible*, cit., 119–121.

32 «... L'art. 23 della Carta sarà sottoposto a un nuovo esame nella sessione del 1831» (art. 68). La costituzione del 1848, invece, rinvia genericamente alla «redazione delle leggi organiche la cui enumerazione sarà determinata da una legge speciale» (art. 115).

1830 bisognava "fare presto" e stabilire di conseguenza le modifiche assolutamente necessarie e "condivisibili". Ma l'esito complessivo della Carta dipendeva molto dal tipo di scelte che sarebbero poi state fatte attuando l'art. 69 e più in generale le numerose norme dal contenuto politico-programmatico. Per certi aspetti tale articolo lasciava aperta, come una ferita o come una promessa, la questione del potere costituente e delle determinazioni politiche della Costituzione. Qui, nell'interpretazione e nell'applicazione concreta, si sarebbero giocate le sorti del nuovo regime politico. I costituenti del 1830 non riuscirono tuttavia a imporre alle istituzioni una chiara direzione di marcia, preferendo rinviare alla prassi e al tessuto convenzionale e, in ultima istanza, alla lotta politica l'esito della vicenda costituzionale. L'art. 69 della Carta non fu pienamente valorizzato per sviluppare ulteriormente le condizioni politiche del regime parlamentare (sistema elettorale, riforma parlamentare ecc.). L'*Ausbau der Verfassung* fu un dato particolarmente carente del regime orleanista.

3. Sovranità della costituzione, sovranità della forza

È nel corso della monarchia censitaria che si rafforza progressivamente la dottrina della Costituzione come fonte di sovranità. Questa concezione, come è noto, è destinata – sotto il nome di «sovranità della costituzione» – ad avere notevoli sviluppi nella storia costituzionale europea. Nel caso francese è interessante cogliere il nesso ambiguo tra idea di "superiorità" della costituzione e debolezza del principio di legittimità nell'ordine politico. Il 7 agosto 1830 il visconte di Chateaubriand, nel pronunciare, di fronte ai Pari, uno dei più grandi discorsi della storia parlamentare francese, censurò il cambiamento dinastico:

> «Vous choisissez un roi aujourd'hui: qui vous empêchera d'en choisir un autre demain? La loi, direz-vous. La loi? c'est vous qui la faites! Il est encore une manière plus simple de trancher la question, c'est de dire: Nous ne voulons plus de la branche aînée des Bourbons. Et pourquoi n'en voulez-vous pas? Parce que nous sommes victorieux; nous avons triomphé dans une cause juste et sainte; nous usons d'un double droit de conquête. Très bien: vous proclamez la souveraineté de la force. Alors gardez soigneusement cette force, car si dans quelques mois elle vous échappe, vous serez mal venus à vous plaindre. Telle est la nature humaine! Les esprits les plus éclairés et les plus justes ne s'élèvent pas toujours au-dessus d'un succès. Ils étaient les premiers, ces esprits, à invoquer le droit contre la violence; ils appuyaient ce droit de toute la supériorité de leur talent, et au moment même où la vérité de ce qu'ils disaient est démontrée par l'abus le plus abominable de la force, et par le renversement de cette force, les vainqueurs s'emparent de l'arme qu'ils ont brisée! Dangereux tronçons qui blesseront leur main sans les servir».[33]

33 Discorso di Chateaubriand alla Camera dei Pari, sabato 7 agosto 1830, in *Le Moniteur Universel*, mercredi 11 août 1830, 883.

Non erano stati i redattori dei giornali parigini a dire, il 27 luglio, che – dopo le ordinanze di Carlo X – l'ordine legale era venuto meno sostituito dal regno della forza? A sua volta Chateaubriand coglieva il punto debole del nuovo regime: «vous proclamez la souveraineté de la force» e così facendo costruite sulla sabbia. Sovranità della costituzione, sovranità della forza: bisognava allontanare o almeno occultare la delicatissima questione della legittimità.

L'opera dei dottrinari, dei primi costituzionalisti, di una buona parte della cultura liberale non riuscì certo a salvare il regime orleanista, ma contribuì in maniera significativa a dar forma a quell'idea di sovranità della costituzione che rappresenta una tappa importante verso la definitiva delimitazione del concetto di sovranità nazionale. La *Charte* è l'alfa e l'omega, la risorsa strategica che si pensa di poter utilizzare per fronteggiare due minacce, lo spettro del potere costituente incarnato dalla sovranità del popolo e quello, ormai depotenziato, della sovranità assoluta del monarca. Era stato Royer-Collard dopo la Restaurazione a ribadire che la sovranità del popolo altro non era che la «souveraineté de la force». Nel 1820 François Guizot affermava l'equivalenza tra ogni forma di sovranità che si pretendesse assoluta, derivata dal popolo o dal diritto divino, e l'usurpazione della forza, per aggiungere poi che la sovranità popolare era una forma di tirannia, ovvero il potere assoluto della maggioranza numerica sulla minoranza.[34] «Je crois à la souveraineté de la raison, de la justice, du droit: c'est là le souverain légitime que cherche le monde et qu'il cherchera toujours; car la raison, la verité, la justice ne résident nulle part complètes et infaillibles».[35] Il diritto e la legittimità si trovano dappertutto e in nessuna parte, perché solo così la società sarà stabile e il potere regolare. Si ritorna dunque alla prima riflessione costituzionale post-rivoluzionaria e da lì si crede di poter ripartire per "addomesticare" la sovranità nella costituzione. Si pensa, insomma, di aver trovato la soluzione per il "paradosso di Clermont-Tonnerre" secondo il quale «... o si esercita la sovranità o si rispetta la Carta ...».[36]

Nei dottrinari – da Royer-Collard a Cousin sino a Guizot – la sovranità della ragione è il punto di convergenza della teoria della rappresentanza e della fondamentale distinzione tra origine ed esercizio della sovranità.[37] Il costituzio-

34 F. Guizot, *Philosophie politique: de la souveraineté*, in F. Guizot, *Histoire de la civilisation en Europe depuis la chute de l'Empire romain jusqu'à la Révolution française*, ed. a cura di P. Rosanvallon, Paris 1985, 309 ss. e 374.

35 F. Guizot, *Du gouvernement de la France depuis la Restauration, et du ministère actuel*, Paris 1820, 201.

36 P. Colombo, *Governo e costituzione. La trasformazione del regime politico nelle teorie dell'età rivoluzionaria francese*, Milano 1993, 373 ss.

37 Su questo aspetto, oltre ai lavori di Rosanvallon già citati, si vedano dello stesso

nalismo del gruppo di Coppet[38] e l'idea di nazione elaborata dagli scrittori contro-rivoluzionari forniscono ai dottrinari gli "ingredienti" essenziali per la loro teoria politica.[39] La sovranità della ragione, come è stato giustamente osservato, possiede la stessa natura e presuppone le stesse condizioni di esercizio della sovranità nazionale. In particolare, ciò che le accomuna è proprio la volontà di collocare la sovranità in una sorta di non-luogo, o quanto meno in «une région suffisament lointaine et éthérée pour que nulle autorité constituée ne puisse se dire elle-même souveraine».[40] È tuttavia nel corso del regime orleanista che tale filosofia politica può ambire a diventare anche dottrina giuridica. Si prende in mano la *Charte* per trovare in essa uno strumento di legittimazione. Per Royer-Collard:

> «Dès qu'il y a une souveraineté, il y a despotisme, dès qu'il y a despotisme, il y a sinon mort sociale, du moins désordre économique profond. Demander où est la souveraineté c'est être despotiste et déclarer qu'on l'est».[41]

Non è sovrano nessuno dei poteri istituiti dalla *Charte*; in tal senso non può esistere un sovrano, ovvero un potere investito di tutti i diritti e senza limiti, benché debba poi esistere una posizione prevalente che – nel caso della *Charte* del 1814 – appartiene al monarca. Il dibattito sul potere costituente durante la Monarchia di Luglio – se si esclude la lineare posizione repubblicana e, per

autore *Les Doctrinaires et la question du gouvernement représentatif*, cit., 421 ss.; *Guizot et la question du suffrage universel au XIXème siècle*, in *François Guizot et la culture politique*, a cura di M. Valensise, Paris 1991, 129–145; *Le sacre du citoyen. Du suffrage universel en France*, Paris 1992; ed inoltre A.-F. Perny, *Le pouvoir constituant sous la monarchie de Juillet*, Paris 1901; M. Barbè, *Etude historique des idées sur la souveraineté en France de 1815 à 1848*, Paris 1904; J. Barthèlemy, *La distinction des lois constitutionnelles*, cit.; Ch. Pouthas, *Guizot pendant la Restauration, préparation de l'homme d'Etat*, Paris 1923, 313 ss.; L. Diez Del Corral, *El liberalismo doctrinario*, Madrid 1984, 4 ed., 221 ss.; G. Bacot, *Carré de Malberg et l'origine de la distinction entre souveraineté du peuple et souveraineté nationale*, Paris 1985, 120 ss.; L. Jaume, *Guizot et la philosophie de la représentation*, in *Droits*, 15, 1992, 141–152; dello stesso autore si veda anche *La raison politique chez Victor Cousin et Guizot*, in *La pensée politique*, 2, 1994, 242–253; e soprattutto *L'individu effacé ou le paradoxe du libéralisme français*, Paris 1997.

38 Sul punto v. *supra* in questo volume *Coppet et la percée de l'Etat libéral constitutionnel*, 201 ss.

39 G. Bacot, *Carré de Malberg et l'origine de la distinction entre souveraineté du peuple et souveraineté nationale*, cit., 120 ss.

40 *Ibidem*, 135. «De ces trois systèmes, il faut d'abord écarter le dernier, comme ne faisant que déplacer la question sans la résoudre. En effet, personne ne nie que les pouvoirs préposés à la tête d'une société politique ne doivent prendre pour guide dans leurs actes la raison et la justice» (D. Serrigny, *Traité de droit public des Français*, cit., t. I, 25).

41 G. Remond, *Royer-Collard. Son essai d'un système politique*, Paris 1933, 39.

diverse ragioni, quella legittimista – rivela lo scarto tra centralità politica e sociologica del sistema censitario (anch'esso visto nella prospettiva meramente funzionale) e la teorizzazione a prevalente coloritura dottrinaria. La Carta del 1830 era nata da una rivoluzione e da una «réunion constituante»[42] e ciò poteva innescare un pericoloso corto circuito con il principio della sovranità del popolo. Nel novembre del 1830 Guizot aveva affermato, con indubbia chiarezza, che «Le principe qui a présidé à notre révolution ne doit pas présider à notre gouvernement». Questa scissione era la chiave di volta del sistema, basato essenzialmente sul concetto negativo di rappresentanza[43] e sull'elettorato come "funzione".

Non è certo un caso che sia lo stesso Guizot, nella veste di ministro della pubblica istruzione, a far istituire a Parigi, nel 1834, la prima cattedra di diritto costituzionale affidandola a Pellegrino Rossi, per affermare la piena legittimità del nuovo regime e rimettere in armonia la lunga durata della storia francese con le istituzioni politiche nate dalla *Charte*. La questione della quasi-legittimità del regime orleanista rendeva urgente una «soluzione» che rimettesse Luigi-Filippo – novello Guglielmo d'Orange – nel solco di una stessa linea, seppur di incerta continuità. La cattedra di diritto costituzionale nasceva così in un clima necessariamente militante.

Nel *Rapport au Roi* di Guizot si legge:

> «L'objet et la forme de l'enseignement du droit constitutionnel sont déterminés par son titre même; c'est l'exposition de la Charte et des garanties individuelles comme des institutions politiques qu'elle consacre. Ce n'est plus là, pour nous, un simple système philosophique livré aux disputes des hommes, c'est une loi écrite, reconnue, qui peut et doit être expliquée, commentée aussi bien que la loi civile ou toute autre partie de notre législation. Un tel enseignement, à la fois vaste et précis, fondé sur le droit public national et sur les leçons de l'histoire, susceptible de s'étendre par les comparaisons et les analogies étrangères, doit substituer aux erreurs de l'ignorance et à la témérité des notions superficielles des connaissances fortes et positives».[44]

42 J. Barthélemy, *La distinction des lois constitutionnelles et des lois ordinaires sous la Monarchie de Juillet*, cit., 25 ss.

43 «La représentation n'existe nulle part dans notre Gouvernement. La Chambre, telle que la Charte l'a conçue, est un *pouvoir*, et non une représentation» (P. De Barante, *La vie politique de Royer-Collard. Ses discours et ses écrits*, Paris 1878, t. I, 228; sul punto si veda il commento di de Barante, *ibidem*, 235).

44 *Rapport au Roi sur la création d'une chaire de droit constitutionnel*, 22 août 1834. Esporre scientificamente la Carta, «comme M. Demante explique le Code civil ...» (*Journal des débats* del 30 novembre 1834), «neutralizzare» la «filosofia», l'«opinione politica» della *Charte*: è questo il paradosso a cui Rossi darà solo parzialmente seguito (cfr. *Mémoire pour MM. Bugnet, Demante, de Portets, du Caurroy et Duranton*, Paris 1834). Sulla cattedra di diritto costituzionale di Rossi,

L'elaborazione del concetto di sovranità della costituzione avrebbe dovuto trovare un supporto politico-filosofico nelle nozioni di ragione, di giustizia, di diritto. La costituzione diventava essa stessa un parametro di ragione e ad essa si assegnava, sorta di "luogo neutrale", l'attributo di entità sovrana per modo che né il principe né il popolo, né la monarchia né la democrazia potessero pretendere l'esercizio del minaccioso potere costituente.[45] Ne derivava un'idea di costituzione autopoietica, sovrana in sé e per sé, come caduta dal cielo. Al *tertium non datur* si contrapponeva una teoria che mettesse il silenziatore sul fragoroso «principio che aveva presieduto alla Rivoluzione». Questa concezione, tuttavia, non è, come si potrebbe pensare, effimera e non dura il tempo della Monarchia di Luglio. Se è vero che le costituzioni successive (dal 1848 al 1875) hanno presupposto il potere costituente del popolo, l'*imprinting* non andrà perduto, e i giuristi e il personale politico orleanista non rinunceranno alla dottrina della sovranità nazionale, spesso riprendendo siffatti argomenti nel mutato contesto.[46] Per loro questa nozione equivarrà a un principio di delimitazione del potere e designerà l'idea della sovranità della costituzione, ovvero della supremazia della norma costituzionale.[47]

Se la Carta del 1830 era nata da un «contratto» fondatore della sovranità nazionale – secondo l'interpretazione affermatasi già nel testo – ne derivava che la sola autorità concepibile fosse quella composta dalla «souveraineté du roi et des deux chambres, faisant la loi, exprimant la volonté nationale».[48] Durante il dibattito sul progetto di legge relativo alla reggenza, nel 1842, il duca de Broglie ricordava che «En appeler de la souveraineté fondée et réglée par la Charte à quelque autre souveraineté, c'est en appeler au nombre, à la force brutale; c'est

mi sia consentito rinviare a L. Lacchè, *Tra politica e diritto, ovvero Rossi e la Monarchia di Luglio*, in *Un liberale europeo: Pellegrino Rossi (1787–1848)*, a cura di Luigi Lacchè, Milano 2001, 69–108, e Id., *La Libertà che guida il Popolo*, cit., 164–173.

45 Si vedano al riguardo le osservazioni di C. Schmitt, *Verfassungslehre*, Berlin 1928, tr. it. *Dottrina della costituzione*, Milano 1984, 21, 80–83, 270. Cfr. inoltre P. Bastid, *Les institutions politiques*, cit., 164; L. Jaume, *Il potere costituente in Francia dal 1789 a De Gaulle*, in *Potere costituente e riforme costituzionali*, a cura di P. Pombeni, Bologna 1992, 33–51 e M. Fioravanti, *Potere costituente e diritto pubblico. Il caso italiano, ibidem*, 55–77.

46 G. Bacot, *Carré de Malberg et l'origine de la distinction entre souveraineté du peuple et souveraineté nationale*, cit., 147 ss.

47 Sulle contraddizioni inerenti a questo duplice uso, si veda O. Beaud, *La souveraineté dans la "Contribution à la théorie générale de l'Etat" de Carré de Malberg*, in *Revue du droit public*, 5, 1994, 1291 ss.

48 Chambre des Pairs, A. Thiers, *Séance du 16 mai 1840*, in *Le Moniteur Universel*, 17 mai 1840, 1081.

prétendre organiser le désordre même et réaliser le néant».[49] E qualche giorno prima era stato il sarcastico Guizot, allora ministro degli esteri, a respingere la teoria dei due poteri, «l'un ordinaire, l'autre extraordinaire; l'un constitutionnel, l'autre constituant; l'un pour les jours ouvrables (permettez-moi cette expression), l'autre pour les jours fériés: on dit une chose inouïe, pleine de dangers et fatale ...». Le rivoluzioni, insomma, non si organizzano: «Soyez tranquilles, messieurs: nous, les trois pouvoirs constitutionnels, nous sommes les seuls organes légitimes et réguliers de la souveraineté nationale. Hors de nous, il n'y a, je le répète, qu'usurpation ou révolution».[50]

L'"assorbimento" della sovranità del popolo nella costituzione sanciva il fatto che la Carta fosse la sola depositaria e per essa, secondo la declinazione inglese – sovente richiamata – i poteri (il Re in Parlamento) costituiti.[51] I giuristi cercarono di fare la loro parte. Anche chi, come Serrigny, criticava il concetto di sovranità della ragione, procedeva poi lungo il sentiero della neutralizzazione del potere costituente visto come forma anomala, latente,[52] o – per dirla con

49 Chambre des Pairs, *Séance du 27 août 1842*, in *Le Moniteur Universel*, 28 août 1842, 1866. Nel passo che precede la citazione si afferma: «... la transaction de 1830 a consommé le partage des pouvoirs publics; le contrat de 1830 a constitué la souveraineté nationale. Si ce grand acte n'est pas absolu, définitif; si par-delà la Charte il existe autre chose que des individus qu'elle protège, des volontés qui lui sont soumises; si notre puissance a d'autres limites que la raison, la justice et la sagesse, la Charte n'est qu'un mensonge, le roi ne règne pas, les Chambres, les corps élus, le corps électoral, tout cela est précaire et provisoire ...».

50 Chambre des Pairs, *Séance du 19 août 1842*, in *Le Moniteur Universel*, 20 août 1842, 1811.

51 «... Maintenant, quelle est la présomption ordinaire dans un gouvernement, dans une constitution où le pouvoir constituant et le pouvoir constitué n'ont pas été distingués? La présomption, la voici d'après ce qui s'est passé en Angleterre et chez nous. Quand la constitution n'a pas distingué un pouvoir constituant et un pouvoir constitué, et qu'il s'agit d'un acte important, quel que soit le caractère, on s'adresse à qui? Aux trois pouvoirs auxquels la constitution a déféré la souveraineté, a déféré les actes les plus importants» (Chambre des députés, *Séance du 20 août 1842*, in *Le Moniteur Universel*, 21 août 1842, 1829).

52 «D'une part, la constitution donnerait le commandement en dernier ressort et le droit de représenter la société politique au pouvoir établi; d'autre part, les volontés individuelles qui ont concouru à le former, voudraient continuer l'exercice anormal d'un droit qu'elles ont abdiqué dans l'intérêt de la communauté. N'est-il pas clair que cette souveraineté latente réservée serait en opposition avec l'établissement de la constitution? On voit par-là comment le pouvoir constituant meurt à l'instant où naît la constitution, pour revivre au décès de celle-ci» (D. Serrigny, *Traité de droit public*, cit., t. I, 37). Charles Hello parimenti osserva: «Havvi oggidì fra noi una unanime riprovazione di questi poteri organizzati ed insieme organizzatori, poteri stanti sempre, poteri inutili se sono

Laferrière – passeggera[53] di esercizio della sovranità. Nell'ordine politico non esiste «d'autre supérieur que la loi constitutionnelle et les pouvoirs déterminés par la Constitution».[54]

Quando Tocqueville – nella prima parte de *La Democrazia in America* – osserva con tono perentorio che «in Francia, la costituzione è un'opera immutabile o considerata tale. Nessun potere la potrebbe cambiare: questa è la teoria riconosciuta»,[55] il nobile normanno delinea la dottrina della sovranità della Costituzione, ma tende ad enfatizzare il carattere formale della Carta insistendo sugli effetti derivanti dalla sua eventuale "modificazione".[56] Nel corso della Monarchia di Luglio si afferma come assolutamente prevalente la distinzione tra leggi costituzionali e leggi ordinarie.[57] Non è un caso che il dibattito sul potere costituente si infiammi soprattutto nei due momenti (Legge sulla paria nel 1831 e Legge sulla reggenza nel 1842) durante i quali si ebbe il timore di veder riemergere quel potere "latente" che si riteneva neutralizzato dalla sua avvenuta incorporazione nel soggetto titolare del potere legislativo. Se la categoria della sovranità della costituzione serviva dunque ad allontanare questo spettro, la strada dell'onnipotenza parlamentare non la si voleva però percorrere se non per necessità, limitandosi quindi al giorno per giorno, eludendo per quanto possibile – come hanno scritto Joseph Barthélemy e Paul Bastid[58] – le grandi questioni e non perseguendo alcun sistema. La distinzione tra i due tipi di legge è alla fine l'unica "teoria" che – in assenza di una procedura speciale di revisione – non leghi le mani (come nell'evenienza drammatica del 1842) al Parlamento con i lacci dell'immutabilità assoluta ricordata da Tocqueville e lasci

inerti, formidabili se sono attivi, e la cui mano piena di tempeste è di continuo aperta sovra i poteri costituiti» (Ch. Hello, *Del regime costituzionale nelle sue relazioni con lo stato attuale della scienza sociale e politica*, Firenze 1850, t. II, 20–21).

53 F. Laferrière, *Cours de droit public et administratif*, Paris 1841–1846, 2 ed., 5.

54 *Ibidem*.

55 A. De Tocqueville, *La democrazia in America*, Milano 1992, lib. I, cap. VI, 103.

56 *Ibidem*, Nota al lib. I, 180–181: «Le leggi del 1830, come quelle del 1814, non indicano alcun mezzo per cambiare la costituzione; ora è evidente che i mezzi ordinari della legislazione non potrebbero essere sufficienti. Da chi il re riceve il potere? Dalla costituzione. Da chi i pari? Dalla costituzione. Da chi i deputati? Dalla costituzione. In che modo dunque il re, i pari e i deputati riuniti potrebbero modificare una legge in virtù della quale soltanto essi governano? Fuori della costituzione essi non sono nulla ... Distruggendo la carta distruggono se stessi ... Così dunque una parte della nostra costituzione è immutabile perché congiunta al destino di una famiglia e il suo complesso è ugualmente immutabile perché non vi sono mezzi legali per cambiarla».

57 J. Barthélemy, *La distinction des lois constitutionnelles et des lois ordinaires sous la Monarchie de Juillet*, cit.

58 Ivi, 45–47; P. Bastid, *Les institutions politiques*, cit., 164.

invece aperta la via della riforma attraverso la, pur cautissima, produzione di leggi "costituzionali" o l'instaurazione di pratiche consuetudinarie. Si potrebbe forse affermare che nuclei distinti di rigidità e di flessibilità convivono e si combinano all'interno di una strategia più articolata di quanto non si usi dire. Ciò in fondo conferma come sia difficile applicare *tout court* siffatte categorie alle Carte francesi (e più in generale alla maggior parte dei documenti costituzionali del XIX secolo). Non sempre giova alla comprensione storico-costituzionale – una volta accertata l'esistenza di un concetto normativo di costituzione – il voler definire fenomeni dalla complessa natura.[59] È evidente che la sovranità nazionale "ritagliata" nella Carta non risolveva né il problema della forma della monarchia costituzionale né quello del regime politico.[60] Dalla «éclatante primauté» del monarca secondo la dizione di Royer-Collard[61] alla Camera elettiva come «pouvoir prépondérant» secondo quella di Duvergier de Hauranne[62] si resta, pur da punti opposti, dentro uno stesso cerchio nel quale perseguire la difficile logica del bilanciamento e dell'equilibrio, la collaborazione / unione dei poteri lungo l'asse monarca–Parlamento. La sovranità della Costituzione era in fondo la formula per sancire l'ideale di uno Stato – quello che più tardi si definirà «liberale di diritto» – in grado di poter separare, nel nome della rappresentanza, valori "universali" (taluni diritti civili) e "privilegi" moderni (i diritti politici sul tronco censitario e capacitario) afferenti al concetto di "interesse". In Francia il regime orleanista era destinato a cadere per mano della forza. E tuttavia tale concezione della sovranità – o se si vuole nonsovranità, almeno per quanto riguarda la dimensione del dualismo "dilatorio"[63] – se in Francia portava la monarchia costituzionale a fallire il suo più realistico "appuntamento" moderno con la costituzione, assegnava a questa un valore che mai aveva potuto possedere sino ad allora e che era destinato a sopravviverle. Paradossalmente, i dottrinari e i "politici costituzionali" separando la costitu-

59 Per la discussione del problema v. A. Pace, *La causa della rigidità costituzionale*, Padova 1996, 2 ed., 33 ss.; J. Varela Suanzes, *Riflessioni sul concetto di rigidità costituzionale*, in *Giurisprudenza costituzionale*, 5, 1994, 3313–3338.

60 Per la discussione del problema v. *supra* in questo volume *Constitución, Monarquía, Parlamento: Francia y Bélgica*, 160 ss.

61 P. De Barante, *La vie politique de Royer-Collard*, cit., t. II, 216–217.

62 P. Duvergier De Hauranne, *De la réforme parlementaire et de la réforme électorale*, Paris 1847, 2 ed., 249.

63 Sul punto v. C. Schmitt, *Dottrina della costituzione*, cit., 55 ss., 80, 402 ss. Per la ridefinizione del problema, v. soprattutto M. Fioravanti, *Potere costituente e diritto pubblico*, cit.; dello stesso autore si veda anche *Le dottrine dello Stato e della costituzione*, in R. Romanelli (ed.), *Storia dello Stato italiano dall'Unità a oggi*, Roma 1995, 408 ss.; G. Zagrebelski, *Storia e costituzione*, in G. Zagrebelski, P. P. Portinaro, J. Luther (edd.), *Il futuro della costituzione*, Torino 1996, 65 ss.

zione dalla sovranità politica, senza poter prevedere, per eterogenesi dei fini, i possibili futuri sviluppi, si ritrovarono per le mani una cosa più grande di loro.[64]

4. La Carta sarà una verità?

Se alla costituzione si riconosce, per le ragioni dette, un valore di "superiorità politica", si può parimenti riconoscerle una qualche forma di "superiorità giuridica"? Per cercare di rispondere a questo interrogativo bisogna affrontare il tema della garanzia della Costituzione. La strada da imboccare sembra obbligata. Il problema è esposto con concisa chiarezza da Tocqueville: se i giudici potessero "sanzionare" le leggi incostituzionali il potere costituente sarebbe allora nelle loro mani.

> «So bene – aggiunge – che rifiutando ai giudici il diritto di dichiarare incostituzionali le leggi, noi diamo indirettamente al corpo legislativo il potere di cambiare la costituzione, poiché esso non trova nessuna barriera legale che lo fermi. Ma val meglio ancora, accordare il potere di cambiare la costituzione del popolo a uomini che rappresentano, sia pure imperfettamente, la volontà popolare, che non ad altri che rappresentano solo se stessi».[65]

Da una parte dunque il potere di «disobbedire alle leggi» attribuito al corpo giudiziario, dall'altra l'«onnipotenza parlamentare», con la conseguente necessità di trovare "limiti"[66] all'interno dell'organizzazione costituzionale. Sono ben note e continuamente ribadite le ragioni che impedirono la formazione di un sistema di controllo di costituzionalità delle leggi, tanto più nel clima ostile della

64 Questo aspetto meriterebbe un approfondimento su scala europea, ovvero su come le ragioni di una difesa "contingente", di segno orleanista e di prevalente elaborazione dottrinaria, abbiano influenzato, in una misura in parte ancora da verificare, i costrutti teorici e le immagini dello Stato liberale di diritto tra Otto e Novecento elaborati da tanta parte della scienza giuridica. Per il caso francese e la configurazione dell'*Etat légal* durante la Terza Repubblica è ora fondamentale M.-J. Redor, *De l'Etat légal à l'Etat de droit. L'évolution des conceptions de la doctrine publiciste française (1879–1914)*, Paris 1992. Si veda inoltre J.-P. Machelon, *La République contre les libertés? Les restrictions aux libertés publiques de 1879 à 1914*, préface de J. Rivero, Paris 1976.

65 A. De Tocqueville, *La democrazia in America*, cit., 103. Sul potere giudiziario come «potere politico» cfr. *infra* in questo volume *Il potere giudiziario come «potere politico»*, 437–445. È inoltre da sottolineare come Tocqueville ricorra all'argomento della carenza di "legittimità" democratica dei giudici, argomento principe nel corso del Novecento per respingere il principio della giustizia costituzionale. Cfr. P. Pasquino, *Sieyès et l'invention de la constitution en France*, Paris 1998, 154. Si veda inoltre A. Laquièze, *Le contrôle de constitutionnalité de la loi aux Etats-Unis vu par les penseurs libéraux français du XIXème siècle*, in *Giornale di storia costituzionale*, 4, 2002, 155–171.

66 Cfr. Ch. Hello, *Del regime costituzionale*, cit., 32.

Francia post-rivoluzionaria.[67] Ragioni complesse, storiche, ideologiche e pratiche[68] hanno allontanato per lungo tempo dagli orizzonti francesi l'affermazione di un sindacato di costituzionalità delle leggi. Quale organo politico poteva essere "superiore" al Legislativo? D'altra parte come assegnare ai giudici – che scontavano la pesante diffidenza post-rivoluzionaria – il più incisivo e delicato dei poteri? Inoltre, perché sottoporre a controllo la legge «espressione della volontà generale» se il suo Autore «ne peut mal faire»?

Senza voler ritornare in questa sede sulla fondatezza di siffatto profilo, è mia intenzione da un lato sottolineare il fatto che proprio tra gli anni Venti e la fine della Monarchia di Luglio si possono rintracciare spunti argomentativi in alcune tipologie di decisione giudiziaria non privi di interesse per il nostro discorso e, soprattutto, mostrare come il «modulo giurisdizionale» di controllo non potendosi affermare come "sistema esterno"[69] resti però al centro delle ipotesi di costruzione dottrinale e storico-concreta di "garanzia politica interna".

Ricerche recenti[70] mostrano come l'ambizione e l'efficacia dell'azione giudiziaria di "controllo" non vadano sottovalutati. È da osservare come la possibilità di eccepire l'incostituzionalità dinanzi ai tribunali dipenda molto, durante il XIX secolo, dalla natura dei regimi politici che si succedono. Se tale possibilità trova alimento nel clima politico della Restaurazione e della Monarchia di Luglio, la nascita della Repubblica e soprattutto il ritorno all'Impero con

67 Per talune esemplificazioni, v. A. Blondel, *Le contrôle juridictionnel de la constitutionnalité des lois*, Paris 1928, 168 ss.; J. Lyon, *Le contrôle de la constitutionnalité des lois en France*, in *Informations Constitutionnelles et Parlementaires*, 105, 1976, 30 ss.; J.-L. Halperin, *Le tribunal de cassation sous la Révolution (1790–1799)*, Paris 1985, t. II, 615.

68 Cfr. M. Cappelletti, *Il controllo giudiziario di costituzionalità delle leggi nel diritto comparato*, Milano 1978, 7 ed.

69 Cfr. L. Jaume, *Benjamin Constant au centre de nos préoccupations*, in *Benjamin Constant en l'an 2000: nouveaux regards*, in *Annales Benjamin Constant*, 23–24, 2000, 29.

70 Seguo qui le conclusioni a cui giungono Ch. Durand, *Les décrets-loi napoléoniens devant la jurisprudence de la Restauration*, in *Etudes offertes à Jean Macqueron*, Aix-en-Provence 1970, 269–277 e soprattutto i lavori di J.-L. Mestre, *Les juridictions judiciaires et l'inconstitutionnalité des ordonnances royales de la Restauration au Second Empire*, in *Revue française de droit constitutionnel*, 15, 1993, 451–461; dello stesso autore si vedano inoltre *La Cour de Cassation et le contrôle de constitutionnalité. Données historiques*, in *La Cour de Cassation et la Constitution de la République*, Actes du Colloque des 9 et 10 décembre 1994, Aix-en-Provence 1995, 35–67; *L'inconstitutionnalité des actes réglementaires de 1814 à 1851*, in *Administration et droit*, a cura di F. Burdeau, Paris 1996,123–133 e di G. Bigot, *L'autorité judiciaire et le contentieux de l'administration. Vicissitudes d'une ambition, 1800–1872*, Paris 1999.

l'istituzione del Senato dotato del potere di opporsi alla promulgazione delle leggi contrarie alla costituzione del 14 gennaio 1852 (artt. 25, 26, 29)[71] ridimensiona in modo decisivo l'ambizione dell'autorità giudiziaria.[72]

I giudici assumono il quadro costituzionale della Restaurazione per interessarsi anzitutto dei decreti imperiali e della ingente massa di regolamenti d'amministrazione[73] e poi delle stesse ordinanze regie. In base alla Carta del 1814 tali ordinanze non possono più sostituirsi – come era avvenuto con i decreti imperiali – alla legge formale, e in mancanza di una previsione costituzionale i giudici cominciano a porre il problema della incostituzionalità di singole disposizioni regolamentari. Nel 1818 Jean-Baptiste Sirey[74] evoca la necessità di un controllo da parte della Cassazione per verificare se le ordinanze siano "costituzionali", cioè conformi alle disposizioni della *Charte* (in particolare agli articoli 14 e 15). Sirey, che distingue molto nettamente la legge dal regolamento e afferma di non voler certo restaurare il potere di registrazione dei Parlamenti di antico regime,[75] denuncia i pericoli di arbitrarietà insiti in un regime costituzionale che non preveda un apposito organo di controllo, distinto dallo stesso Parlamento.[76] È a partire dal 1827 – nella fase più critica del rapporto tra governo del Re e maggioranza liberale in Parlamento – che l'auspicio di Sirey acquista maggiore concretezza attraverso i ripetuti interventi di corti inferiori e talune pronunce della Cassazione.[77] Le famigerate ordinanze del 25 luglio 1830 segnano l'acme del conflitto. La prova di forza e la successiva sconfitta di Carlo X

71 Sui Senati imperiali v. infra, § 5.

72 G. Bigot, *L'autorité judiciaire*, cit., 222–223.

73 Non bisogna dimenticare che la mancanza di un controllo sulla conformità degli atti regolamentari alla legge sia per inerzia del Senato conservatore che – dal 1807 – per la soppressione del Tribunato, consente all'esecutivo di emanare disposizioni derogatorie, specialmente in materia penale e correzionale, aventi forza di legge. Sul potere regolamentare v. M. Verpeaux, *La naissance du pouvoir réglementaire, 1789–1799*, Paris 1991 e la recente analisi di lungo periodo di J.-L. Mestre, *De l'ancien sur l'article 37, alinéa 2, de la Constitution*, in *Revue française de droit administratif*, 2, 2001, 301–318. In ordine al profilo specifico v. Ch. Durand, *Les rapports entre la loi et le règlement gouvernemental*, in Ch. Durand, A. Lanza, *Études sur les rapports entre la loi et le règlement gouvernemental au XIXe siècle*, Aix-en-Provence 1976.

74 G. Bigot, *L'autorité judiciaire*, cit., 179–181.

75 Il reiterato riferimento alla posizione costituzionale dei Parlamenti e alle molteplici funzioni svolte in antico regime è senza dubbio indizio di un discorso non meramente esornativo.

76 «Il codice civile e le leggi attualmente esistenti che non sono contrarie alla presente Carta, restano in vigore sino a che vi si sia legalmente derogato» (art. 68, *Charte* del 1814).

77 Per una dettagliata analisi rinvio ai lavori citati *supra*, nota 70.

rivelano l'esistenza di una parte dell'autorità giudiziaria tutt'altro che acquiescente e nella dinamica della Rivoluzione non bisogna sottovalutare la funzione legittimante dei giudici.[78] Ciò appare evidente nel caso del tribunale di commercio di Parigi[79] che, chiamato a pronunciarsi su una inadempienza contrattuale provocata dalla ordinanza che vietava ai giornali di pubblicare i fogli senza preventiva autorizzazione, dichiara il provvedimento contrario alla Carta e non efficace rispetto alle parti in causa, essendo l'ordinanza non obbligatoria «... pour les citoyens, aux droits desquels elle porte atteinte».[80]

Non stupirà il fatto che durante la Monarchia di Luglio – sia per le benemerenze conquistate sul campo da una parte della magistratura[81] sul finire del regno di Carlo X, sia per la più puntuale disciplina costituzionale[82] – l'autorità giudiziaria prosegua nell'azione di controllo della costituzionalità delle ordinanze regie privando di forza obbligatoria quelle giudicate contrarie alle norme e ai principi costituzionali.

Se il potere regio non incontrasse limiti, se le ordinanze potessero prendere il posto delle leggi – si legge nel 1833 in una pronuncia della Cassazione – il governo rappresentativo istituito dalla Carta «loin d'être une vérité, ne serait qu'un mensonge».[83] La Carta sarà ormai una verità? si chiedevano in fondo le corti giudiziarie richieste di intervenire. Nel 1832, il celebre caso Geoffroy[84]

78 Cfr. J.-L. Bory, *La Révolution de Juillet. 29 Juillet 1830*, Paris 1972, 464.

79 Dupin aîné pubblica, non a caso, l'intera sentenza del tribunale di commercio: A. M. Dupin aîné, *Révolution de Juillet 1830*, cit., 82 ss.

80 Tribunal de commerce, *La Pelouze et Chatelain c. Gaultier-Laguione*, 28 luglio 1830, in *Recueil Sirey*, 1830, II parte, 223. Cfr. J.-L. Bory, *La Révolution de Juillet*, cit., 285–286.

81 Non bisogna tuttavia dimenticare che questo è soltanto un aspetto di una vicenda più complessa. Il nuovo regime orleanista, infatti, non esiterà – seguendo una pratica politica già sperimentata dai regimi precedenti – a realizzare una pesante epurazione nei ranghi della magistratura. Cfr. D. H. Pinkney, *La Révolution de 1830 en France*, cit., 328 e 341; P. M. Pilbeam, *The 1830 Revolution in France*, London 1991, 136. Sulle cifre e sui caratteri generali si veda per tutti J.-P. Royer, *Histoire de la justice en France*, Paris 1996, 479 ss.

82 In particolare attraverso l'art. 13 («Il Re ... fa i regolamenti e le ordinanze necessarie per l'esecuzione delle leggi senza poter mai né sospendere le leggi stesse, né dispensare dalla loro esecuzione ...») e l'articolo 70 («Tutte le leggi e le ordinanze, in ciò che esse hanno di contrario alle disposizioni adottate per la riforma della Carta, sono fin d'ora e restano annullate»).

83 Si veda G. Bigot, *L'autorité judiciaire*, cit., 208–209.

84 Cfr. J. Luther, *Idee e storie di giustizia costituzionale nell'Ottocento*, Torino 1990, 128–131; J.-L. Mestre, *La Cour de Cassation*, cit., 42–43; G. Bigot, *L'autorité judiciaire*, cit., 214–216; P. Alvazzi Del Frate, *Il giudice naturale. Prassi e dottrina in Francia dall'ancien régime alla Restaurazione*, Roma 1999, 211 ss.

conferma il delicato problema della distinzione tra sindacato formale e controllo di merito. L'ordinanza regia (6 giugno 1832) che ordina lo stato d'assedio di Parigi rende applicabile l'art. 103 del decreto imperiale del 24 dicembre 1811 con la conseguenza di assoggettare i civili ai consigli di guerra. Il cittadino Geoffroy ne subisce i rigori e il 18 giugno 1832 viene condannato a morte. Il suo avvocato, Odilon Barrot, importante uomo politico e poi *leader* della Sinistra dinastica, ricorre in Cassazione sostenendo l'incostituzionalità dell'ordinanza per violazione del principio del giudice naturale (artt. 53 e 54 della Carta). La Corte suprema, pur confermando la validità delle leggi e dei decreti relativi allo stato d'assedio, pronuncia però l'incostituzionalità dell'art. 103, restituendo il signor Geoffroy al suo giudice naturale. Il sottile, delicato confine tra decisione politica e soluzione giudiziaria accredita in questo caso l'"ambizione" della magistratura ad operare un controllo di costituzionalità basato sul testo della Carta. Odilon Barrot ebbe modo di ricordare che nella vigenza di una norma come quella denunciata

> «la constitution ne sera qu'une chimère. Une constitution qui ne sera que facultative ... ce ne sera pas une constitution: car une constitution ne vaut quelque chose que si elle est une vérité positive et pratique ...».[85]

L'avvocato Sirey non a caso assegna alla decisione della Corte un posto importante tra i "monumenti" del diritto pubblico. Dopo aver richiamato *en passant* le coraggiose rimostranze degl'antichi Parlamenti, la sentenza – scrive – rimarrà un precedente solenne, «servant à prouver que notre constitution nouvelle n'est pas dépourvue de toute sanction, que les droits et garanties qu'elle stipule en faveur des citoyens ne sont pas à la direction du pouvoir, et n'ont pas été vainement placés sous la sauvegarde de l'autorité judiciaire».[86]

L'azione incisiva delle corti si spingerebbe (ma è prospettiva da approfondire) sino alla formazione, benché empirica e non sistematica, di una sorta di quasi-controllo di costituzionalità delle leggi, soprattutto riguardo ad alcuni aspetti della disciplina legislativa dell'espropriazione per pubblica utilità o agli articoli del Codice penale (291–294) che, stabilendo la sorveglianza del governo sulle associazioni religiose, vengono censurati perché contrari al dettato dell'art. 5

85 «... la cour rendra un service, et le plus grand de tous; elle ramenera le Gouvernement à la loi, elle fera échouer, par une résistance patriotique et généreuse, toute atteinte à la constitution du pays ... Voilà, Messieurs, ce qui est profondement triste. Si vous ne pouvez faire justice, s'il est vrai qu'il n'y a aucun moyen légal de protéger un citoyen condamné à mort par un tribunal que la constitution défendait d'établir, il faudra se voiler la tête et désespérer à jamais de la légalité dans notre pays» (Cour de Cassation, Geoffroy, 29 giugno 1832, in *Recueil Sirey*, parte I, 401 ss.).

86 *Ibidem*, 401.

della *Charte*.[87] La dialettica che si instaura tra le corti e la Cassazione, con le prime intenzionate a riaffermare la «verità» della Carta anche con riferimento alle leggi e la Cassazione molto più riservata e attenta nel depotenziare l'ambizione delle corti inferiori, accompagna il duplice atteggiamento, di favore e di contrasto allo stesso tempo, che si ritrova anche in ambito dottrinale.[88] Se c'è più ampio consenso nell'ammettere l'eccezione di costituzionalità rispetto ai decreti imperiali e alle ordinanze, è ovviamente lo scoglio del sindacato della legge a dividere i giuristi. La ricordata posizione di Tocqueville – come pure quella di Charles Hello o di Armand Dalloz o di altri giuristi – rivela un sottofondo argomentativo destinato a lasciare una traccia profonda; parimenti, anche l'atteggiamento di un Berriat-Saint-Prix, secondo cui «toute loi inconciliable avec le texte de la charte est inconstitutionnelle» e che si rifà al modello americano per affermare che «les juges, lorsqu'ils auront à opter entre le texte de la loi et celui de la Constitution, devront faire du dernier la base de leur jugement», non nasconde però un "doppio scoglio", ovvero il timore che i giudici non usurpino il potere legislativo rifiutandosi di applicare leggi regolari o viceversa non si tirino indietro dinanzi alla necessità di dichiarare incostituzionale una legge.[89]

La natura del regime politico, il sostegno dell'opinione pubblica liberale, l'"ambizione" e l'autostima delle corti inferiori aiutano a comprendere come il periodo compreso tra il 1814 e il 1848 sia il più favorevole ad un possibile sviluppo di un empirico quasi-controllo di costituzionalità. L'antefatto napoleonico, il passaggio repubblicano e la nascita del Secondo Impero in effetti confermano *a contrario* come senza certe condizioni e premesse – pur restando invariato il quadro normativo post-rivoluzionario – sia impossibile immaginare una soluzione alternativa.

87 «Ognuno professa la propria religione con una libertà eguale ed ottiene per il proprio culto la stessa protezione».

88 Rinvio a G. Bigot, *L'autorité judiciaire*, cit., 217 ss. e soprattutto a J.-L. Mestre, *La Cour de Cassation*, cit., 47 ss., con ampi riferimenti in ordine alle diverse posizioni dottrinali. Si veda inoltre P. Laroque, *Les juges français et le contrôle de la loi*, in *Revue du droit public*, 33, 1926, 728.

89 F. Berriat-Saint-Prix, *Commentaire sur la Charte constitutionnelle*, Paris 1836, 119 ss. «Ce sont – scrive Barthélemy all'inizio del Novecento – les objections que l'on adresse encore à l'introduction en France du système de l'inconstitutionnalité des lois» (*La distinction des lois constitutionnelles et des lois ordinaires sous la Monarchie de Juillet*, cit., 21).

5. La garanzia "politico-giurisdizionale" della costituzione

Se il Senato dell'anno VIII risponde anche ad una logica di «desacralizzazione della legge»,[90] non è da escludere che la reintroduzione del Senato nel 1852 con poteri addirittura accresciuti rispetto al suo antenato si debba anche al disegno di riportare all'interno di un organo politico il meccanismo di controllo delle leggi togliendo ogni tentazione a quei giudici che avevano maturato nei decenni precedenti una "cultura" della costituzionalità.[91] Il Senato del Secondo Impero – «potere ponderatore», «custode del patto fondamentale e delle libertà pubbliche» – è investito formalmente di poteri esorbitanti: esercita il potere costituente,[92] mantiene o annulla tutti gli atti che gli sono deferiti come incostituzionali dal Governo o per via di petizione dai cittadini (art. 29), può opporsi alla promulgazione delle leggi,[93] provvede, in caso di scioglimento del Corpo legislativo, con misure di urgenza a tutto ciò che è necessario per il funzionamento del Governo (art. 33). Se i giuristi e i politici della monarchia costituzionale censurarono l'assoluta inefficacia del meccanismo di controllo di quel primo

90 M. Morabito, D. Bourmaud, *Histoire constitutionnelle et politique de la France (1789–1958)*, Paris 1998, 5 ed., 145. Sulle origini del Senato conservatore v. la recente sintesi di L. Scuccimarra, *El sistema de excepción. La construcción constitucional del modelo bonapartista (1799–1804)*, in *Fundamentos*, 2, 2000, 295 ss.

91 Jean-Louis Mestre riporta le posizioni di giuristi come Dalloz, Serrigny, Dufour, Foucart che, pur con varie sfumature, insistono, durante il Secondo Impero, sul ruolo dei giudici in materia di costituzionalità degli atti regolamentari. Così facendo – anche se durante il regime napoleonico non sarà possibile trovare una decisione giudiziaria di controllo – si vuole velatamente riconfermare ai giudici uno spazio che il regime, con la reintroduzione del Senato, ha inteso ridurre al minimo. Cfr. J.-L. Mestre, *Les juridictions judiciaires*, cit., 459–461, e dello stesso autore, *La Cour de Cassation*, cit., 60–62.

92 Il Senato regola con Senato-consulto – sanzionato e promulgato dall'Imperatore – la costituzione delle colonie e dell'Algeria, tutto ciò che non è stato previsto dalla Costituzione e che è necessario al suo funzionamento, interpreta il significato degli articoli della Costituzione che danno luogo a discordanti interpretazioni (artt. 27 e 28, Cost. 12 gennaio 1852), può inoltre proporre modifiche alla Costituzione (art. 31). Ogni modifica alle basi fondamentali dovrà essere sottoposta al suffragio universale (art. 32).

93 «Il Senato si oppone alla promulgazione: 1) delle leggi che fossero contrarie o attentassero alla Costituzione, alla religione, alla morale, alla libertà dei culti, alla libertà individuale, all'eguaglianza dei cittadini davanti alla legge, all'inviolabilità della proprietà e al principio dell'inamovibilità della magistratura; 2) di quelle che potessero compromettere la difesa del territorio» (art. 26). Per l'analisi delle attribuzioni del Senato v. la critica coeva di F. Berriat-Saint-Prix, *Théorie du droit constitutionnel français. Esprit des constitutions de 1848 et de 1852 et des sénatus-consultes organiques …*, Paris 1851–1853.

Senato imperiale,[94] allo stesso modo l'esperienza negativa del Secondo Impero fece allontanare durante la Terza Repubblica ogni possibilità di affidare il controllo costituzionale delle leggi ad un organo politico. Una delle più importanti figure del regime, quel Baroche a lungo presidente del Consiglio di Stato, ebbe a dire che il Senato, non essendo una Camera legislativa, aveva un compito ben più elevato, sebbene poi fosse proprio l'«immensità del potere» a «paralizzare» i senatori.[95]

Il fallimento del controllo di costituzionalità delle leggi esercitato dal Senato ripropone il problema del rapporto tra valore normativo della costituzione e strumenti di garanzia. Paul Duez nel 1929, riflettendo, come molti dei giuristi francesi, sul principio del controllo giurisdizionale delle leggi per fronteggiare il «dispotismo delle maggioranze parlamentari»,[96] definisce *a priori* il controllo

94 Basti pensare alla severa autocritica dell'estensore del testo dell'anno VIII, Daunou, resa pubblica durante la Restaurazione: *Essai sur les garanties individuelles que réclame l'état actuel de la société*, Paris 1819, 215–217. Daunou aveva suggerito nell'art. 24 del suo progetto di costituzione dell'anno III di affidare la conservazione delle istituzioni a un *jury constitutionnaire*. Sui progetti inediti di Daunou v. A. Dauteribes, *Daunou et le modèle du régime représentatif*, in G. Conac e J.-P. Machelon (edd.), *La Constitution de l'an III. Boissy d'Anglas et la naissance du libéralisme constitutionnel*, Paris 1999, 115 e 131. Tuttavia, come è stato fatto notare di recente, «l'objectif poursuivi par Danou n'était plus le même: en 1798, il mettait l'accent sur l'équilibre politique; en 1818, seule l'intéresse la défense des libertés individuelles, menacées par les gouvernements de la Restauration» (J.-P. Clement, *Aux sources du libéralisme français: Boissy d'Anglas, Daunou, Lanjuinais*, Paris 2000, 68).

95 Cfr. al riguardo l'ampio studio di A. Ashworth, *Le contrôle de la constitutionnalité des lois par le Sénat du Second Empire*, in *Revue du droit public*, 1, 1994, 45–102.

96 La giuspubblicistica francese tra la fine del XIX secolo e i primi decenni del seguente ha ampiamente còlto e analizzato il fenomeno del «risveglio dei poteri politici delle nostre corti» (per riprendere l'espressione utilizzata da Edouard Lambert nel suo celebre *Le gouvernement des juges et la lutte contre la législation sociale aux Etats-Unis. L'expérience américaine du contrôle judiciaire de la constitutionnalité des lois*, Paris 1921, tr. it. Milano, 1996, 1) auspicando, pur non senza dubbi e riserve (per es., da posizioni diverse, Larnaude, Duguit, Esmein, Carré de Malberg), un intervento volto a superare non solo gli ostacoli (i divieti rivoluzionari: tit. II legge 5 agosto 1790; tit. 3, cap. 5, art. 3 della Costituzione del 3 settembre 1791 ...) posti a base del diritto pubblico francese ma soprattutto l'ostacolo per eccellenza, ovvero l'assetto costituzionale del 1875 (v. R. Carrè De Malberg, *La loi, expression de la volonté générale*, préface de G. Burdeau, Paris 1931, rist. Paris 1984). Cfr., per i profili essenziali, G. Jèze, *Le contrôle juridictionnel des lois*, Paris 1924; M. Barthélemy, *Le contrôle juridictionnel des lois en France*, Paris 1929; Ch. Eisenmann, *La justice constitutionnelle et la Haute Cour constitutionnelle d'Autriche*, Préface de H. Kelsen, Paris 1928, in part. 24 ss.; Ch. Eisenmann, L. Hamon, *La juridiction constitutionnelle en droit français*

esercitato dal Senato e ricorda – sulla scia di Sieyès – come in base alla costituzione dell'anno VIII la produzione della legge rispondesse ad una logica processuale: da un lato il Tribunato investito della funzione propositiva, dall'altro il Corpo legislativo deliberante, tra i due il Senato conservatore[97] a fungere da corte di cassazione nell'ambito politico.[98] Non bisogna dimenticare come tra la fine del XVIII e il corso del XIX secolo il problema della garanzia della Costituzione[99] non sia identificato con quello del controllo delle leggi realizzato in forma giudiziaria. Difendere la Costituzione è un concetto ben più esteso e vago e può essere raffigurato solo in parte con l'immagine del custode della Costituzione.[100] Un dato però deve essere subito evidenziato, e cioè che una stessa logica accomuna una congerie – difficilmente riconducibile a

(1875–1961), in *Verfassungsgerichtsbarkeit in der Gegenwart*, hrsg. v. Hermann Mosler, Köln, Berlin 1962, 229–291; P. Cruz Villalon, *La formación del sistema europeo de control de constitucionalidad (1918–1939)*, Madrid 1987; E. Pisier, *Léon Duguit et le contrôle de la constitutionnalité*, in *Mélanges Duverger*, Paris 1987, 189–202; L. Hamon, *Les juges de la loi. Naissance et rôle d'un contre pouvoir: le Conseil Constitutionnel*, Paris 1987; S. Gambino, *Sistema delle fonti e controllo di costituzionalità. Il caso francese. Parte I: profili storici-dogmatici*, Torino 1988; M. Verpeaux, *Le contrôle de la loi par la voie d'exception dans les propositions parlementaires sous la IIIe République*, in *Revue française de droit constitutionnel*, 4, 1990, 688–698; M. Cappelletti, *Le pouvoir des juges*, Paris, Aix-en-Provence 1990; M.-J. Redor, *De l'Etat légal à l'Etat de droit*, cit.; R. L. Blanco-Valdés, *El valor de la constitución. Separación de poderes, supremacía de la ley y control de constitucionalidad en los orígenes del estado liberal*, Madrid 1994, tr. it. *Il valore della costituzione. Separazione dei poteri, supremazia della legge e controllo di costituzionalità alle origini dello Stato liberale*, Padova 1997, 244 ss.; E. Maulin, *Le principe du contrôle de la constitutionnalité des lois dans la pensée de R.Carré de Malberg*, in *Revue française de droit constitutionnel*, 21, 1995, 79–105.

97 Sull'originario progetto di Sieyès e sul rapporto tra *jury législatif* e *Collège des Conservateurs*, v. adesso M. Lahmer, *La constitution américaine dans le débat français: 1795–1848*, Paris 2001, 270 ss.

98 P. Duez, *Le contrôle juridictionnel de la constitutionnalité des lois en France. Comment il convient de poser la question*, in *Mélanges Maurice Hauriou*, Paris 1929, 211–249. Sui pericoli insiti nel controllo di costituzionalità delle leggi quanto alla possibile opposizione tra elemento giuridico (costituzione come regola giuridica sottoposta a sanzione) e elemento politico v. M.-J. Redor, *De l'Etat légal à l'Etat de droit*, cit., 174: «Si les publicistes souhaitent éviter la confrontation du juridique et du politique, c'est à la fois pour préserver une certaine cohérence de l'ordre juridique, son auto-suffisance en quelque sorte, et pour garder à leur spécialité l'autorité de la compétence technique».

99 Cfr. D. Rousseau, *La garantie de la constitution*, in *Liberté, libéraux et constitutions*, a cura di J.-P. Clement, L. Jaume, M. Verpeaux, Paris, Aix-en-Provence 1997, 97–105.

100 C. Schmitt, *Der Hüter der Verfassung*, Berlin 1969 (1931), tr. it. *Il custode della costituzione*, Milano 1981, 23.

unitarietà – di proposte e di soluzioni: è la logica che definirei politico-giurisdizionale la quale, non potendo affermarsi sotto forma di *judicial review*, è fatta interagire prevalentemente con la dinamica costituzionale dei poteri.

Marcel Gauchet ha studiato il problema del «potere supplementare» durante il decennio rivoluzionario. Tra la volontà del legislativo e l'azione dell'esecutivo, tra il dogma dell'unità sovrana del corpo politico della nazione e la costanza rivoluzionaria del medesimo principio (malgrado talune apparenti *défaillance*), tra la filosofia della rappresentanza e la sua riflessività, si incunea un tipo di proposta istituzionale destinata a soccombere – con l'eccezione "disgraziata" del Senato conservatore – e che, tuttavia, suggerisce un altro modo di leggere la vicenda dei fondamenti del costituzionalismo liberale francese scossi alla radice dalla tensione tra la dimensione teorica e l'impossibilità pragmatica.

In quel decennio l'immaginario costituzionale è contrassegnato da una fantasia sbrigliata, da una straordinaria fucina di complessi congegni istituzionali.[101] Il "travestimento" è di gran moda: ecco allora in decine di progetti apparire consigli di censori, tribuni, efori, senati revisori, poteri conservatori, alla ricerca

101 Oltre al lavoro di Marcel Gauchet, *La Révolution des pouvoirs. La souveraineté, le peuple et la représentation, 1789–1799*, Paris 1995, cfr. anche E. Zweig, *Die Lehre vom Pouvoir Constituant. Ein Beitrag zum Staatsrecht der französischen Revolution*, Tübingen 1909, 421 ss.; C. Schmitt, *Il custode della costituzione*, cit., 9 ss.; P. Bastid, *Sieyès et sa pensée*, Paris 1970 (1939), 431–433; L. Mannori, *Uno Stato per Romagnosi. I. Il progetto costituzionale*, Milano 1984, 546 ss.; F. Brunel, *Aux origines d'un parti de l'ordre: les projets de constitution de l'an III*, in *Mouvements populaires et conscience sociale, XVIe–XIXe siècles*, a cura di J. Nicolas, Paris 1985, 687–696; G. Robbers, *Emmanuel Joseph Sieyès – Die Idee einer Verfassungsgerichtsbarkeit in der Französischen Revolution*, in *Festschrift für Wolfgang Zeidler*, hrsg. von W. Fürts, R. Herzog, D. C. Umbach, Berlin, New York 1987, t. I, 247–263, con particolare riferimento alla recezione tedesca; M. Pertué, *La censure du peuple dans le projet de Constitution de Condorcet*, in *Condorcet, mathématicien, économiste, philosophe, homme politique*, a cura di P. Crépel e Ch. Gilain, Paris 1989, 322–332; J. Luther, *Idee e storia*, cit.; M. Levinet, *Le problème du contrôle de la loi lors de l'élaboration de la constitution de 1793*, in *Revue du droit public et de la science politique en France et à l'étranger*, 3, 1991, 697–732; P. Colombo, *Governo e costituzione*, cit., 510 ss.; M. Pertué, *Les projets constitutionnels de 1793*, in *Révolution et République. L'exception française*, a cura di M. Vovelle, Paris 1994, 174–199; S. Luzzatto, *L'Autunno della Rivoluzione. Lotta e cultura politica nella Francia del Termidoro*, Torino 1994, 304 ss.; M. Barberis, *Thermidor, le libéralisme et la modernité politique*, in *1795. Pour une République sans Révolution*, a cura di R. Dupuy e M. Morabito, Rennes 1996, 134 ss.; P. P. Portinaro, *Il grande legislatore e il custode della costituzione*, in *Il futuro della costituzione*, cit., 22 ss.; R. L. Blanco-Valdés, *Il valore della costituzione*, cit., 258 ss.

di quell'ordine e di quella stabilità costituzionale che la Rivoluzione non sembra poter mai raggiungere. A ogni grande snodo del dibattito costituente (estate-autunno del 1789, 1791, primavera del 1793, termidoro ecc.) un numero sorprendente di oscuri e improvvisati legislatori o di personalità di navigata esperienza propone di dar vita, sotto varie forme, ad un multiforme terzo potere, protettore, conservatore, di sorveglianza, di censura, di riforma.

In questo ambito appare però assolutamente fuorviante assumere la categoria moderna della giustizia costituzionale[102] come spazio di riflessione del decennio rivoluzionario. Si rischierebbe infatti di assegnare a quei progetti (anche al più noto di essi, ovvero a quello di Sieyès) uno statuto che essi non possiedono se non per singoli dettagli ed elementi, spesso confusi tra loro. Semmai questo dibattito interessa proprio perché mostra la difficoltà di passare dai riferimenti ideali della libertà degli Antichi *en travesti* alla dialettica liberal-repubblicana dei Moderni.

In particolare non bisogna confondere – malgrado le suggestioni e analogie più o meno apparenti – il problema della attivazione di un potere giudiziario di sindacato costituzionale[103] con il richiamo allusivo ad una più vaga e polimorfica logica giudiziaria in grado di offrire un determinato modulo organizzativo: non è così difficile pensare ad «un tribunale degli altri poteri» in perfetta simmetria con il dispositivo della cassazione, ovvero, per altri aspetti, a quel *topos* settecentesco del tribunale dell'opinione che pare realizzare un compromesso tra la volontà sovrana e un giudizioso esercizio della rappresentanza.

In questo panorama l'autore che meglio di ogni altro rappresenta l'evoluzione di un'idea e al tempo stesso ne segnala le *impasses* è ovviamente l'abate Sieyès. Mi riferisco in particolare alla sua "misteriosa" proposta di istituire una *jurie constitutionnaire*[104] benché il nostro abbia individuato questo profilo problema-

102 Come si può vedere in molti degli studi dedicati al problema delle origini della giustizia costituzionale.

103 Diversamente bisogna utilizzare una troppa ampia e generica locuzione per riferirsi ad ogni procedura legale messa in atto per proteggere la costituzione. In tal senso v. H. Mosler, *Introduzione* a *Verfassungsgerichtsbarkeit in der Gegenwart*, cit., XII e G. Stourzh, *Vom Widerstandsrecht zur Verfassungsgerichtsbarkeit: zum Problem der Verfassungswidrigkeit im 18. Jahrhundert*, Graz 1974.

104 «Je demande d'abord un *jury de constitution*, ou, pour franciser un peu plus le mot de jury, et le distinguer dans le son de celui de juré, une *jurie constitutionnaire*». (*Opinion de Sieyès, sur plusieurs articles des titres IV et V du projet de Constitution, prononcée à la Convention le 2 thermidor de l'an troisième de la République*, Paris, an III, 7). Sulla terminologia utilizzata dall'abate v. P. Bastid, *Sieyès et sa pensée*, cit., 433. Cfr. anche B. Nicolle, *Aux origines du contrôle de*

tico sin dalla vigilia rivoluzionaria[105] e abbia cominciato a rifletterci durante l'Ottantanove. L'abate ricompare nel dibattito costituente con uno di quei *coup de théatre* che ne hanno accresciuto la fama di oracolo e di «premier architecte politique». La Convenzione è già avanti nell'esame del progetto elaborato dalla Commissione degli Undici allorché Sieyès il 2 termidoro, nella sua solitaria ricerca della soluzione, fa un nuovo, inaspettato e poco gradito intervento in aula.[106]

L'abate è certamente tra i più consapevoli della necessità di un "soggetto" che svolga una funzione regolatrice e di conservazione della *machine* costituzionale. A questo scopo non giova la dinamica legata al veto reale che interferisce con l'Assemblea nazionale né si può ammettere che la non giuridicizzabile spinta insurrezionale funzioni da potere legale di regolazione. All'inizio della Rivoluzione Sieyès affida al potere costituente organizzato sotto forma di una convenzione nazionale il "giudizio" sul conflitto.[107]

È tuttavia nei discorsi del 2 e del 18 termidoro dell'anno III che Sieyès definisce e sviluppa i termini della sua proposta la quale, pur inserendosi nell'ambito di una

constitutionnalité: la jurie constitutionnaire de Sieyès (1795), Mémoire D. E. A., Paris 1990.

105 «... Mais si votre législature elle-même, si les différentes parties de cette première constitution ne s'accordent pas entre elles, qui sera le juge suprême? Car il en faut toujours un, ou bien l'anarchie succède à l'ordre» (E.-J. Sieyès, *Qu'est-ce que le Tiers Etat?*, Paris 1988, chap. V, 133). Sull'apporto di Sieyès durante il dibattito costituente dopo il 1789 si veda L. Jaume, *Garantir les droits de l'homme: 1791–1793*, in *The Tocqueville Review – La Revue Tocqueville*, XIV, 1, 1993, 49–65.

106 Per una puntuale ricostruzione del ruolo di Sieyès nelle dinamiche politiche e costituzionali tra la primavera e l'estate del 1795 nonché sulla proposta, appena abbozzata, di Durand de Maillane di un *Jury constitutionnel* rinviamo al recente lavoro di R. Martucci, *L'ossessione costituente. Forma di governo e costituzione nella Rivoluzione francese (1789–1799)*, Bologna 2001, 274 ss.

107 *Dire de l'abbé Sieyès, sur la question du veto royal, à la séance du 7 septembre 1789*, Paris, s. d. Sulle posizioni di Sieyès prima dell'anno III, cfr. P. Bastid, *Sieyès et sa pensée*, cit., 430 ss. e più recentemente le belle pagine di S. Mannoni, *Une et indivisible. Storia dell'accentramento amministrativo in Francia*, Milano 1994, t. I, 284 ss. In una annotazione autografa, non datata, a margine del discorso sul veto reale Sieyès scrive «qu'il est rare qu'un appel au peuple ne devient pas un appel à la guerre civile» osservando che il veto dovrà trovarsi «au dehors, dans un jury constitutionnaire» (*ibidem*, 294). Sulla posizione critica di Sieyès rispetto al veto sospensivo e l'appello ai baliaggi v. anche R. Martucci, *1789, la Repubblica dei foglianti. Dal re d'antico regime al primo funzionario dello Stato*, in *Storia Amministrazione Costituzione*, 1, 1993, 97–98; M. Gauchet, *La Révolution des pouvoirs*, cit., 62 ss. Sulla sostanziale continuità del costituzionalismo liberale di Sieyès, v. P. Pasquino, *Il pensiero di Sieyès*, in E.-J. Sieyes, *Opere e testimonianze politiche*, t. I, *Scritti editi*, vol. I, a cura di G. Troisi Spagnoli, Milano 1993, 7–8.

riflessione comune sulla difesa della costituzione e sul controllo del suo corretto funzionamento, riveste una indubbia originalità.[108]

Sieyès nel suo primo discorso muove da una mera constatazione: nel progetto presentato dalla Commissione degli Undici manca la parte relativa alla garanzia, vero e proprio *casse-tête* del dibattito rivoluzionario. Per riportare la sovranità – trasformatasi in "totalità" sconfinata e mostruosa durante il Terrore – «nei suoi giusti limiti»[109] l'abate ritiene si debba riflettere sull'organizzazione del potere[110] inteso come movimento complesso tendente all'unità di azione, in breve accordare l'unità (per evitare l'anarchia) con la divisione (per impedire ogni forma di dispotismo). Sieyès sembra qui "anticipare" i tratti organizzativi di quella che sarà la costituzione dell'anno VIII. La macchina[111] artificiale fondata sul principio della divisione del lavoro e dell'interesse specializza il processo legislativo a cui contribuiscono diversi e autonomi organi (tribunato, "governo", legislatura) tendenti ad una "unità organizzata" che presuppone la fondamentale teoria della distinzione tra potere costituente e potere costituito. Il Corpo legislativo, come un tribunale giudiziario, riceve la questione da giudicare e deve dar "ragione", moderare e decidere, deliberando, sul rapporto di irriducibile diversità che si instaura tra governanti ("governo") e governati (tribunato).[112] Il legislatore-giudice cerca di garantire che l'ordine politico sia il più possibile tagliato sulla misura dell'ordine civile.[113] Tale meccanica si deve però innestare

108 Di recente la giuria costituzionale di Sieyès – a testimonianza del fatto che non tutto è stato detto sull'argomento – ha attirato l'attenzione critica, pur da punti di vista differenti, di due dei più importanti rappresentanti francesi della storia delle idee politiche e della storia e teoria costituzionale: si vedano M. Troper, *Sieyès et le jury constitutionnaire*, in *La République. Etudes offerts à Pierre Avril*, Paris 2001, 265 ss. e L. Jaume, *Sieyès et le sens du jury constitutionnaire: une reinterpretation*, in *Droits*, 36, 2003, 114–134.

109 *Opinion de Sieyès, sur plusieurs articles des titres IV et V du projet de constitution, prononcée à la Convention le 2 thermidor de l'an troisième de la République*, cit., 7. In traduzione italiana si veda l'edizione a cura di G. Troisi Spagnoli in *Opere e testimonianze politiche*, cit., t. I, vol. II, *Opinione di Sieyès su alcuni articoli dei titoli IV e V del progetto di costituzione pronunciata alla Convenzione il 2 termidoro dell'anno III (20 luglio 1795) della Repubblica*, 792–793.

110 Sulla "riabilitazione" costituzionale del "governo" come volontà e deliberazione e sulle influenze (Thouret, Necker ...) in Sieyès v. la sintesi di L. Compagna, *Gli opposti sentieri del costituzionalismo*, Bologna 1998, 239 ss.

111 Su questo concetto v. adesso le osservazioni di S. Mannoni, *La dottrina costituzionale di Sieyès*, in *Quaderni fiorentini*, 29, 2000, 40.

112 Sull'accentuato antivolontarismo di Sieyès v. L. Jaume, *Sieyès et le sens du jury constitutionnaire: une reinterpretation*, cit., 207 ss., che ricostruisce puntualmente la filosofia della deliberazione e del giudizio elaborata dall'abate francese.

113 Cfr. P. Bastid, *Sieyès et sa pensée*, cit., 424–425.

sul tronco della logica dell'equilibrio costituzionale[114] e deve poter risolvere l'originario problema del potere costituente. È in questo contesto istituzionale che l'"architetto" Sieyès introduce la giuria costituzionale, ovvero un «corpo di rappresentanti, con missione speciale, incaricati di esprimersi sui reclami contro ogni attacco alla Costituzione».[115] Volendo anzitutto reagire alla logica dell'onnipotenza legislativa e della sua rappresentanza politica,[116] tale tribunale, nella sua veste di «dépositaire-conservateur de l'Acte Constitutionnel»,[117] è chiamato a pronunciarsi contro tutte le possibili violazioni. È nel discorso del 18 termidoro che Sieyès riduce la competenza ma amplia lo spettro di intervento del *jury*. Se la costituzione è un corpo di leggi obbligatorie (perché altrimenti non serve a nulla) allora «bisogna chiedersi dove risiederà il guardiano, la magistratura di tale codice ...». La giuria, definita nei suoi meccanismi e nelle sue molteplici funzioni,[118] deve dunque fungere da «tribunale di cassazione nel-

114 Sieyès – come è noto – conserva la sua posizione critica verso il "sistema di equilibrio" ascritto alla tradizione costituzionale inglese e, per altri versi, americana. Tuttavia – come dimostrato di recente con notevole acume – il progetto dell'abate per l'anno III (e poi, pur nelle mutate condizioni, per l'anno VIII) non era estraneo ai meccanismi della *balance des pouvoirs*. Al riguardo si rinvia a M. Lahmer, *La constitution américaine dans le débat français: 1795–1848*, cit., 213 ss., anche per cogliere l'indubbia influenza della teoria costituzionale di James Harrington sull'opera di Sieyès (249 ss.).

115 V. *Opinione di Sieyès su alcuni articoli dei titoli IV e V del progetto di costituzione pronunciata alla Convenzione il 2 termidoro dell'anno III (20 luglio 1795) della Repubblica*, cit., 796. «C'est un véritable corps de représentans que je demande, avec mission spéciale de juger les réclamations contre toute atteinte qui seroit portée à la constitution» (*Opinion de Sieyès, sur plusieurs articles des titres IV et V du projet de Constitution, prononcée à la Convention le 2 thermidor de l'an troisième de la République*, cit., 11).

116 Su questa costante preoccupazione, v. P. Bastid, *Sieyès et sa pensée*, cit., 418 ss.

117 Art. I del progetto di Sieyès: *Opinion de Sieyès, sur les attributions et l'organisation du jurì constitutionnaire. Proposée le 2 thermidor, prononcée à la Convention nationale le 18 du même mois, l'an III de la République*, Paris, an III, 20.

118 «En d'autres termes, je considère le jury constitutionnaire, 1° comme tribunal de cassation dans l'ordre constitutionnel; 2° comme atelier de propositions pour les amendemens que le temps pourroit exiger dans la constitution; 3° enfin, comme supplément de juridiction naturelle aux vides de la juridiction positive» (*Opinion de Sieyès sur les attributions et l'organisation du jurì constitutionnaire. Proposée le 2 thermidor, prononcée à la Convention nationale le 18 du même mois, l'an III de la République*, cit., 3–4). Cfr. J. Luther, *Idee e storie*, cit., 39 ss.; P. Colombo, *Governo e costituzione*, cit., 515 ss.; M. Morabito, D. Bourmaud, *Histoire constitutionnelle*, cit., 116–118. Non bisogna dimenticare che la proposta di Sieyès ha uno dei suoi punti di maggiore interesse nel ruolo che assegna alla giuria nella dinamica costituzionale tra maggioranza e minoranza. Sul punto v. le osservazioni di R. L. Blanco-Valdés, *Il valore della costituzione*, cit.; J. Varela Suanzes, *Constitución y ley en los origenes del estado liberal (A propósito del libro de R. L. Blanco Valdes,*

l'ambito costituzionale» che tenga conto della natura speciale dell'atto costituzionale:[119] essa pronuncia sentenze e gl'atti dichiarati incostituzionali sono «nulli e come non avvenuti».[120] La giuria, formata da 108 membri (di cui un terzo da rinnovarsi ogni anno) scelti per cooptazione dai deputati uscenti, è una macchina «pesante», il luogo della memoria e della stabilizzazione di un notabilato rivoluzionario – sorta di nuova aristocrazia repubblicana – che secondo Sieyès in prima battuta dovrebbe provenire per terzi dalle tre assemblee: Costituente, Legislativa, Convenzionale. Questa volta sono gli atti dei consigli legislativi (Anziani, Cinque-Cento), delle assemblee elettorali, delle deliberazioni del tribunale di cassazione a dover passare sotto il controllo di legalità della giuria.[121]

Il complesso edificio suggerito da Sieyès viene aspramente censurato da Faure, Berlier, Louvet e Thibaudeau[122] che ritorcono contro l'abate gl'argomenti richiamati per sostenere la bontà del suo progetto. L'argomento fondamentale è efficace quanto antico: *Quis custodiet ipsos custodes?*[123] Thibaudeau paventa che un "tribunale" come il *jury*, al di fuori di ogni prevedibile possibilità di controllo, possa addirittura diventare un potere mostruoso, sovraordinato agl'altri.

El valór de la constitución), in *Quaderni fiorentini*, 24, 1995, 519 ss.; P. Rolland, *La garantie des droits*, in *La Constitution de l'an III ou l'ordre républicain*, a cura di J. Bart, J.-J. Clère, C. Courvoisier, M. Verpeaux, Dijon 1998, 78–81. Thibaudeau, nella sua critica al progetto di Sieyès, utilizza l'argomento della minoranza come «fazione»: «... c'est la première fois que l'on a proposé d'établir une institution aussi contraire aux principes, aussi favorable aux factions, aussi destructive de l'ordre social; elle ne pourrait convenir qu'à un peuple chez lequel il serait convenu que c'est la minorité qui a toujours raison et qui doit faire la loi» (*Opinion de Thibaudeau, Convention Nationale, Séance du 24 thermidor An III*, in *Le Moniteur universel*, 1332).

119 «La magistrature civile vous paroîtroit-elle pouvoir remplir une aussi haute mission? Pensez au sage décret par lequel vous avez interdit aux juges de citer devant eux les administrateurs, pour raison de leurs fonctions; à plus forte raison vous ne leur accorderez pas la puissance de citer devant eux les premiers corps politiques de l'état. Non, on ne peut méconnoître assez l'importance de l'acte constitutionnel, pour le réduire à n'être qu'un titre du code civil» (*Opinion de Sieyès sur les attributions et l'organisation du jurì constitutionnaire. Proposée le 2 thermidor, prononcée à la Convention nationale le 18 du même mois, l'an III de la République*, cit., 3).

120 Per la prima volta l'atto dichiarato incostituzionale è sanzionato come nullo. Cfr. M. Battaglini, *Contributi alla storia del controllo di costituzionalità delle leggi*, Milano 1957, 62.

121 M. Troper, *Sieyès et le jury constitutionnaire*, cit.

122 Cfr. M. Gauchet, *La Révolution des pouvoirs*, cit., 178 ss.

123 V. *infra* in questo volume *Il potere giudiziario come «potere politico»*, 444–445.

«Se il tribunale costituzionale, le cui funzioni saranno determinate dalla Costituzione, oltrepassa i suoi limiti chi reprimerà la sua usurpazione? Io vi confesso che ho cercato una risposta e che non ne ho trovato alcuna che mi soddisfi».[124]

Thibaudeau, che ritiene già sufficiente il gioco di controbilanciamenti previsti dal progetto di costituzione dell'anno III (il Consiglio dei Cinquecento che solo propone le leggi, il Consiglio degli Anziani che ha un veto assoluto, il potere di reclamo del direttorio esecutivo), vede nella giuria di Sieyès un organo dannoso perché farebbe venir meno la coerenza del sistema senza però offrire una garanzia contro i pericoli propri del "governo degli uomini".[125]

In questo denso dibattito confliggono, senza poter ancora trovare un punto di equilibrio, le due principali tradizioni del costituzionalismo francese: la cd. «tradizione repubblicana» e la via del liberalismo politico-costituzionale.[126] Per Thibaudeau e per l'ortodossia repubblicana la sola garanzia possibile è quella interna, basata su una efficace separazione dei poteri e sulla logica dell'equilibrio nell'ambito della democrazia rappresentativa. I poteri costituzionali, in virtù dell'interesse a conservare sé stessi,[127] fanno il «loro gioco» e così facendo

124 «... Si le jury constitutionnaire, dont les fonctions seront déterminées par la constitution, en passe les limites, qui est-ce qui réprimera son usurpation? Je vous avoue que j'ai beau chercher une réponse, je ne trouve point de satisfaisante» (*Opinion de Thibaudeau*, cit., 1330). Cfr. R. Blanco-Valdés, *Il valore della costituzione*, cit., 301–302.

125 «Voilà comment tout se lie, tout se tient et se balance dans le travail de la commission; je persiste à dire que c'est dans cette organisation même que se trouve toute garantie, et il est sensible que si on veut placer un jury constitutionnaire sur cet édifice, on en détruit l'harmonie, l'intention et l'effet, et on court les risques de l'écraser sous le poids d'une machine qui ne lui a point été adaptée, d'une pièce de rapport qui ne fait point partie de son ensemble». (*Opinion de Thibaudeau*, cit., 1333). Sull'inutilità di attribuire alla giuria un diritto di sanzione, essendo questa percepita come organo legislativo supplementare, si veda M. Lahmer, *La constitution américaine dans le débat français: 1795–1848*, cit., 241–242. Sul punto si veda il poco noto articolo di A. Lezay-Marnezia, *Sur le jury constitutionnaire de Sieyès*, in *Journal de Paris*, 22 Thermidor – 9 août 1795, 1239.

126 In tal senso v. l'eccellente analisi di P. Rolland, *La garantie des droits*, cit., 29–84.

127 «Ainsi, pour prévenir la confusion ou l'usurpation des pouvoirs, il faut donner à ceux qui les exercent des moyens tellement suffisans pour résister aux tentatives dirigées contre eux, qu'ils soient forcés à se respecter mutuellement par le sentiment de leur force et de leur dignité. Il faut que dans l'organisation du gouvernement chacune de ses parties soit établie et posée de manière à retenir toutes les autres dans leur place; il faut, pour ainsi dire, opposer l'ambition à l'ambition ...» (*Opinion de Thibaudeau*, cit., 1332). È trasparente l'influenza – come è stato fatto notare da Pasquale Pasquino, *Il pensiero politico di Sieyès*, cit., 28 – del celebre articolo 51 de *Il Federalista*: «Ma la maggiore garanzia contro la possibilità che il potere finisca, poco per volta, per concentrarsi tutto nel

garantiscono lo standard di costituzionalità e se del caso esisterà una sola condizione esterna, ovvero quella garanzia morale che può derivare dall'amore del popolo per la libertà e la costituzione.[128] Per Sieyès e la tradizione liberale il metodo giurisdizionale – mutuato dall'ordine civile – potrebbe assicurare un multiforme sistema di garanzia esterna della Costituzione. Per gli uni un organo terzo, configurato come potere, non potrebbe essere imparziale e sarebbe peggiore del rimedio; se poi avesse i tratti di una autorità morale esso non disporrebbe dei mezzi per far cessare il conflitto. Per gli altri la giuria costituzionale riuscirebbe a combinare la natura giudiziaria e quella politica di rappresentante investito dalla legislatura[129] venendo così sottoposto a controllo. In un caso la garanzia della costituzione è vista attraverso il problema dell'organizzazione dei poteri e il principio maggioritario, nell'altro sono la protezione dei diritti individuali e il principio di opposizione e di minoranza a balzare in primo piano.

A ben vedere tale dibattito rivela la complessità del discorso liberale all'interno delle dinamiche della Rivoluzione francese. La posizione assunta da Thibaudeau si avvicina ai fondamenti del «liberalismo della bilancia», mentre quella di Sieyès è integrabile, per riprendere la fortunata modellistica di Bernard Manin, nella tradizione del «liberalismo della regola»[130] che necessita di una istanza superiore esogena in grado di far valere giuridicamente la prescrizione del limite, della *boundary-line*.[131]

medesimo settore, è quella di dare a coloro che sono responsabili di ciascun settore i mezzi ed il personale interesse necessari a resistere ai soprusi ed agli abusi degli altri settori … L'ambizione deve essere usata come antidoto all'ambizione» (A. Hamilton, J. Madison, J. Jay, *Il Federalista*, a cura di M. D'Addio e G. Negri, Bologna 1997, 457–458). Ma, in ultima istanza, non si fa che ritornare a Montesquieu (al suo libro XI, capitolo IV dell'*Esprit des Lois*), ovvero all'idea che il «potere arresti il potere».

128 «Les gardiens les plus sûrs et les plus naturels de toute constitution sont les corps dépositaires des pouvoirs, ensuite tous les citoyens» (*Opinion de Thibaudeau*, cit., 1332). Cfr. P. Rolland, *La garantie des droits*, cit., 76–78.

129 Il deputato della Charente Eschassériaux – che almeno in parte sostiene il progetto di Sieyès – osserva come la giuria costituzionale «n'a de puissance que pour ramener toujours à la loi constitutionnelle et n'en a aucune pour la renverser» (*Convention Nationale, Séance du 24 thermidor An III*, in *Le Moniteur universel*, anno III, 1329–1330).

130 Vedi ampiamente B. Manin, *Les deux libéralismes: la règle et la balance*, in *La Famille, la loi, l'Etat. De la Révolution au code civil*, a cura di I. Thery e Ch. Biet, Paris 1989, 372–389.

131 Detto altrimenti, si può parlare anche di una peculiare contrapposizione tra il modello meccanicista e il modello normativo. Sul punto v. M. Troper, *La máquina y la norma. Dos modelos de constitucion*, in *Doxa*, 22, 1999, 331–347.

Il progetto di Sieyès, malgrado un primo parziale sostegno,[132] fu respinto all'unanimità, con la vittoria completa dei suoi critici. La complessità e l'ambiguità del progetto – ovvero il voler mettere insieme, come rilevato da Berlier, questioni capitali ed eterogenee – hanno finito per fare il gioco degli avversari. Il progetto dell'abate non oltrepassa un modello di garanzia che è ancora fortemente radicato nell'immaginario virtuoso della *polis* e assume le forme di una super-magistratura che ha – come una divinità *hindu* – troppe braccia, la cassazione e la censura, la revisione e l'iniziativa, il tribunale dei diritti dell'uomo incaricato di giudicare secondo equità e così via.[133] Nella riflessione di Sieyès – e più tardi nell'autocritica di costituzionali termidoriani come Daunou, Constant, Mme de Staël – c'è senza dubbio un gusto del paradosso e della sfida: presentare un modello di «Stato di diritto» nel momento in cui la classe politica è già ossessionata dalle circostanze e dalla minaccia di dover ricorrere alla forza – l'esatto contrario del diritto – per salvare e stabilizzare un ben individuato regime repubblicano.[134]

Sia il Consiglio degli Anziani nella costituzione dell'anno III che il Senato conservatore dell'anno VIII pur rivelando una stessa teorica preoccupazione si allontanano però da Sieyès e specie il Senato è destinato a giocare un ruolo puramente formale di legittimazione del governo napoleonico e a gettare nient'altro che discredito su quell'idea di controllo "politico" propugnata dall'"oracolo della Rivoluzione".[135] Si può dire che la sconfitta di Sieyès rappresenti in Francia – a parte la fallimentare esperienza dei senati napoleonici – il primo e ultimo grande tentativo di creare un potere neutro con evidente

132 Si è fatto opportunamente notare come il progetto di Sieyès sia in realtà assai meno "isolato" di quanto possa sembrare, inserendosi e anzi dando più compiuta forma al dibattito rivoluzionario sul "potere neutro". Cfr. P. Colombo, *Governo e costituzione*, cit., 517–518.

133 Di «evidente macchinosità» parla M. Fioravanti, *Costituzione*, Bologna 1999, 117; «Un farraginoso organismo di garanzia» è il giudizio di R. Martucci, *L'ossessione costituente*, cit., 282.

134 Cfr. G. Conac, *La convention thérmidorienne: épisode réactionnaire ou transition novatrice?*, in J. Bart, J. J. Clère, C. Courvoisier, M. Verpeaux (edd.), *La constitution de l'an III*, cit., 263 ss. Marcel Morabito ha còlto efficacemente il dilemma della costituzione dell'anno III: essa deve poter vivere nella continuità dei *principi* rivoluzionari e repubblicani ma la stabilità non può essere assicurata dal diritto, ovvero da «... une perspective strictement mécanique, étrangère aux réalités politiques» (*Les nouveautés constitutionnelles de l'an III*, in R. Dupuy, M. Morabito (edd.), *1795. Pour une République sans Révolution*, cit., 177).

135 Anche se lo stesso Sieyès ha poi visto nel *Collège des Conservateurs* un corpo nel quale far prevalere più la dimensione politica dell'iniziativa che quella "conservatrice" della logica giurisdizionale. Cfr. P. Bastid, *Sieyès et sa pensée*, cit., 446.

natura politico-giurisdizionale.[136] Malgrado ciò è da sottolineare come la "logica giurisdizionale" sopravviva sotto altre forme, anche se la dimensione del tribunale, del giudizio e della soluzione del conflitto suggeriscono più interrogativi che soluzioni. Non sarà forse l'ambiguo concetto di "ragione" – tanto caro ai dottrinari – a fare della rappresentanza dei migliori, dei proprietari, degli individui consapevoli delle proprie capacità, dei virtuosi e dei probi un ingrediente imprescindibile dell'antropologia costituzionale del XIX secolo? È certo significativo che Carré de Malberg nel 1927 continui ad osservare che «la conscience des représentants est le tribunal de la constitutionnalité des lois».[137] E nel «tribunale dell'opinione»[138] non ritorna ancora – tra i luoghi più affollati dell'immaginario sette-ottocentesco – la funzione del giudicare? Non era ovviamente più il popolo ad essere evocato, ma al suo posto l'opinione pubblica delle idee e delle intelligenze. Ma nonostante ciò rimaneva l'ambiguità del "tribunale dell'opinione popolare" come guardiano della costituzione. Non stupisce allora che gran parte dei testi – quasi a voler tenere insieme l'idea del legislativo virtuoso e del «tribunale dell'opinione» – ne affidino il deposito alla fedeltà degli organi costituzionali, alla vigilanza dei padri di famiglia, alle spose e alle madri, all'affetto dei giovani cittadini, al coraggio di tutti i Francesi, al patriottismo e al valore delle guardie nazionali (Costituzioni del 1791, 1793, 1795, 1830, 1848).[139]

L'appello retorico alla lealtà, alla virtù è certamente nobile, ma è sempre la costituzione "malfatta" – per ritornare a Constant e al nostro punto di partenza – a far temere che essa resti senza difese di fronte ai probabili abusi. Constant nei *Fragments* si chiede se una costituzione possa garantire da sé la sua esisten-

136 Gauchet parla di «Une philosophie judiciaire de la représentation» (*La Révolution des pouvoirs*, cit., 168 ss.).

137 R. Carré De Malberg, *La constitutionnalité des lois et la Constitution de 1875*, in *Revue politique et parlementaire*, 1927, 344. Cfr. D. Rousseau, *La garantie de la constitution*, cit., 98–100.

138 Nell'Ottocento «La véritable sanction des lois constitutionnelles résidait dans le contrôle de l'opinion publique sans cesse tenue en éveil grâce à la liberté de la presse» (J. Barthélemy, *La distinction des lois constitutionnelles*, cit., 21). Il tema del «tribunale dell'opinione» in rapporto allo sviluppo e alle dinamiche politico-costituzionali dei regimi rappresentativi moderni è tanto importante quanto poco indagato sotto il profilo giuridico-istituzionale. Gli studi citati *supra* di Lucien Jaume hanno senza dubbio il grande merito di aver posto l'accento sul fondamento filosofico del liberalismo con particolare riguardo alla «fonction de juger». Un aspetto, questo, fondamentale che riveste, a mio avviso, anche molteplici conseguenze di ordine più strettamente costituzionale.

139 Cfr. P. Pasquino, *Gardien de la Constitution ou justice constitutionnelle? Carl Schmitt et Hans Kelsen*, in M. Troper, L. Jaume (edd.), *1789 et l'invention de la constitution*, Paris 1994, 143.

za,[140] ovvero se la divisione dei poteri, con la contrapposizione degl'interessi, sia sufficiente a impedire che il legislativo e l'esecutivo compiano abusi che finiranno per distruggere la Costituzione. L'influenza di Necker, del *Des circonstances actuelles* di Madame de Staël (oltre che quella fondamentale di Sieyès)[141] su Constant è evidente: solo prevedendo legami, connessioni, interessi[142] comuni, dipendenza reciproca, sarà possibile unire e intrecciare i poteri.[143] E tuttavia questa macchina ha bisogno di un soggetto costituzionale che prevenga e sappia regolare i possibili conflitti. Il «pouvoir neutre et préservateur» di Constant individua il problema centrale del costituzionalismo repubblicano:[144] il monismo e i difetti intrinseci delle costituzioni di età rivoluzionaria che erano stati generatori di conflitti, abusi e illegalità. Tale potere viene configurato come neutro (rispetto al rapporto legislativo-esecutivo); è inoltre preservatore perché ha lo scopo di conservare, in caso di conflitto, la *machine* costituzionale, operando quindi come una sorta di valvola di sicurezza.[145] Constant costruisce tale potere repubblicano «terzo» e «imparziale» con «materiali» che – e non è affatto paradossale – sono desunti più dal «deposito» storico della monarchia costituzionale (ereditarietà, facoltà di scioglimento del legislativo, facoltà di destituzione del potere esecutivo) che dall'universo concettuale del discorso repubblicano, pur nell'ambito della legittimità legale della nazione. Constant ritiene che questo terzo potere, dovendo arbitrare la competizione e far rispettare le regole del gioco, sia il naturale custode degli interessi superiori dello Stato. Questa funzione in linea di principio "neutralizzata", apolitica, è nella sua essenza profondamente politica, e il potere neutro non sarà affatto una contraddizione in termini rispetto alle "azioni positive" del monarca.[146]

140 B. Constant, *Fragments d'un ouvrage abandonné sur la possibilité d'une constitution républicaine dans un grand pays*, a cura di H. Grange, Paris 1991, 361.

141 Cfr. N. King, E. Hofmann, *Les lettres de Benjamin Constant a Sieyès*, in *Annales Benjamin Constant*, 3, 1983. Non bisogna dimenticare d'altra parte il rapporto intellettuale col J. C. L. Sismondi delle *Recherches sur les constitutions des peuples libres*, edizione e introduzione di M. Minerbi, Genève, 1965 e dell'*Histoire des républiques italiennes du Moyen Age*, Zurich 1808.

142 Sui poteri costituzionali e sul concetto di interesse v. B. Constant, *Fragments*, cit., 375 ss. e M. Barberis, *Benjamin Constant*, cit., 179 ss.

143 Cfr. D. Rousseau, *La garantie de la constitution*, cit., 102 ss. Si vedano inoltre i lavori di H. Grange, *Les idées de Necker*, Paris 1974 e *Introduction* a B. Constant, *Fragments*, cit.

144 Sulla complessa dialettica repubblica / monarchia tanto in Sieyès che in Constant, v. P. Bastid, *Benjamin Constant et sa doctrine*, Paris 1966, t. II, 918.

145 Su tutto ciò, si rinvia alle importanti considerazioni di M. Barberis, *Benjamin Constant*, cit., 173 ss.

146 Questo profilo non ha trovato a mio avviso a tutt'oggi la sottolineatura che merita. Ne dà parzialmente conto P. Bastid, *Benjamin Constant*, cit., 625. Sul

La definizione ulteriore della teoria del potere neutro negli scritti successivi al 1814 è una logica conseguenza della riflessione già maturata in età repubblicana. Il ritorno alla forma monarchica consente a Constant di «riportare» il concetto di «pouvoir neutre et préservateur» all'interno della più favorevole «condition monarchique».[147] Le attribuzioni legali e "razionali" possono ora essere affidate al *pouvoir royal*. La descrizione è ben nota: il *pouvoir royal* è il potere neutro; il *pouvoir ministeriel* un potere attivo. Il monarca-orologiaio interviene «dall'esterno» quando il «mouvement général» si inceppa: «... quand ces ressorts dérangés se croisent, s'entre-choquent et s'entravent, il faut une force qui les remette à leur place».[148]

Se il 2 termidoro dell'anno III Sieyès aveva detto che il limite più grande del progetto esaminato era l'assenza di uno strumento di garanzia della costituzione, allo stesso modo Constant scriverà nel 1815 che «Le vice de presque toutes les constitutions a été de ne pas avoir crée un pouvoir neutre, mais d'avoir placé la somme totale d'autorité dont il doit être investi l'un des pouvoirs actifs».[149] Non è questa la sede per considerare la complessa architettura del potere neutro e preservatore nell'opera di Constant, tra repubblica e monarchia. Il mio discorso si limita al seguente profilo: il recupero, per altri fini, della logica "politico-giudiziaria" di Sieyès all'interno dell'ordine costituzionale. Mentre nel

punto v. *supra* in questo volume *Coppet et la percée de l'Etat libéral constitutionnel*, 222 ss.

147 «N'oublions donc jamais cette grande vérité, cette vérité qui établit l'unique supériorité de la monarchie, mais de la monarchie constitutionnelle seulement, sur le gouvernement républicain, dans lequel il a été impossible jusqu'ici de séparer le pouvoir exécutif du pouvoir suprême, et de résister à l'un sans ébranler l'autre ...» (B. Constant, *Observations sur le discours prononcé par S. E. le ministre de l'intérieur en faveur du projcvorret de loi sur la liberté de la presse* (1814), in B. Constant, *Œuvres*, cit., 1248–1249). Solo considerando l'intero percorso di formazione del concetto di potere neutro e preservatore è possibile cogliere il carattere strutturale della proposta di Constant, non limitata quindi, secondo l'interpretazione schmittiana, al prevalente bisogno borghese di uno spazio costituzionale "neutralizzato". Cfr. questa interpretazione in L. Diez Del Corral, *El liberalismo doctrinario*, cit., 113 ss.

148 B. Constant, *Principes de politique applicables à tous les gouvernements représentatifs et particulièrement à la constitution actuelle de la France* (1815), cit., 1079.

149 *Ibidem*, 1080–1081. Paolo Colombo ha notato come questa posizione di Constant sia anticipata da Daunou: v. *Governo e costituzione*, cit., 511. Constant, d'altra parte, nel 1815 non fa altro che riprendere i passaggi presenti nei *Fragments*: «Le vice de la plupart des constitutions a été de ne pas créer un pouvoir neutre, mais de placer la somme d'autorité dont il doit être investi, tantôt dans les mêmes mains que le pouvoir exécutif, tantôt dans les mêmes mains que le pouvoir législatif».

disegno di Sieyès è la logica giudiziaria a inglobare il fine di politica costituzionale, ovvero difendere (conservare ed emendare) la costituzione in quanto norma minacciata da atti incostituzionali, nel progetto di Constant è nel campo del politico e del discrezionale[150] che è chiamata ad operare la logica giudiziaria, allo scopo di difendere il corretto funzionamento del sistema (rapporto tra legislativo ed esecutivo).

Come il potere giudiziario separa i contendenti e si pronuncia sulle loro pretese, allo stesso modo – ma rispondendo a caratteri peculiarissimi – quando i poteri pubblici si dividono e sono pronti a danneggiarsi reciprocamente occorre «une autorité neutre qui fasse à leur égard ce que le pouvoir judiciaire fait à l'égard des individus. Le pouvoir préservateur est, pour ainsi dire, le pouvoir judiciaire des autres pouvoirs».[151] Questa celebre formula, tuttavia, non deve far dimenticare che c'è una differenza sostanziale. Mentre gli individui sono deboli di fronte al giudiziario, il potere preservatore si trova a dover fronteggiare poteri ben più forti e per questa ragione deve agire rapidamente infliggendo solo le "punizioni" che attengono alla sfera politica della responsabilità, con lo scioglimento dell'assemblea o la destituzione dell'esecutivo, o il più delle volte minacciando soltanto una di queste azioni.[152] Resta però l'obiezione eterna di Thibaudeau: *quis custodiet custodem?* Constant risponde – non so con quanta convinzione – a questa domanda dicendo che per il modo con il quale tale potere è costituito – si tratti di membri eletti a vita, muniti di ingenti mezzi economici e ineleggibili a ogni altra carica o del monarca ereditario «esterno» all'oggetto del comando,

150 In B. Constant, *Fragments*, cit., la nozione di *discrétionnaire* riveste una indubbia centralità. Non è che «... Constant non vede la soluzione intravvista dal Sieyes dei discorsi di Termidoro ...» (M. Barberis, *Divisione dei poteri e libertà da Montesquieu a Constant*, in *Materiali per una storia della cultura giuridica*, 1, 2001, 105), è piuttosto l'evoluzione del sistema costituzionale a convincere Constant della necessità di dare un senso diverso al problema.

151 B. Constant, *Fragments*, cit., 390–391.

152 Su questo profilo fondamentale, riemerso con urgenza in età termidoriana, cfr., tra i lavori più recenti, H. Grange, *Necker, Madame de Staël et la Constitution de l'an III*, in *Approches des Lumières. Mélanges Jean Fabre*, Paris 1974; dello stesso autore si veda anche *De l'influence de Necker sur les idées politiques de Benjamin Constant*, in *Annales Benjamin Constant*, 1982, 73–80; L. Jaume, *L'esprit de Coppet et l'organisation du pouvoir*, in J. Bart, J.J. Clère, C. Courvoisier, M. Verpeaux (edd.), *La constitution de l'an III ou l'ordre républicaine*, cit., 122–141; M. Morabito, *Necker et la question du «Chef de l'Etat»*, in *Coppet, creuset de l'esprit libéral*, cit., 41–54; L. Jaume, *Necker: examen critique de la Constitution de l'an III*, in J. Bart, J.J. Clère, C. Courvoisier, M. Verpeaux (edd.), *La constitution de l'an III*, cit., 167–182; H. Grange, *Mme de Staël et la Constitution de l'an III: avant et après*, *ibidem*, 183–199; L. Jaume, *Le concept de "responsabilité des ministres" chez Benjamin Constant*, in *Revue française de droit constitutionnel*, 42, 2000, 227–243.

posto «au dessus des agitations et des orages»[153] – e per le prerogative assegnatigli esso non ha interesse e non trae alcun vantaggio dal suo intervento "giudiziario".[154]

Sieyès o Constant? È evidente che una contrapposizione di questo tipo sarebbe artificiosa e riduttiva. Sieyès e Constant, mi pare invece di poter dire: nelle riflessioni dei due più grandi pubblicisti francesi a cavaliere dei due secoli si elaborano infatti, pur con esiti diversi, i fondamenti e si delineano le potenzialità e i pericoli della garanzia politica della costituzione. Sieyès e Constant, per semplificare qui la più complessa articolazione del discorso costituzionale, hanno lasciato tracce profonde ed hanno influenzato in vari modi le proposte successive.[155] A ben vedere, i due scrittori ci ricordano quanto sia difficile e, per certi aspetti, addirittura fuorviante ricercare una *summa divisio* tra natura giurisdizionale e politica della garanzia costituzionale.[156]

153 «Le dépositaire du pouvoir suprême, siégeant au haut de la hiérarchie politique, modérant les mouvemens de tous les pouvoirs, rétablissant l'harmonie entre eux, et du haut de sa sphère, au-dessus des agitations et des orages, dissipant ces orages et appaisant ces agitations» (B. Constant, *De l'état constitutionnel de la France*, dans *La Renommée*, n. 1, mardi, 15 juin 1819, dans *Recueil d'articles. Le Mercure, la Minerve et la Renommée*, tomo II, Introduzione, note e commenti di E. Harpaz, Genève 1972, 1232–1233).

154 Cfr. le ottime sintesi di D. Rousseau, *La garantie de la constitution*, cit., 104–105 e L. Jaume, *L'individu effacé*, cit., 185 ss.; Id., *Le concept de "responsabilité des ministres" chez Benjamin Constant*, cit.

155 Si pensi, per limitarci a qualche esempio, alla singolare e acuta riflessione del costituzionalista e poligrafo portoghese Pinheiro-Ferreira (S. Pinheiro-Ferreira, *Principes du droit public constitutionnel, administratif et des gens, ou Manuel du citoyen sous un gouvernement représentatif*, Paris 1834, t. I, 108, n. 182; 350–369, note 590–627; t. III, 800 ss. («Sans un pouvoir conservateur, il ne saurait y avoir indépendance, ni harmonie, ni équilibre entre les autres pouvoirs de l'état», *ibidem*, t. I, 350). Pinheiro si riferisce alla costituzione imperiale del Brasile del 1824 e a quella del Regno portoghese del 1826: si vedano le sue *Observaçoes sobre a Constituiçao do Imperio do Brazil, e sobre a Carta constitucional do Reino de Portugal*, Paris 1835, 2 ed., 44–45; al corso di Pellegrino Rossi (P. Rossi, *Cours de droit constitutionnel professé à la Faculté de droit de Paris …*, Paris 1866–1867, t. IV, *leçon XCII*) o alle notazioni di Prevost-Paradol (L.-A. Prevost-Paradol, *La France nouvelle*, cit., 145 ss.) sul potere conservatore e/o neutro in una monarchia costituzionale o alle osservazioni di Félix Berriat-Saint-Prix sul Senato come «pouvoir conservateur» e «cour de cassation politique» (*Théorie du droit constitutionnel français. Esprit de la constitution de 1848 précédé d'un essai sur le pouvoir constituant*, Paris 1851, 39 ss.).

156 Si vedano le osservazioni di F. Fernandez Segado, *El modelo francés de control politico de la constitucionalidad de las leyes. Su evolución*, in *Revista de la Facultad de derecho de la Universidad Complutense*, 75, 1989–1990, 303–334.

Alla fine, gli insuccessi dei Senati conservatori, della funzione "preservatrice" della monarchia costituzionale, del dualismo repubblicano hanno confermato i timori manifestati dai due nostri scrittori: ché la logica legislativo-centrica (in tutte le sue forme e diverse gradazioni) o l'autocrazia non intendono sottostare, al di là dei buoni propositi, né a "giurisdizioni" *extra* o *intra-constitutionem* né ad àrbitri né a guardiani,[157] ché, per riprendere l'allegoria richiamata da Thibaudeau, il mondo non poteva essere sorretto da un elefante che poggiasse su una tartaruga che, a sua volta, stesse sopra qualcos'altro e così all'infinito, rinviando sempre ad un grado superiore la soluzione del problema.[158] Non fa meraviglia che il tema della fallibilità della garanzia fosse così ben presente alla riflessione post-termidoriana di Constant: «[...] les abus du pouvoir préservateur ... peuvent être terribles; aucune garantie constitutionnelle ne peut être établie contre eux. On ne peut donner une garantie à la garantie elle-même».[159] Constant va oltre Sieyès e cerca di spostare l'aporia della logica politico-giurisdizionale dall'esterno (la giuria costituzionale di Sieyès) all'interno del gioco dei poteri, recuperando la tradizione dell'ordine repubblicano alla Thibaudeau ma rivestita – nel mutare delle condizioni e dopo il patente fallimento di quell'ordine "trasformato" dalla spada di Napoleone – con il manto d'ermellino della monarchia, arrivando a dare poi forma compiuta alle preoccupazioni del costituzionalismo liberale in tema di garanzia dei diritti e delle libertà. Per riprendere una formulazione già utilizzata, potremmo dire che proprio in Constant il liberalismo politico del limite e quello costituzionale della separazione dei poteri realizzano una serie di significative connessioni a testimonianza della complessità del liberalismo post-rivoluzionario.

Si tratta comunque di un confronto sui fondamenti costituzionali dell'ordine politico moderno capace, per alcuni suoi tratti, di individuare con severa lucidità

157 Cfr. M. Barberis, *Benjamin Constant*, cit., 185–187 e P. Pasquino, *Gardien de la Constitution ou justice constitutionnelle?*, cit.

158 «Ainsi chez un peuple des Indes, la croyance vulgaire est, dit-on, que le monde est porté par un éléphant, et cet éléphant par une tortue; mais quand on vient à demander sur quoi repose la tortue, adieu l'érudition. Cette image est parfaitement applicable à l'objet que nous traitons. La garantie de la République est dans la division des pouvoirs et dans une bonne organisation; la garantie des pouvoirs est dans le jury constitutionnaire; mais quand on demande où est la garantie du jury pour lui-même, et celle des pouvoirs contre ses usurpations, on ne sait plus que répondre.» (*Opinion de Thibaudeau*, cit., 1330). Un giurista della Terza Repubblica come Barthélemy potrà osservare che «toute organisation d'une sanction juridique, quelque parfaite qu'elle soit, aboutit comme à un couronnement inéluctable, à un organe qui n'en a pas d'autre au-dessus de lui» (*Notes parlementaires*, in *Revue de droit public*, XIV, 1907, 97).

159 B. Constant, *Fragments*, cit., 451. Il capitolo 15 del libro VIII si intitola «Des garanties contre les abus du pouvoir préservateur».

i termini di un dilemma che non può non lasciarci ancora oggi esitanti, tra vecchi e nuovi idoli,[160] tra i pallidi bagliori della sovranità della costituzione e della sovranità della forza.

160 Per alcune vive suggestioni rinvio soprattutto al dibattito francese. Qui mi limito solo a ricordare il numero 64, mars–avril del 1991 di *Le débat*, con interventi di M. Guénaire, L. Favoreu, D. Rousseau, M. Troper e in particolare di Stéphane Rials, *Entre artificialisme et idolâtrie. Sur l'hésitation du constitutionnalisme*, 163–181. Per ulteriori spunti si veda il numero 32 del 2000 di *Droits* e specialmente il saggio di E. Desmons, *Le normativisme est une scolastique (Brèves considérations sur l'avènement de la démocratie spéculaire présenté comme un progrès)*, 21–32.

Governo rappresentativo e principio parlamentare: le *Chartes* francesi del 1814 e 1830

1. Una società alla ricerca del proprio governo

Tra i temi ricorrenti della storia costituzionale francese è da annoverare quello dell'instabilità delle istituzioni politiche e dei mutevoli, provvisori, equilibri costituzionali, destinati, prima o poi, a venir meno. La questione appare strettamente connessa alla difficoltà estrema di "costituzionalizzare" la Rivoluzione; questa, per certi versi, può essere paragonata ad una potente dinamo capace di produrre e conservare energie tanto forti da abbisognare almeno un secolo per poter essere "imbrigliate" e ricevere così una durevole "direzione" (Furet 1990, 12; Jainchill, Moyn 2004, 138 ss.). Per riprendere la bella metafora che ha accompagnato i lavori di questo Convegno, la deriva, sia come strumento per governare la nave sia, una volta fuori uso, come situazione di difficoltà e di perdita della rotta, è un'immagine che calza perfettamente all'esperienza transalpina. La Rivoluzione disvela ai Francesi un futuro che essi stessi stentano a capire ed interpretare (Luzzatto 2004). Questa "energia" – se non ha certo impedito la nascita di uno straordinario laboratorio di forme, modi, tecniche di organizzazione del potere e di instaurazione dell'ordine politico (Redslob 1918, 186) – ha tuttavia forgiato quel complesso *discorso* strutturale sulla mutevolezza, sulle "patologie" e sull'instabilità costituzionale destinato ad incunearsi ben dentro il nostro più ravvicinato orizzonte temporale.

Non sorprende il fatto che tanti uomini politici e tanti intellettuali si siano interrogati, in maniera finanche ossessiva, sulle ragioni che avrebbero impedito alla Francia di raggiungere una condizione di stabilità e di equilibrio nell'ordine costituzionale. Gli argomenti addotti sono numerosi ed eterogenei. I legittimisti piangono nostalgicamente la fine dinastica dei Borboni, Tocqueville coglie la crisi morale dell'orleanismo e medita sulle illusioni della Seconda Repubblica (Cassina 2004), François Guizot scrive sopra le macerie della Monarchia di Luglio, avendo di fronte la "compiutezza" della *Glorious Revolution* (1849 e 1850). Per Ernest Renan molto si deve al fatto che in Francia la concezione filosofica della libertà ha prevalso sulla concezione storica: «C'est que la souveraineté du peuple ne fonde pas le gouvernement constitutionnel. L'État, ainsi établi à la française, est trop fort, loin de garantir toutes les libertés, il absorbe toutes les libertés; sa forme est la Convention ou le despotisme» (1872, 240). Prevost-Paradol, quasi alle soglie della Terza Repubblica, lo dirà con formula efficace: «[...] la Révolution française a fondé une société, elle cherche encore son gouvernement» (1868, 296). E questa ricerca non è mai stata tanto pressante e necessaria come dopo la Restaurazione.

C'è chi come Walter Bagehot ha chiamato in causa, seguendo una tradizione risalente, il "carattere francese" perché inadatto al governo costituzionale: gli insuccessi a catena gli fanno sorgere a metà dell'Ottocento il sospetto che «[...] un numero così grande di bancarotte suggerisca un po' d'inadeguatezza al commercio [...]» (1997, 94–95) e che l'eccesso di ingegno – di ingegneria costituzionale si direbbe oggi – sia poco adatto a fortificare i principi costituzionali e a radicarne le istituzioni.

Se il tema della "monarchia impossibile" come chiave di lettura della storia delle *Chartes* (1814–1830) e del «momento inglese» (Rosanvallon 1994, 179–180) segnala questioni profonde legate a caratteri e atteggiamenti di lungo periodo presenti nella cultura politica francese, non manca chi, come Odilon Barrot – nelle Memorie scritte durante il Secondo Impero – si rifiuta di considerare il regime parlamentare alla stregua di una irraggiungibile chimera:

> «Le gouvernement parlementaire n'est pas plus impossible en France que chez nos voisins, et les essais que nous en avons faits, bien loin de prouver que cette forme de gouvernement est une source inévitable de révolutions, prouvent, au contraire, qu'en elle, pourvu qu'elle soit loyalement pratiquée, est le seul moyen de concilier la stabilité du pouvoir avec les responsabilités et les agitations qu'entraîne tout régime représentatif: la vérité est que les deux gouvernements tombés en 1830 et 1848, non-seulement n'ont pas péri par les institutions parlementaires, mais qu'ils en ont vécu; l'un, seize, l'autre, dix-huit ans...» [1876, 276–277].

2. Il nome e la cosa

Se il governo rappresentativo sembra avere origini e vita tutt'altro che scontate in Francia, può apparire singolare che la tesi storiografica a lungo prevalente e, a ben vedere, ancora oggi capace di orientare analisi e ricerche, sia invece quella che individua nel periodo ricompreso tra il 1814 e il 1848 il momento di sviluppo e di "maturazione" del regime parlamentare. Il problema da discutere invero non riguarda tanto l'affermazione filosofica e costituzionale del principio parlamentare, quanto piuttosto l'idea secondo la quale prenderebbe forma, già a partire dai primi anni della Restaurazione, una modalità sufficientemente organica e coerente di governo parlamentare. Se per parlamentarismo, inteso come regime o governo liberale, intendiamo – secondo la classificazione tradizionale delle forme moderne di governo (parlamentare, presidenziale, collegiale / direttoriale) – quello nel quale il governo è ritenuto, in solido, politicamente e giuridicamente responsabile del suo programma davanti ad un parlamento eletto (in tutto o in parte) che gli affida, attraverso un vincolo maggioritario revocabile, il potere di "guidare" le Camere (e quindi la nazione in esse rappresentata), non sarà facile collocare dentro questo schema e *con questi termini* i fenomeni osservabili nel periodo esaminato.

L'uso rigido delle classificazioni e dei modelli intesi come figurini in grado di poter "vestire" qualsiasi corpo si porta con sé il rischio di appiattire e uniformare le culture storiche, le strutture mentali e antropologiche, in ultima istanza quell'indefinibile *esprit* che dà *forma e sostanza* a un determinato sistema politico-costituzionale (v. *supra* in questo vol. *La costituzione belga del 1831*, 80–82; Manca 2000). L'impiego di una categoria come governo parlamentare è indispensabile come riferimento concettuale e definitorio, strumento critico-interpretativo, modalità di delimitazione di un campo semantico. Tuttavia considerare un modello solo come dato normativo che definisce e prescrive una regola (regolarità) in senso gerarchico, originaria o derivata, da sovrapporre all'esperienza storico-concreta, appare un percorso non privo di pericoli (cfr. Giannini 1950, XXII, con i rilievi di Elia 1970, 634 ss.). D'altra parte, sono spesso i protagonisti e gli osservatori di un determinato periodo a ricercare, invocare, descrivere, interpretare, "recepire" un insieme di regole, di principi e di valori finendo per assegnare ad essi, inevitabilmente, un significato precettivo. La storia costituzionale continentale, tra la fine del XVIII e tutto il XIX secolo, è ricca di "momenti inglesi". Nella Francia della Restaurazione il "modello inglese" è imperante, onnipresente, è il mito per eccellenza (sia in positivo che in negativo) ma – come è noto – nel complicato gioco di specchi, fatto di osservazioni e di influenze, che si svolge a partire dal Settecento, lo sguardo Oltre Manica è non di rado fonte di fraintendimenti e di interpretazioni abusive (Schiera 1998). La costituzione britannica "immaginaria" è al centro della scena e può essere richiamata nella sua vaghezza (Rosanvallon 1994, 62) offrendo un quadro rassicurante: quintessenza della costituzione storica, senza però dimenticarne gli accorti interventi razionalizzatori, ha assicurato prosperità alla nazione inglese e stabilità alla sua forma di governo capace di conciliare ordine e libertà. Se il modello inglese è una sorta di arsenale dal quale attingere argomenti e motivi di riflessione per introdurli nel dibattito e nella lotta politica in Francia (da Constant a Vitrolles, da Chateaubriand a Guizot ...), preponderanti sono le visioni immaginarie che spesso fanno vedere delle istituzioni inglesi solo aspetti esteriori. L'anglofobo Fievée è impietoso: «Noi crediamo di poter imitare la costituzione inglese; ma la conosciamo? Noi non conosciamo di questa costituzione che ciò che si vede; è come giudicare di primo acchito un edificio per la sola parte che si innalza dalle fondazioni» (1815–1819, prima parte, Lettera I^a^, 3). Ancora una volta si ripropone il dualismo, tanto importante per capire il problema delle forme di governo tra Settecento e Ottocento, ricordato da John Stuart Mill. Da un lato coloro che «valutano una costituzione (con le debite differenze al riguardo dal punto di vista dell'importanza) con lo stesso occhio con cui si soffermerebbero a prendere in esame una macchina a vapore o una trebbiatrice»; dall'altro quelli «che la considerano invece come un prodotto spontaneo e vedono nella scienza politica una filiazione per così dire della storia naturale» (1946, 10).

La complessità di un fenomeno in sé controverso non può di conseguenza essere affrontata con un approccio teso a "ipostatizzare" categorie e modelli che acquistano pieno valore nella dimensione storica. Costantino Mortati ha còlto efficacemente il problema: «[...] conviene accingersi ad analizzare il problema delle forme di governo nelle concrete soluzioni che ne ha dato l'evoluzione storica: è questo il solo modo di evitare un'analisi meramente terminologica e nominalistica, che può permettere forse schematizzazioni logicamente impeccabili ma prive di una effettiva rispondenza con la concreta realtà del diritto» (1962, 82–83). L'anacronismo è, viceversa, un pericolo sempre in agguato. Le classificazioni dei regimi politici devono essere contestualizzate sia in chiave storica che funzionale (Eisenmann 1968; Troper 1989; Lauvaux 2000): così, quello che chiamiamo regime presidenziale non è un'"invenzione" definitiva del costituzionalismo americano della seconda metà del XVIII bensì il prodotto di una lunga e complessa evoluzione storica; sappiamo, parimenti, quanto il "governo di gabinetto" nell'esperienza britannica risponda a principi e logiche che si affermano e si stabilizzano con una certa regolarità solo nel corso di un altrettanto lungo processo storico (Baranger 1999; Rotelli 2002). Gli esempi potrebbero continuare e il discorso vale appieno per l'esperienza francese.

Non bisogna dimenticare il fatto che l'odierna classificazione dei regimi "puri", incentrata sul dualismo tra regime parlamentare e presidenziale, si è andata consolidando sul finire dell'Ottocento, a partire dalle riflessioni di Bagehot. È quella una distinzione che ha origini e ragioni storicamente determinate: risulta allora fuorviante applicarla *tout court* alla realtà costituzionale tra la fine del '700 e almeno la prima metà dell'800 quando invece la classificazione dei regimi costituzionali risponde a linguaggi e categorie diversi, ovvero all'antitesi tra il sistema di bilanciamento / ponderazione dei poteri e il principio di unità legislativa o di specializzazione (Lahmer 2001, 383 ss.), nel solco di un dibattito destinato a durare a lungo anche in prosieguo di tempo (Bonini 1999, 48 ss.).

La formula governo parlamentare è poco utilizzata (e ancora meno quella di regime parlamentare) durante la Restaurazione e quando vi si fa ricorso è piuttosto come sinonimo o specificazione generica di governo rappresentativo, cioè di un tipo di regime liberal-costituzionale informato ad una pur ridotta distribuzione delle funzioni e a un certo grado di equilibrio interorganico dei poteri (tra legislativo ed esecutivo). Spesso l'uso di governo parlamentare – in termini di elaborazione teorica e di pratica concretizzazione – viene enfatizzato nei grandi affreschi elaborati in età successiva, come nel caso della *Histoire du gouvernement parlementaire* di Prosper Duvergier de Hauranne, e diventa di uso comune più ci si addentra nell'età della Terza repubblica. È forse da notare, invece, che lo stesso Duvergier, protagonista della scena politica francese durante l'età orleanista, utilizza il termine *gouvernement représentatif* (1838) o parla, in termini prescrittivi, di *réforme parlementaire* (1847).

Come si diceva, la formula costantemente richiamata è quella di governo rappresentativo (o, per altri aspetti, di monarchia rappresentativa), utilizzata sia dagli autori che difendono la prerogativa regia (come governo del re) sia da coloro che vorrebbero una più marcata influenza "parlamentare". Ma sono di uso comune espressioni ancora più vaghe, come *gouvernement de la Charte* o *selon la Charte*, governo o regime costituzionale, governo ministeriale ecc.

In tutti questi casi il rapporto tra la *parola* e la *cosa* è nient'affatto univoco, e il parlamentarismo – diversamente da quanto sostenuto da Mirkine-Guetzevitch – non appare una conseguenza naturale, logica e quasi automatica dell'applicazione sincera del sistema rappresentativo (1954, 63). Nel caso francese (ma il discorso si potrebbe allargare ad altre esperienze europee) il termine dal quale muovere ci sembra obbligato: è appunto il regime rappresentativo, in quanto formula usata tra il 1814 e il 1848 dalla maggior parte degli autori (per esempio Constant, Chateaubriand, Guizot ecc.). Quello che qui definisco il *principio parlamentare* è piuttosto il *problema*, il *discorso* teorico-pratico affermato, discusso, contrastato; è, in ultimo, l'insieme delle forze e degli orientamenti che mirano a dare una *specificazione* e un determinato indirizzo al governo rappresentativo.

3. Il *prix* Rossi e le radici di un canone storiografico

Alain Laquièze – in un importante e recente studio (2002) – ha ben ricostruito i termini e l'esito del *concours* Rossi del 1903. Tale premio era stato istituito per volontà della vedova di Pellegrino Rossi la quale aveva lasciato un cospicuo legato alla Facoltà giuridica di Parigi. Come è noto, l'esule italiano ottenne nel 1834, con l'aiuto di François Guizot e non senza contestazioni, la cattedra di diritto costituzionale, diventando così il primo studioso ad insegnare questa nuova disciplina in Francia (Lacchè, *Tra politica e diritto*, 2001; Id., 2002, 164–173). Il tema del concorso era il seguente: «Le régime parlementaire en France sous Louis XVIII et Charles X – Rechercher comment ont été introduits et appliqués à cette époque les principes et les usages du gouvernement de cabinet». La commissione esaminatrice conferì il premio *ex aequo* a due candidati, Joseph Barthélemy – destinato a diventare uno degli studiosi più rappresentativi e influenti della Terza Repubblica (Beaud 2000) – e Louis Michon. Il tema e l'esito del concorso, come dimostra Laquièze, si sono rivelati molto importanti sia per il dibattito suscitato sia per la notevole influenza esercitata sull'insieme degli studi costituzionalistici, ovvero per diffondere ed affermare presso il mondo accademico francese (e non solo) l'idea di una repentina e sostanziale affermazione del regime parlamentare in Francia all'inizio della Restaurazione. Del resto, il titolo del concorso, per come è concepito, appare in sintonia con gli sviluppi e con le dinamiche politico-costituzionali della Terza Repubblica, e non lascia grandi margini di dubbio: il regime parlamentare viene asseverato come una realtà durante il regno dei Borboni e si tratta perciò di analizzarne i modi di realizzazione, nel solco di una convinzione diffusa presso i maggiori pubblicisti dell'epoca, a cominciare da Adhémar Esmein, e volta a ritrovare il senso di una continuità nello sviluppo francese del regime parlamentare, non senza qualche sguardo "nostalgico" verso l'istituzione monarchica (orleanista).

Gli studi premiati, quello di Louis Michon e soprattutto il lavoro di Joseph Barthélemy, pubblicati tra il 1904 e il 1905, erano destinati a incidere sul modo stesso di interpretare il periodo delle «origini del regime parlamentare», codificando, pur con risultati di diverso spessore scientifico, un *canone* storiografico di lunga durata (Laquièze 2002, 19 ss., per l'analisi degli orientamenti). Non è un caso che un'altra tesi coeva dedicata allo stesso tema, quella di Joseph Bonnefon (1905), nella quale si discute l'impostazione di Barthélemy e si evidenziano invece i limiti del parlamentarismo e del cd. governo di gabinetto nel regime della Carta del 1814, abbia ricevuto un'attenzione assai minore. Mettendo a confronto le tesi di fondo di Barthélemy e di Bonnefon si vede come, pur in presenza di alcuni tratti comuni, è differente il presupposto dei due lavori: ciò che per il primo è un dato di partenza (l'esistenza del regime parlamentare, definito in maniera incerta) (Laquièze 2002, 15), per il secondo è oggetto di analisi critica, a cominciare dal principio di responsabilità politica del ministero. È la sostanziale linearità di sviluppo a rappresentare la chiave di lettura prevalente: la fase 1814–1830 vista come «periodo di formazione» e quella del 1830–1848 come «periodo di applicazione e di sviluppo del regime parlamentare» (per es. Capitant 1933, 38 ss.). É altrettanto interessante osservare come proprio nella fase descritta si cominci ad utilizzare in maniera sempre più sistematica il termine «regime parlamentare», particolarmente caro al vocabolario francese, per richiamare la più complessiva esperienza del "parlamentarismo alla francese" (Giannini 1950, II).

Gli orientamenti storiografici più recenti seguono in realtà un approccio più problematico. La storia costituzionale comparata, contribuendo ad allargare gli orizzonti segnati dalle storie nazionali, conferma le differenze e le singole peculiarità ma permette anche di far convergere le analisi sul tema complesso del rapporto tra costituzionalizzazione e parlamentarizzazione, rapporto nel quale i due processi non sono necessariamente lineari, coincidenti e paralleli, tanto più se si assume come campo di osservazione le esperienze europee monarchico-costituzionali (per es. Manca 2001; Manca, Lacchè 2003; Kirsch 1999; Hummel 2002). Nel caso francese il costituzionalismo del 1814–1848 oscilla tra il dato originario e fondativo della cd. monarchia limitata (o costituzionale pura) che assegna al sovrano il monopolio del «pouvoir d'Etat» e un regime di bilanciamento dei poteri a esecutivo monarchico, dualistico, ma con forti profili di incompiutezza (Rials 1987; Laquièze 2002; Lacchè 2002). La storia del principio parlamentare in Francia deve fare i conti, da un lato con la fluidità della categoria del governo rappresentativo – con una gamma di posizioni e di azioni costituzionali che lascia aperte diverse strade –, dall'altro con l'insieme delle dinamiche politiche e socio-economiche caratterizzanti la prima metà del XIX secolo. Se nel periodo esaminato possiamo vedere all'opera, senza dubbio, tecniche e meccanismi atti a fondare una monarchia parlamentare, è altrettanto vero che il regime politico non è una conquista definitiva e soprattutto inevitabile.

4. La «monarchia costituzionale» e il problema del governo parlamentare (1814–1848)

Le Carte francesi del 1814 e del 1830 vengono rubricate sotto la generica nozione di "monarchia costituzionale". Il problema definitorio, tuttavia, va ben oltre questa prima approssimazione e rappresenta per il caso francese un significativo *problema costituzionale*. Quella che è stata chiamata la «monarchia impossibile» non riesce a conquistare un preciso statuto giuridico e sconta una "vaghezza" di impianto che deriva dalla difficoltà di concepire il rapporto tra monarchia e costituzione all'interno della teoria dei regimi politici. La monarchia, per la sua natura storica, simbolica, politica, dovrebbe essere l'architrave, il motore e il momento di sintesi dell'ordine costituzionale: e tuttavia, malgrado gli sforzi compiuti, fallisce in Francia il suo appuntamento moderno con la costituzione.

Dopo i tentativi di costituzionalizzazione del 1789–1791, la monarchia riappare nel 1814 nella forma della "monarchia limitata", ovvero di un regime nel quale il sovrano che si autolimita conserva una posizione di supremazia rispetto ai poteri che derivano le loro attribuzioni dalla Carta *octroyée*. «Il governo stabilito dalla Carta è, tra tutti i governi a *istituzioni rappresentative*, il solo nel quale il potere monarchico sia *principio* dell'organizzazione sociale e *fonte* della vita politica» (His 1829, 4–5). Nel 1824 Royer-Collard osserva come non sia sufficiente definire il governo «una monarchia mista, chiamata Governo rappresentativo, nel quale la Camera elettiva concorre con il monarca e una Camera ereditaria alla formazione della legge e alla direzione degli affari pubblici [...]». È il «potere regolatore» quello che imprime al governo il carattere dominante. Nel caso francese è il re della Carta che conserva «un eclatante primato tra i poteri che lo affiancano. Solo rappresenta l'unità morale della società; solo agisce, solo comanda, solo è l'autore della legge la cui iniziativa gli è riservata in via esclusiva. Quest'ultima circostanza esprime il fatto che gli altri poteri non sono per lui che dei limiti; benché siano dei limiti viventi e in grado di attivarsi ...» (de Barante 1863, I, 216–217) [Tutte le traduzioni in italiano sono dell'autore. N. d. R.]. Royer-Collard, sin dai primi passi della monarchia restaurata – assieme ai dottrinari della sua generazione, de Serre e Jordan – aveva condiviso le preoccupazioni di Necker e dei *monarchiens* in ordine al necessario rafforzamento del potere esecutivo.

I temi dell'equilibrio, della moderazione e del compromesso sono senza dubbio fortemente collegati al disegno costituzionale della monarchia. Si concorda nel dire che tale forma è di difficile realizzazione, basata com'è su congegni delicati e complessi (alla stessa stregua della cultura politica "complessa" del liberalismo) che devono essere posti in movimento con sagacia ed una spiccata capacità di visione politica. Il figurino del governo misto accompagna lo sviluppo della monarchia costituzionale ma esso è richiamato per lo più in modo stereotipato, per la referenza nobile d'Oltre Manica, o piuttosto perché d'uso comune, indicando una più o meno generica forma di collaborazione dei poteri «[...] con la partecipazione degli elementi aristocratico e popolare agli atti più importanti ...» (Serrigny 1846, I, 100). Ma il riferimento al carattere misto del governo – che sarà richiamato durante la Monarchia di Luglio come forma di "compromesso" tra diversi princìpi – non è sufficiente di per sé a tradurre gli ideali dell'equilibrio e della moderazione in una forma autonoma e compiuta di regime politico.

La storia costituzionale francese mostra uno sviluppo della forma monarchica che dalla "monarchia limitata" della *Charte* del 1814 – pur in presenza di un difficile ed esitante processo di "parlamentarizzazione" – perviene ad un atto di re-distribuzione dei poteri nel 1830, atto che conserva al re il potere esecutivo (con il depotenziamento del potere regolamentare rispetto alla primazia della legge) ma in una logica di riequilibrio complessivo a vantaggio della Camera eletta. Lungo questo percorso qui appena abbozzato – cui non è estraneo il mutamento dei paradigmi della legittimità politica – resta centrale il problema della natura costituzionale del potere monarchico. La celebre e complessa teoria del potere neutro (cfr. *supra* in questo volume *Coppet et la percée de l'État libéral constitutionnel* 219 ss.) – come è noto – viene descritta in molti luoghi dell'opera di Benjamin Constant e risponde ad una stessa esigenza che si presenta in forme e condizioni diverse tra l'età direttoriale e la restaurazione monarchica. Non bisogna dimenticare che le formule più coerenti sono da un lato quella, d'origine repubblicana, di «potere neutro e preservatore» e dall'altro la formula, utilizzata al momento della Restaurazione, di «potere neutro e intermediario». Il sovrano «preservatore» è l'organo dell'unità nazionale e della continuità dello Stato: forte della sua «maestà» e «imparzialità» incarna il «potere pubblico», è l'«essere a parte, superiore alle differenze di opinioni», il guardiano che garantisce l'equilibrio in caso di eccezione, quando la collaborazione tra i poteri è minacciata. Ma il potere «intermediario» investe il monarca anche del compito, storicamente arduo, di "pacificare" – attraverso la sua neutralità – un paese profondamente diviso tra visioni diverse del futuro (oltre che del passato), sovrintendendo alla formazione e allo sviluppo di un sistema costituzionale in grado di "disciplinare" la lotta politica (nel suo legame con l'opinione), di garantire un governo coeso e responsabile politicamente (nel senso allora in uso), permettendo forme di dissenso e di pluralismo. Il potere preservatore, fondando un governo che risponda dei suoi atti alla nazione, contribuisce a tenere in equilibrio ordine e libertà, garantendo, in ultima istanza, il principio e il fine di un sistema costituzionale ben inteso: la sfera di sicurezza dei cittadini.

Ridimensionata solo in parte la concezione della monarchia limitata, Constant pensa che il potere neutro non possa essere racchiuso in Francia, al momento della Restaurazione (quando il sistema costituzionale è ancora tutto da costruire), nella sola sfera dell'*auctoritas*. Il monarca deve poter, se necessario, esercitare tutte le sue *potestates*. Il potere regio è una risorsa in termini di neutralità, ma, all'occasione, deve avere la forza legale per essere realmente «preservatore» e «intermediario». Il re potere neutro deve avere la capacità e la volontà – e qui sta il problema – di tenere in equilibrio l'opinione e il "potere ministeriale", le Camere e la funzione di governo, individuando il punto variabile di compromesso. Il re – si potrebbe forse dire – ha il difficile compito di fissare il mutevole punto di equilibrio tra la costituzione formale e la costituzione materiale.

I re della Carta del 1814 non hanno tuttavia assunto (se non in qualche momento Luigi XVIII) la categoria del «potere neutro» come guida per il loro operato. Si trattava di una *interpretazione* della monarchia costituzionale che presupponeva – come nel caso inglese – lo sviluppo di una più solida cultura politica e che aveva quindi bisogno di tempo per diventare prassi di governo. Il concetto metteva in luce – come nessun altro – la grande complessità di una *macchina* costituzionale che aveva bisogno per ben funzionare di un capo dello Stato ambivalente: al di sopra delle lotte politiche contingenti, ma severo e attento «regolatore» del sistema costituzionale. Il rischio che la nozione constantiana venisse strumentalizzata (come infatti avvenne tra il 1815 e il 1816) era elevato finendo per semplificare e banalizzare una ricostruzione ingegnosa e in grado di dare un «senso» alla monarchia costituzionale (Antonetti 1998, 148–149).

Non è un caso che tale concetto torni alla ribalta – anche se con elementi nuovi – alla vigilia della rivoluzione e durante la Monarchia di Luglio. Di solito la formula «Il re regna ma non governa» viene vista come una sintesi del pensiero di Thiers. Non bisogna però dimenticare il contesto e l'articolazione della sua elaborazione che precede le giornate di Luglio. Thiers segue ormai la logica della «monarchia rappresentativa» (*Le National*, 8 gennaio 1830, p. 1, col. 3) fondata sul nesso di reciprocità e di «contrappeso» tra due *veti*: il diritto del re di sciogliere la Camera, il diritto della Camera di chiedere le dimissioni del ministero. Thiers – polemizzando con gli *ultras* – ritiene la prerogativa regia un effetto della Carta intesa come atto «contrattuale». Solo dal febbraio 1830 il direttore del «Le National» fissa i termini della teoria secondo cui il «re regna ma non governa». La filiazione constantiana (Thiers 1831, 6–7) è evidente, e tuttavia la diversità del contesto e la natura particolare della lotta politica portano Thiers a utilizzare la teoria del «potere neutro» all'interno di una più pronunciata dinamica parlamentare prefigurando una più chiara scissione del potere esecutivo tra potere di riserva del sovrano e «potere attivo» del ministro e, di conseguenza, il diritto della Camera-maggioranza a partecipare, con il suo potere di *veto*, alla scelta dei ministri. Il potere esecutivo viene esercitato dal ministro: «[...] in una parola, egli governa, e poiché ha la fiducia delle camere, non esistendo altrimenti, non fa che le cose che esse approvano ... Così, il re regna, i ministri governano, le camere giudicano» (*Le National*, 4 febbraio 1830, p. 2, col. 1).

La Carta orleanista istituisce su basi di eguaglianza i due fondamentali poteri dello Stato ma senza riuscire a sciogliere né il nodo teorico della monarchia costituzionale né il problema del regime parlamentare. Paradossalmente, mentre la monarchia del 1814 è coerente rispetto al testo della *Charte*, il documento del 1830 – per l'ambiguità insita nelle origini del nuovo regime "bastardo", monarchico ma con inserzioni "repubblicane" – è reticente su troppe questioni a cominciare da quella fondamentale dello statuto giuridico del governo e della sua responsabilità. La Carta del 1830 che avrebbe dovuto in teoria risolvere le due questioni più controverse della Restaurazione non recepisce *nel testo*, se non in maniera molto parziale, il dibattito che sul finire degli anni Venti e alla vigilia della Rivoluzione aveva posto con decisione il problema del ruolo del monarca, il rapporto di "unione e collaborazione" tra il ministero e la maggioranza parlamentare, i meccanismi costituzionali di risoluzione del conflitto tra gli organi. I costituenti del 1830 non sono riusciti a dare alle istituzioni una chiara direzione di marcia, preferendo rinviare alla prassi e al tessuto convenzionale e, in ultima istanza, alla lotta politica l'esito della vicenda costituzionale. Il 1830, malgrado il riconoscimento del processo di parlamentarizzazione della monarchia, non può risolvere i problemi e fare tesoro del dibattito della Restaurazione. Questo limite – che molto inciderà sulle mancate riforme degli anni Quaranta –

si riverbera sul pieno e definitivo sviluppo del regime parlamentare. La Carta del 1830 aveva affrontato il problema del riequilibrio dei poteri, ma la teoria della "continuità" sostanziale rispetto al testo del 1814 finì per far passare in secondo piano l'adeguamento costituzionale dell'istituto del governo e della responsabilità dei ministri e dei funzionari. In epoca orleanista ci si poteva giovare – a differenza che nel 1814 – dell'esperienza maturata lungo tutta la Restaurazione. L'art. 69 della Carta non fu valorizzato (cfr. le critiche di Pinheiro-Ferreira 1833, 15 e 84–85) per sviluppare ulteriormente le condizioni politiche del regime parlamentare (sistema elettorale, riforma parlamentare ecc.). La Monarchia di Luglio restò, si potrebbe dire, in mezzo al guado: senza poter ovviamente tornare indietro ma incapace di raggiungere la sponda di un equilibrato ed efficiente regime parlamentare.

Sul finire degli anni Trenta torna a farsi sentire la questione che aveva accompagnato la dinamica costituzionale della Restaurazione: in caso di contrasti tra i poteri, chi doveva avere l'ultima parola? La Camera eletta o il re? Il tema della sovranità si intrecciava strettamente col problema della forma monarchica e del regime politico. La soluzione suggerita tra il 1814 e il 1830 era, per gli *ultras*, che fosse il re ad avere l'ultima parola *selon la lettre de la Charte*; per i liberali invece l'ultima parola del re doveva comunque tenere presente il *concorso* dell'opinione rappresentata dalla Camera *selon l'esprit de la Charte*. Questa seconda tesi alla fine prevalse e divenne *senso comune* nel 1830. Tuttavia, la domanda conserva intatto il suo significato anche rispetto all'età orleanista. La vicenda politico-costituzionale del 1838–1839 offre importanti spunti di riflessione. Nel dicembre 1838 si forma contro il secondo gabinetto Molé una coalizione (guidata da Thiers, Guizot, de Broglie, Odilon Barrot) che accusa il ministro di essere il "prestanome" di Luigi-Filippo e di governare indipendentemente dal "concorso" parlamentare. L'*Adresse* si rivela ancora una volta lo strumento per fissare le posizioni dei soggetti politici e del Ministero. In questo caso la commissione che redige l'indirizzo di risposta al discorso del trono è formata in prevalenza da uomini della coalizione ed è ispirata da Thiers. Il dibattito del gennaio 1839 è l'occasione per una polemica aspra contro Molé che si difende con grande energia, riuscendo a parare i colpi più insidiosi e a far emendare il testo dei paragrafi dell'*Adresse* nel senso meno sfavorevole per il Ministero. Molé riuscì a prevalere in Parlamento ma le successive elezioni del marzo 1839 diedero la maggioranza agli uomini della coalizione (Deslandres 1932, 180 ss.) mettendo fine al ministero del 15 aprile 1837. Tale vicenda suscitò un vivace dibattito sulle prerogative costituzionali, sulla forma della monarchia costituzionale e sulla natura del regime politico.

5. Prosper Duvergier de Hauranne: realtà e apparenza del governo rappresentativo-parlamentare

Prosper Duvergier de Hauranne – che nel 1834 aveva abbandonato la sponda della "resistenza" per poi diventare nel 1838 uno dei promotori della *coalition* – è da annoverare tra i più lucidi interpreti dell'evoluzione giuridico-costituzionale della monarchia orleanista. I suoi articoli del 1838 si inseriscono nel vivo della polemica ma possiedono anche una valenza teorica più generale. Il quadro di riferimento non può che essere il sistema istituzionale che discende dalla *Charte* del 1830 con al centro il principio della necessaria collaborazione / "unione" dei poteri. Tale convinzione, che è comune anche ai sostenitori della prerogativa regia, risente della tradizionale e generica teoria del governo misto, ma cerca anche di enucleare una vera e propria dottrina del governo rappresentativo. Se dunque tale sforzo comune esiste, è anche vero però che nel passaggio dalla teoria della collaborazione a quella della risoluzione del conflitto istituzionale emergono i due campi di interpretazione del «regime parlamentare», l'uno ovviamente incentrato sulla prevalenza del "principio parlamentare", l'altro sulla riattualizzazione del "principio monarchico". Un regime come quello rappresentativo, basato sulla necessaria collaborazione dei poteri, può tollerare conflitti solo su questioni di grande rilevanza politico-costituzionale e deve poterli risolvere in breve tempo. La domanda della Restaurazione è in parte modificata ma nell'essenziale resta: chi deve avere l'"ultima parola" in caso di conflitto? Duvergier contesta la teoria "consultativa" – creduta morta dopo il 1830 – che assegna al re l'onnipotenza e alle camere un semplice diritto di controllo e di consiglio (1838, 24). Dovrà pertanto essere la Camera dei deputati a sciogliere il conflitto, essendo questa più *rappresentativa* delle due altre componenti, ovvero il re e la Camera dei pari. Viceversa, autori come His, Fonfrède o Pepin – più o meno «ispirati» dallo stesso Luigi Filippo – assegnano la posizione risolutiva al monarca secondo la formula del "governo del re". Qui emerge ancora una volta il problema del *testo* della Carta. Non averlo modificato nel 1830 – almeno negli articoli relativi al rapporto tra il sovrano e il governo – dava adito a interpretazioni di tipo letterale: i ministri erano un'emanazione del potere regio e non governavano che sotto la sua direzione.

Duvergier invece prefigura un governo parlamentare nel quale il ministero sia il legame vivente tra i poteri. «Per dirlo in una parola, il ministero rappresenta il re nell'ambito delle camere, le camere nel gabinetto del re» (*Ibidem*, 15). E la scelta dei ministri sarà dunque il risultato del "concorso" delle Camere con il re. Non bisogna però perdere di vista una costante del regno orleanista che ha giocato un ruolo primario nella configurazione del regime politico. Il «re regna ma non governa» di Thiers deve fare i conti con le condizioni che accompagnano la fondazione e lo sviluppo del nuovo ordine costituzionale. Quando Cherbuliez scrive che «ieri, questo principe era cittadino, ragionava come un cittadino; domani, sarà re e penserà come un re», mette in luce un profilo importante perché distingue il fondamento "elettivo" e popolare della Monarchia di Luglio dal problema dell'esercizio delle prerogative inscritte nella Carta e nell'eredità simbolica e consuetudinaria che resta appannaggio della monarchia continentale.

Il "personalismo", se riferito a Luigi Filippo, individua almeno due aspetti, l'uno "biografico", legato alla personalità del duca d'Orléans, l'altro istituzionale connesso all'assetto che la Carta del 1830 perpetua nei suoi elementi essenziali. L'immagine satirica del re-pera non deve far pensare ad un monarca senza qualità; al contrario, Luigi Filippo per esperienza, capacità, gusto della politica, un certo cinismo, è portato ad intervenire direttamente nell'arena politica. Basta passare in rassegna le prassi invalse nella formazione, nel funzionamento e nella crisi dei Ministeri per rendersi conto del ruolo tutt'altro che defilato del sovrano. Ci possono essere momenti e condizioni più favorevoli ad affermare un principio di potere esecutivo duale, ma Luigi Filippo è quasi sempre impegnato a contrastare personalità che non gli vanno a genio (si pensi a de Broglie o a Thiers) facendo leva su presidenze fittizie e su politici di assoluta fedeltà (de Montalivet, Molé ecc.) (Pouthas 1954). Probabilmente agli aspetti caratteriali bisogna affiancare il forte investimento dinastico: Luigi Filippo sa di essere il fondatore di un regime e il grave, irrisolto problema della legittimità – nonché la costante minaccia dell'opposizione antidinastica – lo spingono ad andare nella direzione opposta a quella indicata dalla teoria della irresponsabilità del monarca. D'altra parte, l'abolizione dell'ereditarietà della paria – come avevano osservato in molti – favoriva di fatto il rafforzamento del potere personale di Luigi Filippo. Non è un caso se presto si torna a rileggere la Carta, pur modificata, dal punto di vista del "principio monarchico". Così l'ottuagenario barone Roederer nel 1835 nega l'esistenza di un'autonoma e "legale" entità esecutiva distinta dal «governo del re». Mentre tutto ciò che riguarda il consiglio dei ministri è puramente «fattuale», solo il re è a ben vedere «di diritto» presidente del gabinetto. L'obiettivo di Luigi Filippo deve essere quello di assicurare stabilità alla monarchia costituzionale superando gli opposti estremismi del carlismo e della democrazia. «Nessun atto della sua autorità può essere indifferente; tutto ciò che non giova alla corona profitta ad uno dei due partiti opposti, spesso ad entrambi» (1835, 33). Roederer invoca un monarca che, pur dovendo conservare una costituzione minacciata, non può far leva, come in Gran Bretagna, su un sistema politico condiviso. Se la cittadella costituzionale è "assediata", il re deve guidare la controffensiva. Regnare significa, per Roederer, fare nello Stato ciò che nessun altro può fare con pari successo: «aggiungere personalmente all'autorità delle leggi le influenze morali» (*Ibidem*, 39).

È evidente il riferimento alla formula del "regnare" che sembra poter discriminare il campo del parlamentarismo da quello della monarchia costituzionale. In realtà, i contorni sono molto più sfumati di quanto si possa pensare. Anche il ricordato dibattito del 1839 sul governo personale del re e sui ministri-cortigiani non riesce a definire in modo sufficientemente univoco i termini del problema. È vero che Duvergier de Hauranne rivendica il ruolo della maggioranza parlamentare in un ben inteso sistema di governo rappresentativo. Quando la maggioranza si pronuncia contro l'insieme degli atti e lo spirito generale del governo, questo deve ritirarsi (1838, 12). Tuttavia, non è casuale il fatto che Duvergier invochi, nell'esatto suo significato, la teoria del «potere neutro» di ascendenza constantiana. Il monarca gode non solo di attributi simbolici e cerimoniali: deve poter disporre anche delle sue fondamentali prerogative. In tal senso Duvergier non nega al sovrano un diritto di *influenza* sulla direzione politica, ma essa deve esercitarsi più sull'insieme che sui dettagli – ovvero sul piano delle grandi scelte – e i ministri dopo aver rispettosamente ascoltato le obiezioni del re mantengono libertà di azione sino al giorno della loro uscita dal governo (1841, p. XCIV). Di fronte ad un monarca troppo «interventista» de Hauranne ne invocherà uno più «discreto»: «[...] è cosa buona e necessaria che la sua opinione personale appaia il meno possibile, e non lo faccia scendere nell'arena dei partiti» (*Ibidem*). Questo però non significa affermare – come Guizot vorrebbe far credere – che il re «non può far niente» perché, secondo la Carta, il monarca è investito di prerogative costituzionali che presuppongono un pensiero e una volontà. Sia il potere di scioglimento della Camera che il potere di far dimettere il ministero rispondono del tutto legittimamente a questa logica (Capitant 1933, 41–45).

Le diverse posizioni si riavvicinano se si guarda all'uso comune di un termine come quello di *influenza*, un concetto chiave – ancorché sfuggente – per capire la funzione monarchica nella sua lunga e faticosa trasformazione costituzionale nell'Europa del XIX secolo. Guizot, in molti passaggi delle sue opere e, in particolare, dei *Mémoires*, insiste molto sul significato da dare all'espressione «potere personale». Guizot ammette una certa predisposizione caratteriale di Luigi Filippo all'«interventismo» politico. Celebre è il giudizio comparativo sulla condotta di Luigi Filippo e del genero Leopoldo I, re dei Belgi: quanto l'ingerenza del primo era «apparente», tanto la prudenza del secondo sapeva tradursi in una concreta «influenza personale» (1867, VIII, p. 95). Guizot rifiuta però l'idea che il «personalismo» del re abbia mai assunto i tratti di un comportamento extra-legale. Più volte Guizot ha censurato la tesi di chi avrebbe voluto un «trono vuoto» e un re fannullone. Ma ciò che Duvergier contesta non sono né l'influenza né le prerogative del monarca, bensì l'eccesso di sovraesposizione politica del sovrano che rischia di distruggere poco a poco quei salutari schermi e finzioni che fanno funzionare il regime rappresentativo. Guizot ha però ragione quando osserva che tutti i limiti posti alle attribuzioni della *royauté* o la disciplina la più rigorosa e completa della responsabilità dei ministri non potranno mai impedire al monarca di esercitare la sua influenza. «Laddove la monarchia costituzionale è esistita, la persona del monarca, le sue opinioni, i suoi sentimenti, le sue volontà non sono mai stati indifferenti, e i più indipendenti, i più esigenti dei ministri li hanno sempre tenuti in gran conto» (Guizot 1881, XXXVII–XXXVIII). Scrivere, come fa Charles Hello, che «il re influisce sul governo, non governa» (1850, II, p. 162) significa ribadire un principio di prudenza e di funzionalità del governo rappresentativo; ma ciò che emerge dall'esperienza orleanista è invece la difficoltà di pensare e definire la misura e il grado di ripartizione dell'influenza politica necessaria a mantenere in equilibrio i poteri dello Stato.

Se questo equilibrio non riesce a prodursi in maniera stabile e profonda non lo si può imputare al solo "personalismo" che – come altri fattori – ne è al contempo causa ed effetto. Ancora una volta Duvergier de Hauranne si rivela uno dei critici più lucidi dell'evoluzione del regime orleanista avendo compreso come non sia sufficiente l'*apparenza* del regime costituzionale e come, al contrario, ci sia bisogno di determinate *condizioni politiche* per la nascita e la durevole affermazione del regime rappresentativo a carattere parlamentare. Tre sono le condizioni invocate da Duvergier nel 1847: che la corona «coperta» da un ministero che «governa» resti nell'alta sfera in cui la costituzione l'ha posta; la Camera elettiva, indipendente e gelosa della sua prerogativa, sia di fatto e di diritto il reale centro del governo e il potere preponderante; le elezioni siano libere e producano una camera veramente rappresentativa del paese. «Al di fuori di queste condizioni, *si può avere l'apparenza del governo rappresentativo; ma non la realtà*» (1847, 249, corsivo nostro).

I segnali al riguardo sono contraddittori. Da un lato una forte instabilità ministeriale (17 ministeri in 18 anni), soprattutto sino al 1840; dall'altro una notevole ristrettezza nel reclutamento dei ministri. I governi sono infatti formati da un piccolo nucleo di professionisti della politica (una sessantina circa): in maggioranza parlamentari aventi in comune una forte identità sociale e professionale (trattandosi in gran parte di funzionari, avvocati, professori). Una diecina di personaggi domina la scena politica e il succedersi dei governi solo in rari casi corrisponde ad un vero e proprio mutamento di strategia politica. Prima del programma vengono gli uomini; la lotta politica, specialmente dopo il 1835, tende a personalizzarsi in maniera decisa. Non di rado l'analisi costituzionalistica che muove dall'osservazione diretta degli avvenimenti conduce ad una sorta di "dover essere" del regime parlamentare: da ciò deriva l'insistenza sull'omogeneità di una maggioranza parlamentare stabile («sistematica») capace di procedere insieme sulle grandi questioni e sotto la guida di veri *leader*, mettendo da parte se necessario l'amor proprio e gli egoismi di parte; su un'opposizione altrettanto coesa; sul principio di responsabilità politica correttamente inteso. Le «condizioni politiche» a cui fa riferimento Duvergier rinviano in ultima istanza al reclutamento del personale politico e al sistema elettorale, il che significa mettere in discussione "le regole del gioco" che fanno funzionare un tipico sistema notabiliare di canalizzazione del consenso in sintonia con un asfittico "paese legale".

Conservatori come Fonfrède o Pepin muovono dai "mali" della rappresentanza parlamentare – la debolezza dei "partiti", il particolarismo degli interessi, il localismo, il trasformismo, il legame politico-istituzionale dei deputati-funzionari – per ribadire un tipo di equilibrio che poggia anzitutto sul monarca: infatti, mentre questi rappresenta l'interesse generale del paese, i deputati al più sarebbero espressione dei singoli collegi. Emerge un regime di bilanciamento dei poteri ad esecutivo monarchico, nella convinzione che lo stretto rapporto tra monarca e governo (affermato dal *testo* della Carta) debba contrastare – in funzione "conservatrice" – la pretesa della Camera elettiva di "assorbire" il potere esecutivo e di assumere una posizione di preponderanza in contraddizione col principio del "concorso" e dell'equilibrio dei poteri. Queste considerazioni sono condivise dai conservatori ministeriali alla Guizot e di volta in volta dalla "palude" parlamentare – si tratti del *tiers parti* di Dupin o di esponenti del centro sinistra – che cercano di adattare la realtà ad un modello di monarchia rappresentativa che, basato sulle fragili fondamenta della *sovranità nazionale*, non vuole modificare le *condizioni politiche*, il regime elettorale anzitutto e con esso la forma della rappresentanza.

È stridente il confronto tra la teorica dottrinaria sottesa all'individuazione di «tutti gli elementi del potere legittimo disseminati nella società» (Guizot 1850, II, p. 150) al fine di enucleare la «ragione pubblica» e la realtà concreta dei procedimenti e dei mezzi di selezione del personale politico-parlamentare. Il problema dell'allargamento del "paese legale" è dapprima appannaggio della sinistra del "movimento", per poi diventare il terreno privilegiato di incontro di forze politiche in realtà lontane per strategia e obiettivi. La riforma parlamentare e la riforma amministrativa sono due facce della stessa medaglia. Malgrado la legge elettorale del 1831 avesse previsto alcune incompatibilità tra la funzione di deputato e lo *status* di funzionario, il parlamento della Monarchia di Luglio fu caratterizzato da una fortissima presenza di funzionari (Tudesq 1997; Manca 2000). A partire dal 1839 il tema dei funzionari-deputati entra a pieno titolo nell'*agenda* del dibattito politico. Léon Faucher denuncia gli effetti negativi di un sistema di *morcellement* della rappresentanza che fa prevalere gli interessi particolari e al contempo li assoggetta al dispotismo corruttore della centralizzazione. E poiché i ministeri sono instabili, è naturale che i deputati-funzionari guardino soprattutto al dato istituzionale permanente, ovvero alla corona e alla corte. «Non è possibile introdurre un gran numero di funzionari pubblici nella Camera senza snaturare il carattere della rappresentanza nazionale» (1839, 5). Nel corso degl'anni Quaranta le riforme sono invocate da un numero crescente di parlamentari e in più di una occasione la composita minoranza che sostiene, per ragioni diverse, la duplice riforma, elettorale e parlamentare, si avvicina all'obiettivo. Dopo le elezioni del 1 agosto 1846 (Higonnet 1967) che avevano assicurato una forte maggioranza al governo Soult-Guizot, l'opposizione accentuò il programma riformatore. Nel gennaio 1847 il *De la réforme parlementaire et de la réforme électorale* di Duvergier de Hauranne ne diventa il più efficace manifesto. Lo scrittore liberale delinea ormai il dilemma della Monarchia di Luglio: o si procede sulla via delle riforme (parlamentare, elettorale ecc.) che sole consentirebbero di far prosperare un *vero* regime rappresentativo, oppure si rischia il deperimento e una crisi fatale. Il progetto presentato il 6 marzo abbassa il censo da 200 a 100 franchi e aggiunge una lista di capacità. Ciò vuol dire concedere l'elettorato a 200.000 nuovi elettori. Si tratta di una riforma tutt'altro che rivoluzionaria ma che avrebbe potuto tracciare un sentiero per un graduale rinnovamento del quadro istituzionale. È fin troppo nota la sprezzante risposta data da Guizot a Garnier-Pagès che nel corso del dibattito preconizza l'avvento del suffragio universale: «Non vi è giorno per il suffragio universale. Non vi è giorno in cui tutte le creature umane, qualunque esse siano, possano essere chiamate ad esercitare dei diritti politici. La questione non merita che mi distragga in questo momento da ciò che ci occupa» (*Le Moniteur Universel*, 23 marzo 1847, p. 616; Rosanvallon 1991). Il contemporaneo rigetto della proposta di riforma parlamentare presentata da de Rémusat (1962, IV, 115 ss.) chiudeva ogni spiraglio ad un possibile cambiamento. I riformisti, sconfitti in parlamento, continuarono a lottare nel paese, con i banchetti, i raduni, le associazioni.

> «É la prima e naturale missione dei governi di essere conservatori. Noi siamo dei conservatori tanto più decisi perché succediamo a una serie di rivoluzioni, e ci sentiamo incaricati di ristabilire in Francia l'ordine, la durata, il rispetto dei poteri, delle leggi, dei principi, delle tradizioni, di tutto ciò che assicura la vita regolare e lunga delle società ...» [Archives Nationales, 42 AP 297, *Lettera* (privata) di Guizot a Pellegrino Rossi, Parigi venerdì 7 maggio 1847].

Queste parole di Guizot – come sappiamo – non hanno avuto il dono della profezia.

6. Le tecniche del parlamentarismo, il problema della responsabilità politica dei ministri, il nodo del governo parlamentare

Il costituzionalismo della Restaurazione ha riposto poca fiducia nella capacità del testo scritto di creare la regola costituzionale in grado di prevedere e governare la pluralità dei contesti e delle situazioni possibili. Le *Chartes* sono testi laconici, vaghi, talvolta molto carenti nel definire la misura dei rapporti e del controllo tra parlamento ed esecutivo (Laquièze 2000).

In particolare si nota una sorta di contraddizione tra, da un lato, lo sviluppo essenzialmente fattuale, *empirico* della strumentazione di controllo del parlamento sull'attività del governo e, dall'altro, si vedono gli effetti limitati prodotti sul piano della concreta responsabilità ministeriale e quindi sulla stabilizzazione della forma di governo, dovendosi ciò, probabilmente, ad una complessa pluralità di fattori quali la natura e il ruolo della monarchia, la genetica difficoltà di articolazione "partitica" delle forze politiche, la carenza di unità e solidarietà nel ministero ecc. I cosiddetti diritti di interrogazione, di interpellanza o di inchiesta non trovano alcun riconoscimento esplicito nelle Carte, neanche in quella del 1830. Il controllo finanziario (bilancio) ha un riferimento testuale ma il suo sviluppo va ben oltre gli angusti confini tracciati dalla Carta. Nel corso della Restaurazione, già dai primi anni, si affermano i principi fondamentali del controllo finanziario quando ministri delle finanze sono il barone Louis, il conte Corvetto, il conte Villèle. L'ordinanza del 14 settembre 1822 stabilisce la regola dell'unità di bilancio (spese ed entrate) e la sua annualità. Ma già la legge del 25 marzo 1817 (articolo 151) aveva introdotto il voto parlamentare delle spese ministero per ministero, aprendo una strada importante che giunge sino alla Terza Repubblica. Nella logica del governo rappresentativo – ovvero di un governo basato sul principio della pubblicità – bisognava poter verificare nel più ampio dettaglio possibile l'insieme del bilancio. Nel 1829 questo fu votato non più per aggregazione, ma per sezioni. Durante la Monarchia di Luglio, nel 1831, si introduce la suddivisione per capitoli; nel 1848 furono 338 i capitoli votati.

Il dibattito sulla legge annuale di bilancio divenne l'occasione per discutere della politica del governo, senza però che si arrivasse a mettere in discussione la responsabilità ministeriale. Anche la rivendicazione parlamentare del cd. "rifiuto del bilancio" – sostenuta con forza da Thiers e da Constant nella crisi del 1830 – non ebbe rilevanza costituzionale durante il regime orleanista.

Nel corso della Restaurazione, invece, si conquistano uno spazio significativo alcuni strumenti di controllo parlamentare non previsti dalla Carta o, se previsti, "riformulati" sul piano della prassi. Basti pensare all'istituto della petizione (art. 53 *Charte* 1814) utilizzato per sollecitare i ministri a dar conto in aula della loro attività, benché spesso senza alcun esito (Barthélemy 1904, 234 ss.; Dionnet 2003). Diverso il caso dell'*adresse*, modernizzazione del diritto di rimostranza del parlamento nei confronti del monarca. Previsto da una legge del 1814 (13 agosto), non ebbe conseguenze particolari se non dopo il 1821 allorché la discussione e il voto dell'*adresse* – quale risposta al discorso del trono – divennero l'occasione per muovere critiche al governo (e pur indirettamente al sovrano). La storia parlamentare francese è caratterizzata da alcuni *adresse* importanti, a partire da quello dei 221 diretto contro la politica di Polignac e di Carlo X e quello del gennaio 1839 promosso dalla innaturale *coalition* (Guizot, Thiers, Barrot) contro il ministero Molé accusato di dare manforte alla politica personale di Luigi Filippo.

Meno efficaci si sono rivelate altre tecniche di controllo come l'interpellanza (Laquièze 2002) e l'inchiesta parlamentare. La prima era apparsa agli inizi della Monarchia di Luglio e consisteva – sul modello inglese – in una domanda posta da un parlamentare, seguita da un dibattito che si chiudeva col voto di un ordine del giorno. L'interpellanza non sortì grandi effetti anche perché non poteva essere proposta senza il consenso della maggioranza; i ministri interpellati si riservavano il diritto di non rispondere; il voto finale non ebbe mai rilevanza politica. Il diritto d'inchiesta si affermò nel corso della Monarchia di Luglio, ma anche in questo caso senza poter incidere in maniera davvero significativa sull'indirizzo politico dei ministri.

La Carta del 1814, nella sua laconicità, non contempla, se non in forma generale, il principio della responsabilità politico-parlamentare dei ministri (artt. 13, 55, 56). Eppure, sin dal 1814 è subito evidente il rilievo che tale principio riveste per la configurazione del governo rappresentativo. Il dato testuale, come è noto, non è di grande aiuto poiché riprende l'originario carattere "penale" e individuale dell'*impeachment* britannico, con il potere di accusa per le ipotesi "estreme" di tradimento e di concussione riservato alla Camera bassa e il giudizio attribuito alla Camera alta.

Abbiamo di fronte ministri del re o *anche* ministri responsabili *in qualche modo* verso la maggioranza parlamentare? Dare una risposta univoca a questa domanda è obiettivamente difficile. Nel periodo 1814–1848 non si è affermato in Francia, su base convenzionale, un meccanismo che in via "automatica" e "obbligatoria" costringa il governo a dimettersi non appena venga meno il sostegno maggioritario delle Camere.

Il voto contrario di un ramo del parlamento su singoli provvedimenti, taluni anche qualificanti dal punto di vista politico generale, non determina di per sé le dimissioni del Ministero, durante i due regimi politici delle Carte. È invece Casimir Périer all'inizio della Monarchia orleanista a fare un uso sistematico della questione di fiducia (marzo 1831 – ottobre 1832). Tale ricorso non fu estraneo neppure al Ministero Mortier (1834) ma non divenne un' "istituzione" per il resto del nuovo regime politico. In generale si può dire che il voto contrario del parlamento giocò un ruolo limitato e "indiretto" nel determinare la caduta dei governi e soltanto dopo il 1830. Nel periodo considerato, tuttavia, la meta di una compiuta formalizzazione giuridico-politica della responsabilità rimane lontana.

L'assenza di una regola sufficientemente stabile – poi affermatasi nel regime parlamentare più o meno razionalizzato – sembrerebbe pertanto escludere la possibilità di parlare di «regime parlamentare» almeno per il periodo della

Restaurazione. Se, al contrario, si è parlato e si parla di «regime parlamentare» è a dire il vero più per affermare un'origine, un momento di avvio che per sostenere la tesi di una compiutezza del sistema parlamentare. Non è sufficiente, infatti, ritrovare alcune tecniche costituzionali dall'indubbio sapore «parlamentare» (compatibilità tra l'essere ministro e parlamentare; libero accesso dei ministri alle Camere e correlativo diritto di parola; controfirma ministeriale; principio di unità e di omogeneità del consiglio dei ministri; forme di "controllo" del Parlamento sull'azione ministeriale: dall'*adresse* alla discussione e al voto di bilancio ...) per arrivare a tale conclusione. Guizot, nelle sue Memorie, paragona il governo parlamentare a una delicatissima pianta di serra (*Mémoires*, 1867, VIII, p. 98). Esso in effetti non è semplicemente la somma aritmetica di tecniche e di princìpi. C'è un *quid* difficile da definire che ne informa l'*esprit*. Negli anni della monarchia costituzionale è possibile cogliere una forte *tensione* volta a riconoscere nella responsabilità politica dei ministri il problema costituzionale *par excellence* e dalla cui soluzione dipende, in ultima istanza, la definizione della forma di governo.

7. Benjamin Constant: «Quando avremo ciò che non abbiamo ancora ...»

Se la Carta è ambigua e lacunosa, la pubblicistica della Restaurazione è invece straordinariamente ricca, quasi a voler "colmare" la vaghezza del dettato costituzionale. In Benjamin Constant la questione della responsabilità è collegata strettamente all'idea di «potere neutro» che gli permette di configurare come duale il potere esecutivo, imputando alla responsabilità ministeriale gli atti che costituiscono un «cattivo uso» del potere legale (1815, 460; Jaume 2000; Laquièze, *Le modèle anglais*, 2000). Constant tende a vedere tale responsabilità nell'ottica tradizionale dell'accusa penale e tuttavia mostra di riconoscere molto bene il carattere "politico" insito nell'accusa riguardante azioni che sono per loro natura imprevedibili e discrezionali e che richiedono un apprezzamento altrettanto "politico" e discrezionale da parte delle assemblee. Constant conosce bene la pratica inglese del voto di fiducia, ma non pensa di introdurla in Francia perché non intende assegnare alle assemblee una prerogativa che andrebbe a confliggere con il «potere neutro» del monarca e in particolare con il potere di "libera" scelta dei ministri. Il problema è un altro:

> «Quando avremo ciò che non abbiamo ancora, ma che è assolutamente indispensabile in ogni monarchia costituzionale, intendo dire, un ministero che agisca di concerto, una maggioranza stabile, e una opposizione ben distinta da questa maggioranza, nessun ministro potrà restare al suo posto, se non ha per sé la maggioranza dei voti, a meno di appellarsi al popolo attraverso nuove elezioni. E allora, queste nuove elezioni saranno la pietra di paragone della fiducia accordata a questo ministro» [1815, 463].

«Quando avremo ciò che non abbiamo ancora», scrive Constant. Si tratta di un profilo molto importante perché evidenzia il legame necessario tra la natura della monarchia, le condizioni della cultura politica (maggioranza / opposizione, ruolo dei "partiti", unità e omogeneità del Ministero) e lo sviluppo del regime parlamentare.

8. Il problema del principio parlamentare tra limiti strutturali e dinamiche concrete

I tre piani analizzati (laconicità/ vaghezza delle Carte; *décalage* tra principî e strumenti, rappresentazioni e fatti; analisi politico-costituzionali di grande rilievo che rivelano la presa di coscienza della natura e dei caratteri essenziali del regime parlamentare, senza però che questa dimensione del "dover essere" possa diventare compiutamente sangue e nervi del sistema) coesistono e spesso interferiscono fra loro. Tre limiti – già evidenziati – contribuiscono, in particolare, a "spiegare" la mancanza di un legame produttivo tra mezzi di controllo parlamentare e praticabilità del principio di responsabilità ministeriale. Il ruolo del monarca costituzionale è decisivo: ho parlato, non a caso, di «incerti confini della monarchia costituzionale». Si tratti del monarca *selon la Charte* del 1814 (istitutore-detentore *ab origine* del potere di indirizzo politico) o del "personalismo" di Luigi Filippo (il re regna e spesso governa), il risultato non cambia (pur nella diversificazione del regime politico): carenza di autonomia e coesione dei Ministeri, collegialità solo in alcuni casi raggiunta, debolezza istituzionale, spirito di deferenza se non di subordinazione, paradosso della responsabilità: anziché "coprire" il monarca irresponsabile, i ministri tendono spesso a "coprirsi" dietro lo schermo dell'inviolabilità sovrana.

Il sistema di organizzazione e di funzionamento dei gruppi politici risente di vari fattori: inesperienza (*apprentissage*) durante la Restaurazione, mancanza di omogeneità, esistenza di "partiti" anti-sistema durante il regime orleanista (legittimisti, bonapartisti, repubblicani), natura notabilare delle aggregazioni. Questi problemi si collegano in maniera indissolubile alla logica del sistema elettorale censitario che rispecchia la filosofia politico-morale della *rappresentanza* nella quale gran parte dei liberali – pur con sfumature *diverse* – si riconoscono pienamente (Lacchè 2002). In Francia (come in altre esperienze europee del XIX secolo) il regime elettorale tende a trasformarsi in *sistema politico-amministrativo* assecondando quella radicata tradizione nazionale che individuava nella centralizzazione un complesso e coerente strumento di mediazione locale (i *bourgs pourris* francesi, la "corruzione" elettorale ecc.) e di necessario raccordo con la sfera della rappresentanza politica (Lacchè, *Il telegrafo*, 2002). L'*esprit de localité* – che differenzia profondamente le regioni francesi – non è un effetto bensì una condizione di partenza. Anche nei collegi più "grandi" conta la personalità dei candidati e la campagna elettorale non può che essere personalizzata, discreta, basata sui vari livelli di influenza dei notabili.

«Quando avremo ciò che non abbiamo ancora», scrive Constant. E, tuttavia, malgrado i limiti denunciati, non possiamo dimenticare alcune dinamiche importanti. Chi conquista la maggioranza della Camera dei deputati tende ad accentuare la natura "parlamentare" del regime. In fondo, l'atteggiamento degli *ultras* della *Chambre introuvable* (Corciulo 1979 e 2000; De Waresquiel 1992) tra il 1815 e 1816 ha una qualche eco nel comportamento dei liberali a partire dal 1827, dalla caduta del ministero Villèle. Ciò significa che la lotta politica è parte integrante e "produttiva" del quadro costituzionale. Chi ha ottenuto la maggioranza nella Camera elettiva fa leva sul carattere parlamentare e dualistico; chi è sulla difensiva tende a ritrovare nel monarca un soggetto dotato di prerogative il cui esercizio può ricondurre la maggioranza entro un ambito più consono allo schema "monistico" tracciato dalla *Charte*. È evidente che il dibattito di fine anni Venti rimette *ultras* e liberali nelle loro "naturali" posizioni, ma questo carattere non abbandonerà – seppure con forme ulteriori e diverse – il sistema costituzionale in Francia anche dopo il 1830.

Certo è che, pur con le incertezze ricordate, l'insistenza sulla legislazione elettorale e su quella relativa alla stampa – che accompagna i principali snodi politici della Restaurazione – mostra distintamente la convinzione che sia possibile governare e "durare" solo con il sostegno dell'opinione (fatta prosperare dalla libertà di stampa).

Un altro aspetto merita di essere sottolineato: il controllo del parlamento (Mahul 1830, 476) – attraverso la contesa elettorale e le infornate di pari – è la condizione essenziale per influire sulla natura del regime. Pur in assenza di un compiuto regime parlamentare, ci si comporta "come se" esso fosse operante in tutti i suoi principali ingranaggi. Ma non bisogna dimenticare che nessun voto di sfiducia – in quanto tale – fa cadere un governo della Restaurazione e lo scioglimento della Camera resta la manifestazione della prerogativa regia, anche se in alcuni casi è evidente e decisivo l'atteggiamento ripetutamente ostile del parlamento (per es. in occasione della caduta del secondo Ministero Richelieu nel 1821). In altri casi il Ministero ricorre al monarca per chiedere lo scioglimento della Camera nella quale esiste una maggioranza solidale ma attraverso tale atto si intende contrastare il progressivo affermarsi della minoranza (Villèle nel 1824 e nel 1827). Le elezioni rivestono allora un ruolo decisivo e diventano l'"appello al paese" per arbitrare la contesa politica. Il re non può essere "partigiano" e "neutrale": l'intelligenza politica gli è richiesta per ben interpretare il sentimento dell'*opinion*. In un regime a tendenza parlamentare il monarca non può utilizzare sistematicamente i mezzi legali per cambiare il risultato voluto dall'opinione, pena una crisi costituzionale dagli esiti incerti. Il regime parlamentare è al contempo, si potrebbe dire, il «campo da gioco» (la forma del regime rappresentativo) e la «partita» da giocare (principio parlamentare) (Guizot 1881, XV): si tratta di una sovrapposizione, questa, destinata a durare nel tempo.

Bibliografia

Antonetti G., *La monarchie constitutionnelle*, Paris 1998

Bagehot W., *Napoleone III. Lettere sul colpo di Stato francese del 1851*, a cura di M. Griffo, Roma 1997

Baranger D., *Parlementarisme des origines. Essai sur les conditions de formation d'un exécutif responsable en Angleterre (des années 1740 au début de l'âge victorien)*, Paris 1999

Barante P. de, *La vie politique de M. Royer-Collard. Ses discours et ses écrits*, Paris 1863, 2 voll.

Barrot O., *Mémoires posthumes*, Paris 1876, tome IV

Barthélemy J., *L'introduction du régime parlementaire en France sous Louis XVIII et Charles X*, Paris 1904

Beaud O., *Joseph Barthélemy ou la fin de la doctrine constitutionnelle classique*, in *Droits*, 32, 2000, 89–108

Bonini F., *Amministrazione e Costituzione: il modello francese*, Roma 1999

Bonnefon J., *Le régime parlementaire sous la Restauration*, Paris 1905

Capitant R., *Régimes parlementaires*, in *Mélanges R. Carré de Malberg*, Paris 1933, poi Vaduz, Topos Verlag, Paris 1977, 31–57

Cassina C., *«Vincere la demagogia con la democrazia». Il 1848 e le sue illusioni*, in *Giornale di storia costituzionale*, II, 8, 2004

Constant B., *De la responsabilité des ministres*, in *Œuvres complètes*, IX, 1, Tübingen 2001 (1815)

Corciulo M. S., *Le istituzioni parlamentari in Francia. Cento Giorni e seconda Restaurazione (1815–1816)*, Napoli 1979

– *La «Chambre Introuvable» e i princìpi del regime parlamentare (agosto 1815 – settembre 1816)*, in *L'istituzione parlamentare nel XIX secolo. Una prospettiva comparata. Die parlamentarische Institution im 19. Jahrhundert. Eine Perspektive im Vergleich*, a cura di A. G. Manca e W. Brauneder, Bologna, Berlin, 2000, 119–137

Deslandres M., *Histoire constitutionnelle de France de 1789 à 1870*, t. II, *De la chute de l'Empire à l'avènement de la troisième République (1815–1870)*, Paris 1932

De Waresquiel E., *Un paradoxe politique: la Chambre «introuvable» et la naissance du parlementarisme français (octobre 1815 – avril 1816)*, in *Commentaire*, 15, 1992, 409–416

Dionnet J.-P., *La contribution de la pétition à l'évolution politique dans l'histoire contemporaine: évocation d'une difficile intégration*, in *Droits*, 37, 2003, 173–189

Duvergier de Hauranne P., *Des principes du gouvernement représentatif et de leur application*, Paris 1838

– *De la politique extérieure et intérieure de la France*, Paris 1841

– *De la réforme parlementaire et de la réforme électorale*, Paris 1847

– *Histoire du gouvernement parlementaire en France. 1814–1848, précédée d'une introduction …*, Paris 1857–1872

Eisenmann Ch., *Essai d'une classification théorique des formes politiques*, in *Politique*, 1968, 8 ss.

Elia L., *Governo (forme di)*, in *Enciclopedia del diritto*, Milano 1970, vol. XIX, 634–675

Faucher L., *Des fonctionnaires députés. A M. Odilon Barrot*, 20 février 1839

Fievée J., *Correspondance politique et administrative, commencée au mois de mai 1814*, Paris 1815–1819

Furet Fr., *Réflexions sur l'idée de tradition révolutionnaire dans la France du XIXe siècle*, in *Pouvoirs*, 50, 1990, 5–13
Giannini M. S., *Prefazione* a Burdeau (Georges), *Il regime parlamentare nelle costituzioni europee del dopoguerra*, Milano 1950 (1932)
Guizot Fr., *De la démocratie en France (Janvier 1849)*, Paris 1849 (tr. it. *Della democrazia in Francia (gennaio 1849)*, introduzione di M. Griffo, Firenze 2000)
– *Pourquoi la Révolution d'Angleterre a-t-elle réussi? Discours sur l'histoire de la Révolution d'Angleterre*, Paris 1850
– *Histoire des origines du gouvernement représentatif en Europe*, Paris 1851
– *Mémoires pour servir à l'histoire de mon temps*, Paris 1858–1867
– *Mélanges politiques et historiques*, *Préface*, Paris 1881
Hello Ch., *Del regime costituzionale nelle sue relazioni con lo stato attuale della scienza sociale e politica*, Firenze 1850
Higonnet P. L. R., Higonnet T. B., *Class, Corruption and Politics in the French Chamber of Deputies, 1846–1848*, in *French Historical Studies*, 5, 1967, 204–224
His Ch.-H., *De la Monarchie représentative*, Paris 1829
Hummel J., *Le constitutionnalisme allemand (1815–1918): le modèle allemand de la monarchie limitée*, Paris 2002
Jaume L., *Le concept de «responsabilité des ministres» chez Benjamin Constant*, in *Revue française de Droit constitutionnel*, 42, 2000, 227–243
Jainchill A., Moyn S., *French Democracy between Totalitarianism and Solidarity: Pierre Rosanvallon and Revisionist Historiography*, in *The Journal of Modern History*, 76, 2004, 107–154
Kirsch M., *Monarch und Parlament im 19. Jahrhundert. Der monarchische Konstitutionalismus als europäischer Verfassungstyp – Frankreich im Vergleich*, Göttingen 1999
Lacchè L., *Tra politica e diritto, ovvero Rossi e la Monarchia di Luglio*, in *Un liberale europeo: Pellegrino Rossi (1787–1848)*, a cura di L. Lacchè, Milano 2001, 70–108
– *La Libertà che guida il Popolo. Le Tre Gloriose Giornate del luglio 1830 e le Chartes nel costituzionalismo francese*, Bologna 2002
– *Il telegrafo di Stendhal. Politica ed elezioni nel «Lucien Leuwen» ai tempi della Monarchia di Luglio*, in *Giornale di storia costituzionale*, 4/II semestre, 2002, 217–233
Lahmer M., *La constitution américaine dans le débat français: 1795–1848*, Paris 2001
Laquièze A., *Le Parlement, organe de contrôle du gouvernement dans la France de la Restauration et de la Monarchie de Juillet*, in *L'istituzione parlamentare nel XIX secolo*, cit., 175–191
– *Le modèle anglais et la responsabilité ministérielles selon le groupe de Coppet*, in *Coppet, creuset de l'esprit libéral. Les idées politiques et constitutionnelles du Groupe de Madame de Stäel*, a cura di L. Jaume, Aix-en-Provence 2000, 158–176
– *Les origines du régime parlementaire en France (1814–1848)*, Paris 2002
Lauvaux Ph., *Propositions méthodologiques pour la classification des régimes*, in *Droits*, 32, 2000, 109–120
Luzzatto S., *Ombre rosse. Il romanzo della Rivoluzione francese nell'Ottocento*, Bologna 2004
Mahul A., *Tableau de la Constitution politique de la monarchie française selon la Charte, ou Résumé du droit public des Français, accompagné du texte des lois fondamentales et des documents authentiques*, Paris 1830
Manca A. G., *Introduzione* a *L'istituzione parlamentare nel XIX secolo*, cit., 9–45
– *I funzionari-deputati tra Parlamento e amministrazione in una prospettiva comparata*, in *Ibidem*, 391–429
Id. – Lacchè L. (a cura di), *Parlamento e Costituzione nei sistemi costituzionali europei ottocenteschi. Parlament und Verfassung in den konstitutionellen Verfassungssystemen Europas*, Bologna, Berlin 2003
Michon L., *Le gouvernement parlementaire sous la Restauration*, Paris 1905

Mill J. St., *Considerazioni sul governo rappresentativo*, Milano 1946 (1861)

Mirkine-Guetzevitch B., *Le costituzioni europee*, Milano 1954 (1951)

Mortati C., *Corso di lezioni di diritto costituzionale italiano e comparato, Forme di governo*, raccolte da S. Fois, Roma 1962

Pinheiro-Ferreira S., *Observations sur la Charte constitutionnelle de la France, extraites du cours de droit public de M. le commandeur Silvestre Pinheiro-Ferreira, ministre d'état de S. M. T. F.*, Paris 1833

Pouthas Ch., *Les ministères de Louis-Philippe*, in *Revue d'histoire moderne et contemporaine*, I, janvier–mars, 1954

Prevost-Paradol L.-A., *La France nouvelle*, Paris 1868

Redslob R., *Die parlamentarische Regierung in ihrer wahren und in ihrer unechten Form. Eine vergleichende Studie über die Verfassungen von England, Belgien, Ungarn, Schweden und Frankreich*, Tübingen 1918

Rémusat Ch.-Fr.-M. de, *Mémoires de ma vie*, t. IV, *Les dernières années de la monarchie, révolution de 1848, la Seconde République, 1848–1851* ..., a cura di Ch. H. Pouthas, Paris 1962

Renan E., *La monarchie constitutionnelle en France*, in *Revue des Deux Mondes*, 1er novembre 1869, poi in *La réforme intellectuelle et morale*, Paris 1872, 3 ed.

Rials S., *Essai sur le concept de monarchie limitée (autour de la Charte de 1814)*, in *Révolution et contre-révolution au XIXème siècle*, Paris 1987, 88–125

Roederer P.-L., *Adresse d'un constitutionnel aux constitutionnels*, Paris 1835

Rosanvallon P., *Guizot et la question du suffrage universel au XIXème siècle*, in *François Guizot et la culture politique de son temps*, a cura di M. Valensise, Paris 1991, 129–145

– *La Monarchie impossible. Les Chartes de 1814 et de 1830*, Paris 1994

Rotelli E., *La forma di governo britannica fra 1689 e 1784*, in *Storia Amministrazione Costituzione*, 10, 2002, 45–126

Schiera P., *La costituzione inglese fra storia e mito*, in *Il modello costituzionale inglese e la sua recezione nell'area mediterranea tra la fine del'700 e la prima metà dell'800*, a cura di A. Romano, Milano 1998, 39–58

Serrigny D., *Traité du droit public des Français, précédé d'une introduction sur les fondements des sociétés politiques*, Paris 1846, 2 tomi

Thiers A., *La monarchie de 1830*, Paris 1831

Troper M., *Les classifications en droit constitutionnel*, in *Revue de droit public*, 1989, 945 ss. (tr. it. in *Per una teoria giuridica dello Stato*, Napoli 1998, 233–246)

Tudesq A.-J., *La liberté contre la liberté. Le débat sur les incompatibilités parlementaires*, in *Liberté, libéraux et constitutions*, a cura di J.-P. Clément, L. Jaume e M. Verpeaux, Paris 1997, 33–41

La razionalizzazione ottocentesca: il problema dell'affermazione del modello parlamentare nell'età delle *Chartes*

1. Quale razionalizzazione

Con il mio intervento siamo dunque giunti al "momento" della *razionalizzazione* o della *stabilizzazione* del modello parlamentare. Questo titolo mi è stato proposto come tema di fondo da trattare in questa sede: è un titolo "problematico" (come cercherò di dire), ma da me accolto di buon grado proprio come stimolo alla riflessione.

Si tratta di una terminologia che può essere utilizzata, a patto però che, per il contesto e per l'ambito cronologico considerati, si compia uno sforzo di problematizzazione.

Sul titolo infatti aleggia la categoria del "parlamentarismo razionalizzato" applicata, soprattutto, a partire dalle costituzioni europee posteriori al 1919 quando la tradizione del parlamentarismo ottocentesco, fluido, mobile, a forte caratterizzazione consuetudinaria e convenzionale, inizia a subire quelle prime metamorfosi che poi raggiungeranno una veste più consueta nel secondo dopoguerra: forme costituzionali rigide, maggiore diversificazione dei sistemi, "codificazioni" dottrinali riconducibili, anche per l'impatto crescente della modellistica politologica, a strutture più omogenee.[1] Il tema della razionalizzazione dei sistemi parlamentari rischia quindi di suscitare percorsi a ritroso, alla ricerca di improbabili genealogie e di "precedenti" più o meno anacronistici.

Per l'esperienza francese possiamo richiamare un canone storiografico che ha molto influito sulla stessa definizione del campo di indagine: le origini e l'affermazione del regime parlamentare. Il *concours* Rossi nell'edizione del 1903[2] aveva infatti per oggetto il seguente tema: «Le régime parlementaire en France sous Louis XVIII et Charles X – Rechercher comment ont été introduits et

1 Per es. B. Mirkine-Guetzevitch, *Le costituzioni europee*, Milano 1954 (1951), 28.

2 Le vicende del *prix* Rossi e le origini del canone storiografico del regime parlamentare sono state ben analizzate da A. Laquièze, *Les origines du régime parlementaire en France (1814–1848)*, Paris 2002.

appliqués à cette époque les principes et les usages du gouvernement de cabinet». Il tema dava dunque per acquisiti sia l'esistenza del regime parlamentare sia lo sviluppo di principi e usi del governo di gabinetto a partire dalla *Charte* del 1814. Il risultato del concorso, vinto *ex aequo* da due giovani studiosi, Louis Michon e Joseph Barthélemy – quest'ultimo destinato a diventare uno dei costituzionalisti più rappresentativi e influenti della Terza Repubblica[3] –, si è rivelato molto importante, per il dibattito che ne seguì e per aver contribuito a diffondere ed affermare presso il mondo accademico francese (e non solo) l'idea di una repentina e sostanziale affermazione del regime parlamentare in Francia sin dai primi passi della *Charte*.

Il titolo del concorso appare in sintonia con gli sviluppi e con le dinamiche politico-costituzionali della III Repubblica, ed appare fortemente prescrittivo: il regime parlamentare viene affermato come una realtà durante il regno dei Borboni e si tratta perciò di analizzarne i modi di realizzazione, nel solco di una convinzione diffusa presso i maggiori pubblicisti dell'epoca, a cominciare da A. Esmein, e volta a rintracciare il senso di una continuità – ma con risultati "monistici"[4] – nello sviluppo francese del regime parlamentare, non senza qualche sguardo "nostalgico" verso l'istituzione monarchica (orleanista).

Gli studi premiati, quello di Louis Michon e soprattuto il lavoro di Joseph Barthélemy, pubblicati tra il 1904 e il 1905,[5] erano destinati a incidere sul modo stesso di interpretare il periodo delle «origini del regime parlamentare», codificando, pur con risultati di diverso spessore scientifico, un "canone" storiografico di lunga durata.[6] Non è un caso se la tesi di J. Bonnefon,[7] che pure partecipò al *prix*, discutendo l'impostazione di Barthélemy e mostrando i limiti del parlamentarismo e del cd. governo di gabinetto nel regime della Carta del 1814, attirò una più limitata attenzione. Mettendo a confronto i diversi assunti si vede come, pur in presenza di ovvii tratti comuni, sia differente la premessa: ciò

3 A questo autore è stata dedicata una corposa tesi dottorale: F. Saulnier, *Joseph Barthélemy 1874–1945. La crise du constitutionnalisme libéral sous la IIIe République*, Paris 2004. Si vedano però, specie per l'esperienza di Barthélemy a Vichy, O. Beaud, *Joseph Barthélemy ou la fin de la doctrine constitutionnelle classique*, in *Droits*, 32, 2000, 89–108 e S. Rials, «*Malum metaphysicum*». *Faiblesses ordinaires en temps d'épouvante (Vies parallèles à Vichy)*, in *Droits*, 39, 2004, 148 ss.

4 Su questa evoluzione posso rinviare al contributo di J.-P. Machelon, *De l'orléanisme au monisme parlementaire: la IIIe République*, in *La Costituzione francese – La Constitution française*, a cura di M. Calamo Specchia, Torino, 2009, 149–160.

5 J. Barthélemy, *L'introduction du régime parlementaire en France sous Louis XVIII et Charles X*, Paris 1904; L. Michon, *Le gouvernement parlementaire sous la Restauration*, Paris 1905.

6 Per l'analisi degli orientamenti v. A. Laquièze, *Les origines*, cit., 19 ss.

7 J. Bonnefon, *Le régime parlementaire sous la Restauration*, Paris 1905.

che per Barthélemy è un dato di partenza (l'esistenza del regime parlamentare, definito in maniera incerta),[8] per Bonnefon è un dato da sottoporre a vaglio, a cominciare dalla centralità del principio di responsabilità politica del governo. È una sostanziale linearità di sviluppo a rappresentare la chiave di lettura prevalente: la fase 1814–1830 percepita come "periodo di formazione" e quella del 1830–1848 come "periodo di applicazione e di sviluppo del regime parlamentare".[9] È indubbio il fatto che nel periodo di vigenza delle Carte si cominci ad utilizzare in maniera più significativa la formula "regime parlamentare", particolarmente caro al vocabolario transalpino, per richiamare la più complessiva esperienza del "parlamentarismo alla francese".[10]

L'approccio che identifica nella "parlamentarizzazione" il vettore esclusivo della *costituzionalizzazione* appare, a mio avviso, incompleto. Anche l'esperienza francese, pur così singolarmente importante nel contesto europeo per la fondazione di un "modello" costituzionale, deve essere considerata nella prospettiva di una storia costituzionale comparata che contribuisce ad ampliare i confini delle storie nazionali. Tale prospettiva segnala le differenze e le singole peculiarità ma permette anche di far convergere le analisi proprio sul tema del rapporto tra costituzionalizzazione e parlamentarizzazione: questi due processi non sono necessariamente lineari, coincidenti e paralleli, tanto più se si assume come terreno di osservazione le esperienze europee monarchico-costituzionali.[11] Questo approccio permette anche di misurare meglio la logica dei *Sonderwege* che per lungo tempo ha indirizzato le analisi dei sistemi costituzionali.

Nel caso francese il costituzionalismo del 1814–1848 oscilla tra il dato originario e fondativo della cd. monarchia limitata (o costituzionale pura) che riconosce al sovrano il monopolio del «pouvoir d'Etat» e un regime di bilanciamento dei poteri a esecutivo monarchico, dualistico, ma con forti profili di incompiutezza.[12]

8 A. Laquièze, *Les origines*, cit., 15.

9 Per es. R. Capitant, *Régimes parlementaires*, in *Mélanges R. Carré de Malberg*, Paris 1933, poi Vaduz, Paris 1977, 31–57.

10 M. S. Giannini, *Prefazione* a G. Burdeau, *Il regime parlamentare nelle costituzioni europee del dopoguerra*, Milano 1950.

11 Per alcune pratiche di ricerca cfr. A. G. Manca e W. Brauneder (a cura di), *L'istituzione parlamentare nel XIX secolo. Una prospettiva comparata. Die parlamentarische Institution im 19. Jahrhundert. Eine Perspektive im Vergleich*, Bologna, Berlin 2000; A. G. Manca, L. Lacchè (a cura di), *Parlamento e Costituzione nei sistemi costituzionali europei ottocenteschi. Parlament und Verfassung in den konstitutionellen Verfassungssystemen Europas*, Bologna, Berlin 2003; M. Kirsch, *Monarch und Parlament im 19. Jahrhundert. Der monarchische Konstitutionalismus als europäischer Verfassungstyp – Frankreich im Vergleich*, Göttingen 1999; J. Hummel, *Le constitutionnalisme allemand (1815–1918): le modèle allemand de la monarchie limitée*, Paris, 2002.

12 S. Rials, *Essai sur le concept de monarchie limitée (autour de la Charte de 1814)*, in

2. Il regime rappresentativo come problema

La storia del principio parlamentare in Francia deve fare i conti da un lato con la fluidità della categoria del governo rappresentativo – con una gamma di posizioni e di azioni costituzionali che lascia aperte diverse strade –, dall'altro con l'insieme delle dinamiche politiche e socio-economiche caratterizzanti la prima metà del XIX secolo. Se nel periodo esaminato possiamo vedere all'opera, senza dubbio, tecniche e meccanismi atti a fondare una monarchia parlamentare, è altrettanto vero che il regime politico non è una conquista definitiva e soprattutto "inevitabile". Il nostro strumentario concettuale non sempre è il più idoneo a cogliere questo tipo di problema. Non si dovrebbe infatti dimenticare che l'odierna classificazione dei regimi "puri", incentrata sul dualismo tra regime parlamentare e regime presidenziale, si è andata consolidando sul finire dell'Ottocento, a partire dalle riflessioni di Bagehot. È quella una distinzione che ha origini e ragioni storicamente determinate e può essere quindi fuorviante applicarla *tout court* alla realtà costituzionale tra la fine del Settecento e (almeno) la prima metà dell'Ottocento quando invece la classificazione dei regimi costituzionali[13] risponde a linguaggi e categorie diversi, ovvero all'antitesi tra il sistema di bilanciamento/ponderazione dei poteri e il principio di unità legislativa o di specializzazione,[14] nel solco di un dibattito destinato a durare a lungo anche dopo.[15]

Non si deve neppure dimenticare che la formula governo parlamentare è poco utilizzata (e ancora meno lo è quella di regime parlamentare) durante la Restaurazione e quando vi si fa ricorso è piuttosto come sinonimo o specificazione generica di governo rappresentativo, cioè di un tipo di regime liberal-costituzionale informato ad una pur ridotta distribuzione delle funzioni e a un certo grado di equilibrio interorganico dei poteri (tra legislativo ed esecutivo).[16]

Révolution et contre-révolution au XIXème siècle, Paris 1987, 88–125; A. Laquièze, *Les origines*, cit.; L. Lacchè, *La Libertà che guida il Popolo. Le Tre Gloriose Giornate del luglio 1830 e le Chartes nel costituzionalismo francese*, Bologna 2002.

13 Sulla questione cfr. M. Troper, *Les classifications en droit constitutionnel*, in *Revue de droit public*, 1989, 945 ss. (tr. it. in *Per una teoria giuridica dello Stato*, Napoli 1998, 233 ss.); Ph. Lauvaux, *Propositions méthodologiques pour la classification des régimes*, in *Droits*, 32, 2000, 109 ss.

14 M. Lahmer, *La constitution américaine dans le débat français: 1795–1848*, Paris 2001, 383 ss.

15 F. Bonini, *Amministrazione e Costituzione: il modello francese*, Roma 1999, 48 ss.

16 «La Restauration a donc pratiqué un parlementarisme très particulier, non de domination parlementaire, mais d'équilibre et c'est l'état des choses et non les calculs des auteurs de la Constitution qui en a décidé ainsi» (M. Deslandres, *Histoire constitutionnelle de France de 1789 à 1870, t. II, De la chute de l'Empire à l'avènement de la troisième République (1815–1870)*, Paris 1932, 119).

Spesso l'uso di governo parlamentare – in termini di elaborazione teorica e di pratica concretizzazione – viene enfatizzato nei grandi affreschi dipinti in età successiva, come nel caso della *Histoire du gouvernement parlementaire* di Prosper Duvergier de Hauranne,[17] e diventa di uso comune più ci si addentra nell'età della III Repubblica. È forse da notare, invece, che lo stesso Duvergier, acuto osservatore della scena politica francese già durante l'età orleanista, utilizza nel 1838 il termine *gouvernement représentatif* o parla nel 1847, in termini prescrittivi, di *réforme parlementaire*.[18]

La formula maggiormente richiamata è quella di governo rappresentativo (o, per altri aspetti, di monarchia rappresentativa), utilizzata sia dagli autori che difendono la prerogativa regia (come governo del re) sia da coloro che vorrebbero una più marcata influenza "parlamentare". Ma sono di uso comune espressioni ancora più vaghe, come *gouvernement de la Charte* o *selon la Charte*, governo o regime costituzionale, governo ministeriale.

Nel caso francese (ma il discorso si potrebbe allargare ad altre esperienze europee) la scelta della categoria lessicale da cui muovere ci sembra obbligata: è appunto quella del regime rappresentativo. In altra sede ho operato una distinzione tra principio parlamentare e governo rappresentativo.[19] Quello che ho chiamato il "principio parlamentare" è piuttosto il "problema", il "discorso" teorico-pratico affermato, discusso, contrastato; è, in ultimo, l'insieme delle forze e degli orientamenti che mirano a dare una "specificazione" e un determinato indirizzo al governo rappresentativo.

3. Dalla deriva ad una razionalizzazione "storicistica"?

In un precedente, proficuo, convegno barese[20] venne assunta la metafora marinaresca della deriva per cercare di cogliere alcune dinamiche peculiari della storia costituzionale francese. Si trattava di un'immagine dal respiro classico,[21] immagine ben scelta perché "ambigua": strumento per governare la nave ma anche, una volta messo fuori uso, rappresentazione di grave difficoltà e di per-

17 P. Duvergier de Hauranne, *Histoire du gouvernement parlementaire en France. 1814–1848, précédée d'une introduction*, Paris 1857.

18 P. Duvergier de Hauranne, *Des principes du gouvernement représentatif et de leur application*, Paris 1838; Id., *De la réforme parlementaire et de la réforme électorale*, Paris 1847.

19 V. *supra* in questo volume *Governo rappresentativo e principio parlamentare*, 303 ss.

20 I cui atti sono stati pubblicati nel numero monografico del *Giornale di storia costituzionale*, 8, II, 2004, *La "deriva parlamentare" nella storia costituzionale francese*.

21 Cfr. C. M. Moschetti, *Gubernare navem, gubernare rem publicam. Contributo alla storia del diritto marittimo e del diritto pubblico romano*, Milano 1966.

dita della rotta. L'immagine del Giano bifronte offre, non a caso, un quadro suggestivo delle *Chartes* costituzionali e, più in generale, del costituzionalismo europeo ottocentesco. Le *Chartes* hanno almeno due facce che riflettono l'ambiguità del disegno costituzionale della Restaurazione: da un lato l'autorità tradizionale, il volto del principio monarchico, la *lettre* del testo, l'aspetto formale, dall'altro le libertà figlie della Rivoluzione, il volto del principio rappresentativo, l'*esprit* del testo, l'elemento materiale e consuetudinario.

È indubbio che dalla Rivoluzione in poi i Francesi sono alla ricerca di una rotta e di un porto sicuro. L'età della Restaurazione trova – come dirà Victor Hugo ne *Les Miserables* – un paese stanco nel quale «tutti chiedono un letto», un asilo. I francesi vogliono pace e riposo dopo venticinque anni di straordinarie vicessitudini. I francesi sono stanchi ma la ritrovata libertà politica – malgrado la tutela esercitata dalle potenze alleate sino al 1818 – ridà vigore alla verità della parola dopo gli anni del silenzio e della diffidenza.[22] Anni che non erano tuttavia passati invano, facendo intravedere per la prima volta, dalla Rivoluzione, un *discorso pubblico della libertà*, con le varie "famiglie" di liberali e di conservatori moderati destinate a svolgere un ruolo di primo piano.

In genere l'attenzione viene incentrata soprattutto sulla *Charte* del giugno 1814, ma non bisogna dimenticare che il costituzionalismo della Restaurazione non si esaurisce con essa. Tra il 1814 e il 1815 infatti troviamo testi più effimeri, ma non per questo da dimenticare, come la Costituzione senatoriale del 6 aprile 1814, l'Atto Addizionale del 22 aprile 1815 e i progetti del giugno-luglio 1815 elaborati dalla Camera dei deputati.[23] Si può forse parlare di un *corpus* costituzionale relativamente coerente e omogeneo sotto il profilo della forma monarchica e di taluni meccanismi astrattamente intesi (suffragio censitario, bicameralismo di tipo aristocratico, sanzione regia della legge, diritto di scioglimento della Camera elettiva, responsabilità dei ministri di natura prevalentemente "penale" ecc.). Esiste un nocciolo duro di idee e di principi condivisi dai liberali e dai conservatori moderati tanto da far dire a Guizot – con un lessico tipicamente dottrinario – che la Carta «était écrite d'avance dans l'expérience et la pensée du pays; elle sortit naturellement de l'esprit de Louis XVIII revenant d'Angleterre, comme des délibérations du Sénat secouant le joug de l'Empire; elle fut l'œuvre

22 «Nessuna parola torna tanto frequente negli scrittori dell'epoca, sia ultrarealisti che liberali, quanto quella della "stabilità", che oscilla dal sogno di una quiete senza tempo a quella di un moto matematicamente regolato e scandito, di una regola di autodisciplina della nazione» (A. Omodeo, *Studi sull'età della restaurazione. La cultura francese della Restaurazione. Aspetti del cattolicesimo della Restaurazione*, Torino 1974, 48).

23 Su questo aspetto v. in questo volume *supra Constitución, Monarquía, Parlamento: Francia y Belgica*, 130 ss.

de la nécessité et de la raison du temps».[24] Tuttavia, se l'analisi di questi aspetti fa giustamente pensare ad una condivisa cultura costituzionale, nondimeno bisogna osservare la diversità di "ispirazione" delle costituzioni sotto il profilo, assai rilevante per il funzionamento concreto di quei meccanismi, della legittimità "costituente", di ordine storico-provvidenziale o al contrario di natura volontaristico-popolare.

In questo contesto si potrebbe parlare, ricorrendo ad un ossimoro, di una prima razionalizzazione "storicistica" per segnalare il tentativo di "correggere" la rigidità della costituzione artificiale – o, per usare un'espressione di M. Troper, correggere le basi dell'identità costituzionale francese – fondata sulla preminenza dell'indirizzo politico. Nel 1814 solo una prospettiva "eclettica" sembra poter ispirare un testo costituzionale. Resta però di improbabile soluzione il problema delle "premesse" – d'ordine storico-politico – che possano dare unità e coerenza alla costituzione. Se la costituzione-atto, cioè frutto di un disegno costituente e razionale, appare l'unica Costituzione possibile in Francia, l'appello alla storia tende però a rafforzarsi. Proprio dalla impossibilità di conciliare la storia con la Rivoluzione era seguito il disperato progetto di salvare la monarchia di antico regime impiantandola nello spazio ostile della sovranità popolare. B. Constant, pur restando in sostanza fedele ad una idea razionale di costituzione, cercherà di trovare un punto di equilibrio tra la ragione e la storia. Già negli scritti direttoriali la dottrina della perfettibilità pone a livello generale il problema della aderenza tra idee e istituzioni, con il tempo a fare da bilanciere. Nei *Principes* del 1806 Constant mostra di condividere la riflessione sulla storia quale fondamento della teoria politica. «Le temps, dit Bacon, est le grand réformateur. Ne refusez pas son assistance. Laissez-le marcher devant vous, pour qu'il aplanisse la route. Si ce que vous instituez n'a pas été préparé par lui, vous commanderez vainement ...».[25] Al principio della Restaurazione Constant tenderà a "correggere" il dato razionale («Les constitutions se font rarement par la volonté des hommes») con quello della storia («Le temps les fait»). "Fare" la costituzione appare ormai una forma specifica della razionalità, ma una volta costituiti i poteri è bene lasciare il giusto spazio alle «deux puissances réformatrices»,[26] il tempo[27] e l'esperienza.

24 F. Guizot, *Mémoires pour servir à l'histoire de mon temps*, Paris 1858–1867, I, 36.

25 B. Constant, *Principes de politique*, ed. Hofmann, Genève 1980, 412.

26 B. Constant, *Réflexions sur les constitutions, la distribution des pouvoirs et les garanties, dans une monarchie constitutionnelle*, Paris 1814.

27 «Tant qu'on n'a pas essayé d'une constitution par la pratique, les formes sont une lettre morte: la pratique seule en démontre l'effet et en détermine le sens. Nous n'avons que trop abattu l'édifice sous prétexte de le reconstruire: profitons désormais des lumières qui ne s'acquièrent que par les faits, afin de pourvoir

Tale discorso non può essere ricondotto semplicemente alla concezione della costituzione storica. Il discorso viene spostato dalla mera contrapposizione costituzione razionale / costituzione storica, ad una prospettiva assai più complessa senza la quale è difficile immaginare il processo di razionalizzazione della monarchia costituzionale. Il concetto di "macchina costituzionale" vive nella storia, ma opera nel quadro di un disegno razionale (*pouvoir neutre*, responsabilità dei ministri, seconda Camera, governo rappresentativo ecc.), con il modello inglese a fare da principale, ma controverso, paradigma. Controverso perché all'apparenza l'intreccio tra il linguaggio empirico e la razionalizzazione della forma costituzionale appare – e anzi sembra dover essere – quello riconducibile all'esperienza d'oltremanica. Si vedrà però subito la difficoltà di conciliare un modello a forte impianto storicistico che istituzionalizza la dinamica delle forze sociali nell'organizzazione del governo misto a sovranità "frazionata" (le tre forme "pure" di Stato) e la concezione post-rivoluzionaria a predominante razionalistica che ha nel suo codice genetico l'idea forte della sovranità "assoluta" (lo spazio nuovo della sovranità popolare al posto della sovranità monarchico-tradizionale). Insomma, temperare il costituzionalismo meccanicistico e necessariamente "artificiale" facendo appello ad uno incentrato sulla logica storico-naturale dei contropoteri[28] è compito arduo. Nel complicato gioco di specchi, fatto di osservazioni e di influenze, che si svolge a partire dal Settecento, lo sguardo è non di rado fonte di fraintendimenti e di interpretazioni abusive.[29] Ma la costituzione britannica – al di là della sua reale utilizzabilità pratica nel dibattito francese – diventa il paradigma della costituzione storica, un modello peculiare – si potrebbe dire – di "*perfectibilité constitutionnelle*" improntato al principio della moderazione: evitare, perciò, ogni innovazione violenta e quindi pericolosa, così come ogni atteggiamento ostinato di chiusura. «Chaque parti, depuis vingt-cinq ans, a repoussé et regretté tour à tour la constitution anglaise, suivant qu'il était vainqueur ou vainçu [...] On dirait que la constitution anglaise, ou plutôt la raison, en France, est comme la belle Angélique dans

graduellement à tous les besoins partiels, avec mesure, avec lenteur, à l'aide du temps, le plus doux et le plus puissant des auxiliaires» (B. Constant, *Principes de politique applicables à tous les gouvernements représentatifs et particulièrement à la constitution actuelle de la France* (1815), in *Œuvres*, texte présenté et annoté par Alfred Roulin, Paris 1957, 1126).

28 Sul punto si veda l'efficace sintesi di M. Barberis, *Constant e Montesquieu: liberalismo e costituzionalismo*, in *Sette studi sul liberalismo rivoluzionario. Con una introduzione metodologica e un'appendice bibliografica*, Torino 1989, 219 ss.

29 Sul problema dell'interpretazione della costituzione inglese v. le belle e suggestive pagine di P. Schiera, *La costituzione inglese fra storia e mito*, in *Il modello costituzionale inglese e la sua recezione nell'area mediterranea tra la fine del '700 e la prima metà dell'800*, a cura di A. Romano, Milano 1998, 39 ss.

la comédie du *Joueur*: il l'invoque dans sa détresse, et la néglige quand il est heureux».[30]

Vitrolles, nelle sue Memorie, descrive il diffondersi dell'anglomania della Restaurazione come si trattasse di un'epidemia, di una febbre contagiosa.[31] La costituzione britannica sembra poter offrire – secondo un'immagine stereotipata e necessariamente vaga[32] – un quadro rassicurante da cui trarre un buon numero di "insegnamenti": la quintessenza della costituzione storica, ma non priva di taluni accorti interventi razionalizzatori, la prosperità della nazione inglese e la stabilità delle sue istituzioni, la forma di governo in grado di conciliare ordine e libertà. L'esame della costituzione britannica permette anche di riconoscerne il pregio più importante, lungo una linea di sviluppo che in Francia corre da Necker a Constant: la efficace combinazione-intreccio del potere legislativo e del potere esecutivo, nella logica dei contropoteri. «Ce problème de la solution duquel dépendaient et la stabilité des gouvernements et le repos des peuples, a été résolu par les Anglais».[33]

Per certi versi il regime politico della *Charte* è il più ravvicinato e arduo tentativo di "razionalizzazione storicistica" di quell'esperienza costituzionale britannica che funge proprio in quei decenni da inevitabile punto di riferimento e da "modello". Ma si può "razionalizzare" la storia? Questo dilemma accompagna la nascita e lo sviluppo del regime politico-parlamentare. Il "momento inglese" diventa così il "momento francese" della "scrittura" di una costituzione che cerca, con inevitabili ambiguità, di restaurare un ordine politico monarchico all'interno di una organizzazione dei poteri che guarda alla logica del bilanciamento. Il riferimento, reale o immaginario, alla costituzione britannica dovrebbe consentire di raggiungere anche in Francia una condizione di combinazione / intreccio del potere legislativo e del potere esecutivo.

Ma se il modello inglese è un arsenale dal quale attingere argomenti e motivi di riflessione per introdurli nel dibattito e nella lotta politica in Francia (da Constant a Vitrolles, da Chateaubriand a Guizot ...), preponderanti sono le

30 G. de Staël, *Considérations sur les principaux événements de la Révolution française*, in *Œuvres posthumes*, Paris 1861, réimpression Genève 1967, III, 104.

31 E.-F.-A. Arnaud de Vitrolles, *Mémoires de Vitrolles*, texte intégral établi par E. Forgues, présenté et annoté par P. Farel, Paris 1950–1952, II, 53–54.

32 P. Rosanvallon, *La Monarchie impossible. Les Chartes de 1814 et de 1830*, Paris 1994, 62.

33 Anonimo, *D'une des principales causes de l'inactivité du gouvernement*, in *Le Censeur*, 4, 1814, 133: «Un des problèmes les plus difficiles que la politique présentât à résoudre était de constituer le pouvoir législatif et le pouvoir exécutif, de manière que l'un formât toujours un obstacle aux usurpations de l'autre, sans que de leur action et de leur résistance il pût jamais résulter un choc assez fort pour mettre l'un des deux en péril».

visioni "immaginarie" che spesso fanno vedere delle istituzioni inglesi solo aspetti esteriori. L'anglofobo Fievée è impietoso e riporta alla realtà: «Nous croyons pouvoir imiter la constitution anglaise; la connaissons-nous? Nous ne connaissons de cette constitution que ce qui se voit; comme on ne juge, au premier aspect, un bâtiment que par la partie qui s'élève au-dessus des fondations».[34] Ma non dobbiamo credere che lo scetticismo sia prerogativa dei soli scrittori realisti. Lo stesso argomento poteva essere utilizzato da Royer-Collard, per ragioni anche tattiche, in un celebre discorso del 1816, per mostrare la grande diversità di "premesse" e di condizioni tra il regime della *Charte* e la mitica costituzione inglese.[35] Bisognava, insomma, tramutare i francesi in inglesi, esercizio impossibile oltre che, ovviamente, indesiderato.

4. L'armonia laboriosa e il potere neutro

L'«harmonie laborieuse»[36] tra i poteri che altrove rendeva possibile il governo costituzionale non era in Francia a portata di mano. Il nodo strategico della configurazione e dell'articolazione del potere esecutivo, tra *pouvoir d'Etat* e *gouvernement*, era inevitabilmente intrecciato col problema stesso della «monarchia costituzionale». Questa appare, ancora una volta, la strada maestra per affrontare il problema del governo parlamentare tra il 1814 e il 1848. Anche per questa ragione la "razionalizzazione parlamentare" è soprattuto una costruzione e un'esperienza, mai un dato "posto" dalle Carte.

Questi documenti del 1814 e del 1830 vengono rubricati sotto la generica nozione di "monarchia costituzionale". Il problema definitorio, tuttavia, va ben oltre questa prima approssimazione e rappresenta per il caso francese un significativo "problema costituzionale". La monarchia, per la sua natura storica, simbolica, politica, dovrebbe essere l'architrave, il "motore" e il momento di sintesi dell'ordine costituzionale: e tuttavia, malgrado gli sforzi compiuti, fallisce in Francia il suo "appuntamento" moderno con la costituzione.

34 J. Fievée, *Correspondance politique et administrative, commencée au mois de mai 1814*, Paris 1815, prima parte, lettera I, 3.

35 «... Si vous voulez substituer le gouvernement anglais à notre Charte française, donnez-nous donc la constitution physique et morale de l'Angleterre; faites donc que l'histoire d'Angleterre soit la nôtre; mettez dans notre balance politique une aristocratie puissante et honorée ...» (P. de Barante, *La vie politique de M. Royer-Collard. Ses discours et ses écrits*, Paris 1863, I, 217).

36 L'espressione è di F. Guizot, *Pourquoi la Revolution d'Angleterre a-t-elle réussi? Discours sur l'histoire de la Révolution d'Angleterre*, Paris 1850, 114. Cfr. A. Kahan, *Guizot et le modèle anglais*, in *François Guizot et la culture politique de son temps*, Colloque de la Fondation Guizot-Val Richer, a cura di M. Valensise, Paris 1991, 219–231.

Dopo i tentativi di costituzionalizzazione del 1789–1791, la monarchia riappare nel 1814 nella forma della "monarchia limitata", ovvero di un regime nel quale il sovrano che si autolimita conserva una posizione di supremazia rispetto ai "poteri" che derivano le loro attribuzioni dalla Carta *octroyée*. «Il governo stabilito dalla Carta è, tra tutti i governi a *istituzioni rappresentative*, il solo nel quale il potere monarchico sia *principio* dell'organizzazione sociale e *fonte* della vita politica».[37] Nel 1824 Royer-Collard osserva come non sia sufficiente definire il governo «una monarchia mista, chiamata Governo rappresentativo, nel quale la Camera elettiva concorre con il monarca e una Camera ereditaria alla formazione della legge e alla direzione degli affari pubblici ...». È il «potere regolatore» quello che imprime al governo il carattere dominante. Nel caso francese è il Re della Carta che conserva «un eclatante primato tra i poteri che lo affiancano. Solo rappresenta l'unità morale della società; solo agisce, solo comanda, solo è l'autore della legge la cui iniziativa gli è riservata in via esclusiva. Quest'ultima circostanza esprime il fatto che gli altri poteri non sono per lui che dei limiti; benché siano dei limiti viventi e in grado di attivarsi ...».[38] Royer-Collard, sin dai primi passi della monarchia restaurata – assieme ai dottrinari della sua generazione, de Serre e Jordan – aveva condiviso le preoccupazioni di Necker e dei *monarchiens* in ordine al necessario rafforzamento del potere esecutivo.

La storia costituzionale francese mostra, come è noto, uno sviluppo della forma monarchica che dalla «monarchia limitata» della *Charte* del 1814 – pur in presenza di un difficile processo di «parlamentarizzazione» – perviene ad un atto di re-distribuzione dei poteri nel 1830, atto che conserva al re il potere esecutivo (con il depotenziamento del potere regolamentare rispetto alla primazia della legge) ma in una logica di riequilibrio complessivo a vantaggio della Camera eletta. Lungo questo percorso – cui non è estraneo il mutamento dei paradigmi della legittimità politica – resta centrale il problema della natura costituzionale del potere monarchico.

Non è certo un caso se la celebre e complessa teoria del "potere neutro" di Benjamin Constant – probabilmente una delle più importanti ed equivocate riflessioni del primo Ottocento costituzionale – raggiunge la sua "maturazione" negli anni della *Charte*.[39] Una riflessione, presente e riarticolata in molti luoghi dell'opera dello studioso svizzero, che cerca di rispondere ad una stessa esigenza che si presenta in forme e condizioni diverse tra l'età direttoriale e la restaurazione monarchica. Non bisogna dimenticare che le formule più coerenti sono

37 Ch.-H. His, *De la Monarchie représentative*, Paris 1829, 4–5.

38 P. de Barante, *La vie politique de M. Royer-Collard*, cit., 216–217.

39 Su questo profilo v. *supra* in questo volume *Coppet et la percée de l'Etat libéral constitutionnel*, 222.

da un lato quella, d'origine repubblicana, di «potere neutro e preservatore» e dall'altro la formula, utilizzata al momento della Restaurazione, di «potere neutro e intermediario». Il sovrano «preservatore» è l'organo dell'unità nazionale e della continuità dello Stato: forte della sua «maestà» e «imparzialità» incarna il «potere pubblico», è l'«essere a parte, superiore alle differenze di opinioni», il guardiano che garantisce l'equilibrio in caso di eccezione, quando la collaborazione tra i poteri è minacciata. Ma il potere «intermediario» investe il monarca anche del compito, storicamente arduo, di «pacificare» – attraverso la sua neutralità – un paese profondamente diviso tra visioni diverse del futuro (oltre che del passato), sovrintendendo alla formazione e allo sviluppo di un sistema costituzionale in grado di «disciplinare» la lotta politica (nel suo legame con l'opinione), di garantire un governo coeso e responsabile politicamente (nel senso allora in uso), permettendo forme di dissenso e di pluralismo. Il potere preservatore, fondando un governo che risponda dei suoi atti alla nazione, contribuisce a tenere in equilibrio ordine e libertà, garantendo, in ultima istanza, il principio e il fine di un sistema costituzionale ben inteso: la sfera di sicurezza dei cittadini.

Ridimensionata solo in parte la concezione della monarchia limitata, Constant pensa che il potere neutro non possa essere racchiuso in Francia, al momento della Restaurazione (quando il sistema costituzionale è ancora tutto da costruire), nella sola sfera dell'*auctoritas*. Il monarca deve poter, se necessario, esercitare tutte le sue *potestates*. Il «potere regio» è una risorsa in termini di neutralità, ma, all'occasione, deve avere la forza legale per essere realmente «preservatore» e «intermediario». Il Re potere neutro deve avere la capacità e la volontà – e qui sta il problema – di tenere in equilibrio l'opinione e il «potere ministeriale», le Camere e la funzione di governo, individuando il punto variabile di compromesso. Il Re – si potrebbe forse dire – ha il difficile compito di fissare il mutevole punto di equilibrio tra la costituzione formale e la costituzione materiale.

Il concetto metteva in luce – come nessun altro – la grande complessità di una "macchina" costituzionale che aveva bisogno per ben funzionare di un capo dello Stato ambivalente: al di sopra delle lotte politiche contingenti, ma severo e attento «regolatore» del sistema costituzionale. Il rischio che la nozione constantiana venisse strumentalizzata (come infatti avvenne tra il 1815 e il 1816) era elevato finendo per semplificare e banalizzare una ricostruzione ingegnosa e in grado di dare un «senso» alla monarchia costituzionale.[40] In realtà, la teoria del *pouvoir neutre* di Benjamin Constant intendeva descrivere e organizzare le dinamiche costituzionali partendo dalla monarchia come "risorsa" per "razionalizzare" il sistema.

40 G. Antonetti, *La monarchie constitutionnelle*, Paris 1998, 148–149.

Non è neppure un caso se tale concetto torna alla ribalta – anche se con elementi nuovi – alla vigilia della rivoluzione e durante la Monarchia di Luglio. Di solito la formula «Il Re regna ma non governa» viene vista come una sintesi del pensiero di Thiers. Non bisogna però dimenticare il contesto e l'articolazione della sua elaborazione che precede le giornate di Luglio. Thiers segue ormai la logica della «monarchia rappresentativa»[41] fondata sul nesso di reciprocità e di «contrappeso» tra due "veti": il diritto del Re di sciogliere la Camera, il diritto della Camera di chiedere le dimissioni del ministero. Thiers – polemizzando con gli *ultras* – ritiene la prerogativa regia un effetto della Carta intesa come atto «contrattuale». Solo dal febbraio 1830 il direttore del *National* fissa i termini della teoria secondo cui il «Re regna ma non governa». La filiazione constantiana[42] è evidente, e tuttavia la diversità del contesto e la natura particolare della lotta politica portano Thiers a utilizzare la teoria del potere neutro all'interno di una più pronunciata dinamica parlamentare prefigurando una più chiara scissione del potere esecutivo tra potere di riserva del sovrano e «potere attivo» del ministro e, di conseguenza, il diritto della Camera-maggioranza a partecipare, con il suo potere di "veto", alla scelta dei ministri. Il potere esecutivo viene esercitato dal ministro: «... in una parola, egli governa, e poiché ha la fiducia delle camere, non esistendo altrimenti, non fa che le cose che esse approvano ... Così, il re regna, i ministri governano, le camere giudicano».[43]

La Carta orleanista istituisce su basi di eguaglianza i due fondamentali poteri dello Stato ma senza riuscire a sciogliere né il nodo teorico della monarchia costituzionale né il problema del regime parlamentare. Paradossalmente, mentre la monarchia del 1814 è coerente rispetto al testo della *Charte*, il documento del 1830 – per l'ambiguità insita nelle origini del nuovo regime "bastardo", monarchico ma con inserzioni "repubblicane" – è reticente su troppe questioni a cominciare da quella fondamentale dello statuto giuridico del governo e della sua responsabilità. La Carta del 1830 che avrebbe dovuto in teoria risolvere le due questioni più controverse della Restaurazione non recepisce "nel testo", se non in maniera molto parziale, il dibattito che sul finire degli anni Venti e alla vigilia della Rivoluzione aveva posto con decisione il problema del ruolo del monarca, il rapporto di «unione e collaborazione» tra il ministero e la maggioranza parlamentare, i meccanismi costituzionali di risoluzione del conflitto tra gli organi. I costituenti del 1830 non sono riusciti a dare alle istituzioni una chiara direzione di marcia, preferendo rinviare alla prassi e al tessuto convenzionale e, in ultima istanza, alla lotta politica l'esito della vicenda costituzionale.

41 *Le National*, 8 janvier 1830, 1, col. 3.
42 A. Thiers, *La monarchie de 1830*, Paris 1831, 6–7.
43 *Le National*, 4 février, 1830, 2, col. 1.

Il 1830, malgrado il riconoscimento del processo di parlamentarizzazione della monarchia, non può risolvere i problemi e fare tesoro del dibattito della Restaurazione. Questo limite – che molto inciderà sulle mancate riforme degli anni Quaranta – si riverbera sul pieno e definitivo sviluppo del regime parlamentare. La Carta del 1830 affrontò il problema del riequilibrio dei poteri, ma la teoria della «continuità» sostanziale rispetto al testo del 1814 finì per far passare in secondo piano l'adeguamento costituzionale dell'istituto del governo e della responsabilità dei ministri e dei funzionari. In epoca orleanista ci si poteva giovare – a differenza che nel 1814 – dell'esperienza maturata lungo tutta la Restaurazione. L'art. 69 della Carta non fu valorizzato[44] per sviluppare ulteriormente le condizioni politiche del regime parlamentare (sistema elettorale, riforma parlamentare etc.). La Monarchia di Luglio restò, si potrebbe dire, in mezzo al guado: senza poter ovviamente tornare indietro ma incapace di raggiungere la sponda di un equilibrato ed efficiente regime parlamentare.

Sul finire degli anni Trenta torna a farsi sentire la questione che aveva accompagnato la dinamica costituzionale della Restaurazione: in caso di contrasti tra i poteri, chi doveva avere l'ultima parola? La Camera eletta o il re? Il tema della sovranità si intrecciava strettamente col problema della forma monarchica e del regime politico. La soluzione suggerita tra il 1814 e il 1830 era, per gli *ultras*, che fosse il re ad avere l'ultima parola *selon la lettre de la Charte*; per i liberali invece l'ultima parola del re doveva comunque tenere presente il "concorso" dell'opinione rappresentata dalla Camera *selon l'esprit de la Charte*. Questa seconda tesi alla fine prevalse e divenne *senso comune* nel 1830.

5. Parlamentarismo e responsabilità ministeriale

Le *Chartes* sono testi laconici e carenti nel definire la misura dei rapporti e del controllo tra parlamento ed esecutivo.[45] In particolare si nota una contraddizione tra lo sviluppo essenzialmente fattuale, *empirico*, della strumentazione di controllo del parlamento sull'attività del governo e gli effetti limitati prodotti sul piano della concreta responsabilità ministeriale e quindi sulla stabilizzazione della forma di governo, dovendosi ciò, probabilmente, ad una complessa pluralità di fattori quali la natura e il ruolo della monarchia, la genetica difficoltà di articolazione "partitica" delle forze politiche, la carenza di unità e solidarietà

44 V. per es. le critiche di S. Pinheiro-Ferreira, *Observations sur la Charte constitutionnelle de la France, extraites du cours de droit public de M. le commandeur Silvestre Pinheiro-Ferreira, ministre d'état de S. M. T. F*, Paris 1833, 15 e 84–85.

45 A. Laquièze, *Le Parlement, organe de contrôle du gouvernement dans la France de la Restauration et de la Monarchie de Juillet*, in *L'istituzione parlamentare nel XIX secolo*, cit.

nel ministero. I cosiddetti diritti di interrogazione, di interpellanza o di inchiesta non trovano alcun riconoscimento esplicito nelle Carte, neanche in quella del 1830.

Il controllo finanziario (bilancio) ha un riferimento testuale ma il suo sviluppo va ben oltre gli angusti confini tracciati dalla Carta. Nel corso della Restaurazione, già dai primi anni, si affermano i principi fondamentali del controllo finanziario quando ministri delle finanze sono il barone Louis, il conte Corvetto, il conte Villèle. L'ordinanza del 14 settembre 1822 stabilisce la regola dell'unità di bilancio (spese ed entrate) e la sua annualità. Ma già la legge del 25 marzo 1817 (articolo 151) aveva introdotto il voto parlamentare delle spese ministero per ministero, aprendo una strada importante che giunge sino alla Terza Repubblica. Nella logica del governo rappresentativo – ovvero di un governo basato sul principio della pubblicità – bisognava poter verificare nel più ampio dettaglio possibile l'insieme del bilancio. Nel 1829 questo fu votato non più per aggregazione, ma per sezioni. Durante la Monarchia di Luglio, nel 1831, si introduce la suddivisione per capitoli; nel 1848 furono 338 i capitoli votati.

Il dibattito sulla legge annuale di bilancio divenne l'occasione per discutere della politica del governo, senza però che si arrivasse a mettere in discussione la responsabilità ministeriale. Anche la rivendicazione parlamentare del cd. "rifiuto del bilancio" – sostenuta con forza da Thiers e da Constant nella crisi del 1830 – non ebbe rilevanza costituzionale durante il regime orleanista. Nel corso della Restaurazione, invece, si conquistano uno spazio significativo alcuni strumenti di controllo parlamentare non previsti dalla Carta o, se previsti, "riformulati" sul piano della prassi. Basti pensare all'istituto della petizione (art. 53 *Charte* 1814) utilizzato per sollecitare i ministri a dar conto in aula della loro attività,[46] benché spesso senza alcun esito. Diverso il caso dell'*adresse*, modernizzazione del diritto di rimostranza dei *Parlements* nei confronti del monarca. Previsto da una legge del 1814 (13 agosto), non ebbe conseguenze particolari se non dopo il 1821 allorché la discussione e il voto dell'*adresse* – quale risposta al discorso del trono – divennero l'occasione per muovere critiche al governo (e pur indirettamente al Sovrano). La storia parlamentare francese è caratterizzata da alcuni *adresse* importanti, a partire da quello dei 221 diretto contro la politica di Polignac e di Carlo X e quello del gennaio 1839 promosso dalla innaturale *coalition* (Guizot, Thiers, Barrot) contro il ministero Molé accusato di dare manforte alla politica

46 J. Barthélemy, *L'introduction du régime parlementaire*, cit., 234 ss.; J.-P. Dionnet, *La contribution de la pétition à l'évolution politique dans l'histoire contemporaine: évocation d'une difficile intégration*, in *Droits*, 37, 2003, 173–189. Per una sintesi efficace v. M. Morabito, D. Bormaud, *Histoire constitutionnelle et politique de la France (1789–1958)*, Paris 1998, 181 ss.

personale di Luigi Filippo.[47] Meno efficaci si sono rivelate altre tecniche di controllo come l'interpellanza[48] e l'inchiesta parlamentare. La prima era apparsa agli inizi della Monarchia di Luglio e consisteva – sul modello inglese – in una domanda posta da un parlamentare, seguita da un dibattito che si chiudeva col voto di un ordine del giorno. L'interpellanza non sortì grandi effetti anche perché non poteva essere proposta senza il consenso della maggioranza; i ministri interpellati si riservavano il diritto di non rispondere; il voto finale non ebbe mai rilevanza politica. Il diritto d'inchiesta si affermò nel corso della Monarchia di Luglio, ma anche in questo caso senza poter incidere in maniera davvero significativa sull'indirizzo politico dei ministri.

Il "gruppo di Coppet" aveva avviato per tempo con il capostipite Necker una riflessione originale sul tema cruciale del rapporto responsabilità/governo. La "reinvenzione" francese del concetto di responsabilità era invero carica di significati e di prospettive. Per Necker la responsabilità poggiava anzitutto su quella figura retorico-contestativa che veniva nel Settecento identificata col "tribunale dell'opinione pubblica". Surrogato di un corpo rappresentativo – come noterà la figlia Madame de Staël[49] – l'opinione pubblica è vista come una sorta di alta istanza "giudiziaria" di fronte alla quale persino i re devono "rendere conto". Il ministro, "uomo pubblico" che governa in nome del sovrano, deve "avere credito". E avere credito significa guadagnare "fiducia". Non stupisce che il Necker banchiere/ministro utilizzi così agevolmente un lessico tipicamente "economico", da *Commercial Society*. «Il credito – scriverà sempre sua figlia – è dunque la vera scoperta moderna che ha legato i governi coi popoli. Il bisogno di credito obbliga i governi a rispettare la pubblica opinione; ed allo stesso modo che il commercio ha incivilito le nazioni, il credito che da esso deriva ha reso necessarie delle forme costituzionali qualsivoglia ...».[50] Nessun altro orientamento intellettuale ha saputo cogliere, nell'Europa continentale, il senso più profondo della responsabilità ministeriale meglio del "gruppo di Coppet". Necker, anche dopo le disillusioni del 1789, restò convinto che la coppia inviolabilità/responsabilità fosse una grande risorsa della condizione monarchica in grado di separare la responsabilità dei ministri dalla *puissance* e dalla

47 Cfr. M. Deslandres, *Histoire constitutionnelle de France de 1789 à 1870, t. II*, cit., 180 ss. Sul dibattito costituzionale innescato dalle vicende politico-parlamentari del 1838–39 rinvio all'analisi di Prosper Duvergier de Hauranne in questo volume, *supra Governo rappresentativo e principio parlamentare*, 314–319.

48 A. Laquièze, *Les origines*, cit.

49 G. de Staël, *Considerazioni sui principali avvenimenti della Rivoluzione francese*, intr. di A. Omodeo, Milano 1943 (1818), 99.

50 *Ibidem*, 96.

sovranità dello Stato. L'esperienza britannica, inevitabile punto di riferimento, rivelava un percorso di "differenziazione funzionale" tra la responsabilità penale (le "arcaiche" procedure di *impeachment* e di *atteinder*) e la responsabilità "politica". Tra il 1714 e i primi decenni dell'Ottocento la responsabilità penale diventò l'assoluta eccezione, mostrando come lo sviluppo del "parlamentarismo" sia anche un processo di "civilizzazione" costituzionale e di "depenalizzazione" dei comportamenti e degli atti dei ministri che pretendano di definire una concezione del bene comune. Constant, come è noto, saprà fare tesoro, pur con alcune inevitabili incompiutezze, della riflessione neckeriana impostando la più significativa teorica della responsabilità nel costituzionalismo del primo Ottocento. Il pensatore svizzero trae i materiali dall'esperienza inglese che ha "sterilizzato" il "veto" regio, potenziato i legami tra esecutivo e legislativo, distinto tra gli atti illegali arbitrari e il cattivo uso del potere legale dei ministri, definito la responsabilità in termini di acquisto o perdita di "fiducia / credito" nei confronti della nazione e dell'opinione pubblica. Attraverso l'ingegnosa teoria del "potere neutro", che riporta il discorso all'interno della più favorevole condizione monarchica, Constant "giurisdizionalizza" la responsabilità e pensa di poter risolvere il dilemma originario: costringere l'esecutivo a "rendere conto" senza alterare la dignità del governo e la *puissance d'Etat*, conciliando stabilità e mutamento. Se Madame de Staël notava come «En Angleterre, quand le ministre n'a plus la majorité dans le Parlement, il quitte sa place», Constant è ben consapevole che il sistema "parlamentare" francese, appena istituito tra il 1814 e il 1815, è altra cosa e in questo contesto è indispensabile rivalorizzare il monarca come "giudice" supremo dei conflitti tra i poteri.[51]

Nonostante l'importanza di questa riflessione, non meraviglia il fatto che la Carta del 1814 (ma anche quella del 1830), contempli, in forma laconica, un incerto principio di responsabilità dei ministri (artt.13, 55, 56). Non manca certo la consapevolezza del rilievo che esso riveste per la configurazione del governo rappresentativo ma il dato testuale, come è noto, non è di grande aiuto poiché "indeciso" tra dimensione "penale" e potenzialità "politiche". Ci troviamo di fronte ministri del re o "anche" ministri responsabili "in qualche modo" verso la maggioranza parlamentare? Dare una risposta univoca a questa domanda è

51 Su questi profili v. in particolare A. Laquièze, *Le modèle anglais et la responsabilité ministérielle selon le groupe de Coppet*, in *Coppet, creuset de l'esprit libéral. Les idées politiques et constitutionnelles du Groupe de Madame de Staël*, a cura di L. Jaume, Paris, Aix-en-Provence 2000, 157–176; L. Jaume, *Le concept de "responsabilité des ministres" chez Benjamin Constant*, in *Revue française de droit constitutionnel*, 42, 2000, 227–243; Id., *Tra concetto e idea-forza: l'opinione pubblica secondo Necker*, in L. Lacchè, a cura di, *Opinione pubblica. Storia, politica, costituzione dal XVIII al XX secolo*, 6, II, 2003, *Giornale di storia costituzionale*, 129–144.

obiettivamente difficile. Nel periodo 1814–1848 non si è affermato in Francia, su base convenzionale, un meccanismo che in via "automatica" e "obbligatoria" costringa il governo a dimettersi non appena venga meno il sostegno maggioritario delle Camere.

Il voto contrario di un ramo del parlamento su singoli provvedimenti, taluni anche qualificanti dal punto di vista politico generale, non determina di per sé le dimissioni del ministero, durante i due regimi politici delle Carte. È invece C. Périer all'inizio della Monarchia orleanista a fare un uso sistematico della questione di fiducia (marzo 1831 – ottobre 1832). Tale ricorso non fu estraneo neppure al ministero Mortier (1834) ma non divenne un'"istituzione" per il resto del nuovo regime politico. In generale si può dire che il voto contrario del parlamento giocò un ruolo limitato e "indiretto" nel determinare la caduta dei governi e soltanto dopo il 1830. Nel periodo considerato, tuttavia, la meta di una compiuta formalizzazione giuridico-politica della responsabilità rimase lontana.

Guizot, nelle sue Memorie, paragonerà il governo parlamentare ad una delicatissima pianta di serra.[52] In effetti tale forma di governo non consiste nella semplice somma aritmetica di tecniche e di princìpi. C'è un *quid* difficile da definire che ne informa l'*esprit*. Si può dire che alcune tecniche di "razionalizzazione" cominciano a muovere i primi passi ma, come abbiamo visto, non basta mutuare alcuni elementi del "discorso" costituzionale britannico per costruire una compiuta "esperienza" francese. B. Constant è ben consapevole del fatto che mancano ancora "pezzi" fondamentali del sistema. «Quando avremo ciò che non abbiamo ancora, ma che è assolutamente indispensabile in ogni monarchia costituzionale, intendo dire, un ministero che agisca di concerto, una maggioranza stabile, e una opposizione ben distinta da questa maggioranza, nessun ministro potrà restare al suo posto, se non ha per sé la maggioranza dei voti, a meno di appellarsi al popolo attraverso nuove elezioni. E allora, queste nuove elezioni saranno la pietra di paragone della fiducia accordata a questo ministro ...».[53]

6. Una "razionalizzazione" incompiuta

Constant dunque coglie acutamente la distanza tra i limiti strutturali e le dinamiche concrete evidenziando la necessità di uno sviluppo che sappia legare assieme, in una sintesi originale, la natura della monarchia, le condizioni della cultura politica (maggioranza / opposizione, ruolo dei «partiti», unità e omogeneità del ministero), i contenuti del regime parlamentare.

52 F. Guizot, *Mémoires*, cit., 1867, VIII, 98.

53 B. Constant, *De la responsabilité des ministres*, in *Œuvres complètes*, IX, 1, Tübingen 2001 (1815), 463.

I limiti ricordati contribuiscono a "comprendere" le ragioni che rendono meno produttivo il rapporto tra mezzi di controllo parlamentare e praticabilità del principio di responsabilità ministeriale. Gli «incerti confini della monarchia costituzionale» segnano il principale campo problematico. Si tratti del monarca *selon la Charte* del 1814 (istitutore-detentore *ab origine* del potere di indirizzo politico) o del "personalismo" di Luigi Filippo (il Re regna e spesso governa), il risultato non cambia (pur nella diversificazione del regime politico): carenza di autonomia e coesione dei ministeri, collegialità solo in alcuni casi raggiunta, debolezza istituzionale, spirito di deferenza se non di subordinazione, paradosso della responsabilità: anziché "coprire" il monarca irresponsabile, i ministri tendono spesso a "coprirsi" dietro lo schermo dell'inviolabilità sovrana.

Non a caso il dibattito costituzionale di epoca orleanista continua a ruotare attorno alla posizione e al ruolo del Monarca nei suoi legami col Parlamento. In una monarchia "semi-legittima" nata dalle barricate parigine, Luigi Filippo, re per volontà "popolare", si rivela più "sovrano" che "cittadino", rivalorizzando l'eredità simbolica e consuetudinaria appannaggio della monarchia continentale.[54] Cittadino sì, ma pur sempre re. Il suo congenito "personalismo" (un sovrano tutt'altro che privo di qualità), un forte investimento dinastico (la fondazione di un regime e il grave, irrisolto problema della legittimità), la minaccia dell'opposizione antidinastica sono condizioni poco favorevoli. Se Duvergier de Hauranne prefigurava un governo parlamentare nel quale il ministero fosse il legame vivente tra i poteri – «per dirlo in una parola, il ministero rappresenta il re nell'ambito delle camere, le camere nel gabinetto del re»[55] – la realtà rivela prassi di formazione, funzionamento e crisi dei ministeri che raramente consentono di affermare un potere esecutivo duale, depotenziato da strategie che fanno leva su "antipatie" (nei confronti di de Broglie o di Thiers) e su "governi dei marescialli" e presidenze fittizie (de Montalivet, Molé ecc.).[56]

Duvergier non nega al sovrano un diritto di *influenza* sulla direzione politica, ma essa deve esercitarsi più sull'insieme che sui dettagli – ovvero sul piano delle grandi scelte – e i ministri dopo aver rispettosamente ascoltato le obiezioni del re mantengono libertà di azione sino al giorno della loro uscita dal governo.[57]

54 Una riflessione paradigmatica è quella proposta dall'anziano barone Roederer nel 1835: cfr. *infra* in questo volume «*Gouverner n'est point administrer. Régner est encore autre chose que gouverner*», 355 ss.

55 P. Duvergier de Hauranne, *Des principes du gouvernement représentatif*, cit., 15.

56 M. Deslandres, *Histoire constitutionnelle de France de 1789 à 1870*, t. II, cit., 242 ss.; Ch. Pouthas, *Les ministères de Louis-Philippe*, in *Revue d'histoire moderne et contemporaine*, I, janvier–mars, 1954.

57 P. Duvergier de Hauranne, *De la politique extérieure et intérieure de la France*, Paris 1841, p. XCIV.

De Hauranne ne invoca uno più «discreto»: «... è cosa buona e necessaria che la sua opinione personale appaia il meno possibile, e non lo faccia scendere nell'arena dei partiti».[58] Questo però non significa affermare – come Guizot vorrebbe far credere – che il re «non può far niente» perché, secondo la Carta, il Monarca è investito di prerogative costituzionali che presuppongono un pensiero e una volontà. Sia il potere di scioglimento della Camera che il potere di far dimettere il ministero rispondono del tutto legittimamente a questa logica.[59] Le diverse posizioni si riavvicinano se si guarda all'uso comune di un termine come quello di *influenza*, un concetto chiave – ancorché sfuggente – per capire la funzione monarchica nella sua lunga e faticosa trasformazione costituzionale nell'Europa del XIX secolo. Guizot, in molti passaggi delle sue opere e, in particolare, dei *Mémoires*, insiste molto sul significato da dare all'espressione «potere personale». Guizot ammette una certa predisposizione caratteriale di Luigi Filippo all'«interventismo» politico. Celebre è il giudizio comparativo sulla condotta di Luigi Filippo e del genero Leopoldo I, re dei Belgi: quanto l'ingerenza del primo era «apparente», tanto la prudenza del secondo sapeva tradursi in una concreta «influenza personale».[60] Guizot rifiuta però l'idea che il «personalismo» del re abbia mai assunto i tratti di un comportamento extralegale. Più volte Guizot ha censurato la tesi di chi avrebbe voluto un «trono vuoto» e un Re fannullone. Ma ciò che Duvergier contesta non sono né l'influenza né le prerogative del monarca, bensì l'eccesso di sovraesposizione politica del sovrano che rischia di distruggere poco a poco quei salutari schermi e finzioni che fanno funzionare il regime rappresentativo. Guizot ha però ragione quando osserva che tutti i limiti posti alle attribuzioni della *royauté* o la disciplina la più rigorosa e completa della responsabilità dei ministri non potranno mai impedire al monarca di esercitare la sua influenza. «Laddove la monarchia costituzionale è esistita, la persona del monarca, le sue opinioni, i suoi sentimenti, le sue volontà non sono mai stati indifferenti, e i più indipendenti, i più esigenti dei ministri li hanno sempre tenuti in gran conto».[61] Scrivere, come fa C. Hello, che «Il Re influisce sul governo, non governa»[62] significa ribadire un principio di prudenza e di funzionalità del governo rappresentativo; ma ciò che emerge dall'esperienza orleanista è invece la difficoltà di pensare e definire la misura e il grado di ripartizione dell'influenza politica necessaria a mantenere in equilibrio i poteri dello Stato.

58 *Ibidem*.
59 R. Capitant, *Régimes parlementaires*, cit., 41–45.
60 F. Guizot, *Mémoires*, cit., 1867, VIII, 95.
61 F. Guizot, *Mélanges politiques et historiques*, *Préface*, Paris 1881, XXXVII–XXXVIII.
62 Ch. Hello, *Del regime costituzionale nelle sue relazioni con lo stato attuale della scienza sociale e politica*, Firenze 1850, II, 162.

Se questo equilibrio non riesce a prodursi in maniera stabile e profonda non lo si può imputare al solo «personalismo» che – come altri fattori – ne è al contempo causa ed effetto. Duvergier de Hauranne è tra i più lucidi osservatori dell'evoluzione del regime orleanista avendo compreso come non sia sufficiente l' "apparenza" del regime costituzionale e come, al contrario, ci sia bisogno di determinate "condizioni politiche" per la nascita e la durevole affermazione del regime rappresentativo a carattere parlamentare. Tre sono le condizioni invocate da Duvergier nel 1847: che la corona «coperta» da un ministero che «governa» resti nell'alta sfera in cui la costituzione l'ha posta; la Camera elettiva, indipendente e gelosa della sua prerogativa, sia di fatto e di diritto il reale centro del governo e il potere preponderante; le elezioni siano libere e producano una camera veramente rappresentativa del paese. «Al di fuori di queste condizioni, si può avere l'apparenza del governo rappresentativo; ma non la realtà».[63] I segnali al riguardo sono contraddittori. Da un lato una forte instabilità ministeriale (17 ministeri in 18 anni) – soprattutto sino al 1840 –, dall'altro una notevole ristrettezza nel reclutamento dei ministri. I Governi sono infatti formati da un piccolo nucleo di professionisti della politica (una sessantina circa): in maggioranza parlamentari aventi in comune una forte identità sociale e professionale (trattandosi in gran parte di funzionari, avvocati, professori). Una diecina di personaggi domina la scena politica e il succedersi dei governi solo in rari casi corrisponde ad un vero e proprio mutamento di strategia politica. Prima del programma vengono gli uomini; la lotta politica, specialmente dopo il 1835, tende a personalizzarsi in maniera decisa. Non di rado l'analisi costituzionalistica che muove dall'osservazione diretta degli avvenimenti conduce ad una sorta di «dover essere» del regime parlamentare: da ciò deriva l'insistenza sull'omogeneità di una maggioranza parlamentare stabile («sistematica») capace di procedere insieme sulle grandi questioni e sotto la guida di veri *leader*, mettendo da parte se necessario l'amor proprio e gli egoismi di parte; su un'opposizione altrettanto coesa; sul principio di responsabilità politica correttamente inteso. Le «condizioni politiche» a cui fa riferimento Duvergier rinviano in ultima istanza al reclutamento del personale politico e al sistema elettorale, il che

63 P. Duvergier de Hauranne, *De la réforme parlementaire*, cit., 249. È interessante notare come, per esempio, Guizot, nelle sue Memorie, individui le condizioni del governo parlamentare in una prospettiva formale e *interna* al sistema: «J'ai considéré les grandes conditions de ce régime: l'homogénéité politique du cabinet; son intimité avec le parti qu'il a pour allié politique dans les Chambres; son travail continu pour rallier ce parti et pour faire prévaloir, auprès de la couronne comme dans les Chambres, une seule et même politique; l'harmonie ainsi librement établie entre les grands pouvoirs publics, comme leur plus sûr moyen de crédit et de force: telles sont les lois essentielles du gouvernement parlementaire» (*Mémoires*, cit., VIII, 97).

significa mettere in discussione «le regole del gioco» che fanno funzionare un tipico sistema notabiliare di canalizzazione del consenso in sintonia con un asfittico «paese legale».

Emerge un regime di bilanciamento dei poteri ad esecutivo monarchico, nella convinzione che lo stretto rapporto tra monarca e governo (affermato dal "testo" della Carta) debba contrastare – in funzione "conservatrice" – la pretesa della Camera elettiva di «assorbire» il potere esecutivo e di assumere una posizione di preponderanza in contraddizione col principio del «concorso» e dell'equilibrio dei poteri. Queste considerazioni sono condivise dai conservatori ministeriali alla Guizot e di volta in volta dalla «palude» parlamentare – si tratti del *tiers parti* di Dupin o di esponenti del centro sinistra – che cercano di adattare la realtà ad un modello di monarchia rappresentativa che, basato sulle fragili fondamenta della "sovranità nazionale", non vuole modificare le "condizioni politiche", il regime elettorale anzitutto e con esso la forma della rappresentanza.

Il sistema di organizzazione e di funzionamento dei gruppi politici risente di vari fattori: inesperienza (*apprentissage*) durante la Restaurazione, mancanza di omogeneità, esistenza di "partiti" anti-sistema durante il regime orleanista (legittimisti, bonapartisti, repubblicani), natura notabilare delle aggregazioni. Questi problemi si collegano in maniera indissolubile alla logica del sistema elettorale censitario che rispecchia la filosofia politico-morale della *rappresentanza* nella quale gran parte dei liberali – pur con sfumature diverse – si riconoscono pienamente. In Francia (come in altre esperienze europee del XIX secolo) il regime elettorale tende a trasformarsi in «sistema politico-amministrativo»[64] assecondando quella radicata tradizione nazionale che individuava nella centralizzazione un complesso e coerente strumento di mediazione locale (i *bourgs pourris* francesi, la "corruzione" elettorale ecc.) e di necessario raccordo con la sfera della rappresentanza politica.[65]

Malgrado i limiti di sistema, non possiamo neppure dimenticare che l'età delle *Chartes* è per la Francia il primo grande laboratorio[66] nel quale si fanno

64 Nel 1839 Léon Faucher dirà: «... Non è possibile introdurre un gran numero di funzionari pubblici nella Camera senza snaturare il carattere della rappresentanza nazionale» (*Des fonctionnaires députés. A M. Odilon Barrot*, 20 février 1839). Sul sistema dei deputati-funzionari cfr. Patrick L. R. Higonnet, Trevor B. Higonnet, *Class, Corruption and Politics in the French Chamber of Deputies, 1846–1848*, in *French Historical Studies*, 5, 1967, 204 ss.; A.-J. Tudesq, *La liberté contre la liberté. Le débat sur les incompatibilités parlementaires*, in *Liberté, libéraux et constitutions*, a cura di J.-P. Clément, L. Jaume e M. Verpeaux, Paris 1997, 33 ss.; A. G. Manca, *I funzionari-deputati tra Parlamento e amministrazione in una prospettiva comparata*, in *L'istituzione parlamentare*, cit., 391.

65 L. Lacchè, *Il telegrafo di Stendhal. Politica ed elezioni nel «Lucien Leuwen» ai tempi della Monarchia di Luglio*, in *Giornale di storia costituzionale*, 4, II, 2002, 217–233.

66 Sulla Francia come laboratorio di forme, modi, tecniche di organizzazione del

strada alcune dinamiche importanti per affermare la logica del parlamentarismo. Per esempio, chi conquista la maggioranza della Camera dei deputati tende ad accentuare la natura «parlamentare» del regime. In fondo, l'atteggiamento "strumentale" degli *ultras* nella cd. *Chambre introuvable*[67] tra il 1815 e il 1816 ha una qualche eco nel comportamento dei liberali a partire dal 1827, dalla caduta del ministero Villèle. Ciò significa che la lotta politica è parte integrante e «produttiva» del quadro costituzionale. Chi ha ottenuto la maggioranza nella Camera elettiva fa leva sul carattere parlamentare e dualistico; chi è sulla difensiva tende a ritrovare nel monarca un soggetto dotato di prerogative il cui esercizio può ricondurre la maggioranza entro un ambito più consono allo schema «monistico» tracciato dalla *Charte*. È evidente che il dibattito di fine anni Venti rimette *ultras* e liberali nelle loro «naturali» posizioni, ma questo carattere non abbandonerà – seppure con forme ulteriori e diverse – il sistema costituzionale in Francia anche dopo il 1830.

Certo è che, pur con le incertezze ricordate, l'insistenza sulla legislazione elettorale e su quella relativa alla stampa – che accompagna i principali snodi politici della Restaurazione – mostra distintamente la convinzione che sia possibile governare e «durare» solo con il sostegno dell'«opinione» (fatta prosperare dalla libertà di stampa).

Un altro aspetto merita di essere sottolineato: il controllo del Parlamento[68] (attraverso la contesa elettorale e le infornate di pari) è la condizione essenziale per influire sulla natura del regime. Pur in assenza di un compiuto regime parlamentare, ci si comporta «come se» esso fosse operante con tutti i suoi principali ingranaggi. Ma non bisogna dimenticare che nessun voto di sfiducia – in quanto tale – fa cadere un governo della Restaurazione e lo scioglimento della Camera resta la manifestazione della prerogativa regia, anche se in alcuni casi è evidente e decisivo l'atteggiamento ripetutamente ostile del parlamento (per es. in occasione della caduta del secondo ministero Richelieu nel 1821). In altri casi

potere e di instaurazione dell'ordine politico insiste R. Redslob, *Die parlamentarische Regierung in ihrer wahren und in ihrer unechten Form. Eine vergleichende Studie über die Verfassungen von England, Belgien, Ungarn, Schweden und Frankreich*, Tübingen 1918, 186.

67 M. S. Corciulo, *Le istituzioni parlamentari in Francia. Cento Giorni e seconda Restaurazione (1815–1816)*, Napoli 1979; Id., *La «Chambre Introuvable» e i princìpi del regime parlamentare (agosto 1815 – settembre 1816)*, in *L'istituzione parlamentare*, cit., 119–137; E. de Waresquiel, *Un paradoxe politique: la Chambre «introuvable» et la naissance du parlementarisme français (octobre 1815 – avril 1816)*, in *Commentaire*, 15, 1992, 409–416.

68 A. Mahul, *Tableau de la Constitution politique de la monarchie française selon la Charte, ou Résumé du droit public des Français, accompagné du texte des lois fondamentales et des documents authentiques*, Paris 1830, 476.

il ministero ricorre al monarca per chiedere lo scioglimento della Camera nella quale esiste una maggioranza solidale ma attraverso tale atto si intende contrastare il progressivo affermarsi della minoranza (Villèle nel 1824 e nel 1827). Le elezioni rivestono allora un ruolo decisivo e diventano l'«appello al paese» per arbitrare la contesa politica. Il re non può essere «partigiano» e «neutrale»: l'intelligenza politica gli è richiesta per ben «interpretare» il sentimento dell'*opinion*. In un regime a tendenza parlamentare il monarca non può utilizzare sistematicamente i mezzi legali per cambiare il risultato voluto dall'opinione, pena una crisi costituzionale dagli esiti incerti. Il regime parlamentare è al contempo, si potrebbe dire, il «campo da gioco» (la forma del regime rappresentativo) e la «partita» da giocare (principio parlamentare):[69] si tratta di una sovrapposizione, questa, destinata a durare nel tempo.

7. Tra monarchia e parlamentarismo: cicli, fallimenti, memorie

Il patrimonio di idee, dibattiti e concetti elaborati durante l'età delle Carte costituzionali non si dissolve nel 1848. Se la monarchia, alla fine, perderà in Francia il suo appuntamento con la modernità costituzionale, il "parlamentarismo" – che ha le sue radici nei trentacinque anni della monarchia costituzionale – riprenderà più avanti la sua strada, non senza difficoltà e con profonde trasformazioni.

Sul grande tema dell'instabilità – o del *roman*, come dirà Prevost-Paradol[70] – delle istituzioni politiche e sui "cicli" costituzionali pesano molti elementi a cominciare dalla difficoltà di "costituzionalizzare" la Rivoluzione[71] e le sue straordinarie "energie". A sua volta, il tema della «monarchia impossibile» come chiave di lettura della storia delle *Chartes* (1814–1830) e del «momento inglese»[72] segnala questioni profonde legate a caratteri e atteggiamenti di lungo periodo presenti nella cultura politica francese. Non sorprende quindi il fatto che tanti uomini politici e tanti intellettuali si siano interrogati, in maniera finanche ossessiva, sulle ragioni che avrebbero impedito alla Francia di raggiungere una condizione di stabilità e di equilibrio nell'ordine costituzionale. Gli argomenti addotti sono numerosi ed eterogenei. I legittimisti lamenteranno con nostalgia la caduta dei Borboni, Tocqueville rifletterà sulla crisi morale dell'or-

69 F. Guizot, *Mélanges politiques*, cit., XV.

70 L.-A. Prevost-Paradol, *La France nouvelle*, Paris 1868, 295.

71 Cfr. F. Furet, *Réflexions sur l'idée de tradition révolutionnaire dans la France du XIXe siècle*, in *Pouvoirs*, 50, 1990, 5 ss.; A. Jainchill, S. Moyn, *French Democracy between Totalitarianism and Solidarity: Pierre Rosanvallon and Revisionist Historiography*, in *The Journal of Modern History*, 76, 2004, 107 ss.

72 P. Rosanvallon, *La Monarchie impossible*, cit., 179–180.

leanismo e sulle illusioni della Seconda Repubblica,[73] François Guizot scriverà sopra le macerie della Monarchia di Luglio, avendo di fronte la "compiutezza" della *Glorious Revolution*.[74] Walter Bagehot chiamò addirittura in causa il "carattere francese" in quanto, a suo dire, inadatto al governo costituzionale: gli insuccessi a catena gli fecero sorgere nel 1851 il sospetto che «...un numero così grande di bancarotte suggerisca un po' d'inadeguatezza al commercio ...»[75] e che l'eccesso di ingegno – di ingegneria costituzionale si direbbe oggi – fosse poco adatto a fortificare i principi costituzionali e a radicarne le istituzioni.

Prevost-Paradol, quasi alle soglie della Terza Repubblica, userà una formula efficace: «...la Révolution française a fondé une société, elle cherche encore son gouvernement»,[76] per interrogarsi poi sulla storia istituzionale degli ultimi decenni. Le crisi erano una lunga prova per raggiungere infine un porto sicuro o erano invece il sintomo di una malattia incurabile? Per Ernest Renan molto dipendeva dal fatto che in Francia la concezione "filosofica" della libertà avesse prevalso sulla concezione "storica": «C'est que la souveraineté du peuple ne fonde pas le gouvernement constitutionnel. L'Etat, ainsi établi à la française, est trop fort, loin de garantir toutes les libertés, il absorbe toutes les libertés; sa forme est la Convention ou le despotisme».[77]

La monarchia, come condizione «favorevole» per sviluppare il governo parlamentare, restò a lungo nei pensieri e nelle preoccupazioni. François Guizot nelle sue *Mémoires*, trascorsi ormai vent'anni dalla fine del regime orleanista, osserverà come nella monarchia costituzionale e nel regime parlamentare si avesse la possibilità di raggiungere un obiettivo fondamentale: «unir fortement dans son gouvernement la stabilité du pouvoir au mouvement de la liberté» assicurando inoltre la prima e indispensabile base della libertà politica attraverso la «responsabilité habituelle du pouvoir».[78] Anche Odilon Barrot, nelle sue *Memorie*, vorrà riaffermare positivamente il carattere *fondatore* della monarchia costituzionale (malgrado gli errori compiuti): «Le gouvernement parlementaire n'est pas plus impossible en France que chez nos voisins, et les essais que nous en avons faits,

73 C. Cassina, *«Vincere la demagogia con la democrazia». Il 1848 e le sue illusioni*, in *Giornale di storia costituzionale*, 8, II, 2004, 121–134.

74 F. Guizot, *De la démocratie en France (Janvier 1849)*, Paris 1849 (tr. it. *Della democrazia in Francia (gennaio 1849)*, introduzione di M. Griffo, Firenze 2000); Id., *Pourquoi la Révolution d'Angleterre a-t-elle réussi?*, cit.

75 W. Bagehot, *Napoleone III. Lettere sul colpo di Stato francese del 1851*, a cura di M. Griffo, Roma 1997, 94–95.

76 L.-A. Prevost-Paradol, *La France nouvelle*, cit., 296.

77 E. Renan, *La monarchie constitutionnelle en France*, in *Revue des Deux Mondes*, 1er novembre 1869, poi in *La réforme intellectuelle et morale*, Paris 1872, 3 ed., 240.

78 F. Guizot, *Mémoires*, cit., VIII, 98.

bien loin de prouver que cette forme de gouvernement est une source inévitable de révolutions, prouvent, au contraire, qu'en elle, pourvu qu'elle soit loyalement pratiquée, est le seul moyen de concilier la stabilité du pouvoir avec les responsabilités et les agitations qu'entraîne tout régime représentatif: la vérité est que les deux gouvernements tombés en 1830 et 1848, non-seulement n'ont pas péri par les institutions parlementaires, mais qu'ils en ont vécu; l'un, seize, l'autre, dix-huit ans ...».[79] I fallimenti a catena non dovevano far prevalere i «théoriciens profonds du despotisme» che ogni volta insinuavano che la macchina parlamentare fosse troppo complicata per le mani brutali della Francia.[80]

Non saranno dei «tipi ideali» (come osserva giustamente Pierre Machelon nel suo contributo sulla Terza Repubblica) – tanto più se anacronisticamente calati in contesti storici e in esperienze istituzionali complesse[81] – a determinare aprioristicamente la direzione di marcia della *Repubblica parlamentare*.[82] Come sappiamo, da un'iniziale assemblea "monarchica" si passerà, per incidenti, compromessi e soluzioni "organizzative" inattese, da un potenziale "orleanismo" costituzionale a quel "parlamentarismo assoluto"[83] che diventerà, tra luci ed ombre, la formula stessa dell'esperienza costituzionale della III Repubblica.

Non era obiettivo di questo intervento riflettere sul lascito del "modello parlamentare" nato dalle *Chartes* e sulla sua dimensione "produttiva" nella storia costituzionale francese. Di certo, al centro del dibattito restarono le questioni cruciali del regime parlamentare e dei suoi difficili equilibri. Ben altre "razionalizzazioni" erano di là da venire.

79 Odilon Barrot, *Mémoires posthumes*, Paris 1876, IV.

80 L.-A. Prevost-Paradol, *La France nouvelle*, cit., 327–328. «Quelles que soient ses lacunes et ses traverses, ce régime saura bien prendre ou reprendre, là où il sera nécessaire au triomphe de la liberté politique, la place qui lui appartient» (F. Guizot, *Mémoires*, cit., VIII, 99).

81 Una opportuna messa in guardia in O. Rudelle, *Constitution et Parlement sous la Troisième République*, in *Parlamento e Costituzione*, cit., 357 ss.

82 Per questa visione si rinvia soprattutto a O. Rudelle, *La République absolue*, Paris 1986.

83 V. la classica ricostruzione di R. Carré de Malberg, *Contribution à la théorie générale de l'Etat spécialement d'après les données fournies par le Droit constitutionnel français*, Paris 1920, II, 122 ss. Cfr. adesso la bella edizione italiana dell'opera di Carré de Malberg, *La loi, expression de la volonté générale* (1931) (*La legge espressione della volontà generale*, Milano 2008), con una densa introduzione di M. Calamo Specchia.

«Gouverner n'est point administrer. Régner est encore autre chose que gouverner». Le retour d'un vieillard: P.-L. Roederer et le problème du «gouvernement» pendant la Monarchie de Juillet (1835)

1. Le dernier mot d'un infatigable vieillard

À la fin de 1834, un pamphlet anonyme au contenu provocateur est publié à Paris. En février 1835, le pair de France Pierre-Louis Roederer confirme en être l'auteur (ainsi que tout le monde le sait déjà et l'affirme). L'"aveu" de Roederer est cependant une façon de "relancer"»: il accompagne en effet, ainsi qu'un important *Avant-Propos*, la deuxième édition de ce texte. L'auteur entend justifier son œuvre en répondant aux critiques. C'est ainsi que la polémique se rallume et, pendant environ deux mois, elle sera suivie par un débat dans la presse et dans les lieux consacrés à la politique. Le titre – *Adresse d'un constitutionnel aux constitutionnels*[1] – révèle en réalité assez peu. Le véritable sujet de ce texte est, ainsi que nous le verrons, le délicat problème de la nature constitutionnelle du *Conseil du cabinet et de la Présidence de ce Conseil.*[2]

C'est Roederer lui-même qui nous dit qu'à l'origine son intention était de «remettre sous les yeux de plusieurs membres des deux Chambres que je supposais dans les mêmes principes que moi, et, comme moi, dans l'intention de les opposer, le cas échéant, à des doctrines que je crois funestes». L'auteur n'avait pas l'intention de s'adresser au public et c'est pour cette raison que l'œuvre n'avait pas été mise en vente. Mais, les journaux l'ayant amplement diffusée, Roederer qui, au cours de sa longue activité, n'a jamais sous-estimé

1 *Adresse d'un constitutionnel aux constitutionnels. Par M. Le Cte Roederer, pair de France*, seconde édition, Paris, Typographie de Firmin Didot Frères, Imprimeurs de l'Institut de France, Rue Jacob, n° 24, février 1835.

2 *Du Conseil du Cabinet et de la Présidence de ce Conseil* est le titre du mémoire dont Roederer est l'auteur (Archives Nationales, 29 AP 80, *Papiers Roederer*).

l'importance de l'opinion publique[3] pour la formation de la majorité nationale – a décidé de se soumettre ouvertement «à l'autorité de ce public; autorité fort différente de celle des journaux, autorité qui plane également sur les journaux et sur les écrivains».[4] C'est à cette autorité que Roederer, en dernier, transmet ses inquiétudes, puisque son seul objectif a été de courir au secours de la couronne. «Je l'ai vue dans un péril imminent, et je me suis hâté, sans guide, sans conseil, sans suggestion, de me déclarer entre ceux qui ne la laisseraient pas sans secours».[5] À vrai dire, il aurait saisit l'occasion de s'adresser à la Chambre des pairs pour que sa «voix octogénaire» soit écoutée, mais les circonstances l'ont persuadé d'accélérer son intervention.

La question que l'on se pose spontanément est simple: qu'est-ce qui a poussé cet octogénaire énergique qui a tant vécu – emblème vivant de ces dernières cinquante années tumultueuses de la vie française – à se jeter, à ses risques et périls, dans l'arène politique avec une brochure dont le contenu provocateur a suscité la colère, les critiques et l'ironie (même les moins bienveillantes) d'une bonne partie des forces politiques et de la presse libérale la plus influente?

2. Le retour

Certes, la personnalité de l'auteur a une grande importance. Roederer, après la Seconde Restauration, a dû se retirer de la vie publique dans son domaine normand de Bois-Roussel. Patriarche bourgeois maussade, il a cultivé ses liens familiaux et a écrit de médiocres comédies. En 1830, il a retrouvé un certain mordant, mais il apparaît, presque à tous, comme un survivant. Du reste, ce robin de Metz a derrière lui un tel *cursus honorum* que l'on peut difficilement penser qu'il puisse avoir encore un avenir. Conseiller du parlement de sa ville, animateur habile des comités patriotiques, député de l'Assemblée constituante, membre du Club des Jacobins, procureur-général-syndic de la Seine, essayiste et journaliste influent du «Journal de Paris», putschiste de Brumaire, conseiller

3 Sur le circuit «sociologique» qui naît, dans la réflexion de Roederer, du rapport entre sentiment général, *faiseurs d'opinion* et opinion publique cf. F. Sofia, *Ancora «dal modello francese al caso italiano»: gli appunti di P. L. Roederer per la costituzione cisalpina (1801)*, in *Clio*, 3, 1986, 403, 420; R. Bach, *Conduire l'opinion publique en 1796: Roederer et les métamorphoses de la physiocratie*, in *Opinion*, éd. P. E. Knabe, Berlin 2000, 265–275, essai qui en réalité réfléchit plus sur les origines physiocratiques que sur la pensée de Roederer; et surtout L. Jaume, *Échec au libéralisme. Les Jacobins et l'État*, Paris 1990 (qui cite le texte de Roederer du 1796 sur la *théorie de l'opinion publique*); Id., *Tra concetto e idea-forza: l'opinione pubblica secondo Necker*, in *Giornale di storia costituzionale*, 6, II, 2003, 139–141.

4 *Avant-Propos*, *Adresse*, cit., I–II.

5 *Ibidem*, II.

d'État, ministre des finances à Naples, commissaire extraordinaire, il a également attaché son nom à des œuvres ou des entreprises intellectuelles du niveau de *De la Députation aux États Généraux* (1788), *Du Gouvernement* (1795) ou du *Journal d'Économie Publique, de Morale et de Politique* (1796). Acteur controversé de certains moments décisifs de l'histoire française – il suffit de penser au 10 août ou au coup d'État bonapartiste –, cet idéologue cultivé a su conjuguer la réflexion théorique et l'action politique. Il n'a pas eu la chance d'entrer dans le Panthéon restreint des "héros" de la Révolution – en raison aussi de sa prédilection pour les rôles plus "techniques" que "politiques" – mais on ne peut nier qu'il occupe une position de premier ordre.[6]

C'est seulement après la révolution de Juillet que Roederer gagne à nouveau une position. Certes, il est trop tard. Il sent qu'il doit "rattraper" les quinze années perdues. Des événements et de l'affection le lient à Louis-Philippe et aux Orléans. Philippe Égalité a contribué à le sauver après le 10 août 1792; c'est avec une certaine assiduité que le messinois a fréquenté le futur roi à partir des années vingt. Les espoirs du nouveau régime politique – ainsi que nous le verrons – sont aussi les siens: il entrevoit la fondation d'un *système* en mesure d'assurer et de concilier ordre et liberté, les deux idées que la Révolution n'avait pas réussi à faire coexister. Roederer le vieillard pense avoir encore beaucoup à dire et à faire: pourquoi ne pas exploiter son expérience, pourquoi Louis-Philippe ne voudrait-il pas l'écouter, lui qui n'a plus rien à demander? Il recommence à écrire avec vigueur, presque avec acharnement. Des notes, des mémoires, des conseils, tout peut servir à la besogne pour consolider et *conserver* la monarchie orléaniste: voici alors les réflexions sur la notabilité, la pairie, l'élargissement prudent du cens électoral, la propriété, la liberté de la presse.[7] En 1830, il est de nouveau à l'"action": il est nommé maire d'Essay, Guizot le fait élever à la pairie dans l'enfournée du 11 octobre 1832[8] (après qu'il a échoué aux élections de la Chambre des députés), le 22 octobre 1832 il retrouve son siège à l'Institut, classe des sciences morales et politiques. L'idéologue a-t-il retrouvé la place qui lui revient parmi les *faiseurs d'opinions*?

6 Sur le rapport entre pensée et action, ainsi que sur les événements biographiques et intellectuels, nous renvoyons ici à K. Margerison, *P.-L. Roederer: Political Thought and Practice During the French Revolution*, Philadelphia, The American Philosophical Society, 1983; Th. Lentz, *Roederer*, Préface de J. Tulard, Metz 1989.

7 Cf. en particulier P.-L. Roederer, *Œuvres du comte P.-L. Roederer* … publiées par … le baron A. M. Roederer, Paris 1853–1859, vol. VIII. Voir aussi AN, 29 AP 78, *Papiers Roederer, Politique. Gouvernement. Administration.*

8 Arch. Nat., CC 497, f. 346r.

3. L'Objet de ce Mémoire

> « Objet de ce Mémoire. Attaque à la prérogative royale relativement au Conseil de Cabinet. Une idée fausse travaille maintenant une multitude d'esprits contre les droits et les intérêts de la couronne. C'est que le conseil privé du Roi doit être individualisé dans la personne de son Président, et que ce conseil et ce président doivent être indépendants de l'action du Roi. Trois personnes tâchent d'accréditer ce système: 1° le Ministère; 2° le Président de la Chambre des Députés; 3° les journaux républicains. Je vais présenter leur opinion revêtue autant qu'il se pourra de leurs propres paroles ».[9]

C'est donc là la synthèse du sujet que Roederer entend développer dans sa brochure. C'est le «péril imminent» qui, à son avis, menace les fondements de la monarchie orléaniste et qui dénature sa forme institutionnelle. Le risque concerne la forme de gouvernement, la prérogative royale et en dernière instance le problème de la "parlementarisation" du système constitutionnel. Il s'agit d'enjeux bien importants. Ainsi que nous le verrons, Roederer sera critiqué de plusieurs parts et l'un des arguments qui reviendra le plus souvent sera celui de la complète «inactualité» de ce mémoire téméraire. Mais en effet, que peut-on attendre de ce vieillard, manquant peut-être de lucidité, qui a mis sa plume au service du nouveau prince? Le jugement de Talleyrand, son ancien ami, est péremptoire: Roederer a écrit *De la Députation aux États Généraux* cinquante ans à l'avance et *l'Adresse d'un Constitutionnel* cinquante ans en retard.[10] Le *Journal des Débats* dira que l'article aurait dû être publié en 1810 …

On pourrait se débarrasser facilement du texte du juriste de Metz en le condamnant à une incompréhension totale de la modernité constitutionnelle que les Glorieuses Journées ont enfin imposée à la France. Il se peut que son œuvre soit moins impromptue et naïve qu'il ne semble. Mais procédons par ordre.

Nous avons fait fausse route, observe Roederer dès le début. «Nous avons constitué une monarchie représentative. Ils veulent toute autre chose». Ce sont avant tout les doctrinaires qui ont fortement contribué à la construction de la «démocratie aux extrémités» et de l'oligarchie doctrinaire au centre et qui propagent leur «jésuitisme éclectique» comme étant la réponse à tous les maux de la France. Et c'est justement le gouvernement qui est devenu leur principal souci. Des manœuvres, des voix, des bizarreries, des distributions de ministères remplissent les journaux. Cependant, en agissant ainsi, les solidaires de l'oligarchie se croient investis du pouvoir de faire et défaire un conseil, de nier les droits de la couronne, de violer ouvertement la Charte. Guizot et Thiers ont clairement exprimé leur *système* au cours des séances parlementaires

9 Arch. nat., 29 AP 80, *Papiers Roederer, Du Conseil du Cabinet*, cit., 1.

10 Cit. de Th. Lentz, *Roederer*, cit., 211.

du 5 et 6 décembre 1834. Deux idées sont à la base de leur réflexion: «La première, c'est que les ministres doivent, à chaque renouvellement de chambre, obtenir une adhésion *formelle et authentique* de la Chambre à ce qu'ils appellent leur doctrine ou système. La seconde, c'est que ces ministres doivent avoir un président de leur choix, et tenir avec lui des conseils indépendants de l'action, même de l'intervention du Roi».[11]

Dupin aîné aussi, leader du tiers parti et président de la Chambre des députés, avait manifesté la nécessité d'une présidence indépendante. «M. Dupin – observe Roederer – ne prétend pas comme les doctrines ministérielles, constituer une oligarchie gouvernante sous l'autorité de la Chambre représentative. Son intention est de préparer à la Royauté des volontés plus éclairées. Cette intention non seulement est irréprochable, elle est même louable; mais le moyen d'une présidence indépendante et d'un conseil délibérant sans la participation du Roi, est irréfléchi».[12] Enfin, ce sont certains journaux républicains (en particulier le *Messager* e le *National*) qui prétendent que l'exercice effectif du pouvoir est du ressort du ministère rendu indépendant par l'action royale.

Bien que provenant de positions très différentes, l'objectif – comme nous le verrons – semble commun. Comment répondre à ces prétentions? *En retournant à la Charte*, avant tout. La Constitution ne fonde pas ni suppose un conseil de cabinet, un ministère ou un président. Une chose est le fait, une autre le droit. C'est le roi qui dirige le gouvernement et il ne peut subir l'usurpation de huit ou dix chefs «quand la Charte n'en veut qu'un». La *lettre de la Charte* est univoque, écrit notre auteur, il suffit d'en rappeler les dispositions. Mais *l'esprit de la Charte* est également une source d'interprétation fondamentale. La séparation des pouvoirs, ainsi qu'il résulte de l'ordre constitutionnel, est un argument décisif. En particulier, le droit, qui revient au monarque, de dissoudre la Chambre des députés représente la clef de voûte du système. «Sur la personne du Roi repose donc le droit que la nation s'est réservé contre l'abus que la Chambre pourrait faire de son autorité. Le Roi est, si on peut le dire, le *moniteur* que la nation a préposé comme intéressé à l'exercice de ce droit; c'est son procureur général: il doit être au-dessus de toute atteinte pour que le droit de la nation soit en sûreté, pour que l'envahissement du pouvoir exécutif par le pouvoir législatif soit impossible».[13] Le pouvoir de nommer et de révoquer les ministres de la part du souverain représente une ultérieure garantie. S'il n'en était pas ainsi, comme Roederer le craint, les ministres pourraient utiliser leur influence – s'ajoutant à celle de la Chambre – «pour égarer les collèges électoraux, intercepter, dénaturer,

11 P.-L. Roederer, *Adresse*, cit., 5.

12 Arch. Nat., 29 AP 80, *Papiers Roederer, Du Conseil du Cabinet*, cit., 19.

13 P.-L. Roederer, *Adresse*, cit., 10.

oblitérer les griefs de la Royauté et trahir le vœu de la Charte».[14] Roederer nie à la racine l'existence juridique du Conseil (du Roi). La Charte est silencieuse, elle ne fixe pas le nombre des ministres, ne les fait pas se réunir en un conseil, ne leur attribue aucun président, il n'y a pas de responsabilité commune. Le Conseil dépend du chef de l'État, unique dépositaire du pouvoir exécutif. Les ministres sont *autonomes* dans le domaine de l'administration. Dans celui des *affaires d'État*, ils peuvent même se réunir, «mais c'est un fait et non une assemblée légale des ministres».[15] Pour Roederer, le gouvernement est un conseil privé; il en va de même pour la présidence selon la libre détermination du monarque parce que celui-ci est président de droit.[16] Le roi peut consentir, mais il n'en découle pas un droit permanent ou une institution politique. «Les ministres réunis sont avec le Roi, quand il le veut, le conseil du *gouvernement du Roi*». Comme dans tout conseil, on discute et l'opinion du roi peut même ne pas être approuvée par la majorité, mais l'argument commun devient un «fait du *gouvernement*» et est valable s'il reçoit la signature du roi et du ministre responsable. Le roi peut renvoyer les ministres, s'il pense que l'acte est compromis par leur opposition; les ministres contraires peuvent démissionner, le ministre qui signe est en tout cas responsable.

Le roi, chef suprême de l'État, exerce son autorité souveraine avant tout dans le domaine de la politique étrangère. C'est là que la majesté est une ressource importante qui doit pouvoir s'exercer de façon "personnelle", en soutenant, si nécessaire, l'orientation du gouvernement et du ministre des affaires étrangères. «Ces relations de prince à prince sont un des moyens les plus sûrs et souvent les plus efficaces d'entretenir, de rétablir au besoin, des relations pacifiques et amicales. Rien ne peut priver un Roi constitutionnel d'un moyen où son habilité peut si utilement s'employer au service de la patrie».[17] De même, les ministres ne peuvent avoir un *système*, c'est-à-dire des *principes* différents de ceux exprimés par le roi. Ils n'ont, par conséquent, pas le droit de demander ou de provoquer sur leurs *systèmes* l'opinion de la Chambre des Députés, lorsque celle-ci est renouvelée. «Une telle démarche blesse la constitution dans la prérogative royale, dans la dignité de la Chambre et dans le droit sacré que la nation s'est réservé à elle-même».[18] Les ministres ne peuvent donc – selon Roederer – faire appel à la majorité de la Chambre des députés car la nation serait obligée de

14 *Ibidem*, 11.
15 *Ibidem*, 16.
16 Sur le problème du *cabinet* et de sa présidence, est maintenant fondamental, même pour la discussion historiographique, le volume de A. Laquièze, *Les origines du régime parlementaire en France (1814–1848)*, Paris 2002, chap. V–VI.
17 P.-L. Roederer, *Adresse*, cit., 19.
18 *Ibidem*, 25.

juger entre le roi et les ministres. Le rapport existant entre les ministres et la Chambre doit donc être *dépolitisé*, sinon on court le risque de compromettre la prérogative royale.

Mais les ministres objectent: comment peut-on administrer et gouverner sans avoir une majorité parlementaire?

«Sans doute il faut l'avoir. Mais comment? En l'acquérant. Il faut l'obtenir de sa confiance en vos actes et en vos paroles; il faut la gagner avec le temps, mais non y prétendre d'emblée, d'une convention formelle conclue sans examen et par correspondance de système. Les observateurs qui connaissent un peu les qualités et les défauts du caractère français, sa mobilité et sa noblesse, sa légèreté et sa franchise, doutent que les majorités liées, systématiques, de combinaison et de calcul, puissent jamais se former, ou du moins prendre de la consistance en France comme chez un peuple voisin».[19] Dans l'anthropologie constitutionnelle de Roederer, il n'y a pas de place pour les "majorités systématiques". Les députés *uti singuli* reçoivent – selon la logique des notables – le mandat d'être eux-mêmes et non celui de s'engager pour un système ou un parti.

L'exemple anglais lui-même – si souvent cité – ne s'adapte pas au cas français, ou mieux il finirait par renforcer la thèse de Roederer. Au fond, Louis-Philippe se trouve dans la même position que Guillaume III: un roi qui «a fait ses affaires lui-même; il a fait la guerre en personne à ses ennemis ...». En Angleterre, les rapports du roi avec le conseil de cabinet relèvent du fait et non du droit et le fait change selon les rois, les ministres, les circonstances. «En Angleterre c'est à l'usage, c'est au besoin qu'il appartient de régler ce que sera le conseil habituellement, ce qu'il sera dans quelques circonstances, toujours sans déroger à la prérogative royale: c'est là le principe que doit suivre la France».[20] Il est naturellement plus utile pour Roederer de s'adresser au passé (Guillaume III) de l'histoire anglaise qu'au présent du *Reform Bill* et du progressif effacement de l'autorité royale.

Il ne faut pas oublier le contexte, rappelle l'auteur de l'*Adresse*. L'objectif de Louis-Philippe est de donner une certaine stabilité à la monarchie constitutionnelle. En face de lui, il trouve un passage étroit entre le carlisme et la démocratie. «Son autorité ne peut faire aucun acte indifférent; tout ce qui ne profite pas à la couronne profite à l'un des deux partis opposés, souvent même à tous deux». C'est pourquoi le choix des ministres n'est pas simple. En Angleterre, le roi a

19 *Ibidem*, 28.

20 *Ibidem*, 33. Sur le problème, souvent simplifié, de la responsabilité ministérielle et de la forme du gouvernement dans l'histoire britannique, v. D. Baranger, *Parlementarisme des origines. Éssai sur la condition de la formation d'un exécutif responsable en Angleterre (des années 1740 au début de l'âge victorien)*, Paris 1999; E. Rotelli, *Forme di governo nelle democrazie nascenti. 1689–1789*, Bologna 2005; A. Torre, *Regno Unito*, Bologna 2005.

l'opportunité de s'adresser aux *whigs* ou aux *tories* (ou à ce que ceux-ci sont devenus) parce qu'il sait bien ce qu'ils pensent et ce qu'ils ont l'intention de faire. En va-t-il de même en France? Les "partis" sont-ils tout aussi "intelligibles"? Le roi ne devrait-il pas au contraire craindre des actions qui pourraient favoriser les mouvements "antisystème"? En France, le roi – dans ce contexte historique précis – doit pouvoir défendre ses droits, les intérêts permanents, héréditaires, «en qui l'œil du maître est tenu en éveil par les entrailles du père de famille».[21]

4. Le roi règne et gouverne

L'intervention de Roederer a au moins deux dimensions, l'une contingente, l'autre "structurelle". D'un côté nous retrouvons à l'arrière-plan – même au travers des excès de l'interprétation de l'auteur – la profonde ambiguïté qui caractérise la fondation du régime orléaniste et qui est confirmée par le texte même de la Charte de 1830. Un texte qui naît d'une révolution (par la suite adroitement «'apprivoisée' par les libéraux modérés et les conservateurs), qui renvoie à certaines conditions politiques et idéologiques de nature «démocratique» (les promesses contenues dans l'art. 69) et qui toutefois n'entend pas résoudre, de façon plus nette, le problème du gouvernement et en particulier le rapport entre la monarchie, le gouvernement et la représentation parlementaire. Le texte de 1830, en raison de l'ambiguïté inhérente aux origines du nouveau régime «bâtard», monarchique mais ayant de fortes insertions «républicaines», est réticent sur trop de questions (comme du reste la grande partie des constitutions du XIXe siècle), en commençant par la question fondamentale du statut juridique du gouvernement et de la responsabilité ministérielle. Il suffit de suivre les principales articulations politiques et constitutionnelles (et en ce qui concerne les années trente, les événements de 1834–1835 et, en 1838–1839, ceux qui aboutiront à la formation de la coalition contre le gouvernement Molé) pour s'apercevoir que le régime parlementaire est encore loin d'être une *vérité*.[22] Les événements politiques, la personnalité de Louis-Philippe, le contexte international constituent les coordonnées inéluctables pour un discours en aucune façon linéaire sur le problème de la forme de gouvernement. La catégorie même de l'orléanisme, et pour ce qui nous intéresse, de ce qu'on appelle souvent

21 P.-L. Roederer, *Adresse*, cit., 34.

22 Pour une lecture historique et critique du problème des origines du gouvernement parlementaire entre 1814 et 1848 en France v. en particulier S. Rials, *Essai sur le concept de monarchie limitée (autour de la Charte de 1814)*, in *Révolution et contre-révolution au XIXe siècle*, Paris 1987, 88–125; A. *Laquièze, Les origines du régime parlementaire en France (1814–1848)*, cit.; L. Lacchè, *La Libertà che guida il Popolo. Le Tre Gloriose Giornate del luglio 1830 e le "Chartes" nel costituzionalismo francese*, Bologna 2002.

l'exécutif orléaniste court à son tour le risque de devenir une simplification. En conclusion, la brochure de Roederer est moins inactuelle et "hors de propos" qu'on veut le dire. L'auteur n'est pas simplement un Cottu ou un Madrolle;[23] son analyse va au-delà de la donnée contingente. Ce seront des auteurs royalistes comme His ou néo-orléanistes comme Fonfrède ou Pépin qui confirmeront la *vérité*, au cours de la monarchie de Juillet, du "gouvernement du roi".

Après la mort prématurée d'un président du conseil comme le banquier Casimir Perier, à partir de la fin de 1832, la scène politique est marquée par une tension constante, une fluctuation entre des gouvernements à présidence monarchique (souvent masqués par les "maréchaux", de Soult à Mortier) et des gouvernements qui essaient d'affirmer une orientation politique autour des principales personnalités, surtout le triumvirat hétérogène composé par Thiers, Guizot, de Broglie. Ce sont les démissions de De Broglie (doctrinaire mal vu par Louis-Philippe) qui, au mois d'avril 1834, accentuent ce climat de manœuvres personnelles, de mouvements parlementaires et de programmes monarchiques à l'intérieur duquel trouve place la "defense" de Roederer. Bien que les élections du 21 juin 1834 aient porté un coup très dur à la gauche, la Chambre n'est pas en mesure d'exprimer une volonté ferme et univoque. Le gouvernement de Broglie du 12 mars 1835 – qui sous certains aspects représente la limite *ad quem* de la polémique déclenchée par Roederer – devra conduire la *résistance* et faire approuver les tristement célèbres lois de septembre.

Dans la conclusion de sa brochure, Roederer synthétise, avec un langage oraculaire et axiomatique, le sens de son intervention:

> «"Gouverner n'est point administrer. Régner est encore autre chose que gouverner". Administrer, c'est assurer les services publics par ses propres œuvres ou par celles des subordonnés. Gouverner, c'est régler les difficultés d'administration, quand elles intéressent le pouvoir et que des oppositions en font des affaires d'État. Régner, c'est non seulement gouverner selon les lois de l'État, c'est aussi agir dans les circonstances qui le permettent ou l'exigent; c'est faire ce que nul autre dans l'État ne peut faire avec le même succès; c'est ajouter personnellement à l'autorité des lois les influences morales. Administrer est le fait des ministres, chacun dans son département. Gouverner est le fait du Roi, avec un, au moins, de ses ministres, avec plusieurs, avec tous, avec d'autres encore que ses ministres, quand le Roi le veut. Régner, c'est faire concourir les relations personnelles avec les puissances étrangères, à établir et conserver d'utiles intelligences; c'est dans les crises de guerre civile ou étrangère, payer de sa personne et monter à cheval ...».[24]

Ainsi que nous le savons, Roederer a consacré – au cours de sa longue carrière – une attention constante au thème fondamental de l'architecture et de l'articulation du pouvoir exécutif. Ce n'est pas par hasard que dans l'*Avant-Propos*, il

23 Sur le magistrat royaliste Charles Cottu (1778–1849) et sur l'écrivain Antoine Madrolle (1792–1861) v. L. Lacchè, *La Libertà che guida il Popolo*, cit., 61.

24 P.-L. Roederer, *Adresse*, cit., 39–40.

rappelle ces cinquante années de fréquentation.[25] Dans *Du Gouvernement*[26] datant de 1795, il avait réfléchi de façon organique à ce sujet, en contribuant même au cours des années suivantes, au climat culturel idéologique,[27] à la difficile tentative – en large mesure manquée – de "réhabiliter"[28] l'exécutif. Sa lecture critique de la constitution de l'An III représente la tentative lucide de prévoir de plus grands équilibres et des interrelations entre les pouvoirs.[29] Le gouvernement devait acquérir à nouveau la dimension de la "pensée", devait être en mesure d'exprimer une volonté créatrice distincte du pouvoir exécutif/action et "supérieure" à celui-ci. Roederer, sur la ligne tracée par Sieyès, distinguait entre le *pouvoir de procurer et diriger* et celui d'*ordonner et surveiller*, ce dernier étant l'expression d'un processus collectif d'élaboration.[30]

25 «Une connaissance de cinquante années m'intéresse, il est vrai, aux destinées de la personne qui est à la tête du pouvoir exécutif » (*Ibidem*, *Avant-propos*, cit., IV). Outre que du plus célèbre *Du Gouvernement* (V. note suivante), Roederer est l'auteur d'articles et de discours significatifs: cf. par exemple *Discours … sur l'essence du pouvoir exécutif et sur les bases du système administratif, prononcé dans la séance du 10 août 1791*, Paris s. d.; *De l'Usage à faire de l'autorité publique dans les circonstances présentes, extrait corrigé et augmenté de N. XXVII, XXVIII et XXIX du Journal d'économie publique, suivi d'un Traité de l'émigration*, Paris, Desenne, prairial an V – juin 1797.

26 P.-L. Roederer, *Du Gouvernement*, à Paris, de l'Imprimerie du Journal de Paris, 3 thermidor, an III. Dans ce texte, Roederer refond les articles publiés par le *Journal de Paris* afin d'examiner et de critiquer les aspects retenus les plus faibles du *plan* élaboré par la Commission des Onze. Cfr. K. Margerison, *P.-L. Roederer*, cit., 126 et suiv.

27 L. Scuccimarra, *La Repubblica dei Savants. Conflitto politico e ideologie nella Francia di brumaio*, in *Annali di storia moderna e contemporanea*, IX, 2003, 67.

28 Cf. M. Morabito, *Le chef de l'État en France*, Paris 1996, 2 éd., 50; Id., *Il comando negato. Rivoluzione francese e potere esecutivo*, Roma, Manduria 1997, 74 et suiv.; L. Scuccimarra, *La sciabola di Sieyès. Le giornate di brumaio e la genesi del regime bonapartista*, Bologna 2002, 89–95.

29 P. Colombo, *Governo e costituzione. La trasformazione del regime politico nelle teorie dell'età rivoluzionaria francese*, Milan 1993, 497 et suiv.; S. Mannoni, *Une et indivisible. Storia dell'accentramento amministrativo in Francia, I, La formazione del sistema (1661–1815)*, Milan 1994, 393 et suiv.; M. Gauchet, *La Révolution des pouvoirs. La souveraineté, le peuple et la représentation, 1789–1799*, Paris 1995, 157; pour la contribution fondamentale de l'"école de Coppet" à la réflexion libérale sur le problème du pouvoir exécutif, v. L. Jaume, *L'esprit de Coppet et l'organisation du pouvoir exécutif*, dans *La Constitution de l'an III ou l'ordre républicain*, par J. Bart, J.-J. Clère, C. Courvoisier, M. Verpeaux, Dijon 1998, 122–141; Id., *Necker: examen critique de la Constitution de l'an III*, dans *La Constitution de l'an III. Boissy d'Anglas et la naissance du libéralisme constitutionnel*, sous la dir. de G. Conac, J.-P. Machelon, Paris 1999, 167–182; H. Grange, *Mme de Staël et la Constitution de l'an III: avant et après*, *Ibidem*, 183–199.

30 Arch. Nat., 29 AP 79, f. 82, cit. par F. Sofia, *Ancora «dal modello francese al caso italiano»: gli appunti di P.-L. Roederer*, cit., 415. Pour Roederer «Le pouvoir exé-

5. «La démocratie occupe les extrémités du gouvernement, le système tend à l'établir au centre»

Dans *l'Adresse d'un constitutionnel*, Roederer laisse entrevoir le fil conducteur qui relie sa proposition "inactuelle" à la réflexion de l'époque révolutionnaire. Régner redevient – selon la logique prérévolutionnaire – volonté (*gouverner*) mais aussi action (*agir*), c'est-à-dire faire tout ce que dans l'État personne d'autre ne peut faire «avec le même succès». Le Roederer orléaniste nous avoue qu'il a une grande inquiétude: les institutions administratives «sont si purement et si absolument démocratiques, qu'il suffirait d'un esprit audacieux dans une présidence du cabinet indépendante du Roi, pour proposer avec quelque apparence de bonne foi une loi de conversion de la monarchie en république». Notre octogénaire affronte donc une question fondamentale du régime de Juillet, à savoir le problème d'une monarchie entourée des institutions républicaines.[31] Toutefois, malgré le style excessivement pompeux concernant les "dangers imminents", il saisit – ainsi qu'il l'avait fait avec clairvoyance entre thermidor et l'époque napoléonienne – les liens entre l'administration, l'exécutif et le gouvernement.[32] Roederer appréhende une coïncidence d'intérêts entre ceux qui, tout en partant de concepts idéologiques très différents, veulent transformer la monarchie en une république démocratique ou en une fédération de démocraties. Parce que en France, selon lui, la démocratie «tient déjà l'état par les pieds; le système lui livrerait la tête. On peut emprunter une figure plus juste: la démocratie occupe les extrémités du gouvernement, le système tend à l'établir au centre. La démocratie, ai-je dit, occupe les extrémités: et en effet nos institutions municipales, districtales et départementales ne remplissent-elles par les conseils des trois degrés de conseillers à la nomination desquels le roi n'a aucune part?».[33] La stratégie a changé: on prépare la démocratie en partant de la périphérie, des institutions locales, des écoles. Le spectre est la désarticulation de l'unité de l'État incarnée par la monarchie "nationale" et "populaire". Déjà en 1788 – bien que dans un contexte très différent – le publiciste de Metz s'était fait l'interprète d'une forte exigence d'unité en appréhendant des assemblées provinciales agissant comme «des républiques différentes».[34] Il suffirait, maintenant, en 1835, de former deux chambres avec les organes

cutif est essentiellement composé de deux parties; l'administration qui agit & opère, le gouvernement qui dirige, ordonne & surveille» (*Du Gouvernement*, cit., 2).

31 L. Lacchè, *La Libertà che guida il popolo*, cit., *passim*.

32 Pour quelques suggestions v. P. Colombo, *Governo e costituzione*, cit., 529.

33 Arch. nat., 29 AP 80, *Papiers Roederer, Du Conseil du Cabinet*, cit., 28–29.

34 P.-L. Roederer, *De la députation aux états généraux*, s. l., novembre 1788. Sur ce point v. les observations de S. Mannoni, *Une et indivisible*, cit., t. I, 234–236.

actuels des conseils d'arrondissement et des conseils généraux pour transformer la France en une république fédérative.

Cette crainte est sans doute exagérée. Roederer, l'un des principaux auteurs de la loi du 28 pluviôse an VIII[35] – véritable constitution administrative de la France postrévolutionnaire – analyse les institutions politiques et administratives locales dans le but de souligner l'importance de la dimension élective qui attribuerait aux extrémités une dangereuse indépendance par rapport au centre. Toutefois, nous savons que, si d'un côté la législation orléaniste, appelée à l'application de l'art. 69 c. 7, veut légitimer, au moyen des élections, le pouvoir municipal et les conseils locaux, elle suit en même temps le parcours bien rodé de la tutelle, du contrôle et de la méfiance de la part du législateur.[36] Une analyse attentive montre l'extrême complexité structurelle du rapport centre / périphérie.[37] Louis Blanc, dans son *Histoire de dix ans*, considère le système local du règne de Louis-Philippe comme oligarchique et centraliste. Le maire continue d'être nommé par le roi ou par le préfet, selon la population de la commune, à condition qu'il soit choisi parmi les membres du conseil communal. Le législateur a multiplié les interdictions et les sanctions. Le gouvernement dispose d'un remarquable pouvoir discrétionnaire pour dissoudre les conseils et révoquer les maires au moyen d'ordonnances royales. Le contrôle des préfets reste l'axe du système.[38] Les lois de décentralisation ne concernent que le cadre communal et non le cadre départemental; elles ont, en outre, peu de répercussions sur les pouvoirs discrétionnaires des ministres qui tendent en revanche à s'étendre.[39] Certes, il ne faut pas sous-estimer le fait que les électeurs "locaux" (en grande partie censitaires) sont au nombre de presque trois millions par rapport aux deux cent mille électeurs nationaux.[40] La *politique au village* est un élément important et

35 À ce sujet v. G. Thuillier, *Le système administratif d'après Roederer*, in *La revue administrative*, 41, 1988; S. Mannoni, *Une et indivisible*, cit., t. I, 412 et suiv.

36 Cfr. F. Burdeau, *Histoire de l'administration française du 18e au 20e siècle*, Paris 1989, 113 et suiv.; 186–193; 231 et suiv.

37 S. Mannoni, *Une et indivisible. Storia dell'accentramento amministrativo in Francia*, t. II, *Dalla contestazione al consolidamento*, Milan 1996, *passim.*

38 F. Burdeau, *Histoire de l'administration française*, cit., 193.

39 F. Burdeau, *Histoire du droit administratif (de la Révolution au début des années 1970)*, Paris 1995, 151 suiv.; Id., *Pouvoir administratif et droit public français. III. L'épanouissement du pouvoir ministériel sous la monarchie de Juillet*, in *Giornale di storia costituzionale*, 5, I, 2003, 50.

40 S. Mannoni, *Une et indivisible*, t. II, cit., 139; P. Rosanvallon, *Le Sacre du citoyen. Du suffrage universel en France*, Paris 1992. Cf. A.-J. Tudesq, *Institutions locales et histoire sociale: la loi municipale de 1831 et ses premières applications*, in *Annales de la Faculté des lettres et des sciences humaines de Nice*, 9–10, 1969, 327–363; P. Vigier, *Élections municipales et prise de conscience politique sous la monarchie de Juillet*, in *La France au XIXe siècle: études historiques, Mélanges offerts à Ch.-H. Pouthas*, Paris

c'est l'élargissement du suffrage à ce niveau qui pose le problème de la démocratie locale.

La monarchie apparaît ainsi coincée entre le phénomène de la démocratie qui «occupe les extrémités du gouvernement» et celui de l'«oligarchie doctrinale» qui veut affirmer, selon Roederer, le principe de l'indépendance du gouvernement et de la présidence autonome du conseil. Dans ce contexte, face à la montée de la démocratie et à la tentative d'affirmer un gouvernement "parlementaire" au caractère totalement oligarchique, la royauté apparaît être le dernier obstacle s'opposant à «la tyrannie des Chambres et du gouvernement coalisés».[41] Les ministres, devenus des courtisans de la Chambre, pourraient réussir à "confondre" les pouvoirs que la Charte, ainsi que toutes les constitutions des peuples civils, ont plus ou moins voulu séparer. Le spectre est terrible. «J'ai vu dans un avenir plus ou moins éloigné poindre, dans cette confusion des pouvoirs, les trente tyrans d'Athènes, le sénat de Venise, le comité de salut public de la Convention; tyrannies collectives plus redoutables que les tyrannies de despotes isolés».[42] Voulons-nous peut-être que cinquante ans de révolutions et deux siècles d'études et de lumières nous conduisent à une telle situation? C'est pour cette raison, par amour de la vérité et en tant qu'homme public et citoyen que Roederer a décidé de s'adresser aux *constitutionnels*. Et pourtant, observe l'auteur, nous avons «un prince ... né pour la Charte ...»; «... trouvez un prince mieux adapté à la Charte, et je confesserai que je me suis trop occupé du nôtre et pas assez d'elle».[43] On ne peut penser que la Charte «n'ait laissé aucun moyen d'utilité aux rois sages, éclairés, appliqués, bienfaisants; je ne croirai point qu'elle oppose un obstacle insurmontable à l'exercice de leurs plus heureuses facultés ...». La monarchie est donc une grande ressource institutionnelle, d'autant plus que celui qui en est investi a le talent extraordinaire d'un Louis-Philippe. Mais le paradigme cité par Roederer est paradoxalement celui de Napoléon. L'illustre vieillard rappelle comment Bonaparte, revenu d'Égypte, l'avait chargé de parler avec Sieyès[44] du modèle à adopter pour faire sortir la nation de la crise. Roederer exposa au général le projet de l'abbé: instituer un «jury conservateur en permanence » ayant une pluralité d'attributions. Le jury aurait dû être présidé

1973; et surtout C. Guionnet, *L'Apprentissage de la politique moderne. Les élections municipales sous la monarchie de juillet*, Paris 1997; L. Lacchè, *La Libertà che guida il Popolo*, cit., 136–138.

41 Arch. nat., 29 AP 80, *Papiers Roederer, Du Conseil du Cabinet*, cit., 35.

42 P.-L. Roederer, *Adresse*, *Avant-Propos*, cit., III–IV.

43 *Ibidem*, V.

44 Sur les rapports entre Roederer et Sieyès cf. Th. Lentz, *Roederer*, cit., 11, 146 et suiv. Sur le culte précoce pour l'abbé, v. R. Martucci, *L'ossessione costituente. Forma di governo e costituzione nella Rivoluzione francese (1789–1799)*, Bologna 2001, 74.

par un Grand Électeur ayant le droit de nommer les trois consuls détenant le pouvoir exécutif, les ministres, les ambassadeurs et les généraux, «sans pouvoir exercer lui-même aucune de ces fonctions». Bonaparte resta consterné. «Est-ce que je vous entends bien? me demanda-t-il: on me propose une place où je nommerais tous ceux qui auront quelque chose à faire, et où je ne pourrai me mêler de rien!».[45] Bonaparte critiqua âprement la proposition de Sieyès. «Je ne ferai pas un rôle si ridicule – répondit-il –. Je veux être consul avec Sieyès et Roger Ducos, ou rien. Plutôt rien, que d'être ridicule ...».[46]

«Si j'entends bien la doctrine du jour – glosa Roederer – le Roi de France serait précisément le Grand Électeur dont Napoléon n'a pas voulu le rôle».[47] Ce rapprochement entre Napoléon et Louis-Philippe n'apparaît pas complètement hors de propos à l'auteur de l'*Adresse*. Le nouveau dynaste est l'emblème du gouvernement civil comme Bonaparte l'a été du gouvernement militaire. Comment – se demande Roederer – un prince aussi vertueux, valeureux, populaire, modéré peut-il rester «spectateur oisif et indifférent des désordres publics»? On ne peut demander à ce roi d'être un « fainéant », un « cochon à l'engrais » – aurait dit Napoléon[48] – obligé de jouer le rôle du simple observateur.

Le croquis de la monarchie constitutionnelle esquissé par Roederer semble évoquer certaines idées et préoccupations de Royer-Collard. Le père noble, austère et capricieux des doctrinaires remarquait – en réfléchissant sur le singulier événement de la *Chambre Introuvable* – que le jour où le gouvernement aurait dû dépendre seulement des volontés de la majorité de la Chambre, la Charte et la royauté auraient perdu leur sens, en ouvrant ainsi la voie à la "république". En 1824, le grand orateur avait observé qu'il ne suffisait pas de définir le gouvernement comme une monarchie mixte, appelée gouvernement représentatif, dans lequel la Chambre élective concourt avec le monarque et une chambre héréditaire à la formation de la loi et à la direction des affaires publiques. C'est le «pouvoir régulateur» qui imprime au gouvernement son caractère dominant. Et dans le cas français, c'est le roi de la Charte qui garde une «éclatante primauté» parmi ses pouvoirs. Le roi seul représente l'unité morale de la société, lui seul agit, commande, il est l'auteur de la loi. Les autres pouvoirs

45 P.-L. Roederer, *Adresse*, *Avant-Propos*, cit., VII.

46 Ainsi que nous le savons, les mémoires de Roederer sont une source importante pour comprendre l'opposition de Bonaparte au projet de Sieyès. Sur ce point, et plus en général, sur le modèle constitutionnel de Brumaire, v. Th. Lentz, *Roederer*, cit., 117 et suiv.; P. Colombo, *Governo e costituzione*, cit., 286 et suiv., 576, nt. 30.

47 P.-L. Roederer, *Adresse*, *Avant-Propos*, cit., VIII.

48 Il s'agit d'expressions utilisées par Bonaparte et reprises par la suite dans le débat politique de la monarchie constitutionnelle. Sur les témoignages de Roederer, Thibaudeau, Fouché et sur l' «héliocentrisme constitutionnel», v. L. Scuccimarra, *La sciabola di Sieyès*, cit., 165 et suiv.

sont des limites, même s'ils sont vivants et en mesure d'agir.[49] Royer-Collard, dès les premiers pas de la monarchie restaurée – ainsi que les doctrinaires de sa génération, de Serre et Jordan – avait repris les préoccupations de Necker et des disciples du "cercle de Coppet" sur le renforcement nécessaire du pouvoir exécutif.[50] Au cours des années vingt, plus particulièrement en 1827, il avait formulé, ses raisons stratégiques ayant changé, un point de vue selon lequel le Parlement exerçait le «concours» et le «pouvoir indirect» sur l'action du «gouvernement du roi».[51] Mais déjà au cours du délicat débat sur le statut de la pairie – à partir de l'été 1831 – Royer-Collard avait replacé au centre de sa réflexion le sujet de la primauté de la royauté, pour arriver au problème de la nature ambiguë du nouvel ordre constitutionnel. «Allons au cœur du problème: la démocratie royale, qu'elle daigne ou pas de conserver son phantasme de monarchie, est ou sera bientôt la démocratie pure; l'abolition de la pairie implique rapidement cette conséquence».[52]

Roederer craint que le risque ne soit imminent, que la monarchie ne puisse se transformer en une "république" entendue, il est vrai, plus comme une condition "démocratique et parlementaire" que comme une forme constitutionnelle. On pourrait penser que la position de Roederer est totalement réactionnaire, une pleine réaffirmation du *monarchisches Prinzip* dans le processus de rééquilibre des pouvoirs effectué après la révolution de 1830 et établi de façon ambiguë par la Charte orléaniste. L'histoire de la monarchie de Juillet (mais non seulement, bien sûr) montre cependant la permanence de l'enjeu de la nature constitutionnelle du pouvoir monarchique.[53] La théorie constantienne du « pouvoir neutre » est partie intégrante de cette réflexion. Selon Roederer, le souverain doit être « préservateur » plus qu'«intermédiaire»;[54] c'est un pouvoir

49 P. de Barante, *La Vie politique de M. Royer-Collard. Ses discours et ses écrits*, Paris 1863, t. I, 216–217. Cf. aussi J. Barthélemy, *L'Introduction du régime parlementaire en France sous Louis XVIII et Charles X*, Paris 1904, 192 et suiv.; G. Rémond, *Royer-Collard. Son essai d'un système politique*, Paris 1933, 47, 77–79; L. Lacchè, *La Libertà che guida il Popolo*, cit.

50 B. Yvert, *Aux origines de l'orléanisme. Les doctrinaires, «Le Globe» et les Bourbons*, in D. Roldan (sous la dir.), *Colloque Guizot, les doctrinaires et la presse (1820–1830)*, Paris 1994, 41.

51 Cf. V. E. Starzinger, *The Politics of the Center. The* juste milieu *in Theory and Practice, France and England, 1815–1848*, New Brunswick, London 1991, 38–39.

52 Cit. de L. Lacchè, *La Libertà che guida il Popolo*, cit., 140.

53 Pour un aperçu général cf. M. Kirsch, *Monarch und Parlament im 19. Jahrhundert. Der Monarchische Konstitutionalismus als europäischer Verfassungstyp – Frankreich im Vergleich*, Göttingen 1999.

54 Il s'agit de catégories élaborées par Benjamin Constant à partir de l'époque directoriale. Sur ce point, nous renvoyons *supra* dans ce volume *Coppet et la percée de l'État libéral constitutionnel*, 219 ss.

régulateur, c'est un moniteur. En février 1830, Adolphe Thiers avait repris la théorie de Constant en la transfigurant dans la célèbre formule «le roi règne mais ne gouverne pas». Le roi règne, les ministres gouvernent, les Chambres jugent.[55] Roederer repousse cette formulation qui sépare plus nettement – par rapport à ce qu'avait fait Constant – «régner» et «gouverner». Le pouvoir exécutif doit effectivement rester dans la disponibilité du souverain qui, seulement au niveau factuel, pourra le faire exercer par les ministres responsables sans que puisse exister au préalable une majorité «systématique». L'"inactualité" de Roederer consiste à refuser le système des veto croisés (du roi et de la Chambre) qui caractérise un certain type d'équilibre entre les pouvoirs, en attribuant à la nation le rôle du "juge"; la fusion des pouvoirs – selon la logique empirique du gouvernement du cabinet – devient *confusion des pouvoirs*. Le monarque doit pouvoir empêcher que le législatif envahisse le pouvoir exécutif, qu'il l'assujettisse en violant la prérogative royale. Le centre du système constitutionnel n'est pas la Chambre élective mais le roi qui règne et gouverne.

On pourrait dire que Roederer repousse dans sa totalité l'idée du "régime parlementaire". Mais dans ce cas aussi, nous courrons le risque de considérer réelle l'existence d'une forme de gouvernement achevée et organique. Si nous y regardons de près, les différentes positions se rapprochent par leur utilisation commune d'un mot tel qu'influence, un concept clé – bien qu'ambigu – pour comprendre la fonction monarchique au cours de sa longue et difficile transformation constitutionnelle dans l'Europe du XIXe siècle. Il suffit de lire Prosper Duvergier de Hauranne, un constitutionnaliste comme Charles Hello, le François Guizot des années quarante («Le trône n'est pas un fauteuil vide»), pour remarquer cet aspect.[56] Il en résulte un régime de balance des pouvoirs à exécutif monarchique,[57] selon la conviction d'après laquelle le rapport étroit entre le monarque et le gouvernement (affirmé par le *texte* de la Charte) devrait s'opposer – dans une fonction conservatrice – à la prétention de la Chambre élective d' «absorber» le pouvoir exécutif et d'avoir une position de prépondérance en contradiction avec le principe du «concours» et de balance des pouvoirs. Ces considérations sont partagées par des conservateurs ministériels dans le style de Guizot et tour à tour par le «marécage» parlementaire – qu'il s'agisse du tiers parti de Dupin ou des exposants du centre gauche – qui essayent d'adapter la réalité à un modèle de monarchie représentative qui, fondé sur les bases fragiles de la *souveraineté nationale*, ne veut modifier ni les *conditions politiques*, le régime électoral surtout, ni les formes de la représentation.

55 *Le National*, 4 février 1830, 2, col. 1.
56 Cf. L. Lacchè, *La Libertà che guida il Popolo*, cit., 188 et suiv.
57 A. Laquièze, *Les origines du régime parlementaire en France*, cit., 22.

Pour Roederer, il ne suffit pas que le roi règne et *influence* le système politico-constitutionnel. Dans ce contexte historique et institutionnel, le renvoi à la figure apologétique du prince parfait est en fonction du pouvoir exécutif, et donc de la détermination de la volonté politique, dans le cadre d'un «concours» successif avec la chambre élue. Pour les uns (et pour Roederer en particulier) l'impulsion part du monarque, pour les autres elle vient du "bas". Un roi "conservateur" (des équilibres obtenus et de la stabilité dynastique) est utile et nécessaire, surtout pour s'opposer à la démocratie du bas (la "république") en empêchant la confusion (l'oligarchie au centre) entre la majorité parlementaire et un système collégial de gouvernement à direction présidentielle, en raison aussi du fait qu'en France les conditions historiques et politiques qui pourraient conseiller une différente évolution du système n'existent pas encore.

6. Pagès de l'Ariège et un «homme d'un autre temps»: anatomie d'une polémique

En janvier-février 1835, J.-P. Pagès, député de l'Ariège, perspicace commentateur du journal *Le Temps*,[58] offre une intéressante représentation de la situation politique contemporaine.[59] Presque dès le début du régime orléaniste, Casimir Perier avait su imposer un *leadership* fort et déterminé,[60] mais au cours des années suivantes – et de façon très évidente entre 1834 et 1835 – la politique s'était révélée une simple question de tactique et de finesse. Le centre parlementaire apparaît désormais être le "lieu politique" des opinions et des intérêts

58 Fondé en 1829 par Jacques Coste et par l'ancien préfet Baude, avec le *patronage* de quelques dizaines de députés (parmi les fondateurs et les collaborateurs nous trouvons Perier, Guizot, de Broglie, Dupont de l'Eure, La Fayette) dans le but de rapprocher les opinions de la *gauche* et du *centre-gauche*.

59 Né à Seix (Ariège) en 1784, avocat à Toulouse, essayiste (auteur de plusieurs articles juridico-économiques de l'«Encyclopédie Moderne»), journaliste. Pendant la Restauration, il était entré en contact avec d'importants représentants de l'opposition (La Fayette, Constant, Laffitte) en collaborant aux journaux tels que le "Constitutionnel", la "Minerve", la "Renommée". Député du collège de Saint-Girons de 1832 à 1842. Pendant la monarchie de Juillet, il fonda le journal d'opposition (journal du soir) "La Patrie". En 1817, il avait publié les *Principes généraux du droit politique dans leur rapport avec l'esprit de l'Europe et avec la monarchie constitutionnelle*, Paris 1817. En 1836, il réalisa une nouvelle édition du *Cours de politique constitutionnelle* de Benjamin Constant. Libéral de gauche, en 1847 il fut réélu à la Chambre dans le collège de Saint-Girons et en 1848 il prit part à la Constituante où il devint membre du *Comité de Constitution*. En 1849 il se retira de la vie publique.

60 J.-P. Pagès, *Réflexions politiques. Des progrès de l'opposition*, "Le Temps", 26 janvier 1835.

liés au ministère.[61] En l'absence d'un véritable "système ministériel", le gouvernement est obligé de transiger sur tout. La fragmentation de l'échiquier parlementaire rend difficile la recomposition d'une majorité. Les ministres sont des "chapeaux sur des places vides": les gouvernements meurent avant de naître.[62]

En février 1835, ont lieu deux débats de même sorte mais dont les résultats sont à l'opposé. L'un, auprès de la Cour d'Assise de la Seine, appelle sur le banc des accusés *La Gazette de France*, journal légitimiste accusé d'avoir soutenu la thèse selon laquelle Louis-Philippe règne et gouverne et est donc responsable de toute action. La Cour condamne le gérant pour le crime de «mépris du roi».[63] Dans un autre procès contre le journal républicain *Le National*, la défense invoque justement la brochure de Roederer en affirmant qu'elle est la contre-preuve du fait que l'on peut dire les mêmes choses (que le *roi règne et gouverne*) avec des résultats bien différents. Antoine Madrolle lui-même avait été condamné lorsqu'il avait soutenu la théorie du coup d'état en faisant appel à l'art. 14 de la Charte. L'un des fondateurs du journal, Armand Carrel, rappelle au cours du procès, comment l'année 1830 aurait dû fonder un système à partir du "bas", à savoir à partir du corps électoral, pour ensuite "rejoindre" les Chambres et le roi. Cela n'a pas eu lieu: au contraire, le système marche du haut vers le bas: c'est la négation du gouvernement représentatif.[64] Les mots sublimes et efficaces de Carrel convainquent dans ce cas le jury qui acquitte le gérant.

La question constitutionnelle est donc stratégique, elle traverse les institutions, le système politique, les cours de justice. Aucune surprise donc, si Pagès, dans un article du 9 février, aborde le sujet du rapport entre monarchie et gouvernement. L'auteur cite la théorie du pouvoir neutre mais considère que la distinction entre pouvoir royal et pouvoir exécutif est problématique car le pouvoir royal n'aurait plus de base solide. Pagès interprète le concept de pouvoir neutre – bien différemment de comme il apparaît dans la complexe théorisation de Constant[65] – comme un «pouvoir nul». En réalité, selon l'auteur de l'article, le pouvoir n'aurait jamais été neutre, pas même dans la si souvent citée Angleterre. Le pouvoir royal est par sa nature supérieur à tous les pouvoirs constitués.

61 J.-P. Pagès, *Le ministère et la Chambre*, "Le Temps", 12 janvier 1835.

62 J.-P. Pagès, *L'échiquier parlementaire*, "Le Temps", 2 février 1835. Dans cet article, Pagès offre une intéressante vue d'ensemble du système politique français de l'époque, des doctrinaires aux députés fonctionnaires aux hommes d'affaires, de l'opposition légitimiste à l'opposition radicale, dynastique, au tiers parti jusqu'à la «jeune opposition constitutionnelle».

63 "Constitutionnel", 4 mars 1835.

64 Supplément au "Bons Sens", 26 février 1835.

65 D'habitude la théorie de Constant est banalisée, en perdant ainsi la profondeur historique et théorique qu'elle possède. Il manque encore, à notre avis, une lecture d'ensemble et pleinement convaincante de la doctrine du pouvoir neutre.

«Si le pouvoir ministériel le gêne, il renvoie ses ministres; si le pouvoir représentatif le blesse, il dissout les assemblées représentatives; si le pouvoir judiciaire le choque, il détruit ses arrêts par le droit de grâce. Ainsi la royauté, plus puissante que tous les corps sociaux, peut trouver des puissances rivales, mais ne saurait rencontrer de pouvoir égal au sien».[66] Toutefois le pouvoir royal ne peut agir qu'à travers le pouvoir ministériel et celui-ci ne peut lui-même agir qu'à travers la volonté du pouvoir royal. Penser qu'un ministre doit exécuter tout ce que le roi commande serait une absurdité comme penser qu'un roi est tenu de satisfaire tout ce qu'un ministre désire.[67] Dans le gouvernement représentatif, le choix d'un ministre est la manifestation de la pensée du souverain, mais il ne faut pas oublier que «... un homme est un système, et quand le roi choisit un homme, il adopte, en dépit de lui-même, le système dont cet homme est la personnification».[68] Un roi "moderne" ne peut *résister* aux *desiderata* pondérés de la nation. Et si le choix d'un ministre est une déclaration politique, un monarque doit savoir que ce choix aura des conséquences. Ainsi, le fait d'avoir choisi les doctrinaires – qui entre 1815 et 1820 avaient été les conseillers du mouvement réactionnaire et entre 1826 et 1830 les propagandistes les plus téméraires de la liberté contre le pouvoir – avait été une erreur.[69] «Ainsi, le pouvoir royal peut rassurer ou effrayer un pays, se consolider ou se compromettre par le choix des ministres». Et les ministres sans envergure et sans capacités font descendre le souverain sur le terrain de l'administration la plus mesquine.

En Angleterre le pouvoir ministériel est un grand pouvoir parlementaire. En France, au contraire, le ministère n'est que la réunion de huit hommes dans un cabinet, nommés, gardés et révoqués par le roi. «Les majorités se sont liées à un cabinet, mais n'ont jamais formé un cabinet». Mais dans la session actuelle, les ministres ont recherché le plein soutien parlementaire. Ils ne l'ont pas obtenu et maintenant ils dépendent encore plus du roi. Le fait est qu'en France on ne peut appliquer tout court les principes anglais. «Nous devons apprécier seulement l'intervention de la royauté dans le gouvernement, tel qu'il existe en France et en 1835. Ici c'est toujours la royauté qui fait les ministres; ce sont les ministres qui font les majorités, et, depuis la restauration, les chambres n'ont jamais décidé le choix d'un seul cabinet».[70] En France les ministres sont isolés, il n'existe pas de

66 J.-P. Pagès, *Si la royauté doit intervenir dans le gouvernement*, in "Le Temps", 9 février 1835.

67 Dès la Restauration, Pagès avait réfléchi, quand bien même selon une logique surtout "négative", sur le problème de la responsabilité ministérielle: *De la responsabilité ministérielle et de la nécessité d'organiser le mode d'accusation et de jugement des ministres*, Paris mars 1818.

68 J.-P. Pagès, *Si la royauté doit intervenir dans le gouvernement*, 9 février 1835, cit.

69 *Ibidem*, 16 février 1835.

70 *Ibidem*.

conseil parce qu'il n'existe pas d'idée commune. Et «L'homme isolé fait acte de dévouement; le conseil fait preuve de sagesse». Une véritable opinion collective ne peut se former qu'aux réunions auxquelles le roi n'assiste pas. «C'est là le conseil des ministres, l'unité ministérielle, le symbole de la volonté parlementaire dans la sincérité du gouvernement représentatif». Mais l'opinion du conseil peut se former seulement après avoir discuté avec le roi. Dans ce cas, le roi intervient nécessairement dans le gouvernement qui devient alors une sorte de conseil privé. Il existe deux niveaux: dans un cas le conseil *gouverne*, dirigé par son président; dans l'autre le roi *règne*. Chacun a ses prérogatives et, dans la séparation, continuent d'être présents les principes fondamentaux de l'inviolabilité et de la responsabilité.

S'il s'agit là des opinions essentielles de Pagès, nous pouvons donc comprendre pour quelle raison la brochure de Roederer devint tout de suite l'objet de son attention, de quelques sarcasmes et surtout de réflexions politico-constitutionnelles de quelque intérêt. «Une brochure fort curieuse est depuis quelques jours lancée au milieu du monde politique sous le titre d'*Adresse d'un constitutionnel aux constitutionnels*».[71] L'œuvre n'est pas vendue, mais «diffusée», entourée par un halo de mystère. C'est peut-être l'œuvre d'une *camarilla*, même si l'on accuse le comte Roederer de l'avoir écrite. Le travail s'articule entièrement autour de la maxime: *Le roi règne et gouverne*. Pagès dit, non sans ironie, que l'auteur s'est arrêté au gouvernement *selon Louis XIV*: le ministère doctrinaire est jugé trop hostile à l'influence du roi et des personnages tels que Thiers, Guizot, Persil apparaissent comme des usurpateurs de la prérogative, presque des républicains ...

Roederer a accepté de porter le fardeau, mais il est évident que les idées exprimées sont complètement partagées par la cour. En effet les partisans à la Chambre de ce texte sont les "courtisans". Le scandale suscité, les pétitions, les discussions, les protestations étaient fondées. «On voyait dans cette publication un 18 fructidor timide, tenté par la voie de la publicité, un coup d'état en raisonnements et en aphorismes absolutistes; c'était la charte toute entière transformée en un vaste article 14, au profit de la monarchie élue».[72] Guizot et le ministère ont tout de suite demandé un démenti immédiat, même si les protestations des doctrinaires – sourit Pagès – ne servent à rien. La brochure est malgré tout une œuvre de talent, mais un sophisme reste toujours un sophisme. Roederer est un homme d'un autre temps: il a été trop de choses pour pouvoir donner des leçons sur le gouvernement représentatif. La balance des pouvoirs, les limites aux différentes prérogatives, les immunités parlementaires, les garanties

71 J.-P. Pagès, *Opposition de la cour contre les doctrinaires*, "Le Temps", 21 février 1835.

72 J.-P. Pagès, *La Chambre, le ministre et le pamphlet courtisan*, "Le Temps", 22 février 1835.

des corps de l'État sont des concepts qui lui échappent. «Le gouvernement représentatif veut des hommes à lui; ceux-là seuls peuvent le comprendre».[73] Salvandy, Dupin aîné, de Broglie ont avancé leurs critiques. Mais c'est la faute de ces ministres qui, après avoir accepté la présidence du maréchal Soult, subissent aujourd'hui la présidence encore plus dérisoire du maréchal Mortier. «A-t-on oublié que M. Persil a professé publiquement le principe fondamental du livre de M. Roederer: *Le roi règne et gouverne?*».

C'est au cours de la dernière semaine de février 1835 que le pamphlet "anonyme" devient l'objet d'une ample discussion. Roederer est une cible facile. On fait remarquer qu'il s'agit pour lui d'une sorte de fétichisme monarchique.[74] Les doctrinaires demandent un désaveu de la brochure.[75] L'homme de l'école impérialiste s'est arrêté à l'âge d'or de la monarchie administrative.[76] Même pire, c'est le «Cottu de la nouvelle dynastie»:[77] et dans l'espace de cinq ans seulement, on est passé de la *Monarchie de 1830* de Thiers à une sorte de monarchie "orientale". De plus, il n'est pas très difficile de fouiller dans la longue carrière de Roederer, en commençant par les épisodes liés au 10 août 1792.[78] En somme, c'est une vieille girouette.[79] Mais il n'est même pas nécessaire de remonter aussi loin: en 1830, l'auteur avait écrit un *Mémoire au Roi*[80] où il soutenait des thèses bien différentes et maintenant il ne fait que reprendre les mots de Persil, homme politique important, avocat, magistrat et ministre de la justice hostile à la présidence du conseil.[81]

L'attaque de Roederer s'adresse au gouvernement représentatif en tant que tel et c'est sur ce terrain qu'il doit être réfuté. Le ministère est le lien vivant entre le pouvoir royal et les Chambres: «il émane à la fois de tous deux. Il n'appartient exclusivement ni à la royauté ni à la Chambre. Sans la nomination royale, point

73 J.-P. Pagès, *Si les Chambres doivent intervenir dans le gouvernement*, "Le Temps", 23 février 1835.

74 "Le Constitutionnel", 23 février 1835.

75 Apparu par la suite dans le "Moniteur" le 23 février sous forme semi-officielle. Cf. *Ibidem*.

76 "Journal des Débats", 22 février 1835.

77 "Le Bons Sens", 23 février 1835.

78 "Le Temps", 23 février 1835. Mais le journal est obligé de démentir (24 et 26 février) sur demande de Roederer.

79 "Le Constitutionnel", 4 mars 1835. Voir aussi le Marquis de Bartillat, *Observations d'un Indépendant à un Constitutionnel*, Paris 1835, 3 mars, 3. Pagès lui-même ne se dispense pas, de façon subtilement ironique, d'utiliser l'argument de l'incohérence de Roederer: *De l'Adresse d'un Constitutionnel aux Constitutionnels*, "Le Temps", 9 mars 1835.

80 P.-L. Roederer, *Au Roi*, Paris, le 19 octobre 1830, (Paris), impr. de A. Firmin-Didot.

81 "Le Courrier", 1 mars 1835.

de ministres; sans l'indication tacite et sans l'assentiment des Chambres, point de ministres non plus ...».[82] Le concours est possible seulement à travers les ministres et c'est seulement à travers une communication continue que les Chambres peuvent participer à la «direction des affaires publiques ...». La théorie de Roederer est bien autre chose: «C'est le système consultatif au lieu du système représentatif; c'est la monarchie administrative au lieu de la monarchie constitutionnelle et parlementaire».[83]

La réplique de Roederer – comme nous le savons – ne se fait pas attendre: il publie à nouveau l'essai et en déclare cette fois la paternité, en ajoutant une préface. Parmi les critiques reçues, ce n'est qu'à Pagès qu'il reconnaît le droit de réplique. «Je reconnais dans M. Pagès de l'Ariège un écrivain distingué; j'ai l'habitude de couper dans *le Temps* les articles qu'il y insère,[84] et j'en fais une collection séparée ...».[85] *Le Temps*, à son tour, offre à Pagès la possibilité «de continuer cette lutte sur le principe même de notre constitution».[86] Dans l'article du 2 mars, le député récapitule les positions de Roederer et rappelle avec sarcasme que les titres dont Roederer se targue, pair de France et comte, ont bien peu de valeur.[87] Pagès estime que la théorie de l'omnipotence parlementaire – récemment évoquée par Guizot[88] afin que la Chambre s'approprie du gouvernement – est une caractéristique de l'histoire anglaise où se réalise, jusqu'aux réformes de Lord Grey, une «usurpation aristocratique». En France, en revanche, elle produirait d'autres effets parce que ici seule la chambre élue pourrait «envahir» le gouvernement et par conséquent «l'omnipotence parlementaire française serait toute plébéienne, toute démocratique. La France formerait dès lors une république monarchique». Les doctrinaires travaillent à la démocratie sans s'en rendre compte. En France, la prérogative a une plus grande extension «parce que l'usage ne l'a pas circonscrite et qu'elle n'a pas les mêmes adversaires ...». Le ministère ne doit pas être nécessairement pris au sein de la majorité, «mais il est indispensable qu'il soit l'expression de la pensée de la

82 "Journal des Débats", 22 février 1835.

83 *Ibidem*. «Dans notre gouvernement, tout est conseil, tout est consultation et tout aussi est transaction». Et tout ministère divisé et sans leader «diminue la Chambre devant le Roi, ... diminue le Roi devant la chambre, ou ce qui est pire encore, s'efface pour le laisser voir et le mettre face à face avec la chambre, ce qui est la perte de la constitution ...», "Journal des Débats", 27 février 1835.

84 Ainsi qu'on peut en effet le voir in Arch. nat., 29 AP 80, *Papiers Roederer*.

85 P.-L. Roederer, *Adresse*, *Avant-Propos*, cit., XI.

86 *De l'adresse d'un constitutionnel aux constitutionnels*, "Le Temps", 1 mars 1835.

87 *De l'adresse d'un constitutionnel aux constitutionnels*, "Le Temps", 2 mars 1835.

88 «Un doctrinaire qui croit savoir et faire de la politique, parce qu'il sait et fait de l'histoire, a longtemps préconisé ce qu'on appelle dans la Grande Bretagne *l'omnipotence parlementaire*» (J.-P. Pagès, *Si les Chambres doivent intervenir dans le gouvernement*, "Le Temps", 3 mars 1835).

majorité. C'est là ce qui rétablit l'harmonie entre les corps politiques».[89] Ce qui est fondamental, c'est que les principes incarnés par les ministres donnent l'assurance à la Chambre sur l'ensemble de l'activité du gouvernement. «Aussi le roi nomme les ministres, le roi les destitue, mais la chambre signale les ministres qu'il faut nommer, et marque l'heure où ils doivent être révoqués. Prévenir ce vœu est d'un grand roi, l'apprécier est d'un prince habile ...».[90]

Pagès accuse Roederer de changer les principes selon l'avantage. Pourquoi, demande-t-on, le pair de France n'a-t-il pas publié l'*Adresse* lorsque Casimir Perier usurpait la prérogative et en revanche accuse-t-il aujourd'hui les doctrinaires? «Ne serait-ce pas que les doctrinaires déplaisent et que Casimir Perier convenait? Pour moi, dont la politique ne varie ni de jour à jour, ni de brochure à brochure, je voulais la charte telle qu'elle est ...».[91] Les préoccupations de Roederer sur le conseil des ministres et sur la présidence sont dictées par des sophismes et des erreurs de formulation. «Si le savant publiciste eût réfléchi avant d'écrire, il aurait vu que les ministres ne peuvent rien par eux-mêmes, que chacun de leurs actes est nécessairement soumis à l'action, et par conséquent à l'intervention du roi; qu'aucune manifestation du gouvernement, exécutive ou législative, ne peut avoir lieu sans la signature du monarque; et qu'avant de faire connaître sa volonté, le prince peut s'entourer de toutes les lumières désirables; qu'il peut les puiser dans son conseil et hors de son conseil ...».[92] La naissance de la nouvelle présidence de Broglie (12 mars) est selon Pagès la dernière image d'une pièce, d'un spectacle ridicule. Le jésuitisme éclectique – censuré par Roederer – est retourné au pouvoir, mais il sera bientôt abandonné par tous.[93]

Mais laissons le dernier mot à Roederer. «... je demande au public la parole après M. Pagès; je lui répondrai, s'il y a lieu, par une nouvelle brochure ...».[94] L'ancien conseiller de Metz se mit certainement au travail, il recueillit de la documentation et prit des notes.[95] Nous ne trouverons cependant pas cette réponse, pas même anonyme. Roederer meurt la nuit du 17 décembre 1835.

89 *Ibidem.*
90 *Ibidem.*
91 *De l'adresse d'un constitutionnel aux constitutionnels*, "Le Temps", 9 mars 1835.
92 *Ibidem.*
93 J.-P. Pagès, *Du nouveau ministre*, "Le Temps", 18 mars 1835.
94 P.-L. Roederer, *Adresse*, *Avant-Propos*, cit., XI–XII.
95 Cf. Arch. nat., 29 AP 80, *Papiers Roederer.*

Chapter IV
Constitutional developments and discourses: the Italian experience

Responsabilità ministeriale

1. Le origini del lemma

Il *Dictionnaire critique de la langue française* dell'abate Jean-François Feraud (Marseille, 1787–88, t. III, 456) attribuisce a Jacques Necker, ministro del re di Francia, l'introduzione, nel lessico politico-istituzionale, del termine *responsabilité* («Responsabilité est un mot de M. Necker»). *The Oxford English Dictionary* (t. VIII, 542) data al 1787 l'uso del sostantivo *responsability* attribuendone la paternità all'Hamilton del *The Federalist* (art. n. 63). Di certo, nel breve intervallo tra il *Compte rendu au roi* del 1781 e il *De l'administration des finances de la France*, il banchiere ginevrino rivela "pubblicamente" le gravi condizioni finanziarie della Francia mostrando le responsabilità della cattiva amministrazione. «Responsabile», «responsabilità», dopo secoli di vita opaca, cominciano ad acquisire un significato che la Rivoluzione riempirà di contenuti e di contraddizioni. La *responsabilité des ministres* è, quasi ossessivamente, una della formule più reclamate e discusse. Dall'alto verso il basso, dai ministri sino all'ultima guardia campestre il "potere" deve rendere conto di quello che ha fatto o ordina di fare. L'azione politica e amministrativa è sempre "a tempo", è una catena sottoposta al principio di responsabilità. «La Società ha il diritto di chiedere conto a ogni agente pubblico della sua amministrazione» (art. 15, *Dichiarazione dei diritti dell'uomo e del cittadino*, 26 agosto 1789). È attorno a quegli anni che i dizionari cominciano a registrare queste nuove parole e i relativi concetti.

I materiali di costruzione della categoria «responsabilità ministeriale» sono eterogenei e non riescono a trovare una sistemazione coerente. L'idea di fondo – che ha come retropensiero il deprecato «dispotismo ministeriale» di antico regime – è che i ministri debbano «avere paura» (Saint-Just). Le leggi del 1791, la costituzione del 3 settembre, il codice penale dello stesso anno fondano un corpo composito. A prima vista il codice genetico della responsabilità "alla francese" sembra recepire i principi guida dell'esperienza britannica: inviolabilità del monarca, responsabilità dei ministri, controfirma obbligatoria di tutti gli atti mediante i quali si esercita la prerogativa regia. Ma non è certo sufficiente la scrittura dei principî per dar vita agli stessi esiti. Potere esecutivo e potere legislativo in realtà si fronteggiano l'un l'altro, secondo una rigida separazione dei poteri, ma ad armi impari, dando vita ad un sistema che respinge alla radice la logica dell'equilibrio e del bilanciamento. Il vero codice genetico della responsabilità ministeriale del 1791 ha come "formato" quello giuridico-penale. La prima esperienza dell'Assemblea legislativa rivela il tentativo di estendere oltremodo le figure giuridiche della responsabilità per ottenere incerti obiettivi politici.

L'articolazione dei poteri nella costituzione dell'anno III, a cominciare dal problema del rapporto tra direttori e ministri, allontana ancor di più la Francia dalle logiche complesse, anche se solo immaginate, della responsabilità ministeriale.

2. Tra lessico e cultura: la responsabilità nell'Italia del Triennio

La responsabilità dei funzionari pubblici diventa base tralatizia di «garanzia sociale» nelle costituzioni italiane del triennio «giacobino» (Cost. Bologna 1796, art. XXII, Dichiarazione dei diritti; Cost. del popolo ligure, 1797, art. 2; Cost. repubblica cispadana, 1797, Dichiarazione dei diritti, art. XI; costituzioni del 1797 e 1798 repubblica cisalpina; Cost. repubblica romana 1798, Dichiarazione dei diritti, art. 22). L'influenza della costituzione dell'anno III sugli «esercizi» di assetto costituzionale delle repubbliche italiane si porta dietro il *lessico della responsabilità* sviluppato nella Francia post-rivoluzionaria ma anche l'*impossibilità* di dar vita, come del resto nel modello originario, a una cultura istituzionale della responsabilità politica. Giuseppe Compagnoni, nella sua *pedagogia costituzionale* che ben rappresenta temi e culture circolanti allora tra la Francia e l'Italia, sottolinea l'inevitabile carattere *esecutivo* della responsabilità del governo secondo la più stringente logica «assolutistica» della sovranità. Il rapporto tra il popolo e il governo nella «democrazia rappresentativa» si articola attorno alle coppie sovrano / esecutore, padrone / servo, principale / agente. Compagnoni coglie però bene le contraddizioni della costituzione francese del 1791 informata ad un pericoloso dualismo: inviolabile come rappresentante della nazione, il monarca è però «oggetto» di responsabilità come «primo funzionario pubblico».

> «I Francesi, che sono stati i primi a ristabilire in Europa il governo monarchico secondo i veri principj, nella costituzione del 1791 aveano dichiarato il re inviolabile, e responsabili soltanto i suoi ministri. Ma intanto questi ministri si doveano eleggere, e congedare dal solo re. Come mai tanti valentuomini, che componevano l'Assemblea nazionale, non si accorsero della contraddizione? La responsabilità emana dalla natura della cosa: chiunque assuma un'amministrazione pagato, deve renderne conto. Che se voleasi questo conto dai ministri, ostinandosi a non vedere nel re che una volontà costantemente conforme alla legge, era almeno necessario, che la Nazione potesse efficacemente influire sul congedo de' ministri. Perché riserbarsene soltanto il gastigo dopo la prevaricazione! voleano fare del re una cosa sacra, e ne facevano un essere malefico» (Compagnoni 1797, 177–178).

La democrazia rappresentativa, affermata dalla costituzione dell'anno III, e non i degenerati governi misti all'inglese, doveva dunque rappresentare il modello per l'Italia. Un modello, come è noto, che contiene a sua volta, come in una scatola cinese, elaborazioni mentali assai diverse, dall'«ordine plurale» al governo elitario.

La costituzione della repubblica italiana del 1802 segue, vieppiù complicato, lo schema della costituzione dell'anno VIII che, per certi versi, riassume il discorso sulla responsabilità dei pubblici funzionari post-rivoluzionaria giungendo però ad esiti ulteriori: da un lato il meccanismo privilegiato della *garanzia amministrativa* (art. 75), dall'altro il rafforzamento della procedura di responsabilità penale di fronte alla giurisdizione speciale dell'Alta Corte (artt. 72–74). In questa prospettiva, però, occorre tenere presente la logica profonda che sta alla base della costituzione del governo di brumaio: dietro l'apparenza di complesse dinamiche costituzionali e attraverso la moltiplicazione e il depauperamento rappresentativo delle assemblee legislative i poteri reali sono ben serrati nelle mani del primo console. Nel 1804 Vincenzo Cuoco, riprendendo le critiche all'astratto costruttivismo "giacobino", scorge nella rifondazione ereditaria del potere esecutivo, accompagnata dalla responsabilità dei ministri, la via per una possibile conciliazione tra la libertà e l'Impero (Cuoco 1924, 104). E nel *Saggio storico sulla rivoluzione di Napoli* aveva preso atto della necessità "realistica" di governare le diverse nazioni che formavano la società italiana attraverso la *leadership* dei savi resa possibile dal sostegno decisivo dello Stato napoleonico. Un modello, si capisce, nel quale non c'era spazio per un "discorso politico della responsabilità".

3. Il dibattito della Restaurazione e i suoi echi italiani

La "reinvenzione" francese del concetto di responsabilità era invero carica di significati e di prospettive. Per Necker la responsabilità si appoggia anzitutto su quella figura retorico-contestativa che è il «tribunale dell'opinione pubblica». Surrogato di un corpo rappresentativo – come noterà la figlia Madame de Staël (1818, 99) – l'opinione pubblica è vista come una sorta di alta istanza «giudiziaria» di fronte alla quale persino i re devono «rendere conto». Il ministro, "uomo pubblico" che governa in nome del sovrano, deve «avere credito» (Necker 1792). E avere credito significa guadagnare «fiducia». Non stupisce che il Necker banchiere / ministro utilizzi così agevolmente un lessico tipicamente «economico», da *Commercial Society*. «Il credito – scriverà sempre sua figlia – è dunque la vera scoperta moderna che ha legato i governi coi popoli. Il bisogno di credito obbliga i governi a rispettare la pubblica opinione; ed allo stesso modo che il commercio ha incivilito le nazioni, il credito che da esso deriva ha reso necessarie delle forme costituzionali qualsivoglia (de Staël 1818, 96). Nessun altro orientamento intellettuale sa cogliere, nell'Europa continentale, il senso più profondo della responsabilità ministeriale meglio del "gruppo di Coppet". Necker, anche dopo le disillusioni del 1789, resta convinto che la coppia inviolabilità/ responsabilità sia una grande risorsa della condizione monarchica in grado di separare la responsabilità dei ministri dalla *puissance* e dalla sovranità dello Stato.

L'esperienza britannica, inevitabile punto di riferimento, rivelava un percorso di "differenziazione funzionale" tra la responsabilità penale (le arcaiche procedure di *impeachment* e di *attainder*) e la responsabilità "politica". Tra il 1714 e i primi decenni dell'Ottocento la responsabilità penale diventa l'assoluta eccezione, mostrando come lo sviluppo del parlamentarismo sia anche un processo di civilizzazione costituzionale e di depenalizzazione dei comportamenti e degli atti dei ministri che pretendano di definire una concezione del bene comune. Benjamin Constant, come è noto, saprà fare tesoro, pur con alcune inevitabili incompiutezze, della riflessione neckeriana impostando la più significativa teorica della responsabilità nel costituzionalismo del primo Ottocento. Il pensatore svizzero trae i materiali dall'esperienza inglese che ha sterilizzato il veto regio, potenziato i legami tra esecutivo e legislativo, distinto tra gli atti illegali arbitrari e il cattivo uso del potere legale dei ministri, definito la responsabilità in termini di acquisto o perdita di fiducia/credito nei confronti della nazione e dell'opinione pubblica. Attraverso l'ingegnosa teoria del «potere neutro», che riporta il discorso all'interno della più favorevole condizione monarchica, Constant giurisdizionalizza la responsabilità e pensa di poter risolvere il dilemma originario: costringere l'esecutivo a «rendere conto» senza alterare la dignità del governo e la *puissance d'Etat*, conciliando stabilità e mutamento. Se Madame de Staël notava come «en Angleterre, quand le ministre n'a plus la majorité dans le Parlement, il quitte sa place», Constant è ben consapevole che il sistema "parlamentare" francese, appena istituito tra il 1814 e il 1815, è altra cosa e in questo contesto è indispensabile rivalorizzare il monarca come «giudice» supremo dei conflitti tra i poteri (Constant 1815).

È invece sufficiente leggere la *Monarchia nazionale rappresentativa* di Romagnosi per comprendere quanto l'ideario concettuale in Italia resti lontano, al momento della Restaurazione, dalla cultura liberal-costituzionale. L'impossibilità di configurare un percorso di sviluppo della responsabilità «politica» – nel senso constantiano del termine – è legata alle radici rivoluzionarie innervate dalla concezione napoleonica dello Stato "pedagogico", istitutore del sociale, per certi versi autentica forma "razionalizzata" dell'assolutismo settecentesco. Quell'impossibilità è dunque legata alla centralità di una mediazione tecnocratico-amministrativa che non rompe i legami con i modelli di costruzione corporata del sociale tipici dell'antico regime. In questo contesto non si riesce a immaginare un legame politico-fiduciario tra l'esecutivo monarchico, l'opinione pubblica e le istituzioni rappresentative.

Questo *imprinting*, culturale prima ancora che istituzionale, valorizza invece il circuito della "giuridicizzazione" della responsabilità. Due costituzioni, ben diverse per caratteri e natura, la costituzione del Regno di Napoli del 1815 e la costituzione delle Province Unite del 1831, riprendono lo schema contenutistico della costituzione del 1802. La riarticolazione della responsabilità del potere esecutivo, sia nel senso della forma monarchica che di quella repubblicana, non va oltre il modulo assorbente del penale. Non stupisce certo il fatto che la lingua parlata registri appena la dimensione ministeriale, italianizzi i francesismi e ignori in quei decenni il possibile significato politico-giuridico della responsabilità (per es. D'Alberti di Villanuova 1797–1805; Cardinali 1827; Bernardoni 1829). Nell'Italia della Restaurazione "senza costituzioni" il fragile e confuso costituzionalismo che vi circola in brevi interludi "dinamici" – i cosiddetti moti risorgimentali – non si preoccupa tanto delle forme e del problema della legittimità: la costituzione è un bene in sé, essa ha forza in quanto ideologia, è una tavola di valori che subordina i fatti alle idee. La costituzione è un punto di partenza e non un punto di arrivo. La costituzione di Cadice o la costituzione siciliana del 1812 sono dunque "idee di costituzione". Eppure vi sarebbero state parecchie ragioni a consigliare una lettura approfondita del grande laboratorio spagnolo del primo Ottocento proprio sul tema della responsabilità. Santorre di Santarosa nel suo progetto del 1821–22 combina assieme la cultura dell'*impeachment* con il diritto del Parlamento di far «rendre compte de tous les actes du pouvoir exécutif» (art. 96). Ma malgrado il tentativo di radicamento delle istituzioni rappresentative, come nel caso napoletano del 1820–21, l'esito fallimentare di quel biennio accentuò la diffidenza dei governi e non di rado anche la critica dei moderati verso un parlamentarismo privo di tradizioni che non fossero quelle che riconducevano agli antichi Stati. La sostanziale ineffettività delle esperienze costituzionali era lo specchio di una fragilità strutturale. Né la breve stagione della monarchia consultiva, a prevalente valenza politico-territoriale, né i progetti infrastatuali degli anni Quaranta nel segno di un indefinito discorso "federalistico" acceleravano, negli Stati, lo sviluppo della cultura rappresentativo-parlamentare.

4. Gli anni Quaranta: pubblico criticante e responsabilità del potere

Gli anni Quaranta sono però anni cruciali, utili per tracciare, ancora prima del '48, una linea di confine. Le monarchie italiane senza costituzione sono – direbbe Madame de Staël – monarchie «senza credito» e quindi senza fiducia, governi che non possono «rispettare l'opinione pubblica» e collegarsi alla "nazione". Proprio in quegli anni comincia ad emergere quella sfera pubblica – fondata sui presupposti della comunicazione sociale: la nazione dei lettori e del pubblico criticante – che funge da terreno di *collegamento* tra esperienze distinte ed eterogenee. Ludovico di Breme, in una lettera a Sismondi del 1818, coglieva nell'ostacolo frapposto ad ogni tipo di comunicazione commerciale e letteraria la vera strategia politica dei «restauratori»: l'intenzione dei Principi era di isolare i sudditi come in un arcipelago. «Voilà un sujet à traiter sous le titre *Du danger des communications sociales au 19e siècle. Par un ami de l'ordre*» (Di Breme 1966, 532). L'opinione pubblica e la nazione sono dunque le strutture decisive per collegare i soggetti negli Stati e tra gli Stati. Rispetto a questa evoluzione, non pochi intellettuali – si pensi per es. al "secondo" Romagnosi – *déracinés* a partire dalla Restaurazione, cominciano a rappresentarsi come *faiseurs d'opinion*. L'ampliamento di scala, da regionale a nazionale, apre prospettive in parte inedite e si comincia a codificare un'idea di pubblico. Nel 1846, Massimo D'Azeglio, in margine ai *Casi di Romagna*, osserva acutamente: «quando in una nazione tutti riconoscono giusta una cosa e la vogliono, la cosa è fatta; e in Italia il lavoro più importante per la nostra rigenerazione si può far con le mani in tasca» (D'Azeglio 1846, 84). Nel 1844 Cesare Balbo aveva invitato i governi a diventare più «desiderabili» per attrarre le migliore energie e per costruire una «egemonia nazionale» (Balbo 1844, 217 ss.).

Non sorprende che gli incunaboli del costituzionalismo italiano siano incentrati in grandissima misura sul nesso libertà di stampa, opinione pubblica, governo costituzionale / monarchia rappresentativa. Non è difficile cogliere l'affioramento di quella cultura liberal-costituzionale che ha radici britanniche ma "forma francese", filtrata attraverso Constant, Rossi, Hello e altri scrittori orleanisti. La responsabilità dei ministri è uno dei fondamenti del governo rappresentativo perché

> «mantiene un giusto temperamento tra la potenza del Principe, e quella dei parlamenti chiamati a tutelare i diritti e gl'interessi della nazione. Se il Principe con la sanzione, o col divieto delle leggi, con la scelta dei magistrati e dei pubblici ufficiali, con la convocazione e lo scioglimento del parlamento, mantiene la sua suprema autorità su tutte le parti del pubblico reggimento, i deputati della nazione con chieder conto ai Ministri di tutti, senza eccezione, gli atti che a quello appartengono, fanno sì che in tutte le sue parti si mantenga vivo quello spirito, che lo tiene in armonia coi voti e coi desiderii della nazione. Per tal modo si impedisce che non si alteri quell'ordinamento di poteri che è proprio della monarchia rappresentativa.»

In questo modo si impediscono gli atti contrari ai diritti politici riconosciuti dalla coscienza comune e «consacrati dalla costituzione» (Boncompagni 1846, 33–34). In pochi mesi, tra la fine del 1847 e la primavera del 1848, lo scenario *nazionale* cambia decisamente. Le monarchie «senza credito» devono prendere la strada del modello «censitario-rappresentativo» di impianto liberale. La costituzione, rapidamente, «consacra» l'avanzata nazionale dell'opinione pubblica, imita modelli stranieri coniugandoli ai contesti, si conquista «credito».

5. Dal '48 agli anni Cinquanta: la scoperta della responsabilità politica

A leggere i testi delle costituzioni del 1848, il tema della responsabilità viene incardinato sull'asse di alcuni principî comuni. I ministri, di nomina regia, sono responsabili; la persona del re è sacra e inviolabile. «Gli atti di ogni genere sottoscritti dal Re non hanno vigore se non contrassegnati da un ministro segretario di stato, il quale perciò solo se ne rende risponsabile» (Costituzione del Regno delle Due Sicilie, art. 72). I ministri hanno libero accesso in Parlamento e il diritto di essere ascoltati. «Hanno l'obbligo, quando sieno invitati, a dare gli schiarimenti, che all'assemblea sembrassero opportuni» (Statuto del Granducato di Toscana, art. 61). La responsabilità che emerge in forma esplicita è quella giuridico-penale: i ministri potranno essere processati e puniti nei casi previsti da apposita legge. Questa «determinerà i casi di tale responsabilità, le pene, le forme dell'accusa e del giudizio» (Statuto fondamentale del governo temporale degli Stati della Chiesa, art. 54). Le carte del 1848 intendono "temperare" la monarchia "costituzionalizzata" attraverso il governo rappresentativo. Gli articoli che nelle varie costituzioni definiscono il problema della responsabilità rappresentano un dato di partenza che deve essere letto alla luce dell'*origo constitutionis* (la *lettre*) ma anche in rapporto ai profili evolutivi (l'*esprit*). Ancora una volta la fonte britannica viene passata attraverso il filtro, talvolta distorcente, del costituzionalismo continentale con al centro le *Chartes* francesi (1814 e 1830) e la costituzione belga del 1831, ma spesso con differente *esprit* e con esiti originali.

Il 1848 afferma in Italia le prime esperienze costituzionali, fatte di dottrine, lotte parlamentari, prassi: inizia una brevissima (per la gran parte della penisola) difficile ma decisiva stagione che segnerà un punto di non ritorno. La vita costituzionale consente di consolidare logiche e dinamiche rappresentative che vengono così messe alla prova per la prima volta. La responsabilità ministeriale si rivela uno dei più delicati contrafforti. Cesare Balbo ha ben compreso che il regime rappresentativo vive di interdipendenze e di finzioni. Una delle grandi invenzioni del costituzionalismo britannico è che il «Re non può far male»: tanto più è inviolabile la persona del re tanto più è esposta quella dei ministri. Non si può non «ammirare questa istituzione, questo mezzo termine, questo ritrovato» (Balbo 1857, 220) della civiltà che unisce nella monarchia rappresentativa i vantaggi della monarchia e della repubblica. Ma non bisogna cadere nell'equivoco della neutralizzazione politica del sovrano. Ripercorrendo le figure del «potere neutro» Balbo ricorda la centralità strategica della monarchia. La responsabilità penale – che, tra l'altro, è di ardua attivazione – non può diventare inopinatamente uno scudo per i ministri. Il ministro costituzionale deve essere devoto alla nazione in generale e al principe in particolare: «egli è, nella macchina rappresentativa, parte di quel congegno speciale che si chiama potere del principe, ed a questo deve servire principalmente, con questo cooperare» (ivi,

398). Nell'elogio dottrinario dello schema del governo misto-rappresentativo la responsabilità non deve però essere una semplice finzione. Nessun scrittore del '48 italiano coglie e soprattutto sintetizza meglio di Pietro Peverelli le dinamiche della responsabilità retta da due principî: l'accordo vero, cosciente e sincero, tra il monarca e i ministri, l'influenza dell'opinione pubblica "rappresentata" in grado, in alcune circostanze, di impedire o obbligare i ministri. «Sebbene quindi l'art. 65 attribuisca al re il diritto di nominare e revocare i suoi ministri, pure per l'applicazione delle altre disposizioni dello Statuto, che vi hanno correlazione, questo diritto non è né assoluto né illimitato, ma è necessariamente influenzato dalla maggioranza della Camera dei deputati» (Peverelli 1849, 135). Questa influenza non può essere né diretta né esplicita: il parlamento non può chiedere la revoca dei ministri ma può rifiutare la sua approvazione alle leggi non conformi alle idee politiche della maggioranza. Sono le dimissioni e l'appello al popolo a tenere in equilibrio il sistema e rendere mera, remota eccezione la messa in stato d'accusa. La monarchia rappresentativa ha dunque un vantaggio congenito

> «in guisa che i ministri della Corona debbono interpretare i voleri della pluralità e uscir dell'ufficio quando venga lor meno il concorso parlamentare, ognun vede come l'opinione pubblica non intermetta mai di vegliarne gli andamenti, come in ogni tempo si precluda la via ai piccoli arbitrî, si compongano i conflitti fra camera e governo e come si apra l'adito ai mutamenti nella cosa pubblica col semplice scambio dei ministri che consigliano il capo dello stato. In una repubblica presidenziale si comprenderà ancora una rivoluzione; essa diventa inutile nella monarchia» (Carutti 1852, 242).

Non mancheranno certo i tentativi per attuare la "giuridicizzazione" della responsabilità attraverso leggi organiche costituzionali. I progetti del deputato Sineo presentati sin dal 1849 al parlamento subalpino ne danno il tono; ma la tendenza è a separare, ovvero a cogliere anche nella procedura penale la sua prevalente dimensione politica (Pessina 1849; Melegari 1857). La responsabilità penale ha un rilievo più simbolico che effettivo e diventa assoluta *extrema ratio* quanto più un sistema costituzionale comincia a camminare sulle proprie gambe. Il lessico si diffonde rapidamente. Straordinaria è la capacità di registrazione dei neologismi di quel *Dizionario politico popolare* torinese che coniuga e traduce sarcasticamente nel linguaggio democratico le nuove categorie dell'esperienza costituzionale. «Responsabilità. "Chi rompe paga": è questo un proverbio da taverna, ma non certo da gabinetto. Nei gabinetti quel proverbio va rivoltato così: chi rompe è pagato. I ministri si dicono *responsabili* de' loro atti. Ma questa non è più che una frase, finché non sia stata proposta ed emanata una legge sulla responsabilità ministeriale, che determini gli atti che cadono sotto la penalità, stabilisca la penalità stessa, ordini il resoconto degli atti ministeriali, il processo, il giudizio» (*Dizionario popolare* 1851, 199).

I dibattiti sullo statuto del governo e sulla responsabilità riecheggiarono nelle aule parlamentari, dal Piemonte alla Toscana, da Roma a Napoli sino alla Sicilia, con esiti provvisori e limitati ma tutt'altro che banali. Solo il regime subalpino seppe però diventare *esperienza*. «Qui si assalgono, qui si difendono, e qui si feriscono e si uccidono i ministeri e rinascono altri via via» (Balbo 1857, 308). Balbo lo scoprì sulla propria pelle in quei primi anni di *apprentissage*. Pellegrino Rossi fu assassinato, il ministero democratico Guerrazzi-Montanelli si trovò al centro di ben note traversie. Nella storia subalpina – malgrado il grande esperimento cavouriano – e poi nella vicenda nazionale, la responsabilità politica non fu mai un incontroverso *punto di arrivo*: essa rimase un *problema*, cruciale, giacchè dalla sua "soluzione" dipendeva l'assetto e l'evoluzione della forma di governo. La non casuale vaghezza e duttilità della formula costituzionale della responsabilità – strutturale nel costituzionalismo della Restaurazione – era in realtà un programma, da interpretare e riempire di contenuti.

Fonti

Balbo C., *Delle speranze d'Italia*, ed. seconda, Capolago 1844

– *Della monarchia rappresentativa in Italia. Saggi politici di Cesare Balbo. Della politica nella presente civiltà abbozzi del medesimo autore*, Firenze 1857

Bernardoni G., *Elenco di alcune parole oggidì frequentemente in uso, le quali non sono ne' vocabolari italiani*, Roma, ed. prima romana con aggiunte, 1829

Boncompagni C., *Della monarchia rappresentativa*, Torino 1846

Cardinali F., *Dizionario portatile della lingua italiana*, Bologna 1827, 2 voll.

Carutti D., *Del governo libero*, Torino 1852

Compagnoni G., [1797], *Elementi di diritto costituzionale democratico*, a cura di Italo Mereu e Daniela Barbon, Bologna 1985

Constant B., [1815], *De la responsabilité des ministres*, in B. Constant, *Œuvres complètes*, IX, 1, a cura di O. Devaux e K. Kloocke, Tübingen 2001

Cuoco V., [1802], *Saggio storico sulla rivoluzione di Napoli*, a cura di A. de Francesco, Roma, Manduria 1998

– [1804], *Napoleone Imperatore*, in «Il giornale italiano», 30 maggio – 2 giugno 1804, in V. Cuoco, *Scritti vari*, Bari 1924, I, 104

D'Alberti di Villanuova F., *Dizionario universale critico enciclopedico della lingua italiana*, Lucca, 1797–1805, voll. 6

D'Azeglio M., *Degli ultimi casi di Romagna*, Italia, s. e., s. l., 1846

De Stäel G., [1818], *Considerazioni sui principali avvenimenti della Rivoluzione francese*, intr. di A. Omodeo, Milano 1943

Di Breme L., *Lettere*, raccolte e annotate da P. Camporesi, Torino 1966

Dizionario politico popolare [1851], a cura di P. Trifone, introduzione di L. Serianni, Roma, Salerno editore, s. d.

Melegari L. A., *Sunti delle lezioni di diritto costituzionale ...*, Torino 1857

Necker J. [1792], *Du pouvoir exécutif dans les grands États*, in *Œuvres complètes*, Paris 1821, t. VIII

Pessina E., *Manuale del diritto pubblico costituzionale*, Napoli 1849

Peverelli P., *Comenti intorno allo Statuto del regno di Sardegna*, Torino 1849

Romagnosi G.D. [1815], *Della costituzione di una monarchia nazionale rappresentativa: la scienza delle costituzioni*, ed. a cura di G. Astuti, introduzione di F. Patetta, Roma 1937

Bibliografia

Amson D., *La responsabilité politique et pénale des ministres de 1789 à 1958*, in *Pouvoirs*, 1, 2000, 31–60

Azimi V., *Aux origines de la responsabilité ministérielle*, in *1791. La première constitution française*, a cura di J. Bart et alii, Paris 1993, 216–269

Baranger D., *Parlementarisme des origines. Essai sur les conditions de formation d'un exécutif responsable en Angleterre (des années 1740 au début de l'âge victorien)*, Paris 1999

Brunot F., *Responsabilité*, in *Grammatical miscellany offered to Otto Jaspersen on his 70. birthday*, 1930, 401–404

Henriot J., *Note sur la date et le sens de l'apparition du mot "responsabilité"*, in *Archives de philosophie du droit, La responsabilité*, 22, 1977, 59–62

Jaume L., *Tra concetto e idea-forza: l'opinione pubblica secondo Necker*, in L. Lacchè, a cura di, *Opinione pubblica. Storia, politica, costituzione dal XVIII al XX secolo*, n. 6/II semestre 2003, *Giornale di storia costituzionale*, 129–144

– *Le concept de "responsabilité des ministres" chez Benjamin Constant*, in *Revue française de droit constitutionnel*, 42, 2000, 227–243

Lacchè L., *Coppet et la percée de l'État libéral constitutionnel*, in *Coppet, creuset de l'esprit libéral. Les idées politiques et constitutionneles du Groupe de Madame de Staël*, sous la dir. de L. Jaume, Paris 2000, 135–155 (*supra*, 201–226)

Laquieze A., *Le modèle anglais et la responsabilité ministérielle selon le groupe de Coppet*, in *Coppet, creuset de l'esprit libéral*, cit., 157–176

Mannori L., *Uno Stato per Romagnosi. I, Il progetto costituzionale*, Milano 1984

– *La crisi dell'ordine plurale. Nazione e costituzione in Italia tra Sette e Ottocento*, in AA.VV., *Ordo iuris. Storia e forme dell'esperienza giuridica*, Milano 2003, 137–180

Morabito M., *Necker et la question du «chef de l'État»*, in *Coppet, creuset de l'esprit libéral*, cit., 41–54

Proschwitz G., von, *Responsabilité: l'idée et le mot dans le débat politique du XVIIIe siècle*, in *Actes du Xe Congrès de linguistique et philologie romanes*, Paris 1965, 385–397

L'ordine costituzionale liberale nel XIX secolo. Fondamenti e caratteri

1. Radici

L'obiettivo primario di questo contributo consiste nel ricostruire, in chiave sintetica, il dato generale degli elementi strutturali che sembrano fondare l'esperienza del costituzionalismo considerato, anzitutto, nella sua dimensione di ordine costituzionale all'interno del problema delle matrici culturali e della consistenza istituzionale del liberalismo italiano.

Il costituzionalismo liberale ottocentesco affonda le sue principali radici dottrinali e istituzionali nella cultura-madre del costituzionalismo "rivoluzionario" del XVII e XVIII secolo. Forma un grosso ramo dell'«albero» che chiamiamo costituzionalismo; ne ripensa e analizza criticamente i risultati, respinge alcuni profili, ne sviluppa e valorizza altri. Non si tratta quindi di un legato univoco, di un patrimonio che si possa accogliere come un tutto unitario. Per il contesto italiano definiremo come costituzionalismo liberale quel movimento intellettuale e quei processi storico-concreti che sfociano in una dimensione costituzionale nell'ambito di uno sviluppo cronologico che per mera convenzione occupa il secolo che corre dagli anni delle Restaurazioni alla crisi del primo dopoguerra. E, tuttavia, se questa dimensione temporale può essere considerata in termini di sostanziale unitarietà, nello stesso tempo il nostro obiettivo risiede soprattutto nel cogliere i presupposti e i fondamenti del costituzionalismo liberale, soprattutto nella fase precedente l'affermazione dello statualismo costituzionale che rappresenta al tempo stesso uno sviluppo e un superamento della prima fase del costituzionalismo liberale (1815–1880 ca.).

Questo movimento si mette alla ricerca di un punto di equilibrio e di un difficile compromesso, quasi a voler temperare la potenza profetica delle inedite energie che le dinamo rivoluzionarie tra '600 e '700 hanno accumulato nel contesto del più ampio processo di evoluzione e di articolazione tipologica dello Stato moderno. Si ha l'impressione che nel frangente del costituzionalismo rivoluzionario le diverse esperienze (in special modo nel triangolo atlantico dell'Inghilterra, dell'America e della Francia) abbiano prodotto categorie, linguaggi, soluzioni che il lungo Ottocento vorrà o potrà metabolizzare solo in parte e in chiave sostanzialmente eclettica. Nel periodo preso in esame, inoltre, rimangono fermi i pilastri originari del costituzionalismo moderno (garanzia dei diritti e delle libertà; limite e organizzazione della sovranità) ma ciò che è oggetto di ripensamento e di nuova *balance* sono alcuni orizzonti che appaiono radicali o almeno tali potenzialmente. Si tratta, dunque, non di tornare indietro (cosa certo possibile a livello teorico e dottrinale) quanto piuttosto di combinare assieme e di governare quell'insieme di principi e di regole politico-giuridiche in grado di dare soluzione all'incontro, fonte di tensioni e di contraddizioni, tra le libertà/garanzie dei moderni e un principio stabile e progredente di ordine costituzionale. La dimensione propria del costituzionalismo liberale italiano non può prescindere da alcuni «formanti» quali l'immediata dominazione francese sino all'età napoleonica, il perdurare di presenze «straniere» e la frammentazione politico-istituzionale nell'età della Restaurazione, l'avvio e lo sviluppo del risorgimento nazionale, il carattere proprio degli strati borghesi, il complesso processo di *building state* (comprensivo di questioni nazionali e internazionali, a cominciare dalla presenza del pontefice temporale), il dibattito dottrinale sulle scelte istituzionali compiute e sulla costruzione dello Stato liberale di diritto che trova nel Vittorio Emanuele Orlando degli anni Ottanta l'artefice del principale paradigma scientifico teso a rileggere e rifunzionalizzare la stessa cultura del costituzionalismo liberale. Nella fase storica oggetto di questo contributo ad emergere con maggiore evidenza sembrano essere, almeno sino all'unificazione, più le «politiche costituzionali» e la «costituzione come ideologia» che non una organica costellazione concettuale di tipo giuspubblicistico. Tale rispondenza ai canoni scientifici del «diritto costituzionale» sarà più forte e visibile nel contesto rinnovato che unisce il problema della costituzione al processo di edificazione dello Stato nazionale.

2. Oltre la *Révolution*

Il costituzionalismo liberale segue in Italia una linea di sviluppo che è più vicina, per ragioni storiche, all'esperienza francese postrivoluzionaria. Per vicinanza è da intendere anzitutto una prossimità di tipo culturale e istituzionale, nel senso che l'età delle costituzioni in Italia ha un avvio significativo negli anni del cd. «triennio giacobino». E' in questi anni che scorgiamo l'influenza della costituzione dell'anno III sui complicati «esercizi» di assetto costituzionale delle repubbliche italiane, alla ricerca di un ordine che sarà trovato più sul piano delle forze reali (esercito e amministrazione) che su quello del rendimento e delle culture istituzionali. Si è però alla ricerca del «governo migliore» e il «modello» francese – che è a sua volta un complesso palinsesto testuale e ideologico – pone senza dubbio il problema tutto moderno della scrittura della costituzione-atto e della sua natura conformativa. L'art. 16 della Dichiarazione dei diritti dell'uomo e del cittadino del 1789, «Toute Société dans laquelle la garantie des Droits n'est pas assurée, ni la séparation des Pouvoirs déterminée, n'a point de Constitution», rappresenta una tessitura di principi imprescindibili che potranno, come in un gioco di specchi, rinviare a loro volta immagini del costituzionalismo atlantico, britannico e americano, per lo più filtrato attraverso questo primo dimensionamento di impianto francese.

La democrazia rappresentativa affermata dalla costituzione dell'anno III – e non i degenerati governi misti all'inglese – doveva rappresentare per il primo «costituzionalista» italico Giuseppe Compagnoni il modello per l'Italia (*Elementi di diritto costituzionale democratico* [1797], a cura di I. Mereu e D. Barbon, Bologna, Analisi, 1985).

Un modello politico-costituzionale che poteva contenere a sua volta elaborazioni mentali assai diverse, dall'«ordine plurale» al governo elitario. La pedagogia costituzionale è, in questa fase, il principale approccio «costituzionalistico» e ben rappresenta temi e culture circolanti allora tra la Francia e l'Italia. Non mancano elementi di differenziazione nell'esperienza delle cosiddette repubbliche sorelle, pur in presenza di un *modus operandi* che privilegia formule costruttiviste e «uniformatrici» in campo istituzionale. Si pensi, per esempio, alla costituzione partenopea del 1799 elaborata da Mario Pagano con i suoi Efori e Censori e una organizzazione dei poteri che rappresenta, a parte la Francia, un *unicum* nel contesto europeo o ancora alla costituzione della repubblica italiana del 1802 che segue, vieppiù complicato, lo schema della costituzione francese dell'anno VIII. Vista nella prospettiva dell'imperialismo napoleonico, la costituzione del governo di brumaio rivela, dietro l'apparenza di complesse dinamiche costituzionali e attraverso la moltiplicazione e il depauperamento rappresentativo delle assemblee legislative, i poteri reali ben serrati nelle mani del primo console. Nel 1804 Vincenzo Cuoco, riprendendo le critiche all'astratto costruttivismo «giacobino», scorge nella rifondazione ereditaria del potere esecutivo, accompagnata dalla responsabilità dei ministri, la via per una possibile conciliazione tra la libertà e l'Impero (V. Cuoco, *Napoleone Imperatore*, in «Il giornale italiano», 30 maggio – 2 giugno 1804, in V. Cuoco, Scritti vari, Bari, Laterza, 1924, I, 104). Proprio Cuoco aveva preso atto nel *Saggio storico sulla rivoluzione di Napoli* della necessità realistica di governare le diverse «nazioni» che formavano la società «italiana» attraverso la leadership dei savi resa possibile dal sostegno decisivo dello Stato napoleonico. Un modello nel quale la pedagogia costituzionale difficilmente poteva conciliarsi con lo spirito più genuino del costituzionalismo. In un raro scritto del 1815 l'esule Pellegrino Rossi e futuro costituzionalista tracciava un lucido bilancio di un'epoca letta in chiave «progressiva»: «Il regno d'Italia, benchè troppo soggetto alla dominazione francese, e non ancora ben mondo d'ogni macchia rivoluzionaria, offriva ciononostante uno spettacolo abbastanza grato a un italiano, perchè aveva infine una costituzione, un'amministrazione propria, un'armata, un tesoro, quell'insieme in una parola, che costituisce uno stato separato: col tempo la dominazione francese poteva diminuire, le istituzioni migliorarsi, l'insieme consolidarsi: non era al certo una stoltezza lo sperare che alfine, alcune almeno di quelle parti d'Italia, che erano si mostruosamente attaccate alla Francia, potessero più naturalmente e convenevolmente unirsi al regno d'Italia. In somma se non potevasi ancora godere, vi era almeno qualche ragione di sperare, e più vi era da sperare pei figli nostri» (*Autodifesa. Risposta alle imputazioni diffuse contro di lui dopo la fuga da Bologna*, Genthod 14 luglio 1815, 10–11, in Bibliothèque Publique Universitaire, Ginevra).

Al momento della Restaurazione uno spirito militante e originale come Gian Domenico Romagnosi elabora quel vasto disegno – rimasto allora in gran parte inedito – di filosofia «costituzionale» che individua nella «Monarchia nazionale rappresentativa» il polo attorno cui costruire una complessa scienza delle costituzioni (*Della costituzione di una monarchia nazionale rappresentativa: la scienza delle costituzioni* [1815], ed. a cura di G. Astuti, introduzione di F. Patetta, Roma, Reale Accademia d'Italia, 1937). La costituzione politica come limite è valida se riesce ad armonizzare le diversi parti, a disciplinare il regime, a garantirne l'esecuzione. Ma in Romagnosi quella che lui chiama la «compotenza» non può fare a meno della nuova grande forza morale che è l'opinione pubblica in grado, se illuminata e savia, di legare la società civile a quella politica nonché a diventare il potere predominante della macchina costituzionale verso cui devono convergere i poteri governativi e quelli popolari. La monarchia di Romagnosi ha, come in certe riflessioni di Benjamin Constant, un fondamento repubblicano e non può assolutamente guardare in direzione della costituzione inglese (o ad una forma «autoctona» anglofila quale quella siciliana del 1812) che viene rappresentata come costituzione di impronta feudale e nobiliare. Nella singolare architettura romagnosiana vediamo riaffiorare quell'immaginifico linguaggio che a partire dal tumultuoso decennio rivoluzionario aveva cercato di individuare lo spazio di un «potere supplementare» che potesse conciliare la volontà del legislativo e l'azione dell'esecutivo, il dogma dell'unità sovrana del corpo politico della nazione e la logica razionalizzata dell'equilibrio o della *balance*.

Malgrado gli sforzi operati sul registro del costituzionalismo, la Monarchia nazionale rappresentativa di Romagnosi è una possibile sintesi di una stagione che non lascia in eredità all'Italia, al momento della Restaurazione, un insieme organico di principi costituzionali, come nel caso di Benjamin Constant in Francia. Essa rimane legata alle radici rivoluzionarie innervate dalla concezione napoleonica dello Stato pedagogico, istitutore del sociale, per certi versi autentica forma razionalizzata dell'assolutismo settecentesco. La centralità di una mediazione tecnocratico-amministrativa non rompe i legami con i modelli di costruzione corporata del sociale tipici dell'antico regime e in questo contesto non si riesce ancora ad immaginare un legame politico-fiduciario tra l'esecutivo monarchico, l'opinione pubblica e le istituzioni rappresentative.

3. L'ordine costituzionale dei privati e il regno della legge

L'Italia della Restaurazione si ritrova «senza costituzioni» e il fragile costituzionalismo, evocato dai «liberali» e operante in brevi interludi «dinamici» – i cosiddetti «moti risorgimentali» – è ben poco supportato da una elaborazione dottrinale: in realtà, la costituzione appare come un bene in sé (a prescindere da forma e contenuti), possiede forza in quanto ideologia, è una tavola di valori che tende a subordinare i fatti alle idee. La costituzione di Cadice o la costituzione siciliana del 1812 – allora richiamate o «recepite» – sono dunque idee di costituzione. E malgrado il tentativo di impiantare istituzioni rappresentative, come nel caso napoletano del 1820–21, l'esito fallimentare del biennio accentuò la diffidenza dei governi e non di rado anche la critica dei moderati verso un parlamentarismo privo di tradizioni che non fossero quelle che riportavano agli antichi Stati. La sostanziale ineffettività delle esperienze costituzionali era lo specchio di una fragilità strutturale. Né la breve stagione della «monarchia consultiva», a prevalente valenza politico-territoriale, né i progetti infrastatuali degli anni '40 nel segno di un indefinito discorso «federalistico» (la «costituzione» di Gioberti) acceleravano, negli Stati, lo sviluppo della cultura rappresentativo-parlamentare.

Sarebbe tuttavia un approccio parziale quello che volesse leggere i fondamenti del costituzionalismo liberale solo attraverso i testi costituzionali. Non bisogna infatti dimenticare quella vicenda dell'ordine giuridico ottocentesco, liberal-borghese, che trova nel codice civile – ovvero il *Code Napoléon* quale suo paradigma *par excellence* – la sua più autentica costituzione materiale. Lo spazio del codice civile possiede un'indubbia vocazione «costituzionale» ed una forte pretesa di stabilità e di autonomia. Il XIX secolo principia, nel "modello francese" (che avrà ampia risonanza europea), con un costituzionalismo debole o puramente imperiale e con un ordine costituzionale dei privati straordinariamente forte. Sulla scia dell'individualismo proprietario, la dimensione costituzionale accentua, a partire dall'età napoleonica, la logica del privatismo. Il binomio al centro della scena non è più quello libertà / eguaglianza, dirompente nella fase più radicale della Rivoluzione, ma libertà / proprietà, con l'*égalité* neutralizzata dall'antropologia del possesso e la *liberté* resa possibile nella sfera dell'*homo oeconomicus*. La garanzia costituzionale (e quindi il costituzionalismo) può operare principalmente nell'ambito delle libertà economiche, impallidisce quanto più ci si allontana dall'antropologia del proprietario maschio e maggiorenne. La logica del codice è, al tempo stesso, la logica della legge. Questo tipo di «regno della legge», con le sue ben radicate mitologie, è ben diverso dal *rule of law* di matrice anglosassone. Il legicentrismo determina una progressiva scissione tra legge e costituzione, tra legge e diritti. La legge *par excellence*, il codice civile, ha, in tal senso, impoverito la teoria costituzionale dei diritti.

Non ci meraviglia che il filone più sostanzioso del costituzionalismo liberale del primo Ottocento trovi, a livello europeo, in Benjamin Constant lo scrittore che, muovendo proprio dall'esperienza rivoluzionaria e napoleonica, censura il legislatore onnipotente e considera la costituzione «un acte de défiance puisqu'elle prescrit des limites à l'autorité [...]». Limitare la sovranità, e dunque il potere, significa tracciare anzitutto la linea invalicabile della «libertà dei moderni» che garantisce i cittadini «contre le pouvoir». Ma ciò non basta. Constant coglie lucidamente i pericoli del privatismo. Il governo rappresentativo non sana del tutto la irriducibile distanza tra governanti e governati, così come la divisione dei poteri è inutile se i poteri finiscono per non limitare la prorompente autorità sociale. La libertà degli antichi assicurava la partecipazione al potere sociale ma col rischio che gli uomini cedessero a poco prezzo i diritti e i godimenti individuali. La libertà dei moderni, ovvero la libertà individuale che offre il benessere e l'indipendenza privata, rischia di annullare quella politica. L'uomo moderno «costituzionale», invece, ha bisogno di entrambe le libertà, ovvero di combinarle assieme. E' questa l'alchimia del costituzionalismo liberale di matrice individualistica che Constant elabora durante l'età napoleonica e codifica nella sua celebre conferenza su «La libertà degli antichi comparata a quella dei moderni» (1819). In questo costituzionalismo del soggetto – da Constant a Tocqueville a Stuart Mill – cogliamo la tensione tra la necessaria difesa dell'individuo attraverso le garanzie e il pericolo dell'esorbitanza di un potere sociale che, sotto varie forme a cominciare dalla forma-Stato, minaccia lo stesso ordine dei privati.

4. L'opinione pubblica, la nazione, la costituzione

Se in ambito continentale il costituzionalismo liberale si esprime essenzialmente attraverso la stagione «anglofila» delle *Chartes constitutionnelles* francesi, l'innovativa esperienza belga del 1831, il variegato *Frühkonstitutionalismus* di area tedesca, è in Italia il quarto decennio del secolo quello che apre nuovi orizzonti. «... Il credito – aveva scritto la figlia del banchiere ginevrino Necker – è dunque la vera scoperta moderna che ha legato i governi coi popoli. Il bisogno di credito obbliga i governi a rispettare la pubblica opinione; ed allo stesso modo che il commercio ha incivilito le nazioni, il credito che da esso deriva ha reso necessarie delle forme costituzionali qualsivoglia...» (G. de Staël, *Considerazioni sui principali avvenimenti della Rivoluzione francese*, Milano, Ispi, 1943 (1818), 96).

Le monarchie italiane senza costituzione sono – direbbe Madame de Staël – monarchie «senza credito», governi che non possono «rispettare l'opinione pubblica» e collegarsi alla nazione. Ma proprio in quegli anni comincia ad emergere quella sfera pubblica – fondata sui presupposti della comunicazione sociale: la nazione dei lettori e del pubblico criticante – che funge da terreno di collegamento tra esperienze distinte ed eterogenee. L'opinione pubblica e la nazione sono dunque le strutture decisive per collegare i soggetti negli Stati e tra gli Stati. L'ampliamento di scala, da regionale a nazionale, apre prospettive in parte inedite e si comincia a codificare un'idea di pubblico. Massimo D'Azeglio nella sua celebre *Proposta d'un programma per l'opinione nazionale italiana* (Firenze, 1847) costruisce la figura dell'opinione pubblica – di cui invoca il ruolo decisivo – come forza morale trasparente. E' proprio la necessità di uscire definitivamente dalla stagione della forza materiale segnata dalle società segrete e dal loro sterile settarismo, a spingere verso mezzi capaci di influire sull'opinione pubblica che è la prima dispensatrice della forza morale. D'Azeglio intravede – specie dopo il programma di Pio IX – la possibilità per il partito moderato di non essere più percepito come fazione ma come Opinione nazionale italiana. L'obiettivo, certo difficile, è dunque quello di integrare nell'opinione pubblica nazionale quell'insieme di identità diverse che caratterizzano la nazione plurale degli Italiani. In questi anni l'opinione pubblica invocata e abbozzata dal moderatismo liberale ha ancora una dimensione più «pre-politica» che costituzionale. La sua struttura di *civil society* guarda anzitutto allo sviluppo di una classe borghese di stampo europeo che unifica ceti e dimensioni sociali rivolte al progresso materiale (dalle ferrovie alle leghe doganali) e alla distinzione per merito e per «capacità di innovazione».

Ma il *governo con il pubblico* è la strada per arrivare al *governo con la costituzione*. Non sorprende che gli «incunaboli» del costituzionalismo italiano siano incentrati in grandissima misura sul nesso libertà di stampa, opinione pubblica, governo costituzionale / monarchia rappresentativa. Non è difficile cogliere l'affioramento di quella cultura liberal-costituzionale che ha radici britanniche ma «forma francese», filtrata attraverso Constant, Rossi, Hello e altri scrittori orleanisti. In pochi mesi, tra la fine del 1847 e la primavera del 1848, lo scenario nazionale cambia decisamente. Le monarchie «senza credito» devono prendere la strada del modello censitario-rappresentativo di impianto liberale. La costituzione, rapidamente, consacra l'avanzata nazionale dell'opinione pubblica, «imita» modelli stranieri coniugandoli ai contesti, si conquista credito. Il 1848 afferma in Italia le prime esperienze costituzionali, fatte di dottrine, lotte parlamentari, prassi: inizia una brevissima (per la gran parte della penisola) difficile ma decisiva stagione che segnerà un punto di non ritorno. La vita costituzionale consente di consolidare logiche e dinamiche «rappresentative» che vengono così messe alla prova per la prima volta.

5. Caratteri del costituzionalismo liberale italiano (nel contesto europeo)

5.1 Un tentativo definitorio

Nell'aprire la nuova stagione, il movimento politico-costituzionale del 1848 contribuisce in maniera significativa a dare un primo *imprinting* al costituzionalismo italiano. Anzitutto la vicenda storica: dalle ceneri del 1848–49 resterà in piedi solo l'esperimento sabaudo. Spesso si è portati a ritenere che la forza del Regno di Sardegna come motore dell'unificazione risieda anzitutto in un esercito moderno e in uno stato amministrativo ben funzionante. A nostro avviso la vera forza risiede prima di tutto nella tenuta e nello sviluppo della costituzione, del Parlamento e del rapporto con l'opinione pubblica (nazionale). La dinastia sabauda (e la classe dirigente che la sostiene) acquistano meriti e credito più che per concedere lo Statuto (*obtorto collo* lo fanno tutti i sovrani), per mantenerlo vivo una volta passato il Quarantotto. Questa è la decisione fondamentale da cui discendono molte conseguenze.

Il costituzionalismo liberale si sviluppa nell'alveo dottrinario del costituzionalismo moderno inteso come teoria e pratica istituzionale di limitazione e regolazione politico-giuridica dei poteri pubblici di governo allo scopo di garantire ambiti di autonomia definiti da diritti e libertà, con l'obiettivo di progettare e decidere equilibri storico-concreti che mutano dinamicamente nel corso del tempo. L'Italia, dunque, fa il suo ingresso definitivo nel percorso plurale del costituzionalismo moderno, in un momento specifico. La costituzione del '48 è scritta ma è il risultato di un dibattito che a lungo ha fatto perno sullo schema della monarchia cetuale e consultiva. La costituzione «antica» di Gioberti – storicamente segnata da una determinante di tipo pattizio-federativo che viene dalla tradizione municipale – non è del tutto estranea ai liberali moderati che rileggono la costituzione inglese come modello per una graduale transizione verso la monarchia costituzionale rappresentativa.

5.2 Il costituzionalismo liberale «storicistico»

Bisogna fare i conti con la costituzione-atto, ma l'appello alla storia suggerisce la ricerca di un fattore di temperamento. Si cerca di «correggere» la rigidità della costituzione artificiale, fondata sulla preminenza dell'indirizzo politico come atto di sovranità, rileggendola alla luce di una «razionalizzazione» storicistica. Al principio della Restaurazione Constant aveva detto che «Les constitutions se font rarement par la volonté des hommes» perché «Le temps les fait» (*Réflexions sur les constitutions, la distribution des pouvoirs et les garanties, dans une monarchie constitutionnelle*, Paris, H. Nicolle, 1814). Il discorso viene spostato dalla mera contrapposizione costituzione razionale / costituzione storica, ad una prospettiva assai più complessa senza la quale è difficile immaginare il processo di razionalizzazione e di «funzionalizzazione» della monarchia costituzionale.

5.3 Le ambivalenze del costituzionalismo «concesso» e la costituzione «progrediente»

Il costituzionalismo liberale italiano nasce, come quello francese o tedesco o portoghese, dalla stagione dell'*octroi*, ovvero delle costituzioni concesse dai monarchi. Attraverso questa modalità il sovrano cerca di riportare nel suo raggio d'azione l'idea della costituzione-atto. Cerca così di sterilizzare il più terribile dei poteri, il potere costituente del popolo. Nella seconda metà del XVIII secolo *We the People, Nous la Nation* hanno definito – pur con forme ed esiti differenti – un nuovo ordine concettuale destinato a segnare in maniera indelebile le moderne dottrine della costituzione. E' il popolo che si auto-definisce e si auto-rappresenta come totalità, come unità politica consapevole di esistere e di avere una capacità politica di agire. Tutti i corpi «estranei» – ovvero «altri» rispetto alla nazione – non possono più esistere se non annullandosi nella sovranità popolare. Il costituzionalismo liberale intende invece ricondurre questo percorso all'interno di una forma complessa di legittimazione. Il principale artefice dello Statuto albertino del 4 marzo 1848, il conte Borelli, dirà a Carlo Alberto, titubante ma consapevole della situazione: «bisogna darla [la costituzione], non lasciarsela imporre; dettare le condizioni, non riceverle; bisogna avere il tempo di scegliere con calma i modi e l'opportunità, dopo aver promesso di impiegarli» (G. Falco (a cura di), *Lo Statuto albertino e la sua preparazione*, Roma, Capriotti, 1945, 180).

Il costituzionalismo liberale muove da testi che sembrano guardare più al passato che al futuro. Il lessico utilizzato è arcaico, evoca franchigie feudali, organismi cetual-territoriali, liberi Comuni. E' un lessico medievaleggiante che richiama la diplomatica dell'epoca, stilemi e formule antichissime, concezioni di Antico Regime. E' un lessico complesso che copre un'area semantica al cui interno troviamo l'idea di privilegio, i concetti di concessione, imposizione, ma anche di disposizione e di accordo. E' «Con lealtà di Re e con affetto di Padre» che Carlo Alberto concede il suo Statuto. Il re-patriarca ha inteso trovare «un mezzo il più sicuro di raddoppiare coi vincoli d'indissolubile affetto che stringono all'itala Nostra Corona un Popolo». «Perciò di Nostra certa scienza, Regia autorità, avuto il parere del Nostro Consiglio, abbiamo ordinato ed ordiniamo in forza di Statuto e Legge Fondamentale, perpetua ed irrevocabile della Monarchia» (Statuto del Regno di Sardegna, 4 marzo 1848).

Costituzione-atto ma mediante «concessione», forma arcaica ma con contenuti riconducibili ai diversi percorsi dell'ordine liberal-costituzionale. Tale ambivalenza è uno dei tratti forti di questo costituzionalismo liberale. Ma tale carattere deriva soprattutto dall'apparato ermeneutico che si forma nel dibattito teorico e nella lotta politico-parlamentare. Il liberale Karl Theodor Welcker aveva scritto, nel contesto del *Frühkonstitutionalismus* tedesco, che le costituzioni ottriate non sono «vere» costituzioni. Esse, semmai, lo diventano quando il popolo le accoglie con favore: «... solo l'accettazione e la garanzia reciproca, su basi contrattuali, libera e sincera le rende una costituzione». Nel momento in cui il sovrano concede, come rappresentante del potere costituente, la legge costituzionale, questa non potrà più essere revocata.

Il recupero tardivo del modello della Charte del 1814 – la «più monarchica», come fu definita nel '48 italiano – non impedì ai liberali piemontesi di leggere lo Statuto come la fonte di un assetto costituzionale progressivo. Esemplare l'interpretazione immediata e autorevole del conte di Cavour che, nel celebre articolo del 10 marzo apparso ne «Il Risorgimento», osserva che, una volta intrapresa la strada dell'«autolimitazione», il potere unilaterale «il Re non [lo] possiede più. Un ministro che gli consigliasse di farne uso, senza consultare la nazione, violerebbe i principii costituzionali, incorrerebbe nella più grave responsabilità». Il *King in Parliament*, nella lettura dualistica che fu da allora proposta, servì a delineare – all'interno di un testo come lo Statuto che veniva dopo il costituzionalismo orleanista e la carta belga – una struttura rigida – il patto – che avrebbe dovuto limitare e contemperare le ragioni e gli interessi contrapposti offrendo garanzie reciproche. Cavour conosceva bene il dibattito e il conflitto politico-costituzionale che aveva portato alla costituzione orleanista del 1830 e alla sconfitta della lettura *ultra-royaliste* che si era trincerata dietro il baluardo della *lettre* e della Carta come atto giuridico unilaterale. Al contrario i liberali avevano fatto leva soprattutto sull'*esprit* – visto dalla sponda anglofila – e sul fatto che la Carta aveva istituito un certo grado di collaborazione tra il principio monarchico e il principio rappresentativo incarnato dalla camera dei deputati. «La parola irrevocabile, come è impiegata nel preambolo dello Statuto, è solo applicabile – osservava sempre Cavour – letteralmente ai nuovi e grandi principi proclamati da esso, ed al gran fatto di un patto destinato a stringere in modo indissolubile il popolo e il Re. Ma ciò non vuol dire che le condizioni particolari del patto non siano suscettibili di progressivi miglioramenti operati di comune accordo tra le parti contraenti. Il Re, col concorso della nazione, potrà sempre nell'avvenire introdurre in esso tutti i cambiamenti, che saranno indicati dall'esperienza e dalla ragione dei tempi».

La costituzione non è dunque il punto di arrivo, al contrario è il punto di partenza per lo sviluppo del governo monarchico rappresentativo. La *Charte* del 1814 è il modello per la forma della Costituzione, ma i liberali hanno poi in mente il *framework* dinamico e sostanziale della Charte orleanista del 1830 e la costituzione belga del 1831 che presuppone un accordo costituzionale nel segno di una rappresentanza plurale.

5.4 La sovranità della costituzione e il potere costituente

Quella che solitamente viene chiamata «onnipotenza parlamentare», ovvero la capacità di decisione politico-costituzionale riconosciuta al costrutto *King in Parliament*, non può essere scollegata, anche per l'esperienza italiana, dalla teoria della «sovranità della costituzione». Ancora una volta i liberali italiani – a cominciare dai primi pubblicisti subalpini (Balbo, Boncompagni, Cavour, Peverelli, Carutti, Melegari, Pescatore, tra gli altri) – parlano inglese, enfatizzano l'esperienza e la cultura britannica, ma poi agiscono soprattutto «alla francese». Ciò significa aver meditato e valorizzato quelle dottrine che si sviluppano in Francia tra la Restaurazione e soprattutto l'età orleanista. La *Charte* era diventata l'alfa e l'omega, la risorsa strategica da richiamare per fronteggiare quelle che per i liberali sono due distinte e potenziali minacce, lo spettro del potere costituente rivendicato dalla sovranità del popolo e quello della sovranità assoluta del monarca. In particolari sono i dottrinari francesi – Royer-Collard, Cousin, Guizot, Rossi – ad affermare che la sovranità della ragione è il fondamento di un costituzionalismo moderato e di una forma di governo *well balanced*. Nella loro riflessione convergono, in maniera eclettica, il costituzionalismo alla Benjamin Constant e l'idea di nazione elaborata dagli scrittori contro-rivoluzionari. Alla fine non è sovrano da solo nessuno dei poteri istituiti dalla Costituzione. Essa finisce col diventare un parametro di ragione e ad essa si assegna, sorta di «luogo neutrale», l'attributo di entità sovrana per modo che né il principe né il popolo, né la monarchia né la democrazia potessero pretendere l'esercizio del temibile potere costituente.

5.5 La dimensione istituzionale del costituzionalismo liberale

L'obiettivo del costituzionalismo di età liberale è perseguire la logica del bilanciamento e dell'equilibrio, la collaborazione / unione dei poteri lungo l'asse monarca-parlamento.

La cultura liberale pensava di poter «prevenire» le pericolose infatuazioni offrendo strumenti critici, aggiornati, adeguati allo stato della più moderna civilizzazione. Cesare Balbo traccia nel 1847 l'autobiografia di una generazione: la sua «parte» è quella dei liberali o progressisti «meno estremi, meno puri, che nominano sé stessi liberali di mezzo, o liberali moderati; e che così sono pur nominati da tutti, perché questa denominazione è necessaria, è inevitabile, perché sola esprime il fatto relativo dello star in mezzo alle altre due parti...», ovvero dei conservatori puri e dei liberali più radicali (*Dell'uso delle parole moderazione, opinione moderata e parte moderata. Lettera al signor****, Torino 19–23 giugno 1847, in Id., *Lettere di politica e letteratura edite ed inedite di Cesare Balbo precedute da un discorso sulle rivoluzioni*, Firenze, Le Monnier, 1855, 460).

Il partito moderato, scrive il conte di Cavour a Victor Cousin «...s'efforce d'opérer le progrès sans recourir aux moyens révolutionnaires...» (Lettera del 4 febbraio 1846, in C. Cavour, *Epistolario*, a cura di C. Pischedda, III, 1844–1846, Firenze, Olschki, 1973, 274–275).

E' anche per questo che la categoria della «parlamentarizzazione» non descrive in maniera esaustiva la logica istituzionale del costituzionalismo liberale. Se per parlamentarismo, inteso come regime o governo liberale, intendiamo – secondo la classificazione tradizionale delle forme moderne di governo (parlamentare, presidenziale, collegiale / direttoriale) – quello nel quale il governo è ritenuto, in solido, politicamente e giuridicamente responsabile del suo programma davanti ad un parlamento eletto (in tutto o in parte) che gli affida, attraverso un vincolo maggioritario revocabile, il potere di guidare le Camere (e quindi la nazione in esse rappresentata), non sarà facile collocare dentro questo schema e con questi termini i fenomeni osservabili nel periodo esaminato.

Allora, più che di governo parlamentare, bisognerebbe parlare del principio parlamentare come problema, come cifra da leggere all'interno del campo da gioco che trova nel governo rappresentativo la formula più ampia e più elastica. Il parlamentarismo – diversamente da quanto viene ancora sostenuto – non appare una conseguenza naturale, logica e quasi automatica dell'applicazione sincera del sistema rappresentativo. Principio parlamentare e governo rappresentativo sono invece i termini compresenti ma non convergenti di una vicenda complessa.

Piuttosto sembra emergere e strutturarsi un regime di bilanciamento dei poteri ad esecutivo monarchico, nella convinzione che lo stretto rapporto tra monarca e governo (affermato dal testo dello Statuto, artt. 5, 6 e 65) debba contrastare – in funzione «conservatrice» – la pretesa o la tendenza della Camera elettiva ad «assorbire» il potere esecutivo ed assumere una posizione di preponderanza in contraddizione col principio del «concorso» e dell'equilibrio dei poteri.

La monarchia costituzionale è la forma prevalente di ordine politico per tutto il XIX secolo, uno spazio concettuale che nel corso dell'Ottocento assume caratteri e condizioni diversi pur muovendo da ragioni e presupposti comuni. Gli esiti però non sono scontati. Per comprendere la funzione monarchica nella suo processo di adattamento costituzionale è fondamentale il concetto di influenza, un concetto chiave, ancorché sfuggente. Basta leggere le riflessioni dei costituzionalisti liberali per rendersi conto di questo aspetto. La fortunata formula dell'orleanismo francese, il «re regna ma non governa», deve essere letta in questa prospettiva. Già Benjamin Constant, al momento della Restaurazione, aveva rivalorizzato le potenzialità costituzionali della «condizione monarchica». Nella sua lucida riflessione sul «potere neutro» – non di rado malintesa –

concepito sia come «potere neutro e preservatore» che come «potere neutro e intermedio» – il sovrano è l'organo dell'unità nazionale e della continuità dello Stato, organo che incarna la «puissance publique». Il re potere neutro dovrebbe avere la capacità e la volontà – e qui sta il problema – di tenere in equilibrio l'opinione e il «potere ministeriale», le Camere e la funzione di governo, individuando il punto variabile di compromesso.

Mediare tra queste due grandi forme di legittimità indipendenti, il sovrano e la «rappresentanza dei moderni», è dunque il compito storico del XIX secolo e in particolare del costituzionalismo liberale. La non casuale vaghezza e duttilità della formula costituzionale – strutturale nel costituzionalismo della Restaurazione – era in realtà un programma, da interpretare e riempire di contenuti. E, a ben vedere, la difficile separazione fra regnare e governare è anche il grande tema della storia italiana.

6. Dal liberalismo del soggetto allo statualismo liberale

Queste matrici istituzionali e culturali troveranno – come è stato giustamente osservato (Fioravanti) – il più lucido sistematore in Vittorio Emanuele Orlando, a cominciare da uno dei suoi grandi saggi giovanili, gli *Studi giuridici sul governo parlamentare* (1886). Se guardiamo, in conclusione, il costituzionalismo liberale da questo osservatorio possiamo cogliere l'avvio e il primo consolidamento di una strategia ideologica e discorsiva incentrata sul trasferimento allo Stato-persona della piena titolarità di una sovranità opportunamente ridefinita. L'obiettivo non è solo quello «classico» del costituzionalismo liberale, ovvero limitare / regolare i poteri pubblici e garantire i diritti; ora si tratta di assicurare un valore centrale nell'antropologia liberale: la stabilità del costrutto sociale reso «persona» attraverso il diritto e la sua capacità di conformarne i poteri a guisa di organi. Negli anni del parlamentarismo e dei nuovi paradigmi scientifici, appare in crisi una certa retorica della costituzione, l'ottimismo – spesso anglofilo – per le intrinseche virtù organiche del governo parlamentare, per la mano invisibile dei pesi e dei contrappesi. Il costituzionale come politica / ideologia liberale – così era stato dai tempi di Benjamin Constant – ha perduto la sua spinta. Costruito lo Stato con il sangue dei martiri, la generazione nuova degli Orlando assume per sé la missione del *nation building*. Lo Stato liberale di diritto viene vincolato all'idea storica della nazione e delle sue generazioni, per cercare di depotenziare sia la mera forza del numero che l'ingerenza della politica. Questa può trovare il suo cuore pulsante nel parlamento, ovvero in quel suo modo di essere che poggia sul circuito «fazionario» che lo controlla, lo trasforma in una ipertrofica macchina legislativa, ne orienta in modo patologico il suo «comitato», il ministero, ne depotenzia la responsabilità, si autoalimenta di personalismi e localismi e si scarica sull'amministrazione e sulla giustizia. Nel riflettere sul governo parlamentare come forma politica non si poteva restare alla superficie (la crisi), ma occorreva scavare più nel profondo osservando le forze operanti nella società incapaci di tradursi in unità politica e fondamento costituzionale dello Stato. L'evoluzione della forma politica rivelava in realtà le dimensioni del conflitto in seno al corpo sociale e alle sue forze. E' in questi anni giovanili che Orlando costruisce, saggio dopo saggio, il mosaico che edifica la sua teoria giuridica dello Stato rappresentativo moderno inteso come Stato liberale di diritto. La fondazione dello Stato giuridico (e con esso della scienza deputata a sistemare e custodire le strutture di diritto pubblico che legano lo Stato alla società) è il risultato di una complessa e razionale concettualizzazione. Lo storicismo savignyano e la coscienza popolare depotenziano l'idea della sovranità popolare e del volontarismo politico, passando dall'indicibile potere costituente alla legge (propria / impropria) come forma che può solo dichiarare i rapporti giuridici che ad essa preesistono. Ma lo Stato-persona non si può «spiegare» e rappresentare attraverso la società e le forze che in essa operano. Lo Stato giuridico deve essere sottratto all'incandescenza del reale e alla dimensione del conflitto. L'autonomia di volontà della persona / Stato ha come corollari un'idea storicistica di diritto, una sovranità propria, un meccanismo di rappresentanza / designazione dei capaci, una forma bilanciata di governo parlamentare (di «gabinetto»). L'operazione orlandiana postula una soggettività statale dotata di autonomia giuridica che sterilizza ogni dimensione originaria e attribuisce dimensione organica alle forze sociali sottoposte al vaglio di una razionalità amministrativa di tipo moderno. Non a caso lo Stato amministrativo diventerà la forma tipica della sovranità dello Stato nel pieno esercizio dei suoi poteri.

Se nell'ottica del costituzionalismo liberale ogni forma di atomismo può indebolire la parte nobile e stabile della costituzione (Corona, esecutivo 'monarchico', prerogativa militare), il celebre *Torniamo allo Statuto* di Sidney Sonnino non riuscirà a fine secolo a reinventare una tradizione che già nel marzo del 1848 Cavour aveva inteso rifiutare. Il patto tra il popolo e il re sancito dalla ermeneutica dottrinale e consacrato dalla prassi istituzionale aveva in sé un forte potenziale di sviluppo in senso «parlamentare». Ma, nello stesso tempo, il regime di bilanciamento dei poteri ad esecutivo monarchico poteva essere piegato a logiche «monocratiche» sull'asse degli artt. 5, 6 e 65 dello Statuto.

Lo statualismo liberale non riuscirà a trovare il punto di equilibrio tra la sovranità dello Stato (con i suoi corollari di saldezza e stabilità) e le garanzie dell'individuo. Il problema delle libertà individuali e del pluralismo politico e sociale – visto perlopiù dalla sponda «patologica» del fascismo – è in realtà un problema strutturale, costitutivo della statualità in Italia e del rapporto autorità / individuo. Lo Stato liberale di diritto riconosce le conquiste del costituzionalismo ma ha difficoltà a fare i conti con il dissenso politico e sociale che nasce al fuori dalla dimensione dello Stato monoclasse. L'ordine costituzionale liberale è fatto anche di zone grigie nelle quali operano lo stato d'eccezione e il governo dell'emergenza. Dal liberalismo del soggetto allo statualismo liberale: è questa la parabola del secolo lungo del costituzionalismo liberale, tra progressi e reazioni.

Bibliografia

Colombo P., *Con lealtà di Re e con affetto di padre. Torino, 4 marzo 1848: la concessione dello Statuto albertino*, Bologna 2003

Costa P., *Lo Stato immaginario. Metafore e paradigmi nella cultura giuridica italiana fra Ottocento e Novecento*, Milano 1986

Fioravanti M., *Appunti di storia delle costituzioni moderne*, Torino 1995

Fioravanti M., *La scienza del diritto pubblico. Dottrine dello Stato e della costituzione tra Otto e Novecento*, Milano, 2001

Fioravanti M., *Costituzionalismo. Percorsi della storia e tendenze attuali*, Roma, Bari 2009

Fioravanti M., *Per una storia della legge fondamentale in Italia: dallo Statuto alla Costituzione*, in Id., *Il valore della Costituzione. L'esperienza della democrazia repubblicana*, Roma, Bari 2009, 3–40

Ghisalberti C., *Le costituzioni «giacobine» (1796–1799)*, Milano 1957

Ghisalberti C., *Stato e Costituzione nel Risorgimento*, Milano 1972

Ghisalberti C., *Modelli costituzionali e Stato risorgimentale*, Roma 1987

Ghisalberti C., *Stato nazione e costituzione nell'Italia contemporanea*, Napoli 1999

Lacchè L., *Tra universalismo e uniformità: la Rivoluzione del diritto e l'Europa*, in *Amicitiae Pignus*, Studi in ricordo di Adriano Cavanna, Milano 2003, t. II, 1289–1309

Lacchè L., *Il canone eclettico. Alla ricerca di uno strato profondo della cultura giuridica italiana dell'Ottocento*, in *Quaderni fiorentini per la storia del pensiero giuridico moderno*, 39, 2010, 153–228

Manca A. G., *Il Sonderweg italiano al governo parlamentare (a proposito delle acquisizioni della più recente storiografia costituzionale italiana)*, in *Quaderni fiorentini*, 2004–2005, 33–34, 1286–1333

Mannori L., *Uno Stato per Romagnosi. I. Il progetto costituzionale*, Milano 1984

Mannori L., *Il governo dell'opinione. Le interpretazioni dello Statuto Albertino dal 1848 all'Unità*, in *Memoria e Ricerca*, 35, 2010, 83–104

Matteucci N., *Organizzazione del potere e libertà. Storia del costituzionalismo moderno*, Torino 1988

Matteucci N., *Costituzionalismo*, in Id., *Lo Stato moderno. Lessico e percorsi*, Bologna 1993, 127–168

Rotelli E., *Forme di governo delle democrazie nascenti, 1689–1799*, Bologna 2005

Rotelli E. (a cura di), *Le costituzioni di democrazia. Testi 1689–1850*, Bologna 2008

Schiera P., *Profili di storia costituzionale. I – Dottrina politica e istituzioni*, Brescia 2011

Il "discorso" costituzionale nell'opera di Giuseppe Pisanelli

1. Premessa

> «Rimanendo qui [a Napoli] io credo di spendere la mia umile opera nel miglior modo che mi è possibile. L'accoglienza che hanno le mie lezioni mi assicura delle buone intenzioni di questa gioventù e che le mie parole non saranno senza frutto» (Museo Centrale del Risorgimento, Roma, sc. 816, n. 34/6, in Confessore 1979, 108).

Così scrive Pisanelli all'amico Giuseppe Massari, in una lettera del 17 febbraio 1862, illustrandogli la breve esperienza di professore di diritto costituzionale nel rifondato ateneo napoletano.

È difficile mettere a fuoco e ricomporre l'immagine di Pisanelli "costituzionalista". Tale immagine sembra anzi offuscarsi di fronte alle attività più consuete e celebrate, a cominciare dal processualista e dall'artefice della codificazione. Il riferimento al discorso costituzionale nell'opera del giurista salentino vuole anzitutto sottolineare un più vasto àmbito di intervento e di riflessione, in una prospettiva di ricerca rivolta più all'intreccio delle pratiche discorsive che ad una vera e propria specializzazione disciplinare. Pisanelli non è costituzionalista nel senso tecnico-professionale o propriamente disciplinare; lo è invece se tale riferimento individua il *punto di intersezione* tra diritto e politica, tra la dimensione dell'agire politico e i problemi di ordine costituzionale in un significato che trascenda i limiti più angusti dell'assetto statutario. Il Pisanelli costituzionalista conferma la caratura di *giureconsulto pratico*, senza recidere le radici che lo legano alla cultura più vivace e più ricca della penisola italiana. Egli appartiene ad una generazione assorbita completamente dal progetto di *State building* intrecciato all'ancor più delicato processo di costruzione dell'identità nazionale: la sua è un'opera che si rintraccia più nel disegno complessivo che nel singolo dettaglio.

Nel contesto di una scienza costituzionale che, alla metà del secolo, stenta ancora in Italia ad acquisire una qualche autonomia, per Pisanelli il termine costituzionale non è un mero sinonimo di analisi e commento del testo fondamentale attraverso il quale disciplinare e organizzare le libertà e i pubblici poteri. In tal senso, l'opera di Pisanelli si inserisce in una prospettiva nella quale è impossibile separare la scienza giuridica dalla prassi politica: un «libro unitario» (Ungari 1967, 7) guida sempre i suoi interventi. I *luoghi costituzionali* di Pisanelli rivelano una topografia che esula dal discorso disciplinare: si tratti del codice, dell'unificazione legislativa, dei principi dell'ordinamento giudiziario, dei diritti e delle garanzie, del rapporto Stato / Chiesa, è sempre il disegno complessivo che acquista una forte dimensione costituzionale.

Nel mentre insegna diritto costituzionale a Napoli, Pisanelli è immerso nella lotta politica. L'impegno assunto gli impone di restare nella capitale regnicola, ma questo dovere lo sente, in ultimo, come un limite. È il seggio parlamentare la vera cattedra di Pisanelli. Giustamente lo Stolfi (1919, 40) suggerì di ricercare «le dottrine e le idee» della generazione di giuristi che ha posto le basi dell'ordinamento dello Stato italiano negli Atti parlamentari. Anche per Pisanelli sembra valere questa osservazione: il suo discorso costituzionale è attingibile solo seguendo il dialogo incessante ed essenziale tra il giurista (avvocato e professore) e il legislatore, tra la politica del diritto e la cultura giuridica nazionale.

2. «La felice mutazione delle nostre sorti politiche»: l'insegnamento del diritto costituzionale a Napoli (1861–1862)

La riorganizzazione dell'Ateneo napoletano ad opera di Francesco De Sanctis – nei pochi giorni in cui questi ricoprì la carica di direttore dell'Istruzione pubblica (24 ottobre – 6 novembre 1860) – assegna alla Facoltà giuridica un indubbio rilievo e rappresenta un'interessante "sperimentazione" destinata a lasciare ampia traccia negli sviluppi successivi dell'ordinamento nazionale. Il decreto di nomina del 29 ottobre 1860 – dopo quello di "epurazione" di due giorni prima – segnala nomi di grande prestigio, si direbbe il meglio della vivacissima cultura giuridica napoletana, temprata in larga misura, come ebbe a scrivere Pisanelli a Casimiro De Lieto (Torino 24 gennaio 1850, in M. C. R., sc. 173, n. 37/6, in Confessore 1979, 91), dagli «agri giorni dell'esilio»: infatti, leggere i nomi di Paolo Emilio Imbriani (Storia del diritto), di Pasquale Stanislao Mancini (Diritto internazionale), di Giuseppe Pisanelli (Diritto costituzionale), di Roberto Savarese (Diritto romano), di Giovanni Manna (Diritto amministrativo), di Antonio Scialoja (Economia pubblica) ... significa richiamare alla memoria almeno un trentennio di studi e di lotte politiche. L'autonomia di impostazione, rispetto alla legge Casati, è evidente nell'assetto della nuova Facoltà ed è una conferma del produttivo innesto della «cultura meridionale con la generale cultura italiana e ancora col movimento della cultura europea» (Russo 1928, 26).

Pisanelli ebbe un ruolo primario nella rifondazione della Facoltà dopo aver, tra il dicembre del 1859 e il gennaio del 1860, contribuito, su istanza di Farini e di Selmi, a dare nuovo vigore alle università emiliane (Canevazzi 1922, 221–222 e 1925, 182–202). Pisanelli partiva per Napoli nella convinzione, condivisa da De Sanctis, che gli esuli avrebbero potuto svolgere un ruolo fondamentale nella terra d'origine, prossima a far parte della nazione. La Facoltà di Giurisprudenza dovette poi fare a meno di alcune delle figure più prestigiose che rinunciarono, per vari motivi, all'incarico: Mancini, in realtà più avvocato e uomo politico che professore, restò formalmente ad insegnare a Torino sulla cattedra di diritto internazionale; Scialoja abbandonò la cattedra torinese di economia politica per intraprendere la carriera ministeriale. Del resto, in una lettera (28 ottobre 1860) al fratello Bertrando, Silvio Spaventa aveva osservato: «De Sanctis ha abbattuto l'Università che ci era, e che era un orrore, e ne ha creato un'altra, buona se vuoi, ma puramente nominale e di pompa, perché è ben dubbio che i nominati vogliano poi fare davvero i professori» (Spaventa 1923, 335).

Pisanelli, già consigliere di Luogotenenza dal 1860, non fece mancare il suo nome alla nuova Facoltà e cominciò a professare l'insegnamento del diritto costituzionale. «Non era lo Stato italiano che da Torino ordinava l'organizzazione statale degli studi – ha scritto il Russo –. Ma era lo Stato vivo, maturatosi nascostamente in quei seminari di sapere e di umanità che eran gli Studi privati a Napoli e nelle province, il quale veniva alla luce e chiedeva di essere riconosciuto ufficialmente [...]» (1928, 27; sulla riorganizzazione desanctisiana v. Casavola 1961, 36–41; Talamo 1965, LI–LVI; Cortese 1972, 8–21; soprattutto Genovese 1994, 118 ss.; Lovato 1999).

Ancora una volta il pensiero corre a quello straordinario crogiolo di scuole private, di indirizzi metodologici, di pratiche professionali, di difficili esperienze politiche che fu la Napoli degli anni Trenta e Quaranta (Cfr. Zazo 1926; Oldrini 1973 e 1991, 387–410; soprattuto Mazzacane 1994, 77–113; Beneduce 1996), prima dell'ultima diaspora. Pisanelli è certamente figura centrale ed emblematica di questo lungo percorso: da Napoli a Parigi a Torino, per giungere infine di nuovo a Napoli dove gli studi giuridici risorgevano su un terreno già reso fertile dalla precedente provvida stagione.

Pisanelli aveva vissuto le tappe fondamentali del più recente moto "costituzionale" italiano: il '48–'49 a Napoli, poi gli anni di fondazione del sistema costituzionale subalpino,[1] infine la stagione dell'unità e dell'unificazione. Il ritorno di Pisanelli e il varo della cattedra di diritto costituzionale rappresentano anche simbolicamente la fine di un'epoca e il preannuncio, carico di

1 «Io non conosco nel continente un altro paese che meglio del Piemonte ritragga la serietà e la rettitudine dei felici abitatori dell'Inghilterra» (Pisanelli 1856, 181). Sull'ambiente culturale torinese e sul ruolo degli esuli, v. Caballo, Rossini 1961, 3–50; Romeo 1974, 165 ss.; Furiozzi 1979; Giannandré 1991, 157–176; Nada 1993, 47–69; Levra 1997, 88 ss.; Martucci 1999, 32 ss.

esitante ottimismo, di un'età in cui realizzare finalmente le speranze di più generazioni. Nel Pisanelli costituzionalista del 1861–1862 percepiamo l'eco del suo *alter ego* del '48 e autentico maestro della *intellighenzia* napoletana, ovvero quel Roberto Savarese che allora «imprese [...] ad insegnare il diritto costituzionale, quasi come compimento del suo insegnamento della giurisprudenza. Sono ormai pochissimi quelli che si ricordano di quelle lezioni, dirò quasi fuggitive; ma essi – osserva Enrico Cenni – ponno attestare di che maraviglia furono compresi vedendosi lanciati in mare così vasto, sotto la scorta di così fido pilota» (1876, 40–41; Beneduce 1996, 183 ss.; soprattutto Lovato 1999, 53 ss.). Enrico Pessina, ricordando Roberto Savarese e Pisanelli, parlò, non a caso, di «intenti scientifici comuni» (1913, vol. II, 133). Nel solco tracciato nel 1848, riconquistate le libertà costituzionali, occorreva ritessere la trama del *discorso costituzionale*. Savarese, ripercorrendo le vie del costituzionalismo antico e poi moderno, individuava taluni punti critici nell'incontro non sempre coerente tra le idee della costituzione inglese e la monarchia accentratrice dell'Europa continentale, nella pretesa realtà della «bilancia de' poteri», nella distruzione «di ogni gerarchia di ordini politici» e «come questa condizione di cose palleggiasse incessantemente la società tra l'anarchia ed il dispotismo, sia di un solo sia della maggioranza parlamentare; come a cessare tanto disordine non fosse altra via che la ricostruzione della gerarchia politica degli ordini nello Stato» (Cenni 1876, 40).

La cattedra di Pisanelli risponde a forti contenuti *politici* e *simbolici*. Per certi aspetti – al di là delle più evidenti differenze – l'avvio dell'insegnamento di diritto costituzionale al momento dell'Unità lascia trasparire taluni punti di contatto con l'istituzione in Francia, nel 1834, della prima cattedra di diritto costituzionale affidata a Pellegrino Rossi (Lacchè 2001, 67–108; 2002, 164–173). L'affermazione della piena *legittimità* del nuovo ordine politico-costituzionale è al centro di un comune progetto. Del resto gli insegnamenti più politicamente sensibili come il diritto costituzionale (anche se "mascherato" come diritto pubblico "interno": è il caso torinese) o l'economia politica hanno avuto, sino all'Unità, una vita difficile (se si eccettua, pur con taluni limiti, il caso sabaudo dalla seconda metà degli anni '40) (Pene Vidari 2003, 5 ss.). Era «un tempo in cui del diritto pubblico, gloria nostra in antico, si era perduta quasi la nozione, perché ne era stato proibito, come delitto di Stato, lo studio» (Zanichelli 1893, 472).

In particolare il "costituzionale" appare anzitutto con le sembianze di una politica e di un'ideologia della costituzione. Il testo costituzionale ha un valore in sé, quasi indipendente dagli specifici contenuti: è l'affermazione di una idea, di una rivendicazione, di un regime politico dagli ancora incerti confini, di una indispensabile *retorica della costituzione*. Come nel 1848, adesso, all'interno del processo stesso di formazione del Regno d'Italia (Colao 2003, 199 ss.; Mongiano

2003), l'insegnamento del diritto costituzionale diventa l'occasione per un forte messaggio politico-ideologico, ovvero che professare quel "diritto" è possibile soltanto laddove vige un pur minimale regime costituzionale o almeno laddove si stanno costruendo le basi per arrivare alla sua fondazione, difendendo l'unità appena raggiunta e purtuttavia minacciata da forze centrifughe (Giannini 1949, 91). Nella Prolusione al corso di diritto costituzionale pronunciata a Bologna il 18 aprile 1860 da un altro illustre giurista napoletano, Enrico Pessina, è proprio l'insegnamento parigino di Pellegrino Rossi a compendiare «lo spirito della scuola novella, la comune dottrina dei moderni pubblicisti» (p. 20). Pessina nel 1860 – come più tardi Pisanelli a Napoli – era stato chiamato a ricoprire, oltrechè la cattedra di diritto penale, anche l'insegnamento di diritto costituzionale da quel Cesare Albicini (allora ministro dell'istruzione pubblica e delle finanze nell'ambito del governo provvisorio presieduto dal Commissario Massimo d'Azeglio) che proprio nel 1861 sarà chiamato su quella stessa cattedra dando così inizio alla "scuola bolognese" (Zanichelli 1893, 467; Piretti 1987, 197). «L'Italia – osserva Pessina – entra l'ultima nella via del moderno reggimento costituzionale; ma il reggimento costituzionale sarà una verità per l'Italia», quella verità che invece la Francia di Luigi Filippo aveva tradito, malgrado le promesse contenute nella *Charte* del 1830 (1860, 23).

Pisanelli che nel 1861 aveva rinunciato alla cattedra di diritto penale nell'Ateneo torinese (Pene Vidari 2003, 21), accetta di salire su quella napoletana e, per riprendere le parole di Pessina, di «parlar la parola della libertà d'innanzi ad una eletta gioventù italiana» (1860, 5). La cattedra di diritto costituzionale rinasceva a Napoli – come nell'anno precedente in altre parti d'Italia (per le cattedre v. Lanchester 1994, 323 ss.; Lanchester 2004, 42 ss.) – in un clima necessariamente "militante" e "politico", al di fuori di qualsiasi logica "concorsuale". «L'installazione in questo Ateneo di una cattedra di Dritto costituzionale, prova essa sola la felice mutazione delle nostre sorti politiche», poteva affermare Pisanelli pronunciando il suo discorso inaugurale nel gennaio del 1862. «Noi possiamo, noi dobbiamo discutere la sua [dello Stato] legittimità e i termini dei suoi poteri; rilevare i diritti de' cittadini e le garentie ad essi dovute» (1862, 5). Pisanelli coglie il *momento* del dibattito politico a Napoli. Il discorso costituzionale riprende vigore, investe l'opinione pubblica. Nelle assemblee, nella stampa la vita politica è oggetto vivo, è linfa necessaria. Ma tutto ciò non è privo di rischi: i partiti avversi si riorganizzano, scatenando le passioni. Tutto ciò deve restar fuori «dalla soglia di quest'Aula» (*ibidem*, 6). Pisanelli si misura con le «buone intenzioni di questa gioventù», ma il compito è difficile. Sa che la sua opera è da compiersi nel Parlamento, ma per "spirito di servizio" rimane a Napoli. «Nondimeno io sarei partito ieri stesso se non fossi qui legato per tutto questo mese dalle lezioni per cui non posso assolutamente mancare. Se io parto ci saranno altre lezioni di diritto costituzionale, ossia si aprirà una fucina rivoluzionaria» (Lettera a Giuseppe Massari, Napoli 7 marzo 1862, in M. C. R., sc. 816, n. 34/7, in Confessore 1979, 109).

3. Unità nazionale, Stato e unificazione giuridica

Se il corso di Pisanelli ha un altro punto di contatto con quello professato da Rossi[2] negli anni '30, è la condivisione di alcuni principi-guida, ovvero l'eguaglianza dinanzi alla legge e l'unità nazionale (Rossi 1866, t. I, *Leçon d'ouverture*, LXXIII–LXXIV), realizzati attraverso il processo di centralizzazione. Pur essendo diversi i contesti e le ragioni ideologiche da cui muovono i due autori, è però significativo il fatto che il dato "strutturante" sia proprio quello dell'unità attorno allo Stato-nazione. La prolusione di Pisanelli è intitolata significativamente *Lo Stato e la nazionalità*, cioè le fondamenta su cui edificare il diritto costituzionale dell'Italia unita. La scienza, dice il giurista salentino, deve proclamare la «necessaria corrispondenza fra lo Stato e la Nazionalità» (Pisanelli 1862, 6). La dimensione progettuale del processo di *State building* non sfugge certo ad uno dei suoi maggiori artefici. Pisanelli è da annoverare infatti tra i personaggi di maggior spicco di quella generazione di esponenti della Destra storica che ha cercato di definire l'intero assetto politico-istituzionale del nuovo Stato. Non sorprende neppure che nella prolusione pisanelliana si distingua l'eco della celebre prelezione *Della nazionalità come fondamento del dritto delle genti* tenuta a Torino, nel 1851, da Pasquale Stanislao Mancini (tra i lavori più recenti cfr. Jayme 1988; Storti Storchi 1989, 302 ss.; Mansel 1991, 439–470; Treggiari 1990, 145–164; Cammisa 1996, 39–51; Nishitani 1998, 37 ss.; Halperin 1999; Storti Storchi 2001, 53–94; Pene Vidari 2002). Tuttavia, se nel 1851 la nazionalità è per Mancini, in una prospettiva antihegeliana (v. soprattutto Di Ciommo 1993), un *prius* legittimante della sovranità statuale e dei rapporti giuridici tra Stato e cittadino (Colao 2001, 274; Costa 2001, 211 ss.), nella prolusione pisanelliana lo Stato sembra assumere una più marcata centralità concettuale e paradigmatica, destinata poi a segnare nel profondo la storia del progetto costituzionale italiano. Dieci anni più tardi, nel 1872, il costituzionalista e internazionalista Augusto Pierantoni pronuncerà, dalla cattedra napoletana, – con evidenti echi pisanelliani – *La famiglia, la nazione, lo Stato. Introduzione al corso di diritto costituzionale*.

Pisanelli muove da una sintetica ricostruzione storica del concetto di Stato, dall'antichità all'età moderna. Individua, secondo stilemi piuttosto abusati, gli "estremi" di tale sviluppo: la concezione antica aveva conculcato la personalità

2 Pisanelli esprime il seguente giudizio su Pellegrino Rossi: «un pensatore così profondo, e sì spietatamente tolto all'Italia nel punto in cui la sua patria avea maggior uopo del suo alto intelletto» (1856, 153).

dell'individuo, la concezione moderna, in particolare quella di matrice rousseauiana, aveva annullato lo Stato. «La riabilitazione adunque delle ragioni dello Stato è dimandata dallo stesso principio di libertà ch'è il sospiro potente di questo secolo; né il diritto pubblico avrà salda base finché non riconosca ad un tempo e non ponga in armonia le ragioni dell'uomo individuo e quelle dello Stato» (Pisanelli 1862, 12). Lo Stato gli appare la forma, la *personificazione* dell'unità sostanziale di un popolo. Lo Stato-nazione diventa la sintesi necessaria della storia di un popolo – di *tutto* un popolo –, della sua uniformità di costumi, della lingua, delle memorie patrie. «La omogeneità delle idee, dei costumi, delle aspettative, della lingua, delle lettere, delle scienze, sono tali e sì potenti legami che uniscono in un fascio le anime tutte di un popolo e scolpiscono sul fronte di questo il carattere di una persona morale; la quale però non si concreta né s'individua che nella unità dello Stato» (*Ibidem*, 18). Nel 1853, nel suo *Elogio di Vincenzo Gioberti*, Pisanelli aveva osservato: «Ciascun popolo ha in effetto un genio, una complessione, un'indole propria e speciale; onde s'ingenera la personalità nazionale; la quale spira manifesta nella unità della sua storia e della sua lingua, e si rivela non dubbiamente in quella comunione di dolore e di gioia, di memorie e di speranze, che mostra comune ai figli d'una medesima patria la sventura e la gloria, il passato e l'avvenire» (*Ibidem*, 21).

Parimenti, nel lavoro sui giurati, partecipando alla prima fase di costruzione dei paradigmi giuspubblicistici che definiranno poi il "campo teorico" e le immagini dello Stato-persona in Italia (Costa 1986), Pisanelli aveva scritto che l'idea di comunanza civile si poteva attingere «in una suprema fantasticazione».

> «Siffatta fantasticazione, divenendo sempre più astratta e più comprensiva, s'incarna di mano in mano nella persona del principe o nel concetto dello Stato; ed al principe ed allo Stato, costituendosi essi come rappresentanti di tutte le comuni utilità, de' diritti e de' poteri comuni, si sentono rannodati tutti i cittadini. Allora la patria dell'uomo è il paese su cui il principe impera, lo Stato a cui esso appartiene [...] (La società) perché sia compiuta, dee spaziare tra tutti coloro che sortirono la medesima origine, corsero gli stessi pericoli, ebbero dolori e glorie indistinte, ed a cui la natura stessa destinò timori e speranze comuni; ed identificarsi per tal modo con quella unità naturale, che sola corrisponde pienamente all'anelito della patria e lo compie, la nazione [...]. Il vicinato ed il municipio si sente, lo Stato s'immagina, ma la nazione si intende. Il senso insomma ci porge la prima notizia della comunanza a cui apparteniamo, la fantasia la feconda e la ingrandisce, la ragione la sviluppa e la reca a compimento. Così l'uomo che dapprima ha sentito come proprii i beni e i danni della sua famiglia e del comune, avverte anche in appresso come proprii i vantaggi e i disastri dello Stato, della nazione; in guisa che di mano in mano egli si stima socio de' communicipii, de'regnicoli, de'connazionali» (Pisanelli 1856, 124).

La prospettiva dello statualismo liberale (Fioravanti, *Appunti*, 1995; *Lo Stato di diritto*, 1995, 161–177) è dunque il dato di partenza: lo Stato liberale di diritto rappresenta il tentativo di trovare un punto di equilibrio tra l'unità e la sovranità dello Stato (con i suoi corollari di saldezza e stabilità) e le garanzie dell'individuo, anzitutto la sicurezza dei beni e della persona (*liberty and property*). La via dell'unità nazionale è per Pisanelli l'unica possibile: è l'unità politica dello Stato. La generazione di Pisanelli vive questa fase difficile, finanche drammatica, sul confine scomodo che separa ma al tempo stesso unisce *necessità* e *volontà*. Perseguire l'unità significa dover costruire un assetto *costituzionale* in grado di conservare e rafforzare i legami connettivi dello Stato in via di formazione. La cultura di Pisanelli evidenzia significativamente una parabola comune a numerosi uomini politici della Destra: da simpatie autonomistiche e neoguelfe (per es. Pisanelli 1853) alla *scelta* unitaria e uniformatrice (Confessore 1979, 14 ss.). Questo passaggio, in verità, non è un salto da un estremo all'altro. È piuttosto sul terreno della *mediazione* – dote di cui Pisanelli non difettava di certo (Solimano 2003, 51) – e del partito moderato che si cerca di trovare un punto di equilibrio tra il centro come luogo del primato politico e l'autonomia amministrativa quale espressione di forze e tradizioni locali. Il *progetto costituzionale dell'unità* ha dalla sua la coerenza del modello e l'efficacia sperimentale. L'autonomismo neoguelfo napoletano ricerca soluzioni alternative, ma finisce col diffidare esso stesso «della capacità dei gruppi di potere territoriale di gestire in maniera autonoma dal potere governativo centrale il potere locale» (Cianferotti 1998, 164).

I liberali dell'unificazione perseguono un programma unitario che opera a più livelli. Anzitutto quello contingente e immediato della *necessità*: il che significa dare saldezza allo Stato centralizzato per fiaccare le resistenze e le spinte centrifughe nel momento cruciale dell'unità. Ma, al di sopra, troviamo il livello della *volontà*: la convinzione che quel modello di Stato sia una «scelta obbligata per l'individualismo liberale» (Mannoni 1996, vol. II, XIII). L'unità del Regno è – dice Pisanelli ministro guardasigilli in una ben nota circolare – «la più salda garentia della nostra unità nazionale» (*Circolare del ministro guardasigilli Pisanelli ai procuratori generali presso le corti d'Appello*, Torino, 24 gennaio 1863, in D'Addio 1966, 779–780). Il concetto di «patria comune» è l'opzione di modernità che si contrappone alle «passioni municipali», alla propaganda «in senso federativo». La varietà delle leggi, la «babele legislativa» (Pisanelli 1872, 6) richiama alla memoria le antiche divisioni, ma soprattuto – come si legge nella Relazione sul progetto di unificazione legislativa – «tende a perpetuarle, accarezzando le consuetudini locali, le rivalità di provincia, gl'istinti municipali, cioè le forze con cui era tenuta divisa l'Italia e che sono ancor oggi la speranza dei nostri nemici» (D'Addio 1966, 250; Cammarano 1993, 141). Solo sulla norma generale, comune a tutti, può fondarsi la certezza dell'eguaglianza. Un biografo scrisse «Che fu suo assioma fondamentale *Libertà per tutti e Legge eguale per tutti*» (Stampacchia 1880, 173). I paradigmi ottocenteschi della cultura continentale sono alla base delle comuni preoccupazioni: l'accentramento, il costituzionalismo, i codici, il diritto amministrativo. Il richiamo all'unità e all'uniformità è a tratti ossessivo, ma storicamente fondato. L'unificazione legislativa è una «forza irresistibile», ma non una forza cieca e fatale, è un «concetto che ha per base ragionamenti chiari e perspicaci, che ha per iscopo di evitare danni certi e perenni, di conseguire benefizi immancabili» (Atti Parlamentari, Camera dei deputati, *Discussioni*, tornata del 14 febbraio 1865, 8210).

Lo Stato liberale nasce all'insegna del *radicalismo* dei moderati (cfr. per es. Ruffilli *Governo*, 298; *Lo stato liberale*, 325 ss.; *L'Unità d'Italia*, 487 ss.). È questo un paradosso che si spiega con il carattere oggettivamente *rivoluzionario* dell'unità italiana. A ciò si accompagnano un culto a volte astratto e superficialmente livellatore, schemi che devono poi, anche drammaticamente, piegarsi di fronte ad ostacoli di vario segno che rallentano o impediscono il processo unitario. In Pisanelli è possibile scorgere l'ambivalenza del disegno di unificazione (v. Romanelli 1988, 7 ss.): l'impaziente desiderio di unitarismo, ma anche la capacità di discernere i vari livelli di intervento. Non manca nella sua impostazione un certo gradualismo (Confessore 1979, 31), la consapevolezza di dover tenere distinto il piano delle autonomie da quello del primato politico. «Ma per la verità – afferma nel 1865 – non crediamo che si debba unificare ad ogni modo e per forza. Noi abbiamo per fermo che si debbano estendere a tutto il regno quelle istituzioni che reputiamo utili» (A. P., Camera dei deputati, *Discussioni*, tornata del 15 febbraio 1865, 8244). E un esempio di ciò si scorge nei progetti pisanelliani in tema di ordinamento giudiziario (Genovese 1994, 145–149).

Il "piemontesizzato" Pisanelli, moderato di scuola napoletana, lascia spesso trasparire – si tratti del problema dell'Unità (morale) del paese o del rapporto Stato / Chiesa – un sentimento di partecipazione verso quel poderoso travaglio intellettuale che a Napoli aveva salde radici (cfr. Anzilotti 1920, 255–276, 299–303; Lopez 1962; Tessitore s. d; Cianferotti 1998). Il dottrinarismo insito nella dialettica necessità / volontà doveva fare i conti con una domanda reale di unità intesa a meglio rispettare le condizioni e i caratteri propri delle regioni italiane. Qui si stringevano i nodi della storia nazionale in un viluppo destinato a segnare profondamente tutto il suo svolgimento. La generazione del "miracolo" era, in realtà, chiamata a confrontarsi, sin dal principio, con un concetto di politica sempre pragmaticamente divisa tra *decisione* e *mediazione*.

4. Codice, costituzione, monarchia rappresentativa

Il *discorso costituzionale* di Pisanelli si definisce a partire anzitutto dal principio di unità. Ma una parte considerevole di tale discorso, nella topografia pisanelliana, non può che identificarsi con lo *spazio del codice civile*, secondo quella tradizione che ha visto nel codice napoleonico il modello di riferimento. «Voi vedete nel codice francese sviluppato l'elemento politico. Questo sviluppo potete avvertirlo nelle relazioni di famiglia; ed anche meglio in quella parola che appare quasi nuova, e che ha un gran significato, il *diritto dei terzi*. Voi vedete che ogni Codice nuovo, ogni legislatore ai dì nostri si occupa di questo diritto: esso significa il sentimento della comunanza civile, il diritto della società; è il diritto privato irradiato dal diritto pubblico, è il diritto dell'uomo membro di una civile società» (A. P., Camera dei deputati, *Discussioni*, tornata del 14 febbraio 1865, 8212). Il diritto del codice civile possiede un'indubbia vocazione costituzionale ed una elevata pretesa di stabilità e di autonomia. I principi informatori, le fonti del diritto, i concetti di cittadinanza, di libertà, di eguaglianza, di proprietà, di volontà – per non ricordare che i pilastri – sono, nella prospettiva dello statualismo liberale, una *parte* primaria della costituzione materiale dello Stato. La certezza del diritto e l'eguaglianza formale sono garantite dal diritto dello Stato e in particolare dal codice civile che stabilisce le "regole del gioco" (per i rinvii cfr. Lacchè 1995, 256 ss.). E la proprietà è la condizione per essere ammessi a partecipare al "gioco" stesso. «Basta volgere un semplice sguardo al codice civile – osserva Pisanelli – per convincersi che la proprietà sia il subbietto proprio di quel codice» (Mancini, Pisanelli, Scialoja, 1875, vol. I, 494–495).

Se il catalogo dei diritti – nella prospettiva dell'ordine giuridico borghese – è scolpito nelle ampie pieghe del codice civile, alla costituzione vera e propria Pisanelli riserva il compito, più limitato, di determinare «l'organamento dei pubblici poteri» (Pisanelli 1862, 6). La scienza costituzionale «investiga e fissa le fondamenta, l'ampiezza, i termini del potere e della libertà, che sono i due elementari fattori degli ordini politici» (*Ibidem*). Potere e libertà sono dunque i concetti elementari degli ordinamenti politici: ma il vero problema risiede nella delicata opera di contemperamento che è propria di ogni regime genuinamente costituzionale. Già nella riflessione sulla nazionalità Pisanelli aveva posto l'accento sulla necessaria armonia tra le ragioni dell'individuo e le ragioni dello Stato. Questa riflessione ritroviamo nel *costituzionalismo pratico* di Pisanelli, quale emerge soprattutto dai dibattiti parlamentari. «Lo Statuto – afferma nel luglio del 1864 – deve interpretarsi nel suo insieme, sulla scorta dello spirito che lo ha dettato, dei tempi a mezzo ai quali è stato promulgato, col sussidio degli usi e delle consuetudini che hanno preso vigore accanto al regime costituzionale, alla monarchia rappresentativa» (A. P., Camera dei deputati, *Discussioni*, tornata del 6 luglio 1864, 5994). Il ministro della giustizia condivide con i costituzionalisti subalpini degli anni '50 l'idea della centralità della monarchia rappresentativa quale forma di compromesso e di accordo tra i diversi principi (l'autorità e la legittimità ereditarie e il potere elettorale) che animano gli ordinamenti razionalizzati della Restaurazione, a cominciare dall'esperienza francese del 1814 e soprattutto del 1830. Come scrive infatti Boncompagni, la monarchia rappresentativa è «l'ordinamento fra tutti meglio adattato ad assicurare così le ragioni delle singole persone, come quelle dello Stato e della potestà che lo governa»

(1846, 3). Questo concetto, sviluppato dalla pubblicistica subalpina nelle prime opere di Boncompagni, di Balbo, di Peverelli, di Carutti, di Melegari (Ghisalberti, *Il sistema rappresentativo*, 189–217; *L. A. Melegari*, 219–248; *La monarchia rappresentativa*, 291–306; Sartoretti 1996, 67–105; Pene Vidari 2003), ritroviamo riecheggiato nell'opera di Pisanelli, con evidenti impliciti riferimenti ai costituzionalisti francesi: in particolare Benjamin Constant, Charles Hello e Pellegrino Rossi (Lacchè 2002).

La concezione politico-filosofica dello Stato-nazione che Pisanelli traeva dalle più profonde radici del pensiero di scuola napoletana e la teoria della monarchia rappresentativa in senso parlamentare costituiscono i due poli principali del "costituzionalista". La vena eclettica è quindi presente in Pisanelli, ma sempre temperata e orientata dalla consapevolezza della storicità degli avvenimenti. Il regime costituzionale ha ascendenze francesi, ma il modello ideale rimane quello inglese:

> «Così accadde che in Inghilterra si mantenessero costantemente, l'uno accanto dell'altro, temperandosi a vicenda, quegli elementi che nel Continente furono in perpetua lotta, e dei quali l'uno fu soffocato dall'altro; l'elemento monarchico, l'aristocratico e il democratico, di cui furono primi rappresentanti appunto quei minori patrizii che si dissero cavalieri. E quindi avviene che colà si osservi quella graduale ed incessante esplicazione degli ordini sociali, che avvalorata dalla salda tempra dei felici abitatori di quel regno, rende stabile l'acquisto di ogni incremento civile, agevole ed immancabile ogni ulteriore progresso, e porge il maraviglioso spettacolo di veder congiunti insieme, nel seno della medesima società, senza turbarsi, ed egualmente pregiati» (Pisanelli 1856, 6).

5. Teoria e prassi del liberalismo: Pisanelli e le "franchigie costituzionali"

In Pisanelli possiamo scorgere anche un altro profilo dell'organizzazione dei poteri nella storia costituzionale italiana. L'immagine della monarchia rappresentativa sembra incentrata sulla "supremazia" ideale del parlamento, secondo un'interpretazione che da Cavour in poi ha avuto una forte eco nella pubblicistica subalpina (Perticone 1960; Ghisalberti 1986, 67 ss.; Merlini 1995, 4). Proprio in tema di interpretazione statutaria Pisanelli ricorda la «giurisprudenza costante del parlamento subalpino». Il riferimento agli usi e alle consuetudini, alla sistematica del testo, allo spirito e ai tempi rivela una decisa connotazione parlamentare. Il ministro guardasigilli, quando deve intervenire sullo spinoso problema delle inchieste parlamentari, ricorda «che lo spirito con cui si è inaugurato fra noi questo sistema è arra della mutua fiducia con cui sono riguardati finora i varii poteri dello Stato» (A. P., Camera dei deputati, *Discussioni*, 7 luglio – 11 agosto 1863, 1328). In un'altra occasione di dibattito, il giurista pugliese, nel 1864, afferma che «il pensiero e la diligenza maggiore che deve avere un ministro è quello di evitare qualunque conflitto fra i poteri dello Stato;

a questo deve intendere, ma senza pregiudizio certamente delle sue opinioni e delle prerogative del Parlamento, delle quali, lo dichiaro, io sono stato, sono e sarò sempre consequentissimo» (A. P., Camera dei deputati, *Discussioni*, 27 giugno – 22 luglio 1864, 6177).

Tale immagine ha il suo contrappunto nella condizione di *necessità* costantemente invocata per derogare all'ordinario rapporto tra Parlamento e governo. Proprio la vicenda della legge sull'unificazione legislativa testimonia come, su questioni cruciali, e sulla base di argomentazioni politicamente forti (l'assoluta urgenza, lo spostamento della capitale ecc.) il Parlamento fosse chiamato a sacrificare – su una linea di dubbia legittimità costituzionale – la sua principale prerogativa a vantaggio del potere esecutivo. Nelle stesse parole del relatore Pisanelli che parla di «lieve deviazione, se tant'è che deviazione alcuna vi sia» (*Relazione della commissione della camera sul progetto di legge per l'unificazione legislativa*, 12 gennaio 1865, A. P., Camera dei deputati, Documenti, n. 276–A, in Aquarone 1960, 258) si può leggere un sentimento che accomuna molte delle discussioni politiche e parlamentari di quegli anni e che ha per protagonista un rapporto ambiguo tra regola ed eccezione e, in ultima analisi, il delicato problema dell'*effettività* delle "franchigie costituzionali" nel nuovo Stato (sul punto v. adesso Latini 2005).

La pagina drammatica del brigantaggio meridionale è un difficile banco di prova. Se c'è un'accusa davvero bruciante e tale da suscitare reazioni sdegnate è proprio l'accusa di seguire l'esempio dei Borboni, di derogare al principio del giudice naturale,[3] di reintrodurre modi polizieschi che richiamano alla memoria l'*empara* borbonica.

> «Come mai da quelle disposizioni può risultare l'opinione che il Governo volesse riprodurre l'empara? Certamente gli onorevoli deputati che hanno mossa quest'accusa non ignorano che cosa era l'empara. Essa, signori, era un'offesa alla magistratura, un'offesa alla libertà dei cittadini; era l'espressione del concetto politico di tutto il Governo borbonico, il quale come ho detto fin da principio, intendeva a soffocare ogni sentimento generoso, ogni desiderio di libertà. Un cittadino tradotto per reati politici innanzi ai tribunali veniva assoluto. Ebbene, la decisione dei magistrati era lacerata, egli rimaneva cionostante in carcere, e rimaneva a disposizione del ministro di polizia» (A. P., Camera dei deputati, *Discussioni*, tornata del 5 gennaio 1864, p. 2593; 12 gennaio, 2712–2713).
>
> «Ma al deputato Crispi – replica sempre Pisanelli – è sfuggita la grande differenza che intercede fra i provvedimenti eccezionali che usavano i Borboni e quelli

3 A.P., Camera dei deputati, *Discussioni*, tornata del 5 gennaio 1864, 2589–2590. Sul dibattito relativo all'art.71 dello Statuto (principio del giudice naturale) e sull'interpretazione proposta da Pisanelli, v. Martucci 1980, 20 ss., 162–164 e Molfese 1974, 303–304. Per una sintesi delle vicende legate al brigantaggio postunitario, si veda Adorni 1997, 281–319.

adottati dal Governo italiano. Ferdinando II adoperava anch'egli i tribunali militari e le Giunte, ma tutti i provvedimenti di quel Governo erano informati ad un principio, il principio del dispotismo» (A. P., Camera dei deputati, *Discussioni*, tornata del 5 gennaio 1864, 2587).

I perseguitati dei Borboni si chiamavano Poerio, Conforti, D'Ondes-Reggio, Crispi.[4] Le misure del governo italiano, con la legge Pica, sono dirette contro Ninco-Nanco e Crocco. Un liberale come Pisanelli – che ha subìto le conseguenze dell'abuso politico – pensa che la minaccia sia grande, tale da mettere in pericolo la sopravvivenza del nuovo Regno e che l'unico modo per venirne a capo sia quello di utilizzare anche mezzi straordinari. Questa vicenda, come è stato osservato, ha molto contribuito a definire impropriamente il rapporto tra ordine e legalità, lasciando nell'ordinamento italiano tracce pressoché indelebili (Sbriccoli 1990, 173 ss.; Lacchè 1990). Invocare l'emergenza – affrontando solo in superficie le ragioni profonde del malessere nelle regioni meridionali – poteva essere una facile scappatoia. Le libertà costituzionali dovevano fare i conti con il problema dell'ordine pubblico e con una concezione differenziata – quasi una doppia legalità – dei diritti e delle garanzie. Non a caso, nel dicembre del 1863 Pasquale Stanislao Mancini – che tanto si era impegnato per limitare le "improvvisazioni" della legge Pica – denunciava un regime eccezionale che, mantenuto nelle sole regioni meridionali, appariva la negazione dell'unità italiana, riservando ad esse l'arbitrio e lasciando al resto d'Italia «i tesori della libertà, i diritti e le prerogative che l'accompagnano» (cit. da Mele 2002, 27). Si evidenziava così lo scarto tra la "teoria", ovvero il discorso politico-parlamentare di segno "liberale", e la prassi che scopriva un nesso innegabile tra la tradizione borbonica e la legislazione emergenziale italiana.

Del resto, la vicenda legata al brigantaggio meridionale e ai mezzi repressivi adottati per sconfiggerlo è rubricata, dai liberali moderati, proprio sotto la categoria strategica dell'emergenza e del conseguente stato di necessità. Si violava l'ordine liberale, ma solo in via temporanea, per potere affermare alla fine le libertà e le garanzie statutarie. Restaurare la legalità, ma attraverso i dettami della ragion di Stato; educare alla libertà, anche con la repressione, le province meridionali: questo, da ultimo, il programma. Le contraddizioni e i pericoli non sfuggivano certo agli artefici di siffatta politica, ma i valori dell'unità e gli interessi politici dovevano prevalere. In una nota riservata del gennaio 1864, richiestagli dal Presidente del Consiglio Minghetti per ragguagliare la legazione italiana a Londra (Martucci 1980, 304–312), il guardasigilli Pisanelli tracciava un elogio incondizionato della politica penale e criminale attuata dal

4 Una efficace "biografia collettiva" del partito moderato napoletano, che ha i suoi leader in Silvio Spaventa e in Pisanelli, si può leggere in una replica dello stesso Spaventa a Bertani, nella tornata dell'8 dicembre 1861: cfr. Musella 1994, 13.

governo nel Meridione. La "leggenda nera" della giustizia borbonica diveniva il facile bersaglio da colpire. Eppure, non vi era accenno alcuno né alla legge Pica, né alle sue proroghe. Obiettivo del documento era del resto quello di evidenziare i progressi dell'azione di governo in tema di giustizia con argomenti e prove che la legazione italiana potesse sottoporre al governo inglese alla vigilia dell'apertura della sessione parlamentare e dei probabili attacchi del partito *tory* contrario all'unità politica italiana.

Pisanelli si è dunque trovato in prima linea nella attuazione delle politiche per combattere il brigantaggio. Le lettere e le circolari inviate ai procuratori generali rivelano il suo atteggiamento. Il richiamo ai procuratori affinché sorveglino i giudici di mandamento sospettati di scarso impegno o di collusioni; l'invito rivolto al clero al fine di «contribuire cogli espedienti morali e colle dottrine alla repressione del brigantaggio»; la richiesta all'autorità giudiziaria di collaborare con i comandi militari sottolineando al tempo stesso la centralità delle giunte provinciali di pubblica sicurezza, insieme ad altre prese di posizione (Martucci 1980, 81, 134–135, 256–257, 262–263, 289–290, 291–292; Molfese 1974, 245, 271, 291), ci offrono un'immagine del Pisanelli politico che – nel difficile contesto appena ricordato – stenta a collimare con l'immagine del giurista liberale.

L'intervento di D'Ondes Reggio, nella tornata del 12 gennaio 1864, è un duro *j'accuse* contro il guardasigilli Pisanelli:

> «Onorevole guardasigilli, ella è anche professore di diritto costituzionale a Napoli; di grazia, se ella salirà di nuovo alla cattedra, ed un suo discepolo le chiederà: negare la difesa è contro lo Statuto, è contro a leggi superiori allo Statuto, le leggi eterne del giusto o dell'onesto: che cosa risponderà? Ella è stato egregio avvocato: se tornerà all'esercizio di quella nobile professione, e verrà un antico suo cliente, lo pregherà di difenderlo innanzi a una giunta, dicendole: sono innocente, vi sono quattro o cinque specchiati uomini che possono testimoniare in favore della mia innocenza: risponderà ella: a produr questi testimoni siete impedito dalla mia legge? Oh ella sarebbe allora confuso e umiliato e sentirebbe anche qualche rimorso (Rumori)» (A. P., Camera dei deputati, *Discussioni*, tornata del 12 gennaio 1864, 2711).

Il *discorso costituzionale* di Pisanelli sconta, dunque, l'asprezza del paradosso liberale, dal cielo della teoria alle insidie della politica. Con coerenza e riconosciuta onestà, Pisanelli non si è tirato indietro, operando sia al livello "alto" della lotta parlamentare, sia a livello "basso", regionale e di collegio, attraverso una vasta rete di amici e clienti il cui ruolo si rivela fondamentale nell'opera di mediazione. «Io credo che questa politica, cioè quella che rifugge dalle passioni e dagli estremi, la quale non ha che per guida unica la legge, sia la politica a cui un Governo serio debbe attenersi, non solamente nell'interesse della stabilità del Governo, ma nell'interesse del paese e dei suoi destini. Oltre la legge, io non ho mai avuto, e non avrò mai altra guida ai miei passi» (A. P., Camera dei deputati, *Discussioni*, 18 aprile – 31 maggio 1864, 4409). La legge dello Stato è formalmente il cardine del sistema costituzionale. Il distacco del potere legislativo dal potere giudiziario è sancito storicamente dalla cassazione, «propugnacolo della loro mutua indipendenza», che impedisce al giudice «di surrogare alla legge il proprio arbitrio». E sotto questo aspetto la «Corte di Cassazione è una garanzia importantissima dei governi costituzionali: il suo scopo è di mantenere inviolato l'articolo terzo dello Statuto, il quale dichiara che il fare le leggi spetta soltanto al Re ed al Parlamento» (A. P., Camera dei deputati, *Discussioni*, tornata del 20 febbraio 1864, 8389–8390).

Il Pisanelli subalpino aveva insistito, nel suo brillante e influente saggio dedicato al tema politico-costituzionale della giuria, sulla necessità dell'indipendenza del giudice dal potere esecutivo. Del resto, la sua riflessione sul ruolo dei giurati e sulla prospettiva di un'auspicabile estensione del loro intervento anche ai reati comuni, testimoniava di quella "sana" diffidenza che i sostenitori sinceri dell'istituto mostravano per la magistratura togata di prevalente nomina governativa (Padoa Schioppa 2000, 851–864). Ispirandosi a Benjamin Constant, Pisanelli individuava nella stampa, nell'opinione pubblica e nella responsabilità dei ministri i mezzi fondamentali per frenare gli arbitrî del governo, essendo però ben consapevole di quanto fosse facile per il potere esecutivo «frangere tali freni»; perciò «è prepotente bisogno di questi tempi che i giudizii sieno ordinati in guisa da rendere certa per quanto è possibile la indipendenza del giudice» (Pisanelli 1856, 149); la giuria, purché non influenzata dal governo, acquistava pertanto un valore strategico e diveniva la chiave di volta per garantire sino in fondo i "freni" dell'ordinamento costituzionale: la libertà di stampa e con essa l'opinione pubblica e il corretto funzionamento del governo rappresentativo.

Qualche hanno più tardi la *posizione costituzionale* del potere giudiziario nella concezione pisanelliana si accosta di più alla funzione "esecutiva", pur nel sostanziale rispetto del principio di indipendenza: ne conseguono, come è facile immaginare, attriti e contraddizioni. Nella ricordata circolare del gennaio 1863, Pisanelli, appena diventato ministro guardasigilli, invita i procuratori del re a vigilare su quegli organi di stampa che facendo appello alle passioni municipali e suscitando le antiche divisioni minacciano la sopravvivenza del nuovo Regno garante della raggiunta unità politica. «Lo zelo e il patriottismo dei membri dell'ordine giudiziario – osserva Pisanelli – danno assicuranza al ministro che la magistratura sarà per cooperare, nella cerchia delle sue attribuzioni, alla difesa della grande opera dell'unità nazionale da tanto tempo desiderata, ottenuta a prezzo di tanti sacrifici, con tanto senno mantenuta, ed il cui compimento segnerà una delle più memorabili pagine negli annali d'Italia» (*Ibidem*, 779). La difesa dell'unità nazionale ritorna con tutta la sua forza d'urto, quella «forza irresistibile» a cui anche la dialettica dei poteri, di matrice liberale, deve sacrificare, in taluni momenti, dogmi e dottrine. Al limite, l'indipendenza della magistratura può diventare un ipotetico luogo di "neutralità". «Vi sono, signori, alcuni principii i quali debbono mantenersi inviolati nell'interesse di tutti i partiti. Tale è il principio dell'indipendenza del potere giudiziario. L'ufficio del magistrato deve presentarsi come un campo sereno a cui possano rivolgersi con fiducia tutti i partiti» (A. P., Camera dei deputati, *Discussioni*, tornata del 7 maggio 1864, p. 4176). Il magistrato, come pubblico impiegato, deve essere libero di votare per chi vuole, ma «in egual modo io credo che un impiegato del Governo e soprattutto un magistrato non può preservare la dignità del suo ufficio, l'imparzialità del suo Ministero, se non tenendosi alieno da quelle brighe troppo attive che sogliono accadere nelle lotte elettorali nelle quali egli scapita come uffiziale del Governo, con danno del Governo stesso».[5]

Quel Pisanelli che nella prolusione al corso di diritto costituzionale invocava il «sindacato della scienza» e incitava i suoi studenti e se stesso a spogliarsi, sulla soglia dell'aula, di ogni passione, appare forse più lontano. Ma in fondo è proprio la mediazione coerente tra politica e diritto ciò che fa del *discorso costituzionale* di Pisanelli un interessante e utile punto di osservazione su una fase decisiva della storia politica e costituzionale italiana.

Bibliografia

Adorni D., *Il brigantaggio*, in *Storia d'Italia*, Annali 12, *La criminalità*, Torino 1997

Anzilotti A., *Neoguelfi ed autonomisti a Napoli dopo il Sessanta (1920)*, in *Nuova Rivista Storica*, IV, 1920

Aquarone A., *L'unificazione legislativa e i codici del 1865*, Milano 1960

Beneduce P., *Il corpo eloquente. Identificazione del giurista nell'Italia liberale*, Bologna 1996

Boncompagni C., *Della Monarchia rappresentativa*, Torino 1846

Caballo E., Rossini R., *Esuli meridionali a Torino nel Decennio*, Torino 1961

Cammarano F., *Nazionalizzazione della politica e politicizzazione della nazione. I dilemmi della classe dirigente nell'Italia liberale*, in *Dalla città alla nazione. Borghesie ottocentesche in Italia e in Germania*, a cura di M. Meriggi e P. Schiera, Bologna 1993

Cammisa F., *Unificazione nazionale e formalismo giuridico*, Napoli 1996

Canevazzi G., *Camillo De Meis insegnante a Modena. Lettere inedite di lui, dei fratelli Spaventa, di Terenzio Mamiani e di altri*, in *L'Archiginnasio*, 1922

– *Giuseppe Pisanelli per le Università di Modena e di Bologna, 1859–1860*, in *L'Archiginnasio*, 1925

5 A. P., Camera dei deputati, *Discussioni*, tornata del 3 novembre 1864, 6423. Come ha dimostrato Musella 1996, 46, «Il partito moderato, bisognoso come tutti i partiti di una organizzazione che lo legasse alla società civile e che trasmettesse al centro la domanda politica proveniente dai propri elettori, utilizzò soprattutto le istituzioni come canali per il controllo e l'acquisizione del consenso. Il ruolo politico della magistratura e della prefettura e di tutti gli organi dell'amministrazione fu inaugurato dunque dagli uomini della Destra». Sulla politicizzazione della magistratura italiana dopo l'Unità, v. la sintesi di Saraceno 1994, 539 ss.; v. *infra* in questo volume *Il potere giudiziario come "potere politico"*, 430 ss.

Casavola F., *Professori di Napoli 1860*, in *Labeo*, 7, 1961
Cenni E., *Della mente e dell'animo di Roberto Savarese. Studio*, Napoli 1876
Cianferotti G., *Storia della letteratura amministrativistica italiana.* I. *Dall'Unità alla fine dell'Ottocento. Autonomie locali, amministrazione e costituzione*, Milano 1998
Colao F., *L'idea di "nazione" nei giuristi italiani fra Ottocento e Novecento*, in *Quaderni fiorentini per la storia del pensiero giuridico moderno*, 30, 2001
– *Due momenti della storia costituzionale italiana nella cultura giuridica tra Ottocento e Novecento: la «formazione del Regno d'Italia» e la «trasformazione dello Stato» dall'età liberale al fascismo*, in *Costruire lo Stato, costruire la storia. Politica e moderno fra '800 e '900*, a cura di A. De Benedictis, Bologna 2003
Confessore O., *Giuseppe Pisanelli. Lettere inedite con saggio introduttivo*, Milano 1979
Cortese N., *Francesco De Sanctis ed il riordinamento dell'Università di Napoli dell'ottobre 1860*, Napoli 1972
Costa P., *Lo Stato immaginario. Metafore e paradigmi nella cultura giuridica italiana fra Ottocento e Novecento*, Milano 1986
– *Civitas. Storia della cittadinanza in Europa*. III. *La civiltà liberale*, Bari 2001
D'Addio M., *Politica e magistratura (1848–1876)*, Milano 1966
Di Ciommo E., *La nazione possibile. Mezzogiorno e questione nazionale nel 1848*, Milano, Angeli, 1993
Fioravanti M., *Appunti di storia delle costituzioni moderne. Le libertà fondamentali*, Torino 1995
– *Lo Stato di diritto come forma di Stato. Notazioni preliminari sulla tradizione europeo-continentale*, in *Saperi della borghesia e storia dei concetti fra Otto e Novecento*, a cura di R. Gherardi e G. Gozzi, Bologna 1995
Furiozzi G. B., *L'emigrazione politica in Piemonte nel decennio preunitario*, Firenze 1979
Genovese F. A., *La riforma delle Facoltà di Giurisprudenza e l'introduzione dell'ordinamento giudiziario nelle Università italiane (1859–1865)*, in *Università e professioni giuridiche in Europa nell'età liberale*, a cura di A. Mazzacane e C. Vano, Napoli 1994
Ghisalberti C., *Il sistema rappresentativo nella pubblicistica subalpina dopo il '48*, in *Stato e costituzione nel Risorgimento*, Milano 1972
– *L. A. Melegari e i costituzionalisti dell'Unità*, Ibidem
– *Storia costituzionale d'Italia 1848/1948*, Bari 1986
– *La monarchia rappresentativa nel pensiero di Cesare Balbo*, in *Rassegna storica del Risorgimento*, LXXXII, 1995
Giannandrè R., *Mancini e l'ambiente degli esuli napoletani a Torino*, in *P. S. Mancini. L'uomo lo studioso il politico*, a cura di O. Zecchino, Napoli 1991
Giannini M. S., *Gli studi di diritto costituzionale in Italia (1848–1948)*, in *Rassegna di diritto pubblico*, I, 1949
Halperin J.-L., *Entre nationalisme juridique et communauté de droit*, Paris 1999
Jayme E., *P. S.Mancini. Il diritto internazionale privato tra Risorgimento e attività forense*, Padova 1988
Lacchè L., *La giustizia per i galantuomini. Ordine e libertà nell'Italia liberale. Il dibattito sul carcere preventivo (1865–1913)*, Milano 1990
– *L'espropriazione per pubblica utilità. Amministratori e proprietari nella Francia dell'Ottocento*, Milano 1995
– *Tra politica e diritto, ovvero Rossi e la Monarchia di Luglio*, in *Un liberale europeo: Pellegrino Rossi (1787–1848)*, a cura di L. Lacchè, Milano 2001
– *La Libertà che guida il Popolo. Le Tre Gloriose Giornate del luglio 1830 e le «Chartes» nel costituzionalismo francese*, Bologna 2002
Lanchester F., *Momenti e figure nel diritto costituzionale in Italia e in Germania*, Milano 1994
– *Pensare lo Stato. I giuspubblicisti nell'Italia unitaria*, Roma, Bari 2004

Latini C., *Governare l'emergenza. Delega legislativa e pieni poteri in Italia tra Otto e Novecento*, Milano 2005

Levra U., *Dallo Statuto alla Convenzione di settembre*, in *Il Senato nell'età moderna e contemporanea*, Roma, Istituto poligrafico e Zecca dello Stato, 1997

Lopez P., *Enrico Cenni e i cattolici napoletani dopo l'Unità*, Roma 1962

Lovato A., *Diritto romano e scuola storica nell'Ottocento napoletano*, Bari 1999

Mannoni S., *Une et indivisible. Storia dell'accentramento amministrativo in Francia*, Milano 1996, 2 tomi

Mansel H.-P., *Mancini, Mittermaier und die nationalsozialistische Rechtslehre. Zwei Skizzen*, in *P. S. Mancini*, cit.

Martucci R., *Emergenza e tutela dell'ordine pubblico nell'Italia liberale. Regime eccezionale e leggi per la repressione dei reati di brigantaggio (1861–1865)*, Bologna 1980

– *L'invenzione dell'Italia unita, 1855–1864*, Milano 1999

Mazzacane A., *Pratica e insegnamento: l'istruzione giuridica a Napoli nel primo Ottocento*, in *Università e professioni giuridiche*, cit.

Mele F., *Un codice unico per un'Italia nuova. Il progetto di codice penale di Pasquale Stanislao Mancini*, Roma 2002

Merlini S., *Il governo costituzionale*, in *Storia dello Stato italiano dall'Unità a oggi*, a cura di R. Romanelli, Roma 1995

Molfese F., *Storia del brigantaggio dopo l'Unità*, Milano 1974

Mongiano E., *Il "voto della Nazione". I plebisciti nella formazione del Regno d'Italia (1848–60)*, Torino 2003

Musella L., *Individui, amici, clienti. Relazioni personali e circuiti politici in Italia meridionale tra Otto e Novecento*, Bologna 1994

Nada N., *Gli emigrati meridionali a Torino nel decennio di preparazione*, in *Bollettino storico-bibliografico subalpino*, XCI, 1993

Nishitani Y., *Mancini und die Parteienautonomie im Internationalen Privatrecht. Eine Untersuchung auf der Grundlage der neu zutage gekommenen kollisionsrechtlichen Vorlesungen Mancinis*, Heidelberg 1998

Oldrini G., *La cultura filosofica napoletana dell'Ottocento*, Bari 1973

– *La missione filosofica del diritto nella Napoli del giovane Mancini*, in *P. S. Mancini*, cit.

Padoa Schioppa A., *Pisanelli e la giuria penale*, in *Grundlagen des Rechts. Festschrift für Peter Landau zum 65. Geburtstag*, Hrsg. von R. H. Helmholz, P. Mikat, J. Müller und M. Stolleis, Paderborn, München, Wien, Zürich 2000

Perticone G., *Il regime parlamentare nella storia dello Statuto albertino*, Roma 1960

Pene Vidari G. S., *Un secolo e mezzo fa (22 gennaio 1851): la lezione torinese di Pasquale Stanislao Mancini sulla nazionalità*, in *Studi piemontesi*, 2, 2002

– *Considerazioni sul contributo degli esuli risorgimentali al rinnovamento della Facoltà giuridica torinese*, in *Rivista di storia del diritto italiano*, LXXVI, 2003

Pessina E., *Prolusione al corso di diritto costituzionale pronunciata nella Regia Università di Bologna il 18 aprile 1860 dall'avvocato Enrico Pessina professore di diritto penale nell'Università medesima*, Bologna 1860

– *La scuola storica napoletana nella scienza del diritto (1882)*, in *Discorsi varii*, Napoli 1913

Piretti M. S., *Cesare Albicini e la scuola bolognese di diritto costituzionale: la «Rivista di diritto pubblico» (1889–1893)*, in *Quaderni fiorentini*, 17, 1987

Pisanelli G., *Elogio di Vincenzo Gioberti letto nell'Accademia di filosofia italica il dì 2 gennaio 1853*, Torino 1853

– *Dell'istituzione de' giurati*, Torino 1856

– *Lo Stato e la nazionalità. Discorso inaugurale alle lezioni di diritto costituzionale letto nella Regia Università di Napoli il dì 30 gennaio 1862*, Napoli 1862

– *Dei progressi del diritto civile in Italia nel secolo XIX*, Milano 1872
Pisanelli G., Scialoja A., Mancini P. S., *Commentario del codice di procedura civile dei signori Pisanelli, Scialoja e Mancini coordinato e ridotto dall'avvocato e professore di diritto D. Galdi*, Napoli 1875
Romanelli R., *Il comando impossibile. Stato e società nell'Italia liberale*, Bologna 1988
Romeo R., *Dal Piemonte sabaudo all'Italia liberale*, Bari 1974
Rossi P., *Cours de droit constitutionnel professé à la Faculté de droit de Paris*, Paris 1866
Ruffilli R., *Governo, Parlamento e correnti politiche nella genesi della legge 20 marzo 1865*, in *Istituzioni società stato*, Bologna 1989, vol. I
– *Lo stato liberale in Italia*, ibidem, vol. II
– *L'Unità d'Italia e lo Stato liberale*, Ibidem
Russo L., *Francesco De Sanctis e la cultura napoletana (1860–1885)*, Venezia 1928
Saraceno P., *Il reclutamento dei magistrati italiani dall'Unità al 1890*, in *Università e professioni giuridiche*, cit.
Sartoretti C., *La scienza del diritto costituzionale in Italia nella seconda metà dell'Ottocento: le lezioni di Luigi Amedeo Melegari, in Diritto e società*, I, 1996, 67–105
Sbriccoli M., *La penalistica civile. Teorie e ideologie del diritto penale nell'Italia unita*, in *Stato e cultura giuridica in Italia dall'Unità alla Repubblica*, a cura di A. Schiavone, Bari 1990
Solimano S., *"Il letto di Procuste". Diritto e politica nella formazione del codice civile unitario. I Progetti Cassinis (1860–1861)*, Milano 2003
Spaventa S., *Dal 1848 al 1861. Lettere, scritti, documenti*, a cura di B. Croce, Bari 1923
Stampacchia L., *Giuseppe Pisanelli. La biografia e il suo progetto del codice civile*, seconda edizione, Lecce 1880
Stolfi N., *Trattato di diritto civile, Parte generale*. I. *Fonti, disposizioni preliminari e transitorie*, Torino 1919
Storti Storchi C., *Ricerche sulla condizione giuridica dello straniero in Italia dal tardo diritto comune all'età preunitaria. Aspetti civilistici*, Milano 1989
– *Ludovico Casanova e le sue Lezioni di diritto internazionale*, in *Giuristi liguri dell'Ottocento*, a cura di G. B. Varnier, Genova 2001
Talamo G., *Introduzione a F. De Sanctis, Epistolario*, Torino 1965
Tessitore F., *Aspetti del pensiero neoguelfo napoletano dopo il Sessanta*, Napoli, s. d.
Treggiari F., *P. S. Mancini: Nationales Recht und Recht der Nationalität*, in *Nation und Staat im Internationalen Privatrecht…*, a cura di E. Jayme e H.-P. Mansel, Heidelberg 1990
Ungari P., *L'età del codice civile. Lotta per la codificazione e scuole di giurisprudenza nel Risorgimento*, Napoli 1967
Zanichelli D., *Cesare Albicini*, in *Studi politici e storici*, Bologna 1893, 461–478
Zazo A., *Le scuole private universitarie a Napoli dal 1799 al 1860*, in A. Monti, A. Zazo, *Da Roffredo di Benevento a Francesco De Sanctis. Nuovi studi sulla storia dell'insegnamento superiore a Napoli*, Napoli 1926

Il potere giudiziario come «potere politico» in Attilio Brunialti

1. I «primi passi» di Brunialti

> «L'amore sincero alla libertà, alla verità, alla giustizia che ci riscalda il petto fin dalla prima adolescenza, lo studio delle costituzioni d'Europa e d'America, l'esame delle condizioni del governo democratico e dei probabili effetti suoi, i pericoli, alla fine, che crediamo sovrasteranno in un non lontano avvenire anche a questa bella terra che ci fu madre, ecco i motivi che ci spinsero, ecco le cause che ci guidarono in queste nostre ricerche».

Con queste parole Attilio Brunialti conclude, nel 1871, il saggio *Libertà e democrazia. Studi sulla rappresentanza delle minorità.*[1] Parole che, senza dubbio, già definiscono gli obiettivi scientifici del giurista vicentino, disegnando un suo primo ideale programma.

Brunialti, nato a Vicenza il 2 aprile 1849,[2] è dunque poco più che ventenne, e rivela una precoce[3] attitudine intellettuale coltivata, soprattutto, alla scuola di

1 Milano 1871, 474.

2 Morirà a Roma il 2 dicembre 1920. Per il profilo biografico, si vedano, in particolare, S. Rumor, *Gli scrittori vicentini dei secoli decimottavo e decimonono*, Venezia 1905, vol. I, 272–302; G. D'Amelio, *Brunialti Attilio*, in *Dizionario biografico degli italiani*, Roma 1972, vol. XIV, 636–638; F. Piodi, *Attilio Brunialti e la scienza della pubblica amministrazione*, in *Rivista trimestrale di diritto pubblico*, 1976, 675 ss.; G. Cazzetta, *Una costituzione «sperimentale» per una società ideale. I modelli giuridico-politici di Attilio Brunialti*, in *Quaderni fiorentini per la storia del pensiero giuridico moderno*, 15, 1986, 307–353; I. Porciani, *Attilio Brunialti e la «Biblioteca di Scienze Politiche». Per una ricerca su intellettuali e Stato dal trasformismo all'età giolittiana*, in *I giuristi e la crisi dello Stato liberale in Italia fra Otto e Novecento*, Napoli 1986, 191–229; R. Camurri, *Rappresentanza degli interessi e organizzazione del consenso: Attilio Brunialti 1882–1919*, in *Venetica*, 7, 1987, 5–29; Id., *Gli esordi di Attilio Brunialti nella scienza politica italiana (1869–1884)*, in *Ricerche di storia politica*, 2, 1987, 5–23.

3 Il 14 giugno 1868 l'ancora studente Brunialti tiene una conferenza, nell'Accademia Olimpica di Vicenza, intitolata *Sul suffragio delle donne*. Dell'anno successivo è la conferenza *Del carattere politico di Machiavelli*. Sui relativi manoscritti, cfr. R. Camurri, *Gli esordi di Attilio Brunialti*, cit., 5–8.

Fedele Lampertico e del giovane Luigi Luzzatti (1841–1927) che – come ci racconta lo stesso Brunialti – «guidò i primi miei passi nello studio delle scienze politiche».[4] L'Ateneo padovano di allora affiancava al più modesto GianPaolo Tolomei,[5] personalità di primo piano della cosiddetta scuola lombardo-veneta: l'«egregio uomo di Stato» (Luzzatti), Fedele Lampertico, Angelo Messedaglia. Brunialti conseguì la laurea il 14 agosto del 1870 in un ambiente di studi nel quale l'insegnamento politico-amministrativo – grazie soprattutto agli sforzi di Messedaglia – aveva conquistato un più definito statuto accademico e scientifico.[6] Brunialti ebbe dunque la ventura di seguire i «primi passi» della moderna scienza politica ed amministrativa in Italia e di familiarizzarsi con il lessico del diritto costituzionale, cogliendone presto quei complessi legami che saranno, un decennio dopo, al centro del grande progetto della *Biblioteca di Scienze Politiche*.[7]

Il magistero di Luzzatti ha un peso significativo nella formazione di Brunialti. La *Prelezione al corso di diritto costituzionale*[8] del professore padovano evidenzia temi e orientamenti destinati ad influire profondamente sullo studente vicentino. In Luzzatti[9] il giovane Brunialti può trovare un'impostazione non dog-

4 A. Brunialti, *Libertà e democrazia*, cit., 54. Brunialti dedica questo studio a Luzzatti e a Lampertico. Il legame del giovane vicentino con i suoi due «maestri» è ben diverso. Difficile e contraddittorio quello con Luzzatti, a seguito anche di iniziali incomprensioni (v. *Lettera di Attilio Brunialti a Fedele Lampertico*, Padova 25 giugno 1870); più solido e politicamente produttivo il legame con Lampertico. Su tutto questo, cfr. R. Camurri, *Gli esordi di Attilio Brunialti*, cit., 12–14.

5 I. Porciani, *Attilio Brunialti*, cit., 212.

6 A. Brunialti, *Le scienze politiche nello stato moderno*, in *Biblioteca di Scienze Politiche*, serie I, vol. I, parte prima, Torino 1884, 67–68.

7 Sulla Biblioteca, oltre agli autori citati (nt. 2), v. P. Schiera, *Amministrazione e costituzione: verso la nascita della scienza politica*, in *Il pensiero politico*, XV, 1982, 74 ss. e R. Gherardi, *L'arte del compromesso. La politica della mediazione nell'Italia liberale*, Bologna 1993, 54–63. Non bisogna però dimenticare il grande contributo dato da Brunialti all'*Enciclopedia giuridica italiana* di cui curò ben 54 voci: cfr. M. S. Piretti, *La rappresentanza politica. Una lettura attraverso alcune voci dell'Enciclopedia giuridica italiana*, in *Enciclopedia e sapere scientifico. Il diritto e le scienze sociali nell'Enciclopedia giuridica italiana*, a cura di A. Mazzacane e P. Schiera, Bologna 1990, 402.

8 *Del metodo nello studio del diritto costituzionale*, Padova 1867. Luzzatti insegnò diritto costituzionale nell'Università di Padova a partire dal 1866.

9 Sul rapporto intellettuale tra Brunialti e Luzzatti, v. G. Cazzetta, *Una costituzione «sperimentale»*, cit., 319–320; I. Porciani, *Attilio Brunialti*, cit., 220. Su Luzzatti cfr. F. Catalano, *Luigi Luzzatti, la vita e l'opera*, Milano 1965; G. Are, *Luigi Luzzatti e il socialismo della cattedra*, in *Alle origini dell'Italia industriale*, Napoli 1974; P. Pecorari, *Luigi Luzzatti e le origini dello «statalismo» economico nell'età della Destra storica*, Padova 1983; R. Camurri, *Gli esordi di Attilio Brunialti*, cit.; R. Gherardi, *L'arte del compromesso*, cit., 63 ss. e *passim*; *Luigi Luzzatti e il suo tempo*, Atti del Convegno internazionale di studio, Venezia, 7–9 novembre 1991,

matica, supportata da un approccio storico e «sperimentale» allo studio delle istituzioni politiche e costituzionali. La predominante vena eclettica è al tempo stesso segnale di «confusione» disciplinare,[10] ma anche vitalissimo *momento* della cultura italiana impegnata, ancora per lungo tempo, in un difficile sforzo di chiarimento metodologico.[11] Dall'insegnamento luzzattiano Brunialti assume il nesso inscindibile tra costituzione e libertà e soprattutto la predilezione per lo studio comparato[12] delle costituzioni, studio che funge da «laboratorio» empirico per l'ordinamento italiano in via di trasformazione. Il «modello» inglese, in tale contesto, diventa l'*exemplum* obbligato di un tipo di sviluppo storico-costituzionale in sintonia con i più importanti cambiamenti della società.

Brunialti – come si diceva poc'anzi – mostra di aver assimilato precocemente i principali temi del dibattito politico-costituzionale degli anni '60 e '70. In *Libertà e democrazia*, saggio scritto nel 1870, Brunialti inaugura la sua riflessione, mai più interrotta, sul problema della rappresentanza dei "più capaci", delle cosiddette "minorità", in una società già esposta allo spettro del "dispotismo della maggioranza". La rappresentanza proporzionale, in una teorizzazione integralmente tributaria delle fonti classiche del liberalismo europeo (Constant, Tocqueville, Mill, Laboulaye ecc.), appare lo strumento per dar vita ad una «democrazia temperata e costituzionale».[13] Nel Brunialti dei primi anni '70, impegnato in Corsi liberi di diritto costituzionale comparato,[14] membro dell'«Associazione per lo studio della rappresentanza proporzionale» (1873),[15] segretario della

raccolti da P. L. Ballini e P. Pecorari, Venezia, Istituto Veneto di Scienze 1994, in particolare i saggi di Ghisalberti e Pombeni.

10 M. S. Giannini, *Gli studi di diritto costituzionale in Italia*, in *Rassegna di diritto pubblico*, IV, 1949, 88 ss.

11 Su eclettismo e *medietas*, si rinvia, per più ampie notazioni, a L. Lacché, *La giustizia per i galantuomini. Ordine e libertà nell'Italia liberale: il dibattito sul carcere preventivo (1865–1913)*, Milano 1990, 66–67 e soprattutto a R. Gherardi, *L'arte del compromesso*, cit.

12 «In ogni scienza, e in politica soprattutto, nulla contribuisce al progresso con maggiore potenza delle giuste osservazioni che vi introduce uno spirito pratico e dello studio comparativo dei fatti [...]» (A. Brunialti, *Libertà e democrazia*, cit., 9).

13 *Ibidem*, 28.

14 Nel dicembre 1872 Brunialti inaugura, all'Università di Roma, un corso di diritto costituzionale comparato con la prelezione *Le Istituzioni politiche della Svizzera*. Su questo corso, si veda la recensione di Filippo Serafini in *Archivio giuridico*, X, 1872, 424–425.

15 Attraverso questa Associazione venne a contatto con Palma, Saredo, Genala, Bonghi, Mancini, Minghetti, Cairoli e Messedaglia. Sulla ricostruzione del dibattito, v. G. Cazzetta, *Una costituzione «sperimentale»*, cit., 315 ss. Notizia dell'Associazione è data da C. Caristia, *Per una riforma elettorale*, in *Studium*, 1910, cit. da M. S. Piretti, *Santi Romano, la rappresentanza politica e la revisione della legge elettorale*, in *I giuristi e la crisi*, cit., 360. Per più ampi riferimenti, Id.,

Società geografica italiana (1874), esponente della Sinistra (dal 1876 è segretario particolare di Depretis), scorgiamo già molti dei profili della sua attività scientifica e politica che caratterizzeranno anche i decenni successivi.

2. Il *testo* del 1870 e il *contesto* della politica giudiziaria nella prima età liberale

Il nostro giovane giurista pubblica, nel 1870, nella rivista-laboratorio[16] *Archivio giuridico* il breve saggio *La funzione politica del potere giudiziario*. Questo primo scritto – che sarà la prova, a distanza di tempo, di un impegno abbastanza coerente e duraturo[17] – acquista, per più di una ragione, un significato particolare e degno di nota. Se la lettura complessiva dell'opera di Brunialti svela taluni dei limiti della cultura e della scienza giuridica italiane, tra metodo eclettico, prospettive organicistiche e fragilità di un moderatismo liberale dalle incerte e controverse radici,[18] si deve però sottolineare – in ordine al tema cruciale del potere giudiziario – una capacità di analisi poco corrente nel 1870 e sostenuta da una concettualizzazione non priva di ingenuità ma attentissima, nell'essenziale, a cogliere i veri problemi dell'«emergenza» giudiziaria nell'Italia del tempo.

La questione della rappresentanza e l'evoluzione dei sistemi elettorali: il dibattito politico e giuridico italiano nel secondo Ottocento, in *Ricerche di storia politica*, 1, 1986, 9–43; Id., *L'Associazione per lo studio della rappresentanza proporzionale in Italia, 1872–1885*, in *Gli aspetti sociali delle istituzioni rappresentative*, a cura di V. Conti e E. Pii, Firenze 1987, 93–105; Id., *La giustizia dei numeri. Il proporzionalismo in Italia (1870–1923)*, Bologna 1990.

16 Tale riferimento è in P. Beneduce, *Il corpo eloquente. Identificazione del giurista nell'Italia liberale*, Bologna 1996, 45 (e *passim*). La rivista, fondata a Bologna da Pietro Ellero nel 1868 e già nel 1869 diretta da Filippo Serafini, «può essere considerata come un laboratorio nel quale si sperimentava un'opera esemplare di nominazione – cioè di reclutamento, inclusione e assoggettamento – di forze, interlocutori e orizzonti di problemi che confluiranno in una sorta di giacimento "originario" da cui la nuova scienza giuridica nazionale trarrà non pochi aspetti del suo profilo e del suo personale intellettuale». Nei primi anni '70 Brunialti collabora all'*Archivio giuridico*. Risale al 1871 (VII, 431 ss.) la recensione del libro di G. Padelletti, *Teoria delle elezioni politiche*, Napoli 1871.

17 Brunialti lo cita, come suo unico precedente saggio, nel libro IV, dedicato al potere giudiziario, de *Il diritto costituzionale e la politica nella scienza e nelle istituzioni*, Torino 1900, vol. VII, II della seconda serie della *Biblioteca di Scienze Politiche e Amministrative*, 485.

18 Sul genuino liberalismo di Brunialti, ma operante nella "società ideale", armonica, "interna" del diritto pubblico, e sugl'esiti conservatori della sua proposta, cfr. G. Cazzetta, *Una costituzione «sperimentale»*, cit., *passim*. Sulle «ambiguità» di Brunialti, si veda inoltre I. Porciani, *Attilio Brunialti*, cit., 223 ss.

Nel 1870 siamo nel pieno di quel dibattito che si suole rubricare sotto la voce «politica (governo) e magistratura (giustizia)», dibattito carico di molteplici significati e valenze. Tale àmbito gode di un vero e proprio statuto storiografico e, ormai, di una messe considerevole di importanti studi.

Forse si fa fatica ad ascoltare la voce di Brunialti in un coro di ben altra potenza. Sotto la ricordata rubrica possiamo censire, tra numerosi altri, il tono tagliente di Francesco Carrara che attribuisce mitologicamente alla figura del pubblico ministero le sembianze del terribile Briareo dalle cento mani, il «figlio della politica» che aspira a ridurre «i magistrati alla abietta condizione che Pellegrino Rossi così al vivo dipinse con il motto *machines à sentences* [...]».[19] Ma si pensi, per esempio, anche ai puntuali interventi critici del più «oscuro» Giuseppe Musio, giudice e senatore, che, sin dai primi anni Sessanta, si «specializza» sulla controversa questione dell'ordinamento giudiziario. Ne deriva un'interpretazione dello Statuto volta a legittimare un ordine giudiziario «[...] che sia posto in antagonismo col potere ministeriale e sia una guarentigia della nazione contro lo stesso potere»,[20] e dunque ordine autonomo e indipendente che deve essere quindi liberato dal giogo imposto da quelle leggi «incostituzionali» – a cominciare proprio dalla legge sull'ordinamento giudiziario del 1859 pubblicata in virtù dei pieni poteri concessi al governo – che perpetuano la soggezione della magistratura all'esecutivo.

Tra il 1865 e i primi anni '70 il coro di critiche si irrobustisce: professori, avvocati, giudici, parlamentari, taluni ex-guardasigilli (De Foresta e Conforti), settori della stampa censurano l'ordinamento e la sua concreta «gestione» in tema di inamovibilità, di trasferimenti, di promozioni, di controlli, di esercizio

19 F. Carrara, *I discorsi di apertura*, in *Opuscoli di diritto criminale*, Lucca, 1874, vol. IV, 44–45. Sulle funzioni del pubblico ministero e la riflessione di Carrara, si vedano l'ampio studio monografico di L. Lampa, *L'azione penale nel XIX secolo. La titolarità soggettiva della funzione d'accusa*, tesi di dottorato in storia del diritto italiano, 1996; Ead., *Le ministère public et ses fonctions en Italie, après l'Unification (1861–1913)*, in *Le pénal dans tous ses Etats. Justice, Etats et Sociétés en Europe (XIIe–XX siècles)*, a cura di X. Rousseaux e R. Lévy, Bruxelles 1997; Ead., *La magistratura e la giustizia. Il dibattito sul pubblico ministero (XIX–XX sec.)*, in *Annali dell'Università degli Studi di Macerata*, Milano 2000, 148–226. Più in generale, v. le osservazioni di M. Sbriccoli, *Politica e giustizia in Francesco Carrara*, in *Francesco Carrara nel primo centenario della morte*, Milano 1991, 441–449.

20 G. Musio, *Sul riordinamento giudiziario. Studi*, Ancona 1862, cit. da M. D'Addio, *Politica e magistratura (1846–1876)*, Milano 1966, 66. Sulla personalità di Musio, cfr. L. Lampa, *La magistratura e la giustizia*, cit. Di Musio sono da ricordare, almeno per gli anni '60, *Di una novella legge organica dell'ordinamento giudiziario. Nuovi studi*, Firenze 1868 e *Sulla legge organica giudiziaria del 6 dicembre 1865. Note del senatore Musio*, in *Gazzetta dei tribunali di Genova*, 14, 21, 28 marzo, 14 aprile 1868 (quest'ultimo pubblicato da M. D'Addio, *Politica e magistratura*, cit., 577 ss.).

dell'azione disciplinare. Alla lunga serie di infruttuosi progetti ministeriali e parlamentari di riforma[21] – comunque parziali e inidonei a modificare la filosofia ispiratrice dell'ordinamento giudiziario – fanno da contrappunto energici interventi ministeriali che segneranno, nel 1869, attraverso l'azione del guardasigilli Michele Pironti[22] (già procuratore generale presso la corte di appello di Napoli) l'acme di quella politica della Destra (nella *pratica*, e non solo, mai contraddetta successivamente dalla Sinistra) che aveva dato l'*imprinting* al rapporto tra potere politico (governo) e ordine giudiziario, nel tentativo di

21 Per la ricostruzione dell'intera vicenda, sono da ricordare soprattutto M. D'Addio, *Politica e magistratura*, cit.; P. Marovelli, *L'indipendenza e l'autonomia della magistratura italiana dal 1848 al 1923*, Milano 1967. Si vedano, inoltre, per i vari orientamenti storiografici e l'evoluzione interpretativa, P. Ungari, *Studi sulla storia della magistratura*, in *Storia contemporanea*, I, 1970, 379–391; E. R. Papa, *Magistratura e politica. Origini dell'associazionismo democratico nella magistratura italiana (1861–1913)*, Padova, Venezia 1973; P. Piasenza, *L'irresponsabilità politica della magistratura nello stato liberale. Il Piemonte e lo Statuto*, in *Materiali per una storia della cultura giuridica*, V, 1975, 533–633; A. Pignatelli, *I controlli politici sul giudice dallo Stato liberale al regime fascista*, in *Politica del diritto*, VI, 1975, 103–126; G. Neppi Modona, *Sciopero, potere politico e magistratura, 1870/1922*, Bari 1979; C. Guarnieri, *L'indipendenza della magistratura*, Padova 1981; G. Rebuffa, *La funzione giudiziaria. Lezioni introduttive*, Torino 1986; P. Saraceno (a cura di), *I magistrati italiani dall'Unità al fascismo. Studi biografici e prosopografici*, Roma 1988; A. Giuliani, N. Picardi, *La responsabilità del giudice*, Milano 1987; N. Picardi, *La riforma giudiziaria in Italia fra il XIX e XX secolo*, in *I progetti di riforma del processo civile (1866–1935)*, Milano 1988; P. Saraceno, *Parlamento e magistratura tra Siccardi e Rattazzi*, in *Il Parlamento italiano. Storia parlamentare e politica dell'Italia, 1861–1988*, Milano 1988, vol. I, 67–68; C. Guarnieri, *Magistratura e politica in Italia. Pesi senza contrappesi*, Bologna 1992, 83–87; P. Saraceno, *Le «epurazioni» della magistratura in Italia. Dal regno di Sardegna alla Repubblica: 1848–1951*, in *Clio*, XXIX, 1993, 509–523; Id., *Storia della magistratura italiana. La magistratura nel Regno di Sardegna*, Roma 1993; Id., *Il reclutamento dei magistrati italiani dall'Unità al 1890*, in A. Mazzacane e C. Vano (a cura di), *Università e professioni giuridiche in Europa nell'età liberale*, Napoli 1994, 537–588; C. Guarnieri, *L'ordine pubblico e la giustizia penale*, in *Storia dello Stato italiano dall'Unità a oggi*, a cura di R. Romanelli, Roma 1995, 365 ss.; A. Sciumè, *«Quando la politica entra dalla porta, la giustizia fugge impaurita dalla finestra»: giudici e sentimento della giustizia in Italia dall'Unità al primo Novecento*, in *Europäische und amerikanische Richterbilder*, hrsg. von A. Gouron, L. Mayali, A. Padoa Schioppa, D. Simon, Frankfurt am Main 1996, 165–193; C. Storti Storchi, *La dignità e l'autonomia del giudice nelle opinioni del ceto giuridico lombardo sull'intervento del pubblico ministero nelle cause civili (1860–1875)*, ivi, 195–250; C. Castellano, *Tra Francia e Italia. L'ordinamento giudiziario della Restaurazione in Piemonte e nelle Due Sicilie*, in *Magistrati e potere nella storia europea*, a cura di R. Romanelli, Bologna 1997, 111–146; C. Guarnieri, *Magistratura e sistema politico nella storia d'Italia*, ivi, 241–271.

22 M. D'Addio, *Politica e magistratura*, cit., 76 ss. e 216 ss.

«ridurre la giustizia ad un puro momento del potere esecutivo».[23] Occorre, certo, rivedere questa prospettiva unidirezionale (classe politica *vs.* classe giudiziaria) alla luce delle ricerche prosopografiche e delle conseguenti analisi che rivelano, nella prima età post-unitaria, una significativa osmosi tra l'alta magistratura politicizzata, di prevalente «estrazione» risorgimentale, e il corpo politico, con punti di incontro e di integrazione nel Parlamento e in capo alla funzione del ministro guardasigilli.[24]

Il saggio di Brunialti si inserisce nel contesto appena accennato ed è davvero singolare il fatto che esso sia stato interpretato equivocando – come è stato già evidenziato[25] – sul suo reale significato. «Ma sul continente, come potemmo già intravedere, le cose stanno diversamente. Il magistrato non che è un delegato del potere esecutivo, il potere giudiziario è una funzione del governo, a lui spetta bensì il mantenimento dell'ordine e della giustizia ma lo spirito che lo informa è, o deve essere quello del governo».[26] Questo passaggio di Brunialti ha ovviamente – come si desume dalla lettura dell'intero scritto – il senso di censurare quell'*habitus* continentale che fa del potere giudiziario un mero strumento degli altri poteri: «[...] la giustizia stessa è pressoché in balìa dell'amministrazione, e dipendente dal potere esecutivo».[27]

Non sembra tuttavia questo il profilo più interessante dell'articolo di Brunialti. In tal senso, si tratterebbe di uno fra i tanti, tributario di una polemica su «politica e giustizia» che, come detto, coinvolge in quegl'anni un gran numero di pubblicisti. Ciò che davvero interessa è il *punto di osservazione* dal quale Brunialti affronta la questione del potere giudiziario: il suo non è un discorso *tecnico* sui limiti dell'ordinamento giudiziario italiano – come fanno quasi tutti gli altri scrittori – rivolto, in fondo, a cogliere una sorta di *superficie*,

23 *Ibidem*, 239.

24 Il merito è – come noto – da ascrivere a P. Saraceno, *Alta magistratura e classe politica dalla integrazione alla separazione*, Roma 1979. Per le altre ricerche di Saraceno v. *supra*, nt. 21.

25 L'equivoco, in M. D'Addio, *Politica e magistratura*, cit., 244, è stato poi riproposto tralatiziamente da G. D'Amelio, *Brunialti Attilio*, cit., 637, da S. Lanaro, *Il Plutarco italiano: l'istruzione del "popolo" dopo l'Unità*, in *Storia d'Italia*, *Annali*, 4, *Intellettuali e potere*, Torino 1981, 581, da U. Allegretti, *Profilo di storia costituzionale italiana. Individualismo e assolutismo nello stato liberale*, Bologna 1989, 491. Nel Brunialti del 1870 non v'è traccia né dell'autoritarismo della Destra nei riguardi della magistratura, né di una riduzione della vita costituzionale al momento dell'esecutivo. Su questi aspetti, si vedano, per opportune osservazioni, G. Cazzetta, *Una costituzione «sperimentale»*, cit., 338–339 e I. Porciani, *Attilio Brunialti*, cit., 201–202.

26 A. Brunialti, *La funzione politica del potere giudiziario*, in *Archivio giuridico*, V, 1870, 415.

27 *Ibidem*, 408.

ovvero il quadro positivo del sistema giudiziario. Brunialti, nella sua «ingenuità» giovanile,[28] vuole ritrovare gli strati profondi dell'assetto di potere, le radici storiche, i paradigmi.

Prima di poter considerare in àmbito continentale il problema di quella che oggi definiremmo la rilevanza «politica» dell'attività giurisdizionale, Brunialti sente di dover muovere dalla questione preliminare dell'*architettura costituzionale* del potere giudiziario. Nel 1870 Brunialti è dunque testimone di una concezione dell'ordinamento che, pur dovendo fare i conti con i profondi cambiamenti intervenuti, respinge ormai la logica (assolutistica) del giudice-ingranaggio quale espressione ideal-tipica del giurista. Il giudice deve operare in una sfera di *autonomia costituzionale* e non dipendere *integralmente* dal primato della mediazione politico-legislativa.

3. Mediocrità del giudice, infallibilità della legge

Il dato *storico-costituzionale* rappresenta il *punto di osservazione* di Brunialti. Laddove altri si limitano a voler «aggiustare» l'ordinamento giudiziario, Brunialti è anzitutto attratto dalla genealogia del potere giudiziario, a cominciare dalla dottrina della separazione dei poteri.[29] Non sorprende che il costituzionalista vicentino faccia il suo esordio ricordando la teoria montesquiviana accennata nel celebre capitolo sesto ("Della costituzione dell'Inghilterra"), libro undicesimo de *Lo Spirito delle leggi*. La ricorda per evidenziarne il carattere puramente «teorico», «una semplice verità d'osservazione»: l'assolutezza, al contrario, ingenera – come dimostra il caso francese – uno stato continuo di guerra, un «attrito perpetuo»[30] tra i poteri, con esiti comunque fatali alla libertà: da un lato le barricate, dall'altro il dispotismo.

Brunialti, dunque, riprende il solito *topos* negativo della Francia rivoluzionaria che, equivocando Montesquieu e seguendo «l'errore di Rousseau»,[31] ha fatto

28 Non sfuggirà il fatto che taluni aspetti del saggio di Brunialti anticipano, con esiti però diversi, l'impostazione di Lodovico Mortara in *Lo Stato moderno e la giustizia* (1885), Napoli, 1992 e in altri successivi saggi. Come ha scritto Alessandro Pizzorusso (*Prefazione*, 9), «Lodovico Mortara è stato uno dei pochi studiosi italiani dei problemi della giustizia [...] che abbiano cercato di inquadrarli nel sistema generale del diritto pubblico, cominciando con lo stabilire la più esatta collocazione che il potere giudiziario debba venire ad assumere in base alla costituzione vigente [...]».

29 Sul «potere giudiziario» nell'ambito della dottrina della separazione dei poteri, cfr. l'antologia di scritti a cura di A. Pizzorusso, *L'ordinamento giudiziario*, Bologna 1974, 67ss.

30 A. Brunialti, *La funzione politica*, cit., 404.

31 *Ibidem.*

dell'assolutezza la parola d'ordine delle sue teorie politiche.[32] Certo, Montesquieu non aveva affatto riflettuto sul processo di formazione del governo di Gabinetto quale peculiarità del sistema inglese, capace di svelare, più di ogni altra, la assoluta «relatività» del principio di separazione.[33] Parimenti, l'ambiguo tratteggio del «potere giudiziario» nell'opera del *président à mortier* del Parlamento di Bordeaux lascia aperte numerose questioni circa la «compatibilità» tra la natura della «monarchia moderata» (governo misto), che incontra limiti nelle tanto invocate «leggi fondamentali del Regno» e nell'azione dei corpi intermedi, e la celebre immagine del giudice «bocca della legge», «essere inanimato», parte di un potere giudiziario separato dagl'altri due poteri (ed è questo l'unico vero riferimento, ne *L'Esprit des Lois*, al concetto di separazione), ma «invisibile e nullo».[34] Se, come è stato osservato,[35] la *mediocrità* è per i giudici, secondo Montesquieu, una virtù, è tuttavia l'*infallibilità* rousseauiana[36] della legge, quale espressione della volontà generale, a mutare le coordinate della concezione «assoluta» del potere politico.

Mediocrità del giudice, infallibilità della legge: ecco i paradigmi fondamentali alla base della rivoluzione (francese) dei poteri. Le tappe, a cominciare forse dalla legge del 16–24 agosto 1790,[37] sono note. Il dato che qui interessa è la definizione di un figurino – da assumere, certo, con cautela – che Brunialti, costituzionalista ai primi passi, disegna in controluce. La sua riflessione sulla *funzione politica* del potere giudiziario ha per oggetto la *posizione costituzionale*

32 Anziché osservare la massima di Mounier: «Perché i poteri sieno per sempre divisi, non occorre già che essi siano separati assolutamente» (*ibid.*). Brunialti riprende tale impostazione, ma con una più evidente sottolineatura critica verso Montesquieu, in *Il diritto costituzionale e la politica nella scienza e nelle istituzioni*, cit., Torino 1896, vol. VII, I, 301–302. Su questi profili, cfr. in questo volume *supra Coppet et la percée de l'Etat libéral constitutionnel*, 216 ss.

33 Cfr., in particolare, Ch. Eisenmann, *L'"Esprit des lois" et la séparation des pouvoirs*, in *Mélanges Carré de Malberg*, Paris 1933, 163–192; R. Derathé, *Note* a *Lo spirito delle Leggi*, Milano 1989, 574–575; M. Troper, *Montesquieu e la separazione dei poteri negli Stati Uniti*, in *Materiali per una storia della cultura giuridica*, 1, 1990, 71–85.

34 Ch.-L. de Secondat de Montesquieu, *Lo spirito delle leggi*, cit., lib. XI, cap. VI. Sul punto, v. G. Tarello, *Per una interpretazione sistematica de "L'esprit des Lois"*, in *Materiali per una storia della cultura giuridica*, 1, 1971, 40 ss. Più in generale, A. Marongiu, *Il posto del potere giudiziario nella dottrina settecentesca della divisione dei poteri*, in *Studi Esposito*, Padova 1972, vol. I, 679 ss.

35 M. Cappelletti, *Montesquieu abandonné? Développement et legitimité de la "justice constitutionnelle"*, in *Le pouvoir des juges*, Aix-Marseille, Paris 1990, 259–261.

36 J.-J. Rousseau, *Il contratto sociale*, con un saggio introduttivo di R. Derathé, Torino 1966, lib. II, capp. VI–VII.

37 Sulle molteplici implicazioni sottese a questa legge, si rinvia., anche per i riferimenti bibliografici, a L. Lacchè, *L'espropriazione per pubblica utilità. Amministratori e proprietari nella Francia dell'Ottocento*, Milano 1995, 37–39.

dei giudici nei principali «modelli» e, in ultima istanza, il tema fondamentale della «sterilizzazione politica del giudiziario»[38] nella maggior parte dei sistemi continentali, a cominciare da quello francese.

Il figurino si può affrettatamente riassumere con il *tipo* del giudice-funzionario, burocrate chiamato ad applicare, sillogisticamente,[39] la legge, mero esecutore di un comando formalisticamente inteso e operante nel quadro di un sistema delle fonti del diritto che nega alla giurisprudenza, in via teorica, valore creativo. Che tale modello debba essere letto in chiave di sviluppo storico e dunque relativizzato, è evidente;[40] e tuttavia esso designa una *dislocazione* del giudiziario che ne depotenzia la *portata* – diremmo la *significatività politica* – rispetto alla lunga esperienza che ha preceduto il moderno processo di trasformazione del concetto stesso di sovranità. Come dirà Max Weber, «non è sicuro che, nei paesi di diritto codificato, sia sufficiente imporre a un giudice burocratico la corona di "creatore" per trasformarlo in un profeta giuridico».[41]

4. La legge e il governo costituzionale

Dallo Statuto, figlio anch'esso della concezione «francese» – osserva Brunialti – non ci si poteva attendere che una formula ambigua bell'e pronta per legittimare la teoria dei due poteri.[42] Ma questa tara costituzionale, perfettamente inserita nel ricordato processo, è tanto più grave quanto più lascia senza difese il *luogo* della giurisdizione.[43] L'*infallibilità* della legge è, astrattamente intesa, un fattore necessario di garanzia, il fondamento stesso del governo costituzionale. Brunialti deve, *malgré lui*, togliere di bocca le parole a Rousseau. «La legge è una creazione

38 G. Tarello, *Orientamenti della magistratura e della dottrina sulla funzione politica del giurista-interprete*, in *Politica del diritto*, III, 1972, 461.

39 Cfr. F. Roselli, *Il sillogismo giudiziale nella giurisprudenza italiana dell'Ottocento*, in *Politica del diritto*, IX, 1980, 631–693.

40 Si veda la sintesi efficace di R. Romanelli, *Introduzione. Magistratura e potere nella storia moderna*, in *Magistratura e potere*, cit., 15. Cfr. anche L. M. Diez-Picazo, *Il modello europeo di magistratura: un approccio storico*, *ibid.*, 29 ss. e G. Alpa, *L'arte di giudicare*, Bari 1996, 3 ss.

41 M. Weber, *Economia e società*, Milano 1961 (1922), vol. II, 199.

42 Brunialti prende ad esempio il pur lodevole corso di Ludovico Casanova: *Del diritto costituzionale*, Genova, 1859–1860. Per la discussione della teoria, v. A. Brunialti, *Il diritto costituzionale*, cit., I, 318 ss., dove segue soprattutto P. Grippo, *Il potere giudiziario in rapporto alla costituzione dello Stato*, Napoli 1881, e II, 489 ss.

43 Osserva giustamente U. Allegretti, *Profilo*, cit., 488 – sottolineando soprattutto lo sforzo, tardo, di Racioppi e Brunelli per «rivoltare» il significato delle singole norme dello Statuto (artt. 68 ss.) in senso garantista – che tale sforzo «non riflette la condizione d'assieme della vicenda liberale, né nell'applicazione legislativa né nella prassi [...]».

della volontà nazionale, ne è anzi come dicemmo la sintesi».[44] Sin qui il dogma legicentrico è davvero insuperabile, su esso poggia l'intero sistema costituzionale della Destra storica.[45] Ma la legge, aggiunge Brunialti, una volta creata diviene indipendente dalla sua volontà creatrice. «Il principe dei logici», J. Stuart Mill, osserva: «nessuna costituzione, nessuna legge poter pretendere ad un valore assoluto, essendo le qualità del legislatore quelle che decidono del suo valore». La *méfiance du pouvoir législatif* deve dunque guidare, paradossalmente, lo stesso legislatore.

> «Di cotesto ragionamento emana la necessità di un potere destinato a limitare in tutte le sue manifestazioni, in tutte le sue forme, la sovranità popolare in favore della sovranità della legge. Né siffatto potere può essere una creazione del legislativo, come quello che deve anzi nascere gemello colla nozione stessa della legge. Una sola adunque è la via aperta al legislatore per giungere allo scopo, *mettere accanto al suo un altro potere non inferiore, non dipendente, il potere giudiziario*».[46]

Se la legge deve essere *infallibile* (nei limiti accennati da Brunialti), i giudici non possono essere *mediocri*, a pena di degradare il governo costituzionale a dato puramente nominale. I tribunali devono poter togliere ai «funzionarii ed ai partiti politici la interpretazione. A che pro' altrimenti mettere sopra ogni cosa la sovranità delle leggi, e adottare le forme della libertà parlamentare, se nella pratica troviamo invece una gerarchia subordinata sì, ma che alla sua volta tende naturalmente a sostituire i suoi diritti a quelli della comunità per cui pretende di esistere?».[47]

5. «Gli è così insomma che l'Inghilterra e gli Stati Uniti fecero del potere giudiziario un vero potere politico»

> «G. Meyer ha notato, – scriverà Brunialti a fine secolo – che l'originaria identità della giustizia e dell'amministrazione è un principio del diritto europeo. Ogni organo dello Stato aveva un tempo funzioni finanziarie, di polizia, militari e giudiziarie. Non vi era una costituzione giudiziaria distinta dalla costituzione politica, bensì l'attività giudiziaria aveva un'assoluta prevalenza ed assorbiva talmente l'intera attività dello Stato, che il concetto fondamentale della potestà pubblica si poteva designare colla parola *jurisdictio* e tutti i funzionari poterono aver titolo di giudici».[48]

44 A. Brunialti, *La funzione politica*, cit., 406.
45 Cfr. C. Ghisalberti, *Per una storia costituzionale dell'Italia liberale*, in *Stato e costituzione nel Risorgimento*, Milano 1972, 63.
46 A. Brunialti, *La funzione politica*, cit., 407 (corsivo mio).
47 *Ibidem.*
48 Brunialti cita dal *Lehrbuch des deutschen Verwaltungsrechts*, Leipzig 1884, vol. I, 17 ss. (*Il diritto costituzionale*, cit., II, 550).

Il saggio di Brunialti del 1870, pur senza esplicitarlo, segue proprio questa linea di indagine «archeologica»: un tempo, prima che si affermasse sul continente il principio astratto di separazione dei poteri, il *giudicare* era il *luogo naturale* del potere politico. Il *comando* non era disgiunto dal *giudizio*.[49] La *jurisdictio* rappresentava il processo stesso del potere.[50]

> «Quando si esamina – aveva scritto Tocqueville – la costituzione che aveva un tempo il potere giudiziario presso la maggior parte delle nazioni europee, si resta impressionati da due cose: l'indipendenza di questo potere e l'estensione delle sue attribuzioni. Non solo le corti di giustizia decidevano quasi tutte le cause tra privati; ma in moltissimi casi facevano da arbitri fra l'individuo e lo Stato [...] Per tutti i popoli d'Europa vi erano e vi sono ancora molti diritti individuali, collegati generalmente con il diritto generale di proprietà, che erano posti sotto la salvaguardia del giudice e che lo stato non poteva violare senza il permesso di quest'ultimo. *Questo potere semipolitico era la principale differenza tra i tribunali d'Europa e tutti gli altri* [...]».[51]

Tocqueville – vivendo in Francia e nel «secolo dell'amministrazione» – ha descritto efficacemente e con il consueto acume il processo di trasformazione della *potestas publica* in Europa. La «costituzione del potere giudiziario» è ormai entrata nella stagione della *mediocrità*. Ma Tocqueville sa bene che quel «potere semipolitico» occupava – non senza problemi, certo – il *luogo* della «salvaguardia dei diritti individuali».

Brunialti muove anch'egli dal problema della «costituzione del potere giudiziario». «Più geloso della propria indipendenza e delle libertà sue è per noi quel popolo che assiduo veglia alla integrità del suo potere giudiziario, e studiosamente ne serba intatte le attribuzioni, di quello che l'altro che cercando continuamente accrescere i diritti del suo corpo legislativo, riesce alla fine ad una onnipotenza, che per essere di molti non è meno tiranna, né dannosa meno a libertà».[52] È partendo da questa premessa che Brunialti mette in campo la scienza comparata delle costituzioni per sottolineare l'antica «unità» «dei popoli d'Europa», quando l'organizzazione politica e sociale non era stata oggetto di

49 Su questo fondamentale profilo di storia del potere e della sua concettualizzazione giuridica, è d'obbligo riferirsi a L. Mannori, *Giustizia e amministrazione tra antico e nuovo regime*, in *Magistrati e potere*, cit., 39–65. Dello stesso autore, per un maggiore approfondimento, v. *Per una «preistoria» della funzione amministrativa. Cultura giuridica e attività dei pubblici apparati nell'età del tardo diritto comune*, in *Quaderni fiorentini per la storia del pensiero giuridico moderno*, XIX, 1990, 323 ss.; *Il sovrano tutore. Pluralismo istituzionale e accentramento amministrativo nel Principato dei Medici (secc. XVI–XVIII)*, Milano 1994.

50 P. Costa, *Iurisdictio. Semantica del potere politico nella pubblicistica medievale (1100–1433)*, Milano 1969.

51 A. De Tocqueville, *La democrazia in America*, a cura di G. Candeloro, Milano 1992, 724–725 (corsivo mio).

52 A. Brunialti, *La funzione politica*, cit., 407.

radicali mutamenti. Il giurista vicentino, però, più che guardare al passato in quanto tale, sembra rivolgere lo sguardo a quelle esperienze che non avrebbero subìto con altrettanta forza l'aggressione dei princìpi ispirati al binomio *infallibilità / mediocrità*: ricerca, attraverso la comparazione, le tracce e le permanenze di un passato che era stato più «comune» di quanto non dovesse apparire dopo la fine del XVIII secolo. Riprende, quindi, lo stereotipo delle «genti del mezzodì» da contrapporre alle razze anglosassoni. Presso i continentali la costituzione rischia d'essere «un pezzo di carta *octroyé*»[53] che rende nominali le libertà, anche le più sacre, e che i re e i popoli possono calpestare e interpretare a loro piacimento. «Ma v'hanno popoli che saggiamente evitano così fatali pericoli, *facendo del potere giudiziario un vero potere politico*».[54]

Ecco allora che l'Inghilterra e gli Stati Uniti diventano – secondo uno stilema corrente[55] – gli esempi di una provvida organizzazione dei poteri. Le costituzioni anglosassoni non hanno seguìto la via «continentale»: al contrario, hanno dato al potere giudiziario una estensione «[...] che agli occhi dei continentali violava quella assoluta separazione: gli è in omaggio a codesta verità, che l'anglosassone riconosce questo potere, solo interprete della costituzione, e l'amministrazione soggetta al pari del più semplice cittadino al potere dei tribunali: *gli è così insomma che l'Inghilterra e gli Stati Uniti fecero del potere giudiziario un vero potere politico*».[56]

Il *rule of law* è l'idea fondamentale del costituzionalismo inglese:[57] il regno della legge si estende sia sui poteri dello Stato che sui cittadini. «Il potere giudiziario nella posizione che gli assegna il *common law* è ad un tempo custode della giustizia e della libertà, potentissimo freno ad ogni possibile esorbitanza, esteso tanto, quanto si estende la sovranità medesima della legge».[58] L'illustrazione che Brunialti fa della formazione del sistema inglese è del tutto conforme alla ricostruzione liberal-conservatrice di Fischel e soprattutto di Gneist. Il rilievo nei confronti di Bagehot (tesi dell'onnipotenza del parlamento) mostra subito

53 *Ibidem*, 408.

54 Ivi (corsivo mio).

55 Sulla storia delle istituzioni inglesi come punto di riferimento per la «costituzione armonica», v. G. Cazzetta, *Una costituzione «sperimentale»*, cit., 333–334.

56 A. Brunialti, *La funzione politica*, cit., 401 (corsivo mio).

57 Prima ancora – osserva Brunialti equivocando in parte l'insegnamento di Walter Bagehot – «della grande potenza del parlamento» (*ibid.*, 409). Brunialti cita l'edizione francese: *La constitution anglaise*, Paris 1869. Bagehot in realtà incentra il suo saggio sulla «componente efficiente» della costituzione inglese (la «fusione» tra esecutivo e legislativo nel governo di Gabinetto) e sulla «componente nobile» (monarchia e *lords*), tralasciando l'analisi del potere giudiziario (v. G. Rebuffa, *Un'idea di Costituzione. Walter Bagehot e la regina Vittoria*, introduzione a W. Bagehot, *La costituzione inglese*, Bologna 1995 (1872)).

58 A. Brunialti, *La funzione politica*, cit., 409.

l'influenza dello Gneist[59] critico di Blackstone e meno sensibile alle radici parlamentari delle libertà inglesi.

> «L'egida e la garanzia delle libertà individuali e dei diritti del popolo inglese, non istà solamente in un parlamento e nelle istituzioni municipali, ma, e in principal modo, nel regime di quel *common law*, «*le cui sorgenti sono inesplorabili come quelle del Nilo*», nella indipendenza assoluta e sincera della magistratura e del giurì, nella sovranità infine, che tale ella deve essere ed è colà veramente, del potere giudiziario, competente per le questioni di diritto pubblico, non meno che per quelle di diritto privato».[60]

Il *selfgovernment* è nelle mani – come osserva Fischel[61] – di *gentlemen* indipendenti che esercitano la giurisdizione (i famosi *Justices of the Peace*) secondo il *common law* e non secondo le istruzioni di un ministro qualunque. Paese aristocratico, ma libero, l'Inghilterra ha dunque una costituzione che riposa anzitutto sul potere dei tribunali che abbraccia tutta la sfera del diritto. Da

59 Rudolph von Gneist aveva pubblicato nel 1863 la *Geschichte und heutige Gestalt der englischen Communalverfassung*. Brunialti cita l'edizione Paris, Bruxelles 1867–1870, in 5 volumi: *La constitution communale de l'Angleterre, son histoire, son état actuel ou le self-government*. Per il profilo che qui interessa, v. G. Schmidt-Eichstaedt, *Staatsverwaltung und Selbstverwaltung bei Rudolf von Gneist*, in *Die Verwaltung*, 8, 1975, 345 ss.; B. Sordi, *Giustizia e amministrazione nell'Italia liberale. La formazione della nozione di interesse legittimo*, Milano 1985, 86 ss. e *passim*; Id., *L'influenza tedesca*, in *Le riforme crispine*, vol. II, Archivio Isap n. 6, Milano 1990, 533–574; M. Stolleis, *Geschichte des öffentlichen Rechts*, Frankfurt a. M. 1992, t. II, 385–388; Id., *Autogoverno: una indagine semantica*, in *Saperi della borghesia e storia dei concetti fra Otto e Novecento*, a cura di R. Gherardi e G. Gozzi, Bologna 1995, 254. Brunialti ritornerà sul problema del rapporto tra *rule of law* e trasformazione del diritto inglese proprio con riferimento all'opera di Gneist, *Das englische Verwaltungsrecht der Gegenwart in Vergleich mit den deutschen Verwaltungssystemen*, Berlin 1857, pubblicata nella *Biblioteca di scienze politiche e amministrative*, II serie, vol. 3, 1, Torino 1896 assieme al saggio di M. Vauthier, *Il governo locale dell'Inghilterra*, premettendo loro *Il diritto pubblico inglese e la sua trasformazione* (sul Brunialti divulgatore in Italia di Gneist, v. anche I. Porciani, *Attilio Brunialti*, cit., 194). In questo lavoro, Brunialti evidenziava le principali linee evolutive, dal *Reform Bill* del 1832 sino alle riforme amministrative di segno «centralizzatore» a partire dagli anni '70. Un accenno al ruolo dei *Boards* è anche in *Il diritto costituzionale*, cit., II, 551. Sul giudizio di Brunialti, v. B. Sordi, *Giustizia*, cit., 90–91; P. Beneduce, *«Punto di vista amministrativo» e Stato di diritto: aspetti del germanesimo dei giuristi italiani alla fine dell'Ottocento*, in *Annali dell'istituto storico italo-germanico in Trento*, X, 1984, 185 ss., anche in relazione all'opera di Carlo Francesco Ferraris; Id., *Culture dei giuristi e "revisione" orlandiana: le immagini della crisi*, in *I giuristi e la crisi*, cit., 102–103.

60 A. Brunialti, *La funzione politica*, cit., 411. La citazione (corsivo nel testo) è tratta da Lord Hale, *History of the Common law*.

61 Brunialti cita l'edizione francese dell'opera di Fischel. L'opera era già stata tradotta in italiano: *Storia della costituzione inglese*, Milano 1866, 2 voll.

Fortescue[62] a Henry Hallam[63] a Thomas Macaulay[64] il potere giudiziario appare essere il guardiano del *common law*, la pietra angolare della libertà inglese. È dalla società che emergono i giudici delle alte corti: indipendenti, sostanzialmente inamovibili, ben retribuiti, forti di uno *status* sociale che attribuisce loro maestà e dignità.

> «Dal giudice di pace, il magistrato del *selfgovernment* infino ai giudici delle supreme corti di Westminster, il potere giudiziario inglese gode adunque di una grandissima indipendenza, di una autorità che si estende al diritto pubblico non meno che al privato: indipendenza ed autorità, nelle quali è pur forza riconoscere coi celeberrimi legisti e trattatisti inglesi una delle più ferme basi del vivere libero, una delle barriere più salde non solo contro le pretese dell'amministrazione altrove così esorbitanti, ma anche contro le tendenze dominatrici del potere legislativo».[65]

Brunialti inizia il suo «viaggio» in Gran Bretagna ma deve concluderlo, prima di far ritorno in patria, negli Stati Uniti. Il filo rosso è sempre quello della centralità costituzionale della *jurisdictio* (*ius quia justum*). Se in Inghilterra il *gubernaculum* è stato progressivamente «addomesticato» dal Parlamento e dalle istituzioni giudiziarie, è negli Stati Uniti che la costituzione rigida è assurta a strumento per razionalizzare la *fundamental law*[66] diventando la *lex superior*[67] che limita e vincola i poteri (*checks and balances*) e restituisce al potere «custode del diritto»[68] – nella logica del *law finding* – una essenziale funzione *politica* di freno e di contrappeso.

Negli Stati Uniti Brunialti scorge, pur nella profonda novità dell'assetto istituzionale, il «completamento» del «modello» inglese. Sono stati i discendenti

62 *De laudibus legum Angliae*, IX, 29, ed. critica di S. B. Chrimes, Cambridge 1949.

63 Brunialti cita l'edizione italiana: *Storia costituzionale di Inghilterra dal cominciamento del regno di Enrico VII alla morte di Giorgio II*, prima traduzione italiana di Vito d'Ondes Reggio, preceduta da un suo avvertimento sulla medesima e da un suo discorso sul reggimento politico in Europa [...], Torino 1854, 4 voll.

64 Th. Macaulay, *The History of England*, Leipzig 1849–1861.

65 A. Brunialti, *La funzione politica*, cit., 413. Di Brunialti cfr. anche *Il governo parlamentare in Inghilterra ed in Italia*, in *Biblioteca di scienze politiche*, serie I, vol. III, Torino 1886, LXIV–LXV. Sulla clausola «quamdiu se bene gesserint» («during good behaviour») e il principio di indipendenza, a partire dall'*Act of Settlement* (1701), cfr. L. M. Diez-Picazo, *Il modello europeo*, cit., 23 ss.; J. M. Jacob, *I giudici inglesi*, in *Magistrati e potere*, cit., 67 ss.

66 Cfr. N. Matteucci, *Introduzione* a Ch. H. McIlwain, *Costituzionalismo antico e moderno*, Bologna 1990 (1947).

67 Sulla nozione di *lex superior*, v. E. S. Corwin, *L'idea di "legge superiore" e il diritto costituzionale americano*, Venezia, s. d.; M. Cappelletti, *Le contrôle juridictionnel des lois en droit comparé*, in *Le pouvoir des juges*, cit., 183 ss.

68 N. Matteucci, *Costituzionalismo*, in *Dizionario di politica*, a cura di N. Bobbio e N. Matteucci, Torino 1976, 272.

dei *pilgrim fathers* (Hamilton, Madison, Marshall ...), «uomini eminentemente pratici», a «dare forma più precisa e manifesta a questa azione del potere giudiziario, porre fra la costituzione e la legislazione una autorità, che dicesse al legislatore "la costituzione sancita dal popolo è tua legge come è la mia, è la *lex legum* sicché nessuno può attentarsi violarla"».[69] Il *judicial review* rende i giudici federali i sommi sacerdoti che venerano l'«arca santa, dove il popolo custodisce le sue libertà e cui nessuno, *foss'anche il legislatore medesimo ha diritto di mettere le mani*».[70] La giustizia è la compagna della libertà, ne è il limite naturale: «in apparenza è un limite, in realtà ne è lo scudo e la garanzia più sicura: *la vera libertà non è che il regno del diritto*».[71]

6. Attilio Brunialti e il (potere) giudiziario come «vero potere politico»

Al di là della scolastica e semplificante contrapposizione tra i «popoli del mezzodì» e i popoli nordici, la riflessione di Brunialti sulle peculiarità del tracciato storico e culturale delle diverse costituzioni individua questioni di indubbio rilievo. In Inghilterra e negli Stati Uniti «tutto finisce con un processo: il cittadino che fra lui e le sue libertà vede innalzarsi una legge qualsiasi, può esclamare "noi abbiamo dei giudici, vedremo chi à ragione"». Ma «da noi», continua Brunialti, tutto ciò non è possibile. «Da noi», nell'impossibilità di perseguire la «via legale» del *due process*, per fare un banchetto, pubblicare un giornale, aprire una chiesa «anziché ricorrere presso i tribunali contro il ministero che ricusa questo diritto, si fa una rivoluzione: costa più che un processo, e quel che peggio è sempre la libertà che ne paga le spese».[72]

A parte gli stereotipi e le modellizzazioni, intravediamo nel breve saggio del giovane – ma non certo sprovveduto – giurista l'individuazione di problemi che nel 1870 sembrano occultati dal profilo tecnico o dalla lotta politica. L'ordinamento giudiziario del 1865 costringe l'ordine dei magistrati in uno spazio

69 A. Brunialti, *La funzione politica*, cit., 413. La citazione è tratta da E. Laboulaye, *Histoire des Etats-Unis*, Paris 1868, 6 ed., vol. III, *La constitution des Etats-Unis, 1783–1789*, lezione XVIII. Brunialti segue alla lettera il discorso di Laboulaye sul potere giudiziario nella costituzione americana. «Les Américains n'avaient aucun exemple pour se guider. Les premiers, ils ont fait du pouvoir judiciaire un véritable pouvoir politique; les premiers, ils ont compris le rôle de la justice dans un pays libre. C'est une vérité nouvelle qu'ils ont trouvée, et qui a été jusqu'ici peu comprise en Europe» (470).

70 A. Brunialti, *La funzione politica*, cit., 414 (corsivo mio). Su questo aspetto, si veda il fondamentale saggio di M. J. C. Vile, *Constitutionalism and the Separation of the Powers*, Oxford 1967.

71 A. Brunialti, *La funzione politica*, cit., 415. La citazione è tratta sempre da E. Laboulaye, *Histoire*, cit., 498.

72 A. Brunialti, *La funzione politica*, cit., 417.

troppo angusto. Non è solo, evidentemente, per la decisa volontà della Destra di gestire la «politica giudiziaria». È anzitutto l'assetto complessivo dei poteri che determina un tale effetto e ne indica la direzione. In fondo, il ceto politico non «controlla» il senso di marcia del sistema *costituzionale*. Un giurista «medio» come Brunialti sente che le ragioni non sono sempre visibili alla superficie, e occorre quindi scavare più in profondità. Il binomio *infallibilità / mediocrità* è il risultato della più grande torsione che il sistema giuridico moderno abbia subìto e la principale causa della conseguente – non definitiva – divaricazione in àmbito occidentale.

Brunialti ricerca, come tanti altri giuristi, la soluzione in un *altrove* che si dipinge di mito e di improbabili armonie. Ma, in ultima istanza, il vero nodo da sciogliere è e resta la praticabilità del *governo limitato*. A partire da questa riflessione emerge l'idea della costituzione come garanzia dei diritti e delle libertà: e proprio la prospettiva del garantismo è uno dei punti più deboli del costituzionalismo francocentrico rispetto a quello anglosassone e in particolare a quello americano. Il legicentrismo virtuoso, pur ancorato a parametri costituzionali, ha determinato una scissione tra legge e costituzione, tra legge e diritti. La legge *par excellence*, il codice civile, ha impoverito la teoria costituzionale dei diritti.[73] Bisognava, invece, poter *diffidare* della *suprema potestas* rappresentata dal legislatore *infallibile*. Ma per realizzare il principio del governo limitato e

73 La letteratura più recente suggerisce questo percorso di ricerca. Mi limito a ricordare di M. Fioravanti, *Appunti di storia delle costituzioni moderne*, Torino 1995 e *Lo Stato di diritto come forma di Stato. Notazioni preliminari sulla tradizione europeo-continentale*, in *Saperi della borghesia e storia dei concetti fra Otto e Novecento*, a cura di R. Gherardi e G. Gozzi, Bologna 1995, 161–177; di B. Clavero, *Lo spazio dei diritti e la posizione dei giudici tra costituzione e codice*, in *Materiali per una storia della cultura giuridica*, 1, 1989, 95–129 e *Los derechos y los jueces*, Madrid 1989; inoltre G. Zagrebelski, *Il diritto mite. Legge diritti giustizia*, Torino 1992; M. Taruffo, *Il modello burocratico di amministrazione della giustizia*, in *Democrazia e diritto*, 3, 1993, 249–263; S. Mannuzzu, *Il paradosso del giudice. Giustizia e divisione dei poteri*, *ibidem*, 3–4, 1995, 83–95; S. Rodotà, *Magistratura e politica in Italia*, in *Governo dei giudici. La magistratura tra diritto e politica*, a cura di E. Bruti Liberati, A. Ceretti, A Giasanti, Milano 1996, 17–30; E. Scoditti, *Riforma costituzionale e giurisdizione*, in *Democrazia e diritto*, 1, 1997, 1–72; M. R. Ferrarese, *Magistratura e diritti: virtù passive e stato attivo*, *ibid.*, 111–131; G. Palombella, *Giudici, diritti e democrazia*, *ibidem*, 241–264; L. Ferrajoli, *Giurisdizione e democrazia*, *ibidem*, 285–304; R. Romanelli, *Introduzione*, cit.; A. Damien, *Pouvoir judiciaire et vertu. Les trois tentations du magistrat*, in *Archives de philosophie du droit*, 42, 1997, 233–239; M. Luciani, *Giurisdizione e legittimazione nello Stato costituzionale di diritto (ovvero: di un aspetto spesso dimenticato del rapporto fra giurisdizione e democrazia)*, in *Politica del diritto*, 3, 1998, 365–382; A. Pizzorno, *Il potere dei giudici. Stato democratico e controllo della virtù*, Bari 1998, 15 ss.

scacciare la «mano sacrilega» dal «santuario di Temide»[74] la *mediocrità* doveva essere rimessa in discussione.

Quel tipo di equilibrio costituzionale non può esistere – come sappiamo bene oggi[75] – senza un potere giudiziario *policy making*. Brunialti l'ha compreso nel 1870 ma lo dirà più esplicitamente alla fine del secolo;[76] per il momento prefigura il giudiziario come «vero potere politico» e va a toccare i nervi scoperti di una questione che in Italia (e non solo) viene identificata con la dizione «politica e magistratura». Nel 1870 Brunialti, osservando la costituzione «ideale» anglosassone, costruisce il suo concetto di funzione politica del potere giudiziario.

Il giudiziario – riprendendo qui l'insieme delle indicazioni disseminate da Brunialti nel testo – deve essere «non inferiore a» e «non dipendente dagl'altri poteri». I giudici devono essere, come quelli inglesi e americani (pur nella diversità di statuto), realmente inamovibili, garantiti nel proprio ruolo, forti di una *status* sociale (l'autorità dei giudici inglesi) che li metta al sicuro da pressioni di ogni genere. La *funzione politica* consiste nella *posizione costituzionale* e nella *estensione* del potere giudiziario. È un potere *custode* della giustizia e della libertà («il migliore dei guardiani»), «custode della costituzione equilibrata» anche contro il re, il governo e il parlamento, *freno* contro ogni «possibile esorbitanza», *esteso* tanto quanto si estende la sovranità della legge.

La *funzione politica* allontana il giudice dalla *mediocrità* ed evidenzia conseguentemente il problema della legge separata dai diritti, non più *infallibile*,

74 «S'intende perciò come i tramutamenti a cui il ministro Pironti è addivenuto, abbiano destato qualche inquietudine, come se il governo volesse estendere la mano sacrilega nel santuario di Temide e far dei tribunali un cieco istrumento della politica, che è quanto dire di un partito», articolo non firmato apparso sul numero del 5 settembre 1869 di *L'opinione* col titolo *L'inamovibilità* (in M. D'Addio, *Politica e magistratura*, cit., 802).

75 Cfr. N. Matteucci, *Costituzionalismo*, cit., 272: «Questo spostarsi dell'equilibrio costituzionale dal legislativo al giudiziario, questo nuovo rapporto fra il potere e il diritto, segna certo una rottura con la nostra tradizione politica più recente; *una rottura che non è ancora pienamente chiara ed evidente alla nostra cultura politica. Questo era necessario, proprio per l'avvento della democrazia*» (il corsivo è mio).

76 Brunialti segue la traccia utilizzata nel 1870: «Quanto più riusciremo ad assicurare l'autorità e l'indipendenza del potere giudiziario e con esse l'impero della legge, tanto più sicuramente raggiungeremo i massimi intenti di un governo libero [...] Sino a che il potere giudiziario non si consideri come uno dei grandi poteri dello Stato, noi possiamo dire, che la libertà non è guarentita, che le istituzioni parlamentari non funzionano regolarmente, che la prepotenza e l'arbitrio dei governi assoluti non sono scomparsi, ma rifioriscono nei gabinetti onnipotenti, nelle assemblee invadenti, nelle autorità locali prepotenti, nell'amministrazione arbitraria [...]» (*Il diritto costituzionale*, cit., p. I, 325–326).

custodita dal potere giudiziario.[77] Un governo parlamentare, ricorda Brunialti a conclusione del suo saggio, senza tribunali liberi «non è che uno scherzo di cattivo genere».[78] Attraverso Brunialti è possibile intravedere un tratto importante del diversificato processo di formazione del potere giudiziario contemporaneo: da un lato la concezione «giudiziaria» dei diritti, dall'altro la concezione «legale». In questa fase le due concezioni sembrano allontanarsi, formando due poli coerentemente distinti. Il punto di vista di Brunialti non è, come si è potuto constatare, di ordine «democratico». Idealizza il «governo dei giudici» di stampo anglosassone per fondare un'idea di potere giudiziario che possa funzionare, in Italia, da argine alle «esorbitanze» della imminente «ondata democratica». Non può certo interessargli il problema del «Quis custodiet ipsos custodes?».[79] Un dato, però, gli è ben chiaro: una costituzione non può essere equilibrata senza assegnare un certo grado di *funzione politica* al potere giudiziario. Brunialti immagina probabilmente un potere *conservatore*,[80] in una prospettiva che è coerente con le dottrine del liberalismo «puro». Ma è – come si può capire – la nozione stessa di *funzione politica* ad aprire prospettive inimmaginabili, anche se l'idea della costituzione equilibrata rimane come limite e cornice generale.

77 Brunialti citerà De Reu, *Du pouvoir judiciaire dans le canton de Vaud*, Lausanne 1861, 7: «Eppure "non è possibile rilevare l'inconseguenza della maggior parte delle costituzioni per ciò che riguarda il potere giudiziario. Le relazioni e i discorsi degli oratori lo presentano come il palladio della libertà; poi dimenticano il punto di partenza e lo confinano in una sfera di azione isolata, nel diritto privato, quasi fosse nel meccanismo costituzionale elemento inutile, senza dirette relazioni cogli altri poteri dello Stato, che sono in costante rapporto tra loro"» (*Il diritto costituzionale*, cit., p. I, 319).

78 A. Brunialti, *La funzione politica*, cit., 417.

79 Si rinvia, in particolare, a M. Cappelletti, *Giudici irresponsabili?*, Milano 1988; *The Judicial Process in Comparative Perspective*, Oxford 1989; *Quis custodes custodiet? Etude de droit comparé sur la responsabilité des autorités judiciaires*, in *Le pouvoir des juges*, cit., 115 ss.; A. Giuliani, N. Picardi, *La responsabilità del giudice*, cit.; R. Guastini, *Le garanzie dei diritti costituzionali e la teoria dell'interpretazione*, in *Analisi e diritto 1990*, Torino 1990, 113–114.

80 L'influenza di Laboulaye è ancora una volta percepibile. Cfr. *Histoire des Etats-Unis*, cit., 496–497, sulla funzione moderatrice della giurisdizione nel regime democratico.

Argumente, Klischees und Ideologien: Das „französische Verwaltungsmodell“ und die italienische Rechtskultur im 19. Jahrhundert

1. Die „Modelle“, die kulturellen Beziehungen und die Geschichte der Verwaltungssysteme

Die italienische Rechtsentwicklung des 19. Jahrhunderts wird üblicherweise in zwei Phasen unterteilt: eine erste, längere Phase, in der der französische Einfluß vorherrschte, und eine zweite, in der in zunehmendem Maße Deutschland zum Vorbild wurde. Diese Schematisierung gründet sich auf eine Einteilung nach den übernommenen Ideen, dem Gebrauch von „Modellen“, „Idealtypen“ und mehr oder weniger ideologischer Interpretation. Die „Modelle“ versuchen ein System, eine Institution oder eine Regel in „objektiver“ Weise zu verallgemeinern, um auf diese Weise die Wege der Imitation, Rezeption, „Transplantation“ und des Austausches zu untersuchen. Allerdings sind die damit verbundenen möglichen Schwierigkeiten und besonders die unvermeidlichen Vereinfachungen bekannt.

Ein Historiker, der die Beziehungen zwischen den nationalen Rechtssystemen des 19. Jahrhunderts untersuchen will, ist also zu methodologischer Vorsicht angehalten. Diese Zurückhaltung darf auch bei demjenigen nicht fehlen, der – wie in unserem Fall – einige Gesichtspunkte der kulturellen Bande erläutern will, die Italien im Laufe des 19. Jahrhunderts im Bereich der Verwaltungsinstitutionen und der Verwaltungsrechtswissenschaft mit Frankreich verbunden haben – oder auch nicht. Die Frage nach dieser Partnerschaft bezieht sich nicht wie üblich – sozusagen „klassischerweise“ – auf das 19. Jahrhundert als Jahrhundert des *Code civil*, sondern als Jahrhundert der Institutionen, der Justiz und des Verwaltungsrechts, das sich in vielfacher Hinsicht als widersprüchlich und paradox erweist.

Kann man hier von einem einheitlichen „französischen Modell“ ausgehen und für das 19. Jahrhundert als Abgrenzungskriterium die Ereignisse der italienischen Geschichte heranziehen? Diese Frage kann man berechtigter- und begründeterweise stellen, aber sie abstrakt zu beantworten, würde bedeuten, dem vorgegebenen und vorhersehbaren Bild französischen Einflusses und italienischer Rezeption verhaftet zu bleiben.

Die Frage, ob ein „französisches Rechtsmodell" existiert, oder besser, ob man dieses Modell einheitlich definieren kann, ist alt. Sicherlich wechseln die Perspektiven je nach Fachrichtung, dem politischen und sozialen Kontext und den untersuchten Zeiträumen. Lange sah man im *Code Napoléon* das Ereignis, das die Bildung des „Modells" am stärksten geprägt und die Entwicklung in Italien beeinflußt hat.[1] Aber so bedeutend dieses Ereignis für die Rechts-, Politik- und Sozialgeschichte gewesen ist, für das angebliche „Modell" reicht es nicht aus. Der Bereich der Verwaltung und des Verwaltungsrechts ist viel zu sehr fragmentarisch und blieb unberührt von dieser Kodifikation, die sich als gelungene Synthese aus Elementen römischer Rechtstradition und den Grundlagen des moderneren naturrechtlichen Systems, aus nationalem Recht und einigen universalistischen Prinzipien, aus dem Ziel politischer Emanzipation der Gesellschaft und dem mäßigenden Einfluß der herrschenden Klassen präsentierte. Die verwaltungsrechtliche Diskussion hat keine solchen tragfähigen Bezugspunkte. Möglicherweise ist es deshalb schwieriger, darin paradigmatische Gesichtspunkte sowie die Parallelen und Rezeptionswege aufzudecken.

2. Das „französische Modell" in Italien: kultureller Eklektizismus und wissenschaftliche Autonomie

Mit der französischen Herrschaft in Italien[2] vom Ende des 18. Jahrhunderts bis zur napoleonischen Epoche wurde ein eigenes Organisationssystem im Bereich

1 Vgl. G. Astuti, *Il Code Napoléon in Italia e la sua influenza sui codici degli Stati italiani successori*, in *Tradizione romanistica e civiltà giuridica europea*, Neapel 1984, Bd. 2, 711–802; P. Ungari, *L'età del codice civile. Lotta per la codificazione e scuole di giurisprudenza nel Risorgimento*, Neapel 1967; R. Sacco, *Modèles français et modèles allemands dans le droit civil italien*, in *Revue internationale de droit comparé*, 2, 1976, 225–234; C. Ghisalberti, *Unità nazionale e unificazione giuridica in Italia. La codificazione del diritto nel Risorgimento*, Bari 1979, 132 ff.; M.T. Napoli, *La cultura giuridica in Italia. Repertorio delle opere tradotte nel secolo XIX*, Neapel 1987, Bd. 1, 38 ff.; A. Cavanna, *L'influence juridique française en Italie au XIXe siècle*, in *Revue historique des Facultés de droit et de la science juridique*, 15, 1994, 87–112; sowie den Band: R. Schulze (Hg.), *Französisches Zivilrecht in Europa während des 19. Jahrhunderts*, Berlin 1994.

2 Zu den grundlegenden Aspekten vgl. C. Capra, *L'età rivoluzionaria e napoleonica in Italia, 1796–1815*, Turin 1978; J. Godechot, *Originalità e imitazione nelle istituzioni italiane d'epoca giacobina e napoleonica*, in *Dagli Stati preunitari d'antico regime all'unificazione*, N. Raponi (Hg.), Bologna 1981, 191–205; C. Zaghi, *L'Italia di Napoleone dalla Cisalpina al Regno*, Turin 1986; Ch. Dipper/W. Schieder/R. Schulze (Hg.), *Napoleonische Herrschaft in Deutschland und Italien – Verwaltung und Justiz*, Berlin 1995.

der politischen und administrativen Institutionen eingeführt. Frankreichs militärische Macht, der abstrakte Charakter des Rationalismus, die Werte und Mythen der Revolution, die sich wechselseitig beeinflußten, prägten auf Dauer die Realität jedes einzelnen der italienischen Staaten. Das Verwaltungssystem, ohne jeden Zweifel extrem unitarisch und zentralistisch, sollte eine buntgewürfelte Mischung aus Traditionen, Kulturen und besonderen Erfahrungen ersetzen. Die Verfassungen, das Gesetz vom 28. Pluviôse des Jahres VIII und der *Code civil* – hierin bestanden die Pfeiler der staatlichen Neuordnung.

Das napoleonische System gründete sich im einzelnen auf eine zentralisierte Verwaltung mit hierarchischer und bürokratischer Aufgabenverteilung und auf den *Code civil*, der den „verfassungsmäßigen" Spielraum der Autonomie der bürgerlichen Gesellschaft verwirklichen sollte. Die Zentralisierung der Verwaltung, die staatliche Intervention bis hinein in unterste Ebenen, die Rationalisierung von Verwaltungsmechanismus und Institutionen, die sicherlich auch dem *Ancien Régime* nicht unbekannt waren, gehörten zu den bedeutendsten Elementen der napoleonischen Maßnahmen. Das Bild einer kompakten, als Pyramide aufgebauten Verwaltung, die – nach der berühmten Metapher von Roederer und Chaptal – Gesetz und die Regierungsanordnungen über eine Vollzugskette bis in die letzten Verzweigungen des Gesellschaftssystems mit der Geschwindigkeit elektrischen Stroms ausführen sollte, veranschaulicht die Vorstellung eines Vorgehens, das einheitlich, stark, effektiv und weitverzweigt sein sollte.

Diese und einige andere Merkmale lassen den Umriß dessen erkennen, was man für gewöhnlich das „französische Verwaltungsmodell" nennt. Das zwischen 1800 und 1870 verbreitete Bild eines Italien, das sich dem französischen Einfluß öffnete, hat – soviel ist sicher – seine Ursprünge im napoleonischen Italien. Aber erst im Laufe der folgenden Jahrzehnte läßt sich die Verwurzelung der Institutionen nach französischem Muster in ihrem ganzen Ausmaß erkennen. Ein Urteil darüber kann hier nur partiell und begrenzt erfolgen, auch wenn versucht wird, die Hauptlinien dieser Entwicklung zu erfassen.

Die Rezeption im institutionellen Bereich bezog sich nicht auf das ganze „Modell", sondern nur auf einige seiner Mechanismen. Seit der Restauration konnte diese Rezeption keinen ideologischen Charakter mehr besitzen, sondern zeichnete sich durch pragmatische und funktionelle Aspekte aus. Einige Herrscher der Restaurationszeit faßten den Entschluß, bestimmte institutionelle Elemente des französischen Systems zu bewahren oder zu übernehmen, weil sie die Überlegenheit seiner Rationalität und Effizienz schätzten. Man darf nicht vergessen, daß die intellektuellen Gesellschaftsschichten ebenso wie die Schichten, die für einige der revolutionären Prinzipien empfänglich waren, glaubten, daß die französischen Reformen Mittel zur Verwirklichung der aufklärerischen Reformbestrebungen waren, vor allem im Hinblick auf die politische Zentralisierung, das Prinzip der Gewaltenteilung und den Kampf gegen die Kleinstaaterei.

Während der Restauration wurden die politisch-ideologischen Aspekte dieser Reformbestrebungen zurückgewiesen und bekämpft, doch „moltissime sono le istituzioni utili", die bewahrt werden sollten, wie Donato Tommasi an Ferdinand de Bourbon schrieb.[3] Auf diese Weise konnte einiges vom französischen Erbe auf die Institutionen einiger Staaten der Voreinheitszeit übergehen, dies allerdings nicht als Teile eines „Modells", da hierfür ein ausdrücklicher politischer Wille erforderlich gewesen wäre. Nicht zufällig haben die Modernisierungsmechanismen der administrativen und konsultativen Monarchie mit Modifikationen, Anpassungen und Verbesserungen[4] überlebt, auch wenn die Verfassungsstruktur verschwand. Die „Organtransplantation" war in einer Phase der Kompromisse bei denjenigen Institutionen erfolgreich, die mit der administrativen Monarchie „kompatibel" waren.

Es ist sicherlich nicht leicht, Ausmaß und Effektivität dieser pragmatischen Rezeption zu beurteilen. Einige Staaten bewahrten die Merkmale des Polizeistaats nach österreichischem Vorbild, andere übernahmen einige typische Elemente des Rechtsstaats, in anderen wiederum blieb, wie bereits gesagt, der französische Einfluß vorherrschend. Die Verwaltungsorganisation des Königreichs Beider Sizilien ist dafür ein bezeichnendes Beispiel. Die Einrichtung der Verwaltungsgerichtsbarkeit, deren Grundlagen 1817 geschaffen wurden,[5] hatte

3 Vgl. R. Feola, *La monarchia amministrativa. Il sistema del contenzioso nelle Sicilie*, Neapel 1984, 143.

4 C. Ghisalberti, *Contributi alla storia delle amministrazioni preunitarie*, Mailand 1963; G. Landi, *L'influenza della legislazione e della tradizione napoleonica sugli organi di giustizia amministrativa e di controllo degli Stati italiani*, in *Atti del Convegno Napoleone e l'Italia*, Rom 1973, 157–172; R. Moscati. *La tradizione dell'accentramento napoleonico negli Stati italiani della Restaurazione*, ebd., 265 ff.; C. Ghisalberti, *Der Einfluß des napoleonischen Frankreichs auf das Verfassungs- und Verwaltungssystem Italiens*, in *Deutschland und Italien im Zeitalter Napoleons*, A. von Reden-Dohna (Hg.), Wiesbaden 1975; ders., *Dall'antico regime al 1848*, Bari, 1978; G. Galasso, *La nuova borghesia, la „monarchia amministrativa" e i governi restaurati*, in *Dagli Stati preunitari* ... (Fn. 2), 207–222; R. Feola (Fn. 3); E. Rotelli, P. Aimo, *Il sistema napoleonico del contenzioso amministrativo dalla Francia all'Italia*, in *Amministrare*, 1, 1990, 5–21; P. Aimo, *Le origini della giustizia amministrativa. Consigli di prefettura e Consiglio di Stato nell'Italia napoleonica*, Mailand 1990.

5 Über die Verwaltungsgerichtsbarkeit im Königreich Beider Sizilien vgl. C. Ghisalberti, *Per la storia del contenzioso amministrativo nel Regno meridionale*, in *Contributi alla storia* (Fn. 4), 67–144; G. Landi, *Istituzioni di diritto pubblico del Regno delle Due Sicilie (1815–1861)*, Mailand 1977, Bd. 2, 938 ff.; R. Feola (Fn. 3); L. Mannori, *I contenziosi amministrativi degli Stati preunitari italiani e il modello francese. Riflessioni e spunti per un possibile studio comparato*, in *Jahrbuch für europäische Verwaltungsgeschichte*, 2, 1990, 139–171.

unter anderem das Ziel, dem einzelnen weitestgehende Garantien im Konflikt mit der Staatsgewalt zu gewähren. Das hatte deutliche Auswirkungen in einem Staat, der die Verwaltung zum Hauptinstrument der Regierung sowie zur sozialen Schlichtung gemacht hatte. Das Vorbild der französischen Epoche hatte sicherlich Bedeutung, doch ist die Verwaltungsgerichtsbarkeit von 1817 in ihrer Funktionalität und ihren Garantieerklärungen weit über die Errungenschaften der napoleonischen Epoche hinausgegangen.

In diesem Zusammenhang muß auch die frühe Entwicklung der modernen Verwaltungsrechtswissenschaft in Italien hervorgehoben werden. Giandomenico Romagnosi veröffentlichte 1814 in Mailand die *Principi fondamentali di diritto amministrativo onde tesserne le istituzioni.*[6] Der Gebrauch des Begriffs „Verwaltungsrecht" ist bedeutsam in einem Werk, das neben der Kenntnis des französischen Diskussionsstands – in gewisser Hinsicht – auch neue Konzeptionen und bemerkenswerten Weitblick offenbart. Das Werk Romagnosis zeugt von dialektischer Vorgehensweise, kultivierter Rezeption und origineller Umsetzung. Hier vermutet man das Echo der französischen Juristen – Merlin, Bonnin, Locré, Jourdain usw. –, die sich bereits mit der Beziehung zwischen „politischer Form" und Verwaltungsrecht befaßt hatten, doch ist die französische Rechtskultur immer sorgfältig innerhalb der umfassenden Wahrnehmung des großen lombardischen Juristen unterschieden worden. Aus dieser Perspektive läßt sich selbst das neapolitanische Gesetz über die Verwaltungsgerichtsbarkeit (21. März 1817) nur dann wirklich verstehen, wenn man den Einfluß von Romagnosis frühzeitigen Überlegungen zur Trennung von aktiven Verwaltungsorganen und Organen der Verwaltungsjustiz berücksichtigt. Und dabei darf man nicht vergessen, daß das Werk Romagnosis und die neapolitanischen Reformen den ersten großen Werken von De Cormenin, De Gérando und Macarel vorausgegangen sind.

So beeinflußten sich die juristische Diskussion in der Lombardei und das Werk des süditalienischen Gesetzgebers gegenseitig; auf dieselbe Weise erweiterte die Blüte der napoleonischen Verwaltungswissenschaft den Horizont um eine reichhaltige Arbeit von hohem Niveau. Die Rechtsentwicklung in jedem Staat der Voreinigungszeit läßt sich nicht nur auf ein patriotisches Bewußtsein zurückführen;[7] dahinter verbirgt sich möglicherweise auch die Neigung eines

6 Über den Rechtspublizisten Romagnosi vgl. den grundlegenden Beitrag von L. Mannori, *Uno Stato per Romagnosi*. I. *Il progetto costituzionale*; II. *La scoperta del diritto amministrativo*, Mailand 1984–1987.

7 Niccola Nicolini schrieb 1812: „Non è già che io non tenga in alta venerazione i nomi di Locré, di Merlin, di Sirey. Ma noi, prima delle leggi nuove, non eravamo certo senza leggi né giurisprudenza" (N. Nicolini, *Della corte suprema di giustizia nelle sue relazioni con le antiche istituzioni del Regno. Discorso* [...], Neapel 1841 (1812)).

großen Teils der italienischen Rechtskultur, sich an der gerade herrschenden institutionellen Kultur zu orientieren: Man favorisiert ein gemäßigtes Programm,[8] einen Eklektizismus[9] französischer Herkunft, der indessen mit der italienischen Situation übereinstimmen muß.

Das „französische Modell“ steht im Zusammenhang mit der kulturellen Hegemonie einer Sprache, einer Literatur und einer Welt voller symbolischer Bezüge. Die juristische Literatur, mit dem Neapel der Restauration als Zentrum der italienischen Rechtskultur, zeugte vom französischen Einfluß – und sei es nur hinsichtlich ihrer Dimensionen – besonders im Bereich der exegetischen Kommentare, der Arbeit der Anwälte und der Rechtsprechungsanalyse. Doch war die Hauptstadt des Königreichs Beider Sizilien in Italien auch einflußreichstes Zentrum von Historismus, Hegelianismus und Staatsphilosophie. Übersetzungen, kulturelle Betrachtungen waren nicht wortgetreu, tendierten vielmehr dazu, die Originale nach einem bestimmten Plan zu „verraten“.[10] In Neapel übersetzte man Bonnin, Dalloz, Sirey, De Gérando und Macarel,[11] doch die große Masse der süditalienischen Verwaltungsrechtswissenschaftler interessierte sich offenbar zumeist für das französische „politische Projekt“, das auf Übereinstimmung und mögliche „Kontinuität“ hinsichtlich der Reformen des 18. Jahrhunderts hin untersucht wurde.

Das Werk Giovanni Mannas,[12] des größten neapolitanischen Verwaltungsrechtswissenschaftlers, spiegelt diese Haltung deutlich wider: Die Verwaltungs-

8 Victor Molinier bemerkte 1842: „L'Italie, cette terre toujours féconde en hautes intelligences, qui cultive la science avec amour, nous offrira des hommes trop peu connus en France, et dont les travaux peuvent être placés en face de ceux qu'a produits l'Allemagne. Pendant que l'école de Paris vulgarise les doctrines toujours exactes mais souvent sèches et nébuleuses de la Germanie, il nous conviendrait, à nous hommes du midi, d'importer en France de l'Italie». (*Cours d'introduction générale à l'étude du droit. Discours d'ouverture*, in *Revue de législation et de jurisprudence*, 15, 1842, 365–386).

9 Zu den unterschiedlichen Aspekten vgl. E. Genta, *Eclettismo giuridico della Restaurazione*, in *Studi in onore di Mario E. Viora*, Rom 1989, 351–375.

10 P. Beneduce, *„Traduttore-traditore“. Das französische Zivilrecht in Italien in den Handbüchern der Rechtswissenschaft und -praxis*, in *Französisches Zivilrecht* (Fn. 1), 205–248. Im Bereich des Verwaltungsrechts spricht Francesco Dias bezeichnenderweise von der „Notwendigkeit der Bücherpiraterie […]“ (*Corso completo di diritto amministrativo ovvero esposizione delle leggi relative all'amministrazione civile ed al contenzioso amministrativo*, Neapel 1854, Bd. 1, XII. Zu diesem Aspekt vgl. L. Martone, *La scienza amministrativa nel Regno delle Due Sicilie (1815–1848). Diritto e politica*, in *Rivista trimestrale di diritto pubblico*, 30, 1980, 1068, der als Ahnherren der „Bücherpiraterie“ den gemäßigten Nicola Comerci nennt.

11 Vgl. M.T. Napoli (Fn. 1), 126 ff.

12 Vgl. G. Rebuffa, *La formazione del diritto amministrativo in Italia. Profili di amministrativisti preorlandiani*, Bologna 1981, 33 ff.; O. Abbamonte, *Potere pubblico e*

tätigkeit wurde als bevorzugtes Instrument betrachtet, um die letzten Überreste des Feudalsystems zu beseitigen, wirtschaftliche Expansion zu garantieren, den neuen Klassen Freiräume zu gewähren und die formell absolutistischen Züge des Staates einzuschränken, ohne den gefährlichen Weg des Konstitutionalismus gehen zu müssen.

Hervorzuheben ist noch ein weiterer bedeutender Aspekt, der vielfältige Auswirkungen auf die spätere Entwicklung hatte. Was beim „französischen Verwaltungsmodell" ins Auge fällt, sind die „politischen" Elemente des Bruchs mit dem *Ancien Régime*, aber das heißt nicht, daß das „Modell" zum Vorbild juristischer Projekte genommen wurde. Das „französische Modell" war vor allem als generelles Schema von Bedeutung, um den Entstehungsprozeß des modernen Staats zu erklären.[13] Das französische Verwaltungsrecht konnte zwar Anregungen und Stoff zum Nachdenken liefern, doch läßt sich ihm gegenüber in Italien eine Haltung erkennen, die man als motivierten Skeptizismus bezeichnen konnte. Die französischen Juristen befaßten sich entweder mit der Gesetzeskommentierung oder mit der Suche nach Prinzipien und Kriterien dogmatischer Klassifizierung.[14] Demgegenüber schenkten die italienischen Juristen gegen Mitte des Jahrhunderts – unter ihnen besonders Giovanni Manna – dem geltenden Recht und der nationalen Rechtsprechung, die gegenüber der französischen deutlich weniger Prestige und Bedeutung hatte, weniger Aufmerksamkeit. Manna schrieb: „Per lo che senza far menzione alcuna di questo o di quell'altro diritto positivo, né dell'amministrazione di questa o di quell'altra nazione, ci faremo a descrivere la indole invariabile di ciascuna delle tre parti dell'amministrazione generale, secondo che sorge dell'essenza e dallo scopo ultimo di ogni società politica."[15] Das Verwaltungsrecht, das sich in den italienischen Staaten gerade festigte, entfernte sich *de facto* vom sogenannten „französischen Modell", es war im Vergleich zu demjenigen jenseits der Alpen weniger praxisorientiert und konkret, stärker der Lehre und der „Philosophie" und weitaus weniger der Rechtsprechung verpflichtet.

Kommentare zu jedem Gesetz fehlten auch in Italien nicht – man denke zum Beispiel an die neapolitanische Literatur zur Verwaltungsgerichtsbarkeit. Doch fehlte im noch nicht vereinigten Italien die Verwaltungsorganisation, mit der man in Frankreich bereits Erfahrung hatte, insbesondere im Bereich der Ver-

privata autonomia. Giovanni Manna e la scienza amministrativa nel Mezzogiorno, Neapel 1991.

13 Diese Sichtweise wird auch von anderen süditalienischen Schriftstellern geteilt, wie z. B. G. Rocco, *Corso di diritto amministrativo*, Neapel 1850–1856, 3 Bde.

14 Einen Überblick bietet L. Lacchè, *L'espropriazione per pubblica utilità. Amministratori e proprietari nella Francia dell'Ottocento*, Mailand 1995, 90 ff.

15 G. Manna, *Principii di diritto amministrativo*, Neapel 1876 (1860), Bd. 1, 60.

waltungsjustiz.[16] Den in genügender Zahl vorhandenen italienischen Juristen fehlte es folglich zur erforderlichen Klarheit und Effektivität in ihrem Rechtssystem und ihrer Rechtsterminologie – von begrenzten Ausnahmen abgesehen – an der unerläßlichen Unterstützung durch Rechtsinstitutionen.

3. Die Ideologie des „Negativmodells" oder eine falsche Zielscheibe

Gerade der fragmentarische Charakter der Rezeption des „französischen Modells" in Italien hatte trotz der weiten Verbreitung der französischen Literatur und Rechtsprechung eine fortschreitende Distanzierung zur Folge. Wenn Frankreich, wie Meucci schrieb, diejenige Nation war, „da cui noi derivammo la generalità delle nostre istituzioni amministrative [...]",[17] und wenn in einigen Staaten der Voreinigungszeit die kulturelle Hegemonie Frankreichs noch mit dem Glauben an die Überwindung des absolutistischen Staates verbunden war, schien dieser Einfluß mit dem Übergang zum Einheitsstaat endgültig zum Niedergang verurteilt zu sein. „Quanto alle istituzioni dell'amministrazione centrale, il sistema di egemonia seguito nella istaurazione del regno portò di necessità l'applicazione de' sistemi francesi, adottati già nella legislazione sarda, ma che ora si vanno modificando sotto l'influenza delle idee e delle tradizione nazionali e sotto quello della opportunità locale [...]."[18]

Das „französische Modell" wurde sogar für einige der einflußreichsten Verwaltungsrechtswissenschaftler zum Negativmodell. Die Gründe für diese Haltung sind vielfältig. Insbesondere zeigt sich darin die Tendenz, die italienischen Institutionen als aus den französischen Institutionen abgeleitete Erscheinungen zu betrachten und damit die Fehler der Gesetzgebung und der nationalen Verwaltungsorganisation der Rezeption des „französischen Modells" anzulasten. Die „Prototypen" wurden in Erinnerung gerufen, um zunächst den „Ausdehnungs"-Prozeß des piemontesischen Systems auf die alten Staaten der Voreinigungsszeit und ferner die Gesetzgebung des vereinigten Italien zu kritisieren. Das piemontesische System wurde zumindest teilweise als „Kopie" des französischen Systems betrachtet, ohne daß die „nationalen" Entwicklungen und der wirkliche Einfluß der „Modelle" richtig bewertet worden wären.[19]

16 M. S. Giannini, *Profili storici della scienza del diritto amministrativo*, in *Quaderni fiorentini per la storia del pensiero giuridico moderno*, 2, 1973, 222.

17 L. Meucci, *Istituzioni di diritto amministrativo*, 4. Aufl., Turin 1898 (1. Aufl. 1879), 12. Zu Meucci vgl. G. Rebuffa (Fn. 12), 173 ff.

18 L. Meucci (Fn. 17), 17.

19 Vgl. A. Petracchi, *Le origini dell'ordinamento comunale e provinciale italiano. Storia della legislazione piemontese sugli enti locali dalla fine dell'antico regime al chiudersi dell'età cavouriana (1770–1861)*, Venedig 1962, Bd. 1, 383–384.

Aber was wurde an den französischen Verwaltungsinstitutionen (und indirekt an den italienischen Institutionen) kritisiert? Eine kleine Bestandsaufnahme davon findet sich etwa im Werk De Gioannis Gianquintos. Die ausländischen Modelle entsprächen nicht „all'indole della nostrana civiltà", betont der sardische Jurist, sie seien „mal conformi al carattere italiano".[20] Der „juristische Nationalismus" habe leichtes Spiel, wenn man sich an die Vortrefflichkeit der römischen Rechtstradition erinnere; unter Berufung auf den Historismus Savignys betrachtete er das Rechtssystem als Ergebnis eines langsamen, organischen Entwicklungsprozesses.[21] Der Eklektizismus[22] sei demgegenüber eine Schwächeerscheinung. „[...] L'Ordinamento d'Italia debbe avere un proprio tipo ideale, dev'essere una cosa viva e nostrana, non già un affastellamento di ciarpe esotiche [...] Nel sistema francese domina troppo la onnipotenza dello Stato: v'ha troppo d'ingerimento del potere centrale, v'ha troppo di unità assorbente, troppo di sindacato, sotto la cui bella vita individua [...]".[23] „La centralizzazione è la Francia [...]",[24] fügte Gianquinto hinzu und meinte damit, daß diese kein Vorbild für Italien sein könne. Der administrative Despotismus, die fehlende Verantwortlichkeit der Beamten und die Verwaltungsgerichtsbarkeit seien nur unvermeidbare Folgen der Zentralisierung.

Aus den Worten Gianquintos lassen sich unschwer einige Ansichten französischer Liberaler, insbesondere Tocquevilles, heraushören „La centralizzazione ... puro gallicismo [...]":[25] Damit berief er sich auf eine genau bestimmte

20 G. de Gioannis Gianquinto, *Corso di diritto pubblico amministrativo ...*, Pisa 1877, Bd. 1, IX. 1864 hielt Gianquinto an der Universität von Pavia eine Antrittsvorlesung mit dem Titel: *Diritto amministrativo d'Italia informato al carattere nazionale, e necessità di emanciparne la sposizione teorica dalle influenze prevalenti de' metodi stranieri*, Pavia 1864. Vgl. G. Rebuffa (Fn. 12), 73 ff.

21 „Il diritto è un organismo, né già un artificioso meccanismo" (G. de Gioannis Gianquinto (Fn. 20), XXXI).

22 „E fin quando eclettici fra le leggi amministrative del Belgio e della Francia, tentammo accoppiare alcuni instituiti della liberta provinciale del primo con principii di concentramento dell'altra, riuscimmo più liberali, ma meno logici dei Francesi, più avviluppati e meno sinceri dei Belgi! E non copiammo noi dalla Costituzione Francese dell'anno VIII, che minava di già i fondamenti della pubblica libertà, la guarentigia costituzionale dei pubblici funzionari? [...] Noi venimmo in tali tempi, e in tali viviamo, che il diritto amministrativo italiano sia addivenuto come stanza dell'usuraio, in che tu vedi schierati i pegni d'ogni fatta di persone e stati [...] Vergogniamoci, Italiani, figli dell'antica terra classica del diritto, di rifare le nostre leggi amministrative scimmiottando i Codici stranieri! [...]" (ebd., X–XI). Eine gemäßigtere Haltung vertrat Saverio Scolari, *Del diritto amministrativo*. 2. Aufl., Pisa 1866.

23 G. de Gioannis Gianquinto (Fn. 20), LI.

24 Ebd., XLVI.

25 Ebd., XLIII.

Genealogie. Der Verwaltungsdespotismus, der nach Ansicht Tocquevilles[26] mit einem Repräsentativsystem auf der Basis von Freiheit und Gesetz unvereinbar sei, schien das Übel zu sein, das in Italien das liberale Konzept zu entstellen drohte. Mythische Überhöhung der alten örtlichen und städtischen Autonomie, stereotype und oberflächliche Verherrlichung des englischen *self-government*, ein illusionärer *proprio tipo ideale* der neuen Staatsorganisation wie auch eine eigene Konzeption der Institutionen und des Verwaltungsrechts waren in dieser Art von Pamphlet enthalten. Tocqueville hatte andererseits die „Besonderheit" des französischen Verwaltungsrechts scharf kritisiert,[27] indem er maßlos übertrieben dessen „autoritäre" Zuge hervorhob, ohne auf der anderen Seite die gleichwohl existierenden „Garantien" und die verdienstvolle Arbeit des *Conseil d'État* zu würdigen.

Die Rezeption Tocquevilles trug zur Entstehung einer sehr ideologischen und „negativen" Deutung dessen bei, was der Aristokrat aus der Normandie als „une des formes de l'État nouveau du monde" bezeichnet hatte.[28] Diese Deutung fand in Italien großen Anklang. Die Kritik am Zentralismus und an der gleichmacherischen Tendenz des Einheitsstaats gründete sich auf der Analyse der positiven Gesetzgebung. Dies führte zu einer sonderbaren Kluft zwischen bestehendem Verwaltungssystem (dem „realen" System von 1860 bis 1870) und dem „Idealtypus" der Verwaltung.

Das Verwaltungsrecht, so wie es in den meisten Arbeiten der italienischen Juristen behandelt wurde,[29] sollte eher der Beschränkung staatlicher Macht und der Wahrung der Privatinteressen als der Legitimation staatlicher Machtansprüche dienen. Es handelte sich um ein „privates" Verwaltungsrecht,[30] nicht so sehr wegen seines konzeptionellen Aufbaus,[31] sondern vielmehr wegen seiner Tendenz, insbesondere in Fragen der Wirtschaftsfreiheit das System der Prinzipien und Regeln, die für sämtliche öffentlichen und privaten Rechtssubjekte

26 Vgl. besonders seinen Bericht für die *Académie des sciences morales et politiques* über das Buch von M. Macarel, *Cours de droit administratif*, in *Etudes économiques, politiques et littéraires*, Paris 1866, Bd. 9.

27 Im Sog der französischen liberalen Tradition. Vgl. L. Lacchè, *Regard Outre-Manche. Le jury spécial d'expropriation et les logiques du droit administratif français au début du XIXe siècle*, in *Jahrbuch für europäische Verwaltungsgeschichte*, 8, 1996, 135–151.

28 A. de Tocqueville (Fn. 26).

29 Jedoch mit einigen wichtigen Ausnahmen, wie etwa das Werk Giuseppe Mantellinis. Vgl. G. Rebuffa (Fn. 12), 117 ff.

30 Ebd., S. 15 ff. Einen Überblick bietet G. Azzariti, *Dalla discrezionalità al potere*, Padua 1989.

31 Vgl. S. Cassese, *Le basi del diritto amministrativo*, Turin 1989, 44; M. D'Alberti, *Diritto amministrativo comparato. Trasformazioni dei sistemi amministrativi in Francia, Gran Bretagna, Stati Uniti, Italia*, Bologna 1992, 126.

gelten sollen, aus dem Gemeinen Recht abzuleiten. Gleichrangigkeit, konzeptionelle „Stabilität“, ein universaler Anspruch und die Idee von möglichst wenig Staat wurden gegen die Idee eines „willkürlichen“, instabilen[32] und asymmetrischen Verwaltungsrechts und die Konzeption eines „Eingriffs“-Staats ins Feld geführt.

Am Beispiel der „Justiz in der Verwaltung“[33] wird deutlich, wie widersprüchlich die Haltung des Gesetzgebers und der italienischen Juristen gegenüber dem „französischen Modell“ war. Die Juristen und Politiker, die 1865 für die Aufhebung der Verwaltungsgerichtsbarkeit kämpften, setzten italienische und französische Gerichtsbarkeit gleich, kannten also offensichtlich nicht die Unterschiede zwischen beiden Systemen. Dazu zählte vor allem die bedeutende Rolle, die der Staatsrat in Frankreich zwischen Julimonarchie und Zweitem Kaiserreich beim Aufbau eines immer effektiveren und „umfassenderen“ Systems zur Wahrung der Einzelinteressen in den Auseinandersetzungen mit der öffentlichen Gewalt spielte.[34]

Die Einführung des *juge unique* 1865 – nach dem „belgischen Modell“[35] – schien mit den Ansichten der herrschenden Lehre übereinzustimmen. Doch in Wirklichkeit hatten der Gesetzgeber wie auch die Rechtswissenschaft nur eine oberflächliche und schematische Vorstellung vom Verwaltungsrecht jenseits der Alpen. Im Namen des liberalen Dogmas vom *juge unique* verwarf man 1865 ein System der Verwaltungsgerichtsbarkeit, dessen genaue Funktionsweise man gar nicht kannte. Dennoch verhinderte die Aufhebung der Verwaltungsgerichtsbarkeit nicht das Eindringen begrifflicher Kategorien, die vom französischen Staatsrat entwickelt worden waren.[36] Die Reform Crispis 1889–1890 sollte das Projekt von 1865 – das bereits von liberalen Juristen kritisiert wurde – vervoll-

32 „Mi sconfortava ancora più lo spettacolo della instabilità della nostrana legislazione amministrativa, addiventata quasi una tela di Penelope, che muta e rimuta gli ordinamenti e gl'istituti con un'altalena degnissima dei Francesi …“ (G. de Gioannis Gianquinto (Fn. 20), CXLVIII).

33 Vgl. besonders M. S. Giannini/A. Piras, *Giurisdizione amministrativa e giurisdizione ordinaria nei confronti della pubblica amministrazione*, in *Enciclopedia del diritto*, Mailand 1970, Bd. 19, 229 ff.; F. Benvenuti, *Giustizia amministrativa*, ebd., 589 ff.; S. Sambataro, *L'abolizione del contenzioso nel sistema di giustizia amministrativa*, Mailand 1977; B. Sordi, *Giustizia e amministrazione nell'Italia liberale. La formazione della nozione di interesse legittimo*, Mailand 1985; *Le riforme crispine*, Bd. 2, *Giustizia amministrativa*, Archivio I. S. A. P., n. s. 6, Mailand 1990, besonders L. Mannori, *L'influenza francese*, 575–616.

34 Vgl. P. Sandevoir, *Études sur le recours de pleine juridiction*, Paris 1964; F. Burdeau, *Histoire du droit administratif (de la Révolution au début des années 1970)*, Paris 1995.

35 Vgl. J.-C. Escarras, *Les expériences belge et italienne d'unité de juridiction*, Paris 1972.

36 M. S. Giannini (Fn. 16), 236.

ständigen, indem es die „gerichtliche“ Wahrung der „Interessen“ einer Abteilung des Staatsrats zuwies, der der Tradition des französischen Anfechtungsprozesses besonders verpflichtet war. Wenn sich daher das Reformprojekt Crispis auch theoretisch an den deutschen und österreichischen Modellen der frühen 70er Jahre orientierte, so hatte die 1890 eingeführte Ordnung viel mehr Gemeinsamkeiten mit dem französischen System. Kurzum, man konnte angesichts dieser kulturellen Orientierungsversuche sagen, daß man das eine wollte, während man *de facto* das andere tat, indem man vom französischen Modell nur einige Elemente übernahm und sich damit Probleme im Gesamtzusammenhang einhandelte.

Aufgrund ihrer Orientierung an der Vergangenheit zeichnete sich die Reform von 1890 durch einen vorhersehbaren kulturellen Rückstand aus: Sie führte einen beamteten Richter ein, mit einem unbestreitbar „administrativen“ Anklang und mit eigentümlich widersprüchlichen Befugnissen.[37] Gerade der „Verrat“ des (bereits mehrdeutigen) Systems von 1865 führte in Italien zum Bruch zwischen erklärten Zielen und erzielten Ergebnissen. Man hat zu Recht von dem „schlechten Gewissen“ der italienischen Juristen gesprochen, die die Probleme der Aufgabenverteilung durch die Wahrung des legitimen Interesses zu lösen versuchten,[38] d. h. auf einem dogmatischen Sonderweg, der den übrigen europäischen Verwaltungsstrukturen unbekannt war. Die Hypothek des liberalen Dogmas vom *juge unique* lastete auf dem Gewissen der Juristen in solchem Maße, daß sie als Zielscheibe ihrer Polemik das französische System wählten, das, wenn auch hintergründig,[39] zum konkreten Bezugspunkt geworden war.

4. Gegensätze und Vorbilder: „Politikbesessenheit“, die Wende durch Orlando und die juristische Methode

In der Zeit von 1800 bis 1870, die für gewöhnlich der kulturellen Hegemonie Frankreichs „zugerechnet“ wird, scheint der Einfluß des dort entwickelten „Modells“ – zumindest im Bereich der Institutionen und des Verwaltungsrechts – widersprüchlich und begrenzt zu sein.[40] Die Tatsache, daß ein Großteil der

37 Zu diesem Problemkreis vgl. die Beobachtungen von L. Mannori, *L'influenza francese* (Fn. 33), 596 ff.

38 B. Sordi, *Giustizia e amministrazione* (Fn. 33); ders., *Uno sguardo all'Europa: il legislatore del 1889 di fronte ai modelli continentali di giustizia amministrativa*, in *Studi per il Centenario della Quarta Sezione*, Rom 1989, 173–202.

39 Jedoch muß noch einmal auf den Ausnahmefall Giuseppe Mantellini hingewiesen werden. Vgl. G. Rebuffa (Fn. 12), 166; B. Sordi, *Giustizia e amministrazione* (Fn. 33), 177.

40 Vgl. dazu S. Cassese (Fn. 31), 15 ff.

Verwaltungsrechtswissenschaftler wie auch der Gesetzgeber selbst sich vor allem damit befaßt haben, das „französische Modell“ zu kritisieren, bisweilen die Ebene einfacher Rezeption zu betonen und die Tragweite anderer Umstände zu bagatellisieren oder gar zu leugnen, selbst wenn sie erwiesen und unleugbar war, scheint einzigartig zu sein und verdient besondere Aufmerksamkeit.

In den ersten Jahrzehnten nach der staatlichen Einigung neigten die liberalen Juristen dazu, die Unterschiede zwischen theoretischem Programm und erreichten Resultaten zu betonen, also enttäuscht auf die Distanz zwischen den Institutionen des neuen Staates und den Idealen der liberalen Doktrin hinzuweisen.[41] Das „französische Modell“ erschien vor allem aus dieser besonderen Sicht als negativ. Die Kritik am „Modell“, die meist stereotyp und ohne genauere Kenntnis der tatsächlichen Entwicklung in Frankreich geschah, beinhaltete eine mehr oder weniger versteckte Kritik an den italienischen Institutionen. In anderen Bereichen diente das konstitutionelle und parlamentarische System (der Julimonarchie) in Frankreich als Bezugspunkt und Bindeglied zu den Erfahrungen in England. Und man darf nicht die Rolle vergessen, die Frankreich unter Napoleon III auf militärischem und diplomatischem Gebiet im schwierigen Einigungsprozeß Italiens gespielt hat.

In den 70er und 80er Jahren des 19. Jahrhunderts läßt sich ein bedeutender Wandel in der italienischen Kultur und ihrer Einstellung gegenüber der französischen Kultur feststellen, der sich vor allem auf den politischen Bereich erstreckte. Auch diesmal wurde das „französische Modell“ zumeist als Negativmodell erwähnt, doch hatten sich Horizont und Perspektive grundlegend geändert. Nicht mehr die Zentralisierung bildete den Kern der Debatte, sondern das Verhältnis zwischen Recht und Politik, genauer gesagt zwischen Verwaltung, Politik und Parlamentarismus.

Die italienische Interpretation von Taine und Renan nahm eine kritische Haltung gegenüber Frankreich ein, das in weniger als einem Jahrhundert mehr als zehnmal seine Verfassung geändert hatte, ohne eine „dauerhafte“ Form zu finden.[42] Die Maßlosigkeit des allgemeinen Wahlrechts, der abstrakte, von Rousseau inspirierte Konstitutionalismus, die nationale Souveränität – kurzum, die Revolution, die nicht enden wollte – seien die tönernen Füße des französischen Giganten. Der französisch-preußische Krieg von 1870 habe die mangelnde Eignung Frankreichs, auch auf kulturellem Gebiet, bewiesen und umgekehrt

41 Über das Fehlen einer juristischen und politischen Kultur der herrschenden Klassen in Italien vgl. F. Benvenuti, *Mito e realtà nell'ordinamento amministrativo italiano*, und G. Miglio, *Le contraddizioni dello Stato unitario*, in *Unificazione amministrativa ed i suoi protagonisti*, F. Benvenuti / G. Miglio (Hg.), Vicenza 1969.

42 H. Taine, *Les origines de la France contemporaine. L'ancien régime*, Paris 1880, II. Vgl. besonders L. Mangoni, *Una crisi fine secolo. La cultura italiana e la Francia fra Otto e Novecento*, Turin 1985.

den endgültigen Aufstieg Deutschlands zur Großmacht besiegelt. Das Echo der französischen Niederlage war in Italien noch lange Zeit zu vernehmen.[43] Wie konnte Preußen in kurzer Zeit zur treibenden Kraft des deutschen Wiederaufstiegs werden? Diese Frage, die den gesamten kulturellen Bereich mitumfaßte, stellten sich viele Italiener. Man denke nur an die Pandektistik, den Kathedersozialismus, die Staatsphilosophie, die technologische Revolution und zahlreiche andere Erscheinungen.[44] Deutschland wurde zum Vorbild. Das Frankreich von 1870 – das Land der Kommune, der Dritten Republik – erschien als ein den Erschütterungen der „Demokratie" wehrlos ausgelieferter Staat. „[...] dopo aver reso all'Europa l'eminente servigio di svegliarla quando sonnecchiava, ora [Frankreich] la disturba col far fracasso mentre ella vuole studiare, lavorare, ordinarsi e progredire saggiamente." Die französische Hegemonie schien seitdem der Vergangenheit anzugehören. Es war Zeit, „l'ideale francese di un processo vorticoso, di una democrazia plebea" aufzugeben, um „lavorare di conserva colla Germania al trionfo della Democrazia armonica e del Progresso regolare".[45] Aus diesen Worten Nicola Marsellis, eines gebildeten Offiziers, läßt sich die Tragweite des Wandels ermessen. Wenn die *Destra storica* Cavours den politisch-konstitutionellen Idealen des französischen Mittelweges treu geblieben war, so wandte sich die *Sinistra* im Gegenzug sehr schnell und mit besonderer Aufmerksamkeit der deutschen Realpolitik zu. Der – antifranzösische – Dreibund-Vertrag von 1882 bestätigte die neue politische Hegemonie.

Im Modell „Deutschland" sah man Gegenpol und Alternative zum „französischen Modell". Unter den italienischen Juristen hat der junge sizilianische Professor Vittorio Emanuele Orlando[46] diese Vorstellung mit ausgesprochenem Scharfsinn beschrieben. Die zeitliche Abfolge ist wichtig. In den frühen 80er

43 Die Niederlage machte eine Befreiung Italiens von der politisch-militärischen „Vormundschaft" Frankreichs möglich. Vgl. dazu F. Chabod, *Storia della politica estera italiana dal 1870 al 1896*, Bari 1971, Bd. 1, 23 ff.

44 Zum Vordringen der deutschen Kultur in Italien vgl. S. Cassese, *Cultura e politica del diritto amministrativo*, Bologna 1971, 16 ff.; R. Romeo, *La Germania e la vita intellettuale italiana dall'Unità alla prima guerra mondiale* (1971), in *L'Italia e la prima guerra mondiale*, Bari 1978; G. Cianferotti, *Il pensiero di V. E. Orlando e la giuspubblicistica italiana fra Ottocento e Novecento*, Mailand 1980, 29 ff.; A. Massera, *L'influenza della cultura tedesca sulla prolusione orlandiana*, in *Rivista trimestrale di diritto pubblico*, 39, 1989, 937–967; B. Sordi. *L'influenza tedesca*, in *Le riforme crispine*, Bd. 2, *Giustizia amministrativa* (Fn. 33), 533–574; M.T. Napoli (Fn. 1), 8 ff.

45 N. Marselli, *Gli avvenimenti del 1870–71*, Turin 1871, Bd. 2, 208. Vgl. F. Chabod (Fn. 43), 36 ff.

46 Aufschlußreich ist der Vergleich der unterschiedlichen Beurteilungen von M. Fioravanti, *La vicenda intellettuale del ‚giovane' Orlando (1881–1897)*, Florenz 1979 und G. Cianferotti (Fn. 44).

Jahren entwickelte Orlando die Kerngedanken der Debatte: *La riforma elettorale* (1883), *La decadenza del sistema parlamentare* (1884) und *Studi giuridici sul governo parlamentare* (1886). Die Beiträge Orlandos betrafen den Kern einer Debatte mit weitaus größeren Dimensionen. Spaventa, Bonghi, Jacini, Minghetti, Mosca und Turiello befaßten sich, wie andere Autoren auch, mit denselben Problemen. Der Einfluß Renans und Bluntschlis auf den jungen Orlando ist besonders bemerkenswert. Die rein konstitutionelle Monarchie, die Ablehnung des Prinzips der Gewaltenteilung, die Kritik am allgemeinen Wahlrecht, an der zentralen Stellung des Parlaments und an der Rolle der Parteien bildeten Hauptthemen der Debatte. Bei diesen Themen nahm man, negativ, Bezug auf das „französische Modell" der Dritten Republik und, positiv, auf das Deutschland Bismarcks.[47] Wieder einmal verbarg sich hinter der Präsentation des französischen Modells ein ideologisches Ziel: Es war das „Antimodell". Ein Kapitel in einem der einflußreichsten Werke[48] von Rudolf von Gneist trägt die Überschrift „Die Negation des Rechtsstaats in dem Staatswesen Frankreichs". Durch die Regierung der Parteien, die parlamentarische Allmacht, die Ablehnung der Monarchie werde Frankreich in „politischer" Hinsicht geschwächt, da es der Gefahr einer absoluten Herrschaft ausgesetzt sei.

Die Bezugnahmen auf das „französische Modell" betrafen immer die revolutionären Prinzipien: das Dogma der Gewaltenteilung, die politische Vertretung, das Wahlrecht, das Versammlungsprinzip usw. Orlando schrieb, dasselbe „modello costituzionale inglese non era a noi pervenuto direttamente, ma attraverso il modo con cui era stato inteso (o frainteso) in Francia, a cominciare dall'esposizione fattane dal Montesquieu, per finire poi confuso e frammisto nel più complesso e paradossale conglomerato di dottrine, di scuole, di tendenze politiche che la storia ricordi, ed il cui urto determinò in Francia una dozzina di rivoluzioni in meno di un secolo!".[49] Orlando ist dem alten Thema der politischen Instabilität Frankreichs treu geblieben.

47 Ohne jedoch bestimmte wichtige konzeptionelle Unterschiede zu übersehen, vgl. G. Cianferotti (Fn. 44), 104 ff.

48 Der Rechtsstaat und die Verwaltungsgerichte in Deutschland, Nachdr. d. 3. Aufl. 1879, Darmstadt 1958, 158. Zum Einfluß Gneists in Italien vgl. B. Sordi, *Giustizia e amministrazione* (Fn. 33), 86–100; ders., *L'influenza tedesca* (Fn. 44), 540 ff. Allgemeiner sind die Beobachtungen von M. Fioravanti, *Giuristi e costituzione politica nell'Ottocento tedesco*, Mailand 1979, 213 ff.

49 V. E. Orlando, *Prefazione a Diritto pubblico generale. Scritti varii (1881–1940) coordinati in sistema*, Mailand 1954, XIV. Ein Vergleich zwischen den Ansichten Orlandos und einer Lesart der Französischen Revolution, wie sie von Carré de Malberg vorgeschlagen wurde, wäre interessant. Zur Verwaltungsdebatte im Frankreich der Dritten Republik vgl. den Überblick von H. S. Jones, *The French State in Question: Public Law and Political Argument in the Third Republic*, Cambridge 1993.

Die „Politikbesessenheit", die „demokratischen Exzesse", die „zügellose" Herrschaft von Volkssouveränität und sozialem Konflikt erhielten – im Laufe der 80er Jahre – ein Gegengewicht durch die Stärkung von Exekutive und Verwaltung. Und gerade die Verwaltung schien den Schlußstein des Rechtsstaats zu bilden, die einzige konkrete Antwort, die die Legitimierung der herrschenden Klassen ohne den Rückgriff auf das allgemeine Wahlrecht zuließ. Der „administrative Germanismus"[50] wurde zum Bezugsmodell, aber auch diesmal mit besonderen italienischen Abwandlungen und Ansichten, mit immer noch beachtlicher Kluft zwischen Ideologie und juristischer und institutioneller Praxis.

Nachdem die Ursachen der Krise – der Mangel an Zusammenhalt und Homogenität des neuen Staates – aufgedeckt worden waren, nachdem aufgrund klarer Entscheidungen Alternativmodelle ausgearbeitet worden waren, blieb die schwierige Arbeit der Schaffung und Verteidigung des „Rechtsstaates". Der junge Vittorio Emanuele Orlando gab diesem Programm seine endgültige Form. Dies läßt sich bereits in seinen Antrittsvorlesungen von 1885 und 1886 feststellen,[51] doch die eigentliche „orlandische Wende" leitete er 1889 mit seiner Antrittsvorlesung in Palermo ein. Sie trug den Titel: „I criteri tecnici per la ricostruzione giuridica del diritto pubblico".[52]

Das „Manifest" Orlandos interessiert uns hier besonders wegen seiner Bezüge zur französischen Verwaltungstradition. Das große Vorhaben der italienischen

50 Neben den bereits zitierten Werken vgl. C. Mozzarelli / S. Nespor, *Giuristi e scienze sociali nell'Italia liberale. Il dibattito sulla scienza dell'amministrazione e l'organizzazione dello Stato*, Padua 1981; P. Beneduce, *„Punto di vista amministrativo" e Stato di diritto: aspetti del germanesimo dei giuristi italiani alla fine dell'Ottocento*, in *Annali dell'Istituto storico italo-germanico in Trento*, 10, 1984, 119–194; B. Sordi, *Giustizia e amministrazione* (Fn. 33), 100 ff.; sowie den Sammelband *Deutsche Rechtswissenschaft und Staatslehre im Spiegel der italienischen Rechtskultur während der zweiten Hälfte des 19. Jahrhunderts*, R. Schulze (Hg.), Berlin 1990.

51 *Ordine giuridico e ordine politico*, Antrittsvorlesung an der Universität von Modena vom 4. Dezember 1885; *Sulla necessità di una ricostruzione giuridica del Diritto Costituzionale*, Antrittsvorlesung an der Universität von Messina vom 12. Dezember 1886.

52 Es handelte sich um die Antrittsvorlesung (vom 8. Januar 1889) der Vorlesung im Verwaltungs- und Verfassungsrecht an der Universität von Palermo. Der Text wurde veröffentlicht in *Archivio giuridico*, 62, 1889, 107–124. Vgl. M. Fioravanti (Fn. 46); G. Cianferotti (Fn. 44); vgl. besonders die Artikel von Mangoni, Beneduce und Cianferotti im Sammelband *I giuristi e la crisi dello Stato liberale in Italia fra Otto e Novecento*, A. Mazzacane (Hg.), Neapel 1986; G. Rebuffa, *I lessici e il tempo delle prolusioni di Vittorio Emanuele Orlando*, in *Rivista trimestrale di diritto pubblico*, 4, 1989, 919–936; G. Azzariti, *La prolusione orlandiana e la scienza del diritto amministrativo anteriore al 1889*, ebd., 968–994; G. Cianferotti, *La prolusione di Orlando. Il paradigma pandettistico, i nuovi giuristi universitari e lo Stato liberale*, ebd., 995–1024.

Juristen war die Wiederherstellung des öffentlichen Rechts. Orlando war in der Tat der Ansicht, daß die Wissenschaft des öffentlichen Rechts vollständig neu zu begründen sei. Die Tatsache, daß Orlando als Negativbeispiel die französische Wissenschaft nannte, ist bezeichnend. Die Verordnung, mit der der erste Lehrstuhl für Verfassungsrecht in Frankreich eingeführt wurde, verpflichtete den Amtsinhaber zur Kommentierung der Verfassung von 1830.[53] „Ecco subito l'eccesso del criterio esegetico", bemerkt Orlando. Die Verfassungen dieser Art „consistono in una strana accozzaglia di definizioni astratte, di massime generalissime [...]".[54] Daher waren die grundlegenden Theorien der neuen Wissenschaft ein Resultat „da questo mostruoso accoppiamento di una metafisica presuntuosa col pedestre commento di un infelice documento legislativo".[55] Von dem übertriebenen exegetischen Ansatz bleibe, trotz der unbestreitbaren Fähigkeiten einiger Spezialisten, auch die verwaltungsrechtliche Literatur nicht verschont.[56] Orlando wies hin auf die Schwäche der wissenschaftlichen Kriterien und der Klassifikation, der sich die französischen Verwaltungsrechtler bedienten.

Exegetische und philosophische Exzesse, Ablehnung aller systematischen Kriterien – die Spezialisten des öffentlichen Rechts „sono troppo filosofi, troppo politici, troppo storici, troppo sociologisti e troppo poco giureconsulti [...]".[57] Die Wissenschaft des öffentlichen Rechts müsse ihre eigenen Methoden entwickeln. Überspitzte Philosophie und Exegese-Verfahren hätten aus der Wissenschaft des öffentlichen Rechts ein regelloses, unzusammenhängendes und eklektisches Sammelsurium gemacht. Die juristische Methode dürfe den übrigen (philosophischen, politischen, exegetischen usw.) Methoden nicht länger untergeordnet werden: „Ciò che noi censuriamo, ciò che è stato esiziale al fisiologo sviluppo del diritto pubblico [...] è l'aver dimenticato che altro è diritto, altro filosofia, altro scienza del diritto, altro cognizione delle leggi [...]." Der Weg, auf dem das öffentliche Recht wieder seiner wahren Bestimmung zugeführt werden könnte, war sehr einfach – zumindest nach den Worten Orlandos: „cioè che il diritto pubblico si consideri, nel modo stesso che il diritto privato, come un complesso di principi giuridici sistematicamente coordinati".[58]

53 Zum ersten Pariser Lehrstuhl (1834), den Pellegrino Rossi innehatte, vgl. P. Lavigne, *Le comte Rossi, premier professeur de droit constitutionnel français*, in *Histoire des idées et idées sur l'histoire. Études offertes à Jean-Jacques Chevallier*, Paris 1979, 173–178.

54 V. E. Orlando, *I criteri* (Fn. 52), 111.

55 Ebd., 112.

56 Aber Orlando verschonte mit seiner Kritik auch die deutsche Literatur nicht, der er exzessiven Gebrauch exegetischer und philosophischer Methoden vorwarf.

57 V. E. Orlando, *I criteri* (Fn. 52), 110.

58 Ebd., 122.

Bezeichnend ist der Umstand, daß sich Orlando niemals direkt auf italienische Juristen bezog. Dieses Schweigen ist eine implizite Verurteilung der bisherigen Kritik an der französischen Tradition.[59] Der Vortrag von 1889 war auch ein „Vernichtungsschlag".[60] Der Vorschlag Orlandos konzentrierte sich ganz auf den Prozeß der Wiederherstellung, der sich als Gegenentwurf zur „Methode" seiner Vorgänger darstellte: Da diese Exegese, Eklektizismus, Naturrecht und das Abstraktum eines „proprio tipo ideale" den positiv verankerten Institutionen vorgezogen hätten, müsse sich die Revisionstätigkeit auf ein juristisches System, auf wissenschaftliche Spezialisierung und Formalismus, auf pandektistische Kategorien und auf die Begriffsordnung des Privatrechts und schließlich auf die Anerkennung des „existierenden Staates", d. h. der „sovranità di poteri costituiti" stützen.[61]

Die grundsätzliche Trennung „nel procedimento logico, fra diritto e politica, fra ordine giuridico e ordine politico"[62] war eines der grundlegenden methodischen Prinzipien der neuen italienischen Schule des öffentlichen Rechts. Die logisch-juristische Vorgehensweise, entwickelt aus der begrifflichen Ordnung der Pandektisten, garantierte den wissenschaftlichen Formalismus. Der Rechtswissenschaftler wurde zum Wächter über die rechtliche Form. Das Bestreben, jede Möglichkeit von Instabilität und Konflikt im System und in den rechtlichen Beziehungen auszuschließen, stützte sich auf übermäßige „Verstaatlichung"[63] und auf eine extrem „verrechtlichte" Regierungsweise.

In den Jahren, in denen in Frankreich die *École scientifique de droit*[64] entstand und die Soziologie die Gesellschaft als das Zentrum aller Überlegungen ent-

59 Orlando beschrieb die Phasen vor und nach der Einigung als Stadien der „Kindheit" des Staates. Die Mittel der Rechtspublizisten „erano per sé stessi così scarsi da escludere la possibilità di uno studio scientifico adeguato [...] Tradizioni storiche mancavano [...] In tali condizioni, dunque, il nuovo Stato d'Italia altro non poteva che imitare e copiare; e come si era fatto per le istituzioni adottate cosi si fece per la loro ricostruzione scientifica, ricorrendo a letterature straniere, ma soprattutto a quella francese" (*Prefazione* (Fn. 49), XIII–XIV). Über diesen „Gemeinplatz" des 19. Jahrhunderts vgl. z. B. P. Turiello, *Governo e governati in Italia*, Bologna 1882 (Turin 1980, 4–5).

60 Zu den Aspekten, die die „Präorlandianer" nicht berücksichtigt haben, vgl. R. Rebuffa (Fn. 12), 214. Zur historiographischen Bewertung der „orlandischen Wende" vgl. M. Fioravanti, *La scienza italiana di diritto pubblico del diciannovesimo secolo: bilancio della ricerca storiografica*, in *Ius commune*, 10, 1983, 201–204.

61 V. E. Orlando, *I criteri* (Fn. 52), 123.

62 V. E. Orlando, *Programma*, in *Archivio di diritto pubblico*, 1, 1891, 7.

63 Zur Rekonstruktion der Argumente, die in der italienischen Literatur zum öffentlichen Recht vorgebracht wurden, vgl. P. Costa, *Lo Stato immaginario. Metafore e paradigmi nella cultura giuridica italiano fra Ottocento e Novecento*, Mailand 1986.

64 G. Cianferotti (Fn. 44), 210 ff.

deckte,[65] richtete Orlando seinen Blick nach Frankreich, dessen Wunden verheilt waren und das seine Macht durch die effiziente Verwaltungsorganisation, die ihm von dem „genio napoleonico" geblieben war, hatte aufrechterhalten können. „Spettacolo veramente mirabile codesto, di una nazione rovinata dai suoi principi e dai suoi uomini di Stato, e salvata della gerarchia poggiante sull'umile funzionario, forte di quella routine così spregiata e derisa dagli esprits forts del liberismo!"[66]

Angesichts einer schwachen bürgerlichen Gesellschaft und einer widersprüchlichen Realität wurden juristische Methode und Bürokratie, auch vom ideologischen Standpunkt aus, zu bevorzugten Instrumentarien, mit denen sich die Vorherrschaft des Staates bewahren und die politische Einheit konsolidieren ließen. Vielleicht können „deutsches" und „französisches Modell" so betrachtet schließlich in Italien zu einem Ausgleich gelangen, mag dieser auch schwierig und provisorisch sein.

65 L. Mangoni (Fn. 42), 110 ff.

66 V. E. Orlando, *Principii di diritto amministrativo*, Florenz 1892, 271–272.

L'opinione pubblica nazionale e l'appello al popolo: figure e campi di tensione

1. Un'idea di opinione pubblica, idee di costituzione

Il mio intervento[1] propone una rapida riflessione sulle figure dell'opinione pubblica e dell'appello al popolo nel periodo dei plebisciti per l'unificazione italiana. Si tratta di "figure" retoriche, di concetti che rivelano significativi campi di tensione. Il profilo che in particolare suscita la mia attenzione non è tanto quello della "forma" plebiscito e della vicenda italiana del 1860 – oggetto specifico di questo Convegno – quanto piuttosto la *dimensione costituzionale* ovvero la questione dell'opinione pubblica rispetto ad almeno due temi cruciali e di vasta portata: la formazione del consenso e della volontà politica, la legittimazione costituzionale.

Del resto, il tema può essere riletto partendo da più angoli visuali. Potrei dire da quello del "dopo", ovvero dalla "sponda" del 1911 (o più in generale del dibattito sulla formazione del Regno d'Italia e sulla sua unità costituzionale) oppure dal punto di vista del "prima", cioè almeno dagli anni '40 dell'Ottocento. Il "dopo" evoca in particolare quel dibattito, a predominanza "continuistica",[2] che si è sviluppato a partire dalla discussione parlamentare degli anni '80 per culminare nel 1911 (in occasione delle celebrazioni per i 50 anni della nascita del regno), "innescato" da un celebre scritto dell'internazionalista Dionisio Anzilotti.[3]

La discussione di inizio secolo verteva sulla qualificazione giuridica del procedimento di formazione dello Stato italiano: mero ingrandimento del Regno di

1 Il presente contributo conserva i caratteri della relazione orale con l'aggiunta dell'apparato bibliografico.
2 P. Pombeni, *Autorità sociale e potere politico nell'Italia contemporanea*, Padova 1993, 31 ss.
3 Sul punto v. adesso L. Passero, *Dionisio Anzilotti e la dottrina internazionalistica tra Otto e Novecento*, Milano 2010, 313 ss.

Sardegna (tramite annessioni) o invece "fusione" tra gli Stati prima esistenti dando così vita ad una entità statale nuova?

In questa sede però ritengo più utile partire dal "prima" e quindi dai decenni che precedono, nel percorso risorgimentale, la fase dell'unificazione "plebiscitaria" del 1860.

Per cogliere il "prima" occorre probabilmente ritornare più indietro e per restare sul Continente europeo, al caso francese della crisi della monarchia assoluta di fine Settecento.

Nel corso del XVIII secolo prende forma, soprattutto nella Francia delle *causes célèbres*, una suggestiva figura retorica: il «tribunale dell'opinione pubblica», «un tribunale – come scrive Jacques Necker – dinanzi al quale tutti gli uomini che attirano su di sé degli sguardi sono costretti a comparire: là, l'opinione pubblica, come dall'alto di un trono, conferisce premi e corone, fa e disfa le reputazioni».[4] Per il ministro del re di Francia, banchiere e *uomo pubblico*, l'appello all'opinione è anche un modo per cercare di riempire il vuoto minaccioso che la monarchia ha creato attorno a sé, isolandosi dalla nazione, per ridare così linfa vitale a un corpo politico indebolito.[5] Più che il prodotto di un'autonoma sfera pubblica borghese emergente dalla società civile, questo "tribunale", dotato di universalità, razionalità, oggettività, segnalerebbe uno spazio nuovo di «invenzione politica»[6]

4 J. Necker, *De l'administration des finances de la France*, s. l., 1784, t. I, XLIX.

5 Sull'importante articolazione del problema dell'opinione pubblica nell'opera e nell'azione politica di Necker v. in particolare H. Grange, *Les idées de Necker*, Paris 1974; J.-D. Bredin, *Necker et l'opinion publique*, in *Coppet, creuset de l'esprit libéral*, a cura di L. Jaume, Paris 2000, 25–40; L. Jaume, *Tra concetto e idea-forza: l'opinione pubblica secondo Necker*, in *Opinione pubblica. Storia, politica, costituzione dal XVII al XX secolo*, a cura di L. Lacchè, numero monografico del *Giornale di storia costituzionale*, 6/II semestre, 2003, 129–144.

6 Mi riferisco, in particolare, alle tesi avanzate da Keith Michael Baker in vari contributi volti, tra l'altro, a discutere l'uso del paradigma *habermasiano di "sfera pubblica"* (J. Habermas, *Strukturwandel der Öffentlichkeit*, Neuwied 1962, tr. it. *Storia e critica dell'opinione pubblica*, Bari 2001 (1971)) nel contesto della Francia prerivoluzionaria. Cfr. *Politics and Public Opinion under the Old Regime: Some Reflections*, in J. R. Censer, J. D. Popkin (eds.), *Press and Politics in Pre-Revolutionary France*, Berkeley, Los Angeles 1987, 204–246; *Politique et opinion publique sous l'ancien régime*, in *Annales E. S. C.*, 1, 1987, 41–71; *Inventing the French Revolution*, Cambridge 1990 (in tr. francese *Au tribunal de l'opinion. Essais sur l'imaginaire politique au XVIIIe siècle*, Paris 1993, 219–265); *Defining the Public Sphere in Eighteenth-Century France: Variations on a Theme by Habermas*, in *Habermas and the Public Sphere*, a cura di C. Calhoun, Oxford 1992, 181–211. Sempre nell'ambito di questo dibattito, arricchitosi nel corso degl'anni Novanta, si vedano inoltre i saggi di Mona Ozouf: *"Public Opinion" at the End of the Old regime*, in *The Rise and Fall of the French Revolution*, ed. by T. C. W. Blanning,

dotato di una propria legittimità ed autorità, rivelatosi alla fine incompatibile con lo spazio tradizionale "incorporato" dalla persona del sovrano.

Dell'esistenza di un'istanza del *pubblico* davanti alla quale comparire per essere "sottoposti" ad un "giudizio" su temi di interesse comune potremmo trovare sviluppi e applicazioni ulteriori nel corso del XIX secolo.[7] Ma mentre in Gran Bretagna la funzione critica procede, pur non senza gravi difficoltà (basti pensare, per esempio, al problema della libertà di stampa e della pubblicità degli atti di governo), di pari passo con l'evoluzione "pluralistica" di una funzione

Chicago, London 1996; *L'opinion publique*, in *The French Revolution and the Creation of a Modern Political Culture*, I, *The Political Culture of the Old Regime*, ed. by K. M. Baker, Oxford, 1987, I, 419–434; *Le concept d'opinion publique au XVIII siècle*, in *L'Homme régéneré. Essais sur la Révolution française*, Paris 1989. Sono da segnalare anche i lavori di J. A. W. Gunn, *Public Spirit to Public Opinion*, in *Beyond Liberty and Property. The Process of Self-Recognition in Eighteenth-Century political thought*, Kingston 1983, 260–315; B. Nathans, *Habermas's 'Public sphere' in the Era of the French Revolution*, in *French Historical Studies*, 16, 1990, 620–644; A. J. La Vopa, *Conceiving a Public: Idea and Society in Eighteenth-Century Europe*, in *Journal of Modern History*, LXIV, March 1992, 79–116; J. D. Popkin, *The Concept of Public Opinion in the Historiography of the French Revolution: A Critique*, in *Storia della Storiografia*, XX, 1991, 77–92; D. Goodman, *Public Sphere and Private Life: Toward a Synthesis of Current Historiographical Approach to the Old Regime*, in *History and Theory*, XXXI, 1992, 1, 1–20; A. Cottereau, P. Ladrière (a cura di), *Pouvoir et légitimité. Figures de l'espace public*, Paris 1992; C. Calhoun (ed.), *Habermas and the Public Sphere*, cit.; F. Schneider, *Öffentlichkeit und Diskurs. Studien zu Entstehung, Struktur und Form der Öffentlichkeit im 18. Jahrhundert*, Bielefeld 1992; gli articoli di D. Gordon, D. A. Bell e S. Maza in *French Historical Studies*, 17, 1992, 882–956, sul tema *The Public Sphere in the Eighteenth Century*; J. R. Censer, *The French Press in the Age of Enlightenment*, London, New York 1994; L. Brooke, *Reason and Passion in the Public Sphere: Habermas and the Cultural Historians*, in *Journal of Interdisciplinary History*, XXIV, 1998, 1, 43–67; P.-E. Knabe (éd.), *Opinion*, Berlin 2000; H. Barker, S. Burrows (eds.), *Press, Politics and the Public Sphere in Europe and North America, 1760–1820*, Cambridge 2002; A. Briggs, P. Burke, *A Social History of the Media. From Gutenberg to the Internet*, Cambridge, Oxford 2000, tr. it. *Storia sociale dei media. Da Gutenberg a Internet*, Bologna 2002. Nell'ambito della storiografia italiana ricordo i saggi di Edoardo Tortarolo: *«Opinion publique» tra Antico regime e Rivoluzione francese. Contributo a un vocabolario storico della politica settecentesca*, in *Rivista storica italiana*, CII, 1990, 1, 5–23; *Opinione pubblica*, in *L'Illuminismo. Dizionario storico*, a cura di V. Ferrone e D. Roche, Roma, Bari, 1997, 283–291; *Public Opinion and the Italian Enlightenment. Approaches to a Historical Vocabulary*, in P.-E. Knabe (éd.), *Opinion*, cit., 33–44 e la recente complessiva analisi critica di L. Scuccimarra, *La trasparenza del politico. Habermas e il paradigma della 'sfera pubblica', in Opinione pubblica. Storia, politica, costituzione*, cit.

7 Rinvio a L. Lacché, *Introduzione* e Id., *Per una teoria costituzionale dell'opinione pubblica. Il dibattito italiano (XIX sec.)*, in *Opinione pubblica. Storia, politica, costituzione*, cit.

politico-costituzionale istituzionalizzata (circuito politico-parlamentare), in Francia la metafora essenzialmente contestativa del "tribunale" precede e surroga il dato istituzionale e si esprime nel corso del Settecento come critica del *public éclairé*.

Surrogato di un corpo rappresentativo – come noterà la figlia di Necker, Madame de Staël[8] – l'opinione pubblica è vista come una sorta di alta istanza "giudiziaria" di fronte alla quale persino i re devono *rendere conto*. Il ministro, *uomo pubblico* che governa in nome del sovrano, deve *avere credito*. E avere credito significa guadagnare *fiducia*. Non stupisce che il Necker banchiere / ministro utilizzi così agevolmente un lessico tipicamente "economico", da *Commercial Society*. Scriverà sempre sua figlia:

> «il credito è dunque la vera scoperta moderna che ha legato i governi coi popoli. Il bisogno di credito obbliga i governi a rispettare la pubblica opinione; ed allo stesso modo che il commercio ha incivilito le nazioni, il credito che da esso deriva ha reso necessarie delle forme costituzionali qualsivoglia».[9]

Nessun altro orientamento intellettuale sa cogliere, nell'Europa continentale, il senso più profondo della responsabilità ministeriale meglio del "gruppo di Coppet".[10] Questo orientamento ha scarse possibilità di trovare ricezione in ambito italiano al momento della Restaurazione dove, a differenza della Francia "costituzionalizzata" dei Borboni, la via è quella di una monarchia *senza rappresentanza moderna*.

E' infatti sufficiente leggere la *Monarchia nazionale rappresentativa* di Romagnosi per comprendere quanto l'ideario concettuale in Italia resti lontano, al momento della Restaurazione, dalla cultura liberal-costituzionale.[11] L'*impossibilità* di configurare un percorso di sviluppo della responsabilità "politica" – nel senso constantiano del termine – è legata alle radici rivoluzionarie innervate dalla concezione napoleonica dello Stato *pedagogico*, istitutore del sociale, per certi versi autentica forma *razionalizzata* dell'assolutismo settecentesco. Quell'impossibilità è dunque legata alla centralità di una mediazione tecnocratico-amministrativa che non rompe i legami con i modelli di costruzione corporata

8 A.-L.-G. De Staël, *Considerazioni sui principali avvenimenti della Rivoluzione francese* (1818), introduzione di A. Omodeo, Milano 1943, 99.

9 *Ibidem*, 96.

10 L. Lacchè, *Coppet et la percée de l'État libéral constitutionnel*, *supra*, 220; A. Laquièze, *Le modèle anglais et la responsabilité ministérielle selon le groupe de Coppet*, *ibidem*, 157–176.

11 G. D. Romagnosi, *Della costituzione di una monarchia nazionale rappresentativa: la scienza delle costituzioni* (1815), a cura di G. Astuti, Roma 1937. Cfr. L. Mannori, *Uno Stato per Romagnosi.* I: *Il progetto costituzionale*, Milano 1984.

del sociale tipici dell'antico regime. In questo contesto non si riesce a *immaginare* un legame *politico-fiduciario* tra l'esecutivo monarchico, l'opinione pubblica e le istituzioni rappresentative.

Nell'Italia della Restaurazione "senza costituzioni" il fragile e confuso costituzionalismo che vi circola in brevi interludi "dinamici" – i cosiddetti "moti risorgimentali" – non si preoccupa tanto delle forme e del problema della legittimità: la costituzione è un bene in sé, essa ha forza in quanto *ideologia*, è una tavola di valori che subordina i fatti alle idee. La costituzione è un punto di partenza e non un punto di arrivo. Malgrado il tentativo di radicamento delle istituzioni rappresentative, come nel caso napoletano del 1820–21,[12] l'esito fallimentare di quel biennio accentuò la diffidenza dei governi e non di rado anche la critica dei moderati verso un parlamentarismo privo di tradizioni che non fossero quelle che riconducevano agli antichi Stati. La sostanziale ineffettività delle esperienze costituzionali era lo specchio di una fragilità strutturale. Né la breve stagione della "monarchia consultiva", a prevalente valenza politico-territoriale, né i progetti infrastatuali degli anni '40 nel segno di un indefinito discorso "federalistico" acceleravano, negli Stati, lo sviluppo della cultura rappresentativo-parlamentare.

Gli anni '40 si rivelarono però anni cruciali, utili per tracciare, ancora prima del '48, una linea di confine. Le monarchie italiane senza costituzione sono – direbbe Madame de Staël – monarchie "senza credito" e quindi senza fiducia, governi che non possono «rispettare l'opinione pubblica» e collegarsi alla "nazione". Proprio in quegli anni comincia ad emergere quella sfera pubblica – fondata sui presupposti della *comunicazione* sociale: la nazione dei lettori e del pubblico *criticante* – che funge da terreno di *collegamento* tra esperienze distinte ed eterogenee. Nel 1818 Ludovico di Breme, in una lettera a Sismondi, coglieva nell'ostacolo frapposto a ogni tipo di comunicazione commerciale e letteraria la vera strategia politica dei "restauratori": l'intenzione dei Principi era di isolare i sudditi come in un arcipelago: «Voilà un sujet à traiter sous le titre Du danger des communications sociales au 19e siècle. Par un ami de l'ordre».[13]

12 Cfr. per esempio I. Fernández Sarasola, *Poder y libertad: los orígines de la responsabilidad del Ejecutivo en España (1808–1823)*, Madrid 2001; P. Colombo, *Costituzione come ideologia. Le rivoluzioni italiane del 1820–21 e la costituzione di Cadice*, in J. M. Portillo Valdés, *La Nazione cattolica. Cadice 1812: una costituzione per la Spagna*, Manduria 1998, 131–157.

13 L. Di Breme, *Lettere*, raccolte e annotate da P. Camporesi, Torino 1966, 532. Il tema dell'isolamento dell'intellettuale negli Stati italiani della Restaurazione è còlto efficacemente da L. Mannori, *La crisi dell'ordine plurale. Nazione e costituzione in Italia tra Sette e Ottocento*, in AA. VV., *Ordo Iuris. Storia e forme dell'esperienza giuridica*, Milano 2003, 137–180. Come è noto, Marino Berengo

2. L'opinione pubblica (moderata) per la nazione degli Italiani

L'opinione pubblica e la nazione sono dunque le strutture decisive per *collegare* i soggetti negli Stati e tra gli Stati. Rispetto a questa evoluzione, non pochi intellettuali – si pensi per esempio al "secondo" Romagnosi – *déracinés* a partire dalla Restaurazione, cominciano a rappresentarsi come *faiseurs d'opinion*. L'ampliamento di *scala*, da regionale a nazionale, apre prospettive in parte inedite e si comincia a codificare un'idea di *pubblico*. Nel 1846, Massimo d'Azeglio, in margine agli *ultimi casi di Romagna*, osserva acutamente: «quando in una nazione tutti riconoscono giusta una cosa e la vogliono, la cosa è fatta; e in Italia il lavoro più importante per la nostra rigenerazione si può far con le mani in tasca».[14] Nel 1844 Cesare Balbo aveva invitato i governi a diventare più *desiderabili* per attrarre le migliori energie e per costruire una *egemonia nazionale*.[15]

Se è probabilmente vero che «Nella nostra storia preunitaria mancano tracce significative di un fenomeno socialmente diffuso come in Inghilterra, politicamente dirompente come in Francia, o precocemente concentrato sul tema della nazione come in Germania»,[16] la forza dell'opinione è però già una notevole conquista della fase cruciale del Risorgimento.

Già nel *pamphlet* sui casi di Romagna, d'Azeglio lanciò l'idea della «congiura al chiaro giorno». Bisognava superare la sterile strategia insurrezionale che nulla poteva contro la potenza militare dell'Austria, pronta a soccorrere gli arretrati Stati italiani e a imporre la reazione. Nella sua celebre *Proposta d'un programma per l'opinione nazionale italiana*[17] d'Azeglio costruisce la figura dell'opinione pubblica – di cui invoca il ruolo decisivo – come *forza morale trasparente*. E' proprio la necessità di uscire definitivamente dalla stagione della *forza materiale* segnata dalle società segrete e dal loro sterile settarismo, a spingere verso mezzi capaci di influire sull'opinione pubblica che è la prima dispensatrice della forza

ha ricostruito le dinamiche della formazione, nel primo Ottocento, di un ceto di intellettuali che, esclusi dagli uffici governativi, operano all'interno di una vivace imprenditoria editoriale di tipo moderno. Cfr. M. Berengo, *Intellettuali e organizzazione della cultura nell'età della Restaurazione*, in *La Restaurazione in Italia: strutture e ideologie*, Roma 1976, 297–307 e in particolare il classico *Intellettuali e librai nella Milano della Restaurazione*, Torino 1980.

14 M. d'Azeglio, *Degli ultimi casi di Romagna*, s. l. 1846, 84.

15 C. Balbo, *Delle speranze d'Italia*, 2ª ed., Capolago 1844, 217 ss.

16 G. Civile, *Per una storia sociale dell'opinione pubblica: osservazioni a proposito della tarda età liberale*, in *Quaderni storici*, 2, 2000, 469.

17 Firenze, 1847.

morale.[18] D'Azeglio intravede – specie dopo il programma di Pio IX – la possibilità per il partito moderato di non essere più percepito come "partito" ma come *Opinione nazionale italiana.*[19] «Una forza però è necessaria, ed abbiam dichiarato che crediamo si debba cercarla nel consenso dell'opinion pubblica».[20] «Quest'opinione tuttavia non dev'essere considerata in astratto; e troviamo che in concreto è composta di classi, di ceti e d'individui disponenti di maggiore o minor potenza secondo l'autorità, il grado, la ricchezza, i talenti, la scienza ec. d'ognuno. E' chiaro che tanto più sarà grande l'influenza dell'opinione pubblica, e potrà più facilmente concretarsi in fatti importanti, quanto più saranno potenti gl'individui che la professano».[21] L'obiettivo, certo difficile, è dunque quello di integrare nell'opinione pubblica nazionale quell'insieme di identità diverse che caratterizzano la nazione *plurale* degli Italiani.[22] Bisogna far convergere il più grande numero possibile di Italiani su poche, concrete, utili proposte riformatrici. Riprendendo il grande tema settecentesco dell'opinione pubblica come "tribunale", d'Azeglio ritiene che guadagnare la fiducia dei popoli sia la sfida del liberalismo italiano «grazie alla nuova via di moderata e prudente riserva».[23] Non a caso egli chiede a questa opinione pubblica «d'esaminare e conoscere la nostra causa, giudicarla, e proclamare un giudicio del quale ci teniamo sicuri».[24] «Intesi ad agire unicamente sull'opinione pubblica, più sarà pubblica la nostra azione, e più raggiungerà il suo scopo; volendoci appoggiare al consenso universale, più il suo voto sarà espresso apertamente, più ci darà forza».[25]

In questi anni l'opinione pubblica invocata e "abbozzata" dal moderatismo liberale ha una dimensione più "pre-politica" che costituzionale. La sua struttura

18 M. d'Azeglio, *Proposta d'un programma*, cit., 4. Cfr. D. Orta, *Prodromi di un'opinione pubblica*, in V. Castronovo (a cura di), *La nascita dell'opinione pubblica in Italia. La stampa nella Torino del Risorgimento e capitale d'Italia (1848–1864)*, Roma, Bari 2004, 99; M.T. Pichetto, *La "congiura al chiaro giorno" di Massimo d'Azeglio*, in *Potere e circolazione delle idee. Stampa, accademie e censura nel Risorgimento italiano*, a cura di D. M. Bruni, Milano 2007, 91–108; G. Martellini, M.T. Pichetto, *Massimo d'Azeglio. Vita e avventure di un artista in politica*, Milano 1990; D. M. Bruni, *Opinione pubblica e lotta politica nella riflessione di Massimo d'Azeglio a cavallo del 1848*, in M. L. Betri (a cura di), *Rileggere l'Ottocento. Risorgimento e nazione*, Torino 2010, 111; M. Meriggi, *Opinione pubblica*, in *Atlante culturale del Risorgimento. Lessico del linguaggio politico dal Settecento all'Unità*, a cura di A. M. Banti, A. Chiavistelli, L. Mannori, M. Meriggi, Roma, Bari 2011, 160.

19 M. d'Azeglio, *Proposta d'un programma*, cit., 5.

20 *Ibidem*, 17.

21 *Ibidem*, 18.

22 L. Mannori, *La crisi dell'ordine plurale*, cit., 177.

23 M. d'Azeglio, *Proposta d'un programma*, cit., 19.

24 *Ibidem*, 25.

25 *Ibidem*, 29.

di *civil society* guarda anzitutto allo sviluppo di una classe borghese di stampo europeo che unifica ceti e dimensioni sociali rivolte al progresso materiale (dalle ferrovie alle leghe doganali) e alla distinzione per merito e per "capacità di innovazione".[26] D'Azeglio ha ben compreso che i sovrani – nel mondo "nuovo" delle comunicazioni rapide rappresentate dal telegrafo e dalla stampa – si illudono di potere governare contro l'opinione pubblica, e quindi senza giustizia e con malafede. L'artista guadagnato alla politica si rivolge tanto ai principi che dovrebbero comprendere quali sono i loro veri interessi (non certo la mera reazione), che ai popoli conquistati dalla forza trasparente, concreta e moderata dell'opinione pubblica.

«Dal 1841, epoca da cui si potrebbe quasi asserire abbia preso movimento ed influenza l'opinione liberale moderata ... Quale ostacolo si opporrà a queste irresistibili idee che da ogni parte ci arrivano, e come sottrarvisi potrebbero ancorchè il volessero i popoli d'Italia? S'insinuano queste idee ora per mezzo di quei progressi intellettuali e morali, cui partecipano tutte le nazioni civili; or pei benefizi del progresso dei loro governi stessi; or per l'influenza dell'alta industria e di quei commerci che rannodano tutti gli interessi quasi in un sol corpo, dal quale partono, nel quale ritornano tutte le vene della pubblica ricchezza; or secondate dalle inevitabili applicazioni dei principii dell'economia politica; or finalmente dalla confidenza dei popoli nella generosità e saviezza dei principi».[27] La loro "parte" era, per dirla con Cesare Balbo, quella dei liberali o progressisti «meno estremi, meno puri, che nominano sé stessi liberali di mezzo, o *liberali moderati*; e che così sono pur nominati da tutti, perché questa denominazione è necessaria, è inevitabile, perché sola esprime il fatto relativo dello star in mezzo alle altre due parti ...», ovvero dei conservatori puri e dei liberali più radicali.[28] Il partito moderato, scriveva il conte di Cavour a Victor Cousin nel 1846, «... s'efforce d'opérer le progrès sans recourir aux moyens révolutionnaires ...».[29]

26 Cfr. R. Romanelli, *Nazione e costituzione nell'opinione liberale prima del '48*, in *Passato e presente*, 46, 1999, 167–168.

27 M. Castelli, *Saggi sull'opinione politica moderata in Italia*, Italia 1847, 146–147.

28 C. Balbo, *Dell'uso delle parole moderazione, opinione moderata e parte moderata. Lettera al signor****, Torino 19–23 giugno 1847, in Id., *Lettere di politica e letteratura edite ed inedite di Cesare Balbo precedute da un discorso sulle rivoluzioni*, Firenze 1855, 460.

29 Lettera del 4 febbraio 1846, in C. Cavour, *Epistolario* a cura di C. Pischedda, III, 1844–1846, Firenze 1973, 274–275. Per una analisi della struttura concettuale del moderatismo v. S. La Salvia, *Il moderatismo in Italia*, in *Istituzioni e ideologie in Italia e in Germania tra le rivoluzioni*, a cura di U. Corsini, R. Lill, Bologna 1987, 169–330. Per taluni aspetti cfr. L. Lacchè, *Il* canone eclettico. *Alla ricerca di uno* strato profondo *della cultura giuridica italiana dell'Ottocento*, in *Quaderni fiorentini per la storia del pensiero giuridico moderno*, 39, 2010, 153–228 e la sintesi di A. Chiavistelli, *Moderati/Democratici*, in *Atlante culturale del Risorgimento*, cit., 126–129.

I pubblicisti come d'Azeglio hanno certamente meditato e hanno saputo adattare al contesto italiano l'insegnamento che abbiamo attribuito al gruppo di Coppet e alle sue radici neckeriane. E' stato probabilmente Benjamin Constant l'autore continentale che, all'inizio del XIX secolo, ha meglio compreso l'essenza dell'opinione pubblica («pouvoir représentatif de l'opinion») nella teoria liberal-costituzionale, valorizzando il circuito pubblicità-libertà di stampa-governo d'opinione. «Ce ne sont point les formes des constitutions qui les conservent; il n'y a point de durée pour une constitution, sans opinion publique, et il n'y a point d'opinion publique, sans liberté de la presse. Quand cette liberté est étouffée, les grands corps de l'Etat sont des masses isolées de la nation, sans vie et sans force véritable ...».[30] Qualche anno prima lo scrittore svizzero aveva detto che «L'opinion publique est la vie des Etats. Quand l'opinion publique ne se renouvelle pas, les Etats dépérissent et tombent en dissolution».[31] In Italia è attraverso Romagnosi che si arriva più o meno consapevolmente a Filangieri e soprattutto alla fonte originaria, a Jacques Necker[32] e alla sua celebre rappresentazione di quel tribunale, considerato anzitutto come figura retorica nel quale siede trionfante l'opinione pubblica «invisibile ed inesorabile potenza, che senza tesori, senza guardie e senza armate si fa ubbidire dai magistrati, dalle città, dalle nazioni, e giunge a comandare persino nelle reggie».[33] Ma l'opinione dei *moderati*, l'opinione che diventa fattore civile, è quella che, come osserva Sismondi, deve stare in equilibrio con la «saviezza nazionale», perché l'«... opinione instabile, passeggera e capricciosa, è un tiranno onde convien diffidare non meno che d'ogni altro tiranno».[34]

3. Il governo costituzionale e la responsabilità

Il *governo con il pubblico* è la strada per arrivare al governo con la *costituzione*. Non sorprende che gli "incunaboli" del costituzionalismo italiano siano incentrati in grandissima misura sul nesso libertà di stampa, opinione pubblica, governo costituzionale / *monarchia rappresentativa*. Non è difficile cogliere l'affioramento

30 B. Constant, *Observations sur le discours prononcé par S. E. le ministre de l'Intérieur en faveur du projet de loi sur la liberté de la presse* (1814), in *Œuvres*, texte présenté et annoté par A. Roulin, Paris 1957, 1261.

31 B. Constant, *Principes de politiques* (1806), édition par E. Hofman, texte établi d'après les manuscrits de Lausanne et de Paris avec une introduction et des notes, Genève 1980, 137.

32 L. Jaume, *Tra concetto e idea-forza: l'opinione pubblica secondo Necker*, cit.

33 G. D. Romagnosi, *La scienza delle costituzioni ... opera postuma*, Torino 1849, 106.

34 J.-Ch.-L. Simonde de Sismondi, *Studi intorno alle costituzioni dei popoli liberi*, Capolago 1839, 161.

di quella cultura liberal-costituzionale che ha radici britanniche ma "forma francese", filtrata attraverso Constant, Rossi, Hello e altri scrittori orleanisti. La responsabilità dei ministri è uno dei fondamenti del governo rappresentativo perché «mantiene un giusto temperamento tra la potenza del Principe, e quella dei parlamenti chiamati a tutelare i diritti e gl'interessi della nazione. Se il Principe con la sanzione, o col divieto delle leggi, con la scelta dei magistrati e dei pubblici ufficiali, con la convocazione e lo scioglimento del parlamento, mantiene la sua suprema autorità su tutte le parti del pubblico reggimento, i deputati della nazione con chieder conto ai Ministri di tutti, senza eccezione, gli atti che a quello appartengono, fanno sì che in tutte le sue parti si mantenga vivo quello spirito, che lo tiene in armonia coi voti e coi desiderii della nazione. Per tal modo si impedisce che non si alteri quell'ordinamento di poteri che è proprio della monarchia rappresentativa».[35]

In questo modo si impediscono gli atti contrari ai diritti politici riconosciuti dalla coscienza comune e «consacrati dalla costituzione».[36] In pochi mesi, tra la fine del 1847 e la primavera del 1848, lo scenario *nazionale* cambia decisamente. Le monarchie "senza credito" devono prendere la strada del modello "censitario-rappresentativo" di impianto liberale. La costituzione, rapidamente, "consacra" l'avanzata nazionale dell'opinione pubblica, imita modelli stranieri coniugandoli ai contesti, si conquista "credito".

In Italia i primi scrittori costituzionali (subalpini) seguono tale via identificando l'ordine rappresentativo con la preponderanza del giudizio dell'opinione pubblica in tutte le cose relative al governo.[37] Il governo costituzionale è forte se procede in pieno accordo e in armonia con l'opinione pubblica.[38] Romagnosi – ampiamente citato – ricordava il legame tra la legge, il governo e l'opinione. «Quando l'opinione pubblica precede il governo, la esecuzion della legge riesce pronta e completa».[39] Diversamente tra la legge e la sua applicazione si produce una *distanza* che deve essere riempita con «idee intermedie».

L'obiettivo degli scrittori moderati degli anni '40 e '50 è dunque quello di "costituzionalizzare" l'opinione pubblica nel governo rappresentativo (e in maniera non certo univoca nella forma del governo parlamentare). L'opinione pubblica è il vapore, è il fluido, la condizione per l'esistenza e il funzionamento

35 C. Boncompagni, *Della monarchia rappresentativa*, Torino 1846, 33–34.

36 *Ibidem*, 34.

37 C. Boncompagni, *Della monarchia rappresentativa*, Torino 1848, 65.

38 P. Peverelli, *Comenti intorno allo Statuto del regno di Sardegna*, Torino 1849, 87–89; D. Carutti, *Dei principii del governo libero*, Torino 1852, 242.

39 G. D. Romagnosi, *La scienza delle costituzioni*, cit., 108.

di un sistema rappresentativo.[40] In questo schema i proto-costituzionalisti subalpini di quegl'anni collegano la *forza* dell'opinione pubblica al problema della volontà politica. E' interessante notare come l'espressione *appello al popolo* sia utilizzata per designare il meccanismo "rappresentativo-parlamentare" dello scioglimento sovrano della camera eletta e il rinvio, appunto, alle elezioni politiche.

A leggere i testi delle costituzioni del 1848, il tema della responsabilità viene incardinato sull'asse di alcuni principî comuni. I ministri, di nomina regia, sono responsabili; la persona del re è sacra e inviolabile: «Gli atti di ogni genere sottoscritti dal Re non hanno vigore se non contrassegnati da un ministro segretario di stato, il quale perciò solo se ne rende risponsabile».[41] I ministri hanno libero accesso in Parlamento e il diritto di essere ascoltati: «Hanno l'obbligo, quando sieno invitati, a dare gli schiarimenti, che all'assemblea sembrassero opportuni».[42]

Le carte del 1848 intendono "temperare" la monarchia *costituzionalizzata* attraverso il governo rappresentativo. Gli articoli che nelle varie costituzioni definiscono il *problema* della responsabilità rappresentano un dato di partenza che deve essere letto alla luce dell'*origo constitutionis* (la *lettre*) ma anche in rapporto ai profili evolutivi (l'*esprit*). Ancora una volta la fonte britannica viene passata attraverso il filtro, talvolta distorcente, del costituzionalismo continentale con al centro le *Chartes* francesi (1814 e 1830) e la costituzione belga del 1831, ma spesso con differente *esprit* e con esiti originali.

Il 1848 afferma in Italia le prime *esperienze costituzionali*, fatte di dottrine, lotte parlamentari, prassi: inizia una brevissima (per la gran parte della penisola) difficile ma decisiva stagione che segnerà un punto di non ritorno, appunto quello del *regime politico costituzionale*. La *vita costituzionale* consente di consolidare logiche e dinamiche "rappresentative" che vengono così messe alla prova per la prima volta. La responsabilità ministeriale si rivela uno dei più delicati contrafforti. Cesare Balbo ha ben compreso che il regime rappresentativo vive di interdipendenze e di finzioni. Una delle grandi *invenzioni* del costituzionalismo britannico è che il *Re non può far male*: tanto più è inviolabile la persona del re tanto più è *esposta* quella dei ministri. Non si può non «ammirare questa istituzione, questo mezzo termine, questo ritrovato» della civiltà che unisce nella monarchia rappresentativa i vantaggi della monarchia e della

40 C. Balbo, *Della monarchia rappresentativa in Italia. Saggi politici di Cesare Balbo. Della politica nella presente civiltà, abbozzi del medesimo autore*, Firenze 1857, 244–245.

41 Costituzione del Regno delle Due Sicilie, art. 72.

42 Statuto del Granducato di Toscana, art. 61.

repubblica. Ma non bisogna cadere nell'equivoco della *neutralizzazione politica* del sovrano.[43]

Nell'elogio dottrinario dello schema del governo misto-rappresentativo la responsabilità non deve però essere una semplice "finzione". Nessun scrittore del '48 italiano coglie e soprattutto sintetizza meglio di Pietro Peverelli le dinamiche della responsabilità retta da due principî: l'accordo *vero*, cosciente e sincero, tra il monarca e i ministri, l'*influenza* dell'opinione pubblica "rappresentata" e capace, in alcune circostanze, di "impedire" o "obbligare" i ministri: «Sebbene quindi l'art. 65 attribuisca al re il diritto di nominare e revocare i suoi ministri, pure per l'applicazione delle altre disposizioni dello Statuto, che vi hanno correlazione, questo diritto non è né assoluto né illimitato, ma è necessariamente influenzato dalla maggioranza della Camera dei deputati».[44]

Questa influenza non può essere né diretta né esplicita: il parlamento non può chiedere la revoca dei ministri ma può rifiutare la sua approvazione alle leggi non conformi alle idee politiche della maggioranza. Sono le dimissioni e l'appello al popolo a tenere in equilibrio il sistema e rendere mera, remota eccezione la messa in stato d'accusa. La monarchia rappresentativa ha dunque un vantaggio congenito:

> «in guisa che i ministri della Corona debbono interpretare i voleri della pluralità e uscir dell'ufficio quando venga lor meno il concorso parlamentare, ognun vede come l'opinione pubblica non intermetta mai di vegliarne gli andamenti, come in ogni tempo si precluda la via ai piccoli arbitrî, si compongano i conflitti fra camera e governo e come si apra l'adito ai mutamenti nella cosa pubblica col semplice scambio dei ministri che consigliano il capo dello stato. In una repubblica presidenziale si comprenderà ancora una rivoluzione; essa diventa inutile nella monarchia».[45]

I dibattiti sullo statuto del governo e sulla responsabilità riecheggiarono nelle aule parlamentari, dal Piemonte alla Toscana, da Roma a Napoli sino alla Sicilia, con esiti provvisori e limitati ma tutt'altro che banali. Solo il regime subalpino seppe però diventare *esperienza*: «Qui si assalgono, qui si difendono, e qui si feriscono e si uccidono i ministeri e rinascono altri via via».[46]

43 C. Balbo, *Della monarchia rappresentativa in Italia*, cit., 398.

44 P. Peverelli, *Comenti intorno allo Statuto del regno di Sardegna*, cit., 135. Cfr. R. Ferrari Zumbini, *Tra idealità e ideologia. Il Rinnovamento costituzionale nel Regno di Sardegna fra la primavera 1847 e l'inverno 1848*, Torino 2008; C. Ghisalberti, *Stato e costituzione nel Risorgimento*, Milano 1972; A. Chiavistelli, *Dallo Stato alla nazione. Costituzione e sfera pubblica in Toscana dal 1814 al 1849*, Roma 2006.

45 D. Carutti, *Del governo libero*, cit., 242.

46 C. Balbo, *Della monarchia rappresentativa in Italia*, cit., 308.

Balbo lo scoprì sulla propria pelle in quei primi anni di *apprentissage*. Pellegrino Rossi fu assassinato, il ministero democratico Guerrazzi-Montanelli si trovò al centro di ben note traversie.

Il canone costituzionale per cui nel Governo di gabinetto un ministro ha "diritto" di restare al potere, finché sia sorretto da una adeguata *influenza* parlamentare, si fonda sulla presunzione che tale armonia tra l'esecutivo e il legislativo sia indizio dell'adesione del paese. Che cos'è l'"appello al popolo" se non una forma istituzionalizzata di appello all'opinione pubblica che è il *sancta sanctorum* del "governo di opinione"?

Qui però ci muoviamo in uno spazio che si allontana da quell'*Appel au peuple* che è, come è noto, la dizione più comunemente usata per designare le ratifiche nel "modello" napoleonico.[47] Il discorso retorico dell'opinione pubblica "nazionale" e "costituzionale" viene costruito attorno alla figura del Re in Parlamento nella forma della monarchia rappresentativa.[48]

4. L'opinione pubblica e la sovranità della ragione

I primi incunaboli del pensiero costituzionale liberale moderato ed "egemonico" registrano il problema e le tensioni innescate dalle vicende del 1848–1860. Il problema è, appunto, sintetizzato dalla formula "il voto della nazione" o suffragio nazionale.[49] Questa dinamica, con le sue accelerazioni e con i suoi arresti, con elementi di "casualità" e con elementi di "regia" e di "razionalità" tutt'altro che secondari, delinea i campi di tensione tra costituzione, opinione pubblica e appello al popolo.[50] La costituzione non è più una ideologia, ma è concretamente lo Statuto albertino (una carta formalmente ottriata); l'opinione

47 Cfr. C. Cassina, *Il bonapartismo o la falsa eccezione. Napoleone III, i francesi e la tradizione illiberale*, Roma 2001; Id., *Parole vecchie, parole nuove. Ottocento francese e modernità politica*, Roma 2007; Id., *Alle origini del plebiscito «dei moderni»*, in *Giornale di storia costituzionale / Journal of Constitutional History*, 18, 2008, II semestre, n. monografico *Politiche del Popolo*, a cura di L. Scuccimarra, 89–110; Id., *L'istituto plebiscitario in Francia. Appunti per un profilo storico (1792–1969)*, in *Vox Populi? Pratiche plebiscitarie in Francia Italia Germania (secoli XVIII–XX)*, a cura di E. Fimiani, Bologna 2010, 59–86.

48 C. Ghisalberti, *La monarchia rappresentativa nel pensiero di Cesare Balbo*, in *Stato Nazione e Costituzione nell'Italia contemporanea*, Napoli 1999, 144.

49 E. Mongiano, *Il "voto della Nazione". I plebisciti nella formazione del regno d'Italia (1848–60)*, Torino 2003.

50 Utili osservazioni in E. Fimiani, *Introduzione: «il breve conclusivo monosillabo»*, in *Vox Populi?*, cit., 32–34; Id., *Per una storia delle teorie e delle pratiche plebiscitarie nell'Europa moderna e contemporanea*, in *Annali dell'Istituto storico italo-germanico*, 21, 1995, 297–313.

pubblica si identifica in prevalenza con un ben determinato corpo elettorale; l'appello al popolo è *la cosa* (prima ancora che la *parola*) del plebiscito. In questo contesto / processo si intrecciano due linee che danno conto della problematicità dello sviluppo costituzionale italiano. Potremmo parlare di uno scarto tra il "sistema dei plebisciti" e il regime elettorale censitario / capacitario che alimenta il circuito della volontà politica. Si può dire che il plebiscito *dei moderni* nasca come prima, necessaria, benché approssimativa traduzione di un esercizio quantomeno diffuso del potere sovrano. Il suo ingresso nella politica moderna, non a caso, avviene contestualmente ai due eventi che hanno segnato la nascita del mondo occidentale contemporaneo: la rivoluzione americana (Massachusett e New Hampshire) e la rivoluzione francese.

In occasione del precoce voto parmense del maggio 1848, si legge: «Più non sono, né più debbono tornare quei tempi i quali impedivano che la pubblica opinione si manifestasse; ora che a nessuno è interdetto di esporre liberamente e civilmente il proprio voto, assai meno è interdetto a molti, ad una Città, ad un Popolo».[51] L'appello al popolo, in questa prospettiva, deve essere "inclusivo", deve esprimere la volontà della nazione. Si fa uso di un largo suffragio «che in astratto dava pieno riconoscimento alla sovranità popolare, ma che nei fatti chiamava direttamente ad esprimersi talora senza particolare cognizione di causa, cittadini che non avevano esperienza alcuna del voto, né politico, né amministrativo».[52] Viceversa, "l'appello al popolo" nell'ordinario circuito della volontà politica è "esclusivo", limitato, legato anzitutto al censo.

Tra il 1848 e l'unificazione scorgiamo questo doppio movimento, questo doppio livello di manifestazione della volontà della "nazione". Gli studi più recenti – che hanno opportunamente "preso sul serio" il fenomeno – mostrano, attraverso il "sacro" dei "plebisciti", una indubbia dimensione partecipativa, popolare, celebrativa dell'unità nazionale che si rivela, anche attraverso specifici linguaggi e rappresentazioni, attorno al capo della nazione.[53] Sorge allora spontanea la domanda: come si poteva conciliare l'uso del suffragio universale a fini "plebiscitari" con la pratica del modello "orleanista"[54] (censitario-liberale)? La legge elettorale sarda del 17 marzo 1848 univa profili timocratici, alfabetizzazione, età, genere maschile: nel 1848 erano in possesso dei diritti politici

51 Cit. da E. Mongiano, *Il "voto della Nazione"*, cit., 257.

52 *Ibidem*, 75.

53 In particolare G. L. Fruci, *Il «suffragio nazionale». Discorsi e rappresentazioni del voto universale nel 1848 italiano*, in *Contemporanea*, 8, 2005, 597–620; Id., *Il sacramento dell'unità nazionale. Linguaggi, iconografia e pratiche dei plebisciti risorgimentali (1848–1870)*, in *Il Risorgimento*, Annali 22, a cura di A. M. Banti, P. Ginsborg, Torino 2007, 567–605.

54 Cfr. L. Lacchè, *La libertà che guida il Popolo. Le Tre Gloriose Giornate del luglio 1830 e le "Chartes" nel costituzionalismo francese*, Bologna 2002.

77.366 cittadini maschi di età superiore ai 25 anni, su una massa di un milione circa di cittadini maggiorenni.[55] L'uso del suffragio universale maschile, appello per chiedere al popolo il "voto della nazione" nel 1848, nel 1860 e nelle successive occasioni – senza però che tale congegno potesse realmente retroagire sul circuito parlamentare della volontà politica – rivelava il principale campo di tensione interno a quel *doppio movimento* o *doppio livello di legittimazione*. L'*opinione pubblica nazionale* era il *vapore* del processo di unificazione, ma il ricorso al suffragio universale non poteva essere fonte, per i liberali, di legittimazione della classe dirigente italiana. Al contrario, nel *Dizionario politico popolare* (1851), di ispirazione popolare / democratica, si identifica invece l'opinione *pubblica* con il popolo. «O popolo! Sia veramente *tua* la tua opinione, ed allora sarà vero che la voce del popolo è voce di Dio».[56] D'altra parte, sono ben noti i dubbi di Cavour sull'uso del suffragio universale per fondare la nazione.[57]

Verrebbe allora da dire che quando si tratta di assumere la decisione "costituente"[58] (senza poterlo dire) occorra la volontà di "tutti", ma quando invece bisogna indicare chi rappresenta (unitariamente) la nazione (e quindi governa), "pochi" lo possano fare. I plebisciti sono strumenti di autodeterminazione che nella vicenda italiana legittimano situazioni di fatto, più o meno consolidate,[59] ed operano al livello della politica internazionale. Nondimeno, quella compresenza di tecniche di legittimazione resta un campo di tensione nel profilo teorico e nelle esperienze del costituzionalismo liberale.

Proprio per smussare gli angoli di questo campo di tensione, il ricorso al sintagma opinione pubblica può costituire, in qualche caso, una sorta di punto mediano tra la visione censitaria del suffragio e la scelta di una legittimazione "unanimistica" tipica del discorso plebiscitario. Come aveva scritto d'Azeglio nel 1847, l'«... opinione ... è composta di classi, di ceti e d'individui disponenti di

55 R. Martucci, *Storia costituzionale italiana. Dallo Statuto albertino alla Repubblica (1848–2001)*, Roma 2002, 85.

56 *Dizionario politico popolare*, a cura di P. Trifone, introduzione di L. Serianni, Roma s. d., 167.

57 E. Mongiano, *Il "voto della Nazione"*, cit., 206. Di un uso del suffragio universale in chiave antigiacobina e antirivoluzionaria ma anche antibonapartista da parte di Cavour ha scritto acutamente C. Pavone, *Appunti sul principio plebiscitario*, in *La virtù del politico*, a cura di G. Carbone, Venezia 1996, 162.

58 Su questo tema cruciale v. M. Fioravanti, *Potere costituente e diritto pubblico. Il caso italiano, in particolare*, in *Potere costituente e riforme costituzionali*, a cura di P. Pombeni, Bologna 1992, 55–77.

59 Cfr. G. S. Pene Vidari, *Considerazioni sui plebisciti italiani del 1860*, in *Rivista di storia del diritto italiano*, LXXXIII, 2010, 5–24.

maggiore o minor potenza secondo l'autorità, il grado, la ricchezza, i talenti, la scienza ec. d'ognuno ...».[60] Ma l'opinione pubblica, aveva osservato Sismondi, esprime «più i sensi e le opinioni dell'aristocrazia intellettuale, che quella della democrazia».[61] L'opinione è nondimeno fondamentale per l'esistenza del governo rappresentativo. E tuttavia, come aveva osservato il Boncompagni, in uno dei più importanti incunaboli del costituzionalismo liberale italiano, un conto era l'opinione "volgare", apparente, licenziosa, un conto quella "vera", imparziale, libera, illuminata, perseverante.[62] Questa dialettica tra l'"opinione", quella "vera", antisettaria, dei moderati e progressisti, e le altre "opinioni", avrebbe ben presto mostrato i limiti del '48 liberale. Massimo d'Azeglio anche questa volta fu tra i più lucidi a cogliere, sin dal 1847, i pericoli di un'opinione pubblica / moltitudine adulata e condotta dalle parole d'ordine dei democratici. Specie dopo l'armistizio di Salasco, appariva sempre più importante conquistare lo spazio pubblico della comunicazione politica. Le piazze e i tumulti (ed ora i parlamenti) apparivano luoghi nei quali i "pochi" avrebbero potuto avere la meglio sulla maggioranza silenziosa, tanto più se sostenuti da un giornalismo[63] che rischiava di ergersi a potere autonomo, strumento di lotta politica, e non più al servizio della genuina opinione pubblica. La stampa e il giornalismo, proprio nella temperie che precedè il 1848, assunsero un ruolo politico-costituzionale che mai avevano potuto svolgere, in quei termini, sino ad allora, mostrando da subito la straordinaria potenza ma anche, agli occhi dei moderati, limiti e pericoli[64] «Io, veda, caro Torelli – scriveva d'Azeglio – ho gran cura della mia riputazione – il solo bene che abbia – e perciò studio l'opinione pubblica e disprezzo la popolarità. So che mi farò buon nome facendo ciò che approva l'opinione pubblica – quella grande di tutti i tempi – e non quello che chiedono le ragazzate effimere di pochi».[65]

60 M. d'Azeglio, *Proposta d'un programma*, cit., 19.

61 J. Ch. L. Simonde de Sismondi, *Studi intorno alle costituzioni dei popoli liberi*, Capolago 1839, 110.

62 C. Boncompagni, *Della monarchia rappresentativa*, cit., 68 ss.

63 M. d'Azeglio, *Del giornalismo*, in Id., *Scritti e discorsi politici*, a cura di M. de Rubris, III, 1853–1865, Firenze 1938. Sul punto v. D. M. Bruni, *Opinione pubblica e lotta politica nella riflessione di Massimo d'Azeglio a cavallo del 1848*, cit., 122 ss.; D. Maldini, *La stampa moderata e democratica*, in V. Castronovo (a cura di), *La nascita dell'opinione pubblica in Italia*, cit., 15.

64 Cfr. più in generale F. Della Peruta, *Il giornalismo dal 1847 all'Unità*, in V. Castronovo, N. Tranfaglia (a cura di), *La stampa italiana del Risorgimento*, Roma, Bari 1979, 287–356; V. Castronovo, *Stampa e opinione pubblica nell'Italia liberale*, in V. Castronovo, N. Tranfaglia (a cura di), *La stampa italiana nell'età liberale*, Roma, Bari 1979, 5–68.

65 C. Paoli (a cura di), *Lettere di Massimo d'Azeglio a Giuseppe Torelli*, Milano 1870, 13, cit. da D. Maldini, *La stampa moderata e democratica*, cit., 11.

Nel 1846 l'idea di opinione pubblica identificava, per i liberali moderati, uno spazio dotato di una valenza "positiva" (sinonimo di "giudizio di ragione"); possedeva una forte valenza nazionale, ovvero sovralocale; una *forza morale congruente con la libertà dei moderni*; era infine un "contenitore" in grado di tenere insieme classi, ceti, individui. Si trattava dunque di una struttura retorico-discorsiva che è condizione del sistema rappresentativo, senza poter essere identificata completamente con esso. In questo percorso costruito dai liberali subalpini (e non solo) l'opinione pubblica era stata messa al centro del nuovo spazio costituzionale e con esso della nuova nazione.

Il riferimento all'opinione pubblica nazionale è uno degli argomenti concettuali e retorici per allontanare e depotenziare il pericolo di un *autonomo* momento "costituente" tra il 1848 e il 1860. L'opinione pubblica non è *volontà* "assoluta", sciolta da vincoli; se è poi nazionale, diventa "storicità", temperamento, limite "costituzionale".

Il potere costituente – scrive Balbo in *Della monarchia rappresentativa in Italia* – distrugge l'idea secondo cui la sovranità risiede nei tre poteri e quindi «la rappresentanza nazionale non risiede né può risiedere in nessuno dei tre poteri detti, ma in tutti e tre; che nessuno di questi solo, ma tutti e tre si debbono chiamare Parlamento; e che in questo Parlamento solo può e debbe risedere la potenza del fare e disfare le leggi e di mutare la costituzione dello Stato, quella potenza che è opportunamente ed esattamente chiamata *onnipotenza parlamentare*».[66] La modellistica britannica si intreccia con la teoria dottrinaria dei Guizot e dei Royer Collard che cerca di fondare un regime in grado di associare l'ordine alla libertà. Come conciliare il principio della libertà con una autorità stabile? A quali condizioni rappresentare la società e garantire un governo forte?

Su questa linea di pensiero, la natura *democratica* della sovranità, che si esprime attraverso il potere costituente, è vista come una forza bruta, un fiume in piena che non sembra riconoscere né argini, né barriere, che abbatte il pluralismo dei poteri, livella le condizioni, riduce lo spazio di autonomia degli individui, contesta le differenze e i ranghi sociali. I liberali cercano in vari modi di «neutralizzare» la sovranità poiché sanno per esperienza diretta che questa tende a concentrare il potere in un solo «luogo». La topografia liberale si fonda su una pluralità di luoghi del potere, divisi eppure collaboranti, moderatori l'uno dell'altro, rivolti ad uno stesso fine. Sono stati soprattutto i dottrinari, nel corso della Restaurazione, a qualificare la sovranità in termini prevalentemente negativi, trattandosi per loro di una «controversia teologico-giuridica».[67]

66 C. Balbo, *Della monarchia rappresentativa*, cit., 209.
67 A. Omodeo, *Studi sull'età della Restaurazione. La cultura francese nell'età della Restaurazione*..., Torino 1974, 2 ed., 66.

E' nell'ambito della monarchia censitaria che si è formata progressivamente la dottrina della costituzione come fonte di sovranità. Questa concezione, come è noto, era destinata – sotto il nome di «sovranità della costituzione» – ad avere significativi sviluppi nella storia costituzionale europea. Era stato Royer-Collard dopo la Restaurazione ad affermare l'equivalenza tra sovranità del popolo e «sovranità della forza». Nel 1820 François Guizot richiamava l'analogia tra ogni forma di sovranità che si pretendesse assoluta, derivata dal popolo o dal diritto divino, e l'usurpazione della forza, per aggiungere poi che la sovranità popolare era una forma di tirannia, ovvero il potere assoluto della maggioranza numerica sulla minoranza.[68] «Io credo alla sovranità della ragione, della giustizia, del diritto: sta qui il sovrano legittimo che il mondo cerca e che cercherà sempre; poiché la ragione, la verità, la giustizia non si trovano in nessun luogo complete e infallibili».[69] Il diritto e la legittimità si trovano dappertutto e in nessun luogo, perché solo così la società sarà stabile e il potere regolare. Si ritorna dunque alla prima riflessione costituzionale post-rivoluzionaria e da lì si crede di poter ripartire per "addomesticare" la sovranità nella costituzione. Si pensa, insomma, di aver trovato la soluzione per il «paradosso di Clermont-Tonnerre» secondo il quale «... o si esercita la sovranità o si rispetta la Carta ...».[70]

Nei dottrinari – da Royer-Collard a Cousin sino a Guizot – la sovranità della ragione è il punto di convergenza della teoria della rappresentanza e della fondamentale distinzione tra origine ed esercizio della sovranità.[71] Il costituzionalismo del gruppo di Coppet e l'idea di nazione elaborata dagli scrittori controrivoluzionari forniscono ai dottrinari taluni «ingredienti» per elaborare – a modo loro – una teoria politica.[72] La sovranità della ragione possiede la stessa natura e presuppone le stesse condizioni di esercizio della sovranità nazionale. In particolare, ciò che le accomuna è proprio la volontà di collocare la sovranità in una sorta di non-luogo, o quanto meno in una »regione« sufficientemente lontana.[73] Non è certo casuale che tale filosofia, nel corso del regime orleanista,

68 F. Guizot, *Philosophie politique: de la souveraineté*, in Id., *Histoire de la civilisation en Europe depuis la chute de l'Empire romain jusqu'à la Révolution française*, ed. a cura di P. Rosanvallon, Paris 1985, 309 ss. (*Présentation* di Rosanvallon) e 374.

69 F. Guizot, *Du gouvernement de la France depuis la Restauration, et du ministère actuel*, Paris 1820, 201. Sul carattere trascendente della sovranità in Guizot v. C. Lefort, *Introduction* a F. Guizot, *Des moyens de gouvernement et d'opposition dans l'état actuel de la France*, Paris 1988 (1821), 31.

70 P. Colombo, *Governo e costituzione. La trasformazione del regime politico nelle teorie dell'età rivoluzionaria francese*, Milano 1993, 373 ss.

71 Su questo profilo rinvio a L. Lacchè, *La libertà che guida il Popolo*, cit.

72 G. Bacot, *Carré de Malberg et l'origine de la distinction entre souveraineté du peuple et souveraineté nationale*, Paris 1985, 120 ss.

73 *Ibidem*, 135. Cfr. anche D. Roldán, *Charles de Rémusat. Certitudes et impasses du libéralisme doctrinaire*, prefazione di P. Rosanvallon, Paris 1999, 133 ss.

ambisca a diventare anche una dottrina giuridica. Ci si rifugia nella *Charte* per puntellare il nuovo regime. «Chiedere dov'è la sovranità – dice Royer-Collard – significa essere e dichiararsi a favore del dispotismo».[74] Non è sovrano nessuno dei poteri istituiti dalla *Charte*; in tal senso non può esistere un sovrano, ovvero un potere investito di tutti i diritti e senza limiti.

La costituzione diventava essa stessa un parametro di ragione e ad essa si assegnava, sorta di «luogo neutrale», l'attributo di entità *sovrana* per modo che né il principe né il popolo, né la monarchia né la democrazia potessero pretendere l'esercizio del minaccioso potere costituente.[75]

5. A mo' di epilogo

Nel 1883 Agostino Bertani, intervenendo in Parlamento contro la legge sul giuramento politico, allora in discussione, notava come, finalmente, lo Statuto non potesse più dirsi "plebiscitario". «Ella vedrà – gli rispose il Presidente Farini – che nei plebisciti si è votato per l'Italia e la monarchia costituzionale di Vittorio Emanuele». Sulla scia di questo dibattito, il costituzionalista Attilio Brunialti intervenne prontamente con un saggio intitolato *La Costituzione italiana e i Plebisciti*.[76] Un altro studioso di costituzioni, l'on. Augusto Pierantoni,[77] aveva ribadito in aula la natura *ottriata* dello Statuto.[78] Per un Bertani che negava la natura plebiscitaria della costituzione, c'era un Brunialti che si domandava: «come può essere che lo Statuto sia *ottriato* e la costituzione plebiscitaria?».[79] Questo interrogativo consentiva al costituzionalista veneto di ripercorre le tappe che avevano portato alla formazione dello Stato italiano. Brunialti metteva a confronto l'esperienza francese con quella italiana. «I francesi uccisero la libertà, i nostri la consacrarono, e ne garantirono l'esistenza; quelli furono un'arma in mano ad un sovrano assoluto, questi diedero una sanzione giuridica al sentimento nazionale, e più per le Potenze straniere, che per noi e per il nostro diritto pubblico. La costituzione italiana veniva ad essere il risultato di una

74 G. Remond, *Royer-Collard. Son essai d'un système politique*, Paris 1933, 39.

75 Si vedano al riguardo le osservazioni di C. Schmitt, *Verfassungslehre*, Berlin 1928, tr. it. *Dottrina della costituzione*, Milano 1984, 21, 80–83, 270.

76 In *Nuova antologia*, XXXVII, 1883, 322–349.

77 Su Augusto Pierantoni v. L. Lacchè, *«Celebrato come una gloria nazionale». Pietro Sbarbaro e il "risorgimento" di Alberico Gentili*, in AA., *Alberico Gentili. Atti dei Convegni nel quarto centenario della morte*, Milano 2010, vol. II, *passim*, in part. 233.

78 L. Lacchè, *Le carte ottriate. La teoria dell'octroi e le esperienze costituzionali nell'Europa post-rivoluzionaria*, in *Giornale di storia costituzionale*, 18, II, 2009, 229–254.

79 A. Brunialti, *La Costituzione italiana e i Plebisciti*, cit., 323.

affermazione della coscienza nazionale, affermata giuridicamente coi plebisciti ... Per gli italiani che formarono il regno lo Statuto non è un atto unilaterale, non è ottriato o largito dal principe; bensì un patto nazionale, stretto tra il principe e il popolo, una condizione *sine qua non* posta alla monarchia».[80] Dall'autoritario plebiscito bonapartista al plebiscito nazionale e *convenzionale*. «La Costituzione italiana non è adunque ottriata come la piemontese, e non si raccoglie tutta nello Statuto. Questo ne contiene le disposizioni essenziali; ma come vi sono in esso disposizioni che non hanno più valore, così vi sono principii non scritti nello Statuto, i quali non si potrebbero violare impunemente. *Ottriata* nell'origine, lo Statuto piemontese diventando, insieme alle consuetudini che lo svolsero e completarono, la costituzione italiana, assunse un prevalente carattere *convenzionale*, e dal 1861 in poi si è sviluppato come una costituzione *storica*, adattandosi sempre più alle tradizioni, al temperamento, ai bisogni progressivi del popolo italiano».

Se Brunialti propone una lettura di "discontinuità" tra lo Statuto "ottriato" e la "costituzione" *convenzionale* nata dai plebisciti, nondimeno, in sintonia con la visione liberal-moderata, descrive e respinge nettamente la cultura costituzionale dei repubblicani incardinata sulla centralità del popolo "atomistico", sull'idea del potere costituente.[81] Ma, pur respingendo tale teoria, «La *monarchia costituzionale* non può dipendere perciò dalla volontà di un corpo elettorale, o di un Parlamento, né da quella stessa del Sovrano».[82] La costituzione-patto non nasce dalla sola volontà di un corpo elettorale o dagli stessi organi costituzionali, ma si sviluppa attraverso la *storia*.

La tesi di Brunialti sulla "discontinuità" del processo unitario e costituzionale restò "minoritaria" rispetto alla dottrina prevalente che istituzionalizzò invece il *canone della continuità* (Santi Romano, Ranelletti e altri, ma non Orlando e, per ragioni diverse, Anzilotti) e della fusione per successive "annessioni".[83] Ciò che però lega i diversi interventi è la costante affermazione di uno *spazio di costruzione dello Stato nazionale* che respinge o depotenzia la dimensione "volontaristica" di quell'*appello al popolo* che si è rivelato alla scena della *politica moderna* nel corso del Settecento "rivoluzionario". Ernest Renan, proprio a

80 *Ibidem*, 339.
81 *Ibidem*, 342.
82 *Ibidem*, 343.
83 F. Colao, *L'"idea di nazione" nei giuristi italiani tra Ottocento e Novecento*, in *Quaderni fiorentini per la storia del pensiero giuridico moderno*, 30, 2001, 255–360; Id., *Due momenti della storia costituzionale italiana nella cultura giuridica tra Ottocento e Novecento: la "formazione del regno d'Italia" e la "trasformazione dello Stato" dall'età liberale al fascismo*, in *Costruire lo Stato, costruire la storia. Politica e moderno fra '800 e '900*, a cura di A. De Benedictis, Bologna 2003, 183–247.

ridosso dell'ultimo appuntamento plebiscitario di Luigi Napoleone Bonaparte, si chiede: «Il sovrano investito attraverso plebiscito della pienezza dei diritti popolari, può essere parlamentare?».[84] «Può la pratica plebiscitaria sposarsi con le forme del governo parlamentare?».[85]

Una domanda, questa, che identifica il campo di tensione che attraversa la vicenda dei "plebisciti" italiani, la formazione *empirica* dello Stato, la sua dimensione costituzionale, la formalizzazione operata dai giuristi tra Otto e Novecento. «Così, è sicuramente vero che la fase di trapasso all'unità nazionale fu lunga e tormentata, differenziata per zone e regioni, con un concorso delle classi dirigenti locali, e delle popolazioni che furono chiamate a esprimersi con i plebisciti, certamente non irrilevante; ma è altrettanto certo che il complesso di quelle azioni non si espresse mai in una volontà che intendesse valere davvero come atto di fondazione di un nuovo Stato ...».[86]

Protagonisti della vicenda, almeno per la dottrina giuridica di inizio Novecento, non furono alla fine né l'opinione pubblica nazionale, né gli stessi "appelli al popolo". L'elemento unificatore, esso solo *costituente*, non potè che essere – secondo il paradigma organicista[87] – il preesistente Stato sovrano istitutore della "nazione" e di una unità politica altrimenti resa fragile da elementi eterogenei, parziali, "locali".[88] Nel 1883 Brunialti così concludeva il suo saggio sui plebisciti cogliendo la tensione di fondo: «L'on. Bertani può forse sofisticare ancora sul carattere dei plebisciti, sulla natura dello Statuto, sulla indeterminatezza del concetto di costituzione. Ma la moderna generazione non lo comprende più. Nata e cresciuta in libero paese ha più vigoroso e preciso il senso della libertà vera; non la toccano i fortissimi sentimenti, ma neanche le passioni e gli errori che accompagnarono e non riuscirono ad impedire il nostro risorgimento. Questa generazione non riconosce queste libertà costituzionali dal principe, e non è disposta a lasciarle compromettere dalla piazza ...».[89]

84 E. Renan, *La Monarchie constitutionnelle en France*, in *Revue des Deux Mondes*, novembre 1869, 90, cit. da C. Cassina, *Alle origini del plebiscito «dei moderni»*, cit., 107.

85 C. Cassina, *Alle origini del plebiscito «dei moderni»*, cit., 107.

86 M. Fioravanti, *Le dottrine dello Stato e della costituzione*, in *Storia dello stato italiano dall'Unità a oggi*, a cura di R. Romanelli, Roma 1995, 410.

87 F. Colao, *L'"idea di nazione"*, cit., 286.

88 M. Fioravanti, *Le dottrine dello Stato e della costituzione*, cit., 411.

89 A. Brunialti, *La Costituzione italiana e i Plebisciti*, cit., 349.

Per una teoria costituzionale dell'opinione pubblica. Il dibattito italiano (XIX sec.)

1. Come l'araba fenice

«Addotta talvolta come testimonio di fatto, talvolta come giudice, talaltra ancora come maestra di verità, la pubblica opinione è una autorità, di cui nessuno può facilmente definire la vera competenza ... Tutti la invocano, ma ben pochi conoscono i segni e i caratteri per cui sicuramente riconoscerla ...» (C. F. Gabba 1881, 25). Così l'"enciclopedico" Gabba, filosofo del diritto, civilista e "sociologo" (cfr. P. Beneduce 1998, 821; S. Cingari 2001, 63–64) evidenzia – parlando dalla cattedra fiorentina del «Cesare Alfieri» – il carattere sfuggente di una "nuova" parola, di un concetto e di una categoria-contenitore che a partire dagli anni '70 del XIX secolo ha iniziato ad attirare l'attenzione di una composita schiera di studiosi italiani. Sulla stessa linea il costituzionalista Ignazio Brunelli – agli inizi del Novecento – afferma essere «non nuovo» il tema (1906, 8), offrendo un elenco di chi l'ha già fatto oggetto di studî. «Ciò non ostante noi non sappiamo dire che cosa sia realmente questa decantata pubblica opinione. Anzi ci è persino lecito chiederci se realmente essa esiste, o non sia piuttosto un nome vano al quale non corrisponda qualche cosa di concreto» (*Ibidem*, 10). Scipio Sighele, invece, trae dalla sostanziale indefinibilità del soggetto un motivo per spiegare lo scarso numero di analisi disponibili (1899, 88). Nel 1895 Antonio Teso afferma che forse di nessun concetto si parla tanto quanto dell'opinione pubblica, divenuta ormai una vera parola "magica", al pari di popolo, libertà, democrazia. Tuttavia se ne parla senza sapere bene cosa essa sia e ciò «dipende [...] dalla indeterminatezza di significato delle parole del linguaggio politico, da cui proviene la varietà di sensi che ad esse si sogliono attribuire, ciò che non può a meno d'esser causa di grande confusione» (1895, 6).

Questo dibattito italiano di fine secolo, sulle piste del moderno concetto di opinione pubblica, non ha ricevuto finora una particolare attenzione. Pur non rivestendo un carattere di marcata originalità – anche se Franz von Holtzendorff (1880), per esempio, polemizza e dialoga a distanza con Saverio Scolari (1871) –, nondimeno individua una soglia concettuale assai stimolante per cogliere la complessa fenomenologia della *pubblicità* politico-rappresentativa in una fase di grande significato, tra l'ottimismo della raggiunta istituzionalizzazione e i timori precoci per l'emergente dimensione della "crisi". In tal senso, tale studio può offrire utili indicazioni di natura anche metodologica in relazione agli oggetti e agli strumenti propri della storia costituzionale e in particolare al nodo essenziale che, attraverso mille sfaccettature, consiste nel rapporto tra la dimensione fluida del «linguaggio politico» e il difficile ma robusto cammino della formalizzazione giuridica.

Gli autori italiani fanno iniziare il loro "naturale" percorso ricostruttivo – quasi sempre in maniera tralatizia – da scrittori come Romagnosi o Sismondi. Senza dover riandare alle fonti inglesi e francesi del XVII e XVIII secolo, se non per richiami indiretti e perlopiù stereotipati, recuperano più il tema settecentesco del "tribunale dell'opinione pubblica" che quello antico / moderno dell'opinione "regina del mondo" (cfr. W. Gunn 1995). Attraverso Romagnosi si arriva più o meno consapevolmente a Filangieri e soprattutto alla fonte originaria, a Jacques Necker (cfr. L. Jaume 2003) e alla sua celebre rappresentazione di quel tribunale, considerato anzitutto come figura retorica (cfr. K. M. Baker 1993; S. Maza 1987), nel quale siede trionfante l'opinione pubblica «invisibile ed inesorabile potenza, che senza tesori, senza guardie e senza armate si fa ubbidire dai magistrati, dalle città, dalle nazioni, e giunge a comandare persino nelle reggie» (G. D. Romagnosi 1849, 106). Non è casuale il riferimento ai due autori citati: entrambi, pur paradigmatici di due ben diversi approcci al problema della monarchia costituzionale (rappresentativa), descrivono la fase di transizione dalla "retorica" dell'opinione pubblica come istanza di *giudizio* propria dell'*intelligenza umana* alla sua istituzionalizzazione come "potere predominante" (di cui però diffidare in termini di validità) (Romagnosi; cfr. Mannori 2003), ma anche come fattore civile, da far maturare e illuminare, e da mettere in equilibrio con la «saviezza nazionale», perché l'«... opinione instabile, passeggera e capricciosa, è un tiranno onde convien diffidare non meno che d'ogni altro tiranno» (S. Sismondi 1839, 161). Nella duplice analisi si intravedono il dover essere dell'opinione pubblica, fluido senza il quale nessun governo costituzionale, il governo dei moderni, può ben vivere e prosperare, ma anche i fattori concretissimi di degenerazione e di intrinseca relatività che rischiano di tramutarla in una inesorabile macchina di conformismo se non di vero e proprio dispotismo della maggioranza. Nella seconda metà del secolo gl'echi da John Stuart Mill e da Tocqueville (v. J. Habermas 2001, 156 ss.; N. Matteucci 1980, 428) sono evidenti, ma saranno invece – lo si vedrà – autori come Bluntschli o Gneist ad esercitare la più duratura e vasta influenza.

L'opinione pubblica sembrerebbe così bipartita, tra un'immagine razionale, còlta, borghese, proto-liberale, omogenea e astrattizzante delle "origini" e una già critica, segnata dalla rapida decadenza e dalla crisi incipiente dell'oggetto di analisi. C'è da chiedersi, tuttavia, quanto questa opinione pubblica – analizzata in Italia tra la metà dell'800 e gl'inizi del '900 da autori tanto diversi per competenze e spessore scientifico – coincida, in che misura, in quali termini, con quali trasformazioni, con la *public opinion* o l'*opinion publique* di ascendenza sei-settecentesca. Come è stato giustamente osservato (G. Civile 2000) si rischia di passare da una sorta di "età dell'oro" (a sua volta ben lontana dal poter essere vista in termini di "unitarietà") a quella di una rapida discesa lungo il crinale della decadenza senza che si possa ritrovare nei discorsi e nelle pratiche un'accezione univoca di pubblico, o di sfera pubblica (il modello liberale di una sfera pubblica borghese), e tanto meno di *opinione pubblica* (cfr. A. Cottereau, P. Ladrière 1992; C. Calhoun 1996). «Nella nostra storia preunitaria mancano tracce significative di un fenomeno socialmente diffuso come in Inghilterra, politicamente dirompente come in Francia, o precocemente concentrato sul tema della nazione come in Germania» (G. Civile 2000, 469). Non si corre solo il rischio di leggere la vicenda italiana come inevitabilmente tarda e "anomala", ma anche di fare dell'opinione pubblica un fenomeno privo di valenza analitica. Recentemente il difficile rapporto tra costituzione e nazione, nel tramonto dell'ordine plurale della "società di società" (a cavallo tra il '700 e i primi decenni dell'800), è stato acutamente osservato attraverso la lente offerta dalla nozione di pubblico (formato prevalentemente da lettori liberi e raziocinanti) e di opinione pubblica, mostrando le peculiarità, le *impasse* e certi paradossi della vicenda "italiana" (L. Mannori 2003). Il *Nachmärz* nostrano impone una decisiva accelerazione – in termini di linguaggi e di pratiche – ma non può che muovere dall'enorme problema di ricondurre il pluralismo delle "società" e delle opinioni entro un nuovo ordine, da legare in maniera indissolubile ad un nuovo spazio pubblico costituzionale-rappresentativo, con al centro il ruolo cruciale, ma tutto da definire, di un'opinione pubblica nazionale.

A ben vedere il caso italiano, a partire dalla metà dell'Ottocento – quando cominciano ad essere riconoscibili elementi importanti di trasformazione (P. Pombeni 1994, 82 ss.) – senza poter essere caratterizzato da un fattore genetico "forte", realizza un intreccio del tutto peculiare. La sua "opinione pubblica" è al contempo problema di qualche consistenza sociologica, di sicura valenza politico-costituzionale e di indubbio rapporto con il processo di *Nation building*. Nella formazione di una "sfera pubblica nazionale" convivono quindi elementi genetici e fattori di transizione e di cambiamento. Nel momento stesso in cui un'opinione pubblica "deve" prendere forma – come autentica questione nazionale – identità sociali e politiche, nuove rispetto al "modello classico", si affacciano sulla scena, con specifiche dimensioni pratiche e proprie reti di partecipazione e di controllo. Nella storia italiana, si potrebbe dire per semplificare, *non c'è tempo* per la piena esplicazione del modello classico (individuato da Habermas), sia come mera trasposizione da un secolo all'altro, senza riconoscere cesure e mutamenti, sia come possibilità di universalizzazione del modello.

In Italia convivono e si sovrappongono quelle che in teoria potrebbero essere individuate come singole "fasi": la fase "ottimistica" dell'opinione pubblica intesa come istanza "esterna" e superiore di giudizio-controllo; quella "interna" della rilevanza "costituzionale" nell'ambito del sistema di governo rappresentativo (il cd. governo di opinione) (J.-Ph. Heurtin 1999); l'ultima, infine, che più rivela i fattori di tensione e di potenziale conflitto. Nei decenni indagati queste diverse caratterizzazioni formano un solo universo concettuale e coloro che ne fanno oggetto di studio ricorrono spesso, non a caso, a differenti registri interpretativi, si tratti dell'osservazione sociologica, dell'analisi politico-costituzionale, dell'applicazione della teoria giuridica dello Stato liberale, ecc.

È nel corso del XIX secolo che il discorso acquista una vera dimensione europea, allorché il governo rappresentativo viene visto *naturaliter* come governo di opinione e la libertà di stampa come strumento di pubblicità, di trasparenza, di comunicazione e di controllo. «C'est dans l'art de conduire l'opinion, ou d'y céder à propos, que consiste la science de gouverner dans les temps modernes», aveva osservato Madame de Staël seguendo le orme paterne (1818, Chap. XIII, 174). Non bisogna però confondere l'idealizzazione politica del modello classico dell'opinione pubblica con la storia stessa dei modi, dei processi e dei circuiti di formazione e sviluppo della sfera pubblica in momenti e contesti diversi. Certamente lo sviluppo ottocentesco di sistemi politici a tendenza parlamentare contribuisce a ridefinire la soglia concettuale tra pubblico e privato generalizzando le forme di articolazione del rapporto tra lo Stato e la società civile. Il luogo del dibattito istituzionalizzato però si deve via via confrontare con nuovi soggetti, attori, parole d'ordine, discorsi politici, pratiche sociali che rivelano una nozione più ricca di opinione pubblica.

2. Tentativi tipologici

L'assunto della indeterminatezza e dell'indefinibilità dell'opinione pubblica non solo non dissuade dal proporre definizioni ma per certi versi finisce coll'alimentare una vera e propria "sfida" lessicologica. I vari autori si provano a coglierne i contorni essenziali, non dopo aver discusso e ricusato le opinioni altrui. Se non è facile individuare tipologie e modelli, sembra tuttavia utile cercare di raggruppare le varie tesi ricostruttive sotto alcune "categorie" principali, senza ovviamente escludere che in molti casi sarebbe possibile operare ulteriori accostamenti se non riscontrare vere e proprie sovrapposizioni.

2.1 Opinione illuminata / opinione mediocre. Il vero e il fallibile

Sotto questa dizione possiamo far rientrare, in realtà, vari atteggiamenti. Più che le sole radici illuministiche del XVIII secolo, si scorgono qui i caratteri dell'approccio liberal-aristocratico (per es. A. S. Kahan 2001). Il "discorso della capacità" – uno dei cardini della cultura liberale ottocentesca su scala europea – è il principale metro di valutazione. Il pericolo del numero e il modo conseguente di articolare e praticare la politica rappresentano gli spettri di un'opinione pubblica come potere delle masse. John Stuart Mill, lettore di Tocqueville e di Wilhelm von Humboldt, parla di "governo mediocre", di spirito di conformismo e di uniformità, di un'Europa nata dalla diversità di carattere e di cultura, che ora però rischia di «diventare un'altra Cina» (1890, 67). Questa opinione pubblica già governa le società e si avvia a predominare nell'augusto recinto degli Stati. La fede nel progresso e nella ragione sembra cedere all'immagine ossessiva della società polverizzata, atomistica, senza più legami e doveri di obbedienza. Il problema della maggioranza rappresenta solo una faccia della medaglia: nell'altra c'è quello speculare delle minoranze. «Non vi sono più poteri abbastanza autonomi ed indipendenti, che avendo il coraggio d'opporsi alla forza numerica delle maggioranze, possano prendere sotto il loro patrocinio e la loro salvaguardia le opinioni e le tendenze che sono in minoranza». «... il contrappeso e correttivo necessario di questa tendenza dovrebbe essere l'individualità sempre più spiegata e decisa dei grandi pensatori» (*Ibidem*, 61–62, 68–69).

I pericoli del governo di maggioranza sono presenti nella pubblicistica italiana (v. anche L. Fracassetti 1893, 6), basti pensare ancora una volta alla recezione dell'ultimo Sismondi (l'opinione pubblica esprime «più i sensi e le opinioni dell'aristocrazia intellettuale, che quella della democrazia», 1839, 110) o ai timori manifestati da un Luigi Palma: a chi chiedere protezione per le minoranze? «Alla stampa? È dominata dalla maggioranza. All'opinione pubblica? È formata dalla maggioranza» (1885, 36). L'opinione pubblica è nondimeno fondamentale per l'esistenza del governo rappresentativo. Ma – come aveva osservato il Bon-Compagni, in uno dei più importanti incunaboli del costituzionalismo liberale italiano, – un conto era l'opinione "volgare" (le passioni non temperate dalla ragione e dalla riflessione sono volgari), apparente, licenziosa, un conto quella "vera", imparziale, libera, illuminata, perseverante (1848, 68 ss.). Se l'opinione pubblica e i partiti, in quanto fenomeni sociali, sono il risultato della cooperazione intellettuale di molte persone, «hanno però e devono necessariamente avere il loro primo germe e il primo impulso in pochi individui, e talvolta persino in uno solo». Anche nel campo politico l'opinione pubblica ha bisogno del concorso dei molti e dell'iniziativa dei pochi (C. F. Gabba 1881, 89–90).

In tal senso, ritorna il problema del "governo delle opinioni". L'uomo di Stato è spesso invocato come il migliore interprete dell'opinione pubblica.

La posizione influente di Gneist rafforza questa idea, sulla scia di Hegel che lascia al politico il compito di riconoscere l'opinione, altrimenti non determinabile dallo scienziato che dovrà limitarsi ad additarne genesi, sviluppo, valore ed organi (cfr. la critica di L. Minguzzi, 1893, 30 e le osservazioni di I. Brunelli 1906, 23). Se gli scrittori inglesi sono visti per lo più come fautori dell'opinione pubblica, «Tra i tedeschi, invece, e specialmente tra i seguaci della teoria del così detto "governo giuridico", annoveriamo i più focosi avversarii» (I. Brunelli 1906, 34). Von Gneist in particolare mostra di temere una società che difetta di "senso giuridico" (cfr. K. Luig 1992, 23–24). Se le spinte egoistiche che guidano l'individuo nella sfera privata venissero lasciate a se stesse ne nascerebbe un tale caos «che niuno potrebbe supporre che un re od un ministro possa lasciare il Governo *alla somma di codeste idee*, ossia *all'opinione pubblica*» (R. von Gneist 1891, 1277; cfr. le osservazioni di I. Artom 1891, 1135).

Se la società deve quindi organizzarsi e disciplinarsi mediante organi universalmente riconosciuti dalla cultura liberale come "fattori" dell'opinione pubblica (stampa, associazioni, elezioni, partiti politici), nondimeno lo spettro della parzialità e del conflitto appare essere un ostacolo alla piena affermazione del *Rechtsstaat*. Lo "Stato giuridico", specialmente nella sua veste di Stato fondato sull'amministrazione, rappresenta il più grande tentativo compiuto dai giuristi europei (con importanti articolazioni italiane) per costruire un modello di governo della società prevalentemente anti-democratico (nel senso ottocentesco del termine), riducendo al massimo attriti e tensioni e salvaguardando una determinata idea di ordine politico-giuridico (per tutti cfr. F. Tessitore 1988; M. Fioravanti 1979 e 2001). Giorgio Arcoleo individua la debolezza dell'opinione pubblica nella sua stessa natura: essa obbedisce all'impulso, «manca di limiti, di responsabilità, di leggi ...» (1907, 121–122).

Il tema antichissimo della fallibilità dell'opinione – che i filosofi contrappongono a ragione – attraversa per intero questo indirizzo e dalle pagine di Gneist e Bluntschli, pur con profonde differenze, s'afferma in Italia con echi e segni evidenti. Se tuttavia l'opinione non è in sé infallibile, se oscilla, se il suo giudizio è spesso formato senza che ci sia una vera conoscenza delle cose, se può essere turbata da passioni e condotta ad arte all'errore, resta pur sempre un'importante forza morale con la quale fare i conti. Bluntschli la considera «La più grande forza extraufficiale, la di cui influenza fin da un secolo nel mondo civilizzato è sicuramente aumentata ... Anche i suoi dispregiatori non possono negare la sua potenza, e qualunque uomo di Stato moderno è nella necessità di dover calcolare questa "nuova grande forza"» (1879, 154). «Perciò l'uomo di Stato non deve dispregiare la pubblica opinione, quantunque non sempre l'approvi. Egli deve averle riguardo non per la sua verità ma per la sua forza. Egli deve adoperarsi d'illuminare la pubblica opinione quando gli è contraria per pregiudizî, e correggerla quando è erronea» (*Ibidem*, 156).

Proprio gl'uomini politici, gli statisti, sono considerati "coefficienti" dell'opinione pubblica, come dimostrerebbero gli esempi relativi al barone von Stein in Germania, di O'Connor in Irlanda, di Cavour in Italia (A. Teso 1895, 21). Anche quando la criticano, i grandi ministri gli rendono omaggio, come nel caso di un Peel e soprattutto di un Bismarck. Cavour ne sarebbe invece il perfetto interprete, capace di preparare il terreno, di guidare l'opinione. «Lo stato costituzionale deve essere necessariamente in armonia colla pubblica opinione, senza alcuna cieca subordinazione, senza alcuna illimitata soggezione. Camillo di Cavour la tenne costantemente come la sua bussola, e la seguiva quando la stimava giusta od era necessario seguirla» (A. Brunialti 1896, 330). Cesare Balbo definisce i grandi uomini di Stato «macchinisti del sistema rappresentativo, i quali l'abbiano governato sapientemente a pro della nazione mostrandosi giusti e perspicaci estimatori dell'opinione pubblica e forti guidatori di essa» (1857, 245). Il governo di gabinetto (allorché si realizza o pare realizzarsi), considerato dal punto di vista dell'opinione pubblica, appare così come il tentativo di mediare tra la spinta "democratica" della maggioranza e la conservazione dell'individuale, delle superiorità sociali, del principio di designazione-selezione nel determinare l'inevitabile prevalenza dei migliori e dei più capaci.

2.2 L'opinione e il ceto medio

Ma governare l'opinione significa per Bluntschli aver coscienza del fatto che essa non è né l'opinione dei detentori del potere né quella dei sapienti. «Essa è principalmente la opinione delle *classi medie*, le quali si permettono un giudizio indipendente e comunemente lo esprimono. Essa si forma nella società, nello scambievole commercio degli uomini ...» (1879, 155). Questa posizione però non va esente da critiche. Lo stesso Bluntschli – secondo l'Holtzendorff – aveva sfumato la sua teoria in *Die Politik als Wissenschaft* (1876) rispetto alla voce pubblicata nel 1862 nel *Deutsches Staats-Wörterbuch* diretto dallo stesso giurista zurighese e da Brater (vol. VII, 345–347). La classe media non appare il crogiuolo «in cui si fondono i sentimenti troppo raffinati delle classi superiori con gli istinti materiali e rozzi dei ceti più umili, come il punto d'incontro che raccoglie i suoi elementi da ambedue le parti, come la risultante meccanica di un sistema di forze» (L. Minguzzi 1893, 24–25). Inoltre, così facendo, Bluntschli non avrebbe fatto altro che spostare il centro di manifestazione dell'opinione pubblica, trasportandolo dal ceto dei dotti al ceto medio in quanto tale non rappresentativo dell'intera società (I. Tambaro 1904–1908, 851). Inoltre «mentre il giudizio dell'elemento dotto e intellettuale della società sarà generalmente obbiettivo e spassionato, altrettanto non potrà dirsi del giudizio del ceto medio che sarà animato dall'interesse proprio» (I. Brunelli 1906, 19).

Questa discussione – che rivela tra l'altro l'enorme difficoltà di dare una risposta adeguata al problema della legittimazione delle classi dirigenti – fa parte del tentativo italiano, tipicamente eclettico, di ritrovare in modelli stranieri, presunti o reali fattori di organizzazione organica e coesiva nel rapporto Stato / società. Si pensi per esempio all'insistenza – spesso con speculare intento polemico nei riguardi del "modello francese" (L. Lacchè 1998) – con la quale si richiamano le forme di governo / controllo delle società locali in Inghilterra per opera della mitica *gentry*. O ancora al modello tedesco della scienza (*Deutsche Wissenschaft*) come "fattore costituzionale" e al *Bildungsbürgertum* come insieme di ceti chiamati a dirigere i processi di edificazione e di sviluppo nazionale (P. Schiera 1987; R. Gherardi 1993; A. Mazzacane / C. Vano 1994). Basti ricordare l'influente concezione elaborata da Gaetano Mosca incentrata sull'immagine di una "classe media" colta, nuova "aristocrazia" capace di assumere attivamente la funzione egemonica di "classe politica" e di rappresentanza istituzionale. Se l'opinione pubblica deve fondarsi sul consenso più generale ed essere stabile, «deve avere [anche] per suo natural fondamento la cultura, la capacità a giudicare di una data cosa. Abbiamo troppo dimenticato la cultura, la capacità, il sapere come fonte di diritto ...» (G. A. Pugliese 1898, 10).

2.3 L'opinione e la tirannide borghese

La parzialità è anche l'argomento che spinge Pietro Ellero a parlare di un'opinione pubblica fittizia, strumento ulteriore della *tirannide borghese*. Essa è l'opera di un ceto «sopraffattore», «non è già ispirata dalla dottrina e dalla speranza de' savi, che sono da essa derisi; né sopra tutto manifesta il sentimento intimo e reale della nazione, che ne subisce il fascino senza parteciparvi» (1879, 420–421). Attraverso il monopolio della stampa e in particolare del mezzo suo più efficace, il giornalismo politico, si attua la direzione del pensiero nazionale e risiedono qui «... gli autori dell'opinione pubblica; la cui genesi, se si volesse rintracciare, non è altro, che un bisbiglio de' crocchi borghesi». In tal senso, la conquista dell'opinione «è una condizione essenziale di vita delle dominazioni borghesi e delle monarchie costituzionali».

2.4 La folla, il pubblico e l'opinione

Per Scipio Sighele l'opinione pubblica si impone anche quando non è formata dal consenso più generale delle menti colte di un paese (R. Bonghi 1873, 444; G. A. Pugliese 1898); inoltre anche il pensiero dei savi può essere figlio di un'impressione improvvisa, erronea o rettificabile (e adduce come esempi l'influenza dell'opinione pubblica dopo la sconfitta di Adua e il mutato atteggiamento nell'*affaire* Dreyfus). Ciò che conta è studiare il modo in cui essa si forma «e da quali strane e oscure leggi psicologiche è governata» (S. Sighele 1899, 93). Nel 1898 Gabriel Tarde aveva pubblicato un saggio su *Le Public et la Foule* e in contemporanea (disputando però sul primato) Sighele (e l'agguerrita pattuglia di positivisti italiani) studiano in maniera analitica ogni forma di manifestazione collettiva.

Per vari aspetti, un autore come Sighele sancisce il definitivo passaggio dell'opinione dalle concezioni liberal-aristocratiche all'approdo "massificato". Nell'antichità esistevano folle ma non pubblici. Era stata la rivoluzione della stampa a far nascere un pubblico, ovvero individui legati, anche a distanza, da un'idea e da un sentimento comuni, cioè da una invisibile coesione mentale. Se per Sighele (1897) e per Gustave Le Bon (1895) la loro è un'epoca contrassegnata dalle folle, per Tarde si dovrebbe parlare di un'«era dei pubblici». Se la folla è un organismo semplice, barbaro, atavico, il pubblico è una collettività civile e moderna. Tuttavia secondo Sighele folla e pubblico in realtà convivono, potendo l'una elevarsi, l'altra degenerare. E ancora una volta la stampa e il giornalismo possono suggestionare, plasmare, guidare il pubblico verso obiettivi e "oggetti d'odio" (caso Dreyfus).

2.5 L'opinione pubblica e la coscienza popolare

Per superare l'*impasse* rappresentata dalla "parzialità" di ogni concettualizzazione dell'opinione pubblica, è nel riferimento alla coscienza popolare – e in buona misura al paradigma savigniano – che si cerca di trovare una via di uscita. Se la legge deve essere l'espressione organica della società, quale sarà l'organo universale capace di interpretare la coscienza giuridica della nazione? Per Saverio Scolari non potrà che essere la tanto disputata opinione pubblica. Essa è infatti di tutti e di nessuno allo stesso tempo. «Né v'ha dubbio che concorrano a formarla tutti i membri della società; perché, qualunque sia la coltura e la operosità di un individuo, egli agisce sulla mente e sull'animo di chi lo avvicina o gli sta d'intorno ...» (1871, 702–703). L'opinione popolare è quindi adattissima all'ufficio legislativo. La legge non può essere fatta ad arbitrio dell'una o dell'altra parte della società. «Donde l'avvertimento ... che siano aperte tutte le vie, tutti i modi consentiti e protette tutte le azioni, per le quali i cittadini possano contribuire alla formazione e allo svolgimento di questo poderoso organo dell'autorità politica» (*Ibidem*, 705). Scolari individua tre fattori legislativi (opinione popolare, elezione, deputazione) come momenti di un processo unico. Negli Stati liberi il Parlamento non possiede la potestà legislativa ma esercita piuttosto una speciale funzione.

Come è noto, è Vittorio Emanuele Orlando lo scrittore che in Italia elabora in maniera compiuta la teoria dell'atto legislativo come atto "esterno". Il diritto non dipende da una mera manifestazione di volontà. Applicando l'insegnamento savigniano, Orlando ritiene il diritto una «manifestazione organica della vita dei popoli». Il diritto, che vive nella profondità e nella dimensione temporale, è "popolare" o non è; esso è obiettivamente frutto di invenzione, di scoperta, mai di "creazione". Di conseguenza anche la legge in senso proprio non è che una "forma", poiché il "contenuto" «non è opera di alcuna assemblea, né di alcun altro *potere* politico» (V. E. Orlando 1886, 377. Cfr. anche V. E. Orlando 1912, 175 ss.). L'assemblea agisce come *organo* dello spirito pubblico «ed è una qualità che divide con le altre forme con cui la "pubblica opinione" fa sentire la sua voce ...» (*ibidem*, 378). Nell'ambito della teorica della "resistenza legale" Orlando considera l'opinione pubblica («come si dice con frase non bella ma oramai imposta dall'uso») il principale mezzo morale di resistenza popolare. «Nel suo più alto significato, essa esprime la migliore e più genuina manifestazione dello spirito pubblico; essa è la viva voce della comunità e come tale, forma l'inevitabile fondamento di ogni governo, anche se rigorosamente dispotico» (V. E. Orlando 1890, 1110).

L'opinione pubblica è dunque una manifestazione, pur discussa e discutibile, «dell'esistenza effettiva d'una volontà comune» (V. E. Orlando 1905–06, 433). L'opinione, che «... risponde alla coscienza politica ed alla teoria della sovranità popolare, si fa valere di per sé, indipendentemente dalla elezione» (*ibidem*, 524). La concezione popolare della legge e il ruolo organico dell'opinione pubblica come espressione dello spirito pubblico, "intermedia" tra la coscienza popolare e l'intervento positivo della scienza (V. E. Orlando 1886, 378) rappresentano, come vedremo, profili importanti nella costruzione giuridica del governo rappresentativo (M. Fioravanti 2001, 77 ss.).

L'Holtzendorff nel 1879 aveva criticato lo Scolari per aver ridotto ad una stessa cosa «la opinione del popolo e la sua coscienza giuridica» (S. Scolari 1892, 135). Secondo Scolari se una differenza esiste, essa concerne la forma attraverso la quale si manifestano ma non l'oggetto. «La teoria politica della opinione pubblica proietterà la sua luce su quella della coscienza giuridica del popolo; le quali teoriche si potranno distinguere bensì l'una dall'altra, ma sono intimamente legate per le sostanziali relazioni dei loro obietti» (*ibidem*, 172). Del resto il nesso tra consuetudine e opinione pubblica viene egualmente evidenziato. «La consuetudine rappresenta la voce della coscienza popolare nella vita giuridica, l'opinione pubblica nella vita politica ... Il diritto consuetudinario può trovare nella pubblica opinione in virtù della stessa comunione di origine, un aiuto potentissimo, cioè la forza senza cui l'idea stessa di diritto è inconcepibile» (A. Longo 1892, 44–45). Non è un caso che la definizione più ricorrente dell'opinione pubblica sia quella tratta da Erskine May, si riferisca alla "mitica" costituzione inglese e in particolare alla fondamentale condizione che distingue la libertà inglese dalla democrazia:

> «La pubblica opinione è espressa non dal coro clamoroso della moltitudine, ma dalle voci misurate di tutte le classi, di tutti i partiti, di tutti gli interessi. Essa è dichiarata dalla stampa, dalla borsa, dal mercato, dal circolo, dalla società intera. Essa è sottoposta ad altrettanti freni e contrappesi come la Costituzione medesima; e più che la volontà popolare, rappresenta la coscienza nazionale» [1866, 294].

La ricerca di un'opinione pubblica generale, stabile, nazionale, su fatti o persone che abbiano attinenza ad un pubblico interesse è alla fine il principale terreno di incontro (per es. C. Bon-Compagni 1848, 78; G. D. Romagnosi 1849, 105; A. Villa Pernice 1891, 189; L. Minguzzi 1893, 30; A. Brunialti 1900, 845; I. Tambaro 1904–08, 852). Si tratti della coscienza popolare o della coscienza nazionale, il risultato non cambia in maniera decisiva. Quel richiamo a Erskine May – a un'opinione pubblica *made in Great Britain*, «che non è il numero, che non è la legge, che non è la forza, ma l'assieme di tutto questo ...» (A. Brunialti 1881, 363) – tuttavia rivela una questione dirimente: le eminenti qualità politiche del popolo inglese, «che altri potranno imitare da lungi, ma giammai raggiungere» (A. Brunialti 1886, XCIII).

3. Per una teoria dell'opinione pubblica nello Stato costituzionale

Un problema fondamentale è quello che concerne la natura dell'opinione pubblica, ovvero in quale misura sia un fenomeno sociale, politico o giuridico. Livio Minguzzi si ripromette di studiare l'opinione – analizzata per lo più dalla scienza sociale – nell'ambito dello Stato costituzionale (1893, 6–7). Saverio Scolari, invece, a differenza dei filosofi, non considera l'opinione pubblica dal punto di vista del problema della competenza e della credibilità, bensì lo esamina come *forza politica*, indifferente quindi al vero e al falso, al bene e al male (1892, 135). In tal senso ritiene *The American Commonwealth* di James Bryce (1888) il migliore esempio di analisi condotta secondo i principi della scienza politica (A. Laquièze 2003).

Naturalmente i postulati del metodo orlandiano, della distinzione / armonizzazione tra ordine giuridico e ordine politico, hanno nel frattempo lasciato il segno e un concetto-soglia come quello di opinione pubblica non può non suscitare un particolare interesse. Il costituzionalista Minguzzi cerca di "integrare" l'opinione pubblica nel sistema di governo rappresentativo. Non la si può considerare – come fa la «scuola del governo giuridico» e Gneist in particolare – l'antitesi del *Rechtsstaat*, sancendo l'assoluto divorzio tra l'opinione e il governo dello Stato. In realtà non c'è un'opposizione invincibile tra l'organismo costituzionale «ed un'equa prevalenza dell'opinione pubblica. Il vero problema è fissare i limiti del potere dell'opinione pubblica nel governo costituzionale» (1893, 54). Voler dare carattere e valore giuridico allo Stato costituzionale è una tendenza «a noi venuta dalla Germania, ove ha in certo modo un carattere di opposizione e di resistenza alle idee democratiche ...» (*ibidem*, 135), anche se ha prodotto alcuni effetti benefici, ovvero reagire contro l'eccessiva indeterminatezza dei principi del governo costituzionale e l'illimitata ingerenza delle maggioranze. Tuttavia, identificando opinione pubblica e volontà nazionale, Minguzzi concepisce lo Stato costituzionale come diverso dallo Stato di diritto poiché si basa non solo sulla legge ma anche sul consenso continuo dei cittadini. «... lo Stato costituzionale ... per soddisfare veramente e pienamente alla propria, deve rendere anche conto continuamente ai cittadini dell'opera sua e meritarsene l'approvazione» (*ibidem*, 108). Se l' opinione pubblica «non può entrare nell'ordine giuridico di uno Stato», non per questo deve essere esclusa «dagli elementi veri e proprii dello Stato costituzionale» (*ibidem*, 133) che non esiste senza un vero regime di pubblicità e di discussione.

Resta il problema dell'uso dei concetti politici, che «non possono avere il rigore che è proprio del diritto». Ma se non tutti i principî – si chiede Minguzzi – possono tradursi nel dato statutario, «cessano forse per questo di essere veri e proprii elementi costitutivi del governo rappresentativo?». Forse che in ogni trattato di diritto costituzionale non si prenda sul serio l'azione dei partiti? «Lo stesso avviene dell'opinione, che sebbene incapace di espressione giuridica, non è meno per questo un vero e proprio elemento costitutivo dello Stato costituzionale» (*ibidem*, 136). Il rapporto tra il governo e l'opinione non può essere tradotto in determinazioni legislative, ma forma pur sempre un concetto dotato di un vero contenuto giuridico e fonte di una norma necessaria e permanente (*ibidem*, 137).

4. L'opinione pubblica tra diritto e politica: potere, forza, influenza

L'opinione pubblica – è convinzione comune – esercita una grande influenza, è indubitabilmente una forza politica, ma è, di più, un "potere"? L'approccio "materiale" della scienza politica e la stessa opzione metodologica del diritto costituzionale tornano ad affrontarsi. Potere preponderante per Romagnosi, forza extra-ufficiale per Bluntschli, potere di governo per Bryce, l'opinione pubblica sembra potersi conquistare una posizione istituzionale.

Per Vittorio Emanuele Orlando, tuttavia, se è bene avere coscienza dell'opinione come forza politica (e lo scrittore siciliano, specie agli inizi, è assai attento al concetto di forza quale fattore istituzionale), come uno dei mezzi morali di resistenza collettiva, nondimeno è errato ritenere che possa annoverarsi a vero potere dello Stato, giacché ciò necessita di organizzazione giuridica (1890, 1112). Altrimenti si annacqua «il concetto di *potere pubblico*, la cui caratteristica è il manifestarsi in un *pubblico istituto* ...» (1905, 75). Di diverso avviso – e non fa meraviglia – è Attilio Brunialti. Per il costituzionalista vicentino l'opinione pubblica è – a cominciare dalla Gran Bretagna – «un vero potere dello Stato, che agisce in modo organico al pari degli altri, e determina quell'intima unione tra il parlamento e il paese, che è scarsa o manca nel continente d'Europa» (1896, 329). Il fatto che non possa assumere espressione giuridica non è decisivo; è, come dice il Minguzzi, «un vero e proprio elemento costituzionale ordinario». Il passo è breve per farne un potere dello Stato, insieme ai tre poteri classici e a quello elettorale. Ignazio Tambaro, discutendo le tesi di Minguzzi e di Brunialti, nega infine tale carattere. «L'opinione pubblica, adunque, unitamente alla pubblicità e ai partiti politici, costituisce il complesso degli elementi cioè che hanno una base evolutiva, diretta ad agevolare l'azione degli elementi giuridici, che sono, alla loro volta, costitutivi» (1904–1908, 853).

5. L'opinione pubblica nel regime rappresentativo

È stato probabilmente Benjamin Constant l'autore continentale che, nel XIX secolo, ha meglio compreso l'essenza dell'opinione pubblica («pouvoir représentatif de l'opinion») nella teoria liberal-costituzionale, valorizzando il circuito pubblicità-libertà di stampa-governo d'opinione. «L'opinion publique est la vie des Etats. Quand l'opinion publique ne se renouvelle pas, les États dépérissent et tombent en dissolution» (B. Constant 1806, 137). In Italia i primi scrittori costituzionali seguono tale via identificando l'ordine rappresentativo con la preponderanza del giudizio dell'opinione pubblica in tutte le cose relative al governo (C. Bon-Compagni 1848, 65). Il sistema costituzionale funziona quanto più c'è equilibrio e sintonia tra le istituzioni e l'opinione pubblica. Come si è già visto, l'uomo di Stato non può ignorare i moti dell'opinione, quali essi siano, anche se non dovrà riceverli passivamente. Il governo costituzionale è forte se procede in pieno accordo e in armonia con l'opinione pubblica (per es. P. Peverelli 1849, 88; D. Carutti 1852, 242; M. Minghetti 1881, 633; L. Minguzzi 1893, 56 ss.). Romagnosi – ampiamente citato – ricordava il legame tra la legge, il governo e l'opinione. «Quando l'opinione pubblica precede il governo, la esecuzion della legge riesce pronta e completa» (1849, 108). Diversamente tra la legge e la sua applicazione si produce una distanza che deve essere riempita con «idee intermedie». Nella pubblicistica italiana lo specchio verso il quale rivolgere lo sguardo è la costituzione inglese. Nell'isola l'enorme influenza dell'opinione «coincide col definitivo prevalere del governo parlamentare (fine del secolo XVIII)» (V. E. Orlando 1890, 1113). Il governo rappresentativo è anzitutto «un governo a base di discussione e di pubblicità ...» (1895, 449). Per Minguzzi l'opinione pubblica (come coscienza pubblica) è la trama sulla quale lo Stato costituzionale ordisce la sua opera quotidiana e continua. «Perciò è presente in tutti i singoli momenti della sua operosità, involge, abbraccia, investe interamente il regime costituzionale; non vi è parte, non vi è atto di esso in cui questo elemento non debba entrare» (1893, 90). Se il sistema rappresentativo può essere paragonato ad una macchina – aveva osservato Cesare Balbo –, allora l'opinione pubblica ne rappresenta il vapore (1857, 244–245).

La *presenza* dell'opinione pubblica nel governo costituzionale viene riscontrata in due ambiti principali: da un lato come «intervento legale … chiamata a terminare le contese de' poteri costituzionali e ad esercitare il suo legittimo impero» (L. Minguzzi 1893, 92), dall'altro come insieme di organi e di "fattori". Le crisi parlamentari sono il principale terreno di intervento. Il canone costituzionale per cui nel Governo di gabinetto un ministro ha diritto di restare al potere, finché sia sorretto da una maggioranza parlamentare, si fonda sulla presunzione che tale armonia tra l'esecutivo e il legislativo sia indizio dell'adesione del paese. Che cos'è l'"appello al popolo" se non una forma istituzionalizzata di appello all'opinione pubblica? Si entra qui nel *sancta sanctorum* del "governo di opinione". Solo che dovrà essere la pubblicità, la discussione, la comunicazione a far penetrare il "Paese" nei meandri di una disarmonia, di uno scollamento, di un conflitto che rappresentano dimensioni "ordinarie" del sistema.

Naturalmente la vera questione diventa "chi fa chi", ovvero chi è il massimo interprete dell'opinione pubblica, dei suoi movimenti, dei suoi sentimenti? In tale contesto ci si imbatte nell'ambiguità strutturale, genetica, della forma di governo e nella sua incompiutezza, approdo ricercato ma all'apparenza irraggiungibile. L'attribuzione e la gestione delle due prerogative-cardine del governo rappresentativo (scioglimento della camera eletta, dimissione dei ministri) diventano il terreno disputato del *government by opinion*. Non è un caso che insistentemente, nelle esemplificazioni, si richiamino le esperienze di capi di governo (Cavour, Bismarck, Palmerston, Peel, Disraeli, Guizot …) – afferenti, per la verità, ad una gamma davvero ampia di contesti e di situazioni istituzionali – che di monarchi per la loro capacità, reale o presunta, di interpretare e guidare l'opinione pubblica. Così, per esempio, al disastro di Guizot e Luigi Filippo nel '48 francese si contrappone l'azione saggia dei due primi Leopoldo del Belgio (1857, 1871, 1884). È però soprattutto la figura del capo dello Stato ad attirare l'attenzione degli studiosi. Ritorna il tema – presente in tanta riflessione costituzionale anglo-europea – della superiorità della monarchia sulla repubblica in ordine alla durata, stabilità, *performance* istituzionale del capo dello stato ereditario. Anche in questo caso si tratta di cogliere gl'impulsi profondi, le ragioni costitutive della coscienza collettiva. Lo schema della "monarchia popolare" (F. Mazzonis 1996; P. Colombo 1999; P. Colombo 2001) è perfettamente centrato sul rapporto monarchia / opinione pubblica. Nessuno meglio di Walter Bagehot autore di *The English Constitution* (1867) ha rilevato – scrive Attilio Brunialti che dedica un capitolo del suo trattato al problema del rapporto tra capo dello Stato e opinione pubblica – «questa influenza reciproca della Corona e della pubblica opinione nella monarchia costituzionale» (1900, 253). La nazione si divide in partiti, il Parlamento in gruppi e camarille, la società sulla base di interessi economici e materiali: solo la monarchia, simbolo visibile dell'unità e della potenza dello Stato-persona, «è al di fuori e al di sopra di tutti, ordinariamente nascosta come un mistero, qualche volta splendida agli occhi della folla» (*ibidem*, 254). Il riferimento a una certa interpretazione della teoria constantiana del "potere neutro" (in questo volume *supra Coppet et la percée de l'Etat libéral constitutionnel*) è trasparente, ma lo sfondo reale è la crisi di fine secolo e le *impasse* del sistema costituzionale italiano. Secondo Brunialti in nessun altra nazione come in Italia, il Re ha forse esercitato la sua personale influenza sulla pubblica opinione sino ad essere in parecchie occasioni «interprete fedele della pubblica opinione, che provocò, secondò, approvò l'opera sua, contro Gabinetti fiacchi, imprevidenti o colpevoli, contro maggioranze servili e compiacenti, in una parola contro tutti gli altri poteri dello Stato» (*ibidem*, 256).

6. Gli organi dell'opinione pubblica e il problema della rappresentanza

Se esiste dunque un'opinione pubblica "costituzionale", chiamata a svolgere un intervento "legale", integrabile, in varia misura, nel gioco delicatissimo di equilibri e incastri tra legislativo ed esecutivo, nondimeno irrisolto appare il problema del duplice statuto: resta infatti apertissimo il problema del ruolo di "fluido" costituzionale. Per certi aspetti, per riprendere uno spunto iniziale, nell'Ottocento costituzionale italiano ritroviamo le due dinamiche che, semplificando, pervadono il settecento inglese e francese: in un caso la nascita e la prima evoluzione del *government by opinion* (parlamentare?) segnalano i cardini dell'opinione pubblica "governante", nell'altro, invece, è il profilo retorico-discorsivo, di contestazione e di "tribunale", a evidenziare la crisi del potere legittimo. Questo secondo profilo non scompare e passa, profondamente trasformato, dall'età dell'oro a quella del dubbio che contrassegna l'età liberale.

Il pluralismo costituzionale ottocentesco proprio del regime rappresentativo è inscritto in un discorso del potere (anche con evidenti incrostazioni "assolutiste") che scorge negli organi dell'opinione pubblica (pubblicità, stampa, associazioni, riunioni, partiti ecc.) potenziali e forti minacce e nello stesso tempo non ignora il discorso della "contestazione" che fa dell'opinione pubblica l'istanza alla quale anche le istituzioni devono rendere conto. La contraddizione è altrettanto visibile nello statuto dell'assemblea politica. Il parlamento è retoricamente e spesso convintamente inteso come arena pubblica dove ricomporre le "parti" nel "tutto", luogo di legittimazione politico-costituzionale della classe dirigente e di dialogo-direzione permanente nel rapporto Stato-società civile (F. Cammarano 1990 e 1999; F. Soddu, 2001).

Eppure è altrettanto netta l'immagine dottrinale e reale che lo trasforma di significato e di valore. Da un lato la ricorrente diffidenza liberale verso le tentazioni "assolutistiche" delle assemblee e le derive fazionarie. Proprio l'opinione pubblica può essere un freno dell'«opinione legale»: «A questo mirano e la libertà assicurata ai cittadini di pubblicare le proprie opinioni, e di censurare gli atti sanciti dai legislatori, e la facoltà fatta al Principe di sciogliere i parlamenti elettivi» (C. Bon-Compagni 1848, 77). Dall'altro opera il problema fondamentale della rappresentanza, vero e proprio *casse-tête* nella tensione politico-costituzionale presente nel codice genetico del liberalismo. Questo scoglio teorico e pratico non è facilmente aggirabile. «La rappresentanza presuppone la selezione dei capaci per affidar loro l'esercizio delle più alte funzioni della vita pubblica. Meno questo presupposto è d'accordo coi fatti, e più fa difetto la ragion d'essere di questo istituto; il quale così, per una fatale necessità, decade o si corrompe» (V. E. Orlando 1895, 456). In tal senso l'assemblea politica "legislatrice" è solo una delle forme di esercizio concreto dello spirito pubblico, dovendo anzi trovare elementi di rafforzamento, ma anche di limite, nei diversi organi dell'opinione pubblica.

E, in effetti, parlare dell'opinione pubblica significa in concreto parlare dei suoi "organi". Anche in questo caso si potrebbe vedere come, a seconda degli autori, le venga assegnato un certo grado di intervento. A ben vedere, però, c'è quasi unanimità nel fare della pubblicità, delle riunioni, delle associazioni, dei partiti e soprattutto della stampa i suoi "coefficienti" essenziali.

Tuttavia, nella vita concreta dello Stato liberale di diritto nessuna di queste articolazioni dell'opinione pubblica ha avuto vita facile. La stampa – chi non lo afferma! – è il palladio assoluto delle libertà pubbliche, la libertà delle libertà. Diventa anche «... l'inestimabile correttivo dell'onnipotenza parlamentare che così facilmente diviene prepotenza. Per essa le minoranze non rappresentate o imperfettamente rappresentate nel Parlamento, impotenti davanti alle maggioranze governanti, possono fare appello alla ragione pubblica, conquistare la opinione pubblica ...» (L. Palma, *Corso* 1885, 155). Ma Tocqueville, come è noto, ama la stampa più per il male che impedisce che per il bene che produce: potenza straordinaria «così stranamente mescolata di bene e di male, senza la quale la libertà non potrebbe vivere e con la quale l'ordine si mantiene a malapena» (Tocqueville 1835, 195). Venuto meno il regime preventivo, quello di repressione non ignora tecniche che a fatica convivono coi principî teorici del liberalismo. I partiti politici (cfr. P. Pombeni 1992 e 1994; G. Quagliariello 1990) diventano il principale vettore della *politica*, nondimeno – in quanto soggetti "privati" volti ad acquisire crescente rilevanza "pubblica" – minacciano la cittadella fortificata (dai giuristi) dello Stato-persona, possono far degenerare il governo di gabinetto in – è il caso di dire – "governo di partito", rischiano inoltre di trascinare la monarchia nell'arena politica. Anche in questo caso lo Stato costituzionale, se non corre ai ripari, può venir preso in ostaggio dall'opinione pubblica che si trasforma in "Stato nello Stato", in una parola essere alla mercé di una società frammentata e inorganica. Le associazioni, infine, non hanno fondamento costituzionale e non di rado diventano lungo l'Ottocento una mera questione di ordine pubblico e di politica della sicurezza (cfr. G. Brunelli 1989; M. Meriggi 1992; F. Sofia 2001). Solo l'opinione pubblica illuminata, istruita, capace, necessariamente elitaria, può in fondo aspirare ad un ruolo ordinatore nel contesto delle sempre più complesse e conflittuali relazioni tra lo "Stato dei giuristi" e la "sociocrazia" annunciata dall'allargamento del suffragio, allorché la linea separatrice tra statualità e socialità, tra pubblico e privato, ha perso gran parte della sua originaria valenza critico-razionale.

Con queste credenziali non meraviglia che l'opinione pubblica "costituzionale", con l'ausilio dei suoi organi, rappresenti, quale concetto-soglia, un illuminante campo di tensioni tra politica e diritto, Stato e società, istituzioni liberali e istanze democratiche. Nel 1895, un oscuro conferenziere, l'avvocato e poi deputato Antonio Teso, descriveva così il problema:

> In Italia purtroppo l'opinione pubblica non sa ancora farsi valere adeguatamente, e ciò per la scarsezza di educazione politica che rende le classi popolari indifferenti e noncuranti degli interessi generali dello Stato o schiave dei pregiudizi più strani ed eccessivi, per il disamore che spinge molta parte delle classi elevate a tenersi fuori della vita pubblica, per la mancanza di un logico e saldo ordinamento delle parti politiche, ma soprattutto perché la stampa periodica non vi ha ancora acquistata quell'autorità e quella diffusione che possiede in altri paesi [1895, 32].

È una diagnosi che non manca, ancora oggi, di sollecitare le nostre riflessioni.

Bibliografia

Arcoleo G., *Diritto costituzionale. Dottrina e storia*, Napoli 1907, 3 ed.

Bagehot W., *The English constitution*, London 1867, tr. it. *La Costituzione inglese*, Bologna 1995

Baker K. M., *Au tribunal de l'opinion. Essais sur l'imaginaire politique au XVIIIe siècle*, Paris 1993

Balbo C., *Della monarchia rappresentativa in Italia*, Firenze 1857

Beneduce P., s.v. *Gabba Carlo Francesco*, in *Dizionario biografico degli Italiani*, Roma 1998, 819–822

Bluntschli J. J., *La politica come scienza*, versione dal tedesco per G. Trono, Napoli 1879

Bon-Compagni C., *Della Monarchia rappresentativa*, Torino 1848

Bonghi R., *Discorso alla camera dei Deputati*, tornata del 14 maggio 1873, in *Discorsi parlamentari* ..., Roma 1918, vol. I

Brunelli I., *Della pubblica opinione nello Stato moderno*, Torino 1906

Brunialti A., *La costituzione inglese negl'ultimi cinquant'anni (1830–1880)*, in *Le moderne evoluzioni del diritto costituzionale. Saggi e letture*, Milano 1881

– *Prefazione. Il Governo parlamentare in Inghilterra ed in Italia*, in *Biblioteca di Scienze politiche*, diretta da Id., Torino 1886, vol. III

– *Il diritto costituzionale e la politica nella scienza e nelle istituzioni*, in *Biblioteca di scienze politiche e amministrative*, diretta da Id., Torino 1896, vol. I; 1890, vol. II
Calhoun C. (a cura di), *Habermas and the Public Sphere*, Cambridge, London 1996, 4 ed.
Cammarano F., *Il progresso moderato. Un'opposizione liberale nella svolta del'Italia crispina (1887–1892)*, Bologna 1990
– *Storia politica dell'Italia liberale. L'età del liberalismo classico, 1861–1901*, Bari 1999
Carutti D., *Dei principii del governo libero*, Torino 1852
Cingari S., *Antologia e introduzione critiche ai testi*, in A. Zanfarino, *Politica costituzionale e scienza sociale alle origini della "Cesare Alfieri"*, Firenze 2001
Civile G., *Per una storia sociale dell'opinione pubblica: osservazioni a proposito della tarda età liberale*, in *Quaderni storici*, 2/2000, 469–504
Colombo P., *Il re d'Italia. Prerogative costituzionali e potere politico della Corona (1848–1922)*, Milano 1999
– *La «ben calcolata inazione»: Corona, Parlamento e ministri nella forma di governo statutaria*, in *Storia d'Italia*, Annali 17, *Il Parlamento*, Torino 2001, 67–90
Constant B., *Principes de politiques* (1806), édition par E. Hofman, texte établi d'après les manuscrits de Lausanne et de Paris avec une introduction et des notes, Genève 1980
Cottereau A., Ladrière P. (a cura di), *Pouvoir et légitimité. Figures de l'espace public*, Paris 1992
Ellero P., *La tirannide borghese*, Bologna 1879
Fioravanti M., *Giuristi e costituzione politica nell'Ottocento tedesco*, Milano 1979
– *La scienza del diritto pubblico. Dottrine dello Stato e della costituzione tra Otto e Novecento*, Milano 2001, 2 tomi
Fracassetti L., *L'opinione pubblica*, Udine 1893
Gabba C. F., *Dell'origine e dell'autorità della pubblica opinione*, in *Intorno ad alcuni più generali problemi della scienza sociale. Conferenze*, 2ª serie, Firenze 1881
– *Origini e vicende dei partiti politici*, in *Ibidem*
Gherardi R., *L'arte del compromesso. La politica della mediazione nell'Italia liberale*, Bologna 1993
Gneist R. von, *Lo Stato secondo il diritto ossia la giustizia nell'amministrazione politica*, prima traduzione dal tedesco col consenso dell'autore del sen. Isacco Artom, in *Biblioteca di Scienze politiche* diretta da Attilio Brunialti, Torino 1891
Gunn J. A. W, *Queen of the world: opinion in the public life of France from the Renaissance to the Revolution*, Oxford 1995
Habermas J., *Storia e critica dell'opinione pubblica* (1962), Roma, Bari 2001
Heurtin J. Ph., *L'espace public parlementaire. Essai sur les raisons du législateur*, Paris 1999
Holtzendorff F. von, *Wesen und Werth der Öffentlichen Meinung*, München 1880
Jaume L., *Tra concetto e idea-forza: l'opinione pubblica secondo Necker*, in *Giornale di storia costituzionale*, 6, II, 2003
Kahan A. S., *Aristocratic Liberalism. The Social and Political Thought of Jacob Burckhardt, John Stuart Mill and Alexis de Tocqueville*, with a new afterword by the author, New Brunswick, London 2001
Laquièze A., *L'opinion publique des juristes*, in *Giornale di storia costituzionale*, 6, II, 2003
Le Bon G., *Psychologie des foules*, Paris 1895
Longo A., *Della consuetudine come fonte del diritto pubblico costituzionale ed amministrativo*, Palermo 1892
Luig K., *Monarchia sociale o democrazia sociale. Osservazioni sulla dottrina dello Stato di R. von Gneist (1816–1895)*, in *I concetti fondamentali delle scienze sociali e dello Stato in Italia e in Germania fra Otto e Novecento*, a cura di Raffaella Gherardi e Gustavo Gozzi, Bologna 1992, 13–36

Mannori L., *La crisi dell'ordine plurale. Nazione e costituzione in Italia tra Sette e Ottocento* in *Giornale di storia costituzionale*, 6, II, 2003
Matteucci N., *Opinione pubblica*, in *Enciclopedia del diritto*, Milano 1980, vol. XXX, 420–430
May Th. Erskine, *Histoire constitutionnelle de l'Angleterre depuis l'avénement de George III, 1760–1860*, traduite et précédée d'une Introduction par C. de Witt, Paris 1866, t. II
Maza S., *Le tribunal de la nation: les mémoires judiciaires et l'opinion publique à la fin de l'ancien régime*, in *Annales E. S. C.*, 1, 1987, 73–79
Mazzacane A., Vano C. (a cura di), *Università e professioni giuridiche in Europa nell'età liberale*, Napoli 1994
Mazzonis F. (a cura di), *La Monarchia nella storia dell'Italia unita. Problematiche ed esemplificazioni*, in *Cheiron*, a. XIII, 25–26, 1996
Meriggi M., *Dalla Restaurazione all'età liberale. Per una storia del concetto di associazione in Italia*, in *I concetti fondamentali*, cit., 87–106
Mill J. S., *La libertà*, in *La libertà nello Stato moderno*, vol. V, Biblioteca di Scienze Politiche diretta da A. Brunialti, Torino 1890
Minghetti M., *I partiti politici e la ingerenza loro nella giustizia e nell'amministrazione* (1881), in *Scritti politici*, a cura di Raffaella Gherardi, Roma 1986
Minguzzi L., *La teoria della opinione pubblica nello Stato costituzionale. Saggio*, Torino, Roma 1893
Orlando V. E., *Studi giuridici sul governo parlamentare*, in *Archivio giuridico*, XXXVI, 1886, poi in *Diritto pubblico generale. Scritti varii (1881–1940) coordinati in sistema*, Milano 1954
– *Teorica giuridica delle guarentigie della libertà*, in *Biblioteca di Scienze politiche*, diretta da A. Brunialti, vol. V, Torino 1890
– *Del fondamento giuridico della rappresentanza politica*, in *Revue de Droit Public et de la Science Politique*, III, 1895, poi in *Diritto pubblico generale*, cit.
– *Principii di diritto costituzionale*, Firenze 1905
– *Diritto costituzionale. Diritto pubblico interno. Lezioni* .... redatte da A. Campobassi, Roma 1905–1906
– *Teorica della legislazione e del governo, anno 1911–1912*, Roma 1912
Palma L., *Corso di diritto costituzionale*, vol. III, parte III, Firenze 1885
– *Questioni costituzionali*, volume complementare del Corso di diritto costituzionale, Firenze 1885
Peverelli P., *Comenti intorno allo Statuto del Regno di Sardegna*, Torino 1849
Pombeni P., *Il problema del partito politico nella riflessione della scienza politica italiana (1870–1914)*, in *I concetti fondamentali*, cit., 107–135
– *Partiti e sistemi politici nella storia contemporanea*, Bologna 1994
Pugliese G. A., *La pubblica opinione*, in *Rivista di giurisprudenza*, XXI, 1898, 5–13
Quagliariello G. (a cura di), *Il partito politico nella Belle époque: il dibattito sulla forma-partito in Italia tra '800 e '900*, Milano 1990
Romagnosi G. D., *La scienza delle costituzioni ... opera postuma*, Torino 1849
Schiera P., *Il laboratorio tedesco. Scienza e politica nella Germania dell'Ottocento*, Bologna 1987
Scolari S., *Istituzioni di scienza politica*, Pisa 1871
– *Il regno e la sociocrazia in Italia*, Venezia 1892
Sighele S., *La delinquenza settaria: appunti di sociologia*, Milano 1897
– *L'opinione pubblica*, in *Mentre il secolo muore*, Palermo 1899
Sismondi J. Ch. L. Simonde de, *Studi intorno alle costituzioni dei popoli liberi*, Capolago 1839
Soddu F., *Il ruolo del Parlamento nella costruzione dell'Italia politica e amministrativa*, in *Storia d'Italia*, Annali 17, *Il Parlamento*, cit., 91–123

Sofia F., *Il diritto di associazione nella crisi di fine secolo: l'Italia in una prospettiva comparata*, in *Cheiron. La morte del re e la crisi di fine secolo*, a cura di M. Malatesta, 35-36, 2001, 85–138

Staël G. de, *Considérations sur les principaux événements de la Révolution française* (1818), in *Œuvres posthumes de Madame la baronne de Staël-Holstein précédées d'une notice sur son caractère et ses écrits*, Genève 1967 (ristampa dell'edizione Paris 1861)

Tambaro I., *Opinione pubblica* in *Il Digesto Italiano* ..., vol. XVII, Torino 1904–1908

Tarde G., *L'opinion et la foule. Gabriel Tarde, théoricien de l'opinion*, introduction par Dominique Reynié, Paris 1989

Tessitore F., *Crisi e trasformazioni dello Stato. Ricerche sul pensiero giuspubblicistico italiano tra Otto e Novecento*, Milano 1988, 3 ed.

Teso A., *L'opinione pubblica. Conferenza*, Roma 1895

Tocqueville A. de, *La democrazia in America*, Lib. II, cap. III (1835), Milano 1992

Villa Pernice A., *L'opinione pubblica*, conferenza tenuta al Circolo filologico di Milano e al Circolo filologico di Firenze, Milano 1891, ora pubblicata in appendice a Maifreda G., *Governo e rappresentanza degli interessi. Angelo Villa Pernice (1827–1892)*, Soveria Mannelli 2001, 231–241

Lo Stato giuridico e la costituzione sociale. Angelo Majorana e la giuspubblicistica di fine secolo

1. Un giurista di famiglia

«Angelo Majorana è una mente lucida, un ingegno vivido e pronto, un carattere specchiato: niuna meraviglia se amici e avversari gli riconoscono i suoi meriti e il diritto alla sua fortunata ascensione».[1] Così Alfredo Frassati, il grande direttore de «La Stampa» di Torino, giudica l'allora ministro del Tesoro (1906–1907) conosciuto per caso nel 1898 nella stazione di Catania mentre entrambi attendono il treno per Roma. Angelo Majorana morirà a soli 44 anni nel 1910, al culmine della sua carriera politica e istituzionale. Una vita breve, ma ricca di avvenimenti, attività, impegni. La sua precocità intellettuale – caratteristica che condivide con i fratelli educati dal padre Salvatore al culto dello studio, della scienza, dell'etica civile[2] – è il presupposto per l'avvio di un percorso che seguirò nel periodo maggiormente legato al suo ingresso e alla sua "collocazione" scientifica ed accademica nella giuspubblicistica di fine secolo. È sempre un'operazione un po' arbitraria quella di "fotografare" una parte, una sezione, pur ampia, della vicenda intellettuale di un personaggio complesso, a più dimensioni, qual è stato senza dubbio Angelo Majorana. Come è evidente dal titolo non mi occuperò dell'amministratore locale o dell'uomo politico, ma certo occorre tenere conto di questa sua vocazione "attiva" – legata all'idea di un notabilato civile e di un felice impegno politico – che ha sicuramente radici nella formazione e nella visione del mondo, per dir così, che Majorana esprime anche nei suoi lavori di ricerca.

Le due domande di fondo che ispirano il mio contributo possono essere così formulate: che "posto" occupa Angelo Majorana nella giuspubblicistica italiana

1 L. Frassati, *Un uomo, un giornale. Alfredo Frassati*, Roma 1982, vol. III, parte I, 171.

2 Cfr. G. Majorana, *Il Grand Tour. Lettere alla famiglia 1890*, premessa di Angelo Majorana, introduzione di Giuseppe Giarrizzo, a cura di Anna Maria Palazzolo, Palermo 2000.

di fine secolo, sia dal punto di vista accademico che, soprattutto, del merito scientifico? Quali sono i temi forti che lo hanno motivato alla riflessione e al dibattito? Sono due domande alle quali, allo stato della ricerca, non è facile né scontato rispondere, come cercherò di dire.

La precocità intellettuale, abbiamo detto. Un marchio di famiglia. Angelo, nato a Catania nel 1865, si laurea a Roma in Giurisprudenza nel 1881 con una tesi sulla teoria della sovranità. Ha sedici anni. Nello stesso anno si laurea anche Vittorio Emanuele Orlando, ventunenne. Questo riferimento al giurista palermitano, come vedremo, non è certo casuale. Nel 1883 Majorana consegue la libera docenza in diritto costituzionale presso l'Università di Catania. Nel concorso di Messina del 1887 viene dichiarato eleggibile e dal 1889 è ordinario a Catania, la sua Università. Quando dico "sua" penso anche al predominio accademico che i Majorana Calatabiano, guidati dal padre Salvatore, valente economista, già ministro dell'agricoltura, dell'industria e del commercio in due governi Depretis e senatore del Regno, esercitano sul *Siculorum Gymnasium*. Nell'arco di un ventennio Salvatore e i tre figli Angelo, Giuseppe professore di statistica ed economista, Dante studioso di diritto amministrativo, saliranno sulle cattedre dell'Ateneo etneo, di cui saranno anche presidi e rettori. Predominio, a dire il vero, diarchico perché i Majorana lo devono condividere con l'altra grande dinastia catanese, quella dei Carnazza.[3] Li accomunano però le strategie dinastiche e un raffinato *mix* di locale e di globale, come si direbbe oggi. Basta leggere il carteggio di famiglia che accompagna i viaggi in mezza Europa di Giuseppe Majorana, delegato del governo italiano in due importanti conferenze internazionali tenutesi a Berlino e Madrid nel 1890, per comprendere questa duplice dimensione: dalla provincia ai più grandi orizzonti attraverso una cultura di assoluto livello europeo, mediata da una competenza linguistica che, in quel contesto, non sorprende.

2. La tradizione del diritto costituzionale in Italia

Gli anni '80 del secolo rappresentano – nella storia della giuspubblicistica italiana – un tornante. Anzitutto per lo sviluppo stesso delle discipline che ad essa si ricollegano. Nel 1861 i professori ordinari di diritto costituzionale sono 6, quelli di diritto amministrativo 3. Nel 1882 sono raddoppiati. Tra l'unità d'Italia e il 1880 si svolge un solo concorso per il diritto costituzionale, ed è quello vinto

3 L'ambiente accademico e scientifico catanese di quegl'anni è ben tratteggiato da G. Speciale, *Antologia giuridica. Laboratori e rifondazioni di fine Ottocento*, Milano 2001, 18 ss.

da Luigi Palma che insegna a Roma dal 1874 ed è, come ricorda Angelo Majorana nel suo primo lavoro, «il mio esimio maestro».[4] Le prime cattedre di diritto costituzionale sono state istituite dai governi provvisori del 1860 nel segno di una vera e propria "ideologia della costituzione". Il testo statutario sabaudo – la "nuova" Costituzione del Regno – doveva essere studiato, illustrato, volgarizzato. Questa *retorica della costituzione* ricorda, per certi versi, la nascita della cattedra parigina conferita nel 1834 da François Guizot a Pellegrino Rossi.[5] All'interno del processo di formazione del Regno d'Italia, l'insegnamento del diritto costituzionale diventa l'occasione per un messaggio politico-ideologico: l'Italia è entrata finalmente nel novero dei regimi liberali e rappresentativi. Enrico Pessina nel 1860 viene chiamato da Cesare Albicini[6] (allora ministro dell'istruzione pubblica e delle finanze nel governo provvisorio presieduto dal Commissario Massimo d'Azeglio) a ricoprire a Bologna anche l'insegnamento di diritto costituzionale.[7] «L'Italia – osservava Pessina – entra l'ultima nella via del moderno reggimento costituzionale; ma il reggimento costituzionale sarà una verità per l'Italia».[8] Con le stesse finalità Giuseppe Pisanelli ricopre nel 1861 la cattedra di diritto costituzionale nell'Ateneo napoletano[9] e lo stesso fa Francesco Sulis a Pavia a partire dal 1860.[10] Queste cattedre nascono in un clima più "militante" che scientifico e al di fuori di qualsiasi logica "concorsuale".

Tra la fine degli anni '60 e il decennio successivo si comincia a definire un primo quadro significativo della scienza costituzionalistica italiana: dal 1866

4 A. Majorana, *Del parlamentarismo. Mali – Cause – Rimedii*, Roma 1885, 18.

5 Su questa vicenda v. L. Lacchè, *Tra politica e diritto, ovvero Rossi e la Monarchia di Luglio*, in *Un liberale europeo: Pellegrino Rossi (1787–1848)*, a cura di Luigi Lacchè, Milano 2001, 70–108; Id., *La Libertà che guida il Popolo. Le Tre Gloriose Giornate del luglio 1830 e le Chartes nel costituzionalismo francese*, Bologna 2002, 164–173.

6 Che nel 1861 sarà chiamato su quella stessa cattedra dando così inizio alla cosiddetta "scuola bolognese" (cfr. D. Zanichelli, *Cesare Albicini*, in *Studi politici e storici*, Bologna 1893, 467 e soprattutto M. S. Piretti, *Cesare Albicini e la scuola bolognese di diritto costituzionale: la «Rivista di diritto pubblico» (1889–1893)*, in Quaderni fiorentini per la storia del pensiero giuridico, 17, 1987, 197; A. De Benedictis, *Costituzione e Stato moderno. Politica, storia e diritto nella scienza del costituzionalista risorgimentale Cesare Albicini*, in Ead. (a cura di), *Costruire lo Stato, costruire la storia*, Bologna 2003, 119–140.

7 Cfr. la *Prolusione al corso di diritto costituzionale pronunciata nella Regia Università di Bologna il 18 aprile 1860 dall'avvocato Enrico Pessina professore di diritto penale nell'Università medesima*, Bologna 1860.

8 *Ibidem*, 23.

9 V. in questo volume, *supra*, *Il "discorso" costituzionale nell'opera di Giuseppe Pisanelli*, 407–411.

10 F. Lanchester, *Pensare lo Stato. I giuspubblicisti nell'Italia unitaria*, Roma, Bari 2004, 194.

Luigi Luzzatti tiene cattedra a Padova,[11] l'allievo Brunialti[12] sarà a Torino dal 1879 e nello stesso anno il siciliano Giorgio Arcoleo comincia a insegnare a Napoli. Di Luigi Palma si è detto. Gli anni '80 segnano un passaggio importante. Si susseguono molti concorsi e si affaccia sulla scena con la sua giovanile sicurezza l'astro di Vittorio Emanuele Orlando che vince la cattedra a Modena nel 1885, due anni dopo risulta primo nel concorso messinese e nel 1889 giunge nella sua Palermo. Nel concorso modenese la commissione gli riconosce «un pregio comune, ingegno acuto, trattazione sobria e dottrina quasi sempre attinta a buone fonti e con diligenza».[13] Nello stesso anno Angelo Majorana sale sulla cattedra catanese, dopo l'insuccesso nel concorso di Modena e la dichiarazione di eleggibilità in quello di Messina del 1887.[14] Gli anni Ottanta vengono identificati – e per certi versi non potrebbe essere diversamente – con i lavori giovanili di Orlando e con le sue prese di posizione di ordine metodologico. In pochi anni, dalle prolusioni di Modena e di Messina,[15] Orlando giunge a definire l'8 gennaio 1889 il problema de *I criteri tecnici per la ricostruzione giuridica del diritto pubblico*.[16]

11 Risale a questa fase la prolusione luzzattiana intitolata *Del metodo nello studio del diritto costituzionale: prelezione al corso di diritto costituzionale* letta nella R. Università di Padova il 13 dicembre 1867, Padova 1867.

12 Su Brunialti e i suoi inizi rinvio in questo volume *supra* a *Il potere giudiziario come "potere politico"*. 428–429.

13 Il passaggio della relazione in Lanchester, *Pensare lo Stato*, cit., 50.

14 *Ibidem*, 50–51.

15 *Ordine giuridico e ordine politico*, prolusione letta nella Università di Modena, 4 dicembre 1885; *Sulla necessità di una ricostruzione giuridica del Diritto Costituzionale*, prolusione letta nella Università di Messina, 12 dicembre 1886.

16 Il testo fu pubblicato nell'Archivio giuridico, 62, 1889, 107–124. Cfr. M. Fioravanti, *Popolo e Stato negli scritti giovanili di Vittorio Emanuele Orlando*, in Id., *La scienza del diritto pubblico. Dottrine dello Stato e della costituzione tra Otto e Novecento*, Milano 2001, 133 ss.; G. Cianferotti, *Il pensiero di V. E. Orlando e la giuspubblicistica italiana fra Ottocento e Novecento*, Milano 1980; A. Mazzacane (a cura di), *I giuristi e la crisi dello Stato liberale in Italia fra Otto e Novecento*, Napoli 1986, in particolare i saggi di Mangoni, Beneduce e Cianferotti; G. Rebuffa, *I lessici e il tempo delle prolusioni di Vittorio Emanuele Orlando*, in *Rivista trimestrale di diritto pubblico*, 4, 1989, 919–936; G. Azzariti, *La prolusione orlandiana e la scienza del diritto amministrativo anteriore al 1889*, ivi, 968–994; G. Cianferotti, *La prolusione di Orlando. Il paradigma pandettistico, i nuovi giuristi universitari e lo Stato liberale*, ivi, 995–1024; in questo volume, *supra*, *Argumente, Klischees und Ideologien*, 458 ss.; L. Lacchè, *Il* canone eclettico. *Alla ricerca di uno* strato profondo *della cultura giuridica italiana dell'Ottocento*, in *Quaderni fiorentini per la storia del pensiero giuridico moderno*, 39, 2010, 176 ss., 223 ss.

3. Lo Stato giuridico, tra Majorana, Orlando e i tedeschi

La ricostruzione giuridica del diritto pubblico è la grande impresa (tautologica) che i giuristi italiani si avviano a intraprendere, partendo dall'assunto che la scienza del diritto pubblico deve essere rifondata. Eccesso esegetico e filosofico, negazione del criterio sistematico; i cultori del diritto pubblico «sono troppo filosofi, troppo politici, troppo storici, troppo sociologisti e troppo poco giureconsulti ...».[17] La scienza del diritto pubblico deve quindi individuare le fondamenta della sua *specificità*. Le estremizzazioni, invece, ne hanno fatto un insieme disordinato, incoerente, eclettico. «Ciò che noi censuriamo – dice Orlando –, ciò che è stato esiziale al fisiologo sviluppo del diritto pubblico [...] è l'aver dimenticato che altro è diritto, altro filosofia, altro scienza del diritto, altro cognizione delle leggi ...». Il mezzo per ricondurre il diritto pubblico al suo vero fine è, almeno in teoria, semplicissimo: «cioè che il diritto pubblico si consideri, nel modo stesso che il diritto privato, come un complesso di principi giuridici sistematicamente coordinati».[18]

La proposta orlandiana è incentrata su un processo di ricostruzione che condanna l'esegesi, l'eclettismo, il giusnaturalismo privatistico, un «proprio tipo ideale», astratto, di istituzioni politiche. L'opera di revisione deve invece fondarsi sul sistema, sullo specialismo e sul formalismo scientifico, sulle raffinate categorie pandettistiche e sull'ordine concettuale del diritto privato, e ancora sull'accettazione dello «Stato esistente», cioè della «sovranità di poteri costituiti».[19]

La netta distinzione, «nel procedimento logico, fra *diritto* e *politica*, fra ordine *giuridico* e ordine *politico*»[20] dovrà essere uno dei fondamentali principi metodici della nuova scuola italiana di diritto pubblico. Dunque, per ricapitolare: tono deciso, distinzione tra giuridicità e politicità, rivendicazione di identità e di autonomia, *discorsi* sul metodo come parte integrante di una strategia disciplinare.

Gli anni di Orlando e di Majorana sono insieme gli anni del *parlamentarismo* e dei nuovi paradigmi scientifici. Al centro sta il problema dello Stato posto di fronte alla costituzione e alla società. Per molti è finito il tempo della *retorica della costituzione*, dell'ottimismo – spesso anglofilo – per le intrinseche virtù organiche del governo parlamentare, per la *mano invisibile* dei pesi e dei contrappesi. Il *costituzionale* come *politica / ideologia liberale* – così era stato dai

17 V. E. Orlando, *I criteri*, cit., 110.
18 *Ibidem*, 122.
19 *Ibidem*, 123.
20 V. E. Orlando, *Programma*, in *Archivio di diritto pubblico*, 1, 1891, 7.

tempi di Benjamin Constant[21] – sembrava perdere dinamismo. Da Spaventa a Bonghi, da Minghetti a Turiello a Mosca,[22] con accenti e colori diversi, l'*ingerenza della politica* appare il grande spettro minaccioso. Tale "invasione" ha il cuore pulsante nel parlamento, ovvero in quel suo modo di essere che poggia sul circuito "fazionario" che lo controlla, lo trasforma in una ipertrofica macchina legislativa, ne orienta in modo patologico il suo "comitato", il ministero, ne depotenzia la responsabilità, si autoalimenta di personalismi e localismi e si scarica sull'amministrazione e sulla giustizia. Non ci meraviglia che in questi primi anni '80 anche il giovanissimo Angelo Majorana si cimenti, nel suo primo lavoro monografico, col tema caldissimo del *parlamentarismo* seguendo lo schema minghettiano. Bisogna avere contezza di un fenomeno di "decadenza" che rischia di creare un fossato verso la società, di disunire i poteri dello Stato e far perdere saldezza alle istituzioni rappresentative. Ma denunciare solo significherebbe assecondare un «convenzionalismo comune».[23] Occorre invece rintracciare le cause e proporre infine i rimedi. Con giudizio di sintesi, non privo di buon senso, Majorana osserva:

> «Così pure non partecipo alle elegie sui mali dei partiti: le irritazioni sociali fatte regola di vita, gli intelletti eminenti sottratti al servigio della cosa pubblica, la considerazione partigiana sostituita alla universale. Credo che il principio del governo rappresentativo sia buono in sé stesso e possa realizzarsi comecchè non perfettamente. Amo la lotta dei partiti, sebbene trascini una serie inevitabile di mali, i quali del resto sarebbero più intensi in ogni altro governo; non amo quella delle persone. Qui riconosco il male, non là [...] Piacemi insomma la lotta, quando sia informata a saldi e larghi concetti. Il male del parlamentarismo a me pare si riduca e riassuma nella strana sostituzione dell'individuo all'ente, del gregario al partito. Il partito sovente non esiste che come bandiera sotto cui passi merce di contrabbando; (p. 90) allora è fazioso quando è accolta da fazioni.

21 Si rinvia in questo volume, *supra*, *Coppet et la percée de l'Etat libéral constitutionnel*.

22 Evidente – oltre che con Orlando – il "confronto" di Majorana con Gaetano Mosca, scrittore che giudica audace e originale. «Si può dissentire da lui (ed io in molte cose dissento); ma non si può fare a meno di apprezzare molto questo valente che, affidandosi alle sue forze, trascurando il convenzionalismo degli scrittori politici, investiga ed arriva alle più audaci conseguenze» (A. Majorana, rec. a *Le Costituzioni moderne, Saggio*, Palermo 1887, in *Antologia giuridica*, 2, fasc. 1–2, 1887, 125). Tra i punti di dissenso le proposte di Mosca in materia di Consiglio privato della Corona e di Camera Alta. Cfr. L. Borsi, *Classe politica e costituzionalismo. Mosca Arcoleo Maranini*, Milano 2000, 69 ss.; M. Fioravanti, *Gaetano Mosca e Vittorio Emanuele Orlando: due itinerari paralleli (1881–1897)*, in *La scienza del diritto pubblico*, I, cit., 187 ss.

23 A. Majorana, *Del parlamentarismo. Mali – Cause – Rimedii*, cit., 20. Sulla relativizzazione della figura del Gabinetto in Majorana v. L. Borsi, *Storia nazione costituzione. Palma e i 'preorlandiani'*, Milano 2007, 127.

Prevale la Camera al Senato, meno come istituzione che come accolta di individui più potenti. Questa maggiore potenza è costituita dalla possibilità di scalzare il ministero: il quale dal suo canto, per legge di conservazione, è costretto a lisciare e favorire i suoi giudici. È l'individuo colui che parla molto, che sollecita aumenti di spese per il suo collegio e favori per gli elettori, che fa ressa per il portafoglio o il segretariato generale: non il parlamento che, avendo l'ascendente sulla cosa pubblica, ne facciano il malgoverno che si lamenta: sono gli individui parlamentari. Non si condanni adunque il regime rappresentativo, e non si aspiri a radicali mutamenti.»[24]

Un anno prima, nel 1884, Orlando aveva pubblicato un breve saggio intitolato *La decadenza del sistema parlamentare*[25] nel quale discuteva, al pari di Majorana, il tema all'ordine del giorno. Nel suo contributo il giurista palermitano rifletteva sul governo parlamentare come forma politica. Non era sufficiente fermarsi alla superficie (la crisi), ma occorreva scavare più nel profondo osservando le *forze* operanti nella società incapaci di tradursi in unità politica e fondamento *costituzionale dello Stato*. L'evoluzione della forma politica rivelava in realtà le dimensioni del conflitto in seno al corpo sociale e alle sue *forze*. È in questi anni giovanili che Orlando costruisce, saggio dopo saggio, il mosaico che edifica la sua teoria giuridica dello Stato rappresentativo moderno[26] inteso come Stato liberale di diritto. La fondazione dello *Stato giuridico* (e con esso della scienza deputata a sistemare e custodire le strutture di diritto pubblico che *legano* lo Stato alla società) è il risultato di una complessa e razionale concettualizzazione. Lo storicismo savignyano e la coscienza popolare depotenziano l'idea "titanica" della sovranità popolare e della volontà politica, dall'indicibile potere costituente alla legge (propria / impropria) come forma che può solo dichiarare i rapporti giuridici che ad essa preesistono. Ma lo Stato-persona non si può "spiegare" e rappresentare attraverso la società e le *forze* che in essa operano. Lo Stato giuridico deve essere sottratto all'incandescenza del reale e alla dimensione del conflitto. L'autonomia di volontà della *persona* / Stato ha come corollari un'idea storicistica di diritto, una sovranità *propria*, un meccanismo di rappresentanza / designazione dei capaci, una forma di governo (di gabinetto) come fusione e non separazione dei poteri. L'operazione orlandiana postula una soggettività statale dotata di autonomia "giuridica" che sterilizza ogni dimensione costitutiva (anzitutto il contratto) e attribuisce dimensione organica alle forze sociali sottoposte al vaglio di una razionalità amministrativa di tipo

24 A. Majorana, *Del parlamentarismo. Mali – Cause – Rimedii*, cit., 89–90.

25 In *Rassegna di scienze sociali e politiche*, II, 1884, 589–600. Questo saggio viene analizzato da M. Fioravanti, *Popolo e Stato negli scritti giovanili di Vittorio Emanuele Orlando*, cit., 92–94.

26 Su questa espressione v. L. Borsi, *Nazione Democrazia Stato. Zanichelli e Arangio Ruiz*, Milano 2009, 402 ss.

moderno. Lo Stato amministrativo diventa allora la forma più perfezionata della piena sovranità dello Stato nell'esercizio dei suoi poteri.

La riflessione sullo *Stato giuridico* è parimenti centrale nella prima riflessione di Majorana. Il giurista catanese preferisce questa traduzione di *Rechtsstaat* a quella utilizzata da Isacco Artom – *Lo Stato secondo il diritto* – nell'edizione italiana della celebre opera di Gneist.[27] L'idea non gli sembra nuova, sebbene riconosca l'importanza dei risultati raggiunti dalla dottrina tedesca che mostra di conoscere in maniera approfondita. Dalla formulazione filosofica kantiana alla ricostruzione teorica di von Mohl[28] sino alla sistemazione di Gneist, Gerber, Laband, Rönne ecc., non sfugge a Majorana il carattere intimamente ideologico: «Sarebbe anzi studio di molto momento il vedere come in Gneist le preoccupazioni politiche si sieno fatte valere in una teorica che da esse apertamente vorrebbe prescindere».[29] Il più «recente restauratore della dottrina», Rudolf von Gneist, ne traccia una storia millenaria che culmina infine con la monarchia costituzionale. Non sfuggono a Majorana le celebri pagine in cui Gneist si scaglia contro i principî e le pratiche francesi, ovvero *La negazione del governo giuridico nello Stato francese*. Il governo dei partiti, la *toute-puissance* parlamentare, la negazione del *monarchische Prinzip* indeboliscono, nel "politico", la Francia esponendola al rischio del governo assoluto.

Per Majorana il *Rechtsstaat* – nozione dalla straordinaria capacità di adattamento che con audacia e originalità Orlando ha cercato di applicare al governo parlamentare – non è una forma, o un tipo o una specie perché ogni Stato è giuridico. Esso, più propriamente, è un *sistema*. Per questa ragione il suo studio non può limitarsi al solo diritto costituzionale o alla sola politica, «ma deve spaziare nel largo campo della *Scienza politica*, intesa come *Dottrina Generale dello Stato*».[30] Un'analisi che non può essere solo giuridica, se con ciò si intende la scienza politica come complesso che studia assieme la dimensione morale,

27 *Il sistema dello Stato giuridico*, in *Antologia giuridica*, 3, fasc. 5–8, 1889, 377. Ci si riferisce a Rudolf von Gneist, *Lo Stato secondo il diritto, ossia La giustizia nell'amministrazione politica*, opera tradotta (*Der Rechtsstaat und die Verwaltungsgerichte in Deutschland*) nel 1884 (Bologna, Zanichelli) da Isacco Artom. Sull'influenza di Gneist in Italia, v. B. Sordi, *Giustizia e amministrazione nell'Italia liberale. La formazione della nozione di interesse legittimo*, Milano 1985, 86–100; Id., *L'influenza tedesca*, in *Le riforme crispine*, vol. II, *Giustizia amministrativa*, Archivio I. S. A. P., n. s. 6, Milano 1990, 540 ss. Più in generale, le riflessioni di M. Fioravanti, *Giuristi e costituzione politica nell'Ottocento tedesco*, Milano 1979, 213 ss.; G. Cianferotti, *Il pensiero di V. E. Orlando*, cit., 106–107.

28 Di cui cita *Die Geschichte und Literatur der Staatswissenschaften: in Monographien dargestellt*, Erlangen 1855–1858, I, 15–18.

29 A. Majorana, *Il sistema dello Stato giuridico*, cit., 379.

30 *Ibidem*, 385.

economica e giuridica della statualità. Elementi, questi, non separati o in antitesi, ma in armonia fra loro.[31]

Il "metodo" di Majorana non segue, sotto il profilo "filosofico", gli *input* che provengono dalla Germania. Riconosce, nella sua impostazione "moderata", l'efficacia e la necessità del "metodo giuridico" dei tedeschi ma non il "fine". Majorana infatti distingue tra la grande elaborazione tedesca della *Rechtsstaatslehre* e i sistemi e i criteri politici che se ne possono far discendere.[32]

Già nel libro sul parlamentarismo il costituzionalista catanese operava il distinguo tra l'apparato concettuale della grande dottrina tedesca e il suo dottrinarismo. «Io non partecipo – osserva – al feticismo per le cose germaniche ...».[33] L'esito politico era a suo avviso – forse semplificando il quadro ma non sbagliando nell'impostazione di fondo – «mal celata antipatia per le idee democratiche e certa tendenza all'autoritarismo ...».[34] Se il parlamentarismo era un estremo, il *costituzionalismo* (secondo il lessico di Majorana) era l'altro. E qui questo *ismo* segnalava non la centralità della monarchia costituzionale pura ma l'evoluzione del *monarchische Prinzip* corredato del *vollziehende Gewalt*[35] che aveva posto sotto tutela il *Reichstag* e determinato una violazione dello spirito della costituzione rappresentativa.[36]

Ciò che corrisponde, *mutatis mutandis*, alla prolusione orlandiana del 1889, Majorana lo fa a Catania due anni prima, salendo la cattedra. È allora che legge la sua prolusione intitolata *La tutela del diritto nel governo rappresentativo*.[37] La vocazione del diritto costituzionale – che è materia giuridica e politica – è «di

31 L'autore cita, come riferimento, le considerazioni generali del *Trattato di economia politica* del padre.

32 A. Majorana, *L'imperatore Guglielmo I e lo Stato costituzionale germanico. Discorso pronunziato dall'Avv. Prof. Angelo Majorana nell'Aula Magna dell'Università di Catania l'11 marzo 1888*, aggiuntavi un'appendice *Sui presupposti della dottrina dello Stato giuridico (Rechtsstaat)*, Catania 1888, 21.

33 A. Majorana, *Del parlamentarismo. Mali – Cause – Rimedii*, cit., cap. IV, *Del costituzionalismo germanico*, 87.

34 *Ibidem*, 72. «Quello che vi ha di caratteristico nelle moderne teoriche germaniche – a parte del contributo veramente importante arrecato alla scienza nel campo amministrativo – è l'avversione alla democrazia. E qui non parlo dello Gneist, che sovra ogni altro com'aquila vola: ma di coloro che si servono delle sue teoriche a fine politico ...» (86).

35 In Germania il «governo è così vero potere, che ha la sua *ausführende Gewalt* e la *vollziehende* ben pure; per cui rimane fermo, anzi imminente, e provvede sempre l'azione dello Stato, per il migliore asseguimento dei fini di esso. Or di così fatto Governo il principe è il solo Capo: in diritto e in fatto» (A. Majorana, *L'imperatore Guglielmo I e lo Stato costituzionale germanico*, cit., 15).

36 A. Majorana, *Del parlamentarismo. Mali – Cause – Rimedii*, cit., 75–78.

37 *La tutela del diritto nel governo rappresentativo. Prolusione letta inaugurando il suo corso di lezioni* da Angelo Majorana Prof. straord. di diritto costituzionale nell'Università di Catania, Catania 1887.

dare norme e limiti giuridici alla politica». Questa prospettiva si integra con la tradizione del costituzionalismo liberale, con il *liberalismo della regola*.[38]

Va bene dire che lo Stato è giuridico. Ma che significa essere sottoposti al diritto? E che cosa si intende per diritto?

> «Soprattutto non si dà del diritto quell'ampia nozione che si dovrebbe. Dimenticasi come la ragione politica, la morale e l'economica non solo sieno armoniche, ma reciprocamente si integrino con quella giuridica. Per amore di antinomie si è fatto un distacco, fra il fondamento politico dei governi e le loro guarentigie giuridiche: distacco illogico, dovendo la buona politica essere dal diritto determinata e difesa, e non potendo questo, nonché imporre, consentire una cattiva politica. Da ciò segue non di rado, nelle trattazioni teoriche, un formalismo vacuo, e nelle pratiche conclusioni si hanno encomii di quei sistemi e di quei metodi di governo, conformi bensì talvolta alle leggi positive del luogo, ma non sempre conformi ai dettati di un diritto più liberale e forse più vero.
>
> Ciò malgrado, riconosco che l'*indirizzo giuridico* è quello che oggi deve seguirsi nello studio del diritto costituzionale, spogliandosi dalle unilateralità e supplendo alle deficienze degli scrittori germanici. Le istituzioni politiche odierne devesi cercare di migliorarle, adattandole alla ragione dei tempi. Ed oggi, conseguitasi la libertà politica, che sembrava ed era il precipuo bisogno sociale, ciò che da ogni parte si chiede è che il diritto dei cittadini in tutte le forme di loro attività, così molteplici e così grandemente accrescentesi, sia tutelato. Il governo dello Stato si considera quale deve essere: cioè la rappresentanza di tutti i cittadini, non la espressione di una parte, sia pur maggioranza. Le lagnanze che muovonsi contro ai nostri governi sorgono appunto dal dubbio che essi male adempiano a questa tutela del diritto.»[39]

La funzione eminente dello Stato è dunque la tutela del diritto. Lo sviluppo del principio di eguaglianza sollecita a sua volta la funzione del governo rappresentativo di cui la tutela è il principio fondamentale.[40] Seguendo il concetto kantiano del diritto come limite, come coesistenza reciproca, Majorana evidenzia il tema della limitazione giuridica delle potestà pubbliche. Il sillogismo da proporre è il seguente:

> «Scopo dello Stato è la tutela del diritto. I governanti, abbandonati a sé, hanno l'impulso ad eccedere, cioè a violare il diritto. Il limite costituzionale infrena i governanti. Guarentisce dalla violazione del diritto. Giova al raggiungimento del fine dello Stato. – È da questo richiesto.»[41]

Il governo rappresentativo è quello nel quale, in principio, i diritti di libertà sono garantiti a tutti. Se la inevitabile maggioranza dei più "capaci"[42] ha una qual

38 B. Manin, *Les deux libéralismes: la règle et la balance*, in I. Théry e Ch. Biet (a cura di), *La famille, la loi, l'Etat: de la Révolution au Code civil*, Paris 1989, 372–389.

39 A. Majorana, *La tutela del diritto nel governo rappresentativo*, cit., 8.

40 *Ibidem*, 12.

41 *Ibidem*, 14.

42 Sul concetto di capacità in Majorana, posto a confronto con la riflessione di

certa prevalenza, ciò non può avvenire a discapito dei diritti poiché questa si esercita solo «sul mero e proprio indirizzo politico del governo».[43] Majorana, con piglio positivista, usa formulare "leggi storiche". Una in particolare è centrale nella sua idea di progresso della società,[44] ovvero che «in ragione del progresso sociale il campo del lecito si viene sempre restringendo e viceversa si vien sempre più allargando quello del diritto».[45] Nello Stato di diritto i rapporti, i fenomeni sociali e politici, le relazioni di fatto si rivestono del diritto come della sua forma tipica.

La prima forma di sviluppo si è consolidata, nel moderno, attraverso il diritto privato codificato. La seconda, di sistema, passa attraverso le *garanzie giuridiche*. La *questione sociale* esprime infine le legittime richieste del riconoscimento giuridico degli interessi di alcune classi sociali. I governi rappresentativi apprestano sufficienti garanzie per ciò che si riferisce ai rapporti politici, ma devono perfezionarsi per dare garanzie giurisdizionali nel nuovo campo dei rapporti giuridici. «La giustizia amministrativa, per molti, non è che la vanguardia della *giustizia sociale*».[46]

Majorana dice di osservare e di constatare i fatti, senza approvare o biasimare (per il momento). E i due grandi fatti sono l'evoluzione dei governi parlamentari in senso democratico (tanto da far pensare che anche in Germania la speciale figura

Luigi Rossi, v. ora G. P. Trifone, *Il diritto al cospetto della politica. Miceli, Rossi, Siotto Pintòr e la crisi della rappresentanza liberale*, Napoli 2010, 133 ss.

43 A. Majorana, *La tutela del diritto nel governo rappresentativo*, cit., 17.

44 Già nel saggio – sviluppo della sua tesi di laurea – *Del principio sovrano nella costituzione degli Stati. Studio storico-critico*, Roma 1886, aveva formulato, suggerita dalla teoria comtiana degli "stadi", la legge del progresso storico verso il "giuridico": «Il pensiero umano, riflesso sulla costituzione degli Stati, dall'iniziale *preordinamento religioso* è passato, progredendo, al riconoscimento dei precetti morali, ha oscillato alternativamente e cumulativamente fra i precetti morali e la *convenienza politica*; spesso ha fatto molti e lunghi passi all'indietro, abbandonandosi al *fatalismo dinamico*; finalmente si è posto sulla via del più sicuro progresso, affermando il necessario *fondamento giuridico* delle istituzioni politiche».

45 A. Majorana, *La tutela del diritto nel governo rappresentativo*, cit., 19.

46 *Ibidem*, 22. Sul punto v. *Il sistema dello Stato giuridico*, cit., 554 ss. Nel saggio *L'evoluzione storica dei rapporti tra la legislazione e la giurisdizione* (Bologna 1889, 140, estr. dall'*Archivio giuridico*, vol. 43, fasc. 4–5) Majorana cerca di sviluppare la "legge storica" «secondo cui si succederebbero (colla forma dei corsi e dei ricorsi) due sistemi diversi: la sentenza, rigida esecutrice della legge; la sentenza, modificatrice e creatrice della legge. Ho creduto, anzi, di poter notare che la tendenza odierna sia ad allontanarsi dalla prima forma ed avvicinarsi alla seconda, in ispecial modo mercè l'arbitrato, le azioni popolari, la giurisdizione volontaria e nuovi democratici modi di nominare i magistrati».

del governo costituzionale sia transitoria di fronte al socialismo impellente)[47] e la questione sociale.

È in questa prospettiva che Majorana sembra voler collocare la sua riflessione dentro uno spazio teorico "mediano", "integrativo" che da un lato cerca di affrontare, *sub specie iuris*, la sfida di una politicità invadente ma necessaria e incomprimibile, dall'altro di assumere il principio del *Rechtsstaat* come effettiva sovranità della legge. Se la via delle riforme politiche non deve illudere, non altrettanto sembra essere «per le guarentigie amministrative, che sono più veracemente giuridiche. Molto vantaggerebbesi a diminuire il campo dell'arbitrio».[48]

Majorana – per dirla in parole povere – non ha paura delle sfide impervie che lo Stato liberale di diritto deve affrontare per garantire l'inesorabile sviluppo del "senso democratico". Lo sguardo verso la Germania è importante ma occorre «rievocare le tradizioni di noi medesimi».[49] Lo Stato giuridico di Majorana non è informato che solo per la parte "positiva" al "germanesimo amministrativo",[50] ma le radici riposano su un terreno autonomo[51] e sincretistico.

> «Ho cercato, nel ricostruire il sistema dello stato giuridico, di fondarmi sulle più pure tradizioni di Kant da un lato, di Romagnosi dall'altro; tenendo conto però delle condizioni sociali e politiche dell'età nostra. Mi sono anche informato alle tradizioni liberali, che sono proprie alla scuola italiana.»[52]

Da un lato è come se il dottrinarismo tedesco si fosse troppo allontanato dalla tradizione del formalismo kantiano e dalla sua prospettiva individualistica, dall'altro troviamo tutta la tradizione della «sistematica del nostro grande Maestro, Romagnosi».[53] E proprio il riferimento costante all'intellettuale pia-

47 A. Majorana, *L'imperatore Guglielmo I e lo Stato costituzionale germanico*, cit., 20.

48 *Ibidem*, 24.

49 *Ibidem*.

50 Oltre ai lavori già citati, v. C. Mozzarelli, S. Nespor, *Giuristi e scienze sociali nell'Italia liberale. Il dibattito sulla scienza dell'amministrazione e l'organizzazione dello Stato*, Padova 1981; P. Beneduce, *"Punto di vista amministrativo" e Stato di diritto: aspetti del germanesimo dei giuristi italiani alla fine dell'Ottocento*, in *Annali dell'Istituto storico italo-germanico in Trento*, 10, 1984, 119–194; B. Sordi, *Giustizia e amministrazione*, cit., 100 ss.; e ancora i saggi raccolti nel volume *Deutsche Rechtswissenschaft und Staatslehre im Spiegel der italienischen Rechtskultur während der zweiten Hälfte des 19. Jahrhunderts*, a cura di Reiner Schulze, Berlin 1990.

51 «I lettori vorranno riconoscere, spero, se non altri, un certo valore logico alla sistematica. E vorranno, spero ancora, riconoscere, in questa, indipendenza di talune teoriche, in buona parte convenzionali e terminate da ragioni politiche che oggi predominano in Germania, né colà soltanto» (A. Majorana, *Il sistema dello Stato giuridico*, cit., 566).

52 A. Majorana, *Il sistema dello Stato giuridico*, cit., 566–567.

53 *Ibidem*, 453.

centino denuncia in maniera chiara una fonte che, come ha ben rilevato Giuseppe Giarrizzo, è un *point de repère* per la formazione della dinastia dei Calatabiano. Già nell'opera del padre Salvatore è possibile cogliere l'impegno «a fondare una 'teoria giuridica delle scienze sociali', [e] che riprende dalla tradizione massonica un'antropologia positiva ed una altrettanto positiva filosofia della storia».[54] E il nume tutelare Romagnosi evoca diversi temi: la "figura" del giureconsulto-filosofo, più "costruttore" che mero "esegeta"; il temperamento di un originario giusnaturalismo sensista con il sentimento della vita del diritto intesa come *socialità;* la filosofia civile e dell'*incivilimento* italiano in rapporto alla giurisprudenza; un'idea di «ragion pubblica economica» che intreccia saperi e pratiche.[55]

Il riferimento, non rituale, ad un autore come Romagnosi, tipicamente "preorlandiano", mostra qui la distanza, ovvero la specificità di Majorana rispetto alle opzioni metodologiche che Orlando diffonde in quegli anni. Non una *ricostruzione giuridica del diritto pubblico*, ma una *teoria giuridica delle scienze sociali*. Gran parte dei saggi che Majorana pubblica tra il 1885 e il 1890 si muovono più sul terreno della teoria generale dello Stato che su quello delle istituzioni del diritto costituzionale.

L'*esprit* liberal-democratico lo conduce a soluzioni coerenti. Critica del parlamentarismo e delle sue patologie, ma centralità del parlamento. Questo significa considerare il governo parlamentare come una specifica figura giuridica.[56] Non segue parimenti i tedeschi, Laband in particolare, quando considerano il bilancio dello Stato una legge puramente formale. Per Majorana invece la legge di bilancio è una "vera" legge con tutte le conseguenze del caso. La soluzione è diversa da quella bismarckiana:

> «Il parlamento, dunque, ha sul bilancio la *plena potestas*, e può modificarlo o rigettarlo, come crede. Su ciò verte grave controversia; ma non mi par discutibile che, astrattamente, il parlamento abbia anche il diritto di rifiutare il bilancio.»[57]

54 G. Giarrizzo, *Una dinastia siciliana*, in G. Majorana, *Il Grand Tour*, cit., 18.

55 Sulla straordinaria presenza di Romagnosi nella cultura italiana del XIX secolo, vero elemento strutturale di quello che di recente ho chiamato il *canone eclettico*, mi permetto di rinviare a L. Lacchè, *Il* canone eclettico. *Alla ricerca di uno* strato profondo *della cultura giuridica italiana dell'Ottocento*, cit. Sui "precursori" del pensiero sociologico, Vico e Romagnosi, v. R. Treves, *Lo studio dei diritti antichi e le origini della sociologia del diritto in Italia*, in Id. (a cura di), *Alle origini della sociologia del diritto*, Milano 1983, 7.

56 A. Majorana, *Il sistema dello Stato giuridico*, cit., 541 ss.

57 A. Majorana, *Teoria costituzionale delle entrate e delle spese dello Stato*, in *Antologia giuridica*, n. 1, fasc. 4–5, luglio – agosto 1886, 379. In *Il sistema dello Stato giuridico*, cit., 531 ss., Majorana critica la teorica orlandiana delle leggi proprie e improprie. Cfr. anche *Il rigetto del bilancio. Nota*, in *Archivio di diritto pubblico*, III, 3, 197–201.

Certo, parliamo di *extrema ratio* e in ogni caso bisogna trovare un bilanciamento tra due principi rilevanti.

> «Il principio costituzionale immanente è quello di far in modo che il parlamento possa esercitare il suo controllo colla maggior possibile serietà ed efficacia. Gli esercizii provvisorii, le strozzate discussioni al Senato, quelle diluite alla Camera, l'importuno criticismo e le colpevoli condiscendenze delle Commissioni di bilancio, dovrebbero proscriversi. Ma in tutto ciò ben poco valgono i teorici precetti costituzionali: occorre lo spontaneo senso dei diritti proprii e del limite, nelle assemblee o nel governo.»[58]

È significativo il fatto che Majorana nel 1888 tenga due discorsi, uno sullo Stato costituzionale germanico e l'altro su *La Rivoluzione francese e la sua influenza costituzionale*. Il professore catanese non teme di essere definito *atomista* quando afferma, seguendo le tre grandi dichiarazioni dei diritti, le due "storiche", inglese (1689) e americana (1774), la "filosofica", quella francese del 1789, che la ragione degli individui preesiste alla società e allo Stato. Majorana, nonostante le esagerazioni della scuola di diritto naturale, riconosce il fondamento universalistico della dottrina dei diritti innati. Lo Stato giuridico deve essere

> «incondizionatamente condizionato al rispetto ed alla guarentigia della *persona umana* e dei suoi più essenziali attributi. Oggi, presso alcune scuole, si è diffuso il mal vezzo di irridere gli universali principii di ragione, che vengono qualificati come vacue ed astratte generalità. Noi non seguiremo certo, per inconscia imitazione, un tale mal vezzo.»[59]

Qui siamo su una linea diversa dal costituzionalismo orlandiano che riconosce all'individuo non *libertà* ma *garanzie* poste dallo Stato senza subordinazioni ai diritti degli individui/*atomi*.

4. La costituzione sociale del diritto e lo Stato giuridico

Se con gli scritti degli anni '80 Majorana persegue l'obiettivo di proporre una teoria liberal-democratica dello Stato giuridico, con quelli dei primi anni '90 – che in buona sostanza concludono l'itinerario di ricerca di Majorana prima

58 A. Majorana, *Teoria costituzionale delle entrate*, cit., 390–391. Il dibattito italiano, tributario anche della prassi e delle riflessioni dottrinali tedesche, fu animato in quegli anni in particolare da Salandra, Arcoleo, Palma, Sciacca, Orlando e Luzzatti: v. in particolare L. Borsi, *Classe politica e costituzionalismo*, cit., 186 ss. e M. Giannetto, *Organizzazione della pubblica amministrazione e legge di bilancio. Facoltà dell'esecutivo, sindacato parlamentare e organi di controllo*, in A. G. Manca e W. Brauneder (a cura di), *L'istituzione parlamentare nel XIX secolo*, Bologna, Berlin 2000, 335–360.

59 A. Majorana, *Il sistema dello Stato giuridico*, cit., 480. L'autore segue la teoria romagnosiana della libertà come padronanza originaria (suità) e come universale condizione dei diritti.

dell'avvio della sua carriera politica che lo porterà in Parlamento e al governo – definisce e sviluppa l'indirizzo *sociologico* della costituzione politica.

Sarebbe sbagliato scorgere nel forte progetto scientifico e ideologico che Orlando propone negli stessi anni una sorta di *caterpillar* capace di eliminare, *d'emblée*, i differenti modi di intendere e di organizzare il diritto costituzionale. Gli scritti degli anni '80, i *Principi* di diritto costituzionale e di diritto amministrativo, la fondazione dell'*Archivio di diritto pubblico* nel 1891, l'avvio del *Trattato di diritto amministrativo* fissano senza dubbio le principali tappe di un disegno organico volto a modificare i presupposti e gli obiettivi della scienza del diritto pubblico in Italia.[60] Ma a questo disegno occorreranno due decenni per diventare *egemonico* (pur lasciando ancora spazi di pluralismo metodologico) e per riuscire a modificare l'assetto complessivo della disciplina, a livello tanto accademico che pratico, a partire dall'età giolittiana, col fine ultimo di costruire una scuola nazionale di diritto pubblico[61] in grado di realizzare la necessaria «coordinazione di lavoro scientifico».[62]

Il rapporto intellettuale tra Majorana e Orlando rappresenta bene, a nostro avviso, questa fase. Il loro percorso è per molti aspetti parallelo. Orlando è nato cinque anni prima di Majorana, ma la precocità di quest'ultimo li avvicina nei rispettivi *cursus* accademici. Tra i due si stabilì una profonda amicizia.[63]

60 Per i limiti del discorso metodologico orlandiano v. soprattutto P. Costa, *Lo Stato immaginario. Metafore e paradigmi nella cultura giuridica italiana fra Ottocento e Novecento*, Milano 1986. Sulle tappe di quello sviluppo v. M. Fioravanti, *La scienza del diritto pubblico*, cit., vol. I.

61 Un cartina di tornasole per leggere questa trasformazione è quella dei concorsi universitari, delle commissioni e dei vincitori di concorso. Cfr. F. Lanchester, *Pensare lo Stato*, cit., 54. Per un concorso in particolare, quello senese del 1892, vinto da Domenico Zanichelli, v. adesso L. Borsi, *Nazione Democrazia Stato. Zanichelli e Arangio Ruiz*, cit., 487 ss.

62 V. E. Orlando, *Programma*, in *Archivio di diritto pubblico*, I, 1, 1891, 4.

63 Il carteggio tra Orlando e Majorana registra una duratura amicizia costruita attorno al lavoro scientifico e alle opzioni culturali, all'impegno accademico (posti, sedi universitarie, gestione dei concorsi, politica ministeriale), al dibattito politico, ai legami familiari. Le diversità di ordine metodologico non impediscono di sviluppare un discorso comune che va oltre la rigidità del "paradigma scientifico". Una raccolta di lettere inedite di Orlando a Majorana è stata pubblicata da S. Majorana, *Cultura, vita accademica e politica nelle lettere di Vittorio Emanuele Orlando ad Angelo Majorana (1888–1910)*, tesi di laurea discussa nell'a. a. 2000/2001, Università di Catania, Facoltà di Scienze Politiche, rel. prof. R. Spampinato, corr. prof. G. Barone. Una selezione è ora edita, a cura di S. Majorana, nell'Appendice al volume *Il "giureconsulto della politica". Angelo Majorana e l'indirizzo sociologico del Diritto pubblico*, a cura di G. Pace Gravina, Macerata 2011, 199–245. Sulle "vite parallele" di Orlando e Majorana v. il bel saggio di G. Pace Gravina, *Angelo Majorana: per una fisiologia del Diritto pubblico*, *ibidem*, 95–126.

Majorana, nella prolusione del 1887, attribuiva, come si è visto, ai tedeschi la paternità della distinzione metodologica tra i criteri di ordine giuridico e quelli di ordine politico nel diritto costituzionale. Un anno dopo giunge la "replica" di Orlando che rivendica un ruolo non proprio secondario nell'aver posto l'attenzione, in Italia, su una distinzione «generalmente non molto osservata». Il «mio carissimo amico Angelo Majorana li ricordava ed applicava, con la solita acutezza, nella sua *Tutela giuridica del Governo rappresentativo*, Catania, 1887, dove, fra l'altro, si constata l'antitesi fra un indirizzo *politico* ed un indirizzo *giuridico* nel diritto costituzionale, attribuendo quest'ultimo agli scrittori tedeschi».[64]

Parlare di Orlando e di Majorana significa anche dover tenere conto del contesto del loro operare. E la Sicilia di quegl'anni è un laboratorio culturale dal respiro più che nazionale. La generazione dei due costituzionalisti è anche quella di Gaetano Mosca, degli altri fratelli Majorana, di Francesco Scaduto, dei Carnazza, di Antonino Longo, di Enrico Cimbali e di molti altri. Una generazione che negl'anni '80 emerge sulla scena nazionale e succede a quella dei Ferrara, dei D'Ondes Reggio, dei Cusumano, di Majorana padre.[65] Il quadro è quello di una cultura vivace che si consolida nelle tre antiche Università isolane, nei circoli giuridici, nelle riviste scientifiche. Commemorando Gaetano Mosca, Santi Romano, allievo di Orlando, osserva, a ragione, come la Sicilia sia stata allora la regione che più contribuì (con Arcoleo, Orlando, Scaduto, Majorana e Mosca) a rinnovare le categorie concettuali del diritto pubblico e delle istituzioni dello Stato unitario. Non si può certo parlare né di una sola scuola né di un solo indirizzo. Anzi, il dato che emerge è quello di un pluralismo scientifico arricchente per alcuni versi, problematico per altri.[66] Negli anni in cui Orlando ribadisce con forza e sicurezza crescenti le basi scientifiche del suo *Methodenstreit*, il panorama "siciliano" non è consonante e anche da ciò, credo, le prolusioni

64 Orlando continuava osservando: «In questo senso, io ammetterò certamente che la constatazione di quell'antitesi e l'aver sostenuta la necessità di ricostruire la nostra scienza su basi più rigorosamente giuridiche possa avere, negli argomenti di che si serve, molti e notevoli riscontri con scrittori di altre scuole e particolarmente tedeschi, ma d'altra parte non credo che quella, dirò così, riscossa giuridica possa propriamente dirsi *tedesca* [...]». Del resto, osservava, queste sue idee erano state accolte in Italia con indifferenza e mal comprese anche quando erano state lodate (V. E. Orlando, *Teoria giuridica delle guarentigie della libertà*, in *Biblioteca di scienze politiche*, diretta da Attilio Brunialti, Torino 1890, vol. V, 921–922. Sul punto F. Tessitore, *Crisi e trasformazioni dello Stato. Ricerche sul pensiero giuspubblicistico italiano tra Otto e Novecento*, Napoli 1963, 170; G. Cianferotti, *Il pensiero di V. E. Orlando*, cit., 197, 202).

65 G. Cianferotti, *Il pensiero di V. E. Orlando*, cit.

66 S. Romano, *Gaetano Mosca*, in *Scritti minori*, vol. I, Milano 1950, 381–382.

orlandiane traggono un ulteriore significato. *Gli studi ausiliari del diritto costituzionale*[67] di Gaetano Mosca mostrano per un verso la necessità di interpretare in maniera adeguata i fatti sociali e le dinamiche del *politico* che determinano i modi di essere del potere e dei regimi come oggetto di indagine della *scienza politica*.[68] Il solo evocare i nomi di studiosi come Salvioli, Vadalà-Papale o D'Aguanno, significa, per un altro verso, mostrare un panorama complesso che si rispecchia, per esempio, nell'attività del *Circolo giuridico*[69] fondato a Palermo nel 1870 da Luigi Sampolo e, dal 1886, nel laboratorio catanese dell'*Antologia giuridica*.[70] Il positivismo (*rectius*: le sue svariate declinazioni), il problema del metodo nelle scienze sociali, la questione sociale e le forme politiche e giuridiche del socialismo, la formazione di campi disciplinari per una visione "globale" della società (sociologia, antropologia, statistica e demografia ecc.) pervadono riflessioni, discussioni, critiche e polemiche negli anni di Angelo Majorana.

Se per Orlando il formante della costituzione è anzitutto lo Stato-persona plasmato dalla nuova scienza del diritto pubblico, per Majorana il polo costitutivo è e resta la società, la sua "costituzione", le sue forze e le sue dinamiche, i suoi modi di essere e di evolvere.[71] Per certi versi si potrebbe dire che il Majorana giurista degli anni '80 lascia il posto al sociologo degli anni '90, lo Stato giuridico fa posto al problema della costituzione sociale. Se questo passaggio è indubbio, sarebbe però eccessivo vedere in ciò una sorta di trasmutazione genetica. In realtà il patrimonio (e quindi la predisposizione metodologica) è già presente, ciò che cambia però è l'accentuazione del punto di vista. Il nucleo è rappresentato dalla riflessione del 1887 su *La tutela del diritto nel governo rappresentativo*: la irriducibilità del diritto costituzionale al solo ordine giuridico. La *dottrina generale dello Stato* deve essere integrata[72] attraverso una

67 *Circolo giuridico*, 17, 1886, 101–110.

68 Cfr. M. Fioravanti, *Gaetano Mosca e Vittorio Emanuele Orlando: due itinerari paralleli (1881–1897)*, cit. e L. Borsi, *Classe politica e costituzionalismo. Mosca Arcoleo Maranini*, cit.

69 Su questa rivista, oltre ai riferimenti nella nota seguente, v. M. L. Sagù, *Alle origini di una rivista siciliana: "Il Circolo Giuridico" di Palermo*, in *Clio*, XX, 1984, 489–504; M. A. Cocchiara, *Vito la Mantia e gli studi storico-giuridici nella Sicilia dell'Ottocento*, Milano 1999, 323–381.

70 Su questa rivista v. lo studio di G. Speciale, *Antologia giuridica*, cit. Cfr. inoltre P. De Salvo, *La cultura delle riviste giuridiche siciliane dell'Ottocento*, Milano 2002, 129–136, 335 ss. per le utilissime schede-indice.

71 In tal senso l'impostazione di Majorana è parte integrante di quella che Pietro Costa ha identificato con la giuspubblicistica di ispirazione sociocentrica: *Lo Stato immaginario*, cit.

72 Il tema dell'"integrazionismo" nel dibattito tra "orlandiani" e "non-orlandiani" è stato colto da P. Costa, *Lo Stato immaginario*, cit., 441 ss.

dottrina generale della società. Majorana riconosce l'efficacia del "metodo giuridico", ma non ritiene che esso possa essere la via esclusiva per una piena comprensione del diritto costituzionale.

Il 1891 segna, senza dubbio, un momento significativo nel percorso intellettuale del giurista catanese. Escono i suoi *Primi principii della sociologia*,[73] un'opera nella quale cerca di «fermare una breve serie di principî fondamentali, attorno a cui possasi raggruppare la materia vasta, molteplice, difforme, diffusa, incoerente financo».[74] In questo lavoro l'autore riprende e sviluppa il concetto della sociologia – il cui oggetto e i cui confini restano incerti[75] – come *dottrina generale della società*.[76] Majorana – che si dice allievo di Filomusi Guelfi nelle ricerche filosofiche – ha respirato un'aria di famiglia particolarmente propizia: la sistematica delle scienze sociali la deve al padre, le applicazioni di ordine quantitativo, le dimostrazioni statistiche al fratello Giuseppe.[77] Seguendo un metodo «quasi matematico», Angelo porta alle estreme conseguenze – con esiti che oggi possono apparire talvolta di dubbio interesse – il tipico modo di procedere del sociologismo evoluzionista fondato su "leggi di sviluppo" culminanti con la Legge per eccellenza del XIX secolo borghese: quella che Majorana pretende di raffigurare come la *Legge assintotica del progresso sociale*. L'accumulazione di materiali i più vari, alla ricerca di una visione globale della società e delle scienze, è un tratto distintivo di questa stagione eroica, controversa, segnata da infinite "infedeltà" interpretative. La nuova scienza di Comte e di Spencer –

73 *I Primi Principii della Sociologia. Libri VI*, Roma 1891.

74 *Ibidem*, 13.

75 «[...] la logica applicata ci ha insegnato da un pezzo che una scienza non può dirsi costituita, se non quando se ne sieno risolute le questioni generali e fondamentali, vale a dire fissato in base ai suoi caratteri differenziali l'oggetto e con questo il campo e i limiti, determinato il posto che occupa nel sistema delle scienze o gruppi di scienze affini, distinte le parti, assegnato il metodo, indicato lo scopo. È dunque un lavoro essenzialmente ed eminentemente critico che si richiede per la sociologia, un lavoro propedeutico di sistemazione, di organizzazione, di orientazione», I. Vanni, *Prime linee di un programma critico di sociologia*, Perugia 1888, poi in *Saggi di filosofia sociale e giuridica*, Bologna 1906, 426–427. Questo importante saggio di Vanni viene recensito nel 1890 su l'*Antologia giuridica*, 4, fasc. 2, 154–155.

76 *I Primi Principii della Sociologia*, cit., 24. L'opera sociologica di Angelo Majorana non sembra aver trovato una puntuale sistemazione nell'ambito della storiografia italiana sulle "origini" della sociologia e delle nuove scienze sociali di fine Ottocento. Cfr. per es. E. R. Papa (a cura di), *Il positivismo e la cultura italiana*, Milano 1985; F. Barbano, G. Sola, *Sociologia e scienze sociali in Italia. 1861–1890. Introduzioni critiche e repertorio bibliografico*, Milano 1985.

77 *I Primi Principii della Sociologia*, cit., 14.

filtrata spesso, più o meno consapevolmente, attraverso gli "italici" Vico e Romagnosi – pretendeva di funzionare come *sintesi* delle scienze sociali.

Un dato deve essere sottolineato: quello che per Orlando è il punto di partenza, per Majorana è, per così dire, il punto di arrivo. Non è casuale il titolo che il nostro autore sceglie per un saggio che affianca, nel 1891, i principi di sociologia: *Forze e forme politiche e la loro valutazione giuridica.*[78] Dieci anni prima, nel 1881, Orlando, non ancora laureato, aveva esordito con un saggio intitolato *Delle forme e delle forze politiche secondo H. Spencer,*[79] pubblicato nella fiorentina «Rivista europea». Allora Orlando aveva trovato nello scritto di Spencer[80] la "soluzione" ad un problema che toccava «le questioni più ardue del diritto pubblico moderno».[81] L'analisi morfologica delle forme di governo operata da Spencer su base "antropologica" poteva risolvere il problema del governo misto di classica ascendenza e modificare «le teorie del diritto pubblico moderno, circa le forme degli Stati e le origini del potere Sovrano».[82] Il punto di osservazione doveva riguardare il livello *profondo* delle *forze* e non quello *superficiale* e contingente delle *forme.* Se queste ultime si trasformano e si diversificano, il principio, il fondamento – ovvero la forza – rimane unico. Il concetto organico di Stato è allora fondamentale per esprimere il sentimento costante del popolo inteso come unità composta da una pluralità di vincoli e di affetti e non, alla Rousseau, come «aggregato accidentale di tanti individui tutti eguali fra loro».[83]

La prospettiva di Majorana, dieci anni dopo, è invece quella della fondazione della *sociologia politica.* Non tutti i fenomeni possono essere assorbiti nel diritto pubblico o nel diritto costituzionale.

> «Invero, proponendoci lo studio del fenomeno nella sua pienezza, non possiamo restringerci al solo profilo giuridico, né in questo costringere tutti gli altri: dobbiamo, invece, dare propria e distinta trattazione ai vari lati del problema, considerandone ciascuno sotto il suo singolo e particolare aspetto; pur curando,

78 A. Majorana, *Forze e forme politiche e la loro valutazione giuridica. Saggio di sociologia politica*, Roma 1891.

79 Poi ripubblicato in *Diritto pubblico generale. Scritti varii coordinati in sistema*, Milano 1940, 557–578. Sulle interpretazioni di questo primo saggio di Orlando v. M. Fioravanti, *Popolo e Stato negli scritti giovanili di Vittorio Emanuele Orlando*, cit., 78–83 e G. Cianferotti, *Il pensiero di V. E. Orlando e la giuspubblicistica italiana*, cit., 39–42. Sulla genesi del lavoro e sulla corrispondenza con Luigi Palma e con Attilio Brunialti v. ivi, 36–37.

80 Pubblicato in francese nel marzo 1881 nella «Revue Philosophique» col titolo, appunto, *Des formes et des forces politiques.*

81 *Delle forme e delle forze politiche secondo H. Spencer*, cit., 557.

82 *Ibidem*, 559.

83 *Ibidem*, 571.

poi, di raggrupparli tutti in una sintesi finale e complessiva. Il fare ciò è ufficio della Sociologia; la quale sotto questo riguardo appalesasi più che altro come un *metodo*, ed in ciò manifesta la sua principale ragione scientifica di essere.»[84]

La sociologia come *metodo* appare dunque lo strumento per ricomprendere l'unità del fenomeno. Le forze devono essere analizzate in tutti i loro elementi costitutivi: struttura, equilibrio ma anche *movimento*. Deve mutare anche l'angolo visuale per leggere le forme di governo:

> «Bisogna riflettere che *gli ordinamenti politici sono dati dalle condizioni sociali* e che il *governo è dato dalla società*. Più che ai governanti vuolsi guardare ai governati; più che al numero ed alla qualità di quelli, al numero ed alla qualità di questi. È un vero rivolgimento che devesi portare al modo con cui, di solito, si procede nella classificazione delle forme di governo.»[85]

Il campo di intervento è dunque anzitutto la società, sotto i profili della gerarchia, della coesione e delle forze di aggregazione. Majorana ne formula, secondo il metodo positivistico, le "leggi di sviluppo". Riflette sul concetto di rappresentanza naturale e di *classe politica*, discutendo le teoriche di Mosca. Accanto e avverso le forze legali agiscono *elementi anomali* (forze, individui che influenzano la gestione "legale" del governo), *ingerenze* anche indebite. Ma, pur non seguendo il concetto darwiniano della selezione naturale, «la sostanza della dottrina della *lotta politica* permane integra.[86] Nella prospettiva sociologica non esiste un solo *Stato giuridico*.

> «Teniamo saldo il principio che ogni Stato, sol perché tale, è giuridico. E ciò non soltanto perché è *organo di diritto*; ma perché, nella sua essenza, è la *costituzione giuridica della società*; ossia comprende quell'ordinamento e quelle sanzioni per cui la società diventa, in modo *pratico e efficace*, un organismo, e le sue parti non vanno disperse in un atomismo dissolvente. Il carattere giuridico, pertanto, si ha in *re ipsa*, nello Stato.»[87]

La valutazione giuridica, di cui Majorana parla nel titolo, si può fare solo per le forze che, nella loro essenza, sono sempre eguali. Ma «le leggi sociologiche hanno universalità ed immanenza, simili alle leggi giuridiche. D'altronde queste non sono che *proiezione* di quelle».[88] Attraverso il meccanismo della rappresentanza emergono *nello Stato* i soggetti e i gruppi che interagiscono nella società dando vita a gerarchie e capacità. La rappresentanza *riconosce* le forze della società e lo Stato può così esprimere la «sovranità imperante» come unità del politico.

84 Majorana, *Forze e forme politiche*, cit., 4. Lo scrittore siciliano segue quella che Icilio Vanni definiva come la terza concezione della sociologia (sintesi delle scienze sociali).

85 *Ibidem*, 7.

86 *Ibidem*, 39.

87 *Ibidem*, 49.

88 *Ibidem*, 50.

Questi interessi *realistici* di Angelo Majorana non sono isolati. Si è detto, per un verso, del fertile ambiente culturale siciliano che si interroga sui tre campi fondamentali, distinti eppur interconnessi, del positivismo, della sociologia e del socialismo. Nel 1894 verrà fondata da quel singolare personaggio che è Giuseppe Fiamingo, insieme a Giuseppe Vadalà-Papale e allo statistico Filippo Virgilii, la *Rivista di sociologia*.[89]

È con la "svolta" del 1891 che il nome di Majorana viene sempre più associato alla "scuola sociologica di diritto pubblico". Non di scuola si tratta, invero, ma di un orientamento che tra gli anni '80 e '90 avvicina di fatto sensibilità diverse e discute la *Methodenstreit* sul diritto costituzionale e sulla definizione dei legami tra sociologia e costituzione politica.[90] Vincenzo Miceli pubblica nel 1890 *Lo studio del diritto costituzionale e la moderna sociologia*[91] nel quale propone un esame del diritto costituzionale rispondente alla nuova «scienza della costituzione politica». Nel 1892 inaugura l'anno accademico a Perugia parlando de *Il diritto costituzionale e la biologia*.[92]

Un apparente paradosso è che un luogo di raccordo tra queste sensibilità è l'«Archivio di diritto pubblico» fondato nel 1891 da Vittorio Emanuele Orlando. Come è stato osservato,[93] questa rivista-progetto, passo ulteriore nel processo di identificazione e decantazione del metodo giuridico nella ricostruzione del diritto pubblico nazionale, non solo non rifiuta la pubblicazione di contributi eterodossi ma, forse a maggior ragione, li assume come termine di paragone sul piano della costruzione dell'oggetto e della specificazione metodologica.[94] Il "diverso" viene apprezzato, appunto, anche come "dimostrazione" di tolleranza scientifica e di apertura.[95] Nel primo numero Guido Jona, un altro esponente

89 Cfr. ampiamente G. Speciale, *Antologia giuridica*, cit., 35–41.

90 Sui diversi indirizzi cfr. G. Cianferotti, *Il pensiero di V. E. Orlando*, cit., 199 ss.

91 Perugia 1890, estr. dagli «Annali della libera Università di Perugia», IV, 1889, vol. II. Negli anni precedenti Miceli aveva pubblicato *La divisione nelle scienze sociali*, in *Rassegna di scienze sociali e politiche*, III, fasc. LV, 1885, 341–356 e *La scienza della costituzione politica della società*, in Ivi, III, fasc. LVIII, 1885, 507–523. Per alcuni aspetti dell'opera di Miceli v. L. Borsi, *Classe politica e costituzionalismo*, cit., 37; P. Costa, *Civitas. Storia della cittadinanza in Europa. 3. La civiltà liberale*, Roma, Bari 2001, 221 ss.; i recenti contributi di G. P. Trifone, *Rappresentanza 'armonica' e crisi del 'mandato politico' in Vincenzo Miceli*, in *Giornale di storia costituzionale*, 16, II, 2008, 129–152; Id., *Il diritto al cospetto della politica. Miceli, Rossi, Siotto Pintòr e la crisi della rappresentanza liberale*, cit.

92 Perugia 1892.

93 M. Fioravanti, *Vittorio Emanuele Orlando e le prime riviste della giuspubblicistica italiana (1891–1903)*, in *La scienza del diritto pubblico*, I, cit., 218 ss.

94 Sempre nella prima annata l'«Archivio» pubblica uno dei "manifesti" del sociologismo di Majorana: *Ipotesi di una legge di embriologia sociale con ispeciali applicazioni alla sociologia politica*, I, 1, 1891, 18–41, 81–98.

95 Così in V. E. Orlando, *La sociologia e la legge del progresso a proposito di una*

dell'*indirizzo sociologico* (ma in realtà diverso dalle opzioni accolte da Majorana), viene chiamato a confrontare i *nuovi indirizzi* della giuspubblicistica italiana espressi dai *Principii di diritto costituzionale* di Orlando e da *Il sistema dello Stato giuridico* di Majorana, entrambi del 1889.[96] Se il pensiero di Orlando – secondo l'analisi di Jona – si sviluppa attorno ai principî della determinazione storicistica del diritto, dell'assoluta autonomia sovrana dello Stato-persona, dell'immanenza dell'ordine giuridico nelle dinamiche del diritto pubblico, nella riflessione di Majorana il diritto è il limite per la tutela della libertà e dell'eguaglianza,[97] la sovranità dello Stato non può essere anteposta agli individui e al contratto sociale, le dinamiche del diritto pubblico non possono prescindere dall'ordine politico e quindi dai rapporti tra la società e le ideologie presenti in un determinato momento storico.

Orlando non tarda però ad offrire il suo diretto punto di vista e poche pagine dopo il confronto operato da Jona recensisce i recentissimi *primi principii della sociologia* di Majorana.[98] Quello che il direttore della rivista vuole mostrare, parlando dell'opera dell'amico catanese, è che la sociologia è una sorta di «vecchio diritto naturale camuffato»[99] che ripropone, in forma aggiornata, attraverso leggi "obbiettive", i temi classici della dimensione metafisica, del contrattualismo, della società atomistica, dell'artificialismo post-rivoluzionario, dell'antistatalismo. Principî, questi, che impedirebbero allo Stato di diventare quella persona *reale* e *positiva* di cui l'Italia nuova e i suoi interpreti, i giuristi, hanno urgentemente bisogno. Semmai Orlando ritiene di un certo interesse, anche se mantiene tutte le sue riserve,[100] l'impostazione sociologica di Majorana sul punto di riuscire «a ridurre a giusta armonia l'elemento giuridico con quello sociologico [...] Lavori notevoli a questo tipo appartenenti sono quelli di Miceli e di Jona sulla *Rappresentanza politica*».[101]

pubblicazione recente (A. Majorana, I primi principii della Sociologia, Libri VI, in *Archivio di diritto pubblico*, I, 1, 1891, 280.

96 G. Jona, *Nuovi indirizzi del diritto pubblico in Italia a proposito di recenti pubblicazioni*, in *Archivio di diritto pubblico*, I, 1, 1891, 99–106.

97 Principio questo che, nella costruzione dei campi disciplinari della scienza politica e della sociologia positivistica, deve fare i conti con l'idea che le aggregazioni sociali producono naturalmente differenze e gerarchie. Sul punto v. P. Costa, *Lo Stato immaginario*, cit., 52.

98 V. E. Orlando, *La sociologia e la legge del progresso*, cit., 280–284.

99 M. Fioravanti, *Vittorio Emanuele Orlando e le prime riviste della giuspubblicistica italiana*, cit., 220.

100 «Va da sé che noi manteniamo le nostre riserve circa la bontà di questo metodo sia per ragioni specialmente relative allo stato attuale del diritto pubblico in Italia sia per ragioni generali dipendenti cioè dal *modo* e dalla *misura* con cui quel metodo va usato» (V. E. Orlando, *La letteratura del diritto pubblico a proposito di recenti pubblicazioni*, in *Archivio di diritto pubblico*, III, 3, 1893, 193).

101 *Ibidem*, 193.

Nel suo ultimo scritto di carattere metodologico,[102] la *Teoria sociologica della costituzione politica*, Majorana riassume tra il 1892 e il 1894 i temi che lo hanno portato ad intrecciare la dottrina generale del diritto costituzionale con la sociologia della costituzione politica. Lo studio *realistico* del potere, nel suo presupposto di sovranità, ne è il suo oggetto.

> «Una siffatta ricerca ci si appalesa fuor di dubbio come *sociologica*. È una gravissima serie di *fenomeni sociali* quelli che si vogliono riconoscere e non meramente *giuridici* o, peggio, *legali*; non genericamente *politici*, né particolarmente *morali* o, tanto meno, *economici*. E perché sociali, sono fenomeni *complessi*; i quali presentano contemporaneamente l'aspetto morale, economico, giuridico, ed assumono, specificatamente, la forma politica.»[103]

La costituzione, alla quale pensa Majorana, è una *struttura* di tipo dualistico che «esprime proprio il momento, il senso del formarsi, del prendere forma dello Stato in rapporto al polo opposto, e connesso, del sociale».[104]

Con il suo saggio del 1894 su una questione di grande attualità, lo stato d'assedio proclamato a seguito dei fatti di Lunigiana e di Sicilia,[105] il liberale Majorana chiude – se così si può dire – un decennio di studi e di attività scientifica. Gli anni successivi, sino alla malattia e alla precoce scomparsa, lo vedranno impegnato con crescente successo nell'attività politico-amministrativa locale e poi nazionale. Da Catania, peculiare laboratorio italiano, vede l'avanzata del socialismo. In una recensione del 1890 al libro di Sidney Webb *Socialism in England*, Majorana coglie l'esito di una legge di tendenza.

> «Non vale il negarlo: nella lotta secolare fra i due fondamentali principii di libertà e di vincolo, di individualità e di collettività, questo scorcio del secolo XIX ha dato e dà la palma al secondo ... le cose cangiarono; si disse che quel concetto di libertà

102 Nel 1893 Majorana pubblica in *La scienza del diritto privato*, I, il saggio *Il nuovo indirizzo del diritto pubblico in rapporto alla sociologia ed al diritto privato*. Sulla partecipazione del giurista catanese allo stimolante foglio fiorentino cfr. P. Grossi, *"La scienza del diritto privato". Una rivista-progetto nella Firenze di fine secolo 1893–1896*, Milano 1988, 104.

103 A. Majorana, *Teoria sociologica della costituzione politica*, seconda edizione completamente rifatta, Torino 1894. Una parte era uscita nell'*Antologia giuridica*, 6, fasc. 5, 1892, 377–409. Per una analisi cfr. C. Dollo, *Angelo Majorana e la Teoria sociologica della costituzione politica*, in G. Cacciatore, M. Martirano, E. Massimilla (a cura di), *Filosofia e storia della cultura. Studi in onore di Fulvio Tessitore*, Napoli 1997, II, 213–226.

104 P. Costa, *Lo Stato immaginario*, cit., 307.

105 A. Majorana, *Lo stato di assedio*, Catania 1894. Questo lavoro fu recensito, tra gli altri, da Giuseppe Fiamingo in *Antologia giuridica*, 8, fasc. 6–7, 1894, 440–441 e da Santi Romano in *Archivio di diritto pubblico*, IV, 1894, 317–318. Sul punto v. G. Astuto, *Crispi e lo stato d'assedio in Sicilia*, Milano 1999, 93 ss. Per un inquadramento dottrinale si veda per tutti C. Latini, *Governare l'emergenza. Delega legislativa e pieni poteri in Italia tra Otto e Novecento*, Milano 2005.

individuale fosse *negativo* e *atonisico*; si volle aspirare a concezioni più vaste e collettive; si credette che meglio si potesse provvedere al bene pubblico, convertendo il metodo, ossia provvedendo, non già ai singoli per il bene del tutto, ma al tutto per il bene dei singoli. Disgraziatamente non è soltanto questione di metodo, ma di sostanza: l'inversione dei procedimenti ha tale importanza da compromettere lo scopo. E' lecito chiedere: dove ci incamminiamo?»[106]

La risposta è ardua, tante sono le *forze* in campo. Ma non ci si deve dissimulare il problema perché bisogna affrontarlo con coraggio per tentare di risolverlo.

Questo appare essere l'orizzonte operativo, *politico*, di Angelo Majorana. Il suo lavoro scientifico non offre soluzioni, ma pone problemi. Al di là dei meriti specifici, ciò che acquista rilievo è la tensione a porre la questione della crisi, della trasformazione, del conflitto anzitutto dal punto di vista della *costituzione sociale*. In un saggio del 1901 il giurista catanese tracciava un bilancio del secolo appena concluso come età, ormai controversa, di crescita e di sviluppo del governo parlamentare. La spinta propulsiva era terminata, ma nondimeno la *crisi* richiedeva al nuovo secolo che «la evoluzione del regime parlamentare [...] dovrà condurre ad un sempre maggiore esercizio diretto della sovranità, da parte della nazione». La tendenza nuova della *socializzazione*, «ossia di rendere collettivo il modo di provvedere alla soddisfazione dei bisogni umani [...]», non poteva non riguardare le istituzioni parlamentari.[107] Diversamente dall'antitesi orlandiana tra ordine giuridico e ordine politico, tra Stato e società,[108] per Majorana erano piuttosto le forme di integrazione nella *costituzione sociale* dello Stato giuridico a dover rappresentare una possibile via di uscita dalla crisi.

Accordare lo *Stato giuridico* ai bisogni contradditorii della società e degli individui per trovare il miglior punto di equilibrio possibile tra *istituzioni* e *forze* è anche la sfida di Majorana: una sfida, in ultima istanza, che nasce dalla straordinaria tensione tra il valore antico della libertà e quello nuovo dell'eguaglianza, tra i diritti dell'individuo e i doveri della società democratica. Una sfida persa con l'avvento del fascismo, ma destinata a segnare tutto il secolo.

106 Rec. a *Sidney Webb, Socialism in England*, London 1890, in *Antologia giuridica*, 4, fasc. 3, 1890, 251. Nella *Nuova Antologia* del luglio 1889 Majorana aveva pubblicato un articolo sul *Socialismo inglese*. Cfr. G. Speciale, *Antologia giuridica*, cit., 118–120. Nel 1902 pubblicherà sotto il titolo di *Psicologia del socialismo* una recensione al libro di E. Ciccotti, *Psicologia del movimento socialista*, Bari 1902, in *Archivio di diritto pubblico e dell'amministrazione italiana*, XI–XII, 1903, 648.

107 A. Majorana, *Il Governo parlamentare all'inizio del secolo XX*, in *La Riforma sociale*, VIII, 1901, 358–359.

108 Cfr. L. Mangoni, *La crisi dello Stato liberale e i giuristi italiani*, in A. Mazzacane (a cura di), *I giuristi e la crisi dello Stato liberale in Italia fra Otto e Novecento*, cit., 32.

Il nome della libertà. Tre dimensioni nel secolo della Costituzione (1848–1948)

1. Una (modesta) proposta

Parlare della parola / concetto *libertà* nel secolo italiano della costituzione è compito temerario, anzi, dirò, impossibile nello spazio di una breve relazione.[1] Per non affogare subito nel *mare magnum* di significati, definizioni e specificazioni propongo di individuare una «via di fuga» che ha il carattere del «nuoto libero» e propone una visione essenzialmente soggettiva.

In particolare cercherò di passare in rassegna tre declinazioni della libertà che mi sembrano aver contrassegnato il secolo di cui parliamo in questo convegno. Non parlerei di categorie ma piuttosto di accentuazioni, di modi di essere, di relazioni, di dimensioni della parola *libertà*. In successione parlerò quindi di *libertà proprietaria*, di *libertà riflessa*, di *libertà degna*. In successione perché è possibile intravedere dei momenti che marcano un'epoca, una fase, e tuttavia solo dalla complessa contaminazione e dalla sovrapposizione dialettica sarà possibile cogliere tratti permanenti e discontinuità.

La parola *libertà* è di quelle che sollecitano cautela e fanno nascere subito la necessità di misure e di limiti. «Libertà! Ecco una parola a cui furono date le più diverse significazioni; una parola di cui si è stranamente abusato, fino al punto di commettere in suo nome i più atroci misfatti. Pertanto poiché gli uomini sogliono annettere ai vocaboli non solo l'idea delle cose che rappresentano, ma anche quelle delle loro passioni, importa definire con esattezza il senso di quella parola che ha commosso, e commove gli animi in tante maniere».[2] Un altro dei nostri primi costituzionalisti ricordava, nella fase genetica del nuovo Stato liberal-costituzionale, che «non vi ha parola più variamente intesa della libertà! Tutte le storie ne trattano, tutte le lingue ne favellano, in suo nome sono avvenuti gli atti più eroici e si sono commesse le scene più nefande; in tutti i luoghi, in tutti i secoli, si sono in nome della libertà abbattute dinastie, teocrazie

1 Conservo i caratteri della relazione orale con l'aggiunta di un apparato bibliografico strettamente funzionale.

2 L. Casanova, *Del diritto costituzionale. Lezioni*, 2 voll., Genova 1859, vol. I, 39.

ed aristocrazie, si sono create nuove società politiche, ed anche nuovi despoti, nuove tirannie».[3]

Di fronte alla vastità dell'orizzonte, appare indispensabile indicare e seguire alcune boe cui aggrapparsi di tanto in tanto per evitare pericoli peggiori e per segnalare, seppure in forma appena abbozzata, le tre dimensioni della libertà appena accennate.

2. La libertà proprietaria

Per tratteggiare questo primo binomio assumo a paradigma la imponente ricognizione che un altro costituzionalista italiano dell'Ottocento ci propone nella sua celebre *Biblioteca*: mi riferisco al volume *La libertà nello Stato moderno* curato da Attilio Brunialti sul finire degli anni Ottanta del secolo.[4] Il grosso tomo contiene una silloge aggiornata ed eclettica della cultura politico-giuridica europea che attraversa e segna il XIX secolo. Dopo una lunga introduzione, Brunialti raccoglie autori e opere che, nel loro insieme, suggeriscono percorsi, retoriche e un "programma" per la libertà nello Stato moderno. Si tratta di un saggio stratigrafico che cerca di individuare i livelli di formazione e di sviluppo del concetto di *libertà* (più al singolare che al plurale) nel secolo in cui l'individualismo giunge a misurarsi in maniera compiuta con la dimensione dello Stato moderno ormai sufficientemente oggettivato. La scelta degli autori mira a segnalare la centralità del tema della libertà individuale come caposaldo vitale, rispetto al quale gli approcci dichiaratamente "anti-individualistici" non giungono a contrapporre individuo e Stato, libertà e dimensione collettiva del sociale. Si possono cogliere le manchevolezze di un modello di libertà proprietaria, ma alla fine la soggettività (economica e politica) non può fare mai a meno della parola *libertà*.

Il percorso di Brunialti corre dal Benjamin Constant della libertà dei moderni al giovane Vittorio Emanuele Orlando e alla Enciclica di Leone XIII sulla libertà umana, passando per l'*On the Liberty* di John Stuart Mill, lo studio "constantiano" di Eduard de Laboulaye *La liberté antique et la liberté moderne* (1863), l'*On civil liberty and self-government* dell'internazionalista e carbonaro tedesco – naturalizzato americano – Francis Lieber, *I limiti della libertà individuale* (annotato da Orlando) di Francis Charles Montague, *L'istituzione regia e la responsabilità ministeriale* di Camillo Montalcini e infine la *Teoria giuridica delle guarentigie della Libertà* del giovane Orlando. Spettro eclettico di un percorso che vuole rappresentare autori "individualisti" e autori che pongono pregiudiziali

3 L. Palma, *Corso di diritto costituzionale*, Firenze 1877, vol. I, 161.

4 *Biblioteca di scienze politiche*, V, Torino 1890.

"antiliberiste". Specchio confuso, segnale di una complessità tutta interna al discorso prodotto dalla cultura liberale.

È indubbio il fatto che uno dei grandi legati delle rivoluzioni settecentesche sia il nuovo linguaggio costituzionale (costituente) che darà sostanza concettuale al costituzionalismo liberale ottocentesco. Ma si ha anche l'impressione che nel frangente del *costituzionalismo rivoluzionario* le diverse esperienze (in special modo nel triangolo atlantico dell'Inghilterra, dell'America e della Francia) abbiano prodotto categorie, linguaggi, soluzioni che il lungo Ottocento vorrà o potrà metabolizzare solo in parte e in chiave sostanzialmente eclettica.[5] Nel corso del XIX secolo rimangono fermi i pilastri originari del costituzionalismo moderno (garanzia dei diritti e delle libertà; limite e organizzazione della sovranità) ma ciò che è oggetto di ripensamento e di nuova *balance* sono alcuni orizzonti che appaiono radicali o almeno tali potenzialmente. Si tratta, dunque, non di tornare indietro (cosa certo possibile a livello teorico e dottrinale) quanto piuttosto di combinare assieme e di governare quell'insieme di principi e di regole politico-giuridiche in grado di dare soluzione all'incontro, fonte di tensioni e di contraddizioni, tra le libertà/garanzie dei moderni e un principio stabile e progrediente di ordine costituzionale.

Sarebbe tuttavia un approccio parziale quello che volesse leggere i fondamenti del costituzionalismo liberale solo attraverso i testi costituzionali. Non bisogna infatti dimenticare quella vicenda dell'ordine giuridico ottocentesco, liberal-borghese, che individua nel codice civile – per semplificare il *Code Napoléon* quale suo più vistoso paradigma – la più autentica *costituzione materiale*. Lo spazio del codice civile possiede un'indubbia vocazione "costituzionale" ed una forte pretesa di stabilità e di autonomia. Il XIX secolo principia, nel "modello francese" (che avrà ampia risonanza europea), con un costituzionalismo debole o puramente *imperiale* e con un ordine costituzionale *dei privati* straordinariamente forte.

Sulla scia dell'individualismo proprietario, la dimensione costituzionale accentua, a partire dall'età napoleonica, la logica del *privatismo*. Il binomio al centro della scena non è più quello libertà/eguaglianza, dirompente nella fase più radicale della Rivoluzione, ma libertà/proprietà, con l'*égalité* neutralizzata dall'antropologia del possesso e la *liberté* resa possibile nella sfera dell'*homo oeconomicus*. La garanzia costituzionale (e quindi il costituzionalismo) può operare principalmente nell'ambito delle libertà economiche, impallidisce quanto più ci si allontana dall'antropologia del proprietario maschio e maggio-

5 Su questo fondamentale atteggiamento antropologico della cultura italiana v. L. Lacchè, *Il* canone eclettico. *Alla ricerca di uno* strato profondo *della cultura giuridica italiana dell'Ottocento*, in *Quaderni fiorentini per la storia del pensiero giuridico moderno*, 39, 2010, 153–228.

renne. La logica del codice è, al tempo stesso, la logica della legge. Questo tipo di "regno della legge", con le sue ben radicate mitologie, è ben diverso dal *rule of law* di matrice anglosassone. Il legicentrismo determina una progressiva scissione tra legge e costituzione, tra legge e diritti. La super-legge, il codice civile, ha, in tal senso, impoverito la teoria costituzionale dei diritti.

Al contempo, non ci meraviglia che il filone più sostanzioso del costituzionalismo liberale del primo Ottocento trovi, a livello europeo, in Benjamin Constant lo scrittore che, muovendo proprio dall'esperienza rivoluzionaria e napoleonica, censura il legislatore onnipotente e considera la costituzione «un acte de défiance puisqu'elle prescrit des limites à l'autorité». Limitare la sovranità, e dunque il potere, significa tracciare anzitutto la linea invalicabile della «libertà dei moderni» che garantisce i cittadini «contre le pouvoir».[6]

Ma ciò non basta. Constant coglie lucidamente i pericoli del privatismo. Il governo rappresentativo non sana del tutto la irriducibile distanza tra governanti e governati, così come la divisione dei poteri è insufficiente se i poteri finiscono per non limitare la prorompente autorità sociale. La libertà degli antichi assicurava la partecipazione al potere sociale ma col rischio che gli uomini cedessero a poco prezzo i diritti e i godimenti individuali. La libertà dei moderni, ovvero la libertà individuale che offre il benessere e l'indipendenza privata, rischia di annullare quella politica. L'uomo moderno "costituzionale", invece, ha bisogno di entrambe le libertà, ovvero di combinarle assieme. È questa l'alchimia del costituzionalismo liberale di matrice individualistica che Constant elabora durante l'età napoleonica e popolarizza nella sua celebre conferenza su «La libertà degli antichi comparata a quella dei moderni» (1819). In questo *costituzionalismo del soggetto* – da Constant a Tocqueville a Stuart Mill – cogliamo la tensione tra la necessaria difesa dell'individuo attraverso le garanzie e il pericolo dell'esorbitanza di un potere sociale che, sotto varie forme a cominciare dalla forma-Stato, minaccia lo stesso ordine dei privati. Ma la libertà può essere minacciata anche da altre forme "sociali" di controllo, dal governo delle opinioni, da una pura determinazione numerica che rischia di condurre a tirannie *au petit pied*.

Nella dimensione della *libertà proprietaria* la misura è l'*avere*, ormai distanziato da *status* predeterminati a livello cetuale. Le due cose possono stare assieme, ma il contrario non è realmente possibile. La *proprietà di sé* è la stella polare della forma giuridica e dello strumento politico. È autonomia, calcolo, ragione: è misura di quel fascio di diritti e doveri che formano la semantica giuridica e politica della proprietà. A ben vedere la *libertà proprietaria* è più del classico e

6 Benjamin Constant, *Principes de politique*, a cura di Etienne Hofmann, 3 tomi, Genève 1980, t. I, libro XVI, cap. 7, 432.

fondamentale binomio *liberty and property* perché ne intende cogliere la densità dell'intreccio. Non è la libertà più la proprietà: è la libertà *piena* che *vive* attraverso la proprietà che, a sua volta, può essere graduata per intensità e pregnanza. La *libertà proprietaria* è la forza vitale del XIX secolo; il binomio libertà / uguaglianza è il programma di un futuro annunciato ma ancora difficile da raggiungere. Tutte le libertà di "prima generazione" sono più efficienti, funzionano appieno, se collegate alla proprietà. L'eguaglianza è funzionale alla *libertà proprietaria*, ma non può regolare la sfera pubblica dove operano i meccanismi ben delimitati del governo rappresentativo. Insomma, la *libertà proprietaria* è liberale ma non democratica.

Quella dimensione ha una forza progrediente, modernizzatrice, civilizzatrice, ordinante sul piano del garantismo dei diritti e delle libertà (astrattamente per tutti) del soggetto ma, al tempo stesso, teme ciò che eccede la *misura* e ridetermina differenze cogenti sul piano concreto, tanto più se questo può portare a sovranità prive di limite e a forme di abuso.

«In un solo, fortunato paese, la libertà – scrive Attilio Brunalti – non patisce eclissi, ma di rozza, illimitata, inconciliabile col vivere civile, si trasforma a poco a poco in una facoltà guarentita dalle leggi, difesa come un patrimonio e si eleva e si esplica nella vita pubblica, preservando dapprima le istituzioni locali, determinando la formazione della rappresentanza e presiedendo a tutto lo sviluppo del sistema parlamentare».[7] Questa è «la libertà operosa, cosciente feconda del cittadino anglo-sassone».[8] In quel contesto – ampiamente mitizzato – la libertà non ha gran bisogno di definizioni ma *vive* nel concreto della storia e della nazione. «Proclamare la libertà di quanti uomini sono al mondo e costringerli a riconoscerla colle armi può essere grande e gloriosa impresa; ma assai più durevole è la libertà conquistata in secoli di lotte, che ciascun cittadino è in grado di comprendere e di apprezzare, che si svolge nella sua vita quotidiana, sa evitare gli eccessi appunto per la coscienza del valore suo, ed è affermata timidamente, con parole modeste, o persino sottintesa, ma trova efficace garanzia in tutto l'ordinamento politico, nelle leggi e nei costumi, nella responsabilità del governo e nelle virtù dei cittadini».[9] La libertà dei liberali alla Brunialti è anzitutto una libertà / ordine, mentre la libertà proclamata e dichiarata dalla Rivoluzione francese è una libertà / programma. Dentro questo dilemma si svolgeranno molte delle vicende del XIX e del XX secolo.

«Sin da principio si era sbagliato il metodo. Gli Inglesi, gli Americani, alcuni cantoni Svizzeri traevano le loro libertà dalla storia, i Francesi vogliono

7 A. Brunialti, *Prefazione. La libertà nello Stato moderno*, in *Biblioteca di scienze politiche*, V, cit., LII.

8 *Ibidem*, VII.

9 *Ibidem*, LXXIV–LXXV.

ricominciarla».[10] L'astrattismo rivoluzionario ha interrotto un processo storico ma i popoli hanno compreso a poco a poco che la libertà non è una «pianta esotica da coltivarsi in serra calda, ma deve crescere nel proprio suolo, secondo le forme a ciascuna più adatte»,[11] libertà che fu assicurata nel concreto dalla forme del governo rappresentativo «svolto in ciascun paese secondo l'esempio inglese e le tradizioni nazionali».[12]

Ecco allora che «legge e libertà sono i due perni dello Stato moderno; la legge senza la libertà è servitù politica e civile; la libertà senza la legge non raccoglie, non concilia, non indirizza, ma stempera nell'anarchia le volontà e le distrugge in un eccesso impotente».[13] Bisogna trovare un punto di equilibrio. Lo stato non è un potere sovraumano; la vita sociale non può essere abbandonata al capriccio degli individui. La riserva di legge è il grande meccanismo del garantismo ma è anche l'"opera aperta" dentro la quale si annidano strumenti di limitazione e di esclusione.

Brunialti – come più in generale la sua generazione di costituzionalisti – diffida della libertà "alla francese" scaturita dalla Rivoluzione e del volontarismo politico che spezza legami e vincoli. Rivolge lo sguardo verso la dimensione storica della nazione. Ma nello stesso tempo mette in guardia dalla statolatria, dal pericolo dello Stato tutore, educatore, lavoratore. Porre la libertà nelle mani dell'amministrazione (tanto più per ragioni di pubblica sicurezza) significa annullare l'individuo che «è l'unico potere sociale, è la stessa civiltà».[14]

Che lo spazio e la garanzia delle libertà siano ridotti nel paradigma ottocentesco della Costituzione italiana, ovvero lo Statuto albertino del 1848, non può sorprenderci. I suoi "arcaismi"[15] sono in linea con la cultura politico-costituzionale del tempo e non serve molto leggere questa vicenda dalla sponda della Costituzione "normativa", "suprema" del lungo XX secolo. Lo Statuto albertino è figlio dei suoi tempi, disorganico sul punto delle libertà, per molti aspetti evanescente. La vera partita si gioca altrove, sul piano applicativo, sulla difficoltà della cultura liberale di farne un effettivo e progrediente strumento di "incivilimento". Costruire lo Stato liberale di diritto è impresa ardua e richiede forti aperture culturali. Il problema delle libertà individuali e del pluralismo politico e sociale è un *problema strutturale, costitutivo* della statualità in Italia e dello stesso rapporto autorità / individuo. I liberali (moderati) stentano a ricondurre il con-

10 *Ibidem*, XCIII.

11 *Ibidem*, CIII.

12 *Ibidem*, CIV.

13 *Ibidem*, XXV.

14 *Ibidem*, CXXV.

15 Sul punto cfr. L. Lacchè, *Le carte ottriate. La teoria dell'octroi e le esperienze costituzionali nell'Europa post-rivoluzionaria*, in *Giornale di storia costituzionale*, XVIII-2, 2009, 229–254.

flitto ad una dimensione dinamica e "positiva"; ne vedono prevalentemente il profilo (proprio del privatismo) del disordine e dell'insicurezza. Lo Stato liberale di diritto, fondato sul principio di legalità, sui meccanismi rappresentativi dell'*Öffentlichkeit*, non può non legittimare il pluralismo delle opinioni ma, alla prova dei fatti, ha difficoltà a "governare" il dissenso che eccede la dimensione dello Stato monoclasse.

Fin da subito il ceto politico dei liberali si trova a dover affrontare il "paradosso della libertà". Lo Stato nazionale è di "diritto" se dà segni di discontinuità rispetto al passato ma la libertà, cardine costituzionale, può essere usata contro "le libertà costituzionali" (e il governo). Che fare allora? E come operare per non cadere in questa trappola? La vicenda sofferta dello Stato liberale in Italia ci pone di fronte il problema dei differenti livelli di legalità che rappresentano un elemento di *imprinting* e un "tratto permanente" del sistema giuridico liberale.[16] Nel 1990, in un volume dedicato alla questione del carcere preventivo nello Stato liberale, parlavo de *La giustizia per i galantuomini*[17] per porre l'attenzione su una aporia originaria del pensiero e della pratica liberale determinata dal campo di tensione ordine / libertà, tra il garantismo retorico della legge e i meccanismi di effettivo funzionamento del sistema penale incentrati soprattutto su due relazioni funzionali: ordinario / straordinario; regola / eccezione. È tra XVIII e XIX secolo che si fa strada un *altro* livello della legalità che tende a separare la prevenzione e la pericolosità sociale dall'ordine giuridico "normale". Questo secondo livello opera spesso "al di là della legge", quella legge che in linea teorica dovrebbe assumere su di sé la totalità della garanzia giuridica. E non di rado questo livello finisce per trovare posto sotto il "tappeto della legalità", come quelle cose sgradite che talvolta vengono celate senza troppi complimenti in un bel salotto borghese.

Il doppio livello di legalità – che mette in crisi l'idea del principio di legalità inteso come un monolite – contribuisce a identificare la tensione che si instaura tra forme e dimensioni diverse della legalità: i codici e le leggi di pubblica

16 Sul concetto del doppio livello di legalità v. M. Sbriccoli, *La penalistica civile. Teorie e ideologie del diritto penale nell'Italia unita*, ora in *Scritti di storia del diritto penale e della giustizia. Scritti editi e inediti (1972–2007)*, Milano 2009, t. I, 524; «Il duplice livello di legalità discerne i "galantuomini" dai "birbanti" destinandoli a differenti *filières* punitive, fa prevalere l'opportunità politica sulla regola giuridica, lo scopo sul diritto. Permette il conseguimento di obiettivi politicamente desiderabili attraverso la compressione di diritti, prerogative e garanzie, tenendo in ombra coloro che di tale compressione portano le responsabilità giuridiche e politiche» (*Caratteri originari e tratti permanenti del sistema penale italiano (1860–1990)*, ivi, 596–597, anche 647, 654–655).

17 L. Lacchè, *La giustizia per i galantuomini. Ordine e libertà nell'Italia liberale: il dibattito sul carcere preventivo (1865–1913)*, Milano 1990.

sicurezza, i codici e le leggi di eccezione, la legge generale e universale e le concrete specifiche applicazioni. Quel concetto descrive i meccanismi che fanno prevalere talvolta l'opportunità politica sulla regola giuridica e sui "principi", comprimendo diritti e garanzie. Questo è, a ben vedere, un nodo interno al "problema penale liberale" che forse ci aiuta a capire meglio anche le traiettorie e le vicende personali di singoli giuristi. Non è tanto la coesistenza, in singoli autori, di pagine "liberali" e pagine "autoritarie", quanto piuttosto il reale dimensionamento dello statuto costituzionale della libertà e dello Stato che attraversa la cultura liberale. Probabilmente non è solo una questione di «affiancamento» (per dirla con Mario Sbriccoli), ma più in profondità abbiamo a che fare con la struttura mentale e operativa dell'ordine liberale. Da strumento *interno* e integrato l'eccezione diventa elemento *esterno*, «spazio di sospensione dell'ordine giuridico».[18]

Per esempio, lo studio delle "zone grigie" nei sistemi penali costruiti lungo il XIX secolo attorno al principio di legalità,[19] ci rivela un paesaggio più complesso e problematico destinato a conservare un significato preciso anche nello sviluppo del penale e della giustizia nelle società democratiche. Tale paesaggio ci permette di cogliere meglio quella sorta di *actio finium regundorum*, evocata dai giuristi, per distinguere lo spazio non controverso del principio di legalità dalla zona ibrida della difesa sociale, del penale amministrativo, delle misure di sicurezza, attraverso forme di attenuazione, deroga, eccezione. Lo Stato liberale, per contrastare antagonisti e *disturbers*, opera sulla linea di confine, crea zone grigie, "zone franche" (rispetto ai postulati del garantismo liberale), "sottrazioni" che però continuano ad avere come termine dialettico il principio di legalità. In questo modo è possibile conservare un legame tra il diritto penale e le libertà pubbliche, legame certo controverso, ma posto all'interno di un ordine giuridico inclusivo.

La parola *libertà*, dunque, non può essere indagata solo attraverso il lessico delle dichiarazioni e delle costituzioni. Ha ragione Francesco Carrara – campione del liberalismo "giuridico" – quando dice che il «giure penale» è il contesto privilegiato nel quale le "grandi parole" vengono scarnificate e sono costrette a vivere nella realtà. Nel *penale* il principio di legalità è posto di fronte alla prospettiva *politica* del liberalismo costituzionale e del garantismo.

18 M. Meccarelli, *Paradigmi dell'eccezione nella parabola della modernità penale. Una prospettiva storico-giuridica*, in *Quaderni storici*, XLIV, 2, 2009, 501.

19 Su questo profilo ha recentemente riflettuto M. Pifferi, *Difendere i confini, superare le frontiere. Le "zone grigie" della legalità penale tra Otto e Novecento*, in *Quaderni fiorentini per la storia del pensiero giuridico moderno*, 36, 2007, 743–798. Cfr. inoltre L. Lacchè, M. Stronati (ed. by), *Beyond the statute law: the "grey" government of criminal justice systems. History and Theory in the modern age*, Macerata 2011.

In Italia, osserva amaramente Carrara nei primi anni Settanta, ci si riempie la bocca della parola libertà evidentemente senza sapere di che cosa si parla, se ogni volta si invoca la legge penale come *farmaco* universale: la prigione è la farmacia, i birri sono i farmacisti. Chi si oppone a questo metodo viene apostrofato come *dottrinario*. Carrara accetta di buon grado tale nome[20] (perché il liberalismo non può che essere una *dottrina*, la «santa *dottrina giuridica*»), purché gli avversari smettano ipocritamente di chiamarsi liberali. Infatti, i falsi liberali, i *liberali religiosi* e i *liberali politici*, sarebbero pronti a secondare qualunque tirannide eretta nel nome della libertà. Per Carrara invece «il vero liberalismo è il liberalismo *giuridico*. I seguaci di questa dottrina (sia pure *dottrina*) sono sempre fedeli alla *sovranità del diritto*, unica sovranità costituita da Dio sulla terra. Ognuno sia libero e sicuro nello esercizio della propria attività finché i suoi atti non *ledono i diritti altrui*. Nessuna coazione violenta, nessuna repressione è *legittima* se non è in modo assoluto necessaria per proteggere un diritto aggredito e violato [...]. Ecco il liberalismo *giuridico*: ecco la sua bandiera ed il suo catechismo; ecco la fede di colui che solo ha diritto di chiamarsi *liberale*, e che solo può vantarsi di combattere sotto la *santa bandiera* della libertà. Per lui la libertà è giustizia. E questa egli non tollera che si conculchi né per fanatismo superstizioso, né per autorità di Governo, qualunque sia, perché Dio ci volle soggetti alla legge perché fossimo liberi. *Legibus subiecti ut liberi esse possimus*».[21]

«Si è detto agli Italiani – commenta Carrara con la sua vena sarcastica – che erano maturi per avviarsi progressivamente al governo di sé stessi, e che perciò si liberavano dal governamentalismo dei vecchi Signori. Ma se ad un governamentalismo, che era preventivo e che assumeva il nome di paterno, si va sostituendo il governamentalismo del giudizio criminale, non so vedere il guadagno del mutato sistema. Dove prima si incappava in un monito del presidente del buon Governo, oggi spessissimo si incappa in qualche mese di prigionia. E' questo un buono avviamento ad assuefare il popolo a governarsi da sé!».[22] In *Libertà e Giustizia*, scritto del 1869, Carrara sottolineava come la monarchia nazionale avesse concesso le libertà politiche «con mano larghissima».[23] Ma queste non erano che un mezzo per raggiungere ampie libertà civili.

20 F. Carrara, *Le tre concubine* (Discorso letto nel R. Istituto Lombardo di Scienze e Lettere alla tornata del 6 novembre 1873), in *Opuscoli di diritto criminale*, vol. IV, Lucca 1874, 495.

21 *Ibidem*, 497.

22 F. Carrara, *Il delitto e il matrimonio ecclesiastico*, in *Opuscoli di diritto criminale*, vol. V, Lucca 1874, vol. V, 130.

23 F. Carrara, *Libertà e giustizia* (parole dette nell'atrio della R. Università di Pisa il 29 maggio 1869 per la commemorazione funebre degli studenti morti a Curtatone e Montanara), in *Opuscoli di diritto criminale*, vol. III, seconda ed. corretta, ampliata e riordinata, 1870, 637.

E, a differenza delle prime, queste ultime non si possono "dare", si devono "fare". Le disillusioni non tardarono quindi ad arrivare. Carrara, nato lucchese, più tardi suddito toscano, infine italiano, chiamerà ironicamente «progressi della libertà civile» tutti quei fatti che ostacolano nel nuovo Regno il godimento delle libertà. «Parve allora che una pioggia d'oro di libertà non mai godute né sognate dovessero rovesciarsi sovra di noi come un torrente di inesauste benedizioni. In qual guisa queste libertà sieno venute altri lo cerchi: io mi tengo stretto allo argomento mio».[24]

3. La «libertà riflessa»

Si potrebbe dire, per semplificare, che il secolo XIX "nasce" dalle parti dell'individualismo proprietario e "muore" dalle parti dello statualismo liberale. Il corposo volume assemblato da Attilio Brunialti sul finire del secolo ci ha mostrato l'intera gamma di una cultura della libertà che, nel secolo sorto all'insegna dell'individualismo, giunge però a doversi misurare sempre più, in maniera controversa, con la dimensione, definitivamente affermata, dello Stato moderno "nazional-costituzionale".

Anche in questo caso prendiamo a "pretesto" un'opera / soglia, i *Diritti di libertà*, pubblicata nel 1926 da Francesco Ruffini a Torino per i tipi di Piero Gobetti. Storico del diritto, tra i fondatori del rinnovato metodo scientifico del diritto ecclesiastico in Italia, il senatore Ruffini, autentico maestro per un'intera generazione di giovani che hanno lasciato una forte impronta nella storia italiana del Novecento, figurerà non a caso tra gli sparutissimi docenti universitari (assieme al figlio Edoardo) che nel 1931 preferirono lasciare l'insegnamento pur di non sottostare al giuramento di fedeltà al regime fascista.

Nella sua Prefazione il professore torinese dice di temere per il popolo italiano il crollo della Costituzione statutaria che, negli ultimi tre quarti di secolo, aveva garantito le libertà costituzionali. L'oggetto del suo studio sono appunto quelli che la scienza definiva felicemente *diritti di libertà*. «Intanto, qui non sarà questione della Libertà, al singolare e con la elle maiuscola. Sibbene di alcune speciali e ben distinte libertà, e cioè di quelle storiche libertà, che l'epica lotta intorno ad esse combattuta per secoli, e la consacrazione ad esse data da alcuni dei documenti più solenni, che la vita dei popoli ricordi, hanno nettamente individuate, conferendo loro fisionomia e denominazione propria. Sono esse le *public liberties* come le chiamano gli Inglesi, oppure i *droits de*

24 F. Carrara, *Progressi della libertà civile* (1873), in *Opuscoli di diritto criminale*, cit., vol. V, 436 e ss.

l'homme et du citoyen, come le dicono i Francesi, oppure i *Grundrechte* e cioè i diritti fondamentali, come le designano i Tedeschi».[25]

Eppure, per un singolare paradosso, gli Italiani stanno perdendo le loro libertà mentre nuovi popoli ne assaporano il gusto. Citando le *Democrazie moderne* di James Bryce, Ruffini ricorda come «... il numero delle democrazie è raddoppiato nel mondo nello spazio di quindici anni. E quello, che delle democrazie egli diceva, vale per più forte ragione ancora del sistema dei Diritti di libertà, i quali ne sono il presupposto».[26] Il fenomeno parla di una espansione geopolitica e di uno sviluppo qualitativo dei diritti, come lascia intravedere la recente costituzione di Weimar, con una parte dedicata ai diritti sociali-economici, vero e proprio programma per il futuro svolgimento legislativo.

In Italia – invece – le "guarentigie" vengono distrutte, cominciando dalla libertà di stampa. E «Stroncata, adunque, da noi in Italia la libertà della stampa, tutte le altre libertà costituzionali furon al tempo stesso automaticamente fiaccate».[27] Un processo che fa uscire l'Italia dal novero degli Stati liberali, andando a braccetto («oh! elegante conciliazione hegeliana dei contrarii, direbbe il filosofo ...»)[28] con la Repubblica russa dei Soviet.

Ruffini assume uno dei più celebri discorsi programmatici di Alfredo Rocco, pronunciato a Perugia il 25 agosto del 1925 nell'Aula dei notari, come paradigma della più generale dottrina politico-giuridica del fascismo.[29] Tale discorso si basa su tre capisaldi: a) la tradizione politica italiana considerata del tutto avversa alle dottrine liberali delle altre nazioni europee; b) la concezione organica dello Stato contrapposta a quella individualistica; c) le pubbliche libertà intese come concessioni graziose dello Stato, anzi semplici *riflessi* del sovrano diritto dello Stato.

La critica di Ruffini investe soprattutto la dimensione culturale e scientifica di quella che potremmo chiamare la *libertà riflessa*. Il vizio dell'impostazione fascista risiede nella completa ricezione della teoria giuridica dello Stato mutuata da quella scienza tedesca che considera i diritti dei cittadini emanazioni, creazioni, concessioni dello Stato, *Reflexrechte*. «Gli stessi diritti dell'individuo, – osserva Rocco – quando vengono riconosciuti, non sono che *riflesso* dei diritti dello Stato».[30] Ruffini allora ricostruisce la genesi della cultura "illiberale" tedesca del diritto pubblico facendola iniziare dal Gerber dei *Diritti Pubblici*

25 Cito da F. Ruffini, *Diritti di libertà*, seconda edizione con introduzione e note di Piero Calamandrei, Firenze 1946, LX e ss.

26 *Ibidem*, 48.

27 *Ibidem*, 63.

28 *Ibidem*, 89.

29 A. Rocco, *La Dottrina del Fascismo e il suo posto nella storia del Pensiero politico*, Milano 1925, («Biblioteca dell'Istituto fascista di cultura»).

30 F. Ruffini, *Diritti di libertà*, cit., 103.

(1852), opera *epochemachend* per lo sviluppo della scienza, ma "sciagurata" per ciò che avvia nell'età bismarckiana. Le grandi parole *Libertà, Civiltà, Umanità* sono irrise come «sonore parolone inglesi e in genere dei paesi occidentali».[31] Se Gerber è l'incomparabile iniziatore, Jellinek ne è il perfezionatore, quaranta anni dopo, con i suoi *Diritti pubblici subiettivi* (1892).

Ripercorrendo l'evoluzione della teoria dell'autolimitazione dello Stato nell'esercizio del suo diritto sovrano, Ruffini stigmatizza il progressivo affievolimento di quei diritti di libertà che si erano storicamente e positivamente affermati. L'*Etat soleil* è posto «al centro di un sistema di infiniti, minuscoli pianeti: gli Individui. Il diritto sovrano dello Stato è la luce propria di quell'astro [...] Fuori di metafora: le possibilità, facoltà, libertà, di cui gli individui possono godere, non sono se non *Diritti riflessi* del *Diritto sovrano* dello Stato».[32] Con il tornante rappresentato dalla costituzione di Weimar, però, è alle viste un paradosso, ovvero che mentre gli stessi Tedeschi si stanno liberando di certi «vecchi e screditati articoli politico-giuridici di scarto», i teorici del nuovo regime fascista, «i nostri novelli pubblicisti», ne diventano i più acritici seguaci facendo come quei «musicanti di provincia [che] rilevano in blocco, senza guardare tanto per il sottile, strumenti, divise e pennacchi smessi da quelli della metropoli».[33]

Al di là della ricostruzione polemica di Ruffini – non certo immune da semplificazioni – ciò che interessa è vedere come il liberale torinese, a metà degli anni Venti, ricorra ai grandi giuspubblicisti italiani per fondare, in contrapposizione ai tedeschi, una teoria giuridica e "liberale" dei diritti di libertà. Se Ruffini affronta a colpi d'ascia le teoriche "germaniche", adotta invece un registro interpretativo più sfumato quando legge la teoria dell'autolimitazione in ambito italiano e non solo dal punto di vista della compressione dei diritti di libertà all'interno della torsione statualistica che accompagna la fondazione e l'evoluzione dello Stato liberale (europeo-continentale) di diritto. Ruffini valorizza la riflessione di Vittorio Emanuele Orlando più legata alla concezione savignyana del diritto come «intimo lavorìo della coscienza sociale, uno spontaneo fenomeno psico-collettivo». Il diritto sta dunque prima dello Stato. «Dunque: preesistenza del Diritto, non solo, ma anche indipendenza e superiorità. Lo *Stato*, come ebbe a dire poi con efficacia il nostro Romano, non sarebbe che una specie del genere *Diritto*».[34] Ruffini evoca l'insegnamento di «un grandissimo maestro», il von Gierke de *I Concetti fondamentali del Diritto dello Stato* (1915) e cita Hans Kelsen, «il più rinomato dei giovani pubblicisti austriaci», per il quale lo Stato non può pensarsi che *sub specie iuris*.

31 *Ibidem*, 112.
32 *Ibidem*, 120.
33 *Ibidem*, 122 e ss.
34 *Ibidem*, 130.

È parimenti interessante il fatto che Ruffini metta in primo piano la teorica di Santi Romano – di cui ricorda il recentissimo impegno come «uno dei diciotto *Soloni*» chiamati a delineare la riforma "fascista" delle istituzioni – una «fra le più limpide e geniali certamente della nostra letteratura pubblicistica».[35] Il "Solone" Romano aveva mostrato mirabilmente, pochi anni prima, come l'ordinamento non fosse racchiuso tutto nel *diritto obbiettivo* posto dallo Stato, valorizzando invece l'idea di un diritto-posizione, un diritto-organizzazione dell'ente sociale Stato. Proprio attraverso questa teoria diventava possibile concepire i diritti di libertà come veri diritti subiettivi pubblici, senza far ricorso ad elementi pregiuridici, metagiuridici o sopragiuridici. Lo Stato quindi nasce già limitato dall'ordinamento giuridico. Il legislatore non è il creatore del diritto nel senso pieno e assoluto della parola e per questo non può annullarlo completamente, come «con grande vigoria, un altro maestro di queste discipline, il Ranelletti, aveva già scritto, che lo Stato "non può sopprimere il diritto e l'ordine giuridico, senza negare e distruggere se stesso"».[36] «Quella dello Stato, vorremmo poter dire, è, per rispetto ai Diritti di libertà dei cittadini, non una limitazione volontaria e da esso acquisita, sì bene una limitazione necessaria e congenita».[37]

Ruffini cerca di allontanare la *libertà riflessa* – prossima all'annullamento da parte del regime – dalla tradizione della giuspubblicistica post-orlandiana. Questo tema meriterebbe ben altro approfondimento ma è interessante notare come il professore dell'Università di Torino cerchi di puntellare il concetto dei diritti di libertà ricorrendo a quella tradizione con una lettura di taglio liberal-individualistico. Le accuse che Rocco muove proprio alla teoria individualistica – voler asservire lo Stato «ai fini individuali di una sola generazione» – vengono respinte da Ruffini attraverso il richiamo, fortemente consapevole della grande minaccia in corso, all'idea di «un vero Stato di diritto» che abbia origine dall'intangibilità e dall'imprescrittibilità dei diritti di libertà.[38]

Il giurista piemontese tiene conto della complessità della teoria dell'autolimitazione in un autore come Orlando. Tuttavia mentre per Ruffini rimane centrale la dimensione propriamente individualistica del liberalismo, per Orlando la limitazione dello Stato non può dipendere da soggettività "atomistiche" poiché è il popolo – storicamente operante in senso savignyano – a coincidere con lo Stato visto come sede di realizzazione e di perfezionamento giuridico-istituzionale. La libertà è strettamente legata allo Stato, anche se compito di questo è registrare e di rivestire di autorità formale e durevole la regola di diritto che si è affermata nella coscienza popolare. In questo senso lo

35 *Ibidem*, 131.
36 *Ibidem*, 135.
37 *Ibidem*, 136.
38 *Ibidem*.

Stato / diritto non può dipendere dal giusnaturalismo individualistico e contrattualistico. L'ordine giuridico ha dunque autonomia rispetto all'ordine politico ma il tema della garanzia delle libertà transita anzitutto attraverso la figura complessa e ambigua dello Stato liberale di diritto. Sono la razionalità oggettiva del diritto e il protagonismo della nuova giuspubblicistica a fungere da limite allo Stato legislatore più che l'espressa dichiarazione dei diritti di libertà.

Ruffini vuole smentire la tesi di partenza di Rocco, ovvero che la tradizione italiana sia avversa al liberalismo europeo di stampo "individualistico". Intende trovare conferma di ciò richiamando il pensiero dei giuspubblicisti italiani (Orlando, Romano e Ranelletti) nella loro feconda elaborazione scientifica a cavaliere tra i due secoli, operando una lettura manichea: da una parte la *Staatsrechtslehre* germanica, dall'altra la dottrina dell'autolimitazione *all'italiana*.

Probabilmente per leggere in maniera più ampia quella che viene chiamata la "torsione autoritaria" dello statualismo liberale bisogna tenere conto anzitutto, specie sul piano del diritto "vivente" delle libertà, l'assoggettamento dell'individuo allo Stato / amministrazione. La dimensione del conflitto sociale che attraversa l'Italia tra Otto e Novecento e il problema del disciplinamento delle dinamiche pluralistiche enfatizza quel "paradosso della libertà" di cui abbiamo parlato poc'anzi come *formante* e non come *accidente* della cultura liberale. La tutela dell'ordine, l'amministrativizzazione delle libertà, le zone grigie che ne derivano (tanto più con il ricorso a strumenti come lo stato d'assedio e a provvedimenti di emergenza) aprono varchi importanti e l'argine dell'autolimitazione non è sempre in grado di tenere il sistema in equilibrio e di garantire le libertà come autentico dominio dell'individuo.

Il riferimento a Santi Romano, ormai impegnato nella Commissione dei Soloni, vuole probabilmente segnalare il cambiamento in atto: partiti da *La teoria dei diritti pubblici subbiettivi* (1891) si giunge alla "svolta" del 1925 che mette al centro un'idea di libertà limitata più dall'amministrazione che dalla legge (e quindi dal "diritto"). In buona sostanza è la soggettività organica e politico-amministrativa dello Stato che Alfredo Rocco *fascistizza* nel discorso del 1925 ad essere assunta come paradigma. In questo modo era possibile lavorare sul registro della continuità: la rivoluzione fascista poteva apparire una riattualizzazione del "ritorno allo Statuto" per sconfiggere la crisi dell'ordine politico parlamentare o, più semplicemente, come il necessario rafforzamento del potere esecutivo e amministrativo (lo "Stato forte") al servizio dell'organismo nazionale per contrastare ogni forma di "particolarismo".

4. La «libertà degna»

I libri possono avere più di una vita. Questo è il caso dei *Diritti di libertà* di Francesco Ruffini. Nella sua prima vita il libro alimentò la cultura liberale dell'antifascismo negli anni duri del regime. Nella sua seconda esistenza, dopo la liberazione, divenne uno dei fondamenti ideali per riannodare il filo spezzato. Il testo di Ruffini è ben presente nelle discussioni, nei temi selezionati e nelle formulazioni tecniche che emergono dai lavori della cd. Commissione Forti, ovvero la «Commissione per studi attinenti alla riorganizzazione dello stato» che operò tra il 1945 e la prima metà del 1946, nelle sue molteplici articolazioni, nell'ambito delle attività del Ministero per la Costituente finalizzate, appunto, a predisporre gli elementi per la preparazione della nuova Costituzione.

La Commissione consegnò nel 1946 all'Assemblea Costituente i tre volumi che raccolgono i principali risultati delle sottocommissioni.[39] Tuttavia, è soprattutto dai lavori preparatori che possiamo trarre utili indicazioni, anche grazie alla trascrizione sintetica degli accesi dibattiti. Si pensi alle considerazioni generali sulla dichiarazione dei diritti e la relazione sui diritti subiettivi politici di Costantino Mortati. O – più ancora in questo caso – alle riflessioni del giovane storico del diritto Guido Astuti, esponente di spicco del partito liberale e futuro giudice costituzionale. Astuti si era formato a Torino alla scuola di Federico Patetta, ma aveva avuto tra i suoi maestri Francesco Ruffini. Non stupisce che Astuti, membro della Prima Sottocommissione «Problemi costituzionali», assieme a Calamandrei, Crisafulli, M.S. Giannini, Jemolo, Mortati, Zanobini e ad importanti figure di magistrato e avvocato (poi anche protagonisti della Costituente), incaricato di "relazionare" sui diritti di libertà, seguisse l'impostazione di Ruffini sottolineando l'involuzione della dottrina pubblicistica tedesca «dimentica della Dichiarazione di Francoforte, e asservita agli scopi della politica prussiana, sotto specie di formali esigenze scientifiche e sistematiche, dal Gerber al Laband, con le impeccabili teorie della sovranità e della autolimitazione dello Stato ridusse i diritti di libertà, esclusi dal sistema dei diritti pubblici subiettivi, alla categoria di diritti riflessi, o di effetti riflessi del diritto sovrano dello Stato».[40] Se una parte non trascurabile della scienza ufficiale italiana aveva recepito incautamente tali teorie per offrirle alla dottrina mussoliniana dello

39 Si tratta dei volumi della Commissione per studi attinenti alla riorganizzazione dello Stato, *Relazione all'Assemblea Costituente*. I. *Problemi costituzionali Organizzazione dello Stato*. II. *Autonomie locali*. III. *Enti pubblici non territoriali Organizzazione sanitaria*, Roma, Stabilimento Tipografico Fausto Failli, 1946, con prefazione di Ugo Forti e introduzione di Rodolfo Ambrosino.

40 G. Astuti, *I diritti di libertà*, *Considerazioni generali*, in *Alle origini della Costituzione italiana. I lavori preparatori della "Commissione per studi attinenti alla riorganizzazione dello stato" (1945–1946)*, a cura di G. D'Alessio, Bologna 1979, 256.

Stato, ci fu chi, tra i pochi studiosi, riaffermò «il valore assoluto e il preciso fondamento dei diritti di libertà, come veri diritti pubblici subiettivi, nell'ambito delle moderne dottrine dello stato di diritto e dell'ordinamento giuridico».[41] Per tutti, appunto, ricordava Francesco Ruffini «che ancora nel 1926 reagì con coraggioso saggio all'astrattismo dogmatico delle teorie di moda, e rivendicò apertamente i diritti di libertà non sulla base di elementi pregiuridici o metagiuridici, bensì individuandone la intrinseca giuridicità in quanto premessa o condizione essenziale ed originaria dell'ordinamento statale, nel momento stesso del suo porsi in funzione di essi, come ordinamento di diritto».[42]

Fu l'azionista Piero Calamandrei, l'inquieto giurista alla ricerca della nuova legalità "costituzionale", a far ripubblicare nel 1946, presso l'editore fiorentino La Nuova Italia (collana «Orientamenti»), l'opera del giurista e storico piemontese. Quando il suo libro apparve, la battaglia per la libertà sembrava perduta ma quella difesa appassionata era un atto di fede e di coraggio. Nel 1925 Ruffini poteva registrare un presente minaccioso e già chiaro ma il peggio doveva arrivare. Gli fu però risparmiato di vedere quella "morte del diritto" che attraverso il nazismo portò alla totale abolizione «della nozione di diritto soggettivo [...] cioè, in sostanza, della stessa rilevanza giuridica della persona: *Kampf wider das subiektive Recht*, che poi voleva dire, nel campo morale, guerra contro la personalità umana».[43] C'erano voluti venti anni per far capire agli Italiani – nota amaramente Calamandrei nel 1946 – che Ruffini aveva ragione.

Ecco perché «Francesco Ruffini è accanto a noi, vivo come allora; anche oggi possiamo trarre dalla sua parola precorritrice un lume per orientarci in quest'alba ancor così ingombra di foschia».[44] Ora si può parlare di *avvenire dei diritti di libertà*. La prospettiva è cambiata. Non più il dilemma tra il giusnaturalismo dei diritti individuali che a tutto preesistono e la loro riduzione a effetto riflesso e successivo della preesistente sovranità dello Stato secondo la logica più ferrea del positivismo giuridico. «Nel momento storico che attraversiamo libertà individuali e stato non si presentano più, come quando il Ruffini scriveva, in posizione di forze antagoniste [...]. Libertà individuale e sovranità popolare si affermano insieme come espressioni di una stessa concezione politica, e insieme troveranno la loro sistemazione giuridica nella costituzione, come due aspetti complementari ed inscindibili della democrazia tradotta in ordinamento positivo».[45] Non più *diffidenza* tra lo Stato sovrano democratico e i diritti di libertà.

41 *Ibidem*, pp. 256 e ss.

42 *Ibidem*, 257.

43 P. Calamandrei, *L'avvenire dei diritti di libertà*, introduzione alla seconda edizione dei *Diritti di libertà* di F. Ruffini, cit., X.

44 *Ibidem*, XI.

45 *Ibidem*, XII e s.

Non ha più molto senso la distinzione tra libertà civili e politiche (i diritti dell'uomo e i diritti del cittadino); Calamandrei preferisce «considerare qui tutti i diritti, che mirano a proteggere l'indipendenza del singolo entro la propria sfera, nella loro funzione *altruistica*, e annoverarli tutti tra le libertà politiche. I diritti di libertà non devono infatti concepirsi, in regime democratico, come il recinto di filo spinato entro cui il singolo cerca scampo contro gli assalti della comunità ostile, ma piuttosto come la porta che gli consente di uscire dal suo piccolo giardino sulla strada, e di portare di lì il suo contributo al lavoro comune: libertà, non garanzia di isolamento egoistico, ma garanzia di espansione sociale. Dove questi diritti sono soppressi, lì veramente, quasi per tentar di nascondersi all'invadente oppressione dell'autorità, l'individuo si rinchiude in sé stesso e perde il senso della solidarietà collettiva».[46]

La distinzione tra libertà degli antichi e libertà dei moderni (spesso letta erroneamente attraverso la dicotomia libertà negativa / libertà positiva) esce ridimensionata se vista dalla prospettiva (annunciata) dell'*homo democraticus* nell'era del costituzionalismo postbellico. È la "nuova" socialità il dato emergente che Calamandrei richiama valorizzando il *Socialismo liberale* di Carlo Rosselli. Il 1789 ha annunciato i diritti di libertà ma nel prosieguo quel potenziale dinamico ha perso slancio. Le libertà sono diventate *statiche*, *chiuse*. Lo spirito del liberalismo e il carattere propulsivo dei diritti si sono impoveriti lungo il XIX secolo per "governare" e contrastare l'avanzata politica dei ceti sociali "subalterni".

Il primo dopoguerra ha lasciato intuire che la giustizia sociale e la libertà individuale possono coesistere e cooperare. L'art. 151 della costituzione di Weimar ne ha dato un primo riconoscimento affermando che «la vita economica deve essere organizzata conformemente ai principi della giustizia, e allo scopo di garantire a tutti un'esistenza degna dell'uomo». La libertà dal bisogno è al centro sia delle sei libertà sociali del liberale Beveridge; sia delle quattro libertà di Roosevelt (*freedom of speach, of religion*; *freedom from want, freedom from pear*). «La libertà dal bisogno, *freedom from want*, è considerata anch'essa come condizione indispensabile per salvaguardare la dignità morale della persona e per permettere la sua partecipazione attiva alla vita politica della comunità democratica».[47] Calamandrei è consapevole del fatto che il nuovo *punto di Archimede* dell'ordine costituzionale che si sta delineando nel dopoguerra risiede nella leva della democrazia sociale, ovvero di un sistema nel quale i diritti politici e i diritti sociali sono messi sullo stesso piano. Ma mentre i diritti politici sono "perfetti", quelli che attengono alla sfera economico-sociale richiedono azioni positive e mezzi adeguati. Ma il *punto* pone un ulteriore, fondamentale, problema: per

46 *Ibidem*, XV e s.
47 *Ibidem*, XXXV e s.

garantire i diritti sociali non si possono sacrificare la libertà individuale e quella politica. Calamandrei assume la costituzione sovietica del 1936 come paradigma. «Qui l'equilibrio tra i diritti politici e i diritti sociali, che è l'ideale di quel reggimento democratico in cui la giustizia sociale è posta come condizione di libertà, è rotto a favore dei diritti sociali, al contrario di quello che avveniva negli ordinamenti cosiddetti "borghesi", in cui i diritti sociali erano sacrificati a quelli politici».[48]

La riflessione pre-costituente di Calamandrei, in margine ai *Diritti di libertà* di Ruffini, coglie uno dei tratti decisivi del costituzionalismo del secondo dopoguerra. «L'innovazione più significativa è affidata al principio di dignità» che permea la Costituzione italiana, la Dichiarazione universale dei diritti dell'uomo, la Legge fondamentale tedesca. «Una svolta è così compiuta, la dignità si presenta come un ineludibile denominatore comune, disegna, insieme, un nuovo statuto della persona e un nuovo quadro dei doveri costituzionali».[49] L'antropologia dell'*homo dignus* – evocata efficacemente da Stefano Rodotà – dà sostanza alla figura della persona umana, libera ed eguale nella dignità. È la «sovrana dignità di tutti i cittadini»[50] nel regime democratico di cui parla Carlo Esposito e che, si afferma, anzitutto, attraverso il lavoro. In uno dei primi interventi nell'aula dell'Assemblea Costituente (11 marzo 1947) Palmiro Togliatti criticò i giuristi che negli ultimi decenni avevano accolto dottrine dannose che attribuivano la sovranità allo Stato e non al popolo dando «quindi ai diritti individuali soltanto un carattere riflesso». Insomma, la *Staatslehre* avrebbe reso inadeguata la scienza giuridica nel momento di scrivere la costituzione democratica. Togliatti enfatizza questo problema, ma sono i giuristi "nuovi" ad offrire, non senza contraddizioni, il vocabolario concettuale e gli strumenti operativi per consentire alla Costituzione di essere il fattore decisivo per costruire il nuovo *ordine*.

Di recente l'editore Sellerio ha ripubblicato il *Processo all'articolo 4*[51] di Danilo Dolci. Il 2 febbraio 1956 il «noto agitatore politico» – come riportava un verbale di polizia – era stato arrestato per aver guidato, a Partinico, un gruppo di braccianti che chiedevano di poter lavorare terre abbandonate, compiendo una sorta di "sciopero alla rovescia". Manifestazione non autorizzata, resistenza a pubblico ufficiale, grida sediziose: è difficile immaginare Danilo Dolci nelle vesti aggressive di un sovvertitore dell'ordine sociale. Questo apostolo della pace e

48 *Ibidem*, XLVIII.

49 S. Rodotà, *Antropologia dell'*homo dignus, *Lectio doctoralis*, in Conferimento della Laurea honoris causa in Scienze della politica a S. Rodotà, Macerata 6 ottobre 2010, 61.

50 C. Esposito, *Commento all'art.1 della Costituzione*, in La *Costituzione italiana. Saggi*, Padova 1954, 9.

51 D. Dolci, *Processo all'articolo 4*, postfazione di P. Beneduce, Palermo 2011.

della fraternità – rimasto sconvolto pochi anni prima dalla morte per fame di un bambino – voleva certamente provocare, come farà molte altre volte, le coscienze di un'Italia che stentava a fare della sua nuova Costituzione il vangelo laico per avviare un vero cambiamento della società, superando le ingiustizie ataviche di un ordine, per molti versi, pre-politico.

Il vero obiettivo dell'azione di Dolci era difendere la Costituzione, chiederne il rispetto. Il processo all'art. 4 – ovvero quella previsione costituzionale che impegna la Repubblica a riconoscere a tutti i cittadini il diritto al lavoro promuovendo le condizioni per renderlo effettivo – è il processo contro Danilo Dolci e altri. Processo che diviene – come succederà altre volte – "di rottura" allo scopo di denunciare la distanza tra il dettato costituzionale e la realtà drammatica del mondo bracciantile in Sicilia. Portati in aula come "delinquenti" comuni, gli imputati ricevono il sostegno di testimoni e avvocati d'eccezione. Da Lucio Lombardo-Radice ad Alberto Carocci, da Norberto Bobbio a Elio Vittorini a Carlo Levi, da Achille Battaglia a Piero Calamandrei, il processo ci svela vividamente il clima di un'epoca. Proprio l'arringa di Piero Calamandrei, l'ultimo ad intervenire per "difendere" gli imputati, illustra bene gli anni nei quali i Danilo Dolci venivano messi in carcere come pericolosi sovversivi. Un'Italia, come osserva il grande giurista toscano, che vive un'età di trapasso nella quale «la funzione dei giudici, meglio che quella di difendere una legalità decrepita, è quella di creare gradualmente la nuova legalità promessa dalla Costituzione».[52] Le grandi speranze suscitate dal documento basilare della nuova Italia sono penetrate nei cuori.

Nella sua arringa Calamandrei ci parla delle *parole* della Costituzione e del tema tanto caro al costituente fiorentino. «La nostra Costituzione è piena di queste grandi parole preannunciatrici del futuro: "pari dignità sociale"; "rimuovere gli ostacoli che impediscono il pieno sviluppo della persona umana"; "Repubblica fondata sul lavoro"; "diritto al lavoro"; "condizioni che rendano effettivo questo diritto"; assicurata ad ogni lavoratore e alla sua famiglia "una esistenza libera e dignitosa" [...]. Grandi promesse che penetrano nei cuori e li allargano, e che una volta intese non si possono più ritirare. Come potete voi

52 *Ibidem*, 308. L'importanza dell'arringa di Calamandrei è stata còlta da P. Grossi, *Lungo l'itinerario di Piero Calamandrei*, in *Rivista trimestrale di diritto e procedura civile*, LXIII, 3, 2009, 883–884. Nello stesso anno, il 23 aprile, Piero Calamandrei partecipò alla prima udienza della Corte costituzionale come capofila di un gruppo di professori e di avvocati per difendere, in altro modo, la Costituzione. Del gruppo facevano parte Giuliano Vassalli, Achille Battaglia, Federico Comandini, Costantino Mortati, Vezio Crisafulli, Massimo Severo Giannini, Francesco Mazzei. Ce lo ricorda G. Vassalli, *Testimonianza*, in *Giornale di storia costituzionale*, n. 11/I, 2006, 56–58.

pensare che i derelitti che hanno udito queste promesse, e che vi hanno creduto e che ci si sono attaccati come naufraghi alla tavola di salvezza, possano ora essere condannati come delinquenti solo perché chiedono, civilmente e senza far male a nessuno, che queste promesse siano adempiute come la legge comanda? Signori Giudici, che cosa vuol dire la libertà, che cosa vuol dire democrazia? Vuol dire prima di tutto fiducia del popolo nelle *sue* leggi».[53]

Come è noto, Calamandrei ci sapeva fare con le parole. Si deve a lui l'immagine efficace della costituzione *presbite*, capace di progettare il futuro ma soggetta al rischio di non essere compresa e "attuata", se non col tempo e a costo di dure lotte, specialmente nella parte sui diritti che trasformava *ab imis* «la scala dei valori di riferimento».[54]

Nel 1926 Francesco Ruffini concludeva il suo saggio ripetendo «la infrangibile sequenza del Machiavelli» nel libro secondo delle *Istorie fiorentine*: «Avete voi considerato [...] quanto sia gagliardo il nome della libertà? Il quale forza alcuna non doma, tempo alcuno non consuma, e merito alcuno non contrappesa».[55] L'impegno per attuare la *libertà degna* è tutt'altro che esaurito. E questo nome gagliardo della libertà deve confrontarsi con minacce ricorrenti e sfide sempre nuove.

53 In D. Dolci, *Processo all'articolo 4*, cit., 308.

54 S. Rodotà, *La libertà e i diritti*, in *Storia dello Stato italiano dall'Unità a oggi*, a cura di R. Romanelli, Roma 1995, 350.

55 F. Ruffini, *Diritti di libertà*, cit., 158.

La *lotta per il regolamento*: libertà politiche, forma di governo e ostruzionismo parlamentare. Dalle riforme Bonghi al regolamento Villa del 1900

1. Premessa

Il lungo periodo preso in esame consiglia una selezione degli aspetti e dei temi da analizzare e valutare alla luce della prospettiva dei «regolamenti parlamentari nei momenti di "svolta" della storia costituzionale italiana». Si possono subito indicare tre temi che emergono con una certa evidenza nel periodo considerato e che possiedono una portata più generale.

Il primo avvalora il rilievo del regolamento parlamentare e più in generale del diritto parlamentare quale laboratorio significativo di "elaborazione" e di "consolidamento" di cambiamenti costituzionali che esaltano la intrinseca dimensione "politica" del tessuto materiale delle regole di autorganizzazione (prassi, consuetudini, convenzioni) e pongono però al tempo stesso il problema della loro "codificazione" e della loro possibile "sclerotizzazione". Il fatto e la regola formano così un insieme problematico (Caretti 2001), un intreccio complesso e non privo di tensioni segnato da un robusto "protagonismo" del "momento" regolamentare. Ne consegue, se solo si volesse ricordarlo, la conferma della rilevanza delle regole del diritto parlamentare (cfr. Negri 1968, 9–10) – direi dell'*ordine parlamentare* (su cui, attraverso Santi Romano, v. Beaud 2001) – per un approccio fecondo e complesso alla storia costituzionale che in esse trova alimento per una sua parte non trascurabile.

Il periodo esaminato enfatizza, in secondo luogo, in un modo che sino alla "crisi di fine secolo" non era emerso con pari virulenza, la capacità o meno delle regole di assicurare, in una dialettica anche accesissima, un equilibrio "accettabile" – tanto per gli attori che per il sistema oggettivamente inteso – tra due esigenze egualmente legittime sia sul piano teorico che su quello del funzionamento concreto di un genuino sistema parlamentare: da un lato un'adeguata funzionalità dei lavori parlamentari secondo le volontà espresse dalla maggioranza governativa, dall'altro il diritto delle minoranze ad esprimere in maniera congrua le proprie ragioni. Due diritti entrano così in collisione in maniera legittima e altrettanto legittimamente si deve ricercare una soluzione dialettica.

Il terzo tema che si può subito segnalare, e che caratterizza in maniera specifica la vicenda che porterà al regolamento del 1900, è la posta in gioco del conflitto parlamentare: il terreno regolamentare finisce, come vedremo, per diventare spazio privilegiato per un conflitto sui *diritti fondamentali*. La *lotta per il regolamento* è parte integrante di un *progetto costituzionale* che ha come obiettivo ultimo la "registrazione" di un determinato assetto della forma di governo e che insiste sul terreno dei *diritti pubblici soggettivi*, ovvero di un sistema di libertà politiche fragili, da rassodare per un verso, da conquistare per un altro.

2. Una duttile "provvisorietà"

Tra i caratteri "permanenti" e i tratti originari (cfr. Sbriccoli 1998) della storia italiana, operante a vari livelli e con diversa funzionalità, è da annoverare senz'altro il carattere della *provvisorietà*: di norme, di istituti, di pratiche. Per i primi cinquant'anni della storia parlamentare statutaria si potrebbe parlare di una *naturale provvisorietà* del tessuto regolamentare. Tale carattere è stato segnalato come un momento necessario di flessibilità in grado di accompagnare l'evoluzione della forma di governo e i relativi equilibri raggiunti nel tempo (Manzella 1977, 50; Caretti 2001, 585) in una cornice costituzionale che l'originario impianto statutario non determinava certo in maniera "assoluta". Due questioni cruciali e controverse si addensarono attorno alla verifica dei poteri e alle tecniche della procedura legislativa. Non di rado le proposte volte a intervenire in maniera organica e radicale sul *corpus* regolamentare finirono per rafforzare il registro della provvisorietà. Tra il regolamento del 1868 e le legislature successive si susseguono Commissioni, progetti, relazioni e talune modifiche che danno vita ad un notevole accumulo di materiali e di proposte – come testimoniato ampiamente dall'opera pioneristica di Mario Mancini e Ugo Galeotti, *Norme ed usi del Parlamento italiano* (1887) – senza però che l'esito voluto possa essere raggiunto. Le quattro sessioni della XIV Legislatura (10 giugno 1886 – 3 agosto 1890) appaiono particolarmente produttive proprio perché viene adottato un criterio differente. La Commissione – composta da nove membri scelti dal presidente della Camera: Bonghi, Boselli, Crispi, Cuccia, Di Rudinì, Ercole, Lazzaro, Marcora, Spaventa – investita a partire dal 21 giugno 1886 del compito di portare a termine i lavori già predisposti nelle precedenti legislature, muove proprio dal fallimento del metodo "massimalista", della "grande riforma", colla rinuncia quindi a perseguire la strada del, sino ad allora, impossibile regolamento definitivo per fare invece del canone della *provvisorietà* la *regola* reputando miglior metodo quello delle «modificazioni e aggiunte al regolamento che l'esperienza mostrerà necessarie» (Astraldi 1932, 48).

Lo strumento per intraprendere questa via fu la costituzione, a partire dal 1887, di una Commissione permanente formata, in questo caso, dagli stessi membri della Commissione del giugno 1886.

Tra il maggio 1887 e il maggio 1888 numerose furono le proposte di modifica elaborate dalla Giunta che ebbe come relatore Ruggero Bonghi, autore di saggi celebri come *I partiti politici nel Parlamento italiano* (1868) o *Una questione grossa. La decadenza del regime parlamentare* (1884) e il cui nome sarà poi accostato, non a caso, al *corpus* regolamentare della Camera. L'ordine della discussione, la disciplina delle questioni sospensive e pregiudiziali, il metodo di votazione, la discussione delle mozioni, gli emendamenti e gli articoli aggiuntivi proposti da singoli deputati furono oggetto di revisione e la Camera nella maggior parte dei casi approvò le proposte della Commissione. Di particolare importanza risulta la disciplina (artt. 70–73), più organica, del diritto di interrogazione e di interpellanza e soprattutto l'introduzione del sistema delle tre letture per la discussione delle leggi. Come si è osservato, il procedimento di discussione e approvazione delle leggi fu senza dubbio uno dei grandi temi del dibattito parlamentare a partire dalle origini della storia parlamentare italiana (Manzella 1977, 50–51; Merlini 1995, 34–35). Le tre letture, pur avendo dalla loro il mitizzato paradigma britannico, avevano suscitato in passato dubbi e difficoltà di vario segno e sostituirle al macchinoso sistema degli Uffici non appariva un'operazione indolore. La proposta del 28 febbraio 1888 invece rientrava a pieno titolo nella logica "sperimentale" che accompagna la XIV Legislatura: se i due sistemi, infatti, avevano dimostrato pregi e difetti, si lasciava adesso alla Camera la libertà di scegliere, di volta in volta, quale dei due metodi apparisse il più opportuno. Il dibattito che seguì in aula (Astraldi 1932, 53) fece vedere ancora una volta il carattere fortemente controverso della scelta operata, anche se alla fine le tre letture poterono riacquistare, dopo la sfavorevole parentesi del 1868–1872, cittadinanza nella Camera dei deputati, pur in alternativa agli Uffici e senza trovare nel prosieguo il successo sperato.

Le importanti modifiche introdotte tra il 1887 e il 1888 posero il problema del coordinamento con il testo in vigore risalente al 1868. Fu l'on. Di Rudinì nella tornata del 19 maggio 1888 a presentare in aula, a nome della Giunta permanente, il nuovo regolamento coordinato. Il regolamento fu di nuovo modificato nel 1891 all'inizio della XVII Legislatura per meglio specificare gli istituti dell'interrogazione, dell'interpellanza e della mozione (*Ibid.*, 56): così il regolamento Bonghi, con i suoi interventi mirati, alcuni dei quali di notevole significato, era destinato a disciplinare la vita parlamentare nel tumultuoso ultimo decennio del secolo. Non si può dire che nel corso degli anni Novanta non vi fossero state proposte di modifica, da parte di singoli deputati e della stessa commissione (cfr. la raccolta di fonti in Tanda 1996), ma l'esito fu quasi sempre negativo.

3. Il canone della *complessità* del sistema regolamentare nella "crisi di fine secolo"

La crisi di fine secolo mise a durissima prova le riforme Bonghi e più in generale l'assetto regolamentare frutto del primo cinquantennio di storia parlamentare. La rottura degli equilibri politico-costituzionali, faticosamente raggiunti, non poteva non investire appieno quel canone della *provvisorietà* (e conseguente duttilità) che aveva accompagnato l'evoluzione del diritto parlamentare della Camera dei deputati. Ciò che aveva consentito un relativo primato della dimensione fattuale nella configurazione delle norme e degli usi regolamentari apparve inadeguato a governare le forti spinte provenienti dalla società, spinte destinate ad incidere profondamente sulla vita politico-parlamentare e sulle stesse dinamiche costituzionali. Ha così inizio la fase della *complessità regolamentare*, che si apre con forza nel 1898 e si concluderà nel 1922, una fase nella quale la vita dei regolamenti parlamentari non ha più una esclusiva legittimità *endogena* (dialettica parlamento/governo/Corona), in quanto è il rapporto con la complessità del sociale – nelle sue più diverse manifestazioni – a incidere sul modo di essere e di agire della regola parlamentare, potenziandone la stessa rilevanza costituzionale.

In questa sede non è possibile affrontare, neanche per sommi capi, il grande tema della storia nazionale che la storiografia ha codificato con l'espressione "crisi di fine secolo".[1] Crisi senza dubbio a più dimensioni che testimonia la debolezza di ogni tentativo "semplicistico" (come osservò bene Croce 1927, 272 ss.) – sia di ordine socio-economico che di ordine politico-costituzionale – volto ad offrire risposte univoche a questioni complesse. La visione "semplice" che discende dal paradigma borghese costitutivo della cultura giuridica e del sapere politico liberale del XIX secolo, fondato sul tranquillizzante binomio Stato/individuo, deve fare i conti con la dimensione spuria, ambigua, ma vitale del "collettivo" (cfr. Marchetti 2006), una dimensione che complica profondamente lo scenario e modifica gli stessi punti di osservazione.

Il Parlamento, sul finire del secolo, è stretto tra vari fuochi (per alcune esemplificazioni v. Levra 2001; Rebuffa 2001) e non gode, da tempo, di buona salute. L'antiparlamentarismo non è sorto invano: moribondo, degradato, corrotto, in preda ad un atomismo particolaristico che indebolisce la parte *nobile* e *stabile* della costituzione (Corona, esecutivo 'monarchico', prerogativa militare), la crisi del Parlamento, inteso come luogo inadeguato a determinare un coerente indirizzo politico, rischia di far deflagrare l'intero sistema istituzionale. Il celebre *Torniamo allo Statuto* di Sidney Sonnino – il principale protago-

1 Sulle diverse interpretazioni e sulla complessiva discussione storiografica più recente rinvio a Guazzaloca 2004, 94 ss.

nista della battaglia parlamentare di fine secolo vista dai ranghi della maggioranza "conservatrice" – è un efficace grido di dolore che condensa umori, sentimenti e ragioni di una parte cospicua della classe liberale che cerca di trovare soluzioni alla crisi del regime rappresentativo insistendo sulla *naturale* centralità dell'istituto monarchico, sulla necessità di una autentica separazione dei poteri e sull'esperimento rischioso, ma indispensabile, del suffragio universale inteso come meccanismo di reale *socializzazione governata* dello Stato e delle sue istituzioni (Nieri 2000; Haywood 1999, 219 ss.; Ballini 2000).

D'altra parte l'immagine scolorita del Parlamento non affascina certo quelle forze politiche e sociali che vi scorgono un mero meccanismo funzionale alla *montée de la démocratie*. Nel 1897 i socialisti rappresentano il 10% dei voti validi (Ballini 1988; Piretti 1996) e la Sinistra nel suo insieme dispone di un'ottantina di seggi. Minoranza, certo, e tuttavia la sua presenza ha anzitutto un valore *qualitativo* (Cambria 1989, I, 69) perché destinata ad incidere fortemente sulle dinamiche parlamentari. Paradossalmente dallo scontro di queste due visioni, poco inclini a cogliere la dimensione costitutiva del fenomeno parlamentare per un autentico sistema "rappresentativo", il Parlamento, almeno per alcuni profili, ne uscirà rafforzato (Isastia 1977, 424–425).

Il corto circuito tra i diversi livelli della crisi e la più lontana (almeno in apparenza) dimensione regolamentare scoppia nel 1899. Nel febbraio il tenente generale e senatore del Regno Luigi Pelloux,[2] liberale proveniente dai ranghi della Sinistra costituzionale, vicino alla Corte ma non privo di una sua visione politica (Manacorda 1967, LXVI; Doglio 1977), presenta un disegno di legge contenente quelli che Umberto Levra ha chiamato i «provvedimenti cosacchi» (1975, 299; 2001, 181), ovvero un *corpus* di interventi repressivi (sui quali v. le sintesi recentissime di Colao 2007 e Latini 2007). Essi "codificano", rendendole "permanenti", le misure emergenziali che negli anni precedenti, in maniera più o meno "temporanea", erano state adottate, sin dal 1894, da Crispi, Di Rudinì (Belardinelli 1976) e dallo stesso Pelloux (con validità sino al 30 giugno 1899) per contrastare le gravi "emergenze" dell'ordine pubblico: le proteste sociali, lo spettro del sovversivismo, l'anarchia, l'antagonismo politico-sindacale. Le più importanti libertà pubbliche (stampa, riunione, associazione) e i diritti dei lavoratori in alcuni settori strategici (ferrovie, poste, telegrafi) venivano fortemente limitati e ricondotti prevalentemente alla discrezionalità dell'esecutivo. Con questo intervento Pelloux modificava ulteriormente le basi programmatiche del suo governo e ritornava sulla strada più marcatamente "repressiva".[3]

2 Sulla figura di Pelloux e sulla sua ascesa al potere v. Levra 1975, 233 ss.

3 Levra 1975, 237 ss., insiste piuttosto sulla assoluta continuità dei due governi del "bifronte" Pelloux, ma per una analisi più convincente del "mutamento" di indirizzo v. Doglio 1977, 327 ss.

Il tentativo di *ordinare* la società complessa di fine secolo, di *neutralizzare* il conflitto socio-economico, di *giuridicizzare* (per mezzo di strumenti perlopiù repressivi) la politica parlamentare, in realtà svelavano, come apparve agli osservatori più lucidi, la sostanziale debolezza (tema, come noto, ampiamente sviluppato da Maranini 1967 nella prospettiva sistemica del "regime pseudo-parlamentare") di una parte della classe dirigente che, sulla scia del Novantotto, intendeva perseguire confuse suggestioni autoritarie indotte da paure e da progetti di "nuovi" equilibri politici incentrati su esecutivi monarchici.

Sostenuto ancora da ampi settori della Sinistra costituzionale, Pelloux ricorse alla tecnica delle tre letture confidando in un ampio consenso della maggioranza (Perticone 1960, 153). Il progetto di legge fu presentato il 16 febbraio 1899 e l'esame ebbe termine il 4 marzo quando venne approvato ad ampia maggioranza il passaggio alla seconda lettura. Il governo mostrò invece segni di indebolimento a seguito dell'ennesima improvvida avventura coloniale in Cina che aveva immediate ricadute sulle linee di politica economica dell'esecutivo. Le dimissioni del primo gabinetto Pelloux, il 3 maggio, aprivano una nuova esperienza di governo, segnata in profondità dall'incisiva influenza sonniniana (Carusi 2003, 420 ss.), che radicalizzava l'azione dell'esecutivo su posizioni di destra-centro (celebre il giudizio di Domenico Farini: «... dal 1876 in poi, non vi fu mai l'uguale di tendenze, origini, propositi conservatori!», 1962, 1499–1550) e con la rinuncia al sostegno organico della galassia della Sinistra liberale (Levra 1975, 324 ss.). A partire dal 1 giugno il disegno di legge, redatto da Sonnino secondo l'orientamento più restrittivo della Commissione parlamentare e giunto alla seconda lettura, teneva a battesimo l'ostruzionismo.

4. Il tempo dell'ostruzionismo

Le vicende sono note: l'estrema Sinistra per impedire l'approvazione della legge utilizzò le norme regolamentari vigenti per prolungare in maniera artificiosa la discussione sollecitando defatiganti appelli nominali, proponendo una selva di questioni pregiudiziali e sospensive, i rinvii alla commissione, un numero enorme di emendamenti sui quali chiedere la verifica del numero legale, sostenendo infine memorabili *tour de force* oratori (Isastia 1977). Il 7 giugno, il principale ispiratore dell'azione di governo, Sidney Sonnino, presentò una modifica al regolamento. L'art. 89 bis (Tanda 1996, 328) attribuiva al Presidente, qualora la discussione generale di un progetto o di un articolo di legge si prolungasse «in modo da turbare il regolare andamento dei lavori parlamentari», la possibilità di chiedere all'aula una deliberazione sul tempo massimo da assegnare ai singoli oratori, nonché di fissare il giorno e l'ora in cui la discussione avrebbe dovuto terminare con la votazione. Le proposte del Presidente avrebbero dovuto essere votate subito dalla Camera per alzata e seduta, senza alcuna discussione o dichiarazione di voto. Inoltre, giunto il termine prestabilito, ogni discussione sarebbe terminata con la votazione. Il 10 giugno Attilio Brunialti presentò una diversa proposta che avrebbe comunque dovuto limitare gli atteggiamenti ostruzionistici: la richiesta di venti deputati per la verifica del numero legale (art. 33), il divieto, per ciascun deputato, di parlare più di venti minuti in seconda lettura (art. 59) e di presentare più di un ordine del giorno (art. 82), la votazione per alzata e seduta in ordine all'interdizione inflitta all'oratore indiscipinato (art. 77) (*Ibid.*, 329–332).

Il dibattito che ebbe luogo in seno alla Giunta per il regolamento, dopo il 10 giugno 1899, fissa con precisione i termini della questione. In particolare la prima seduta, quando si comincia a discutere la proposta Sonnino, mostra come il lavoro in Commissione "raffreddi" il calor bianco della lotta parlamentare e come le posizioni della maggioranza e della minoranza non siano ancora così irrimediabilmente divaricate. L'on. Simeoni «dichiara che il quesito è un solo: quello di sapere se l'ostruzionismo possa elevarsi ad istituto parlamentare, ammesso e rispettato. Egli è per la negativa. Accetterà ogni proposta, che valga ad impedirlo e che si concili col maggior rispetto alla libertà della tribuna» (*Ibid.*, 71). Per la minoranza l'on. Sacchi solleva la questione «se durante una discussione sia possibile ammettere che si muti la forma e le disposizioni del Regolamento» e l'on. Rampoldi ritiene che così si creerebbe un pericoloso precedente «mettendo sempre la minoranza in balìa della maggioranza che potrebbe di volta in volta riformare le norme parlamentari» (*Ibid.*, 71–72). Di fronte alla necessità di intervenire su una situazione eccezionale che rischiava, secondo i membri della maggioranza, di alterare la normale dialettica parlamentare, l'on Ferraris, della minoranza, non esita a riconoscere «che l'istituto dell'ostruzionismo non possa essere in alcun modo consentito perchè sconvolgerebbe tutto il sistema parlamentare» e d'altra parte il relatore di maggioranza, Cambray-Digny, non ha difficoltà a riconoscere che i diritti della maggioranza devono incontrare «limiti ragionevoli» e che le proposte hanno un carattere politico che «imbarazzerà anche la discussione in seno alla Commissione del regolamento». La minoranza non vuole impedire l'esame delle proposte, purché le soluzioni adottate non si applichino alla discussione in corso. Nella seduta del 16 giugno l'on. Sacchi specifica ulteriormente la posizione della minoranza e

> «aggiunge che quando pure si dovesse considerare specialmente la discussione in corso non si può dire che l'ostruzionismo sia introdotto nei costumi parlamentari, dacché mai vi si ricorse per importanti che fossero le leggi; riconosce i diritti della maggioranza ma osserva che questa può eccedere nell'uso di quelli e che se oggi non è più possibile il dispotismo di un principe è ben possibile quello della maggioranza; in concreto si fa ostruzionismo perché si tratta di diritti statutari; una maggioranza potrebbe privare i cittadini del suffragio come ora li vuol privare dell'associazione, e allora la minoranza entra nel diritto di opporre resistenza anche con metodi eccezionali. Prevedendo poi di non poter riuscire ad impedire

che qualche deliberazione di genere abbreviativo si prenda propone questa declaratoria pregiudiziale, sebbene riconosca che la forma odierna dell'onorevole Simeoni sia attenuata di fronte alle proposte sue e dell'onorevole Sonnino: "Le forme abbreviative della discussione non sono applicabili allorché si tratta di disegni di legge che riguardino l'esercizio dei diritti statutari"» [*Ibid.*, 78–79].

Alla fine l'art. 89 bis proposto da Sonnino con le integrazioni "migliorative" di Simeoni e la relazione di maggioranza vengono approvati dalla Giunta per il regolamento senza però che l'aula di Montecitorio possa trarne vantaggio. L'on. Sacchi aveva però còlto nel segno ricollegando in maniera esplicita il divieto di "ghigliottine" alla difesa dei diritti statutari e attribuendo quindi all'ostruzionismo una legittimità di cui la stessa minoranza dubitava. Già contro Crispi l'Estrema Sinistra aveva cominciato ad utilizzare la tattica parlamentare per rallentare i lavori e per criticare la politica del governo. E sin dalla XVII Legislatura si può scorgere l'impegno della Giunta per il regolamento a predisporre soluzioni antiostruzionistiche. Nella XVIII Legislatura Bonghi e altri deputati avevano presentato una modifica delle misure disciplinari contro i deputati "perturbatori" e soprattutto agli inizi della Legislatura seguente la proposta Cibrario e quella "provocatoria" di Cavallotti (che estendeva le sanzioni ai membri del governo e ai deputati sotto inchiesta) (Astraldi 1932, 58–59; Tanda 1996, 21 ss.) rivelavano l'avvio di nuove strategie che dalla primavera del 1899 avrebbero trovato massima realizzazione. La lettera di Andrea Costa a Edoardo Pantano, datata 17 aprile 1899, conferma il carattere concertato e sistematico dell'ostruzionismo:

«Per l'ostruzionismo, di cui parlammo, mi sembra che potremmo fare così. Voi invitate tutti i Vostri, per mezzo dell'*Italia*, a trovarsi in Roma il giorno della riapertura della Camera. Noi facciamo altrettanto. E nel giorno stesso della riapertura teniamo – tutti – un'adunanza e fissiamo le norme dell'ostruzionismo e diamo ai singoli il mandato preciso di trovarsi in Roma in questi o in quei giorni, affinché siano presenti sempre in numero sufficiente per chiedere l'appello nominale o per constatare il numero legale. – Va bene? Rispondimi a Imola – Aff.mo A. Costa. P.S. Scrivo altrettanto al Barzilai. Comunica al Socci!» [cit. da Tanda 1996, 24].

Legittimo o meno, manifesto o occulto, proprio o improprio (Longi, Stramacci 1968, 112–113) l'ostruzionismo, che inneschi o meno un processo di accelerazione delle riforme regolamentari (Tanda 2001, 701), appare nell'esperienza italiana di fine secolo anche un possibile segnale di trasformazione del modo stesso di concepire il lavoro parlamentare: è, se si vuole, anche un indizio di un rafforzato spirito di organizzazione e forse della definitiva crisi dell'atomismo parlamentare.

Gli ultimi dieci giorni del giugno 1899 segnarono la prima grande fase della battaglia parlamentare. Il 20 giugno Pelloux propose e ottenne, nonostante la forte opposizione, che la discussione delle modificazioni al regolamento fosse messa all'ordine del giorno. L'indomani ebbe inizio ma già il 22 la sessione viene prorogata e il 28 l'aula è investita delle due questioni ormai indissolubilmente legate: i provvedimenti politici presentati con decreto da convertire in legge e la proposta di Sonnino e di altri quattordici deputati per formare una Commissione *ad hoc* allo scopo di introdurre nel regolamento le modifiche dimostrate dall'esperienza opportune per il buon andamento dei lavori parlamentari e predisporre inoltre un testo che avrebbe dovuto entrare in vigore provvisoriamente senza discussione e votazione due giorni dopo la presentazione alla Camera (*Atti Parlamentari*, Legislatura XX, seconda sessione, Documenti n. VII-*quinquies*). Nella relazione al Re che accompagnava il famigerato decreto-legge 22 giugno 1899 n. 227, con efficacia esecutiva dal 20 luglio 1899 (registrato con riserva dalla Corte dei Conti), l'ostruzionismo è richiamato come motivo dello stato di necessità. «La situazione creata da queste condizioni impone al Governo il dovere di procurare che la volontà ed il diritto della maggioranza possano, secondo lo spirito degli ordini costituzionali, ottenere la loro legittima prevalenza. Non si può lasciare che una esigua minoranza impedisca alla Camera dei deputati l'esercizio delle sue funzioni» (*Atti Parlamentari*, Legislatura XX, seconda sessione, Documenti n. 143-C; Di Muccio 1987, 34). Nel suo scritto del 16 novembre 1899, «I decreti-legge e il regolamento della Camera», pubblicato nella *Nuova Antologia*, Sonnino subordinerà l'eliminazione del discusso strumento "consuetudinario" della decretazione del governo (Isastia 1977, 442 ss.; Latini 2006) – che affermava essere contrario al corretto funzionamento degli istituti rappresentativi (come ricorderà Ferracciù 1900, 486) – ad una riforma del regolamento che assicurasse la soluzione del problema nei casi di necessità e urgenza «nonostante qualunque più fiera opposizione delle minoranze, e pur rispettando in queste ogni uso ragionevole della libera discussione» (Sonnino 1972, I, 667).

L'ostruzionismo sempre più deciso dell'Estrema depotenziò sia la proposta Franchetti di modifica regolamentare del 29 giugno (Tanda 1996, 86–90) sia la sua iscrizione all'ordine del giorno nella tornata del 30. Il decreto-legge liberticida del 22 giugno – che entrerà in vigore il 20 luglio – aveva spinto i moderati ad abbandonare definitivamente l'atteggiamento di equidistanza. La seduta pomeridiana del 30 giugno fu tra le più drammatiche nell'aula soffocante di Montecitorio. Gli scontri tra i socialisti e i sonniniani non furono solo verbali, come potè provare lo stesso Sonnino colpito da Bissolati (Levra 2001, 189). Il presidente Chinaglia fu aspramente contestato. La sola soluzione possibile era mettere fine alla seconda sessione della XX Legislatura.

Il 14 novembre 1899, con l'inizio della terza sessione, cominciava l'ultimo e decisivo atto della battaglia parlamentare. Sonnino aveva suggerito di andare a nuove elezioni prima di affrontare il nodo del decreto legge e del regolamento (Sonnino, *Diario*, 28 dicembre 1899, 4 gennaio 1900, I, 1972, 414 e 428).

Ma, indebolito sul piano politico (Levra 2001, 190–191), il gabinetto Pelloux dovrà fronteggiare anche le conseguenze della sentenza della prima sezione della Corte di cassazione emessa il 20 febbraio 1900. Era una sentenza che "declassava" il decreto del 22 giugno scorso a mero disegno di legge non discusso né approvato dal Parlamento, decaduto inesorabilmente dopo la chiusura anticipata della sessione, privo pertanto di efficacia giuridica e illegittimo nella sua applicazione dopo il 20 luglio 1899 (cfr. Meccarelli 2005). Studi recenti hanno confermato l'importanza di questa sentenza per l'esito della crisi: risultato non improvvisato, nato da una comunanza di intenti tra alcuni alti magistrati di Cassazione legati a Giolitti e Zanardelli e la politica, non certo esente da errori e contraddizioni, della Sinistra costituzionale per una difesa dei principi liberali legati alle libertà pubbliche e alle garanzie giuridiche. Il presidente Tancredi Canonico (Themelly 1975, 171–175) e il consigliere Luigi Lucchini (anche dalla sua autorevole tribuna scientifica: Sbriccoli 1987) offrirono alla Sinistra moderata un'occasione – di per sé non risolutiva – per uscire da una crisi il cui esito restava incerto (Cambria 1989, I, 79–80; III, 1990, 95–100; Malatesta 2001).

Ancora una volta Sonnino, eletto presidente della Giunta per il regolamento, cercò di dettare i tempi della politica parlamentare. La discussione del "nuovo" disegno di legge sui provvedimenti politici – dopo l'esito infausto della sentenza della Cassazione – fu però l'occasione per rinvigorire l'ostruzionismo, riproponendo lo stesso copione del giugno 1899. Il 21 marzo fa capolino, sotto forma di mozione presentata da Tommaso Cambray-Digny, il meccanismo della modifica provvisoria del regolamento con esecuzione dal secondo giorno dalla presentazione e il 29 marzo, tra le proteste accesissime della Sinistra, il progetto è approvato per alzata e seduta. «Si fa colpo alla Camera», scrive Sonnino nel suo Diario, mentre di Rudinì, già molto critico verso la riproposizione dei provvedimenti politici, e i suoi si mostrano perplessi sull'azione "sonniniana" del governo, incapace di trovare un compromesso con la sinistra liberale. Il Presidente dell'assemblea, Giuseppe Colombo, il giorno seguente fu contestato con epiteti di ogni genere e fu costretto a pur brevissime dimissioni. Lo stesso Giolitti aveva qualificato la manovra del governo una violazione aperta e diretta dello Statuto, tanto più che si affidavano i pieni poteri ad una Commissione nella quale la minoranza non veniva adeguatamente rappresentata. Il deputato di destra Gabriele D'Annunzio intanto lodava il "vitalismo" degli ostruzionisti della Estrema Sinistra (Levra 2001, 163). Il 3 aprile, dopo i veementi discorsi di Giuseppe Zanardelli e del repubblicano Edoardo Pantano, che non riconoscevano validità alla deliberazione del 29 marzo e annunciavano l'abbandono dell'aula (inaugurando un "modello" di lotta politica destinato a proseguire, Martucci 2001, 80–81, 132) di tutti i deputati della Sinistra per protestare contro il «premeditato e preparato colpo di maggioranza, inteso a far votare senza discussione quelle norme regolamentari che sopprimono la libertà della tribuna parlamentare» (Tanda 1996, 31), iniziava l'ultima fase di un confronto sempre più aspro nel quale aleggiava anche lo spettro della convocazione di un'assemblea costituente … (cfr. la ricostruzione in Levra 2001, 191 ss.). La replica formale di Sonnino, che si trincerava dietro il rispetto dell'ordine delle discussioni parlamentari e del ruolo del Presidente dell'assemblea visto come difensore delle libertà di tutti e delle stesse istituzioni rappresentative, non sortiva alcun effetto (Di Muccio, I, 1987, 37). Il 5 aprile il governo ritirava il decreto legge 22 giugno 1899, a ulteriore conferma del legame a doppio filo con la vicenda del regolamento parlamentare.

L'epilogo si compì il 15 maggio, alla ripresa dei lavori. Fu allora che Giolitti, superata definitivamente la sua posizione di "attesa" e di "equidistanza",[4] sottolineò la gravità della situazione (una modifica regolamentare ritenuta illegale dai due quinti dei deputati) e formulò un'ultima proposta conciliativa: da un canto sospendere l'approvazione del verbale della seduta del 3 aprile e dall'altro nominare una commissione di nove membri eletti con voto limitato richiesta di formulare, entro due giorni, soluzioni adeguate mentre i lavori dell'aula restavano sospesi. «Evidentemente nessuna persona ragionevole può volere un regolamento che consenta l'ostruzionismo, ma nessuna persona ragionevole può pretendere che si abbia un regolamento il quale permetta alla metà più uno dell'Assemblea di far tacere a giorno ed ora fissa l'altra metà meno uno dell'Assemblea stessa».

La mozione non venne accolta e Giolitti la ritirò accollando al governo tutto il peso delle proprie responsabilità. La votazione del verbale fu l'ultimo atto del secondo governo Pelloux e ben presto la vittoria di Sonnino si palcsò, come sappiamo, per il suo vero significato: una vittoria di Pirro che produsse invero l'effetto contrario.

Le elezioni del giugno 1900, l'appello al popolo, furono fatali a Pelloux che, pur conservando la maggioranza numerica, dovette constatare l'avanzata delle Sinistre e dei moderati. «Ed allora – osserverà Orlando – il Gabinetto Pelloux fu costretto a dimettersi … Egli è che bisogna liberarsi dal pregiudizio di considerare le forme parlamentari nel precetto semplicista che il Gabinetto può sussistere in quanto ha la maggioranza nella Camera, la verità che un Gabinetto può sussistere senza maggioranza; e può non sussistere con la maggioranza» (Orlando 1912, 66).

La relazione Chimirri che accompagnò le modifiche regolamentari ricorse a due argomenti che già erano stati ampiamente utilizzati (direi teorizzati da

4 Giolitti, nelle *Memorie* 1922, traccia le linee direttrici di quella che sarebbe stata la sua visione politica nella crisi di fine secolo: dall'iniziale attesa verso la svolta autoritaria di Pelloux all'equidistanza dall'ostruzionismo sino alla piena affermazione del "progetto liberale".

Sonnino 1899 (1972)): la libertà della discussione parlamentare era la ragion d'essere delle assemblee ma non poteva impedire l'esercizio di una potestà fondamentale ovvero il diritto della maggioranza a deliberare; i regolamenti parlamentari in vigore in altre nazioni prevedevano misure coercitive contro i perturbatori dell'ordine delle discussioni. Questo argomenti, per la verità, non erano mai stati respinti *a priori* dalla minoranza: il problema era l'uso strumentale delle modifiche proposte per approvare i provvedimenti politici che incidevano fortemente sull'assetto delle libertà costituzionali. Mai, nella storia italiana, il regolamento parlamentare aveva assunto una così piena valenza costituzionale. Per Enrico Ferri (1899 e 1900) il regolamento diventava la legge delle leggi:

> «Il regolamento adunque ha valore fondamentale e costituzionale per l'Assemblea stessa ed esso è l'unico strumento per cui il lavoro dell'Assemblea legislativa può essere legale nella forma, fecondo nella sostanza, coercibile al Paese cui si ponga una determinata norma legislativa; perché è col regolamento che si tutelano i diritti imprescrittibili delle minoranze. Se questi diritti non avessero nel regolamento la loro sanzione, il regime parlamentare sarebbe inesistente nella sostanza ed alla prevalenza della maggioranza si sostituirebbe la sua onnipotenza assoluta senza confini.»

Non la sostanza delle disposizioni ma il metodo autoritario spaventava dunque Ferri e la Sinistra, possibile prodromo di una completa involuzione costituzionale che muoveva da azioni contrarie a qualsiasi legalità di forma. L'on. Sacchi, che già aveva mostrato in modo chiaro nel 1899 la posta in gioco e il fondamento di legittimità dell'ostruzionismo, ribadì in coda alla relazione di maggioranza che il diritto di limitare l'opposizione era giusta «sol quando la maggioranza non miri a restringere i diritti fondamentali di libertà e di suffragio che formano il contenuto essenziale della costituzione politica del Paese. Questo caso avverandosi, la minoranza, che la costituzione vuol difendere, non può più essere giudicata a stregua del regolamento interno dell'Assemblea, ma il diritto di chiedere che il Paese sia chiamato a giudicare in supremo appello se la sua volontà sovrana sia rappresentata dalla maggioranza o dalla minoranza» (cit. da Di Muccio, I, 1987, 41–42).

Il "pacchetto" Sonnino, nato morto, interveniva su una buona parte degli istituti e dei congegni procedurali che erano stati motivo di ostruzionismo: la votazione del processo verbale, la verifica del numero legale, la presentazione di articoli aggiuntivi o emendamenti, lo svolgimento degli ordini del giorno, la votazione per alzata e seduta sulle deliberazioni della Camera relative all'interdizione della parola e soprattutto, come nel modello inglese (Bertolini 1981, pp. 476 ss.; Ghisalberti 1986, 256) la cd. "ghigliottina" (artt. 87-bis, 88-bis, 89-bis), ovvero l'insieme delle misure volte a negare l'accettazione e lo svolgimento di ordini del giorno o emendamenti estranei alla discussione e a limitare ad un massimo di dieci minuti il tempo per ciascun oratore per arrivare sino alla fissazione del giorno e dell'ora in cui la discussione avrebbe dovuto terminare con il voto immediato (Astraldi 1932, 64–66; Di Muccio, I, 1987, 38 ss.).

5. Il regolamento del 1900 come "svolta" della storia costituzionale italiana?

La XXI Legislatura, iniziata con la crisi extraparlamentare del governo Pelloux e con l'incarico al vecchio senatore sabaudo Giuseppe Saracco, riprese il discorso da dove, il 15 maggio, era stato interrotto con il rifiuto della mediazione Giolitti. Uno dei protagonisti della vicenda fu Tommaso Villa, grande avvocato d'affari, già guardasigilli, sodale di Crispi, ed eletto il 28 giugno 1900 a grandissima maggioranza presidente della Camera che già aveva guidato tra il 1895 e il 1897 (v. la bella biografia intellettuale di Montaldo 1999; Montaldo 2001, 203). Divenne così presidente il "trasformista" Villa che nel 1899 aveva dato ampia disponibilità a Sonnino e Pelloux ad assumere quella stessa funzione nel periodo più caldo della lotta parlamentare. Chiusa la XX Legislatura con lo strappo sul regolamento, la nuova non poteva non affrontare in via preliminare questa delicata questione. Il discorso di insediamento del nuovo Presidente, equilibrato e lucido, sancisce l'armistizio tra le parti in lotta: se il regolamento aveva diviso la Camera sino ai tumulti e alla violenza, ora esso doveva unire per ridare vigore e legittimità ad un Parlamento ferito e incerto. Villa (legato a Sonnino) muove da un principio di forte discontinuità rispetto al recente passato. Ogni legislatura, si afferma, ha il diritto di stabilire il proprio regolamento garantendo la libera manifestazione delle idee e del voto.[5] Se in passato era prevalso il principio della continuità ciò era avvenuto per tacito consenso non trovando consacrazione in una disposizione legislativa. Il Presidente sottolinea la complessità del lavoro parlamentare di fronte ad una società che cresce e che pretende risposte. Il progresso sociale e economico non può essere raggiunto se l'autonomia del Parlamento non viene pienamente assicurata. «Ogni convinzione, ogni idea onestamente professata è un'energia. Ogni energia ha un valore, morale od economico, poco importa, ma un valore che non deve essere trascurato mai» (cit. da Di Muccio, I, 1987, 52). Il regolamento avrebbe dovuto essere lo strumento

5 Questa tesi avrà nel 1906 l'avallo autorevole di Santi Romano: ad ogni legislatura il regolamento «cessa allora di aver vita giuridica e, se, come di fatto suole avvenire, la nuova camera si sottopone al regolamento medesimo, ciò dipende da un suo atto di volontà, per lo più tacito, col quale essa si dà delle disposizioni perfettamente identiche nel loro contenuto alle antiche, ma che debbono considerarsi come emanate nel momento in cui essa comincia a funzionare uniformandosi di fatto a quelle disposizioni dimostra di volerle adottare» (246).

per valorizzare queste energie e per consentire lo svolgimento di un leale e libero confronto tra tutte le parti. Per questo Villa propose di istituire una Commissione che entro due giorni avrebbe dovuto presentare uno schema di regolamento. L'on. Pantano, a nome dell'Estrema Sinistra, accolse con favore le parole di Villa che aprivano una nuova stagione, pur manifestando dubbi sul diritto della Camera a darsi ad ogni legislatura il suo regolamento. Tale principio era dettato da circostanze eccezionali e non doveva costituire un precedente.

La Commissione, presieduta dallo stesso Villa e formata da molti dei protagonisti dei dibattiti e delle lotte parlamentari di fine secolo (da Ferri a Giolitti, da Di Rudinì a Pantano, da Chinaglia a Sacchi, da Biancheri a Zanardelli), assolse senza problemi il suo compito. Il valore dei commissari, la loro rappresentatività politica e il consenso diffuso portarono, il 1 luglio 1900, ad una rapidissima discussione e approvazione, dopo che il Presidente-relatore aveva di nuovo, con particolare enfasi, richiamato il principio della *tabula rasa*. Si era insomma lavorato guardando al futuro e non più al passato, ai dissidi recenti e ai motivi di discordia, anche se era evidente la presenza di norme generali che non potevano non figurare in un qualsiasi regolamento parlamentare.

Per questa ragione la Commissione mantenne tutte quelle disposizioni, e non erano poche, che avevano dato buona prova nel passato. Il nuovo regolamento, mediante il ricorso al voto limitato, offriva alla minoranza maggiori garanzie di rappresentatività nelle Commissioni e nelle Giunte, a cominciare dalla Giunta per le elezioni e dall'Ufficio di Presidenza. Si istituzionalizzava inoltre la presenza del Presidente dell'assemblea alla guida della Commissione per il regolamento. Inoltre le Commissioni dovevano riferire entro un termine stabilito, trascorso il quale ogni deputato poteva reclamare dalla Camera il rispetto dei tempi e diversamente si poteva discutere il provvedimento senza l'avviso della Commissione.

Il tema più dibattito fu ovviamente quello che riguardava l'ordine dei lavori parlamentari. Non v'è dubbio che la figura di Villa, che aveva molto tenuto a presentarsi come Presidente *super partes* – tanto più dopo gli esempi discutibili dei suoi immediati predecessori e lungo una tradizione che aveva molto stentato a *depoliticizzarne* la funzione (Ungari 1968, 70 ss.) –, rimise al centro della discussione, con atteggiamento "pretorio", la funzione presidenziale (cfr. Di Muccio 1979; Torre 2000; Iacometti 2001; la recente sintesi in Gianfrancesco 2007) come chiave di volta per il buon andamento dei lavori parlamentari.[6] La tesi che alla fine prevalse, condivisa dallo stesso Villa, individuava nelle attribuzioni "gene-

6 Per un'analisi particolarmente approfondita del ruolo "potenziato" del presidente d'assemblea visto come perno istituzionale per la risoluzione di conflitti "ostruzionistici" insorti tra maggioranza e minoranza, anche in prospettiva comparatistica, v. Chimienti 1920, II, 282–298.

rali" del Presidente una barriera sufficiente a contenere comportamenti e azioni contrari allo spirito dell'ordine parlamentare. Tuttavia, la Commissione aveva ritenuto di dover eliminare «quei mezzucci ai quali si poteva ricorrere per sottrarsi in qualche modo alle sue attribuzioni». Non era più permesso di ricorrere a votazioni nominali per qualunque questione, ma solo quando fosse necessario il voto di proposte complete; il Presidente aveva facoltà di negare l'accettazione e lo svolgimento di ordini del giorno, emendamenti o articoli aggiuntivi redatti in modo sconveniente, relativi ad argomenti affatto estranei all'oggetto della discussione; in tal senso gli oratori non potevano usare mezzi dilatori e il Presidente aveva la facoltà, dopo due richiami, di vietare la parola per il resto della seduta, salvo il diritto di appello alla Camera che decideva per alzata e seduta e senza che si potesse invocare la verifica del numero legale; inoltre il Presidente poteva, in caso di turbamento dell'ordine, dopo i richiami di rito, proporre all'aula l'esclusione per il resto della seduta e nei casi più gravi la censura con l'interdizione sino a otto giorni. Non venne invece accolta dalla Commissione la proposta ulteriore di deferire al potere discrezionale del Presidente, su domanda firmata da cinquanta deputati e con votazione a scrutinio segreto a maggioranza di due terzi, il modo di disciplinare il prosieguo della discussione nei casi di grave turbamento dei lavori. Il Presidente Villa giustificò tale diniego osservando come nel caso di tumulti si abbandonasse lo spazio di un'assemblea funzionante per entrare in una diversa situazione. «Ma, lo ripeto: come potete voi con un articolo regolare l'ostruzionismo violento?». Il Presidente non ha bisogno di ulteriori poteri discrezionali.[7] Come dirà Giolitti durante la discussione, «A mio avviso l'ostruzionismo è impossibile quando il Governo adopera la prudenza necessaria e non crea situazioni violente, e quando il Presidente ha sufficiente autorità e sa valersi dei mezzi che il regolamento mette a sua disposizione».

Il regolamento del 1 luglio 1900 pacificava gli animi, ristabiliva condizioni normali nell'attività parlamentare, sanciva la fine della crisi di fine secolo e apriva una nuova stagione. Il sentimento della "svolta" è ben presente ai protagonisti di questa vicenda e trova riscontro nella memorialistica. Era un regolamento, approvato in maniera regolare e definitivo,[8] che chiudeva la lunga fase della *duttile provvisorietà* e individuava nuovi equilibri, irrigidendo forse il diritto parlamentare e la sua stessa evoluzione (Manzella 1977, 50–51). Non bisogna

7 Sonnino nel 1899 affermò la convinzione che il combinato disposto degli artt. 13 e 77 del regolamento vigente potesse essere interpretato nel senso di attribuire al presidente «tutta quella superiore autorità discrezionale che è manifestamente indispensabile al disimpegno dell'arduo suo ufficio ...» (Sonnino 1972, I, 672).

8 Ugo Galeotti (1902, 6) osserva che «per la sua composizione, in parte frammentaria ed in parte improvvisata, presenta dove lacune, dove ripetizioni, dove spostamenti ...».

però dimenticare che per la prima volta il regolamento parlamentare – come "strumento di decisione" – aveva dovuto fronteggiare una crisi acutissima che aveva come posta in gioco quelle libertà costituzionali, quei *diritti di libertà politica* (Ferracciù 1900, 492), che in Italia avevano fragili radici. La forte "costituzionalizzazione" del regolamento Villa nasceva da questa profonda preoccupazione.

Una certa "retorica" della centralità del Parlamento aleggia nel dibattito che portò al nuovo regolamento e alcuni "segnali", in esso iscritti, lasciano solo intuire quel percorso di "democratizzazione regolata" che sarà la grande sfida dell'età giolittiana. Saranno piuttosto il decreto del 14 novembre 1901 n. 466 sulle attribuzioni del Consiglio dei ministri (Rotelli 1972; Merlini 1995); un uso non più "monarchico-esecutivo" della proroga e della chiusura delle sessioni, l'affermarsi, dal 1906, della convenzione della fiducia preventiva (Rossi 2001), l'introduzione del suffragio universale maschile a stabilire, assieme ad altri fattori, le condizioni istituzionali per uno sviluppo (pur provvisorio) del *continuum* corpo elettorale/rappresentanza parlamentare/governo/indirizzo politico (Montaldo 2001, 204 ss.).

Il regolamento del 1900 fu dunque il regolamento dell'età giolittiana e dell'ultima fase della crisi dello Stato liberale sino alle sostanziali modifiche del 1920–22, ma rappresenterà anche il "blocco regolamentare" destinato a funzionare da paradigma nella successiva "nuovissima" vicenda repubblicana. Ci si è ben interrogati sulle ragioni di questa continuità (Manzella 1977, 51; Caretti 2001, 587–588) e a me pare che la si possa considerare solo avendo ben presente l'assetto complessivo della costituzione materiale italiana nel primo ventennio del secolo. E non v'è dubbio che questa *longue durée* del regolamento del 1900/1922 abbia potenziato *ex post* il canone della "svolta" costituzionale.

Nel 1900 non tutte le voci però cantarono nello stesso coro. Agli opposti estremi troviamo Sidney Sonnino e Arturo Labriola. L'uomo politico toscano colse l'occasione della breve discussione sul testo del nuovo progetto per manifestare la sua preoccupazione: il regolamento, oltre ad assegnare alle minoranze una rappresentanza fuori misura negli Uffici di Presidenza e nelle Giunte, faceva un passo indietro nella disciplina dell'ostruzionismo che era un fenomeno ben diverso dalle singole, sporadiche, azioni dilatorie. «Prevedo – osservava – che purtroppo saremo presto da capo …». Ben diverso, come si può intuire, il giudizio di Labriola. A suo dire il nuovo regolamento rafforzando comunque il potere discrezionale del presidente e in generale le misure antiostruzionistiche poneva le basi per un rinvigorimento della linea conservatrice assicurata da Saracco e probabilmente dallo stesso Villa (Montaldo 2001, 203). «Così, dopo due anni di lotte e di proteste, l'Estrema accettava, contenta o rassegnata, la situazione contro la quale si era tanto fortemente ribellata» (Labriola 1975, 40).

6. La scienza giuridica di fronte ai "nuovi" fenomeni

La crisi di fine secolo vista attraverso la vicenda regolamentare offre, per la prima volta, alla scienza giuridica lo spunto per interrogarsi sul *fenomeno* ostruzionismo e più in generale sul problema dei regolamenti parlamentari. Un'originale figura di studioso del diritto costituzionale, di orientamento sociologico-giuridico [Cianferotti 1980, 200; Lanchester 2004], Antonio Ferracciù, professore a Sassari, Perugia e Siena, autore, a fine secolo, di saggi significativi sulle libertà di riunione e di associazione e su vari istituti parlamentari (regolamenti del Senato, inchiesta, incompatibilità, nomina dei senatori ecc.) pubblica nel 1901 la prima organica riflessione scientifica sulla dimensione giuridica e politico-costituzionale dell'ostruzionismo.[9] Si trattava, per l'Italia, di un fenomeno nuovo, ancor privo di una base scientifica e per questo «in balia completa alle inconsulte e parziali esagerazioni della letteratura giornalistica, le quali andarono determinando ognor più intorno ad esso una serie di giudizi oltremodo unilaterali, punto scientifici, utili solo in quanto le passioni della politica militante fossero meglio e nella più varia maniera riusciti a sollecitare» (Ferracciù 1901, 321; Levra 1975, 332–333, sulla battaglia giornalistica contro l'ostruzionismo).

L'autore, assai critico verso i "provvedimenti politici", riconduce l'analisi giuridica dell'ostruzionismo *proprio* alla natura del governo parlamentare come governo di gabinetto. Ci può essere il caso di una maggioranza *legale* che non è però maggioranza *reale*. In questo caso il dissidio può essere pericoloso e il capo dello Stato può sciogliere la Camera per interrogare direttamente il paese. Ma qual è il fondamento per l'esercizio dell'ostruzione? Ebbene, quando la Corona non intende avvalersi delle sue prerogative (nomina dei ministri e scioglimento della Camera), «laddove d'altro canto risulti chiaramente che il Gabinetto più non rispecchi le tendenze del paese, dal quale la maggioranza parlamentare, incerta o provvisoria o meccanica, siasi allontanata in guisa da non potere più oltre rappresentare l'organo principale della sua volontà politica, trova in tali condizioni giuridico fondamento l'esercizio dell'ostruzione da parte delle minoranze di opposizione, mercè il ricorso legale a tutti quei diritti regolamentari, onde possano procrastinarsi le risoluzioni della materia in discussione, per guisa da lasciar tempo alla volontà del paese di manifestarsi decisa ed energica ed imporsi nello Stato» (Ferracciù 1901, 326). Fedele ad una visione antiformalistica del fenomeno costituzionale Ferracciù scorge nell'ostruzionismo legittimo una «zona grigia» (Ferracciù 1905; Lanchester 1998) ma non antigiuridica (*contra* Santangelo Spoto 1908, 1113; Miceli 1913, 772; Nigro 1918, che parlerà di "teoria di anarchia"). Quando il Sovrano

9 Ippolito Santangelo Spoto nel 1908 continua ad affermare che «Sull'ostruzionismo una bibliografia non esiste» (1107).

«senza una vera necessità di Stato, si rifiuti di accogliere le manifestazioni *legittime* della volontà popolare, che in seno al Parlamento si concretino nelle aspirazioni di una minoranza organicamente compatta ed omogenea, ma soverchiata e schiacciata dalla brutalità di una maggioranza numerica, che non sia alimentata da virtù organica di principi e di tendenze ... In tale evenienza, la *ostruzione* altro non rappresenta che la *sostituzione legittima*, diremmo della coscienza della *vera rappresentanza nazionale* alla coscienza non vera che, nella nuova posizione intervenuta nel funzionamento del Governo parlamentare, di essa siasi fatta il Sovrano per rapporto all'eventuale esercizio della prerogativa accennata di sopra» (Ferracciù 1901, 327).

La coscienza popolare diventa in questo caso la fonte dell'ostruzionismo che assurge pertanto a *diritto*, proprio perché la *base giuridica* della forma di Governo rappresentativo risiede nel *consenso popolare*. È dunque un fenomeno eccezionale[10] ma non antigiuridico. Se il governo rappresentativo è una forza autonoma tra lo Stato e la società, il Parlamento deve sentire l'influenza costituzionalmente decisiva dell'opinione pubblica; deve essere in armonia col corpo sociale «e le *crisi* nel Governo di Gabinetto sono appunto preordinate a conservare inalterata tale armonia». Se dunque è la minoranza a meglio corrispondervi, essa ha il diritto di procrastinare le deliberazioni della maggioranza. L'ostruzionismo "giuridico" – nonostante alcuni dei pericoli segnalati da Sonnino – non è un fenomeno violento a cui ricorrono forze estremiste. Nel 1893, per esempio, l'ostruzione è esercitata dai conservatori britannici contro Gladstone favorevole alla *Home Rule* irlandese. Ferracciù riprende le categorie orlandiane di resistenza e di rivoluzione (Buratti 2006, 166 ss.) e inquadra l'ostruzionismo, a metà tra le due, come *forma speciale di resistenza collettiva legale*. Le preoccupazioni e le obiezioni di Sonnino non lo convincono: si possono introdurre freni e limitazioni ma ciò che conta davvero sono le condizioni politiche generali, il potere più o meno forte dell'opinione pubblica, la diversa configurazione delle parti politiche. Per Sonnino la comparazione – a cominciare dall'autorevole esperienza britannica e americana – mostra la piena legittimità e funzionalità di interventi volti a limitare, soprattutto in virtù del riconoscimento al Presidente d'assemblea di poteri incisivi, azioni ostruzionistiche e dilatorie, specie sul punto della riforma regolamentare (Sonnino 1972, I, 667 ss.). Per Ferracciù, invece, la comparazione rivela come una minoranza ostruzionistica finirà sempre per avere

10 L'autore lo definisce così: «quella forma speciale ed eccezionale di opposizione, che una minoranza parlamentare, entro i limiti assegnati dalle leggi e dai regolamenti costituzionali, esercita contro il gabinetto e la maggioranza, allorché per le condizioni speciali di composizione di quest'ultima e per la riluttanza del Sovrano a valersi delle prerogative più specialmente dirette alla eliminazione del conflitto, a quella riesca impossibile provocare una *crisi*, che sarebbe invece resa necessaria dalla mancata armonizzazione reale ed effettiva della volontà dell'Assemblea con la volontà nazionale» (328).

la meglio, nonostante i freni regolamentari, quando essa è volta a contrastare o ritardare l'approvazione di leggi o provvedimenti che non siano l'espressione della coscienza nazionale. È il caso degli *Home rulers* irlandesi (1881, contro il *Coercion bill* di Gladstone); nel 1890 dei socialisti, liberali e democratici belgi contro il tentativo dei cattolici conservatori di approvare una legge elettorale restrittiva e illiberale (l'opinione pubblica si dimostrò dalla parte della minoranza e il governo dovette dimettersi); nel 1897 dei parlamentari austriaci e tedeschi (Santangelo Spoto 1908, 1111); degli spagnoli nel 1899. Se dunque si rivelano inopportuni e illiberali i freni regolamentari permanenti (d'indole *politica* o *giuridica*) perché possono ostacolare ogni legittima opposizione, sono da ritenersi comunque preferibili i freni *preventivi* d'indole *morale*, a quelli *repressivi* d'indole *politica* o *giuridica*. La correttezza costituzionale è quindi indispensabile. «Non v'ha ormai chi non si mostri convinto che il buon andamento del Governo parlamentare si fonda essenzialmente su una serie di concessioni, di transazioni e di temperamenti reciprocamente riconosciuti, nell'esercizio di lor proprie funzioni, fra i diversi organi principali di cui si compone l'intero organismo statuale e tra le parti diverse eziandio di codesti organi» (Ferracciù 1901, 410). Governi e maggioranze, minoranza e opinione pubblica devono a tal fine cooperare *moralmente e preventivamente* per impedire forme estreme di resistenza. E ciò è possibile quando la maggioranza ha una vera *base d'idee*, è veramente *rappresentativa* e non è invece onnipotenza del numero. Questa analisi critica porta Ferracciù a "spiegare" la crisi di fine secolo attraverso un duplice fenomeno: un Parlamento troppo giovane perché potesse sviluppare gradatamente e con misura le proprie facoltà e che si sentì spesso nel diritto di usurpare le funzioni degli altri organi dello Stato. Ma ciò avrebbe finito paradossalmente col rafforzare oltremodo il Gabinetto.

> «Continua invero e assai funesta è l'invasione che il Gabinetto esercita da un pezzo, in Italia, in quelle attribuzioni e prerogative, specialmente col sistema dei decreti-legge, appoggiandosi all'autorità della Corona, cui giunge talora a scoprire ... Così stando le cose, è naturale che il Gabinetto, in questa marcia progressivamente illiberale, di conquista in conquista, siasi spinto fino al punto di presentare un progetto di riforme statutarie che, ben lungi dallo apparire sufficientemente giustificate da ragioni di politica necessità, significavano invece una evoluzione giuridica in senso inverso, in quanto appalesavano una forte tendenza reazionaria, contraddistinta specialmente dal carattere permanente che la rivestiva» [Ferracciù 1901, 413].

L'autore conclude sul grande male italiano: il distacco tra le istituzioni e la coscienza popolare che si esplica nell'opinione pubblica; ed è un male che coinvolge tanto la maggioranza che la minoranza, perché un'opinione viva, vigorosa, imperiosa, è il frutto della educazione e dei costumi politici del paese.

Di certo, la crisi di fine secolo coincise con un impegno significativo della dottrina italiana nell'esame e nella ricostruzione critica dei diversi aspetti del diritto parlamentare, andando oltre i modelli, inglese, francese e belga, che più avevano influenzato l'elaborazione del sistema nazionale. Nel 1906 Santi Romano affrontando la questione della natura dei regolamenti delle assemblee parlamentari osservava come il tema fosse stato poco trattato e per lo più superficialmente. Muovendo dalla negazione della qualità di norme giuridiche (concetto che poi supererà ampiamente, Cheli 1967, 13; Traversa 1968, 20), anche Romano scorgeva nei regolamenti un "luogo" di sperimentazione, consolidazione e oggettivazione di regole «in modo da renderle adatte ... ad essere assunte nel sistema delle vere norme giuridiche, sia pure consuetudinarie ... Ora ciò che le leggi non fanno, ed è bene che non facciano, può anche darsi che, talvolta, sia suscettibile di formare oggetto di regolamenti parlamentari» (1906, 257). Si può dire che questa conclusione è l'"anteprima" di quella prolusione pisana del 1909 che Romano dedicherà al tema "diceyano", intonso o giù di lì nella riflessione italiana, incentrato sul rapporto tra *Diritto e correttezza costituzionale*. I principi e le regole della *constitutional morality* offrono quella duttilità di cui un complesso sistema costituzionale parlamentare non può fare a meno. Tramite e filtro tra la *morale* e il *diritto*, la correttezza gli appariva quel fluido «senza che la lotta assumerebbe un carattere troppo aspro e non si eviterebbe la frode e l'insidia». Solo dopo la necessaria "sperimentazione" quei principi e quelle regole potevano aspirare a diventare consuetudini apportando elementi di nuova giovinezza alle istituzioni politiche e in particolare salvaguardando la "purezza" e l'autonomia del giuridico (*sub specie iuris constitutionis*) dalla spinta impetuosa e disordinata del sociale (cfr. Fioravanti 1981 (2001, I), 318 ss.).

> «Privata della sua impetuosità e impulsività occasionale e dei suoi fermenti non durevoli, essa può tradursi in norma di correttezza, consolidata maggiormente e, sopra tutto, saggiata dalla lunga pratica, può in seguito divenire consuetudine, ovvero ispirare l'attività del legislatore, ed entrare con l'una o l'altra veste nel tempio del diritto. Severo e solenne tempio, le cui porte invitatrici non vengono mai chiuse, e che attende sempre nuove pietre e nuove colonne, per ingrandirsi e rafforzarsi, ma che non sarà mai difeso abbastanza rigorosamente da tutto ciò che è eccessivamente caduco, o fragile, o volgare. Solo in tal modo il diritto potrà costituire il centro di gravità, intorno al quale, dando e ricevendo vita, potranno equilibrarsi le altre norme sociali in un armonico sistema» [Romano 1909, 285]

Forse Romano pensava anche all'esito della crisi di fine secolo e ai primi anni dell'età giolittiana. Ma il solenne tempio del grande giurista siciliano non era il Parlamento, bensì il diritto. La complessità del giuridico tuttavia doveva fare i conti, dopo la crisi di fine secolo, con un tempio meno severo e solenne segnato da disarmonie e questioni aperte: una politica costituzionale inquieta dinanzi ai dilemmi della democratizzazione del paese.

Bibliografia

Astraldi R., *Le norme regolamentari del Parlamento italiano. Storia, esposizione sistematica e confronti con regolamenti stranieri*, Roma 1932

Ballini P. L., *Le elezioni nella storia d'Italia dall'unità al fascismo. Profilo storico-statistico*, Bologna 1988

– (a cura di), *Sidney Sonnino e il suo tempo*, vol. I, Firenze 2000

Beaud O., *Ordre constitutionnel et ordre parlementaire. Une rélecture à partir de Santi Romano*, in *Droits*, 33, 2001, 73–95

Belardinelli M., *Un esperimento liberal-conservatore: i governi di Rudinì (1896–1898)*, Roma 1976

Bertolini G., *Ostruzionismo parlamentare*, in *Enciclopedia del diritto*, Milano 1981, vol. XXXI

Buratti A., *Dal diritto di resistenza al metodo democratico. Per una genealogia del principio di opposizione nello stato costituzionale*, Milano 2006

Cambria R., *Alle origini del Ministero Zanardelli-Giolitti. L'ordine e la libertà*, in *Nuova Rivista Storica*, LXXIII, 1–2, 1989, I parte, 67–132; LXXIII, 5–6, 1989, II parte, 609–656; LXXIV, 1–2, 1990, III parte, 25–100

Caretti P., *Le svolte della politica italiana nelle riforme dei regolamenti parlamentari*, in *Storia d'Italia*, Annali 17, *Il Parlamento*, a cura di L. Violante, Torino 2001, 583–611

Carusi P., *I governi Pelloux, Sonnino e le elezioni del giugno 1900*, in *Rassegna storica del Risorgimento*, XC, 3, 2003, 415–441

Cheli E., *Potere regolamentare e struttura costituzionale*, Milano 1962

Chimienti P., *Manuale di diritto costituzionale*, Roma 1920, 2 voll.

Cianferotti G., *Il pensiero di V. E. Orlando e la giuspubblicistica fra Ottocento e Novecento*, Milano 1980

Colao F., *Il principio di legalità nell'Italia di fine Ottocento tra «giustizia penale eccezionale» e «repressione necessaria e legale ... nel senso più retto e saviamente giuridico, il che vuol dire anche nel senso più liberale»*, in *Quaderni fiorentini per la storia del pensiero giuridico moderno*, 36, 2007, t. I, 699–742

Croce B., *Storia d'Italia dal 1871 al 1915*, a cura di G. Galasso, Milano 1991 (1927)

Di Muccio P., *Il Presidente della Camera dei deputati nel periodo statutario, 1848–1939*, in *Il Foro Amministrativo*, 9–11, 1979

– *Il regolamento della Camera dei deputati dal 1900 al 1922 (Una cronaca parlamentare)*, in *Bollettino di informazioni costituzionali e parlamentari*, nn. 1 e 2, 1987, 26–116; 67–125

Doglio M., *Pelloux, il ministero dell'interno e la crisi di fine secolo*, in *Nuova rivista storica*, LXI, 3–4, 1977, 307–332

Farini D., *Diario di fine secolo, 1896–1899*, a cura di E. Morelli, Roma 1962

Ferri E., *Battaglie parlamentari: una campagna ostruzionistica*, Milano 1899

– *Ostruzionismo*, Milano 1900

Ferracciù A., *La costituzione italiana nel 1899 e le libertà pubbliche in Italia*, Prolusione al corso libero di Storia delle Costituzioni, letta nella R. Università di Sassari addì 1 febbraio 1900, in *Il Filangieri*, XXV, 1900, 481–502

– *L'ostruzionismo parlamentare davanti al diritto ed alla politica costituzionale*, in *Il Filangieri*, XXVI, 1901, n. 5, 321–343; n. 6, 401–417

– *Il diritto costituzionale e le sue zone grigie (Note ed appunti metodologici)*, in *Annali della Facoltà di Giurisprudenza della R. Università di Perugia*, s. III, vol. III, 1905, 83–126, 145–220

Fioravanti M., *"Stato giuridico" e diritto costituzionale negli scritti giovanili di Santi Romano (1897–1909)*, ora in *La scienza del diritto pubblico. Dottrine dello Stato e della Costituzione tra Otto e Novecento*, Milano 2001, t. I

Galeotti U., *Il Regolamento della Camera dei deputati ...*, Roma 1902

Ghisalberti C., *Storia costituzionale d'Italia, 1848–1948*, Bari 1986

Gianfrancesco E., *Il ruolo dei Presidenti delle Camere tra soggetti politici e arbitri imparziali*, in *Le regole del diritto parlamentare nella dialettica tra maggioranza e opposizione*, a cura di E. Gianfrancesco e N. Lupo, Roma 2007, 11–29

Giolitti G., *Memorie della mia vita*, Milano 1967 (1922)

Guazzaloca G., *Fine secolo. Gli intellettuali italiani e inglesi e la crisi tra Otto e Novecento*, Bologna 2004

Haywood G. A., *Failure of a dream. Sidney Sonnino and the Rise and Fall of Liberal Party, 1847–1922*, Firenze 1999

Iacometti M., *I presidenti di Assemblea parlamentare*, Milano 2001

Isastia A. M., *L'ostruzionismo parlamentare di fine secolo*, in *Rassegna storica del Risorgimento*, LXIV, 4, 1977, 418–448

Labriola A., *Storia di dieci anni, 1899–1909*, Milano 1975 (1910)

Lanchester F., *Pensare lo Stato. I giuspubblicisti nell'Italia unitaria*, Roma, Bari 2004

Latini C., *Governare l'emergenza. Delega legislativa e pieni poteri in Italia tra Otto e Novecento*, Milano 2005

– *La sentenza "dei giornalisti". Repressione del dissenso e uso dei tribunali penali militari durante lo stato d'assedio nel 1898*, in *Inchiesta penale e pre-giudizio. Una riflessione interdisciplinare*, a cura di P. Marchetti, Napoli 2007, 243–277

Levra U., *Il colpo di stato della borghesia. La crisi politica di fine secolo in Italia, 1896/1900*, Milano 1975

– *Il Parlamento nella crisi di fine secolo*, in *Storia d'Italia*, Annali 17, *Il Parlamento*, cit., 163–195

Longi V., Stramacci M., *Il regolamento della Camera dei deputati illustrato con i lavori preparatori*, 1848–1968, Milano 1968

Malatesta M., *Introduzione*, a *La morte del re e la crisi di fine secolo*, in *Cheiron*, a. XVIII, n. 35–36, 2001, 43–83

Manacorda G., *Introduzione* a L. Pelloux, *Quelques souvenirs de ma vie*, Roma 1967

Mancini M., Galeotti U., *Norme ed usi del Parlamento italiano. Trattato pratico di diritto e procedura parlamentare*, Roma 1887

Manzella A., *Il Parlamento*, Bologna 1977

Maranini G., *Storia del potere in Italia, 1848–1967*, Firenze 1967

Marchetti P., *L'essere collettivo. L'emersione della nozione di collettivo nella scienza giuridica italiana tra contratto di lavoro e Stato sindacale*, Milano 2006

Martucci R., *Storia costituzionale italiana. Dallo Statuto albertino alla Repubblica (1848–2001)*, Roma 2002

Meccarelli M., *La questione dei decreti-legge tra dimensione fattuale e teorica: la sentenza della Corte di Cassazione di Roma del 20 febbraio 1900 riguardo al R. D. 22 giugno 1899 n. 227*, in *Historia costituciónal*, revista electrónica, http://hc.rediris.es

– *Le Corti di Cassazione nell'Italia unita. Profili sistematici e costituzionali della giurisdizione in una prospettiva comparata (1865–1923)*, Milano 2005

Merlini S., *Il governo costituzionale*, in *Storia dello Stato italiano dall'Unità a oggi*, a cura di R. Romanelli, Roma 1995, 3–72

Miceli V., *Principii di diritto costituzionale*, Milano 1913

Montaldo S., *Patria e affari. Tommaso Villa e la costruzione del consenso tra Unità e grande guerra*, Roma 1999

– *Il Parlamento e la società di massa (1900–1919)*, in *Storia d'Italia*, Annali 17, *Il Parlamento*, cit., 197–251

Negri G., *Il diritto parlamentare nel quadro del diritto pubblico*, in AA.VV., *Il regolamento della Camera dei deputati. Storia, istituti, procedure*, Roma 1968

Nieri R., *Costituzione e problemi sociali. Il pensiero politico di Sidney Sonnino*, Pisa 2000

Nigro O., *L'ostruzionismo parlamentare e i possibili rimedi: studio di diritto pubblico*, Torino 1918

Orlando V. E., *Teorica della legislazione e del governo. Corso del prof. V. E. Orlando, anno 1911–1912*, Roma 1912
Perticone G., *Il regime parlamentare nella storia dello Statuto albertino*, Roma 1960
Piretti M. S., *Le elezioni politiche in Italia dal 1848 a oggi*, Bari 1996
Rebuffa G., *Teoria e prassi del negoziato parlamentare tra conflitto e consociazione*, in *Storia d'Italia*, Annali 17, *Il Parlamento*, cit., 485–517
Romano S., *Sulla natura dei regolamenti delle Camere parlamentari*, in *Archivio giuridico*, LXXV, 1906, poi in *Scritti minori*, vol. I, *Diritto costituzionale*, Milano 1950, 213–258
– *Diritto e correttezza costituzionale*, in *Rivista di diritto pubblico*, 1909, poi in *Scritti minori*, cit., 271–285
Rossi F., *Saggio sul sistema politico dell'Italia liberale. Procedure fiduciarie e sistema dei partiti fra Otto e Novecento*, Soveria Mannelli 2001
Rotelli E., *La Presidenza del Consiglio dei Ministri: il problema del coordinamento dell'amministrazione centrale in Italia, 1848–1948*, Bologna 1972
Santangelo Spoto I., *Ostruzionismo*, in *Il Digesto italiano*, Torino 1904–1908, 1107–1114
Sbriccoli M., *Caratteri originari e tratti permanenti del sistema penale italiano (1860–1990)*, in *Storia d'Italia. Annali* 14, *Legge Diritto Giustizia*, a cura di L.Violante, Torino 1998, 485–551
Sonnino S., *I decreti-legge e il regolamento della Camera*, in *Scritti e discorsi extraparlamentari, 1870–1902*, a cura di B. F. Brown, Bari 1972, vol. I, 658–675
– *Diario 1866/1912*, vol. I, a cura di B. F. Brown, Bari 1972
Tanda A. P. (a cura e con una introduzione), *Le riforme parlamentari di fine secolo (1886–1900)*, Roma 1996
– *Lineamenti di storia dell'ostruzionismo italiano*, in *Storia d'Italia*, Annali 17, *Il Parlamento*, cit., 697–726
Themelly M., *Canonico Tancredi*, in *Dizionario biografico degli Italiani*, Roma 1975
Torre A., *Il magistrato dell'Assemblea. Saggio sui presidenti parlamentari*, Torino 2000
Traversa S., *La natura giuridica delle norme dei regolamenti parlamentari*, in AA.VV., *Il regolamento della Camera dei deputati*, cit.
Ungari P., *I precedenti storici del diritto parlamentare vigente in Italia*, *Ibid.*

«Personalmente contrario, giuridicamente favorevole». La "sentenza Mortara" e il voto politico alle donne (25 luglio 1906)

1. «Le donne hanno diritto al voto politico»

Nel marzo del 1906 nove maestre di Senigallia e una di Montemarciano, in provincia di Ancona, chiedono l'iscrizione nelle liste elettorali, *come se* fossero cittadini maschi in possesso dei requisiti richiesti dalla legge. Le Commissioni elettorali comunali, dopo qualche titubanza, decidono di inserire i loro nomi nelle liste. Il 28 maggio 1906 la Commissione elettorale provinciale, presieduta dall'avv. Luigi Capogrossi Colognesi,[1] conferma, con un voto espresso a maggioranza, l'iscrizione. Al procuratore del Re presso il Tribunale di Ancona non rimane che presentare ricorso avverso questa deliberazione adducendo argomenti ben sperimentati: le maestre citate non godono dei diritti politici di cui all'art. 1 della legge elettorale T.U. 28 marzo 1895 e, d'altra parte, «dalle disposizioni della stessa legge e dall'intenzione del legislatore risulta essere particolarmente sancita la loro incapacità all'esercizio del diritto elettorale».[2] Il 18 luglio il Procuratore pronuncia la sua requisitoria dopo aver ascoltato la relazione del Primo Presidente. Il giorno 25 la Corte respinge l'appello promosso dal Procuratore. «Così deciso e deliberato in Camera di Consiglio della Corte di Appello di Ancona addì 25 luglio 1906 intervenendo l'Ill.mo signor Comm. Lodovico Mortara Primo Presidente estensore ed i sig. Consiglieri Cav.

1 Su questo avvocato e poeta jesino, v. M. Ciani, *Storia dell'avvocatura anconitana, 1860–1980*, Introduzione di N. Sbano, Ancona 1999.

2 Il testo integrale della sentenza della Corte d'Appello di Ancona si può leggere in un foglio volante intitolato «Le donne hanno diritto al voto politico», stampato a Senigallia nel 1906 o anche nella rivista *La Corte di Ancona. Raccolta di giurisprudenza di tutte le autorità giudiziarie e amministrative*, IV, 1906, 326–334. Il foglio citato è pubblicato da F. Del Pozzo, *Ancona 1906: «Le donne hanno diritto al voto»*, in *Storia e problemi contemporanei*, 4, II, 1989, 109–125, per la citazione 112.

Giacomo Reggiani, Cav. Gioacchino De Rossi, Avv. Giovanni Sabatini, Cav. Carlo D'Angelantonio». La sentenza viene pubblicata tre giorni dopo.

Questa nuda e burocratica trafila procedimentale nulla aggiungerebbe ad una vicenda nazionale che si svolge, come vedremo, tra il 1905 e il 1907, se non fosse per l'esito "rivoluzionario" della sentenza e per la personalità assolutamente *sui generis* del suo estensore.

Da alcuni decenni il suffragismo era diventato una delle bandiere dispiegate dal movimento femminista europeo. Le aule parlamentari avevano cominciato, soprattutto con riguardo al voto amministrativo, a sentire, come di lontano, la flebile voce delle rivendicazioni femminili.[3] In Italia però solo nei primi anni del nuovo secolo la richiesta del voto politico divenne elemento fondamentale dell'emancipazionismo. Nel 1905 i Comitati pro-suffragio lanciarono una vigorosa campagna per invitare le donne munite dei requisiti di età (21 anni) e di cultura (maestre per lo più) a chiedere l'iscrizione nelle liste elettorali dei propri Comuni. Celebre è il manifesto di Maria Montessori (nata a Chiaravalle, cioé tra Senigallia ed Ancona) pubblicato nel febbraio 1906 ed è appena del marzo successivo la petizione al Parlamento con cui Anna Maria Mozzoni, la veterana del movimento femminista nazionale, seguita da altre sodali (tra cui la stessa Montessori), chiedeva il voto, benché solo per alcune "categorie" di donne.

Gaetano Mosca nel febbraio 1906 aveva commentato negativamente l'agitazione che si propagava come un fluido elettrico da una città all'altra (Mantova, Reggio Emilia, Imola, Milano, Caltanissetta, Palermo, Venezia ecc.),[4] giusto a seguito delle temerarie iscrizioni femminili nelle liste elettorali. Ciò avveniva, a detta di Mosca, nelle città dove i socialisti avevano la maggioranza e lo scopo vero non era quello di ottenere il voto bensì di orientare l'opinione pubblica nel senso della riforma elettorale.

È tuttavia assurdo, rileva il grande studioso, ammettere il principio che

> «una legge fondamentale dello Stato, e dirò di più, un principio generale del nostro diritto pubblico, possano essere di punto in bianco annullati per la semplice opera di qualche Commissione elettorale e sulla base di qualche mediocre e cavillosa argomentazione.»[5]

3 Per la ricostruzione della vicenda v. M. P. Bigaran, *Progetti e dibattiti parlamentari sul suffragio femminile: da Peruzzi a Giolitti*, in *Rivista di storia contemporanea*, XIV, 1, 1985, 50–82. Qualche riferimento in L. Martone, *L'incapacità della donna nel sistema giuridico dell'Italia liberale*, in *Democrazia e diritto*, 2–3, 1996, 535 ss.

4 Per un'analisi vedi I. De Bonis De Nobili, *Per il voto alle donne*, Roma 1909; I. Brunelli, *Il suffragio politico femminile ne' suoi criterî giuridici*, Torino 1910, 191 ss.

5 G. Mosca, *Le iscrizioni delle donne nelle liste elettorali politiche*, in *Corriere della Sera*, 27 febbraio 1906.

Più che per il sostegno delle forze politiche progressiste,[6] i comitati femminili si fanno largo un po' dappertutto sollecitando le Commissioni elettorali e imboccando la «via giudiziaria» secondo una strategia già collaudata in Gran Bretagna dopo il *Reform Act* del 1867 e in Francia sul finire del secolo.[7]

Nei primi anni del Novecento, tra le Marche e la Romagna, si intensifica, come nel resto d'Italia, negli ambienti socialisti, repubblicani e radicali il dibattito sul suffragio universale, pur con perduranti margini di ambiguità circa la natura e quindi la sorte della questione femminile. Non è per un caso, comunque, se le famose maestrine di Senigallia,[8] di estrazione sociale modesta,[9] riescono ad ottenere, pur processualmente «tutte contumaci», quello che altre donne avevano negli stessi mesi provato a chiedere – con esito sfavorevole – presso altre Corti d'Appello, da Firenze a Palermo, da Venezia a Cagliari.[10] La differenza fondamentale sta nel fatto che le nostre diplomate hanno avuto la fortuna (provvisoria) di trovare ascolto presso un magistrato come Lodovico Mortara. Si mettano assieme il nome e l'autorità scientifica dell'estensore e l'imprevisto[11] rigetto della richiesta del procuratore del Re per avere contezza dello scalpore, delle reazioni e dei commenti che la decisione, destinata a passare alla storia come "sentenza Mortara",[12] ebbe a provocare. Per qualche mese la

6 Su questo profilo v. soprattutto i lavori di Franca Pieroni Bortolotti, *Alle origini del movimento femminile in Italia, 1848–1892*, Torino 1975 (1963) e *Socialismo e questione femminile in Italia (1892–1922)*, Milano 1974.

7 Cfr. R. Romanelli, *Circa l'ammissibilità delle donne al suffragio politico nell'Italia liberale. Le sentenze pronunciate dalla magistratura nel 1905–1907*, in *Laboratorio di storia. Studi in onore di Claudio Pavone*, a cura di P. Pezzino e G. Ranzato, Milano, 1994, 132.

8 Con riferimento al genere femminile l'area di Senigallia risulta essere nel corso del XIX secolo tra le più scolarizzate delle Marche. Si veda al riguardo A. Palombarini, *Lo scandalo dell'alfabeto. Educazione e istruzione popolare femminile nelle Marche in età moderna*, in *Proposte e ricerche*, 50, 2003, 62–117 e Id., *Educazione e istruzione popolare femminile nelle Marche dell'Ottocento*, ivi, 51, 2003, 134–161. Più in generale, sui rapporti fra istruzione femminile e suffragismo, v. M. P. Bigaran, *Progetti e dibattiti*, cit.

9 F. Del Pozzo, *Ancona 1906*, cit., anche per l'analisi delle reazioni nella stampa locale.

10 Per l'analisi delle sentenze del periodo 1905–1907 v. *infra* par. 5.

11 L'avvocato Capogrossi Colognesi ebbe a dichiarare in un'intervista rilasciata a *Il Giornale d'Italia* (3 agosto 1906): «... non mi pareva facile che la Corte venisse a una conclusione così nuova e, direi quasi, rivoluzionaria. Era quasi un'interpretazione consuetudinaria quella che negava quel voto e io ritenevo che la Corte fosse contraria a un'interpretazione ardita e innovatrice».

12 Sul fatto che Mortara fosse superbamente convinto delle sue idee, soprattutto in qualità di magistrato giudicante, tanto da dare sovente una sua personale e fortissima impronta alle sentenze emesse dal Collegio, v. la testimonianza, non proprio benevola, dell'avvocato A. L. Ferreri, *Ricordi di un vecchio avvocato romano*, Roma 1942, 193 ss.

massima che lo stesso Mortara pubblicò assieme alla sentenza[13] fece discorrere e non poco l'opinione pubblica, ovvero che «Secondo la vigente legge elettorale politica, le donne che possiedono gli altri requisiti di capacità, hanno diritto di essere iscritte nelle liste elettorali». Insomma, nel luglio 1906, *de iure condito*, le donne hanno diritto al voto.[14]

2. Le tre "cattedre" di Mortara

Nato il 16 aprile 1855 a Mantova, figlio del rabbino maggiore – patriota e grande studioso di ebraismo – Lodovico Mortara[15] si era laureato a diciannove anni in procedura civile nella Facoltà di Giurisprudenza di Modena (4 luglio 1874), dopo essere stato allievo al Liceo di Roberto Ardigò. Intrapresa la professione di avvocato nella sua città, Lodovico rivela una non comune competenza che si traduce ben presto in saggi e collaborazioni a importanti riviste giuridiche e imprese editoriali. Nel 1882 consegue a Bologna, su consiglio del concittadino Enrico Ferri,[16] la libera docenza in procedura civile. Nel 1885 pubblica *Lo Stato moderno e la giustizia*, un saggio – come vedremo – di largo respiro, pieno di idee e di proposte di riforma. Nello stesso anno si presenta al concorso per la cattedra di diritto costituzionale di Modena, vinto dal venticinquenne Vittorio Emanuele Orlando. Il trentunenne Mortara invece la cattedra la vince a Pisa nel 1886 per diventare l'anno dopo ordinario a Catania, ma preferendo restare nella città toscana dove ebbe ad insegnare anche il diritto amministrativo e la scienza dell'amministrazione e dal 1888, allorché vi divenne ordinario, per dieci anni, il diritto costituzionale.

Nel 1888 esce il suo *Manuale della procedura civile* (nove edizioni sino al 1922); nel 1890 vedono la luce, per i tipi di Barbera, i due agili e fondamentali *Principii di procedura civile* e *Istituzioni di ordinamento giudiziario*, opere di grande successo

13 In *Giurisprudenza italiana*, III, 1906, col. 389–394.

14 Così, per esempio, l'avvocato A. Casertano, *Le donne hanno diritto al voto*, Napoli 1906.

15 Per il profilo biografico v. G. Mortara, *Appunti biografici su Lodovico Mortara*, in *Quaderni fiorentini per la storia del pensiero giuridico moderno*, 19, 1990, 107–113 e soprattutto i lavori, tra l'altro assai ricchi di notizie inedite, di F. Cipriani, *Le dimissioni del professore Mortara e i «germanisti» del preside Scialoja*, in *Rivista di diritto processuale*, XLV (II s.), 1990, 770–821; Id., *Storie di processualisti e di oligarchi. La procedura civile nel Regno d'Italia (1866–1936)*, Milano 1991, *passim*; Id., *Lodovico Mortara nella storia del diritto italiano*, in *Donne e diritti. Dalla sentenza Mortara del 1906 alla prima avvocata italiana*, a cura di N. Sbano, Bologna 2004, 35–63. Parimenti utile è la *Bibliografia di Lodovico Mortara*, a cura di F. Cipriani e N. Carrata, in *Quaderni fiorentini*, 19, 1990, 121–143.

16 Sulla duratura amicizia con Ferri, v. M. N. Miletti, *Un processo per la Terza Italia. Il codice di procedura penale del 1913, I, L'attesa*, Milano 2003, 345, nt. 74.

e longevità. Questi lavori sanciscono la crescente influenza di Mortara nel campo degli studi della procedura civile nonché la proverbiale capacità di incidere con i suoi interventi sullo stesso lavoro del legislatore impegnato – come spesso capita in Italia – in estenuanti tele di Penelope dal segno più o meno riformatore.[17] Tale influenza non può che accrescersi allorché il nostro giurista assume, assieme al collega pisano Carlo Francesco Gabba, la direzione della *Giurisprudenza italiana*. Vera e propria «rivista-persona», sarà per Mortara la «cattedra» che non abbandonerà mai e dalla quale per quarantacinque anni tirerà le fila del dibattito giurisprudenziale e scientifico.[18] Nel 1898 inizia a pubblicare il monumentale *Commentario del codice e delle leggi di procedura civile* e si trasferisce presso la Facoltà di Napoli.

Nel dicembre 1902 Lodovico abbandona il mondo accademico per diventare consigliere di Cassazione. Nell'ottobre 1905 lo troviamo Procuratore Generale presso la Corte d'appello di Cagliari (con uno stipendio annuo di 12 mila lire) e il 28 marzo 1906 è nominato Primo presidente della Corte d'Appello di Ancona. Dal 14 giugno 1907 è capo di gabinetto del guardasigilli Vittorio Emanuele Orlando. Nel gennaio 1908 fa ritorno a Roma come Avvocato generale presso la Cassazione, ma l'anno dopo è già Procuratore generale presso la Cassazione di Palermo dove rimane quasi due anni e nel frattempo è nominato senatore del Regno. Nel gennaio 1911 è a Firenze e nell'aprile a Roma sempre come Procuratore Generale. Risale al settembre 1915 la sua nomina a Primo Presidente della Corte romana di Cassazione.[19] Guardasigilli dal 23 giugno 1919 al 23 maggio 1920 nei due ministeri Nitti, Mortara viene «epurato» il 1 novembre 1923 e collocato, anticipatamente, a riposo. I suoi più recenti interventi in materia di sindacato giurisdizionale sui decreti-legge (1922) non dovevano risultare in sintonia con i disegni del nuovo esecutivo.[20] Il Regio decreto

17 Sul difficile riformismo tra '800 e '900 v. M. Taruffo, *La giustizia civile in Italia dal '700 a oggi*, Bologna 1980.

18 Sulla fondazione di questa importante rivista da parte del patriota genovese Filippo Bettini v. G. S. Pene Vidari, *Le origini di "Giurisprudenza italiana"*, in *Giurisprudenza italiana*, 2000, 3–11; Id., *Filippo Bettini e la sua raccolta di giurisprudenza*, in *Giuristi liguri dell'Ottocento*, a cura di G. B. Varnier, Genova 2001, 95–124. Sul periodo mortariano cfr. F. Cipriani, S. Mazzamuto, *La «Giurisprudenza Italiana» di Gabba e Mortara (1892–1936)*, in *Giurisprudenza italiana*, vol. CXLIV, parte IV, 1992, col. 497–502.

19 F. Cipriani, *Le dimissioni*, cit., 821.

20 Cfr. N. Picardi, *Lodovico Mortara, magistrato*, in *Giornata Lincea in ricordo di Lodovico Mortara*, Roma 1998, 92–95. Per una ricostruzione della teoria mortariana e della sua evoluzione (dal 1899 al 1922) in materia di decreti-legge v. M. Meccarelli, *La questione dei decreti-legge tra dimensione fattuale e teorica: la sentenza della Corte di cassazione di Roma del 20 febbraio 1900 riguardo al r.d. 22 giugno 1899 n. 227*, in *«Mit den Augen der Rechtsgeschichte: Rechtsfälle –*

3 maggio 1923 n. 1028[21] servì al governo Mussolini per assestare un duro colpo ai vertici potenziali della Cassazione unica. L'attività di avvocato e di consulente[22] lo accompagneranno sino alla morte avvenuta il 1 gennaio 1937.

Non si può certo dire che la vita professionale di Mortara sia stata povera di avvenimenti e di «fuori programma». Avvocato, soprattutto all'inizio e alla fine della sua vita, professore per sedici anni, alto magistrato per altri venti, «uomo politico» e per molti anni autentico *deus ex machina* di progetti e di interventi legislativi in materia di processo (civile e penale), di ordinamento giudiziario, ma anche in molti altri settori della legislazione italiana. Se in questa sede ci interessa anzitutto il Mortara magistrato in occasione della sentenza del 1906, non bisogna dimenticare che il passaggio in magistratura non fu tanto il coronamento di una «vocazione», quanto piuttosto una scelta, poi rivelatasi strategica, dettata da una serie di "disavventure" in ambito universitario. E alcune vicende accademico-concorsuali hanno rivestito un'importanza non secondaria sui successivi sviluppi della scienza processual-civilistica italiana determinando anche le condizioni per un graduale, seppur relativo, oblio dell'opera scientifica di Mortara. Nella memoria della disciplina si è perso o si è inteso perdere il significato della drastica decisione mortariana, ovvero di passare dalla cattedra universitaria che gl'assicurava ormai il predominio scientifico a quella del «modesto ufficio del consigliere di cassazione», come ebbe a dire Carnelutti nel 1947. Le testimonianze e le commemorazioni hanno molto insistito sulla «vocazione» di Mortara per la magistratura, per la «santità della funzione giudiziaria» (Calamandrei), per il bisogno di attuare la giustizia, per

(selbst)kritisch kommentiert», a cura di M. Luminati, U. Falk, M. Schmoeckel, Zürich 2008, 271–294.

21 Tale decreto dava facoltà al governo di collocare a riposo, anche d'ufficio, i primi presidenti e i procuratori generali delle Cassazioni. Sul collocamento a riposo di Mortara – diciotto mesi prima della naturale scadenza – cfr. F. Venturini, *Un «sindacato» di giudici da Giolitti a Mussolini: l'Associazione Generale fra i Magistrati Italiani, 1909–1926*, Bologna 1987, 253. Pietro Saraceno ha rilevato – in alcune sue note pubblicate da F. Cipriani in *Il primo presidente Mortara e i «due illustri rissanti»*, in *Rassegna di diritto civile*, XIV, 1993, 15–16 – come la sostituzione di Mortara con Mariano D'Amelio sia dovuta più che a ragioni politiche, ad una serie di fattori prevalentemente tecnici ed organizzativi. Mi sento però di condividere la tesi avanzata da Cipriani e volta a sottolineare, con argomentazioni pertinenti, i caratteri di quella che appare essere una vera e propria operazione politica. Questa lettura è adesso ulteriormente suffragata dallo studio di O. Abbamonte, *La politica invisibile. Corte di Cassazione e magistratura durante il Fascismo*, Milano 2003, 124 ss.

22 Consulente di altissimo livello come, per esempio, si può vedere dall'elenco dei *Pareri manoscritti di Lodovico Mortara (1924/1928)*, a cura di A. Mortara, in *Quaderni fiorentini*, 19, 1990, 115–120.

una prevalente dimensione empirica e fattuale nel suo modo di essere giurista (Carnelutti).[23] Anche Salvatore Satta che ha avuto il merito di togliere un po' della polvere accumulata sull'opera e sulla figura di Mortara e che ha pubblicato le *Pagine autobiografiche*[24] dello studioso mantovano, pur ponendosi il problema dell'improvviso mutamento di rotta, conferma nondimeno la tesi del «coronamento»:

> «Come abbiamo accennato, è impossibile scoprire il motivo per cui egli si decise al grave passo: ma la causa è evidente ... Con profondo intuito, Mortara si era reso conto che non la legge, ma il giudizio è al centro dell'esperienza, che l'azione non sta nel freddo testo elaborato in tempi magari lontani, ma nell'opera e nella sentenza del giudice. E giudice volle essere, con un'autorità e un coraggio che a noi appaiono mitici. Si badi bene: Mortara giudice ricomprende, nel lungo corso della sua carriera, il Mortara legislatore, il Mortara politico, il Mortara scienziato, poiché la sua opera scientifica è soprattutto opera di giudice.»[25]

L'autore de *Lo Stato moderno e la giustizia*, delle *Istituzioni di ordinamento giudiziario*, del primo volume del *Commentario* dedicato alla teoria della giurisdizione, il direttore della *Giurisprudenza italiana* non poteva non aspirare alla magistratura. Quello che senza dubbio era l'occhiale da sempre inforcato da Mortara per leggere il processo (la giustizia e l'ordinamento giudiziario nello Stato moderno-democratico) diventava così la *causa efficiens*.

Se molto sappiamo sulle ragioni *reali* e *apparenti* che spinsero Mortara ad abbandonare la carriera accademica (che per un giurista della sua taglia non poteva concludersi allora che negli augusti ambienti della Sapienza romana) lo dobbiamo alle ricerche minuziose e alle ipotesi interpretative di Franco Cipriani[26] che consentono di andare oltre le reticenti *Pagine autobiografiche* di Mortara e talune intuizioni (pur erronee) di Satta. Ricostruendo le vicende concorsuali e scientifiche dei primi anni del Novecento Cipriani mostra come non potesse

23 Su queste valutazioni v. F. Cipriani, *Le dimissioni*, cit., 774–776.

24 L. Mortara, *Pagine autobiografiche* (1933), in S. Satta, *Quaderni del diritto e del processo civile*, I, Padova 1969. Sulla riscoperta di Mortara v. G. Tesoriere, *Appunti per una storia della scienza del processo civile in Italia dall'unificazione ad oggi*, in *Rivista trimestrale di diritto e procedura civile*, XXVI, 1972, 1340 ss.

25 S. Satta, *Attualità di Lodovico Mortara*, in *Soliloqui e colloqui di un giurista*, Padova 1968, 470.

26 Oltre ai lavori citati, e al profilo generale pubblicato in questo volume, si debbono ricordare almeno i seguenti lavori di Cipriani: *Le "poche cose" e la lunga vita di Lodovico Mortara*, in *Quaderni Fiorentini*, 19, 1990, 85–105; *Il testamento e il «caro discepolo» del figlio del rabbino di Mantova (Un magistrato barese in casa Mortara)*, in *Rivista trimestrale di diritto e procedura civile*, XLV, 1991, 179–190; *Le peripezie di Carlo Lessona tra Mortara, Chiovenda e Calamandrei*, in *Rivista di diritto processuale*, vol. XLVI, 1991, 754–792; *Il codice di procedura civile tra gerarchi e processualisti*, Napoli 1992.

certo essere Chiovenda e la sua scuola (come pure sospettava Satta) nel 1902 a determinare Mortara nella sua scelta. Le cose andarono diversamente. Chiovenda si stava appena affacciando sulla scena e non poteva ancora essere quello che poi sarebbe diventato. Nel 1899, quando Enrico Galluppi si dimise dall'Università per diventare consigliere di Stato, lasciando vacante la cattedra romana di procedura civile ed ordinamento giudiziario, Mortara era all'apice della carriera e Chiovenda non era ancora abilitato. Se Mortara non poté compiere l'ultimo tratto di strada per entrare nel corpo accademico della Sapienza ciò fu dovuto soprattutto all'abile strategia accademica di Vittoria Scialoja, preside della Facoltà romana nonché riconosciuto caposcuola di una scienza romanistica rinvigoritasi alla fonte della pandettistica tedesca e ben consapevole di poter giocare un ruolo di primissimo piano in campo epistemologico. Cipriani ha ricostruito nei minimi dettagli la strategia[27] che nel giro di pochi anni avrebbe portato Chiovenda, laureatosi con Scialoja, all'ordinariato, il civilista Vincenzo Simoncelli (allievo del guardasigilli Gianturco e dello stesso Scialoja) «comandato» nell'agosto 1900 sulla cattedra romana di procedura (per coprire un «vuoto» pericoloso) e infine il grande giurista di Premosello dapprima sulla cattedra che lo stesso Mortara aveva ricoperto a Napoli (1905) eppoi, chiudendo il cerchio, sulla ambita cattedra romana (1907).

Subìto l'affronto, il primo dei «proceduristi» – uomo intransigente e consapevole del suo valore – preferisce diventare consigliere presso la Cassazione romana;[28] e in tal modo, secondo Cipriani, Mortara riesce comunque ad andare a Roma, non rinunciando al suo primato scientifico e alla sua vocazione di «legislatore». Se il 3 febbraio 1903 Chiovenda pronunciò la celebre prolusione su *L'azione nel sistema dei diritti* (destinata a diventare il «manifesto» della rifondata scienza italiana del processo),[29] nello stesso anno Mortara colse l'occasione – una sentenza della Corte d'Appello di Bologna in materia di esecuzione provvisoria e conseguente inibitoria – per attaccare con foga e sarcasmo un commento del «giovane professore» (nella fattispecie più capro espiatorio che principale bersaglio), inaugurando una stagione di confronto

27 Cfr. in particolare *Le dimissioni*, cit. e *Storie di processualisti e di oligarchi*, cit.

28 Le corti di Cassazione erano cinque: Torino, Firenze, Napoli, Palermo, Roma. La Cassazione romana investita sin dal 1875 di una giurisdizione esclusiva, «Fu elevata più ancora ...» per dignità eminente (L. Mortara, *Istituzioni di ordinamento giudiziario*, Firenze 1919, 3 ed., 219) con la legge 31 marzo 1877 n. 3761 che deferì alle Sezioni Unite la risoluzione dei conflitti di attribuzione fra autorità giudiziaria e autorità amministrativa nonché la cognizione dei ricorsi avverso le decisioni emesse da giurisdizioni speciali a motivo di incompetenza o eccesso di potere. Con la riforma zanardelliana la Cassazione romana acquistò la competenza esclusiva in materia penale (Legge 6 dicembre 1888 n. 5825).

29 Sulla prolusione v. F. Cipriani, *Storie di processualisti e di oligarchi*, cit., 91–92.

polemico che li avrebbe accompagnati per il resto dei loro giorni.[30] Nell'attacco di Mortara c'è già l'atteggiamento psicologico e scientifico-dottrinale che troverà eco, a distanza di trent'anni, nelle *Pagine autobiografiche*. Emerge quella «superba umiltà» còlta acutamente da Satta:[31] è la difesa dei «buoni proceduristi italiani» che pur «non saranno stati aquile d'ingegno né arche di erudizione; ma una mediocre dose di buon senso e di intelligenza, fra tutti insieme, è probabile che l'abbiano posseduta ...»; è la difesa di «poveri empirici discreditati» che tuttavia non ricorrono a formule astruse e inadatte, avendo peraltro «l'abitudine di parlare un linguaggio intelligibile a tutti ...». Al concettualista Chiovenda che «è salito di fresco sulle cattedre di procedura annunciandosi come il primo, e finora unico, cultore di questa scienza con metodo veramente scientifico ...», Mortara, uomo di pianura, ricorda come «... l'umile viandante che percorre passo a passo la bassa uniforme pianura, la vede e la conosce meglio assai dell'illustre alpinista il quale si degna scoprirla dalle sommità inaccessibili che il suo garretto conquistatore ha superate».[32]

L'avanzata dei «germanisti» e il grande rilievo assunto da Mortara nell'«ufficio del legislatore» ha finito per creare un fossato tra metodi e indirizzi dottrinali più largo di quanto sia poi stato nella realtà. È evidente che l'antitesi e il passaggio dall'approccio esegetico dei proceduristi al metodo sistematico dei «germanisti» finisce per rivelarsi alla fine una semplificazione.[33] Se Chiovenda, come dimostra ne *I principii di diritto processuale civile* del 1906, utilizza il sistema come canone ermeneutico, opera prevalentemente a livello della teoria generale del processo, ricostruendone in maniera mirabile istituti, concetti,

30 Sui rapporti, non certo facili, tra Mortara e Chiovenda v. la sintesi equilibrata di B. Cavallone, *«Preferisco il cattivo processo attuale» (Chiovenda, Mortara e il «progetto Orlando»)*, in *Rivista di diritto processuale*, XLIII (II s.), 1988, 1059, nt. 25, anche con riferimento alle opposte valutazioni di G. Tarello, *L'opera di Giuseppe Chiovenda nel crepuscolo dello Stato liberale* (1973), in *Dottrine del processo civile. Studi storici sulla formazione del diritto processuale civile*, Bologna 1989, che enfatizza oltremodo i motivi di disaccordo e di E.T. Liebman, *Storiografia giuridica «manipolata»*, in *Rivista di diritto processuale*, XXIX (II s.), 1974, 100–123, che replicando appassionatamente alle irriverenti (e non sempre convincenti) osservazioni tarelliane, ricorre alla propria testimonianza personale per ricordare i «rapporti di amicizia e di reciproca stima, della cui sincerità Tarello ha torto di dubitare» (104, in nota).

31 *Attualità di Lodovico Mortara*, cit., 469.

32 L. Mortara, *Qualche osservazione intorno ai poteri del giudice d'appello in tema di esecuzione provvisoria*, in *Giurisprudenza italiana*, vol. LV, 1903, Parte prima, sez. II, col. 469–474.

33 Come, più in generale, il cd. passaggio dall'esegesi al sistema, invero sofferto, e ricco di sfumature, forme ed espressioni. Cfr. P. Grossi, *«La scienza del diritto privato». Una rivista-progetto nella Firenze di fine secolo, 1893–1896*, Milano 1988, 15 ss.

categorie, principi, autonomizza scientificamente il basilare concetto di azione, Mortara – che con ispida ironia[34] molto gioca sul suo essere «umile viandante» ed esegeta – si rivela, a cominciare dal *Commentario*, scrittore tutt'altro che privo di spirito critico e di cospicue aperture.[35] È a lui, del resto, che si deve il precoce orientamento pubblicistico del processo civile e i suoi studi costituzionalistici, come vedremo, rivestono nella sua vastissima produzione una posizione affatto marginale. Se le differenze sono meno marcate di quanto le circostanze e certa *vis polemica* hanno finito per far apparire, è indubbio che la questione epistemologica del fenomeno processuale – come il ricordato dualismo fa già intravedere – non è stata rimossa e ha accompagnato, a ben vedere, l'intera vicenda della processualcivilistica italiana sino ai nostri giorni.[36]

3. Mortara e la magistratura

Se nel dicembre 1902 Mortara passa dalla cattedra napoletana alla Cassazione romana è perché due condizioni rendono la cosa possibile. Nel 1901 il Parlamento aveva approvato la legge 31 marzo n. 107 che riformava il procedimento sommario.[37] Mortara – che da anni aveva maturato una sua concezione al riguardo – fu chiamato dal guardasigilli ad elaborare quel regolamento attuativo (r.d. 31 agosto 1901, n. 413) che per un quarantennio resse poi le sorti del processo civile italiano. A seguito dell'ottima prova, il ministro Francesco Cocco-Ortu fece probabilmente intravedere al professore la possibilità di cambiar «mestiere».[38] È dunque il Mortara «legislatore» (e quindi il sommo «procedu-

34 L'alto magistrato De Notaristefani (1920) descriverà il carattere di Mortara «altero, imperioso, sprezzante». Cit. da F. Venturini, *Un «sindacato» di giudici*, cit., 211.

35 F. Cipriani, *Storie di processualisti e di oligarchi*, cit., 116 ss.; P. Grossi, *Scienza giuridica italiana. Un profilo storico, 1860–1950*, Milano 2000, 64 ss.; 88 ss., dove si colgono efficacemente i peculiari punti di vista dei due grandi giuristi.

36 Non è un caso che i lavori di Franco Cipriani abbiano suscitato diverse prese di posizione e un vivace dibattito. Ricordo, per es., i rilievi critici di L. Montesano, *«Storie» recenti su Mortara e Chiovenda e sul «romanesimo» di Vittorio Scialoja «concretato» dai fascisti*, in *Foro italiano*, 1991, V, col. 598–602 (con successiva breve replica di Cipriani); *«Culto della personalità», «prodotti organici» e «pappagalli lusingatori» di Chiovenda in un libro recente*, in *Rivista di diritto processuale*, XLIVII, 1992, 284–295; le argomentate osservazioni di E. Grasso, *Le «Storie» di Franco Cipriani, la conoscenza scientifica del processo e i metodi*, in *Quaderni fiorentini*, 23, 1994, 499–522; la replica di L. Montesano, *Fede in «verità metafisiche» e «assioma valutativo nella dottrina processualcivilistica italiana? (A proposito del saggio di Eduardo Grasso …)*, ivi, 25, 1996, 653–663, con riferimenti ad altre recensioni di Pera, Gambaro, Fazzalari; E. Grasso, *Note a Montesano*, ivi, 665–666.

37 Cfr. F. Cipriani, *Le dimissioni*, cit., 773.

38 Il biglietto inedito con il quale Mortara (4 dicembre 1902) si dichiara ben disposto ad accettare l'ufficio di consigliere della Corte di Cassazione di Roma è

rista») a conquistarsi presso il governo un credito cospicuo e tale da aprirgli agevolmente le porte della Cassazione romana.

Che avvocati e professori di diritto con alle spalle una determinata e variabile anzianità nell'esercizio della professione o nell'insegnamento fossero chiamati a coprire i posti vacanti in magistratura era tradizione antica, ma regolata con qualche organicità da Urbano Rattazzi nel 1859 (l. 13 novembre n. 3781). Tale facoltà era stata utilizzata ampiamente nel periodo 1860–1865 per formare in breve tempo un ordine giudiziario di provata fede risorgimentale e nazionale. L'art. 128 del r. d. 6 dicembre 1865 sull'ordinamento giudiziario riconfermava il meccanismo della nomina governativa prevedendo che in caso di vacanza in un grado della magistratura si potesse ovviare con magistrati del grado inferiore o con avvocati o professori di materie giuridiche con una anzianità di dodici anni.[39] Fu la legge Zanardelli-Cocco Ortu (8 giugno 1890 n. 6878) a prevedere una vera e propria carriera per i magistrati, introducendo il concorso per giovani laureati e limitando l'accesso di avvocati e professori ai soli gradi di presidente di tribunale, consigliere di corte d'appello e consigliere di cassazione e a quelli corrispondenti del pubblico ministero. Pochi, a dire il vero, furono i professori transitati dalla cattedra alle corti di cassazione. Per gl'anni dell'«informata» post-unitaria possiamo ricordare[40] due dei fondatori della «proceduristica» italiana, Matteo Pescatore[41] e Luigi Borsari,[42] nonché la singolare figura del civilista

pubblicato da F. Cipriani, *Storie di processualisti e di oligarchi*, cit., 86. Passano pochissimi giorni e il professore viene nominato consigliere di cassazione con r. d. 14 dicembre 1902. Vale forse la pena di ricordare che Mortara nel saggio del 1885 – *Lo Stato moderno e la giustizia* – si mostra perplesso circa l'efficacia del reclutamento «esterno» (v. l'edizione a cura di A. Pizzorusso, *Lo Stato moderno e la giustizia e altri saggi*, Napoli 1992, 140).

39 Cfr. P. Saraceno, *Alta magistratura e classe politica dalla integrazione alla separazione. Linee di una analisi socio-politica del personale dell'alta magistratura italiana dall'unità al fascismo*, Roma 1979, 65, nt. 39; Id., *Il reclutamento dei magistrati italiani dall'unità al 1890*, in *Università e professioni giuridiche in Europa nell'età liberale*, a cura di A. Mazzacane e C. Vano, Napoli 1994, 563–565; e la puntuale ricognizione storico-normativa di F. Cipriani, *La chiamata in Cassazione per meriti insigni (appunto per la bicamerale)*, in *Il Foro italiano*, V, 3, 1997, col. 57–68.

40 E. Piola-Caselli, *Magistratura*, in *Il Digesto italiano*, vol. XV, parte I, Torino, Utet, 1903–1907, 225, limita a tre, nel periodo compreso tra il 1866 e il 1895, il numero dei consiglieri di cassazione di provenienza accademica. Il numero è in realtà maggiore, anche se di poco.

41 Pescatore divenne consigliere a Milano (1860–1864), su suggerimento di Cavour e restò in magistratura sino al 1879, nel ruolo di avvocato generale presso la Cassazione romana. Cfr. G. Roddi, *Matteo Pescatore, giurista (1810–1879). La vita e l'opera*, Torino 1986, 17 ss.

42 Su questo giurista ferrarese vedi L. Scolari Sellerio Jesurum, s.v., in *Dizionario biografico degli Italiani*, Roma 1971, vol. XIII, 116–117.

maceratese Assuero Tartufari;[43] in un periodo successivo troviamo il penalista e filosofo Tancredi Canonico,[44] il giurista e poligrafo Pietro Ellero,[45] i due civilisti Emidio Pacifici-Mazzoni e Francesco Saverio Bianchi.[46]

Dopo il 1890 possiamo citare solo due nomi, da annoverare tra le maggiori personalità della scienza giuridica italiana dell'epoca: il processualpenalista Luigi Lucchini[47] e appunto il nostro Lodovico Mortara. Se dunque i magistrati ex-professori sono pochi per numero, nondimeno rappresentano un «fenomeno» di indubbio significato. Non bisogna dimenticare, affrontando più in generale il tema, che dagl'anni Sessanta in poi, pur in mezzo a trasformazioni di vario segno, le alte cariche della magistratura (Primi Presidenti e Procuratori generali delle quattro (poi cinque) corti di Cassazione e delle diciotto Corti di appello) sono state in prevalenza appannaggio di personale politico risorgimentale, con una presenza notevole di esuli meridionali. Questi «magistrati-politici», «nati dalle lotte del risorgimento nazionale, non solo popolarono gli alti gradi del corpo giudiziario all'indomani dell'unità, ma restarono spesso ancora per decenni ai vertici delle Corti di appello e di Cassazione ...».[48]

Molti presidenti della Cassazione sono o, come nel caso di Mortara, diventano poi senatori. Nelle ricerche condotte da Pasquale Saraceno l'immagine ricevuta della magistratura italiana, subordinata o peggio asservita all'esecutivo, viene, almeno in parte, ridimensionata,[49] se oltre al quadro ordinamentale si analizza la rete dei rapporti tra il personale giudiziario e gl'organi politico-costituzionali: ne risulta allora una magistratura che come «corpo», forte di una significativa

43 Nel febbraio 1861 il guardasigilli Cassinis lo nomina – mentre insegna diritto civile nell'Ateneo maceratese – sostituto procuratore presso la Corte d'Appello d'Ancona, sezione del Tribunale di Macerata (Biblioteca Comunale di Macerata, Fondo Manoscritti, 933, IV, nn. 16–17–18). Inizia una carriera che lo porterà a Perugia, Modena, Bologna (dove nel 1876 è consigliere di Corte d'Appello), per diventare infine, nel dicembre del 1878, consigliere della Cassazione romana (ivi, nn. 41–52).

44 Magistrato dal 1876, divenne Presidente della Corte di Cassazione di Firenze. Cfr. M. Themelly, s.v., in *Dizionario biografico degli Italiani*, Roma 1975, vol. XVIII, 171–175.

45 Nel 1880 fu nominato dal ministro di grazia e giustizia Villa consigliere presso la Corte di Cassazione di Roma. Nel 1889 diventerà consigliere di Stato. Cfr. C. Vano, s.v., in *Dizionario biografico degli Italiani*, Roma 1993, vol. XLII, 512–520 e G. D'Agostini, s.v., in *Dizionario biografico dei Consiglieri di Stato (1861–1948) (le prime 138 biografie)*, Roma 1994, 182–183.

46 Su Bianchi, consigliere di Cassazione prima a Torino poi a Roma (1880–1883), v. G. Mosca, s.v., in *Dizionario biografico degli Italiani*, Roma 1968, vol. X, 94–95.

47 Vedi *infra* nt. 51.

48 P. Saraceno, *Alta magistratura e classe politica*, cit., 64.

49 Per una analisi più ampia del problema rinvio in questo volume, *supra*, a *Il potere giudiziario come «potere politico»*, 427–445.

presenza in Parlamento e soprattutto in Senato,[50] riesce ad affermare una propria visione della politica giudiziaria e non manca di contribuire alla stessa composizione dei governi cui fornisce non pochi guardasigilli, segretari generali e sottosegretari. Lungo questi decenni a prevalere sarebbe quindi un certo grado di osmosi o integrazione fra personale politico e personale giudiziario.

Il passaggio in Cassazione di Mortara ricalca, per taluni aspetti, quello di Luigi Lucchini nominato consigliere di cassazione nel 1893[51] grazie ai legami che aveva stretto col guardasigilli Zanardelli nella sua funzione di «legislatore», essendone stato il principale collaboratore nei faticosi lavori di elaborazione e stesura del codice penale (nonché nella relazione d'accompagno).

> «Mortara e Lucchini impersonano un nuovo modello di alto magistrato italiano, per molti versi analogo a quello dei grandi magistrati politici della generazione del risorgimento, del quale anzi costituisce il seguito ideale. Come i loro predecessori infatti anche questi magistrati giungono alla carriera giudiziaria, direttamente in posizioni di rilievo, dopo aver dimostrato il loro valore in campo politico e culturale ed essi pure, anche dopo aver indossato la toga del giudice, non si sentono minimamente in dovere di astenersi dal partecipare in prima persona alla vita politica del paese ...»[52]

Il magistrato di estrazione «politica» è il nerbo della magistratura italiana sino alla fine del secolo quando cominciano a giungere in posizioni elevate i primi magistrati reclutati per concorso. Inizia allora il processo che porterà alla piena affermazione di un nuovo modello di magistrato-burocrate che da uditore arriva, per carriera interna, sino ai gradi più elevati.[53] È un segnale di trasformazione, questo, che avvierebbe la separazione tra alta magistratura e classe politica.

50 Per talune conferme, v. A. Meniconi, *I burocrati nel Senato regio*, in *L'istituzione parlamentare nel XIX secolo. Una prospettiva comparata*, a cura di A. G. Manca e W. Brauneder, Bologna, Berlin 2000, 361–389.

51 Lucchini fu procuratore generale a Firenze e poi componente della seconda sezione penale della Corte di Cassazione di Roma proprio negl'anni della crisi di fine secolo. Cfr. M. Sbriccoli, *Il diritto penale liberale. La «Rivista Penale» di Luigi Lucchini, 1874–1900*, in *Quaderni fiorentini*, 16, 1987, 105–183. Sul ruolo di Lucchini nell'ambito degli orientamenti giurisprudenziali della Cassazione romana v. R. Cambria, *Alle origini del ministero Zanardelli-Giolitti. L'ordine e la libertà*, in *Nuova rivista storica*, I–II, 1989, 67–132; V–VI, 1989, 609–656 e soprattutto M. Malatesta, *Magistrati, politici e diritti umani in Italia e in Francia. Un'ipotesi di ricerca*, in *Cheiron*, 35–36, 2001, *La morte del re e la crisi di fine secolo*, 43–82. È forse da notare che anche Mortara agl'inizi degl'anni Ottanta era stato consigliere comunale a Mantova, su posizioni democratiche e "zanardelliane".

52 P. Saraceno, *Alta magistratura e classe politica*, cit., 68.

53 Senza però dimenticare la persistenza e la rilevanza di figure di magistrati che costruiscono, spesso con singolare rapidità, la loro carriera all'ombra di gabinetti e di uffici ministeriali, commissioni extragiudiziarie ed altro. Ne dà adesso ampia e documentata notizia – tra l'età giolittiana e l'avvento del fascismo – O. Abbamonte, *La politica invisibile*, cit.

Mortara magistrato vive, se così si può dire, in una fase di transizione. È, per certi versi, un «magistrato-politico» (anche se bisognerà precisare, nello specifico, il senso di questa espressione), ma al contempo deve confrontarsi con i cambiamenti che proprio in età giolittiana investono la magistratura italiana nel suo insieme. Su questo piano la scelta di entrare a far parte dell'ordine giudiziario, contrassegnata com'è da un'intricata serie di ragioni, si concilia però in maniera perfetta (tanto da farla apparire poi frutto di una «vocazione») con una concezione della giurisdizione e del processo maturata sin dagl'anni giovanili. È stato osservato giustamente che i migliori scritti sul problema dell'organizzazione della giustizia e sul tema inesauribile della «riforma giudiziaria» provengono, nel periodo esaminato, da coloro che hanno coltivato assieme la processualistica e gli studi di diritto costituzionale, secondo un tracciato che il legame accademico tra procedura civile e ordinamento giudiziario rendeva possibile e forse auspicabile.[54] Si possono fare, per es., i nomi di Pescatore, di Bonasi, ma è indubbio che nessuno ha saputo coniugare al pari di Mortara il problema del fondamento epistemologico del processo con quello della giustizia e del suo ordinamento («diritto giudiziario»). Opere come *Lo Stato moderno e la giustizia* (1885), le *Istituzioni di ordinamento giudiziario* (1890), il primo volume del *Commentario* lo dimostrano in maniera solare. Questo dato di fondo è stato còlto con accenti e finalità spesso diversi dai grandi processualisti del Novecento in un quadro di riflessione non sempre rispettoso del momento storico nel quale si inserisce la concezione mortariana.[55] Calamandrei ebbe a dire, con formula efficace ma forzata, che Mortara era arrivato allo studio del processo civile «non salendovi dal diritto privato, ma scendendovi dal diritto costituzionale; cercando in esso non lo strumento per far vincere le cause ai litiganti, ma il mezzo per attuare lo scopo più augusto dello Stato, che è la giustizia».[56] Anche Carnelutti accentuò la lettura dell'opera di Mortara scorgendone il fondatore del filone pubblicistico «copioso nella scuola e perfino impetuoso nella legge italiana ...».[57] Salvatore Satta, vent'anni dopo, ha raffigurato, in una luce più aderente alla *realtà* di Mortara, l'intimo significato di una concezione che è lontana da «prologhi in cielo»: il processo è il divenire

54 Cfr. F. A. Genovese, *Introduzione allo studio dell'ordinamento giudiziario*, Urbino, Edizione l'asterisco, 1996, 20–21, 109.

55 Cfr. G. Tarello, *La riforma processuale in Italia nel primo quarto del secolo. Per uno studio della genesi dottrinale e ideologica del vigente codice italiano di procedura civile* (1977), in *Dottrine del processo civile. Studi storici sulla formazione del diritto processuale civile*, cit., 52.

56 P. Calamandrei, *Lodovico Mortara* (1937), in *Opere giuridiche*, a cura di M. Cappelletti, Napoli, Morano, 1985, vol. X, 158–159.

57 F. Carnelutti, *Scuola italiana del processo*, in *Rivista di diritto processuale*, II, 1947, 244.

dell'ordinamento ed è il giudice che fa vivere la norma. Non meraviglia che Satta ricordi una delle pagine più belle di Mortara, tratta dal primo volume del *Commentario* e resa dalla celebre formula secondo cui «mentre la legge rappresenta la statica del diritto obbiettivo, la giurisprudenza ne costituisce la dinamica».[58]

In tal senso Mortara è da annoverare tra i pochi studiosi dell'età liberale che hanno posto l'accento sulla funzione giurisdizionale come ufficio diretto di sovranità, cioè «vera e alta funzione politica». Nel panorama italiano è forse Attilio Brunialti – non a caso un costituzionalista – l'altro autore che più e approfonditamente ha riflettuto (anche prima di Mortara) sugli strati meno superficiali degli assetti di potere, sulle radici storiche della rilevanza *politica* della giustizia.[59] Mortara è, a mio avviso, «magistrato-politico» soprattutto in questa accezione, avendo piena, matura e costante coscienza[60] del nesso inscindibile tra Stato moderno e apparati di giustizia, specialmente nella prospettiva dello Stato democratico.[61] Ciò lo sollecitava – sin dagli anni Ottanta – ad una

58 *Commentario del Codice e delle Leggi di Procedura civile. Vol. I. Teoria e sistema della giurisdizione civile*, Milano, 2 ed. (s. d.), 76, n. 70.

59 Sul differente esito della visione di Brunialti cfr. *supra* in questo volume *Il potere giudiziario come «potere politico»*, 427 ss.

60 Pizzorusso individua nella «onestà intellettuale» di Mortara, più che nel suo insegnamento pisano di diritto costituzionale e del diritto amministrativo, il presupposto della sua costante ricerca di un'organizzazione giudiziaria efficiente e portatrice di valori di giustizia (*Prefazione* a L. Mortara, *Lo Stato moderno e la giustizia*, cit., 7–8). È lo stesso Mortara ad affermare in *La lotta per l'uguaglianza. Prolusione al Corso di diritto costituzionale fatto per incarico nell'Università di Pisa dal professore Lodovico Mortara ordinario di procedura civile e ord. Giudiziario nell'anno 1888–89*, Pisa 1889 (questa importante e poco nota prolusione è stata ripubblicata nei *Quaderni fiorentini*, 19, 1990, 145–162) di essere lusingato di potersi «giovare degli studi con affetto costante sempre coltivati nel campo di questa scienza ch'io reputo strettamente collegata con quella del diritto giudiziario a cui la mia attività più specialmente è dedicata. Imperocché io stimo che a trattare scientificamente del diritto giudiziario non basti la fredda analisi degli atti di procedura e delle loro forme, o la discussione arida delle fattispecie contenziose; ma si debba risalire alle ragioni somme della giustizia, le quali non possono essere conosciute se non portando indagini accurate e profonde su le discipline del diritto pubblico, dove hanno radice l'essere e lo agire della giustizia, di questa aspirazione e meta suprema della civile convivenza» (cito dall'originale, 3–4).

61 Il discorso pronunziato il 9 dicembre 1912 nell'Assemblea generale della Corte di cassazione di Roma per l'inaugurazione dell'anno giudiziario e intitolato *La giustizia nello Stato democratico* si congiunge idealmente con il volume del 1885 *Lo Stato moderno e la giustizia*, ora ripubblicati nella bella edizione curata da A. Pizzorusso, *Lo Stato moderno e la giustizia e altri saggi*, cit. Nello scritto *Intorno ai problemi dell'ordinamento giudiziario* (1917) è lo stesso Mortara a richiamare questa sua costante preoccupazione: «Dalla prima giovinezza, ormai lontana, la mia meditazione è stata dedicata con particolare affetto all'esame dei problemi,

"rilettura" dell'art. 68 dello Statuto alla luce della teoria del giudiziario quale potere emanante dalla sovranità popolare e in evidente contrasto con la concezione «esecutiva» più tradizionale. Nella sua visione riformatrice la magistratura non può accontentarsi dell'indipendenza; altra cosa è «... *l'autonomia organica* della magistratura come potere dello Stato ... tutta propria del reggimento democratico».[62] L'ingresso nell'alta magistratura non poteva non incidere su talune sue posizioni. Il giurista mantovano rafforza quella «predisposizione all'ufficio del legislatore» che nel 1902 aveva reso possibile il suo ingresso nell'ordine giudiziario. Da magistrato Mortara gioca un ruolo da protagonista in gran parte delle imprese riformatrici e ciò per più di un ventennio, basti pensare ai progetti Orlando del 1908–1909 (quando Mortara è il capo di gabinetto del guardasigilli),[63] alla sfortunata riforma del processo civile del 1912 (giudice unico nei processi civili di prima istanza),[64] al codice di procedura penale dello stesso anno,[65] alle riforme del 1919–1920, alla presidenza tra il 1924 e il 1926 della Sottocommissione C per la riforma del codice di procedura civile.[66]

Non stupisce neppure che Mortara diventi, dopo le iniziali titubanze, un punto di riferimento per l'Associazione Generale fra i magistrati italiani.[67] Nel 1912 è membro del Consiglio Superiore della Magistratura e dopo la travagliata

che già allora udivo dichiarare urgenti, relativi all'ordinamento giudiziario. Ben presto mi resi conto della difficoltà essenziale di codesti problemi: si tratta di determinare e stabilire la posizione e l'assetto della funzione giudiziaria nel moderno regime democratico» (ivi, 197).

62 L.Mortara, *Lo Stato moderno e la giustizia*, cit., 65.

63 Cfr. B. Cavallone, *«Preferisco il cattivo processo attuale» (Chiovenda, Mortara e il «progetto Orlando»)*, cit. V. anche G. Tarello, *La riforma processuale in Italia*, cit., 64 ss.

64 Sulla repentina abrogazione di questa misura e sul ruolo di Mortara, v. F. Venturini, *Un «sindacato» di giudici*, cit., 144 ss.; F. Cipriani, *Storie di processualisti e di oligarchi*, cit., 171 ss. Per le riforme processuali in età giolittiana v. anche V. Colesanti, *Mortara e le riforme processuali. La prima fase (1901–1912)*, in *Giornata Lincea*, cit., 49–64. Sulle proteste del mondo forense, v. F. Tacchi, *Gli avvocati italiani dall'Unità alla Repubblica*, Bologna 2002, 346 ss.

65 Su questo codice si veda adesso l'importante lavoro di M. N. Miletti, *Un processo per la Terza Italia. Il codice di procedura penale del 1913*, cit., con numerosi ragguagli sul ruolo fondamentale di Mortara nella commissione senatoriale, nel dibattito in aula come relatore, nella commissione di coordinamento relativi al progetto di codice Finocchiaro-Aprile. È da sottolineare, inoltre, l'attestazione di un Mortara assai vicino, sul terreno della penalistica, al metodo del positivismo scientifico (ivi, 236) e ad una visione coerente coi temi e le preoccupazioni della «difesa sociale» (ivi, 240, 344–345).

66 Sul Mortara riformatore v., per più ampi riferimenti, F. Cipriani, *Le dimissioni*, cit., 777–780; Id., *Storie di processualisti e di oligarchi*, cit.

67 Su questa vicenda v. F. Venturini, *Un «sindacato» di giudici*, cit., *passim*.

nomina a Primo Presidente della Cassazione di Roma nel 1915,[68] Mortara esercitò una notevole influenza sul progetto associativo della magistratura, non solo per la sua posizione di vertice dell'ordine giudiziario, ma anche in virtù della sua risalente riflessione in tema di riforme giudiziarie e di funzione politica della magistratura. Il giovane Mortara che nel 1885 parlava di «guarentigie e freni per l'autonomia organica della magistratura», non ignorava i pericoli di un'autonomia priva di raccordi istituzionali con gli altri poteri dello Stato. La critica che nel 1912 fa degli effetti prodotti dalle leggi del 1890 e 1907 segnala la preoccupazione per un sistema di autogoverno che a suo dire allontanava e isolava il corpo giudiziario dal popolo e dai fini dello Stato democratico.[69] Di fronte ai problemi della magistratura italiana in età giolittiana – problemi vecchi e nuovi – Mortara disegna, pur non senza dubbi e perplessità, un modello di magistrato «elitario», il più possibile affrancato da lacci burocratici, condizionamenti economici e meccanismi gerarchici, per potersi dedicare alla sua alta funzione forte di un profilo tecnico-professionale di prim'ordine.[70]

68 È Ferdinando Martini nel suo Diario a svelare i retroscena della nomina di Mortara, caldeggiata da Nitti ma osteggiata dal Consiglio dei ministri (10 luglio 1915) malgrado la presidenza di Vittorio Emanuele Orlando. Il 21 luglio 1915 Martini, ministro delle Colonie, annota: «Vi nominammo presidente della Cassazione di Roma il Mortara; nomina che fu e sarà oggetto di molta discussione» (F. Martini, *Diario 1914–1918*, a cura di G. de Rosa, Milano 1966, 486–487, 542). L'art. 2 del r. d. 14 novembre 1901 n. 466 attribuiva al Consiglio dei ministri la nomina degli uffici direttivi delle Corti di Cassazione e delle Corti di Appello. Mortara successe, il 23 settembre 1915, al senatore Oronzo Quarta, collocato a riposo per limiti di età.

69 L. Mortara, *La giustizia nello Stato democratico*, cit., 189 ss. Sul problema v. le equilibrate osservazioni di G. Verde, *Vero e falso sull'autogoverno dei giudici secondo Mortara*, in *Quaderni fiorentini*, 22, 1993, 689–698.

70 L'esito più maturo e complesso del «progetto» mortariano di riforma dell'ordinamento giudiziario è da identificare col disegno di legge presentato in qualità di guardasigilli alla Camera dei deputati il 16 dicembre 1919, ritirato poi nel marzo del 1920 e mai trasmesso al Senato (pubblicato assieme alla relazione nella *Giurisprudenza italiana*, vol. LXXII, 1920, parte IV, col. 1–40). Su questo progetto e sull'evoluzione della concezione mortariana v., per la ricostruzione generale del dibattito, P. Marovelli, *L'indipendenza e l'autonomia della magistratura italiana dal 1848 al 1923*, Milano 1967, 247 ss. Nello specifico v. soprattutto F. Venturini, *Un «sindacato» di giudici*, cit., 213 ss.; le pagine nelle quali F. A. Genovese, *Introduzione allo studio dell'ordinamento giudiziario*, cit., mette a confronto il disegno proposto da Piola-Caselli nel 1907 (*Magistratura*, cit.) e il progetto Mortara del 1919–20. Giovanni Tarello non coglie il significato e la complessità storico-istituzionale della proposta riformatrice di Mortara allorché la definisce di segno autoritario e tale addirittura da prefigurare una scelta di politica del diritto «in funzione di un particolare disegno politico che sarebbe stato fatto proprio, nei primi suoi governi, dal fascismo al potere» (*La riforma processuale in Italia*, cit., 89). Sui problemi della magistratura agl'inizi del Novecento v. anche P. Saraceno,

4. «Un monumento di sottigliezza e di audacia»

Se mi sono soffermato su taluni degli elementi più direttamente riconducibili al magistrato e al «legislatore» è anche per meglio comprendere, in una cornice più ampia e ricca di riferimenti, la famosa sentenza anconetana del 1906. Se la presenza del grande giurista nella città marchigiana è certamente casuale, è assai probabile però che l'ambiente ed il clima politico e culturale in quel contesto territoriale abbiano giocato un qualche ruolo, diremo concomitante, a cominciare, ovviamente, dalle rivendicazioni delle maestre di Senigallia.[71] Mortara restò ad Ancona per poco più di un anno (sino alla nomina, il 14 giugno 1907, a capo di gabinetto dell'amico guardasigilli Vittorio Emanuele Orlando) e, per di più, durante questo breve periodo comunicò per dieci volte al ministro di grazia e giustizia di doversi recare a Roma per partecipare ai lavori di diverse commissioni legislative.[72] Mortara si era trasferito nei pressi di Ancona, in una villa di Falconara. Non sappiamo se e quanto la sua figura di illustre professore e di alto magistrato[73] abbia lasciato tracce nella vita anconetana del tempo e

Retribuzioni e condizioni economiche dei magistrati italiani dall'Unità alla grande guerra, in *I magistrati italiani dall'Unità al fascismo*, a cura di P. Saraceno, Roma 1988, 241–256.

71 È da ricordare inoltre che ad Ancona nel 1905 una laureata in giurisprudenza aveva presentato ricorso in Corte d'Appello contro il rifiuto del Consiglio dell'Ordine degli avvocati di iscriverla nell'albo dei praticanti procuratori. Sul punto v. R. Canosa, *Il giudice e la donna. Cento anni di sentenze sulla condizione femminile in Italia*, Milano 1978, 32–33.

72 F. Cipriani, *Storie di processualisti e di oligarchi*, cit., 127.

73 In occasione del Centenario del giuramento di Mortara in Cassazione (24 gennaio 1903), la Corte suprema e la Cassa Nazionale di Previdenza e Assistenza forense hanno pubblicato una cospicua raccolta di sentenze rese da Mortara in qualità di estensore, e tra queste alcune delle sentenze anconetane a partire dal maggio 1906 (in tema di appello, colpa civile, competenza, giudizio di rinvio, impiegati dello Stato, ipoteca, procedimento civile, servitù, vendita). È una pubblicazione meritoria che conferma la necessità di analizzare e studiare le sentenze (evidenziata per tempo da Gino Gorla: cfr. almeno la raccolta di saggi *Diritto comparato e diritto comune europeo*, Milano, 1981) per penetrare le tecniche ma anche le convinzioni radicate e i valori di fondo di cui un determinato corpo giudiziario nel suo insieme e i singoli protagonisti sono portatori. Per un'attenta riflessione su questa prospettiva di analisi v. O. Abbamonte, *Le ragioni del decidere. Per un possibile studio della giurisprudenza e della mentalità del giudice*, in *Sociologia del diritto*, 2, 2001, 5–44; Id., *La politica invisibile*, cit. Queste osservazioni, se hanno una valenza generale, acquistano però un significato particolare riguardo all'opera di Mortara. Piero Calamandrei ha sottolineato l'importanza del magistero mortariano sull'insieme della giurisprudenza italiana: «... il documento più insigne della sua attività è stata la giurisprudenza, sulla quale ha dominato dall'alto, diffondendo luce fino alle ultime ramificazioni della magistratura, il faro della sua dottrina» (*Lodovico Mortara*, cit., 156–157).

soprattutto nella memoria di un ceto forense ricco – in una città che contava allora quarantamila abitanti – di personalità dall'innegabile profilo nazionale.[74] Sappiamo invece che la sentenza vi ebbe grande risalto, così come nel resto del paese.

Pochi si aspettavano una decisione di quel tenore. Gaetano Mosca confesserà poi di aver sbagliato previsione, ovvero che nessuna corte avrebbe accolto i ricorsi.[75] Vittorio Emanuele Orlando sottolineò subito il significato e il potenziale effetto di una sentenza che:

> «per la natura e il grado di quella giurisdizione e per l'altissimo valore dell'estensore, giustamente stimato come uno dei più forti giuristi dell'Italia contemporanea, basta, pel solo fatto della sua esistenza, ad affermare che la questione, per diritto vigente, può farsi.»[76]

Tutti i commentatori sottolinearono «l'autorità scientifica di chi la redasse ...», e molti restarono colpiti dall'uso degli argomenti addotti, dal ricorso ad una critica serrata e al «rigore severo di una stretta logica giuridica»[77] o, per utilizzare l'espressione di un anonimo scrittore, ad un «monumento di sottigliezza e di audacia»,[78] producendo quella che Alessandro Stoppato definirà negativamente una «sentenza di tendenza».[79]

5. *Infirmitas sexus* e consuetudine interpretativa

La Corte di Ancona intende subito sgombrare il campo affermando di voler esaminare e quindi decidere la questione «colla scorta dei criterî puramente giuridici ed esegetici, senza divagare in discussioni teoriche pertinenti alla scienza ed all'ufficio del legislatore».[80] La decisione riconosce l'esistenza del diritto di voto attraverso un ragionamento serrato, asciutto, senza ricorrere agli *obiter dicta* e agl'argomenti extra-giuridici che contrassegnano le sentenze delle altre Corti.

74 Cfr. Nicola Sbano, *Introduzione*, in *Donne e diritti*, cit., ne offre esemplificazioni significative: si pensi ai nomi di Arturo Vecchini o di Luigi Dari.

75 G. Mosca, *Contro una sentenza*, in *Corriere della sera*, 26 agosto 1906.

76 V. E. Orlando, in *Il Foro italiano*, XXXI, 1906, col. 1060. Queste idee erano state già pubblicate in *La Tribuna*, a. XXIV, giovedì 2 agosto 1906, n. 213, *Le donne hanno diritto al voto politico?*

77 I. Brunelli, *Il suffragio politico femminile*, cit., 231.

78 *Il voto politico alle donne*, in *La provincia di Ferrara*, a. IV, n. 174, martedì 7 agosto 1906.

79 A. Stoppato, *A proposito del voto politico alle donne*, in *Giornale d'Italia*, a. VI, n. 222, 10 agosto 1906.

80 Corte d'Appello di Ancona, 25 luglio 1906, in *Giurisprudenza italiana*, vol. LVIII, 1906, col. 390.

Questo *incipit* – che enfatizza un approccio ermeneutico conforme al metodo giuridico-tradizionale – permette al presidente di partire «all'attacco», per censurare un atteggiamento consolidato. Come sappiamo la sentenza del 25 luglio fa seguito ad una serie di pronunce di altri corti italiane tutte concordi nel negare alle ricorrenti l'iscrizione nelle liste elettorali. Un *leitmotiv* risulta dalla riproposizione, in tutte le forme possibili e immaginabili, dell'argomento dell'*infirmitas sexus*. Il riferimento a profili extra-giuridici in tema di diritti delle donne era in realtà un patrimonio della giurisprudenza italiana, come, per es., dimostra un'altra celebre sentenza, quella della Corte di Cassazione di Torino del 18 aprile 1884 che confermò il divieto di iscrizione all'ordine degli avvocati richiesta e in un primo tempo ottenuta da Lidia Poët, laureata in giurisprudenza (1881).[81] L'*infirmitas sexus* diventava un «contenitore» universale nel quale far rientrare ogni cosa, l'incapacità di autonomia e di giudizio, il decoro, l'ignoranza, la natura «privata», domestica, della condizione femminile e via dicendo.

> «La condizione del sesso maschile – aveva scritto Attilio Brunialti rappresentando un sentire comune – e la conseguente esclusione delle donne è di tutti i sistemi, e di tutte le leggi elettorali: le poche timide eccezioni confermano una regola, indarno contrastata anche nelle società dove la donna ha la stessa educazione degli uomini, gode di eguale libertà e indipendenza sociale, ed affronta in pari condizioni le lotte per la vita.»[82]

> «La meno elevata loro educazione, la maggiore potenza del sentimento religioso, la soggezione domestica, la loro inferiorità nella legislazione civile di molti Stati, sono difficoltà che il tempo vince e si possono dire, in gran parte, scomparse; ma giammai potranno scomparire le difficoltà fisiologiche e mentali, che determinano tutto un diverso indirizzo di occupazioni e di idee, e come rendono la donna meglio adatta a molti uffici familiari e sociali, così ci fanno ritenere che la politica, come il servizio militare, siano esclusivo dominio dell'uomo.»[83]

La Corte di Appello di Firenze fece nel 1906 un uso esemplare di questo canone. Come conseguenza del voto politico riconosciuto alle donne – e argomentando *ab absurdo* – si darebbe «... al mondo civile il nuovo bizzarro spettacolo di un governo di donne con quanto prestigio, decoro ed utilità del nostro paese, è

81 Su questa vicenda v. R. Canosa, *Il giudice e la donna*, cit., 26 ss. e soprattutto F. Tacchi, *Gli avvocati italiani*, cit., 262 ss.

82 A. Brunialti, *Guida allo studio del diritto costituzionale*, Torino, 1882.

83 Id., *Il voto politico alla donna*, in *Nuova Antologia*, XIV, 1879, 220 ss. Sulla stessa linea L. Palma, *Del potere elettorale negli stati liberi*, Milano, 1869, 211 ss.; G. Padelletti, *Teoria delle elezioni politiche*, Napoli 1879; V. E. Orlando, *La riforma elettorale*, Milano 1883. Per una puntuale ricostruzione della dottrina orlandiana in tema di suffragio e dell'insieme degli orientamenti più influenti (Bluntschli, Palma, ecc.) v. G. Cianferotti, *Il pensiero di V. E. Orlando e la giuspubblicistica italiana fra Ottocento e Novecento*, Milano 1980, 51 ss.

facile ad ognuno d'immaginarsi».[84] L'esclusione, invece, è il risultato di una consuetudine interpretativa delle Corti che si fonda su una tradizione consolidata e richiama alcune massime del diritto romano.[85]

L'iscrizione delle ricorrenti nelle liste elettorali da parte delle Commissioni provinciali traeva fondamento dall'art. 24 dello Statuto:

> «Tutti i regnicoli, qualunque sia il loro titolo e grado, sono eguali dinanzi alla legge. Tutti godono egualmente i diritti civili e politici, e sono ammissibili alle cariche civili e militari, salve le eccezioni determinate dalle leggi.»

La Corte anconetana ritiene che la dizione «regnicoli» ricomprenda i cittadini dei due sessi, trovando ulteriore conferma nell'art. 25 dello Statuto laddove si dice che «Essi» – i regnicoli – «contribuiscono indistintamente, nella proporzione dei loro averi, ai carichi dello Stato», visto che non si poteva dubitare del fatto che le donne fossero contribuenti al pari degl'uomini. Se il pronome ricomprendeva entrambi i sessi, identico principio doveva valere anche per l'art. 24, ché, altrimenti, il legislatore per non essere a tal punto incoerente, avrebbe dovuto espressamente escludere le donne.

Tra i critici di Mortara, l'amico Vittorio Emanuele Orlando ritiene che il «sistema della sentenza» assegni all'art. 24 una portata eccessiva. Se Orlando richiama lo spirito dello statualismo liberale, le sentenze delle altre corti e molti commentatori ricorrono piuttosto ad interpretazioni «storiche» dell'art. 24, ovvero che l'intenzione non era di eliminare le diseguaglianze tra i sessi, ma abolire le tracce di privilegi odiosi, sia nei rapporti tra le classi che nell'ambito delle interdizioni religiose.[86]

84 Corte d'Appello di Firenze, 14 agosto 1906, in *Giurisprudenza italiana*, vol. LVIII, 1906, col. 383. La Corte più avanti osserva che l'interpretazione «... che ora si vorrebbe far prevalere e che contraddice alle nostre tradizioni, ai nostri costumi ed alle stesse condizioni fisiologiche della donna che *ob infirmitatem sexus* non ha né può avere quella robustezza di carattere, quella energia fisica e mentale necessaria per disimpegnare come l'uomo le pubbliche cariche, deve essere senza altro respinta». La Corte d'Appello di Torino, 21 giugno 1907, ivi, vol. LIX, 1907, col. 364, adduce come argomento il fatto che «la nostra legislazione conservò un carattere prevalentemente maschile».

85 È ancora il caso della sentenza della corte fiorentina che argomenta il diniego affermando che «... sempre così fu praticato fin dai primi tempi del nostro risorgimento e così fin da quando insieme con lo statuto vige la legge elettorale politica, che in questa parte, nonostante le varie modificazioni subìte, non venne mai cambiata, in modo che trova congrua applicazione alla specie la regola d'ermeneutica legale contenuta nella l. 37, Dig. *De legibus*, I, 3 «si de interpretatione legis quaeritur, in primis inspiciendum est quo iure civitatis retro in eiusmodi casibus usa fuisset: optima est legum interpres consuetudo», regola che perfettamente collima con l'insegnamento di Paolo: «minime sunt mutanda quae interpretationem certam habuerunt» (14 agosto 1906, cit., col. 384).

86 In tal senso per es. Corte di Appello di Brescia, 10 ottobre 1906, in *Foro italiano*,

6. Tra diritti fondamentali e diritti pubblici subiettivi

L'estensore della sentenza anconetana, tuttavia, è perfettamente consapevole del fatto che l'interpretazione dell'art. 24 si trascina dietro un problema di fondamentale importanza. Non è esatto sostenere che le donne non godono dei diritti politici, poiché i *diritti fondamentali* (libertà individuale, inviolabilità del domicilio, libertà di manifestare le proprie opinioni per mezzo della stampa, il diritto di riunirsi pacificamente e senz'armi, artt. 26, 27, 28, 32 dello Statuto), sono certamente comuni ai due sessi.

> «L'errore della proposizione anzidetta ha origine dal falso supposto che siano diritti politici soltanto quelli che si estrinsecano nell'esercizio di pubbliche funzioni o nell'investitura di cariche pubbliche. Il diritto elettorale è a sua volta un diritto politico, il quale alla stregua delle premesse considerazioni spetta a tutti i regnicoli ...»[87]

Questo è uno dei passaggi più importanti della sentenza Mortara. L'illustre giurista fa riferimento ai *diritti fondamentali*, ovvero ad una categoria non accolta, se non in misura marginale, dalla dottrina e dalla giurisprudenza. La posizione di Orlando – come si può capire – è mirabilmente riassuntiva del problema.

> «Queste dichiarazioni generalissime, che si leggono nelle carte statutarie, hanno un valore storico altissimo e solenne, ma un valore esegetico quasi nullo. E la ragione non la diremo all'eminente giurista, che scrisse l'annotata sentenza. Dal lato esegetico, una disposizione legislativa ha valore non in quanto è pura astrazione, ma in quanto è norma concreta, capace d'immediate e reali applicazioni.»[88]

Lo Statuto – come gran parte delle costituzioni del XIX secolo – è caratterizzato da una *normatività debole* e ciò si riflette anzitutto sul riconoscimento e sulla garanzia dei diritti e delle libertà.[89] Resta quindi difficile se non impossibile configurarli come diritti fondamentali dotati di uno status giuridico-costituzionale distinto e peculiare. L'operazione mortariana va in una direzione che la dottrina e la giurisprudenza o avversano o stentano a riconoscere. In fondo la

vol. XXXI, 1906, col. 1316, con commento del primo presidente Giuseppe Favini; Corte d'Appello di Napoli, 5 novembre 1906. Cfr. anche G. Mosca, *Contro una sentenza*, cit.

87 Corte d'Appello di Ancona, 25 luglio 1906, cit., col. 390.

88 V. E. Orlando, in *Il Foro italiano*, cit., col. 1060.

89 Cfr., per i riferimenti essenziali, S. Rodotà, *Le libertà e i diritti*, in *Storia dello Stato italiano dall'Unità a oggi*, a cura di R. Romanelli, Roma 1995, 301 ss.; M. Fioravanti, *Le dottrine dello Stato e della costituzione*, ivi, 408 ss.; P. Pombeni, *La rappresentanza politica*, ivi, 73 ss.; B. Clavero, *Lo spazio dei diritti e la posizione dei giudici tra costituzione e codice*, in *Materiali per una storia della cultura giuridica*, 1, 1989, 95–129.

sentenza *inclusiva* del 1906 individua la linea esterna di una frontiera che lascia fuori dalla cittadella (sempre più assediata) dello Stato liberale di diritto chi per ragioni di genere, censo e capacità non corrisponde ad un preciso modello di cittadinanza politica. Se l'idea costituzionale dei diritti è geneticamente povera, la *normatività forte* è semmai quella realizzata dalla legge dello Stato, la norma concreta e immediatamente «applicativa» che limita, individua, garantisce e disciplina i diritti. Mortara è un giurista del suo tempo e sa bene che il successo della sua operazione passa attraverso l'interpretazione della legge, una volta ricondotta ad unità la distinzione tra diritti civili e diritti di libertà. Orlando non è da meno quando precisa che lo stesso art. 24 dello Statuto «ha potuto ben dire che tutti godono egualmente dei diritti politici: ma certo è che, a prescindere dalla questione femminile, dei maschi stessi quelli ammessi al voto politico rappresentano pur sempre una scarsissima minoranza».[90]

I diritti di libertà – prosegue Orlando – afferiscono alla personalità umana e il loro riconoscimento «non dipende dalle *forme di governo*, ma dagli *stadii di civiltà*». Il diritto elettorale, come pure i diritti per mezzo dei quali si concorre attivamente alla rappresentanza dello Stato sovrano, rivestono invece altra natura. Per Orlando – sulla scia di un autore straordinariamente influente, Kaspar Johann Bluntschli – la rappresentanza non è da considerare un'espressione di autonomia della società: il diritto elettorale è insieme diritto e funzione, ragione ed esercizio di qualcosa che spetta, ma pur sempre una funzione conferita dallo Stato per i fini generali dell'organismo politico.[91]

Per dimostrare tali principi il giurista siciliano non ritiene necessario[92] richiamare le teorie dei diritti pubblici subiettivi elaborate dai giuristi tedeschi, da Gerber a Jellinek; è sufficiente in realtà vedere come il legislatore

> «avverte sicuramente la natura dei rapporti fondamentali, ch'egli è chiamato a regolare; il legislatore, intendo, rappresentato non già da alcune centinaia di deputati e di senatori, ma da tutta la coscienza e da tutto il sentimento giuridico di un popolo, nelle complesse e indefinite manifestazioni della vita di esso.»

Chi dubita che il minorenne – ovvero il soggetto che si trova nella condizione più vicina a quella della donna – sia escluso da tutti i diritti *politici*, pur godendo di tutti i diritti di libertà? E lo straniero non gode di quest'ultimi, senza poter disporre dei primi?

90 V. E. Orlando, in *Il Foro italiano*, cit., col. 1062.
91 V. E. Orlando, *La riforma elettorale*, cit., 52.
92 Afferma ironicamente: «... io potrei atterrire il lettore citando quelle teoriche sui diritti pubblici subiettivi e su la loro classificazione, intorno a cui, formidabilmente armati di sottili e nebulose distinzioni, si sono esercitati e si esercitano i giuristi tedeschi ...» (in *Il Foro italiano*, cit., col. 1063).

Il richiamo orlandiano alle teorie dei diritti pubblici subiettivi[93] e alla teoria dell'atto legislativo come atto «esterno»[94] – questioni cruciali nella configurazione del rapporto tra legge, libertà e «diritti individuali» nell'ambito di una determinata concezione dello Stato liberale – rivela per converso l'«originalità» di Mortara. Nel dibattito dottrinale e politico di quegl'anni, più direttamente connesso alla questione del voto politico delle donne, ritorna spesso il riferimento alla categoria e alla classificazione, tipicamente dogmatica, dei diritti pubblici subiettivi, discussa e «adattata» al contesto italiano, con rilievi e ampliamenti, da Orlando, Santi Romano, Oreste Ranelletti, Luigi Rossi.[95] Contrariamente a quanto sosteneva l'onorevole Mirabelli,[96] il riferimento alla

93 Sulla messa a punto della teorica orlandiana negl'anni della sentenza Mortara è interessante *Diritto costituzionale. Diritto pubblico interno*. Lezioni dette dal Prof. V. E. Orlando, redatte da A. Campobassi, anno 1905–1906, Roma 1906. Come è noto, Orlando è anche il prefatore della traduzione italiana della seconda ed. tedesca del *Sistema dei diritti pubblici subiettivi* di Georg Jellinek, Milano 1912 (la prefazione, *Sulla teoria dei «diritti pubblici subiettivi» di Jellinek*, è stata poi raccolta in *Diritto pubblico generale. Scritti varii (1881–1940) coordinati in sistema*, Milano 1954, 275–285).

94 Il diritto non dipende da una mera manifestazione di volontà. Applicando l'insegnamento savignyano, Orlando ritiene il diritto una «manifestazione organica della vita dei popoli». Il diritto, che vive nella profondità e nella dimensione temporale, è *popolare* o non è; esso è obiettivamente frutto di invenzione, di scoperta, mai di "creazione". Di conseguenza anche la legge in senso proprio non è che una *forma*, poiché il *contenuto* «non è opera di alcuna assemblea, né di alcun altro *potere* politico» (per es. *Studi giuridici sul governo parlamentare*, in *Archivio giuridico*, XXXVI, 1886, poi in *Diritto pubblico generale*, cit., 377; *Teorica della legislazione e del governo, anno 1911–1912*, Roma 1912, 175 ss.).

95 Per una ricognizione delle diverse posizioni dottrinali v. S. A. Di Pisa, *Le dottrine più recenti intorno ai diritti pubblici subbiettivi*, Palermo 1917. Sull'influenza del pensiero di Jellinek nel dibattito italiano, v. M. La Torre, *Jellinek e il sistema dei diritti pubblici soggettivi: il paradiso dei diritti di libertà*, in *Materiali per una storia della cultura giuridica*, XII, 1, 1982, 79–116; Id., *Disavventure del diritto soggettivo*, Milano 1996; G. Valera, *Coercizione e potere: storia, diritti pubblici soggettivi e poteri dello Stato nel pensiero di Georg Jellinek*, in *Saperi della borghesia e storia dei concetti fra Otto e Novecento*, a cura di R. Gherardi, G. Gozzi, Bologna 1995, 53 ss. Per una visione d'assieme G. Oestreich, *Storia dei diritti umani e delle libertà fondamentali*, a cura di Gustavo Gozzi, Roma, Bari 2001. Per l'individuazione dei temi fondamentali della giuspubblicistica italiana tra Otto e Novecento, v. in particolare F. Tessitore, *Crisi e trasformazioni dello Stato. Ricerche sul pensiero giuspubblicistico italiano tra Otto e Novecento*, Milano 1988, 3 ed.; M. Fioravanti, *Giuristi e costituzione politica nell'Ottocento tedesco*, Milano 1979; G. Cianferotti, *La crisi dello Stato liberale nella giuspubblicistica italiana del primo Novecento*, in *I giuristi e la crisi dello Stato liberale in Italia fra Otto e Novecento*, Napoli 1986, 157–170; M. Fioravanti, *La scienza del diritto pubblico. Dottrine dello Stato e della costituzione tra Otto e Novecento*, Milano 2001, t. I.

96 «Oramai la stessa distinzione del Sieyès e del dottrinarismo francese di Hello, di Guizot e di De Broglie, tra diritti *politici* e *civili*, surta per reazione alla causa

teoria del diritto elettorale come diritto subiettivo e quindi come funzione pubblica garantita dallo Stato e assegnata ai più capaci per via di designazione ha orientato anche le proposte dottrinali che cercavano di riconoscere, entro una certa misura, il diritto di voto alle donne. Ignazio Brunelli, per esempio, è tra coloro che applicano la logica del suffragio-funzione ad alcune categorie di donne,[97] così come, del resto, avevano fatto Anna Maria Mozzoni e le sue sodali con la petizione al Parlamento nel 1906. Il carattere «rivoluzionario» della sentenza Mortara risiede proprio nella ricerca di autonomia da quel paradigma[98] predominante che ha accompagnato l'evoluzione dei sistemi politico-costituzionali tra Otto e Novecento, segnando in profondità la lunga e difficile transizione verso i regimi democratici.

7. L'eccezione e la regola

Tutti godono i diritti civili e politici, fatte salve le eccezioni determinate dalle leggi, recita l'art. 24 dello Statuto. «Tali eccezioni – si legge nella sentenza anconetana – devono essere espressamente stabilite e non è permesso indurle dal silenzio della legge, il quale anzi, secondo la regola della buona ermeneutica, la esclude».[99] Dall'art. 24 dello Statuto la *querelle* interpretativa si sposta sul terreno delle «norme concrete». Mentre la legge comunale e provinciale[100] escludeva espressamente le donne dall'elettorato attivo e passivo, la legge elettorale politica non conteneva una disposizione analoga. Infatti l'art. 1 del r. d. 28 marzo 1895 n. 83[101] stabiliva che:

> «Per essere elettore è richiesto il concorso delle seguenti condizioni: 1) di godere per nascita, o per origine, dei diritti civili e politici del regno; 2) di aver compiuto il ventunesimo anno di età; 3) di sapere leggere e scrivere; 4) di avere uno degli altri requisiti negli articoli seguenti 2 e 3.»[102]

democratica, non resiste più al martello della scienza ed alla voce della Storia» (cit. da I. De Bonis De Nobili, *Per il voto alle donne*, cit., 186–187).

97 «... quelle la cui attività, uscendo dalla famiglia, pesa sui rapporti statali e sociali». Ignazio Brunelli, *de iure condendo*, prefigura le diverse categorie di donne ammissibili al voto (*Il suffragio politico femminile*, cit., 348 ss.).

98 Per tutti v. P. Costa, *Civitas. Storia della cittadinanza in Europa, 2. L'età delle Rivoluzioni; 3. La civiltà liberale*, Roma, Bari 2000 e 2001.

99 Corte d'Appello di Ancona, 25 luglio 1906, cit., col. 390.

100 Art. 26 Legge comunale e provinciale 20 marzo 1865, poi art. 22, b), Legge 4 maggio 1898.

101 Così come le leggi precedenti (L. 17 dicembre 1860; 24 settembre 1882).

102 L'art. 2 determinava quali fossero gli elettori per *intellettualità*; il 3, parimenti, quelli per *censo*. Sul sistema elettorale v. M. S. Piretti, *Le elezioni politiche in Italia dal 1848 a oggi*, Roma, Bari 1996 e P. Pombeni, *La rappresentanza politica*, cit.

Il silenzio della legge diveniva quindi il tema della contesa. In particolare la sentenza della Corte d'Appello di Venezia (14 luglio 1906)[103] nel rifiutare l'iscrizione delle istanti nelle liste elettorali aveva contestato l'applicabilità del principio *ubi voluit dixit, ubi noluit tacuit* affermando che questo veniva meno quando era evidente il motivo per il quale il legislatore aveva giudicato opportuno parlare in un caso determinato e non in un altro. Secondo la Corte il legislatore aveva negato espressamente il diritto elettorale alle donne in campo amministrativo perché tale diritto non era del tutto estraneo alla condizione giuridica della donna italiana, come mostravano alcune esperienze preunitarie (in Toscana e Lombardo-Veneto) e le numerose proposte legislative avanzate dopo l'Unità. Ben diverso, invece, il caso dell'elettorato politico giacché per esso non esistevano precedenti. La Corte quindi affermava doversi applicare piuttosto la massima *ubi eadem legis ratio, ibi et eadem legis dispositio* e, in secondo luogo, procedere all'interpretazione *de minori ad maius*: se il legislatore italiano ha dunque ritenuto di non poter accordare alla donna il voto amministrativo, tanto più ha inteso negarle il suffragio politico che ha una rilevanza ben superiore. Le diverse Corti d'appello, inoltre, ponendo l'accento sulla necessità di una interpretazione sistematica,[104] facevano rilevare come l'esercizio di pubbliche funzioni era stato accordato alla donna per mezzo di sole leggi speciali.[105] Vittorio Emanuele Orlando giungeva inoltre a stabilire

> «un'equazione logica tra le seguenti tre proposizioni, di cui le prime due riproducono precise disposizioni legislative: 1° tutti gli elettori politici possono essere elettori amministrativi; 2° le donne non possono essere elettori amministrativi; 3° dunque le donne non possono essere elettori politici.»[106]

La corte di Ancona respingeva sia l'argomentazione *de minori ad maius*, sia la tesi secondo cui la volontà negativa del legislatore espressa nella legge amministrativa si doveva perciò riverberare per necessità logica sulla legge elettorale politica, «argomentando dalla maggiore importanza del voto politico in confronto

103 Cfr. in *Giurisprudenza italiana*, vol. LVIII, 1906, col. 379–380.

104 Secondo Orlando bisognava trovare la soluzione «nel sistema dei principi fondamentali del nostro diritto pubblico interno». Il sistema di diritto e non le singole leggi era il parametro per l'interprete (in *Il Foro italiano*, cit., col. 1061). Al contrario Manfredi Siotto Pintor, *Il diritto della donna italiana al voto politico*, in *Giurisprudenza italiana*, LIX, 1907, col. 60, censurava «il ricorso a tutte quelle indagini e argomentazioni indirette che hanno dilagato con tanta generosa abbondanza».

105 Per es. la legge sulla istruzione pubblica che abilitava la donna all'insegnamento; r.d. 22 maggio 1873 che ammetteva la donna agli impieghi telegrafici; L. 15 giugno 1893 n. 295 sui probiviri; L. 17 luglio 1890 sugli istituti pubblici di beneficenza ecc.

106 *Il Foro italiano*, cit., col. 1061.

all'amministrativo». Si trattava comunque di un motivo facilmente controvertibile, potendosi al contrario sostenere che «... il voto politico è determinato dalle grandi e semplici linee delle idee fondamentali che dividono i partiti ...», mentre quello amministrativo suppone la consapevolezza e la corretta valutazione di problemi complessi. Non giovava neppure il richiamo a tutte quelle leggi che avevano attribuito esplicitamente alle donne alcuni diritti politici. Il riferimento era in alcuni casi non pertinente e in altri – come per l'eleggibilità prevista dalla legge sui probiviri – non si contemplava «un vero e proprio diritto politico, giacché si provvede[va] alla disciplina di rapporti nascenti dal contratto di lavoro ed attinenti in modo esclusivo agli interessi patrimoniali ...».[107]

Pur in assenza di una norma espressa, per rafforzare la tesi secondo la quale l'esclusione delle donne dal voto politico fosse incontestabilmente *ius commune*, i pubblici ministeri, le Corti d'Appello e gl'interpreti cercavano di desumere il divieto dagli artt. 8 e 12 del testo unico elettorale: nel primo caso si teneva conto delle imposte pagate dalla moglie per poter conferire il diritto elettorale al marito (art. 8);[108] nel secondo caso la vedova o la moglie separata legalmente potevano delegare il loro censo, a scopo elettorale, al figlio o al genero (art. 12).[109]

Queste disposizioni mostravano secondo la Corte di Ancona che, in determinate condizioni di famiglia, la legge preferiva che il censo della donna venisse assegnato ai maschi come titolo per il diritto elettorale. Ma esse isolatamente non valevano a dimostrare che alla donna, in qualunque condizione e per qualunque titolo, fosse negato tale diritto.[110] Nella legge per il voto amministrativo erano

107 Corte d'Appello di Ancona, 25 luglio 1906, cit., col. 392.

108 «Per costituire il censo elettorale stabilito al n. 1 dell'art. 3 si computano tutte le imposte dirette pagate allo Stato in qualsiasi parte del Regno. Al padre si tiene conto delle imposte che paga pei beni della sua prole, dei quali abbia il godimento; al marito di quelle che paga la moglie, eccettoché siano personalmente separati per effetto di sentenza passata in giudicato, o pel consenso dei coniugi omologato dal tribunale».

109 «Le imposte dirette pagate da una vedova o dalla moglie separata legalmente dal proprio marito, possono essere computate, pel censo elettorale, a favore d'uno dei suoi figli, o generi di primo e secondo grado da lei designato».

110 Come detto, la Corte di Palermo giustificava il diniego del diritto di voto sulla base del complesso degli artt. 1, 8 e 12 della legge elettorale del 1895 (Sentenza del 9 luglio 1906, in *Giurisprudenza italiana*, 1907, III, c. 58). Lo stesso argomento nelle sentenze della Corte di Appello di Venezia (14 luglio 1906), della Corte d'Appello di Cagliari (19 luglio 1906), di quella successiva della Corte d'Appello di Brescia (10 ottobre 1906), in *Il Foro italiano*, XXXI, 1906, col. 1319, e tutte sul punto della impossibile delegazione, per la donna, dell'esercizio del diritto elettorale. Cfr. anche l'intervento del magistrato Raffaele Garofalo in *Giornale d'Italia*, n. 222, 10 agosto 1906. Più tardi il costituzionalista Ignazio Brunelli, *Il suffragio politico femminile*, cit., 181, affermerà che «La legge elettorale

state riprodotte queste stesse regole, ma non parve al legislatore di aver sanzionato l'interdizione generale dall'elettorato amministrativo in ragione del sesso perché in alcuni articoli successivi si prevedeva espressamente che le donne non fossero né elettori né eleggibili.[111] Nei dibattiti parlamentari che portarono a tali disposizioni tutti quelli che parteciparono alla discussione attaccarono o difesero la clausola proibitiva generale, espressa, ben sapendo che in assenza si sarebbe ammessa al voto la donna in conformità ai principi generali. Le leggi elettorali politiche (1865, 1882, 1895) non accolsero mai il divieto generale esplicito: «la differenza, dal punto di vista esegetico, ha un evidente altissimo valore».[112]

Nel 1907 la Corte di Appello di Roma ritenne giuridicamente infondate le argomentazioni seguite dalle altri Corti italiane (ad eccezione di quella d'Ancona) in merito all'interpretazione degli artt. 8 e 12. Ammettere la possibilità di un'eccezione non espressa e indiretta ai principi di diritto comune significava contraddire apertamente quanto prescritto dall'art. 4 delle disposizioni sulla pubblicazione, interpretazione ed applicazione delle leggi in generale, ovvero «che il *ius singulare*, ossia la deroga alle norme di diritto comune, risulti da una disposizione non implicita né sottintesa, ma espressa».[113] Lo scopo dell'art. 4[114] era, secondo la Corte, evitare che il giudice potesse usurpare le funzioni del legislatore qualora, per supposte ragioni d'analogia, o col pretesto di sottintesi o di non esatta corrispondenza della parola al concetto della legge, pretendesse di attribuire alla disposizione eccezionale un significato più ampio di quello consentito dalla sua locuzione, od ammettesse eccezioni implicite.

politica e la legge comunale e provinciale (anche guardata limitatamente all'ordinamento dell'elettorato e della funzione elettiva) sono due leggi speciali. L'una non è l'altra, e, con l'una, l'altra non si deve interpretare. E molto meno deve la interpretazione autentica, data per la comunale, assumersi a criterio interpretativo della politica ...».

111 Art. 22, Legge comunale e provinciale, T.U. 4 maggio 1898 n. 164: «Non sono elettori né eleggibili a) gli analfabeti; b) le donne; gli interdetti e gli inabilitati ...». Il sistema della delegazione del censo venne introdotto con la legge del 17 marzo 1848 e perpetuato, pur con talune modifiche, dalla successiva legislazione. Il tenore delle disposizioni riguardanti la delegazione derivava dalla legislazione francese e in particolare dall'ordinanza del 5 settembre 1816 (poi confermato dalle leggi elettorali del 1817 e 1820).

112 Corte di Appello di Ancona, 25 luglio 1906, cit., col. 391–392.

113 Corte di Appello di Roma, 18 maggio 1907, in *Giurisprudenza italiana*, LIX, 1907, col. 199, dove si ricorda la tesi di Matteo Pescatore che aveva invece sostenuto che il giudice potesse ricercare la volontà del legislatore anche in tema di diritto singolare o eccezionale.

114 «Le leggi penali e quelle che restringono il libero esercizio dei diritti o formano eccezione alle regole generali o ad altre leggi, non si estendono oltre i casi e tempi in essi espressi».

La «sentenza Mortara» concludeva sul punto del censo di cui agli artt. 8 e 12 della legge elettorale politica affermando che «non vi sono argomenti esegetici i quali conducano necessariamente a ritenere che essa interdica alle donne il diritto elettorale».

8. L'intenzione del legislatore e l'adeguamento del giudice, ovvero dal metodo giuridico-tradizionale al metodo storico-evolutivo

Rimaneva un ultimo argomento da affrontare. I lavori preparatori erano stati invocati per confermare il divieto. Dapprima la Corte di Venezia e poi, nell'agosto 1906, la Corte di Firenze fecero riferimento, in particolare, ad alcune dichiarazioni del relatore Zanardelli[115] e del ministro Crispi (1881–1882) che avrebbero dovuto dissipare ogni dubbio. Secondo Mortara, invece, la richiamata posizione di Zanardelli era a dir poco esorbitante[116] e frutto di una supposizione gratuita, priva poi di qualsiasi fondamento fattuale visto che era tra l'altro contraddetta dagli innumerevoli ricorsi, «e soprattutto difettosa perciò che ad una argomentazione giuridica sostituì una figura rettorica, cioè una iperbole, non idonea a veruna dimostrazione scientifica». L'art. 3 delle disposizioni preliminari al codice civile stabiliva che l'intenzione del legislatore fosse da ricercare nel testo della legge, non fuori di esso. I lavori preparatori potevano essere un sussidio, non una fonte diretta per tale ricerca.[117] Inoltre, nell'ordina-

115 È celebre la lettera che Anna Maria Mozzoni indirizzò all'on. Zanardelli, relatore del progetto di riforma elettorale (1881).

116 Zanardelli aveva sostenuto la contrarietà delle donne ad avere il diritto al voto. Si trattava di un argomento ampiamente utilizzato in dottrina, per es. da C. F. Gabba, *Della condizione giuridica della donna nella legislazione francese, austriaca, sarda. Studio di legislazione comparata*, Milano 1861, 14: «Attribuire alla donna i diritti politici sarebbe farle un regalo a cui essa non aspira e di cui non saprebbe fare uso». Sul punto v. anche G. Padelletti, *Teoria delle elezioni politiche*, cit. Teresa Labriola riconosceva i limiti delle aspirazioni femminili, ma ciò dipendeva dal fatto che la società non consentendo alla donna di partecipare a funzioni di qualche rilievo, finisse per aspirare solo agli uffici sociali consentiti (*Studio sul problema del diritto al voto*, Roma 1904). Sulla figura e sul pensiero di Teresa Labriola in tema di suffragio v. F. Taricone, *T. Labriola. Biografia politica di un'intellettuale tra Ottocento e Novecento*, Milano 1994; G. Conti Odorisio, *La rappresentanza femminile nel pensiero politico di Teresa Labriola*, in *La rappresentanza politica in Europa tra le due guerre*, a cura di C. Carini, Firenze 1995, 375–406.

117 Nel 1904 Mortara ribadiva la necessità di seguire il «metodo esegetico razionale e costante di fronte alla parola della legge» e quindi in particolare l'art. 3 delle Disposizioni preliminari al codice civile. «Stimiamo pericoloso che l'interprete si prefigga la libera indagine della intenzione del legislatore, nelle materie processuali, in cui molte volte questa *intenzione* è figlia di apprezzamenti, e quindi

mento attuale della funzione legislativa, l'opinione dei compilatori della legge restava sempre un indizio incerto «della vera intenzione dell'organo collettivo onde emana la volontà in essa consacrata».[118]

In conclusione la sentenza anconetana si sofferma sulla questione cruciale: l'interpretazione della legge e la misura dell'argomentazione interpretativa da riconoscere al magistrato. La legge è sempre una formula «di precetto generale destinata a governare i bisogni e le contingenze della vita sociale per un tempo illimitato, adattandosi alla variabilità in modo da rispondere sempre al fine di tutela nell'ordinamento civile». Essa non si cristallizza una volta per tutte in una forma primigenia e irriducibile,

> «ma vive la vita stessa della civiltà ed è animata dallo spirito di questa. Indagarne il significato, dichiararne l'intenzione, è compito del magistrato nel tempo in cui sorge la controversia su tale proposta e in relazione al caso dal quale è essa occasionata.»

È possibile che i compilatori di una regola non fossero favorevoli ad un determinato adattamento pratico. Ma il magistrato può legittimamente riconoscere questo adattamento «allorché l'ermeneutica guidata da criteri razionali gli dimostri che il testo lo autorizza». Se c'è un dubbio sull'intenzione del legislatore, esso va sciolto nel senso della libertà, «trattandosi appunto di determinare l'estensione di un diritto politico che qualcuno definì pure diritto naturale, e che sotto questo profilo quasi nessuno contesta appartenere a tutti i soggetti capaci, senza distinzione di sesso».[119]

Per comprendere il valore e il significato della sentenza anconetana del 1906 e ricondurla alla complessità intellettuale del suo principale artefice, bisogna tenere conto di una concezione dell'ufficio dell'interprete e della funzione del giudice che Mortara, nella sua attività scientifica e poi giurisdizionale, ha maturato nel corso del tempo. Mortara è solidamente piantato sul terreno della

male si presta ad essere accertata mediante criterio obbiettivo ... Il campo d'attività del *critico* e quello dell'*interprete* (commentatore o magistrato) deggono rimanere con rigorosa delimitazione separati» (L. Mortara, *Principii di procedura civile*, Firenze 1904, 5 ed., 8–9).

118 Sulla relatività dei cd. "lavori preparatori" cfr. L. Mortara, *Commentario*, cit., vol. I, 81, n. 75. «... in secondo luogo, perché appartiene alla essenza della legge e della sua funzione sociale lo adattarsi alle differenti e mutevoli contingenze della vita collettiva, per mezzo di interpretazioni corrispondenti alle medesime. Ora, inchiodato il senso della legge al pensiero del suo primo compilatore, le si impedirebbe certo di compiere regolarmente siffatta funzione. La volontà della legge è dunque cosa distinta dal pensiero dei suoi redattori».

119 Corte di Appello di Ancona, 25 luglio 1906, cit., col. 393–394. Su questo passaggio cfr. anche A. Sciumè, *I principî generali del diritto nell'ordine giuridico contemporaneo (1837–1942)*, Torino 2000, 188.

legge quale strumento di regolazione e determinazione del rapporto tra Stato e società.

> «L'epoca moderna – scrive nel 1885 –, inaugurando il sistema delle codificazioni, parallelo al concetto politico della divisione dei poteri, ha recato una mutazione radicale e profondissima nell'officio del magistrato. Un criterio positivo, indefettibile, domina la sua azione; la legge è; non si tratta che di applicarla con equanime imparzialità a ciascun caso ...»[120]

Nella prima edizione (1887) del *Manuale della procedura civile* Mortara afferma di procedere, nell'esegesi della legge,

> «secondo il metodo e le raccomandazioni del Laurent: mi guardo cioè, con ogni cura, dal sostituire alla volontà del legislatore (nei casi in cui può essere stabilita con sicurezza) l'idea dell'interprete, anche quando la seconda sia fuor di dubbio migliore della prima. Ma nella critica rivendico pienezza di libertà.»[121]

Come abbiamo visto, è lo stesso Mortara – specie nella sua polemica scientifica con Chiovenda – ad enfatizzare l'immagine del «proceduristа» e dell'«esegeta». Bisogna, però, intendersi sulla portata di questi riferimenti. Quando Satta scrive che per Mortara è il giudizio e non la legge il centro dell'esperienza, fa una giusta osservazione, anche se non bisogna dimenticare l'evoluzione del suo pensiero. La celebre espressione mortariana secondo cui se la legge è la statica, la giurisprudenza è la dinamica del diritto obiettivo, segnala mirabilmente l'accresciuta sensibilità di una parte cospicua della scienza giuridica, tra Otto e Novecento, per l'attività dei giudici chiamati, non senza molte inquietudini, a interpretare la legge con uno sguardo più aperto nei confronti di una società segnata ormai in profondità da progressi materiali e da tumultuose e inquietanti trasformazioni. Non si trattava certo di recidere le solide radici – antiche di un secolo – che legavano l'interprete al terreno della legalità e al «diritto dei moderni»; pur dovendo conservare un sistema delle fonti segnato da dogmi insuperabili, era adesso la vita che esigeva dal giudice il riconoscimento dei propri diritti suggerendogli di «allontanarsi» dal testo normativo. La sentenza Mortara – «rivoluzionaria», pur ricorrendo a «criteri puramente giuridici ed esegetici» – rappresenta senza dubbio uno dei *grands arrêts* della giurisprudenza italiana del periodo.[122]

120 L. Mortara, *Lo Stato moderno e la giustizia*, cit., 77.

121 Cit. da F. Cipriani, *Storie di processualisti e di oligarchi*, cit., 35. È da notare che nelle edizioni successive – e certamente nella quarta del 1903 – la prefazione con il ricordato "programma" viene meno.

122 Lo fa giustamente rilevare P. Grossi, *Scienza giuridica italiana*, cit., 105, cui si rinvia per le pagine sul "modernismo giuridico". Cfr. anche Id., «*Il coraggio della moderazione*» *(Specularità dell'itinerario riflessivo di Vittorio Polacco)*, in *Quaderni fiorentini*, 18, 1989, 197–251.

Un inviato del *Giornale d'Italia*[123] volle intervistare Mortara nella sua villa di Falconara. In questa singolare occasione il magistrato mantovano – al centro dei riflettori della stampa nazionale – ebbe modo di meglio chiarire le sue idee e i suoi propositi. Già in precedenza, nel 1903, Mortara aveva dichiarato di essere contrario[124] – per ragioni di opportunità politica – al voto politico delle donne che in maggioranza erano, a suo parere, ancora impreparate ad esercitare una così importante e delicata funzione. Quando però si trattava di abbandonare ogni pregiudizio personale e di guardare al solo testo della legge, allora – come aveva mostrato nella sentenza – le cose cambiavano. L'ermeneuta, insomma, aveva la meglio sull'uomo privato, rivelando al contempo, quasi che Mortara volesse attutire l'impatto della sua sentenza, la tensione fra la donna vista nella sua sfera intima e familiare, ancora inadatta alla funzione politica, e la donna protesa all'allargamento della cittadinanza e della sfera pubblica. L'intervista è assai utile per capire la concezione che il nostro giurista ha maturato in tema di interpretazione della legge. L'attività del magistrato appare più complessa, aperta com'è alle trasformazioni della società e agl'orientamenti dell'opinione pubblica.[125] Il legislatore, osserva, Mortara non è più il padrone dello Stato, in grado di imporre la volontà a tutti i consociati, bensì «il primo e più alto degli organi destinati al servizio della vita sociale. Perciò è sua funzione, e quindi suo obbligo, adattare la norma giuridica ai bisogni della vita civile». Di conseguenza l'ufficio del magistrato assume, come interprete della legge, un aspetto e un rilievo assolutamente nuovi.

123 Il *Giornale d'Italia*, inizialmente concepito dall'on. Domenico Oliva (col titolo *La Patria*), fu diretto da Alberto Bergamini. Organo di stampa romano volto ad organizzare – col patrocinio di Sidney Sonnino – il "partito moderato-conservatore", diventò in breve tempo una delle più importanti testate nazionali. Cfr., al riguardo, M. S. Piretti, *Il Giornale d'Italia e l'Opposizione Costituzionale*, in Id. (a cura di), *Immagini dal Giornale d'Italia (1923–1960)*, Bologna 1996; Id., *Una voce per l'Opposizione Costituzionale di Sua Maestà. Alle origini del «Giornale d'Italia»*, in *Contemporanea*, II, 4, 1999, 699–712 (dove si può leggere l'originario progetto di Oliva).

124 Nell'intervista Mortara si dichiara personalmente contrario, ma giuridicamente favorevole al voto delle donne.

125 Sul crescente ruolo dell'opinione pubblica tra Otto e Novecento mi permetto di rinviare al volume monografico del *Giornale di storia costituzionale*, 6/II, 2003, *Opinione pubblica. Storia, politica, costituzione (XVIII–XX sec.)*, a cura del sottoscritto. «Nella sua concezione moderna, infatti, – scrive Brunelli nel 1910 – la legge è uno strumento di regolamentazione della società, e di fronte ad essa è funzione del giudice quella di regolatore della vita sociale nei suoi rapporti con la legge ... Il diritto vive e si muove, non solo per opera del legislatore, che lo crea, ma altresì del magistrato che è chiamato ad applicarlo secondo le variabilissime condizioni di tempo, e di luogo, subbiettive ed obbiettive» (*Il suffragio politico femminile*, cit., 289).

«Ecco, le spiegherò meglio – osserva Mortara riprendendo in maniera più articolata l'argomento già richiamato nella sentenza – ... il magistrato non si deve soltanto proporre la ricerca storica del pensiero del legislatore in un tempo più o meno remoto; ma, molto più utilmente, deve domandarsi con quale intenzione l'organo legislativo oggi mantenga in vigore un testo o una formula di legge che può prestarsi ad una interpretazione molto diversa da quella che i suoi compilatori originali s'erano proposti di darle. Se il magistrato può convincersi che l'intenzione del legislatore non sia conforme a quella dei compilatori, egli deve risolvere la indagine sulla intenzione in favore del legislatore di oggi e non già del legislatore del passato. Così il diritto pubblico moderno viene ad affidare al magistrato una funzione non meno nobile ed alta di quella che, prima della codificazione, gli spettava come creatore del diritto mediante la giurisprudenza. Oggi però il magistrato non crea il diritto: ne ricava la parola viva e conforme ai bisogni della vita civile dal testo della legge. Se egli s'inganna nell'interpretare il pensiero del legislatore, questi ne ha tosto il mezzo di eliminare l'interpretazione errata, con l'esercizio diretto della sua funzione.»

Non sono trascorsi invano vent'anni e il Presidente Mortara del 1906 ha senza dubbio allargato e di molto gl'orizzonti di chi si era definito un esegeta «alla Laurent». L'interpretazione serve per intendere la norma a fini applicativi affinché possa corrispondere ai diversi, mutevoli, rapporti della vita,[126] coniugando – in una sola e unificante attività – l'evoluzione dell'ordinamento con un

126 Il passo sopra ricordato (nt. 58) sulla legge / statica e sulla giurisprudenza / dinamica prosegue in questi termini: «Identica è la natura della forza in esse contenuta, poiché nell'una e nell'altra vive e si attua il diritto obbiettivo. Questa forza, però, nella legge è immanente, e la sua energia rimane allo stato potenziale. Nella giurisprudenza, si dispiega operosa e si impone alla obbedienza di coloro i quali avessero cercato di sottrarvisi indebitamente. In codesto sviluppo di attività specifica essa non subisce variazioni di essenza, perché una necessità sociale imprescindibile agguaglia, o per meglio dire unifica, la volontà della legge con quella della sentenza giudiziaria. Ma pur conservandosi una, essa si adatta alle condizioni, ai bisogni, alle opportunità dei singoli casi speciali: e così, nel mentre compie, momento per momento, l'uffizio al quale è destinata, evolve lentamente nel senso medesimo della vita di correlazione civile, e può riuscire modificata, col trascorrere del tempo, nel suo effetto intrinseco, senza che le apparenze esteriori abbiano ricevuto alterazione alcuna» (*Commentario*, cit., vol. I, 77, n. 70). Un attento ed equilibrato sostenitore del metodo storico-evolutivo fu, negli stessi anni, Francesco Degni: *L'interpretazione della legge*, con prefazione di B. Brugi, Napoli 1909, 2 ed. Per inquadrare la "sentenza Mortara" nel contesto delle trasformazioni dei metodi e degli atteggiamenti ermeneutici connessi al cd. orientamento storico-evolutivo, fondamentali le pagine di P. Costa, *L'interpretazione della legge: François Gény e la cultura giuridica italiana fra Ottocento e Novecento*, in *Quaderni fiorentini*, 19, 1990, 394 ss. Un'utile ricostruzione del dibattito che a cavaliere dei due secoli coinvolge in Italia, lungo una linea di confine segnata da «sollecitazioni giusliberiste» di respiro europeo, giuristi come Brugi, Coviello, Simoncelli, Polacco, Ferrara ecc., cfr. M. Meccarelli, *Un senso moderno di legalità. Il diritto e la sua evoluzione nel pensiero di Biagio Brugi*, in *Quaderni fiorentini*, 30, 2001, t. I, in particolare 436 ss.

certo grado di stabilità e di certezza quali presupposti indispensabili della legalità. Mortara fonda la sua decisione su uno strumentario interpretativo che discende dal metodo giuridico-tradizionale ma passando attraverso il vaglio di quello che altrove aveva definito un «metodo critico»;[127] in modo particolare richiama, per affermare o negare determinate proposizioni, gran parte dei procedimenti grammaticali e logici[128] ritenuti necessari per ricercare la volontà del legislatore. Ma il punto d'arrivo è una tipologia interpretativa che si inquadra all'interno del cd. metodo storico-evolutivo; nello specifico, relativizzando il ricorso all'intenzione del legislatore come criterio ermeneutico, Mortara introduce un argomento che rivela la cautela della giurisprudenza nell'ammettere i lavori preparatori ai fini dell'interpretazione.[129]

Il legislatore non è più il «padrone della legge»; questa è un'entità formale che più si allontana dalla volontà del legislatore storico, più il magistrato è «obbligato» ad interpretare per farle conseguire quegli obiettivi di giustizia e di utilità sociale che soli si possono ricavare dall'insieme degl'elementi positivi.[130] In realtà Mortara compie una lettura sistematica delle fonti normative –

127 L. Mortara, *Commentario*, cit., vol. I, Prefazione, VI.

128 Cfr. F. Degni, *L'interpretazione della legge*, cit., 155–160.

129 Mortara «anticipa» prospettive ermeneutiche poi raccomandate dalla dottrina costituzionalistica e dalla Cassazione del secondo dopoguerra allorché leggi «vecchie» dovranno trovare applicazione in un contesto sociale profondamente trasformato. Del resto si tratta di un ridimensionamento che non è estraneo neppure ad un "esegeta" influente quale François Laurent. Cfr. P. L. Chiassoni, *Scuola dell'Esegesi. Progetto di voce per un «Vademecum» giuridico*, in *Materiali per una storia della cultura giuridica*, 2, 2003, 352–353.

130 F. Degni, *L'interpretazione della legge*, cit., 160 ss., è favorevole a questo metodo perché garantisce stabilità, armonia e al tempo stesso evoluzione. Il metodo giuridico-tradizionale è troppo rigido, legalistico, non riesce a tener dietro alla realtà; il metodo del libero diritto va invece troppo oltre, non dando garanzie di certezza. Degni osserva come il metodo storico-evolutivo cominciasse a trovare applicazione in Italia sul finire dell'Ottocento, con Cimbali, Gabba, Vadalà-Papale ed ebbe vasto seguito all'inizio del XX secolo presso giuristi come Filomusi-Guelfi, Fadda, Bensa, Brugi, Ferrara ecc. È inoltre significativo il fatto che Degni individui in Oronzo Quarta e in Lodovico Mortara i due "campioni" del metodo storico-evolutivo «Nella nostra giurisprudenza pratica ...». In particolare, ricordando la sentenza anconetana Degni richiama un lungo passaggio dell'intervista di Mortara nel *Giornale d'Italia* nel quale il magistrato «... determinò, con una esattezza insuperabile di concetti, il criterio fondamentale del metodo storico-evolutivo ...». È da sottolineare, però, il dissenso circa gli effetti dell'«applicazione del metodo storico-evolutivo alla specie risoluta dalla Corte di Ancona ... Il metodo storico-evolutivo può adottare le leggi esistenti alle nuove esigenze ed alle nuove idee quando trova un appoggio nel sistema generale della legislazione, ma non può sostituirsi a questa» (F. Degni, *L'interpretazione della legge*, cit., 176–177).

l'unica possibile per fondare un'interpretazione evolutiva – nel campo del diritto pubblico, attribuendosi, in quanto giudice, il massimo grado di responsabilità.[131] Il magistrato non «crea il diritto», ma ne ricava la «parola viva» individuando la massima di decisione nel testo della legge. Mortara prefigura un modello di giurista-interprete visto come «cauto adeguatore» del diritto:[132] il giudice non potendo più essere un mero dichiaratore-esecutore della legge, è chiamato ad assumere la veste di adeguatore capace di esprimere scelte e valutazioni, pur sempre nei limiti imposti dalle norme positive e dalle tecniche interpretative prescritte dalle Preleggi in una prospettiva di indubbia complessità metodologica.[133]

9. Una sentenza «politico-sociale»?

La sentenza di Ancona e l'intervista di Mortara agl'inizi d'agosto definiscono un approccio interpretativo destinato ad essere censurato dalla Cassazione romana. In realtà, le Corti d'Appello da subito respingono la soluzione affermativa applicando il principio *secundum legem et non de legibus iudex iudicare debet*. Andare oltre significherebbe porsi in una prospettiva *de iure condendo*.[134] La Corte di Firenze ribadisce essere

> «canone inconcusso di una sana ermeneutica che per ricostruire il pensiero del legislatore l'interprete non può né deve tener conto dello sviluppo scientifico del diritto che può aver luogo successivamente all'emanazione della legge della cui interpretazione si tratta, come non deve tener conto delle cambiate condizioni dei tempi e delle nuove esigenze sociali, ma rigido *custos legum*, deve riportarsi all'epoca in cui la legge fu fatta, la quale sempre la stessa rimane come il legislatore la volle a quel tempo finché dal legislatore medesimo non sia modificata né cambiata, non dovendosi mai confondere il progresso della giurisprudenza con quello della legislazione.»[135]

131 Come osservava M. S. Giannini, «È in essa [nell'interpretazione evolutiva] che si manifesta più che in altre specie d'interpretazione la responsabilità di colui che interpreta la legge con particolare autorità, cioè del giudice ...» (*L'interpretazione dell'atto amministrativo e la teoria giuridica generale dell'interpretazione*, Milano 1939, 135).

132 Cfr. C. Luzzati, *La vaghezza delle norme. Un'analisi del linguaggio giuridico*, Milano 1990, 133 ss.

133 Per un inquadramento sistematico v. E. Betti, *Interpretazione della legge e sua efficienza evolutiva* (1959), ora in *Diritto Metodo Ermeneutica. Scritti scelti*, a cura di G. Crifò, Milano 1991, 523–554. Per la critica del concetto di interpretazione evolutiva cfr. invece S. Romano, *Frammenti di un dizionario giuridico*, rist. inalterata, Milano 1953, *ad vocem*, 119–125.

134 Corte di Appello di Venezia, 14 luglio 1906, cit., col. 378.

135 Corte d'Appello di Firenze, 14 agosto 1906, cit., col. 382–383.

In tal senso il magistrato deve essere calmo, sereno, senza preoccupazioni, senza preconcetti, «senza aspirazioni ad un ideale di perfetta eguaglianza ...», lasciando la soluzione del problema all'opera saggia e illuminata del legislatore.

Si capisce come la sentenza Mortara – oltreché per l'oggetto delicatissimo – andasse in tutt'altra direzione, disegnando un diverso approccio ermeneutico. Gaetano Mosca temeva, senza l'intervento del potere legislativo, «una rivoluzione forse più sostanziale di quella che in Italia si compì mercé la Carta albertina e che ebbe la sanzione dei plebisciti».[136] Ciò che per il giudice Mortara era un insieme elegantemente e audacemente congegnato di argomenti e indirizzi interpretativi, diveniva per gl'altri magistrati e per la maggior parte dei commentatori un fatto da lasciare al prudente apprezzamento del legislatore. Non era dunque una questione giuridica, ma una tesi «politico-sociale».[137]

Il ricorso in cassazione avverso la sentenza anconetana concluse la vicenda. Il 12 dicembre 1906 di fronte a un insolito pubblico di signore e signorine, la decisione fu accolta «da dei bene e dei bravo e da un tentativo di applausi».[138] Le due pronunce della Cassazione di Roma,[139] l'una avverso la sentenza anconetana, l'altra conforme a quella veneziana, stabiliscono la seguente massima: «Secondo la vigente legge elettorale politica, le donne non hanno in nessun caso il diritto di essere iscritte nelle liste elettorali». La Cassazione ripercorre tutti gl'argomenti e le soluzioni interpretative, a cominciare dall'art. 24 dello Statuto, considerato solo genericamente quale elemento giustificativo del diniego. Non si può accogliere l'interpretazione suggerita dalla Corte anconetana giacché il diritto all'elettorato trova per le donne un ostacolo proprio nelle «eccezioni determinate dalle leggi», a cominciare dagl'articoli 8 e 12 della legge elettorale. La Corte suprema riproduce l'argomento orlandiano dell'interpretazione sistematica. Non c'era bisogno di una clausola proibitiva perché in realtà le donne erano private del diritto politico in forza del principio dominante «... tutto il diritto pubblico vigente non solo nelle disposizioni scritte, ma anche nelle

136 G. Mosca, *Contro una sentenza*, cit.

137 A. Stoppato, *A proposito del voto politico alle donne*, cit. È interessante notare come la Corte d'Appello di Ancona (senza più Mortara) in una successiva sentenza (6 luglio 1907, in *Giurisprudenza italiana*, vol. LIX, 1907, col. 278) sottolinei come della precedente pronuncia «può conservarsi ricordo solo per la virtù sua politico-sociale di aver vivificato il dibattito su di una questione, sorta nell'orizzonte della vita moderna dello Stato, e di aver additato, se non altro, al legislatore la necessità di una risoluzione della questione stessa con chiare e nette disposizioni di legge».

138 Lo ricorda F. Del Pozzo, *Ancona 1906*, cit., 125.

139 Cassazione di Roma, 12 dicembre 1906 e 15 dicembre 1906, in *Giurisprudenza italiana*, vol. LIX, 1907, III, col. 1 ss. Primo Presidente era il senatore Giovanbattista Pagano Guarnaschelli; pubblico ministero il senatore Oronzo Quarta.

norme, nelle consuetudini e nelle tradizioni sempre riconosciute che le completano e ne formano parte integrante».[140]

La Cassazione ritiene debba essere il legislatore a stabilire il diritto o meno delle donne a godere dei diritti politici che comportino una diretta o indiretta partecipazione ai pubblici poteri dello Stato, stabilendo condizioni, limiti, temperamenti.[141] Con trasparente censura dell'orientamento mortariano, la Cassazione osserva come

> «giudicare altrimenti non è interpretare la legge facendo rientrare nella sua formola nuovi casi e nuove esigenze che virtualmente e come in germe fossero già da esse contenuti, ma è usurpare l'opera legislativa senza che l'innovazione a cui si apre l'adito possa essere giustificata dalla maturità del bisogno che, trattandosi di riforme di ordine pubblico, soltanto il legislatore è in grado di riconoscere, e senza che la medesima innovazione possa essere circondata da quei temperamenti e quelle cautele che si reputassero necessarie e convincenti.»[142]

La questione del voto femminile rileva dunque solo in quanto possa richiedere, *de iure condendo*, l'intervento del legislatore. Nel maggio del 1907 la Cassazione ricorda al magistrato come egli debba

> «interpretare la legge attuale e non quella dell'avvenire: e qui neppure si tratterebbe di adattare la vecchia legge ad una situazione sociale nuova, perché omogenea, ma di fondare un nuovo sistema e creare nuove capacità politiche in assoluto contrasto col passato; il che eccede il potere del giudice il più liberale ed illuminato.»[143]

L'orientamento negativo della Cassazione mostrava come lo *ius commune* restasse quello di sempre,[144] lasciato intatto dallo Statuto del 1848: l'incapacità della donna a partecipare alla vita politica nazionale era un principio storico-consuetudinario, per lo più non scritto, ma presupposto imprescindibile del sistema di diritto pubblico. La consuetudine in questo ambito rivestiva «un grandissimo valore nell'interpretazione delle leggi ...».[145] Cesare Vivante – in una intervista raccolta da Ugo Ojetti sul *Corriere della Sera* – parlando di una giurisprudenza «feroce» e discriminatoria offriva una diversa rappresentazione del magistrato «medio»,

> «obbligato ad orientare le sue interpretazioni sul passato, sulla tradizione, a seguire nel labirinto il tenue filo del diritto romano, logorato ed estenuato dai

140 Cassazione di Roma, 12 dicembre 1906, cit., col. 6.

141 Per una critica della sentenza della Cassazione romana v. il commento di M. Siotto Pintor, *Il diritto della donna italiana al voto politico*, cit.

142 Cassazione di Roma, 12 dicembre 1906, cit.

143 Cassazione di Roma, 20 maggio 1907, in *Giurisprudenza italiana*, vol. LIX, 1907, col. 277.

144 Cfr. Corte di Appello di Roma, 18 maggio 1907, in *Giurisprudenza italiana*, 1908, III, c. 198.

145 Cassazione di Roma, 15 dicembre 1906, cit., col. 8.

secoli ma, *chapeau bas!*, d'una sicura legittimità. Le povere antiquate biblioteche di cui dispone, gli esagerano l'importanza della tradizione, gli velano la visione della vita presente.»[146]

10. La lotta per l'uguaglianza

Di questa «visione della vita presente» non ha mai difettato Lodovico Mortara. Dieci anni dopo, divenuto guardasigilli, sarà l'artefice della legge 17 luglio 1919 n. 1176 con la quale si compie un passo decisivo per riconoscere alla donna la piena capacità giuridica mettendo fine all'arcaico istituto dell'autorizzazione maritale e aprendole le porte delle professioni e degli impieghi pubblici.[147] Nella relazione del ministro che nel 1919 accompagna il suo progetto di riforma giudiziaria si legge che il movimento di trasformazione della società

> «è condizione essenziale, nei paesi retti a libero regime, per acquistare la esatta percezione del giusto e del non giusto, in armonia con le esigenze del tempo e coi bisogni morali e giuridici del popolo; il giusto e il non giusto sono nozioni relative, non assolute e immutabili. Il giurista chiuso fra i codici e le glosse, quando pure sia un'arca di dottrina, rimane fatalmente tagliato fuori dalla realtà della convivenza civile.»[148]

Mortara, in fondo, aveva creduto nel carattere «liberatorio» del pur fragile Statuto albertino. Non si dimentichi che Mortara era il figlio del rabbino maggiore nella Mantova austro-ungarica, ovvero del patriota insigne che aveva guardato con favore al progetto di emancipazione legato alla nascita della nuova Italia. D'altro canto lui stesso, nelle *Pagine autobiografiche*, rammenta come l'essere ebreo sia «un marchio classificatore che non si elimina». Non è certo

146 *Per la capacità giuridica della donna. Un colloquio col professor Vivante*, in *Corriere della Sera*, 30 agosto 1907.

147 Ad eccezione, salvo espressa previsione di legge, degli impieghi che implicano poteri pubblici giurisdizionali o l'esercizio di diritti e di potestà politiche, o che attengono alla difesa dello stato. Non bisogna però dimenticare che lo stesso Mortara si era espresso negativamente sulla presenza professionale delle donne nel foro (v. F. Tacchi, *Gli avvocati italiani*, cit., 297). Sull'opera del guardasigilli (con un breve ma efficace ritratto di Mortara) cfr. le notazioni del prefetto Enrico Flores, già capo di gabinetto di Orlando e di Nitti: *Eredità della guerra (L'opera del primo ministro del dopoguerra)*, Napoli 1925, 199–211. Sul dibattito del 1919 nell'ambito della storia del suffragismo italiano cfr. G. Chianese, *Storia sociale della donna in Italia (1800–1980)*, Napoli 1980; A. M. Galoppini, *Il lungo viaggio verso la parità. I diritti civili e politici delle donne dall'unità ad oggi*, Bologna 1992, 75 ss.; M. P. Bigaran, *Donne e rappresentanza nel dibattito e nella legislazione tra '800 e '900*, in *La sfera pubblica femminile. Percorsi di storia delle donne in età contemporanea*, a cura di D. Gagliani e M. Salvati, Bologna 1992, 63–72; A. Rossi-Doria, *Diventare cittadine. Il voto alle donne in Italia*, Firenze 1996.

148 Cit. da F. Venturini, *Un «sindacato» di giudici*, cit., 215.

casuale che la prolusione pisana al Corso di diritto costituzionale del 1889 fosse consacrata a *La lotta per l'uguaglianza*. La lotta per l'esistenza – l'inesorabile cifra della storia umana – gl'appare «... il fatale risultato delle disuguaglianze fra gli uomini e fra le consociazioni ...»[149] ed è causa perpetua di nuove disuguaglianze e di nuove lotte. Mortara passa rapidamente in rassegna gl'effetti di questa lotta: il dispotismo, il predominio di una classe sull'altra, la divisione in caste, la politica di potenza, uno Stato costruito per l'avidità della dominazione, gl'esseri umani ridotti a *esseri inanimati* della politica. La storia umana vista da questo punto d'osservazione – che, a suo dire, è quello di Hobbes, Schopenhauer, Hartmann – è negatrice di ogni possibilità di uguaglianza. Ma la forza intellettuale ha gradualmente acquisito un grado di autorità e una potenza di mezzi d'azione, «da bastare essa sola per guarentire il trionfo immancabile dell'uomo ...».[150] Si tratta, è vero, di una prospettiva rivolta più al futuro che al presente, e tante sono le resistenze e le reazioni, ma «... è ben lungi dall'apparire una utopia il convincimento che la conquista della forza intellettuale su quella materiale abbia da rendersi nell'avvenire completa e definitiva».[151] La forza intellettuale diventa il parametro su cui costruire la società e l'uguaglianza di diritto ne è l'indispensabile fondamento.

> «L'uguaglianza di diritto non contiene l'uguaglianza di fatto. Anzi il principio della uguaglianza di diritto non ha valore pratico se non in quanto suppone le disuguaglianze di fatto che nell'ordine di natura sono inevitabili. Ma l'uguaglianza di diritto applicata ad uno stato di disuguaglianza di fatto stabilisce una necessaria *tendenza* alla diminuzione di quest'ultima ed una necessaria *aspirazione* al suo totale concellamento. Tendenza ed aspirazione che gli uomini dell'età nostra non possono arrogarsi il diritto di giudicare se e quanto siano nel lontano avvenire realizzabili.»[152]

È da questo tipo di filosofia politica, da questa «forza intellettuale» che la sentenza anconetana del 1906 riceve piena luce. Pur con il senso del limite – giacché Mortara è *uomo* del suo tempo, aristocraticamente liberale e democraticamente *sensibile* ai tempi nuovi della società –, con il dovuto realismo,[153] con il necessario equilibrio e con un punto obbligato di partenza nella uguaglianza di diritto, nell'opera di Lodovico Mortara scorgiamo più da vicino le origini del *costituzionalismo dell'uguaglianza*,[154] vediamo il XX secolo, le tendenze e le aspirazioni ad essere uguali, noi tutti, uomini e donne impegnati sul terreno

149 *La lotta per l'uguaglianza*, cit., 14.
150 *Ibidem*, 18.
151 *Ibidem*, 19–20.
152 *Ibidem*, 26.
153 *Ibidem*, 27–28.
154 Cfr. M. Fioravanti, *Il principio di eguaglianza nella storia del costituzionalismo moderno*, in *La scienza del diritto pubblico*, cit., t. II, 815.

della democrazia costituzionale, quella forma compiuta, ma nondimeno fragile, che cerca il progresso nella incessante tensione tra uguaglianza, libertà e giustizia. Di tutto ciò Mortara era pienamente consapevole.

Il limite, la garanzia, l'arbitro. La Corte e il costituzionalismo

1. La Corte costituzionale e la dimensione storica

Che il cinquantenario di una istituzione come la Corte costituzionale potesse essere l'occasione per riflettere sulla sua storia era scontato. L'occasione, si può dire adesso, non è trascorsa invano. Tra il 2005 e il 2006 una lunga teoria di convegni, seminari, pubblicazioni ha riccamente celebrato l'evento, con risultati, in alcuni casi, eccellenti.[1] Il mezzo secolo è un traguardo di prim'ordine per una istituzione repubblicana e ne segna in maniera definitiva l'ingresso nella "storia". Si offriva il destro per ritornare in maniera critica sulle radici, sulle fondamenta e sulle trasformazioni di una istituzione essenziale per il funzionamento e lo sviluppo di una democrazia costituzionale. Anche il *Giornale di storia costituzionale* – pur dal suo angolo visuale – ha inteso dedicare un numero monografico alla Corte e ai profili storici della giustizia costituzionale.

Nel confronto con una pubblicistica che si preannunciava tecnicamente provvedutissima ed esaustiva, il *Giornale* ha optato per un disegno storico-critico, certamente parziale, ma in grado di affrontare alcuni nodi strategici propri della *storicità* della dimensione *esistenziale* della Corte, sia nel quadro specifico del contesto italiano sia in quello più generale dei *principî* e delle *esperienze*.

Tra le istituzioni consolidate della nostra repubblica la Corte costituzionale – pur così carica di responsabilità e, per dirla con terminologia spiccia, di *poteri* – è probabilmente la meno conosciuta, anche al pubblico più informato e più attrezzato culturalmente (Zagrebelsky 2005, 3).

Invero i profili più problematici della Corte – della sua storia e della sua stessa vita istituzionale – non sono stati certo ignorati sul piano storiografico generale

1 Penso per es. ai tre tomi (e all'allegato cd) di documentazione storica dell'attività della Corte e dei suoi giudici, dalle origini ad oggi, edita dalla Corte stessa: *1956–2006. Cinquant'anni di Corte costituzionale*, con Introduzione di U. De Siervo.

(per es. Massera 1972; Tranfaglia 1973; Mezzanotte 1979; Barile, Cheli, Grassi 1982; D'Orazio 1983; Bonini 1996; Rodotà 1999; Cheli 1999; Cerri 2001; Simoncini 2004) o su quello più "interno" della sempre più ampia manualistica connessa allo sviluppo della giustizia costituzionale. Enzo Cheli, nella *Introduzione* all'importante opera postuma di Livio Paladin *Per una storia costituzionale dell'Italia repubblicana* (2004, 12), coglie bene tuttavia uno dei nodi più delicati sul piano della ricognizione storica del fenomeno costituzionale, ovvero lo scarto tra la «storia degli storici» e la «storia dei giuristi» (come ricorda Simoncini 2006, 295). Questa distinzione segnala senza dubbio un problema di fondo – già discusso da tempo (Bonini 1987; 1995; Paladin 1997) – che proprio nella storia della Corte costituzionale trova un palese banco di prova. Questo profilo "critico" mantiene una sua indubbia rilevanza, sul piano epistemologico e metodologico, e il terreno della storia costituzionale dovrebbe servire come rinnovato laboratorio (per es. Lacchè 2001; Pinelli 2001) nel quale la imprescindibile dimensione giuridico-istituzionale possa realmente confrontarsi con i linguaggi scientifici della storiografia più sensibile e attenta alla complessità del fenomeno costituzionale.

Come è noto, fare la storia di una istituzione come la Corte costituzionale è compito certamente difficile. La Corte "parla" attraverso le sue decisioni e il "segreto" della Camera di consiglio deve per forza di cose creare uno schermo opaco verso l'"esterno". Si potrebbe dire che le condizioni *esistenziali* di funzionamento della Corte – a cominciare dalla vita e dal modo di essere dei giudici – rilevano in misura molto minore delle decisioni assunte. Tuttavia il rischio di una visione integralmente "formalistica" dell'operato della Corte, ancorata in maniera esegetica e parcellizzata alle singole vicende e soprattutto alle singole decisioni (del genere note a sentenza) (Luciani 2006) rischia di riprodurre una sorta di *positivismo giurisprudenziale* che cozza – se assunto a dimensione esclusiva – con la natura e soprattutto con la *realtà* della Corte. Lo stimolante saggio di Gustavo Zagrebelsky su *Principî e voti* mostra in maniera evidente le possibilità offerte da un approccio in grado di tener conto dei diversi registri che contrassegnano la vita di una istituzione tanto complessa. Il rischio di descrivere in astratto un sistema di giustizia (Cheli 1999, 10) è sempre in agguato e la modellistica della giustizia costituzionale non può prescindere da un adeguato lavoro di storicizzazione. Per questo gli sforzi di periodizzazione, pur con i limiti del caso, rappresentano uno stimolo utile per mostrare come i *tempi* di una istituzione che maneggia e bilancia principî, valori e interessi coincidano solo in parte con quelli della contingenza politica, dei conflitti sociali e della incandescenza dei fatti economici: non si può certo prescindere da essi (il contesto) ma non bisogna neppure sottovalutare le *specificità* istituzionali della Corte, ovvero quell'insieme di tradizione, prassi, strategie, uomini che ne fanno la storia.

La giurisprudenza costituzionale, se ha ricevuto la massima e crescente attenzione, come è ovvio che sia, da parte degli studiosi, specie sotto il profilo dogmatico e delle tecniche raffinate di interpretazione, non ha altrettanto sollecitato – almeno in maniera *strutturale* – il punto di vista della metodologia storica. Ciò è dovuto a vari fattori e tra questi la «perdurante vitalità dell'idea della giurisdizione come attività di meccanica applicazione della legge (o di qualunque altra fonte, Costituzione compresa), a lungo assai radicata nei paesi di *civil law*, nei quali per molto tempo ci si è abituati a considerare i mutamenti della giurisprudenza come meri riflessi (registrazioni) delle trasformazioni del diritto positivo, senza connessione con l'evoluzione del quadro sociale, politico, economico» (Luciani 2006). In tal senso, è fondamentale maturare «una piena consapevolezza di ciò che essa (la Corte) fa effettivamente nella specifica contingenza storica nella quale essa opera» (De Siervo 2006, 81).

2. Le domande di fondo

La "storia giudiziaria" nel nostro paese non ha una vera tradizione (Luciani 2006), ampiamente legittimata come in altri contesti (quello americano per primo). Il cinquantenario, a dire il vero, ha prodotto qualche effetto, in termini di testimonianza. Non si tratta di mere ricognizioni "autobiografiche" ma di riflessioni dalla forte valenza istituzionale. Per questa ragione il *Giornale* ha richiesto – anche a titolo di esemplificazione e di banco di prova – ad alcuni protagonisti di rendere testimonianza sul loro lavoro *dentro* o *dinanzi* la Corte. Si voleva, così facendo, richiamare un "genere" letterario che in Italia è poco utilizzato (anche perché gode di relativa legittimazione) per comprendere meglio che cosa è e come funziona una istituzione. In particolare sono stati individuati tre poli tematici principali. Il primo ha riguardato il rapporto tra la Corte e la società "aperta", per riprendere un'idea espressa alla fine degli anni '70 da Peter Häberle con riguardo al Tribunale costituzionale federale tedesco: il Tribunale supremo come strumento di garanzia e organo di attualizzazione della Costituzione intesa quale "contratto sociale" (alla luce della teoria costituzionale pluralista). Quali sono state le percezioni dei rapporti esistenti tra la Corte come istituzione e la società nel suo insieme? Si può parlare di un "sottodimensionamento" della Corte rispetto al ruolo che ha svolto e svolge nella società? È bene che sia così, ovvero che il massimo organo di garanzia resti più "discosto" dagli umori e dall'incandescenza del sociale (lasciando la parola in buona sostanza ai giuristi), oppure si dovrebbe meglio rappresentare la sua funzione in termini di attuazione / valorizzazione della Costituzione? Come si dovrebbe rappresentare lo snodo fondamentale che ha contrassegnato l'attività della Corte, ovvero il rapporto tra tradizione e trasformazione / progresso della società? La Corte infine può svolgere ancora oggi una "funzione educativa" sull'insieme della società?

La seconda questione ha considerato il problema relativo al rapporto tra la Corte e gli altri organi costituzionali. In particolare si voleva indagare la dimensione rinnovata della separazione dei poteri e in particolare il ruolo della Corte come organo di garanzia di fronte ai poteri "politici". Basti pensare al problema del ricorso crescente al conflitto di attribuzione che fa della Corte l'organo di chiusura del sistema riconoscendogli un ruolo arbitrale indispensabile ma come tale esposto alla dimensione conflittuale propria della normale (e talvolta anomala) dialettica tra i poteri. Più in generale questo aspetto "colloca" la Corte – forse più di altri – lungo la linea storica principale del costituzionalismo come cultura (liberale) del limite sottoposta a indubbie tensioni nei sistemi democratici che invece privilegiano, in linea teorica, il dato della legittimazione del potere alla luce del principio democratico.

La terza questione ha preso in esame quel profilo fondamentale che segna il rapporto tra la Corte e la sua giurisprudenza e la cultura giuridica nel suo complesso. Quanto ha inciso (soprattutto negli ultimi decenni) l'azione della Corte sul superamento o sulla revisione delle teorie giuridiche dominanti? Si può parlare di una "cultura giuridica" elaborata dalla Corte nel corso del tempo, pur nella ovvia varietà degli accenti e delle opinioni personali dei giudici? Ovvero, è possibile riconoscere un orientamento culturale che – se posso dire – è "strutturale", indipendente dalla volontà dei singoli e che deriva piuttosto dalla conformazione della Corte (e forse si potrebbe dire delle Corti in termini di "convergenza"), dalla sua peculiare "posizione" costituzionale? Se invece così non è, quanto ha inciso la cultura dei giuristi – intesa come insieme stipulativo di modalità tecniche, contenuti scientifici e valori etico-morali presenti in un determinato momento storico – sulla "cultura della Corte"?

Si tratta di questioni centrali e apertissime, alle quali è impossibile poter dare risposte univoche.

3. La storia complessa della garanzia giurisdizionale della Costituzione

Lo storico non può e non deve appagarsi di idee ricevute, di schemi preconfezionati e tralatizi, di modelli che tendono a uniformare realtà diverse. Il *Giornale di storia costituzionale* ha battuto strade apparentemente ben spianate, senza asperità e ostacoli. Ma uno sguardo critico rivela la necessità di guardare alla storia della garanzia giurisdizionale della Costituzione con occhi anche diversi, a cominciare dal rischio incombente di mitizzazione di alcune esperienze (Grossi 2006). Un esempio di straordinario rilievo (e un insegnamento non superficiale) ci proviene dalla notissima sentenza del 1803 *Marbury v. Madison* posta alle origini del sindacato di costituzionalità. La più universalmente celebre pronuncia della Corte suprema americana è in realtà più citata che letta e non basta l'estrapolazione di qualche passaggio per affermare in maniera definitiva e univoca un principio. A veder meglio le cose, quella sentenza è molto più un *problema storiografico* che un dato acquisito. Il giudice John Marshall, così come i due personaggi che hanno dato il nome alla pronuncia, sono passati alla storia (e il giudice lo meritava pienamente), ma il percorso è stato lungo e affatto lineare. Benedetta Barbisan ricorda il paradosso: la decisione fondatrice del *judicial review of legislation* viene citata dalla Corte per la prima volta solo nel 1887 con qualche riferimento al principio del sindacato e la "manualistica" del tempo è altrettanto riservata. Bisogna allora guardare alle radici più profonde dell'albero per capire qualcosa di più, che quello che non c'era nella Costituzione, che taluni ritenevano essere implicito nella cultura dell'età costituente, aveva bisogno di una vera e propria *costruzione*, meglio ancora di una *invenzione*. Nel 1895 – nell'infuocata polemica in tema di *direct taxes* – la sentenza *Pollock v. Farmers' Loan & Trust Co.* sanciva – per finalità "conservatrici" – una rivoluzione culturale. «Nel momento in cui il diritto, un tempo neutro ed indifferente, si fa prodotto del conflitto sociale, la *Marbury* diventa il crisma con cui ungere misticamente i casi più discussi, la sua forza retorica il condono alla natura controversa delle decisioni più contestate.» (Barbisan 2006, 159). Viene da chiedersi perché proprio la *Marbury* e non altre sentenze. La sua poliedricità funzionale, la sua capacità di offrire una pluralità di *significati* ne avrebbe fatto il paradigma stesso di un *judicial review* che nel 1803 aveva soprattutto una valenza "privatistica" (cfr. anche Zoller 2003; Ahumada Ruiz 2006; Ackermann 2006).

Un capitolo fondamentale dello sviluppo e della concettualizzazione della giustizia costituzionale è quello che identifichiamo con il dibattito mitteleuropeo del primo dopoguerra. È da quella fase che si può dire abbia inizio il secolo della giustizia costituzionale (Zagrebelsky 2006, 33). Anche qui la riflessione critica offre spunti importanti. C'è la tendenza a situare le origini della *Verfassungsgerichtsbarkeit* all'interno di una sorta di laboratorio asettico identificato soprattuto con la dottrina kelseniana della *Reine Rechtslehre*. Eppure, come si può ben vedere dal saggio di Sara Lagi, Hans Kelsen, su invito dello stesso Karl Renner, elabora, tra il 1918 e il 1920, progetti e soluzioni che non possono prescindere da concretissime questioni antiche e di rinnovato valore politico-costituzionale: il rapporto tra il Centro e i *Länder*, la costruzione di una nuova sovranità dello Stato incarnata dall'Assemblea Nazionale dopo il crollo dell'Impero, il superamento delle ipoteche antiparlamentari (del maestro Jellinek, per esempio), la tutela della Costituzione (e quindi della decisione politica ad essa sottesa) in una prospettiva di unitarietà. «La riflessione kelseniana sulla Corte costituzionale, sviluppatasi tra il 1918 e il 1920, che ci appare oggi né organica, né sistematica, né approfondita, sembrava correlata al timore di Kelsen che i Länder attuassero un movimento separatista. In ciò è probabilmente racchiuso il senso della Corte costituzionale kelseniana del 1920: essa e la stessa «procedura d'ufficio» furono allora concepiti come strumenti per proteggere l'intrinseca unità dello Stato che, per Kelsen, era stata sancita dalla rivendicazione della sovranità da parte dell'Assemblea nazionale e riaffermata dalla costituzione approvata il 1° ottobre 1920, che era stata elaborata e infine approvata da un organo unitario, l'Assemblea costituente» (Lagi 2006, 174).

L'immagine della Corte come organo di difesa della democrazia politico-parlamentare ben presente nelle due edizioni di *Vom Wesen und Wert der Demokratie* fanno di Kelsen, senza dubbio, il naturale contraddittore di chi – è il caso di Carl Schmitt – rintraccia in un altro percorso storico e intellettuale le radici e i fondamenti della *custodia della costituzione*. Negli anni Venti e Trenta, attorno alle costituzioni cecoslovacca, austriaca, tedesca e poi spagnola (Cruz Villalón 1987), si delinea lo scenario concettuale e il lessico fondamentale della giustizia costituzionale contemporanea. Il "grande assente" (Meccarelli 2002) diventa un "presente" disputato e fragile. La maggiore coerenza del modello austriaco rispetto a quello "decentralizzato" weimariano – malgrado poi i progetti di Heinrich Triepel (1924) (Schefold 2006) e di Gerhard Anschütz (1926) (Beguin 1982; Le Divellec 2003) – non riesce a risolvere i problemi di fondo. Come è noto, il confronto – ma sarebbe meglio dire il dialogo tra sordi – tra Carl Schmitt e Hans Kelsen nel 1931 (innescato dalle riflessioni del dopoguerra) delinea posizioni e strategie antitetiche. Schmitt vede in *Der Hüter der Verfassung* – lungo un cammino che lo porta ad una reinterpretazione del *pouvoir neutre* di Benjamin Constant e del *pouvoir monarchique* della tradizione orleanista (Guizot) – l'unico garante *democratico* dell'unità della Costituzione, eletto dal popolo e fattore di riequilibrio tra gli organi. Nel tentativo di salvare un concetto di ordine politico antico (attraverso una sua modernizzazione *democratico-plebiscitaria*), Schmitt è ben consapevole dei rischi che una Corte giudiziaria affidataria del controllo di costituzionalità farebbe correre ai principi cardine del *Rechtsstaat* e della *Staatsgerichtsbarkeit* (su questa cfr. Luther 1990). Pronunciarsi su una decisione politica è per lui un atto eminentemente politico che è proprio del legislatore. Per Kelsen – che ha già respinto nel 1928 le principali obiezioni mosse contro la *garantie juridictionnelle de la Constitution* – non c'è differenza di natura tra le decisioni legislative e quelle che discendono dalla giustizia. «"chaque conflit juridique est pourtant un conflit d'intérêts, respectivement de pouvoir, chaque conflit juridique est donc une controverse politique, et chaque conflit qu'il soit d'intérêts, de pouvoir ou politique, peut être résolu comme une controverse juridique" [Kelsen, 2006 (1931), 76]. Ainsi, les contentieux constitutionnels relèvent, pour Kelsen, de la politique juridique.» (Baume 2006, 184).

Anche la complessa esperienza britannica della *Supreme Court* (e delle alti corti di giustizia e dei *Committees*) – solitamente esclusa da ogni tipo di legame con il modello continentale di giustizia costituzionale – può diventare, in una lettura più ampia e non formalistica, un interessante ambito di riflessione perché «... consente di destrutturare la categoria concettuale complessa che si configura nella nozione ampia di "giustizia costituzionale" e di metterne in rilievo alcuni moventi di fondo che, appunto, prescindono aprioristicamente dalla sussistenza di una carta costituzionale scritta. Questi moventi non sono meno autentici quali elementi fondanti la necessità di una giustizia costituzionale, e questa necessità – come ipotizzava Bagehot senza tuttavia spingere il suo pensiero fino ad affermare la necessità di istituire una corte costituzionale *ante litteram* – è ben presente nella storia costituzionale del Regno Unito dall'età vittoriana in poi» (Torre 2006, 264).

4. La volta dell'edificio

Non desta certo meraviglia che le Costituzioni del secondo dopoguerra cerchino di riannodare i fili con le Costituzioni democratiche della prima generazione. I problemi però non mancano e tre questioni in particolare contrassegnano il dibattito costituente: la *lunga durata* degli schemi concettuali del costituzionalismo ottocentesco (dal forte impianto monarchico); la questione della sovranità nello Stato liberale di diritto; la natura caleidoscopica della giustizia costituzionale, una categoria generale che in realtà contiene fenomeni diversi. Questi grandi temi – assieme a molti altri, evidentemente – vengono affrontati e risolti in maniera diversa nelle principali esperienze europee, basti pensare all'Italia, alla Germania e alla Francia. Tradizioni, problemi, atteggiamenti culturali differenti contribuiscono a far nascere "rami" dell'"albero" giustizia costituzionale che, pur accomunati da una stessa linfa, hanno tempi asimmetrici e seguono traiettorie peculiari (Schefold 2006). Nel dibattito costituente italiano Giorgio La Pira – siamo a fine novembre 1947 – afferma: «se vogliamo che il nostro edificio sia completo, è necessario mettere questa volta» (cit. da Bonini 1996, 51). Senza la Corte la casa comune resterebbe senza tetto, un edificio senza volta. Questa metafora architettonica che sarà ripresa da Carlo Lavagna nel 1951 conferma, per un verso, la consapevolezza di una *necessità* ma, per un altro, testimonia la difficoltà di realizzare un dispositivo di chiusura del sistema costituzionale.

Lo *spazio* della giustizia costituzionale, la *posizione*, la *natura* e le *funzioni* delle Corti non erano né univoci né ampiamente legittimati. La previsione della Corte – restando al caso italiano – aveva un indubbio valore rivoluzionario. Nel contesto di costituzioni democratiche rampollate da una manifestazione tanto *forte* del potere costituente e segnate, a livello ideologico, da una decisiva marcatura del primato della *politica*, la giustizia costituzionale doveva conquistarsi una sua fisionomia. Le obiezioni e le perplessità sollevate nel corso del dibattito costituente avverso l'ipotesi di una Corte costituzionale erano accomunate, pur partendo da posizioni ideologiche anche molto distanti, dal timore che la nuova istituzione (per natura, composizione ecc.) fosse inadeguata. Di gran lunga più forte avrebbe dovuto essere la dimensione *politica* della Corte per coloro che intendevano assegnarle un pieno fondamento democratico (lungo il circuito sovranità popolare – partiti – parlamento – legge sovrana); più *tecnica* invece – quindi più *giudiziaria* – per chi ne temeva al contrario la "politicizzazione". In realtà questi timori erano spesso dettati dalla difficoltà oggettiva di *pensare* un organo del tutto nuovo che avrebbe dovuto al tempo stesso salvaguardare la tradizione "classica" del costituzionalismo liberale – il limite e la garanzia – e rendere attuabile l'*indirizzo* costituzionale ispirato dal livello superiore, rigido, dei principi e dei valori. La Corte costituzionale nasceva all'incrocio di due costituzionalismi, quello liberale e quello democratico, ne assumeva i dilemmi, le tensioni, le grandi sfide. La Corte si incuneava, quale snodo essenziale, nella storica tensione tra democrazia politica e Stato costituzionale, tra *voluntas* e *ratio* (Costa 2006, per una sintesi limpidissima). Aveva ragione La Pira quando diceva che senza la Corte costituzionale l'edificio sarebbe rimasto "senza tetto". La giustizia costituzionale è diventata non a caso uno degli emblemi delle democrazie contemporanee (e lo è a livello "estetico" anche quando si tratta di costruire democrazie solo sulla carta) proprio perché rafforzando a livello *costituzionale* la cultura del limite (contro ogni forma di assolutismo politico) e della garanzia (dei diritti, soprattutto dei soggetti più deboli e delle minoranze) ha consolidato lo sviluppo stesso dei principi costituzionali.

La via italiana alla *giustizia nella costituzione* è tra le più interessanti per la sua sostanziale originalità. Ibridazione empirica di modalità e di strumenti, *mixtum compositum* (da subito con la legge n. 1 del 1948) di accentramento e di incidentalità del giudizio, non inquadrabile dentro gli schemi del principio "astratto" di separazione dei poteri (Pasquino 2006), «snodo elastico tra le due sfere, tra la giurisdizione e la politica ...» (Cheli 1999, 31), flessibile nei suoi presupposti di indeterminatezza del testo costituzionale, la Corte italiana è nata ed ha poi cominciato ad operare pragmaticamente in un quadro di riferimento incerto e contraddittorio. La non applicazione dell'art. 28 della legge n. 87 del 1953 – che escludeva ogni valutazione di natura politica e ogni sindacato sull'uso del potere discrezionale del Parlamento – è un chiaro esempio di quanto detto (Pinelli 2006).

Il cinquantenario ha offerto l'occasione per riflettere sull'avvio della Corte come complesso problema storico-giuridico. La tesi dell'«ostruzionismo di maggioranza» – assunta tradizionalmente, sulla scia di Calamandrei e di numerosi altri protagonisti – quale cifra della prima legislatura repubblicana ha molto influito anche sull'inquadramento storico della Corte. Fermo restando il dato politico dell'inattuazione costituzionale, l'anno 1953 è stato percepito più come l'anno della cd. "legge truffa" che delle leggi costituzionali in materia di giustizia costituzionale. È lo stesso Parlamento però ad approvare, a grandissima maggioranza, le leggi attuative. Già Livio Paladin aveva còlto i limiti di una interpretazione puramente "ostruzionistica" (2004, 98) e ricerche ulteriori sembrano confermare quei dubbi (Bisogni 2004, 71 ss.; Simoncini 2006). «Va, perciò, quantomeno corretto un diffuso giudizio sulla istituzione della Corte: questa nuova istituzione repubblicana nasce, certamente, in un contesto politico dominato da un fortissimo contrasto tra maggioranza ed opposizione, probabilmente, nasce tra sospetti e ostilità politiche, *ma, in primo luogo e soprattutto, nasce circondata da una diffusa incomprensione del suo ruolo e da una radicale incertezza sulla sua natura*» (Simoncini 2006, 298). Il confronto politico – senza dubbio rilevante – non offre una spiegazione omnicomprensiva.

5. Quando mancò la luce elettrica

Il racconto della prima udienza della Corte (23 aprile 1956) attraverso la testimonianza del Presidente emerito Giuliano Vassalli evoca quella storica giornata con rara efficacia. La tensione per l'importanza della prima udienza, la posta in gioco (il valore della Costituzione come parametro e quindi l'ammissibilità del sindacato costituzionale degli atti normativi antecedenti), il prestigio dei protagonisti ne fanno una sorta di *pièce* drammaturgica.

Sembra quasi di vedere quel manipolo di "coraggiosi" (destinati alcuni a diventare poi giudici costituzionali) – il capofila Piero Calamandrei, poi Achille Battaglia, Federico Comandini, Costantino Mortati, Vezio Crisafulli, Massimo Severo Giannini, l'avvocato Francesco Mazzei e appunto Giuliano Vassalli – impegnati, finalmente, nella difesa della Costituzione e dei suoi valori. Iniziava nel migliore dei modi, con una sentenza davvero rivoluzionaria (come i più avveduti subito compresero), il cammino della Corte. La morte improvvisa di Giuseppe Capograssi gettò sull'udienza un senso profondo di sgomento; i lavori, in segno di lutto, ripresero così nel pomeriggio. «Verso le 18.30, mentre parlavo io, mancò la luce elettrica e, pure essendo aprile avanzato, l'aula d'udienza precipitò nel buio più profondo. In quel buio e nel generale silenzio, ignorando tutti se e quando la luce sarebbe tornata, dissi, rivolto al presidente, che sarei stato egualmente in grado di continuare il mio discorso. De Nicola stette sopra pensiero uno o due minuti, dopo di che, rivolto a me, disse: "Continui". Io continuai per almeno un quarto d'ora, forse anche venti minuti, nel buio più fitto senza il minimo inceppo né esitazione: trattavo un aspetto penalistico e la preparazione era stata molto approfondita. La luce tornò, fortunatamente, prima che io avessi finito» (Vassalli 2006, 57). La sentenza del 14 giugno 1956 suscitò numerosi commenti e un dibattito significativo nel quale intervennero alcuni dei protagonisti, si pensi a Calamandrei, a Mortati, a Crisafulli (per una accurata ricostruzione cfr. Bartole 2004, 121–131; Casini 2006, che pubblica le memorie superstiti relative alla prima sentenza della Corte).

Non si è riflettuto forse abbastanza sul fatto che questa sentenza e altre che seguiranno rivelano una capacità di cogliere da subito, da parte dei protagonisti, le potenzialità e il *valore della Costituzione*. Mentre il vertice della magistratura ordinaria resta ancorato in una sua *maior pars* alla cultura del positivismo legale; mentre l'avvocatura dello Stato è parimenti restia, per lungo tempo, a vedere nella Costituzione un testo integralmente normativo, mentre una parte cospicua della cultura giuridica scorge nella *programmaticità* del testo costituzionale un limite alla sua applicazione, la Corte, istituzione nuova, senza precedenti e senza tradizione, mostra di aver *compreso* il suo ruolo dandosi una precisa identità costituzionale. Enrico De Nicola, primo prestigioso presidente di un collegio altrettanto prestigioso (Bonini 1996, 126), aveva ricordato non a caso, nel suo discorso inaugurale pronunciato dinanzi al Presidente della Repubblica Giovanni Gronchi, come la Corte avesse dovuto affrontare nei primi mesi (ma il discorso ha una valenza più ampia) «... un compito assai arduo: quello della totale organizzazione interna e della speciale disciplina processuale, con una serie di questioni da risolvere, di ostacoli da rimuovere, soprattutto di precedenti da creare, per la mancanza di quel complesso di utili suggerimenti che il lontano passato – attraverso la tradizione – tramanda al futuro» (De Nicola 1956, 13).

È stato acutamente osservato che la Corte, non potendo proporsi, in quel momento, né come custode dei valori fondamentali né come arbitro tra gli interessi in conflitto (Cheli 1999, 33), ha scelto il ruolo "obbligato" (Bartole 2004, 118) di "motore delle riforme". Svolgendo una funzione di supplenza del potere politico e del legislativo, l'alta giurisdizione ha rivolto lo sguardo anzitutto verso il passato (Onida 1977, 506 ss.) consolidando la sua posizione "riformatrice". Andrea Simoncini ricorda giustamente il celebre passo nel quale il Presidente Gaetano Azzariti, nel corso della conferenza stampa del dicembre 1957, affronta il problema della posizione della Corte nel sistema costituzionale: «Poichè si tratta di un organo nuovissimo, il suo collocamento nel quadro dell'ordinamento può dare luogo a perplessità. Non è certo, agevole rendersi subito conto delle novità. Bisognerà, però, tenere presente che la famosa tripartizione quale è a base della teoria della divisione dei poteri dovuta a Montesquieu non è più sufficiente a caratterizzare nella loro integrità gli ordinamenti presenti dello Stato: perché vi sono degli organi che sono fuori di tutti e tre i poteri: legislativo, esecutivo e giudiziario. Quali sono questi organi? Uno è il Capo dello Stato, l'altro la Corte Costituzionale».[2] Aspetto cruciale questo della *posizione* della Corte (rispetto al quale lo stesso Azzariti si dimostrò molto sensibile, 1958, 446–463), perché dimostra sia lo sforzo per

2 Il testo della conversazione con la stampa raccolto in forma stenografica fu pubblicato nella *Rivista di diritto e procedura civile*, 1957, 1443 (2006).

cogliere gli elementi di novità sia la cautela necessaria per non mettere in allarme i tre tradizionali poteri dello Stato.

La storia della Corte, specialmente nei suoi primi anni, è caratterizzata da un abile pragmatismo: se i Presidenti e i giudici, nei loro discorsi e nei loro scritti, cercano da un lato di "rassicurare" gli altri poteri istituzionali (in ordine a gran parte delle attribuzioni), dall'altro non esitano, pur nel segno di una costante ricerca del punto di equilibrio, ad elaborare tecniche, strumenti, strategie di collaborazione che di fatto hanno come obiettivo la legittimazione crescente della Corte e l'ampliamento dei suoi margini di azione. Su questo aspetto la Corte ha avuto sin dall'inizio le idee chiare (Bartole 2004, 131).

6. Difendere la democrazia da sé stessa

Lo Stato costituzionale rappresenta lo sforzo più alto e (umanamente) riuscito di conciliare la democrazia con il costituzionalismo. La Corte costituzionale ne è uno degli snodi fondamentali: «... tutti sono ormai consapevoli che quest'ultimo [il sistema costituzionale] non sarebbe quello che è – e sarebbe invece un sistema diverso – se in esso non fosse presente la Corte; se in esso non fosse venuto meno quel principio del prepotere assoluto della legge, che gli uomini della Costituente, nel disegno di difendere la democrazia da sé stessa, vollero limitare allorché fissarono il principio garantistico dalla soggezione delle leggi alla Costituzione e della loro sindacabilità in sede di giustizia costituzionale» (Sandulli 1968, 56). La presenza e la *posizione* della Corte hanno una chiara valenza "costituzionalistica". Nella sua storia si inscrive la consapevolezza (contrastata dai critici e dagli scettici) che essa rappresenti un dispositivo volto a limitare il *governo rappresentativo* (come dice Pasquino 2006, l'«ideologia rappresentativa» e i suoi miti). «In sostanza, la presenza di un organo di controllo modifica le basi stesse del governo rappresentativo (o se si preferisce della democrazia): non è più la legge espressa dal Parlamento eletto che è sovrana, ma una pluralità di organi dei quali è "sovrano", in senso stretto, solo il meno capace di esprimere comandi (il corpo elettorale – non bisogna dimenticarsi che anche nella forma pura del governo rappresentativo sono costituzionalmente vietati i mandati imperativi ...». Lo Stato costituzionale è *misto* secondo un significato differente rispetto al passato. «Qui il carattere misto risiede nella diversità del fondamento di legittimità degli organi che esercitano non solo funzioni legislative ma anche funzioni d'indirizzo costituzionale. Il principio elettivo si coniuga con quello della competenza a "dire" ed a proteggere i diritti» (Pasquino 2006, 319). Un terreno interessante di verifica del ruolo della Corte rispetto al concetto di democrazia rappresentativa si può scorgere negli orientamenti giurisprudenziali relativi allo strumento referendario. La democrazia rappresentativa viene "rafforzata" dagli strumenti di democrazia diretta (Salerno 2006).

La giustizia costituzionale è una «funzione repubblicana» (Zagrebelsky 2005, 121), l'"albero di Ulisse" al quale la democrazia ha deciso di incatenarsi sapendo che le sirene sono sempre in agguato: lo strapotere, la logica maggioritaria / quantitativa, la denuncia di ogni vitale compromesso. «Possiamo perciò dire che la giustizia costituzionale non fa parte della democrazia ma serve alla democrazia» (Zagrebelsky 2005, 122).

Ma la Corte non ha svolto solo questa primaria funzione. «... prezioso organo respiratorio che consente il perenne adeguamento di comandi e forme alla sostanza di quei valori, con una visione rinnovata della legge che lascia finalmente alle spalle la vieta nozione di un contenitore vuoto da rispettare ad ogni costo» (Grossi 2006, 48; Id. 2005, 62–63), l'attività della Consulta segnala almeno due profili di grande significato. La Corte opera avendo come punto di riferimento una concezione – che discende naturalmente dalla Costituzione e dall'*interpretatio iuris* – complessa, dinamica, pluralista del diritto còlto allo "stato fluido", attingendo a quel diritto per principi e valori (oltreché per interessi e fatti) che caratterizza le società contemporanee. Così facendo coglie la dimensione più profonda ed effettiva del diritto, la sua più riposta storicità. «Oggi non basta – ha osservato Cesare Ruperto nel 2002 – che le leggi siano approvate da una maggioranza; occorre che risultino ragionevoli e che l'esercizio della legislazione, pur discrezionale, si svolga nei limiti di princìpi indisponibili da parte del legislatore» (Ruperto). E «La ragionevolezza del diritto sta nel punto di equilibrio fra testo e contesto, fra legalità e vitalità, fra lettera della legge e coscienza sociale, fra certezza del diritto e concretezza dell'ordinamento. Il conseguimento di questo punto di equilibrio non può che passare da fonti spontanee e diffuse, a cominciare dall'interpretazione giurisprudenziale, la cui azione rende possibile la formazione di un diritto aderente al massimo grado al divenire sociale, al dispiegarsi della vita economica, al pluralistico e mutevole patrimonio etico di una collettività» (Mazzarella 2006, 138). Il ruolo della Corte – discosta dal principio della democrazia – è stato ben interpretato dai suoi giudici che in cinquant'anni hanno mostrato, partendo da una concezione tutta legalistica del diritto, una sicura capacità ordinatoria, recuperando al giurista un protagonismo a lungo smarrito (Grossi 2006).

7. Nell'officina della Corte

Chi sono i giudici costituzionali, che cosa fanno quando lavorano, da soli o collegialmente, quando ascoltano in udienza i difensori delle parti, quando discutono in camera di consiglio? A queste domande non è difficile rispondere, anche se le risposte non sono univoche. Certamente la Corte è un luogo nel quale personalità di forte caratura intellettuale si trovano, per nove anni, a dover lavorare insieme. Per molti l'esperienza della Corte è stata l'occasione – e non sembri un paradosso – per *comprendere* in profondità l'essenza del giudizio di costituzionalità, talvolta mitizzato, talaltra sottovalutato. Alla fine di tutto, c'è di mezzo una cosa relativamente semplice ma fondamentale: il bilanciamento tra la libertà e l'autorità. La provenienza dei giudici è un dato molto importante che incide in termini di cultura e di sensibilità. Ogni "categoria" si porta dietro "pregi" e "difetti" legati alla professione di origine. Il presidente emerito Mauro Ferri insiste molto sulla politica come *magistra vitae*. Non si tratta solo di riconoscere il dato autobiografico, ma di sottolineare anche una necessità che va oltre, ovvero che il giudice possieda e sviluppi una sensibilità "politica", indispensabile alla sua funzione. Parimenti la "specializzazione" eccessiva dei giudici appare a Ferri un limite vistoso, perché questi devono avere una visione complessiva dell'ordinamento costituzionale. Controverso è anche il peso da attribuire alla figura del presidente della Consulta. Per alcuni non conta più di tanto (Zagrebelsky 2005, 82), per altri è una funzione di rilievo, specialmente nei momenti di incertezza o di crisi (Ferri 2006). Anche la collegialità è un tema centrale. Tutti i giudici concordano sul fatto che il periodo dei nove anni sia lungo (ma Mauro Ferri con ironia osserva che alla fine «ci si affeziona») e molto faticoso. Nove anni di convivenza è un dato da non sottovalutare. Nel collegio si mettono in discussione convinzioni, valori, idee preesistenti; spesso ci si divide per poi riconfermarsi: è la stretta di mano ricordata da Zagrebelsky (2005, 10). Tuttavia se per quest'ultimo la collegialità è un valore in sé, inclusivo, che deve funzionare da regola per evitare il più possibile il «voto decidente» considerato come una sconfitta (Zagrebelsky 2006), per altri la collegialità non deve essere necessariamente sinonimo di unanimità (De Siervo 2006). Si discute, anche animatamente, ma alla fine si decide, se occorre con il voto del presidente (Ferri 2006). La tradizione, il valore del precedente sono importanti (Zagrebelsky 2006, 83–84), ma non mancano neppure *revirement* significativi (Vassalli 2006).

La vita della Corte, come istituzione complessa, non si limita però ai soli giudici. Sarebbe interessante approfondire il ruolo peculiare (non riscontrabile in nessun altro organo giurisdizionale) degli assistenti dei giudici. Il loro contributo è senza dubbio indispensabile ai fini dell'organizzazione e dell'economia del lavoro dei giudici. Le osservazioni al riguardo di Giuliano Vassalli e di Mauro Ferri (ma cfr. anche Ruperto 2005, *Prefazione*) offrono utili spunti di riflessione.

Certamente è mancata sinora una storia dell'avvocatura dinanzi alla Corte. Per tale motivo abbiamo chiesto di rendere una testimonianza anche a chi della Corte è stato protagonista «al di là del banco». Non solo perché l'avvocatura è un modo per testimoniare passione e impegno civile e politico, ma perché l'avvocato chiede alla Corte che gli si risponda (Luciani). «Per la verità, almeno l'esame degli scritti difensivi delle parti sarebbe sempre molto utile, per non dire doveroso, per comprendere la vera sostanza degli interessi e della posta in gioco nei vari giudizi costituzionali. È proprio leggendo quelle difese, poi, che è possibile capire se e dove la Corte sia stata reticente o audace; se e quanto abbia risposto a tutti gli interrogativi postisi nel corso del giudizio; se e in che misura abbia replicato agli argomenti delle parti. Qualche volta, va detto, gli annotatori mostrano di aver considerato la produzione delle parti, e qualche volta alcuni scritti difensivi sono pubblicati nelle riviste specializzate (è quanto è accaduto, in alcune occasioni, in *Giurisprudenza costituzionale*). Anche se vi è qualche segno di una più chiara consapevolezza dell'importanza della questione (v., da ultimo, L. Casini, *La prima sentenza della Corte costituzionale: le memorie processuali*, in *Riv. trim. dir. pubbl.*, 2006, 13 ss., ove si commentano – allegandole – le memorie redatte, appunto, in occasione della prima controversia decisa dalla Corte), tuttavia, l'attenzione per la posizione e per gli argomenti delle parti resta alquanto occasionale e costituisce meno la regola che l'eccezione.» (Luciani 2006, 114).

8. Un mondo comunicante?

Non è utile fare una storia della Corte costituzionale italiana avulsa dalla dimensione sovranazionale. Peter Häberle, riferendosi al ruolo propulsivo delle Corti costituzionali e in particolare della Corte europea di giustizia in materia di diritti fondamentali, ha osservato come esse abbiano fatto in alcuni casi «comparazione giuridica in forma di giudizio». A tal riguardo ha parlato di una «società aperta degli interpreti della costituzione» (Häberle 1999, 202–203).

Angioletta Sperti ricostruisce i principali contributi della comparazione giuridica nell'ambito della giurisprudenza delle Corti costituzionali. «Gli elementi di novità si manifestano, dunque, su un duplice piano: da un lato, su un piano sostanziale, non può negarsi come, in particolare nell'ambito della tutela dei diritti fondamentali, sia individuabile un *common core* di principi e valori costituzionali condiviso dalle principali nazioni; dall'altro, con riferimento agli strumenti ed alle tecniche di interpretazione, la comparazione si presenta sempre più come un «quinto metodo» di interpretazione del diritto» (Sperti 2006, 196; cfr. anche Id. 2005). Le convergenze che è dato constatare devono attirare l'attenzione se appena si considera che in origine vi erano differenze notevoli tra i sistemi di garanzia giurisdizionale della Costituzione, dal punto di vista tecnico e da quello fondamentale del modo di essere dello Stato costituzionale (Zagrebelsky 2006). L'esame del ricorso a precedenti stranieri in alcuni contesti (Stati Uniti, Canada, Regno Unito, Sudafrica) mostra differenti livelli di "apertura" e di volontà "dialogica" delle Corti. Se negli Stati Uniti il ricorso alla comparazione ha una prevalente funzione confermativa del patrimonio costituzionale (contrastata del resto dal Congresso che teme un attivismo giudiziario su scala mondiale), in Canada segnala l'esigenza di "apprendere" da precedenti stranieri, in Sudafrica la doverosità della comparazione (specie nell'ambito dei principi fondamentali in tema di tutela di diritti) trova riconoscimento in una disposizione costituzionale. Di questa tendenza abbiamo un esempio nel tentativo della Corte egiziana – come ci ricorda Tahani Muhammad Al-Gibeli, prima giudice donna in una Corte del mondo arabo – di far rispettare al legislatore egiziano le regole internazionali e le misure stabilite in accordi o trattati internazionali firmati dall'Egitto. «La Corte nutre un'altissima considerazione per le regole internazionali, il cui confronto con le leggi nazionali è decisivo per migliori risultati nella tutela dei diritti e delle libertà, in ogni ambito: nell'ambito delle libertà di espressione, delle libertà di stampa, del diritto alla mobilitazione e al lavoro sindacale, ecc.» (Al-Gibeli 2006, 289–290).

In Italia «la giurisprudenza costituzionale rivela uno scarso riferimento alle pronunce costituzionali straniere. Se si escludono i frequenti ma generici richiami ai principi posti a fondamento di uno «stato democratico», dello «stato di diritto» o accolti nelle «moderne democrazie parlamentari», gli esempi di riferimento alle pronunce costituzionali straniere o ai principi espressi in altre costituzioni nella nostra giurisprudenza costituzionale si rivelano alquanto sporadici e sono spesso giustificabili in base alla specifica sensibilità o alla formazione dei nostri giudici costituzionali. I casi di citazione di precedenti di altre corti supreme sono inoltre in genere solo incidentali ed utili per rafforzare le conclusioni espresse nella motivazione, la quale resta tuttavia fondata su soli principi e disposizioni interni al nostro ordinamento. Inoltre nella nostra giurisprudenza, anche al di fuori di quella costituzionale, è in generale assente ogni riflessione circa l'utilità del diritto comparato ai fini interpretativi ed i problemi posti dal ricorso a tale strumento» (Sperti 2006, 200).

La *respublica jurisconsultorum* dei giudici costituzionali è una prospettiva essenzialmente culturale. Talune analogie con il "mondo comunicante" evocato dal cardinal Giovan Battista De Luca e fondato sulla *communis interpretatio* dei Tribunali supremi di antico regime (Gorla 1981) appaiono suggestive – come ricorda Cesare Ruperto (11–13) – ma la prospettiva di una nuova dimensione della giustizia costituzionale rimane in buona parte da costruire.

9. L'invidia degli Dei

Fare un bilancio generale sui primi cinquant'anni della Corte è arduo e forse temerario. Mi limito solo ad alcune indicazioni che emergono dai saggi pubblicati in questo numero. La storia della Corte è una storia di sostanziale successo, con taluni fallimenti. Non sempre la Corte ha saputo far sua una visione "oppositiva" (Pace 2006), "polemica" (Luciani 2006) del costituzionalismo come limite del potere. La materia radiotelevisiva (e del pluralismo), per fare un esempio, appare un nodo strategico non del tutto risolto e un paradigma delle difficoltà nel rapporto politica – costituzione – giustizia. La Corte però rimane la fondamentale tutrice del primato effettivo della norma costituzionale (De Siervo 2006). Il sistema politico nel suo complesso mostra insofferenza verso i limiti della legalità costituzionale, con elusioni e forzature (De Siervo). Il rapporto tra la Corte e i poteri rappresentativi è regolato da una insopprimibile dialettica, ancorata necessariamente a logiche di *self-restraint* e di *fair play*. «Quando Corte e Parlamento non si parlano, i processi decisionali perdono ogni trasparenza, e sono messe seriamente a repentaglio la certezza e la prevedibilità dei rapporti giuridici» (Pinelli 2006, 326). Le polemiche del resto «... non sono mai mancate sull'attività della Corte costituzionale. Anzi potrebbe dirsi – osservava nel 1981 il presidente Leonetto Amadei in occasione del venticinquesimo anniversario – che la Corte è stata disegnata già sull'onda delle polemiche ...» (Amadei 1981, 64).

D'altra parte la Corte non è né può essere il "conclave divino" di platoniana memoria. I giudici sono essere umani, ben consapevoli del "potere" della Corte. «E che tutto sommato, devo dire, salvo in qualche caso specifico, la Corte ha usato sempre con misura e con grande equilibrio e discrezione. Ricordo quel convegno che si tenne a Bellagio nel 1990 con la Corte francese. Io dissi una battuta su questo potere: stiamo attenti a non creare l'invidia degli Dei. Nel nostro caso la divinità che potrebbe invidiare il nostro potere, è il Parlamento. Nella riforma c'è, mi pare, un tentativo di cambiare la composizione, però io spero, mi auguro – sono stato tra i promotori del Comitato per il referendum – che questa riforma non passi. Alcune proposte distruggono il fondamento della Costituzione» (Ferri 2006, 74). «... ogni volta che la Corte – scrive Ugo De Siervo – non riesce a contenere, se non ad eliminare, prassi ed atti di dubbia compatibilità costituzionale non solo rischia la sostanziale irrilevanza nel sistema istituzionale complessivo, ma si assume una grave responsabilità proprio in riferimento alla complessiva società italiana, già tanto profondamente dubbiosa dell'effettiva vigenza del principio di legalità specie in riferimento ai soggetti ed agli organi più forti. Ma tutto ciò può essere operato dalla Corte solo tramite l'esercizio delle sue specifiche competenze, ampie, incisive, ma certo non illimitate: è una pericolosa tentazione da respingere quella di forzarne i confini, poiché in tal modo la Corte si esporrebbe a pericolosi confronti politici, da cui uscirebbe sicuramente sconfitta. Ma in genere la Corte è non poco prudente nel respingere le pur ricorrenti tentazioni che si sviluppano al suo interno, seppure con varie misure e modalità (è pericolosa la apparente sensazione di onnipotenza in un organo, logicamente privo di controlli esterni, ove non esista un forte senso di autocontrollo). Semmai è nella sapiente utilizzazione delle tecniche processuali e decisorie che un organo giurisdizionale altamente specializzato che la Corte può esercitare le proprie competenze in modo parzialmente espansivo: strada in realtà largamente utilizzata, seppure sempre nel sostanziale rispetto dell'ambito delle competenze determinate dalla costituzione e dalla legge n. 87/1953».

Enzo Cheli ha sottolineato l'importanza di alcuni "condizioni di partenza" per un funzionamento adeguato della Corte: l'indipendenza dal sistema dei partiti; la tempestività dei giudizi; il livello costituzionale delle pronunce; la continuità e la "certezza" giurisprudenziale (Cheli 1999, 25). L'indipendenza della Corte e dei singoli giudici è un argomento essenziale che suscita proposte *de iure condendo*: per es. in merito ad una possibile disciplina dell'incompatibilità alla fine del mandato; o ancora in tema di riduzione del numero dei giudici; di astensione e di ricusazione; di verifica dei poteri; di introduzione del voto separato. Come è noto il dibattito sulla *dissenting opinion* è antico, delicato e piuttosto controverso in dottrina e nelle stesse posizioni dei giudici. Il dibattito ogni tanto riaffiora e non sembra destinato a spegnersi.

Anche la tempestività dei giudizi (Ferri) è tema importante. La storia della Corte conosce un momento di discontinuità, quasi sempre sottolineato con enfasi, durante la presidenza di Francesco Saja allorché si ebbe l'abbattimento dell'arretrato. Anche in questo ambito le esperienze straniere offrono "insegnamenti" utili. Proprio in tema di accesso alla Corte (tema davvero cruciale), l'esperienza tedesca e quella spagnola mostrano significative differenze. Se lo strumento del ricorso individuale è stato in entrambi i casi decisivo per il consolidamento della giurisprudenza, specie in tema di diritti fondamentali, nondimeno esso ha prodotto conseguenze diverse. Se in Germania il sistema è stato accompagnato da interventi "riformatori" e da prassi volte a regolare la procedura di accesso (Schefold 2006), in Spagna il *recurso de amparo* (che nel 2005 ha rappresentato il 97% del totale) ha contribuito ad allungare di molto i tempi dei procedimenti, tanto da sollecitare di recente una proposta di riforma della legge organica del 1979 (Presno Linera 2006). Nel primo caso il cittadino, in qualità di soggetto di un «ulteriore processo costituzionale» dinanzi ad un *Bundesverfassungsgericht* in grado di offrire "prestazioni" accettabili, ha percepito il ruolo della Corte in termini di una (pur fragile) integrazione (Schefold 2006), nel secondo l'inefficienza della regolazione procedurale rischia di diminuire il livello di fiducia dei cittadini per una istituzione, come quella del *Tribunal Constitucional*, che pure ha dato un contributo fondamentale allo sviluppo dello Stato democratico in Spagna (Presno Linera 2006).

Queste realtà offrono ulteriori spunti di riflessione anche in merito ad un profilo funzionale della nostra Corte che negli ultimi anni ha assunto – anche a seguito di riforme costituzionali – una dimensione nuova. La forte erosione del giudizio incidentale di costituzionalità a "vantaggio" delle tecniche di risoluzione dei conflitti fra i poteri dello Stato e soprattutto con riguardo alla accresciuta conflittualità fra Stato e Regioni ha fatto parlare, con «formula sintetica, magari un po' esagerata come molte semplificazioni, [...] di una Corte che si trasforma da "Corte dei diritti a Corte dei conflitti"» (De Siervo 2006, 83). Giustamente però è stato notato che la contrazione del sindacato incidentale può determinare, soprattutto se dettato dall'uso eccessivo di strumenti ordinatori, «un appannamento del ruolo della Corte e la diminuzione della sua capacità di dialogare (anche in funzione "educativa", appunto) con gli altri operatori del diritto e con tutta l'opinione pubblica» (Luciani 2006, 115; cfr. anche Vassalli 2006).

L'ampliamento del ruolo "arbitrale" è però conseguenza dell'aumento della conflittualità tra organi costituzionali e non. Il «moltiplicarsi del contenzioso può essere la spia di un malessere delle istituzioni e di un indebolimento dello spirito di leale collaborazione. L'ottimismo, però, lo ravviso nella giuridicizzazione / formalizzazione dello scontro, che ha il pregio sia di consentire una soluzione diversa da quella della prevalenza del più forte, sia di rendere trasparente – e accessibile al controllo della pubblica opinione – la contesa» (Luciani 2006, 116).

Nel complesso – al di là di alcune questioni aperte – il giudizio sull'attività svolta dalla Corte in questi cinquant'anni è positivo. «A mio avviso – osserva Giuliano Vassalli – la Corte è stata sinora all'altezza dei propri compiti in un mondo che ha visto e vede trasformazioni profonde. Ed è riuscita persino a sopportare, sinora, il peso crescente delle decisioni sui rapporti tra Stato e regioni nonostante le difficoltà createle da un legislatore piuttosto improvvido. Le preoccupazioni di coloro che ai tempi della Assemblea costituente non avrebbero voluto quest'organismo di garanzia si sono rivelate, a mio avviso, infondate. Al contrario, la Corte ha molto aiutato il potere legislativo ed ha contribuito, fin dove possibile, alla tenuta del sistema votato negli anni 1946 e 1947. Tutti riconoscono che per il futuro dell'Italia non si vedono ancora trasformazioni di sicura utilità e sufficientemente chiare». Alessandro Pace non condivide la dubbiosa conclusione di Gustavo Zagrebelsky (*Principî e voti*, 130–131) circa il contributo effettivo della Corte al «patrimonio spirituale vivente del nostro Paese ...», riscontrando invece «una quarantina di decisioni della Corte che, insieme a moltissime altre (centinaia), hanno praticamente guidato il cambiamento del nostro ordinamento adeguandolo ai principi e alle regole della nostra Costituzione». Non senza ombre: soprattutto in quei settori nei quali la Consulta deve fare i conti con i reali assetti di potere. Di certo la "conservazione" della Corte (nella sua costituzione formale e materiale) non è esercizio di "conservatorismo". Bisogna riflettere più di due volte prima di pensare a cambiamenti e riforme che rischierebbero – e paradigmatico è l'esempio del testo di revisione costituzionale del 2005 respinto con referendum nel giugno scorso – di fare della Corte costituzionale un'altra cosa. Ugo De Siervo si domanda allora «se la sorte futura della Corte non dipenda fondamentalmente da un necessario recupero a livello di opinione pubblica del significato e del valore dello Stato costituzionale».

In chiusura di questo contributo mi piace far mie le parole del presidente Cesare Ruperto pronunciate nel 2002: «Concludo osservando che provare ad acquisire continuamente nello spazio della democrazia questo incessante discutere e ridiscutere sulle leggi e sulle dinamiche costituzionali, cioè, in definitiva, sulle regole, sui principî e sui valori, affidandosi alla ricerca di soluzioni che reputiamo "giuste", mi pare che rappresenti un risultato troppo entusiasmante per non essere infaticabilmente e da tutti perseguito. Non so se e quanto ci riusciremo; ma bisogna continuare a pensarci con umiltà e, insieme, con fiducia» (15–16).

Bibliografia

Ackerman B., *Marbury* versus *Stuart*, in *Fundamentos*, 4, 2006, *La Rebelión de las leyes.* Demos *y* nomos*: la agonía de la justicia constitucional*, 151–202

Ahumada Ruiz A., *Marbury* versus *Madison: doscientos años (y más) después*, in *Fundamentos*, 4, 2006, *La Rebelión de las leyes.* Demos *y* nomos*: la agonía de la justicia constitucional*, 109–149

Tahani Muhammad Al-Gibeli, *Lo sviluppo costituzionale in Egitto*, in *Giornale di storia costituzionale*, 1, 11, 2006, 287–291

Amadei L., *Il venticinquesimo anniversario dall'inizio dell'attività della Corte*, ora in *1956–2006. Cinquant'anni di Corte costituzionale*, Roma 2006, t. I, 64–70

Azzariti G., *La posizione della Corte costituzionale nell'ordinamento dello Stato italiano*, in *Studi sulla Costituzione*, Milano 1958, vol. III, 446–463, ora in *1956–2006. Cinquant'anni di Corte costituzionale*, cit., t. I, 107–118

Barbisan B., *L'invenzione della* Marbury v. Madison, in *Giornale di storia costituzionale*, 1, 11, 2006, 145–164

Barile P., Cheli E., Grassi S. (a cura di), *Corte costituzionale e sviluppo della forma di governo in Italia*, Bologna 1982

Bartole S., *Interpretazioni e trasformazioni della Costituzione repubblicana*, Bologna 2004

Baume S., *Les sources légitimes de la juridiction constitutionnelle. La réplique de Hans Kelsen à Carl Schmitt*, in *Giornale di storia costituzionale*, 1, 11, 2006, 177–191

Béguin J.-C., *Le Contrôle de la constitutionnalité des lois en République fédérale d'Allemagne*, Paris 1982

Bisogni G., *Le leggi istitutive della Corte costituzionale*, in De Siervo U., Guerrieri S., Varsori A. (a cura di), *La prima legislatura repubblicana. Continuità e discontinuità nell'azione delle istituzioni*, vol. I, Roma 2004

Bonini F., *Problemi di una storia costituzionale*, in *Rivista di storia contemporanea*, 1987

– *Uno statuto controverso. Considerazioni sulla storia costituzionale*, in *Quaderni costituzionali*, 1995, 95–109

– *Storia della Corte costituzionale*, Napoli 1996

Casini L., *La prima sentenza della Corte costituzionale: le memorie processuali*, in *Rivista trimestrale di diritto pubblico*, 1, 2006, 13–76

Cerri A., *La giurisprudenza costituzionale*, in *Rivista trimestrale di diritto pubblico*, 41, 2001, 1325–1362

Cheli E., *Il giudice delle leggi: la Corte costituzionale nelle dinamiche dei poteri*, Bologna 1999

Costa P., *Democrazia politica e Stato costituzionale*, Napoli 1996

Cruz Villalón P., *La formación del sistema europeo de control de constitucionalidad (1918–1939)*, Madrid 1987

De Nicola E., *La Corte inizia la sua attività*, in *1956–2006. Cinquant'anni di Corte costituzionale*, cit., t. I

De Siervo U., *Riflessioni su un'esperienza di lavoro alla Corte costituzionale*, in *Giornale di storia costituzionale*, 1, 11, 2006, 81–91

D'Orazio G., *La genesi della Corte costituzionale*, Milano 1981

Ferri M., *La ricerca dell'essenziale. Intervista*, in *Giornale di storia costituzionale*, 1, 11, 2006, 65–79

Gorla G., *Diritto comparato e diritto comune europeo*, Milano 1981

Grossi P., *Il diritto tra potere e ordinamento*, Napoli 2005

Grossi P., *Il costituzionalismo moderno fra mito e storia*, in *Giornale di storia costituzionale*, 1, 11, 2006, 25–52

Häberle P., *Colloquio sulla "costituzione europea"*, a cura di P. Ridola, in *Diritto romano attuale*, 2, 1999

Lacchè L., *Tra storia e comparazione*, in *Giornale di storia costituzionale*, 1, 2001, 5–6

Lagi S., *Kelsen e la Corte costituzionale austriaca: un percorso storico-politico (1918–1920)*, in *Giornale di storia costituzionale*, 1, 11, 2006, 165–176

Le Divellec A., *Les Prémices de la justice constitutionnelle en Allemagne avant 1945*, in D. Chagnollaud (a cura di), *Aux origines du contrôle de constitutionnalité XVIIIe–XXe siècle*, Paris 2000, 103– 140

Luciani M., *Costituzionalismo irenico e costituzionalismo polemico*, in www.associazionedeicostituzionalisti.it

Luciani M., *La Corte costituzionale vista "di là dal banco"*, in *Giornale di storia costituzionale*, 1, 11, 2006, 113–117

Luther J., *Idee e storie di giustizia costituzionale nell'Ottocento*, Torino 1990

Massera A., *Materiali per uno studio sulla Corte costituzionale*, in *Rivista trimestrale di diritto pubblico*, a. XXII, 1972, 833–890

Mazzarella F., *Un diritto "allo stato fluido". Note storico-giuridiche su* aequitas *e ragionevolezza*, in *Giornale di storia costituzionale*, 1, 11, 2006, 121–144

Meccarelli M., *Il grande assente? Controllo di costituzionalità e giurisdizione suprema nell'Italia post-unitaria*, in *Giornale di storia costituzionale*, 4/II, 2002, 173–188

Mezzanotte C., *Il giudizio sulle leggi. I. Le ideologie del Costituente*, Milano 1979

Onida V., *Magistratura e Corte costituzionale*, in AA.VV., *Aspetti e tendenze del diritto costituzionale: scritti in onore di Costantinc Mortati*, Milano 1977

Paladin L., *La questione del metodo nella storia costituzionale*, in *Quaderni fiorentini per la storia del pensiero giuridico moderno*, 26, 1997, 243–263

– *Per una storia costituzionale dell'Italia repubblicana*, Bologna 2004

Pasquino P., *Constitutional Adjudication and Democracy. Comparative Perspectives: USA, France, Italy*, in *Ratio iuris*, 11, mars 1998, 38–50

Pasquino P., *Controllo di costituzionalità e forma di governo in Italia*, in *Giornale di storia costituzionale*, 1, 11, 2006, 309–320

Pinelli C., *Diritto e storia costituzionale*, in *Giornale di storia costituzionale*, 1, 2001, 17–19

Pinelli C., *I rapporti fra Corte e Parlamento in mancanza di una politica costituzionale*, in *Giornale di storia costituzionale*, 1, 11, 2006, 321–327

Presno Linera M., *25 años de historia del Tribunal Constitucional español: acordes y desacordes* in *Giornale di storia costituzionale*, 1, 11, 2006, 235–257

Rodotà C., *Storia della Corte costituzionale*, Bari 1999

Ruperto C., *Costituzione e Corte costituzionale: un'esperienza* (2002), in *La Costituzione in mezzo a noi*, a cura e con introduzione di A. de Nitto, Milano 2005, 1–16

Salerno G., *In piedi ... entra il popolo sovrano!*, in *Giornale di storia costituzionale*, 1, 11, 2006, 329–338

Sandulli A. M., *Il dodicesimo anniversario dall'inizio dell'attività della Corte*, in *1956–2006. Cinquant'anni di Corte costituzionale*, cit., t. I

Schefold D., *Corte costituzionale e sistema costituzionale in Germania*, in *Giornale di storia costituzionale*, 1, 11, 2006, 209–234

Simoncini A., *L'avvio della Corte costituzionale e gli strumenti per la definizione del suo ruolo: un problema storico aperto*, in *Giurisprudenza costituzionale*, 4, 2004, 3065–3104

Simoncini A., *L'istituzione della Corte costituzionale e la sua affermazione: una lezione dalla storia*, in *Giornale di storia costituzionale*, 1, 11, 2006, 295–307

Sperti A., *Corti supreme e conflitti tra poteri. Spunti per un confronto Italia–USA sugli strumenti e le tecniche di giudizio del giudice costituzionale*, Torino 2005

Sperti A., *I giudici costituzionali e la comparazione giuridica*, in *Giornale di storia costituzionale*, 1, 11, 2006, 195–208

Torre A., *La Corte suprema del Regno Unito: la nuova forma di una vecchia idea*, in *Giornale di storia costituzionale*, 1, 11, 2006, 259–286

Tranfaglia N., *Per una storia politica della Corte costituzionale*, in *Dallo stato liberale al regime fascista. Problemi e ricerche*, Milano 1973, 185–280

Vassalli G., *Testimonianza*, in *Giornale di storia costituzionale*, 1, 11, 2006, 55–64

Zagrebelsky G., *Principî e voti. La Corte costituzionale e la politica*, Torino 2005

– *Corti costituzionali e diritti universali, Relazione del Presidente emerito G. Zagrebelsky in occasione dell'incontro del 21 aprile 2006 al Palazzo del Quirinale*, in *Rivista trimestrale di diritto pubblico*, 2, 2006, 279–311

Zoller E. (a cura di), *Marbury v. Madison: 1803–2003. Un dialogue franco-américain*, Paris 2003

Il tempo e i tempi della Costituzione

1. "Inadeguatezza" della Costituzione? Per una visione polittica del fenomeno costituzionale

Il mio intervento[1] prenderà in considerazione, selettivamente, solo alcuni dei temi presentati e discussi nel seminario «Dalla Costituzione "inattuata" alla Costituzione "inattuale"? Potere costituente e riforme costituzionali nell'Italia repubblicana». E cercherà di instaurare un dialogo anzitutto con le riflessioni di Massimo Luciani esposte nella sua relazione introduttiva su *Dottrina del moto delle costituzioni e vicende della Costituzione repubblicana* e con i lucidi commenti di apertura di Giuditta Brunelli e Pietro Costa, e infine con le suggestioni di lettura tratte da coloro che sono intervenuti nel corso del seminario. Il tema è così vasto e problematico, come il dibattito ha dimostrato, da richiedere cautela in chi dovrebbe tracciare, seppur parzialmente, qualche linea "conclusiva".

Io vorrei cominciare da un passaggio della relazione di Luciani che non è stato sin qui richiamato e che mi sembra utile per riconfermare un'indicazione metodica che questo seminario ha voluto approfondire. «Il fatto è – osserva Luciani – che nessun discorso sulle costituzioni, sulla misura della loro prescrittività attuale, sulle loro prospettive storiche, insomma sui loro destini, può reggere se non è condotto da una molteplicità di prospettive e con l'ausilio degli apporti di molte discipline. È forte, dunque, la sensazione che la tesi dell'inadeguatezza della Costituzione repubblicana rispetto alle sfide del presente e del prossimo futuro (oltre, nessuno sa ragionevolmente vedere) si appoggi su una serie di semplificazioni teoriche e su una povertà di acquisizioni probatorie che ne segnano negativamente la capacità esplicativa».

Il "discorso" sulla Costituzione è troppo serio per non meritare approcci disciplinari ben integrati. Il dialogo tra costituzionalisti e storici – che il seminario illustra e rende programmatico – registra questa esigenza. L'inadeguatezza

1 Il presente contributo conserva i caratteri dell'intervento orale svolto nella Tavola rotonda conclusiva del Seminario ferrarese con l'aggiunta di un apparato bibliografico essenziale.

presunta della Costituzione segnala probabilmente anche alcune inadeguatezze nell'analisi e nella previsione. Occorre delineare, credo, quello che chiamo un approccio *polittico*.[2] Il nostro "quadro di riferimento" è infatti come un grande polittico che faccia da pala d'altare del tempio costituzionale. Come è noto, i polittici sono composizioni multiple. Al centro l'ancona può raffigurare la Maestà o il Cristo in croce, ma più il polittico è grande e ambizioso più si arricchisce di predelle, cimase, cuspidi, riquadri con immagini di santi, scene di vita, angeli, piccoli paesaggi, racchiusi da possenti cornici dorate. Ora, il lavoro di chi mette al centro dell'indagine scientifica la Costituzione e, più ampiamente, il "fenomeno costituzionale" nella dimensione diacronica e geopolitica, assomiglia in fondo a quello dello storico dell'arte che cerca di ricomporre e ricondurre ad unità i non pochi polittici che la storia ha smembrato tra luoghi di committenza, musei e collezioni. Ogni "pezzo" ha un *senso*, un *valore*, può essere visto a sé stante, ma il "fenomeno costituzionale" è la continua – Luciani parla di "moto" – combinazione / scombinazione delle parti nel tutto, tra passato, presente e futuro. Noi possiamo osservare le "predelle" come elementi dotati di una qualche autonomia, di una "vita" propria, eppure tutto cambia quando, per la fortunata coincidenza dell'avvenuta ricomposizione delle parti isolate, possiamo riammirare un polittico nella sua struttura originaria. Vediamo allora le corrispondenze, il disegno complessivo, potremmo dire la «molteplicità delle prospettive». L'ancona del polittico è diventata per noi la Costituzione (la Maestà) e tutto attorno stanno le forme e le strutture della società, della politica, dell'economia, dell'antropologia, della cultura ... Per leggere il grande "polittico costituzionale" – spesso bifronte – mai come oggi occorre un approccio integrato. Ed una domanda che non si può aggirare è: inadeguata la Costituzione o inadeguato ciò che gli sta intorno?[3]

2. Il tempio, il tempo e i sacerdoti

Non v'è alcun dubbio sul fatto che la Costituzione – ovvero l'insieme di valori, principi e diritti che essa "contiene" nel suo inveramento storico – stia al centro della scena. Noi parliamo dell'esperienza italiana, ma il dibattito sul *Global Constitutionalism* ci rivela da anni scenari e controversie continentali e mondiali. Questo seminario ha fatto emergere domande sull'identità disciplinare, culturale e civile del "costituzionalista", di chi cioè per "professione" osserva, studia e delimita il campo della Costituzione. La sua, per certi versi, è una sorta di professione "religiosa" attraverso la quale viene ammesso al "sacerdozio". La sua Maestà è la Costituzione. Dico questo – con qualche esagerazione – per rilevare

2 Lacchè 2001, 5.
3 Cheli 2012.

tuttavia un'impressione, ovvero che nessun'altra figura di giurista / intellettuale sembra aver instaurato – dopo l'avvento delle costituzioni "forti" del dopoguerra – un legame così stretto e coinvolgente con una "fonte", o meglio, "superfonte" a più dimensioni. Il grido di dolore che da più di uno è stato levato («Noi costituzionalisti non contiamo niente ...»), evoca a mio avviso un sentimento di disagio di fronte allo smarrimento, reale o dichiarato, di senso e di valore della Costituzione.

Questo "atto di fondazione" evoca una dimensione del "sacro". L'abate Sieyès aveva còlto per tempo il profilo "teologico" della messa in opera del potere costituente inteso quale concetto-soglia della "nuova" matrice costituzionale. Questo legame forte tra il costituzionalista e il suo campo di indagine trova, a mio avviso, anche un risvolto sul piano tecnico-dogmatico. Tanto da far ritenere che la elaborazione più raffinata e generale della teoria del diritto sia passata in una prima fase, come un testimone, da ciò che risiedeva saldamente, tra la fine dell'Ottocento e una parte del Novecento, nel campo dei romanisti / civilisti (nel solco della tarda pandettistica), nelle mani della teoria e del diritto che sempre più guardavano allo spazio costituzionale (*judicial review*, *rule of law*, *jurisprudence*). Con, tuttavia, un punto critico tutt'altro che piccolo: un progressivo crescente sbilanciamento verso la giurisprudenza costituzionale e le singole sentenze col rischio di far «perdere le coordinate generali del complessivo costrutto costituzionale».[4]

È fondamentale dunque, come si è fatto in questo seminario, problematizzare il rapporto tra la dogmatica, le categorie concettuali, le «cristallizzazioni culturali»[5] e la dimensione storico-evolutiva. Il rapporto tra *Costituzione e tempo* – soprattutto nell'accezione häberliana di *öffentlicher Prozeß*[6] – riveste caratteri ulteriori e specifici rispetto a quelli che possiamo rubricare sotto la voce «Diritto e tempo». Per restare sul piano fenomenologico e parafrasando Heidegger, si potrebbe parlare di *esistenzialismo costituzionale*, del *senso dell'essere nel tempo di una costituzione*. Luciani ricorda che la costituzione di ascendenza illuministica, essendo un atto di volontà *politica*, ha la pretesa di modellare il reale. Essa vuole plasmare i destini di una comunità politica. Ma questa tensione *ad aeternitatem* si scontra con la sfida della storia e del cambiamento. «Si ha, dunque, che una costituzione non può nascere – senza contraddire se stessa – né come provvisoria né come eterna».[7] Le costituzioni sono sempre e comunque destinate al movimento. La costituzione esiste e viene "gettata nel mondo", opera nel concreto del

4 Cassese 2012, 621.
5 Su questa categoria v. Häberle 2001.
6 Häberle 1978.
7 Martines 1978, 791.

mondo-della-vita. È sulla soglia storica della contemporaneità che all'idea ambigua e controversa di costituzione si comincia ad assegnare un significato più specifico, ponendo il problema della dimensione temporale della costituzione come norma giuridica. Come è noto, la *querelle* sull'esistenza o meno della costituzione (antica) di fronte al moto per "gettare nel mondo" una costituzione di tipo nuovo (atto di volontà, razionale, istitutore di un ordine, a tendenza prescrittiva) è al centro delle grandi rivoluzioni costituzionali, dall'Inghilterra del '600 alla Francia rivoluzionaria, passando per il grande laboratorio americano, seppure con forme ed esiti ben diversi.

Per la prima visione la *costituzione è il tempo*. È la costituzione-tempo. Qui la temporalità storica identifica, costruisce, trasforma le dinamiche e quindi il fenomeno costituzionale. La costituzione si costruisce nella temporalità storica, rappresenta, nel suo progredire, forme e modi di essere della società e delle sue principali strutture.

Per la seconda visione, nella soglia tra moderno e contemporaneo, inizia il cammino della costituzione come vero atto di fondazione, *atto che istituisce un suo tempo* – «tamquam Deus» potremmo dire – tale da incidere anche sulla sua stessa evoluzione (il moto). Nella forma più "radicale" (che spesso, con un po' di semplificazione, ribattezziamo "giacobina") c'è l'idea della costituzione come nuova *religio societatis*. La rivoluzione costituzionale pensa il tempo come ragione e non più come tradizione. Il rapporto tra la Costituzione e il tempo presenta forme di eccedenza rispetto alla classica considerazione del diritto nel «tempo storico».[8]

Queste due visioni, che *in nuce* contengono la dialettica tra costituzione-bilancio e costituzione-programma, si affrontano per tutto l'Ottocento: le costituzioni ottriate e la costituzione liberale e rappresentativa ne sono una complessa testimonianza.[9]

È nel corso del Novecento che la costituzione assume definitivamente una dimensione progettuale organica. Su questo terreno Massimo Luciani usa un'espressione efficace, parla infatti dell'«eccedenza progettuale» della Costituzione italiana. Proprio la ricordata distinzione tra applicazione e attuazione "chiarita" dalla sentenza n. 1/1956 della Corte costituzionale[10] sancisce il riconoscimento della Costituzione come atto che apre «percorsi di sviluppo sociale, indica obiettivi, disegna scenari futuri». Questa eccedenza progettuale – vista

8 Husserl 1998.

9 V. *supra* in questo volume *Granted Constitutions. The Theory of* octroi, 227–257. La prospettiva del carattere politico-programmatico non era però certo sconosciuta alle *konstitutionelle Verfassungen* ottocentesche (Manca 2003).

10 Vassalli 2006; Bartole 2004.

inizialmente attraverso l'acceso dibattito sulla dialettica norme programmatiche / prescrittive – non poteva soddisfarsi con la pur fondamentale applicazione, ma richiedeva l'attivazione del circuito della volontà politica (costituente). La tensione tra la forza progettuale della Costituzione e l'intermittente o, poi, inconcludente, progettualità della politica (con la p minuscola) è stata una questione cruciale per la storia italiana del dopoguerra. La Costituzione incorpora una temporalità eccedente al punto da dovere / volere rinviare al futuro la sua dimensione fenomenologica.

3. I tempi, le generazioni, la Costituzione

Se abbiamo parlato di esistenzialismo costituzionale e di Costituzione e tempo, dovremo però approfondire questa riflessione in una prospettiva nella quale la narrazione si frammenta in temporalità multiple. La settimana scorsa ho partecipato ad un seminario coordinato da Paolo Pombeni sul "peso della storia"[11] nelle ricostruzioni del dopoguerra. Il tempo si declina al plurale: sembrano infatti emergere quattro tempi.

Il primo è il *tempo dell'agire politico*, della politica nuova rappresentata soprattutto dalle forze politico-partitiche. È il tempo che accende il *potere costituente*. Questo è un tempo che parla il linguaggio della rigenerazione, della rifondazione, della ricostruzione. Nel dibattito di quegli anni si intrecciano due immagini: quella delle macerie e quella della fondazione della "casa comune". Le rovine non sono innocue, come osserva Georg Simmel in un saggio del 1911.[12] La rovina è *produttiva* e si può vedere come evento che acquista autonomia ed una precisa capacità di esistenza.[13] Costruire sulle macerie non è semplice, bisogna «sgombrare il campo», come dice Calamandrei. Questo tempo è chiamato a enfatizzare la frattura con il "prima", se non addirittura a costruire "contro". Il potere sovrano determina la Costituzione e si trasforma poi come potere del Parlamento e quindi come legislatore "attuatore".

Ma il *tempo della Costituzione*,[14] come detto, è un tempo nuovo. Come si è già osservato, la Costituzione è figlia del *tempo dell'agire politico costituente* ed è l'architrave per l'attuazione della democrazia pluralista. Ma come atto di fondazione, *atto che istituisce un suo tempo*, essa *deve* poter determinare le

11 *Il peso della storia nella gestione del consenso politico. Italia, Austria, Germania e Francia nel secondo dopoguerra*, 17 gennaio 2013, Istituto storico italo-germanico, Fondazione Bruno Kessler.

12 Simmel 1911, 122.

13 Lacchè 2010a, 155.

14 In questa sede non si può affrontare il tema del *tempo nella Costituzione*. Cfr. Giocoli Nacci 1984.

condizioni per la sua stessa evoluzione (il moto). In questa prospettiva l'attuazione costituzionale non può che essere il punto d'attacco. L'inattuazione non potrà che essere vista come tradimento[15] o, almeno, come dilazione. La *Costituzione* è storicamente determinata ma essa è destinata – una volta "gettata nel mondo" – a diventare movimento, divenendo la "madre" di chi l'ha generata (il *tempo dell'agire politico*). Se l'«uomo del futuro» può essere rappresentato dal legislatore, come ci dice Gerhart Husserl, tanto più ciò deve valere per il costituente in quanto massimo *pianificatore*. La costituzione è una grande «freccia del futuro».[16] Da qui discende anche la centralità della Costituzione del 1948 (con cui tutti devono fare i conti), il suo essere vero «riferimento pivotale»[17] per diventare ordine consolidato e legittimato.

In questa prospettiva, però, non possiamo ignorare altri due "tempi", quello dei giuristi e della scienza giuridica e quello dei giudici.

Qui ritroviamo temi che sembrano riecheggiare "lontani" dibattiti settecenteschi che prefigurano distintamente la tensione tra la durata della costituzione, il posto della sovranità e il moto impetuoso della democrazia, tra l'Ulisse che si fa legare all'albero della nave e il canto delle sirene. È il tema della vita come dimensione del presente e del rapporto di *commitment* tra democrazia e costituzionalismo.[18] Può ogni generazione voler essere libera di legare a sé le seguenti, senza però essere più legata alle precedenti? Per Thomas Jefferson la durata non era garanzia di venerabilità. «La vana presunzione di governare dalla tomba – osservava Thomas Paine – è la più ridicola e oltraggiosa di tutte le tirannidi. L'uomo non ha diritti di proprietà sull'uomo, e nessuna generazione ha diritti di proprietà sulle generazioni a venire».[19]

Questo topos argomentativo (poi "canonizzato" dall'art. 28 della costituzione francese del 1793) è rivolto soprattutto contro la costituzione-tempo e la tradizione, e non contro l'idea di un determinato rapporto tra sovrano e revisione.[20] «... la costituzione si sarebbe attualizzata, nel senso di trovare il proprio fondamento di validità non più nel passato ma nella forza dell'incontro di volontà presenti e future. Ed era appunto del futuro che il moderno costituzionalismo puntava a farsi carico, non senza contraddizioni, attraverso l'*engagement*, lo scambio di auspici e promesse, l'accordo tra individui e fra generazioni, di cui la costituzione sarebbe stato l'esito giuridicamente e politicamente più alto».[21]

15 Calamandrei 1996.
16 Husserl 1998, 52.
17 Bonini 2007, 23.
18 Rubenfeld 2001.
19 Cfr. Elster 1992; Elster 1996; Elster 2004; Holmes 1996; Holmes 1998.
20 Fioravanti 2009a, 77 ss.
21 Persano 2007, 181.

La dimensione "intragenerazionale" è ben presente nel confronto tra culture e "antropologie" dei giuristi negli anni attorno alla Costituente. In un intervento tenuto il 26 ottobre 1945 davanti alla Consulta, Ferruccio Parri osservava: «Io non so, non credo che si possano definire regimi democratici quelli che avevamo prima del fascismo ... [interruzioni, scambio di apostrofi, commenti, rumori]. Non vorrei offendere con queste mie parole quei regimi [commenti, interruzioni, rumori]. Mi rincresce che la mia definizione sia male accetta. Intendevo dire questo: democratico ha un significato preciso, direi tecnico. Quelli erano regimi che possiamo definire e ritenere liberali [Interruzioni, commenti, grida di: Viva Orlando! Vivissimi e prolungati applausi all'indirizzo dell'on. Orlando, grida di: Viva Vittorio Veneto!]».[22] È altrettanto nota la replica di Benedetto Croce che rivendicava allo Stato liberale italiano (1860–1922) una autentica sostanza democratica.

Gli evviva rivolti all'indirizzo di Vittorio Emanuele Orlando, prima della scelta costituente del 2 giugno 1946, evocavano il mondo dello Stato liberale nella sua valenza politica e giuridica. Ma la partita della Costituzione vide la sconfitta, sul piano concettuale, del mondo "antico" della tradizione costituzionale del *Rechtsstaat*, della specifica forma dello Stato liberale di diritto formatosi in Italia tra i due secoli. La scienza italiana del diritto pubblico di Orlando, Ranelletti, Amorth, Amedeo Giannini e molti altri non ha più in mano la giusta bussola per navigare nel mare nuovo della Costituzione. L'11 marzo 1947 Palmiro Togliatti in Assemblea Costituente non dovrà più adottare le cautele di Parri. «Noi siamo responsabili del futuro verso i nostri figli, verso i nostri nipoti. Per questo facciamo una nuova Costituzione, cioè vogliamo fondare un ordinamento costituzionale nuovo, tenendo conto di quello che è accaduto, cioè tirando le somme di un processo storico e politico che si è concluso con una catastrofe nazionale. Questa catastrofe, signori, è stata in pari tempo il fallimento di una classe dirigente, e questa è dunque la vera questione, che sta davanti a noi e che ci deve orientare in tutto il dibattito[23] costituzionale. Il popolo italiano infatti oggi non può [fare] a meno di chiedersi se questa sconfitta che abbiamo subìto, questo disastro nel quale ci hanno gettato, era qualche cosa di inevitabile, legata a uno di quei cataclismi che travolgono popoli e regimi, come furono nel passato le invasioni barbariche [...]. Questa sconfitta non era inevitabile. Colleghi, io sento rispetto, e anche più che rispetto, per gli uomini che siedono in quest'aula e che appartengono ai gruppi che furono parte integrante di questa vecchia classe dirigente [...] però non posso non sentire e non affermare che

22 *Atti della Consulta Nazionale. Discorsi dal 25 ottobre 1945 al 9 marzo 1946*, Roma, Tipografia della Camera dei Deputati, 18.

23 Cfr. Gentile, Grasso 1999.

anche questi uomini portano una parte della responsabilità per la catastrofe che si è abbattuta sul popolo italiano. Perché voi avevate occhi e non avete visto».

Nel corso di questa celebre "requisitoria", Togliatti critica, non a caso, i giuristi italiani che avevano accolto dottrine dannose. «Oserei dire che nel nostro lavoro non ci hanno dato grande aiuto i giuristi. Non se ne abbiano a male i colleghi che esercitano questa nobile professione, che del resto avrebbe potuto essere anche la mia, se la politica non mi avesse traviato ... Negli ultimi venti o trenta anni (...) sono affiorate e sono state accolte, soprattutto nel nostro Paese, dottrine diverse (...) che riconoscono e collocano la sovranità non nel popolo, ma soltanto nello Stato, e danno quindi ai diritti individuali soltanto un carattere riflesso. La scienza giuridica degli ultimi venti anni è stata permeata da queste nuove dottrine, e questo spiega perché, quando abbiamo dovuto scrivere una Costituzione democratica e abbiamo chiesto l'ausilio dei giuristi, essi non sono stati in grado di darci un aiuto efficace ...».[24]

In realtà, come sappiamo bene, la critica di Togliatti è manichea e non distingue tra i due "tempi dei giuristi". Può sembrare un paradosso – ma non lo è – il fatto che i "neoterici" – come Mortati, Crisafulli, Lavagna, Tosato, Esposito, Massimo Severo Giannini ecc. (tutti protagonisti del dibattito costituente e della prima attuazione) – si siano formati durante il fascismo e da lì abbiano cominciato, tra gli anni '30 e '40, a porre le basi per una *nuova dottrina della costituzione*[25] che muove dalla teoria del potere costituente, dalla riflessione sull'indirizzo politico e sulla forma-partito. La generazione orlandiana (che abbraccia almeno due generazioni della giuspubblicistica italiana) prova disagio verso ciò che sta prendendo forma. Nel campo dei giuristi, pur senza la visibilità dello scontro politico, si affrontano infatti visioni e culture diverse della Costituzione. Dalla parte degli uni riaffiora la cultura della costituzione-tempo, progrediente, elastica, elaborata in chiave anticostruttivista dalla *Staatslehre* italiana. Dalla parte degli altri ri-emerge la dottrina della costituzione-atto, manifestazione forte del potere costituente di cui è depositario il popolo sovrano per fondare la democrazia costituzionale. Gli uni hanno bisogno di una costituzione capace di governare una temporalità senza strappi violenti, gli altri vogliono un progetto per costruire il presente e orientare il futuro.[26] La visione degli uni separa diritto e politica, quella degli altri li integra.

Il dibattito sulla qualificazione delle norme costituzionali, certi interventi giurisprudenziali (si pensi alla sentenza del 7 febbraio 1948 della Cassazione

24 Assemblea Costituente, 11 marzo 1947, in *La Costituzione nei lavori preparatori dell'Assemblea costituente*, Roma, Camera dei Deputati, 1970, 328–329.

25 Fioravanti 2001.

26 Costa 2012, 134–137.

penale a sezioni unite), i commenti dottrinali mostrano come la posta in gioco fosse, in ultima istanza, il valore / posizione della Costituzione.[27] L'eccedenza progettuale della Costituzione era proprio ciò che procurava "disorientamento" e suscitava resistenze, anzitutto culturali, da parte di tutti coloro che leggevano il testo con gli occhiali del paradigma statualistico. Riecheggiava la formula che Carl Schmitt aveva affibbiato alla costituzione di Weimar come *dilatorische Formelkompromisse.* Il concetto di «compromesso costituzionale», ampiamente utilizzato in sede costituente, poteva essere interpretato in vari modi e strumentalizzato. Ma normatività piena della Costituzione e progettualità erano due facce della stessa medaglia. In questa prospettiva, l'azionabilità delle norme della Costituzione diveniva il terreno di confronto. Proprio la novità delle norme definite, polemicamente, "programmatiche" e direttive – considerate enunciazioni politico-ideologiche e sociali, sorta di proclami e di promesse per un futuro indeterminato – consisteva nel loro essere indirizzo di politica costituzionale aperto al futuro.

L'istituzione della Corte costituzionale e il dialogo con i giudici furono momenti decisivi per affermare i nuovi e originali caratteri della Costituzione repubblicana.[28] Non fu uno scontro tra "buoni" e "cattivi" – come Luciani sottolinea – ma si trattò piuttosto di un processo di transizione che non poteva non avvertire il "peso della storia". La Corte costituzionale fece valere la supremazia della Costituzione nei riguardi delle altre fonti normative. L'applicazione prendeva così la propria strada, ma l'attuazione sarebbe rimasto il vero problema di fondo.

4. Il quarto tempo

La forte dimensione prospettica della Costituzione ha contrassegnato quelli che possiamo chiamare i primi Trenta anni "gloriosi". In questi decenni le retoriche dell'attuazione e dell'inattuazione sono state le due facce di una stessa medaglia, coniata dall'eccedenza progettuale della Costituzione e dalla sua spinta in avanti. Entrambe sono state *politiche costituzionali* nell'ambito di un gioco complesso. È nel corso degli anni '70 – come ha ben messo in luce Maurizio Fioravanti[29] – che la spinta in avanti comincia a indebolirsi destando la preoccupazione di alcuni padri della Costituzione, a cominciare da Costantino Mortati. Già sul finire degli anni '60 Mortati denunciava il fatto che «la forza di rottura, potenzialmente contenuta nel testo costituzionale, radicalmente innovatore

27 Gregorio 2006.
28 Fioravanti 2007.
29 Fioravanti 2007, 2009b, 20 ss.

rispetto non solo alla ideologia fascista ma anche a quella liberale, non ha trovato forze sufficienti a metterla in opera, sicchè la costituzione materiale, quale si è di fatto realizzata, ha privato di efficacia, non solo e non tanto singoli precetti costituzionali, quanto la sua più profonda essenza».[30] Il problema non risiedeva tanto nelle singole inattuazioni quanto nell'indebolimento *materiale* delle *forze* che quella Costituzione avevano voluto.

Per Massimo Luciani la ragione dell'indebolimento risiede anzitutto nella progressiva delineazione di uno squilibrio. Nella fase di *take-off* – pur con limiti ed episodici scantonamenti – l'applicazione giudiziale della Costituzione e l'azione riformatrice del potere politico-parlamentare hanno avuto uno stesso indirizzo. I problemi sono cominciati quando l'attuazione costituzionale – riservata al circuito della sovranità popolare – ha imboccato con forza crescente la strada delle aule di giustizia. Questo processo avrebbe ingenerato uno squilibrio tra politica e diritto tale da incidere sulla fisiologia dello Stato costituzionale democratico. E ciò avrebbe prodotto l'avvio di un'altra retorica, quella dell'inattualità della Costituzione e della necessità della "grande riforma", destinata a caratterizzare sterilmente gli ultimi venticinque anni della nostra vita costituzionale.

Il quarto tempo, ovvero la quarta delle scansioni temporali evocate all'inizio, è quello che chiama in causa la giurisdizione e i giudici. La crisi della politica (Mortati avrebbe detto delle forze insufficienti) è stata vista come il contrappunto, in Italia, della *montée en puissance* della giurisdizione. Il fenomeno è certamente complesso e dipende – come lo stesso Luciani osserva nella sua relazione – da una pluralità di fattori. L'"aristocratizzazione"[31] per via giurisdizionale della Costituzione mette in discussione il primato della politica democratica e la sua prerogativa in chiave di attuazione. La supplenza della giurisdizione diventa così effetto ed alibi al tempo stesso, fenomeno "necessitato" e accompagnato da prese di posizione della dottrina costituzionalistica. «... basta dire che quella che sembra esaltazione della prescrittività costituzionale è, in realtà, radicale alterazione del modello disegnato dalla Costituzione repubblicana, che è strutturato secondo le linee direttrici prima indicate ed è fortemente caratterizzato dal positivo apprezzamento dell'agire politico, inteso anzitutto come strumento di compimento del percorso di sviluppo della personalità di tutti e di ciascuno tracciato dall'art. 3, comma 2» (Luciani). Il *costituzionalismo polemico* è legato alla ineliminabilità del conflitto che non può essere delimitato dalle aule dei tribunali ma deve restare al centro di una politica politico-parlamentare rigenerata alla quale conservare l'arduo compito di identificare

30 Mortati 1969, 467.
31 Luciani 2011, 5.

tempi e modi del compimento del percorso indicato dalla Costituzione, nel rispetto dei suoi contenuti di valore.

Ho parlato del tempo della giurisdizione come quarto tempo, per sottolineare che nello sviluppo della Costituzione italiana il richiamo ai tempi "al plurale" ci può tornare utile per coglierne le sfasature, le aritmie. Solo in parte, e in alcuni momenti, i tempi nel "tempo storico" della Costituzione procedono in maniera "coordinata". Anzi, come abbiamo visto, le tensioni e i conflitti fanno parte integrante del processo di legittimazione. Non bisogna allora dimenticare che lo *spazio* della giustizia costituzionale, la *posizione*, la *natura* e le *funzioni* della Corte non erano, in origine, né univoci né ampiamente legittimati. Nel contesto di costituzioni democratiche rampollate da una manifestazione *forte* del potere costituente e segnate, a livello ideologico, da una decisiva marcatura del primato della *politica*, la giustizia costituzionale doveva conquistarsi una sua fisionomia. Le obiezioni e le perplessità sollevate nel corso del dibattito costituente avverso l'ipotesi di una Corte costituzionale erano accomunate, pur partendo da posizioni ideologiche anche molto distanti, dal timore che la nuova istituzione (per natura, composizione ecc.) fosse inadeguata. Di gran lunga più forte avrebbe dovuto essere la dimensione *politica* della Corte per coloro che intendevano assegnarle un pieno fondamento democratico (lungo il circuito sovranità popolare – partiti – parlamento – legge sovrana); più *tecnica* invece – quindi più *giudiziaria* – per chi ne temeva al contrario la "politicizzazione". In realtà questi timori erano spesso dettati dalla difficoltà oggettiva di *pensare* un organo del tutto nuovo che avrebbe dovuto al tempo stesso salvaguardare la tradizione "classica" del costituzionalismo liberale – il limite e la garanzia – e rendere attuabile l'*indirizzo* costituzionale ispirato dal livello superiore, rigido, dei principi e dei valori. La Corte costituzionale nasceva all'incrocio di due costituzionalismi, quello liberale e quello democratico, ne assumeva i dilemmi, le tensioni, le grandi sfide. La Corte si incuneava, quale snodo essenziale, nella storica tensione tra democrazia politica e Stato costituzionale, tra *voluntas* e *ratio*.[32] Aveva ragione La Pira quando diceva che senza la Corte costituzionale l'edificio sarebbe rimasto "senza tetto". La giustizia costituzionale è diventata non a caso uno degli emblemi delle democrazie contemporanee (e lo è a livello "estetico" anche quando si tratta di costruire democrazie solo sulla carta) proprio perché rafforzando a livello *costituzionale* la cultura del limite (contro l'assolutismo politico) e della garanzia (dei diritti, soprattutto dei soggetti più deboli e delle minoranze) ha consolidato lo sviluppo stesso dei principi costituzionali.

32 Costa 2006.

La via italiana alla *giustizia nella costituzione* è tra le più interessanti per la sua sostanziale originalità. Ibridazione empirica di modalità e di strumenti, *mixtum compositum* (da subito con la legge n. 1 del 1948) di accentramento e di incidentalità del giudizio, non inquadrabile dentro gli schemi del principio "astratto" di separazione dei poteri,[33] «snodo elastico tra le due sfere, tra la giurisdizione e la politica ...»,[34] flessibile nei suoi presupposti di indeterminatezza del testo costituzionale, la Corte italiana è nata ed ha poi cominciato ad operare pragmaticamente in un quadro di riferimento incerto e contraddittorio. La non applicazione dell'art. 28 della legge n. 87 del 1953 – che escludeva ogni valutazione di natura politica e ogni sindacato sull'uso del potere discrezionale del Parlamento – è un chiaro esempio di quanto detto.[35]

Riflettere sull'avvio della Corte non è un ozioso problema storico-giuridico. La tesi dell'«ostruzionismo di maggioranza» – assunta tradizionalmente, sulla scia di Calamandrei e di numerosi altri protagonisti – quale cifra della prima legislatura repubblicana ha molto influito anche sull'inquadramento storico della Corte. Fermo restando il dato politico dell'inattuazione costituzionale, l'anno 1953 è stato percepito più come l'anno della cd. "legge truffa" che delle leggi costituzionali in materia di giustizia costituzionale. È lo stesso Parlamento però ad approvare, a grandissima maggioranza, le leggi attuative. Già Livio Paladin aveva còlto i limiti di una interpretazione puramente "ostruzionistica"[36] e ricerche ulteriori sembrano confermare quei dubbi.[37] «Va, perciò, quantomeno corretto un diffuso giudizio sulla istituzione della Corte: questa nuova istituzione repubblicana nasce, certamente, in un contesto politico dominato da un fortissimo contrasto tra maggioranza ed opposizione, probabilmente, nasce tra sospetti e ostilità politiche, *ma, in primo luogo e soprattutto, nasce circondata da una diffusa incomprensione del suo ruolo e da una radicale incertezza sulla sua natura*».[38]

È stato acutamente osservato che la Corte, non potendo proporsi, in quel momento, né come custode dei valori fondamentali né come arbitro tra gli interessi in conflitto,[39] ha scelto il ruolo "obbligato"[40] di "motore delle riforme". Svolgendo una funzione di supplenza del potere politico e del legislativo, l'alta giurisdizione ha rivolto lo sguardo anzitutto verso il passato[41] consolidando la sua posizione "riformatrice". Il Presidente della Corte Gaetano Azzariti, nel corso

33 Pasquino 2006.
34 Cheli 1999, 31.
35 Pinelli 2006.
36 Paladin 2004, 98.
37 Bisogni 2004, 71 ss.
38 Simoncini 2006, 298.
39 Cheli 1999, 33.
40 Bartole 2004, 118.
41 Onida 1977, 506 ss.

della conferenza stampa del dicembre 1957, affrontava il problema della posizione della Corte nel sistema costituzionale: «Poichè si tratta di un organo nuovissimo, il suo collocamento nel quadro dell'ordinamento può dare luogo a perplessità. Non è certo agevole rendersi subito conto delle novità. Bisognerà, però, tenere presente che la famosa tripartizione quale è a base della teoria della divisione dei poteri dovuta a Montesquieu non è più sufficiente a caratterizzare nella loro integrità gli ordinamenti presenti dello Stato: perché vi sono degli organi che sono fuori di tutti e tre i poteri: legislativo, esecutivo e giudiziario. Quali sono questi organi? Uno è il Capo dello Stato, l'altro la Corte Costituzionale».[42]

La storicizzazione problematica dell'esperienza costituzionale italiana ci fa vedere meglio, io credo, la struttura *profonda* della questione che Massimo Luciani ha inteso mettere al centro della sua relazione. Alla metà degli anni '70 Nicola Matteucci aveva còlto il tema come questione centrale del costituzionalismo contemporaneo. «Questo spostarsi dell'equilibrio costituzionale dal legislativo al giudiziario, questo nuovo rapporto fra il potere e il diritto, segna certo una rottura con la nostra tradizione politica più recente; una rottura che non è ancora pienamente chiara ed evidente alla nostra cultura politica. Questo era necessario, proprio per l'avvento della democrazia».[43] Struttura originaria o "alterazione" successiva? Probabilmente l'una e l'altra. Le inerzie della ragione politico-rappresentativa hanno determinato uno "squilibrio" o hanno rivelato una Costituzione che vive alla ricerca di un dinamico punto di equilibrio tra il polo della Costituzione indirizzo/programma e la Costituzione-garanzia? È sufficiente il ritorno al circuito – rigenerato come? – della politica e della *legis-latio* per rimettere a posto le cose, per ritornare ad una attuazione "virtuosa", per evitare le "alterazioni"? E quale legislazione, quella del Parlamento o quella, sempre più emergenziale, del governo?

5. Il *senso* della Costituzione e la *melancolia* costituzionale

Ritorno, in conclusione, alla domanda di partenza, alla quale non so dare una risposta. Inadeguata e inattuale la Costituzione o inadeguato e inattuale ciò che gli sta intorno? Il nostro polittico di partenza ci fa vedere immagini che non possono non rendere complessa l'interpretazione dell'intero manufatto. Nel corso del seminario sono state evocate alcune questioni cruciali come, per esempio, il rapporto tra la Costituzione e la "nuova" costituzione economica

42 Azzariti 2006. Il testo della conversazione con la stampa raccolto in forma stenografica fu pubblicato nella «Rivista di diritto e procedura civile», 1957, 1443.

43 Matteucci 1976, 272.

del mondo; gli irrisolti problemi del rapporto tra autorità religiosa e potere "laico"; il movimento tellurico che viene dall'Europa e le fonti multilivello ormai lontane dal ceppo del potere costituente; la complessità dei casi della vita che sono – non dimentichiamolo – il vero oggetto "pointilliste", come ha osservato qui Roberto Bin, della giurisdizione.[44]

Come è stato "amministrato", dunque, il cospicuo patrimonio che i Costituenti ci hanno lasciato? Che uso ne abbiamo saputo fare? Più di sessant'anni di vita corrispondono a più generazioni. Le forze costituenti sono un ricordo storico e i loro più diretti eredi hanno perso ogni presa *materiale* sul testo costituzionale. La formula della "Seconda repubblica" è stato il segnale semantico, ma sostanziale, di una perdita di *senso* della Costituzione. Le ragioni sono profonde e molteplici. La lettura "scettica" o "indifferente" o, al contrario, aggressivamente "difensiva" della Costituzione hanno finito – dentro il discorso inconcludente e stereotipato delle riforme – per mettere in primo piano la dimensione *contingente* mentre nel discorso pubblico la Costituzione perdeva le sue grandi potenzialità. «Più ancora che da calcoli partigiani e veti incrociati, il dibattito sulla Costituzione è impoverito da questo circolo vizioso tra "conservatori" e "innovatori", caricatura dell'antico dibattito sul perché le scelte dei padri debbano vincolare i figli. L'assenza di un legame fra tradizione e mutamento costituzionale nella consapevolezza collettiva ha dunque bisogno di una spiegazione. Possiamo cominciare provando a ricostruire la parabola di significato che certe formule hanno assunto nel discorso pubblico, quali "Costituzione nata dalla Resistenza" e "attuazione della Costituzione"».[45] I padri della Costituzione sono quasi tutti scomparsi, restano i figli e i nipoti. Quale *narrazione* è dunque possibile nella temporalità del post-moderno? Come *esiste* oggi la Costituzione? Ci può bastare la via *ermeneutica*[46] in capo alla scienza giuridica (nel suo complesso) per trovare punti di equilibrio fra testo e contesto, fra certezza del diritto e concretezza di un ordinamento sempre più informato alle dinamiche complesse e "conflittuali" del pluralismo sociale e istituzionale? È questo l'unico modo per far parlare oggi la Costituzione, interpellata dalla realtà? O la Costituzione deve ritrovare – come auspica Luciani – un percorso nel quale l'«attuazione ... possa distinguersi dalla sua applicazione solo se, come accennavo, non si riduce all'occupazione degli spazi di libertà lasciati dalle norme costituzionali, ma si qualifica per la consapevole intenzione di realizzare un voluto costituzionale dinamicamente proiettato nel futuro»?

Talvolta si parla della Costituzione come di una bussola per orientare i naviganti. Dal nostro seminario emerge un quadro contrastato nel quale le

44 Sulla «pressione» dei casi v. Zagrebelski 2008, 190.

45 Pinelli 2012, 118.

46 Zagrebelsky 1996, 77 ss.

stesse categorie dottrinali classiche (a cominciare dal trinomio rigidità/flessibilità/elasticità) appaiono meno produttive di quanto si vorrebbe. «La Costituzione che oggi utilizziamo è fatta di disposizioni scritte, delle relative scelte ermeneutiche, dei regolamenti parlamentari e delle leggi ordinarie che hanno concretato le scelte delle assemblee legislative, delle elaborazioni concettuali che vi si sono sovrapposte, delle convinzioni e prassi poste in essere dagli organi governanti, dalla giurisprudenza spesso additiva e certamente innovativa della Corte costituzionale».[47] I soggetti "manipolatori" – nel senso di rendere vivente la Costituzione e i suoi valori e principi – sono più numerosi del previsto. La generazione del 1947–48 aveva, per motivi politici e culturali, uno sguardo proiettato in avanti. Lo stesso Calamandrei – tutt'altro che tenero rispetto a talune scelte concrete – usò un'immagine "architettonica" molto efficace parlando della necessità che la futura Costituzione accogliesse un principio. «Ma come gli architetti nel costruir l'ala di un edificio che dovrà esser compiuto nell'avvenire, lasciano nella parete destinata a servire d'appoggio certe pietre sporgenti che essi chiamano "ammorzature", così è concepibile che nella costituzione italiana siano inserite ... cosiffatte ammorzature giuridiche ...»[48] (1945, 168).

Ascoltando qui gli interventi che si sono succeduti, ho tratto una percezione che vorrei evocare, in conclusione, con un rinvio allo straordinario ciclo pittorico allegorico sugli effetti del buono e del cattivo governo che Ambrogio Lorenzetti ha lasciato, quasi a metà Trecento, in Palazzo Pubblico alla sua potente committenza senese (e a tutti noi). Catalogo visivo e concettuale di un medioevo urbano, dinamico e costituzionalmente fazioso, il *Buongoverno* è l'alchimia delle virtù che fa uscire o mai cadere la *Città* nella discordia che è esasperazione, sregolata, del conflitto. Nel ciclo pittorico di Lorenzetti è ben presente – come ha dimostrato con grande acume Pierangelo Schiera[49] – la dimensione del *Timor*, di quel sentimento "melancolico" che fa temere per la perdita di un bene caro come la *Pax*. E forse potremmo parlare, anche per i nostri giorni, di *melancolia costituzionale*, di uno stato d'animo dubbioso, in bilico, tra la Costituzione come *bene comune*, *res publica*, e nostro principale "strumento di convivenza" e la doverosa presa d'atto della realtà, con le sue gravi *impasse* e le sue minacce. Non è scontato dare *senso* a ciò che la Costituzione è diventata. Sentiamo echi premoderni che evocano la vicenda della *iurisdictio* in una logica nuova di garanzia; la complessità del mondo e dei casi della vita rendono meno "direzionale" la Costituzione dei costituenti e la Costituzione-arena fa coesistere e confliggere valori, principi e interessi immaginati nel passato ma da

47 Bartole 2004, 445.
48 Calamandrei 1945, 168.
49 Schiera 2006; anche Schiera 1999.

ribilanciare nel presente; percepiamo la necessità di non perdere il legame politico, fondativo, con il potere sovrano, pur nella crisi delle sue forme di attuazione a livello di rappresentanza e sistema politico. *Melancolia costituzionale* significa allora avere piena coscienza di ciò che si ha e di ciò che si può perdere. Non mettiamo contro tradizione e mutamento, perché non è questo il vero problema.

Bibliografia citata

Azzariti G. (2006), *La posizione della Corte costituzionale nell'ordinamento dello Stato italiano*, in *Studi sulla Costituzione*, Milano, 1958, vol. III, 446–463, ora in *1956–2006. Cinquant'anni di Corte costituzionale*, Roma, t. I

Bartole S. (2004), *Interpretazioni e trasformazioni della Costituzione repubblicana*, Bologna: Il Mulino

Bisogni G. (2004), *Le leggi istitutive della Corte costituzionale*, in U. De Siervo., S. Guerrieri, A. Varsori (a cura di), *La prima legislatura repubblicana. Continuità e discontinuità nell'azione delle istituzioni*, vol. I, Roma: Carocci

Bonini F. (2007), *Storia costituzionale della Repubblica*, Roma: Carocci

Calamandrei P. (1995), *Costituente italiana e federalismo europeo* (1945), in *Costruire la democrazia. Premesse alla Costituente*, con un saggio introduttivo di P. Barile, Firenze: Vallecchi

Calamandrei P. (1996), *La Costituzione e le leggi per attuarla* (1955), in *Costituzione e leggi di Antigone. Scritti e leggi di Antigone*, Firenze: La Nuova Italia, 137–232

Cassese S. (2012), *La giustizia costituzionale in Italia: lo stato presente*, in *Rivista trimestrale di diritto pubblico*, 3, 2012, 603–624

Cheli E. (1999), *Il giudice delle leggi: la Corte costituzionale nelle dinamiche dei poteri*, Bologna: 1999

Cheli E. (2012), *Nata per unire. La Costituzione italiana tra storia e politica*, Bologna: Il Mulino

Costa P. (2006), *Democrazia politica e Stato costituzionale*, Napoli: editoriale scientifica

Costa P. (2012), *Il problema del potere costituente in Italia fra Risorgimento e Repubblica*, in F. Bambi (a cura di), *Un secolo per la Costituzione (1848–1948). Concetti e parole nello svolgersi del lessico costituzionale italiano*, Firenze: Accademia della Crusca, 109–137

Elster J. (1992), *Intertemporal Choice and Political Thought*, in G. Loewenstein, J. Elster, *Choice over time*, New York: Russell Sage Foundation

Elster J. (1996), *Lo studio dei processi costituenti: uno schema generale*, in G. Zagrebelsky, P. P. Portinaro, J. Luther (a cura di), *Il futuro della costituzione*, Torino: Einaudi, 209–228

Elster J. (2004), *Ulisse liberato: razionalità e vincoli*, Bologna: Il Mulino

Fioravanti M. (2001), *Dottrina dello Stato-persona e dottrina della Costituzione. Costantino Mortati e la tradizione giuspubblicistica italiana*, in Id., *La scienza del diritto pubblico. Dottrine dello Stato e della Costituzione tra Otto e Novecento*, Milano: Giuffrè, 657–793

Fioravanti M. (2007), *L'attuazione della Costituzione: il ruolo della cultura costituzionale*, in B. Pezzini e M. Baronchelli (a cura di), *La Costituzione della Repubblica italiana. Le radici, il cammino*, Bergamo: Istituto bergamasco per la storia della Resistenza e dell'Età contemporanea, 69 ss

Fioravanti M. (2009a), *Un'eredità delle rivoluzioni: il "modello costituzionale" radicale*, in Id., *Costituzionalismo. Percorsi della storia e tendenze attuali*, Roma, Bari: Laterza

Fioravanti M. (2009b), *Per una storia della legge fondamentale in Italia: dallo Statuto alla Costituzione*, in Id. (a cura di), *Il valore della Costituzione. L'esperienza della democrazia repubblicana*, Roma, Bari: Laterza, 3–40

Gentile F., Grasso P. G. (1999), a cura di, *Costituzione criticata*, Napoli: ESI

Giocoli Nacci P. (1984), *Il tempo nella Costituzione*, Padova: Cedam

Gregorio M. (2006), *Quale Costituzione? Le interpretazioni della giuspubblicistica nell'immediato dopoguerra*, in *Quaderni fiorentini per la storia del pensiero giuridico moderno*, 35, I, 849–913

Husserl G. (1998), *Diritto e tempo. Saggi di filosofia del diritto* (1955), Milano: Giuffrè

Häberle P. (1978), *Zeit und Verfassung* (1974), in *Verfassung als öffentlicher Prozeß. Materialien zu einer Verfassungstheorie der offenen Gesellschaft*, Berlin: Duncker & Humblot, 59–92

Häberle P. (2001), *Per una dottrina della Costituzione come scienza della cultura* (1982), Roma: Carocci

Holmes S. (1996), *Vincoli costituzionali e paradosso della democrazia*, in G. Zagrebelsky, P. P. Portinaro, J. Luther (a cura di), *Il futuro della costituzione*, cit., 167–208

Holmes S. (1998), *Passioni e vincoli: i fondamenti della democrazia liberale*, Torino: Edizioni di Comunità

Lacchè L. (2001), *Tra storia e comparazione*, in *Giornale di storia costituzionale*, I,1, 5–6

Lacchè L. (2010a), *Il* canone eclettico. *Alla ricerca di uno* strato profondo *della cultura giuridica italiana dell'Ottocento*, in *Quaderni fiorentini per la storia del pensiero giuridico moderno*, 39, 2010, 153–228

Lacchè L. (2010b), *Las Cartas Otorgadas. La teoría de l'octroi y las experiencias constitucionales en la Europa postrevolucionaria*, in *Fundamentos*, 6, 2010, 269–305

Luciani M. (2011), *Unità nazionale e struttura economica. La prospettiva della Costituzione repubblicana*, relazione al Convegno annuale AIC su *Costituzionalismo e Costituzione nella vicenda unitaria italiana*, Torino, 28 ottobre, www.associazionedeicostituzionalisti.it

Manca A. G. (2003), *Introduzione*, in A. G. Manca, L. Lacchè (a cura di), *Parlamento e Costituzione nei sistemi costituzionali europei ottocenteschi – Parlament und Verfassung in den konstitutionellen Verfassungssystemen Europas*, Bologna: Il Mulino, Berlin: Duncker & Humblot, 7–27

Martines T. (1978), *Prime osservazioni sul tempo nel diritto costituzionale*, in *Scritti in onore di Salvatore Pugliatti*, vol. III, *Diritto pubblico*, Milano: Giuffrè, 783–888

Matteucci N. (1976), *Costituzionalismo*, in *Dizionario di politica*, a cura di N. Bobbio e N. Matteucci, Torino: Utet, 272

Mortati C. (1969), *Considerazioni sui mancati adempimenti costituzionali*, in *Studi per il XX anniversario dell'Assemblea costituente*, vol. IV, *Aspetti del sistema costituzionale*, Firenze: Vallecchi

Onida V. (1977), *Magistratura e Corte costituzionale*, in AA.VV., *Aspetti e tendenze del diritto costituzionale: scritti in onore di Costantino Mortati*, Milano: Giuffrè

Paladin L. (2004), *Per una storia costituzionale dell'Italia repubblicana*, Bologna: Il Mulino

Pasquino P. (2006), *Controllo di costituzionalità e forma di governo in Italia*, in *Giornale di storia costituzionale*, numero monografico *Storia, giustizia, costituzione. Per i cinquant'anni della Corte costituzionale*, 11,1, 309–320

Persano P. (2007), *La catena del tempo. Il vincolo generazionale nel pensiero politico francese tra* Ancien Régime *e Rivoluzione*, Macerata: eum

Pinelli C. (2006), *I rapporti fra Corte e Parlamento in mancanza di una politica costituzionale*, in *Giornale di storia costituzionale*, numero monografico *Storia, giustizia, costituzione. Per i cinquant'anni della Corte costituzionale*, 11,1, 321–327

Pinelli C. (2012), *L'incivilimento degli italiani e la Costituzione della Repubblica* (2008), ora in Id., *Nel lungo andare. Una Costituzione alla prova dell'esperienza. Scritti scelti, 1985–2011*, Napoli: Editoriale scientifica, 113–128

Rubenfeld J. (2001), *Freedom and Time. A Theory of Constitutional Self-Government*, New Haven, London: Yale University Press

Schiera P. (1999), *Specchi della politica. Disciplina, melanconia, socialità nell'Occidente moderno*, Bologna: Il Mulino

Schiera P. (2006), *Il* Buongoverno *"melancolico" di Ambrogio Lorenzetti e la "costituzionale faziosità" delle città*, in *Scienza & Politica*, 34, 2006, 93–108

Simmel G. (1911), *Die Ruine* (1911), tr. it. *La rovina*, in *Rivista di estetica*, XXI, 8, 1981

Simoncini A. (2006), *L'istituzione della Corte costituzionale e la sua affermazione: una lezione dalla storia*, in *Giornale di storia costituzionale*, numero monografico *Storia, giustizia, costituzione. Per i cinquant'anni della Corte costituzionale*, 11,1, 295–307

Vassalli G. (2006), *Testimonianza*, in *Giornale di storia costituzionale*, numero monografico *Storia, giustizia, costituzione. Per i cinquant'anni della Corte costituzionale*, 11,1, 55–64

Zagrebelsky G. (1996), *Storia e costituzione*, in G. Zagrebelsky, P. P. Portinaro, J. Luther (a cura di), *Il futuro della costituzione*, cit., 35–82

Zagrebelsky G. (2008), *La legge e la sua giustizia. Tre capitoli di giustizia costituzionale*, Bologna: Il Mulino

Chapter V
Comparative constitutional History and European perspectives

Europa *una et diversa*. A proposito di *ius commune europaeum* e tradizioni costituzionali comuni

> «Un principe crede che sarà più grande per la rovina di uno Stato vicino. Al contrario. La situazione è tale in Europa, che tutti gli Stati dipendono gli uni dagli altri. La Francia ha bisogno dell'opulenza della Polonia e della Moscovia, come la Guyenna ha bisogno della Bretagna e la Bretagna dell'Anjou. L'Europa è uno Stato composto da più province» (Ch. L. de Secondat, barone di Montesquieu, Cahiers 1716–1755)

1. Europa in divenire

«Qual è il ruolo dell'Europa in questo mondo trasformato? [...] L'Europa, continente dei valori umanistici, della *Magna Carta*, del *Bill of Rights*, della rivoluzione francese e della caduta del muro di Berlino. Il continente della libertà, della solidarietà e soprattutto della diversità, il che implica il rispetto per le lingue, la cultura e le tradizioni altrui». Questo passaggio della Dichiarazione di Laeken sul futuro dell'Unione europea può offrire una rapida chiave di accesso – retoricamente sostenuta – su alcuni dei nodi fondamentali del difficile[1] processo di "costituzionalizzazione" che impegna l'Europa da lungo tempo e che le due ravvicinate Convenzioni, quella che ha elaborato la Carta dei diritti fondamentali e quella che da un anno sta procedendo al riordino dei trattati secondo una logica sostanzialmente costituzionale, ha messo al centro del dibattito pubblico europeo, nella fase cruciale dell'allargamento a est dell'Unione. L'Europa, nella sua quasi integrale dimensione geo-politica, è chiamata a «condividere un futuro di pace fondato su valori comuni»[2] muovendo dall'originaria, ovvia, condizione di diversità dei suoi popoli. Come si può contribuire al «mantenimento e allo sviluppo di questi valori comuni nel rispetto della

1 Cfr. per es. U. De Siervo (a cura di), *La difficile Costituzione europea*, Bologna 2001.

2 Preambolo della Carta dei diritti fondamentali dell'Unione europea, I cpv.

diversità delle culture e delle tradizioni dei popoli europei, dell'identità nazionale degli Stati membri e dell'ordinamento dei loro pubblici poteri a livello nazionale, regionale e locale»?[3] Il presidente della Convenzione sul futuro dell'Europa Valery Giscard d'Estaing, nel discorso di apertura (26 febbraio 2002), ha posto come condizione per il successo dei lavori l'individuazione di un «concept porteur d'unité pour notre continent et de respect pour sa diversité».[4]

Questo è il nodo fondamentale[5] che l'Unione si trova a dover affrontare in questo momento, ma, a ben vedere, esso identifica prima di tutto la lunga durata di una tensione fondativa dell'identità[6] e dello spazio dell'Europa. La dialettica tra ciò che unisce e ciò che divide e distingue, il divenire nella storia, la ricerca incessante – contrassegnata anche dai «demoni del passato» – di una forma e di un ordine politico, l'individuazione faticosa dei valori e dei principi comuni sono tutti presupposti senza i quali qualsiasi interrogazione aperta all'avvenire appare destinata a restare senza risposta. L'Europa in divenire, *una et diversa*, è anche la paradossale costruzione, lungo un percorso che non sembra mai poter avere fine (ed è bene che sia così),[7] di una "impossibilità".[8]

2. Elementi di complessità

Questa tensione, come si diceva, è antica eppure sempre nuova, pronta ad assumere forme sempre inedite. Essa, per uno storico, è un richiamo quasi irresistibile. Il processo di "costituzionalizzazione" – comunque lo si voglia giudicare – offre a uno storico-giurista la possibilità di riflettere non solo in prospettiva storica sulla costruzione di una identità stratificata e complessa, ma, di più, anche l'occasione per meditare sull'uso di categorie e di punti di vista che tradizionalmente non fanno difetto nella cassetta dei suo ferri del mestiere. Forse mai come negl'ultimi anni la storia del diritto – ovvero di alcuni dei concetti e

3 *Ibidem*, III cpv.

4 Il testo in http://www.european-convention.eu.int. Giscard individua ulteriormente il problema fondamentale nella «difficulté de conjuger un fort sentiment d'appartenance à l'Union européenne, et le maintien d'une identité nationale». Il recente testo (28 maggio 2003) del preambolo, proposto dal Presidium della Convenzione, parla di un'Europa «unita nella sua diversità».

5 Vedi C. Pinelli, *Il momento della scrittura. Contributo al dibattito sulla Costituzione europea*, Bologna 2002, 206.

6 Sul punto v. soprattutto B. De Giovanni, *L'identità dell'Europa*, in S. Guerrieri, A. Manzella, F. Sdogati, *Dall'Europa a Quindici alla Grande Europa. La sfida istituzionale*, Bologna 2001, 19–40.

7 P. Häberle, *Colloquio sulla "costituzione europea"*, a cura di P. Ridola, in *Diritto romano attuale*, 2, 1999, 211.

8 Secondo la ricostruzione di M. Cacciari, *Geo-filosofia dell'Europa*, Milano 1994.

delle figure rappresentative del suo statuto disciplinare – ha potuto beneficiare di un sonoro effetto di ritorno intessuto di richiami, di prestiti, di echi, di allusioni e di veri e propri riutilizzi da parte dei giuristi impegnati intellettualmente nel cantiere europeo e alle prese con paradigmi, scenari, trasformazioni che per certi aspetti elevano il *de profundis* sulle antiche certezze di una scienza fiera, a buon diritto, del suo millenario sapere e delle sue raffinate categorie interpretative. La ricerca di una *nova methodus*[9] è questione annosa; ma senza dubbio le straordinarie accelerazioni innescate da catene di fenomeni che per facile convenzione collochiamo dentro la capiente categoria della "globalizzazione" hanno dato il segno di un movimento in avanti riassuntivo di profondi mutamenti che affondano le proprie radici in tempi più lontani. Lo Stato sovrano nazionale, il legislatore onnipotente, la gerarchia e la natura delle fonti – per accennare solo ai profili più vistosi – individuano il lessico di una modernità giuridica che, senza soluzione di continuità, intere generazioni di giuristi hanno respirato come aria di famiglia. Senza dover qui postulare il tramonto inesorabile o addirittura la fine imminente di questo ben noto scenario (materia più per indovini), certo è che oggi percepiamo come sintesi e punto di arrivo una dimensione della "crisi" che per certi aspetti ha accompagnato fedelmente una buona parte del secolo passato, facendo da costante, sordo contrappunto alla pur lodevole opera di una scienza giuridica impegnata a puntellare un edificio pericolante.

Chi osservi i vastissimi fenomeni accennati e il progetto lento e faticoso di costruire uno spazio pubblico europeo non può non rilevare quanto oggi il giurista che voglia cercare di comprendere il proprio tempo debba impegnarsi per potenziare il proprio strumentario tecnico e culturale. La complessità del nuovo paesaggio[10] richiede una scienza pienamente consapevole del proprio

9 A. Giuliani, *Presentazione* a P. Stein, J. Shand, *I valori giuridici della civiltà occidentale*, Milano 1981, XVIII.

10 Per il profilo analizzato v. soprattutto P. Grossi, *Pagina introduttiva (ancora sulle fonti del diritto)*, in *Quaderni fiorentini per la storia del pensiero giuridico moderno*, 29, 2000, 1–10; Id., *Globalizzazione e pluralismo giuridico (a proposito di:* M. R. Ferrarese, *Le istituzioni della globalizzazione – Diritto e diritti nella società transnazionale*, Bologna 2000), ivi, 551–558; R. Sacco, *Frammentarietà, diversità e unità. Variabilità e storicità del diritto*, in AA.VV., *Diritto generale e diritti particolari nell'esperienza storica*, Atti del Congresso internazionale della Società italiana di storia del diritto, Torino, 19–21 novembre 1998, Roma 2001, 423–433; P. Grossi, *Il periodo medievale e moderno*, ivi, 479–495; S. Mannoni, *Globalizzazione, diritto, Stato*, in AA.VV., *Ordo iuris. Storia e forme dell'esperienza giuridica*, Milano 2003, 359–372; A. Padoa Schioppa, *Il diritto comune in Europa: riflessioni sul declino e sulla rinascita di un modello*, in *Foro it.*, 1996, vol. CXIX, parte V, 14–21; Id., *Verso una storia del diritto europeo*, in *Studi di storia del diritto*, III, Milano 2001, 1–26; A. A. Cervati, *Il diritto costituzionale europeo e la crisi della dogmatica statualistica*,

compito e capace di governare la complessità sistemica del giuridico. Quando parliamo della necessità di un giurista europeo[11] inevitabilmente ci riferiamo a questa dimensione. Il pluralismo, la coesistenza / tensione tra unità e diversità, il confronto continuo devono essere maneggiati con sensibilità appropriate, con spirito critico e capacità di intraprendere strade meno consuete.

Non v'è dubbio che il divenire dell'Europa all'interno delle coordinate comunitarie ha rappresentato, negl'ultimi decenni, il principale terreno di riflessione e di confronto dei giuristi europei. Su questo terreno si sono successivamente incrociati, sovrapposti e spesso confusi distinti concetti di diritto europeo e differenti modi di concepire l'idea di un diritto comune. Si tratta di un problema che ha toccato trasversalmente tutti gli ambiti della scienza giuridica e che ha trovato radicazione soprattutto attraverso la categoria del diritto privato europeo quale dimensione ri-costitutiva di un tessuto, per lo più settoriale, di principi comuni. L'ultimo decennio, tuttavia, ha visto la forte emersione di una prospettiva di "comune" non più incentrata sull'ambito tradizionale del diritto privato ma piuttosto sull'enucleazione-riconoscimento di "tradizioni costituzionali comuni" connesse in maniera forte al cd. processo di "costituzionalizzazione" di cui oggi possiamo cogliere i diversi elementi di complessità.

Il presente contributo vuole ripercorrere queste due dimensioni di diritto comune europeo, distinte, ma evidentemente incidenti sullo stesso terreno, e in vari modi intrecciate e portatrici di determinate visioni del diritto in Europa, sia in termini categoriali che di esperienza storica. Entrambe rispondono a un bisogno profondo di legittimazione, di modelli e valori in grado di *animare* un diritto comunitario che, pur inteso nella sua più ampia estensione, non può affatto rinunciare alla individuazione di più solide fondamenta e di principi connettivi. Le due prospettive sono per molti aspetti complementari e proprio la ricerca di raccordi e di principi comuni può essere vista come uno dei compiti più significativi della scienza giuridica europea. Nello stesso tempo, però, tale dinamica evidenzia elementi potenziali e reali di tensione tra un'idea forte di

in *Diritto romano attuale*, 6, 2001, 21–47; K. Å. Modéer, *La comparazione come critica della cultura giuridica: un discorso tra globalizzazione e regionalizzazione*, in *Le Carte e la Storia*, 2, 2002, 7–16.

11 Per es., da prospettive diverse, F. Ranieri, *Der europäische Jurist. Rechtshistorisches Forschungsthema und rechtspolitische Aufgabe*, in *Ius commune*, XVII, 1990, 9–24, con ampia bibliografia; B. De Witte, C. Forded, *The Common Law of Europe and the Future of Legal Tradition …*, Deventer 1992; P. Häberle, *Colloquio sulla "costituzione europea"*, cit., 210; A. von Bogdandy, *A Bird's Eye View on the Science of European Law: Structures, Debates and Development Prospects of Basic Research on the Law of the European Union in a German Perspective*, in *European Law Journal*, 6, 2000; P. Häberle, *Per una dottrina della Costituzione come scienza della cultura*, Roma 2001, 142 ss.

"ragion civile" (europea) – supportata da una blasonata *traditio* – e una concezione di "ragion pubblica" segnata da elementi di incompiutezza e di indecisione.[12] Proprio il moto "costituzionale" che è sotto i nostri occhi vuole per certi aspetti costruire una prima cornice, simbolica e operativa, in grado di assicurare, attraverso richiami strategici a principi e valori, alcuni punti fermi seppur all'interno di una incessante dimensione processuale. È a ben vedere anche l'incontro tra tempi diversi del diritto e delle sue forme consolidate. Da un lato, c'è un diritto che pare potersi muovere – vedremo in quale modo – lungo la linea di una storia che pur segnata da cesure profonde individua essenzialmente nella tradizione romanistica (riferimento in sé dei più generici) la propria matrice universalizzante e "continua" in ordine alle categorie e alla loro sistematizzazione. Dall'altro, un diritto che per tanti aspetti deriva proprio dalla logica della discontinuità, figlio di trasformazioni epocali a partire dall'età moderna e agganciato infine alle ardite architetture statualistiche con tutti i relativi corollari. Se oggi questo "incontro" appare problematico ma potenzialmente arricchente si deve anche al fatto che molte delle certezze e delle categorie fondamentali che hanno segnato nel profondo la nascita dei sistemi giuridici moderni sono oggetto di una sempre più condivisa riflessione critica. È sul terreno della "crisi" che si aprono spiragli, che si intravede la consapevolezza crescente per una riconsiderazione unitaria di fenomeni giuridici complessi che chiedono all'interprete creatività e sentimento acuito di "globalità". Europa *una et diversa* è per il giurista una grande sfida e un cantiere che mai come in questo momento ha avuto bisogno di una visione forte ed integrata.

3. Alla ricerca di un diritto comune europeo

La nozione di diritto comune europeo è ben lungi dall'essere indiscussa.[13] Anche se nell'uso si riscontra talvolta la tendenza a confondere esperienze e piani di lettura, non si tratta in senso proprio né del diritto espresso nei trattati e nei regolamenti europei, né del diritto in via di armonizzazione attraverso direttive comunitarie, né di un *corpus* genericamente inteso di "diritto europeo" come

12 Questa dimensione "dualista" è stata colta per es. da G. Crifò, *Pandettisti e storicisti nel diritto romano oggi*, in *Diritto romano attuale*, 1, 1999, 25–26. Elementi di discussione, riferiti soprattutto al caso tedesco, anche in R. Schulze, *Un nouveau domaine de recherche en Allemagne: l'histoire de droit européen*, in *Revue historique de droit français et étranger*, 1, 1992, 29–48.

13 Cfr. A. Wijffels, *Alberico Gentili e i fondamenti storico-concettuali del diritto comune europeo*, in AA.VV., *Alberico Gentili nel Quarto Centenario del De Jure Belli*, Atti del Convegno, Milano 2000, 73 ss., con ulteriori riferimenti; A. Padoa Schioppa, *Il diritto comune in Europa: riflessioni*, cit.

sistema, né di una sua specificazione in forma di un "diritto privato europeo" (attuale o futuro). È dunque, per molti aspetti, una nozione "in cerca di autore".[14] Non v'è dubbio però che proprio l'ultimo riferimento rappresenti per molti la chiave di accesso più ravvicinata per dare alla nozione forma e contenuti, in grado di enucleare un complesso di regole materiali, intese anzitutto in senso sussidiario e / o come forma specifica di comparazione. Su questo terreno – che è anche un "luogo" di confronto tra privatisti / romanisti (la congiunzione o meno dipendendo dalle tradizioni disciplinari e accademiche nazionali), comparatisti e, in parte, storici del diritto – è possibile, come del resto è ben noto a tutti, ricostruire e forgiare schemi uniformi, principi comuni (in ambiti settoriali ma pur sempre di rilevantissima consistenza), tecniche di redazione, con un contributo di primissimo piano della scienza giuridica.[15] Questa prospettiva, tuttavia, pur avendo l'ambizione di edificare un discorso "comune" ai principali modelli giuridici europei, deve fare i conti, se non altro, con talune, più o meno esplicite, resistenze e pregiudiziali storico-politiche a riconoscere la possibilità (e di conseguenza l'opportunità) di instaurare un dialogo sulle ragioni e sui caratteri peculiari della tradizione del *common law* e dei sistemi di *civil law*.[16]

Le diversità, vere o presunte, possono rappresentare finanche un ostacolo al naturale processo di unificazione del diritto privato. Possono essere depotenziate, rinchiuse entro margini accettabili, ma esse acquistano un senso solo in relazione al concetto di "comune". Che cos'è comune? Che cosa ricomprende questa qualificazione? Quali i confini? La nozione di "comune" – come sanno bene gli storici del diritto – è in sé una nozione correlativa, presuppone sempre una condizione di diversità (si tratti di diritti particolari, di singolarità, di eccezioni ecc.) interagenti fra di loro, pur all'interno di un ordine giuridico riconducibile, in modi e forme i più diversi, a principi "comuni". È appunto la ricerca dei termini di unità (ma non di uniformità) il problema fondamentale. Su questo terreno l'analisi storico-comparativa acquista una valenza metodologica niente affatto secondaria. È una prospettiva preziosa ma non priva di difficoltà e di trappole.

14 W. Brauneder, *Europäisches Privatrecht, aber was ist es?*, in *Zeitschrift für Neuere Rechtsgeschichte*, 15, 1993, 225–235. Cfr. inoltre *Vers un droit privé européen commun? Skizzen zum gemeineuropäischen Privatrecht*, a cura di B. Schmidlin, in *Zeitschrift für Schweizerisches Recht*, 6, 1994. Per un quadro d'insieme v. anche R. C. van Caenegem, *I sistemi giuridici europei*, Bologna, 2003, 35–47.

15 Per l'essenziale v. l'ampio AA.VV., *Un codice internazionale del diritto dei contratti: i principi Unidroit dei contratti commerciali internazionali*, Milano 1995; O. Lando e H. Beale, *The principles of European Contract Law*, Dordrecht 1995.

16 Sul punto v. *infra*, § 4.2.

4. Modelli e radici dello *ius commune europaeum*

La ricerca del diritto comune europeo ha dunque bisogno di modelli e di radici. Se la nazionalizzazione del diritto di impianto statuale ha imposto frontiere, ha rinserrato i sistemi dentro confini meno permeabili, ha cercato di ricondurre – senza però riuscirci del tutto – il pluralismo dei diritti al monismo di un diritto legificato entro un disegno gerarchico, ha insomma enfatizzato gli elementi identitari di diversità e di specificità, è anche vero che queste trasformazioni acquistano una pluralità di significati solo se comparati alla dimensione comune del diritto che ha caratterizzato la storia europea tra Medioevo ed età moderna. «La disciplina del diritto è stata degradata allo studio dei sistemi giuridici legali nazionali – dirà *von Jhering* nel XIX secolo –; i limiti dello studio del diritto coincidono ora con i limiti politici. Una forma scoraggiante ed indegna per una disciplina giuridica». Gli fa eco, nel secolo scorso, la parola di uno dei più grandi comparatisti, René David: «Cette dégradation de la science du droit me paraissait être désastreuse pour l'avenir de notre société [...]».[17] In tal senso la ricerca della dimensione "comune" risponde specularmente alla coscienza critica di una determinata condizione della scienza giuridica e allo stesso tempo scopre un terreno fertile di enfatizzazione nel dichiarare la crisi dei paradigmi più familiari e nel constatare i limiti del processo di armonizzazione europea del diritto.

L'esperienza europea dello *ius commune* diventa così un crocevia, un punto obbligato di passaggio, ma pone al centro del dibattito la questione centrale dell'interpretazione, ovvero dell'analisi delle forme, dei contenuti, dei confini entro cui leggere un'esperienza plurisecolare, una delle più complesse strutture di *longue durée* della storia giuridica europea.

4.1 *De usu et Authoritate Juris Civilis Romanorum per Dominia Principum Christianorum*

Alludo evidentemente all'opera di un professore di Oxford, Arthur Duck, *civil laywer* del XVII secolo.[18] Tale riferimento concerne più in generale il problema annoso – potremmo dire "costitutivo" – dell'uso e dell'autorità del diritto romano nella storia europea. È un problema questo che riguarda molto da vicino il diritto comune europeo[19] perché a sua volta richiama e definisce la questione dell'interpretazione storica e dogmatica della tradizione romanistica quale matrice culturale imprescindibile per un "nuovo" diritto comune. Per

17 R. David, *Les avatars d'un comparatiste*, Paris 1982, 258.

18 Cfr. A. Wijffels, *Arthur Duck et le ius commune européen*, in *Revue d'histoire des Facultés de droit et de la science juridique*, 1990, 193–221.

19 Come si può vedere nella rivista, pubblicata a partire dal 1993, *Zeitschrift für Europäisches Privatrecht.*

alcuni è possibile scorgere un percorso di "ri-europeizzazione" del diritto e della scienza:[20] per superare le angustie del positivismo legalistico e la frammentarietà di un'"unità" giuridica artificiale imposta da Bruxelles. Lo *ius commune* europeo non può allora che diventare la prova dell'esperibilità di un "altro modo" di organizzare il diritto su base romanistica, quando la *koiné* era facilitata dalla comune formazione e tradizione scientifica, e da una stessa lingua. «Diritto romano e unità giuridica europea: questo tema costituisce un programma» osserva Reinhard Zimmermann. Avere consapevolezza di una cultura giuridica comune europea significa riconoscere che i moderni sistemi giuridici nazionali sono a ben vedere modellati dal diritto romano. La storia del diritto e la comparazione giuridica[21] sono tra gli strumenti fondamentali per riscoprire le nervature nascoste della tradizione dello *ius commune* romanistico e per ripristinare in prospettiva l'unità culturale interrotta dalle codificazioni. La scienza – intesa in senso savignyano – «[...] progetta il nuovo *ius commune europaeum* di nuovo dal centro del diritto privato comune. Perciò la conoscenza del diritto romano e della storia della sua efficacia saranno indispensabili anche in futuro».[22]

20 Sulla questione della europeizzazione della scienza giuridica, centrale nel dibattito tedesco, non si può ovviamente non ricordare il progetto scientifico connaturato all'attività del Max-Planck-Institut für Europäische Rechtsgeschichte di Francoforte sul Meno e al piano dell'*Handbuch der Quellen und Literatur der neueren europäischen Privatrechtsgeschichte*, München 1973 ss. (su cui v. taluni interventi pubblicati nella rivista *Ius commune*). In particolare di H. Coing si possono ricordare *Die ursprüngliche Einheit der europäischen Rechtswissenschaft*, Wiesbaden 1967; Id., *Die europäische Privatrechtsgeschichte der neueren Zeit als einheitliches Forschungsgebiet*, in *Ius Commune*, I, 1967, 1–33; Id., *Europäisierung der Rechtswissenschaft*, in *Neue Juristische Wochenschrift*, 15, 1990, 939–941; *Geschichtliche Grundlagen des Rechts im kontinentalen Europa und im Common Law*, in K.J. Hopt, *Europäische Integration als Herausforderung des Rechts*, Berlin 1991, 17 ss.

21 Cfr. H. Kötz, *Was erwartet die Rechtsvergleichung von der Rechtsgeschichte?*, in *Juristenzeitung*, 47, 1992, 20 ss.

22 R. Zimmermann, *Diritto romano e unità giuridica europea*, in G. di Renzo Villata, G.P. Massetto, A. Padoa Schioppa, *Storia del diritto italiano*, I, Milano 1996, 1–25, in part. 24–25. Di Zimmermann bisogna ricordare almeno l'importante *The Law of Obligations. Roman Foundations of the Civilian Tradition*, Cape Town, Johannesburg 1990, e tra i suoi scritti di natura metodologica e più legati alla prospettiva del diritto comune europeo, *Usus hodiernus Pandectarum*, in R. Schulze, *Europäische Rechts- und Verfassungsgeschichte. Ergebnisse und Perspektiven der Forschung*, Berlin 1991; Id., *Das römisch-kanonische* ius commune *als Grundlage europäischer Rechtseinheit*, in *Juristenzeitung*, 47, 1992, 8 ss.; Id., *Civil Code and Civil Law. The «Europeanization» of Private Law within the European Community and the re-emergence of a European Legal Science*, in *Columbia Journal of European Law*, I, 1994–95, 63–105; Id., *Savigny's Vermächtnis. Rechtsgeschichte, Rechtsvergleichung und die Begründung einer Europäischen Rechtswissenschaft*, in P. Caroni,

Nella prospettiva dell'*Usus hodiernus Pandectarum*, sovente connotata dalla qualifica di "neopandettismo",[23] il diritto romano sembra fluire nel tempo e nello spazio su una linea di ininterrotta continuità come quintessenza di un patrimonio inestinguibile di razionalità, di concetti, di tecniche. Questa presenza forte, "applicativa", organica e autoreferenziale del diritto romano connota un'esperienza a tal punto invasiva ed assorbente da trasformare il segno della storicità nel suo contrario. Ne può derivare una visione a-temporale che anziché cogliere le ragioni e i fenomeni della trasformazione (e quindi del rapporto continuità/discontinuità) fissa in un tempo immoto ciò che invece è mobile, specifico, proprio, singolare, diverso. Il rischio di una lettura uniformatrice è evidente. Il diritto romano è sempre vivo – e non morto come disse Vittorio Scialoja nel 1881[24] – ed è il parametro universale che qualifica e esprime in senso unitario la storia europea del diritto. La presenza di una tradizione romanistica in Inghilterra – pur così peculiare e storicamente complessa,[25] oltrechè controversa – può servire a depotenziare il *problema* dei rapporti tra *common law* e *ius commune*;[26] le codificazioni moderne possono essere lette in chiave di *usus modernus*; la Pandettistica come ritorno alle pretese origini ideali e spirituali del diritto romano.[27]

4.2 Quale *ius commune*?

L'approccio al diritto comune europeo informato ai dettami dell'"uso attuale" del diritto romano rischia, se estremizzato, di portare ad un paradosso:

G. Dilcher, *Norm und Tradition. Welche Geschichtlichkeit für die Rechtsgeschichte? – Fra norma e tradizione. Quale storicità per la storia giuridica?*, Köln, Weimar, Wien 1998, 281–320; *Roman Law, Contemporary Law, European Law. The Civilian Tradition Today*, Oxford 2001. Per una discussione delle tesi di *R. Zimmermann*, v. R. Ogorek, *Die Erbschaft ausschlagen?*, in P. Caroni, G. Dilcher, *Norm und Tradition*, cit., 183–190.

23 Per un'analisi chiarissima ed efficace delle "pretese" della neopandettistica sulla storiografia v. M. Bretone, *La «coscienza ironica» della romanistica*, in P. Caroni, G. Dilcher, *Norm und Tradition*, cit., 36–52.

24 Si veda la lettura puntuale ed equilibrata di G. Crifò, *Pandettisti e storicisti nel diritto romano oggi*, cit., 11–28.

25 Per una sintesi v. R. C. van Caenegem, *I sistemi giuridici europei*, cit., 49 ss.

26 R. Zimmermann, *Der europäische Charakter des englischen Rechts. Historische Verbindungen zwischen civil law und common law*, in *Zeitschrift für Europäisches Privatrecht*, 1993, 4–51; Id., *Diritto romano e unità giuridica europea*, cit., 13 ss.; R. H. Helmholz, *Continental Law and Common Law: Historical Strangers or Companions?*, in *Duke L. Rev.*, 1990, 120 ss. Sul punto v. infra, § 4.2.

27 Cfr. per es. C. A. Cannata, *Usus modernus Pandectarum e diritto europeo (a proposito di:* H. Coing, *Europäisches Privatrecht, I. Älteres Gemeines Recht, München, 1985)*, in *Studia et documenta historiae et iuris*, LII, 1986, 435–442; Id., *Il diritto europeo e*

indebolire la credibilità di una considerazione che è invece ovvia,[28] ovvero poter riaffermare sempre, come storici e giuristi, il carattere fondativo dell'esperienza romana e del suo straordinario patrimonio culturale soprattutto in termini di metodi e strutture e cercare di capire l'insieme delle innumerevoli ragioni che ne hanno fatto la dimensione più *produttiva* nella storia del diritto occidentale dalle origini sino alla titanica impresa della Pandettistica. Costringere però questa esperienza – fondamentale anche in termini di dogmatica e di *interpretatio* – in un archetipo e in un modello "meta-temporale" per farne la misura di tutto è operazione rischiosa e tale da trasformare lo *ius commune* d'origine medievale in una delle manifestazioni risorgenti dello *ius romanum (medii aevi)*.[29] È dunque fondamentale avere piena consapevolezza della storicità[30] dello *ius commune* inteso come "opera aperta",[31] riscrittura incessante dei *doctores* realizzata *sub specie interpretationis* e volta a definire un ordine giuridico tanto nuovo e dinamico quanto più il testo del *Corpus iuris* è antico e fisso. Questa dimensione si riflette sia sulla concezione del problema del diritto

le codificazioni moderne, ivi, LVI, 1990, 309–322; Id., *Usus hodiernus pandectarum, common law, diritto romano olandese e diritto comune europeo*, ivi, 1991, 383–401. S. Schipani, *La codificazione del diritto romano comune*, Torino, 1999, 36: «Con riferimento ai codici moderni, e limitandomi ai civili, mi sembra che, se li esaminiamo senza porci *a priori* all'interno della prospettiva statual-legalista, ci accorgiamo che essi consentirebbero di riaffermare la loro appartenenza al diritto romano comune, che attraverso di essi, permane "sostanza viva" del nostro diritto, base della permanente unità del sistema». Sul rapporto tra la giurisprudenza della Corte europea di giustizia e le categorie del diritto romano v. K. Luig, *The History of Roman Private Law and the Unification of European Law*, in *Zeitschrift für Europäisches Privatrecht*, 5, 1997, 405–427. In generale v. R. Schulze, *Vom Ius Commune bis zum Gemeinschaftsrecht – das Forschungsfeld der europäischen Rechtsgeschichte*, in *Europäische Rechts- und Verfassungsgeschichte*, cit., 3 ss.

28 M. Sbriccoli, *Intervento*, in AA.VV., *Alberico Gentili nel Quarto Centenario del De Jure Belli*, cit., 212.

29 P. Grossi, *Modelli storici e progetti attuali nella formazione di un futuro diritto europeo*, in *Riv. dir. civ.*, 3, 1996, parte I, 281–286.

30 Al riguardo si veda l'importante volume curato da P. Caroni, G. Dilcher, *Norm und Tradition*, cit. Il dibattito incentrato su storicità e "attualità" della tradizione romanistica mette al centro della discussione il problema della rilevanza della ricerca storico-giuridica come elemento di conoscenza ai fini del diritto vigente e del processo di unificazione europea. Si vedano in particolare i contributi di Caroni, Dilcher, Bretone, Grossi (intervento, cit., nt. 29). Di P. Caroni cfr. anche *Der Schiffbruch der Geschichtlichkeit. Anmerkungen zum Neo-Pandektismus*, in *Zeitschrift für Neuere Rechtsgeschichte*, 16, 1994, 85–100. Utili elementi di discussione in G. Crifò, *Pandettisti e storicisti*, cit., 24 ss.

31 Riprendo il riferimento a U. Eco, *Opera aperta*, Milano 1987, 5 ed., da P. Costa, *Storia giuridica: immagini a confronto*, in *Anuario de historia del derecho español*, LXVII, 1997, I, 76.

comune europeo, sia sul modo di interpretare la stessa categoria dello *ius commune*.

È forte la tentazione di richiamare analogie e omologie, specie se si è alla ricerca di "modelli" di riferimento legittimanti il presente.[32] Il "paradiso perduto" rischia di trasformarsi in "paradiso artificiale". La temporalità è la dimensione naturale dello storico, e il tempo dello *ius commune* è tempo compiuto e proprio per questo lo storico ha la possibilità, con gli strumenti e la sensibilità peculiari al suo mestiere, di ben operare per coglierne i tratti che ne fanno un'esperienza unica, per molti aspetti "altra" da noi. Le suggestioni sono invece potenziali vettori di "uniformazione" del passato e di possibili equivoci. E l'Europa *una et diversa* non consente – così ci pare – letture uniformatrici. Fare leva sulla nozione di *ius commune* significa spesso individuare un concetto sin troppo generico, a tal punto da poter significare «un punto di partenza astratto e teorico, un po' come la nozione dello "stato di natura" nelle teorie del diritto naturale nei secoli XVII e XVIII».[33] Se il giurista ricorre legittimamente all'analogia come elemento retorico del discorso, lo storico[34] non può seguirlo su questa strada poiché rischia di perdere la sua funzione di sentinella critica in grado di rifuggire anacronismi, visioni teleologiche e "progressive", e di affermare invece l'*autonomia* epistemologica del passato e lo statuto della *differenza*.[35] Non è possibile quindi "mitizzare" il diritto comune, specie in funzione delle nuove esigenze comunitarie[36] e d'altra parte non si vede come potrebbe diventare un "modello" un'esperienza tanto complessa come quella dello *ius*

32 Su questi profili Paolo Grossi è ritornato a più riprese negl'ultimi anni. Si vedano almeno *Modelli storici e progetti attuali*, cit., 286; Id., *Pagina introduttiva (ancora sulle fonti del diritto)*, cit., 6.

33 A. Wijffels, *Alberico Gentili e i fondamenti storico-concettuali del diritto comune europeo*, cit., 180–181. Sulla pluralità di significati v. R. C. van Caenegem, *I sistemi giuridici europei*, cit., 22.

34 Oltra ai lavori di Paolo Grossi, cfr. M. Sbriccoli, *Intervento*, cit., 217: «Io ho una certa invidia per i giuristi positivi che pensano che gli sia consentito, di fronte ad una realtà storica lontana, di rilevare somiglianze, o magari apparenti identità con processi reali in atto e stabilire a loro piacimento l'esistenza di rassicuranti ricorsi storici. Agli storici questo non è consentito». Pietro Costa parla dell'analogia come «impercorribile scorciatoia» per lo storico (*La cittadinanza fra Stati nazionali e ordine giuridico europeo: una comparazione diacronica*, in G. Bonacchi, *Una costituzione senza Stato*, Bologna 2001, 302).

35 Cfr. A. Hespanha, *Introduzione alla storia del diritto europeo*, Bologna 1999, 9 ss. Si vedano anche gli interventi di Wiegand, A. Padoa Schioppa, Arnaud, Simitis, D. Simon, Stolleis, Giaro pubblicati in *Rechtshistorisches Journal*, 12, 1993, 277 ss.

36 M. Ascheri, *Le fonti e la flessibilità del diritto comune: il paradosso del* consilium sapientis, in M. Ascheri, I. Baumgärtner, J. Kirshner, *Legal Consulting in the Civil Tradition*, Berkeley 1999, 52.

commune, contrassegnata da peculiarissimi fondamenti antropologici e da forme proprie di razionalità.[37] Del resto non bisogna neppure sottovalutare le ragioni profonde della crisi del diritto comune: andrebbero infatti chiarite, più di quanto non sia stato fatto.[38]

Si tratta di questioni di grandissima rilevanza che riguardano anche il problema della definizione-interpretazione di una categoria complessa come quella dello *ius commune*. Non è questa la sede per affrontare un problema di tale portata. Qui si vuole più semplicemente mettere l'accento sul fatto che tale categoria è storiograficamente (e quindi *geschichtlich*) determinata, non scevra quindi da opzioni scientifiche, posizioni ideologiche, precomprensioni e riletture. Basti qui ricordare gli elementi di "contestualizzazione"[39] necessari per comprendere le valenze della ricostruzione straordinariamente creativa di Francesco Calasso e capire la "direzione di senso"[40] che ha inteso assegnare al concetto di unità-sistema del diritto comune. Non si possono non ricordare le rivitalizzanti discussioni che *L'ordine giuridico medievale* di Paolo Grossi,[41] nettissimo nel delineare opzioni metodologiche e presupposti intellettuali, ha fatto nascere tra gli storici del diritto e tra i giuristi più pronti a cogliere il rilievo di quell'operazione culturale.

L'uso della nozione di *ius commune* deve essere accompagnato dalla coscienza di trovarsi di fronte un concetto i cui confini e le cui scansioni spazio-temporali non rispondono ad una logica univoca.[42] "Comune" non può essere sinonimo di unitario,[43] a costo di tradire l'immensa ricchezza che si può scorgere in una

37 Per la discussione di questo aspetto e per i relativi percorsi bibliografici, si rinvia a P. Cappellini, Juris prudentia *versus* scientia iuris*: prolegomeni ad ogni futuro "lessico politico europeo"*, in *Filosofia politica*, 2, 1987, 314–316.

38 A. Padoa Schioppa, *Il diritto comune in Europa: riflessioni*, cit., 16.

39 Oltre a B. Paradisi, *Il problema del diritto comune nella dottrina di Francesco Calasso* (1980), ora in *Studi sul medioevo giuridico*, Roma 1987, II, 1009–1112, è da vedere l'acuta analisi di P. Costa, *"Ius commune", "Ius proprium", "interpretatio doctorum": ipotesi per una discussione*, in *El dret comú i Catalunya*, Actes del IV Simposi Internacional, Barcelona, 27–28 de maig de 1994, Barcelona 1995, 29–42.

40 *Ibidem*, 41–42.

41 Roma, Bari 1995, in part. 5–35. Cfr. anche *Un diritto senza Stato (La nozione di autonomia come fondamento della costituzione giuridica medievale)*, in *Quaderni fiorentini*, 25, 1996, 267–284.

42 V. per es. la discussione ben documentata in T. Giaro, *Europäische Privatrechtsgeschichte: Werkzeug der Rechtsvereinheitlichung und Produkt der Kategorienvermengung*, in *Ius commune*, 21, 1994, 1–43; Id., *Römisches Recht, Romanistik und Rechtsraum Europa*, ivi, 22, 1995, 1–16.

43 «[...] perché è vero che quella lontana esperienza giuridica si è svolta su di un terreno comune, ma non sempre un terreno comune è la stessa cosa che un'esperienza unitaria. Noi possiamo avere un terreno comune, ma quello che c'è sopra, pur vivendo delle stesse risorse e alimentandosi alle stesse fonti, può

esperienza tanto estesa e concettualmente forte da identificarsi per tanti aspetti con la storia stessa del diritto in Europa tra medioevo ed età moderna.[44] Senza dubbio è doveroso partire da un'accezione condivisa e convenzionale di *ius commune*, ovvero di quell'esperienza giuridica plurisecolare in grado di qualificare, in tempi diversi, gli ordinamenti di una buona parte dell'Europa, incentrata sulla grandiosa attività di *interpretatio iuris* realizzata dai *doctores* a partire dai testi romano-giustinianei, anzitutto nell'ambito degli *studia* universitari, integrante una pluralità di fonti autonome coordinate in un ordine giuridico, in una dimensione processuale che la trasforma nel corso del tempo, integrata in età moderna, tra l'altro, dall'attività giurisprudenziale delle grandi corti di giustizia, pur non venendo meno la funzione ordinante della dottrina. Non si può d'altra parte non segnalare quanto il diritto comune, specie se lo sguardo è bifronte, avendo da un lato il problema contemporaneo del "diritto comune europeo", possa ampliare la sua prospettiva spazio-temporale. A ben vedere, è anche questa preoccupazione a orientare, in maniera più o meno riconoscibile, la definizione dello *ius commune* in ordine alla questione dei "confini". In questo caso si può ben dire che, rovesciando il detto di Maitland, *comparison involves history*. La teoria storico-comparativa di Gino Gorla, nel suo itinerario originalissimo di comparatista, ha rappresentato coerentemente un'autentica modalità della scienza giuridica. La luce gettata sull'attività giurisprudenziale-creativa dei Grandi Tribunali in ambito europeo, *iurisprudentia* comune e comunicante, porta ad allargare la tradizionale nozione di *ius commune* facendone un sofisticato contenitore storico-comparativo in cui l'esperienza continentale e quella inglese, tradizionalmente divise da un fossato riempito di pregiudizi e di rimozioni,[45] possono dialogare su uno stesso piano. Non è un caso comunque

assumere forme, fisionomie e ruoli assolutamente diversi» (M. Sbriccoli, *Intervento*, cit., 211).

44 Sui limiti di una visione unitaria della tradizione romanistica in Europa, sia in termini di "sistema" che di "scienza", v. A. Mazzacane, *«Il leone fuggito dal circo»*, cit., 101 ss.

45 Della vasta produzione gorliana si vedano almeno la raccolta *Diritto comparato e diritto comune europeo*, Milano 1981 e *Il diritto comparato in Italia e nel «mondo occidentale» e una introduzione al «dialogo Civil law – Common law»*, Milano 1983. Per il necessario inquadramento dei paradigmi interpretativi v., oltre ai saggi pubblicati in comune dallo stesso Gorla e da Luigi Moccia, di quest'ultimo in particolare *Il legislatore del «diritto comune» continentale (sec. XVI–XVII) nell'opera di Gino Gorla*, in A. Giuliani e N. Picardi, *L'educazione giuridica*, V, *Modelli e scienza della legislazione*, Napoli 1987, 69–108; Id., *La «comparazione» come «pedagogia» giuridica nell'opera di Gino Gorla*, in *Scintillae iuris. Studi in memoria di Gino Gorla*, Milano 1994, t. I, 825–860; Id., *Prospetto storico delle origini e degli atteggiamenti del moderno diritto comparato (Per una teoria dell'ordinamento giuridico «aperto»)*, in *Riv. trim. dir. proc.*, 1996, 181–193. Cfr. inoltre il profilo

che il problema del diritto europeo visto da una delle sponde della Manica finisca per rappresentare un fattore importante per tracciare i limiti spazio-temporali del diritto europeo.[46] Maurizio Lupoi ha proposto una nozione di diritto comune europeo che, diversamente dallo *ius commune doctorum*, sarebbe l'espressione altomedievale della comunanza di *principia* e di *regula* intesi come modelli risolutori dei temi fondamentali della vita giuridica. Quello che abitualmente si considera, pur con modulazioni diverse del rapporto continuità/discontinuità, il punto di partenza dello *ius commune* cambia per Lupoi di segno e diventa il punto d'arrivo, il trauma dell'XI–XII sec., facendo sopravvivere la *comune ley* solo in Inghilterra e ponendo le premesse per «l'incolmabile iato fra *civil law* e *common law*», contribuendo a conformare i caratteri strutturali di un allontanamento.[47]

Che si tratti della presenza multiforme del diritto romano o della persistente natura "comunicante" del fattore giurisprudenziale, o ancora della sopravvivenza inglese di un diritto comune altomedievale, differenti nozioni di diritto comune europeo sono al centro del dibattito in una prospettiva di storia giuridica e di comparazione. Certo, la tentazione di ricorrere al registro della reviviscenza, pur avendo ben presenti differenze e alterità, rimane sempre sullo sfondo. Un dato merita di essere ulteriormente sottolineato: l'Europa del diritto comune europeo appare, pur tra incertezze e dilemmi, più ricca di esperienze, più complessa per articolazioni, più aperta al dialogo. Rimane il problema (vero, falso?) – in chiave prevalentemente di diritto privato europeo – dell'allontanamento o viceversa del mancato avvicinamento, a seconda che si calchi la mano sugl'elementi di alterità o si voglia riconoscere, più opportunamente, la costante presenza di aspetti comuni e di interazioni.[48] Europa irrimediabilmente diversa, osserva tuttavia

ricostruttivo in M. Ascheri, *Gino Gorla tra diritto e storia: per il diritto comune europeo*, in *Riv. trim. dir. proc.*, XLIV, 1990, 945–962 (pubblicato anche in M. Sbriccoli e A. Bettoni, *Grandi Tribunali e Rote nell'Italia di antico regime*, Milano 1993, XI–XXXIII).

46 Ancora utili sono le intuizioni e le piste di ricerca presenti in F. Vassalli, *Osservazioni di uomini di legge in Inghilterra* (1946), poi in *Studi giuridici*, vol. III, t. II, Studi vari (1942–1955), Milano 1960, in part. 580, nt. 2. Fondamentale per comprendere i problemi di metodo e di interpretazione connessi al confronto tra *common law* e *civil law* è adesso il monumentale lavoro di A. Torre, *Interpretare la Costituzione britannica. Itinerari culturali a confronto*, Torino 1997.

47 M. Lupoi, *Alle radici del mondo giuridico europeo. Saggio storico-comparativo*, Roma 1994; Id., *Common law e civil law (alle radici del diritto europeo)*, in *Foro it.*, CXVI, 1993, parte V, coll. 431–440. Sulla monografia di Lupoi si veda la recensione di E. Conte, in *Rivista di storia del diritto italiano*, LXVIII, 1995, 318–323.

48 Cfr. J. L. Halpérin, *Droit comparé et histoire du droit. A proposito di* Pierre Legrand, Le droit comparé ..., in *Quaderni fiorentini*, 30, 2001, t. II, 803–811. Di Halpérin si veda inoltre *Entre nationalisme juridique et communauté de droit*, Paris 1990, 87 ss.

Pierre Legrand[49] negando la possibilità e l'opportunità di far convergere i sistemi, di coordinarli in chiave di *approximation*. L'Europa plurigiuridica, segnata da differenze epistemologiche, mentali, morali, divisa da in-comprensioni, respinge ogni prospettiva "normalizzatrice", specie se da realizzarsi per mezzo di un codice privato europeo.

Che dire, dunque? Che forse per leggere l'Europa *una et diversa* di oggi non è più sufficiente il solo punto di vista del diritto comune europeo nelle varie accezioni ricordate. È per questo che mi accingo a dedicare la "seconda parte" del mio intervento al processo europeo di "costituzionalizzazione", dove l'orizzonte storico-critico può offrire egualmente un contributo alla riflessione in corso.

5. Un *novum ius commune*, ovvero l'altra tradizione del diritto comune europeo

Il 14 febbraio 1996 la mano sanguinaria dell'Eta assassinava a Madrid Francisco Tomás y Valiente, eminente storico del diritto, costituzionalista, giudice e presidente emerito del Tribunale costituzionale spagnolo. Da pochissimi anni era ritornato all'insegnamento universitario, ma, potremmo dire, con occhi e con spirito mutati: l'esperienza come giudice lo aveva sollecitato infatti a rimeditare i lavori scientifici del passato e a intravedere nuove prospettive nel campo della storia costituzionale, terreno a lui congeniale già prima della "parentesi" giurisdizionale. Il suo però era un *back to the future*. Il concetto di rivoluzione costituzionale, la cultura giurisprudenziale, il recupero innovativo dello *ius commune* europeo diventavano categorie referenziali. Tomás prospetta «l'approccio storiografico del diritto costituzionale come *diritto comune del costituzionalismo*, come prosecuzione costituzionale di quello *ius commune*. Il diritto costituzionale sarebbe innanzi tutto un *nuovo diritto comune* e questo potrà essere realmente rilevante per una storia costituzionale».[50] In una confe-

49 P. Legrand, *European Legal Systems are not Converging*, in *Int'l. & Comp. L. Q.*, 52, 1992, 64–78; *Sens et non-sens d'un Code civil européen*, in *Rev. Intern. dr. comp.*, 4, 1996, 779–812, 780 per i riferimenti relativi ai progetti di codice civile europeo; Id., *Uniformità, tradizioni giuridiche e limiti del diritto*, in *Pol. dir.*, 1, 1997, 3–26. V. anche P. Goodrich, *Oedipus Lex: Psychoanalysis, History, Law*, Berkeley 1995. *Contra* soprattutto i volumi curati da B. S. Markesinis, *The Gradual Convergence. Foreign Ideas, Foreign Influences and English Law on the eve of the twenty-first century*, Oxford 1994; Id., *The Coming Together of the Common Law and the Civil Law*, Oxford, Portland 2000.

50 La lettura interpretativa, su cui si basano le mie osservazioni, è quella di B. Clavero, *Tomás y Valiente, storico costituzionale inedito*, in A. Romano, *Il modello costituzionale inglese e la sua recezione nell'area mediterranea tra la fine del '700 e la prima metà dell'800*, Atti del Seminario internazionale di studi in memoria di

renza italiana del 1988 Tomás preannuncia i termini della questione: «L'Europa non è solo un mercato. Si appresta ad essere uno spazio giuridico comune. Rinasce un *novum ius commune*, integrato non soltanto da accordi doganali o direttive di discussa forza cogente, ma in modo preponderante e più profondo dalla coincidenza del regime di alcuni diritti fondamentali riconosciuti e garantiti in costituzioni, trattati e accordi. Su questo suolo dei diritti fondamentali, sostanzialmente eguali in tutti i nostri paesi, i Tribunali costituzionali e la Corte europea dei diritti dell'uomo hanno creato una giurisprudenza comune».[51] Lo *ius commune* romano-canonico era entrato in crisi definitivamente nel corso del XVIII secolo, destinato a perire di morte naturale[52] «per la sua incapacità di *evoluzione costituzionale*,[53] per trovare poi continuità nel *diritto comune* di questo tipo, un diritto che, similmente comune, viene ad essere quello dei diritti di libertà».[54] Le radici del "nuovo" affondano nella cultura giuspolitica e filosofica del XVII e XVIII sec. Età di grandi idee, ma anche di presupposti fragili e di diritti solennemente dichiarati e meno coerentemente garantiti. La cultura giuridica dei diritti ha faticato ad uscire dal sentiero della divinizzazione dello Stato.[55] Sono state soprattutto le costituzioni e con esse le convenzioni e i tribunali europei del secondo dopoguerra ad aver impiantato nel Continente una vera cultura dei diritti. Se oggi sono fondamentali e intoccabili nei loro contenuti essenziali è perché gli Stati sono democratici e realmente impegnati a garantirli.[56] In tal senso, si tratta di una cultura comune dei diritti perché in grado di produrre effetti di imitazione e di emulazione; perché le Corti costituzionali svolgono la loro opera di custodi e interpreti della Costituzione come norma dei diritti; perché al di sopra degli Stati c'è un tribunale comune

Francisco Tomás y Valiente, Messina, 14–16 novembre 1996, Milano 1998, 28. Clavero ha poi dedicato una biografia al giurista valenciano, nella quale dà conto ampiamente della "preoccupazione costituzionale" di Tomás: B. Clavero, *Tomás y Valiente. Una biografía intelectual*, Milano 1996.

51 Cit. da B. Clavero, *Tomás y Valiente, storico costituzionale inedito*, cit., 28–29.

52 F. Tomás y Valiente, *El «ius commune europaeum» de ayer y de hoy*, in *Glossae. Revista de Historia del derecho europeo*, 5–6, 1993–1994, 13–14. Importante è la pubblicazione postuma di alcuni scritti di F. Tomás, *Constitución: escritos de introducción histórica*, con introduzione di B. Clavero, Madrid 1996.

53 B. Clavero, *Tomás y Valiente, storico costituzionale inedito*, cit., 29. Il corsivo è mio.

54 *Ibidem*.

55 Paolo Grossi rileva la centralità dello Stato nella complessiva visione scientifica di Tomás y Valiente, cogliendone alcuni profili di tensione rispetto alle valenze più innovative del costituzionalismo: *Pagina introduttiva* in B. Clavero, *Tomás y Valiente*, cit., XXVI ss.

56 V. A. Romano, *Enunciazione e giustiziabilità dei diritti fondamentali nelle Carte costituzionali europee. Profili storici e comparativi*, Atti di un Convegno in onore di *Francisco Tomás y Valiente*, Messina, 15–16 marzo 1993, Milano 1994.

che protegge i diritti individuali e rettifica gl'eccessi statali. È una scienza dei diritti fondamentali trasformatasi in scienza della giurisprudenza costituzionale.[57]

La cultura del costituzionalismo – come diritto comune attuale[58] – richiamata da Tomás y Valiente è un elemento importante per capire le trasformazioni attraverso una chiave di lettura che fa del "costituzionale" un vero e proprio fattore ordinante dei sistemi giuridici. Tale cultura, pur nascendo dal seno degli Stati moderni si è andata faticosamente affrancando dal mero e indiscusso primato della legge, è stata incastonata dentro lo statuto normativo della costituzione, ha trovato un grado crescente di effettività nella giurisprudenza delle corti costituzionali e conquistato natura eminentemente transnazionale, "oltre" gli Stati, aspirando a diventare *ius commune europaeum*. «Si sta aprendo – osserva *Clavero* – tutta una possibilità di storia costituzionale senza la centralità dello Stato, una storia che non dia per precostituiti gli Stati, capace di affrontarli nella loro più radicale problematica costituente».[59] Certo, non si dovranno dimenticare i caratteri distinti, originari e sopravvenuti, dei "costituzionalismi" che hanno contrassegnato la storia moderna tra Europa e America e di conseguenza la pluralità di effetti prodotti sui relativi ordinamenti. Non si potrà neppure sottovalutare il fatto che una parte cospicua di quella che potremmo chiamare la "teoria costituzionale" di Antico regime – espressa anche attraverso le categorie dello *ius commune* – non si trova dove troppo semplicisticamente le nostre mappe concettuali pretendono di condurci.[60] E proprio il terreno fertile

57 Cfr. F. Tomás y Valiente, *El «ius commune europaeum» de ayer y de hoy*, cit., 14–16. L'autore cita uno scritto di Robert Alexy, verosimilmente la *Theorie der Grundrechte*, Frankfurt am Main 1986. Sulla relativa teoria di Alexy v. G. Bongiovanni, *R. Alexy e il costituzionalismo*, e A. Rotolo, *Morale, diritto e discorso pratico. Il contributo di R. Alexy*, entrambi in G. Bongiovanni, *La filosofia del diritto costituzionale e i problemi del liberalismo contemporaneo*, Bologna 1998, 29–50 e 51–77.

58 L'espressione è utilizzata da B. Clavero, *Tomás y Valiente, storico costituzionale inedito*, cit., 30.

59 Ivi, 31. Importanti gli studi di B. Clavero, *Lo spazio dei diritti e la posizione dei giudici tra costituzione e codice*, in *Materiali per una storia della cultura giuridica*, 1, 1989, 95–129; Id., *Happy Constitution. Cultura y lengua constitucionales*, Madrid 1997; Id., *Constituyencia de derechos entre América y Europa: Bill of Rights, We the People, Freedom's Law, American Constitution, Constitution of Europe*, in *Quaderni fiorentini*, 29, 2000, 87–171.

60 Su questo fondamentale profilo ricordo P. Costa, *Iurisdictio. Semantica del potere politico nella pubblicistica medievale (1100–1433)*, Milano 1969; A. Hespanha, *Représentation dogmatique et projets de pouvoir. Les outils conceptuels des juristes du jus commune dans le domaine de l'administration*, in E.V. Heyen, *Wissenschaft und Recht der Verwaltung seit dem Ancien Régime*, Frankfurt am Main 1984, 3–28; L. Mannori, *Per una "preistoria" della funzione amministrativa: cultura giuridica e attività dei pubblici apparati nell'età del tardo diritto comune*, in *Quaderni fiorentini*,

della *iustitia* e della *iurisdictio* – ovvero lo spazio di "identificazione" del "costituzionale" nell'esperienza medievale destinata a lunghe sopravvivenze – fanno venire in mente suggestioni e cortocircuiti destinati a far riflettere.

Le intuizioni di Tomás maturate nel corso degl'anni Ottanta si sono rivelate tutt'altro che infeconde. Lo storico spagnolo ha potuto soltanto abbozzare il proprio disegno, ma l'idea di fondo riveste una valenza metodologica che la storia costituzionale europea – come vedremo integrata nel processo di "costituzionalizzazione" – e la scienza giuridica farebbero bene a non lasciar cadere nel vuoto. Si potrebbe dire che la *realtà* ha superato l'*immaginazione*.[61] Proprio per questa ragione c'è bisogno di ri-pensare i limiti e i contenuti essenziali dello spazio costituzionale europeo perché questo spinga le radici – come pure si sta cercando di fare – più in profondità di quanto non sia avvenuto finora: una profondità o, se si vuole, uno strato che molto ha a che fare con la cultura del costituzionalismo inteso come *novum ius commune*, un fattore connettivo e ordinante necessario per rispondere efficacemente alla sfide e ai dilemmi del presente.

6. Il *mixtum compositum* e la "costituzione europea"

Nell'ultimo decennio il problema della "costituzione europea", per utilizzare un'espressione controversa, ma fonte di importanti dibattiti,[62] ha assunto una rilevanza dottrinale e politica crescente. Lo scenario complessivo ha subìto profondi cambiamenti e il processo di "costituzionalizzazione" è apparso a

19, 1990, 323–504; A. Hespanha, *Justiça e administração entre o antico regime e a revolução*, in B. Clavero, P. Grossi, F. Tomás y Valiente, *Hispania: Entre derechos propios y derechos nacionales*, Milano 1990, I, 135–204; J. Vallejo, *Ruda equidad, ley consumada: Concepción de la potestad normativa, 1250–1350*, Madrid 1992; A. Hespanha, *La gracia del derecho: economia de la cultura en la edad moderna*, Madrid 1993; L. Mannori, *Il sovrano tutore. Pluralismo istituzionale e accentramento amministrativo nel principato dei Medici (secc. XVI–XVIII)*, Milano 1994; P. Grossi, *L'ordine giuridico medievale*, cit.; L. Mannori, *Giustizia e amministrazione tra antico e nuovo regime*, in R. Romanelli, *Magistrati e potere nella storia europea*, Bologna 1997, 39–65; J. Vallejo, *Acerca del fruto del árbol de los jueces: escenarios de la justicia en la cultura del ius commune, in Anuario de la Facultad de Derecho de la Universidad Autónoma de Madrid*, 2, 1998, 19–46; P. Prodi, *Una storia della giustizia. Dal pluralismo dei fori al moderno dualismo tra coscienza e diritto*, Bologna 2000; B. Clavero, *"Iurisdictio" nello specchio o el silencio de Pietro Costa*, in P. Costa, *Iurisdictio*, cit., XIX–LXXX.

61 Cfr. P. Costa, *Discurso jurídico e imaginación. Hipótesis para una antropología del jurista*, in C. Petit, *Pasiones del jurista. Amor, memoria, melancolía, imaginacíon*, Madrid 1997, 161–190.

62 Per una messa a punto dei temi fondamentali v. C. Pinelli, *Il momento della scrittura*, cit., 183 ss.

taluni come il *medium* più appropriato per riequilibrare l'asse portante di un'Europa nata con un evidente intento politico ma cresciuta tramite una razionalità d'ordine essenzialmente economico[63] (sino all'istituzione di una Banca e di una moneta uniche). Nello stesso tempo il problema della proiezione internazionale dell'Unione, della ricerca di forme condivise di *governance* nel mondo globalizzato, del complesso allargamento verso gli Stati orientali ha contribuito ad accelerare un movimento preannunciato da molteplici segnali.

L'Europa ha bisogno di una "costituzione"? La risposta, come è noto, è tutt'altro che univoca. In fondo la celebre *querelle* tra Dieter Grimm e Jürgen Habermas[64] sul futuro della costituzione era già riassuntiva di gran parte dei temi in discussione e rappresentativa, pur entro una gamma vastissima di graduazioni e di distinguo, dei principali indirizzi interpretativi. Per gli uni bisogna anzitutto dubitare fortemente dell'uso della parola "costituzione", in quanto il diritto comunitario primario derivato dai trattati non può assumere il senso di una "costituzione" così come larga parte della scienza giuridica europea ha inteso esprimerlo. La struttura ordinamentale complessa dell'Unione – fino a che non muteranno i presupposti fondamentali (a cominciare dal *mix* di elementi distinti propri della logica intergovernativa, multinazionale e transnazionale, e delle culture del diritto internazionale, del costituzionalismo e del federalismo) – impedisce di dar vita ad una costituzione in senso proprio. Emergono allora tutti i limiti del "discorso costituzionale": un diritto di autodeterminazione politica che non può risalire ad un atto del popolo, la mancanza di un'identità collettiva intesa come senso di appartenenza, un deficit strutturale di legittimazione democratica. Se questo è il panorama, non è ancora auspicabile la trasformazione dell'Unione europea in Stato federale; nello stesso tempo una costituzione in senso proprio attribuirebbe all'Unione la competenza sulla competenza facendo di essa uno Stato, poiché «[...] la costituzione è in definitiva strettamente connessa allo Stato [...]».[65] In questa prospettiva gradualistica non sarà possibile immaginare un risultato duraturo ed efficace se non partendo da una ponderata revisione razionalizzatrice dell'esistente e soprattutto dall'individuazione del tessuto "materiale" come terreno di progressiva edificazione di un effettivo spazio pubblico europeo.[66]

63 Cfr. A. Anzon, *La costituzione europea come problema*, in *Riv. it. dir. pubbl. com.*, 2000, 657; S. Gambino, *Verso la formazione di un diritto comune europeo: metodo comparatistico e ricerca costituzionale*, in *Pol. dir.*, 1, 2001, 43.

64 Elementi di sintesi in G. Marramao, *L'Europa dopo il Leviatano. Tecnica, politica, costituzione*, in *Una costituzione senza Stato*, cit., 121 ss.

65 D. Grimm, *Una costituzione per l'Europa?* (1994), in G. Zagrebelsky, P. P. Portinaro, J. Luther, *Il futuro della costituzione*, Torino 1996, 367.

66 Per questa posizione in Italia, pur con differenze di accenti e di impostazione, per es. M. Luciani, *Legalità e legittimità nel processo di integrazione europea*, in *Una*

Per chi invece ritiene quantomeno opportuno immaginare un'Europa "costituzionalizzata" in tempi relativamente ravvicinati, non è con i paradigmi tradizionali, per lo più di matrice statualistica,[67] che sarà possibile ridefinire un ordinamento caratterizzato, nella sua evoluzione fluida, da un elevato tasso di originalità. Una struttura tanto complessa non può essere valutata con strumenti "obsoleti" per un verso, inidonei per un altro, ma richiede, specie ai giuristi e alle loro concettualizzazioni, uno sforzo intenso di "immaginazione". È evidente, inoltre, che la parola-concetto "costituzione" qui tenderà ad assumere un significato più "aperto",[68] più dinamico, di integrazione orizzontale, in questo accompagnata dal viatico di una rinnovata teoria della costituzione. In tal senso dell'idea democratico-pluralistica di costituzione si valorizzano gli aspetti ritenuti più consoni alla prospettiva europea. In questa visione da un lato si depotenzia e si delimita l'assolutezza dell'argomento della legittimazione,[69] dall'altro si individua proprio nel processo di integrazione costituzionale il vero motore per la formazione di una condizione minimale di cittadinanza, di identità sociale, di partecipazione politica, di prassi discorsive, verso l'obiettivo di un adeguato spazio pubblico europeo.[70] Nello stesso tempo però *fare la Costituzione* non potrà consistere che in una *consolidazione di segno costituzionale*, perché una costituzione in senso sostanziale esiste già,[71] una consolidazione volta a selezio-

costituzione senza Stato, cit., 71–87; A. Pace, *La dichiarazione di Laeken e il processo costituente europeo*, in *Riv. trim. dir. pubbl.*, 3, 2002, 613–650; F. Bilancia, *Brevi note su costituzione materiale, legalità ed Unione europea*, in A. Catelani e S. Labriola, *La costituzione materiale. Percorsi culturali e attualità di un'idea*, Milano 2001; S. Gambino, *Verso la formazione di un diritto comune europeo*, cit.

67 Per tutti P. Häberle, *Colloquio sulla "costituzione europea"*, cit., 199: «L'assetto costituzionale dell'Europa, e correlativamente il processo di strutturazione di essa, non si possono comprendere con le categorie della *Allgemeine Staatslehre*».

68 G. Zagrebelsky, *Il diritto mite. Legge diritti giustizia*, Torino 1992, 10. Si veda anche L. Ornaghi, *La nuova età delle costituzioni. Da una concezione nazionale della democrazia a una prospettiva europea e internazionale*, Bologna 2000.

69 Per tutti S. Cassese, *Lo spazio giuridico globale*, Roma, Bari 2003, 82–92.

70 J. Habermas, *Una costituzione per l'Europa? Osservazioni su Dieter Grimm*, in *Il futuro della Costituzione*, cit., 369–375; Id., *Perché l'Europa ha bisogno di una costituzione?*, in *Una costituzione senza Stato*, cit., 145–166. Pur con notevoli differenze, v. J. H. H. Weiler, *The Constitution of Europe*, Cambridge, 1999, 324 ss.; Id., *Why Should Europe be a Democracy: The Corruption of Political Culture and the Principle of Constitutional Tolerance*, in F. Snyder, *The Europeanisation of Law. The Legal Effects of European Integration*, Oxford, Portland 2000, 213 ss.

71 Per il dibattito sull'esistenza o meno di una "costituzione" e in base a quali presupposti, v. A. Barbera, *Esiste una «Costituzione europea»?*, in *Quad. cost.*, 1, 2000, 59 ss.; C. Pinelli, *Il momento della scrittura*, cit., 187 ss.; P. Craig, *Constitutions, Constitutionalism and the European Union*, in *Eur. L. J.*, 2, 2001, 136; G. G. Floridia, *Una costituzione per l'Europa. Ma in che senso? (appunti definitori*

nare, semplificare e riordinare il diritto dei trattati e le sue concrete espressioni istituzionali avendo come orizzonte possibile un "testo costituzionale".[72] Se l'obiettivo razionalizzatore è in fondo comune ai diversi orientamenti, è però il "momento della scrittura" quello che li allontana, almeno in questa fase. Mettere per iscritto anche solo ciò che preesiste come tradizione costituzionale comune prescritta dal tempo non è mai un'operazione notarile e passiva.[73] Lo sa bene chi frequenta la storia costituzionale e il risalente fenomeno delle imitazioni, delle influenze, delle "copiature" letterali e addirittura delle recezioni integrali di testi costituzionali.[74] In questa prospettiva, la "costituzione" – intesa anche come meccanismo di integrazione del pluralismo e come processo[75] evolutivo aperto – assumerebbe anche una forte valenza simbolica, emozionale,[76] "comunicativa".

L'impossibilità di prefigurare a breve termine l'Unione europea come Stato ma, ancora di più, l'inverosimiglianza e l'inopportunità di questa soluzione sembrerebbero – a rigor di logica – mettere il processo in atto in un *cul-de-sac*. I critici diranno tuttavia che lo Stato non è più la condizione necessaria per far vivere un ordinamento costituzionale e che ciò discende proprio dalla *cultura costituzionale* che ha gradualmente eroso quel binomio all'apparenza indefettibile. Nel contempo l'ipotesi secondo cui l'Unione avrebbe già una "costituzione" *sui generis* parrebbe rafforzare la via intrapresa. Tuttavia, come spesso capita, sembra più facile dire ciò che l'Unione europea *non è*, piuttosto che ciò che essa *è*. La "crisi" della teoria giuridica legata allo Stato-persona e al concetto di sovranità mette i giuristi in una scomoda posizione: non possono più affidarsi a questi concetti con la stessa sicurezza nutrita nel passato, ma non dispongono ancora di categorie e paradigmi sufficientemente affidabili, condivisi e coordinati. Probabilmente non bisogna aspettarsi un ritorno alla dogmatica "pesante", poiché i tempi nei quali viviamo non sembrano più in grado di sopportarne il peso. Tuttavia, è su questo terreno che si può sperare di costruire qualcosa di più

e di metodo), in *Dir. pubb. comp. eur.*, 2, 2002, 579–595; S. Cassese, *Lo spazio giuridico globale*, cit., 27 ss.

72 Questa espressione è stata utilizzata per la prima volta nella Dichiarazione di Laeken.

73 C. Pinelli, *Il momento della scrittura*, cit., 195–196. Cfr. anche M. Fioravanti, S. Mannoni, *Il «modello costituzionale» europeo: tradizioni e prospettive*, in G. Bonacchi, *Una costituzione senza Stato*, cit., 23–70; A. Pizzorusso, *Il patrimonio costituzionale europeo*, Bologna 2002.

74 Cfr. *supra* in questo volume *La Costituzione belga del 1831*, 80–83.

75 Cfr. A. Spadaro, *Dalla Costituzione come «atto» (puntuale nel tempo) alla Costituzione come «processo» storico. Ovvero della continua evoluzione del parametro costituzionale attraverso i giudizi di costituzionalità*, in *Quad. cost.*, 3, 1998, 343 ss.

76 P. Häberle, *Colloquio sulla "costituzione europea"*, cit. Cfr. F. Politi, *Stato costituzionale e Kulturstaat nel pensiero di Peter Häberle*, in *Dir. pubbl. comp. eur.*, 2, 2002, 463–465.

durevole. Non è un caso che la teoria, la storia e la comparazione stiano ricominciando a tessere un discorso comune e che proprio l'Europa sia il vettore principale e l'"oggetto" di questo "incontro". Lo storico, in particolare, non si meraviglia nel vedere che modelli e principi organizzativi a lui ben presenti siano evocati per svelare l'"arcano" dell'Unione europea e per immaginare possibili sviluppi.

In questo "ritorno al passato" il pluralismo medievale governato dallo *ius commune* dei *doctores*, i soli in grado di coglierne la cifra "unitaria" in mezzo a diversità d'ordine territoriale e soggettivo, si conquista una qualche valenza euristica: il fine sarebbe quello di allargare gli orizzonti, di "avvicinare" mentalità quasi sempre irriducibilmente diverse e aprire un "laboratorio" storico-comparativo nel quale dare "respiro" e profondità a proposte dell'oggi, si tratti del concetto "politologico" di *multilevel constitutionalism*[77] o della suggestiva ma sfuggente metafora della *rete*.[78] Non v'è dubbio che la centralità di principi come quello di sussidiarietà o di adeguatezza, per fare solo un esempio, rispondono anche al tentativo di individuare strumenti per governare, a vari livelli, un sistema-arcipelago e dare una "direzione di senso" a strutture rette da logiche e dinamiche non più riconducibili a universi omogenei.

Del resto, non si deve necessariamente riandare all'esperienza pre-statuale per rispondere al bisogno di "precedenti". Una fondamentale revisione storiografica ha riletto in chiave critica sia il paradigma weberiano che la grande tradizione di scienza europea del diritto pubblico tra XIX e XX artefice della edificazione dello "Stato di diritto".[79] Togliendo le incrostazioni e denunciando

77 Cfr. in particolare I. Pernice, *Multilevel Constitutionalism and the Treaty of Amsterdam: European Constitution-Making Revisited?*, in *C. Mkt. L. Rev.*, 36, 1999, 703 ss.; I. Pernice, F. Meyer, *De la constitution composée de l'Europe*, in *Rev. trim. dr. eur.*, 2000, 623–647. Per una discussione critica di questa teoria v. M. Luciani, *Legalità e legittimità*, cit., 84–85.

78 K. H. Ladeur, *Towards a Legal Theory of Supranationality. The Viability of the Network Concept*, in *Eur. L. J.*, 1997; A. Predieri, M. Morisi, *L'Europa delle reti*, Torino 2001; F. Scharpf, *Verso una teoria della multi-level governance in Europa*, in *Rivista italiana di politiche pubbliche*, 1, 2002; S. Cassese, *Lo spazio giuridico globale*, cit., 21 ss., con ulteriore bibliografia. Sull'uso dell'immagine della rete v. P. Grossi, *Dalla società di società alla insularità dello Stato fra Medioevo ed età moderna*, Napoli 2003, 16 ss. Per un approccio di «teoria dialettica» del diritto v. F. Ost, M. van de Kerchove, *De la pyramide au réseau? Vers un nouveau mode de production du droit?*, in *Revue interdisciplinaire d'études juridiques*, 44, 2000, 1–82; F. Ost, M. van de Kerchove, *De la pyramide au reseau? Pour une théorie dialectique du droit*, Bruxelles 2002. L'uso di queste metafore è stato discusso in una prospettiva interculturale nel n. 49, 2002 della *Revue interdisciplinaire d'études juridiques*, diretta dai due studiosi belgi.

79 È d'obbligo il rinvio a Fioravanti, specialmente le raccolte di saggi M. Fioravanti, *Stato e costituzione. Materiali per una storia delle dottrine costituzionali*, Torino 1993;

le giustapposizioni incombenti sulla genesi e sullo sviluppo del cd. "Stato moderno"; tale orientamento ha permesso di andare oltre lo schermo teorico e retorico della sovranità, mostrando come quegli Stati (moderni) e i loro sovrani abbiano dovuto fronteggiare per lungo tempo caratteri e attributi pluralistici apparentemente "medievali" come il pattizio, il composito, il consociativo, solitamente appannaggio – in età contemporanea – delle categorie riconducibili al federalismo e a quella costruzione peculiarissima che è lo Stato in senso federale. La *respublica composita*, il *mixtum compositum*, la variegatissima tipologia di unioni di stati tornano così al centro dell'attenzione.[80]

Paradossalmente il "futuro della costituzione" e gl'incunaboli del "costituzionalismo antico" sembrerebbero meno lontani di quanto la cronologia lascerebbe intendere. Tuttavia dovremmo riflettere di più sul senso di marcia di questi "avvicinamenti" e interrogarci sulla specularità delle operazioni interpretative e sul significato profondo di questi cortocircuiti. Lo storico, comunque, non può abdicare alla sua funzione critica. L'esperienza dello Stato moderno – è un'ovvietà – non può essere certo racchiusa tra due parentesi.[81] Dovremmo, altrimenti, essere diversi da come siamo e notoriamente il principio di identità ce lo impedisce. È piuttosto su un altro terreno, quello del *novum ius commune* – nell'accezione di Tomás – che il passato e il presente si pongono in una relazione di continuità (oltre che di rilevate differenze nel costituzionalismo post-bellico), rendendo forse più produttivo e intelligibile il dialogo tra giuristi. Più che l'Europa del mercato, dei poteri e delle competenze, è l'Europa dei diritti che "ha bisogno" del passato.

7. La Carta dei diritti e le «tradizioni costituzionali comuni»

Questo "nuovo" diritto comune europeo – forse la risposta più significativa alla crisi dello *jus publicum europaeum* – si è sedimentato nel corso del tempo. Non è un caso che diversi commentatori abbiano impiegato per definire il risultato più vistoso di questo sviluppo – la Carta dei diritti fondamentali dell'Unione

Id., *La scienza del diritto pubblico. Dottrine dello Stato e della Costituzione tra Otto e Novecento*, Milano 2001, 2 tomi.

80 Per la più informata discussione del problema, v. S. Cassese, *Lo spazio giuridico globale*, cit., 55 ss., cui si rinvia anche per gli orientamenti bibliografici. Per una acuta riflessione sul problema della "sovranità ripartita" e dell'esercizio di competenze in ambito comunitario, cfr. E. Cannizzaro, *Esercizio di competenze e sovranità nell'esperienza giuridica dell'integrazione europea*, in *Riv. dir. cost.*, 1, 1996, 75–123. Sul concetto di *commonwealth* v. soprattutto N. MacCormick, *La sovranità in discussione. Diritto, stato e nazione nel «commonwealth» europeo*, Bologna 2003.

81 Lo sottolinea G. Marramao, *L'Europa dopo il Leviatano*, cit., 133.

europea – il riferimento pregnantissimo al *Bill of Rights*.[82] Questa volta senza una *Glorious Revolution*, la Carta avrebbe consolidato «[...] i veri, antichi e incontestabili diritti e libertà del popolo [...]»,[83] in verità i diritti fondamentali già a fondamento dell'Unione, «al fine di sancirne in modo visibile l'importanza capitale e la portata per i cittadini [...]»[84] europei. Rendere più *visibili* i diritti e quindi le tradizioni comuni in un documento unitario e solenne avrebbe assolto ad una funzione ricognitiva, essenzialmente "conservatrice". Peter Häberle ha ricordato il concetto di *Nachführung* ("direzione che si forma attraverso un'evoluzione graduale") coniato in Svizzera come processo per arrivare a chiarificare, sistematizzare e precisare l'esistente, dando maggiore "trasparenza" alla realtà.[85] I valori comuni, derivanti da un patrimonio spirituale e morale, sono dichiarati indivisibili e universali, e proprio il principio di indivisibilità e di non gerarchizzazione è uno degli aspetti innovativi del *Restatement*, a dimostrazione del fatto che la Carta rispecchia una modalità tecnica di elaborazione che si distacca, almeno in parte, dal modo più tradizionale di sistematizzare i diritti.[86] In questa dimensione "propositiva" a forte valenza assiologica e incentrata su un catalogo dei diritti almeno in parte innovativo[87] molti scorgono oltre al più complessivo

82 K. Lenaerts, E. E. de Smuter, *A «Bill of Rights» for the European Union*, in *Com. Mkt. L. Rev.*, 2001.

83 *Bill of Rights*, 13 febbraio 1689. Sul carattere ricognitivo e consolidatorio della Carta v. A. Pizzorusso, *Il patrimonio costituzionale europeo*, cit. Questa interpretazione ha trovato conferma, per es., nelle conclusioni formulate l'8 febbraio 2001 dall'Avvocato generale Antonio Tizzano nella causa *Bectu c. Secretary of State for Trade and Industry* dinanzi alla Corte di Giustizia delle Comunità europee: «Tuttavia anche a non volere entrare qui nell'ampio dibattito già in corso circa gli effetti che, in altre forme e per altre vie, la Carta potrebbe comunque produrre, resta il fatto che essa racchiude enunciazioni che appaiono in gran parte come ricognitive di diritti già altrove sanciti ...» (citato da E. Paciotti, *La Carta dei diritti fondamentali: una novità istituzionale*, in G. Bonacchi, *Una Costituzione senza Stato*, cit., 449). Sulla Carta v. A. Manzella, P. Melograni, E. Paciotti, S. Rodotà, *Riscrivere i diritti in Europa*, Bologna 2001; R. Bifulco, M. Cartabia, A. Celotto, *L'Europa dei diritti*, Bologna 2001; A. Pace, *A che serve la Carta dei diritti fondamentali dell'Unione Europea? Appunti preliminari*, in *Giur. cost.*, 2000, 193 ss.; M. P. Chiti, *La Carta europea dei diritti fondamentali: una carta di carattere funzionale?*, in *Riv. trim. dir. pubbl.*, 1, 2002.

84 Consiglio europeo, allegato IV, *Decisione del Consiglio europeo relativa all'elaborazione di una Carta dei diritti fondamentali dell'Unione europea*, Colonia, 3–4 giugno 1999.

85 P. Häberle, *Colloquio sulla "costituzione europea"*, cit., 2.

86 V. E. Paciotti, *La Carta dei diritti fondamentali: una novità istituzionale*, cit., 446; A. Pizzorusso, *Il patrimonio costituzionale europeo*, cit., 108–109; C. Pinelli, *Il momento della scrittura*, cit., 215 ss.

87 Come si coglie, del resto, dal IV capoverso del Preambolo: «A tal fine è necessario [...] rafforzare la tutela dei diritti fondamentali alla luce dell'evoluzione della

carattere simbolico della Carta, un primo fondamentale presupposto per rafforzare l'Unione sul piano della legittimità dandogli forza espansiva[88] e facendone quindi un probabile «[...] sostanziale parametro di riferimento per tutti gli attori – Stati membri, istituzioni, persone fisiche e giuridiche – della scena comunitaria [...]».[89] La Carta dovrebbe essere – prima ancora che il problema formale del suo *status* e della sua efficacia giuridica venga "risolto" dalla Convenzione sul futuro dell'Europa[90] – il punto costante di riferimento nei lavori di quest'ultimo consesso impegnato nella ridefinizione dei poteri[91] e delle istituzioni europee. Avere sempre presenti i diritti consentirebbe inoltre di ovviare al rischio, altrimenti reale, di separare artificiosamente gl'uni dagl'altri.[92]

Non bisognerà però dimenticare un fatto: ovvero, che la Carta ha contribuito a "codificare" anche la giurisprudenza europea in materia di diritti fondamentali. Questo è un legame importante per la vitalità della "tradizioni costituzionali comuni". La peculiarità dei caratteri istituzionali della Corte di Giustizia, gli strumenti e la tipologia di ricorsi sui quali può contare, la funzione pretoria (non isolatamente però) svolta nell'affermare la supremazia del diritto comunitario e nel rafforzare il sistema giuridico comunitario sono tutti profili ben noti.[93] È dai primi anni '70 che la Corte del Lussemburgo si richiama alla tradizioni costituzionali comuni agli Stati membri e poi alla Convenzione europea

società, del progresso sociale e degli sviluppi scientifici e tecnologici». Cfr. S. Rodotà, *Tra diritti e mercato: una cittadinanza europea possibile*, in *Una Costituzione senza Stato*, cit., 451 ss.

88 G. G. Floridia, *Una costituzione per l'Europa. Ma in che senso?*, cit., 592.

89 Conclusioni dell'Avvocato generale nella causa *Bectu c. Secretary of State for Trade and Industry*, cit.

90 Ma sui vari effetti della Carta, v. in particolare A. Pace, *La dichiarazione di Laeken*, cit., 626–627.

91 J. H. H. Weiler, *Diritti umani, costituzionalismo ed integrazione: iconografia e feticismo*, in *Quad. cost.*, 3, 2002, 521 ss. Cfr. anche L. S. Rossi, *La Carta dei diritti come strumento di costituzionalizzazione dell'ordinamento dell'UE*, ivi, 565 ss.

92 M. Cartabia, *Allargamento e diritti fondamentali nell'Unione europea. Dimensione politica e dimensione individuale*, in S. Guerrieri, A. Manzella, F. Sdogati, *Dall'Europa a Quindici alla Grande Europa*, cit., 126.

93 Cfr. J. H. H. Weiler, *Il sistema comunitario europeo*, Bologna, 1985; E. Stein, *Giuristi, giudici e la creazione di una costituzione transnazionale* (1987), in Id., *Un nuovo diritto per l'Europa. Uno sguardo d'oltreoceano*, Milano, 1991, 17–43; J. H. H. Weiler, R. Dehousse, G. Bebr, *Primus Inter Pares. The European Court and National Courts: Thirty Years of Cooperation*, Firenze 1988; B. De Witte, *The Past and Future Role of the European Court of Justice in the Protection of Human Rights*, in Ph. Alston (a cura di), *The EU and Human Rights*, Oxford 1999, 859 ss.; A. Pizzorusso, *Il patrimonio costituzionale europeo*, cit., 163 ss. Per le prospettive di riforma del sistema giurisdizionale comunitario v. E. Chiti, G. P. Manzella, J. P. Miranda de Sousa, *La Corte di giustizia*, in *Dall'Europa a Quindici alla Grande Europa*, cit., 211–240.

per la salvaguardia dei diritti dell'uomo e delle libertà fondamentali quali presupposti del suo *judicial activism* contribuendo alla formazione di un vitale circuito a tre livelli ordinamentali fra le corti europee e le corti costituzionali.[94]

Se il ruolo svolto dalle istituzioni di giustizia europea e, insieme, il contributo, più o meno convinto delle singole corti costituzionali, hanno trovato un crescente riconoscimento, pare troppo semplicistico affidarsi al carattere retorico e simbolico di quest'ultimo documento che, per molti aspetti, è rivolto all'"esterno", in termini di proiezione identitaria e soprattutto di *fines* di civiltà dell'Europa. La scrittura però non è mai innocua e il rischio di "immobilizzazione" e di "isolamento" dei diritti dal *contesto* è ben presente allo storico.[95] Non è questa la sede per entrare nel merito della sistematica e dei singoli valori ispiratori dei principi che a loro volta fonderebbero i diritti sanciti dalla Carta. Qui interessa un altro aspetto. La Carta, come è stato giustamente osservato, è *anche* uno strumento diretto a «riequilibrare i rapporti fra diritto giurisprudenziale e diritto di formazione legislativa, e a conferire una certezza di tutela relativamente maggiore dei diritti fondamentali nei confronti degli atti dell'Unione».[96] Si tocca allora con mano una delle questioni aperte di questa fase delicatissima della storia comunitaria. La Carta serve per affermare i diritti ai confini dell'Europa o per riportare la Corte dentro un terreno che essa stessa ha delimitato? Questo è un dilemma che riveste rilevanza dentro un orizzonte più vasto. La *scrittura* è "politicamente" necessaria, ma rischia di inserire nei delicati meccanismi di evoluzione elementi di rigidità, non sempre così necessari, proprio in virtù del suo carattere fluido, processuale, "materiale".

Quando Peter Häberle si riferisce al ruolo propulsivo della Corte di giustizia in materia di diritti fondamentali osserva anche come essa abbia fatto «comparazione giuridica in forma di giudizio»[97] elaborando principi generali –

94 Su questi processi si rinvia a C. Pinelli, *Il momento della scrittura*, cit., 119 ss. Per la circolazione dei precedenti tra Corti costituzionali, v. G. Lombardi, *La fase attuale dello «ius publicum europaeum»*, in *Enunciazione e giustiziabilità dei diritti fondamentali nelle Carte costituzionali europee*, cit., 89 ss.

95 V. la discussione in P. Grossi, *Pagina introduttiva (Storia e cronistoria dei "Quaderni fiorentini")*, in *Quaderni fiorentini*, 30, 2001, t. I, 6–12.

96 C. Pinelli, *Il momento della scrittura*, cit., 215. Sul paradosso della Carta, che dovrebbe ridimensionare il potere della Corte comunitaria, ma rischia, in mancanza di un suo valore vincolante, di accrescerne il ruolo creativo, v. L. Azzena, *Prospettive della Carta europea dei diritti e ruolo della giurisprudenza*, in G. F. Ferrari, *I diritti fondamentali dopo la Carta di Nizza. Il costituzionalismo dei diritti*, Milano 2001, 126.

97 Ma sul metodo scarsamente comparativo della Corte di Giustizia v. G. F. Ferrari, *I diritti tra costituzionalismi statali e discipline transnazionali*, in Id., *I diritti fondamentali dopo la Carta di Nizza*, cit., 93 ss.

ispiratori del complessivo ordine giuridico europeo – tratti per lo più dagli ordinamenti degli Stati membri, anche se non sempre con il rigore necessario. E il carattere multinazionale della Corte ha contribuito a farne una «società aperta degli interpreti della costituzione».[98] È fin troppo suggestivo, forse, sentire in queste espressioni, in termini di *novum ius commune*, echi della fraseologia del cardinal Giovan Battista de Luca tanto evocativa del ruolo dei Grandi Tribunali di antico regime e tante volte ricordata da Gino Gorla. Non è un caso però che questi avesse compreso il carattere demistificante che la prospettiva europea imponeva alla ri-lettura – quasi passando per usi interpretativi tipici del *common law* – dell'art. 12 delle Disposizioni preliminari al codice civile del 1942.[99]

La Corte di giustizia ha fatto ricorso ai principi generali derivanti dalle «tradizioni costituzionali comuni agli Stati membri» dando vita ad un *corpus* di decisioni – incentrato fortemente sulla tutela dei diritti fondamentali – che ha poi trovato il riconoscimento e la valorizzazione di cui si diceva.[100] È sul terreno dei principi[101] – derivati più dalle costituzioni che dai codici – e delle «tradizioni costituzionali comuni» che appare dunque possibile elaborare un "nuovo diritto comune" che abbia da un lato carattere "patrimoniale", consolidatorio,[102] che si rivolga cioè al passato e quindi soprattutto alla storia degl'ordinamenti degli Stati membri, e dall'altro sia "comunicante",[103] in grado cioè di guardare al futuro indipendentemente dall'evoluzione del diritto posto dai trattati o, in altra prospettiva, da un Trattato-Costituzione. Per mantenere integra la natura

98 P. Häberle, *Colloquio sulla "costituzione europea"*, cit., 202–203.

99 G. Gorla, *Diritto comparato e diritto comune europeo*, cit., 649 e 700 ss. Sulla persistente lettura statualistica dei principi generali v. per tutti le osservazioni di P. Grossi, *Un diritto senza Stato*, cit., 273 ss.

100 Non sfuggono tuttavia i profili di "arretratezza" della Carta rispetto all'*acquis* giurisprudenziale: cfr. per es. G. di Plinio, *La Carta dei diritti nel processo di integrazione europea*, in G. F. Ferrari, *I diritti fondamentali dopo la Carta di Nizza*, cit., 149 ss.

101 Sull'argomento rinvio a G. Zagrebelsky, *Il diritto mite*, cit., 147 ss.; J. P. Puissochet, *La Cour de Justice et les principes généraux de droit*, in AA.VV., *Congrès des avocats européens, La protection juridictionnelle des droits dans le système communautaire*, Bruxelles 1997, 1 ss.; G. Gaja, *Identifying the status of general principles in European community law*, in AA.VV., *Scritti in onore di G. F. Mancini*, Milano 1998, 445 ss.; A. Pizzorusso, *Il patrimonio costituzionale europeo*, cit., *passim*.

102 Sul punto v. L. Gianformaggio, *Tempo della costituzione, tempo della consolidazione*, in *Pol. dir.*, 4, 1997, 527–551.

103 Sulla *contaminatio* fra sistemi e sulla vicenda inglese che ha portato nel 1998 alla ratifica, con l'*Human Rights Act*, della Convenzione europea dei diritti umani, v. i saggi raccolti in Ph. Alston, *Promoting Human Rights Through Bills of Rights*, Oxford 1999 e E. Ceccherini, *La codificazione dei diritti nelle recenti costituzioni*, Milano 2002, 40 ss.

dinamica dei principi, la funzione interpretativa delle tradizioni e la tensione vitale propria di una complessa dimensione culturale[104] si dovrebbe evitare il rischio di vedere nel processo in atto il "compimento" di un grande disegno dimenticando quanta strada rimane da compiere. Il lavoro di dissodamento e di evidenziazione del «patrimonio costituzionale comune»[105] non è ancora soddisfacente. Una storia costituzionale su scala europea, realmente comparata esiste solo per frammenti.[106] Le storie nazionali continuano ad avere il sopravvento. Le lacune restano vistose. La prospettiva concreta di un *diritto comune del costituzionalismo* non può prescindere da una cognizione più complessa, articolata e rigorosa delle tradizioni comuni, specialmente alla luce dell'allargamento

104 Sul nesso fondamentale tra approccio *kulturwissenschaftlich*, cultura giuridica europea e prospettive del *gemeineuropäisches Verfassungsrecht* è d'obbligo il rinvio a P. Häberle, *Colloquio sulla "costituzione europea"*, cit. e Id., *Per una dottrina della Costituzione come scienza della cultura*, cit. Cfr. anche P. C. Müller-Graff e E. Riedel, *Gemeinsames Verfassungsrecht in der Europäischen Union*, Baden-Baden 1998. Di notevole interesse risulta il saggio di A. A. Cervati, *Il diritto costituzionale europeo*, cit. Per una analisi storico-giuridica del concetto di "cultura" v. le osservazioni di H. Mohnhaupt, *Europäische Rechtsgeschichte und europäische Integration. Kulturelle Bedingungen europäischer Rechtseinheit und vergleichende Beobachtungen*, in *Europäische Rechtsgeschichte und europäische Integration*, Institutet för Rättshistorisk Forskning, Stockholm 2002, 17–57.

105 Sul punto v. l'importante ricostruzione di A. Pizzorusso, *Il patrimonio costituzionale europeo*, cit. Cfr. inoltre *Le patrimoine constitutionnel européen*, Strasbourg 1997; R. Dehousse, *Naissance d'un constitutionalisme transnational*, in *Pouvoirs*, 96, 2001, 19 ss.; M. Fioravanti, S. Mannoni, *Il «modello costituzionale» europeo: tradizioni e prospettive*, cit.; S. Gambino, *Verso la formazione di un diritto comune europeo*, cit.

106 Tra i più recenti progetti collettivi di ricerca segnalo *Europäische Rechts- und Verfassungsgeschichte*, cit.; i volumi curati da A. Romano, *Alle origini del costituzionalismo europeo*, Messina 1991; *Enunciazione e giustiziabilità dei Diritti nelle carte costituzionali europee*, cit.; *Il modello costituzionale inglese e la sua recezione nell'area mediterranea tra la fine del '700 e la prima metà dell'800*, cit.; le ricerche promosse da P. Schiera e M. Kirsch, *Denken und Umsetzung des Konstitutionalismus in Deutschland und europäischen Ländern in der ersten Hälfte des 19. Jahrhunderts*, Berlin 2000; *Verfassungswandel um 1848 im europäischen Vergleich*, Berlin 2001; da G. Manca, *L'istituzione parlamentare nel XIX secolo. Una prospettiva comparata ...*, Bologna, Berlin 2000; *Parlamento e costituzione nei sistemi costituzionali europei ottocenteschi*, Bologna, Berlin 2003; il volume curato da H. Dippel, *Executive and Legislative Powers in the Constitutions of 1848–49*, Berlin 1999. Mi piace infine ricordare due riviste, nate di recente, dedicate alla storia costituzionale europea, una spagnola, pubblicata dal Dipartimento di diritto pubblico dell'Università di Oviedo, *Historia Constitucional. Revista electrónica de Historia Constitucional*, il cui primo numero risale al 2000 (http://constitucion.rediris.es/revista/hc/index.html), l'altra italiana, sorta nel 2001, il *Giornale di storia costituzionale*, semestrale del Laboratorio di storia costituzionale *"A. Barnave"* dell'Università di Macerata, condiretta da *R. Martucci* e dal sottoscritto e pubblicata dall'editore Quodlibet.

dell'Unione a paesi che solo da pochi anni hanno potuto accogliere i valori e i principi fondamentali dello Stato costituzionale. Di fronte ad una Europa allargata, meno omogenea, l'unità e la diversità saranno messi ancora più in tensione. L'odierno processo di consolidamento – di segno essenzialmente empirico più che deliberativo – appare per vari profili necessario. Non si deve tuttavia dimenticare che la nozione di principi generali del diritto europeo (più ancora che del diritto comunitario) non può essere identificata quale mera "estensione" di quella tradizionalmente operante negl'ordinamenti nazionali. Sono state le costituzioni del dopoguerra e l'*interpretatio iuris* delle Corti costituzionali ad offrire un ventaglio creativo o rafforzativo di principi tratti complessivamente dai singoli ordinamenti. Il circuito giurisdizionale di cui si è fatto cenno deve poter continuare a svolgere la funzione propositiva sin qui adempiuta.[107]

Il *novum ius commune* – manifestazione di valori comuni, «nel rispetto della diversità delle culture e delle tradizioni dei popoli, dell'identità nazionale degli Stati membri e dell'ordinamento dei loro pubblici poteri a livello nazionale, regionale e locale»[108] – rischia di disseccarsi se privato di due dimensioni essenziali: la profondità e la complessità di tradizioni comuni nella storia costituzionale europea, l'interpretazione per principi come fattore evolutivo "aperto" e ordinante, a prescindere da artificiose gerarchizzazioni. In fondo la ricerca di un "diritto comune europeo" – quali ne siano le matrici e i presupposti – rinvia in ultima istanza ad una struttura che va *oltre* l'ordine comunitario inteso in senso formale e rimanda ad un circuito virtuoso che impegna una pluralità di soggetti (Stati, corti costituzionali, istituzioni comunitarie, corti europee).[109] Perseguire una prospettiva di equilibrio sostenibile e sperabilmente efficace tra unità e diversità, tra *visibilità* e *profondità* potrebbe consentire all'Europa di avanzare nella sua missione *possibile* grazie ad una visione intimamente legata alla cultura e alla storia quali elementi "costitutivi" di questo "nuovo diritto comune". Mai come oggi il costituzionalismo, pur con tutti i suoi limiti, sembra poter assurgere ad autentico *ius commune europaeum* posto a tutela dei diritti fondamentali. Manteniamone sane le radici affinché l'albero possa continuare a dare buoni frutti.

107 Vedi R. Toniatti, *La via giurisdizionale per la legittimazione dell'Unione europea*, in *Dir. pubbl. comp. eur.*, 2001, 186 ss.

108 Carta dei diritti fondamentali dell'UE, Preambolo, III cpv.

109 Cfr. J. Mertens de Wilmars, *Pluralisme et intégration européenne*, in H. Van Goethem, L. Waelkens, K. Breugelmans, *Libertés, pluralisme et droit. Une approche historique*, Bruxelles 1995.

The Italian Constitutional Tradition and the Debate around a European Constitution

1. The Value of the Constitution

It is in the 1940s that we can identify the origin, in recent Italian history, of the relationship between the idea of "constitution" and the idea of Europe. For in 1941 Altiero Spinelli and Ernesto Rossi wrote the so-called *Manifesto di Ventotene*,[1] a document that saw national states' desire for dominion as the principal reason for the catastrophe that had befallen the world, and federalism as the putative instrument for social and economic reform in Europe. «The general mood today – Spinelli was to write – is already far more disposed than it was in the past towards a federal reorganisation of Europe. The painful experience of the last decades has opened the eyes even of those who refused to see, and has matured many circumstances favourable to our ideal».[2] In 1943 Spinelli, after sixteen years of imprisonment, founded the European Federalist Movement. As a staunch supporter of the idea of federalism,[3] Spinelli had his own distinct vision of Europe. This characteristically "Italian" attitude, which is not lacking in utopian elements, has certainly left its mark on the way in which the process of European formation is regarded.

The idea of Europe accompanies, so to speak, the idea of constitution. In the post-war period Italy had to be rebuilt around values, principles and rules that

1 The authors were held by the Fascist regime on the Mediterranean island of Ventotene.

2 Cf. http://www.altierospinelli.org/manifesto/en/manifesto1944en_it.html.

3 About Spinelli see A. Chiti-Batelli, *L'idea d'Europa nel pensiero di A. Spinelli*, Manduria, Bari, Rome 1989; *Spinelli and Federalism in Europe and in the World*, ed. by L. Levi, Milan 1990. About the important Italian federalist movement see M. Albertini *et al.*, *Storia del federalismo europeo*, Turin, 1973; *Per l'unità europea: dalla Giovine Europa al manifesto di Ventotene*, ed. by G. Spadolini, Florence 1984. About Mario Albertini, great scholar of federalism and the problem of European unity, F. Terranova, *Il federalismo di Mario Albertini*, Milan 2003. On the project of Umberto Campagnolo see *Verso una costituzione federale per l'Europa. Una proposta inedita del 1943*, ed. by M. G. Losano, Milan 2003.

were to a greater or lesser degree shared. The 1948 constitution could not draw, other than in a very limited way, on the constitutional traditions of the liberal State.[4] The collapse of the Fascist regime and the catastrophe of the war had shown the shortcomings both of the path Italy had been taking towards a unitary state and of the spiritual values of the nation. It was the terrible experience of the war and its tragedies, the resistance to Nazi-Fascism and the realisation of the supreme value of liberty that created the premise for a radical rethinking of the Italian nation's conditions of existence. The State and the community had to be rebuilt from scratch, starting with the constitution. There was no sense in which the *Statuto Albertino*, the *graciously conceded* constitution of 1848, initially of the Kingdom of Sardinia, and then of the Kingdom of Italy, could have been used as a foundation for the new State. The Statute, which was an offspring of monarchical constitutionalism, then subsequently disfigured under Fascism, was silenced once and for all in 1946, when the Republic was founded.[5] The 1948 constitution required wholly different foundations. This was the first time in Italian history that the constituent power manifested itself in all its might and inevitably with novel traits, if we compare it to the constituent initiatives of 1848.[6] June 2nd 1946 saw the birth of both the Republic and the Constituent Assembly. The constitution that arose from the work of the Assembly sanctioned the clear primacy of political democracy. The organised forces – the political parties – were able to define a fundamental path projected towards the future. Pluralism was the keystone of the constitutional architecture. At the centre, but not isolated, were the values of the person and human dignity, within their specific social context. It was a constitution that, as regards fundamental principles, was able to produce an efficient synthesis that conferred value on common elements and affirmed the deeper roots of the people of Italy.[7] The value of the constitution lay precisely in the unifying plurality of the values it enshrined.

4 As was the case also with models. Cfr. L. Paladin, *Per una storia costituzionale dell'Italia repubblicana*, Bologna 2004, 47–48.

5 On the Statuto Albertino in the history of the Italian constitutional tradition see now M. Fioravanti, *Costituzione e legge fondamentale*, in *Diritto Pubblico*, 2, 2006, 467 ss.

6 For the earlier history, and the debate on the "constituent process" see P. Pombeni, *La Costituente. Un problema storico-politico*, Bologna 1995.

7 As such, the Italian constitution corresponds well to the concept of a culture-constitution in the acceptation of Peter Häberle, *Colloquio sulla "costituzione europea"*, edited by P. Ridola, in *Diritto romano attuale*, 2, 1999, 211; Id., *Per una dottrina della costituzione come scienza della cultura*, Rome 2001. Cf. F. Politi, *Stato costituzionale e* Kulturstaat *nel pensiero di Peter Häberle*, in *Diritto pubblico comparato ed europeo*, 2, 2002, 463–465.

The fundamental principles were the expression of a conception of democracy that tightly wove together political, social and economic dimensions.

Whilst the "time for politics" would soon split (from 1947, under the fourth De Gasperi government) the protagonists of the *Resistenza*, excluding from the government the now allied communists and socialists, the "time for the constitution" would continue to play an aggregating role.[8] Thus, in Italy, the *space for constitutional legitimacy*[9] had an integrating function that politics had not been able to assume. This attitude helped to bolster the constitution, to render it "neutral",[10] and to overcome, although not without some difficulty, the obstacles raised by the objective internal and international political situation against its creation. It could be said that in Italy the constitution – having survived the first years of total non-implementation and the initial scepticism of those highly left-wing forces[11] – was for a considerable period a place of encounter and inclusion. Only at the onset of the crisis of the founding parties of the Republic (the "bearers" of the constitution) in the early nineties, did the *time for the constitution* enter a further phase marked by constitutional reforms which were called for, promised, but substantially never realised.

The Italian constitution – whose sixtieth anniversary we celebrate this year – is perhaps the post-war constitution that has most strongly accentuated the new profile of liberal-democratic and social constitutionalism in its attribution of a clearly demarcated space to principles and values which were to orient, not without contradictions and difficulties, the long phase of *enactment.*

This is what Giorgio La Pira called the fundamental ("architectural") structure of the constitution, or the pluralistic organic principle «that accords due juridical and constitutional relevance to the person, to the State and to the intermediate groups that exist between the person and the State».[12] The *sphere*

8 On the problem of constitutional implementation, on doctrinal debates and on constitutional jurisprudence see F. Lanchester, *La dottrina costituzionalistica italiana tra il 1948 ed 1954*, in *Continuità e trasformazione: la scienza giuridica italiana fra fascismo e repubblica, Quaderni fiorentini per la storia del pensiero giuridico moderno*, 28, II, 1998, 749 ss.; S. Bartole, *Interpretazioni e trasformazioni della Costituzione repubblicana*, Bologna 2005; M. Gregorio, *Quale costituzione? Le interpretazioni della giuspubblicistica nell'immediato dopoguerra*, in *Quaderni fiorentini*, 35, 2006, 849–913.

9 F. Bonini, *Storia costituzionale della Repubblica. Un profilo dal 1946 a oggi*, Rome 2007.

10 On the effect of the freezing of constitutional work see E. Cheli, *Il problema storico della Costituente*, in *Politica del diritto*, 1973, 490.

11 Cf. for all U. De Siervo, *La mancata riforma delle istituzioni politiche*, in *La prima legislatura repubblicana. Continuità e discontinuità nell'azione delle istituzioni*, edited by U. De Siervo et alii, Rome 2004, vol. I, 3–15.

12 G. La Pira, *Il valore della Costituzione*, in *I cattolici democratici e la Costituzione*, edited by N. Antonetti, U. De Siervo, F. Malgeri, Bologna 1998, 1171.

of rights played – as the more lucid members of the constituent assembly had plainly grasped – a guiding role. The institution of the Constitutional Court in 1955 and its activities in successive decades represented the crucial moment for affirming the effective primacy of the constitutional act.[13]

The 1948 constitution thus founded a strong tradition. The first part of the text, in particular, had the merit of recalling and safeguarding the values of a society that needed to recast itself and to grow within the pluralism of democracy. It established a real *constitutional culture* along with an articulated *culture of rights*.[14] If we were to ask "the man in the street" to talk about the constitution he would probably not be able to do so very precisely. If, however, we were to ask him if he identified with the values, the principles and the rights contained therein, the answer would tend to be "yes". And this is what, in spite of everything, continues to *legitimise* the constitution.

2. The Italian Constitutional Tradition and Common Constitutional Traditions

This new Italian constitutional tradition emerged in its original form as part of the process of twentieth century European constitutional reform. The constitutional state affirms democratic values, rights and freedoms, it promotes them, it guarantees them. This type of state retains national peculiarities but it can no longer act as the exclusive and all-absorbing stage for the life of citizens.[15] The ravages of totalitarianism had made the risks connected with state idolatry all too plain. The sense of national belonging was not diminished but the supranational dimension was immediately apprehended as the terrain for building, starting with forms of economic partnership, reciprocal links and limitations. As we know, Europe took its first steps in the conviction – widely shared by the founding states – that peace could only become a reality for the future if new forms of interdependence were consistently promoted. Piero Calamandrei, in 1945, wished the future constituent assembly to assume a strong democratic character which would itself nurture an *appetitus foederationis*. «The central principle of democracy lies in solidarity more than in liberty: *in «interdependence» rather than in independence.* For this reason, if the Italian people succeeds in giving itself in the constituent assembly a truly democratic internal

13 Refer to Luigi Lacchè (ed. by), *Storia giustizia costituzione. Per i cinquant'anni della Corte costituzionale*, *Giornale di storia costituzionale*, 11, I, 2006.

14 For a discussion on this theme see *Il valore della Costituzione italiana*, *Giornale di storia costituzionale*, 16, II, 2008.

15 On this theme see E. Cheli, *Lo Stato costituzionale. Radici e prospettive*, Naples 2006; P. Costa, *Democrazia politica e Stato costituzionale*, Naples 2006.

system, with this it will have created an organism that is *internationally sociable*, that is, willing and able, through the natural development of the principles that animate it, to recoil from nationalism and to feel that solidarity between peoples that drives them to look for agreements and bonds in an international community that is larger than the nation».[16]

This capacity for supranational projection is stated in a far-sighted article in the Italian constitution, art. 11. which reads «Italy repudiates war as an instrument offending the liberty of the peoples and as a means for settling international disputes; it agrees to limitations of sovereignty where they are necessary to allow for a legal system of peace and justice between nations, provided the principle of reciprocity is guaranteed; it promotes and encourages international organizations furthering such ends.». In this article we can hear the echo of the pacifist case but it also recalls the original federalist inspiration.[17]

There is no doubt that the crucial problem in the construction of Europe, and one that has become increasingly urgent as the Union has proceeded along its path, has been that of reconciling two concepts – unity and diversity[18] – that in the modern history of power have always proved hard to reconcile. The President of the Convention on the Future of Europe, the ex-President of France, Valery Giscard d'Estaing, in his opening address (26 February 2002) defined as a condition for the success of the draft the identification of a «concept porteur d'unité pour notre continent et de respect pour sa diversité».[19] This was to acknowledge a primordial tension in the very identity[20] of Europe. The dialectic between what unites and what divides, the search for political form, the identification of common values and principles are thus elements that should be brought to the fore.

The great legal historian, Francisco Tomàs y Valiente, president of the Spanish Constitutional Court, assassinated in 1996 by Basque terrorists, had spoken in

16 P. Calamandrei, *Costituente italiana e federalismo europeo*, in *Costruire la democrazia. Premesse alla Costituente*, with an introductory essay by P. Barile, Florence 1995, 167.

17 On the stance of the *partito d'azione*, of the *partito repubblicano* and on the opinion of Piero Calamandrei refer to A. Cassese, *Politica estera e relazioni internazionali nel disegno emerso alla Assemblea Costituente*, in *Scelte della Costituente e cultura giuridica. II. Protagonisti e momenti del dibattito costituzionale*, ed. by U. de Siervo, Bologna 1980, 516–517.

18 Cf. *supra* in this volume *Europa una et diversa. A proposito di* ius commune europaeum *e tradizioni costituzionali comuni*, 659 ss.

19 The text in http://www.european-convention.eu.int. Giscard identified the fundamental problem in the «difficulté de conjuger un fort sentiment d'appartenance à l'Union européenne, et le maintien d'une identité nationale».

20 On this see especially B. de Giovanni, *L'identità dell'Europa*, in S. Guerrieri, A. Manzella, F. Sdogati, *Dall'Europa a Quindici alla Grande Europa. La sfida istituzionale*, Bologna 2001, 19–40.

the eighties about constitutionalism as a new *ius commune*[21] made up in particular of certain fundamental rights that are recognised and guaranteed by the jurisprudence of constitutional courts and of the European Court of Human Rights. The Court of justice referred to general principles deriving from «constitutional traditions that are common to member States», thus generating a series of decisions focused on the protection of fundamental rights. It was in the ambit of principles and "common constitutional traditions" that it was possible to develop a "new *ius commune*", and this on two levels: on the one hand, a "heritage" that consolidated the past and which was therefore rooted primarily in national traditions, and on the other a *space of communication*, which made it possible to look to the future independently of the evolution of law as defined by treaties or, from another perspective, by a Constitution-Treaty. This tilling of the ground, and this task of highlighting the "common constitutional heritage"[22] was a stimulating prospect. In this context, history and constitutional comparison were able to offer an important contribution even if, on a European scale, much still needed to be done.[23] The concrete prospect of a *ius commune of*

21 F. Tomás y Valiente, *El «ius commune europaeum» de ayer y de hoy*, in *Glossae. Revista de Historia del derecho europeo*, 5–6, 1993–1994, 13–14. Cfr. B. Clavero, *Tomás y Valiente, storico costituzionale inedito*, in ed. by A. Romano, *Il modello costituzionale inglese e la sua recezione nell'area mediterranea tra la fine del '700 e la prima metà dell'800*, Milan 1998, 28. Peter Häberle has spoken since the early 90s of *gemeineuropäisches Verfassungsrecht*. Cfr. P. Häberle, *Colloquio sulla "costituzione europea"*, cit., 211. For a perspective on the history of European law – considered from the Italian viewpoint – see the works of A. Padoa Schioppa, *Italia ed Europa nella storia del diritto*, Bologna 2003; Id., *Storia del diritto in Europa. Dal medioevo all'età contemporanea*, Bologna 2007.

22 For all see A. Pizzorusso, *Il patrimonio costituzionale europeo*, Bologna 2002; P. Grossi, *L'Europa del diritto*, Rome, Bari 2007.

23 Amongst the volumes that over the last two decades have brought into focus the question of constitutional history on a European scale I refer, for example, to *Europäische Rechts- und Verfassungsgeschichte. Ergebnisse und Perspektiven der Forschung*, ed. by R. Schulze, Berlin 1991; the volumes edited by Andrea Romano, *Alle origini del costituzionalismo europeo*, Messina 1991; *Enunciazione e giustiziabilità dei diritti fondamentali nelle Carte costituzionali europee. Profili storici e comparativi*, Atti di un Convegno in onore di Francisco Tomás y Valiente, Messina, 15–16 March 1993, ed. A. Romano, Milan 1994; *Il modello costituzionale inglese e la sua recezione nell'area mediterranea tra la fine del '700 e la prima metà dell'800*, Milan 1998; research work promoted by P. Schiera and M. Kirsch, *Denken und Umsetzung des Konstitutionalismus in Deutschland und europäischen Ländern in der ersten Hälfte des 19. Jahrhunderts*, Berlin 2000; *Verfassungswandel um 1848 im europäischen Vergleich*, Berlin 2001; by G. Manca, W. Brauneder, *L'istituzione parlamentare nel XIX secolo. Una prospettiva comparata*, Bologna, Berlin 2000; by G. Manca, L. Lacchè, *Parlamento e costituzione nei sistemi costituzionali europei ottocenteschi*, Bologna, Berlin 2003; the volume edited by H. Dippel, *Executive and Legislative Powers in the Constitutions of 1848–49*, Berlin 1999. Contributions

constitutionalism could not flourish, however, without a more complex, articulated and rigorous analysis of common traditions, in terms also of *Sonderwege*, especially in the light of the broadening of the Union to include countries that had only recently been able to welcome the fundamental values and principles of a constitutional state. The expression *common constitutional traditions* – coined by the jurisprudence of Luxembourg and adopted by European "legislators" – posed the problem of identifying two dimensions: the dimension of historical tradition[24] and the common dimension. Popular sovereignty, constitutional rigidity, the inviolable character of fundamental liberties, judicial review and the reinforced role of judges should serve as some of benchmarks of those traditions.

Courts of justice absorbed the heritage of principles and guarantees which were common to member States, and they enriched and developed it. The events relating to the Union's Charter of Fundamental Rights, however, revealed all the difficulties that were inherent in the moment of *writing*. Constitutional traditions were shown to be particularly vital so long as they operated within the ambit of the various supreme Courts, offering themselves as a sort of general principles of community law and an efficient *integration engine*. This system of constitutional traditions seemed best able to express its dynamism through the effectiveness of *interpretatio iuris*, which had the capacity to operate separately from the parallel evolution of law founded on treaties. I shall thus refer to the *autonomy* of constitutional tradition that needs to be safeguarded but not frozen, precisely in order to correspond better to the unity/diversity dialectic. We are talking about common traditions, not singular traditions nor those which can simply be recorded in a list. If the purpose of drafting laws is above all to create

by M. Stolleis, *Concepts, models and traditions of a comparative European constitutional History*, in *Themis*, 6, 2003, 155–163; H. Dippel, *Modern Constitutionalism. An introduction to a history in need of writing*, in *Tijdschrift voor Rechtgeschiedenis*, 1 2, 2005, 153–169; P. Brandt, M. Kirsch, A. Schlegelmilch (editors), *Handbuch der europäischen Verfassungsgeschichte im 19. Jahrhundert. Institutionen und Rechtspraxis im gesellschaftlichen Wandel, I: Um 1800*, Bonn 2004; A. von Bogdandy, P. Cruz Villalon, P. M. Huber, *Grundlagen und Grundzüge staatlichen Verfassungsrechts*, I, *Handbuch Ius Publicum Europaeum*, Heidelberg 2007. – Amongst the scientific initiatives that at European level have dealt with the theme of constitutional history, I recall the review published in Oviedo, *Historia Constitucional. Revista electrónica*, 2000 (http://constitucion.rediris.es/revista/hc/index.html) and the *Giornale di storia costituzionale*, six-monthly review, founded at the University of Macerata nel 2001 by Luigi Lacché, Roberto Martucci and Luca Scuccimarra (edizioni università di Macerata).

24 On the question of defining common constitutional traditions from the point of view of the identities of European peoples, see C. Pinelli, *Le tradizioni costituzionali comuni ai popoli europei fra apprendimenti e virtù trasformative*, in *Giornale di storia costituzionale*, 9, I, 2005, 11–20.

harmony (especially in a Europe with twenty-seven member states), we should not forget that, in the last resort, the search for a "European *ius commune*" refers to a structure that goes *beyond* the community order in the formal sense, and refers back to a virtuous circle that involves a plurality of entities (States, constitutional courts, community institutions, European courts).[25] *Pluralism* of sources and forms better reflects the *complexity* of the material European constitution. Pluralism, in my view, is a better expression of the *profundity* of common constitutional traditions. The attempt to give greater *visibility* to the architecture of a European constitution highlighted the difficulty in *declaring* and stating constitutional principles intended as a common heritage. Pluralism, complexity, profundity, visibility: it is by starting from these concepts that we can best examine the problem of the European constitution.

3. The name and the thing. The quest for the European constitution

As is well known, the Presidency Conclusions of June 2007 issued a mandate to the Intergovernmental Conference to develop a Reform Treaty that would modify existing treaties. On that occasion the following statement was issued: "The constitutional concept, which consisted in repealing all existing Treaties and replacing them by a single text called "Constitution", is abandoned".[26] The Treaty, signed in Lisbon on 18 December 2007, applied the mandate thus putting an end to the use of the word "constitution", which had inflamed the European debate from the Nice Treaty onwards. Regarding the body of jurisprudence of the Court of Justice, an authoritative part of Italian doctrine[27] had for some time recognised the existence of a European constitution founded on treaties and on Court decisions quite apart from the existence of any unitary text. The Laeken Declaration of 2001 and the start of the constituent process that led to the "Treaty that adopts a Constitution for the European Union" had shifted the axis of the discussion. We thus witnessed a strong *investment* in the use of constitutional vocabulary that suggested – in Italy this was viewed favourably if not enthusiastically – new horizons. The constituent process was primarily supposed to rationalize and simplify the jungle of treaties, to rectify the Union's so-called "democratic deficit", to recognize and strengthen

25 Cfr. J. Mertens de Wilmars, *Pluralisme et intégration européenne*, in H. Van Goethem, L. Waelkens, K. Breugelmans, *Libertés, pluralisme et droit. Une approche historique*, Bruxelles 1995, 13 ss.

26 Brussels European Council, 21–22 June 2007, General Observations, par. 1, in http//www.consilium.europa.eu /ueDocs/cms_Data/docs/pressData/en/ec/94932.pdf.

27 For a summary R. Calvano, *La Corte di giustizia e la costituzione europea*, Padova 2004.

European identity. The word "constitution" could have restored dynamism to a European politics that was suffering from an identity crisis.[28]

Those who between 2001 and 2002 initiated the European "constitutional project" by using the vocabulary and semantics of constitutionalism may not have been fully aware of the possible impact of their rhetoric.[29] That idea of constitution was so rich in references and implications that it proved to be both too ambiguous and too strong. Reference to the category of *convention*, the idea of *making a constitution* recalled traditions that were burdened with history and symbolism. A consequence of this, furthermore, was a paradoxical gap between the use of *words* and the sense of *things*: a constitutional treaty was being forged – consisting of a consolidation – but the intention was for it to be a "constitutional text".[30] The material that was selected and consolidated certainly did not entirely possess the traits of a constitution; the technique that was adopted made prevalent use of the logic of EU legislation and the language of international law. This use of words, however, did foster a constitutional vision. This way of proceeding, which inevitably had the nature of a compromise, ended up by engendering misunderstandings amongst those who *strongly wanted* the constitution, and those who *did not want it* because that would have meant certain very precise things. Anyone familiar with the debate on the idea of a constitution in Europe in the early nineteenth century knows that the use of words was not only descriptive but also performative.[31] Using the syntagm *Charte constitutionelle* rather than a "revolutionary" word such as *constitution* had a precise meaning[32] in the France of 1814, just as the term *Landständische Verfassung* did in the Germany of 1815, or likewise *Statuto costituzionale* in the Italy of 1848. The *Constitutional Treaty* or *Treaty-constitution* sought to fuse heterogeneous material elements and juridical methods by means of a strong rhetorical and symbolic dimension which, when faced with reality, was not able to survive.

This dimension exploited the construction of a common identity that drew to a large extent on the language of constitutionalism of States. The reader may recall the two Preambles, the three catalogues of values the Treaty contained, and the introduction of classical symbols: flag, motto, anthem and feast of the

28 C. De Fiores, *Il fallimento della Costituzione europea. Note a margine del Trattato di Lisbona*, 10/04/2008, at www.costituzionalismo.it.

29 I highlighted the effects of "constituent" rhetoric in *Il ratto d'Europa*, in *Giornale di storia costituzionale*, 9, I, 2005, 5–7.

30 This expression was first used in the Laeken Declaration. Cfr. J.-Ph. Feldman, *Existe-t-il un constitutionnalisme européen?*, in *Droits*, 45, 2007, 163–175.

31 I made a reference to "doing things with words" in *Una Convenzione per l'Europa*, in *Giornale di storia costituzionale*, 3, I, 2002, 6.

32 See *supra* in this volume *Constitución, Monarquía, Parlamento: Francia y Belgica*, 134–136.

Union. It has been correctly observed that «Given the relative lack of courage shown in dealing with the *deficit* of legitimacy of the European institutions, the audacity displayed in evoking a presumed collective identity raises a disturbing doubt, i.e. that they sought to regain in identity what they did not want to concede – addressing the problem in a neo-elitist spirit – in democratic participation».[33] The Lisbon Treaty returned, with perceptible modifications, to the path of reforming the structure of the powers of the Union and their legitimization. But it was precisely in the area of the rhetoric and symbolism of the constitution that the axe fell in the implementation of the mandate of June 2007.

The problem of identity can certainly not be underestimated. It was not by chance that in Italy there was a flare-up in the *controversy* that, by the middle of the nineties, had pitted two great German intellectuals against each other, Dieter Grimm and Jürgen Habermas.[34] The central theme was the relationship between the European *demos* and the idea of constitution. It was a debate that in some way had defined the political agenda and the two principal visions which in Italy ramified to such an extent that they gave rise to what has even been described as a dialogue of the deaf.[35] Those who had warned against the use of the word "constitution" rather than EU law or simply legal order had sought to highlight the incongruity of a "constitutional field of discussion" that was not yet founded on an act of self-determination of the people, on a collective identity or sense of belonging, or on an achieved democratic legitimization. Those, on the other hand, who underlined the originality of the process of European "constitutionalization", stressed the impossibility of referring to the paradigms of the state tradition in order to evoke a wholly different type of "pluralistic" constituent power which was able to clarify from treaties the Union's fundamental principles and values. The process of constitutional integration was to be the real engine that powered the formation of a minimal condition of citizen-

33 S. Dellavalle, *Una legge fondamentale post-costituzionale? Il diritto pubblico europeo alla luce del Trattato di Lisbona*, 04/04/2008, at www.costituzionalismo.it.

34 D. Grimm, *Una costituzione per l'Europa?*, in ed. by G. Zagrebelsky, P. P. Portinaro, J. Luther, *Il futuro della costituzione*, Turin 1996, 339–367; D. Grimm, *La natura del "Trattato che adotta una Costituzione per l'Unione europea"*, in *Quaderni. costituzionali*, 2004, 163 ss.; J. Habermas, *Una costituzione per l'Europa? Osservazioni su Dieter Grimm*, in *Il futuro della Costituzione*, cit., 369–375; Id., *Perché l'Europa ha bisogno di una costituzione?*, in *Una costituzione senza Stato*, ed. by G. Bonacchi, Bologna 2001, 145–166.

35 M. Luciani, *Costituzionalismo irenico e costituzionalismo polemico*, in *Giurisprudenza costituzionale*, 2006 (also at www.associazionedeicostituzionalisti.it).

ship, of social identity, of political participation, of discursive praxis, with a view to building an adequate European public space.[36]

4. Elements of complexity: a challenge for historians and jurists

The constitutional tension of Europe, *una et diversa*, – as already observed – is old, and yet it is also always new, and prone to assume unfamiliar forms. For a historian, this fact exerts an almost irresistible attraction. The process of "constitutionalisation" – however one wishes to judge it – offers the historian-jurist the chance to reflect, and not only from an historical perspective on the construction of a stratified and complex identity. To an even greater extent, however, this process presents us with an opportunity to think about the use of categories and points of view that traditionally are never lacking amongst the tools of the trade. Maybe more than at any time in recent years the history of law – or some of the concepts and figures that represent its disciplinary status – has been able to benefit from the manifold echoes to be discerned in the references, loans, allusions and out-and-out recastings by jurists who are intellectually involved in European projects and who are struggling with paradigms, scenarios and transformations that in some respects sound a *de profundis* over the ancient certainties of a science that is rightfully proud of its venerable knowledge and its refined interpretative categories. The search for a *nova methodus*[37] has been with us for years; but it is beyond dispute that the extraordinary accelerations triggered by a series of phenomena that for the sake of convenience we place within the capacious category of "globalisation" have displayed signs of a forward movement that are reminiscent of deep changes rooted in more distant times. The national sovereign State, the omnipotent legislator, the hierarchy and the nature of sources – to mention only the most visible phenomena – embody the lexicon of a legal modernity that, generation upon generation of jurists have breathed as their native air. Without going so far as to posit the inexorable decline or even the imminent end of this familiar scenario (a task better suited to fortune-tellers), it is certain that today we perceive as a synthesis and point of arrival an aspect of the "crisis" that in certain respects was present for a large part of the last century as a constant, voiceless counterpoint to the otherwise laudable endeavours of a juridical science committed to underpinning a crumbling edifice.

36 On Habermas's "communicative paradigm" see in particular S. Dellavalle, *Una costituzione senza popolo? La costituzione europea alla luce delle concezioni del popolo come "potere costituente"*, Milan 2002.

37 A. Giuliani, *Presentazione* to P. Stein, J. Shand, *I valori giuridici della civiltà occidentale*, Milan 1981, XVIII.

Those who observe these wide-ranging phenomena and the arduous and wearisome task of constructing a European public space cannot help noting how much effort is required by the jurist who is seeking to comprehend his times with a view to strengthening his array of technical and cultural armoury. The complexity of the new landscape[38] requires a science that is fully aware of its task and able to govern the systemic complexity of law. When we speak of a European jurist's[39] need, we are invariably referring to this dimension. Pluralism, coexistence / tension between unity and diversity, and constant comparison must be handled with the appropriate sensibility, with a critical spirit and with the capacity to tread less well-worn paths.

There is no doubt that, in recent decades, Europe's transformation within Community coordinates has represented the principal preoccupation of European jurists. On this ground different concepts of European law and diverse ways of conceiving the idea of a common law successively crossed paths, overlapped and often became confused. This was a problem affecting every area of legal science. The last decade, however, has seen the emergence of a "common" perspective that is no longer focused on the traditional context of private law but rather on the clarification and recognition of "common constitutional tradi-

38 For an analytical profile see especially P. Grossi, *Pagina introduttiva (ancora sulle fonti del diritto)*, in *Quaderni fiorentini per la storia del pensiero giuridico moderno*, 29, 2000, 1–10; Id., *Globalizzazione e pluralismo giuridico (a proposito di:* Maria Rosaria Ferrarese, *Le istituzioni della globalizzazione – Diritto e diritti nella società trans-nazionale*, Bologna 2000), ivi, 551–558; R. Sacco, *Frammentarietà, diversità e unità. Variabilità e storicità del diritto*, in *Diritto generale e diritti particolari nell'esperienza storica*, Rome 2001, 423–433; P. Grossi, *Il periodo medievale e moderno*, ivi, 479–495; S. Mannoni, *Globalizzazione, diritto, Stato*, in AA.VV., *Ordo iuris. Storia e forme dell'esperienza giuridica*, Milano 2003, 359–372; A. Padoa Schioppa, *Il diritto comune in Europa: riflessioni sul declino e sulla rinascita di un modello*, in *Foro italiano*, 1996, vol. CXIX, parte V, 14–21; Id., *Verso una storia del diritto europeo*, in *Studi di storia del diritto*, III, Milan 2001, 1–26; A. A. Cervati, *Il diritto costituzionale europeo e la crisi della dogmatica statualistica*, in *Diritto romano attuale*, 6, 2001, 21–47; K. Å. Modéer, *La comparazione come critica della cultura giuridica: un discorso tra globalizzazione e regionalizzazione*, in *Le Carte e la Storia*, 2, 2002, 7–16.

39 E. g., from different perspectives, F. Ranieri, *Der europäische Jurist. Rechtshistorisches Forschungsthema und rechtspolitische Aufgabe*, in *Ius commune*, XVII, 1990, 9–24, with ample bibiography; B. de Witte, C. Forded, *The Common Law of Europe and the Future of Legal Education*, Deventer 1992; P. Häberle, *Colloquio sulla "costituzione europea"*, cit., 210; A. von Bogdandy, *A Bird's Eye View on the Science of European Law: Structures, Debates and Development Prospects of Basic Research on the Law of the European Union in a German Perspective*, in *European Law Journal*, 6, 2000; P. Häberle, *Per una dottrina della Costituzione come scienza della cultura*, Rome 2001, 142 ss.

tions" that are closely linked to the so-called process of "constitutionalisation", whose various elements we can identify today.

The impossibility of prefiguring the European Union as a State but, even more, the unlikelihood and inappropriateness of this proposition would appear – to the logical eye – to divert the process that is underway into a *cul-de-sac*. Critics, however, will say that a State is no longer the necessary condition for bringing a constitutional system to life and that this fact derives precisely from a *constitutional culture* that has gradually eroded the relationships between state and constitution. At the same time, the hypothesis according to which the European Union already has a *sui generis* "constitution" would seem to reinforce the path taken. However, as often happens, it seems to be easier to say what the European Union *is not*, rather than what it *is*. The "crisis" of legal theory linked to the person-State and to the concept of sovereignty leaves jurists an awkward position: they can no longer trust these concepts as once they did, but nor do they yet have access to categories and paradigms that are sufficiently reliable, shared and coordinated. We can hardly anticipate a return to "heavy" dogma, since the times in which we live no longer seem to be able to bear its weight. Nevertheless, it is on this same terrain that we can hope to build something more lasting. It is not by accident that theory, history and comparative study are starting once again to produce a common language, and that Europe is the main bearer and protagonist of this encounter. The historian, in particular, is not surprised to see that the organisational models and principles that he knows well are evoked to reveal what is "arcane" in the European Union and to imagine possible developments.

In this "return to the past" the medieval pluralism governed by the *ius commune* of the *doctores*, the only ones who could decipher "unity" in the middle of territorial and subjective diversity, takes on a certain heuristic value: the objective is to broaden horizons, to reconcile stubbenly different mentalities and to inaugurate a historical-comparative "workshop" where "breadth" and profundity can be given to today's proposals. This is the concept of *multilevel constitutionalism*[40] or the evocative but elusive metaphor of *network*.[41]

40 Cf. in particular I. Pernice, *Multilevel Constitutionalism and the Treaty of Amsterdam: European Constitution-Making Revisited?*, in *Common Market Law Review*, 36, 1999, 703 ss.; I. Pernice, F. Meyer, *De la constitution composée de l'Europe*, in *Revue trimestrielle de droit européen*, 2000, 623–647. For a critical discussion of this theory see M. Luciani, *Legalità e legittimità nel processo di integrazione europea*, in *Una costituzione senza Stato*, cit., 84–85.

41 K. H. Ladeur, *Towards a Legal Theory of Supranationality. The Viability of the Network Concept*, in *European Law Journal*, 1997; *L'Europa delle reti*, edited by A. Predieri, M. Morisi, Turin 2001; F. Scharpf, *Verso una teoria della multi-level governance in Europa*, in *Rivista italiana di politiche pubbliche*, 1, 2002; S. Cassese,

There is no doubt that the centrality of principles such as those of subsidiarity and adequacy, to give just one example, also reflect the endeavour to identify instruments for governing, at various levels, an archipelago-system and to give a direction to structures supported by a logic and by dynamics that may no longer be ascribed to homogeneous universes.

Moreover, there is no need to return to the pre-state experience in order to respond to the demand for a plausible "precedent". A fundamental historiographical revision has provided a new critical re-reading of both the Weberian paradigm and the great tradition of the European science of public law between the 19th and 20th centuries, which was the creator of the "legally constituted State".[42] By removing the sediment and revealing the overlying juxtapositions regarding the origin and development of the so-called modern State, this orientation has enabled us to pass beyond the theoretical and rhetorical screen of sovereignty, and to show how, for a long time, those (modern) States and their sovereigns had to face pluralistic, apparently "medieval" characteristics and attributes – in contemporary times – of the categories connected with federalism and to that extremely unusual construction of the State as a federal entity. The *respublica composita*, the *mixtum compositum*, the highly varied types of state unions are thus once again centre stage.[43]

Lo spazio giuridico globale, Rome, Bari 2003, 21 ss., with further bibliography. On the use of the image of the network see P. Grossi, *Dalla società di società alla insularità dello Stato fra Medioevo ed età moderna*, Naples 2003, 16 ss. For a «dialectic theory» approach to law see F. Ost, M. van de Kerchove, *De la pyramide au réseau? Vers un nouveau mode de production du droit?*, in *Revue interdisciplinaire d'études juridiques*, 44, 2000, 1–82; F. Ost, M. van de Kerchove, *De la pyramide au reseau? Pour une théorie dialectique du droit*, Bruxelles 2002. The use of these metaphors is discussed within an intercultural perspective in n. 49, 2002 of *Revue interdisciplinaire d'études juridiques*, directed by the two Belgian scholars.

42 Refer especially to M. Fioravanti, above all the collection of essays *Stato e costituzione. Materiali per una storia delle dottrine costituzionali*, Turin 1993; *La scienza del diritto pubblico. Dottrine dello Stato e della Costituzione tra Otto e Novecento*, Milan 2001, t. 2. «Europe is a political whole within which the national States exist. It is *a whole composed of distinct parts* that remain as such, whilst finding more and more significance only within the whole. Europe once again contradicts the tradition of the modern State in its Hobbesian matrix, that requires its parts to be destined, by their nature, either to be absorbed by the whole, or to dissolve it because in reality they contain the seed of a new whole» (M. Fioravanti, *La forma politica europea*, in *Costituzionalismo. Percorsi della storia e tendenze attuali*, Rome, Bari 2009, 145).

43 For a discussion on the question, see S. Cassese, *Lo spazio giuridico globale*, cit., 55 ss., also for bibiographical orientations. For a reflection on the issue of «shared sovereignty» and the exercise of competences in a Community context, cf. E. Cannizzaro, *Esercizio di competenze e sovranità nell'esperienza giuridica dell'integrazione europea*, in *Rivista di diritto costituzionale*, 1, 1996, 75–123. On the con-

Paradoxically, "the future of the constitution" and the incunabula of "ancient constitutionalism" would seem less distant one from the other than chronology would have us believe. We do however still need to reflect more on which direction these "*rapprochements*" are moving, to wonder about just how perspicacious recent interpretations are, and to ponder the deeper meaning of these short circuits. The historian, however, cannot abdicate from his critical role. The experience of the modern world – it goes without saying – clearly cannot be confined between two parentheses.[44] Otherwise, we should be different from what we are, a possibility denied to us by the principle of identity. It is rather on another terrain – that of *novum ius commune* – in the acceptation of Tomás y Valiente – that past and present are seen in a relation of continuity (as well as of noted differences in post-war constitutionalism), perhaps rendering the dialogue between jurists more productive and more intelligible. More than the Europe of markets, powers and competences, it is the Europe of rights that needs the past.

5. What should the "European constitution" be?

The last decade saw the emergence of a plurality of conceptions of the European constitution. The Lisbon Treaty brought to an end – at least for the time being – the "Promethean"[45] attempt to "adopt a constitution for the European Union". François Ost and Michel van de Kerchove spoke of the written constitutions and of the Declarations of rights as the "temps des foundations", viewing them as sacralised times. The European attempt was, however, easily desacralized. As for the popular referenda that in France and in the Netherlands "turned down" the constitution; what did they really turn down? The "too much" or the "too little" of the constitutional Treaty? And what about Ireland which said it was against the Lisbon Treaty? Such questions are not easy to answer, I believe, because there are so many reasons that are concomitant and entangled. If, in the context of Europe, the exercise of constituent power has become a juridical exercise of competence, the constituent legitimacy of the peoples of Europe has turned into a counter-power that could find itself in opposition to the transformation of the Union.[46]

cept of *commonwealth* see especially N. MacCormick, *La sovranità in discussione. Diritto, stato e nazione nel «commonwealth» europeo*, Bologna 2003.

44 Underlined by G. Marramao, *L'Europa dopo il Leviatano. Tecnica, politica, costituzione*, in *Una costituzione senza Stato*, cit., 133.

45 L. Gianformaggio, *Tempo della costituzione, tempo della consolidazione*, in *Politica del diritto*, 4, 1997, 533.

46 E. Maulin, *Le pouvoir constituant dans l'Unione européenne*, in *Droits*, 45, 2007, 82–83.

Italian public opinion tends to look favourably upon Europe, a positive attitude rooted in the history of European integration. In some respects, Europe has represented an added value for Italian economic and social development and in some circumstances it has performed the function – certainly unacceptable for other nations – of "external limitation". Over the last fifteen years, however, we have witnessed the emergence of Euro-sceptic currents prepared to criticize the bureaucratic, supranational and pervasive characteristics of the Union. The adoption of the Euro and the consequent loss of purchasing power of broad social strata have certainly influenced this change of mood.

After Lisbon, as I noted above, the pragmatic path of European construction was followed with renewed vigour or, in other words, the view was taken that a constitution already existed or, conversely, that it could not be allowed to exist, because if Europe became constitutional it would also have to become a federal State. "Constitutional rhetoric" could thus be abandoned in order to revert instead to the path of rationalization, of improvements to the performance of the institutions, of multilevel governance and above all of the mechanisms of legitimization.[47] Along these lines, there was a tendency to stress the "effective force" of the Lisbon Treaty, which was expected to save "nearly the whole substance of the constitutional Treaty...".[48] With a paradox: the idea of constitution was abandoned, but the principle of the "supremacy" (akin to *primauté*) of the community[49] over internal law was committed to writing, a principle traditionally motivated by the Union's Court of Justice on the basis of the qualification of Treaties as a fundamental constitutional Charter of the Community.[50] This European "material constitution", bolstered by the efficiency argument, still fails to solve the dilemma of the justification of supremacy unless in the light of the functional paradigm that evolves within the "competitive social market economy".

It is evident that, following Lisbon, the path of the constitution in the liberal-democratic sense, which was capable of imposing order and unifying, at a given

47 S. Dellavalle, *Una legge fondamentale post-costituzionale?*, cit.

48 J. Ziller, *Il nuovo Trattato europeo*, Bologna 2007, 48, richiamato da L. Patruno, *Lo spirito del tempo e il processo di riforma delle istituzioni europee*, 11/03/2008, inwww.costituzionalismo.it. By the same author also see *Addio "costituzione" europea? I nomi: Trattato, Costituzione; la cosa: il diritto europeo*, 17/07/2007, inwww.costituzionalismo.it. e *Il modello istituzionale europeo e l'idea di Costituzione*, Turin 2006.

49 On the discussion relating to the concept of *primauté* cf. M. Cartabia, *«Unità nella diversità». Il rapporto tra la costituzione europea e le costituzioni nazionali*, in *Una Costituzione per l'Unione Europea*, ed. by G. Morbidelli e F. Donati, Turin 2006, 185 ss.; A. Celotto, T. Groppi, *Diritto UE e diritto nazionale: primauté vs. contro-limiti*, in *Rivista italiana di diritto pubblico comunitario*, 14, 2004, 1309 ss.

50 L. Patruno, *Lo spirito del tempo*, cit.

moment, a political body, was abandoned, in order to restore to centre stage the idea of a *constitutional process* of the Union that is in the *reality of things*. The rhetoric of the constitution led to a discontinuity that triggered a difficult rebalancing process of the Union's structure as regards the *constituent* dimension, in the conviction that a European constitution could be created on the basis of paradigms that were partially or wholly different from the constitutional traditions of the twentieth century. An *ideology of rights* was held to suffice; rights that were ever more separate from powers in the fluidity of multilevel constitutionalism – according to the conceptual scheme that Massimo Luciani defined as *eirenic constitutionalism*[51] – in order to lend substance to the plan for a European constitution. The post-Lisbon phase seems to have brought the process back to the track of "constitutionalism", focusing more on the reasoning of *homo oeconomicus* than on that of *homo politicus*. For the moment, the splitting of the Treaty-constitution syntagm (with the abandonment of the second term) sanctioned, also symbolically, a turning point that may not have been radical but which was nonetheless sufficiently clear in its broad outlines. This tendency sanctioned the prevalence of functional content and, on the level that is of interest to us, brought back the discussion on to the terrain of *pluralism* and *fluidity* of a *material constitutionalism* that rests upon common constitutional traditions.

This prospect, however, in the Italian debate also, leaves the fundamental dilemma unresolved. If the Treaty-Constitution failed because it was the product of an impossible compromise, does the path of *Treaty Reform* (Lisbon) have to be taken up again? Or is the solution to address once again the "erased" problem, which concerns the indissoluble relationship between people, identity, sovereignty,[52] constitution and democracy? Some say that only the realisation of a European *demos* can restore sense to the word "constitution", bridging the democratic deficit in a perspective of profound institutional transformation.[53]

Yet, it is hard to imagine today that this could be a prospect in the near future. Nevertheless, the European project – which in the Italian constitutional context

51 M. Luciani, *Costituzionalismo irenico e costituzionalismo polemico*, cit.: «Occorre rifuggire, insomma, i rischi di un *costituzionalismo irenico* che si limiti a celebrare i trionfi dei diritti fondamentali grazie alla giurisdizione (anzi: alle giurisdizioni) e tornare ad un *costituzionalismo polemico* che si misuri con il potere».

52 For a good attempt at rethinking the concept of sovereignty in a European perspective see A. Jakob, *Neutralizing the Sovereignty Question. Compromise Strategies in Constitutional Argumentations about the Concept of Sovereignty before the European Integration and since*, in *European Constitutional Law Review*, 2006, 375 ss.

53 See C. De Fiores, *Il fallimento della Costituzione europea. Note a margine del Trattato di Lisbona*, cit.

was of unquestionable importance – must start again from an awareness that historians could do much to foster. Constitutions (written or unwritten) have been the instruments and the form – albeit within the diversity of national histories – for mediating between the absolutist logic of power and the natural reasoning of law. There is no history of rights before power nor of power before rights. It is the dialectic, the conflict, the intertwining and the mediation that mark the *relational* dimension of power and rights within a *constitution*. Rights may have a strong historicistic dimension in certain constitutional experiences or a more pronounced declarative value (in some cases absolutely *foundational*) in others, but in no case may they be abstracted from the structures of power, from its forms of organisation and explication. The crux of the matter remains that of the relationship between the governing classes – or their legitimation in constructing "from above" a Europe that is better equipped to respond to the enormous challenges that lie ahead – and the electorates if and when they become involved. The short circuit between a rational and organic design (right or wrong, imperfect or appropriate as the case may be) and the *passions* of democracy and the *demos* – which are nurtured in the main by *reality* and everyday life – stares us in the face.[54]

The limit of the European constitutional structure lies in our not yet having managed to find a convincing *relational nexus* between the moment of recognition of common traditions and the moment of political decision, between the vital force of a constitutionalism of rights and the self-referential character of the cycle of legitimation. Whether the constitution is written or not: that is the question. And that is the point from which we must start anew.

54 L. Lacchè, *Il ratto di Europa*, cit.

Index of Authors

A

Abbamonte O. 452, 582, 589, 594
Ackerman B. 3, 4, 11, 621, 635
Acomb F. 128
Adorni D. 418, 422
Ahumada Ruiz A. 621, 635
Aimo P. 11, 19, 79, 450
Albertini M. 689
Albicini C. 511
Alen A. 78
Alexy R. 675
Al-Gibeli T. M. 631, 635
Allegretti U. 433, 436
Alpa G. 436
Alston Ph. 683, 685
Alvazzi Del Frate P. 281
Amadei L. 632, 635
Amorth A. 645
Amson D. 390
Anschütz G. 622
Antonetti G. 83, 93, 123, 124, 143, 146, 173, 175, 184, 311, 325, 340
Antonetti N. 691
Anzilotti A. 415, 422
Anzon A. 677
Aquarone A. 418, 422
Arcoleo G. 494, 505, 512, 524
Are G. 428
Arnaud A.-J. 669
Arrivabene G. 85, 86
Artom I. 494, 506, 516
Ascheri M. 669, 672
Ashworth A. 285
Astraldi R. 554, 555, 560, 565, 573
Astuti G. 390, 394, 448, 470, 547
Astuto G. 531
Aubert J.-F. 24, 44, 47, 48, 57, 61, 64, 65, 69, 71
Auer A. 20, 24, 48, 51
Azzariti A. 456, 512
Azzariti G. 462, 626, 635, 650, 651, 654
Azimi V. 390
Azzena L. 684

B

Bach R. 355
Bacot G. 158, 272, 274, 484
Bagehot W. 122, 260, 304, 325, 353, 439, 502, 505
Baker K. M. 468, 469, 490, 505
Balayé S. 203
Balbo C. 386, 387, 388, 389, 401, 417, 472, 474, 477, 478, 483, 495, 502, 505
Ballini P. L. 429, 557, 573
Bambi F. 654
Banti A. M. 13, 473, 480
Baranger D. 165, 306, 325, 361, 390
Barbano F. 526
Barbé M. 157, 272
Barbera A. 678
Barberis M. 127, 164, 204, 214, 216, 222, 225, 265, 287, 297, 299, 301, 336
Barbisan B. 621, 635
Barbon D. 389, 393
Barile P. 618, 635, 654
Barker H. 469
Baronchelli M. 654
Barone G. 523
Barrot O. 304, 325 , 353, 354
Bart J. 292, 295, 299, 364, 390
Barthélemy J. 108, 123, 127, 139, 141, 158, 166, 168, 195, 247, 266, 272, 273, 276, 283, 285, 296, 301, 307, 308, 320, 325, 330, 343, 369
Bartole S. 625, 627, 635, 642, 650, 653, 654, 691
Bastid P. 43, 71, 126, 127, 134, 210, 221, 233, 261, 262, 274, 276, 286, 289, 290, 291, 295, 297
Battaglia A. 625
Battaglini M. 292
Baudelaire Ch. 1
Baume S. 622, 635
Baumgartner G. J. 30
Baumgärtner I. 669
Beale H. 664
Beaud O. 160, 274, 325, 330, 553, 573
Beck Varela L. 239
Becquet H. 241
Béguin J.-C. 622, 635

Belardinelli M. 557, 573
Bell D. A. 469
Beltjens G. 113
Beneduce P. 409, 410, 422, 430, 440, 452, 462, 489, 505, 512, 520
Benjamin W. 1
Benvenuti F. 457, 459
Bercé Y.-M. 83, 123
Berengo M. 471, 472
Bergmann G. 47, 65
Bernardoni G. 385, 389
Berriax Saint Prix F. 148, 283, 284, 300
Bertani A. 485
Bertolini G. 564, 573
Bertoni B. 47, 62, 68
Betri M. L. 473
Betti E. 611
Bettini F. 581
Bettoni A. 11, 672
Beugnot A. 140
Beugnot J.-C. 140, 235, 248
Bianchi F. S. 588
Biaudet J.-Ch. 47, 53, 57
Biet C. 154, 211, 294, 518
Bifulco R. 682
Bigaran M. P. 578, 579, 614
Bigot G. 279, 280, 281, 283
Bilancia F. 678
Bin R. 11, 652
Bisogni G. 625, 635, 650, 654
Bivort J.-B. 98, 105, 188, 193
Blanco L. 228
Blanco-Valdés R. L. 286, 287, 291, 293
Blänkner R. 8
Blanning T. C. W. 468
Bloch M. 244
Blockmans W. P. 22
Blom H. W. 22
Blondel A. 279
Bluche F. 136
Bluntschli J. K. 50, 66, 70, 494, 495, 500, 505, 596, 599
Blythe J.-M. 156
Bobbio N. 441, 655
Böckenförde E. W. 80, 102, 189, 233, 239, 241, 242, 249, 250, 255
Boffa M. 126
Boldt H. 116, 254
Bonacchi G. 669, 679, 682, 698
Bonacina G. 240
Bonaparte N.-L. 33
Boncompagni C. 386, 389, 401, 417, 422, 476, 482, 499, 501, 503, 505
Bonghi R. 496, 505, 514, 555
Bongiovanni G. 675
Bonifacio M.V. 203
Bonini F. 306, 325, 332, 618, 623, 626, 635, 644, 654, 691
Bonjour E. 19
Bonnefon J. 134, 168, 235, 262, 308, 325, 330
Bonno G. 128
Borelli G. 227, 232, 399
Bornhak C. 80
Borsari L. 587
Borsi L. 514, 515, 522, 523, 525, 529
Bory J.-L. 281
Bourmaud D. 122, 132, 149, 172, 175, 284, 291, 343
Brandt P. 7, 249, 254, 695
Brauneder W. 6, 12, 80, 264, 325, 331, 522, 589, 664, 694
Bredin J.-D. 221, 468
Bretone M. 667, 668
Breugelmans K. 687, 696
Bridel M. 47, 72
Briggs A. 469
Brooke L. 469
Brown B. F. 575
Brunel F. 221, 287
Brunelli G. 14, 505, 639
Brunelli I. 489, 494, 495, 505, 575, 595, 603, 608
Bruni D. M. 473, 482
Brunialti A. 70, 81, 427, 428, 429, 430, 431, 433, 434, 435, 436, 437, 438, 439, 440, 441, 442, 444, 445, 485, 486, 487, 495, 499, 500, 501, 503, 505, 506, 507, 512, 524, 527, 534, 537, 538, 542, 559, 591, 596
Brunner O. 254
Brunot F. 390
Bruti Liberati E. 443
Bryce J. 61, 65, 499, 500, 543
Buitta A. 47
Buratti A. 570, 573
Burckhardt W. 47
Burdeau F. 11, 128, 279, 366, 457
Burdeau G. 285, 326, 331
Burke P. 469
Burrows S. 469
Busino G. 11

C
Caballo E. 409, 422
Cacciari M. 660
Cacciatore G. 531
Cadet E. 178
Calamandrei P. 543, 547, 548, 549, 550, 551, 552, 590, 594, 625, 644, 650, 653, 654, 693
Calamo Specchia M. 11, 13, 330, 354
Calasso F. 670
Calhoun C. 468, 469, 491, 506
Calvano R. 696
Cambria R. 557, 562, 573, 589
Camerlengo Q. 4
Cammarano F. 414, 422, 503, 506
Cammisa F. 412, 422
Campobassi A. 507
Camporesi P. 389, 471
Camurri R. 427, 428
Candeloro G. 438
Canevazzi G. 409, 422
Cannata C. A. 667, 668
Cannizzaro E. 681, 702
Canonico T. 588
Canosa R. 594, 596
Capefigue J. B. H. 120, 145
Capitant H. 308, 316, 325, 331, 348
Capograssi G. 625
Cappelletti M. 279, 286, 435, 441, 445, 590
Cappellini P. 1, 11, 13, 670
Capra C. 448
Car R. 237, 238
Carbone G. 481
Cardinali F. 385, 389
Caretti P. 553, 554, 568, 573
Carini C. 605
Caristia C. 429
Carnelutti F. 582, 583, 590
Caroni P. 20, 121, 666, 667, 668
Carrara F. 431, 540, 541, 542
Carrata N. 580
Carré de Malberg, 285, 296, 354, 461
Cartabia M. 682, 683, 704
Carusi P. 558, 573
Carutti D. 388, 389, 401, 417, 476, 478, 501, 506
Casanova L. 436, 533
Casavola F. 409, 423
Casertano A. 580
Casini L. 625, 630, 635
Cassese A. 693
Cassese S. 11, 456, 458, 460, 641, 654, 678, 679, 680, 681, 701, 702
Cassina C. 170, 264, 303, 325, 353, 479, 487
Castellano C. 432
Castelli M. 474
Castiau A. 105
Castronovo V. 473, 482
Catalano F. 428
Catelani A. 678
Cavallone B. 585, 592
Cavanna A. 448
Cazzetta G. 11, 14, 121, 427, 428, 429, 430, 433, 439
Ceccherini E. 685
Celotto A. 682, 704
Cenni E. 410, 423
Censer J. R. 468, 469
Ceretti A. 443
Cerexhe E. 78
Cernigliaro A. 11
Cerri A. 618, 635
Cervati A. A. 661, 686, 700
Chabod F. 19, 460
Chagnollaud D. 636
Cheli E. 572, 573, 618, 624, 626, 633, 635, 640, 650, 654, 691, 692
Cherbuliez A.-E. 29, 34, 51, 53, 54, 55, 63, 69
Chevallaz G.-A. 50
Chevallier J.-J. 19
Chianese G. 614
Chiassoni P. L. 610
Chiavistelli A. 13, 473, 474, 478
Chignola S. 126, 231
Chimienti P. 566, 573
Chiovenda G. 584, 585
Chiti M. P. 682, 683
Chiti-Batelli A. 689
Chrimes S. B. 441
Cianferotti G. 11, 414, 415, 423, 460, 461, 462, 464, 512, 516, 524, 527, 529, 569, 573, 596, 600
Ciaurro L. 235
Ciccotti C. 532
Cimbali E. 524
Cingari S. 489, 506
Cipriani F. 580, 581, 582, 583, 584, 586, 587, 592, 594, 607
Civile G. 472, 491, 506
Clavero B. 5, 8, 11, 120, 205, 443, 598, 673, 674, 675, 676, 694
Clément J.-P. 126, 285, 286, 327, 350

Clère J.-J. 292, 295, 299, 364
Cocchiara M. A. 525
Coing H. 121, 666, 667
Colao F. 11, 410, 412, 423, 486, 487, 557, 573
Colenbrander H.T. 85
Colesanti V. 592
Colmet-Daage G. 159
Colombo P. 11, 111, 113, 230, 235, 252, 271, 287, 291, 295, 298, 364, 365, 368, 405, 471, 484, 502, 506
Comandini F. 625
Comerci N. 453
Compagna L. 290
Compagnoni G. 382, 389, 393
Comte Ch. 139
Conac G. 285, 295, 364
Confessore O. 407, 412, 414, 415, 423
Constant B. 125, 126, 153, 154, 155, 163, 165, 169, 203, 204, 205, 206, 207, 209, 210, 211, 212, 213, 214, 215, 216, 218, 219, 221, 222, 223, 225, 227, 237, 253, 259, 261, 297, 298, 299, 300, 301, 310, 322, 325, 335, 336, 339, 340, 346, 369, 384, 389, 394, 396, 398, 402, 417, 475, 501, 506, 514, 534, 536
Conte E. 672
Conti V. 430
Contigiani N. 11
Conze W. 102, 189, 255
Corciulo M. S. 170, 230, 264, 324, 325, 351
Corradini D. 120
Corsini U. 474
Cortese N. 409, 423
Corwin E. S. 441
Costa P. 1, 11, 13, 405, 412, 412, 423, 438, 464, 523, 525, 529, 530, 531, 601, 609, 624, 635, 639, 646, 649, 654, 668, 669, 670, 675, 676, 692
Cottereau A. 469, 491, 506
Cottu Ch. 142, 268
Courvoisier C. 292, 295, 299, 364
Cousin V. 401, 402, 484
Craeybeckx J. 88, 111, 181, 198
Craig P. 678
Craiutu A. 242
Crépel P. 287
Crifò G. 611, 663, 667, 668
Crisafulli V. 547, 625, 646
Croce B. 425, 556, 573, 645
Crosa E. 232
Cruz Villalon P. 286, 622, 636, 695
Cuoco V. 383, 389, 393

D

D'Addio M. 294, 414, 423, 431, 432, 433, 444
D'Agostini G. 588
D'Aguanno G. 525
D'Alberti M. 456
D'Alberti di Villanuova F. 385, 389
D'Alessio G. 547
Dalloz A. 283
Dame F. W. 19
D'Amelio G. 427, 433
D'Amelio M. 582
Damien A. 443
D'Atena A. 78
Daum W. 7
Daunou P.-C.-F. 285
Dauteribes A. 285
David R. 665
D'Azeglio M. 386, 389, 397, 472, 473, 482
De Barante P. 129, 135, 158, 161, 244, 262, 273, 277, 310, 325, 338, 339, 369
De Bartillat A. J. 375
De Bellescize D. 136
De Benedictis A. 233, 423, 486, 511
De Bonis De Nobili I. 578, 601
De Brouckère C. 99
De Capitani F. 27
De Carné L. 84, 117
De Chateaubriand F.-R. 139, 157, 165, 170, 171, 177, 180, 223, 247, 264, 270
De' Cocci D. 108, 195
De Cormenin L.-M. 119, 129, 147, 172
De Fiores C. 697, 705
De Francesco A. 389
De Gerlache E. C. 83
De Gioannis Gianquinto G. 455, 457
De Giovanni B. 660, 693
Degni F. 609, 610
De Gobineau A. 19, 39
Degros M. 19, 64
De Hon Ch. 194
Dehousse R. 686
De Kerchove De Denterghem O. 104, 105, 106, 193

De Laveleye E. 80, 83, 119, 123
De Lichtervelde L. 91, 106
Della Peruta F. 482
Dellavalle S. 698, 699, 704
Delley J.-D. 42, 48
Delperée F. 11, 77, 78, 82, 89, 105, 109, 110, 114, 194
Del Pozzo F. 577, 579, 612
De Meyer J. 110
De Montesquieu Ch.-L. 22
De Nicola E. 625, 626, 636
De Nitto A. 636
De Pascale C. 254
De Potter L. 88, 183
Derathé R. 435
De Rémusat Ch. 135, 242, 319, 327
De Reynold G. 58
De Rosa G. 593
De Rubris M. 482
De Salvo P. 525
De Sanctis F. 408
Descamps E. 94, 186
De Schepper H. 22
De Secondat De Montesquieu Ch.-L. 435, 659
De Seigneux G. M. 34
De Siervo U. 617, 619, 629, 632, 634, 635, 636, 654, 659, 691, 693
Deslandres M. 123, 313, 325, 332, 344, 347
Desmons E. 302
Desmottes P. 172
De Smuter E. E. 682
De Soto J. 131, 132, 230
De Staël G. 127, 162, 205, 206, 208, 213, 214, 216, 217, 219, 220, 336, 344, 345, 383, 389, 396, 470, 492, 508
De Tocqueville A. 10, 19, 22, 23, 26, 27, 35, 36, 37, 38, 39, 53, 54, 56, 64, 73, 276, 278, 438, 456, 503, 508
Deuerlein E. 45
Devaux O. 389
De Vitrolles E.-F.-A. 127, 171, 264, 337
De Waresquiel E. 170, 264, 324, 325, 351
De Witt C. 507
De Witte B. 662, 683, 700
Dias F. 452
Di Breme L. 386, 389, 471
Di Cavour C. B. 252, 400, 401, 402, 474, 481, 495
Dicey A.V. 66
Di Ciommo E. 412, 423
Di Cosimo G. 11
Dierauer J. 55
Diez Del Corral L. 126, 161, 166, 175, 244, 272, 298
Diez-Picazo L. M. 436, 441
Dilcher G. 667, 668
Di Muccio P. 561, 563, 564, 565, 566, 573
Dionnet, 320, 325, 343
Di Pisa S. A. 600
Di Plinio G. 685
Dippel H. 6, 251, 686, 694, 695
Dipper Ch. 448
Di Renzo Villata G. 666
Dobner P. 3, 4
Doe N. 156
Doglio M. 557, 573
Dolci D. 550, 551, 552
Dollo C. 531
Dolt G. 29
Dominicé Ch. 45
Domenichelli L. 109, 111, 113
Domeny De Rienzi L. 264
Donati F. 704
D'Ondes Reggio V. 441, 524
D'Orazio G. 618, 636
Droz N. 71
Druey H. 34
Du Bled V. 41, 49, 95, 98, 104, 185, 187
Dubs J. 45, 47, 51, 52, 61, 63, 66, 67, 69, 70
Duck A. 665
Duez P. 286
Dufour A. 11, 53
Duhamel O. 180
Dumoulin M. 79
Dunoff J. L. 4
Dupin aîné A.-M. 144, 146, 147, 149, 268, 269, 281
Dupret B. 105, 109, 110, 114, 194
Dupuy R. 214, 287, 295
Durand Ch. 279, 280
Dürrenmatt F. 21
Dürsteller J. 62
Duve Th. 8, 11
Duvergier J. B. 266
Duvergier De Hauranne P. 129, 132, 144, 176, 177, 178, 179, 268, 277,

307, 314, 316, 317, 319, 325, 333, 347, 349

E

Eco U. 668
Eeckhout G. 90
Eisenmann Ch. 285, 306, 325, 435
Elia L. 305, 325
Ellero P. 430, 496, 506, 588
Elster J. 644, 654
Ergec R. 111
Erler A. 249
Ermatinger G. 67
Errera P. 91, 97, 103, 104, 106, 113, 114, 189
Escarras J.-C. 79, 457
Esposito C. 550, 646

F

Fader Ch. 94
Falco G. 232, 399
Falk U. 582
Farel P. 127, 337
Farini D. 558, 573
Faucher L. 318, 325, 350
Favoreu L. 302
Fazy J. 55, 60
Fazy-Pasteur M. A. 28
Febbrajo A. 5
Feldman J.-Ph. 697
Feola R. 450
Fernandez Sarasola I. 11, 115, 471
Fernandez Segado F. 300
Ferracciù A. 561, 568, 569, 570, 571, 573
Ferrajoli L. 443
Ferrand A.-F.-C. 232
Ferrara F. 524
Ferrarese M. R. 443, 700
Ferrari G. F. 684, 685
Ferrari Zumbini R. 232, 478
Ferraris C. F. 440
Ferreri A. L. 579
Ferri E. 564, 573, 580
Ferri M. 629, 632, 633, 635
Ferrone V. 469
Fiamingo G. 529, 531
Fiévée J. 128, 305, 306, 325, 338
Filomusi Guelfi F. 526
Fimiani E. 479
Fioravanti Maurizio 1, 7, 11, 13, 121, 151, 152, 208, 252, 274, 277, 295, 403, 405, 413, 423, 443, 460, 461, 462, 464, 481, 487, 494, 498, 506, 512, 514, 515, 516, 523, 525, 527, 529, 530, 572, 573, 598, 600, 615, 644, 646, 647, 654, 679, 680, 686, 690, 702
Fischel E. 440
Fischer-Lescano A. 5
Flauss J.-F. 48
Fleiner F. 45, 47, 62
Fleiner-Gerster T. 23, 51, 72
Flores E. 614
Floridia G. G. 678, 683
Fois S. 327
Fonfrède H. 176
Fontana B. 126, 203
Forded C. 662, 700
Forgues E. 127, 337
Fortescue J. 441
Fracassetti L. 493, 506
Frassati L. 509
Frederking B. 241
Frei K. 57
Fröschl T. 22
Fruci G. L. 480
Furet F. 121, 152, 157, 203, 260, 264, 303, 326, 352
Furiozzi G. B. 409, 423
Furlani S. 79
Fürts W. 287
Fusilier R. 110

G

Gabba C. F. 489, 493, 506, 581, 605
Gagliani D. 614
Gagliardi E. 72
Gaja G. 685
Galasso G. 450, 573
Galdi D. 425
Galeotti U. 554, 567, 573, 574
Galizia M. 79
Gall L. 248
Galoppini A. M. 614
Gambino F. 5, 678
Gambino S. 286, 677, 686
Gangl H. 80
Ganshof Van Der Meersch W. J. 106, 110
García Marín J. M. 13
Garofalo R. 603
Gauchet M. 216, 287, 289, 292, 296, 364
Gemelli C. 98, 188
Gemperle J. 20, 48, 50

Gengel J. 70
Genovese F. A. 409, 415, 423, 590, 593
Genta E. 452
Gentile F. 645, 655
Germann R. E. 48
Gherardi R. 423, 428, 429, 440, 443, 496, 506, 507, 600
Ghisalberti C. 405, 417, 423, 429, 437, 448, 450, 478, 479, 564, 573
Giacometti Z. 47, 51
Gianformaggio L. 685, 703
Gianfrancesco E. 566, 574
Giannandré R. 409, 423
Giannetto M. 522
Giannini A. 645
Giannini M. S. 305, 308, 326, 331, 411, 423, 429, 454, 457, 547, 611, 625, 646
Giaro T. 669, 670
Giarrizzo G. 509, 521
Giasanti A. 443
Gilain Ch. 287
Gilissen J. 80, 81, 84, 86, 89, 90, 91, 92, 94, 96, 98, 100, 101, 108, 112, 113, 114, 119, 195, 255
Gilliard Ch. 46
Ginsborg P. 480
Gioberti V. 398
Giocoli Nacci P. 643, 655
Giolitti G. 563, 567, 574
Girard L. 178
Giscard D'Estaing V. 660, 693
Giuliani A. 432, 445, 661, 671, 698
Glasson E. 159
Godechot J. 448
Goderbauer G. 250
Goodman D. 469
Goodrich P. 673
Gordon D. 469
Gorla G. 594, 631, 635, 671, 685
Gossez R. 178
Götschmann D. 249
Gozzi G. 423, 440, 443, 506, 600
Gouron A. 432
Grange H. 128, 202, 205, 218, 219, 220, 222, 297, 299, 364, 468
Grassi S. 618, 635
Grasso E. 586
Grasso P. G. 645, 655
Gregoire H. 132
Gregorio M. 647, 655, 691
Griffo M. 260, 325, 326, 353
Grimm D. 11, 121, 251, 677, 698
Grippo P. 436
Groppi T. 704
Grisel E. J. 48
Grossi P. 11, 531, 551, 585, 586, 607, 620, 628, 635, 661, 668, 669, 670, 674, 676, 680, 684, 685, 694, 700, 702
Grüner E. 57, 59, 71
Guarnieri C. 432, 432
Guastini R. 445
Guazzaloca G. 556, 574
Guelfi V. 66
Gueli V. 47
Guénaire M. 302
Guerrieri S. 635, 654, 660, 683, 693
Guiglia G. 78
Guionnet C. 367
Guizot F. 109, 122, 124, 129, 130, 139, 140, 145, 146, 157, 164, 171, 172, 175, 180, 239, 240, 248, 264, 269, 271, 275, 303, 316, 317, 318, 319, 322, 325, 326, 334, 335, 338, 346, 348, 352, 353, 354, 401, 484, 511
Gunn J. A. W. 469, 490, 506
Gutiérrez Vega P. 239

H
Häberle P. 8, 619, 630, 635, 641, 655, 660, 662, 678, 679, 682, 684, 685, 686, 690, 694, 700
Habermas J. 20, 468, 490, 506, 677, 678, 698
Haeberli R. 40, 68
Häfelin U. 45, 47
Hallam H. 441
Haller W. 47, 55
Halperin J.-L. 279, 412, 423, 672
Hamilton A. 22, 45, 294
Hamon L. 285, 286
Harismendy P. 108, 112, 196
Harpaz E. 163, 223, 253, 300
Harsin P. 105
Hasselrot B. 216
Hauriou M. 41, 72
Hayem R. 175
Haywood G. A. 557, 574
Heinen A. 232
Heller H. 244
Hello Ch. 143, 175, 179, 275, 276, 278, 283, 317, 326, 348, 349, 417
Helmholz R. H. 424, 667

Henriot J. 390
Herzog R. 287
Hespanha A. M. 11, 669, 675, 676
Heurtin J.-P. 492, 506
Heusler A. 47
Heyen E.V. 675
Higonnet P. L. R. 319, 326, 350
Higonnet T. B. 326, 350
Hilty C. 47, 70
Hintze O. 102, 189, 238, 239, 243 254, 255
Hirschl R. 4
His Ch. H. 129, 160, 176, 243, 326, 339
His E. 34, 47, 58
Hochuli W. 66
Hofmann E. 153, 204, 208, 210, 213, 297, 309, 335, 475, 506, 536
Hofmann H. 239, 240, 244
Hojer C. H. 114
Holmes S. 214, 216, 644, 655
Hopt K. J. 666
Huber P. M. 7, 695
Hummel J. 237, 243, 249, 250, 309, 326, 331
Hungerbühler H. 18
Hüser D. 232
Husserl G. 642, 644, 655
Huyttens E. 82, 85, 91, 92, 93, 94, 96, 97, 100, 101, 102, 107, 113, 119, 186, 187, 191, 192 194, 195
Hymans L. 84, 105, 182, 193

I

Iacometti M. 566, 574
Im Hof U. 27, 46, 47
Iñurritegui J. M. 117
Isastia A. M. 557, 558, 561, 574

J

Jacob J. M. 441
Jacot-Guillarmod O. 48
Jaeger N. 47
Jainchill A. 303, 326, 352
Jakob A. 705
Jardin A. 22, 38, 53, 180
Jasinski B. W. 204
Jaume L. 11, 12, 119, 126, 127, 128, 153, 156, 158, 172, 204, 210, 211, 216, 219, 220, 223, 272, 274, 279, 286, 289, 290, 296, 299, 300, 322, 326, 327, 345, 350, 355, 364, 390, 468, 475, 490, 506
Jay J. 22, 45, 294
Jayme E. 412, 423, 425
Jefferson Th. 644
Jellinek G. 45, 599, 600
Jemolo A. C. 547
Jennings J. R. 127
Jèze G. 285
Joerges Ch. 5
Johnson D. 145
Jona G. 529, 530
Jones H. S. 461
Juste Th. 80, 82, 89, 91, 92, 93, 94, 96, 97, 100, 103, 105, 118, 119, 183, 184, 185, 186, 187, 190, 191, 193, 255

K

Kahan A. 129, 338, 493, 506
Kaufmann E. 68, 161, 240, 249
Kaufmann O. K. 50
Keller A. 11
Kelsen H. 223, 285, 544, 621, 622
King N. 201, 297
Kirsch M. 6, 7, 228, 238, 239, 240, 249, 309, 326, 331, 369, 686, 694, 695
Kirshner J. 669
Kloocke K. 389
Knabe P. E. 355, 469
Knapp B. 44, 46
Kölz A. 48, 55, 57, 58, 59, 60, 63, 67, 68, 71
Koselleck R. 10
Kosfeld A. G. 7
Koskenniemi M. 11
Kötz H. 666

L

Laband P. 45, 516, 547
Laboulaye E. 120, 442, 445, 534
Labriola A. 568, 574
Labriola S. 678
Labriola T. 605
Lacchè L. 1, 2, 7, 12, 51, 52, 53, 55, 57, 62, 121, 160, 234, 245, 253, 255, 262, 267, 274, 307, 309, 323, 326, 331, 332, 345, 350, 362, 363, 365, 367, 369, 370, 390, 405, 410, 416, 417, 419, 423, 429, 435, 453, 456, 468, 469, 470, 474, 480, 484 485, 496, 511, 512, 521, 535, 538, 539, 540, 618, 636, 640, 643, 655, 692, 694, 695, 697, 705

Ladeur K.-H. 5, 680, 701
Ladrière P. 469, 491, 506
Laferriere F. 158, 276
Lagi S. 621, 636
Lahmer M. 286, 291, 293, 306, 326, 332
Lambert E. 285
Lampa L. 431
Lampertico F. 428
Lanaro S. 17, 433
Lanchester F. 411, 423, 511, 512, 523, 569, 574, 691
Landi G. 450
Lando O. 664
Lanza A. 280
Laquièze A. 124, 127, 131, 132, 133, 134, 135, 136, 137, 141, 146, 149, 160, 161, 167, 168, 170, 175, 179, 230, 231, 232, 236, 242, 253, 263, 278, 307, 308, 309, 320, 321, 322, 326, 329, 330, 332, 342, 343, 345, 360, 362, 370, 390, 470, 499, 506
La Pira G. 623, 624, 691
Laroque P. 283
La Salvia S. 474
Lasserre A. 57
La Torre M. 600
Lauber O. 55
Laurent F. 610
Lauvaux P. 78, 82, 102, 160, 189, 242, 306, 326, 332
Lavagna C. 623, 646
Lavigne P. 160, 463
La Vopa A. J. 469
Lebas C. 96
Lebeau J. 92, 105, 184, 192
Le Bon G. 497, 506
Le Divellec A. 622, 635
Ledré Ch. 172
Lefort C. 484
Legrand P. 672, 673
Lemoine E. 180
Lenaerts K. 682
Lentz Th. 357, 358, 367, 368
Leroy M. 77
Levi L. 689
Levinet M. 287
Levra U. 409, 424, 556, 557, 558, 561, 562, 563, 569, 574
Lévy R. 431
Lezay-Marnezia A. 293
Lieber F. 534
Liebman E.T. 585
Lijphart A. 78
Lill R. 474
Lingens H.-K. 11
Loewenstein G. 654
Lombardi A. 48
Lombardi G. 684
Longi V. 560
Longo A. 198, 506, 524
Lopez P. 415, 424
Lorente M. 11
Losano M. G. 689
Loughlin M. 3, 4, 11
Lousse E. 94
Lovato A. 409, 410, 424
Lucas P. 126
Lucchini L. 562, 588, 589
Luciani M. 11, 443, 618, 619, 629, 630, 631, 634, 636, 639, 642, 648, 651, 652, 655, 677, 680, 698, 701, 705
Luig K. 494, 506, 574, 668
Luminati M. 582
Lupo N. 11, 574
Lupoi M. 672
Luscieti B. 20
Lutaud O. 145
Luther J. 277, 281, 287, 291, 622, 636, 654, 655, 656, 677, 698
Luzzatti C. 611
Luzzatti L. 78, 112, 118, 197, 428, 512
Luzzatto S. 221, 287, 303, 326
Lyon J. 279

M

Macarel M. 456
Macaulay Th. 441
MacCormick N. 681, 703
Machelon J.-P. 278, 285, 330, 364
Madison J. 22, 45, 294
Mager W. 238
Mahul A. 142, 172, 267, 324, 326, 351
Maifreda G. 508
Maitland F. W. 671
Majorana A. 508, 511, 512, 514, 515, 516, 517, 518, 519, 520, 521, 522, 523, 524, 525, 526, 527, 528, 529, 530, 531, 532
Majorana G. 509, 521, 526
Majorana S. 517, 521, 526
Majorana S., junior 523
Malatesta M. 508, 562, 574, 589

Maldini D. 482 G. 557
Malgeri F. 691
Manacorda G. 557, 574
Manca A.G. 6, 7, 11, 12, 80, 112, 117, 228, 255, 264, 305, 309, 318, 325, 326, 331, 350, 405, 522, 589, 642, 655, 686, 694
Mancini M. 554, 574
Mancini P.S. 412, 416, 419, 425
Manent P. 126, 203
Mangoni L. 459, 465, 512, 532
Manin B. 154, 211, 294, 518
Manna G. 452, 453
Mannoni S. 11, 84, 151, 182, 197, 221, 289, 290, 364, 365, 366, 414, 424, 661, 679, 686, 700
Mannori L. 11, 13, 287, 390, 405, 438, 450, 451, 457, 458, 470, 471, 473, 490, 491, 507, 675, 676
Mannuzzu S. 443
Mansel H.P. 412, 424, 425
Mantellini G. 456, 458
Manzella A. 554, 555, 567, 568, 574, 660, 682, 683, 693
Maranini G. 558, 574
Marchetti P. 11, 556, 574
Margerison K. 357, 364
Markesinis B.S. 673
Marongiu A. 435
Marovelli P. 432, 593
Marramao G. 677, 681, 703
Marselli N. 460
Martellini G. 473
Marti U. 38, 59
Martin W. 17, 46, 57
Martines T. 641, 655
Martini F. 593
Martirano M. 530
Martone L. 452, 578
Martucci R. 2, 11, 219, 289, 295, 367, 409, 418, 419, 420, 424, 481, 562, 574, 695
Massera A. 460, 618, 636
Massetto G.P. 666
Massimilla E. 531
Mast A. 82, 96, 112
Matteucci N. 23, 54, 151, 208, 405, 441, 444, 490, 507, 651, 655
Maulin E. 286, 703
May Th. Erskine 498, 499, 507
Mayali L. 432
Mayer J.-P. 22, 53
Mayr O. 221
Maza S. 469, 490, 507
Mazzacane A. 409, 424, 428, 432, 462, 496, 507, 512, 532, 587, 671
Mazzamuto S. 581
Mazzarella F. 621, 636
Mazzonis F. 502, 507
McIlwain Ch.H. 441
Mecca G. 11
Meccarelli M. 11, 540, 562, 574, 581, 609, 622, 636
Meisner H.O. 160, 240
Mele F. 419, 424
Melegari L.A. 388, 389, 401, 417
Melograni P. 682
Meniconi A. 589
Mereu I. 389, 393
Meriggi M. 13, 252, 422, 473, 505, 507
Merlini S. 417, 424, 555, 568, 574
Mertens de Wilmars J. 687, 696
Mestre J.L. 142, 279, 280, 281, 283, 284
Messedaglia A. 428
Meucci L. 454
Meyer F. 680, 701
Meyer G. 45, 437
Mezzanotte C. 618, 636
Miceli V. 529, 530, 569, 574
Michon L. 308, 326, 330
Miglio G. 459
Mikat P. 424
Miletti M.N. 580, 592
Mill J. St. 306, 327, 437, 493, 507, 534
Minerbi M. 125, 206, 214, 236, 297
Minghetti M. 501, 507, 514
Minguzzi L. 494, 495, 499, 500, 501, 502, 507
Miranda de Sousa J.P. 683
Mirkine-Guetzevitch B. 80, 81, 113, 116, 307, 327, 329
Miroir A. 111, 112 197
Moccia L. 671
Modéer K. Å 8, 9, 662, 700
Mohl R. 45
Mohnhaupt H. 11, 251, 686
Molfese F. 418, 424
Molinier V. 452
Molitor A. 110, 194
Mongiano E. 410, 424, 479, 480, 481
Monnard Ch. 34
Monnier L. 53
Monnier V. 11, 52

Montague F. Ch. 534
Montalcini C. 81, 106, 109, 534
Montaldo S. 565, 568, 574
Montesano L. 586
Monti A. 425
Morabito M. 11, 122, 128, 132, 149, 172, 175, 214, 218, 220, 287, 291, 295, 299, 343, 364, 390
Morand Ch.-A. 45
Morbidelli G. 704
Morelli E. 573
Morisi M. 680, 701
Mortara A. 582
Mortara G. 580
Mortara L. 434, 580, 581, 583, 584, 585, 586, 587, 588, 589, 590, 591, 592, 593, 594, 597, 605, 606, 607, 608, 609, 610, 614, 615
Mortati C. 306, 327, 547, 625, 646, 647, 648, 655
Mosca G. 496, 514, 524, 578, 595, 598, 612
Moscati R. 450
Moschetti C. M. 333
Mosler H. 286, 288
Moyn S. 303, 326, 352
Mozzarelli C. 462, 520
Mozzoni A. 605
Muller J. D. 48
Müller J. 424
Müller-Graff P. C. 686
Muret J. 34
Musella L. 419, 424
Musio G. 431
Müßig U. 8, 244, 249

N

Nada N. 409, 424
Napoli M.T. 448, 452, 460
Nathans B. 469
Necker J. 205, 208, 217, 218, 219, 381, 389, 468
Negri G. 232, 294, 553, 574
Neidhart L. 45
Neppi Modona G. 432
Nespor S. 462, 520
Nicolas J. 221, 287
Nicolini N. 451
Nicolle B. 288
Niemeyer G. 244
Nieri R. 557, 574
Nigro O. 569, 574
Nilsen P. 8, 9
Nippel W. 155
Nishitani Y. 412, 424
Notarangelo R. 51
Nothomb J.-B. 90, 92, 107

O

Oeschey R. 240
Oestreich G. 238
Ogorek R. 667
Ojetti U. 613
Oldrini G. 409, 424
Olivetti A. O. 47, 62, 68
Omacini L. 205
Omodeo A. 123, 130, 137, 157, 262, 334, 344, 389, 470, 483
Onida V. 626, 636, 650, 655
Orban O. 86, 96, 97, 99, 104, 106, 110, 113, 256
Orlando V. E. 403, 461, 462, 463, 464, 465, 486, 498, 500, 501, 503, 507, 512, 513, 515, 523, 524, 525, 527, 529, 530, 534, 544, 545, 546, 563, 575, 580, 581, 592, 593, 594, 595, 597, 598, 599, 600, 602, 645
Ornaghi L. 678
Orrù R. 78
Orta D. 473
Ost F. 680, 702
Ozouf M. 157, 264, 468, 469

P

Pace A. 11, 77, 277, 631, 678, 682, 683
Pace Gravina G. 11, 523
Pacifici Mazzoni E. 588
Paciotti E. 682
Padelletti G. 66, 70, 430, 596, 605
Padoa Schioppa A. 421, 424, 432, 661, 663, 666, 669, 670, 694, 700
Pagès J.-P. 371, 372, 373, 374, 375, 376, 377
Paine Th. 644
Paladin L. 618, 625, 636, 650, 655, 690
Palazzolo A. M. 509
Palma L. 66, 70, 85, 87, 493, 503, 507, 512, 527, 534, 596
Palombarini A. 579
Palombella G. 443
Paoli C. 482
Papa E. R. 18, 46, 432, 526
Paradisi B. 670
Parri F. 645

Pasquino P. 138, 160, 215, 223, 278, 289, 293, 296, 301, 624, 627, 636, 650, 655
Passero L. 467
Patetta F. 390, 394
Patruno L. 704
Pavone C. 481
Peccolo G. 78
Pecorari P. 428, 429
Pene Vidari G. S. 11, 410, 411, 412, 424, 481, 581
Perin F. 87, 114
Pernice I. 680, 701
Perny A.-F. 157, 272
Perrin F. 172
Persano P. 644, 655
Perticone G. 417, 424, 558, 575
Pertué M. 11, 244, 287
Pescatore M. 401, 587, 604
Pessina E. 388, 389, 410, 411, 424, 511
Petit C. 11, 121, 676
Petracchi A. 79, 454
Peverelli P. 388, 389, 401, 417, 476, 478, 501, 507
Pezzini B. 654
Pezzino P. 579
Pfyffer K. 28
Piasenza P. 432
Picardi N. 432, 445, 581, 671
Picavet C. G. 47
Pichetto M.T. 473
Pierantoni A. 412, 485
Pieroni Bortolotti F. 579
Pifferi M. 540
Pignatelli A. 432
Pii E. 430
Pilbeam P. M. 281
Pinelli C. 11, 618, 624, 632, 636, 650, 652, 655, 656, 660, 676, 678, 679, 682, 684, 695
Pinheiro Ferreira S. 300, 313, 327, 342
Pinkney D. H. 269, 281
Piodi F. 427
Piola-Caselli E. 587, 593
Piras A. 457
Pirenne H. 87, 88, 93, 109, 182, 184, 196, 256
Piretti M. S. 108, 196, 411, 424, 428, 429, 430, 511, 557, 575, 601, 608
Pirro A. 48
Pisanelli G. 407, 408, 409, 410, 411, 412, 413, 414, 415, 416, 417, 418, 419, 420, 421, 422, 423, 424, 425, 511
Pischedda C. 402, 474
Pisier E. 286
Pizzorno A. 443
Pizzorusso A. 434, 587, 590, 679, 682, 683, 685, 686, 694
Politi F. 679, 690
Pombeni P. 429, 467, 491, 503, 507, 598, 601, 643, 690
Popkin J. D. 468, 469
Porciani I. 427, 428, 440
Porret M. 11
Portillo Valdés J. M. 117, 123, 471
Portinaro P. P. 277, 287, 654, 655, 656, 677, 698
Pouthas Ch. 158, 272, 315, 327, 347
Predieri A. 680, 701
Presno Linera M. 633, 636
Prevost-Paradol L.-A. 260, 300, 304, 327, 352, 353, 354
Primicerio L. 78
Prodi P. 18, 676
Prutsch M. J. 239
Pugliese G. A. 496, 507
Puissochet J. P. 685

Q
Quagliariello G. 503, 507
Quarta O. 610, 612

R
Rader D. L. 143
Radiguet L. 136
Raikem J. 194
Ranelletti O. 486, 546, 600, 645
Ranieri F. 662, 700
Ranzato G. 579
Raponi N. 448
Rappard W. 28, 47, 55, 57
Raynaud Ph. 145, 203
Reboul P. 127
Rebuffa G. 241, 432, 439, 452, 454, 455, 456, 462, 464, 512, 556, 575
Redor J. M. 209, 278, 286
Redslob R. 303, 327, 351
Remond G. 158, 161, 169, 272, 369, 485
Renan E. 17, 50, 119, 180, 327, 353, 487
Renner K. 621

Reynié D. 508
Rials S. 132, 134, 135, 137, 160, 230, 233, 234, 235, 242, 262, 302, 309, 327, 330, 331, 362
Ridola P. 636, 690
Riedel E. 686
Ritter G. 254
Rivero J. 278
Robbers G. 287
Robert H. 134, 143, 144, 146, 236, 263
Rocco Alf. 543, 546
Rocco G. 453
Roche D. 469
Roddi G. 587
Rodotà S. 443, 550, 552, 598, 618, 636, 682, 683
Roederer P.-L. 217, 315, 327, 355, 356, 357, 358, 359, 360, 361, 362, 363, 364, 365, 367, 368, 375, 376, 377
Rohmer Ch. 134, 235, 262
Rohr A. 34, 48
Roldan D. 172, 369, 484
Rolland P. 292, 293, 294
Romagnosi G. D. 390, 394, 470, 475, 476, 490, 499, 500, 501, 507, 521
Romanelli R. 277, 415, 425, 432, 436, 443, 474, 552, 574, 579, 598, 676
Romano A. 79, 117, 327, 336, 673, 674, 686, 694
Romano S. 524, 531, 544, 545, 546, 553, 565, 572, 575, 600, 611
Romeo R. 409, 425, 460, 486
Rosanvallon P. 120, 127, 128, 131, 132, 133, 134, 135, 137, 142, 143, 144, 147, 149, 150, 157, 158, 159, 160, 167, 170, 175, 209, 223, 226, 230, 233, 234, 239, 240, 260, 264, 266, 267, 268, 269, 271, 272, 304, 305, 319, 327, 337, 352, 366, 484
Roselli F. 436
Rosselli C. 549
Rossi E. 689
Rossi F. 568, 575
Rossi L. 519, 600
Rossi L. S. 683
Rossi P. 1, 29, 31, 32, 33, 51, 53, 101, 192, 300, 393, 394, 401, 410, 411, 412, 417, 425, 463
Rossi-Doria A. 614
Rossini R. 409, 422
Rotelli E. 251, 306, 327, 361, 405, 450, 568, 575
Roth R. 11
Roulin A. 204, 253, 261, 336, 475
Rousseau D. 286, 296, 297, 300, 302
Rousseau J.-J. 435, 436
Rousseaux X. 431
Roux M. 141, 266
Royer J.-P. 281
Royer-Collard P.-P. 339, 368, 369, 401, 484, 485
Rubenfeld J. 644, 656
Rudelle O. 354
Ruffieux R. 47, 56, 60
Ruffilli R. 415, 425
Ruffini F. 542, 543, 544, 545, 547, 548, 550, 552
Rugge F. 81
Ruperto C. 628, 629, 631, 635, 636
Russo L. 408, 425
Rüttimann J. J. 45, 58, 60

S

Sacco R. 448, 661, 700
Sagù M. L. 525
Saint-Simon Ch. 170
Saladin P. 20, 48, 50
Salerno G. 11, 627, 637
Salvati M. 614
Salvioli G. 525
Sambataro S. 457
Sampolo L. 525
Sand I.-J. 5
Sandevoir P. 457
Sandulli A. M. 627, 637
Santangelo Spoto I. 569, 571, 575
Saraceno P. 425, 432, 433, 582, 587, 588, 589, 593, 594
Sarrans B. 147
Sartoretti C. 425
Satta S. 583
Saulnier F. 330
Sbano N. 14, 580, 595
Sbriccoli M. 11, 81, 117, 419, 425, 431, 539, 554, 562, 575, 589, 668, 669, 671, 672
Scaduto F. 524
Schachtschneider Morier-Genoud A. 48
Scharpf F. 680, 701
Schefold D. 11, 34, 55, 622, 623, 633, 637
Schiavone A. 425

Schieder W. 448
Schiera P. 6, 8, 11, 79, 102, 214, 233, 238, 240, 249, 250, 305, 327, 336, 405, 422, 428, 496, 507, 653, 656, 686, 694
Schindler D. 48
Schipani S. 668
Schlegelmilch A. 7, 695
Schmidlin B. 664
Schmidt-Eichstaedt G. 440
Schmitt C. 102, 222, 224, 230, 240, 241, 244, 255, 257, 274, 277, 286, 287, 485, 622, 647
Schmoeckel M. 582
Schneider F. 469
Schnettger M. 244
Schollenberger J. J. 45, 47
Schulze C. 249
Schulze R. 11, 13, 448, 462, 520, 663, 666, 668, 694
Schumann K. 47, 62
Scialoja A. 416, 425, 667
Sciumé A. 432, 606
Scoditti E. 443
Scolari S. 455, 489, 497, 498, 499, 507
Scolari Sellerio Jesurum L. 587
Scuccimarra L. 2, 11, 284, 364, 368, 469, 479, 695
Sdogati F. 660, 683, 693
Seiler D.-L. 41
Sellin V. 232, 241, 243
Senelle R. 78, 110, 111
Serafini F. 429, 430
Serianni L. 389, 481
Serman W. 178
Serrigny D. 144, 158, 161, 268, 272, 275, 310, 327
Shand J. 661, 699
Sidjanski D. 48
Siegfried A. 47
Sieyes E. 210, 221, 227, 288, 289, 290, 291, 292
Sigg O. 48
Sighele S. 489, 497, 507
Simler I. 19, 20, 50
Simmel G. 643, 656
Simon D. 432, 669
Simon P. 133
Simoncini A. 11, 625, 637, 650, 656
Simoni S. 232
Siotto Pintor M. 602, 613
Sismondi J. C. L. 125, 155, 156, 206, 208, 210, 212, 213, 214, 215, 218, 236, 296, 475, 482, 490, 493, 507
Smend R. 102, 189, 255
Smith A. D. 18
Snyder F. 678
Soddu F. 503, 507
Sofia F. 215, 356, 364, 505, 508
Sola G. 526
Solimano S. 425
Sonnino S. 404, 556, 561, 564, 567, 568, 570, 575
Sordi B. 1, 11, 13, 18, 79, 440, 457, 458, 460, 461, 462, 516, 520
Spadaro A. 679
Spadolini G. 689
Spampinato R. 523
Spaventa S. 409, 425
Speciale G. 510, 525, 529, 532
Sperti A. 630, 631, 637
Spinelli A. 689
Spinosa A. 239
Stahl F. J. 255
Stampacchia L. 414, 425
Starobinski J. 18
Starzinger V. E. 369
Stein P. 661, 683, 699
Steinberg J. 18
Steiner A. 40
Stengers J. 110, 111, 194
Sternberger D. 20
Stolfi N. 408
Stolleis M. 9, 11, 241, 242, 249, 424, 440, 669, 695
Stoppato A. 595, 612
Storti C. 11, 412, 425, 432
Stourzh G. 288
Stramacci M. 560, 574
Stronati M. 11, 540
Sulis F. 511

T

Tacchi F. 592, 596, 614
Taine H. 120, 459
Talamo G. 409, 425
Tallichet E. 70
Tambaro I. 499, 501, 508
Tanda A. P. 555, 558, 559, 560, 561, 563, 575
Tanquerel Th. 48
Taradel A. 79
Tarde G. 497, 508

Tarello G. 120, 435, 436, 585, 590, 592, 593
Taricone F. 605
Tartufari A. 588
Taruffo M. 443, 581
Terranova F. 689
Teso A. 495, 505, 508
Tesoriere G. 583
Tessitore F. 415, 425, 494, 508, 524, 600
Teubner G. 4, 5
Themelly M. 562, 575, 588
Théry I. 154, 211, 294, 518
Thibaudeau A.-C. 292, 293, 294, 301
Thiers A. 144, 146, 148, 167, 268, 274, 312, 327, 341, 370
Thom M. 11
Thompson P. 201
Thonissen J.-J. 95, 97, 98, 101, 103, 104, 106, 186, 187, 190, 192, 193
Thuillier G. 366
Tielemans F. 99, 105, 189
Togliatti P. 550, 646
Tomás y Valiente F. 6, 673, 674, 675, 676, 694
Toniatti R. 687
Torre A. 11, 361, 566, 575, 623, 637, 672
Tortarolo E. 469
Tosato E. 646
Trachtman J. P. 4
Tranfaglia N. 482, 618, 637
Traversa S. 572, 575
Treggiari F. 412, 425
Treves R. 521
Triepel H. 622
Trifone G. P. 519, 529
Trifone P. 389, 481
Tripp M. L. 60
Troisi Spagnoli G. 289, 290
Trono G. 505
Troper M. 7, 11, 223, 290, 292, 294, 296, 302, 306, 327, 332, 335, 435
Troxler P. I.V. 34, 55
Tudesq A.-J. 128, 318, 327, 350, 366
Tulard J. 132, 230, 357
Tully J. 4
Turiello P. 464, 514

U
Ullrich H. 251
Umbach D. C. 287
Ungari P. 121, 408, 425, 432, 448, 566, 575
Uyttendaele M. 78, 111

V
Vadalà-Papale G. 525, 529
Valensise M. 129, 145, 272, 327, 338
Valera G. 600
Vallejo J. 676
Van Berchem R. 60
Van Caenegen R. C. 8, 664, 667, 669
Van de Kerchove M. 680, 702
Vandenpeereboom E. 83, 89, 97, 99, 100, 102, 108, 109, 118, 183, 189, 190, 191, 195, 196
Van Den Steene W. 90
Vanderlinden J. 98
Van de Weyer S. 85
Van Goethem H. 687, 696
Van Impe H. 96
Van Kalken F. 88, 89, 91, 104, 107, 111, 112
Van Muyden B. 57
Vanni I. 526, 528
Vano C. 11, 13, 423, 432, 496, 507, 587, 588
Varela Suanzes-Carpegna J. 7, 10, 11, 126, 156, 165, 226, 277, 291
Varnier G. B. 425, 581
Varsori A. 635
Vassalli G. 551, 625, 629, 634, 637, 642, 656, 672
Vauthier M. 440
Vec M. 8
Velu J. 103, 106, 110, 111, 256
Venturini F. 582, 586, 592, 593, 614
Verde G. 593
Verpeaux M. 126, 280, 286, 292, 295, 299, 327, 350, 364
Vico G. B. 521
Vigier Ph. 147, 366
Vile M. J. C. 442
Villa Pernice A. 499, 508
Villemain A. F. 170, 171, 264
Viola P. 219
Violante L. 573, 575
Virgilii F. 529
Vivante C. 613, 614
von Bogdandy A. 7, 662, 695, 700
Von Gentz F. 249
Von Gerber K. F. 516, 543, 544, 547, 599
Von Gierke O. 544

Von Gneist R. 440, 461, 494, 506, 516
Von Holtzendorff F. 489, 495, 506
Von Mohl R. 516
Von Planta P. C. 41
Von Protschwitz G. 390
Von Reden-Dohna A. 450
Von Rotteck K. 227, 235, 241, 251
Vormbaum Th. 11
Vovelle M. 287

W
Wachsmann P. 160
Waelkens L. 687, 696
Wahl R. 254
Waitz G. 45
Waleffe B. 110
Walker N. 3
Webb S. 531
Weber M. 436
Weiler J. H. H. 4, 11, 678, 683
Weishaupt M. 19
Weitzel J. 249
Welcker K. Th. 227, 235, 241, 251, 400
Wertenschlag R. 48
Widmer S. 17
Wigny P. 106
Wijffels A. 11, 663, 665, 669
Wild H. 28, 55
Wind M. 4
Witte E. 88, 111, 181, 198
Wodon L. 106
Wunder B. 238

Y
Yvert B. 161, 369

Z
Zaghi C. 448
Zagrebelski G. 277, 443, 617, 618, 621, 628, 629, 630, 634, 637, 652, 654, 655, 656, 677, 678, 685, 698
Zanfarino A. 506
Zanichelli D. 410, 411, 425, 511
Zanobini G. 547
Zazo A. 409, 425
Zeldin Th. 127
Ziller J. 704
Zimmermann R. 666, 667
Zinniker O. 27
Zoller E. 81, 621, 637
Zweig E. 287